W9-AAX-796

# Welcome to ...

# CERTIFIED LEARNING IN COSMETOLOGY®

## Principles of Education

# cosmetology

# Principles of Education

A Journey of Learning©

cosmetology

# Dedication ...

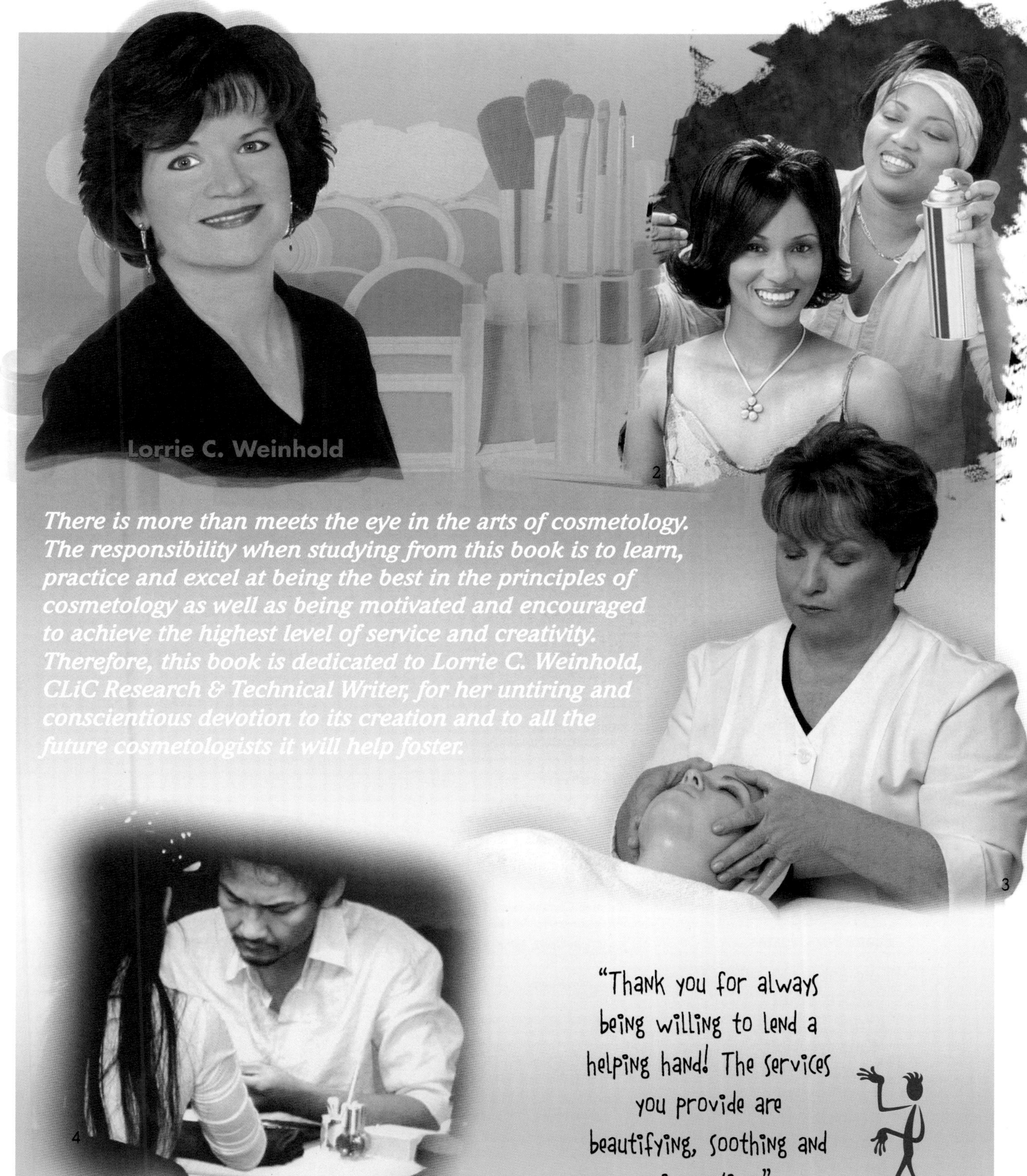


*There is more than meets the eye in the arts of cosmetology. The responsibility when studying from this book is to learn, practice and excel at being the best in the principles of cosmetology as well as being motivated and encouraged to achieve the highest level of service and creativity. Therefore, this book is dedicated to Lorrie C. Weinhold, CLiC Research & Technical Writer, for her untiring and conscientious devotion to its creation and to all the future cosmetologists it will help foster.*

"Thank you for always being willing to lend a helping hand! The services you provide are beautifying, soothing and rejuvenating."

©

## CLiC ART DEPARTMENT:
Layout, Design and Illustration

Senior Graphic Artist
**Rae L. Kauffman**

Graphic Artists
**Artemus D. Tuisl**
**Janelle C. Klitsch**

## SPECIAL ACKNOWLEDGEMENTS

Photographer
**John Dalton**
**Randy L. Donatelli**

Illustration
**Laura Gelsomini**

Editor
**Lori R. McFerran**

Index
**Potomac Indexing, LLC**
www.potomacindexing.com

Contributing Writers
**John Mascarini-**
The Business of Beauty

**Theresa Andrews-**
Art of Makeup

Subject Matter Editors
**Alice Thiel**
**E. Desire McGarity**
**Lisa Beamer**
**Margie Wagner-Clews**
**Theresa Andrews**
**Trang Nguyen**
**Vickie Servais**

Proofreader
**Diane M. Grustas**

CLiC Photo Shoot Contributors
**Alice Thiel**
**Arnaz Dotivala**
**Kathryn Wilt**
**Lauren Doyle**
**Lesa Beamer**
**Nirmala Modi**
**Randy Rick**
**Shelbi Harmes**
**Trang Nguyen**
**Van Thuy Luu**


# COSMETOLOGY / page(picture number)

### Hairdesign Contributors:

**Alyse Tuccio – The Brown Aveda Institute**
352(3), 446(1)

**Amber Cebula – Cloud 9 Salon**
212(1)

**Analyn Cruz – The Aveda Institute**
231(2)

**Arica Diaz – Kathy Adams Salon**
218(1)

**Attitudes A Salon**
20(2)

**Barbara Lhotan**
185(3)

**Belinda Baker**
27(4), 29(2)

**Bella Capelli Salon**
183(8), 192(6), 208(2), 325(4)

**Ben DeCordova**
9(2), 18(5), 26(1), 44(3), 70(1), 171(2,5), 172(4), 178(2), 182(1)

**Blaine Fasnacht**
71(1)

**Bob Steele Artistic Team**
28(4), 352(1)

**Bob Steele Hairdressers**
44(2), 70(2), 176(1)

**Brenda Petty**
33(1)

**Brian Nelson – Chazio's Salon**
214(1)

**Britnee Huffman – The Ohio Academy Paul Mitchell Partner School**
229(2)

**Brooke Barker – The Brown Aveda Institute**
203(1)

**Capitol School of Hairstyling**
218(2)

**Carmen Carmen Salon**
183(1), 189(2,10), 192(3), 204(1), 230(2), 326(1), 352(4)

**Carmen Carmen Salon & Spa Artistic Team**
28(2,5), 159(9), 171(1), 187(2), 302(1), 342(1)

**Casal's de'Spa & Salon**
192(5), 214(2)

**Ces't Moi Salon**
325(1)

**Cindy Freeze – Kathy Adams Salon**
201(1)

**Cloud 9 Hair Salon**
189(1), 215(5)

**Currie Hair, Skin & Nails**
183(4,7), 185(2), 193(5), 215(1)

**Debra Woods – By Grace Styling Salon**
214(5)

**Debra Woods – Total Connection**
175(5), 221(1)

**Denise Endsley – Sheer Professional Salon**
342(2)

**Dina Culotta – Ladies & Gentlemen Salon & Spa**
327(2)

**D.J. Moran-Grund International**
189(3)

**Duncan Lai**
36(1), 44(1), 183(6), 187(1)

**Elon Salon**
7(6), 192(2), 200(1), 211(3), 216(1), 230(4)

**Frederick's Salon & Spa**
170(6), 179(1), 189(7), 213(1), 219(4), 230(6), 325(3), 352(2), 548(1)

**Glynn Jones Salon**
9(1), 172(1), 189(4,8), 193(2), 325(2)

**Identity Salon & Spa**
762(5)

**Joanna Simms**
326(2)

**John Roberts Artistic Team**
20(1,3), 159(2,3,7,8), 344(1)

**Jean-Philippe pages for Oro Vision Magazine**
193(6)

**Jenniffer & Co.**
189(11)

**Jerry Oliver – Cloud 9 Salon**
214(3)

**Jessica Davison – Kathy Adams Salon**
201(2)

**Jessica Russo – The Ohio Academy Paul Mitchell Partner School**
327(1)

**Katresha Cartwright – A Classic Touch**
18(1)

**Keely Martinez – Tangles Salon**
183(2)

**Kenneth's Hair with Style**
181(2), 207(3)

**Kevin Hazzard – A Perfect You**
211(2)

**Kim Lane – Ladies & Gentlemen Salon & Spa**
7(1,3), 194(1), 195(1), 210(1)

**Kinyetta Ford – The Ohio Academy Paul Mitchell Partner School**
219(2)

**Kristen Ball – The Brown Aveda Institute**
35(2)

**Kristen Weber – The Brown Aveda Institute**
212(6)

**Ladies & Gentlemen Salon & Spa**
18(3), 174(1), 177(1), 181(5), 189(5), 196(1), 205(1), 219(5), 230(5), 343(2)

**Lauren Mesojedec – The Brown Aveda Institute**
209(2)

**Laurie Aubrey – Tangles Salon**
212(3)

**Leslie Cook – Tangles Salon**
7(5), 183(5), 203(2), 209(1), 228(2), 230(1)

# COSMETOLOGY / page(picture number)

**London Hair Salon**
32(3)

**Marijana Bosiljcic – Bella Capelli Sanctuario**
159(4)

**Metro Salon**
214(4)

**Michael & Michael Salon**
215(4)

**Michelle Azouz – Tangles Salon**
212(2)

**Paige Berry – The Brown Aveda Institute**
215(2)

**Pat Helmandollar – Savvy Salon & Spa**
228(1)

**Patrick Bradley – True Perfection**
186(1)

**Pat's Hair Design**
170(3), 193(4)

**Philip Battaglia – Focus Salon**
396(2)

**Randy Rick**
39(1), 180(1), 187(3), 218(3) 226, 335(1), 361(1)

**Robin Cook – Tangles Salon**
212(4), 219(1), 229(1)

**Ron Hawkins**
170(2), 172(3), 173(1), 178(1), 223(1)

**Rosa Lee – The Brown Aveda Institute**
230(3)

**Salon Visage Artistic Team**
200(2), 398(1)

**Salon 124**
193(1)

**Sammy Jones**
175(3)

**Sandra Carr – Sheer Professionals Salon**
201(4), 211(1)

**Sanita Elliot – Bradcon International**
189(6)

**Savvy Salon & Spa**
181(7), 187(4)

**Shannan DeTullio – Bella Capelli Sanctuario**
159(5)

**Sheer Professionals Salon**
191(3), 533(3)

**Shortino's Salon & Day Spa**
29(5), 159(6), 185(4), 212(5)

**Stacy Aquila – Ladies & Gentlemen Salon Spa**
302(2)

**Susan Snow**
219(3)

**Sylvia's Colour & Design**
177(2)

**Tangles Salon**
175(1,2), 183(3), 194(2), 201(3), 207(5), 208(4)

**The Aveda Institute – Rachael Plassemeyer**
28(6)

**The Brown Aveda Institute**
193(3)

**The Hair Benders International Design Team**
208(1), 502(3)

**The Hair Benders International Dream Team**
208(3), 302(3)

**The Oak Street Hair Group**
181(8), 185(1)

**The Ohio Academy**
1(3,4), 174(4), 175(4), 181(1), 188(1), 189(9), 200(3), 207(4), 215(3)

**Thresa Loudin – Sheer Professionals Salon**
159(1)

**Traci Johnson – Total Eclipse Day Spa**
3(2), 34(1)

**Urban Euphoria**
207(1)

**Ursula-Shear Creations**
172(2)

**Val Gecik – Attitudes A Salon**
302(4)

**Vanis Salon & Spa**
203(3)

**Vince D'Attilio**
18(4), 32(1), 171(3)

**Yellow Strawberry Global Salon**
192(1), 207(6), 216(2)

## Makeup Contributors:

**Alice Thiel**
3(3), 444, 445(1), 447(2), 456(2), 457, 467, 470(3), 472-475, 584(1)

**Amy Hoegler – Ladies & Gentlemen Salon & Spa**
181(5), 196(1), 230(5)

**Angel Krsacok – Ladies & Gentlemen Salon & Spa**
327(2)

**Angie Mamone – Cloud 9 Salon**
212(1), 214(3)

**Ashley Brown – Savvy Salon & Spa**
228(1)

**Betty MeKonnen – Tangles Salon**
7(5)

**Bianca Marcia – Attitudes A Salon**
20(2), 302(4)

**Carly Tomsic – Ladies & Gentlemen Salon & Spa**
302(2)

**Cindy Freeze – Kathy Adams Salon**
201(1)

**Chloe Gomez – The Ohio Academy Paul Mitchell Partner School**
229(2), 327(1)

**Darin Wright – The Hair Benders International Dream Team**
208(3), 302(3)

**Gina Patrice – Sheer Professional Salon**
159(1), 342(2)

**Gina Payne – Focus Salon**
396(2)

**Homa Safar – The Aveda Institute**
231(2)

**Jody Keeney – Ladies & Gentlemen Salon & Spa**
7(1,3), 194(1), 195(1), 210(1)

**Melisa McDonald – Kathy Adams Salon**
201(2), 218(1)

**Suzanne Ferreri – Casal's de Spa & Salon**
214(2)

## Nail Contributors:

**Lesa Beamer**
180(3), 181(3,6), 622(7-10), 676(1,2), 677, 685(5), 689(1), 709(1)

**Nikki Oxley at** funkyfingers001@yahoo.co.uk
180(2)

**Nirmala Modi**
181(4), 622(5,6,11), 660(3,5), 677(4), 695(1), 699(1)

**Trang Nguyen/Odyssey Nail Systems**
1(1), 3(4), 7(2,4), 9(3), 34(3), 170(4), 171(4), 174(3), 177(3), 179(2), 190(3-5), 207(2), 231(3), 296(2), 614(3), 620(2,3), 621(1,2), 622(1), 629(1), 643(1,2), 652(1), 654(1), 655(1), 658(1), 660(2,4,6), 661(2), 666(1), 668-669, 670(1), 671-673, 675, 680-681, 685(1-4), 687(1), 691(1), 697(1), 703(1), 705(1), 707(1), 711(1), 713(1), 715(1), 717(1), 719(1), 736(2), 759(1,2)

"A special thanks to all the professionals who shared their artwork, products and scientific information to educate and inspire future cosmetologists. Your photographs demonstrate the variety of effects that can be achieved through creativity and dedication!"

# PHOTOGRAPHY / page(picture number)

**Amber Products**
78(1), 135(1), 422(1), 445(2,4,5), 448(1,4), 449(1,2), 450(1,3,4), 451(1-3), 453(2), 454, 455(1), 456(1), 458(1), 464(1), 465(1), 469(3), 470(1), 471(1), 488(1), 489(3), 495(1), 497(1,2), 499(2), 500(1), 501, 502(1,2), 506(1), 507(1), 508(1), 510(2,4), 511(1,2), 519(1,2), 582(2,3)

**Andres Aquino**
68(1), 762(1-4)

**Belvedere USA Corporation**
447(1), 466(1), 468(1,2), 469(1,2), 470(2), 471(2)

**Berks Foot Ankle Surgical Associates, Inc.**
**Dr. Kevin T. Naugle, DPM**
600(2), 614(1)

**Breathe CLEAN, LLC** www.breatheclean.com
95(2)

**Brion Price Photography**
172(5)

**Burmax Company, Inc.**
238(1), 239(1), 445(3), 448(2,3), 450(2), 451(4,5), 506(2), 582(1), 624(1,2), 625(2), 626(1), 633(1,3), 638(1) 639(4), 661(1)

**Charlene Products, Inc.**
163(3-6)

**Chip Foust for** www.universalsalons.com
3(2), 18(1), 34(1), 172(2), 175(5), 211(2), 214(5), 221(1)

**Clean & Easy**
489(1,2), 499(1,3), 500(2-4), 509(1), 510(1,3), 511(3)

**Courtesy of Softsheen-Carson® Professional**
348(1,2), 349(1,2), 355(1)

**Danderm**
77(1), 80(3), 82(1), 150, 155(1), 162(1), 164, 165, 166(1-3), 167, 343(1), 356(1), 396(1), 414(1), 422(2-5), 423-433, 434(1,2), 435(1), 436(1), 437(1,2), 438-440, 441(1-4), 494(1), 514, 600(1), 601(1-3), 602(1), 606, 607(1), 608(1,3), 609, 610(1,2), 611(2-4), 612(1,2,4), 613, 614(4), 615(1),

**Edward Tytel**
33(1)

**e.l.f. Cosmetics** www.eyeslipsface.com
3(1), 9(4), 526(1), 527(1), 532(2), 533(2), 535(1,2,4), 536(2,4), 537(1), 539(2,5), 543(2), 544(1-3), 545(1,2), 546(3), 547(3), 550(1,3), 552(2), 553(3), 554(2), 556(1), 560(1), 562, 567, 578(2,4)

**EnVogue Lashes LLC**
526(2,3), 578(1,3), 579(1,4), 581(1,2)

**European Touch** www.europeantouch.com
663(1), 664(1,2)

**Flexx-Rap, Inc.**
90(1), 625(3)

**Flowery Beauty Products, Inc.**
622(2,4), 633(2,5), 634(2), 642(2), 645(1)

**Hollywood Beauty Supply**
662(2), 663(2)

**ImagiNail Corporation**
9(5), 170(1), 174(2), 190 (2), 191(4), 192(4), 207(7), 527(3), 530(3), 532(1), 566(1), 620(1), 623(2)

**Iredale Mineral Cosmetics, Ltd. – Kevin Sprague**
1(2), 191(2), 249(1), 527(2,4), 530(1), 531(3), 533(1,4), 535(3,5), 536(3), 538, 539 (1,3,4), 540, 541, 542(1), 543(1), 544(4), 546(1,2,4-6), 547(1,2,4), 548(2-4), 549, 550(2,4-6), 551, 552(1), 553(1,2), 554(1,3), 555, 556(2), 736(1)

**Jack Cutler Photography**
71(1), 219(3)

**Jonathan Martin**
27(4), 29(2)

**King Research, Copyright 2005 King Research, Inc.**
76(1), 84(1), 86(1), 87(1), 91(1), 239(2), 255(1), 647(1)

**Modern Solutions, Inc.**
88(1), 95(1), 627(1)

**NovaLash Eyelash Extensions by Sophia Navarro**
579(2,3,5,6), 580(1)

**Odyssey Nail Systems & Tokyo Fashion Week**
9(6), 231(1,4)

**OPI**
34(2), 191(1), 296(1), 623(1), 632(1), 640(2), 642(3,4), 654(5), 656(1,2), 657(3), 658(2), 661(3) 662(1),

**Paul Spinak**
175(3)

**Qosmedix**
77(2), 86(2), 391(1), 534(1), 625(1), 629(2), 638(2), 654(4)

**Regis/Paul Finkelstein**
35(1)

**Robert Sargent**
44(3), 70(1), 171(2,5), 182(1)

**Sani-Care Salon Products, Inc.**
www.sanicareonline.com
89(1), 91(2)

**Sarkli-Repêchage, Ltd.**
453(1), 542(2)
**All photographs© 1980-2008 Sarkli-Repêchage Ltd., All Rights Reserved.**

**Sean Sharp**
186(1)

**Silk Touch Nail Files PWAI, LLC**
http://www.zipafoil.com
633(4)

**Spilo Worldwide**
86(3), 537(2), 626(2), 628(1), 638(3,4), 639(1,3), 645(3,4), 654(2)

**Star Nail International**
190(1), 536(1), 622(3), 627(2), 629(3,4), 634(1,3), 636(1), 639(2), 640(1), 642(1,5), 643(3), 643(3), 645(2), 648(1), 651(1,3), 654(3), 655(2), 657(1,2,4), 659(1), 660(1), 682(1)

**The Procter and Gamble Company**
160(1), 163(1,2)

**Tom Carson**
1(3,4), 7(1,3,5,6), 9(1), 170(3,6), 171(1), 172(1), 174(1,4), 175(1,2,4), 177(1,2), 179(1), 181(1,2,5,7,8), 183(1-5,7,8), 185, 187(4), 188(9), 189(2,4,5,7-11), 191(3), 192(1-3,6), 193(1-5), 194, 195(1), 196, 200(1,3), 201(1-3), 203(2,3), 204(1), 205(1), 207(1,3-6), 208(2,4), 209, 210, 211(3), 212, 213, 214(2-4), 215, 216(1,2), 218(1), 219(1,2,4,5), 228(1,2), 229(1,2), 230, 325(1-4), 326(1,2), 327(1,2), 352(2,4), 396(2), 533(3), 548(1)
**All photographs© 2009 Tom Carson, All Rights Reserved.**

**Tom Carson**
20(1-3), 28(2,4-6), 29(5), 35(2), 159, 187(2), 200(2), 201(4), 203(1), 208(3), 231(2), 302(1-4), 342(1,2), 344(1), 352(1,3), 398(1), 446(1)
**All photographs© 2007 Tom Carson, All Rights Reserved.**

**Tom Carson**
18(3,4), 32(3), 70(2), 149(1), 176(1), 189(1), 192(5), 208(1), 211(1), 214(1), 343(2), 502(3), 762(5)
**All photographs© 2003 Tom Carson, All Rights Reserved.**

**Tom Carson**
44(2)
**All photographs© 2002 Tom Carson, All Rights Reserved.**

**William Marvy Company**
89(2), 239(3), 626(3)

**WR Medical Electronics Co.**
650, 651(2,4)

**YongFeng Enterprises, Ltd.**
89(3)

## Illustrator:

**Laura Gelsomini**
18(2), 19(1,2), 21 (1-3), 22(1,2), 23, 24(1), 25(1), 27(1-3,5-7), 28(1,3), 29(1,3,4), 30(1), 31, 32(2), 33(2-5), 35(3), 58, 59, 80(1,2), 170(5), 187(5), 197-199, 303, 345, 441(2), 461(1,2), 463(1,2), 465(2), 491, 492(1), 528(1,2), 529, 530(2,4,5), 531(1,2,4), 570, 571, 573(1), 576, 577, 608(2), 610(3), 611(1), 612(3), 614(2), 742

# Foreword ...

**Sir Isaac Newton once said, "If I have been able to see further, it was only because I stood on the shoulders of giants."** This profound statement represents one of the guiding principles of the Certified Learning in Cosmetology® (CLiC) system. There is much to be learned and discovered by "standing on the shoulders of giants." It is only by studying the discoveries and accomplishments of leaders who came before us that we can prepare for the future.

**The CLiC system provides a broad cosmetology education with a focus on three key areas:**
1- A basic cosmetology foundation
2- An introduction to artistic concepts and visual inspiration to nurture creativity
3- Effective interpersonal, sales and retail techniques

**Although the professional cosmetology industry is continually evolving, the fundamentals remain unchanged.** The basis of cosmetology is an understanding of human biology combined with scientific and mathematical theories used to create desired results. Building on the basic concepts of cosmetology, we explore artistic and visual inspiration in order to develop and nurture creativity. Throughout the foundational and artistic learning process, successful interpersonal sales and retail skills are introduced and practiced. These skills are paramount to the personal satisfaction and financial success of the professional cosmetologist.

**CLiC is a visually stimulating and inspirational system, focused on preparing students to be salon-ready upon completion of their studies.** Master hairdesigner and international award winner Randy Rick is the creative force behind the revolutionary CLiC system. Always a step ahead, Mr. Rick developed the CLiC system of learning to elevate the artistic, practical and marketable skills of today's students. Through the CLiC program, he shares his vast international knowledge and experience with you ... the professional cosmetologist of the future!

CLiC to a dynamic future in cosmetology!

CLiC™ INTERNATIONAL

# The CLiC Education Team ...

The CLiC Education Team represents over 100 years of combined cosmetology and nail industry education, experience and wisdom. The team includes international award winners, top educators, stylists, salon and beauty school owners, operations managers and owners/operators of highly successful beauty industry businesses.

## Randy Rick
### - artist, teacher, champion, and creator of the CLiC System

Having won more than 75 national and international honors and awards, Randy Rick is one of America's most awarded hairdesigners. He is also the former owner of a beauty school, as well as full-service beauty salons. This industry background, combined with his artistic genius, makes Mr. Rick expertly qualified to share his educational vision for the future of the beauty industry.

**Here are just a few of the many national and international honors awarded to Randy Rick:**

**America's Cup Championship**
- * Gold Medal Evening Style
- * Gold Medal Consumer Day Style
- * Silver Medal Progressive Style
- * Overall High Point Scorer

**N.C.A. Wahl Clipper Cutting Championship**
- * Gold Medal

**National and International Awards**
- High Point Scorer – U.S.A. World Team, Spain
- International World Supreme Champion, New York
- International Team Champion, New York
- World Wig Champion, Brussels, Belgium
- Oscar d'Elegance, Brussels, Belgium
- Vienna Cup, Vienna, Austria
- Midwest Gold Trophy Champion
- Coiffure Creation Competition, Hawaii
- Three-time Diamond Shield Champion
- Grand Master Champion
- Golden Curl Champion
- New York Gold Champion
- Mid-south Gold Trophy Champion
- National Beauty Show Champion

**U.S.A. Midwest Beauty Show**
- * Grand Prix Founder's Award
- * Gold Medal Champion

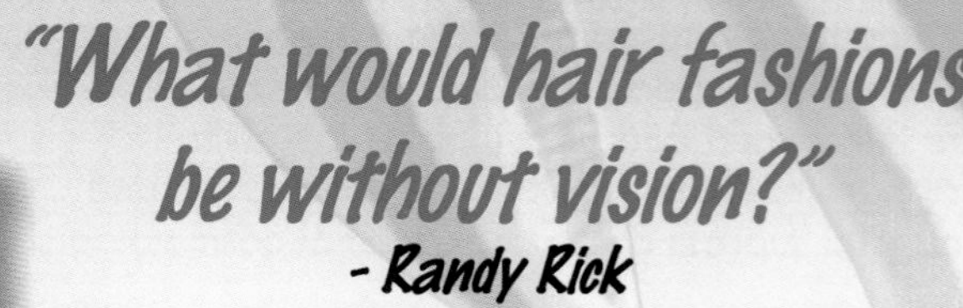

"What would hair fashions be without vision?"
- Randy Rick


**International Beauty Show, New York**
- * Gold Medal Day and Evening Styles
- * Gold Medal Team Championship

**Hair World Coiffure Championship Washington, D.C.**
- * Gold Medal Ladies' Consumer Fashion
- * Gold Medal Ladies' Hair by Night
- * Overall Gold Medal Winner - National Vera Slater Coiffure Championship

**N.C.A. Team Trainer for U.S.A. World Cup Team**

**Two Time N.C.A./U.S.A. World Team Member**

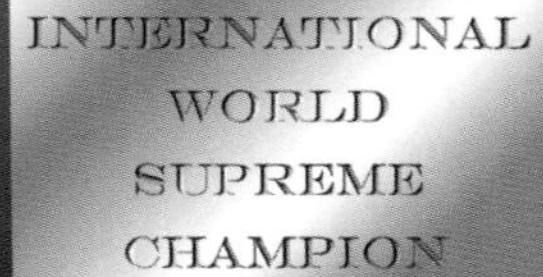


RANDY RICK

# Introduction to CLiC...

**You are about to begin an exciting journey into the world of cosmetology.** The Certified Learning in Cosmetology® (CLiC) system will be your road map, leading you to realize the rewards of becoming a successful, professional cosmetologist.

**The CLiC system is designed to enhance fundamental cosmetology education by incorporating artistic inspiration and successful salon service and retail skills.** The learning modules cannot possibly cover all cosmetology art fashions, but will always encourage freedom of expression and innovation to adapt to future trends.

**This revolutionary system focuses on meeting your educational needs with a solid, competency-based cosmetology curriculum.** Each CLiC module is designed to develop manual dexterity, professional perception, tactile sensitivity and the artistic vision used in the industry. Each module will take you through our competency-based learning system, which will progress from simple to complex skill levels, utilizing the methods of practice, experimentation and testing.

**The CLiC educational system is presented in individual learning modules, each consisting of a complete program.** The module system enables you to focus on individual disciplines, by offering courses for certified specialization in each field. This ensures the opportunity to learn and develop the skills needed for a rewarding and profitable career in the cosmetology field of your choice.

For additional information, contact:

CLiC INTERNATIONAL®
396 Pottsville/Saint Clair Highway
Pottsville, PA 17901 USA
1.800.207.5400 USA & Canada
001.570.429.4216 International
1.570.429.4252 Fax
info@clicusa.com
www.clicusa.com

# The Cast of Characters . . .

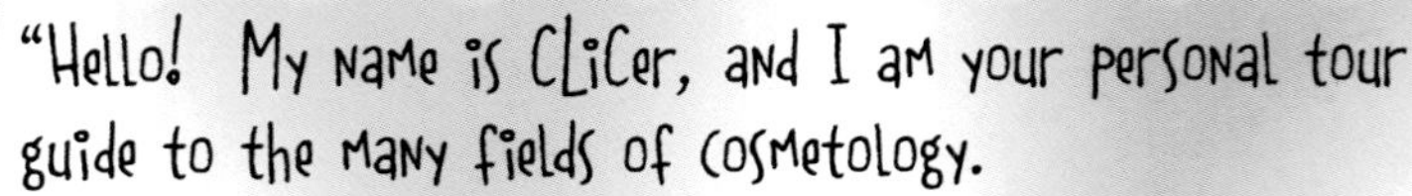

"Hello! My name is CLiCer, and I am your personal tour guide to the many fields of cosmetology.

In this book, we will be studying the arts of Cosmetology. I will lead and encourage you as we explore the many facets of hair-, nail- and skin-care. I will give you tips, ideas and reminders for each of the topics to assist you during the learning process.

Welcome! I am excited to have you join me for this journey of learning."

## Regulatory Alert

Whenever you see the **Regulatory Alert** icon, it will remind you and your instructor to check governmental regulations about the subject on the page. The rules and regulations for cosmetology vary according to geographic location. Place a sticker, from the back of the book, over the shadow if there are governmental regulations that must be followed in your area.

## The 3Rs

At the conclusion of your services there are three important steps you should consistently follow. **Retail** professional products to your customers for home maintenance. **Re-book** future appointments to encourage regular visits. Ask for **referrals** to broaden your customer base. By following the 3Rs they will improve your income and profitability as a professional cosmetologist.

## CLiCer's Sales Pointers

As you will learn throughout this book, selling and financial skills will be just as important to your success in the salon as your actual knowledge and skills in the field of cosmetology services. Whenever you see this icon with CLiCer's hand, pay special attention to the **sales pointers** you are given. Combining sales skills with cosmetology art skills will create a dynamic force for your salon success!

# Introduction to Cosmetology ...

Today, cosmetology artists are exploring new frontiers in learning. As the world becomes increasingly high-tech and a broader range of international services and concepts of cosmetology techniques are being developed, a wider representation of information must be included in our educational manuals.

We believe the "CLiC Visual Learning Concept" is the new language of cosmetology education.

**Cosmetology is a global career** and requires a universal foundation of education to express a greater representation of the new arts, multicultural techniques and modern technologies. This strong educational foundation will help guide you on a journey full of life-long learning and exploration, which will ultimately equal to your success. Today's educated consumers expect the very latest of diverse services in order to meet the demands of their active lifestyle. Creativity, being the cornerstone of our industry, is only fostered when new foundations of education are employed.

**It is our desire to stimulate your creative abilities,** as well as establish balance between the theoretical and practical information required for the state board examination with the latest technologies in the cosmetology industry.

**Cosmetology is a universal art** that enhances an individual's appearance thereby creating a positive experience to those you serve.

**And finally, we should all take responsibility** and play our part to help save our Earth by making wise **"Go Green"** choices to facilitate improvement to our environment. Using products containing "natural" ingredients, purchasing recycled materials and/or saving energy by installing cost efficient light bulbs are some of the avenues used in making this an environmentally safe place to live.

*To the advancement of cosmetology -*
*May I wish you all the very best*
*in your new career!*
*Randy Rick!*

# Table of Contents . . .

## 1 HISTORY OF COSMETOLOGY 17



## 2 PROFESSIONAL SKILLS 41



## 3 SALON SAFETY 75



## 4 ANATOMY 97

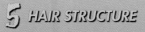

# Table of Contents . . .

## 5 HAIR STRUCTURE 141



## 6 ART PRINCIPLES 169



## 7 HAIR AND SCALP TREATMENTS 233



## 8 COSMETOLOGY CHEMISTRY 277

# Table of Contents ...

# Table of Contents ...

# Table of Contents ...

## 17 NAIL TREATMENTS 619



## 18 THE BUSINESS OF BEAUTY 721

"We have a lot of material to cover ... so let us get started! I will be your personal tour guide as you study, learn and practice the skills needed for a successful and rewarding career as a professional cosmetologist."

barber beehive

cultural fashion

invention

pompadour

rouge

1

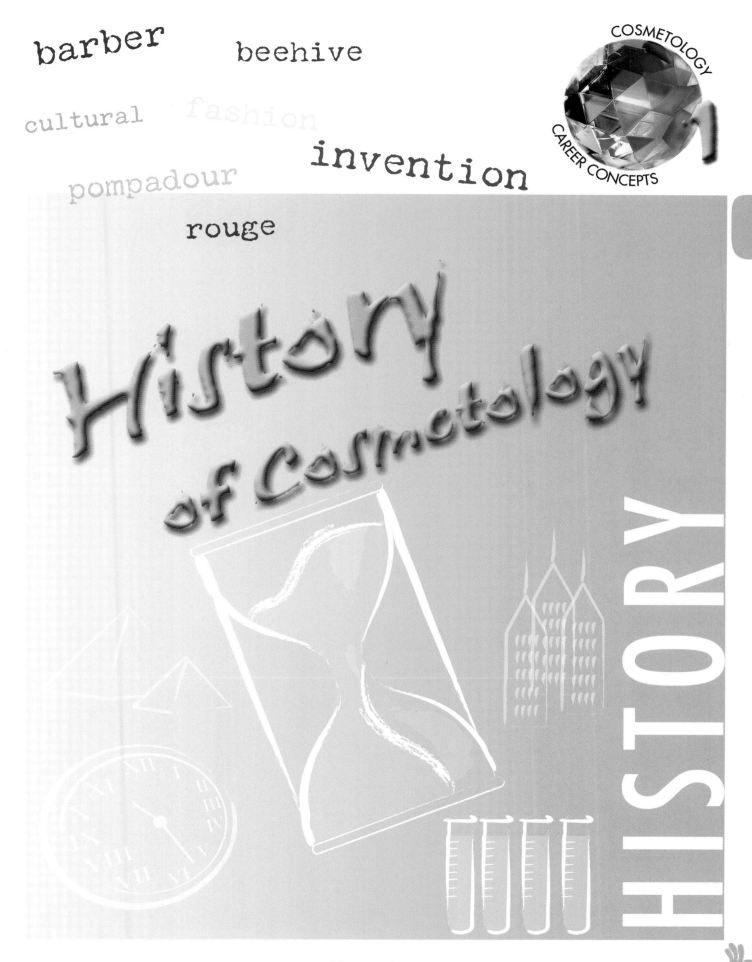

# History of Cosmetology

HISTORY

# Terminology . . .

*Did you ever hear the terms listed below? These words were used in the beauty industry when it was just beginning... the industry that became the foundation for hairdesigners of today. Some of the terms have been rooted forever in our minds, and are often still being used.*



**Bangs** is a term used to describe the hair along the frontal hairline when it is cut to a certain length and rests on the forehead. Today this term is appropriately referred to as the **"fringe area."**

**Beauty Parlor** is a term that originated in the 1900s for a place of business where hairdressers or stylists provided hair and cosmetic services to customers.

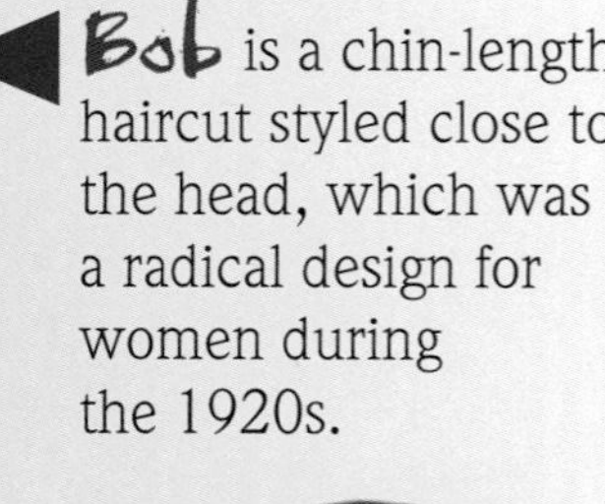

**Bob** is a chin-length haircut styled close to the head, which was a radical design for women during the 1920s.

**Bouffant** describes the hairstyles of the late 1950s to early '60s that had great fullness and height.

**Chignon** is a selected amount of hair that is twisted or rolled along the perimeter of the nape or positioned in back of the head as a bun.

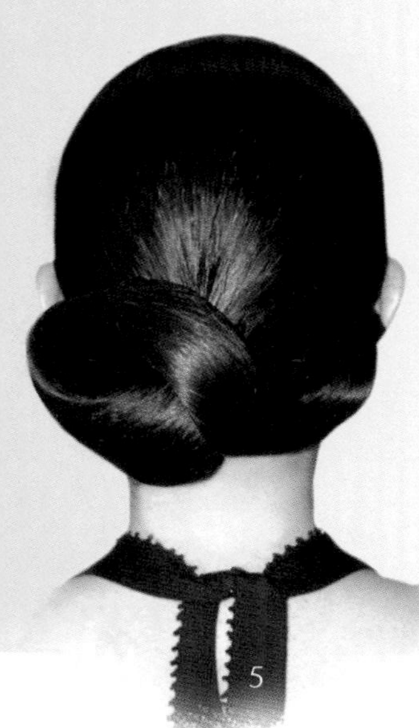

# Terminology . . .

**Finger Waves** are a series of ovaloid shapes created either vertically, horizontally or diagonally into the hair in alternating directions.

**Hairdresser**, comparable to today's sylist, is a cosmetologist that performs hair-care services such as cutting, designing, perming and coloring in a licensed facility.

**Pageboy** is a hairstyle that was popular in the 1960s and '70s, where the hair is cut chin-length and styled with the ends curled toward the face in a series of c-curls.

1

**Shag** is a hairstyle of the 1970s, where the hair is cut in multiple layers creating a "feathered" appearance when styled.

2

**Unisex** refers to a fashion or an establishment that is suitable for both females and males.

1

# History of Hair . . .

"The hair is the richest ornament of women."
Martin Luther (1483-1546) German Theologian

Hair has always played a significant role in our lives, whether used for **protection** as in the Stone Age or to make a ***fashion statement*** as in the Victorian Age. Hair is a valuable asset and throughout time has taken on various forms, textures and colors. There are endless possibilities with hairdesigning and they continue to multiply as we move forward through each generation. With changes brought about by technological advances and cultural impact along with the influence of fashion, ***the beauty industry will continue to evolve and inspire us.***

## Cultural Influences

As early as research will take you, hair has been a central cultural representation of us. Hairstyles from different cultures were **designed to portray a person's age, social or marital status, religious beliefs, tribal affiliation or vocation.** Hairstyles have symbolized aspects of civilization such as cornrows representing cultivation, or hair treatment reflecting mourning (sometimes the dead were honored by shaving off or tearing out all the hair from the head, or by ignoring grooming hair-care altogether). Marital status was depicted by wearing veils or ornamental jewels, or for some, wearing elaborate wigs. Religious beliefs were sometimes manifested through hair by requiring the growth of long side locks or facial hair, or shaving the head completely.

# History of Hair . . .

## Victorian Era 1800s

During this period, women smoothed their hair with oils and styled it in loose elegant curls with short bangs. Hairnets were used to encase the curls. Styling by **a hairdresser** became popular with the fashionable hairstyle having a center part with curls situated beside a **coiled chignon** (chi-gnon), and sometimes adorned with flowers. Men wore their hair short accented with some type of facial hair such as a moustache, sideburns or a beard.

## Late 1800s

During the late 1800s, hair was considered **a woman's "crowning glory"** and was rarely ever cut with the exception of when someone was suffering from a serious illness. Sometimes the hair was worn naturally or with loose curls or in a large loop. By the **1890s, the pompadour** (pom-pa-dour) became an optional hairstyle, where the hair was swept back from the forehead and piled high on top of the head. Parisian hairdresser **Marcel Grateau** introduced hot heated tongs to create loose waves around the head (the marcel wave). This came close to imitating a woman's natural curl. Pale skin was considered a mark of diplomacy and makeup was frowned upon with the exception of actresses that wore rouge and powder.

1

2

3

Marcel Grateau

1

## Edwardian Era

### 1900s – 1910s

This period of time was often referred to as the **"Beautiful Age"** due to a crest of luxury living for a privileged few. The **"Gibson Girl"** was a popular hairstyle for many different types of women because it showcased confidence and independence. Hair was loosely finger waved and combed over an existing piece of hair or hairpiece, which was situated on top of the head. The remaining length of hair was then coiled and secured onto the hairpiece.

Many new innovative hairstyles were born in this era due to the **invention of electricity and hair-care equipment.** To obtain a youthful appearance, ladies would discreetly purchase face creams and rouge from beauty salons.

# History of Hair ...

*1910s - 1920s*

During **World War I,** women went to work in artillery plants to help the war effort. For safety and practical reasons the women wore their hair off the shoulders in **soft waves tied back with a scarf or headband.**

Young girls of this era usually wore their hair down, flowing over their shoulders. **Cosmetic products** became increasingly popular with the availability of makeup for home use. It became **socially acceptable to wear rouge, powder and lipstick** as long as it was cosmetically pleasing for the woman.

# 1920s The Roaring Twenties

This era opened with an air of freedom sporting the **close-fitting bob, the birth of jazz and an increased demand for cosmetics.** Women's ability to vote and earn money brought on a new independence and attitude that would drastically change their views. The **"bob" hairstyle was a radical new move** that represented the independence and convenience of the new-found woman. The bob was cut to contour a woman's face, and was colored to be individually flattering. This free-spirited 1920s woman also accentuated her facial features by wearing powder, deep red or orange rouge and lipstick and crafted thin, sloping black eyebrows.

## 1930s - The Great Depression

The bob started to grow out in length creating more versatility in hairdesign. A **soft, feminine style was favored by most women consisting of finger waves** throughout the entire head with pin curls along the perimeter of the forehead. Movie stars such as **Jean Harlow and Greta Garbo** had great influence in the hair and fashion trends of this time along with the effects resulting from constant modifications on perming and coloring products and techniques. Mothers even had their daughter's hair curled to imitate **Shirley Temple's famous "banana" curls.** Eyebrows were tweezed into fine lines using an eyebrow pencil for detail; red or orange lipstick was applied creating full lips; red or deep coral polish was applied to long fingernails; and natural eyelashes were curled or false lashes were applied.



1

PIN CURL

## 1940s

In this era women imitated the hairstyles of movies stars much like in the 1930s, but were also influenced by the **World War II pin-up girls**. Women wore their hair **shoulder length. Rollers** were predominately the method of choice to set the hair and hairnets were used to keep the style in place. Women either parted their hair on the side or in the middle, allowing it to lay flat or with a slight wave. Some women would wear their hair in a **roll around the nape to the ears** leaving the **bangs** exposed at the forehead. Makeup application was minimal due to the war and shortage of supply, but when worn, rouge was a natural rose or pink color; eyebrows were naturally defined; multiple red shades were used for lipstick to create soft full lips; and nails were polished in dark red or plum.

## 1950s

A favored style for men at this time was hair **greased back with long sideburns** and dovetails that tapered to the nape of the neck. Another style for men was the short, tightly cropped **crew cut**. For women, a popular style was the hair waved throughout the crown area with a series of defined curls along the perimeter and a small flat bang situated along forehead. The teenage girl – with her poodle skirt and saddle shoes – wore the simple but stylish ponytail along with pink lipstick.

Weekly salon appointments were made for women to maintain **heavily sprayed sets** consisting of rollers and pin curls. Hair was pulled up or teased into a cone shape in a popular bouffant hairstyle called the **"beehive"** that could be worn for a full week without shampooing the hair. Makeup was applied heavier than in previous eras with emphasis placed on the eyes and lips by lining them with color.

## 1960s

During the **"Rock 'n' Roll" and "Hippie" era** ... a whole new persona formed for both men and women characterized by hair **grown long and natural**, untouched by any chemical product. Men allowed their sideburns and beards to grow out. In a statement of pride for their heritage, African-Americans wore their hair naturally curly in a revival of the **natural afro style**. Another influence over the hair and fashion industry was First Lady **Jacqueline Kennedy, and her "flipped-up" slightly full hairstyle.** The **bouffant** was still in fashion from the late 1950s, but the hair was cut short in the nape and remained long in the crown area to provide the length necessary to re-create the beehive. The **"pageboy"** was another favored bouffant design with the hair cut chin-length and styled with the ends curled toward the face in a series of c-curls.

# History of Hair . . .

## 1970s

The new rage of the 1970s was making its mark with a **feathered, layered cut** known as the **"wingback or shag style."** The hair was cut in progressive lengths and styled away from the face. Actress **Farrah Fawcett** was known for bringing this style to the forefront. As **"wash and wear"** hair and precision cutting impacted hairdesign choices, the first **unisex (male & female)** salons were opened, along with unisex hairstyles. The **"pageboy"** continued to be favored, but the hair was smoothed and styled to naturally move toward the face. In the later part of this generation, **spiked, punk styles** in fluorescent colors appeared in London and New York along with the tightly cropped **pixie**, a short layered design.

## 1980s

**BIG hair was the rage!** Instead of smooth, straight hair, styling products such as mousse, gel and hairspray were used to create big, messy hairdesigns. **Michael Jackson and Madonna** were the influences for women and men in this generation. **Spiral perms and reverse curl techniques** jumpstarted a permanent wave revolution. What is known as the **five o'clock shadow — short hair stubbles** over men's faces as a result of infrequent shaving — soon became popular. The **buzz or clipper cut** also known as the **"flat top"** with short, clean lines was popular and easy to maintain for men. For African-Americans, the **soft curl permanent,** which chemically altered the natural curl into larger more manageable curls or waves, was the favored hairstyle.

# History of Hair ...

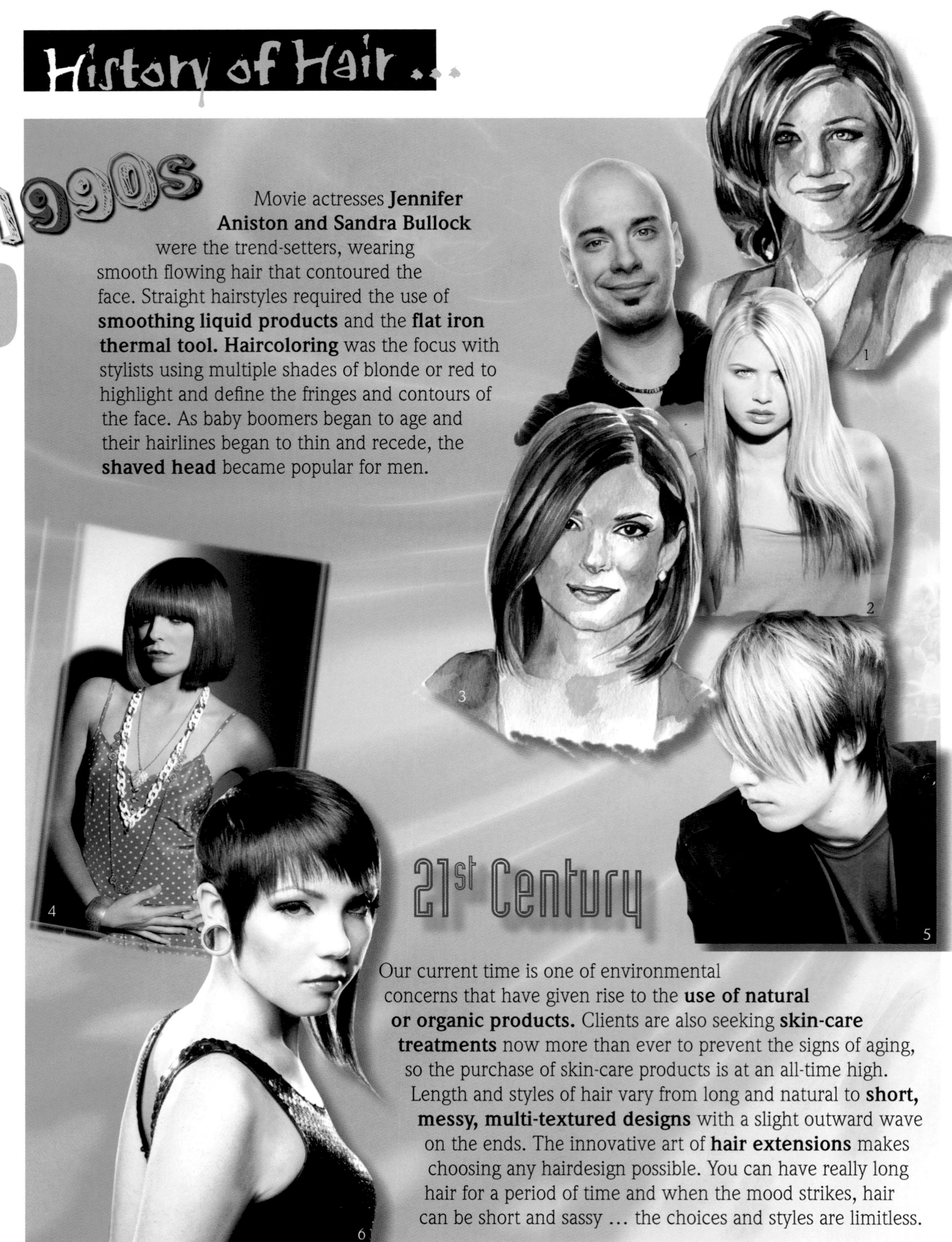

## 1990s

Movie actresses **Jennifer Aniston and Sandra Bullock** were the trend-setters, wearing smooth flowing hair that contoured the face. Straight hairstyles required the use of **smoothing liquid products** and the **flat iron thermal tool. Haircoloring** was the focus with stylists using multiple shades of blonde or red to highlight and define the fringes and contours of the face. As baby boomers began to age and their hairlines began to thin and recede, the **shaved head** became popular for men.

1

2

3

4

5

6

## 21st Century

Our current time is one of environmental concerns that have given rise to the **use of natural or organic products.** Clients are also seeking **skin-care treatments** now more than ever to prevent the signs of aging, so the purchase of skin-care products is at an all-time high. Length and styles of hair vary from long and natural to **short, messy, multi-textured designs** with a slight outward wave on the ends. The innovative art of **hair extensions** makes choosing any hairdesign possible. You can have really long hair for a period of time and when the mood strikes, hair can be short and sassy ... the choices and styles are limitless.

# History of Hair . . .

## Future

The beauty industry is a **highly competitive field made up of professionals** that want to succeed. Anything is achievable for the future as **new products are being formulated, new trend-setting designs** are being developed and ideas for building a **successful business** are being generated. Keep an open and flexible mind and always be a step ahead to imagine and create the newest hairstyle trend, technique or product.

# Industry Development ...

***The beauty industry's remarkable growth has been achieved due to the numerous innovators of today and of the last century and their ingenious ability and determination. It is through these people that the hair-care industry has developed and advanced into a multi-billion-dollar global business!***

In order to instill a degree of professionalism in the beauty industry and create communication amongst fellow hairdressers, a business journal called **"The American Hairdresser" was started in 1877 by Charles Ossenbrunner.** The name of the magazine would later change to "**American Salon**." In its earliest years, the pamphlet offered the hairdresser business guidelines, but later it became the journal for the most current hair trends and education.

**In 1880, a German hairdresser named Franz Ströher** designed wigs and toupees from human hair and began to sell them. This formed the foundation for the development of **The Wella Corporation,** a haircolor, perm and hair products manufacturer still operating today.

The **National Cosmetology Association,** formerly known as The Hairdealers Association, **was formed in 1888**. Three years later a cosmetology academy opened its doors to the public in Chicago, and was the **first educational school of hairdressing**. Also at this time, beauty expert **Martha Matilda Harper** opened the first combination beauty parlor and factory, which manufactured her hair tonic (shampoo). She was also the first to open a franchise shop in another location.

Around **1905, Madam C.J. Walker, an African-American, was selling her "Wonderful Hair Grower"** products door-to-door. In 1911, she built her own factory to mass produce her products and opened her own beauty parlors and school in 1916.

Madam C.J. Walker

# Industry Development . . .

Max Factor Sr.

At the turn of the 20th century, salons were referred to as **"beauty parlors or toilet parlors"** and the cost of a shampoo and style service was $1.25. Opening a beauty establishment was becoming a growing trend and a smart choice for people interested in making some fast money. Thousands of new products, techniques, equipment and services were being discovered by multiple entrepreneurs and innovators marketing to hair parlors around the country. **Max Factor Sr.** introduced his **cosmetic line** of rouges and face creams at the St. Louis World's Fair in 1904.

In 1907, **Eugene Schueller**, a French pharmacist, developed the first synthetic hair dye called "Aureole" color and later formed **L'Oreal USA**, a subsidiary of L'Oreal Group.

A German hairdresser named **Karl Nessler in 1906** created the electric permanent wave machine to produce permanent curls in the hair. **Helena Rubinstein** opened **her cosmetic business** in New York in 1912. Around this time, styling stations with mirrors, moveable manicure tables and adjustable barber chairs were produced to accommodate the hairdresser and client within beauty establishments.

Karl Nessler

Leo J. Wahl

The **International Beauty Show** got its start in 1917 as a showcase for the **newest style trends and cosmetic products** of that time. **Leo J. Wahl** developed the electromagnetic hair clipper and applied for a patent on October 14, 1919. He began to manufacture the clipper at the Wahl Manufacturing Company. In 1921, he received his patent for the clipper and renamed the manufacturing plant the **Wahl Clipper Corporation.**

# Industry Development . . .

**Numerous innovators brought forth their new revelations for the American consumer:**

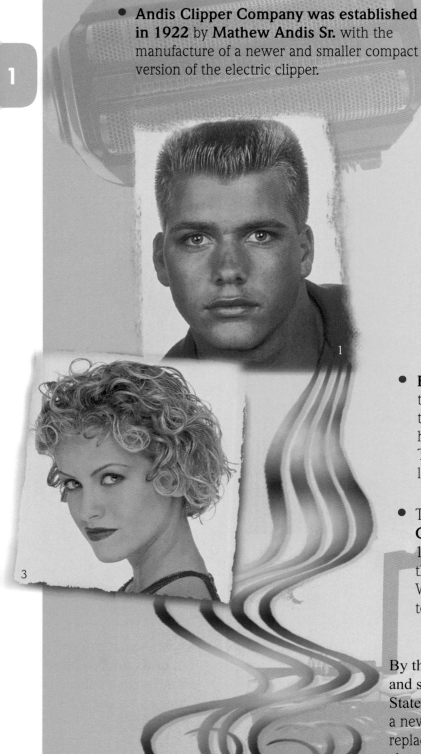

- **Andis Clipper Company was established in 1922** by **Mathew Andis Sr.** with the manufacture of a newer and smaller compact version of the electric clipper.

1

2

Mathew Andis Sr.

3

- **Belvedere**, a manufacturing company that produced a new shampoo sink that was comfortable for the client to rest his or her head upon, opened in 1927. The company is still operating today as the largest salon furniture manufacturer.

- The National Mineral Co., founded by **Gerald S. Gidwitz and Louis Stein** in 1927, produced personal care products. As the company's success increased after World War II, the firm changed its name to **"Helene Curtis."**

By the 1930s, **Wella** was manufacturing and selling its products in the United States. The **Zotos Company** developed a new method of permanent waving that replaced the use of electricity, with a chemical heat that produced curls or waves.

# Industry Development...

**Larry Gelb,** a chemist from New York, introduced a new European permanent haircolor called **Clairol** to the United States. Brothers **Charles and Joseph Revson,** along with chemist **Charles Lachman,** created nail enamel like no other thus building the foundation for their company called **Revlon**, a manufacturer of cosmetics and personal care products sold around the world.

Taking care of the hands, nails and feet through manicures and pedicures was becoming a profitable segment of business for the hairdresser. Manufacturers were **marketing multiple shades (popular color was red) of nail lacquer** through promotional ads in magazines or posters located in salon windows or on walls. Manufacturers became proficient at using movie stars' images to increase their product sales. **Beauty parlors were visited by women whereas barber shops serviced the men.**

Fashion trends were becoming increasingly influenced by hairstyles and vice versa. The improved, non-clogging valve of the **aerosol hairspray can** was developed by **Robert H. Abplanal** in 1953, which increased sales and became a necessity in cementing the hairstyles of this era.

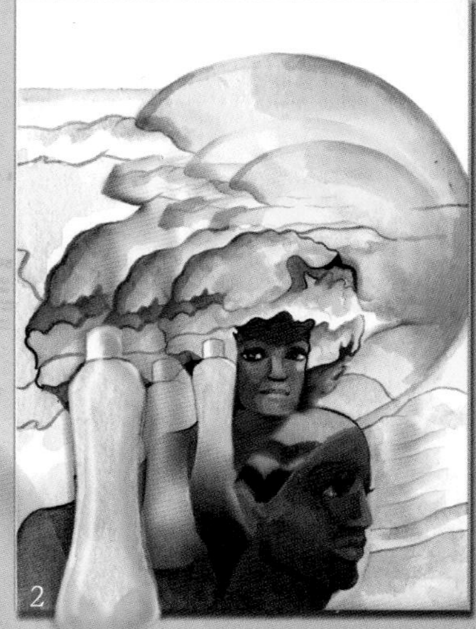

*The **Johnson Products Company**, opened by **George Johnson in 1954**, developed **the first hair relaxers for African-American hair**.*

**The Redken Laboratories was founded in 1960 by Paula Kent**, an actress, and **Jheri Redding**, an entrepreneur, businessman and hairdresser and together they developed the first professional hair-care products that incorporated science with hair. Educating stylists about the chemistry of hair and skin became a necessity so they could reccommend the correct product and better serve their clients. Ms. Kent gained full ownership of the company by 1965 and Mr. Redding went on to develop another professional hair-care line called **Nexxus in 1979**.

Paula Kent

Vidal Sassoon

**In 1963, a celebrity hairstylist Vidal Sassoon** created his signature cut by reinventing the **"classic bob" haircut** in a geometric design using sharp, angular lines. He became the **"modernist stylist"** and a key influence in the marketing side of hairdesign by turning the beauty industry into a multi-million-dollar business.

# Industry Development . . .

**Soft Sheen** was started as a hair conditioner and setting lotion for African-American hair and was created in the basement of the home of **Edward and Bettiann Gardner** in 1964. Soft Sheen became a success with the introduction of multiple new products in the ensuing years and was eventually acquired by L'Oreal USA in 1998.

**In the 1980s,** the hair industry gave birth to many innovative brands that changed the landscape of the professional beauty industry forever. Some of the companies that assisted in the development were **Nexxus**, formed by the visionaries Jheri and Stephen J. Redding, **Matrix** founded by Arnie and Sydell Miller, **Goldwell** owned by Kao Professional Salon Services, and **Paul Mitchell** operated by John Paul DeJoria, etc.

**Nail-care industry giants emerged in the early 1980s** producing "state of the art" products used for manicures, pedicures and artificial nail services. Cosmetologists and nail technicians now had the opportunity to attend advanced educational classes, participate in nail competitions and increase their sales due to these technological and scientific innovations.

Today, the renowned expert in the nail industry is **Mr. Trang Nguyen of Odyssey Nail**. He has triumphed in the nail competition arena and become a **World Champion** more than once. Mr. Nguyen is educating others within the field by sharing his knowledge and exceptional nail artistry skills so that they too can compete for, and win, nail industry awards worldwide.

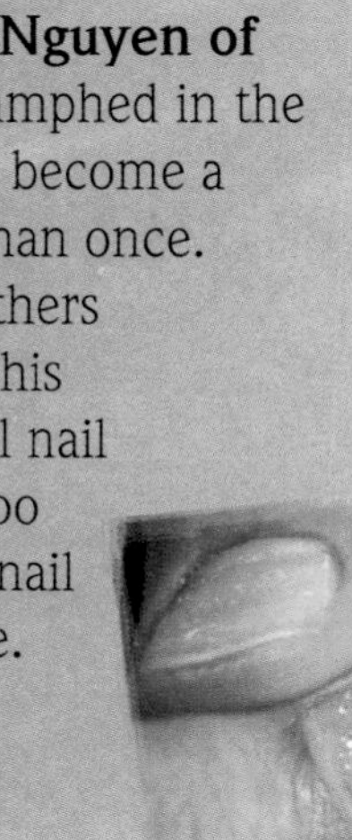

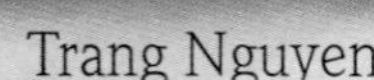

Trang Nguyen

# Industry Development...

The **Regis Corporation** is a **"universal leader"** of cosmetology education, hair-care salons and hair restoration centers. **Myron Kumin started Regis** in 1958 by acquiring his parents' chain of salons that were located in department stores. Myron removed the salons from the department stores and established them into self-supporting businesses relocated within shopping malls. **In 1987, Regis hired Paul D. Finkelstein as the company's new president.** Through Mr. Finkelstein's leadership and restructuring strategies, Regis has grown into a multi-billion-dollar company with a combination of over 13,500 salon and restoration centers worldwide.

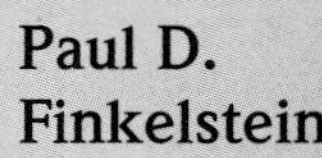

**Paul D. Finkelstein**

In **1993, Redken** was acquired by L'Oreal USA and was relocated to New York. **American Crew**, the first major hair-care system for men, was introduced in 1994 by a hair-care leader **David Raccuglia** and his associate **Terry Lane**. They launched the men's grooming company into a beauty industry that was lacking in men's quality hair-care and grooming products.

**L'Oreal purchased Matrix in 2000**, and went on to acquire other cosmetic companies. L'Oreal continues to develop and manufacture hair- and skin-care products as well as haircolor and fragrances for the professional and the consumer. Also in the beginning of the 21st century, the computer age fully hit the beauty industry with the Internet used as a great marketing tool for all beauty businesses.

James Gamble and William Procter

**In 2003, Procter & Gamble** gained a majority of Wella Corporation's interests. Procter & Gamble was founded in 1837 by two brothers-in-law, **William Procter and James Gamble**, and is a multinational manufacturer of commercial and consumer products.

# Job Opportunities . . .

**NOTE:** Most of the job opportunities below require a cosmetology license and/or advanced educational training or a separate course of study depending on the particular field of interest.

*There are unlimited job opportunities for employment within the innovative world of the beauty industry. The* ***list of career possibilites,*** *covering every facet of today's cosmetology marketplace, seems endless. This is* ***a profession that requires creativity and imagination*** *– along with hard work – to reach success. With a wide selection of jobs to choose from, the student can be selective as to what is suitable for his or her personality and technical skills. The list below provides a summary of choices within the beauty industry.*

1

**Barber:** The barber **performs most of the same services as a cosmetologist** with the exception of nail-care treatments. The barber specializes in cutting with a straight razor and advanced clipper cutting techniques.

**Color Consultant:** The color consultant works with the individual that requests recommendations to enhance his or her appearance. The consultant **uses a color chart to select and match colors that will accentuate the person's natural skin tone and eye color**. The next step is to choose a wardrobe, a proper haircolor and makeup colors that complement the complete body image. A successful color consultant must have artistic expression and good judgment of color. Color consultants typically work in a cosmetic or clothing department store, or for makeup companies.

**Cosmetologist:** Cosmetologists, also known as hairdressers or stylists, **provide services consisting of, but not limited to, cutting, designing, perming and coloring the hair**. The cosmetologist promotes and markets home care maintenance to each client to take care of his or her hair outside of the salon. Cosmetologists are capable of performing manicures, pedicures, scalp treatments, facials, application of makeup, and cleaning and styling of wigs and/or extensions or hairpieces. The opportunity to become a manager or owner of a salon or salons is another option if a person desires to enter the world of business.

# Job Opportunities . . .

**Cruise Ship Stylist:** A cruise ship stylist is a **cosmetologist working in a salon located on a ship**. This person performs the same services as a cosmetologist would. Cruise line personal care positions consist of the cosmetologist, manicurist, esthetician and massage therapist. As an employee of a cruise ship line, benefits include seeing the world, consistently having new clients and working in stretches of only six months.

**Educator:** An educator or instructor is **licensed to teach students all phases of the cosmetology industry** in an ideal classroom setting. The educator provides the necessary technical and practical skills for all hair-, nail- and skin-care services. An instructor must possess excellent people skills and classroom management principles.

**Electrologist:** An electrologist **is educated in the science of permanent hair removal,** commonly referred to as electrology. The electrologist is able to conduct a complete consultation along with an analysis to provide a treatment plan that addresses the client's hair type and areas of removal.

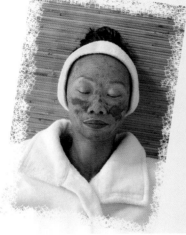

**Esthetician:** The esthetician or skin-care specialist **provides comprehensive facial treatments** along with recommendations for follow-up home care maintenance. This person performs **a consultation and skin analysis, and a facial treatment consisting of cleansing, toning, exfoliating and moisturizing.** In addition, the esthetician is educated in hair removal services consisting of tweezing or waxing as well as makeup application, from basic to corrective colors. An esthetician may be an existing cosmetologist that acquired advanced skin-care education or an individual that is exclusively educated and licensed in all areas of the skin-care industry.

# Job Opportunities . . .

**Film and Theater Hairstylist:** In this specialized area, the **cosmetologist must read and analyze the actor's script to become familiar with all the scenes and events** and how each will affect the actor's appearance. The cosmetologist should possess excellent color vision and creativity, as well as be able to accept criticism and suggestions from the directors, producers and actors. It is recommended for the cosmetologist interested in film or theater to acquire advanced education in practical hair skills.

1

**Film and Theater Makeup Artist:** A makeup artist that **creates prosthetic effects and applies makeup for theatre, television and film**. This person works with cosmetics to beautify and color the face and body to complement the script. It is recommended that someone interested in this type of work enhance his or her learning and practical skills by seeking advanced makeup and color courses. Other job options for the makeup artist are working at photo shoots for modeling agencies or on models for the runway.

**Massage Therapist:** The massage therapist or practitioner **performs advanced soft tissue massage through the use of his or her hands on the body** in a professional establishment. This career requires higher education in human anatomy and the art of massage.

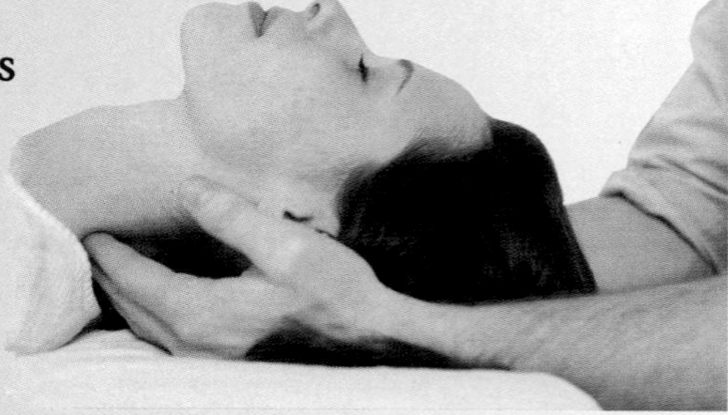

**Nail Technician:** A nail technician is specifically **educated to only treat the nails of the hands and feet**. The technician provides basic nail treatments such as manicures and pedicures, in addition to advanced nail- and foot-care services such as artificial nail application, paraffin treatments and spa specialty services. A cosmetologist may perform all nail-care services.

# Job Opportunities . . .

**Platform Artist:** The platform artist **applies his or her practical skills on models in front of an audience on a stage**. This person is the cosmetology educator that teaches licensed cosmetologists at trade shows or events. The demonstrator is an expert in the beauty industry and showcases his or her talents to peers. The platform artist will typically work with a manufacturer to promote a certain brand of products.

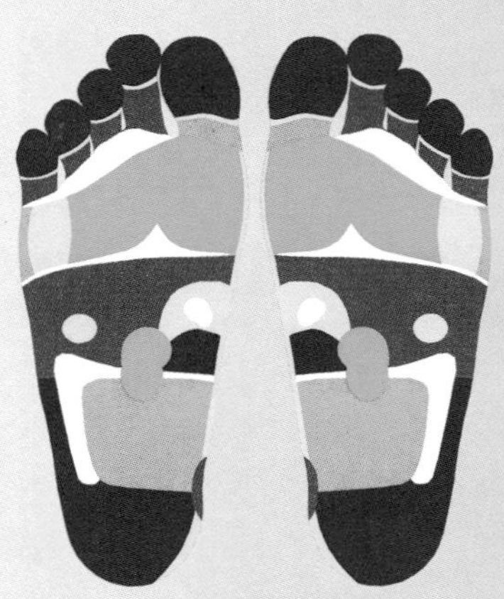

**Reflexologist:** The reflexologist is **educated specifically on human anatomy and location of the reflexes in hands and feet**. This person must have knowledge of each reflex and its stimulating effects and the results on a particular part of the body. A reflexologist may be an existing cosmetologist that completed advanced studies in reflexology or an individual that is exclusively educated and licensed in all areas of reflexology.

**Sales Representatives:** A sales representative or consultant **markets and sells cosmetic products, materials, equipment or furniture within the cosmetology industry**. A cosmetology license is not required, but excellent marketing, business and people skills as well as knowledge of the product are a must. This job requires a tremendous amount of travel to sell the products to other companies, manufacturers and salons/spas. The sales representative must also have good analytical skills to prepare reports and sales figures.

"Always keep up with the most current technological advances in your field of study by attending trade shows, classes and seminars."

# History of Cosmetology REVIEW QUESTIONS

## FILL-IN-THE-BLANKS

| | |
|---|---|
| A. | Afro |
| B. | Barber |
| C. | Beehive |
| D. | Bob |
| E. | Crowning Glory |
| F. | Educator |
| G. | Edwardian Era |
| H. | Electric Clipper |
| I. | Finger Waves |
| J. | Flat Top |
| K. | Gibson Girl |
| L. | Hair |
| M. | Marcel Waves |
| N. | Marital Status |
| O. | Permanent Wave Machine |
| P. | Pompadour |
| Q. | Sales Representative |
| R. | Shag |
| S. | Unisex |
| T. | Victorian Age |

1. ________ is a fashion or an establishment suitable for both female or male.
2. ________ was created by Karl Nessler in 1906 to produce permanent curls in the hair.
3. ________ has played a major role in our lives, whether used for protection or as a fashion statement.
4. ________ performs most of the same services as the cosmetologist with the exception of nail-care treatments.
5. ________ was in the 1800s when women wore long loose curls situated beside a coiled chignon enclosed in a hairnet.
6. ________ is a hairstyle of the 1970s consisting of multiple layers creating a "feathered" appearance.
7. ________ a popular bouffant style worn in the 1950s that had a cone shape appearance.
8. ________ a new radical haircut of the 1920s and later reinvented by Vidal Sassoon.
9. ________ markets cosmetic products, materials, equipment or furniture within the cosmetology industry.
10. ________ is a natural curly style worn by African-Americans in the 1960s.
11. ________ developed by Leo J. Wahl and manufactured in the Wahl Clipper Corporation.
12. ________ was what women's hair was considered during the late 1800s.
13. ________ a series of soft waves consisting of ovaloid shapes that was popular during the 1930s.
14. ________ is a style that was loosely waved and combed over an existing hairpiece and situated on top of head.
15. ________ was depicted by wearing veils, ornamental jewels or elaborate wigs.
16. ________ was a period of time referred to as the "Beautiful Age" in the 1900s to 1910s.
17. ________ was worn in the 1890s when women wore their hair high on top of the head and swept back from forehead.
18. ________ is a short haircut worn in the 1980s by men and is usually called the "clipper cut."
19. ________ were created by Marcel Grateau using heated tongs that produce loose waves in straight hair.
20. ________ is licensed to teach students in all phases of the cosmetology industry.

STUDENT'S NAME DATE GRADE

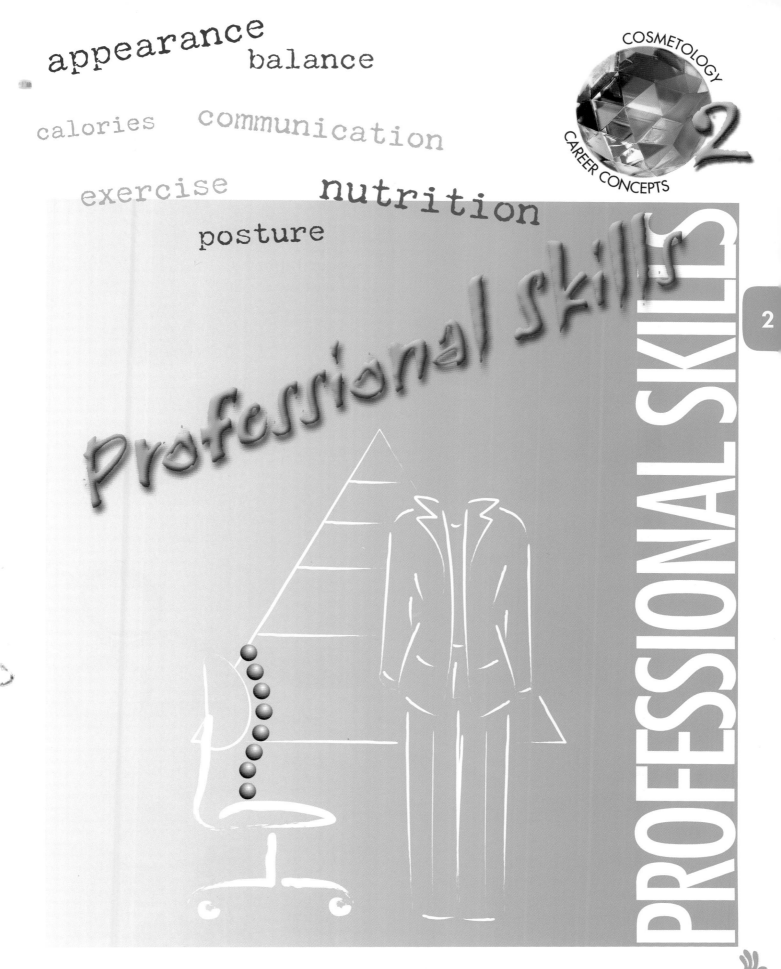

appearance balance

calories communication

exercise nutrition

posture

2

# Professional Skills

# PROFESSIONAL SKILLS

# Terminology ...

*The terms listed below are some of the words used to support the process of learning how to create a good career image and maintain optimum health. Developing a professional appearance as well as forming a proper nutrition and exercise program is a great marketing strategy in building a successful career.*

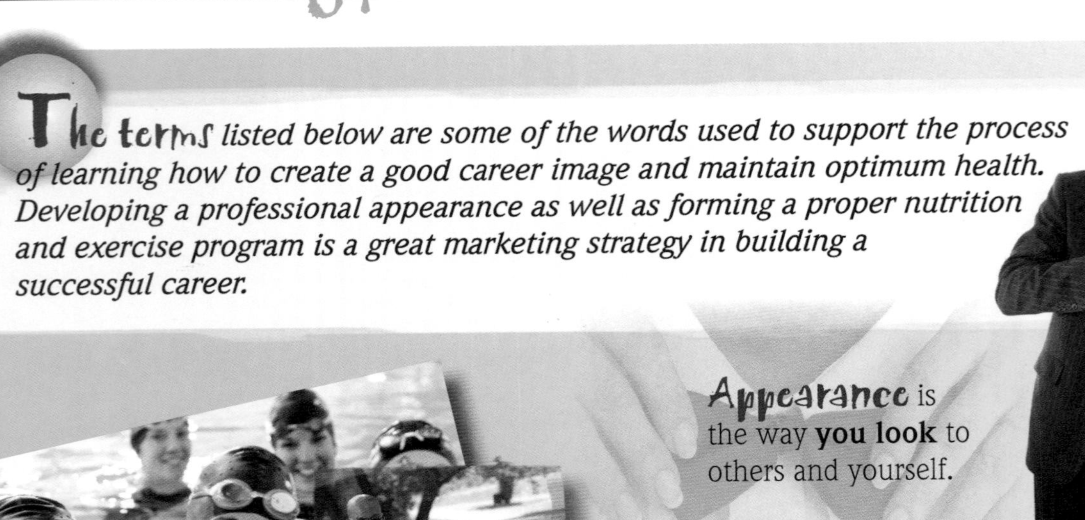

**Appearance** is the way **you look** to others and yourself.

**Activity** is physical movement or the process of doing something.

**Ergonomics** is the scientific design or method of safety, productivity and comfort in a workplace.

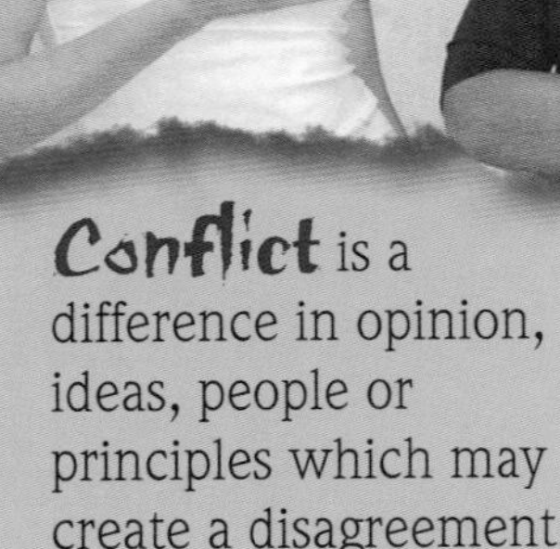

**Conflict** is a difference in opinion, ideas, people or principles which may create a disagreement.

**Fiber** is plant matter that aids in digestion and is found naturally within whole grains, vegetables and fruits.

# Terminology . . .

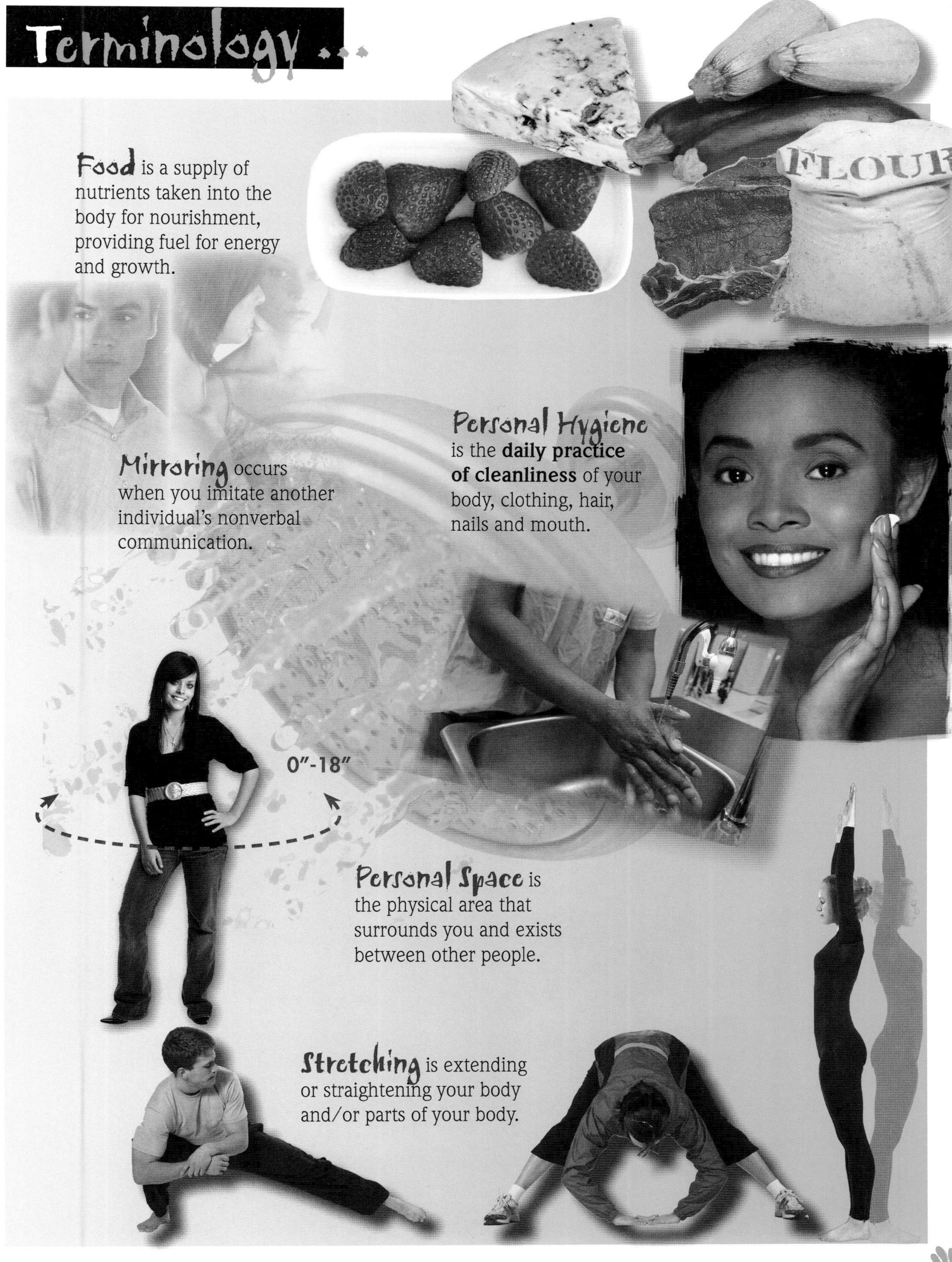


**Food** is a supply of nutrients taken into the body for nourishment, providing fuel for energy and growth.

**Mirroring** occurs when you imitate another individual's nonverbal communication.

**Personal Hygiene** is the **daily practice of cleanliness** of your body, clothing, hair, nails and mouth.

**Personal Space** is the physical area that surrounds you and exists between other people.

**Stretching** is extending or straightening your body and/or parts of your body.

# Introduction ...

*This chapter provides the basis for the professional to learn the skills necessary for a* ***proper presentation*** *as well as the* ***physical aspect of taking care of oneself****. Since this is the BEAUTY industry, we need to apply that beauty to ourselves and become a* ***true professional****, not only in our technical attributes, but also in how we appear.*

2

As you set foot into the salon, the clients are looking to you for the professional image that best portrays their personality. Your appearance **silently supports your beliefs** in setting the example of the beauty industry for the clients. Customers have a tendency to choose the professional that closely resembles their own image ... providing a safe and secure feeling that the professional will give a successful service. By being conscious of our fashion choice, hairstyle, makeup application and manicured nails, we are demonstrating a powerful passion for the beauty industry.

**Become the leader** and determine if your professional attire, hairstyle, makeup and nails are the best representation of the industry.

# Introduction . . .

In addition to your appearance, the **development of ethical socialization** is also a major requisite to building a successful career. Learning technical skills along with social skills will create a strong client base. **People skills** are the socially interactive behavior between you and all other people with whom you come in contact with. **Actively listening to the customer's concerns** about his or her beauty needs, as well as conversing with the client in a warm manner shows a dedicated cosmetologist. It is all about making the client feel welcomed (greeting) and providing an environment that is friendly and caring.



## Two Components of People Skills:

1) **Human relations** is **building a relationship** between you, the client and co-workers ... basically anyone you come in contact with whether personally or professionally. To create a relationship, you need **good communication and listening skills, an understanding of the client's needs and a compassionate, caring attitude for each human being.**

2) **Ethics** (eth-ics) are a **person's morals or beliefs** by which he or she lives and works. Your ethical manner is shown through **your behavior toward others**, such as being courteous, helpful and respectful. Always stay on top of your career by attending ongoing education classes, seminars or trade shows regularly.

"Let this chapter inspire you to potentially change your life as well as the people you come into contact with during your career!"

# Professional Image ...

**Your professional image** *is the manner in which you* ***present yourself both physically and emotionally*** *within a business setting. How we present ourselves – our image – can either have a* ***positive or negative impact on the client.*** *It is important for the professional to exemplify a positive influence by projecting a well-kept and professional fashion sense. This will gain you the confidence and respect of both your customers and co-workers.*

2

**The four areas that influence a professional image are:**
Appearance, Personal Hygiene, Conduct and Communication.

1) **Appearance** is the way **you look** to others and yourself. Who do you see when you think of a successful professional? Do you picture a doctor, lawyer or a business owner? What do these people have in common that creates a professional appearance? It is important to maintain a professional appearance and apply good manners when dealing with customers.

**Appropriate clothing choices** will allow you to show off your personality and individuality while still feeling comfortable.

- **Professional work attire** may consist of "business-type or fashion choice" attire including dress pants, blouse, non-revealing skirts/dresses or collared shirts with long or short sleeves. Also, some salons/spas request uniform dress attire or color-coded clothing.
- **Inappropriate work attire** would be shorts, flip-flops, tank tops, stained, dirty or ripped clothing, jeans, T-shirts or shirts with improper messages or logos.

"It is a nice feeling when someone pays you a compliment ... 'You look very nice today, Emily!'"

**Hygiene** (hy-giene) is the art of practicing healthful living. The two types of hygiene are personal and public.

2) **Personal Hygiene** is the **daily practice of cleanliness** of your body, clothing, hair, nails and mouth.

As a cosmetologist, you will be **working closely with clients**; therefore, it is important not to be offensive, but to be clean, well-groomed and smelling fresh every day. Make sure your teeth are clean and your breath smells fresh, use deodorant and wear your hair in a fashionable style. Check that clothes are clean and well-pressed, fingernails are manicured, and makeup is soft and subtle.

Personal Space 0"-18"

**Personal space** is the physical area that surrounds you and exists between other people. This physical area has a distance of 0 to 18 inches (0cm to 46cm), starting at your body, extending outward. Cosmetologists work within an individual's personal space, so personal hygiene is of utmost importance to avoid being offensive to the client.

In the beauty industry, it is important that you **set the example** and become your own source of advertisement. The most valuable way to apply and support what beauty is all about ... **become what you learned! You should be an image of a true professional!**

**Public hygiene** is **practicing sanitation guidelines** to ensure the safety and welfare of the clients and environment in which you work. **Public hygiene is equally as important as personal hygiene.** Your local regulatory agency sets up standards of sanitation and safety guidelines to follow in a salon/spa setting. The presentation of your work station is just as important as your appearance and personal hygiene because your area of service is still a representation of you. **Maintain a clean, neat and safe work station.** Make sure all **tools are properly sanitized, stored and organized in a clean, safe area.** All hair and debris should be removed from the floor immediately after each service.

"Market Yourself . . . be your own source of advertisement!"

2

3) **Conduct** is your personal behavior and represents your **attitude toward others**. It is the manner in which you choose to **control what you are feeling**. In a workplace environment, it is essential that you present yourself in a respectful and polite manner ... and to demonstrate ethical behavior.

## Good workplace conduct

- Demonstrate good ethical behavior
- Respect clients and co-worker's boundaries
- Be positive and sincere
- Be prompt and ready for each appointment service
- Go "above and beyond" what is expected of you
- Discuss conflicts in private
- Be attentive to others' needs

## Poor workplace conduct

- Discrimination
- Sexual harassment
- Pilfering (stealing)
- Poor attendance and tardy arrival to work
- Loud voice; arguing/yelling
- Inappropriate language
- Ignoring customers
- Being unclean or messy
- Smoking in the workplace
- Chewing gum, eating or talking on cell phone while servicing client
- Inappropriate dress attire

4) **Communication** is the process through which **people exchange information** … it is the way in which you listen and interact with another person or group of people. This is an essential part of your conduct and should exemplify a caring and committed personality.

**Communication begins the moment you greet your client.** Good communication is the basis for customer service satisfaction, which leads to client trust and loyalty, resulting in client retention. **Client retention** is the foundation for a strong and steady client base. Learn to **listen and understand** what your client is communicating. Effective communication requires the professional to alternate between the role of sender and receiver.



## The three types of communication used are active listening, verbal communication and nonverbal communication.

**Active listening** is the main component for all communication skills. When actively listening, the **listener focuses on what the speaker is communicating.** At the appropriate time, the listener will provide the speaker with a response according to what was spoken. This response is to be interpreted in the form of questions and/or clarifications.

### Four Steps to Active Listening

1) **Focus** on the speaker; pay attention, concentrate and look at the speaker.

2) **Sense** is using your eyes and ears to take in the information.

3) **Understand** is comprehending what the speaker is saying and doing.

4) **Paraphrase** is using your own words to summarize what the speaker said to you.

# Communication . . .

**Verbal Communication** *is sending a message* ***using words****. To be effective in your verbal communication, use only specific language and avoid slang and jargon.* ***Slang*** *is* ***informal words*** *that are typically inappropriate for professionals to use, such as* ***"ain't" or "gonna."*** *Jargon is words or phrases that are exclusive to the profession in which you are educated. Example: "Would you like your hair* ***graduated at the lower occipital area****?"*

Use an effective voice when speaking with clients to enhance your communication skills. The way you sound when verbally communicating is just as important.

**The following characteristics of an effective voice will enhance your communicational skills:**

- Speak clearly.
- Use an appropriate pace.
- Use a pleasant pitch.
- Use inflections in your voice.
- Adjust your volume according to your environment.

**Nonverbal communication** is **unspoken language** consisting of **eye contact, facial expressions and body language**. For most people who identify with the Western cultures, **eye contact is a sign of respect**. It expresses interest and concern in what the speaker is saying.

Interpreting **facial expressions** helps us gather important information about the individual. Smiling, frowning or eyebrows raised are facial expressions from thoughts and emotions. **Smiling is the universally recognized expression** for happiness, feeling attractive, sociable, sincere and competent.

**Body language** is the communication cues provided by the **movement and position of your body. Body positions** such as crossed arms, slouching, hanging your head low or even your posture may suggest negative responses. **Body movements** are signals of an individual's emotional state, such as rubbing or tapping a finger indicates that the person is impatient or nervous.

During communication, sometimes conflicts can occur between customer and professional, especially if **a service or the topic being discussed is not agreeable** to both people. **Conflict** is a difference in opinion about an idea, people or principles, which in turn may create a disagreement or argument.

## Some Strategies Recommended to Resolve Conflict

- Address the conflict directly, confidentially and quickly.
- Speak using a normal tone of voice and remain calm.
- Focus and be responsible for your own feelings; avoid blaming others.
- Set limits for unacceptable behavior.
- Express your willingness to compromise.

**Stress or anxiety** is a common **emotional response to demanding situations** such as having a lot of tasks to complete, experiencing a life altering event or ignoring problems.

## To cope with stress, try the following:

Find a solution to the problem.

Participate in deep breathing exercises or meditation.

Perform exercise or yoga.

Communicate through your stress with a friend or family member.

Request help from a professional counselor.

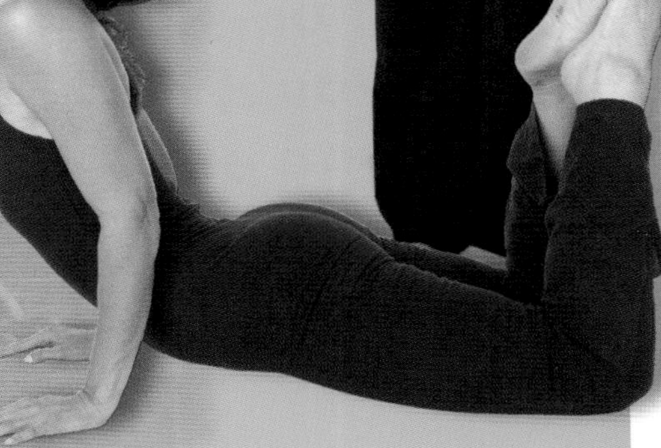

# Communication . . .

**P**araphrasing *(par-a-phras-ing) is* ***rephrasing what the speaker told you****, but in your own summarized version.* ***Active listening plays a key role*** *when paraphrasing because the professional basically needs to repeat back what the client just communicated to him or her. This builds a* ***relationship of trust*** *between you and the customer. As you paraphrase to the client, try to always begin your rephrasing with the word,* ***"you."*** *Example: The cosmetologist says, "You would like your hair cut to the shoulder, and shorter around the face, correct?"*



**"This is how much hair I would like cut off from my length ... about an inch."**

**"I understand you would like no more than an inch cut from the length of your hair, correct?"**

# Servicing the Client ...

What makes certain cosmetologists "unique" when servicing their clients? Why do they have a larger client base? What makes the client "loyal" to a particular cosmetologist?

The Answer: **It is All About the Client and How He or She is Treated!**

## The two necessary components in servicing your customers are etiquette and compassion.

**Etiquette** is guidelines of polite behavior within a social setting, professional environment or group.

**Compassion** is caring for others, which includes a strong desire to help people in need.

2

**"Interesting Statistics"**
A survey taken by one of our professional trade magazines has sent out some alarming results. In the survey, clients who regularly visit a professional salon were asked why they visit a certain salon versus another.

The following are the results in order of importance to the client:

1) I like the professional who services me. He/she is **courteous, kind, punctual, listens to my needs and takes a personal interest in me. She/he respects me and I trust her/him** to give me honest and professional advice.

2) Salon atmosphere – The **salon makes me feel comfortable.** The **music is not too loud**, it is **free of smoke and odors** and **is safe.** The salon offers a "quality of life" feeling.

3) Price – The prices on the salon's menu are **affordable** to my entire family.

4) Parking – The salon's location offers **convenient parking** either on the premises or close by. It is safe and free of charge.

5) Salon location – The salon is located **close to my residence.** I do not wish to travel more than 3-5 miles from my home.

6) I **like the end results** of my hair (including cut, style, color, perm, etc.).

**According to this survey, the No.1 or most important reason people visit a salon was:**
**On-time service, respect, manners and trust!**
**And the least important reason was:**
**The client liked her hairstyle, cut or color!**

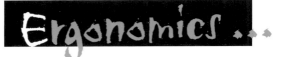

# Ergonomics ...

***The cosmetologist**, nail technician and esthetician's job requires that he or she **stands or sits for long periods of time performing repetitive movements or motions**. It is only a matter of time before the body wears down and work injuries ensue. **Cumulative Trauma Disorder (CTD)** is a painful condition caused by direct pressure, vibration or repetitive movements of particular muscles. Characteristics of CTD are numbness, pain, and wasting and weakening of muscles, which is especially noticeable in the wrists and arms.*

2

**Ergonomics** (er-go-nom-ics) is the **scientific design or method of safety, productivity and comfort in a workplace** along with the equipment to create better overall human performance.

**Ergonomics** is important to your health and well-being as well as your job performance. The science of ergonomics has helped **pave the way for new innovations** in the design of special chairs, desks and methods of movement that help keep your muscles from becoming weak or injured.

Many applications of ergonomic science have been used in our everyday lives. Look around and you will notice mouse pads, chairs, keyboards, pens – even musical instruments – have all been reconfigured to make life more efficient and less painful. The beauty industry has also developed many innovations in furniture design, hand tools and spacial design elements to be more functional to our work environment.

## Bending

Ergonomics is not just represented in products, furniture or equipment; it is also **proper and efficient actions or movements.** Examples might be bending at the knees instead of the waist when lifting heavy objects or positioning yourself at the proper distance from your computer monitor.

Bending at the waist to pick up objects may injure your back.

Bending at the knees puts less strain on your back muscles, thus it is the ergonomically correct way to lift objects.

*Since all professionals communicate to their clients through **body language**, using correct body posture communicates confidence to clients. Most importantly, it helps prevent long-term back, neck or shoulder strain and injury.*

## Hunching

Whether sitting to perform a facial or washing hair at a shampoo bowl, **avoid hunching** over the client, as this will place a strain on the shoulder and back muscles. Try to maintain good posture at all times. **Good Posture** keeps the bones aligned and allows the muscles, joints and ligaments to function properly no matter what activity is being performed.

## Correct Standing Posture

Correct standing posture means placing your weight evenly on both feet and aligning your head directly over your shoulders, with your shoulders directly over your hips and your hips directly over your knees and feet.

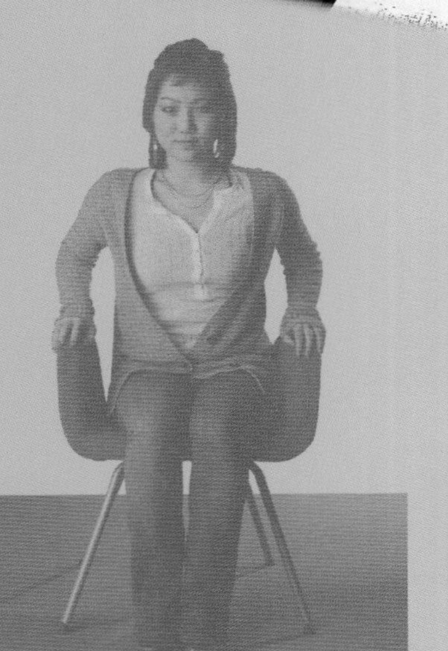

## Correct Seated Posture

Correct seated posture means placing your feet flat on the floor aligned with your knees. Make sure your knees are angled down below your hips. Sit up straight at a 90-degree angle and rest your shoulders, neck and head in line with your hips. Do not "hunch" your shoulders forward as this will put pressure on your back and neck.

# Ergonomics ...

Part of having a good posture is **taking care of the feet.** The objective is ensuring **maximum comfort** while working or even exercising. To protect yourself from toenail disorders or diseases, keep feet clean and dry. To avoid pain and injury, **wear shoes that fit well and provide level body support.**

"Remember, good hygiene and good nutrition help create healthy, attractive hands, feet and nails!"

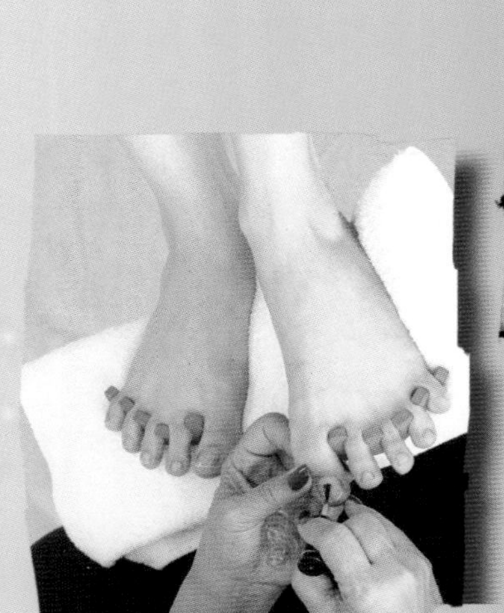

2

A **toe box** is the front part of a shoe, and if adequate, has enough space to wiggle your toes. This type of shoe prevents your toes from pushing and rubbing up against the inside of the shoe throughout the day.

INCORRECT

Shoes with **low heels provide level body support and balance.** This helps to keep a good posture. A **high-heeled shoe creates uneven balance** and applies pressure to the knees and toes. The results may include back and knee discomfort or pain.

CORRECT

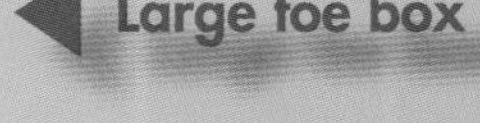


Large toe box

**Postural defects** *can develop over time from consistent improper posture while sitting or standing. You can discover postural defects by examining for figure flaws. Consider upper and lower body proportions and how they relate to one another. The position of a person's head in relation to his/her shoulders, along with spinal curve and a forward angle or tilt of the head could indicate postural defects.*



## The following are some common postural defects:

**Scoliosis** (sco-li-o-sis) is an unnatural side-to-side curvature of the spine. Indicators of scoliosis are uneven shoulder positions or leg length differences.

**Flat back syndrome** is the absence of normal spinal curves. This may be seen in men and women who have degenerative arthritis or have had corrective surgery for scoliosis. It causes the body to stoop forward, and in extreme cases, makes standing difficult.

# Posture ...

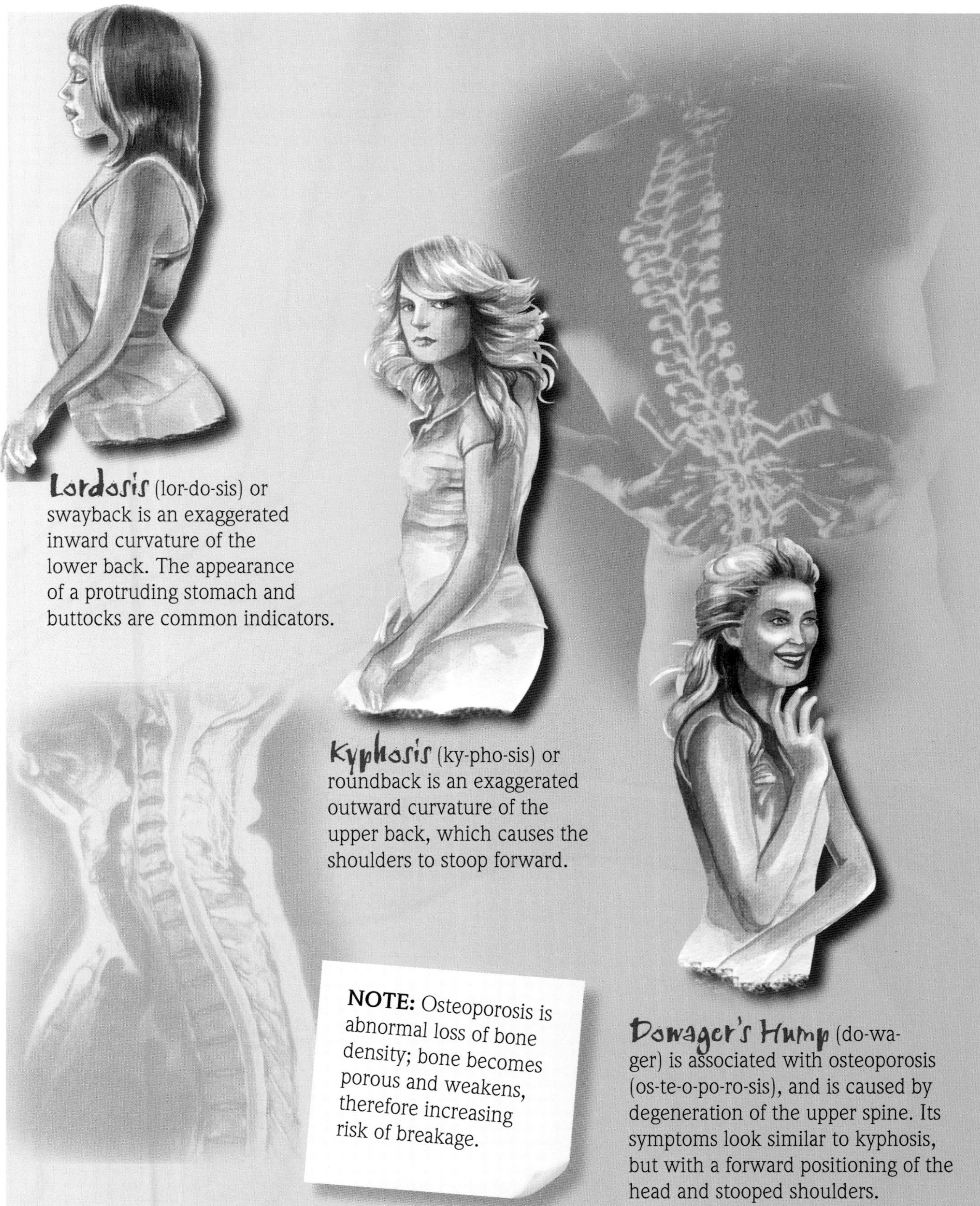

**Lordosis** (lor-do-sis) or swayback is an exaggerated inward curvature of the lower back. The appearance of a protruding stomach and buttocks are common indicators.

**Kyphosis** (ky-pho-sis) or roundback is an exaggerated outward curvature of the upper back, which causes the shoulders to stoop forward.

**NOTE:** Osteoporosis is abnormal loss of bone density; bone becomes porous and weakens, therefore increasing risk of breakage.

**Dowager's Hump** (do-wa-ger) is associated with osteoporosis (os-te-o-po-ro-sis), and is caused by degeneration of the upper spine. Its symptoms look similar to kyphosis, but with a forward positioning of the head and stooped shoulders.

2

# Nutrition . . .

**The human body** *needs to take in nutrients in order to survive.* ***Nutrition*** *is the study and process of the* ***foods consumed and used by an individual.*** *Proper nutrition, obtained through your diet, provides cellular growth, fuel to perform physical activities and assists in the prevention of disease. The United States Department of Agriculture, in cooperation with nutrition.gov, a globally accessed online resource, provides useful information on nutritional guidelines for maintaining a healthy lifestyle.*

2

The standard food guide for proper eating is called the **Food Nutrition Guide**. This guide is made up of six food categories: **Grains, Vegetables, Fruits, Milk, Fats/Oils and Meats/Beans**.

The guide is based on a 2,000-calorie-a-day diet and is an easy way to help maintain nutrition through proper balance of the six food groups.

Try to maintain a **balance** between all six food groups to acquire and support optimal health.

### Why balance is important!

Your body is like a machine; it needs **proper maintenance to perform** its everyday tasks. If you consume less of one food group your body may lack the nutrients it requires, which may lead to fatigue or a lowered immune system. If you consume more of one food group your body may react in other ways such as weight gain or fatigue.

### EXERCISE

Write down your food intake, type of exercise and amount of rest from yesterday. Then compare to the guidelines listed below for maintaining a healthy lifestyle.

- Did you take in all your six food groups?
- Did you eat approximately 2,000 calories or less?
- Did you exercise?
- Did you drink enough water? Divide body weight by 16 with the resulting number being the amount of 8-ounce glasses consumed daily (refer to Chapter 12 Skin)
- Did you get the recommended 8 hours of sleep?

"For further information on nutrition, fitness, supplements and food safety, go to http://www.nutrition.gov."

## Food Nutrition Guide For Healthy Living

**NOTE:** When grocery shopping, buy fresh ... purchase from the perimeter of the store as opposed to the inside aisles where all the processed food is placed. Some stores place their organic food products in one separate section; look for it.

# Nutrition . . .

**Whole Grains** are made from the germ, bran and endosperm – the nourishing part of plant seed – of a whole kernel. **Fiber** is plant matter that aids in digestion and is an important part of your daily intake of healthy foods. **Fiber** is found naturally in whole grains, vegetables and fruits, mechanically it is called **refining. Refined grains** contain no fiber, B vitamins, or iron, and are therefore less healthy for the body. The purpose of refining is to provide finer grain texture and a longer shelf-life.

2

### Some examples of grains are:

**Whole grain products include:** (listed first in ingredients)

- Brown rice
- Bulgur – wheat that is dried and cracked into tiny pieces
- Graham flour
- Oatmeal
- Whole-grain corn
- Whole oats
- Whole rye
- Whole wheat
- Wild rice

**Refined grain products include:**

- White bread
- White flour
- White rice

### How can I tell if an item is a whole grain product?

- Look on the product for a healthy whole grain claim
- Look for whole grains listed as the first ingredient on the nutrition label
- Foods labeled multigrain, stone-ground, seven-grain, 100 percent wheat, cracked wheat, and bran are **not** necessarily considered to be whole grain products.

Nutritional experts recommend that a properly balanced diet requires **half** of your grain foods to be whole grains.

**The proper amount of grains in your diet depends on your physical activity, age and gender.**

| | | | | | |
|---|---|---|---|---|---|
| Children (4-8 yrs) | 4-5 ounces* | Girls | 5 ounces* | Boys | 6 ounces* |
| Women | 6 ounces* | Men | 7 ounces* | | |

***One ounce is equal to 1 slice of bread, ½ cup of cooked rice or pasta, or 1 cup of cereal**

# Nutrition . . .

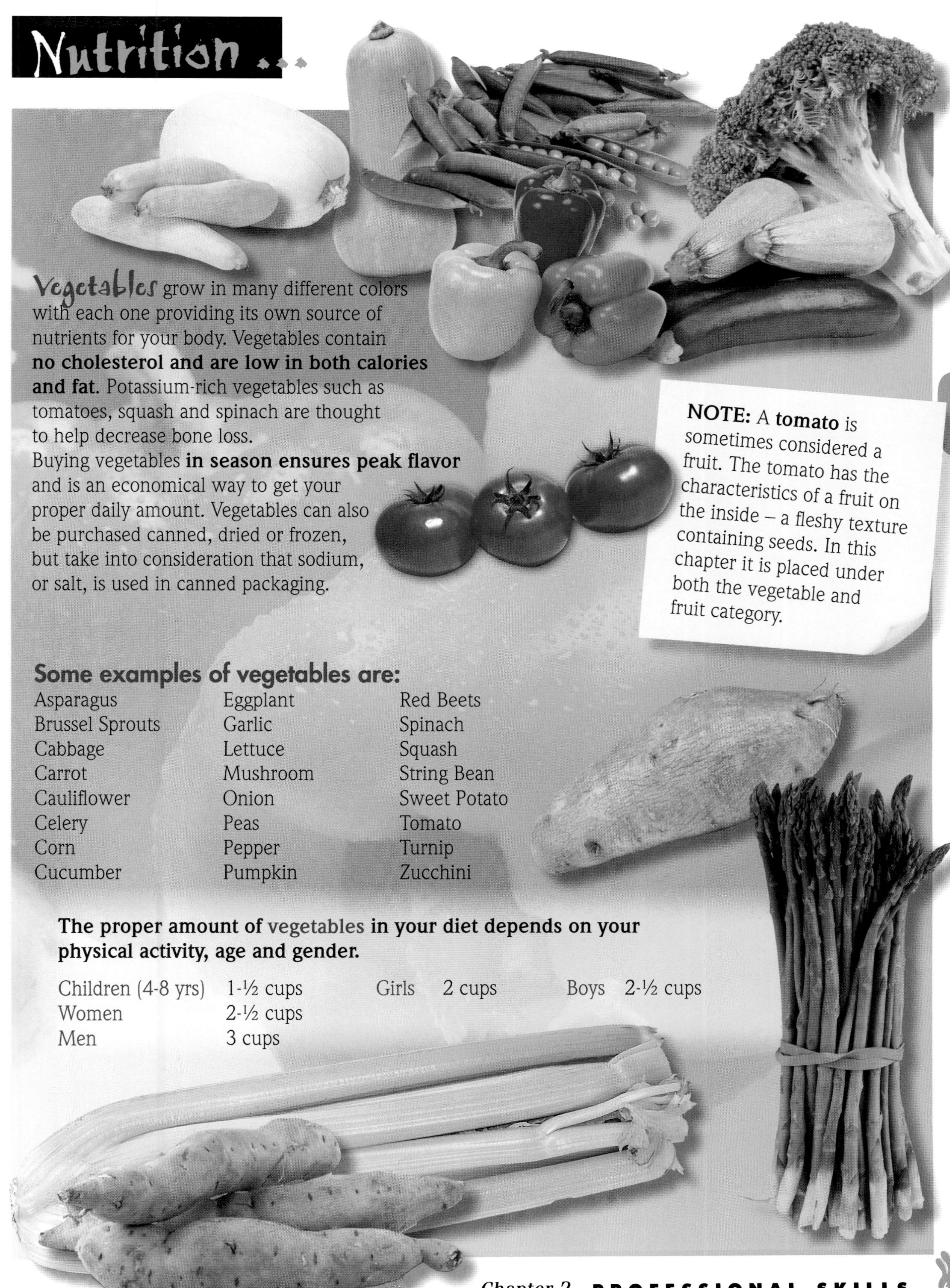

**Vegetables** grow in many different colors with each one providing its own source of nutrients for your body. Vegetables contain **no cholesterol and are low in both calories and fat.** Potassium-rich vegetables such as tomatoes, squash and spinach are thought to help decrease bone loss.

Buying vegetables **in season ensures peak flavor** and is an economical way to get your proper daily amount. Vegetables can also be purchased canned, dried or frozen, but take into consideration that sodium, or salt, is used in canned packaging.

**NOTE:** A **tomato** is sometimes considered a fruit. The tomato has the characteristics of a fruit on the inside – a fleshy texture containing seeds. In this chapter it is placed under both the vegetable and fruit category.

2

## Some examples of vegetables are:

| | | |
|---|---|---|
| Asparagus | Eggplant | Red Beets |
| Brussel Sprouts | Garlic | Spinach |
| Cabbage | Lettuce | Squash |
| Carrot | Mushroom | String Bean |
| Cauliflower | Onion | Sweet Potato |
| Celery | Peas | Tomato |
| Corn | Pepper | Turnip |
| Cucumber | Pumpkin | Zucchini |

**The proper amount of vegetables in your diet depends on your physical activity, age and gender.**

| | | | | | |
|---|---|---|---|---|---|
| Children (4-8 yrs) | 1-½ cups | Girls | 2 cups | Boys | 2-½ cups |
| Women | 2-½ cups | | | | |
| Men | 3 cups | | | | |

# Nutrition . . .

**Fruit** is the ripe, edible part of a plant that contains the seeds and is usually sweet or sour. Fruits are available in many different forms such as fresh, dried, canned and frozen, and are an excellent source of fiber, vitamins and phyto-chemicals, which are non-nutritive plant chemicals that have disease-preventative properties.

**NOTE:** Eating dried fruits is a good way to meet your daily fruit goals, plus they are easy to carry and store. (¼ cup of dried fruits = ½ cup of regular fruit.)

Some examples of fruit are:

| | | | | |
|---|---|---|---|---|
| Apple | Cantaloupe | Grape | Orange | Pomegranate |
| Apricot | Cherry | Guava | Papaya | Raspberry |
| Avocado | Coconut | Honeydew | Peach | Rhubarb |
| Banana | Cranberry | Kiwi | Pear | Strawberry |
| Blackberry | Fig | Lemon/Lime | Pineapple | Tomato |
| Blueberry | Grapefruit | Mango | Plum | Watermelon |

**The proper amount of fruit in your diet depends on your physical activity, age and gender.**

| | | | | | |
|---|---|---|---|---|---|
| Children (4-8 yrs) | 1-½ cups | Girls | 1-½ cups | Boys | 1-½ cups |
| Women | 1-½ cups | Men | 2 cups | | |

**Milk** group comprises of **yogurt, cheese and milk.** Your body depends on calcium to keep your muscles, teeth and bones strong. Foods rich in calcium aid in preventing osteoporosis, which is a slow deterioration of the bones. Dairy products provide the body with protein, potassium, calcium, phosphorus, vitamins A, B-12, and D, riboflavin and niacin. When used as part of a low-calorie diet plan, milk can help burn fat within the body. **No longer included** in the milk group are cream cheese, butter and cream.

**NOTE:** If you are lactose-intolerant – which means that you cannot digest milk products – there are many lactose-free products, such as soy milk, available along with calcium supplements. Discuss this with a nutritionist to maintain a balanced diet.

**The proper amount of milk in your diet depends on your physical activity, age and gender.**

| | | | | | |
|---|---|---|---|---|---|
| Children (4-8 yrs) | 2 cups | Girls | 3 cups | Boys | 3 cups |
| Women | 3 cups | Men | 3 cups | | |

**Oils are fats** that become slippery when turned to liquid at room temperature. Oils are derived from plants and fish and are normally consumed through foods such as nuts, fish, cooking oil and salad dressings. Oils are a major source of essential fatty acids and vitamin E, both of which are needed for optimum health.

## Fats

The three types of fats are **saturated, monounsaturated and polyunsaturated.** An excess of saturated fats raises the LDL cholesterol levels ("bad" cholesterol) in the bloodstream. Limiting saturated fats in your diet will help protect against heart disease. Many oils are high in **monounsaturated** or **polyunsaturated** fats and low **in saturated fats such as peanut, olive, flaxseed and sesame seed oils.**

2

## Hydrogenation occurs when fats are chemically altered into trans fats or fatty acids.

Trans fats are turned into a solid fat, as in vegetable shortening, which is used in cooking and for extending the shelf-life of food. Trans fats act like saturated fats in the bloodstream and therefore are considered unhealthy.

**NOTE:**
A tablespoon of oil contains 120 calories.

## Some examples of oils/fats are:

| Liquid Oils | | | Solid Fats |
|---|---|---|---|
| Almond Oil | Cottonseed Oil | Safflower Oil | Butter |
| Canola Oil | Flaxseed Oil | Sesame Oil | Chicken Fat |
| Coconut Oil | Lemongrass Oil | Soybean Oil | Pork Fat (lard) |
| Corn Oil | Olive Oil | Sunflower Oil | Shortening |
| | Peanut Oil | | Stick Margarine |

**The proper amount of oils in your diet depends on your physical activity, age and gender.**

| | | | | | |
|---|---|---|---|---|---|
| Children (4-8 yrs) | 4 Tsp | Girls | 5 Tsp | Boys | 5 Tsp |
| Women | 5 Tsp | Men | 6 Tsp | | |

# Nutrition . . .

**Meat and Beans** provide protein, which contain many substances such as enzymes, hormones and antibodies that are important to all living cells. These substances are necessary for daily maintenance and functioning of the body. Proteins are important for growth and repair of the tissue and are obtained from foods such as meat, eggs, fish and legumes. Soy is a popular choice for health-conscious individuals due to its high nutritional value. Soy is derived from the soy bean, which is high in protein and polyunsaturated fat, and is cholesterol free.

**NOTE: Tofu** (to-fu) is a soft bean curd containing alpha-linolenic acid (ALA), an essential fatty acid that changes into omega-3 acids in the body. Omega-3 acids are essential to human health but are not manufactured by the body.

## Some examples of meats/beans are:

| Beans | Poultry | Fish | Nuts | Meats | Eggs |
|---|---|---|---|---|---|
| Black-eyed Pea | Chicken | Catfish | Almond | Beef | Chicken |
| Kidney Bean | Duck | Flounder | Cashew | Ham | Duck |
| Lentil | Goose | Haddock | Hazelnut | Lamb | |
| Pinto Bean | Turkey | Salmon | Peanut | Pork | |
| Soy Bean | | Tuna | Pecan | | |
| Split Pea | | | | | |
| Tofu | | | | | |
| White Bean | | | | | |

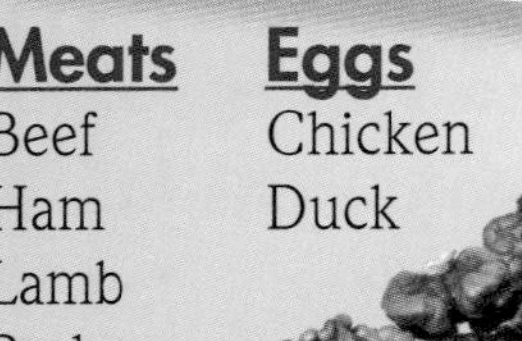

## To follow a healthy diet and maintain low fat and calorie levels follow these tips:

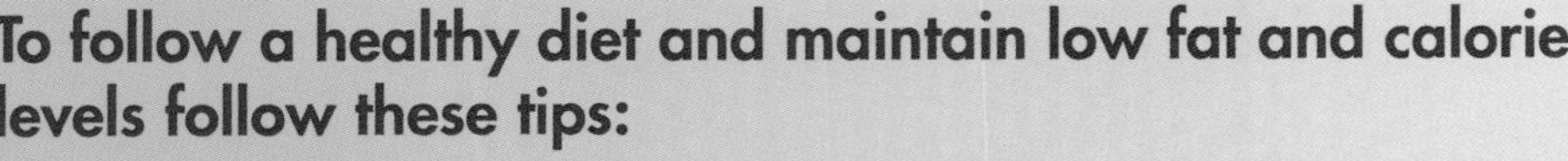

- Choose less fatty meats that are low in cholesterol.
- Reduce your intake of gravies and sauces that contain high amounts of fat and sodium.
- Drain off any fat that appears during cooking.
- Trim away excess fat from meats, poultry and remove the chicken skin.
- Check nutrition labels on packaged food items for hidden calories.
- Eat fish, as it is high in omega-3 fatty acids, which are heart healthy.

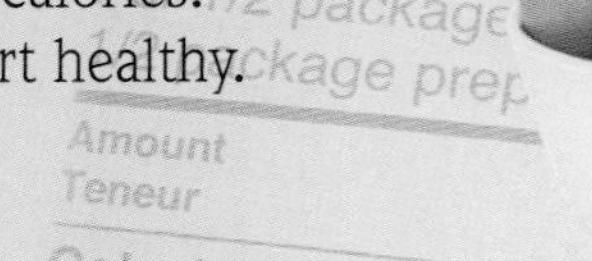

**The proper amount of meat and beans in your diet depends on your physical activity, age and gender.**

| | | | | | |
|---|---|---|---|---|---|
| Children (4-8 yrs) | 3-4 ounces | Girls | 5 ounces | Boys | 5 ounces |
| Women | 5 ounces | Men | 6 ounces | | |

# Nutrition . . .



**Vitamins and Minerals** are organic compounds required through diet and/or supplements. They encourage maintenance of health, growth and reproduction. It is advised to get a certain amount of daily vitamins and minerals through nutrition, and what is not received through food, get in supplement form; pill or, for fast absorption, liquid. Most of the vitamins and minerals necessary for the body are found in every level of the nutrition guide.

### Some essential vitamins and minerals with their benefits:

| Vitamin | Food Group | Benefits |
|---|---|---|
| Vitamin A | Milk, vegetable, fruit, protein | Vision, growth, reproduction and healthy skin |
| Vitamin B | Grains, fruit, milk, protein | Aids in food absorption, promotes energy, maintains metabolism |
| Vitamin D | Milk | Builds strong teeth and bones. A good natural source of vitamin D is sunshine |
| Vitamin E | Fats/oils, protein, grains | Antioxidant (protects against cell damage) |
| Folate | Fruits, grains, vegetable, protein | Promotes growth, blood cell production and resistance to infection |
| Riboflavin | Grains, milk, protein | Supports vision, health of skin and metabolism |
| Thiamine | Protein, grains | Aids in nervous system function and releases energy |

| Minerals | Food Group | Benefits |
|---|---|---|
| Calcium | Protein, milk, vegetable | Builds strong bones and teeth, clots blood, supports muscle contraction and signals nerve impulses |
| Iron | Grains, fruit, protein, vegetable | Prevents anemia by building red blood cells and delivers oxygen in the body |
| Magnesium | Grains, protein, fats/oils, vegetable | Produces muscle contraction, aids in metabolism and supports nervous system |
| Potassium | Grains, fruit (bananas), protein, milk, vegetable | Maintains fluid balance, heart muscle contractions and nerve transmission |

# Exercise ...

**Another aspect** *of maintaining good health is to be physically active every day.* ***Activity*** *is physical movement or the process of doing something.* ***Exercise*** *is considered a physical activity requiring your body's energy and movement. It is intended to strengthen the heart muscle, body muscles, maintain a healthy weight and boost the immune system.*

2

**Balancing** physical activity and proper nutrition is essential to maintaining a healthy body. Performing a minimum of 30 minutes of moderate to vigorous physical activity daily is an ideal goal to acquiring good health.

**Examples of physical activity:**

| **Moderate** | **Vigorous** |
|---|---|
| Bicycling (10 mph or less) | Aerobics |
| Dancing | Basketball |
| Gardening | Bicycling (14-15 mph) |
| Golfing | Running/jogging (5 mph) |
| Hiking | Swimming (freestyle laps) |
| Walking (3 ½ mph) | Walking (4 ½ mph) |
| Weight lifting (light) | Weight lifting (heavy) |

1

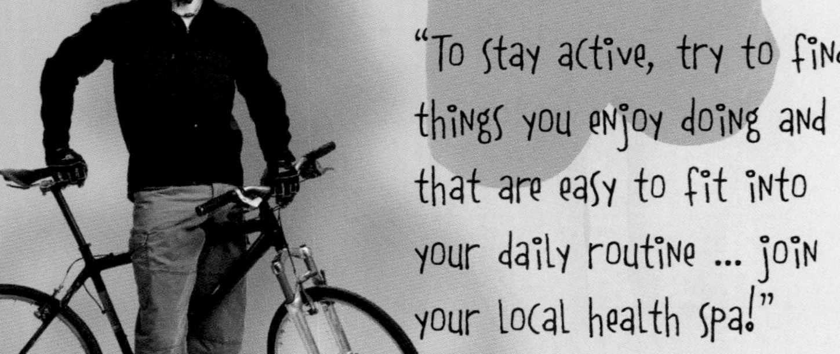

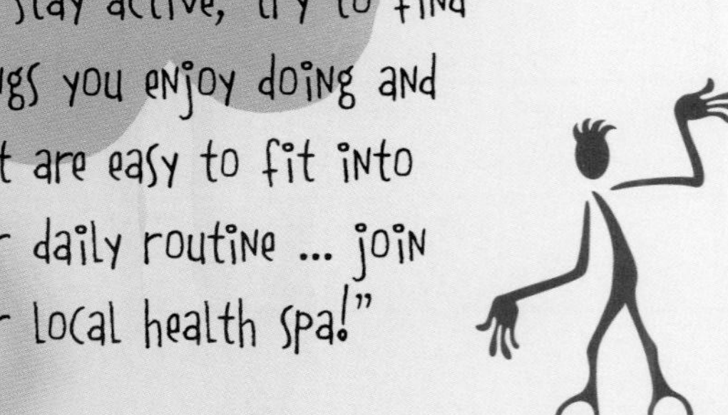

"To stay active, try to find things you enjoy doing and that are easy to fit into your daily routine ... join your local health spa!"

©

# Exercise . . .

**Calories** (cal-o-ries) are units of energy that are burned off by your body during physical activity. Time, type and intensity of exercise will increase the calories burned. There are three components to staying physically fit: **strength, flexibility and endurance. Endurance** is achieved when the body is regularly engaged in physical activity, which promotes a strong heart and stable breathing.

**NOTE:** It takes approximately 30 minutes of vigorous walking to burn an average of 230 calories, which is about the equivalent of one small candy bar.

## Example of calories burned during the following activities:

**Moderate (30 minutes)**

Bicycling (10 mph or less) - 145
Dancing - 176
Gardening - 165
Golfing - 165
Hiking - 185
Stretching - 90
Walking (3 ½ mph) - 140
Weight lifting (light) - 110

**Vigorous (60 minutes)**

Aerobics - 480
Basketball - 471
Bicycling (over 14-15 mph) - 590
Running/jogging (5 mph) - 590
Swimming (freestyle laps) - 590
Walking (4 ½ mph) - 460
Weight lifting (heavy) - 440

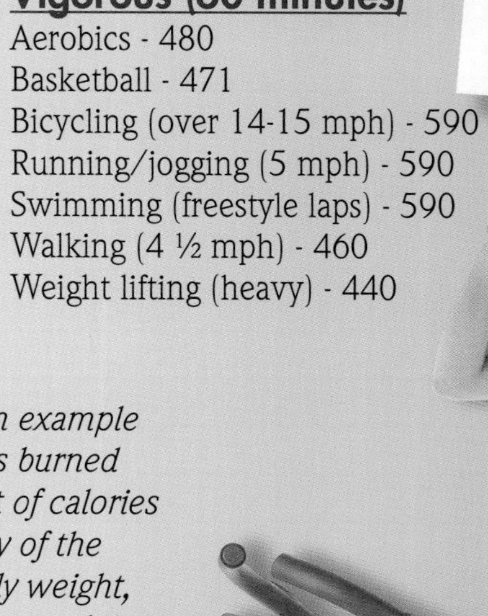

**Disclaimer:** *This chart is **only** an example of the possible amount of calories burned during exercise. The true amount of calories burned is affected by the intensity of the workout, a person's body weight, gender, age and time spent doing the physical activity.*

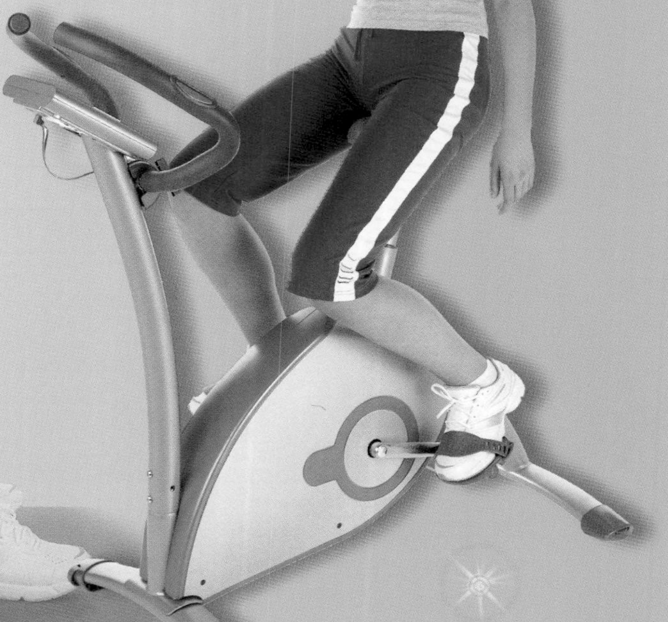

2

# Ideal Weight...

**Ideal weight** *is* ***a healthy*** *weight that is maintained through daily activity and proper nutrition. Extra weight or fat places a person at an increased risk for high blood pressure, high cholesterol, heart disease and diabetes and other weight-related conditions. Weight puts more strain on the heart, contributes to less physical activity and a decrease in proper nutritional consumption.*

**NOTE:** Always check with a medical care professional when starting any increase in activity or change in your dietary intake.

2

| Height with Ideal Weight for Women | | | Height with Ideal Weight for Men | |
|---|---|---|---|---|
| **Height** | **Ideal Weight** | | **Height** | **Ideal Weight** |
| 5'0" | 113-126 | | 5'2" | 131-141 |
| 5'1" | 115-129 | | 5'3" | 133-143 |
| 5'2" | 118-132 | | 5'4" | 135-145 |
| 5'3" | 121-135 | | 5'5" | 137-148 |
| 5'4" | 124-138 | | 5'6" | 139-151 |
| 5'5" | 127-141 | | 5'7" | 142-154 |
| 5'6" | 130-144 | | 5'8" | 145-157 |
| 5'7" | 133-147 | | 5'9" | 148-160 |
| 5'8" | 136-150 | | 5'10" | 151-163 |
| 5'9" | 139-153 | | 5'11" | 154-166 |
| 5'10" | 142-156 | | 6'0" | 157-170 |
| 5'11" | 145-159 | | 6'1" | 160-174 |
| 6'0" | 148-162 | | 6'2" | 164-178 |
| | | | 6'3" | 167-182 |
| | | | 6'4" | 171-187 |

**Disclaimer:** *The chart above is based on a medium frame size. If individual is of a small frame size, deduct 9 to 10 pounds from medium size weight. If of a large frame size, add 9 to 10 pounds from medium size weight.*

2 1

# Healthy Weight . . .

**Another reliable source of information** to determine if you are at a healthy weight is checking your **"body mass index" or BMI. Body mass is body fat** and the body mass index formulates your approximate amount of fat. **BMI** is a mathematical equation that uses a person's height in meters divided by the weight in kilograms (kg/m[2]).

**Measurement of waist size or circumference** also is considered when determining a healthy weight, and if you are at risk of developing any weight-related conditions. A man with a waist measurement of more than 40 inches is at high risk, and a woman is at high risk if her waist circumference is more than 35 inches. (This, of course, excludes pregnant women.) To measure the waist accurately, wrap a tape measure around the bare waist above the hip bone making sure the tape is close against the skin, but not restricting your breathing.

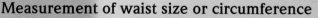

| Body Mass Index | Weight | Waist is Less Than or Equal to 40 inches (men) or 35 inches (women) | Waist is Greater Than 40 inches (men) or 35 inches (women) |
|---|---|---|---|
| 18.5 or less | Underweight | n/a | n/a |
| 18.5 – 24.9 | Normal | n/a | n/a |
| 25.0 – 29.9 | Overweight | Increased | High |
| 30.0 – 34.9 | Obese | High | Very High |
| 35 – 39.9 | Obese | Very High | Very High |
| 40 or greater | Extremely Obese | Extremely High | Extremely High |

"If you want to learn about your BMI and weight loss, refer to www.projectweightloss.com"

**Disclaimer:** *The charts shown on this page and previous page are examples and are not to replace any advice or recommendations given by your medical care professional. These charts are to inspire a healthier you. These are adult charts; there are separate charts for evaluating a child's or teenager's ideal weight.*

# Exercise ...

**Standing** or sitting for long periods of time can become tiresome for the body. At the salon, you will feel a lot fresher if you take time between clients to stretch, restore and revitalize. Follow the examples listed below to renew your energy.

## B-R-E-A-T-H-E

Taking time to breathe voluntarily rather than involuntarily is crucial for reducing tension.

- Sit comfortably, preferably away from others. Block out outside noises.
- Relax your entire body. Focus only on your breath, and work toward breathing through your nose. Make each inhale and exhale long, deliberate and deep.
- Do this for five minutes a day and feel the benefits. This is powerful!

## Head and neck rolls

Try this exercise as a quick, easy tension reducer.

- Stand still and erect or sit comfortably with feet on the floor and your back straight.
- Inhale, and then as you exhale, gently drop your chin forward towards your chest.
- Inhale and slowly roll your left ear toward your shoulder, dropping the opposite shoulder toward the floor to maintain alignment. Hold the pose, and exhale as your neck releases.
- Breathe fully and gently as you drop your chin back down to your chest and repeat the stretch on the right side to loosen these muscles.

**Stretching** is extendin... straightening your body and/or parts of your body ...ulate blood circulation and restore movement to ...scles.

### ...der shrugs

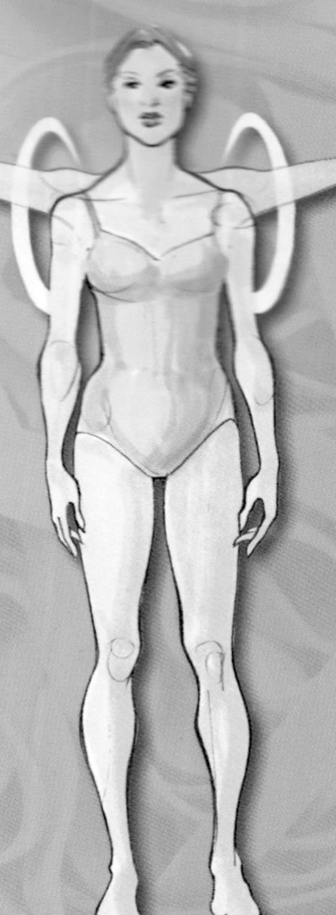

This relaxing stretch helps improve flexibility in the upper back, shoulders and arms while relieving tension in the neck and shoulders.

- Stand still and erect.
- Start moving your shoulders from back to front, making small circles in a fluid motion. Repeat ten times.
- Reverse circular motion of your shoulders, rotating from front to back for ten repetitions.
- Modify this stretch by lifting the arms until they are fully extended to the sides and rolling back to front and front to back. Make increasingly larger arm circles.

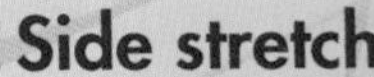

### Side stretch

This stretch strengthens the arms, waist and upper body, and helps align the spine.

- Stand straight with your feet about hip-width apart, and extend the crown of your head up towards the ceiling.
- Keep your feet stationary and inhale as you raise your arms overhead, palms together. Exhale, relaxing your shoulders.
- Keep shoulders relaxed and inhale. As you exhale, bend from the waist to the left. Hold for a few breaths, inhaling and exhaling easily.
- Return to center and inhale. Exhale as you bend to the right. Breathe gently as you briefly hold the pose on this side.
- Return once again to the center on an inhale, exhaling as you drop your arms gently down to rest at your sides.
- Repeat at least twice; you will notice a deeper stretch the second time around.

Professional Skills

REVIEW QUESTIONS

## FILL-IN-THE-BLANKS

| | |
|---|---|
| A. | Active Listening |
| B. | Calcium |
| C. | Calories |
| D. | Conduct |
| E. | Conflict |
| F. | Dowager's Hump |
| G. | Ergonomics |
| H. | Ethics |
| I. | Milk |
| J. | Mirroring |
| K. | Nutrition |
| L. | Paraphrasing |
| M. | People Skills |
| N. | Personal Hygiene |
| O. | Professional Image |
| P. | Refining |
| Q. | Saturated |
| R. | Slang |
| S. | Toe Box |
| T. | Tofu |

2

1. ________ is rephrasing what the speaker told you.
2. ________ is the mechanical removal of the grain's germ and bran.
3. ________ are the socially interactive behavior between the professional and clients.
4. ________, monounsaturated and polyunsaturated are the three types of fats.
5. ________ is a mineral that builds strong bones and teeth.
6. ________ occurs when you imitate an individual's nonverbal communication.
7. ________ are a person's morals by which they live and work.
8. ________ occurs when the listener focuses on what the speaker is communicating.
9. ________ is the scientific design or method of safety, productivity and comfort in the workplace.
10. ________ are units of energy that are burned off by your body during physical activity.
11. ________ is informal words that are typically inappropriate for professionals to use in communication.
12. ________ is the manner in which you present yourself both physically and emotionally within the workplace.
13. ________ is associated with osteoporosis and is caused by degeneration of the upper spine.
14. ________ is the daily practice of cleanliness of your body, clothing, hair, nails and mouth.
15. ________ is your personal behavior and represents your attitude towards others.
16. ________ is the study and process of the foods consumed and used by an individual.
17. ________ is a difference of opinion on an idea, people or principles, which may turn into an argument.
18. ________ group is comprised of yogurt, cheese and milk.
19. ________ is a soft, soy bean curd, providing protein in the body.
20. ________ is the front part of a shoe that has enough space to allow toes to wiggle.

STUDENT'S NAME ______________________ DATE __________ GRADE __________ bacteria contagious

immunity mitosis

purification

parasites

Cosmetology Career Concepts 3

3

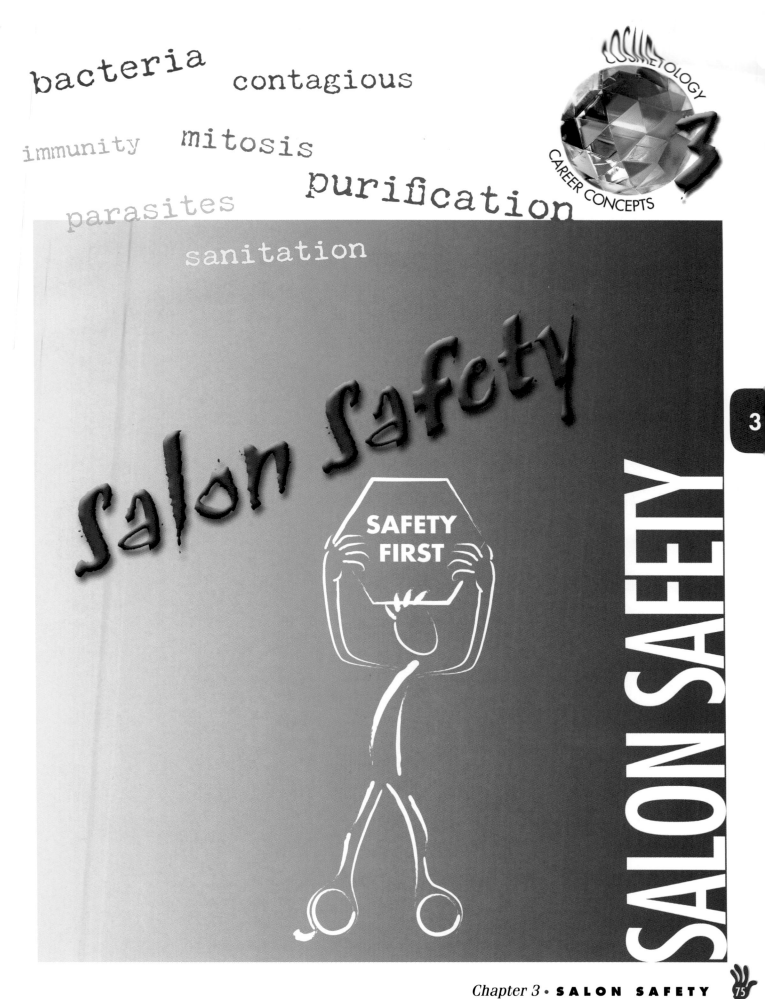

# Terminology...

The following terms are common words used within the cosmetology industry. Because health concerns are so important when working with the public, these terms provide us with the knowledge necessary in avoiding the spread of disease. This chapter will increase your knowledge on the causes and types of diseases. A list of guidelines is provided for the health and safety of the customer as well as the professional.

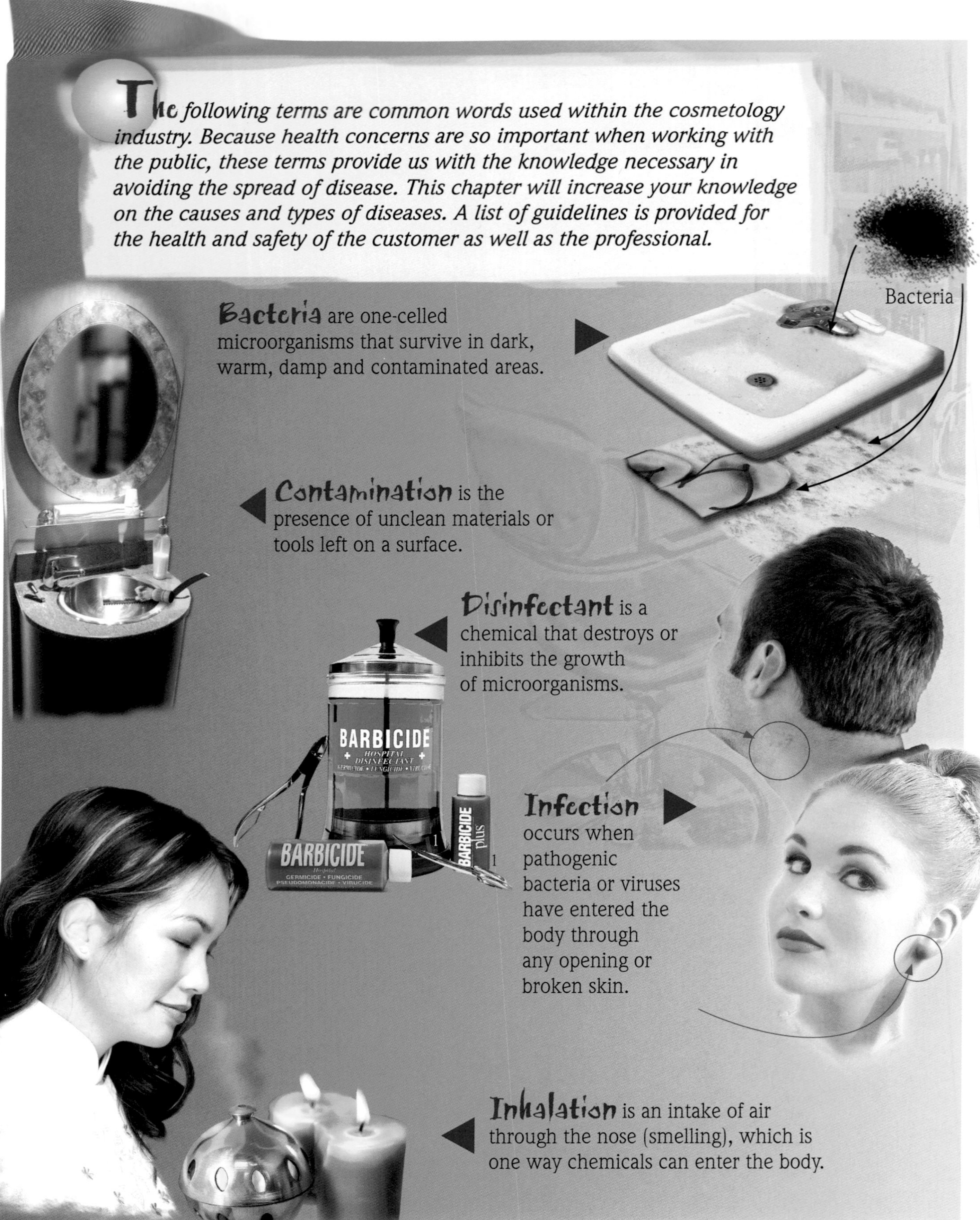


**Bacteria** are one-celled microorganisms that survive in dark, warm, damp and contaminated areas.

**Contamination** is the presence of unclean materials or tools left on a surface.

**Disinfectant** is a chemical that destroys or inhibits the growth of microorganisms.

**Infection** occurs when pathogenic bacteria or viruses have entered the body through any opening or broken skin.

**Inhalation** is an intake of air through the nose (smelling), which is one way chemicals can enter the body.

# Terminology...

**Material Safety Data Sheet (MSDS)** provides employers and employees with the proper information and procedures in handling, working with and storing chemicals in the workplace.

**Occupational Safety + Health Administration (OSHA)** sets and enforces standards for employee training and education and supporting continued improvements within the workplace.

**Overexposure** is excessive contact with a substance, which may result in an allergic reaction, sensitivity or other unwanted side effects.

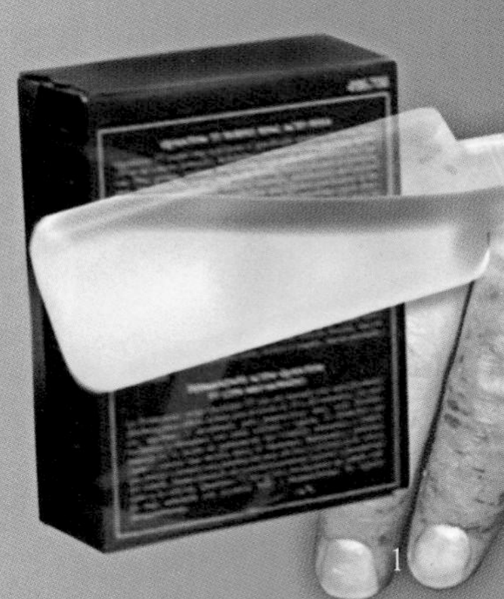

**Personal Protective Equipment (PPE)** provides a barrier between potential blood spills and areas of the body; examples are gloves and eye protection.

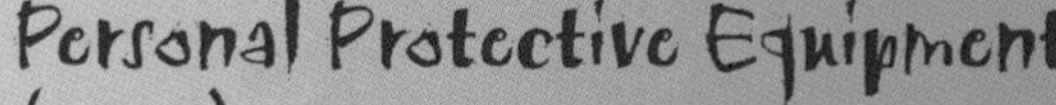

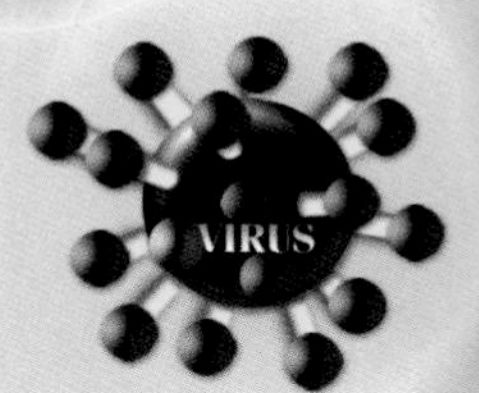


**Viruses** are smaller (submicroscopic) than bacteria and attack the human cells by entering the cell wall.

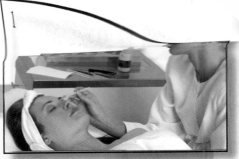

# Problem Causing...

*Cosmetologists, **nail technicians and estheticians** are in an industry that services the public every day. We must take every precaution necessary in guarding ourselves and our clients from contamination.*

## What exactly is contamination?

It is the process of making something **unclean or unsuitable** to be near or touched. As a professional, it is our responsibility to ensure the **welfare and safety** of the client. We must gain the knowledge and follow the required guidelines necessary to prevent the spread of disease.

**Bacteria** (bac-te-ri-a) are one-celled microorganisms that cannot be seen by the human eye (only through a microscope); in fact they are so small that it would take 1,500 to cover a pin's head. Bacteria survive anywhere as long as the condition is favorable as in any **dark, warm, damp and contaminated areas**, and the bacteria will **reproduce (mitosis)** rapidly in this environment. The **active stage** is when reproduction and bacterial growth take place. The bacteria cell will reach a certain size and **divide in half**, creating two bacterial cells. One bacterial cell can reproduce 16,000 cells in 4½ hours! There are over **15,000 identified** forms of bacteria that have both animal and plant characteristics.

Ribosomes
Cytoplasm
Nucleoid
Flagella
Capsule
Cell Wall
Cytoplasmic Membrane
Flagella

## MITOSIS

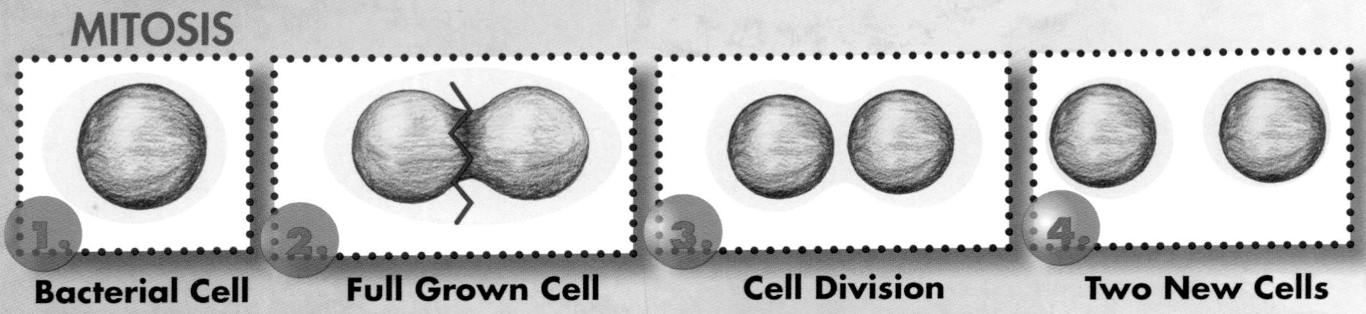


The **inactive stage** is when the bacteria cells meet hostile conditions (decontamination) and reproduction and growth will stop. Some bacteria will produce a **strong outer casing called a spore,** which protects them from disinfectants or hostile conditions. Inside the spore, the **bacteria can remain dormant** (in a restful state) for long periods of time before becoming active again when the environment becomes contaminated.

# Problem Causing...

## The Two Types of Bacteria are:

### Non-Pathogenic

**Non-Pathogenic** (path-o-gen-ic) **bacteria** are **not harmful**, but are actually **helpful in the process of digestion and stimulating the immune system.** They are commonly found in the mouth and intestines and comprise about 70 percent of all bacteria. One example is **saprophytes** (sap-ro-fytes), organisms living on dead or decaying organic matter, which help natural decomposition.

### Pathogenic

**Pathogenic** (path-o-gen-ic) **bacteria** are **harmful** and **cause disease.** These bacteria feed on living matter and are responsible for causing infection. Pathogenic bacteria are also referred to as **germs or microbes.** An example would be **mycobacterium fortuitum furunculosis,** (mi-ko-bac-tere-um for-tu-i-tum fu-run-cu-lo-sis) which is a persistent skin infection causing **boils** below the knees, and triggers concern within podiatry practices.

3

### Three Forms of Pathogenic Bacteria:

- **Cocci** (kok-si) – **circular-shaped** bacteria that produce pus and appear alone or in groups. **Three groups of cocci bacteria are:** **1) Staphylococci** (staph-y-lo-coc-ci) grow in clusters, are pus-forming and produce boils, pustules and abscesses. **2) Diplocci** (dip-lo-coc-ci) grow in pairs, are spherical-shaped and cause pneumonia. **3) Streptococci** (strep-to-coc-ci) grow in curved lines shaped into chains, are pus-forming and produce strep throat and blood poisoning infections.

Cocci

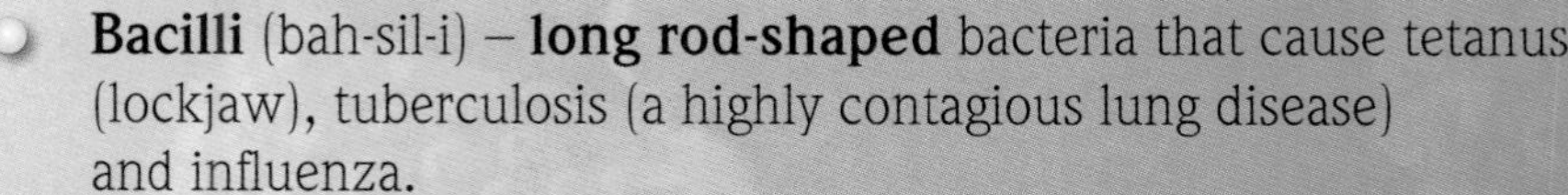

- **Bacilli** (bah-sil-i) – **long rod-shaped** bacteria that cause tetanus (lockjaw), tuberculosis (a highly contagious lung disease) and influenza.

Bacilli

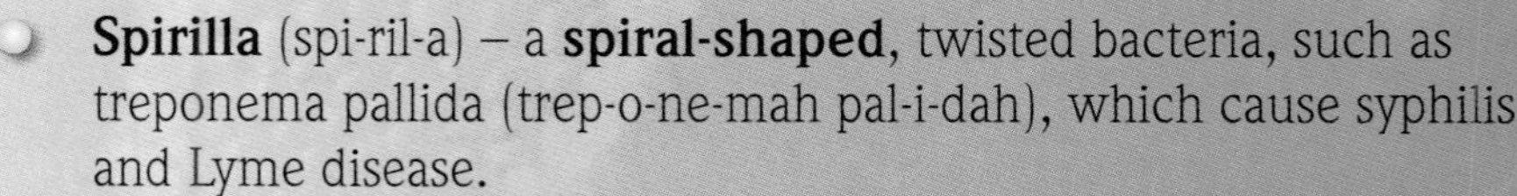

- **Spirilla** (spi-ril-a) – a **spiral-shaped**, twisted bacteria, such as treponema pallida (trep-o-ne-mah pal-i-dah), which cause syphilis and Lyme disease.

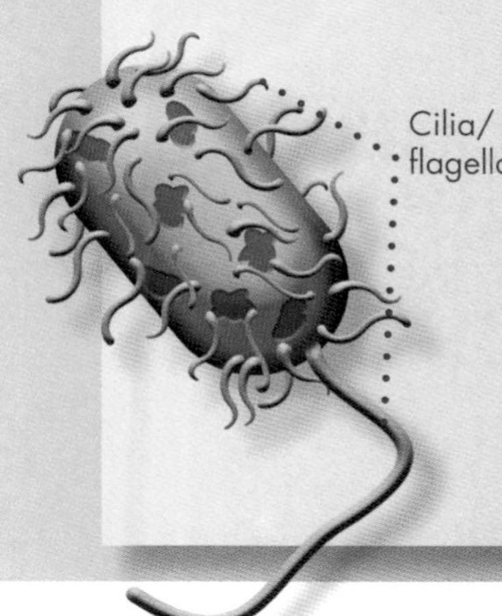

### Bacterial Movement

Only **bacilli** and **spirilla** have the ability to move about. This is done via **hair-like projections** known as **flagella** (flah-jel-ah) or **cilia** (sil-ee-a), which propel the bacteria through liquids. Cocci bacteria do not have these hair-like projections; instead they are spread through dust, air or any substance they settle in.

Spirilla

# Problem Causing . . .

**Anything contagious or communicable** means it can be transferred from one person to another by contact. The following parasitic or viral diseases must never be serviced in the salon. Refer to a medical care professional.

3

**Parasites** (par-a-sites) are pathogenic bacteria, which live on or inside another organism called the **host,** and will survive on that host. These **external insects** survive on your blood whether burrowing under the skin like the **itch mite** or scurrying along the scalp like the **head louse**. (Refer to Chapter 5 for more information).

## The two types of parasites are:

Head louse Itch mite

**Animal parasites** produce diseases such as **scabies (itch mite)** and **pediculosis (head louse).**

Mold

Ringworm fungus on skin

**Plant (vegetable) parasites** produce mold, mildew, yeast and fungus infections, such as **ringworm**, which comes from the parasitic fungus called **dermatophyte** (der-mat-o-phyte).

# Problem Causing . . .

**Viruses** attack human cells by entering the cell wall, growing to maturity and reproducing; often causing the cell's destruction. They are much **smaller than bacteria** (submicroscopic) and can only be seen using a powerful electron microscope. Another difference between bacteria and viruses is that some bacteria can live on their own, while viruses need a host. A common type of virus is influenza.

Flu Virus

## Other types of viruses are:

**Herpes Simplex (HSV)** is characterized by fluid-filled bumps atop a raised, red area. The most common form is a **"cold sore"** or **"fever blister"** that may appear on the lips or mouth. HSV spreads easily by contact.

**Human Hepatitis A, B and C** viruses or bloodborne pathogens **attack the liver.** This can occur through contact with blood or bodily fluids from an infected person. A vaccine is available to help prevent the spread of the hepatitis A and B viruses. There is no vaccine for prevention of hepatitis C.

**Human Immunodeficiency Virus (HIV)** or bloodborne pathogen weakens the immune system by **destroying the white blood cells,** therefore making it difficult to fight infection and other diseases. HIV is contracted through the transfer of blood, bodily fluids and sharing the same needle of an infected person through drug use.

**Acquired Immune Deficiency Syndrome (AIDS)** is the final stage of the HIV virus, which **destroys the immune system.**

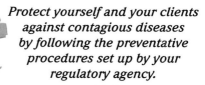

*Protect yourself and your clients against contagious diseases by following the preventative procedures set up by your regulatory agency.*

3

# Infection ...

**Infections** are caused by pathogenic bacteria or viruses that ***enter the body*** in several ways ... through broken skin, the ears, mouth, nose or any opening into the body. An infection occurs when disease-causing microorganisms, which are living cells that can only be seen under a microscope, have invaded a part of the body. These microorganisms grow within the body, producing ***toxins (poisons)*** and causing further harm to the infected tissues.

**Two Classifications of Infection:** A **local infection** is limited to one area of the body such as a boil or pimple containing pus. A **general infection** is when the bacteria and toxins spread throughout the body such as blood poisoning or syphilis.

## Signs of Infection:

- **H** – **Heat:** the infected area feels hot to the touch.
- **A** – **Ache:** the infected area throbs, aches and is painful.
- **R** – **Redness:** the infected area looks red and sore.
- **P** – **Pus:** a thick yellowish liquid found at the site of the infection.
- **S** – **Swelling:** the infected area is inflamed, enlarged or swollen.

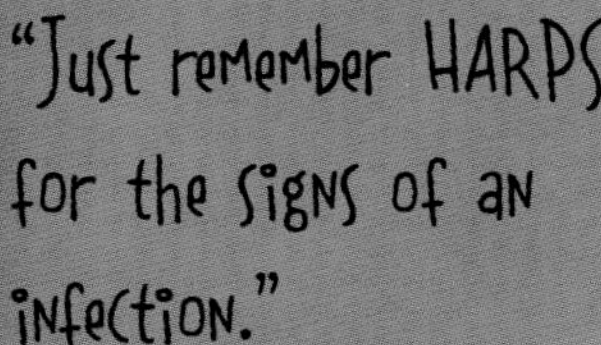

"Just remember HARPS for the signs of an infection."

## Preventative Measures for the Spread of Infection:

- Use an antibacterial soap to wash hands.
- Wash hands before and after service.
- Wash hands after every restroom visit for a minimum of 20 seconds.
- Work with sanitary implements that have been stored in a sanitary receptacle.
- Keep a sanitary and tidy work station.
- Cover open wounds with appropriate dressings.
- Beware of the signs of infection ... **HARPS!**

**Immunity** is the body's ability to **fight or defend** against infection and disease. **Natural immunity** is obtained through inheritance or through hygienic living. **Acquired immunity** is when the body catches and overcomes the disease or an inoculation is offered for the prevention of a disease.

## The body will fight off the bacteria/viruses through:

**Hygienic living** consists of bathing daily, frequent hand washing and the use of deodorant. **Oral hygiene** is brushing your teeth, use of dental floss and using an antiseptic mouthwash.

**Antibodies** remain in your bloodstream and readily fight bacteria. They are a type of protein produced from cells located within the body.

**Vaccines** help produce the **antibodies** to fight a particular disease. Example: **Measles** at one time was a very common virus, but through inoculation it has become practically non-existent.

***If you notice any of the signs of infection, or if your customer mentions symptoms, DO NOT PROVIDE SERVICES! Refer your client to a medical care professional for treatment. This protects you and other salon clients.***

# Sanitation and Disinfection . . .

***In today's world**, preventing the spread of disease has been commercialized and people are exposed to it through the marketing of antibacterial products such as hand wash, gels or wipes. We are also reminded to wash our hands after the use of any public facility. Within the cosmetology industry it is essential that we take the necessary precautions and follow sanitation guidelines to assure that we provide the same respect and safety to our clients as we do ourselves.*

**NOTE:** Medical research has found that antibacterial soaps may be no more effective in combating bacteria than regular liquid soaps. In fact, antibacterial soaps may promote bacterial growth in certain resistant strains.

3

**Contamination** is the presence of unclean materials or tools left on a surface.

**Decontamination** is the removal of any infectious materials on tools or surfaces by following all sanitation and disinfection guidelines.

## Three Levels of Chemical Processes for Controlling Infection:

I Sanitation

II Disinfection

III Sterilization

**Control of Infection** utilizes three levels of chemical processes that will help prevent the spread of, and will kill, most types of pathogenic bacteria.

RA

# Sanitation . . .

## I

**Sanitation** *will remove dirt, reduce the number of pathogenic bacteria and help prevent the growth of microbes, but **will not kill** bacteria.*

### Hand Sanitation

One simple and very easy preventative way of spreading disease is washing your hands. The objective of sanitizing hands is to **significantly reduce** the number of pathogenic bacteria present. The following basic steps will ensure maximum effectiveness when sanitizing hands.

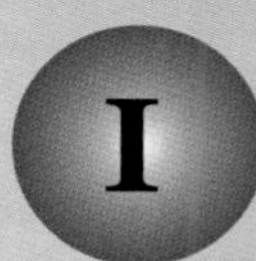

1. Wet hands with warm water and add a liquid soap.

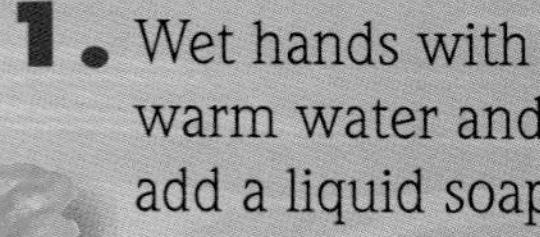

2. Lather hands and rub between each finger and under the nail's free edge. Wash hands for at least 20 seconds for the most effective removal of bacteria and dirt.

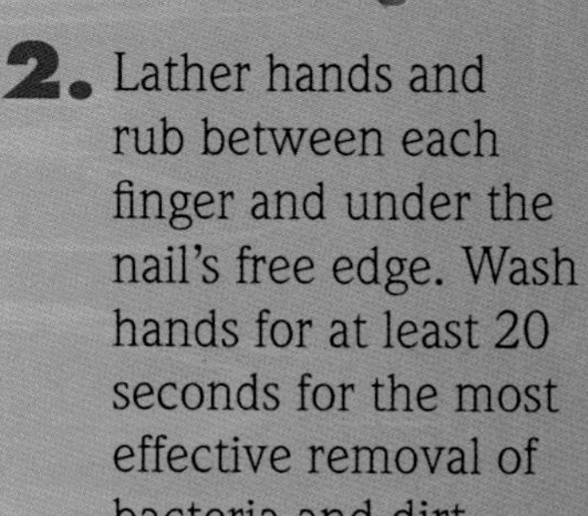

3. Rinse hands thoroughly of all soap residue.

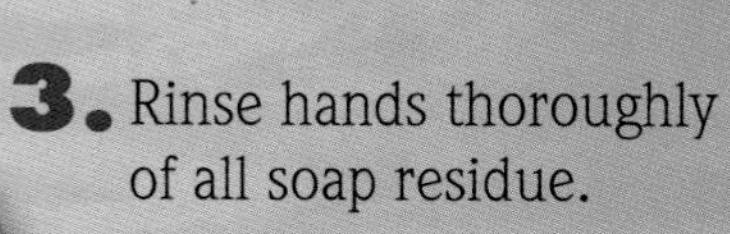

4. Dry hands completely with a clean towel.

**NOTE: DO NOT** use bar soap to wash hands since this form of soap can harbor bacteria.

"Do not take shortcuts for sanitizing and disinfecting. These important procedures are for your own safety, as well as your client's!"

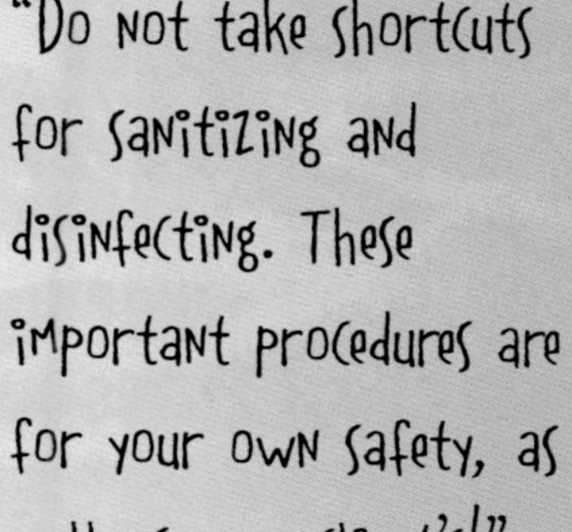

**Antiseptic** is an agent that **prevents or reduces infection** by eliminating or decreasing the growth of microorganisms.
It can be applied **safely to the skin** to cleanse over a superficial wound or assist in the removal of bacteria.

# Disinfection . . .

## II

*Disinfecting is **destroying most** pathogenic bacteria and toxins on non-porous surfaces, implements, work stations, sinks, etc. A disinfectant is a chemical that destroys or inhibits the growth of microorganisms that cause disease. It is **not to be used on skin** or nails. Disinfectants cannot kill bacterial spores.*

## Implement Disinfection

1. Wash and rinse all implements with soap and warm water.
2. Disinfect all non-porous tools such as combs and brushes after each use by immersing completely in disinfectant for a minimum of 10 minutes, or as recommended by manufacturer.
3. Implements should be removed from disinfectant using tongs, a draining basket or gloved hands.
4. Clean implements should be stored in a dry, covered container to protect from re-contamination.
5. Certain buffers, files and manicure sticks that are made from porous material cannot be disinfected – discard after each use or store in Individual Nail kits for each client.
6. Disinfectant solution should be replaced every 24 hours or follow manufacturer's directions.

1

**NOTE:** Never place any type of implement into your mouth or clothes pocket including bobby pins, clips, combs, etc. Implements that drop on the floor are to be discarded, or repeat the disinfectant procedure!

## Product Disinfection

Dispense products from large containers **using a sterile spatula, scoop or pump.** Use tube dispensed products whenever possible or use pipettes (droppers) to remove liquids from bottles. Never double-dip!

3

Soiled cotton, disposable towels or materials **need to be discarded** immediately after use.

2

# Disinfection...

EPA seal: UNITED STATES • ENVIRONMENTAL PROTECTION AGENCY

*A* ***disinfectant*** *product must* ***abide by the effectiveness of its label*** *according to the* ***Environmental Protection Agency (EPA).*** *A manufacturer sends its product(s) to the EPA to verify if it is effective according to the label. The EPA will approve or disapprove the effectiveness of the product. Once the product is tested and proven safe, a registration number and an efficacy label are given.* ***Efficacy*** *(ef-fi-ca-cy) is the ability of the product to produce favorable results. The* ***efficacy label*** *will disclose exactly what results the product will produce.*

RA

## Products Used for Disinfection

**Alcohol** is an extremely flammable, colorless liquid that evaporates quickly. It is slow-acting, therefore less effective than professionally formulated disinfectant systems. A **70-to-90-percent solution of isopropyl or ethyl alcohol** is used on pre-cleaned implements or surfaces.

ALCOHOL

**Quats** is an acronym for **Quarternary** (qua-ter-nar-y) **Ammonium Compounds**, which is a standard name for disinfectants. The chemicals, which are used in the salon, come under the names bactericides, fungicides, virucides. To be sure of the efficacy of an EPA-registered disinfectant, tools must be pre-cleaned and completely immersed in solution (wet sanitizer jar) for 10 to 15 minutes. The disinfectant solution is effective for only 24 hours and must be replaced with a fresh mixture daily.

**Sodium Hypochlorite** (hy-po-chlo-rite) is commonly known as **bleach**. It is a chemical ingredient used in cleansing agents and disinfectants. Bleach solutions are prepared daily at a 5 to 10 percent mixture for safe disinfection of pre-cleaned implements or equipment.

**Phenol** (phe-nol) is a strong, high pH disinfectant. A 5 percent phenol solution is used primarily on metal implements. This is the most expensive form of disinfectant.

CAUTION: Keep this product from contacting the skin and eyes.

# Salon Cleanliness . . .

## Salon Disinfection

- **Everyone** in the salon is responsible for maintaining a clean, orderly environment.
- **Restrooms** should be kept clean, tidy and well stocked with toilet tissue, liquid hand soap and paper towels. All used materials are to be deposited in a covered waste container.
- **Floors** should be swept immediately to remove hair and other debris. Wipe any spills or slippery areas to prevent falling/injury.
- **Towels, robes and capes** should be laundered after each client's use and stored in a closed cabinet.
- **Work stations, shampoo bowls, manicure tables and foot baths** should be sanitized with an **EPA-registered** disinfectant, featuring bactericidal, fungicidal and virucidal efficacy, after each use and allowed to air dry.
- **Foot baths** should be filled with a 10 percent bleach solution and left to sit overnight, at least once a week. Foot baths should also be flushed with water prior to each client's use.
- **No animals/pets** may be allowed on salon premises, except a Seeing Eye dog.
- **Smoking is ONLY** allowed in a designated area outside of salon.

3

## Salon Air Quality

Covered container

- **Dispose of ALL** service waste materials in a covered container. Regularly remove trash material from salon.
- **Change filters** in the heating and cooling systems regularly to avoid the collection of bacteria/molds.
- **Cleanse the air** of dust and vapors with a professional air purification or exhaust system.
- **Keep lids on all containers** to eliminate evaporation of product and confine the odor. Containers **need to be marked,** stating the name of the item inside.

Air Purifier

III **Sterilization** is the **destruction of living microorganisms** on an object or surface. Generally, this procedure is not applied in the salon, but is used within medical facilities.

## Products Used for Sterilization

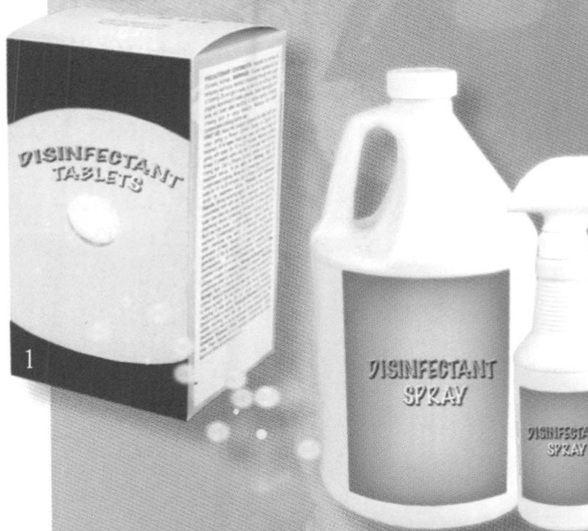

1

**Broad-Spectrum Sterilizers (used in hospitals)** are disinfectants that destroy viruses, fungi and bacteria. They are EPA registered, which means they are capable of getting rid of bacteria, fungi and viruses.

**Ultraviolet Container (dry sanitizer)** contains a lamp or bulb that emits ultraviolet radiation, which destroys germs, viruses, molds and bacteria. In the salon, generally the bulbs are not a high enough wattage to destroy bacteria. Instead, the container is used to store sanitized items, keeping them free from contamination.

2

3

**Autoclave Container** is a strong steel vessel that is used for steam sterilization of nail tools or materials. Implements are placed inside vessel to destroy all bacteria.

# Blood Borne Pathogen...

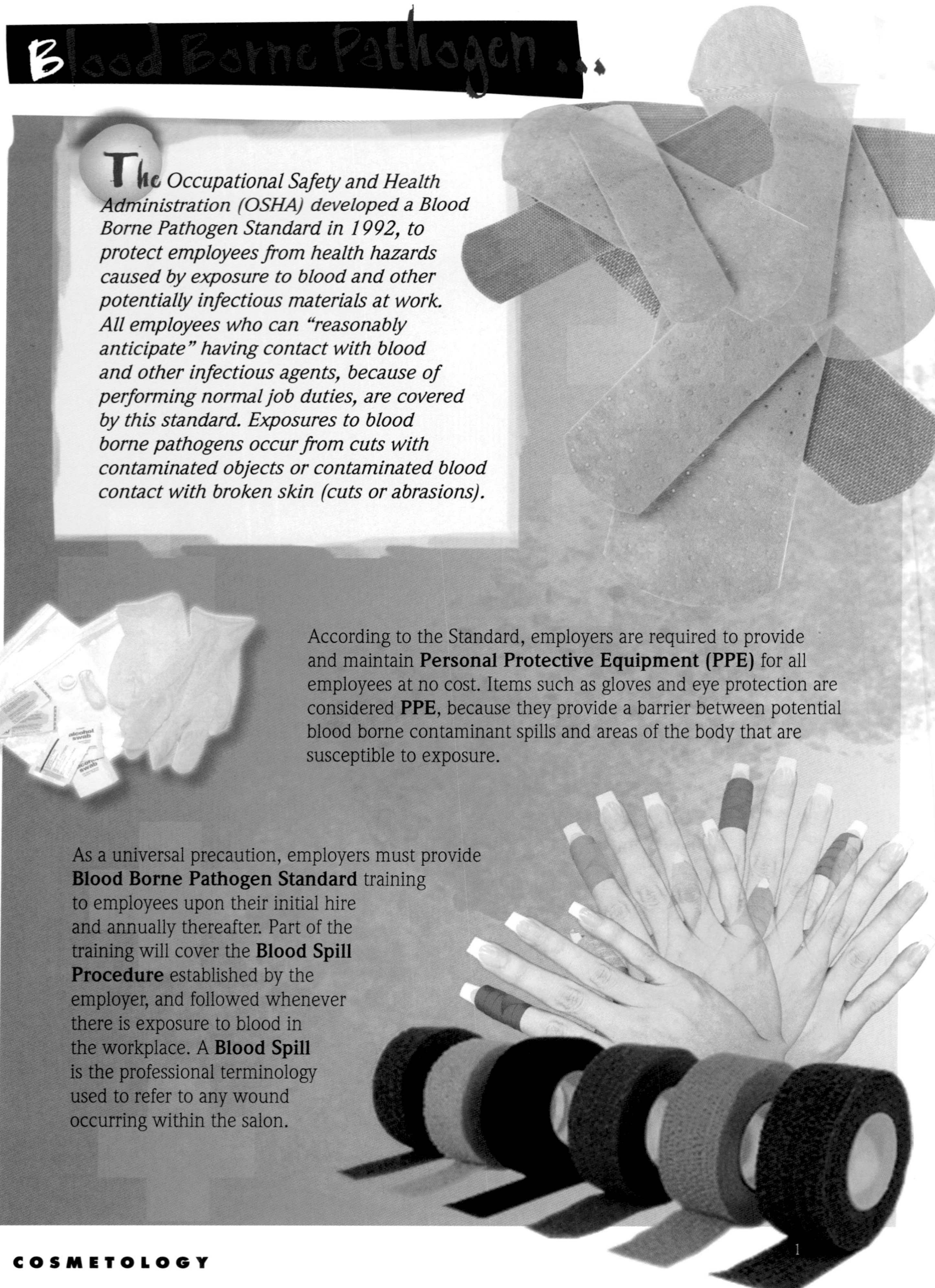

*The Occupational Safety and Health Administration (OSHA) developed a Blood Borne Pathogen Standard in 1992, to protect employees from health hazards caused by exposure to blood and other potentially infectious materials at work. All employees who can "reasonably anticipate" having contact with blood and other infectious agents, because of performing normal job duties, are covered by this standard. Exposures to blood borne pathogens occur from cuts with contaminated objects or contaminated blood contact with broken skin (cuts or abrasions).*

According to the Standard, employers are required to provide and maintain **Personal Protective Equipment (PPE)** for all employees at no cost. Items such as gloves and eye protection are considered **PPE**, because they provide a barrier between potential blood borne contaminant spills and areas of the body that are susceptible to exposure.

As a universal precaution, employers must provide **Blood Borne Pathogen Standard** training to employees upon their initial hire and annually thereafter. Part of the training will cover the **Blood Spill Procedure** established by the employer, and followed whenever there is exposure to blood in the workplace. A **Blood Spill** is the professional terminology used to refer to any wound occurring within the salon.

**The following is a procedural guide to use for blood spills occurring in the salon.**

RA

## Blood Spill Procedures

### Client Injury:

- Stop performing the service. Cleanse your hands with warm water and antibacterial soap, and apply protective gloves.
- Clean injured area with warm water and soap.
- Apply antiseptic and/or styptic cream or lotion to the wound with an applicator.
- Cover the wound with an adhesive dressing.
- Clean and disinfect any contaminated areas of the work station with an EPA-registered or tuberculocidal (phenol-based) disinfectant.
- Dispose of all contaminated materials in a properly marked double bag.
- Proceed with service, avoiding the injured area.

### Employee Injury:

- Stop performing the service. Cleanse your hands with warm water and antibacterial soap.
- Clean injured area with warm water and soap.
- Apply antiseptic and/or styptic cream or lotion to the wound with an applicator.
- Cover the wound with an adhesive dressing.
- Wear a glove or finger wrap if the wound occurred on the hand or finger.
- Clean and disinfect any contaminated areas of the work station with an EPA-registered or tuberculocidal (phenol-based) disinfectant.
- Dispose of all contaminated materials in a properly marked double bag.
- Proceed with service, avoiding the injured area.

"Prevention is the best protection!"

# Safety in Product Use . . .

*As a professional, it is your responsibility to use safe guidelines that will protect both you and the customer. Many of the products in cosmetology can be used safely and without risk by observing proper practices, such as avoiding overexposure.*

Overexposure involves excessively subjecting you or clients to a substance that can produce an allergic reaction, sensitivity or other unwanted side effects. All products have safe and unsafe levels of exposure. Understanding how the product performs and handling products safely are the keys to avoiding overexposure.

## Products may enter the body in three ways:



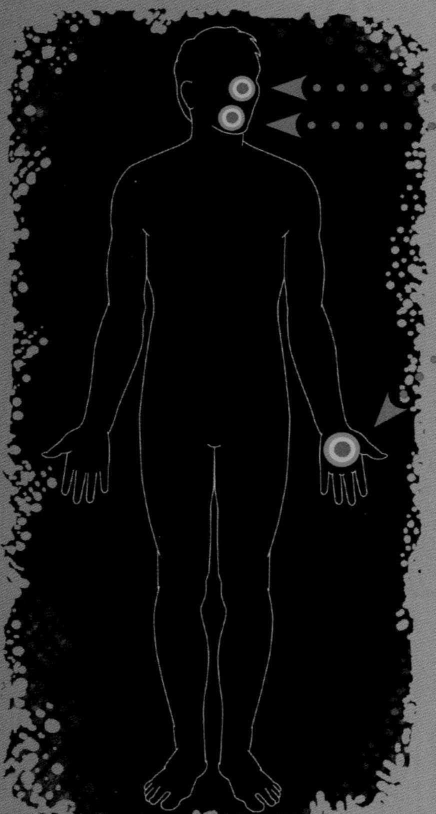

- **Inhalation** (smell)
- **Ingestion** (taste)
- **Skin contact** (touch)

The body will usually indicate if there is any sensitivity to a product by showing some common signs.

Early Warning Signs of Overexposure:
**(DO NOT IGNORE THESE SIGNS)**

**Irritations** of the following:

- Itchy skin, rash or hives
- Watery, red, itchy eyes
- Runny, congested nose
- Dry, scratchy, sore throat

"Be careful in your use of products and processes. Chemicals, UV radiation or viruses may contain carcinogens, which are substances that can cause cancer."

**The Department of Labor set up the regulating agency called the Occupational Safety & Health Administration (OSHA), with the task to assure the safety and health of American workers. This is done by setting and enforcing standards for employee training and education and supporting continued improvements within the workplace.**

**OSHA Hazard Communication Standard CFR 1910.1200** states that information must be available about the characteristics and hazards of the chemicals used, to ensure chemical safety in the workplace.

## OSHA mandates:

**Every chemical** located within the business must have MSDS forms filed in a prominent and available location.

**All products are to have an accurate and clear label with a warning** and a complete chemical inventory list must be available as a quick reference.

# Job Safety and Health

## It's the law!

OSHA

Occupational Safety and Health Administration
U.S. Department of Labor

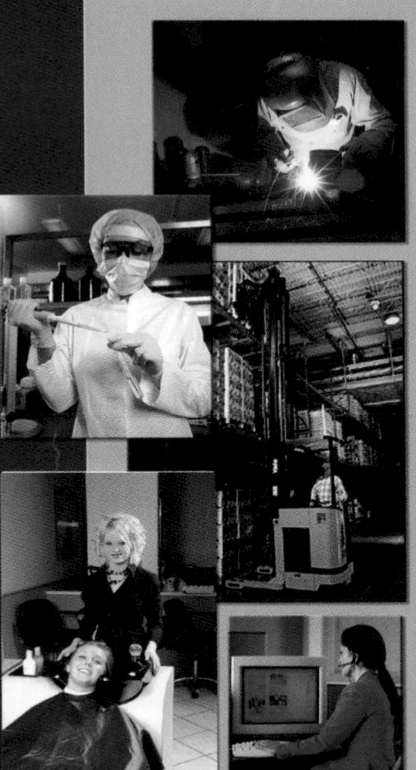

EMPLOYEES:

- You have the right to notify your employer or OSHA about workplace hazards. You may ask OSHA to keep your name confidential.
- You have the right to request an OSHA inspection if you believe that there are unsafe and unhealthful conditions in your workplace. You or your representative may participate in that inspection.
- You can file a complaint with OSHA within 30 days of retaliation or discrimination by your employer for making safety and health complaints or for exercising your rights under the *OSH Act*.
- You have the right to see OSHA citations issued to your employer. Your employer must post the citations at or near the place of the alleged violations.
- Your employer must correct workplace hazards by the date indicated on the citation and must certify that these hazards have been reduced or eliminated.
- You have the right to copies of your medical records and records of your exposures to toxic and harmful substances or conditions.
- Your employer must post this notice in your workplace.
- You must comply with all occupational safety and health standards issued under the *OSH Act* that apply to your own actions and conduct on the job.

EMPLOYERS:

- You must furnish your employees a place of employment free from recognized hazards.
- You must comply with the occupational safety and health standards issued under the *OSH Act*.

**Free assistance in identifying and correcting hazards or complying with standards is available to employers, without citation or penalty, through OSHA-supported consultation programs in each state.**

This free poster available from OSHA –
*The Best Resource for Safety and Health*

**1-800-321-OSHA**
www.osha.gov

OSHA 3165-12-06R

# Safety in Product Use...

**Material Safety Data Sheets (MSDS)** provide employer and employee with the **proper procedure in handling, working with and storing chemicals in the workplace.** MSDS information is made available from the chemical manufacturer or importer for each product used. You can also check with your local product distributor or supplier.

The following is an example of a Material Safety Data Sheet:

## MATERIAL SAFETY DATA SHEET

MSDS-021

Prepared to OSHA, ACC, ANSI, WHMIS & 2001/58 EC Standards | MSDS Revision: 1.0 | MSDS Revision Date: 01/01/2005

### DEFINITION OF TERMS

A large number of abbreviations and acronyms appear on a MSDS. Some of these that are commonly used include the following:

**GENERAL INFORMATION:**

| | |
|---|---|
| CAS No. | Chemical Abstract Service Number |

**EXPOSURE LIMITS IN AIR:**

| | |
|---|---|
| ACGIH | American Conference on Governmental Industrial Hygienists |
| TLV | Threshold Limit Value |
| OSHA | U.S. Occupational Safety and Health Administration |
| PEL | Permissible Exposure Limit |
| IDLH | Immediately Dangerous to Life and Health |

**FIRST AID MEASURES:**

| | |
|---|---|
| CPR | Cardiopulmonary resuscitation - method in which a person whose heart has stopped receives manual chest compressions and breathing to circulate blood and provide oxygen to the body. |

**HAZARDOUS MATERIALS IDENTIFICATION SYSTEM: HMIS**

HEALTH
FLAMMABILITY
REACTIVITY
PERSONAL PROTECTION

**HEALTH, FLAMMABILITY & REACTIVITY RATINGS:**

| | |
|---|---|
| 0 | Minimal Hazard |
| 1 | Slight Hazard |
| 2 | Moderate Hazard |
| 3 | Severe Hazard |
| 4 | Extreme Hazard |

**PERSONAL PROTECTION RATINGS:**

| | |
|---|---|
| A | |
| B | |
| C | |
| D | |
| E | |
| F | |
| G | |
| H | |
| I | |
| J | |
| K | |
| X | Consult your supervisor or S.O.P. for special handling directions. |

Safety Glasses · Splash Goggles · Face Shield & Eye Protection · Gloves · Boots · Synthetic Apron · Full Suit · Dust Respirator · Vapor Respirator · Dust & Vapor Respirator · Full Face Respirator · Airline Hood/Mask or SCBA

Note: the dotted circle indicates that this respiratory protective equipment is required for high concentrations or for large volume spills or releases of product.

**NATIONAL FIRE PROTECTION ASSOCIATION: NFPA**

**FLAMMABILITY LIMITS IN AIR:**

| | |
|---|---|
| Autoignition Temperature | Minimum temperature required to initiate combustion in air with no other source of ignition |
| LEL | Lower Explosive Limit - lowest percent of vapor in air, by volume, that will explode or ignite in the presence of an ignition source |
| UEL | Upper Explosive Limit - highest percent of vapor in air, by volume, that will explode or ignite in the presence of an ignition source |

**HAZARD RATINGS:**

| | |
|---|---|
| 0 | Minimal Hazard |
| 1 | Slight Hazard |
| 2 | Moderate Hazard |
| 3 | Severe Hazard |
| 4 | Extreme Hazard |
| ACD | Acidic |
| ALK | Alkaline |
| COR | Corrosive |
| ~~W~~ | Use No Water |
| OX | Oxidizer |

FLAMMABILITY
REACTIVITY
HEALTH
SPECIAL PRECAU

**TOXICOLOGICAL INFORMATION:**

| | |
|---|---|
| $LD_{50}$ | Lethal Dose (solids & liquids) which kills 5 exposed animals |
| $LC_{50}$ | Lethal concentration (gases) which kil exposed animal |
| ppm | Concentration expressed in parts o million parts |
| $TD_{lo}$ | Lowest dose to cause a symptom |
| $TC_{Lo}$ | Lowest concentration to cause a |
| $TD_{lo}$, $LD_{lo}$, & $LD_o$ or $TC$, $TC_o$, $LC_{lo}$, & $LC_o$ | Lowest dose (or concentration toxic effects |
| IARC | International Agency for Res |
| NTP | National Toxicology Progra |
| RTECS | Registry of Toxic Effects of |
| BCF | Bioconcentration Factor |
| $TL_m$ | Median threshold limit |
| log $K_{OW}$ or log $K_{OC}$ | Coefficient of Oil/Wat |

**REGULATORY INFORMATION:**

| | |
|---|---|
| WHMIS | Canadian Workplace Haz |
| DOT | U.S. Department of Transp |
| TC | Transport Canada |
| EPA | U.S. Environmental Prot |
| DSL | Canadian Domestic S |
| NDSL | Canadian Non-Dom |
| PSL | Canadian Priority S |
| TSCA | U.S. Toxic Substan |
| EU | European Union |

**EC INFORMATION:**

| C | E |
|---|---|
| Corrosive | Explosive |

ABBREVIATIONS:

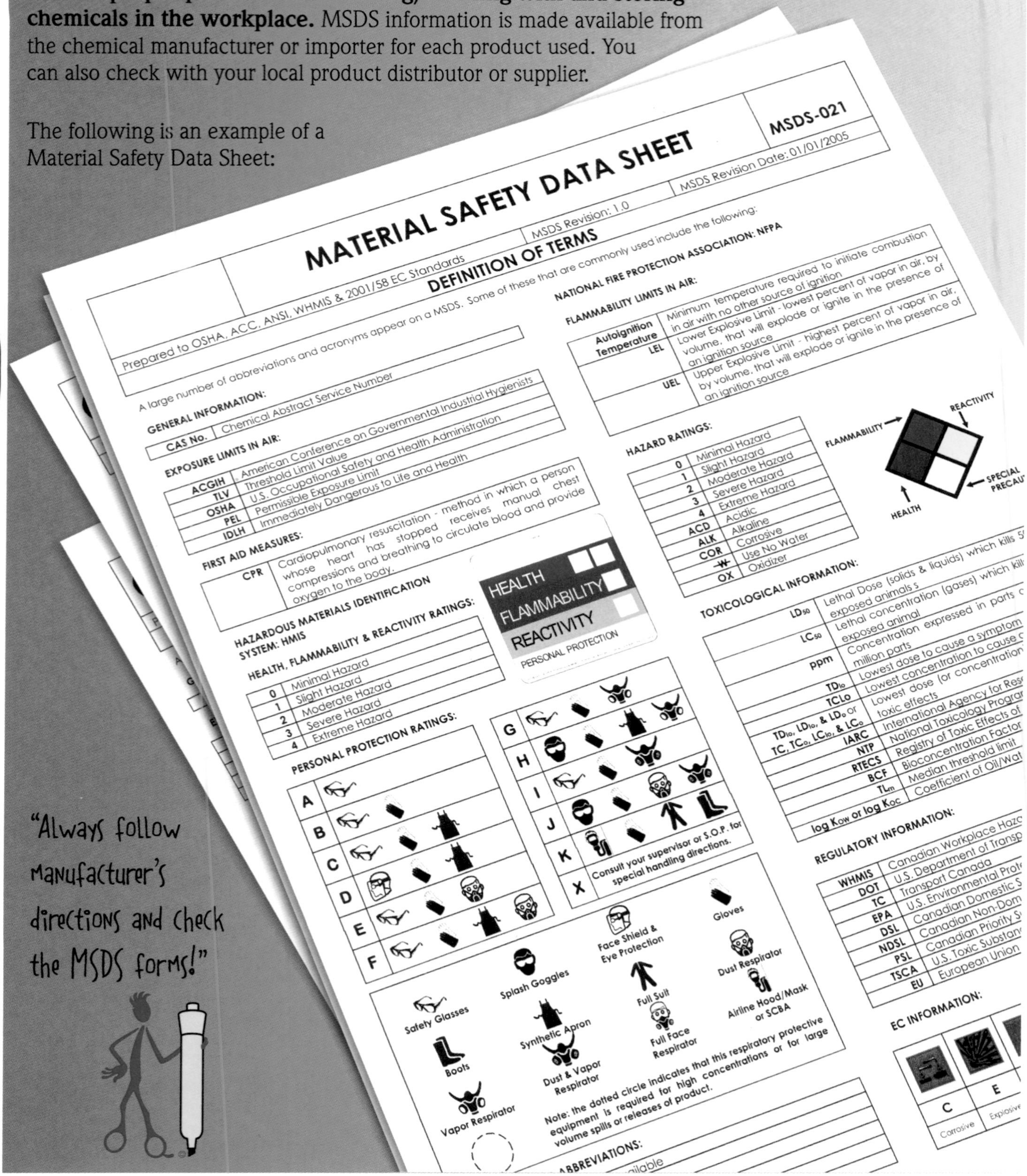

"Always follow manufacturer's directions and check the MSDS forms!"

3

# Air Quality Control...

***Because inhalation** is one of the ways chemicals can enter the body, the salon needs to be free from chemical vapors for the well-being of the client and the cosmetologist. Proper ventilation in the workplace, especially within each individual's "**breathing zone,**" will create a safe environment and help prevent overexposure.*

## Methods to assist in the elimination of vapors and dust:

Filtered air

Unclean air

**FAIR**

* **Air Purification System** takes the existing air within the salon, cleanses the air by filtration and forces it back out into the salon.

**GOOD**

** **Ultraviolet Air Purification System** has become a technologically advanced and healthful way to purify air. Ultraviolet bulbs are installed into existing heating/cooling ductwork, which allows the airflow to pass over the bulbs to purify and cleanse the air.

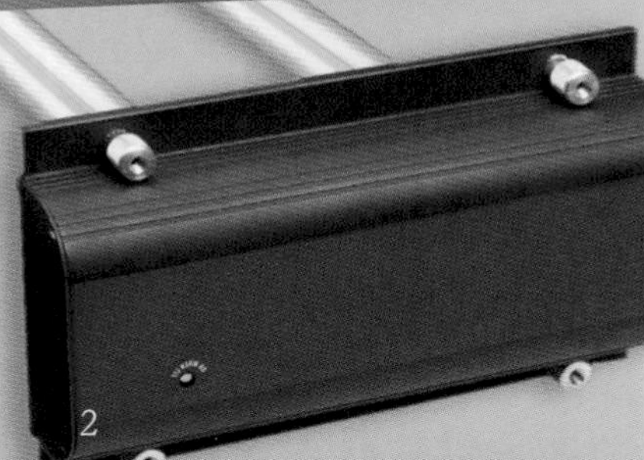


**VERY GOOD**

*** **Ventilation System** will capture any chemical vapors and dust, carry them through the exhaust pipe, and expel the vapors or dust from the building. Fresh air is then brought in from the outside of the building, through an air intake, to replace the air lost. The exhaust pipe and air intake must be separated by a distance of a least 15 feet (4.57 cm).

**EXCELLENT**

**** **Combination of Systems** using exhaust systems with UV and/or air purification systems will provide the ultimate elimination of vapors and dust.

3

# Salon Safety REVIEW QUESTIONS

## MULTIPLE CHOICE

1. The five signs of an infection are heat, ache, redness, pus and?
   A. blisters B. swelling C. scab
2. In what type of environment do bacteria grow and reproduce?
   A. warm and contaminated B. cold and contaminated C. warm and clean
3. To dispense products from large containers, use a?
   A. spatula B. finger C. lid
4. The first step in a blood spill procedure is to?
   A. cover wound B. clean injured area C. stop performing service
5. Which air elimination system expels air outside the salon and brings fresh air back into salon?
   A. air purification B. ultraviolet C. ventilation
6. Which chemical can safely be used on the skin?
   A. antiseptic B. disinfectant C. alcohol
7. Which type of bacteria produces strep throat?
   A. spirilla B. bacilli C. cocci
8. What is the strong outer casing called that covers some bacteria?
   A. shell B. spore C. crust
9. When the body fights off the bacteria or viruses that enter the body it is referred to as?
   A. immunity B. infection C. contamination
10. What happens to the bacterial cell in the reproduction phase?
    A. divides in thirds B. divides in half C. does not divide
11. Which type of bacteria has a spiral shape?
    A. cocci B. bacilli C. spirilla
12. The disease pediculosis comes from the animal parasite called?
    A. itch mite B. head louse C. ringworm
13. How can bacteria enter the body?
    A. mouth B. ears C. both A. and B.
14. What is the thick yellowish liquid at the site of an infection?
    A. pus B. fungus C. blood
15. Which virus attacks the liver?
    A. hepatitis B. herpes simplex C. human immunodeficiency
16. Pathogenic bacteria are also referred to as germs or?
    A. saprophytes B. microbes C. boils
17. Which virus produces fever blisters?
    A. hepatitis B. herpes simplex C. human immunodeficiency
18. Hygienic living consists of daily bathing, frequent hand washing and the use of?
    A. medicine B. deodorant C. tanning beds
19. Which level of controlling infection DOES NOT kill bacteria?
    A. sanitation B. disinfection C. sterilization
20. What type of animal is allowed on the salon premises?
    A. cat B. St. Bernard dog C. Seeing Eye dog

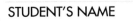

STUDENT'S NAME DATE GRADE

cells circulation

frontalis insertion

myology

massage

temporal

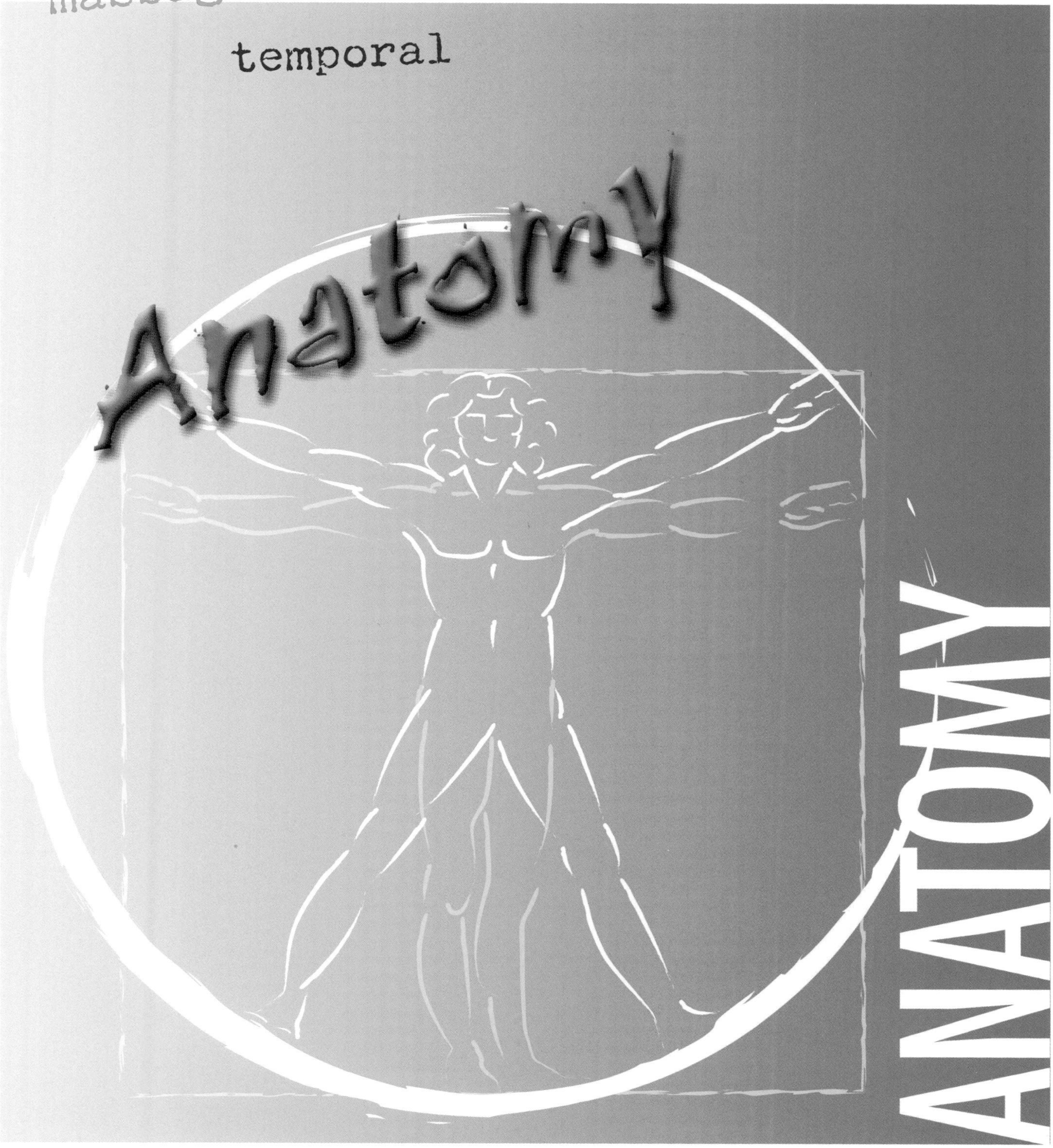

# Anatomy

4

ANATOMY

# Terminology . . .

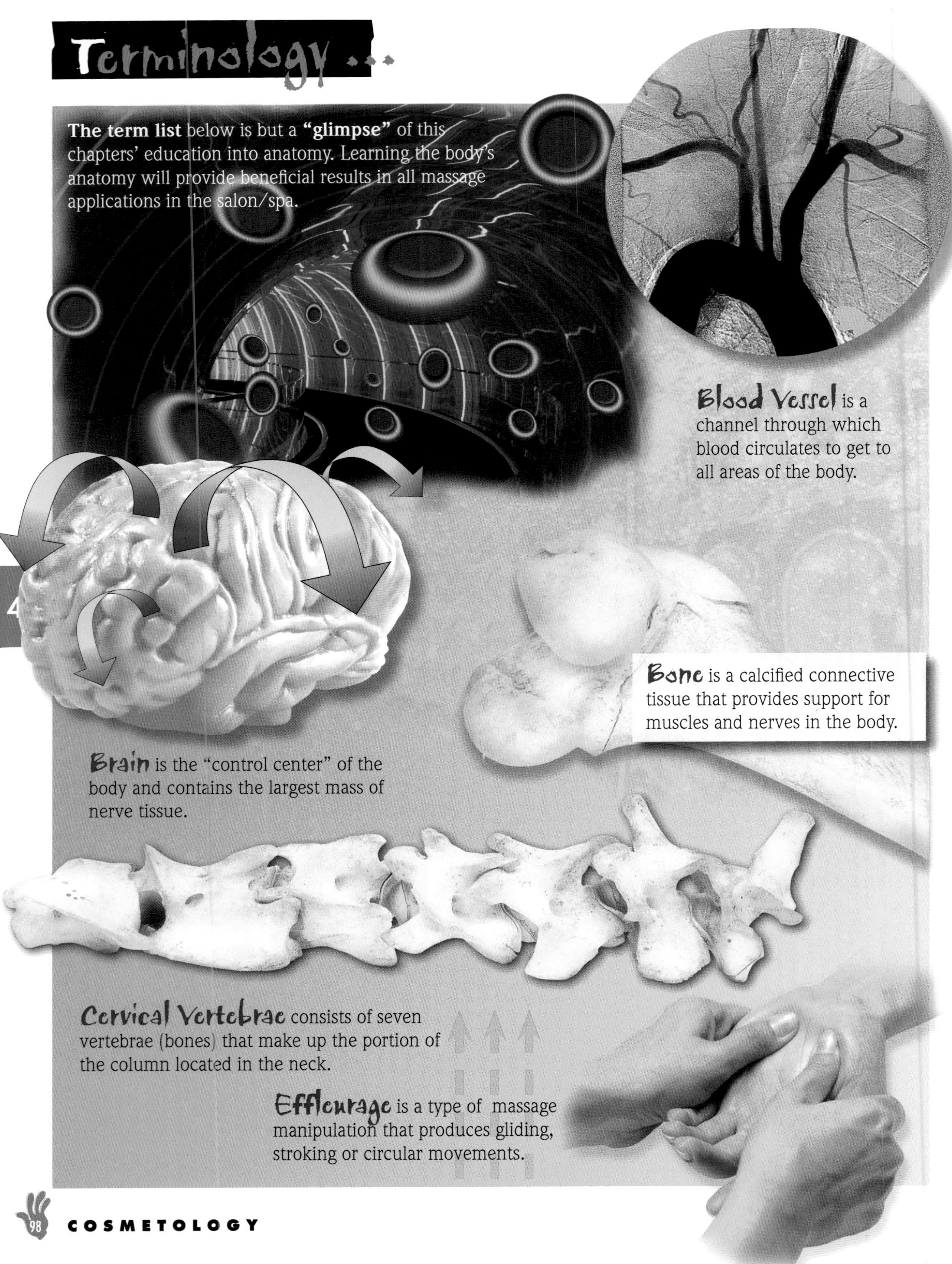

**The term list** below is but a **"glimpse"** of this chapters' education into anatomy. Learning the body's anatomy will provide beneficial results in all massage applications in the salon/spa.

**Blood Vessel** is a channel through which blood circulates to get to all areas of the body.

**Bone** is a calcified connective tissue that provides support for muscles and nerves in the body.

**Brain** is the "control center" of the body and contains the largest mass of nerve tissue.

**Cervical Vertebrae** consists of seven vertebrae (bones) that make up the portion of the column located in the neck.

**Effleurage** is a type of massage manipulation that produces gliding, stroking or circular movements.

# Terminology . . .

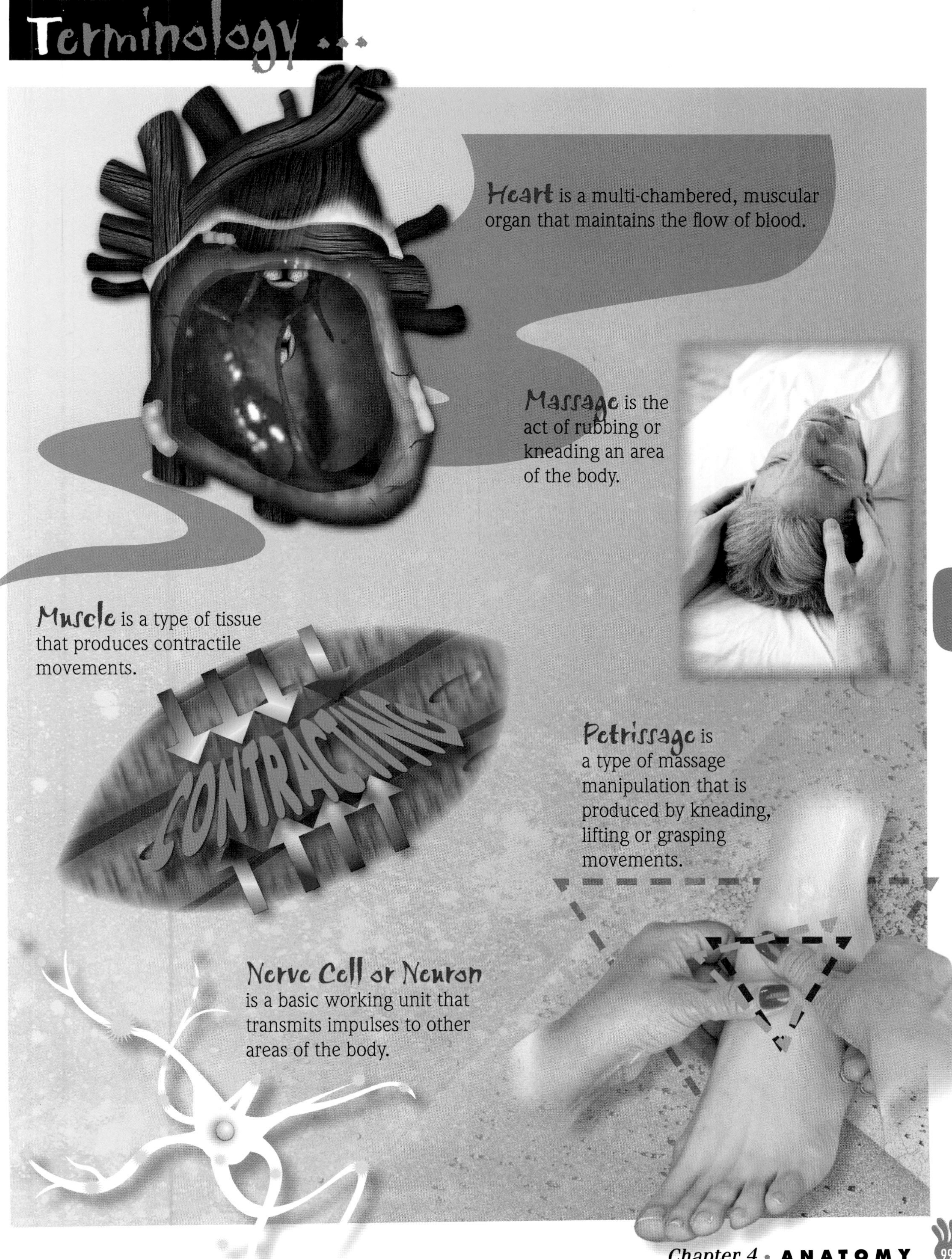


**Heart** is a multi-chambered, muscular organ that maintains the flow of blood.

**Massage** is the act of rubbing or kneading an area of the body.

**Muscle** is a type of tissue that produces contractile movements.

**Petrissage** is a type of massage manipulation that is produced by kneading, lifting or grasping movements.

**Nerve Cell or Neuron** is a basic working unit that transmits impulses to other areas of the body.

4

# Cellular Structure . . .

*As you perform services on the head and face, you will need to understand the basics of **anatomy and physiology. Anatomy** (a-nat-o-my) is the scientific study of the shape and structure of the human body and its parts. **Physiology** (phys-i-ol-o-gy) is the biological study of the body's internal functioning. Knowledge of bodily structures such as bones, muscles, blood and nerves must all begin with a common understanding of the fundamental units of human construction, called cells and tissues. **Histology** (his-tol-o-gy) is the science that deals with the microscopic structures such as cells, tissues and organs and their function within the body.*

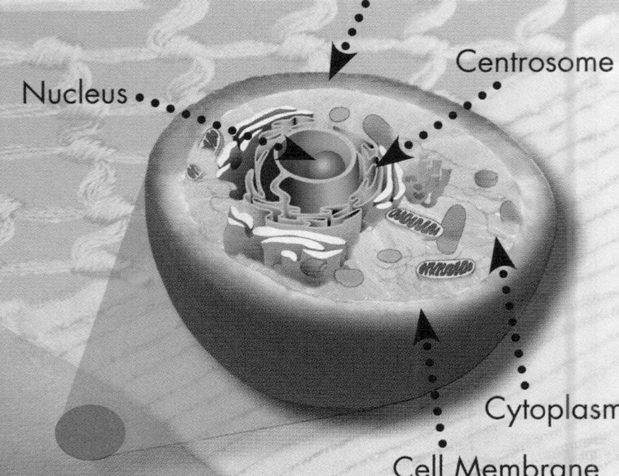


4

**Cells** are the smallest structural units or building blocks of living tissue capable of functioning as independent entities. Cells are made of **protoplasm** (proh-toh-plaz-em) which is a jelly-like, granular material that comprises the living contents of a cell.

## The Components of a Cell

**Cell Membrane** is a thin membrane around the cytoplasm of a cell that controls passage of substances in and out of the cell; can also be called the **"cell wall."**

**Cytoplasm** (seye-toh-plaz-em) is the watery material found between the cell membrane and the nuclear membrane. This contains food substances for cellular growth and repair.

**Centrosome** (sen-tro-sohm) is a specialized region of a living cell situated next to the nucleus, where micro-tubules are assembled and broken down during cell division. This structure facilitates cell division.

**Nucleus** (noo-klee-us) is the central part of the cell, separated by the nuclear membrane that contains **DNA** (deoxyribonucleic [de-ox-y-ri-bo-nu-cle-ic] acid-genetic information) and **RNA** (ribonucleic [ri-bo-nu-cle-ic] acid-manufactures protein), which is responsible for growth and reproduction.

# Cell Metabolism and Tissues ...

*Cells need many things to live, function and reproduce* ***(cells divide in half creating two daughter cells),*** *including an ample supply of nutrients, water, oxygen and the elimination of waste materials.*

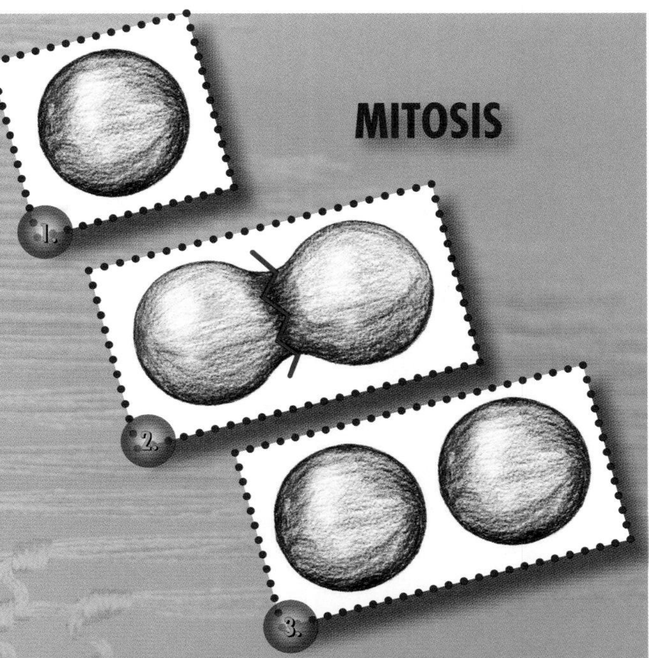


**Cell Metabolism** (meh-tab-o-liz-em) is the method used by living cells to process nutrient molecules and maintain a living state.

**Metabolism can be broken down into two stages:**

1. **Anabolism** (ah-nab-o-liz-em) is the **constructive stage** of metabolism, where complex (large) molecules are built up from small molecules. Throughout this stage, the body stores up energy in the form of oxygen, water and food for cell repair and growth.

2. **Catabolism** (kah-tab-o-liz-em) is the **deconstructive stage** of metabolism, where complex molecules are broken down into small molecules. Throughout this stage, the body releases energy needed for carrying out functions including muscle contraction and digestion.

**Tissues** are **groups of cells** that act together for a specific purpose. Each tissue in the body has a unique function and appearance.

**Types of Tissues:**

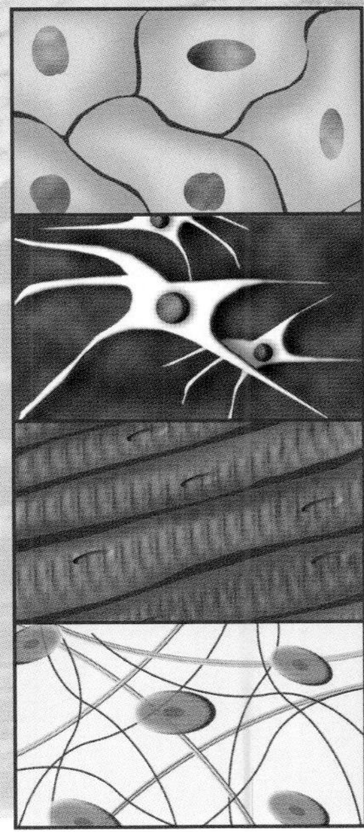

- **Epithelial** (ep-i-the-le-al) **tissue**, such as skin, serves as a protective covering for the body's surfaces and organs.
- **Nerve tissue** carries signals back and forth to the brain to coordinate and manage all bodily functions. Examples of nerve tissues are the brain and spinal cord.
- **Muscular tissue** contracts when stimulated to produce movement of body parts.
- **Connective tissue** is a supporting protective layer that surrounds other tissues and organs. Specialized connective tissues include bones, cartilage, ligaments, blood and fat.

4

# Bodily Organs ...

*We started with the smallest structures in the body: **cells**. Next, we will discover our **organs**, and how they affect the functioning of our complex bodies.*

**Organs** are structural and functional units that are specialized for a particular purpose.

**The following are some of the most vital organs contained within the body:**

- The **brain** is the **"control center"** of the body.
- The **heart** is a multi-chambered, **muscular** organ that **maintains the flow of blood** through the entire circulatory system.
- The **lungs** are two sac-like **respiratory** organs, which **remove carbon dioxide** from the blood while providing it with oxygen.
- The **skin** consists of **membranous** tissue, which covers the body and **protects** all internal structures.
- The **stomach** and **intestines** are the principal organs for **digestion of food.**
- The **kidneys maintain** proper water and electrolyte balance, and **eliminate waste** from the bloodstream.
- The **liver secretes bile** (a substance that aids in the digestion and absorption of fats) and is active in the metabolism of carbohydrates, fats and proteins and **helps to detoxify** poisons from the body.

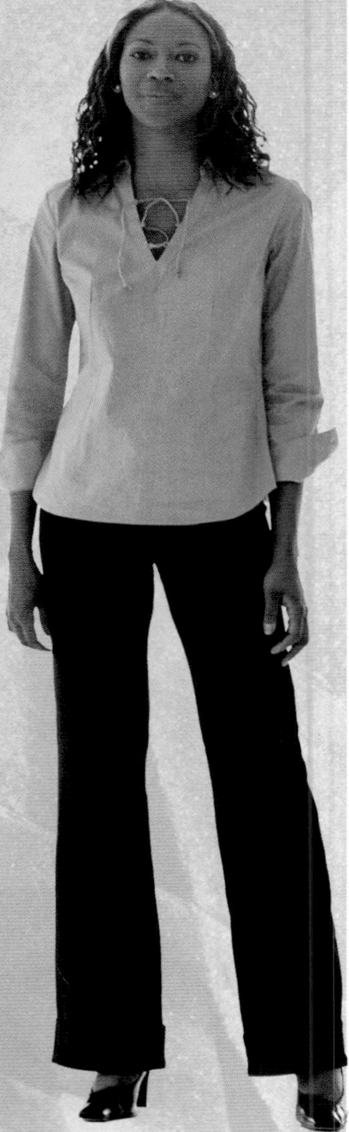

# Bodily Systems . . .

*Just as cells integrate to form the large parts of the body, there are systems within the body that are composed of parts working side by side to accomplish many important tasks.*

**Systems** are a group of interacting or interdependent structures within the body that act together to perform specific functions. The human body consists of **10 different systems.**

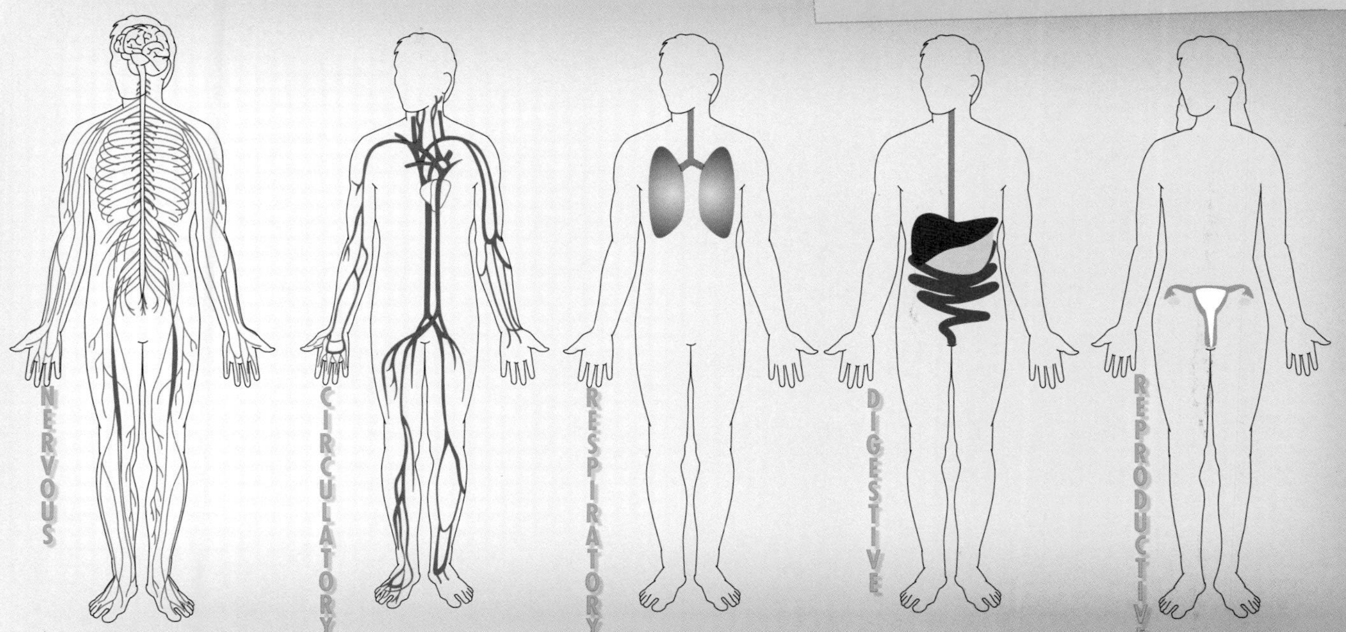


- **Integumentary** (in-teg-u-men-ta-ry) **system** is the **largest system in the body** and is composed of the skin and the structures derived from the skin, such as nails, hair and various glands.
- **Skeletal system** is the bony framework **supporting** the soft tissues and **protecting** the internal organs of the body. It contains **206 bones** that are connected by movable and immovable joints.
- **Nervous system** includes nerves, the spinal cord and the brain. It **regulates and coordinates** all of the body's activities.
- **Circulatory system** contains the heart and the blood vessels, and **moves blood throughout the body**.
- **Muscular system** produces internal and external **movement** and **provides posture** and **support** to the skeletal system. There are more than **500 muscles** in the human body.
- **Respiratory system** consists of organs that **process air** (bringing in oxygen and expelling carbon dioxide) in the body, including the nose, throat and lungs.
- **Digestive or gastrointestinal system** is a series of connected organs, the purpose of which is to **break down, or digest, food.**
- **Reproductive system** is made up of the sexual organs, which allow humans to **develop offspring.**
- **Endocrine system** consists of a group of duct and ductless glands that **regulate bodily functions.**
- **Excretory system** consists of organs that **eliminate waste** from the body. The **kidneys** excrete urine, **skin** eliminates perspiration, **intestines** remove undigested food, **liver** secretes bile and the **lungs** exhale carbon dioxide.

# Bones ...

**People** *usually do not realize the psychological effect a healthy body can have on us.* ***If our hair and face look good ... we in turn will feel beautiful, confident and happy.*** *The body's intricate network of bones, muscles, blood and nerves provide us with shape, contour, color and skin sensitivity of our face and head. The beauty industry offers an endless array of hair, nail and skin care services to assist us with protecting our most exposed asset:* ***our face, hair and hands.***

**Bones** are calcified connective tissue made up of bone cells and **osteocytes** (os-tee-o-sitz). A fibrous connective tissue membrane called the **periosteum** (per-ee-os-tee-um) covers bones.

4

**Ligaments** are bands of cordlike tissue that support the joints, which connect the bones to one another. Bones are important because they provide support for the muscles and nerves, which permit movement of the body.

**NOTE:** Did you know that bone is composed of 25 percent organic material by weight, and that bones produce blood cells? Therefore, even though bones are hard, they are not dead. The bones are **living parts** of the body.

"The scientific study of the anatomy, structure and function of bones is called osteology (os-te-olo-gy)."

# Bones and Joints ...

*Joints are the hinges that hold the skeletal system together by connecting two or more bones. Joints can be movable such as the knees or elbows and other joints have no movement like the skull. The following are the types of joints found within the body.*

**Pivot Joints** are part of the bone that rotates freely. Example: the connection of the radius and ulna in the arm.
**Hinge Joints** are moveable joints that allow movement in only two directions. (bend and straighten). Examples: elbows and knees.
**Ball-and-Socket Joints** feature a rounded end, which fits into a concave socket. Examples: the hip and the shoulder.
**Gliding Joints** move freely using only smooth motions. Examples: the ankle and wrist.
4

# Bones of Head ...

**The *skull*** *is the* ***boney structure*** *that makes up the head and encases the brain.* ***The skull is divided into two areas: cranium and face.***

The cranium (cra-ni-um) covers the **top and sides of the head** and consists of six bones that are affected by massage.

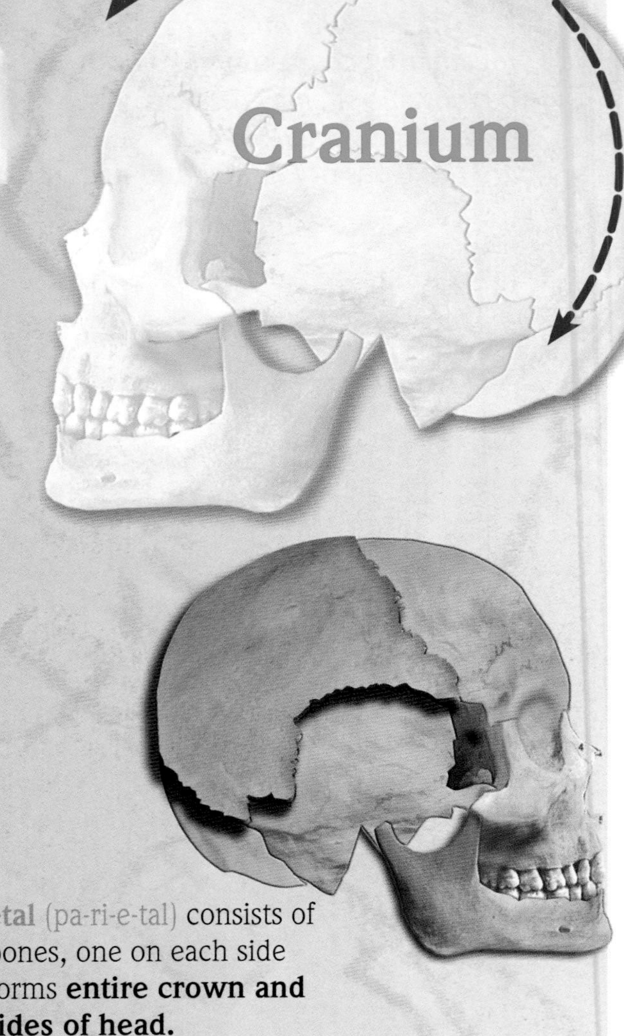


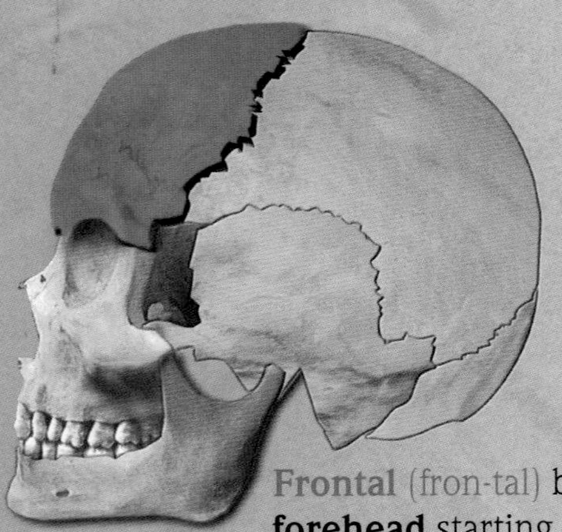

**Frontal** (fron-tal) bone forms the **forehead** starting at top of the eyes, extending to the beginning curve of head.

**Parietal** (pa-ri-e-tal) consists of two bones, one on each side that forms **entire crown and top sides of head.**

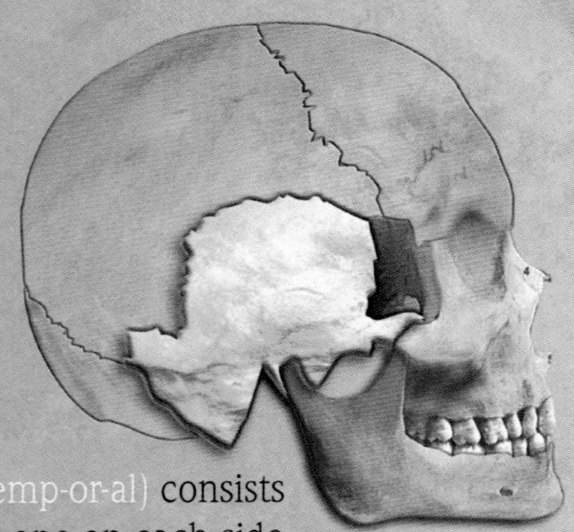

**Temporal** (temp-or-al) consists of two bones, one on each side that forms the **lower sides of head below parietal bones.**

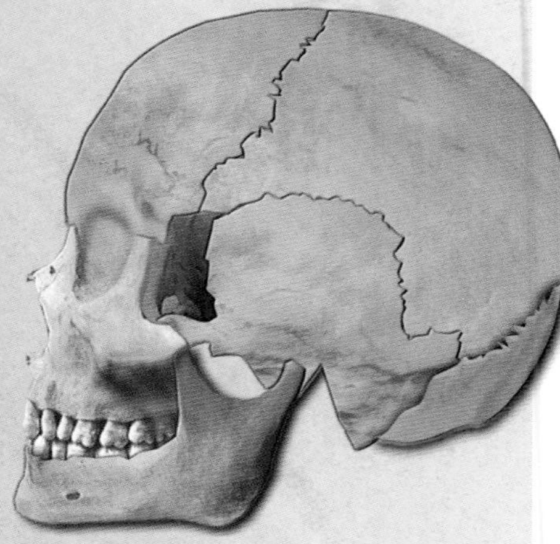

**Occipital bone** (oc-cip-i-tal) covers the **entire back of head,** sits directly above the nape.

"The cranial bones are good reference points when cutting or styling hair."

# Bones of Face . . .

**The face** *consists of 14 bones that cover entire facial area.* ***Listed first are the nine facial bones affected by massage.***

**Lacrimal** (lac-ri-mal) consists of the two smallest bones of the face forming the **front inner area of each eye socket.**

**Nasal** consists of two joining bones to form the **bridge of the nose.**

**Zygomatic** (zy-go-ma-tic) consists of two bones, one on each side of face, that form the **upper part of cheek and lower part of eye socket.**

**Mandible** (man-di-ble) is the largest and strongest bone that forms the **lower jaw.**

**Maxilla** (max-il-la) consists of two bones, one on each side of face, that form the **upper jaw and lower part of cheek.**

4

**Turbinal, Vomer, and Palatine facial bones and Ethmoid and Sphenoid cranial are not touched by massage.**

**Turbinal** (tur-bi-nal) or turbinate bones are spongy, spiral-shaped bones that **form the inside walls of the nasal passage.**

**Ethmoid** (eth-moid) bone forms part of the **nasal cavity and the eye socket's inner wall.**

**Sphenoid** (sphe-noid) bone forms part of the **nasal cavity's roof and walls.**

**Vomer** (vo-mer) is a flat bone that forms the **center of the nasal septum.** The septum divides the nostrils.

**Palatine** (pal-a-tine) consists of two bones that **form the roof of the mouth or palate.**

# Bones of Neck, Chest and Upper Back...

## Neck Bones are:

**Cervical** (cer-vi-cal) **vertebrae** (ver-te-brae) consists of seven vertebrae (bones) that make up the portion of the **spinal column located in the neck.**

**Hyoid** (hy-oid) is a horseshoe-shaped bone located at **base of tongue**, providing support for the tongue muscles; sometimes referred to as the **"Adam's apple."**

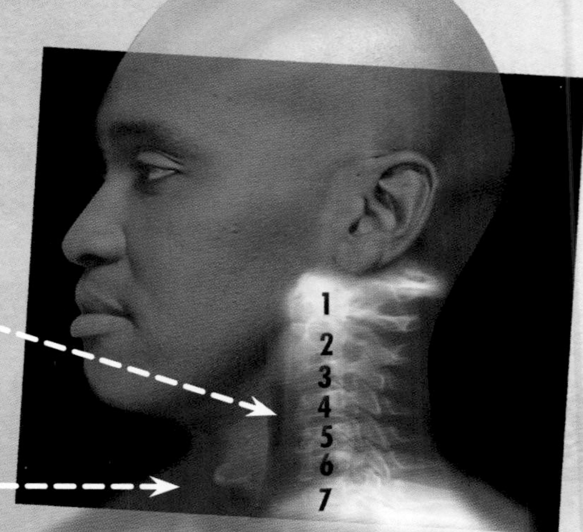


## Chest and Upper Back Bones are:

**Clavicle** (clav-i-cle) is a long bone sometimes referred to as **collarbone** and is located at upper part of chest; **connects the sternum and the scapula.**

**Thorax** (thor-ax) or **thoracic cage** is located between neck and abdomen, commonly known as **chest.**

**Scapula** (scap-u-la) consists of two large, flat bones that form the **back part of the shoulder blades.**

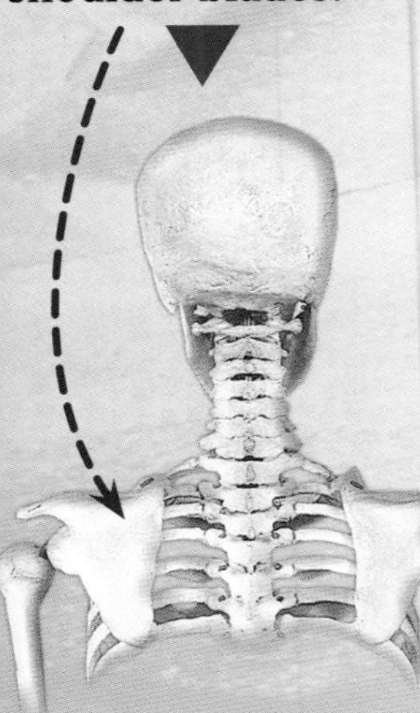

**Sternum** (ster-num) is also known as **breastbone**, a long flat bone **connecting and supporting the ribs.**

**NOTE:** Ribs are bones which are located on the lower part of the thorax. As cosmetologists, we **ARE NOT** licensed to massage that part of the anatomy.

4

# Bones of Arm and Hand . . .

ULNA

RADIUS

HUMERUS

## Bones of the Arm

**Humerus** (hu-mer-us) is the largest upper bone of the arm, located from shoulder to elbow.

**Ulna** is the large inner bone of the forearm.

**Radius** is the shorter of the two bones of the forearm, located on the thumb side.

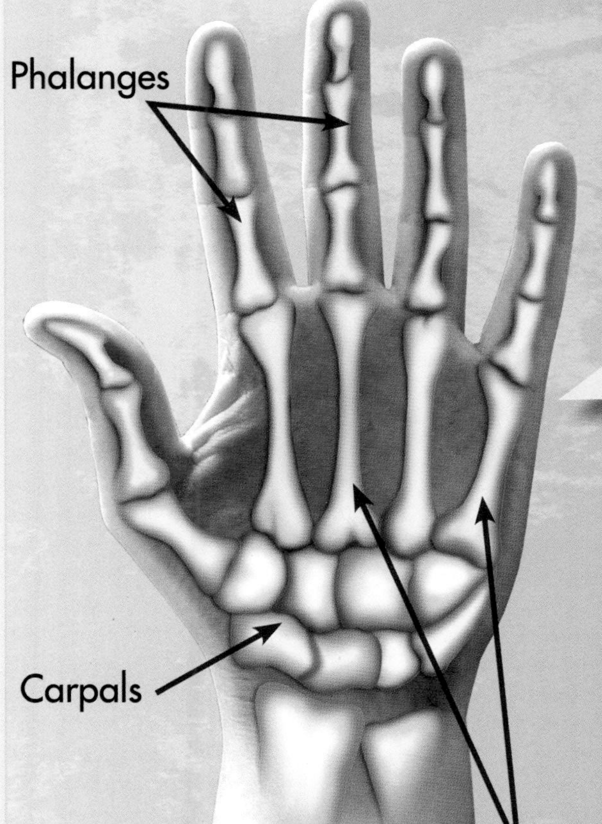


## Bones of the Hand

**Carpals** are the eight small bones, arranged in two rows, which form the wrist.

**Metacarpals** are the five bones of the palm. The heads of the metacarpals are the knuckles.

**Phalanges** (fe-lan-jeze) are the finger bones. There are three phalanges in each finger and two in the thumb, making 14 all together.

"Wow! You have 27 bones in each hand, with 14 of those bones in your fingers alone. That is one reason why your hand and fingers are so flexible."

# Bones of Leg and Foot . . .

*Many people stand or walk during most of their workday, supporting the body's weight with the bones of the legs and feet. To understand how these bones support the upper body, let us take a look at their construction.*

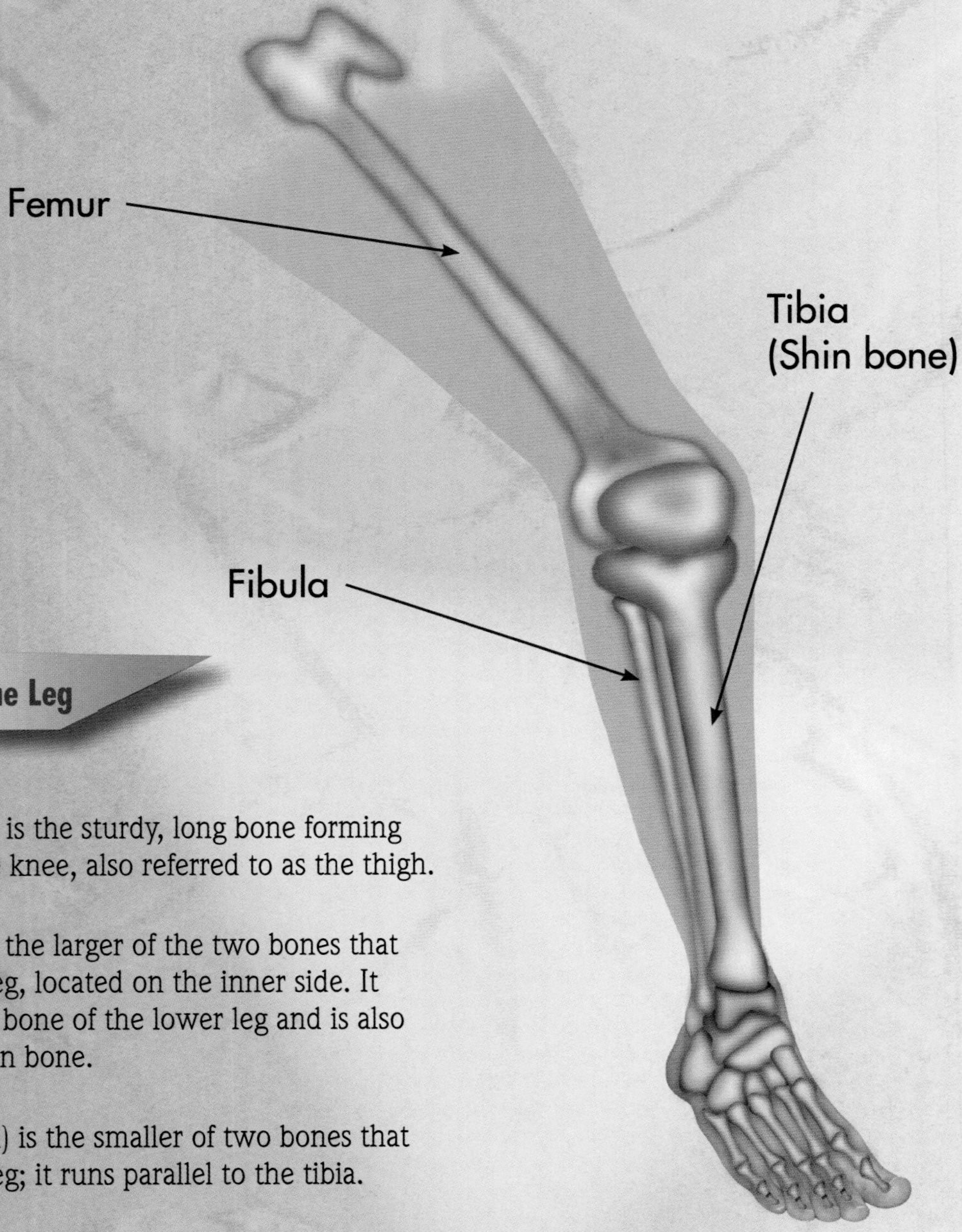

Femur

Tibia (Shin bone)

Fibula

## Bones of the Leg

**Femur** (fe-mur) is the sturdy, long bone forming the leg above the knee, also referred to as the thigh.

**Tibia** (tib-e-a) is the larger of the two bones that form the lower leg, located on the inner side. It is the supporting bone of the lower leg and is also known as the shin bone.

**Fibula** (fib-yu-la) is the smaller of two bones that form the lower leg; it runs parallel to the tibia.

4

# Bones of the Foot . . .

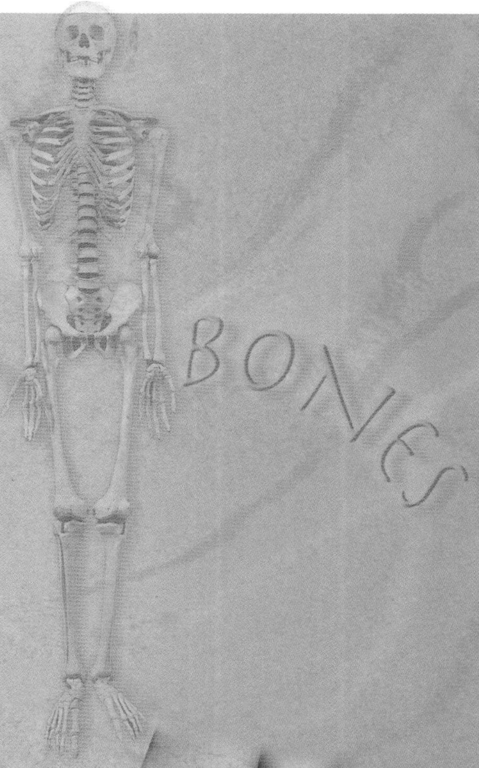

## Bones of the Foot

**Metatarsals** (met-a-tar-sals) include five long, cylindrical bones that form the arch (instep) of the foot.

**Tarsals** (tar-sals) include seven bones in the ankle area. The talus (anklebone) connects with the tibia and fibula to form the ankle joint; the largest of the tarsals, the calcaneus, is the heel bone.

**Phalanges** (fa-lan-jeze) include 14 bones that form the toes. Each toe has three bones, except the big toe, which has two.

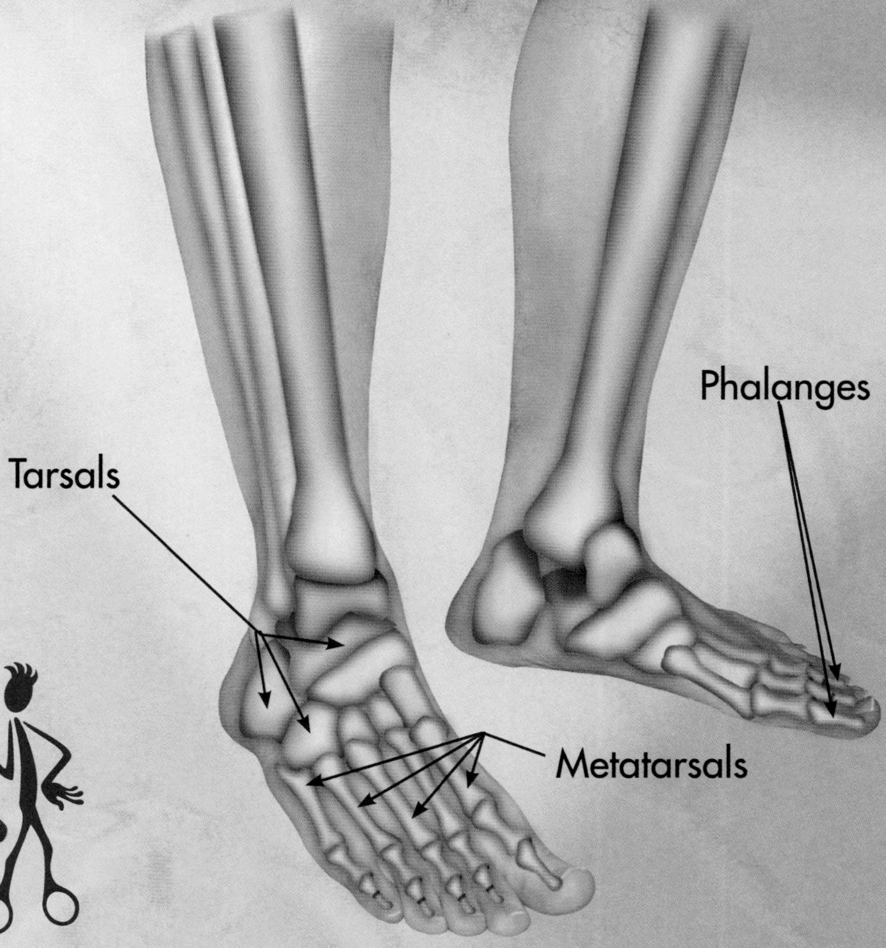

"The 54 bones of the hands and the 52 bones of the feet equal 106 bones, more than 50% of the bones in the entire body! I told you that hands and feet are important."

*Myology (my-ol-o-gy) is the scientific study of the structure, functions and diseases of the muscles.* ***Muscles form the basis for all movement.*** *As you study and understand the muscles of the head and face, and how they coordinate to provide movement, survival and communication, your role in caring for this part of the anatomy becomes more apparent.*

**Muscles** are a form of tissue that **produces contractile** movements. Muscle tissue can be stimulated to contract through nerve impulses, light rays and massage.

## Three Types of Muscles:

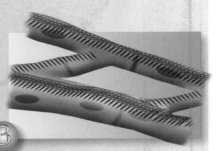

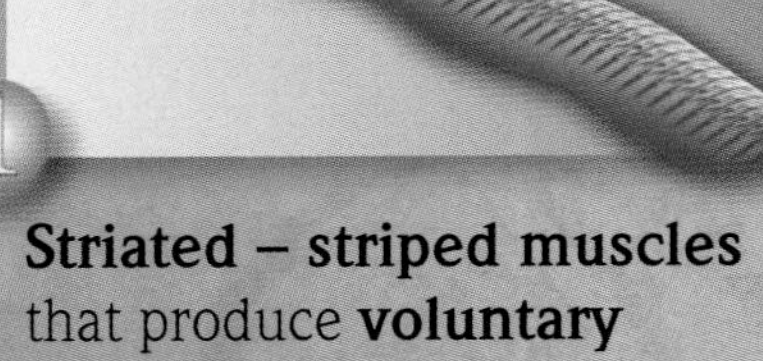

1 **Striated – striped muscles** that produce **voluntary motion**; found in the face, arm and leg.

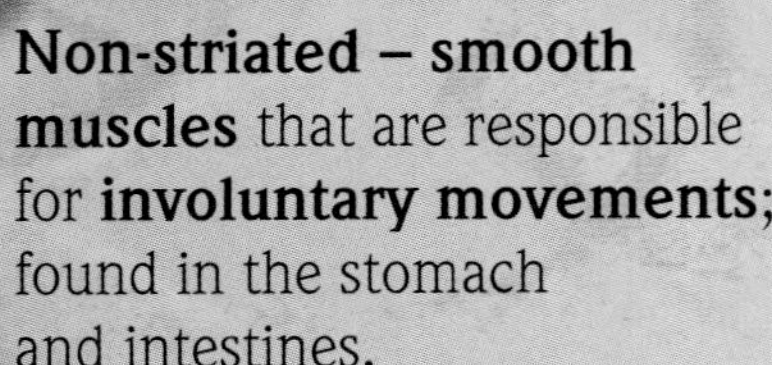

2 **Non-striated – smooth muscles** that are responsible for **involuntary movements**; found in the stomach and intestines.

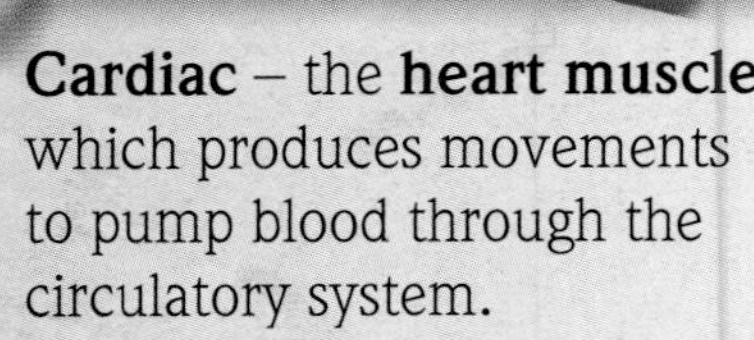

3 **Cardiac** – the **heart muscle**, which produces movements to pump blood through the circulatory system.

4

## Parts of a Muscle:

- **Insertion** is the end of a muscle attached to a movable section of skeleton such as another muscle or movable bone.
- **Belly** is the center of a muscle.
- **Origin** is the end of a muscle attached to an immovable section of skeleton.

# Muscles of Head . . .

The **scalp** or **epicranium** (ep-i-cra-ne-um) is covered by a **large muscle** called **occipito-frontalis** (oc-cip-i-to-fron-ta-lis) or **epicranius.**

**Frontalis** (fron-ta-lis) **muscle encompasses the forehead** and extends into the beginning curve of scalp. This muscle lifts eyebrows and pulls forehead forward causing wrinkles.

**Aponeurosis** (ap-o-neu-ro-sis) is the tendon that connects the occipitalis and frontalis to form the epicranius.

**Temporalis** (tem-po-ra-lis) **muscle** is on the **sides of head,** above the auricularis superior and helps in opening and closing the mouth as in chewing.

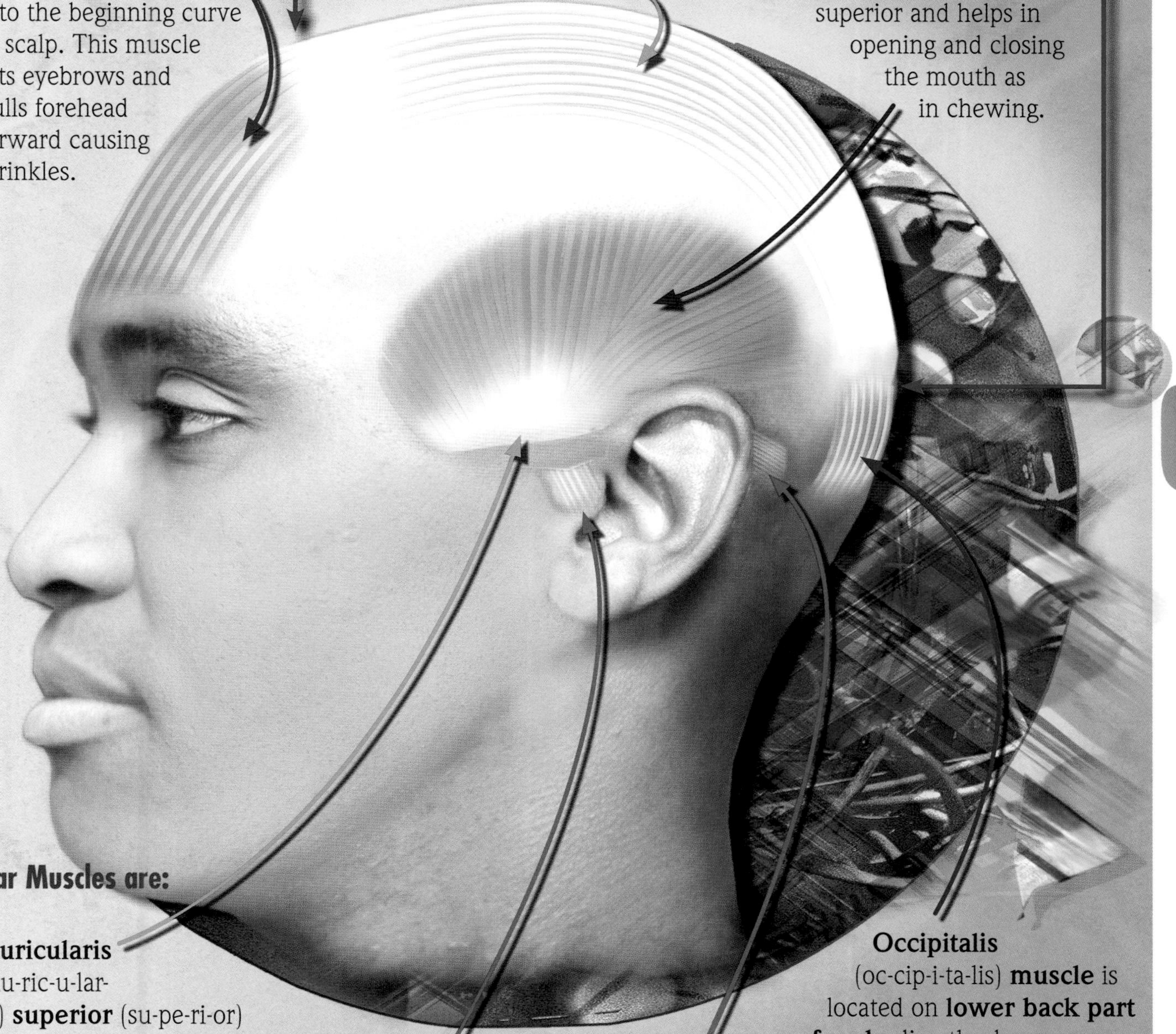

**Ear Muscles are:**

**Auricularis** (au-ric-u-lar-is) **superior** (su-pe-ri-or) **muscle** is located directly **above the ear** and can move the ear upward.

**Auricularis anterior** (an-te-ri-or) **muscle** is located directly in **front of the ear** and can move the ear forward.

**Occipitalis** (oc-cip-i-ta-lis) **muscle** is located on **lower back part of scalp** directly above nape. This muscle pulls scalp back.

**Auricularis posterior** (pos-te-ri-or) **muscle** is located directly **behind the ear** and can move the ear backward.

4

# Muscles of Face . . .

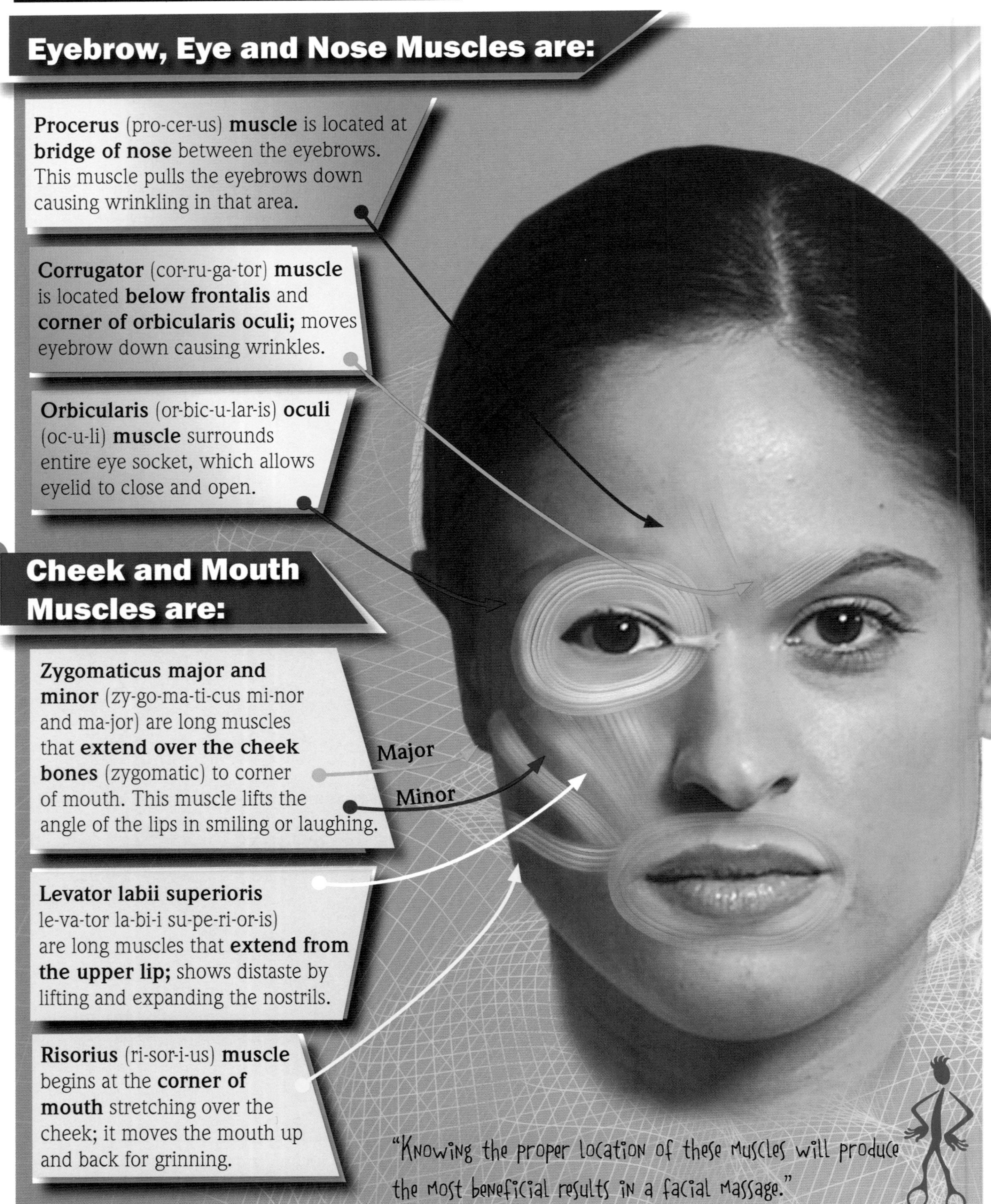

Eyebrow, Eye and Nose Muscles are:
Procerus (pro-cer-us) muscle is located at bridge of nose between the eyebrows. This muscle pulls the eyebrows down causing wrinkling in that area.
Corrugator (cor-ru-ga-tor) muscle is located below frontalis and corner of orbicularis oculi; moves eyebrow down causing wrinkles.
Orbicularis (or-bic-u-lar-is) oculi (oc-u-li) muscle surrounds entire eye socket, which allows eyelid to close and open.
4
Cheek and Mouth Muscles are:
Zygomaticus major and minor (zy-go-ma-ti-cus mi-nor and ma-jor) are long muscles that extend over the cheek bones (zygomatic) to corner of mouth. This muscle lifts the angle of the lips in smiling or laughing.
Major
Minor
Levator labii superioris le-va-tor la-bi-i su-pe-ri-or-is) are long muscles that extend from the upper lip; shows distaste by lifting and expanding the nostrils.
Risorius (ri-sor-i-us) muscle begins at the corner of mouth stretching over the cheek; it moves the mouth up and back for grinning.
"Knowing the proper location of these muscles will produce the most beneficial results in a facial massage."

# Muscles of Face ...

## Cheek, Mouth and Chin Muscles are:

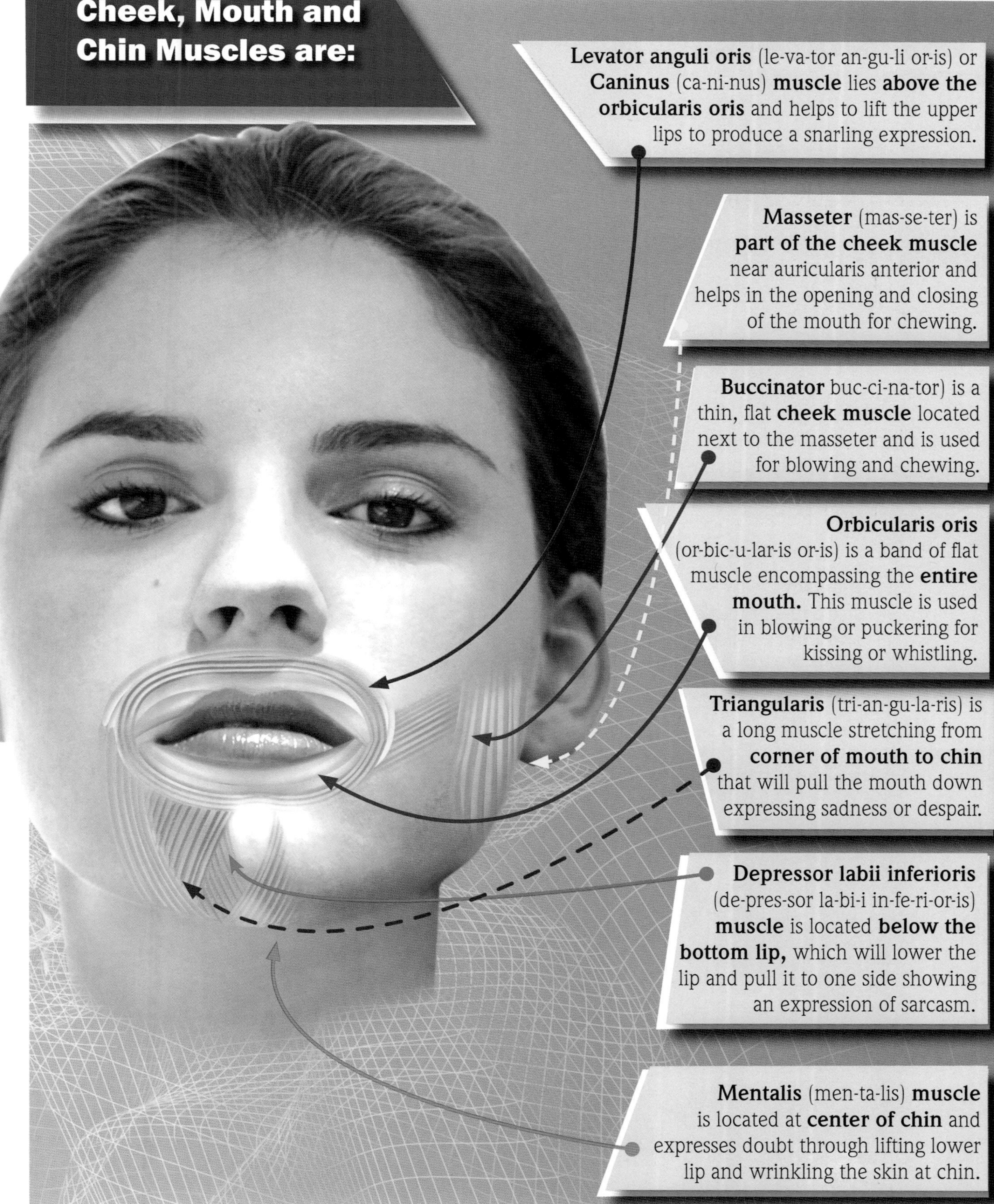

**Levator anguli oris** (le-va-tor an-gu-li or-is) or **Caninus** (ca-ni-nus) **muscle** lies **above the orbicularis oris** and helps to lift the upper lips to produce a snarling expression.

**Masseter** (mas-se-ter) is **part of the cheek muscle** near auricularis anterior and helps in the opening and closing of the mouth for chewing.

**Buccinator** buc-ci-na-tor) is a thin, flat **cheek muscle** located next to the masseter and is used for blowing and chewing.

**Orbicularis oris** (or-bic-u-lar-is or-is) is a band of flat muscle encompassing the **entire mouth.** This muscle is used in blowing or puckering for kissing or whistling.

**Triangularis** (tri-an-gu-la-ris) is a long muscle stretching from **corner of mouth to chin** that will pull the mouth down expressing sadness or despair.

**Depressor labii inferioris** (de-pres-sor la-bi-i in-fe-ri-or-is) **muscle** is located **below the bottom lip,** which will lower the lip and pull it to one side showing an expression of sarcasm.

**Mentalis** (men-ta-lis) **muscle** is located at **center of chin** and expresses doubt through lifting lower lip and wrinkling the skin at chin.

4

# Muscles of Neck, Chest and Upper Back...

## Neck and Back Muscles are:

**Trapezius** (tra-pee-zee-us) **muscle** is located at **back of the neck,** extending down the **upper part of back.** This muscle moves head back, rotates shoulders and swings the arms.

**Sternocleidomastoideus** (ster-no-clei-do-mas-toid-e-us) is a long muscle that stretches from the **back of ear, along side of neck to the collarbone** (clavicle). This muscle moves the head up and down or side to side as in nodding.

4

**Platysma** (pla-tys-ma) is a large muscle stretching from the **chin down to the shoulder** muscle. This muscle moves the lower jaw down expressing sadness.

## Upper Chest Muscle is:

**Pectoralis** (pec-tor-al-is) **major muscle** stretches across the **front of the upper chest** enabling the arms to swing.

# Muscles of Arm and Hand . . .

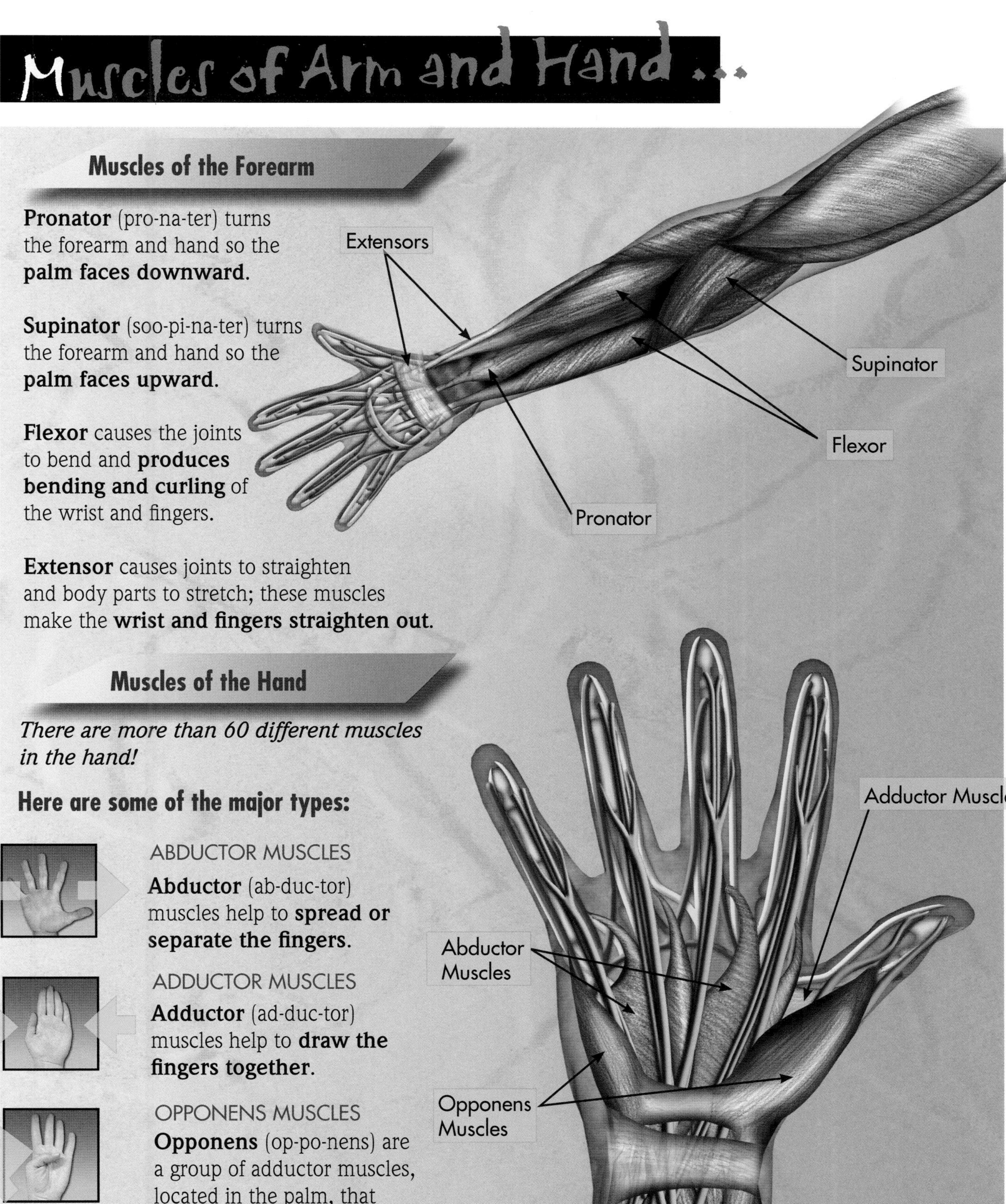


## Muscles of the Forearm

**Pronator** (pro-na-ter) turns the forearm and hand so the **palm faces downward.**

**Supinator** (soo-pi-na-ter) turns the forearm and hand so the **palm faces upward.**

**Flexor** causes the joints to bend and **produces bending and curling** of the wrist and fingers.

**Extensor** causes joints to straighten and body parts to stretch; these muscles make the **wrist and fingers straighten out.**

## Muscles of the Hand

*There are more than 60 different muscles in the hand!*

### Here are some of the major types:

ABDUCTOR MUSCLES

**Abductor** (ab-duc-tor) muscles help to **spread or separate the fingers.**

ADDUCTOR MUSCLES

**Adductor** (ad-duc-tor) muscles help to **draw the fingers together.**

OPPONENS MUSCLES

**Opponens** (op-po-nens) are a group of adductor muscles, located in the palm, that **draw the thumb toward the fingers.**

One of the special features of our hands is the **opposable thumb.** This means that the thumb is placed opposite the rest of the fingers so that even very small objects can be picked up easily through what is called the **pincer grasp.** This is why humans are so skillful with tools.

# Muscles of Leg and Foot...

*Muscles are the fundamental body parts that create motion and movement. Walking, sitting and standing are well-coordinated muscular interactions. As you care for the feet and lower legs, understanding the muscles will assist you in providing outstanding services.*

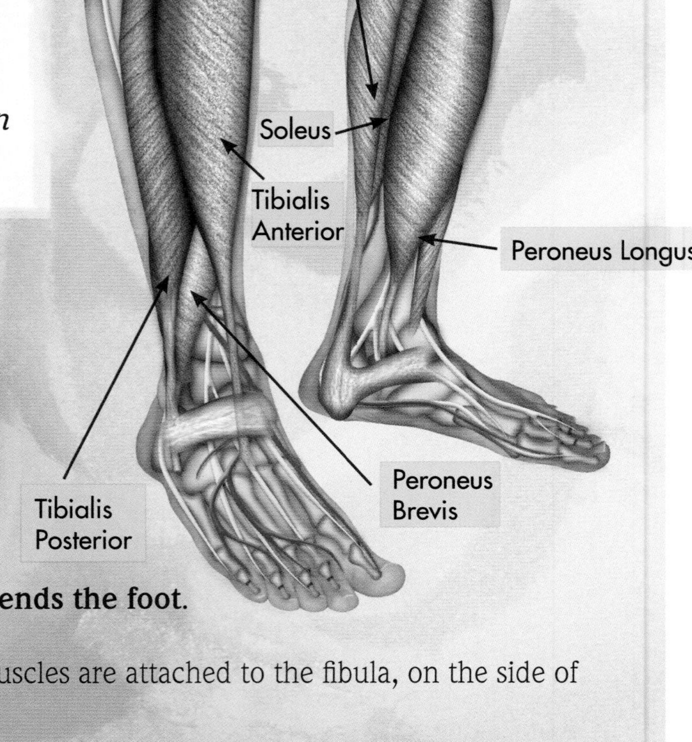


## Muscles of the Lower Leg

**Gastrocnemius** (gas-trok-ne-me-us) is the muscle of the calf of the leg; it **pulls the foot downward.**

**Soleus** (sol-e-us) is a broad, flat muscle located directly in front of the gastrocnemius; it **steadies the leg and bends the foot.**



**Peroneus** (per-one-us) **longus and peronius brevis** muscles are attached to the fibula, on the side of the leg; they help to **rotate and turn the foot.**

**Tibialis** (tib-e-al-is) **anterior** covers the front of the lower leg and **bends the foot up and in.**

**Tibialis posterior** is the key stabilizing muscle of the lower leg and **helps the foot to flex inward.**

## Muscles of the Foot

*The foot muscles are essential for balance while standing upright, and for walking, running, climbing, etc.*

Extensor Muscle
Abductor Muscle
Flexor Muscles
Adductor Muscle

**Listed below are the major muscles of the foot:**

**Abductor** muscles **move a limb away from the body** and **spread the toes.**

**Adductor** muscles **move a limb toward the body** and **draw the toes together.**

**Extensors** provide **straightening or stretching** and **extend the toes.**

**Flexors** help to support the extensors by **keeping toes straight.** Flexors prevent toes from being clawed (having curved, pointed growth).

# Composition of Blood . . .

*Blood is a **nourishing fluid** of normally eight to 10 pints that circulates throughout the body. It has a **sticky consistency and salty taste** and is about 80 percent water. The color of blood is a **vivid red in the arteries** and a **deep red in the veins**. Blood carries away waste products, regulates body temperature, protects the body from evading pathogenic bacteria and nourishes the body cells.*

## The blood is composed of:

**Red blood cells** or **erythrocytes** (e-ryth-ro-cytes) or **red corpuscles** (cor-pus-cles) contain **hemoglobin** (he-mo-glo-bin), an iron supporting protein, which is **responsible for the red color of blood** due to its attraction and delivery of oxygen to the body tissues.

**White blood cells or white corpuscles** or **leukocytes** are **large cells with no color,** but play a necessary role in **protecting the body** against infection by attacking harmful microorganisms.

4

**Platelets** (plate-let) or **thrombocyte** (throm-bo-cyte) are **tiny color-free particles** in the blood that are responsible for the **clotting** or **coagulation** (co-ag-u-lation) of blood. When an injury occurs and the wound is exposed to air, the process of clotting usually develops.

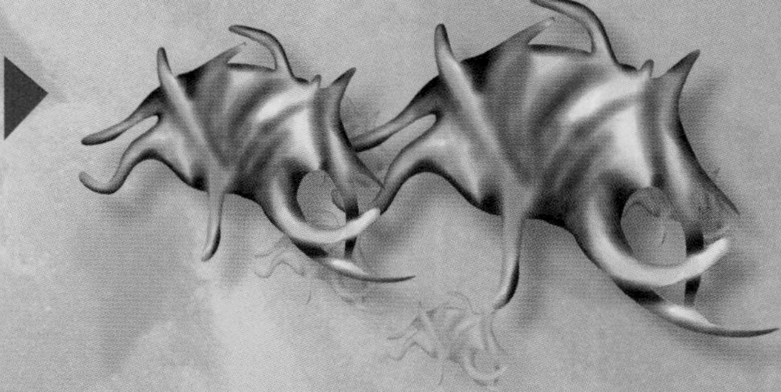

**Plasma** (plas-ma) consists of approximately 90 percent water and is the **yellowish fluid part of blood** that contains the red, white blood cells and platelets. This allows the blood to flow throughout the body providing nutrients and oxygen to all body cells.

# Circulatory System ...

## How does blood travel throughout the body?

"Remember, veins are visible through the skin; arteries are not visible, they are buried deep within the body for protection!"

**Blood vessels** are the channels which blood circulates through to get to all areas of the body. They carry blood to and from the heart and then to other various body tissues.

### Three Principal Types of Blood Vessels:

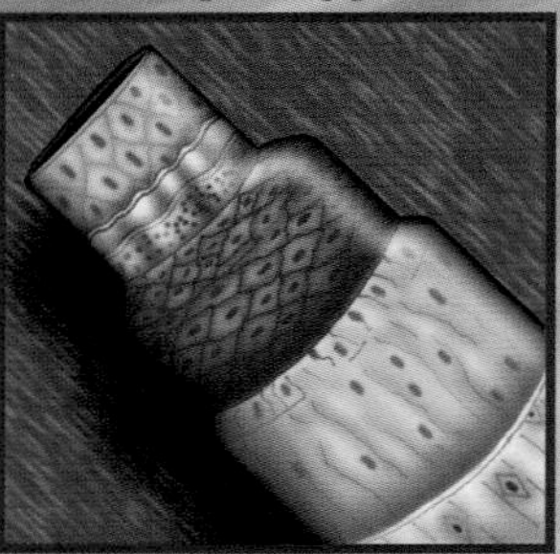

**Arteries** are **muscular, thick-walled vessels** that pulse with each heartbeat because they carry the bright red, purified blood **away from the heart** and the lungs where it receives oxygen.

**Veins** are **thin-walled vessels** that carry the dark blood back from all parts of the body **to the heart** and lungs, to be purified and receive oxygen.

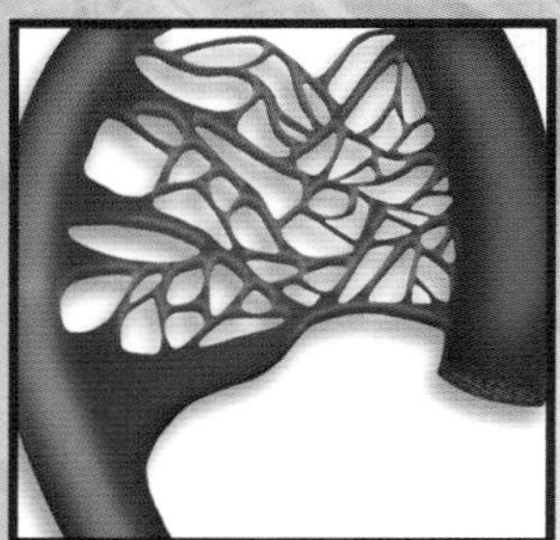

**Capillaries** are **very tiny blood vessels** that connect the arteries and the veins.

4

The circulatory system **comprises the heart, blood vessels, lymph** (limf) **glands, lymph vessels and the blood itself.** Just as the bones are living parts of the body, as are the muscles and nerves, the blood is also a living liquid composed of tissue and is equally important for the healthy function and appearance of the face. The circulatory system is like a fluid highway that carries nourishment and hormones (chemical messengers) to every cell.

# Circulatory System...

**Circulatory system consists of two areas:**

**A** **Blood Vascular** (vas-cu-lar) **System** distributes blood throughout the body by the heart, arteries, veins and capillaries.

Valve

The **heart** is a large **muscular organ** that pumps the blood throughout the body by way of the blood vessels. This extraordinary organ is covered in a fibrous membrane called the **pericardium** (per-i-car-dium). The heart is situated in the center of the chest cavity and weighs about nine ounces and is controlled by the autonomic nervous system and the 10th cranial nerve. The inside of the heart consists of **four chambers and four valves.** The **thin-walled chambers** on the top half of the heart are referred to as the **right and left atriums.** The **thick-walled chambers** on the bottom half of the heart are referred to as the **right and left ventricles.** Between the chambers are arteries that contain **valves** with **open and closed ends**, which permit the blood to travel in one direction. When the heart contracts and relaxes (pumping), blood flows in, travels from the atriums to the ventricles and is then pumped out to be dispersed throughout the body. The **aorta** (a-or-ta) is the **main and largest artery** that is responsible for carrying blood from the left ventricle to other arteries of the heart.

4

**The two systems that account for the regular and uninterrupted circulation of blood are:**

- **Pulmonary circulation** consists of the pulmonary arteries and veins and delivers the blood from the heart to the lungs for purification.
- **General or systemic circulation** sends the blood from the heart to circulate throughout the body then comes back to the heart.

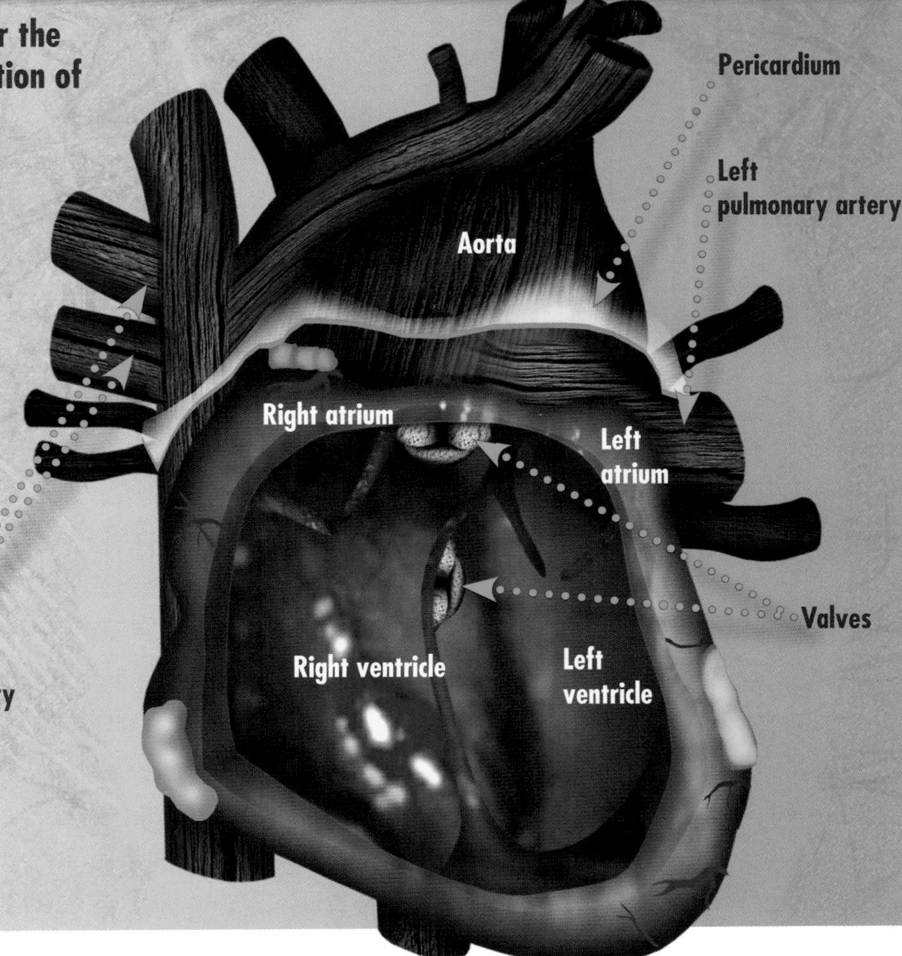

# Circulatory System ...

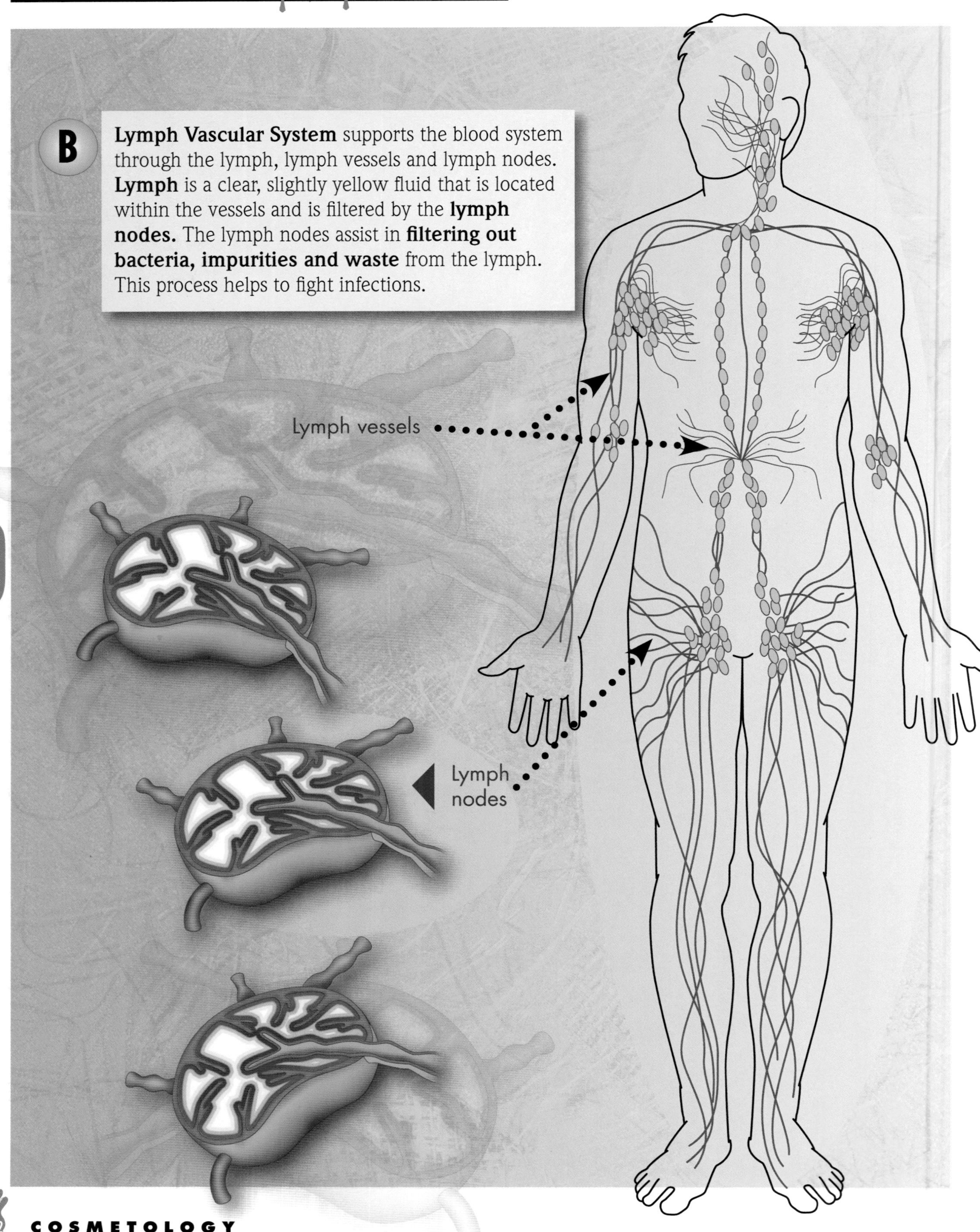


**B** **Lymph Vascular System** supports the blood system through the lymph, lymph vessels and lymph nodes. **Lymph** is a clear, slightly yellow fluid that is located within the vessels and is filtered by the **lymph nodes.** The lymph nodes assist in **filtering out bacteria, impurities and waste** from the lymph. This process helps to fight infections.

# Arteries of Head and Face . . .

***The** main source of blood supply to the head, face and neck are the **common carotid** (car-o-tid) **arteries.** The carotid arteries are divided into two branches, **internal** and **external,** and are located on either side of the neck.*

**Internal carotid artery** blood flows to the nose, internal ear, eyes, eyelids, forehead and brain.

**External carotid artery** blood flows to the neck, face, ear, sides of head and front parts of scalp. This artery subdivides into several of the following branches:

**Facial artery** or **external maxillary artery** delivers blood to the lower area of the face, consisting of nose and mouth.

### Branches of the Facial Artery are:

- **Submental artery** delivers blood to the chin and bottom lip.
- **Inferior labial artery** delivers blood to bottom lip.
- **Angular artery** delivers blood to the sides of nose.
- **Superior labial artery** delivers blood to the top lip and septum (a tissue dividing the nostrils) of nose.

4

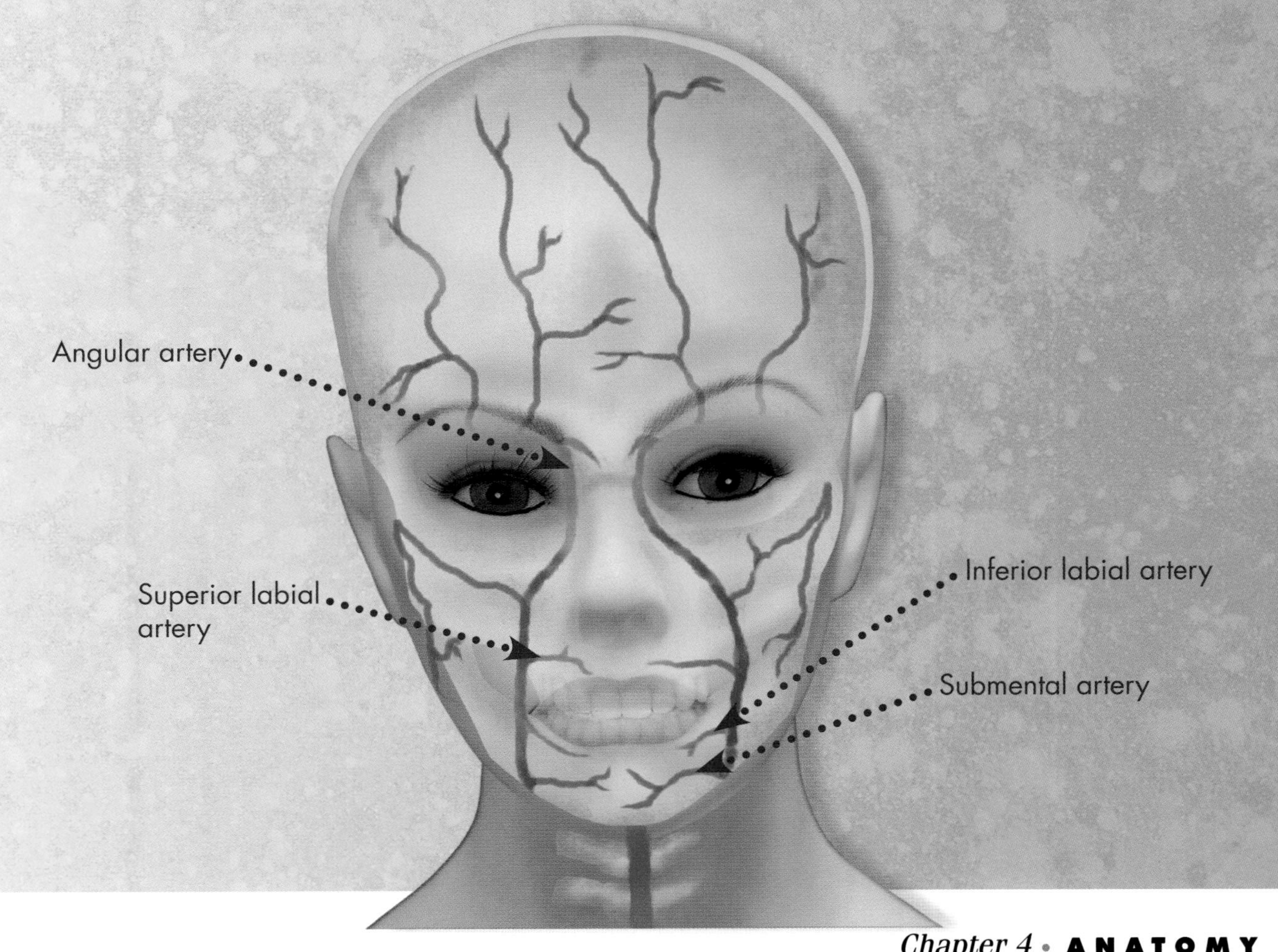

# Arteries of Head and Face . . .



**Superficial temporal artery** *is an extension of the external carotid artery and continues to supply blood to the muscles of top, front and sides of head.*

## Branches of the Superficial Temporal Artery

**Extension of external carotid artery:**

- **Frontal artery** delivers blood to the upper eyelids and forehead.
- **Parietal artery** delivers blood to the sides and crown of head.
- **Transverse facial artery** delivers blood to the masseter (cheek) muscles and skin.
- **Middle temporal artery** delivers blood to the temples.
- **Anterior auricular artery** delivers blood to the front area of the ears.
- **Occipital artery** delivers blood to the scalp and muscles of the crown and back of head.
- **Posterior auricular artery** delivers blood to the skin and scalp area behind and top of ears.

**Extension of internal carotid artery:**

- **Supraorbital artery** delivers blood to the upper eyelids and forehead.
- **Infraorbital artery** delivers blood to the eye muscles.

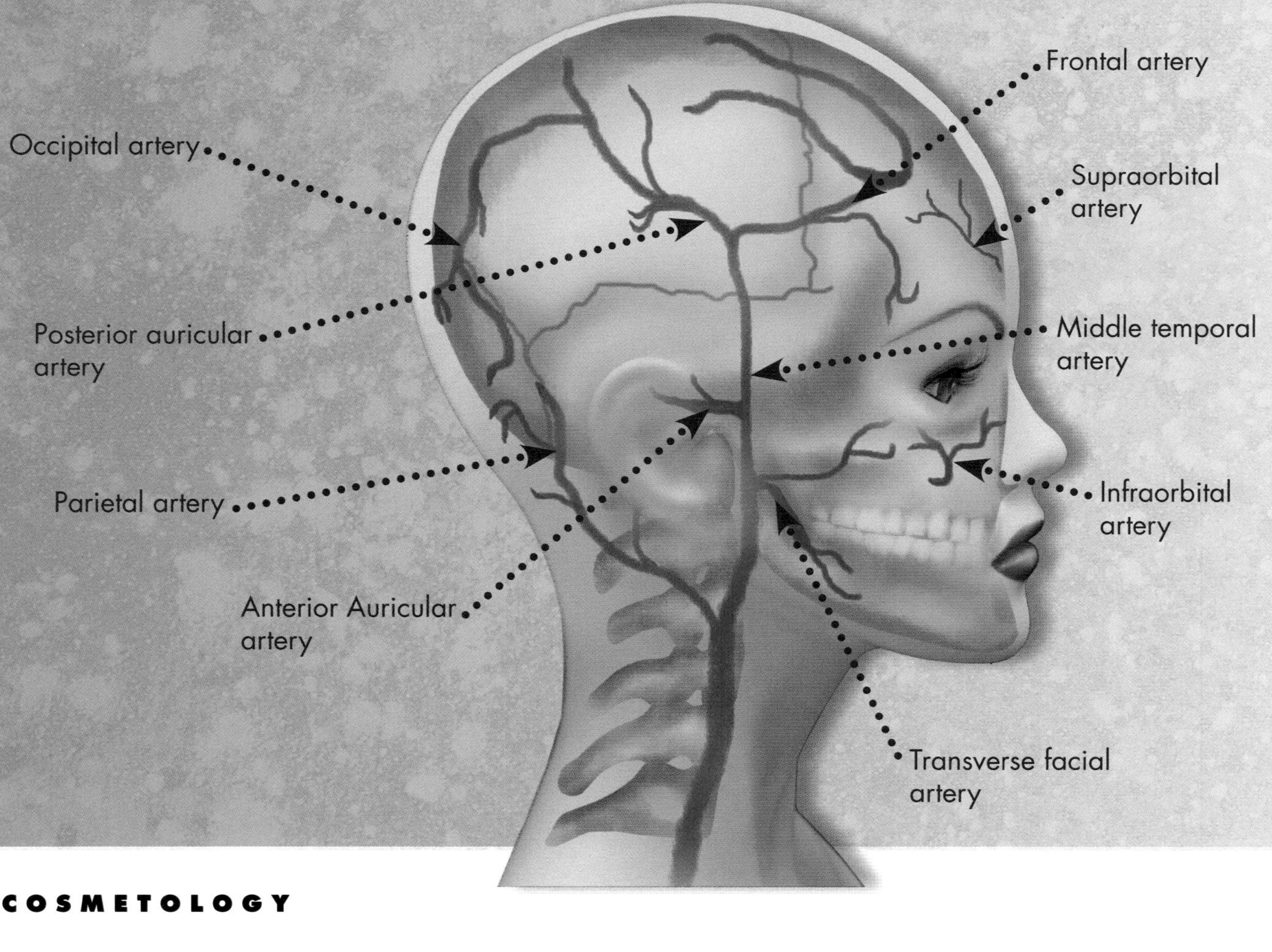

Frontal artery
Occipital artery
Supraorbital artery
Posterior auricular artery
Middle temporal artery
Parietal artery
Infraorbital artery
Anterior Auricular artery
Transverse facial artery

# Veins of Neck . . .

**The neck veins deliver blood from the heart to the neck, face and head.**

**External jugular vein** stretches alongside of neck expanding into head area.

**Posterior external jugular vein** begins in the occipital region and extends down along back of head and neck opening up into the external jugular.

**Anterior jugular vein** stretches mainly along neck opening into the external jugular.

**Internal jugular vein** extends into face, head and along sides to base of neck.

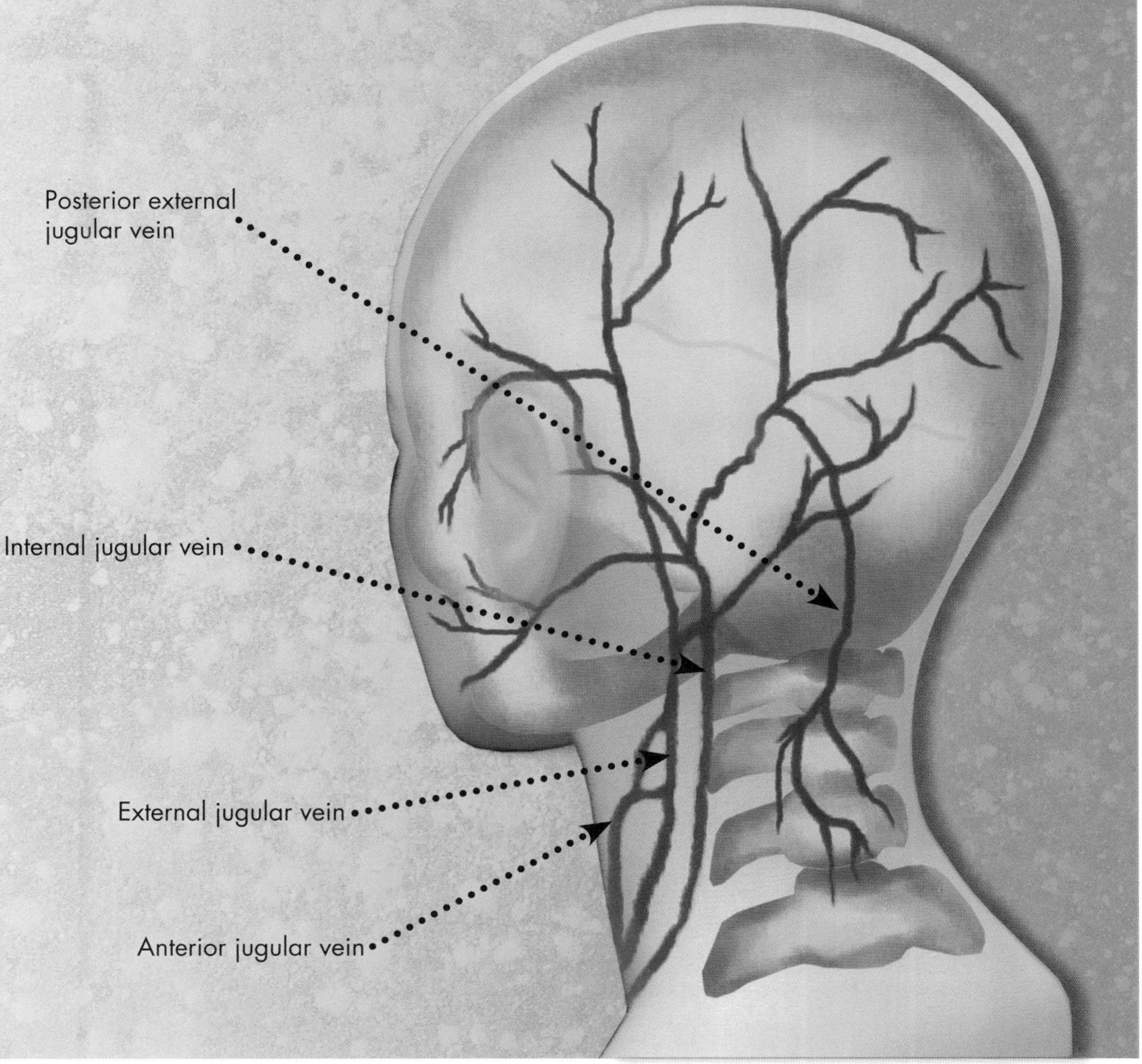

4

# Circulation of Arm and Hand . . .

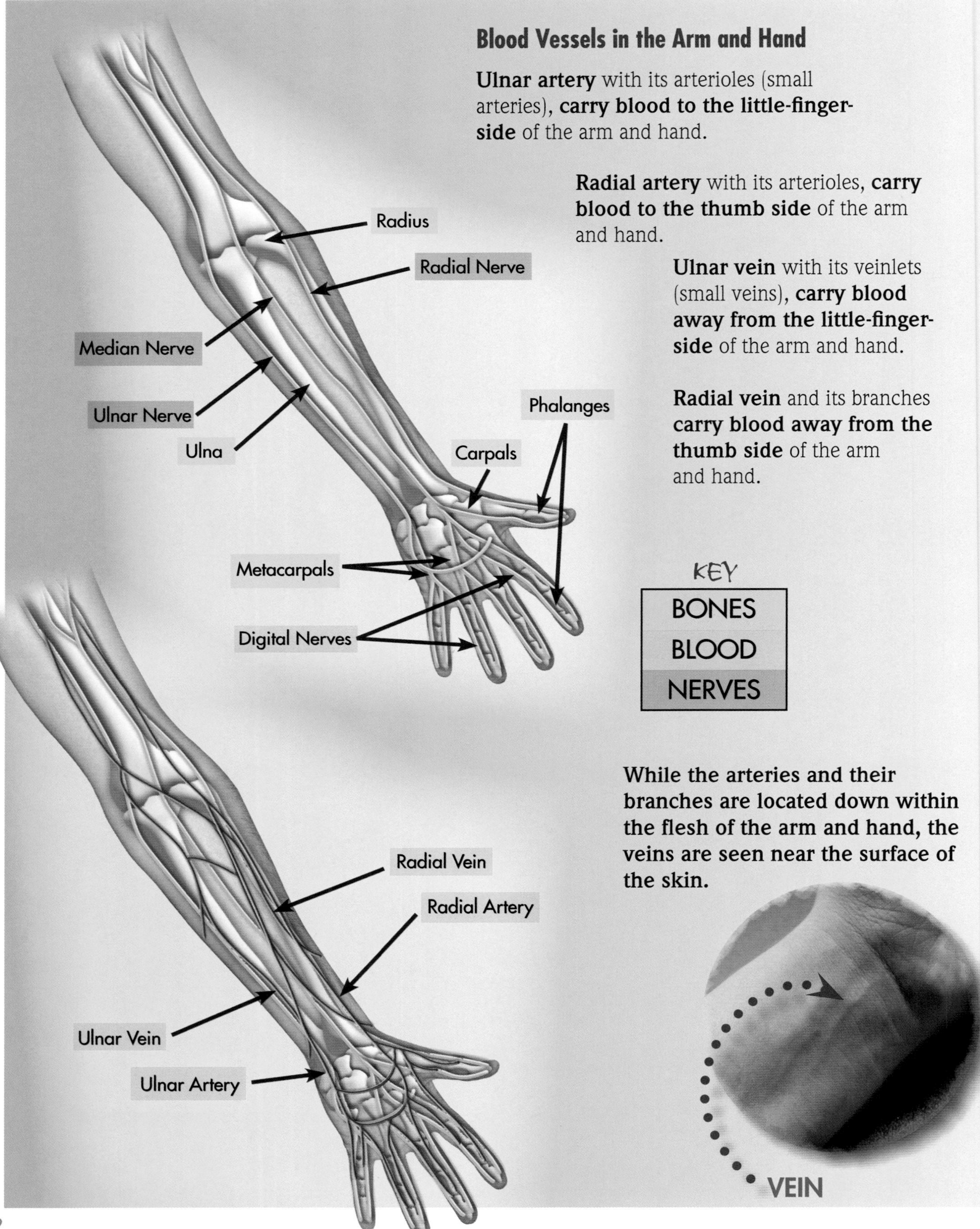


**Blood Vessels in the Arm and Hand**

**Ulnar artery** with its arterioles (small arteries), **carry blood to the little-finger-side** of the arm and hand.

**Radial artery** with its arterioles, **carry blood to the thumb side** of the arm and hand.

**Ulnar vein** with its veinlets (small veins), **carry blood away from the little-finger-side** of the arm and hand.

**Radial vein** and its branches **carry blood away from the thumb side** of the arm and hand.

**While the arteries and their branches are located down within the flesh of the arm and hand, the veins are seen near the surface of the skin.**

# Circulation of the Leg and Foot . . .

*You already know from studying the hand that good circulation is imperative for health, comfort and appearance. The quality of the blood circulation in the feet is extremely significant because the feet are far from the heart and bear the burden of the body's weight. Be aware of circulatory problems in your customers who might be pregnant, diabetic, seriously overweight or elderly. Possible symptoms include unusually cold feet and numbness, tingling or pain in the toes or forefoot. If you suspect problems with foot circulation, suggest that your client discuss this with their medical care professional.*

## Arteries and Veins of the Lower Leg and Foot

The three principal types of blood vessels are **arteries, veins and capillaries.**

**Anterior tibial** (tib-e-al) **artery** is located on the front side of the tibia, nourishing the front of the leg and becoming the **dorsalis pedis.**

**Posterior tibial artery** is located on the back of the tibia, supplying blood to the back of the leg.

**Dorsalis** (dor-sal-is) **pedis artery** brings fresh blood to the foot.

**Anterior tibial vein** is located on the front of the tibia, close to the surface.

**Posterior tibial vein** is behind the tibia, carrying blood away from the back of the leg toward the heart.

**Dorsalis pedis vein** returns blood from the foot.

4

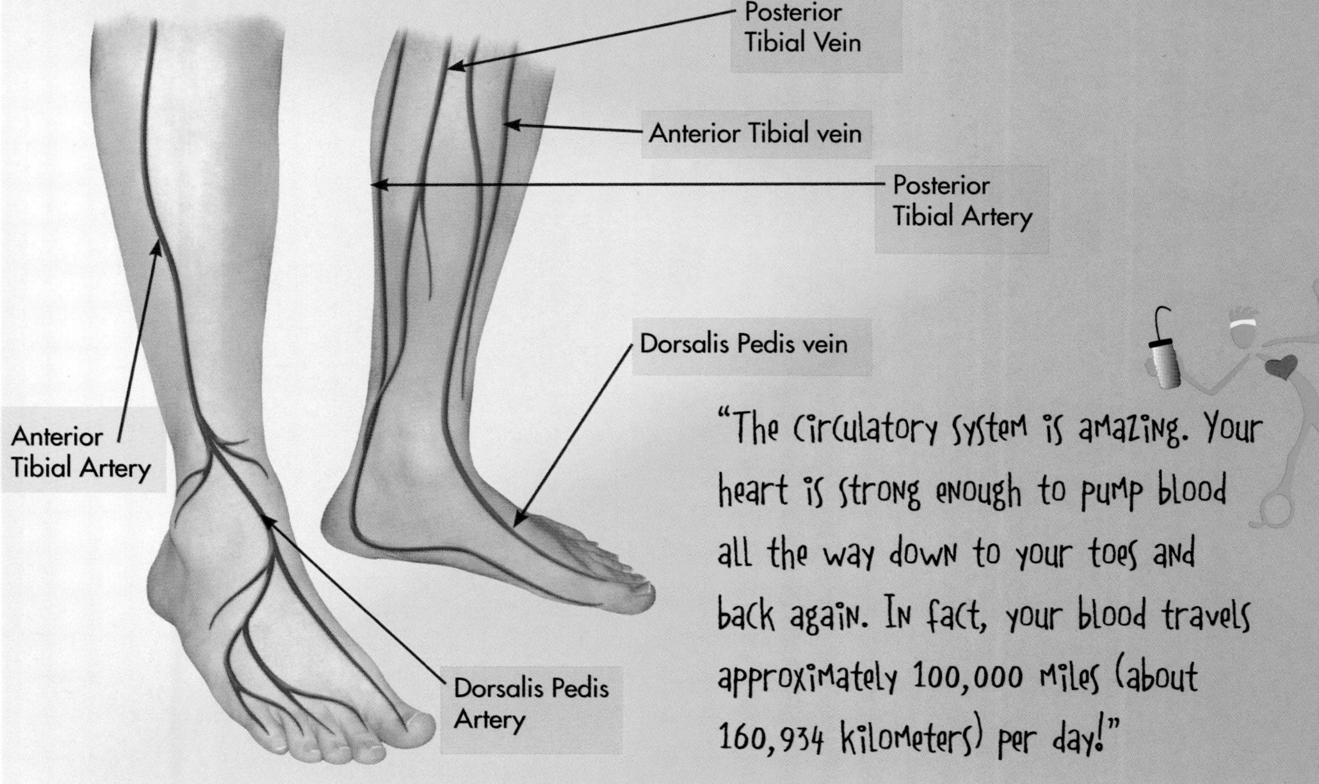
Posterior Tibial Vein
Anterior Tibial vein
Posterior Tibial Artery
Dorsalis Pedis vein
Anterior Tibial Artery
Dorsalis Pedis Artery
"The circulatory system is amazing. Your heart is strong enough to pump blood all the way down to your toes and back again. In fact, your blood travels approximately 100,000 miles (about 160,934 kilometers) per day!"

# Nervous System . . .

***The** nervous system is a **complex network of nerve cells**, continuously **sending and receiving messages** to and from the brain and spinal cord to coordinate body functions.*

**Neurology** (neu-rol-o-gy) is the scientific study of the structure and purpose of the nervous system.

## The Three Components of the Nervous System are:

- **Central nervous system** consists of the spinal cord, spinal nerves, brain and cranial nerves.
- **Peripheral** (pe-rif-e-ral) **nervous system** consists of a group of nerves and nerve cells, **connecting every part of the body** to the central nervous system.
- **Autonomic** (aw-toh-nahm-ik) **nervous system** regulates involuntary body functions, such as those of the **heart and intestines.** This system can be divided into the **sympathetic** and **parasympathetic** systems, which perform in opposition to control heart rate, respiration and blood pressure.

**Sympathetic** (sym-pa-thet-ic) system is activated during stressful periods.

**Parasympathetic** (par-a-sym-pa-thet-ic) system is activated during restful times.

The **brain** is the **largest mass of nerve tissue** in the body; considered the **"control center"** for the nervous system. It is encased by the cranium and generally weighs 44 to 48 ounces. The brain regulates glandular activity, movement, sensation and the ability to think.

Nerve

The **spinal cord** consists of **elongated, off-white nerve fibers** protected by the spinal column. It begins in the **brain** and extends down into the **base of the spine**, containing 31 pairs of nerves that branch out to the muscles, skin and internal organs.

# Nerve Structure . . .

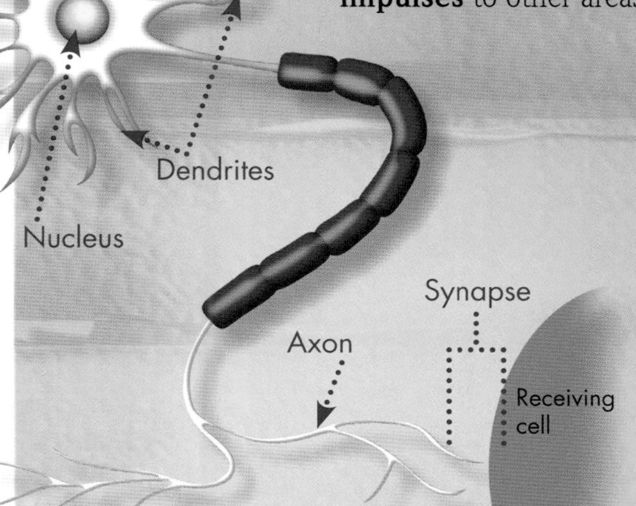


**Nerves** are white cord-like structures made up of one or more bundles of nerve fibers. A **nerve cell** or **neuron** (nu-ron) is a basic working unit that **transmits impulses** to other areas of body, such as muscles, glands or other neurons.

### Nerve cell consists of the following:

- **Nucleus** (nu-cle-us) is the **center** of the nerve cell.
- **Dendrites** (den-drite) are small fibers extending from the cell body that **receive messages** going into the nerve cell.
- **Axon** (ax-on) is a thread-like extension from nerve cell body that **sends impulses outward** to other muscles or glands.
- **Terminal or synapses** (si-napes) are tree-like fibers that extend out from end of axon and **nearly touch** other nerve cells, muscles or glands.

### Three Types of Nerves:

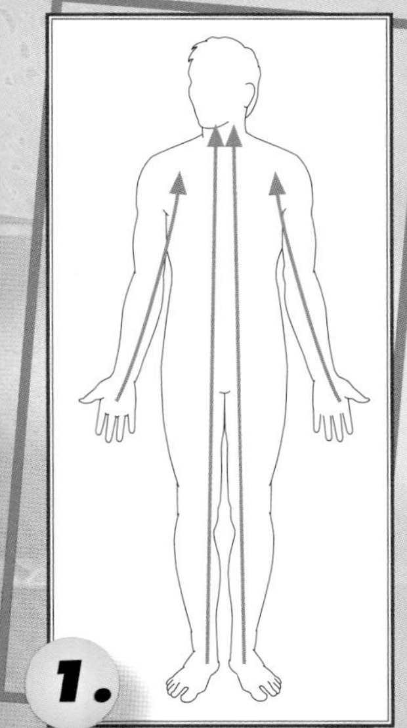

**1. Motor (efferent) nerves**

**send messages** from the central nervous system to the muscles, producing movement. For example, motor nerves cause the arrector pili muscles that are attached to hair follicles to contract and produce goose bumps.

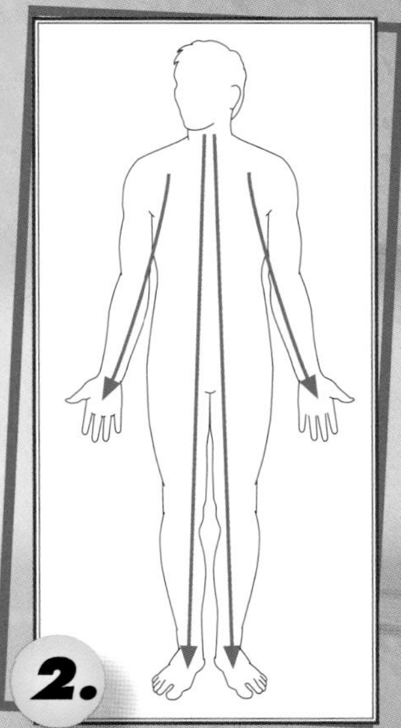

**2. Sensory (afferent) nerves**

**bring messages** to the central nervous system. They also carry sensations of touch, heat, cold, sight and hearing to the brain. Sensory nerve endings also known as receptors are most prevalent in the fingertips and soles of the feet.

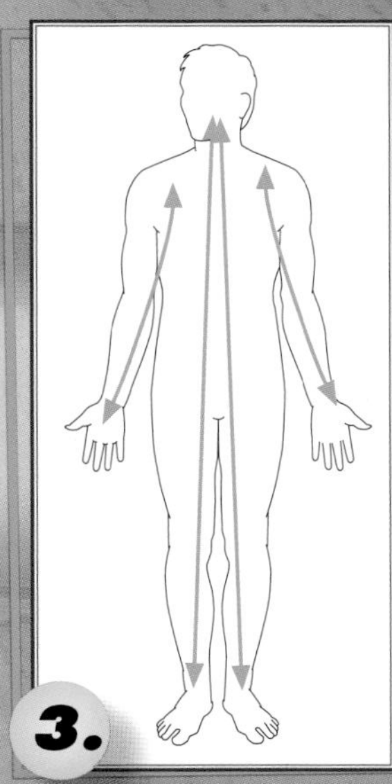

**3. Mixed nerves**

**send and receive messages** from the central nervous system.

4

# Nerves of Head and Face . . .

***The trifacial*** *(tri-fac-ial) or* ***trigeminal*** *(tri-gem-i-nal) nerve is one of the* ***fifth pair of cranial nerves*** *and is the* ***largest of the cranial nerves****. It is the* ***major facial sensory nerve*** *and is responsible for the muscle movement for chewing (masseter muscle).*

**The fifth pair of cranial nerves separates into three branches:**

1. **Ophthalmic** (oph-thal-mic) area consists of the eye region or **top one third of face and head.**
2. **Maxillary** (max-il-lar-y) area consists of upper jawbone, nose and cheek region or **middle one third of face.**
3. **Mandibular** (man-dib-u-lar) area consists of lower jaw region or **lower one third of face and head.**

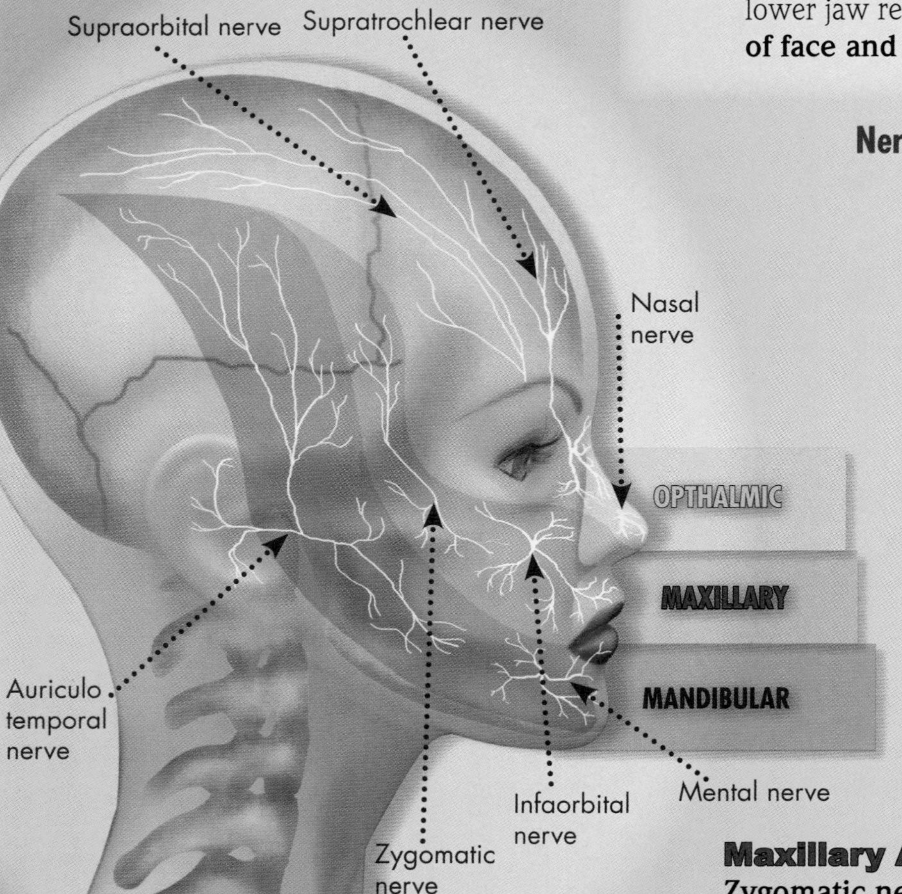


**Nerves affected by massage:**

**Ophthalmic Area**

**Supraorbital** (su-pra-or-bi-tal) **nerve** expands into the skin of scalp, forehead, eyebrows and upper eyelids.

**Supratrochlear** (su-pra-troch-le-ar) **nerve** expands into the skin of upper sides of nose and between the eyes.

**Infratrochlear** (in-fra-troch-le-ar) **nerve** expands into the skin and membrane of nose.

**Nasal nerve** expands into the skin of tip and lower sides of nose.

**Maxillary Area**

**Zygomatic nerve** expands into the muscles of upper area of cheek.

**Infraorbital** (in-fra-or-bi-tal) **nerve** expands into the skin of mouth, top lip, sides of nose and lower eyelids.

**Mandibular Area**

**Auriculotemporal** (au-ric-u-lo-tem-por-al) **nerve** expands into the skin of temple into top of skull and ear region.

**Mental nerve** expands into the skin of bottom lip and chin area.

4

# Nerves of Head and Face . . .

The **seventh pair of cranial nerves, located in the face include the major motor nerves.** It appears in the lower ear region continuing into the muscles of the neck and controls all facial muscles used for expression.

**The Principal Facial Cranial Nerves are:**

**Posterior auricular nerve** involves the lower area of the auricularis posterior muscles (behind the ear).

**Temporal nerve** involves the muscles of the temples, upper cheeks, eyelids, eyebrows and forehead.

**Zygomatic nerve** involves the upper and lower areas of the cheek.

**Buccal nerve** involves the muscles around the mouth.

**Mandibular nerve** involves the muscles of bottom lip and chin.

**Cervical nerves** involve the platysma muscle and both sides of neck.



4

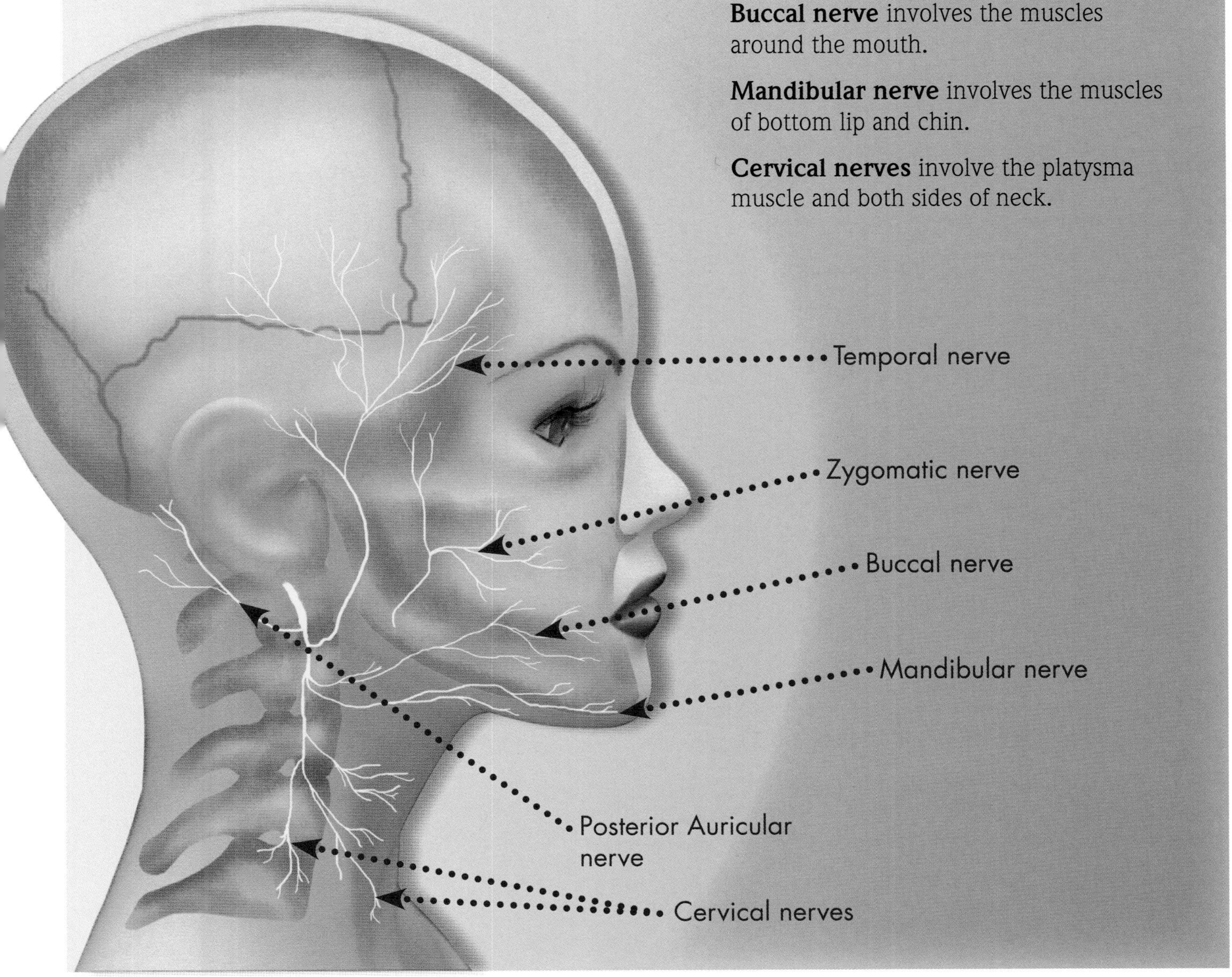

# Nerves of Neck . . .

### The cervical nerves separate into four branches:

**Greater occipital nerve** involves the upper part of the occipitalis muscle located at the back of head.

**Smaller occipital nerve** involves the lower part of the occipitalis muscle located back of head and ears.

**Greater auricular nerve** involves the sides of neck and bottom of ears.

**Cervical cutaneous** (cu-ta-ne-ous) **nerve** involves the sides and front of neck and the **sternum** (breastbone).

**Cervical nerves** begin at the spinal cord and separate to involve the muscles at back of head and neck.

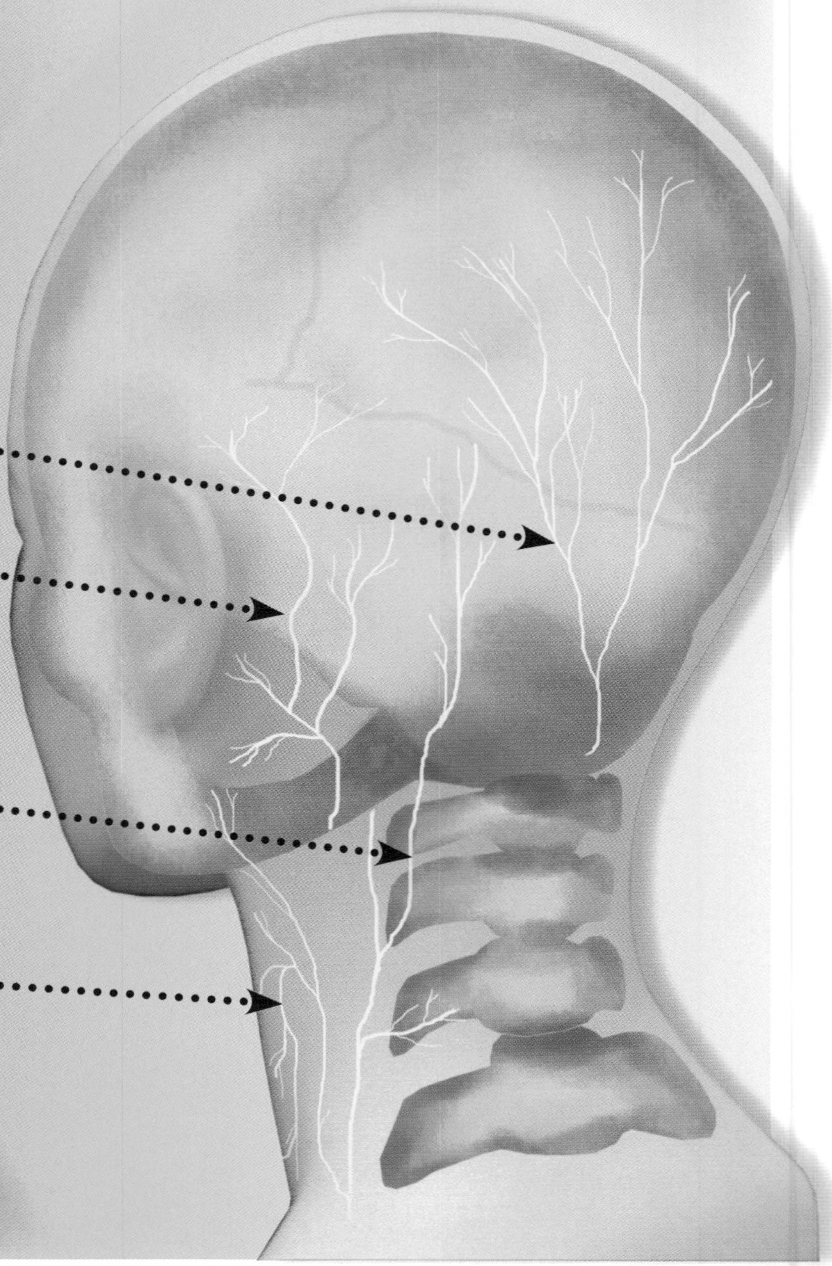

4

Greater occipital nerve

Smaller occipital nerve

Greater auricular nerve

Cervical cutaneous nerve

# Nerves of Arm and Hand ...

## Nerves of the Forearm and Hand

**Ulnar nerve** is located on the little-finger-side of the arm, extending into the palm. It **carries messages to and from the muscles** of the hand, forearms and from the skin of the hands.

**Radial nerve** is located on the thumb side of the arm and extends into the back of the hand.

**Median nerve** is located in the middle of the forearm, extending into the hand. It **supplies impulses to the muscles** of the forearms, hands and to the skin of the hands.

**Digital nerve** is located in the fingers of each hand.

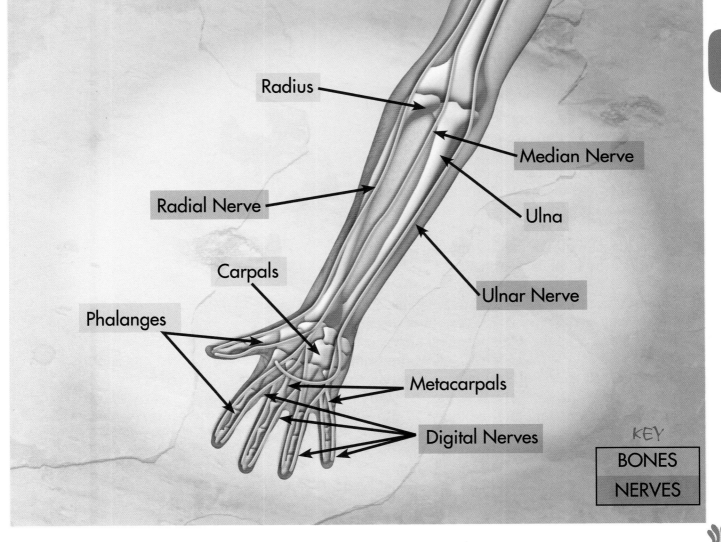



4

# Nerves of Leg and Foot . . .

*One of the most important nerves in the body is the* ***sciatic*** *(si-a-tik)* ***nerve,*** *which begins in the lower back and branches down through the legs into the feet and toes. Clients who are pregnant or who have problems with their lower back, due to injury or other reasons, may experience pain or numbness in their legs and feet from compression of the sciatic nerve. Be careful and gentle when offering pedicure services to these customers, and always make certain that their* ***lower back is supported while they sit,*** *particularly when the chair is in a reclined position.*

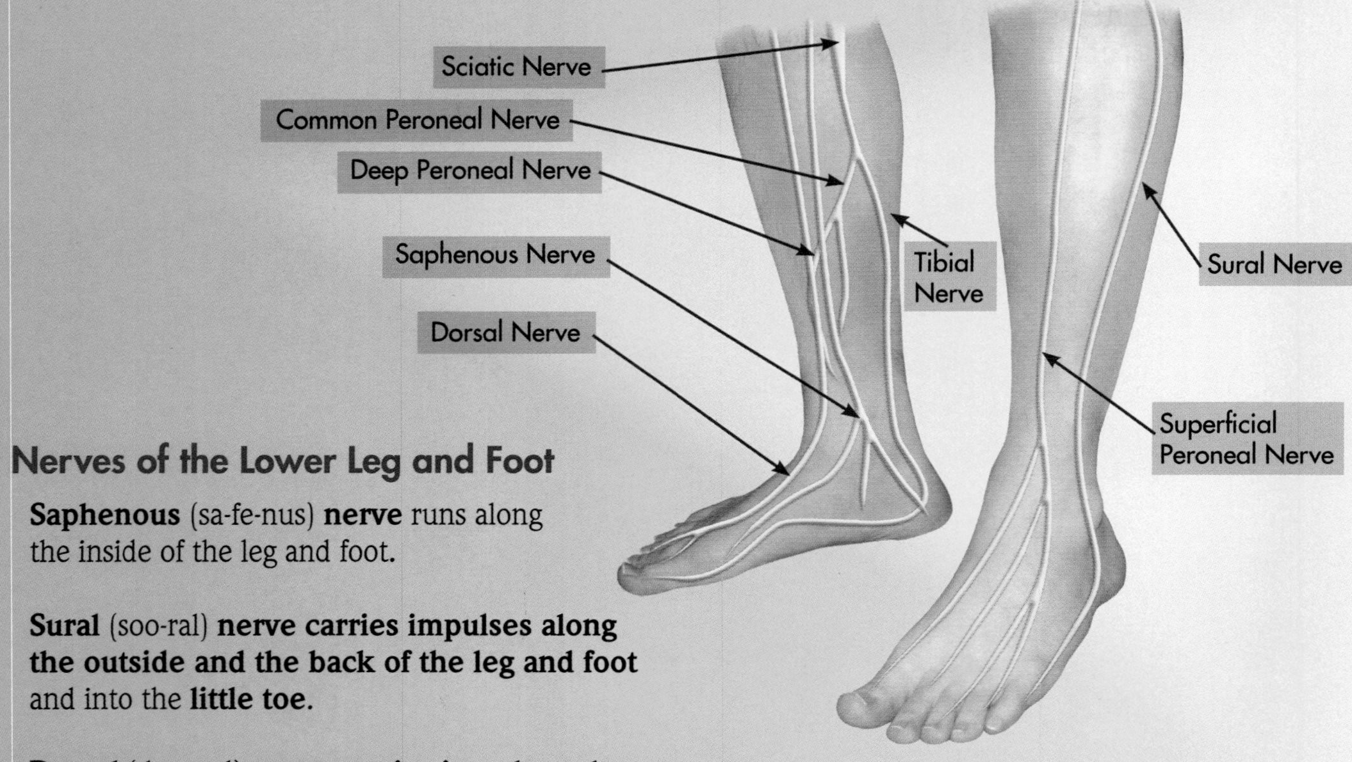


4

## Nerves of the Lower Leg and Foot

**Saphenous** (sa-fe-nus) **nerve** runs along the inside of the leg and foot.

**Sural** (soo-ral) **nerve carries impulses along the outside and the back of the leg and foot** and into the **little toe.**

**Dorsal** (door-sal) **nerve carries impulses along the top of the foot,** to the skin.

**Common peroneal** (per-o-ne-al) **nerve** is one of the two branches of the sciatic nerve. It has two divisions of its own: the **deep peroneal nerve,** or referred to as anterior tibial, which **serves the front of the leg;** and the **superficial peroneal nerve,** lying just under the skin, **which serves the skin of the lower leg, the foot and the toes.**

**Tibial** (tib-e-al) **nerve** is the other major division of the sciatic nerve. It goes down the back of the leg and **supplies nerve impulses to the calf of the leg** and the **sole of the foot.**

***There are more than 50,000 nerve endings in your client's feet. That is why a massage service can be so therapeutic and will add to your total salon ticket!***

# Massage ...

*As a cosmetologist, you will incorporate your sense of touch through the application of massage. To master massage, it is important to have a basic understanding of the anatomy of head, face and neck. A firm, confident touch will allow you to provide the proper benefits of massage, along with the application of essential creams for a smooth, gliding movement across skin or scalp.*

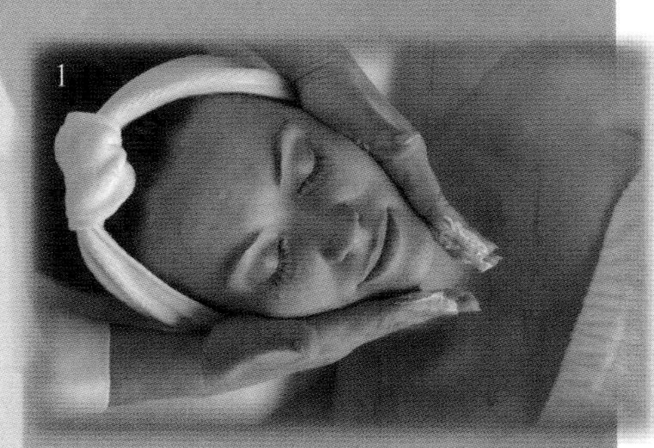

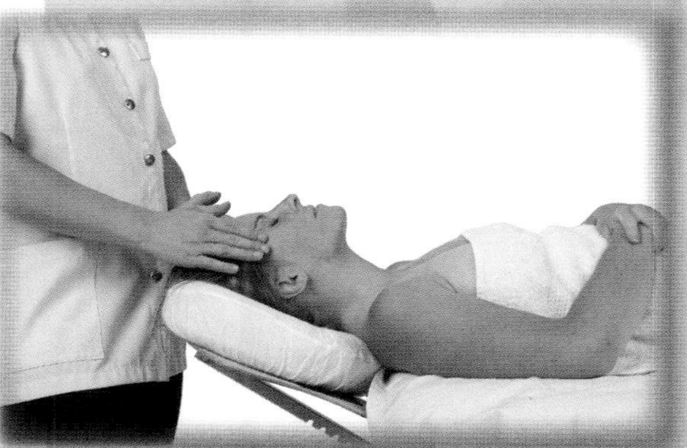

Massage can be traced back to **2000-3000 BCE**, when Egyptians, Greeks, Romans and Asian cultures used massage as a primary source for maintaining health. Massage was one of the oldest forms of **"medicine"** to relieve pain.

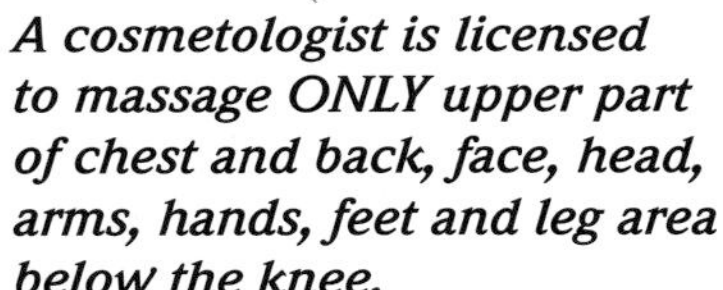


***A cosmetologist is licensed to massage ONLY upper part of chest and back, face, head, arms, hands, feet and leg area below the knee.***

Massage is the **act of rubbing or kneading** an area of the body, manually or mechanically, for medical, therapeutic purposes or to help induce relaxation.

4

# Massage...

The purpose of massage is to **increase blood flow, induce relaxation, reduce stress, and promote contraction of muscles.** Massage provides toning, aids in elimination of toxins from the body and helps to promote overall wellness.

4

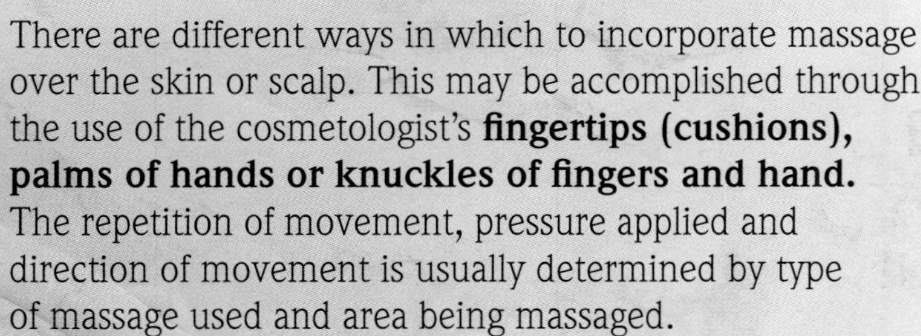

There are different ways in which to incorporate massage over the skin or scalp. This may be accomplished through the use of the cosmetologist's **fingertips (cushions), palms of hands or knuckles of fingers and hand.** The repetition of movement, pressure applied and direction of movement is usually determined by type of massage used and area being massaged.

**CAUTION:** Due to the increase in blood circulation, massage is not recommended for anyone who has had a stroke or who has a heart condition or high blood pressure.

# Motor Nerve Points ...

*Locating motor nerve points is an integral part of a massage. When pressure is applied to these areas of a muscle, contraction of that muscle will occur and produce an early state of relaxation. This area is referred to as the **motor point.** The location of the motor points will vary according to individual's body structure.*

## Facial Motor Nerve Points are:

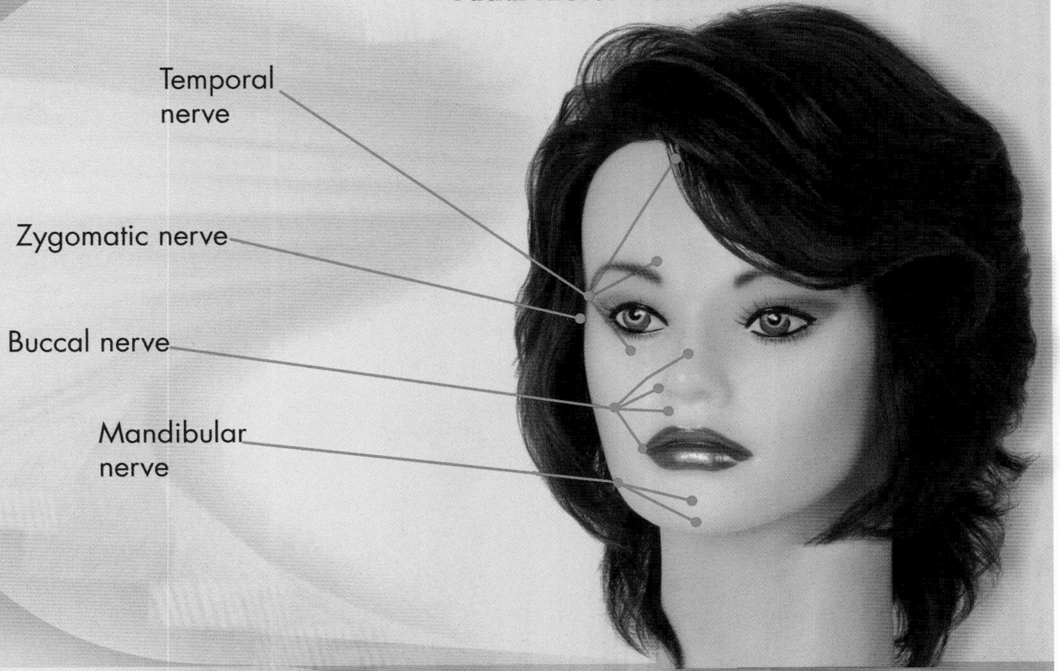

Temporal nerve

Zygomatic nerve

Buccal nerve

Mandibular nerve

## Back of Head and Neck Motor Nerve Points are:

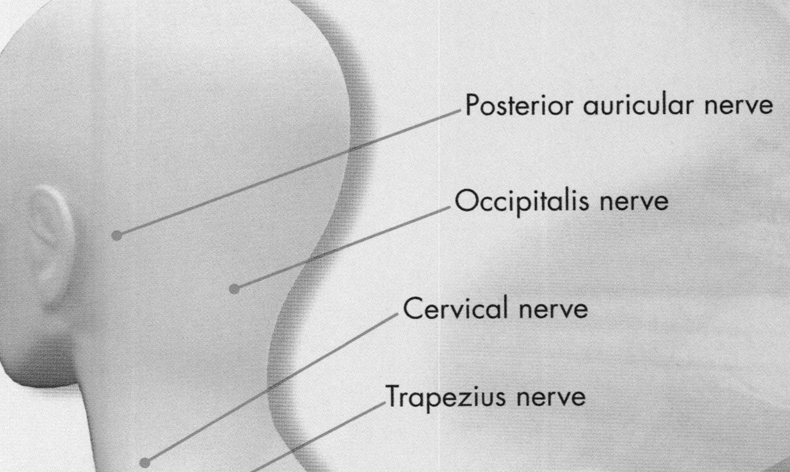

# Manipulations ...

**Direction of Manipulation:**
Generally, the manipulation will move over the skin by following the direction of the muscle (depending on type of massage). Begin by starting at the **insertion of the muscle and moving toward origin of muscle** (follow direction of arrows) to obtain the greatest benefits from the massage.

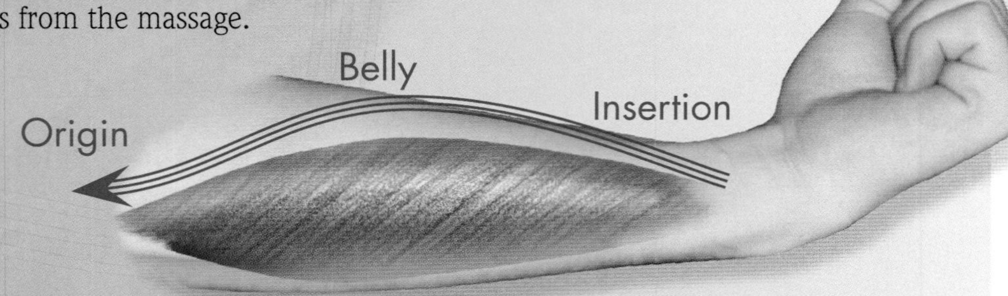


**Types of Manipulations:**



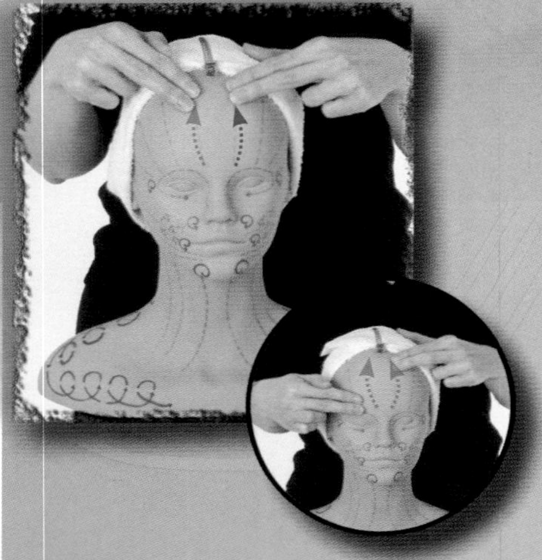

**Effleurage** (ef-le-rahz)**: gliding, stroking or circular** movements applied with a light, slow, consistent motion, using either light or no pressure. The effects of this massage movement are relaxing and gentle and usually start and end a massage procedure.

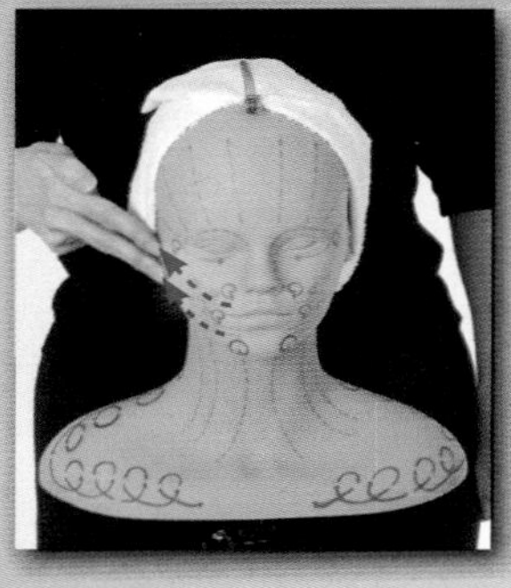

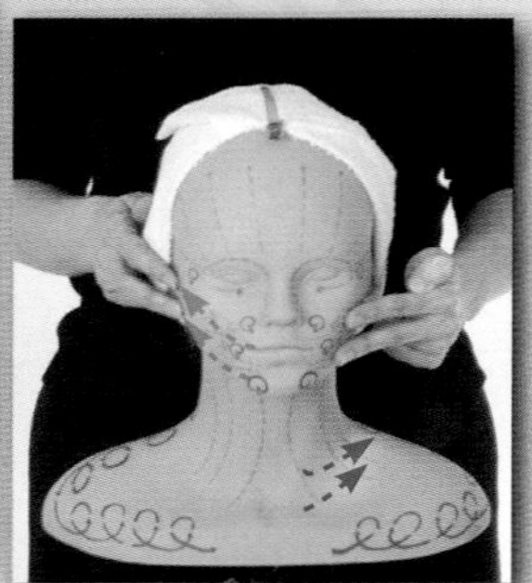

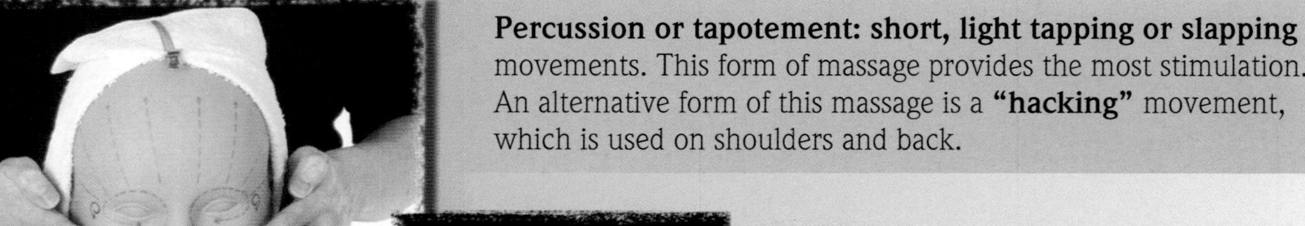

**Percussion or tapotement: short, light tapping or slapping** movements. This form of massage provides the most stimulation. An alternative form of this massage is a **"hacking"** movement, which is used on shoulders and back.

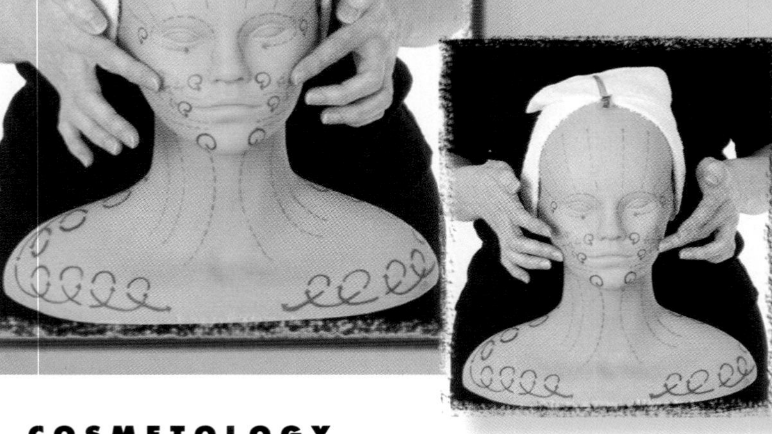

# Manipulations ...

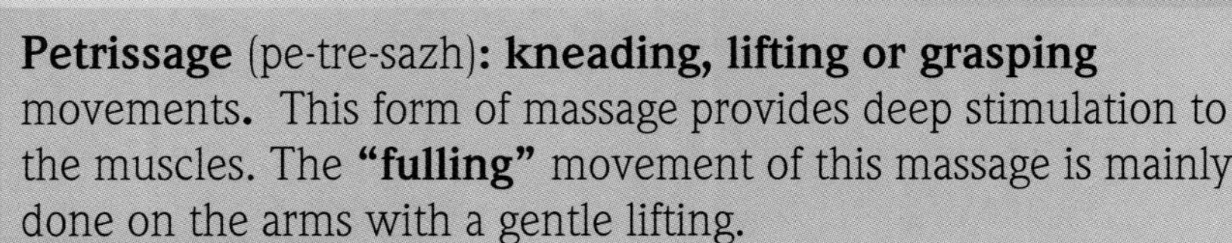

**Petrissage** (pe-tre-sazh)**: kneading, lifting or grasping** movements**.** This form of massage provides deep stimulation to the muscles. The **"fulling"** movement of this massage is mainly done on the arms with a gentle lifting.

4

**Friction: deep rubbing, rolling or wringing** movement applied with pressure, forcing one layer of tissue to press against another layer, therefore flattening or stretching that tissue. The effects of this massage movement are glandular and circulation stimulation.

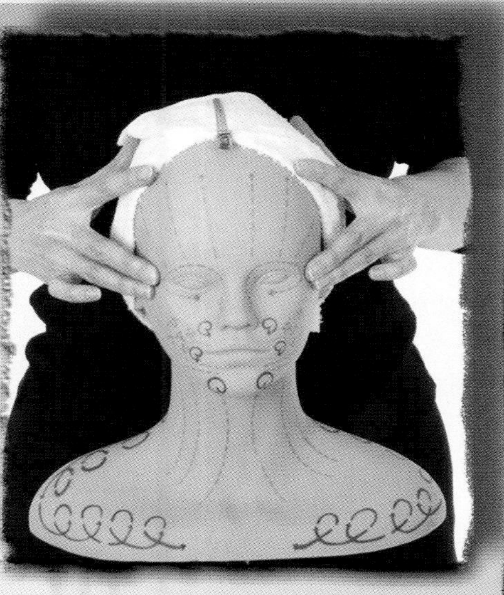

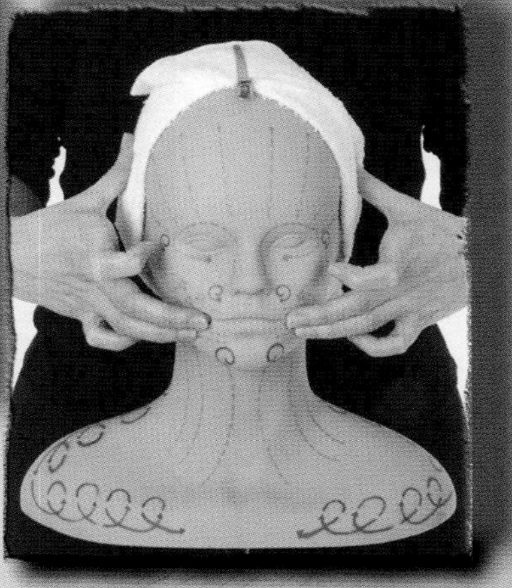

"Massage can be performed once a week as maintenance for healthy skin and scalp."

Anatomy

# REVIEW QUESTIONS

## MULTIPLE CHOICE

1. Which type of tissue serves as a protective covering for the body's organs?
   A. nerve B. epithelial C. connective
2. Which bone covers entire back of head?
   A. occipital B. parietal C. temporal
3. What is the "control center" of the body?
   A. brain B. heart C. spinal cord
4. Which type of manipulation consists of kneading, lifting or grasping?
   A. effleurage B. percussion C. petrissage
5. Which system supports the soft tissues of the body and contains 206 bones?
   A. integumentary B. nervous C. skeletal
6. What bone is the largest and strongest bone of the face?
   A. maxilla B. mandible C. zygomatic
7. What type of blood vessels carry purified blood away from the heart?
   A. capillaries B. arteries C. veins
8. Which end of the muscle is attached to an immovable section of skeleton?
   A. origin B. belly C. insertion
9. What eye muscle allows eyelids to open and close?
   A. orbicularis oris B. orbicularis oculi C. corrugator
10. What part of the nerve cell sends impulses outward to other muscles or glands?
    A. dendrites B. nucleus C. axon
11. Which facial area contains the risorius muscle?
    A. eye B. mouth C. chin
12. Which parts of the blood are tiny color-free particles that are responsible for clotting?
    A. platelets B. white blood cells C. plasma
13. Which bone forms the forehead?
    A. frontal B. parietal C. temporal
14. Which part of cell contains food substances for cellular growth and repair?
    A. nucleus B. centrosome C. cytoplasm
15. What type of nerve brings and sends messages to the central nervous system?
    A. motor B. mixed C. sensory
16. What part of the hand is best used for massage?
    A. finger nails B.topside of hand C. cushions of fingertips
17. Which artery delivers blood to the upper eyelids and forehead?
    A. occipital B. frontal C. parietal
18. Where is the location of the ear muscle auricularis anterior?
    A. front of ear B. above the ear C. behind the ear
19. Which type of muscle is smooth and responsible for involuntary movements?
    A. cardiac B. striated C. non-striated
20. Which organ is multi-chambered, muscular and maintains the flow of blood?
    A. heart B. lungs C. stomach

STUDENT'S NAME DATE GRADE

anagen cortex

melanin papilla

pityriasis

ringworm

whorl

# Hair Structure

HAIR STRUCTURE

5

# Terminology ...

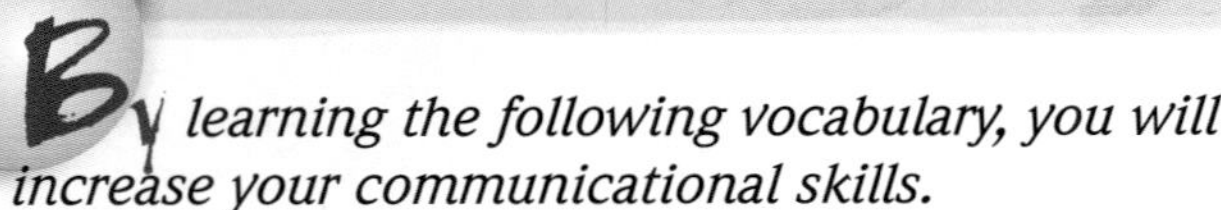

**B**y learning the following vocabulary, you will increase your communicational skills.

**Alopecia** is hair loss in abnormal amounts.

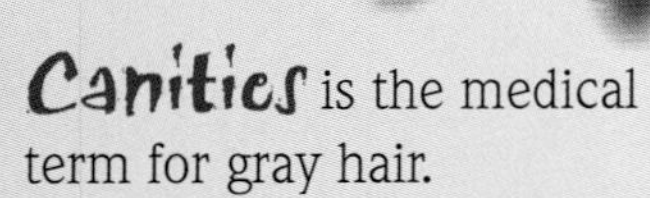

**Canities** is the medical term for gray hair.

**Cuticle** is the tough, outer protective covering.

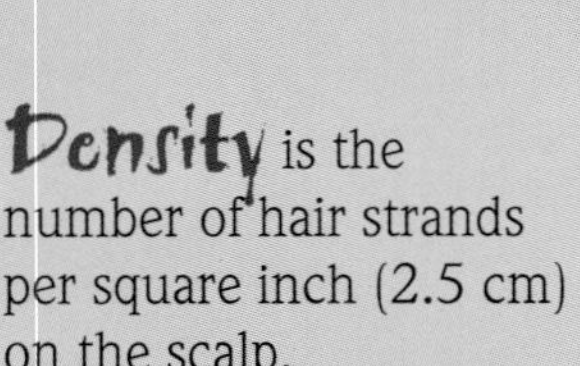

**Density** is the number of hair strands per square inch (2.5 cm) on the scalp.

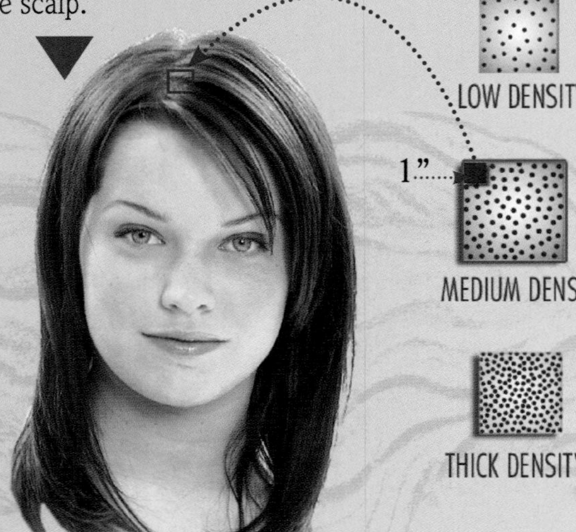


**Eumelanin** is a type of melanin that produces brown to black pigments in the hair.

5

# Terminology...

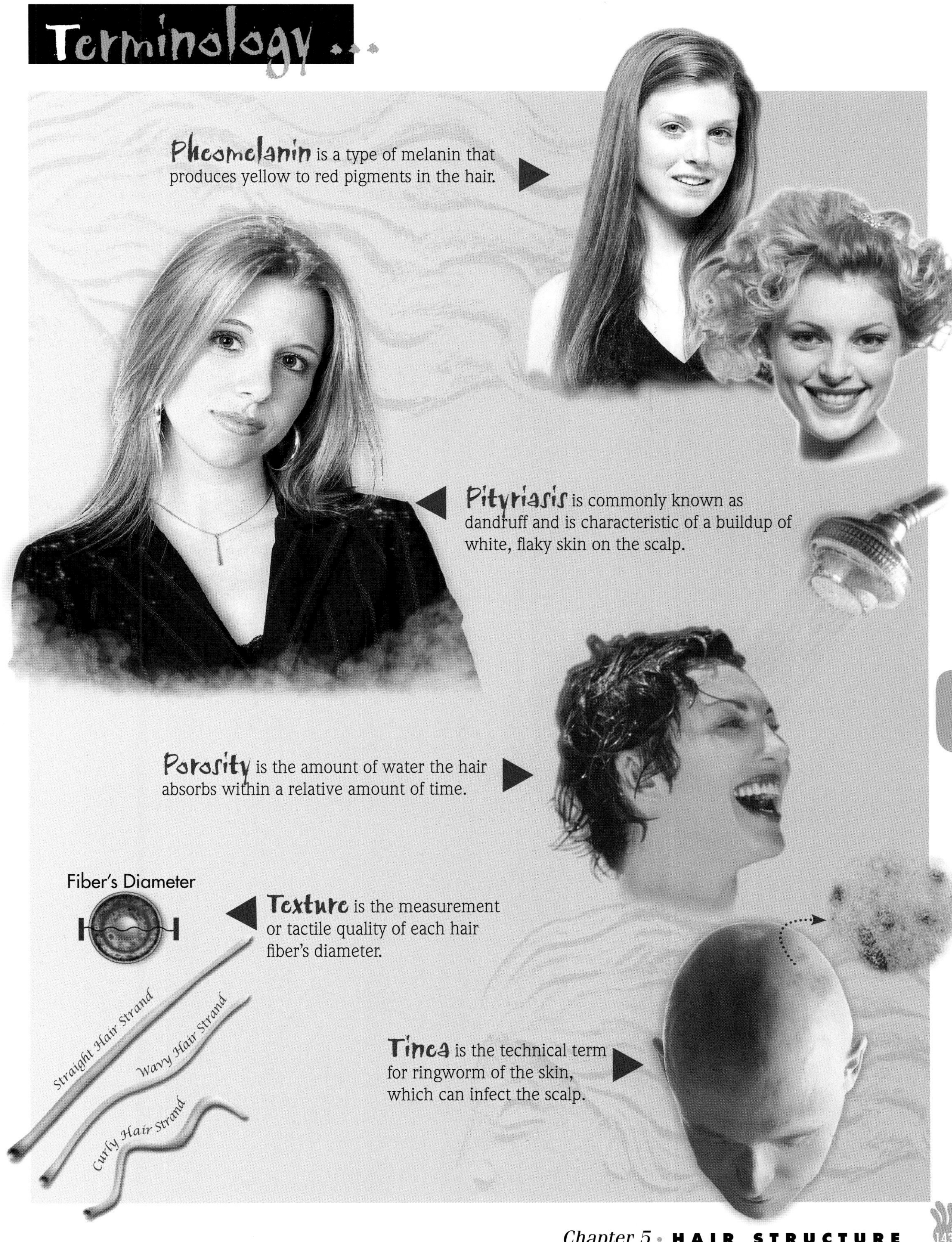


**Pheomelanin** is a type of melanin that produces yellow to red pigments in the hair.

**Pityriasis** is commonly known as dandruff and is characteristic of a buildup of white, flaky skin on the scalp.

**Porosity** is the amount of water the hair absorbs within a relative amount of time.

**Texture** is the measurement or tactile quality of each hair fiber's diameter.

**Tinea** is the technical term for ringworm of the skin, which can infect the scalp.

*Hair is a group of "thread-like" strands growing out from the skin or scalp. Hair is our medium upon which we create our art. It is our means for providing regular hair-care maintenance and/or creative expression, and in the process, enhance a person's beauty. The technical term for the study of hair, disorders, diseases and hair-care is **trichology** (tri-kah-lu-gee).*

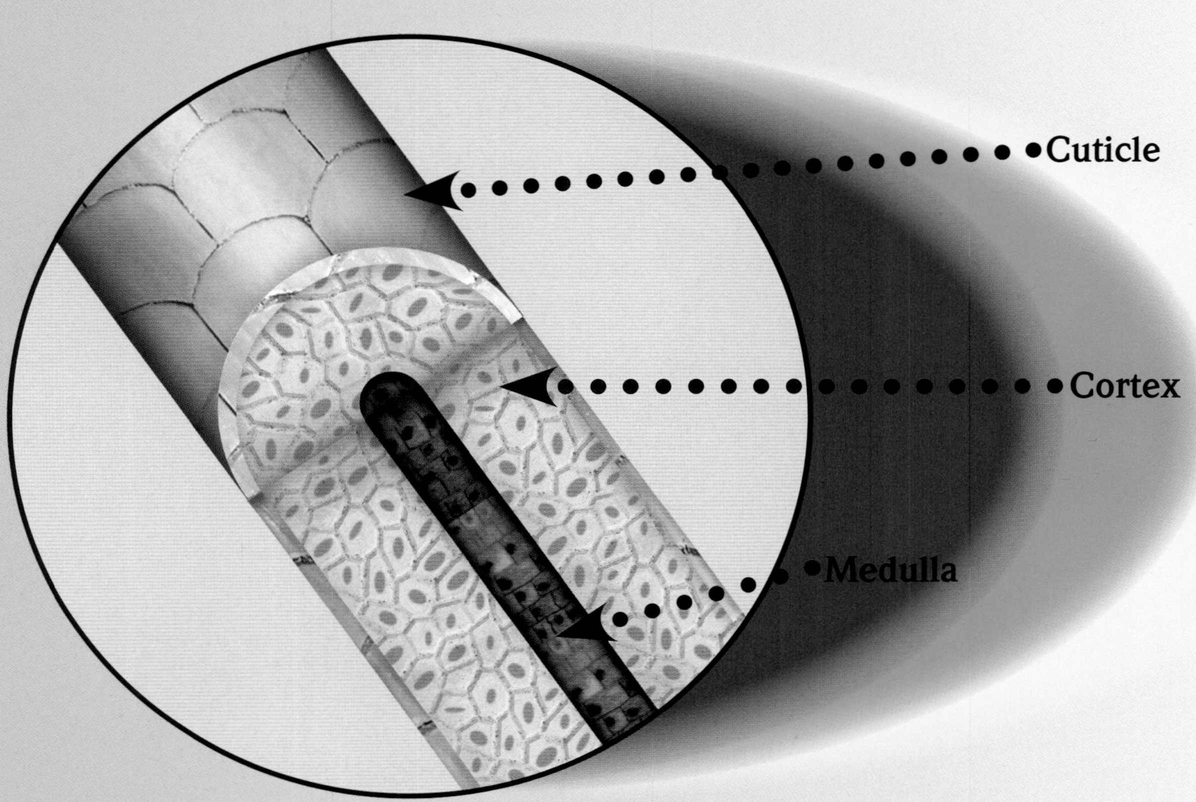


The portion of hair that extends beyond the skin or scalp is the **hair shaft.**

## The hair shaft consists of three layers:

- **Cuticle** is the tough, outer protective covering. This layer is generally made of seven to twelve layers of overlapping scale-like (flat) cells.
- **Cortex** is the soft, elastic, thick, inner layer made up of elongated cells. This layer is responsible for elasticity (stretch) in the hair and it also contains **melanin** or coloring matter.
- **Medulla** is the deepest layer, consisting of round cells. Sometimes it is intermittent or totally absent, which is not known to have any true effect on the hair.

# Hair Root Structure . . .

The portion of hair below skin or scalp is the **hair root.**

## The hair root consists of the following structures:

- **Follicle** is a depression or pocket surrounding the hair root. It determines the angle at which the hair fiber will emerge from the scalp.
- **Bulb** is a rounded club-shaped part at the very end of the root. It is hollowed out and fits over the papilla.
- **Papilla** is a mass of blood and nerves located directly under the hollowed area of the hair bulb. The papilla supplies nourishment for the continued growth of the hair fiber.
- **Arrector pili muscle** is a small involuntary muscle located along the side of the hair follicle. This muscle is responsible for the "goose flesh" or "goose bump" appearance on the skin due to a reaction from cold or fear.
- **Sebaceous glands** are **"oil" glands** and produce the oily substance sebum to the skin or scalp. These glands attach to the sides of the hair follicles.

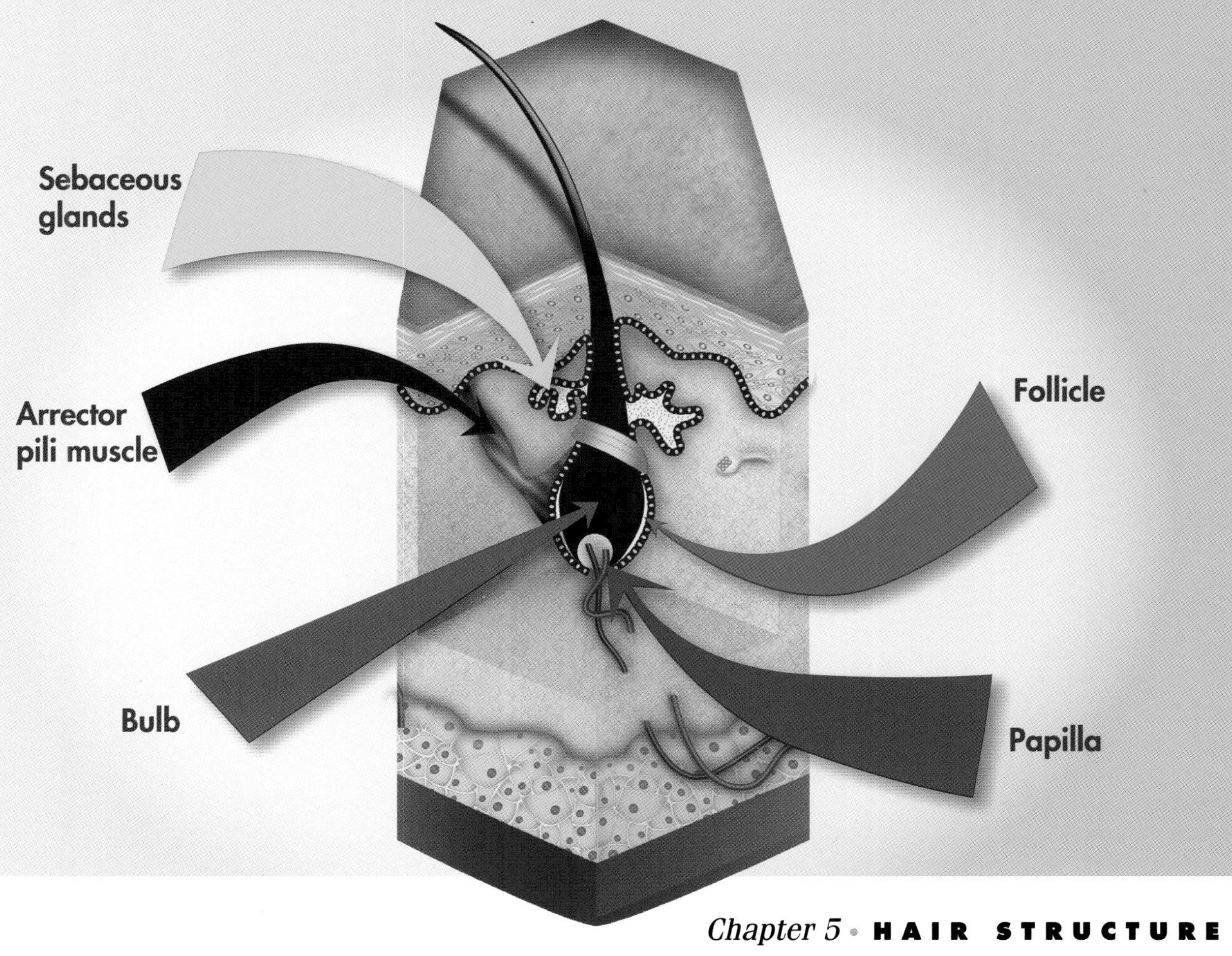


5

# Composition of Hair . . .

*Before we can begin to service hair, we must learn its composition and understand how it reacts to hair-care treatments and chemical services.*

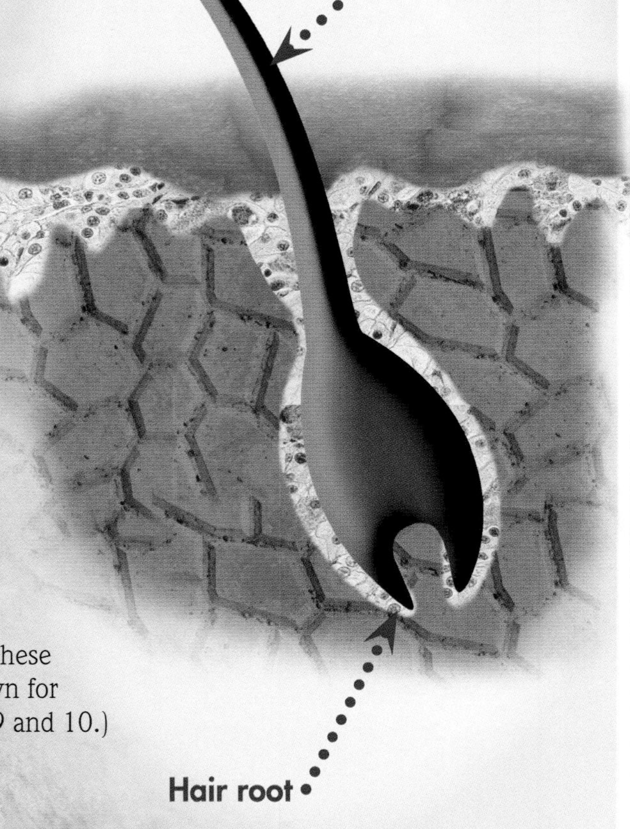


The hair begins to form in the underlying layers (dermis) of the skin. Living cells collect in a pocket of skin located in the dermis layer, which starts the process of building the **hair root.** This pocket is referred to as the **follicle**. The follicle surrounds the entire root, providing a space or a pocket. (If you imagine slipping your hand inside a glove, the follicle is the area that surrounds your hand.) These cells begin to move upward inside this follicle maturing and **keratinizing (hardening)** therefore dying and starting to form the structure (root) of the hair. As this process continues, the hair continues to form and gradually move out of the scalp creating the **hair shaft**, a non-living fiber.

The living cells that start this whole process are composed of a strong, fibrous protein called **keratin.** The protein is derived from the **amino acids** that make up hair and nails. The amino acids link together to form minute protein fibers. Each amino acid consist of the elements, **hydrogen, oxygen, nitrogen, carbon** and **sulfur ... a shorter version of remembering is HONCS!** These elements will play an important role in the chemical breakdown for permanent waving and chemical relaxing. (Refer to Chapters 9 and 10.)

AMINO ACID

H O N C S

Hydrogen—Oxygen—Nitrogen—Carbon—Sulfer

"Remember HONCS are the five elements that make up hair."

5

# Composition of Hair . . .

Amino acids are connected by an **end bond** or **peptide bond** to form long, single chains referred to as a **polypeptide** or an **alpha helix.**

H O N C S

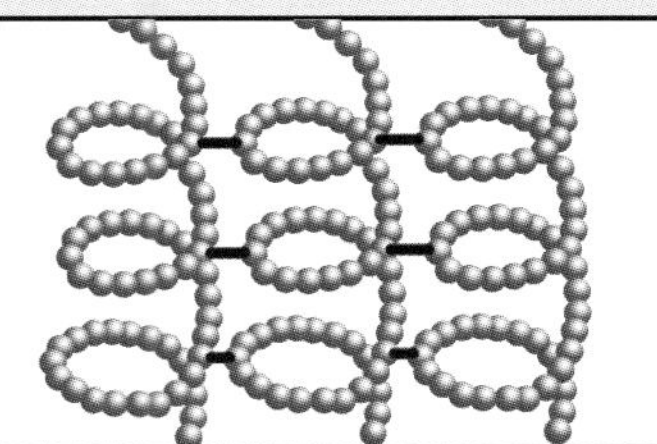

**Three** alpha helix coils twist around each other to form a **protofibril**.

**Nine** protofibrils are packaged together as a **bundle**.

**Eleven** bundles will produce a **microfibril**.

Hundreds of microfibrils are cemented together in a fibrous protein bundle referred to as a **macrofibril**.

This process continues with hundreds of macrofibrils grouped together to create a **cortical fiber**.

The cortical fibers grouped together produce the **cortex**. The dried, dead cells that surround the cortex are the **cuticle scales.**

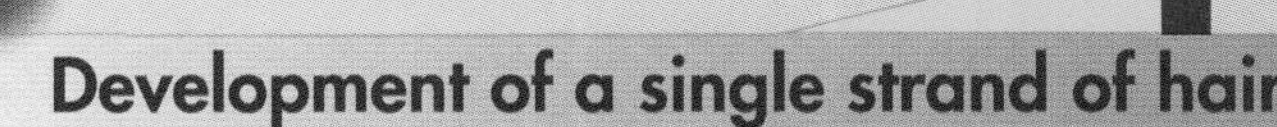


Amino acids
Peptide bond
Polypeptide chain (3)
Protofibril (9)
Microfibril (11)
Macrofibril
Cortical fiber
Cuticle scales

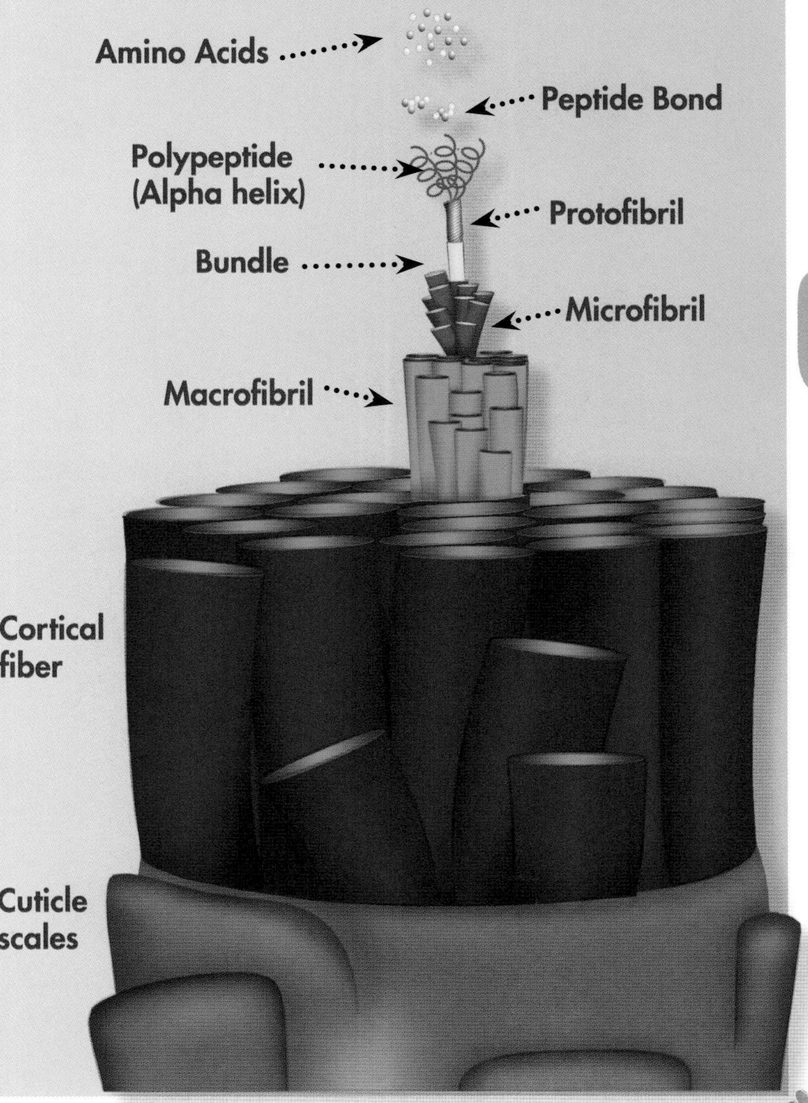


5

# LANUGO

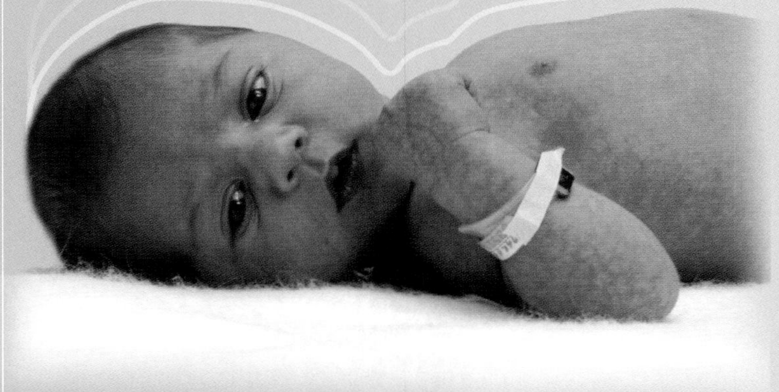

**Lanugo** (la-nu-go) or **vellus** hair is soft, white and downy, usually lacking a medulla and found on any area of the body except palms of hands and soles of feet. This hair is commonly found on newborn babies and women, who retain a larger amount of lanugo hair on their bodies than men.

# TERMINAL

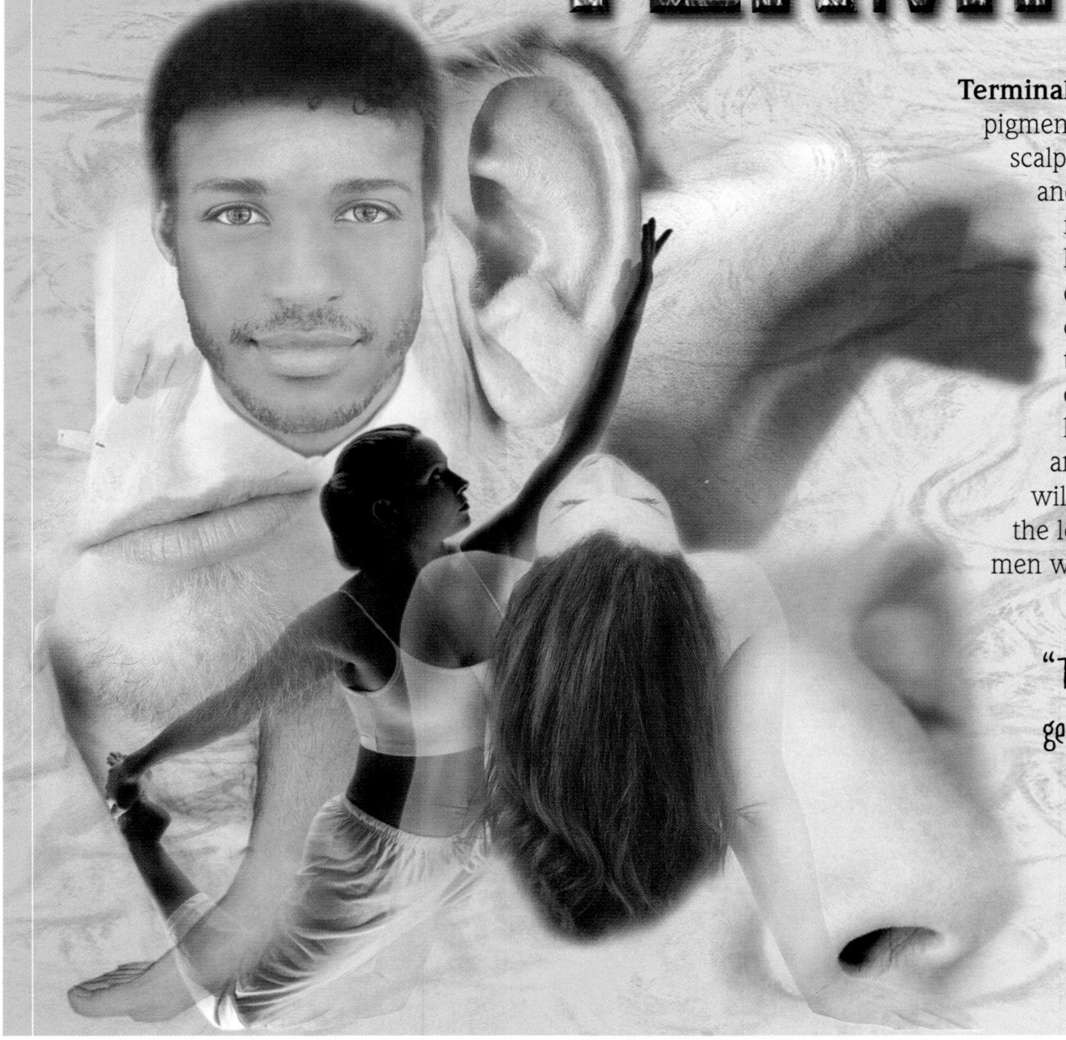

**Terminal** hair is the remaining pigmented hair located on the scalp, arms (underarms), legs and in the nose and ears of men and women. This hair will vary in texture, color, length and can change from vellus hair to terminal hair depending on individual and genetics, hormonal changes (pubic) and age. Generally, women will shave or wax the hair on the legs and underarms and men will shave their facial hair.

"Terminal hair will generally have a Medulla."

5

# Hair Growth . . .

*At varying rates and simultaneously single strands of hair will grow and shed on each individual's head at all times.*

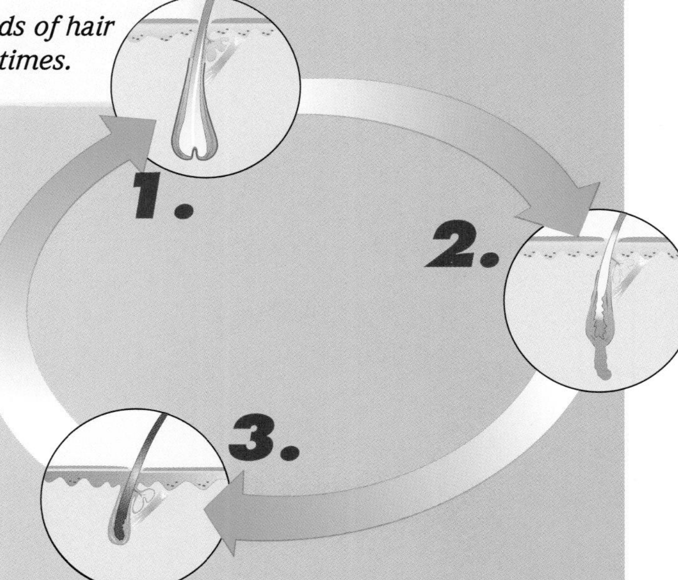


## Three Stages of Hair Growth:

1. **Anagen** (an-a-gen) or **growing stage** is when the hair continues to survive and grow at an average ½ **inch** (1.25 cm) per month, dependent upon each individual and location of hair. **Two to six years** is the life expectancy of hair in this stage, and sometimes as long as 10 years.

2. **Catagen** (cat-a-gen) or **intermediary** (in-ter-me-di-ar-y) **stage** is when the hair stops growing and begins the process of disconnecting from the papilla and follicle. This process may **last two to three weeks.**

3. **Telogen** (tel-o-gen) or **shedding stage** is when the hair cycle ends and hair has shed from the skin or scalp. At the end of this **three to six month** stage, the anagen stage will resume with new hair growth in same hair follicle where hair was shed.

These stages repeat numerous times and in different sequences within our follicles, therefore, at any one point in time we have an average of **90 percent hair on our heads.** The remaining **10 percent hair** is in the telogen stage.

5

## Facts About Hair Growth:

Health can affect hair growth. Lack of vitamins/minerals, certain medications, illness or an injury to skin or scalp can all have an impact.

Normal **daily hair loss** is an average **30 to 50 hair strands**, which are then replaced by new hair.

Hair grows on all areas of the body with the exception of the palms of hands, soles of feet, and lips.

Weather affects hair loss, with more hair being shed during cold months, while warm temperatures will activate the growing stage of hair.

Haircutting or shaving has **no effect** on the growth of hair.

1

# Hair Loss . . .

**Normal hair loss** is the daily shedding of hair included in the three stages of hair growth.

**Abnormal hair loss** is the shedding of hair beyond our daily amount (30 to 50 hair strands) with no replacement of new hair. If this process continues, it may lead to baldness. Hair loss in abnormal amounts is referred to as **alopecia** (al-oh-pee-shah).

## Common Types of Alopecia

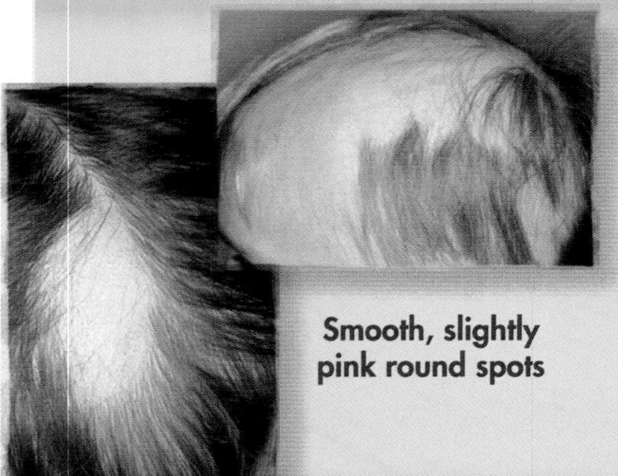

Smooth, slightly pink round spots

**Alopecia Areata** (air-ee-ah-tah) is a patchy loss of hair occurring on scalp or other parts of the body. It is characterized by smooth, slightly pink, irregular or round spots located on any area of the scalp. In severe cases, balding can occur over the entire head, referred to as **alopecia totalis** or over entire body, referred to as **alopecia universalis**. Possible causes are stress induced or an autoimmune disease that attacks the hair follicles. A medical care professional should be contacted for treatment; however, there is no known cure. For more information, go to the National Alopecia Areata Foundation www.naaaf.org

Repetitive pulling or stretching

**Traction Alopecia** is hair loss through **repetitive** and **excessive pulling or stretching** the hair. This commonly occurs when hair is pulled into a ponytail or is tightly twisted into braids, cornrows or long-hairdesigns. This condition may be rectified when trauma to hair is stopped. Refer to medical care professional.

5

Male pattern baldness

**Androgenic** (an-dro-gen-ic) **Alopecia** is male or female pattern baldness The process generally starts with a **thinning of the hairline** (recession areas) and **crown area**, then meeting across the top of head. Hair often remains on the lower perimeter of head giving a horseshoe-shaped appearance. Balding can begin as early as in your teens and is frequently seen by **age 35** with **40 percent** of men and women showing signs of hair loss. Some reasons for balding are genetics, hormonal changes, medication, medical treatments or age. Refer to a medical care professional.

**Telogen Effluvium** is when the hair has been **prematurely pushed** into the telogen (shedding) stage. This disruption to the normal hair growth cycle is usually due to sudden body changes accompanying illness, childbirth (sometimes referred to as **postpartum alopecia**), stress, shock or crash dieting. Continue with the use of professional hair-care products and if condition persists, refer to a medical care professional.

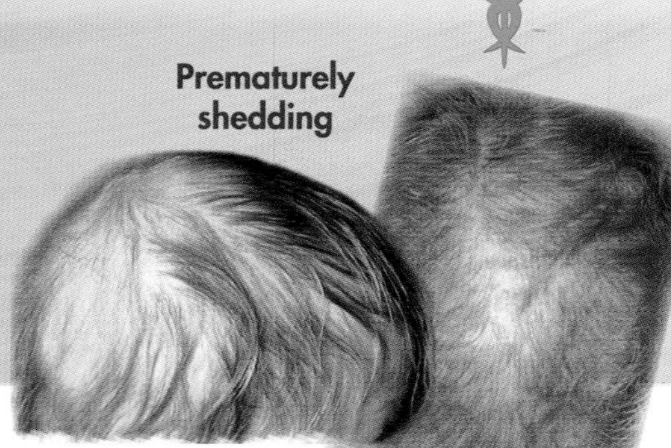

Prematurely shedding

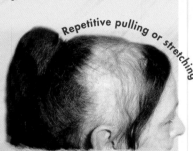

# Hair Loss Treatments . . .

Let us take a step-by-step approach as to how this hair loss process occurs. Hair loss can be caused by any one or a combination of the following factors:

- Heredity
- Toxic substances
- Severe radiation
- Nervous disorder
- Hormonal imbalance
- Illness and infectious disease
- Aging
- Injury and impairment

## Male Hair Loss

Typical male pattern baldness is also known as "Hippocratic Baldness," named in honor of Hippocrates and his own baldness pattern and a lifelong search for a cure. Thinning of hair **normally starts before age 40**, occurring first along the front hairline and crown area then progressing to join into one large area across top of head. In order to inherit baldness, a male needs only **one gene –** either one from the mother's side of the family or one from the father's side.

## Female Hair Loss

Baldness in women usually occurs more evenly throughout the upper two-thirds of the head. A female needs to **inherit two genes** – one from the mother's side of the family and one from the father's side – in order to develop baldness.

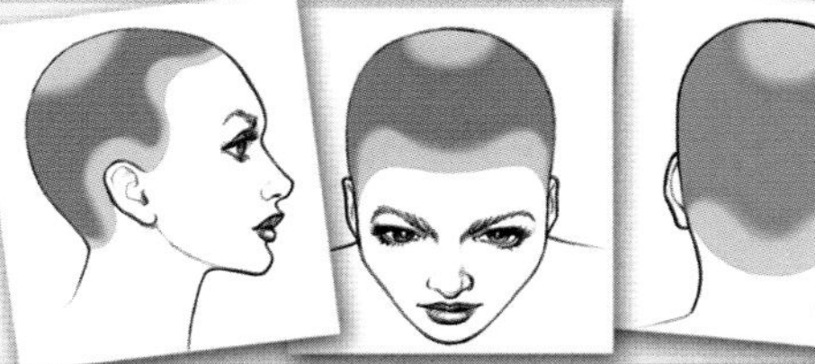

## Male Pattern Hair Loss

According to the **International Society of Hair Restoration Surgery** (www.ishrs.org), an estimated **35 million men in the United States** are affected by male pattern baldness. The male hormone, testosterone causes hair loss in men who carry that one gene. Testosterone is converted to **dihydrotestosterone** (di-hy-dro-tes-tos-ter-one), commonly referred to as **DHT**, which will enter the hair follicles and alter the production of proteins. This ultimately causes hair growth to stop completely.

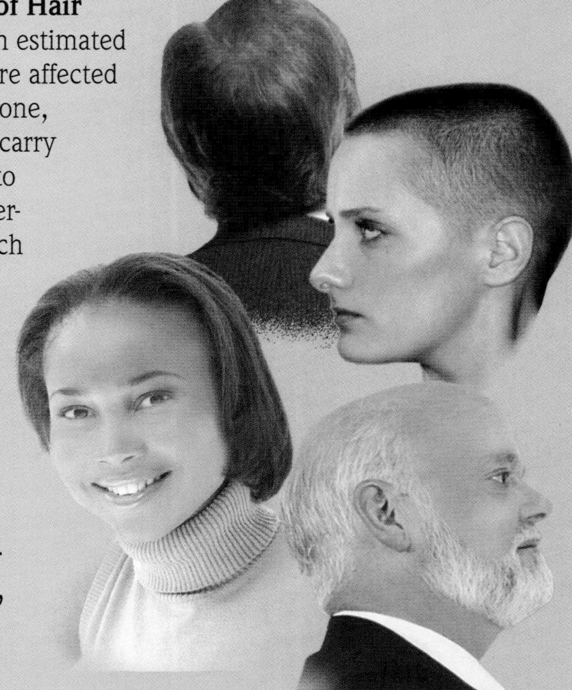

"Since males only have to inherit one gene for baldness, we see more bald males than females."

5

# Hair Loss Treatments...

***Advancements** in medical and scientific technology have provided some exciting treatments for people who experience hair loss. Two of the current most popular treatments are **Rogaine®** (ro-gaine) and **Propecia®** (pro-pee-sha). However, scientific research is ongoing in the area and new treatment alternatives are sure to emerge in the future.*

***"The customer's needs always come first. Make referrals to other professionals for areas beyond your training and knowledge. This added service and caring will help strengthen your customer's loyalty!"***

## Rogaine®

**Minoxidil** (min-ox-i-dil) is the active ingredient in Rogaine and was **approved by the Food and Drug Administration (FDA)** in 1988. It is found to be safe and effective in treating both male and female hair loss or thinning. Originally used to treat high blood pressure, Minoxidil was discovered to also **stimulate hair growth** and thickness by invigorating shrunken hair follicles and increase their size.

Rogaine is a **topical liquid** or **foam** treatment that is applied **twice daily** prior to the use of any styling products. Special care should be taken in conjunction with the use of Rogaine to prevent scalp irritation. Mild shampoo should be used for cleansing and it is recommended to not use this product prior to a chemical service.

**Visit** www.rogaine.com **for additional information.**

## Propecia®

**Finasteride** (fin-as-tur-eyed) is the active ingredient in Propecia and is taken **once daily** in **tablet form**. It **blocks** the formation of **dihydrotestosterone (DHT),** the hormone that causes male pattern baldness. This blockage occurs by disabling the enzyme that is present in and around the hair follicles of balding men. Propecia does not seem to grow hair in areas that are completely bald. The main benefit of finasteride is its ability to reduce or terminate hair loss, or re-grow hair on **thin density** areas of the scalp.

**WARNING:** This product is **not to be taken by women or children**; could cause birth defects in pregnant women if swallowed or in the handling of tablets.

Visit
www.propecia.com
for additional information.

# Surgical Hair Loss Treatments . . .

*If non-invasive hair loss treatments do not meet your needs, there are alternatives to regaining growth of hair. Contact a medical care professional for referral to a hair restoration specialist.*

## The following surgical options are also available:

**Hair Transplantation** or "hair plugs" takes individual hair from a donor site (back of head) and surgically implants it to the hair loss area.

**Skin Flap surgery** is a technique involving the removal of a "flap" of skin with underlying tissue from one area and implanting it at the hair loss area.

## Two Types of Flap Surgeries are:

1. **Pedicle flap** contains tissue with artery-vein blood supply.
2. **Free flap** has no attached pedicle flap; no attached blood supply.

**Alopecia Reduction** or scalp reduction is surgically removing the hair loss area and stretching existing scalp to cover the area removed.

## Two Methods of Stretching Scalp are:

1. **Scalp extender** is a sheet of highly stretchable material inserted under the scalp during alopecia reduction surgery. Material is first stretched and then placed under scalp to expand area. In a period of weeks the extender gradually contracts bringing the scalp along with it.
2. **Scalp expander** is done prior to the surgery. This consists of a balloon-like membrane that is placed under the scalp. It is gradually inflated with a saline fluid over a period of weeks gradually stretching the scalp. This expander is removed during the alopecia reduction surgery.

**Follicular Unit Extraction and Implantation** is surgically removing an entire **follicle unit** from a donor area on the scalp and implanting it in the hair loss area. A **follicle unit** can consist of one to four hair strands, oil glands and arrector pili muscles – the hair follicle's entire support system. This procedure is the latest and innovative hair loss recovery system with continuing research to improve the "natural" look.

"For more detailed information on surgical procedures, visit www.ishrs.org."

5

# Natural Color of Hair . . .

## How do we get the color of our hair?

It all begins with a **melanocyte** (mel-a-no-cyte) cell that consists of a membrane body of **melanosomes,** which contain **melanin** (mel-a-nin). Melanin is the coloring matter that provides us with our natural color to hair and skin.

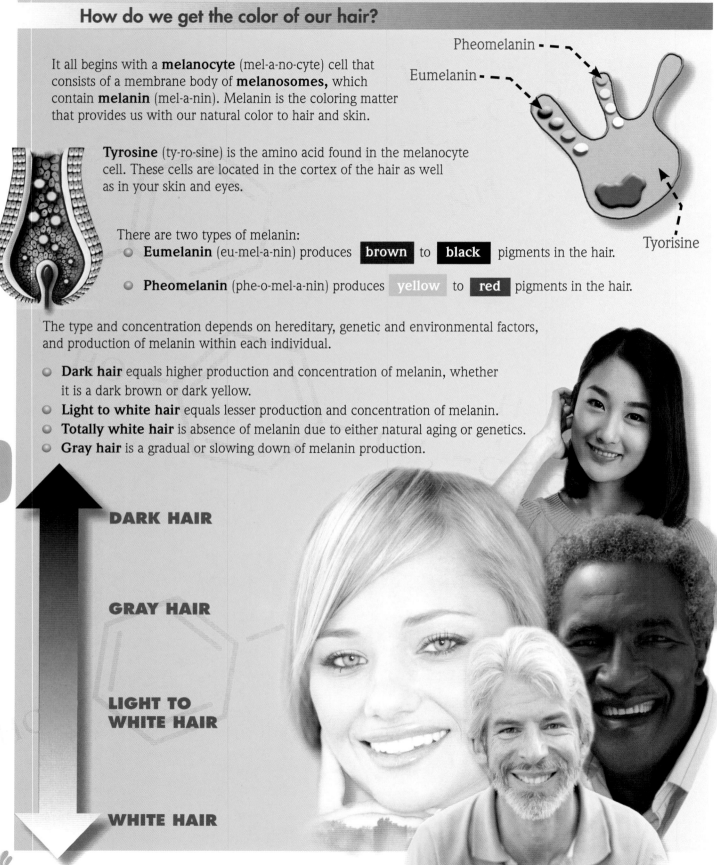

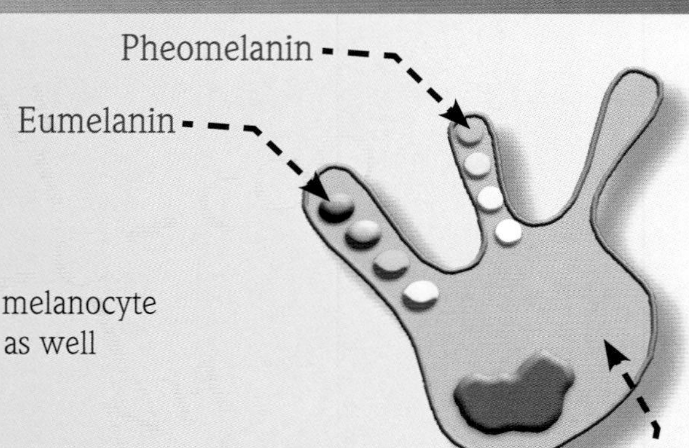


**Tyrosine** (ty-ro-sine) is the amino acid found in the melanocyte cell. These cells are located in the cortex of the hair as well as in your skin and eyes.

There are two types of melanin:

- **Eumelanin** (eu-mel-a-nin) produces **brown** to **black** pigments in the hair.
- **Pheomelanin** (phe-o-mel-a-nin) produces **yellow** to **red** pigments in the hair.

The type and concentration depends on hereditary, genetic and environmental factors, and production of melanin within each individual.

- **Dark hair** equals higher production and concentration of melanin, whether it is a dark brown or dark yellow.
- **Light to white hair** equals lesser production and concentration of melanin.
- **Totally white hair** is absence of melanin due to either natural aging or genetics.
- **Gray hair** is a gradual or slowing down of melanin production.

5

**DARK HAIR**

**GRAY HAIR**

**LIGHT TO WHITE HAIR**

**WHITE HAIR**

# Natural Color of Hair ...

**Gray hair** is partial or slow production of melanin, usually a mixture of white hair with pigmented hair **(ringed hair)** ... gradually all hair fading to white. The medical term for gray hair is **canities** (kah-nish-eez).

"Remember, melanin is also referred to as pigment or coloring matter."

## The Two Types of Canities are:

**Acquired Canities** is when the melanocytes gradually become inactive and production of melanin is slowed down turning hair to a gray color varying in concentration. This usually develops with age and genetics.

**Congenital Canities** can occur before or at birth. **Albinism** is the best example of melanin production slowing down or being totally absent. An albino is genetically afflicted with no coloring matter over his or her entire body.

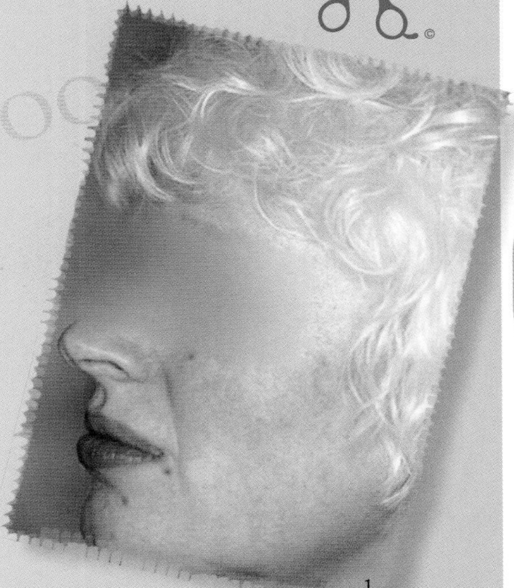

1

5

# Hair Analysis ...

When beginning any hair service, it is important to analyze the client's hair and scalp condition as part of your consultation. The results will predict any unexpected problems that may arise and determine if the requested service can be performed or if a medical solution is required to resolve an issue until the next visit. Analyzing the hair and scalp beforehand will ensure your client a competent service delivery.

## The following are the areas to be analyzed:

### Scalp Condition

**Dry scalp** is usually due to a **lack of sebaceous gland activity** therefore resulting in a flaky, itchy and slightly pink scalp. This can be caused by cold or hot climates, chemicals, and medications and/or aggravated by excessive washing of hair with harsh shampoos.

### Scalp Condition

**Oily scalp** is attributed to **over-stimulated sebaceous glands** and/or poor hygiene, diet or use of improper cleansing products. The results are a greasy sheen over scalp area with an oily coating on hair shaft.

## Growth Patterns at Scalp

5

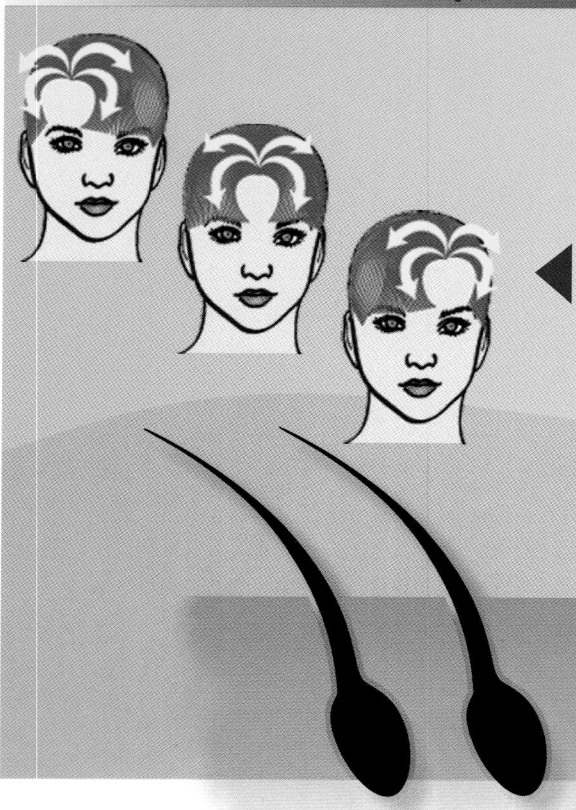

**Whorl** is a patch of hair forming a circular pattern at or near the crown area, normally stronger in children than adults.

**Cowlick** is a tuft of hair that is directed straight out of scalp.

**Hair Stream** is hair growing (follicles are slanted) in the same direction. Hair growing in opposite directions creates a natural part or dividing line.

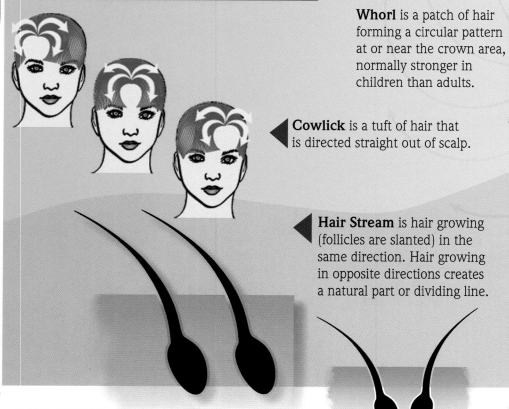

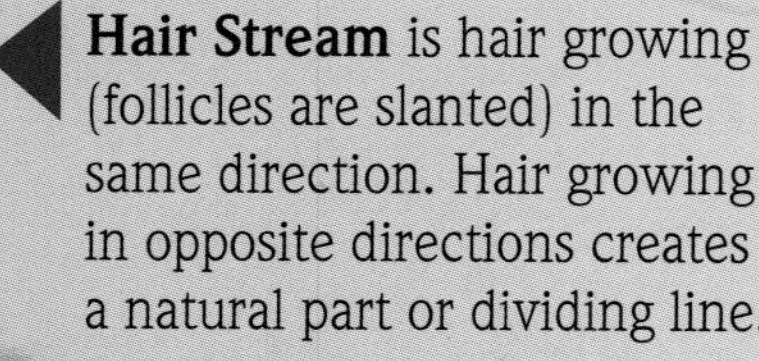

# Hair Analysis . . .

**Texture** is the measurement or tactile quality of each hair fiber's diameter.

**Diameter** refers to the thickness or width of a single hair strand.

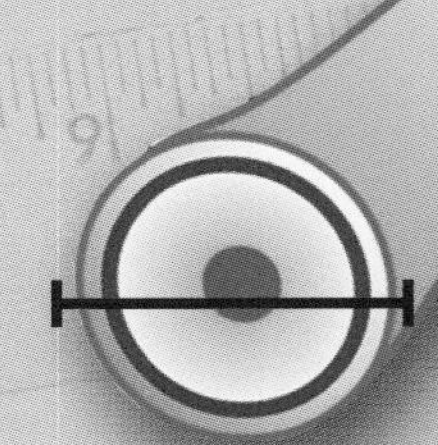

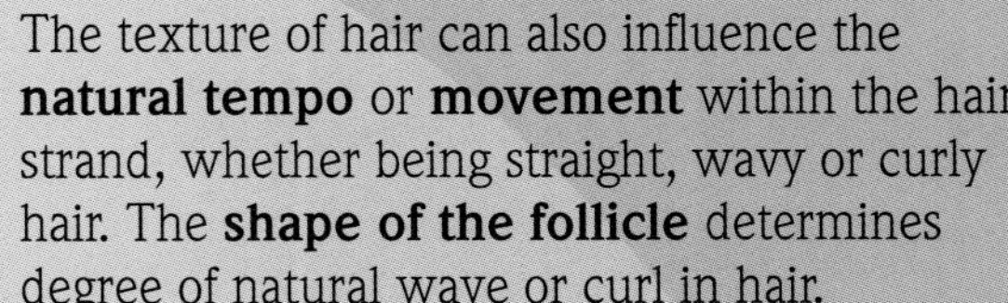


The texture of hair can also influence the **natural tempo** or **movement** within the hair strand, whether being straight, wavy or curly hair. The **shape of the follicle** determines degree of natural wave or curl in hair.

## Three Types of Textures are:

**Coarse** hair has a large diameter or width and feels thick.

**Medium** hair has an average width and thickness.

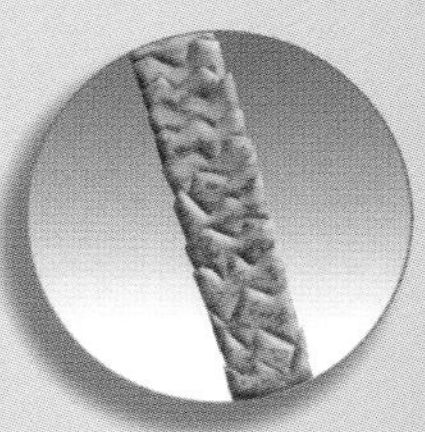

**Fine** hair has a small diameter/ width and feels thin.

## Three Hair Follicles Shapes are:

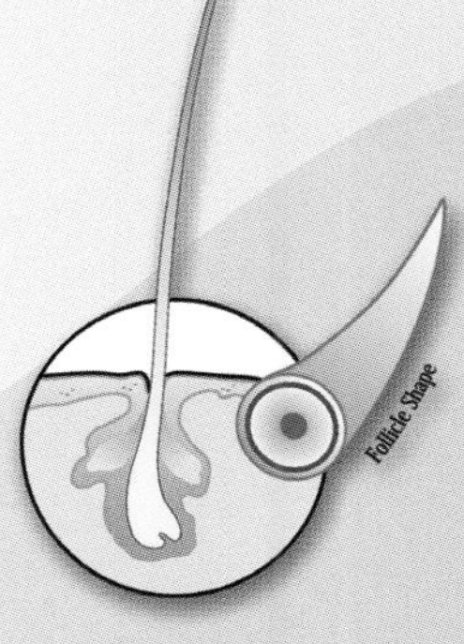


**Round** or **Circular** follicle produces straight hair.

**Large Oval** follicle produces wavy hair.

**Narrow Oval** or **Flat-shaped** follicle produces curly hair.

When determining texture of hair, check a single strand of hair taken from top, both sides and nape of head to make an accurate choice.

# Hair Analysis ...

**Density** is the number of hair strands per square inch (2.5 cm) on the scalp. The average number of hair strands on the scalp is 100,000. This may vary depending upon natural haircolor, heredity, medication or care of hair.

## Three Types of Density are:

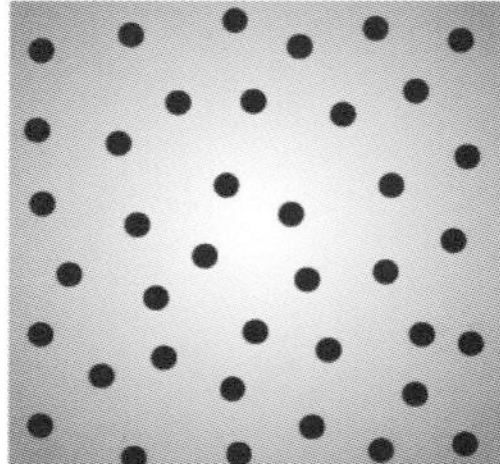

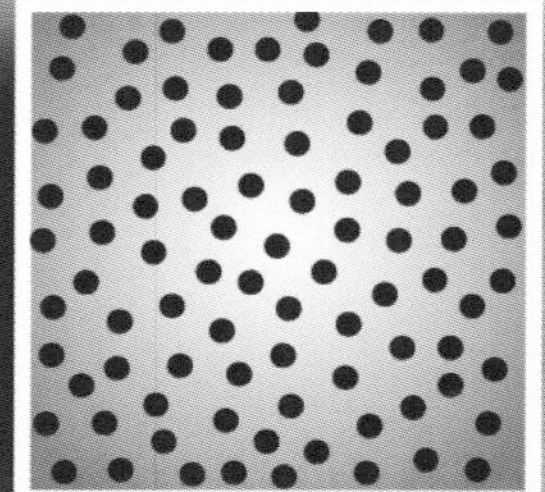

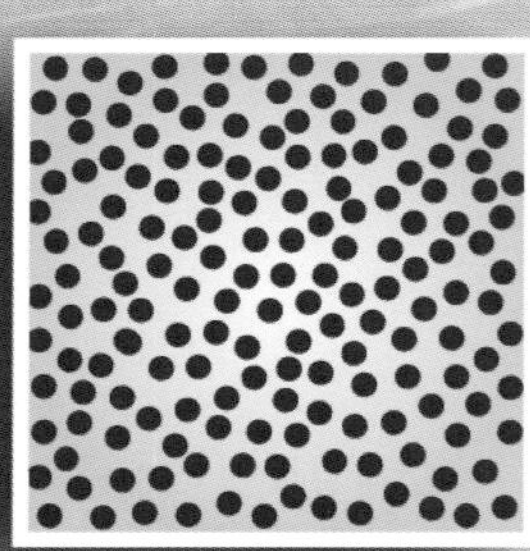

**Thin** has a few amount of hair strands per square inch on the scalp.

**Medium** has an average amount of hair strands per square inch on the scalp.

**Thick** has the most hair strands per square inch on the scalp.

When evaluating density, consider the **distribution** of hair around the head as well. Some areas of the head, such as the hairline, crown and nape areas may have a thin amount of hair with the remaining areas being thicker in density.

The chart below illustrates the average hair density amount for each natural haircolor.

| Natural Haircolor | Amount of Hair on Head |
|---|---|
| Blonde | 140,000 |
| Brown | 110,000 |
| Red | 90,000 |

When analyzing for density, comb or brush through hair and check the crown, hairline, both sides and nape of head.

5

# Hair Analysis . . .

Texture and density are sometimes misinterpreted as having the same meaning, but texture is analyzed by using a single strand of hair whereas density is determined by analyzing all the hair on the head. Keep in mind, a client with coarse texture hair may have a thin hair density or a person with fine texture hair might have a thick hair density. Both texture and density need to be evaluated separately.

# Hair Analysis . . .

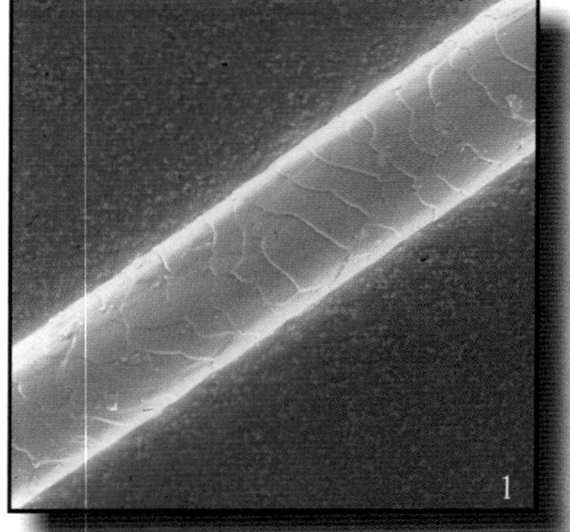
Hair Cuticle

**Porosity** is the amount of water the hair absorbs within a relative amount of time. Much like a sponge, the hair will absorb water, but how long does the hair take to get wet? This is greatly determined by the **condition of the cuticle**. The cuticle is constructed of scales and if these scales are abraded or lifted, the hair will absorb liquids a lot quicker than hair that has cuticle scales lying flat.

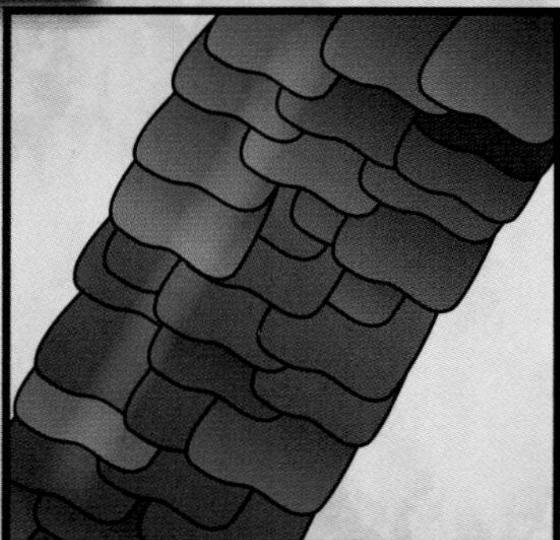
GOOD CUTICLE CONDITION
Smooth cuticle scales

POOR CUTICLE CONDITION
Lifted or abraded cuticle scales

Hair that has been **improperly** maintained or treated with any type of chemicals will have the **cuticle scales raised** to a certain degree. The depth of the lifted scales will be a factor in the water absorption.

5

## Four Types of Porosity are:

- **Resistant** porosity has the **cuticle scales lying flat**, making the amount of liquid absorbed minimal.
- **Normal** porosity has an average amount of absorption, considering it is in **"good condition."** This hair is usually maintained properly by using professional pH hair-care products.
- **Severe** porosity is when the **cuticle scales are raised** due to damage by either chemical services or use of harsh hair-care tools.
- **Irregular** porosity is usually indicated by the **combination of severe porosity** on the ends with **resistant or normal porosity** on the mid-strand. This can be due to heavy use of heating tools, improper chemical services and/or irregular haircut visits.

In checking for type of porosity, take a small sub-section of hair at top, both sides and nape of head; slide fingers down hair shaft, similar to backcombing, till a cushioning of hair appears. The amount of cushioning will determine the degree of raised cuticle scales.

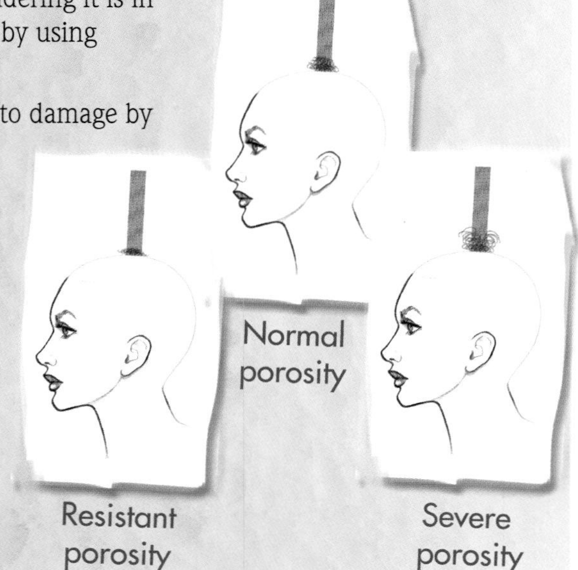

# Hair Analysis ...

**Elasticity** is the capability of the hair strand to stretch and return to its previous form without breaking. The ability of the hair to be stretched and pulled around a roller, perm rod or brush comes from the **twisted fibrils** in the structure of the **cortex**.

## Two Types of Elasticity are:

- **Average** elasticity on **wet hair** generally can be stretched **50 percent of its length** or if hair is **dry**, usually **1/5 its length.**
- **Low** elasticity hair will **break easily** due to the use of harsh hair-care products or being chemically overprocessed.

When analyzing for elasticity, take a single strand of dry hair from top, both sides and nape of head and slightly pull hair. If hair stretches and returns to its shape, much like a rubber band then it has average strength, but if hair breaks or does not return to its original length, then elasticity is considered low.

5

# Disorders of Hair . . .

*A* ***cosmetologist*** *has direct contact with people. We need to have a visual knowledge and understanding as to what hair conditions are contagious and can be transmitted from one person to another. In the following pages, a list is provided with some of the common disorders and diseases of hair and scalp.*

Let us first understand the difference between a disorder and a disease.

**Disorder** is an **ailment** or **illness** that disrupts a normal function of health, usually requiring special scalp or hair-care from either a cosmetologist or medical care professional.

**Disease** is a **bacterial (pathogenic) invasion** of the body that disrupts a normal function of health, generally characteristic of redness, pus and/or fever. Ask client to seek medical attention; no cosmetology service is advised.

**Look for this medical symbol when medical attention is required.**

5

Hair disorders can be caused by a health condition, genetics or improper hair-care. A cosmetologist must be able to recognize signs and symptoms of disorders in order to assist in restoring hair back to normalcy.

**Hypertrichosis** (hi-per-tri-koh-sis) or **hirsutism** (her-soo-tism) is an **excessive growth** of hair in **uncommon areas** of face or body. A common example of hypertrichosis on a woman is terminal hair above lip and/or underneath chin or the hairline hair extending onto cheek or forehead. Removal methods can consist of **waxing**, depilatories or electrolysis.

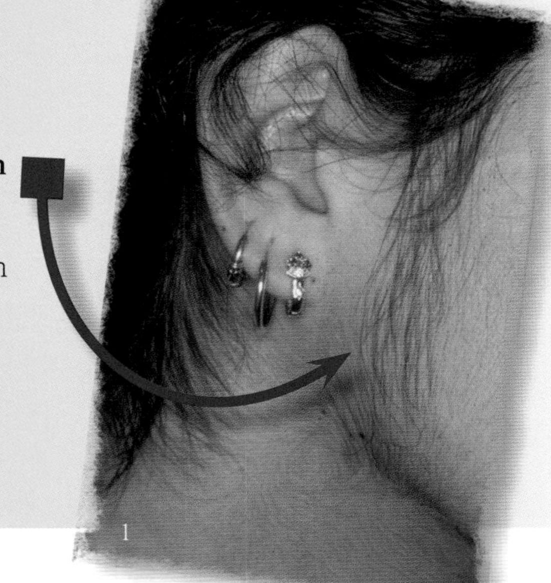

# Disorders of Hair . . .

Split ends

**Trichoptilosis** (tri-kop-ti-loh-sis) is referred to as **split ends.** This occurs when the hair ends are weakened and dried out by excessive exposure to heating tools or chemical services. Regular haircuts every four to six weeks will remove split ends along with the use of thermal protectant liquid tools, which help shield hair ends from the constant use of an airformer and thermal iron. Weekly **conditioning treatments** will also assist in strengthening the hair.

**Fragilitas Crinium** (frah-jil-i-tas kri-nee-um) is known as **brittle hair** and is when hair is susceptible to **breakage**. This hair behaves much the same way as trichoptilosis hair, reacting to the excessive use of heating tools. A suitable home hair-care program of weekly protein **reconstructuring treatments** will prevent breakage and strengthen hair.

**Trichorrehexis Nodosa** (tri-kor-rec-sis no-do-sa) or **knotted hair** has bulges along hair shaft. These thickened areas create a much weakened hair shaft and cause the shaft to **break** at the node. Thermal tool damage due to incorrect use or improperly performed chemical processes may cause the bulges along hair shaft. Consult with cosmetologist to recommend a suitable home hair-care regimen using **reconstructuring treatments** that will assist in strengthening hair and prevent breakage.

**Monilethrix** (mah-nil-ee-thriks) is a condition causing **beaded hair.** The hair is weak before each node and is **easily broken**. Consult with a cosmetologist to recommend a suitable home hair-care regimen using **reconstructuring treatments** that will assist in strengthening hair and prevent breakage.

Bead

5

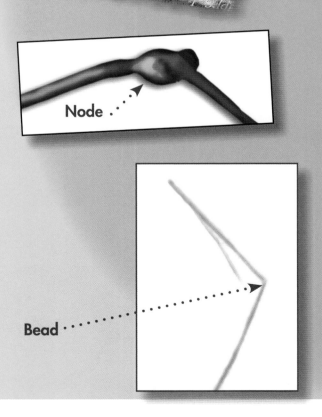

# Disorders of Scalp ...

**Pityriasis** (pit-ih-ry-uh-sus) is commonly known as **dandruff** and is characterized by a buildup of white, flaky skin that is shed from the skin or scalp. The dead skin cells are naturally shed every day, but when dandruff occurs the shedding process is accelerated, usually due to a naturally occurring fungus called **malassezia** (mal-uh-sez-ee-uh), sometimes referred to as **pityrosporum** (pit-i-ros-po-rum) **ovale**. Illness, stress, climate, overactive sebaceous glands or hormonal changes can trigger this fungus into growing in size and amount. This leads to skin cell irritation and production, which forces the old skin cells to rapidly shed and be replaced by new skin.

**NOTE:** Pityriasis is also the term used to describe certain dry, flaking skin conditions on an area of the body.

Treatments are usually available in an anti-dandruff shampoo containing an anti-microbic, such as selenium sulphide, zinc or an antifungal, such as ***ketoconazole**, which is used to fight fungal infections.
(*check with physician before using)

## Two Types of Dandruff are:

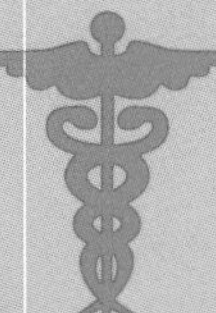

**Pityriasis Captis** (kap-ih-tis) **Simplex** (sim-pleks) is a **dry type** of dandruff and is characterized by white, lightweight flakes that either attach to the scalp in clusters or are scattered loosely within hair and eventually fall to the shoulders. Infrequent shampooing and/or excessive shampooing or use of harsh shampoos can aggravate dandruff.

5

**Pityriasis Steatoides** (stee-uh-toy-deez) is also referred to as **seborrhoeic** (seb-o-ree-ik) **dermatitis**. The skin that normally sheds mixes with an over production of sebum and sticks in clumps to the hair and scalp. This is characterized by large, yellow, bran-like flakes that accumulate onto the scalp or skin. **Do not perform hair service on client**; refer to a medical care professional.

**NOTE:** It is recommended after servicing any client with pityriasis to sanitize your hands and disinfect implements. If there is any sign of swelling, inflammation, broken skin or infection, cosmetologist should not perform hair service; refer to a medical care professional.

# Scalp and Hair Diseases . . .

*Any clients with the following scalp or hair diseases need to be informed and seek a medical care professional.* ***Do not service client.***

**Tinea** (tin-ee-ah) is the technical term for **ringworm**, which is a contagious disease caused by a **fungus parasite** called **dermatophyte** (der-mat-o-phyte). It is characterized by a red ring with white, itchy scales on any area of skin or scalp.

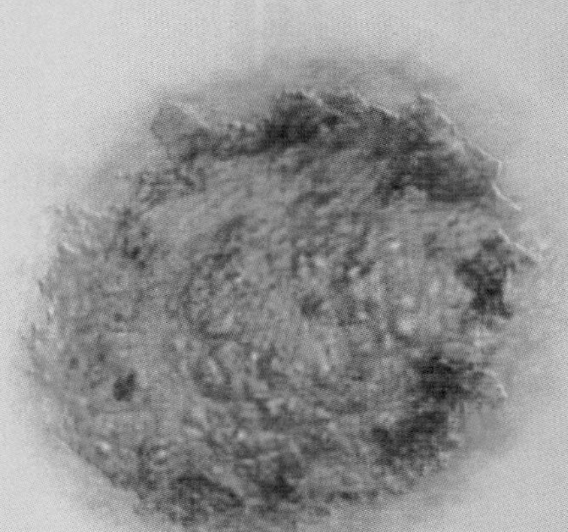

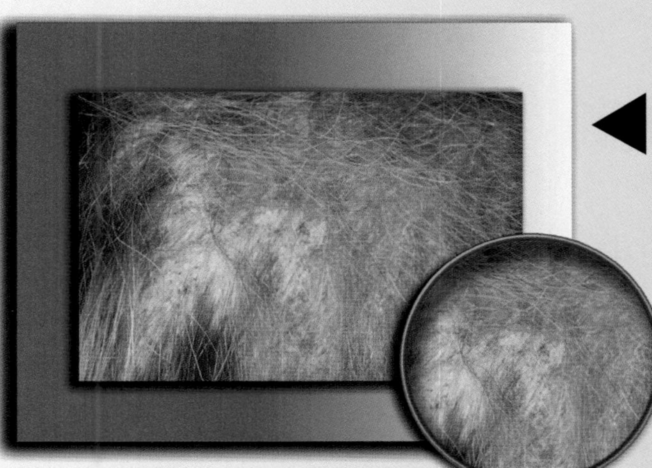

**Tinea Capitis** is a **fungal infection** of the scalp, also known as **ringworm.** The fungus attacks the opening of the follicle at the scalp. The scalp is slightly pink with red spots and a white scaly appearance.

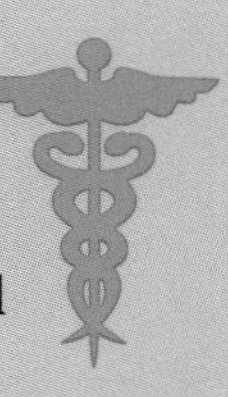

**Tinea Favosa** (fa-vo-suh) or **tinea favus** (fa-vus) is a **fungal infection** of the scalp, also known as **honeycomb ringworm.** This is characterized by a pink scalp with thick, whitish yellow crusts referred to as **scutula** (scu-tu-la), which appear to have a slight odor.

# Scalp and Hair Diseases . . .

**Animal parasites** can be spread with close **prolonged** contact with an infected individual. These parasites are very common with children and crowded areas with frequent skin-to-skin contact, such as child-care facilities or playgrounds.

**Pediculosis** (pe-dik-u-loh-sis) **Capitis** is a condition caused by an animal parasite called the **head louse** (louse is singular and lice is plural). These parasites live off the scalp, surviving on a tiny amount of blood they draw from the scalp. The head louse will lay eggs called **nits** that adhere to the hair shaft. Nits have an appearance similar to dandruff, but the difference is the eggs are fastened to the hair shaft. Head lice are tan or light brown in appearance with the nits being a whitish yellow in color. Lice can create an itchy sensation as they bite the skin or scurry across the scalp producing an irritation or possible infection if left untreated. Head lice crawl or cling to their host; **they do not fly (no wings).**

5

**NOTE:** Lice can survive off the scalp for 10 days and eggs survive up to two weeks. It is important to wash all clothing and bed linen used by an infected person with a water temperature of 130 degrees and place in a hot dryer for at least 30 minutes.

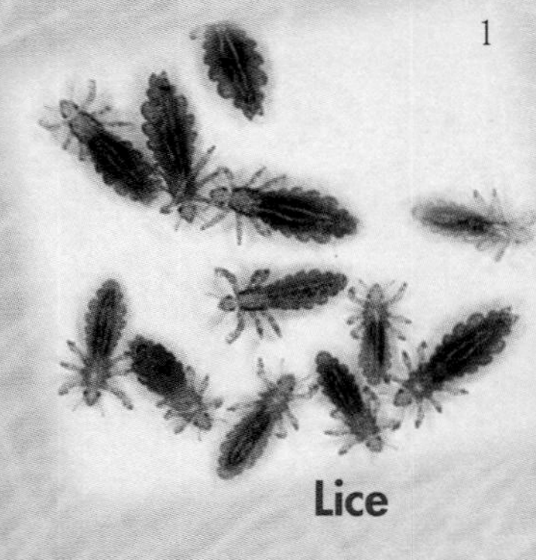
1

Lice

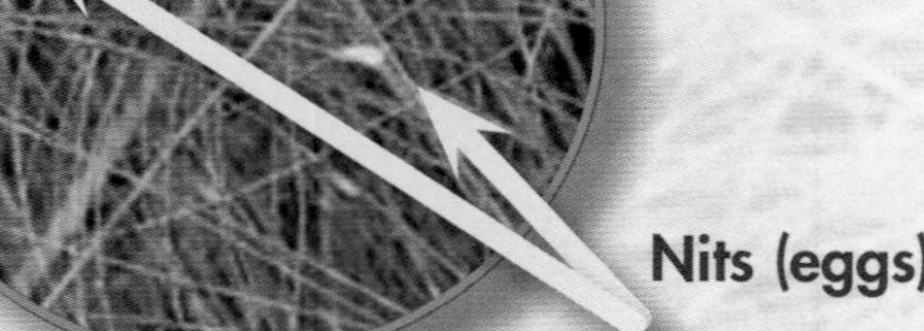
2

3

Nits (eggs)

**Treatment: Do not service client.** Over the counter shampoos and lotions containing the ingredient **pyrethrum** (natural insecticide) can be used to kill lice and nits. A special nit comb will usually be pre-packaged with product to assist in removing eggs from hair shaft. If there is an infection, refer to a medical care professional.

# Scalp and Hair Diseases ...

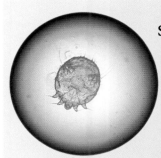

**Scabies** is the condition caused by the **microscopic mite** called **sarcoptes scabei** (sar-kop-tes ska-be-i), also referred to as the **"itch mite."** Measuring only **0.1 mm** in diameter, the mite burrows under the skin creating passages and lays its eggs within the passage. Once an itch mite has infested your skin, it takes about **three to four weeks** until itching and irritation occur, creating the appearance of red bumps, and possible blistering. Scratching is usually intensified mostly at nights and upon bathing. The most desirable areas for the mite to exist are web of fingers or toes, palms, soles, wrists and armpits. Excessive scratching will irritate the skin and lead to possible infection.

Itch Mite

**Treatment: Do not service client!** This condition is treated with over-the-counter dermal cream containing the ingredient **pyrethrum** (py-re-thrum), which is a natural insecticide that can be used to kill the itch mite. The cream is applied over the entire body and left on for eight to 12 hours and then washed off. If a skin allergy or infection occurs, refer to a medical care professional.

**NOTE:** Mites can survive off the skin for 48 to 72 hours, and can live off a person for a month. It is important to wash all clothing and bed linen used by an infected person with a water temperature of 130 degrees and place in a hot dryer for at least 30 minutes.

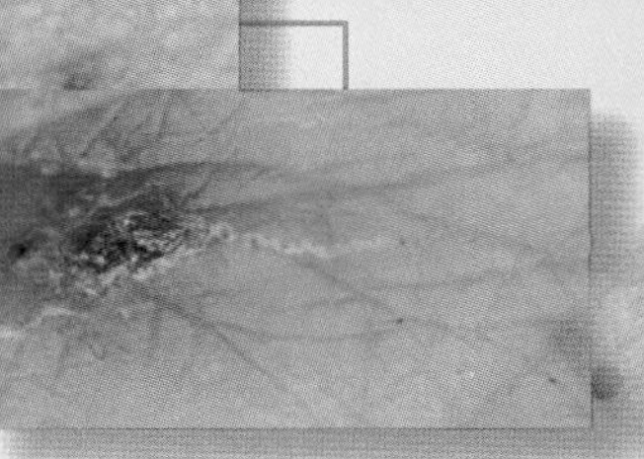

BLISTERING AND RED BUMPS

"Body lice are not the same as head lice."

5

## Hair Follicle Infections

**Furuncle** (fur-un-cle) is a **boil** or **abscess** of the skin located in the hair follicle. It is an infection in the follicle caused by the bacteria **staphylococcus** (staph-y-lo-coc-cus) **aureus** (au-re-us). The infected area can have more than one opening. Some reasons for boils may be ingrown hair, a foreign object lodged in the skin or acne. The area is usually characterized by swelling, inflammation and pus with tenderness and pain. **Do not service client,** refer to a medical care professional.

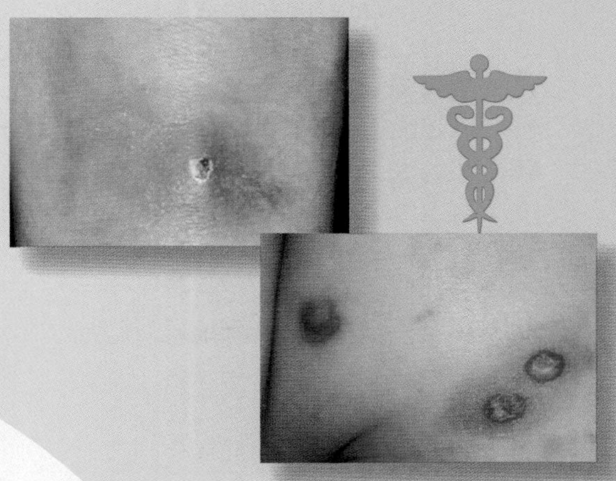

**Carbuncle** (car-bun-cle) is the same as a furuncle, but larger. **Do not service client,** refer to a medical care professional.

# Hair Structure REVIEW QUESTIONS

## MULTIPLE CHOICE

1. A mass of blood and nerves located directly under the hollowed area of the hair bulb is?
   A. keratin B. papilla C. follicle
2. The portion of hair that extends above the skin or scalp is?
   A. hair shaft B. hair root C. hair bulb
3. The tough outer protective covering of hair is?
   A. cuticle B. cortex C. medulla
4. What is the average growth of hair per month?
   A. ¼ inch B. 1 inch C. ½ inch
5. A patchy loss of hair occurring on the scalp is called?
   A. alopecia areata B. traction alopecia C. androgenic alopecia
6. What is the term used for yellow to red hair pigments?
   A. tyrosine B. eumelanin C. pheomelanin
7. A tuft of hair that is directed straight out of scalp is called?
   A. cowlick B. whorl C. hair stream
8. Which hair texture has the largest diameter and will feel thicker?
   A. fine B. medium C. coarse
9. Which type of porosity has cuticle scales lying flat allowing minimal absorption?
   A. severe B. normal C. resistant
10. What is tinea?
    A. dandruff B. ringworm C. head lice
11. Which animal parasite burrows under the skin?
    A. head lice B. itch mite C. ringworm
12. What is the technical term for split hair ends?
    A. hypertrichosis B. hirsuties C. trichoptilosis
13. How far can dry hair be stretched without breaking?
    A. ⅕ its length B. ¼ its length C. ½ its length
14. Which layer of hair is responsible for the elasticity in the hair?
    A. cuticle B. cortex C. medulla
15. What is the average number of hair on the scalp?
    A. 100,000 B. 130,000 C. 150,000
16. Which hair follicle shape produces naturally curly hair?
    A. round B. large oval C. narrow oval
17. What is the technical term for gray hair?
    A. albinism B. canities C. ringed
18. Which layer of hair contains melanin?
    A. cuticle B. cortex C. medulla
19. Which hair loss treatment surgically removes the entire hair loss area?
    A. hair plugs B. alopecia reduction C. follicular unit extraction
20. Which hair loss treatment comes in a pill form?
    A. Propecia® B. Rogaine® C. Minoxidil

STUDENT'S NAME DATE GRADE

element harmony

lines

ornamentation proportion

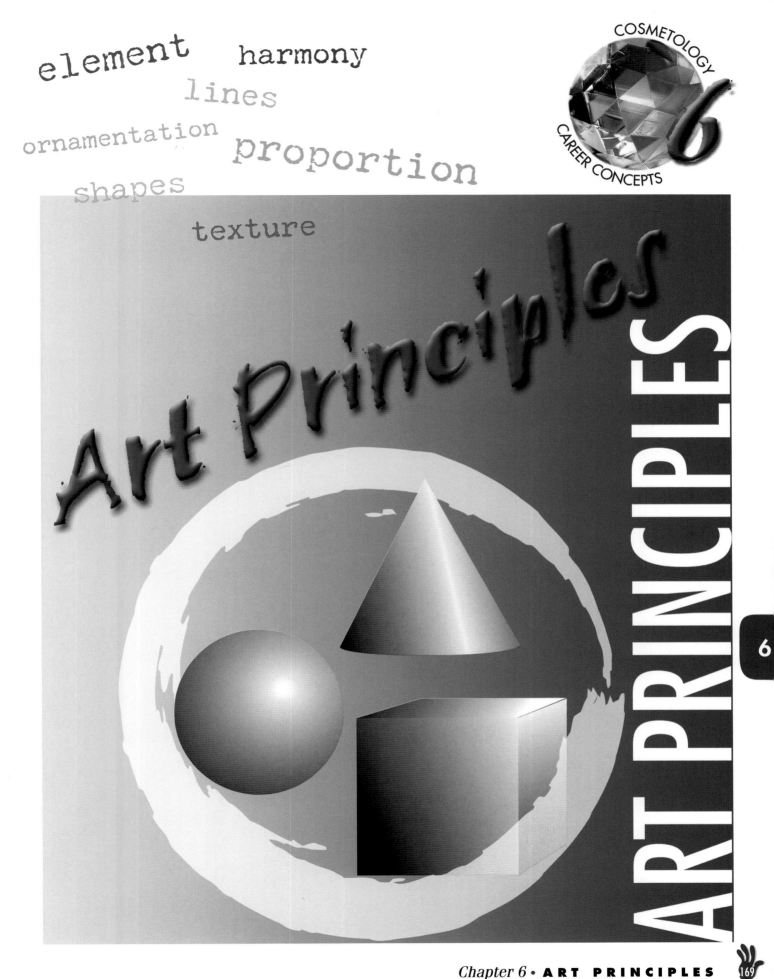

shapes

texture

# Art Principles

# ART PRINCIPLES

6

# Terminology ...

**L**earning the terminology of ***art principles and design elements*** *will help improve your abilities when creating any type of design. The following terms will encourage you to learn more about the art of designing.*

1

**Artistry** is the beauty or imaginative result produced through the creative ability in the arrangement or execution of your art.

2

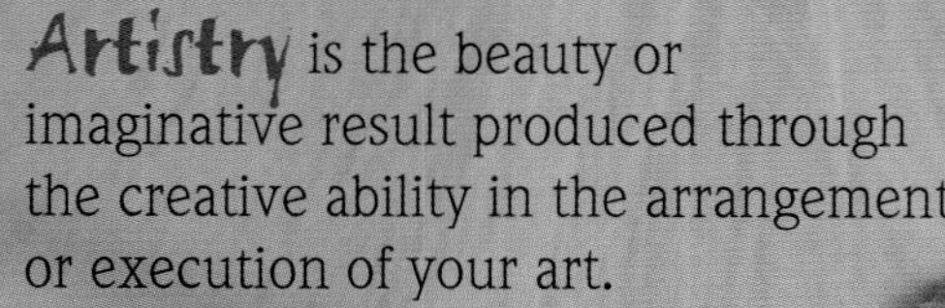

**Color** is a visual sensation experienced when light of varying wavelengths reaches the eye.

4

3

5

**Drawing** is a piece of art created by using pencil, chalk, or pen, applied as shapes, lines, and textures on a surface.

6

**Emotions** are personal feelings invoked by looking at something or someone.

**Medium** is the material or surface on which the artist places his or her creation or design.

6

# Terminology . . .

1

**Movement** is a sense of motion, direction or force within a design.

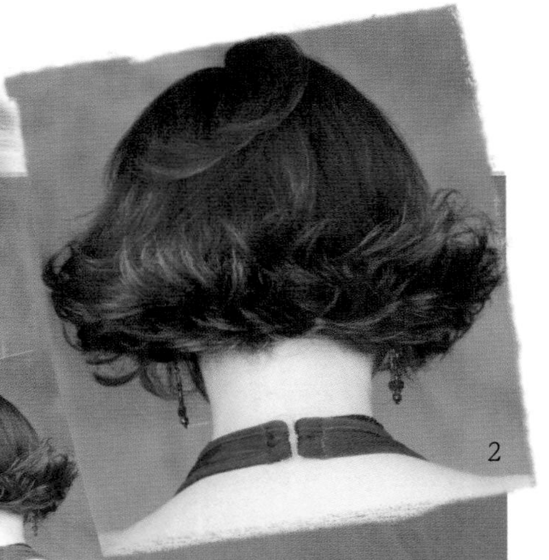

2

3

**Plane** is any flat or level area on a straight or curved surface.

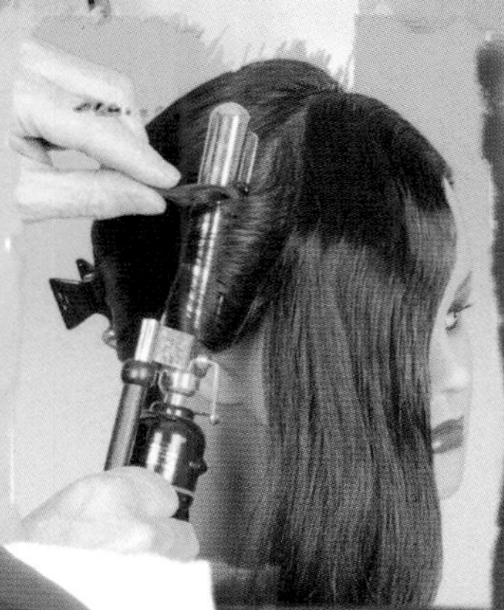

**Practice** is the act of repeating something to gain precision and improve a skill.

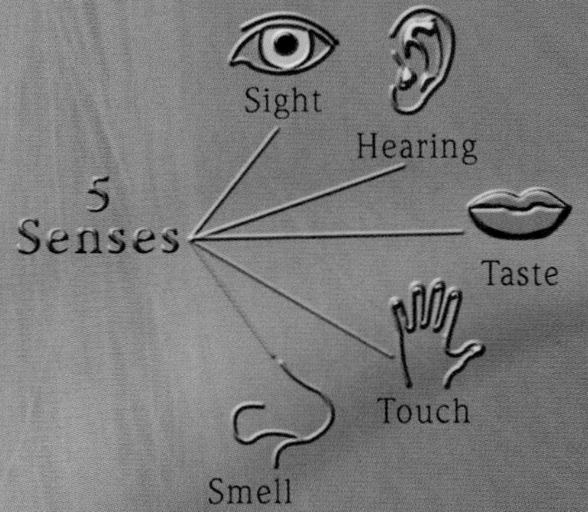

6



4

**Sculpture** is a person's artistic expression in a three-dimensional art form.

5

**Senses** are a person's faculties – including sight, touch, hearing, smell and taste – used to perceive information about the world.

# Art Assessment . . .

**Creative art assessment** *involves design strategies, art principles, the effects of motion and space, and the proper usage of proportions in relationship to size–all of which constitute the visual evidence for decision making and reaching conclusions in a design.*

*"Categories such as time, space, cause and number represent the most general relations which exist between things."*

— **Emile Durkheim, French sociologist** (Paris, 1912).

1

**Science** is conclusion based on careful observation and experimentation, and exploration of truths and facts through methodical study.

2

3

**Art** is the creative use of imagination, skill and craft to produce beauty beyond the ordinary.

**Constructing** is uniting all the art principles, science and materials into a whole or a design.

**Design** is combining elements and art principles to create an end result or finished "appearance."

4

5

# Art Assessment ...

***Artists* observe and examine the attention to detail** *within a painting, a sculpture, hairstyle, nail or a makeup application. Artists refine their creative expressions and skills by perfecting their powers through using four of the five senses* ***(sight, hearing, touch and smell).***

**Using the sense of sight** and learning to **see deep** into your subject matter creates a **visual thinker**! It is important to pay close attention to even the smallest of details, and look for visually stimulating shapes, forms, textures and colors that will help develop your artistic vision. **Repeated practice** of making your design reproduce what the mind's eye has seen will be crucial to the success of the design.

"Learning is 85 percent visual!"

## EXERCISE:

Look at the hairdesign and **list everything you see.** Remember to **look deeply**! Return to this exercise after completion of this chapter and re-evaluate the hairdesign again.

| Inspiration | Design Plan | Creative Design |
| --- | --- | --- |

6

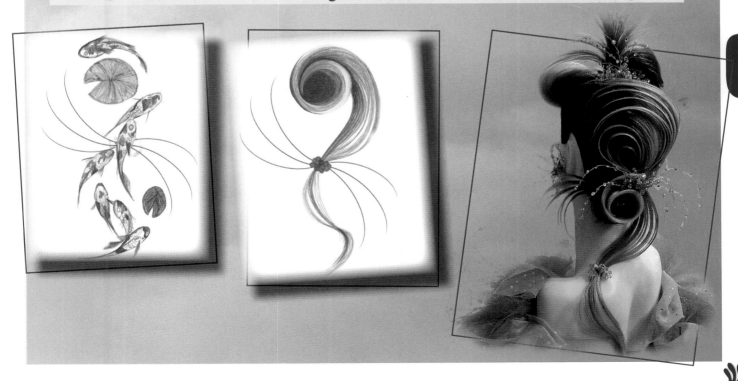

# Art Expression . . .

1

**Vision** – Our biological makeup enables vision to be one of the greatest and best-developed senses we draw upon. Seeing allows us to perceive the discoveries of the world, which helps inspire us to create the best art.

2

**Imagination** – Is the ability of the mind to form thoughts and images, creating the visual picture we see. The artist then transforms these images into a manual skill.

3

**Creativity** – Our genetic coding allows each of us to have unique imaginations and abilities that permit us to express what is seen and envisioned through artistic ideas and concepts.

**Creative art** – Is the ultimate tangible expression of what we have perceived with our mind's eye.

4

6

# Art Expression . . .

*From the moment a client arrives, the **senses are stimulated.** Sharpening the use of each sense will bring a greater level of expertise to the art of designing.*

**For example**, the sense of sight is by far the **most important** for acquiring information. We can explore **shapes, textures, colors and spacial relationships** by employing our sense of sight. The professional needs to **look deeper** to mentally see the form, directional movements and balance of the design. These components affect and impact the body as a whole and the person's lifestyle.

1

Two-dimensional

## Two-dimensional

**When creating art**, the tool of choice (whether it is a pencil, chalk, paints, water colors, etc.) is used to mark a surface such as paper or canvas in the form of lines, shapes, and textures of a design. This type of art is **two-dimensional,** having **only** length and width.

## Three-dimensional

**When creating your hairdesign**, a comb or brush is applied across the scalp or hair surface to create the shapes, lines or textures of a design. This type of art is **three-dimensional,** having length, width and depth.

4

3

Three-dimensional

2

5

## Design Drawing Exercise:

Practice stimulating your sense of sight by following the hairdesign below. Draw the hairdesign on paper using a pencil, and then using a comb or brush; duplicate the hairdesign on a mannequin. Finish by creating your own hairdesign.

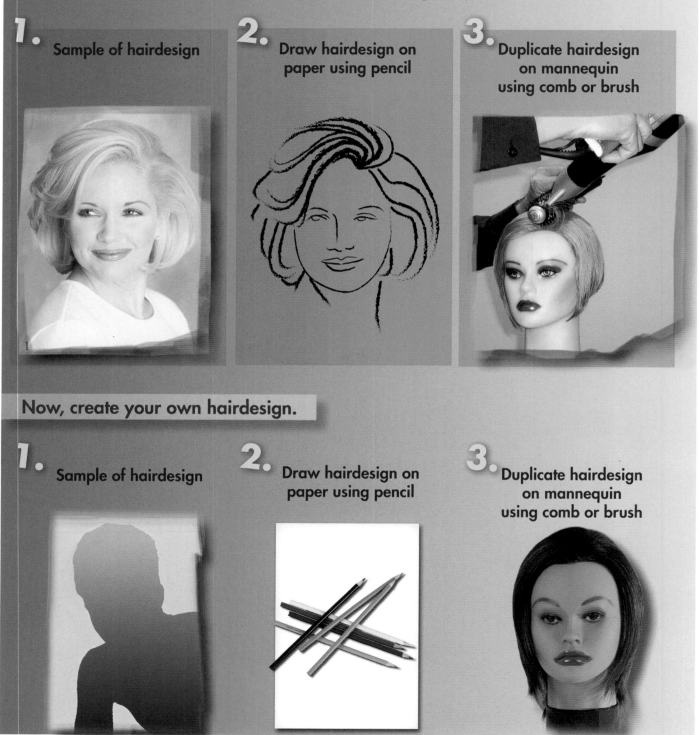

1. Sample of hairdesign

2. Draw hairdesign on paper using pencil

3. Duplicate hairdesign on mannequin using comb or brush

## Now, create your own hairdesign.

1. Sample of hairdesign

2. Draw hairdesign on paper using pencil

3. Duplicate hairdesign on mannequin using comb or brush

# Art . . .

*"Studying the art of hair makes the unseen seen."*
*—By Randy Rick*

**Art** is the **creative use of imagination, skill and craft** to produce beauty beyond the ordinary. Whether we are creating a painting, applying makeup to a face, designing nail art, or creating a hairstyle, the end result is a visual interpretation of our imagination, talents and skills. An individual's fashion choice is an **expression of one's personal taste in art.**

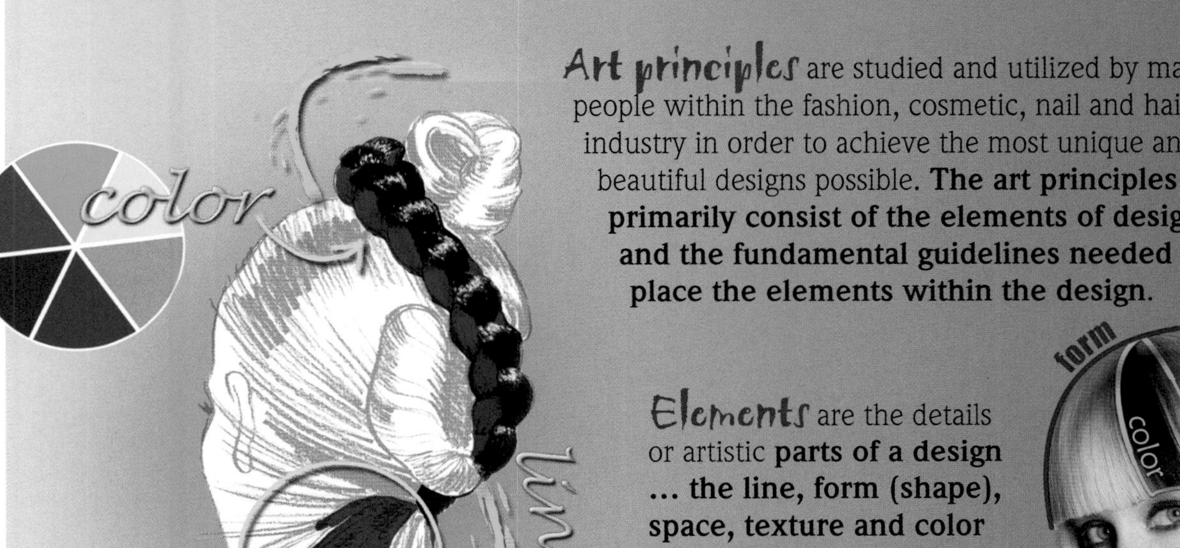


**Art principles** are studied and utilized by many people within the fashion, cosmetic, nail and hair industry in order to achieve the most unique and beautiful designs possible. **The art principles primarily consist of the elements of design and the fundamental guidelines needed to place the elements within the design.**

**Elements** are the details or artistic **parts of a design ... the line, form (shape), space, texture and color** within the art.

**Principles** are the theory behind the application of combining two or more elements to create art or a design. **Principles are proportion, balance, emphasis, rhythm and harmony.**

Once a person is educated and experienced in the principles and elements of design; knowledgeable and calculated risks may be taken to build on this strong art foundation.

# Application of Design ...

**S*cientific* *influences, theories and laws*** *demonstrate how the hair will react when various combinations of principles and elements are applied. Principles move hairdesign from the* ***theoretical concept to the practical actions*** *necessary for creating the finished design. By* ***recognizing, practicing and applying these principles****, the professional will master the art of creation.*

1

**Design** involves two specifically different aspects ... **theory and practical application**. These two aspects are used whether you are deciding on color placement for a makeup application, creating a hairstyle or rebuilding a nail using artificial enhancements.

## The Theoretical Application consists of:

**Concept** is envisioned through the mind's eye. A concept is something thought or imagined that can be evoked by nature, music, art, memory, etc.

2

**Design Plan** is a guide or outline that arranges the elements and principles, which is necessary to perform and complete the design.

# Application of Design ...

## Practical Application consists of:

applying the principles in a design plan using the components, which are then arranged to form the completed design or composition.

**Component** is each individual part or piece that forms the whole design.

**Composition** is the aesthetic arrangement of the components to create a finished design.

# Elements of Design ...

*The elements of design along with the principles and concept are the factors employed to create beautiful and artistic design. The five basic styling elements used in design are **line, form (shape), space, texture and color.** As each of these elements are clarified in the chapter, visualize your design and understand that each individual element will add to the completed art.*

1

All elements are combined within the art, with one particular element that dominates. Total harmony and art expression is achieved when all the elements are placed within the design.

When studying art, it is well established that the quintessential element in drawing is a position in visual space. All artists start with a line when creating their design.

2

3

## How do we create a line?

Let's explore this basic theory ...

A **dot** is the beginning of a line.

A **dot is a point in space** that can be small, medium or large.

As the dot moves along a surface, it creates the **path or direction of a line**. A **line is composed of points or dots in space**.

**Straight or curved lines** are created by shifting the points in various directions. When constructing lines within a hair or nail design or even a makeup application, be aware of the directions and illusions they may create.

# Elements of Design...

**Horizontal lines** extend side to side creating the illusion of width and mass or fullness.

**Vertical lines** extend up and down creating the illusion of length or slenderness.

**Diagonal lines** extend to opposite corners on a slant providing a feeling of dimension or direction.

**Curved lines** are part of the circumference of a circle (arc) creating contour and movement or waves.

1 2 3 3 4 5 6 7 8

Lines may be **bold, light, medium, thick or fine** in appearance to **accentuate or diminish** a part of the design.

6

# Line . . .

**As a line travels,** *it starts to create the* ***outside edge and contour of a shape,*** *which is referred to as a* ***form. Form*** *is the structural outline or* ***silhouette*** *of the design that makes it identifiable from all angles. By darkening an image and following the contours of the design's detailed shape, you create a* ***silhouette*** *(si-le-wet).*

**Dot**

**Traveling Line**

**Line Completing A Straight Form**

**Line Completing A Curved Form**

1

The visual world of design is created when two fields of contrasting lights and/or colors intersect each other. Our mind can create an invisible or continuous line along an edge even though it may not exist. The most noticeable images or shapes travel along the outside perimeters of the head form.

6

When we examine the completed curved form, you will find that our mind's eye sees a round form; however, upon further review, we find the curved form is really a series of straight lines connected together at varying angles or degrees.

Mind's eye sees a circle

"Straight lines connected together at angles create a curved form."

# Shape . . .

A **shape** is made of **multiple traveling lines connected to make straight or curved geometric shapes.**

**Shapes** consist of straight or curved geometric forms such as a square, rectangle, triangle, circle, oval and ovaloid. There are various other straight and curved shapes that are not used as part of the hairdesigning art. The following are the most common shapes used in hairdesigning.

## Straight Shapes:

1

2

3

4

5

**Diamond shape** has two equal triangles placed back to back

**Kite shape** has two unequal triangles placed back to back

**Triangle shape** has three equal sides and three angles

**Square shape** has four equal sides and four angles

**Rectangle shape** has two short ends and two long sides, creating more length than width

## Curvature Shapes:

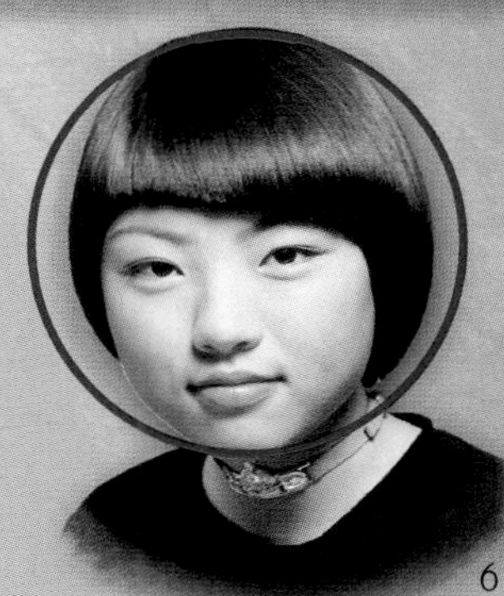
6

7

8

**Circle shape** has equal width or distance from center point to circumference

**Oval shape** has unequal width or distance from center point to circumference

**Ovaloid shape** or oblong has equal or unequal width within an elongated shape that has more length than width



6

# "GESTALT THEORY"

*The word gestalt (ge-stalt) is German, which means **"form."** Gestalt psychologists determined that **our minds want to see organized forms or whole shapes.** During their experimentations they created portions of a shape by using either a dot-to-dot connection or a series of hyphenated lines.*

A **shape** is created by closing all the lines in the outlined area. However, if given only a suggestion of the lines or dots, our mind will automatically define the shape as a whole.

When creating a hairdesign, a combination of shapes (both straight and curvature) is creatively positioned together like a puzzle, thereby creating the (whole) total design – even though we never distinguish the completed design as an actual line.

As hair artists, we will use the "Gestalt Theory" to help us automatically "see" the whole shape or portions of the shapes we are viewing.

**Study the drawings below and determine if your mind will form a closure to create the shapes you are viewing.**

Next, view the hairdesigns on the preceding page to figure out what shape was utilized following the Gestalt theory.

# Virtual Line . . .

A virtual line can connect or create a shape even though it may not exist. When creating a **stable shape** (triangle, square, circle, etc.), you may only be using part of that stable shape in the hair. But the **virtual line extends into the spacial area away from the head**.

OVAL SHAPE

This **principle is referred to as "closure,"** which allows the viewer to see a shape without it being perfectly completed. The principle allows the designer greater freedom of line and form within a design.

Non-existent lines can be in either straight or curved shapes and are illusionary without a physical basis.

SQUARE SHAPE

Looking at the hairdesigns on this page, you will see the **virtual line** that creates the closure to the geometric shape.

DIAMOND SHAPE

RECTANGLE SHAPE

# Space . . .

**Space** is a dimensional area or the area surrounding the design; it is the place that occupies the design or the background. Without adequate space considerations, designs can become too busy and overwhelming to the eye. Less is more in great hair art designs! Dimension creates spaciousness because it provides depth or the illusion of receded areas.

**Negative Space** is an area of the design that is **open and spacious.**

**Positive Space** is part of the design that **occupies a spacial area.**

6

# Dimension . . .

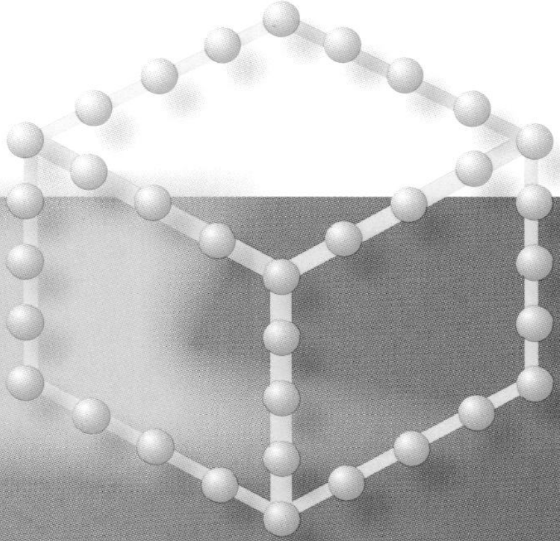

**Dimension** is a measurement of a design in a certain direction, such as length, width or height. In planning your art, we work with three dimensions with each one occupying a different amount of space.

## The three types of art dimensions:

**One-dimensional** has only a single spatial measurement – no depth or width. It starts with a **point/dot,** which has **no dimension**. As the dot moves to create a line, the second dimension begins its creation.

Dot

Line

**Two-dimensional** measures space in two directions, producing designs with **length and width, but no depth**. This is created by using traveling lines.

1 2 4 5

**Three-dimensional** is the measurement of space in three directions: **length, width and depth.** The lines travel into spaces away from the surface, thus creating visual space. A three-dimensional design builds or enhances the medium upon which you are working.

3

"The most exciting and artistic designs are created when a form utilizes the three-dimensional measurements."

©

**Texture** is the visual and tactile quality of the design. We determine the texture of art by using our **sense of touch**, but we also can use our **sense of sight** to indirectly recognize its feel. A design's texture is created by the material or medium, tool and finishing product used.

# The Visual Art of Textures

**Texture** is by far the most dramatic art element in hairdesigning. It is unique because we can see it and feel it, which stimulates two of our senses, **sight and touch**.

When viewing a hairdesign, we recognize shapes and colors. However, the surface of hair embodies many different characteristics. Each individual's hair becomes its own canvas for the hair artist to create his or her masterpiece.

The finish is determined by the hair's composition and how much the finished hair surface is broken up. Words like smooth, wavy, curl, rough, piece, etc. describe the **tactile experience.**

The **visual experience** is viewed in a two-dimensional or three-dimensional field.

**Everything** has some type of texture. Use your visual sense and view the world around you. **Look and see** and then try to use your inborn creative mind's eye to create complementary textures in your hairdesigns.

Hairdesigns become visually exciting when combinations of textures are artistically arranged.

"Remember, try NOT to use more than three different textures in a hairdesign ... less is sometimes more appealing"!

# Hair Texture . . .

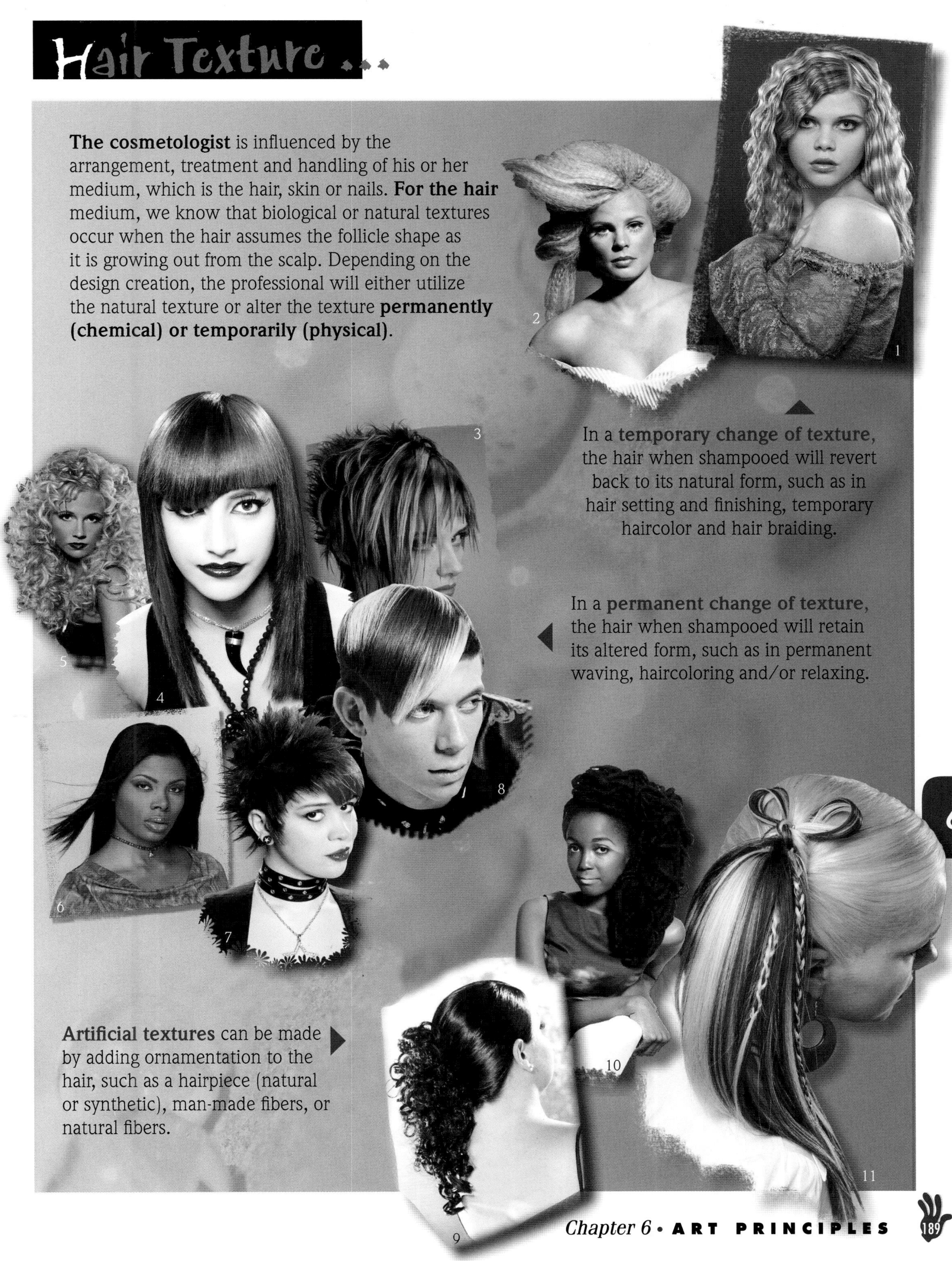

**The cosmetologist** is influenced by the arrangement, treatment and handling of his or her medium, which is the hair, skin or nails. **For the hair** medium, we know that biological or natural textures occur when the hair assumes the follicle shape as it is growing out from the scalp. Depending on the design creation, the professional will either utilize the natural texture or alter the texture **permanently (chemical) or temporarily (physical)**.

In a **temporary change of texture**, the hair when shampooed will revert back to its natural form, such as in hair setting and finishing, temporary haircolor and hair braiding.

In a **permanent change of texture**, the hair when shampooed will retain its altered form, such as in permanent waving, haircoloring and/or relaxing.

**Artificial textures** can be made by adding ornamentation to the hair, such as a hairpiece (natural or synthetic), man-made fibers, or natural fibers.

1 2 3 4 5 6 7 8 9 10 11

# Nail Texture . . .

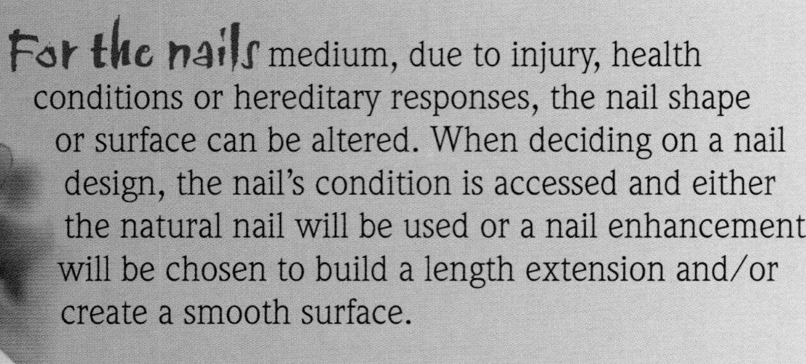

**For the nails** medium, due to injury, health conditions or hereditary responses, the nail shape or surface can be altered. When deciding on a nail design, the nail's condition is accessed and either the natural nail will be used or a nail enhancement will be chosen to build a length extension and/or create a smooth surface.

In a **temporary change of texture**, natural nails with ridges or yellowing are either buffed and/or polished to diminish the appearance of the wavy lines and discoloration.

In a **permanent change of texture**, the nail's shape, surface and length can be altered on length, smoothness and strength with the application of nail enhancements.

1 2 3 4

5

**Artificial textures** occur when rhinestones, tape or acrylic pieces of artwork complement a nail design for nail competition or daily wear.

6

# Skin Texture . . .

**For the skin** medium, the surface may be changed due to certain health conditions, injury or hormonal imbalances. If makeup is to be applied, the technician will access the skin condition to determine the product used for optimal coverage in creating a smooth surface appearance. The makeup design is then influenced by the facial features and your artistic expression.

In a **temporary change of texture**, the skin is covered by a base makeup product to give the illusion of smooth skin and color balance.

In a **permanent change of texture**, the skin is medically altered by the use of chemical exfoliation or plastic surgery procedures.

**Artificial texture** is placing rhinestones, artificial eyelashes or textural paints onto the face as part of the makeup design.

1

2

3

4

6

# Color . . .

**Color** is a visual sensation experienced when light of varying wavelengths reaches the eye. Color helps invoke an **emotional response** to a design. Using the element of color will enhance your design by reinforcing other art principles.

*Color can create value, contrast, illusion, mood, emphasis and dimension.*

1

**Value** is the amount of **light or darkness** in the tone of a particular color.

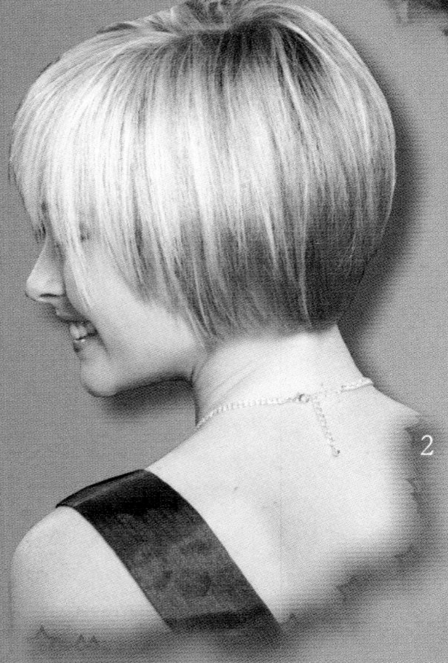

3

2

**Contrast** occurs when two or more **differing colors** are placed close to each other within a nail or hairdesign, or a makeup application.

6

4

5

6

# Color . . .

**Mood** changes according to the **tonal value** of color. Red-based colors create **warmth or vibrancy**. Blue-based colors invoke feelings of **coolness and depth**. Yellow-based colors add **visual lift** using lightness and brightness.

**Illusion** is a visual perception created by the strategic placement of color. Light shades **accentuate** elements and dark colors help them **recede**.

**Dimension** is the use and placement of **contrasting elements** within the design. **Light colors** give the overall design the appearance of being **large, bright and open. Dark colors** have the effect of being **small, recessive, dense and compact.**

**Emphasis** through color gives **prominence** to a component or area of design.

1 2 3 4 5 6

# Art Principles . . .

A **principle** is a basic truth, law or assumption as formulated and accepted by the mind.

Principles will assist in moving the design from the theoretical concept to the practical performance.

## The Principles of Art Design are:

- Proportion
- Balance – symmetry and asymmetry
- Motion
- Harmony
- Emphasis

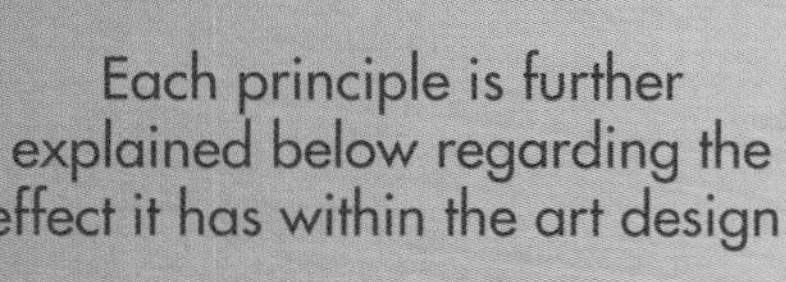
Each principle is further explained below regarding the effect it has within the art design.

2

1

**Proportion** is the direct correlation of size, distance, amount and ratio between the individual characteristics when compared with the whole. It has a **powerful effect on the overall balance of a hairdesign** in relation to the total aesthetic quality of a person's image. Subtle changes that graduate to extreme changes in certain clients should help to create a more balanced relationship.

Your inborn sense of "seeing" will advise you to **observe closely a client's proportions** that regulate his or her size, shape and characteristics. Beauty is all about the arrangement of an individual's characteristics. The following study of body, head and facial shape will help you to control and counterbalance an individual's proportions.

# Body Proportion ...

**Proportion** means that **every part fits with the whole** to create body balance and harmony. Whether creating a hairstyle, makeup application or nail design, every arrangement must look harmonious and graceful, complementing your client's individual traits. The design should appear neither **too large nor too small** in relation to the body's biological proportions.

**Body proportion** has been carefully studied and detailed in its properties by art historians, who consider the human body to be the highest form of art. **Leonardo da Vinci** created an artistic composition called **"The Vitruvian Man,"** which was inspired by the Roman architect **Marcus Vitruvius** (ve-tru-vE-es), who translated the human body's measurements into a method used for creating symmetry in art and architectural design. The drawing became commonly known as the **"Canon of Proportions,"** and is symbolic of the human body's artistic balance and proportion. In our industry, it is recognized as an essential influence in hairdesign.

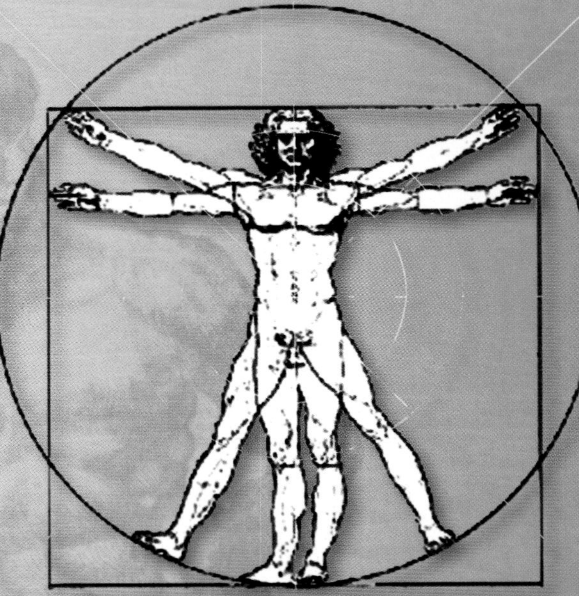

Leonardo da Vinci's *Vitruvian Man*

6

# Body Proportion . . .

*In hairdesign, body proportions are measured using the length and width of the head. Your role as a professional hairdesigner is to determine the **most harmonious style for your client's overall features**. With continued practice, you will develop your intuition for evaluating and balancing proportions to more closely resemble an artist's ideal.*

## The ideal body proportions:

- An **adult's average height** is equivalent to seven or eight head-lengths.
- The maximum **shoulder breadth** is approximately three heads wide.
- **Torso length** is equivalent to the height of two heads.
- The **waist** should equal approximately twice the size of the neck.
- In the human body, the **central point** is naturally the **navel**.
- **Leg length** (hip to toes) is slightly more than half of the body.
- The span from **elbow to wrist** is equal to the size of the foot.

Use these body approximations to assess your client's proportions in your mind. A person will rarely fit these proportions perfectly. For example, the sizes will vary among children, males and females.

Checking to see if your client has a small or large body area compared to the ideal measurements (for instance, short legs or wide shoulders), is the first step in determining what hairdesign will be most appropriate for the shape of his or her body.

# Body Proportion ...

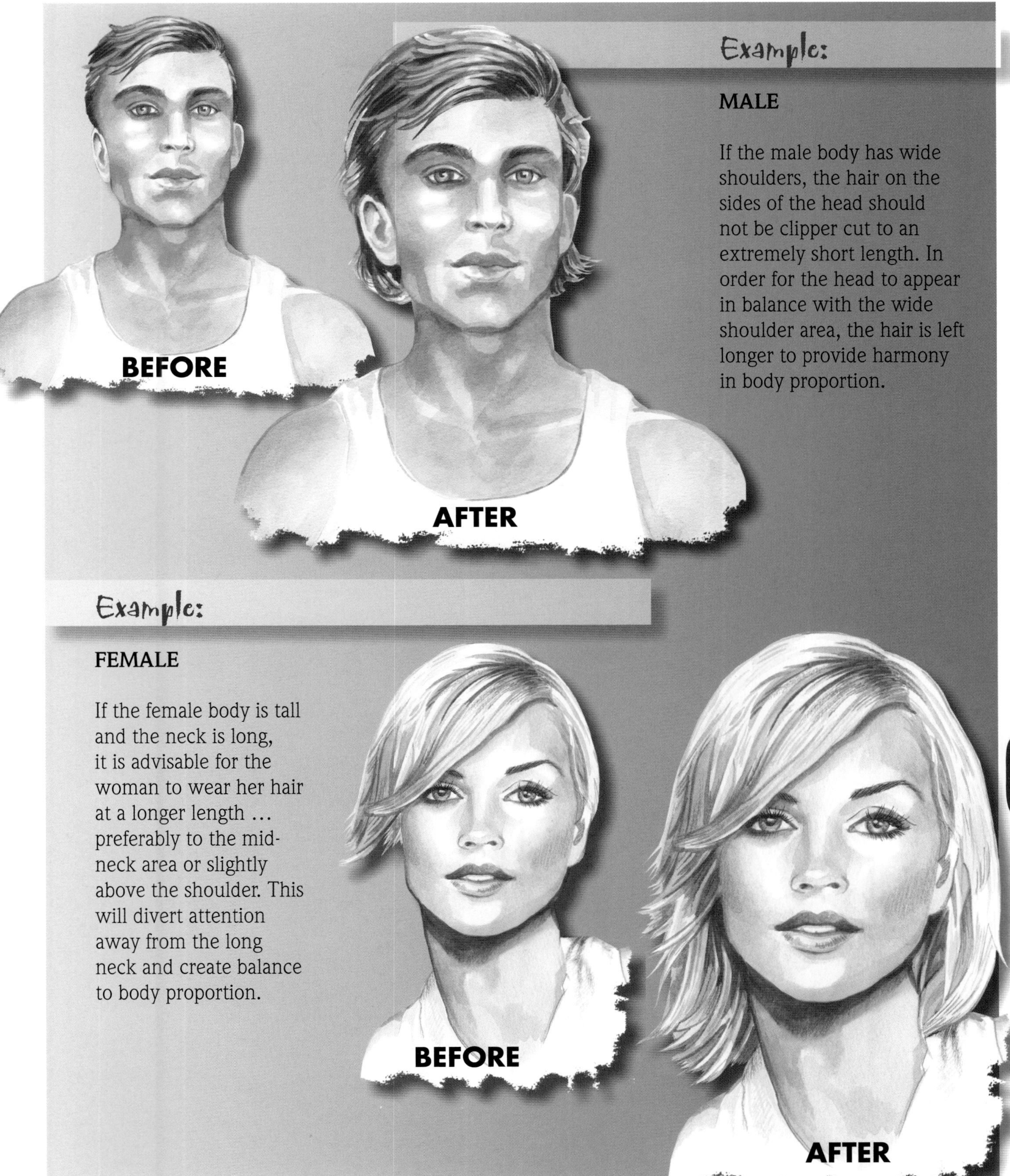


Example:

**MALE**

If the male body has wide shoulders, the hair on the sides of the head should not be clipper cut to an extremely short length. In order for the head to appear in balance with the wide shoulder area, the hair is left longer to provide harmony in body proportion.

Example:

**FEMALE**

If the female body is tall and the neck is long, it is advisable for the woman to wear her hair at a longer length ... preferably to the mid-neck area or slightly above the shoulder. This will divert attention away from the long neck and create balance to body proportion.

6

# Body Proportion ...

**People are all different shapes and sizes.** There are basically three different body types according to the American psychologist William H. Sheldon. In the 1940s, Mr. Sheldon created the Soma Body Types, which categorized the physical body proportions into three general areas.

**All people are considered one of these three major body types:**

- **Endomorph**
- **Ectomorph**
- **Mesomorph**

"Soma is the Greek word used for body."

When creating a hairdesign, consider the entire **body proportion,** whether the client is endomorph, ectomorph or mesomorph. As you greet a client, briefly assess his or her body from both the front and back views and from head to toe.

## Endomorph

(generously rounded or stout and stocky)

The **endomorph** (en-do-morph) **body** is **rounded with short limbs** and the **hips are usually wider than the shoulders.** Many endomorphs have small hands and feet. This body type is prone to weight issues.

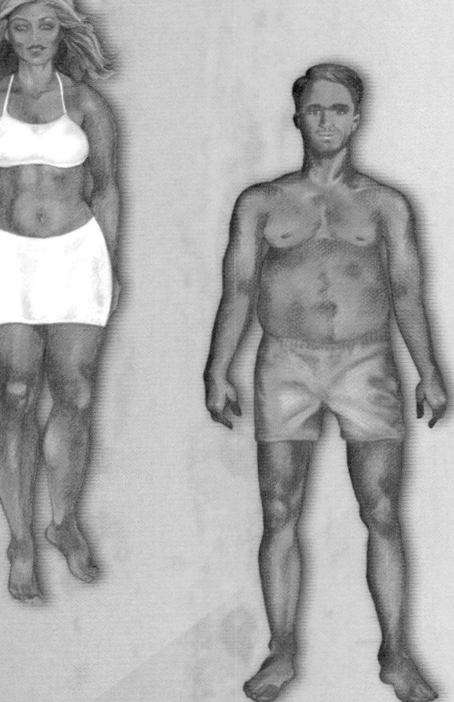

Select angular and unbroken vertical lines in clothing with monochromatic (one-color) themes, dropped waistlines and loose fit to balance out a round body image.

6

# Body Proportion ...

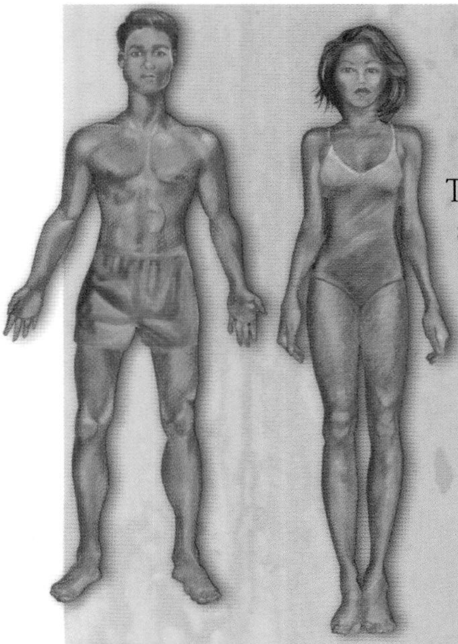

## Ectomorph

(thin and lean)

The **ectomorph** (ec-to-morph) **body** has a **straight, slender frame** consisting of **long, narrow bones.** This type of body has **no muscular bulk;** instead the muscles are long and lean. Endomorphs usually have low body fat and sometimes can be underweight. The endomorph's **hips and shoulders are equal in width.**

To balance out an elongated body, avoid vertical patterns and solid colors. Consider waist-length jackets or belts that create a curvy figure.

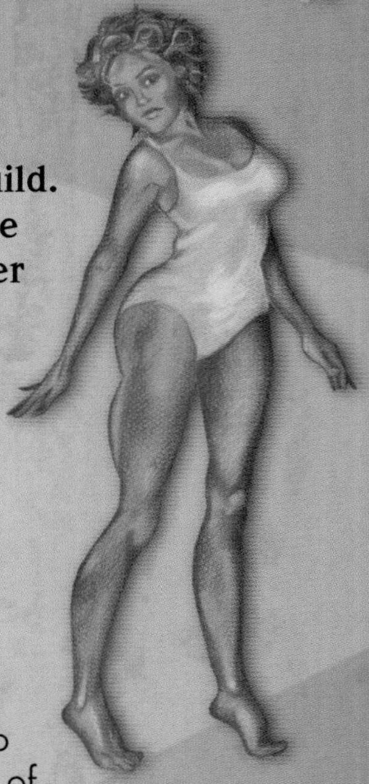

## Mesomorph

(athletic and muscular)

The **mesomorph** (mes-o-morph) **body** is **naturally athletic in build.** The mesomorph's **shoulders are typically wider than his or her hips.** As long as this body type stays active, the mesomorph will encounter few weight issues.

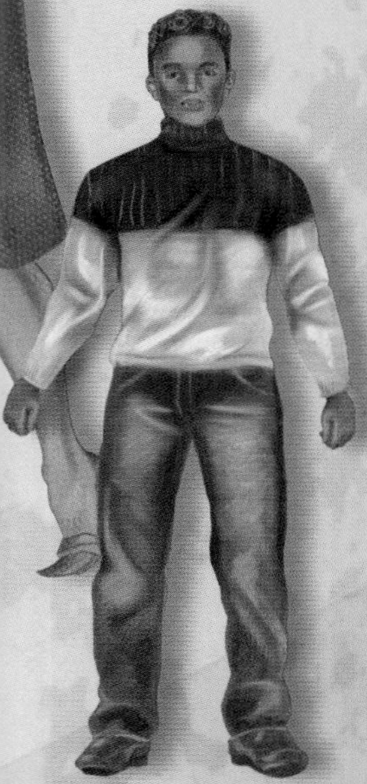

Add volume to the lower half of the body to counterbalance the top. Use clothing with heavy or patterned fabric that flares at the hips. Never choose blouses with boat necks or busy patterns.

The body is best proportioned when the hairdesign does not exceed one-third of the client's total body length (including the head), leaving two-thirds remaining to balance the body image.

6

# Face Shapes ...

**O**nce *you have considered the body, the next step is to focus on the face. To identify a* ***facial shape,*** *the position and prominence of the facial bones are determined. Knowing the client's face shape is crucial in recognizing how to balance the hairdesign.*

**As artists, we create illusions** – whether styling hair to produce a more proportioned face or applying makeup to minimize or enhance a facial feature or forming nail enhancements to provide length to the natural nails.

## There are Seven Face Shapes:

*Oval, Round (circle), Square, Rectangle (oblong), Triangle (pear), Diamond and Inverted Triangle (heart).*

**The oval face shape** has an **ideally balanced** vertical and horizontal proportion for hairdesigning. It tapers in a gentle slope from the widest portion, the forehead, to the narrowest portion, the chin.

Although cultural differences bring their own definition of what is beautiful, stylists may strive to create the illusion of an oval shape for other types of facial shapes. Undesirable features may be made less noticeable, while enhancing the desired attributes.

1

**The round** (circle) **face shape** is almost as wide as it is long. It typically features a wide middle zone, short chin and rounded hairline. Balance the round face with angular hairdesigns.

2

**The square face shape** is equal in width and length. The outer lines are straight vertically and horizontally. Proportion this face by creating a hairstyle that draws the eye away from the strong jawline and softens the frame of the forehead by adding a fringe.

3

6

# Face Shapes . . .

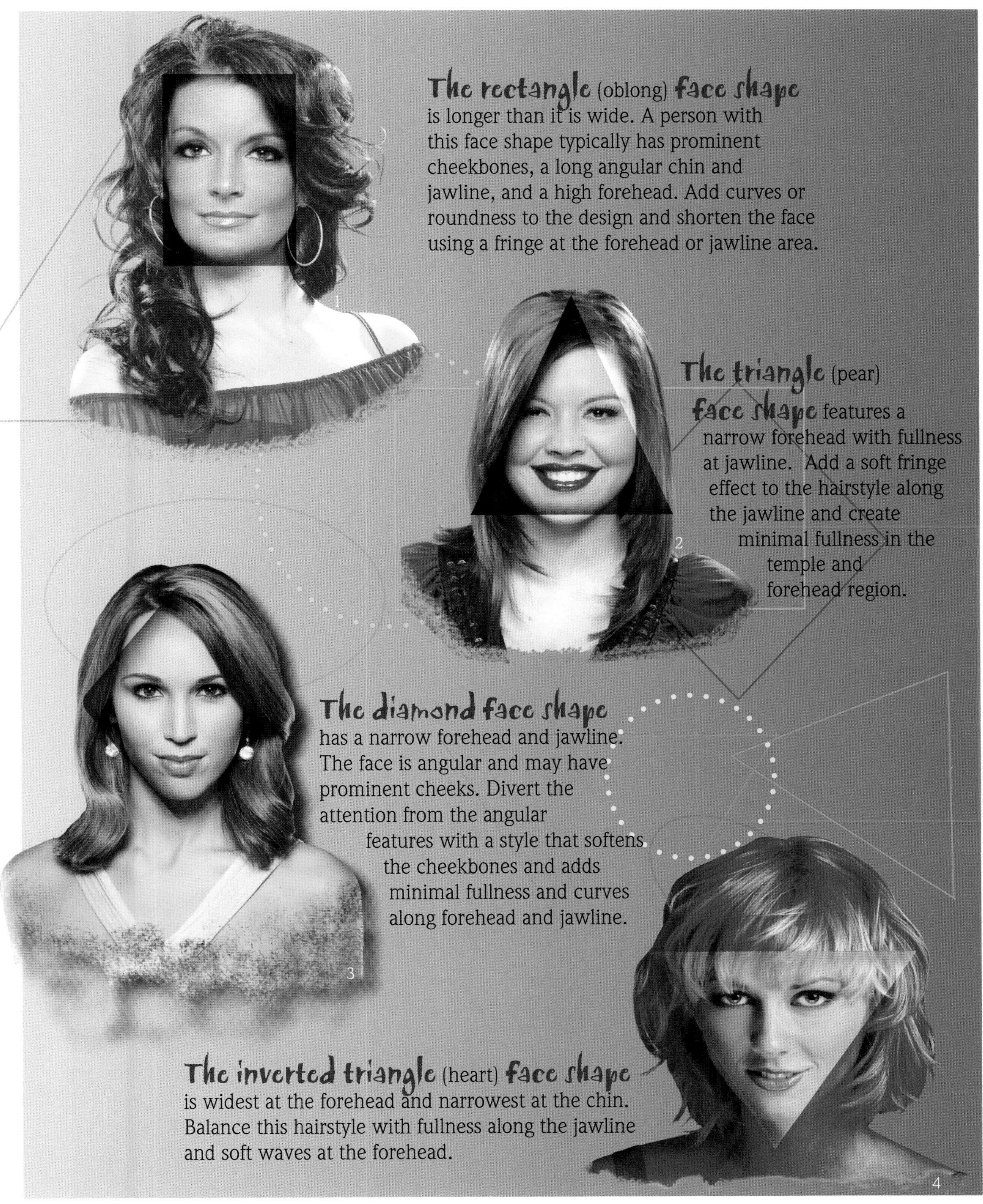


**The rectangle** (oblong) **face shape** is longer than it is wide. A person with this face shape typically has prominent cheekbones, a long angular chin and jawline, and a high forehead. Add curves or roundness to the design and shorten the face using a fringe at the forehead or jawline area.

**The triangle** (pear) **face shape** features a narrow forehead with fullness at jawline. Add a soft fringe effect to the hairstyle along the jawline and create minimal fullness in the temple and forehead region.

**The diamond face shape** has a narrow forehead and jawline. The face is angular and may have prominent cheeks. Divert the attention from the angular features with a style that softens the cheekbones and adds minimal fullness and curves along forehead and jawline.

**The inverted triangle** (heart) **face shape** is widest at the forehead and narrowest at the chin. Balance this hairstyle with fullness along the jawline and soft waves at the forehead.

6

# Face Shapes . . .

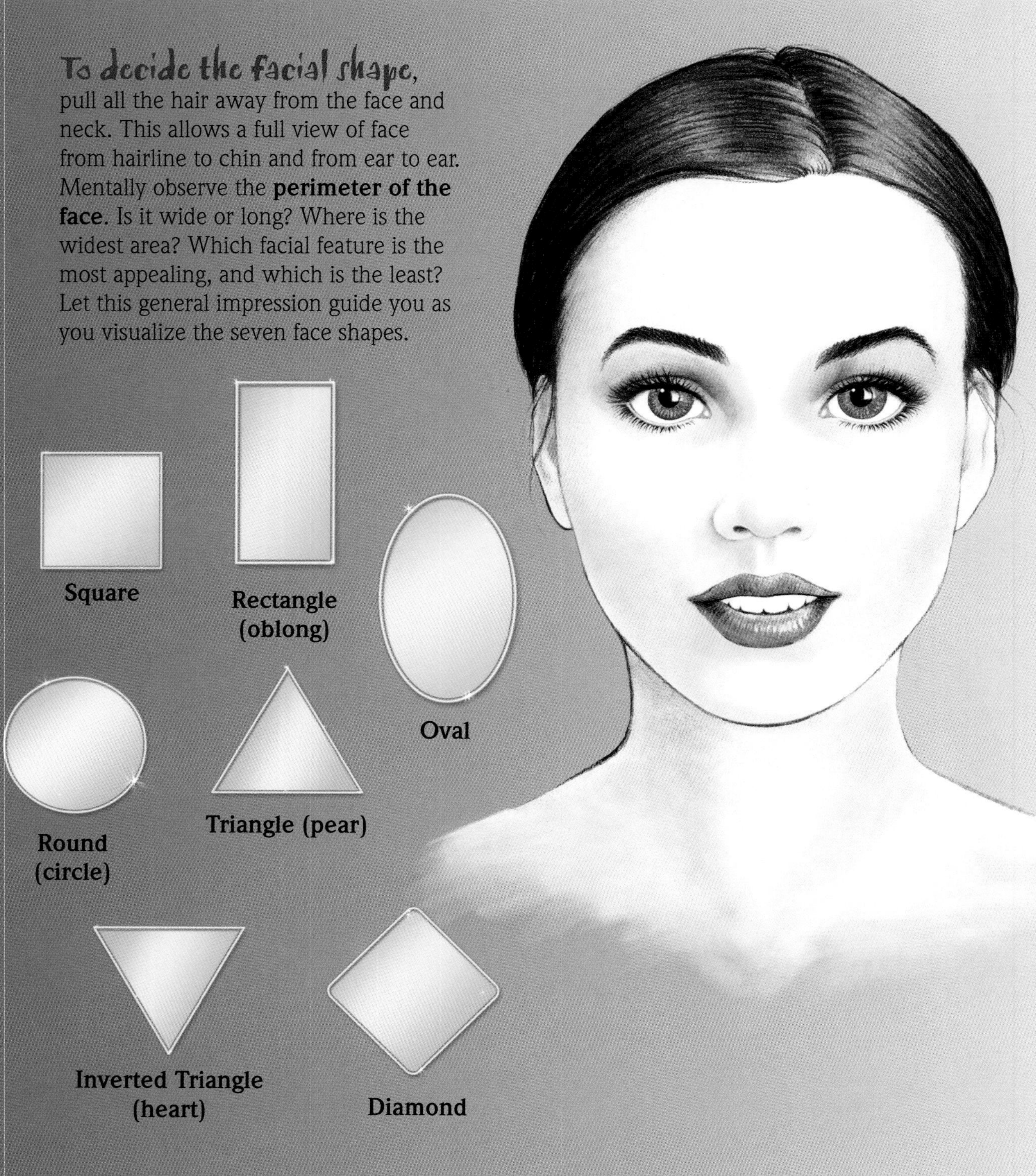


**To decide the facial shape,** pull all the hair away from the face and neck. This allows a full view of face from hairline to chin and from ear to ear. Mentally observe the **perimeter of the face.** Is it wide or long? Where is the widest area? Which facial feature is the most appealing, and which is the least? Let this general impression guide you as you visualize the seven face shapes.

**Exercise:** Pull all hair away from face/neck and look in the mirror. Using a marker, trace the outline of your face onto the mirror. What face shape do you have? Are you wearing the correct hairstyle to complement a proper balance between your face and body?

# Golden Ratio . . .

*To an artist, the mathematical inspiration referred to as the **Golden Ratio** is the key to a well-designed piece of art. This mathematical concept is based on proportions and ratio of design elements that travel from small to large or large to small.*

The Golden Ratio demonstrates that beauty comes from **graceful proportion**, the relationship of a part to the whole. The hair is your medium in which to create the illusion of perfect proportion. **Dividing the components into thirds balances the hairdesign in relation to the entire image** (not just the head) and reinforces the artistic principle of proportion.

The Golden Ratio is what the hairdesigner uses, if even unconsciously, when she **attempts to correct imbalance in the facial structure** by using the hair to create visual harmony.

Look at the ratio or proportion of face to hair in the example above. Think in thirds ... one-third, one-third, and one-third. The model's face is approximately one-third of the total design area. Her hair equals two-thirds of that area, creating the perfect balance for her features. Always follow the 2:3 or 3:2 ratio – two parts face, three parts hair or vice versa.

In this example, the hair is too big for the small body size.

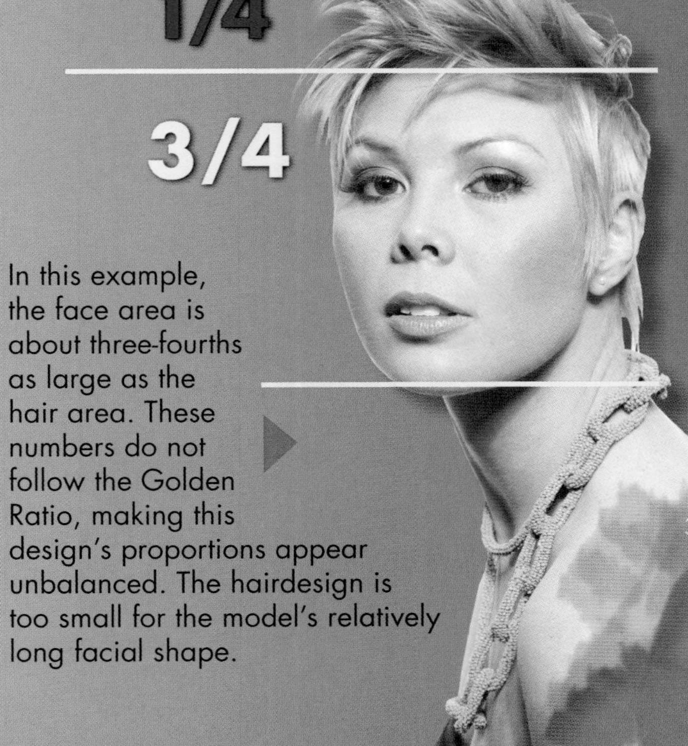


In this example, the face area is about three-fourths as large as the hair area. These numbers do not follow the Golden Ratio, making this design's proportions appear unbalanced. The hairdesign is too small for the model's relatively long facial shape.

6

# Design Plan . . .

**A design plan** *for a hairstyle can be adjusted either direction to accommodate clients of many different sizes. It is from this concept that the term scaling was developed, meaning to sketch shapes, sizes and proportions of a design.*

In hairdesigning, we consider one-dimensional style as having only length, which means individual strands of hair with no elevation.

**Scale** is the proportion of size or mass to the total volume of a hairdesign.

**Scaling** is used to create the general **movement of geometric shapings** by distributing wet hair around the head form.

A design begins with a **one-dimensional shape** that has **only length** and no elevation, and becomes **two-dimensional** by setting the hair into the desired pattern, which now exhibits both **length and width**. When the design is combed or finished into a **three-dimensional form** having **length, width and depth**, it should reflect the scale of the individual's body and facial proportions.

6

# Design Plan . . .

**The principles of hairdesign include a chronological work order with four stages:**

sketch (mold) the design into the desired shape.

**Scale** (proportion) the design into distinct areas or sections (two-dimensional).

**Set** the design (three-dimensional).

1

**Sculpt/comb** the design (three-dimensional).

6

# Balance ...

***Balance** is the visual comparison of **weight used to offset or equalize proportion,** which is achievable by arranging the elements of a design uniformly. It is also important in assuring that some design elements are not over-emphasized. Develop your personal sense of balance in design by observing the artists of today and of the past. Look deeply into the paintings, sculptures and drawings ... observe fashions and even floral arrangements. Then study and practice your skills by following the principle of balance to create your own design.*

## The principle of balance will help in these areas of design:

- Symmetrical/Asymmetrical balance within the hairdesign
- Symmetrical/Asymmetrical balance of hair with the body

Designers use a **center or axis point of reference to view balance** within the hairstyle and in relationship to the body. This axis point of the head occurs by dividing the face horizontally and vertically with an imaginary line.

The axis point of reference on **the body** will fall approximately around the navel or hip area, depending upon the person's body structure.

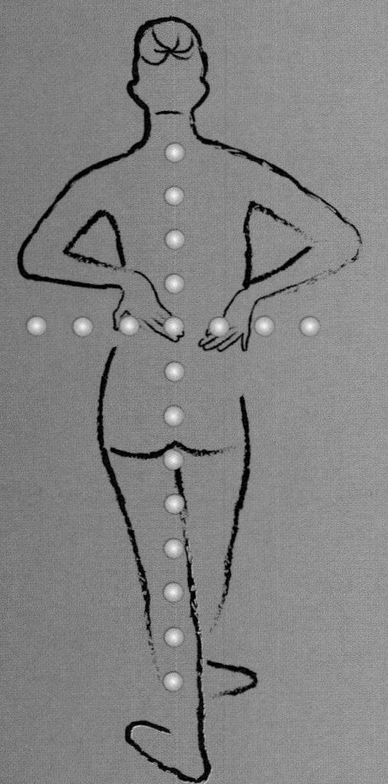

**On the straight (front) view**, the axis point of reference on the head occurs where the lines intersect around the nose. The axis point of reference on the **head in the profile view** occurs where the lines intersect around the top of the ear.

Once the axis is identified, you can then use the principles of balance to create a hairdesign.

# Symmetry . . .

## There are three considerations regarding balance for your hair creation.

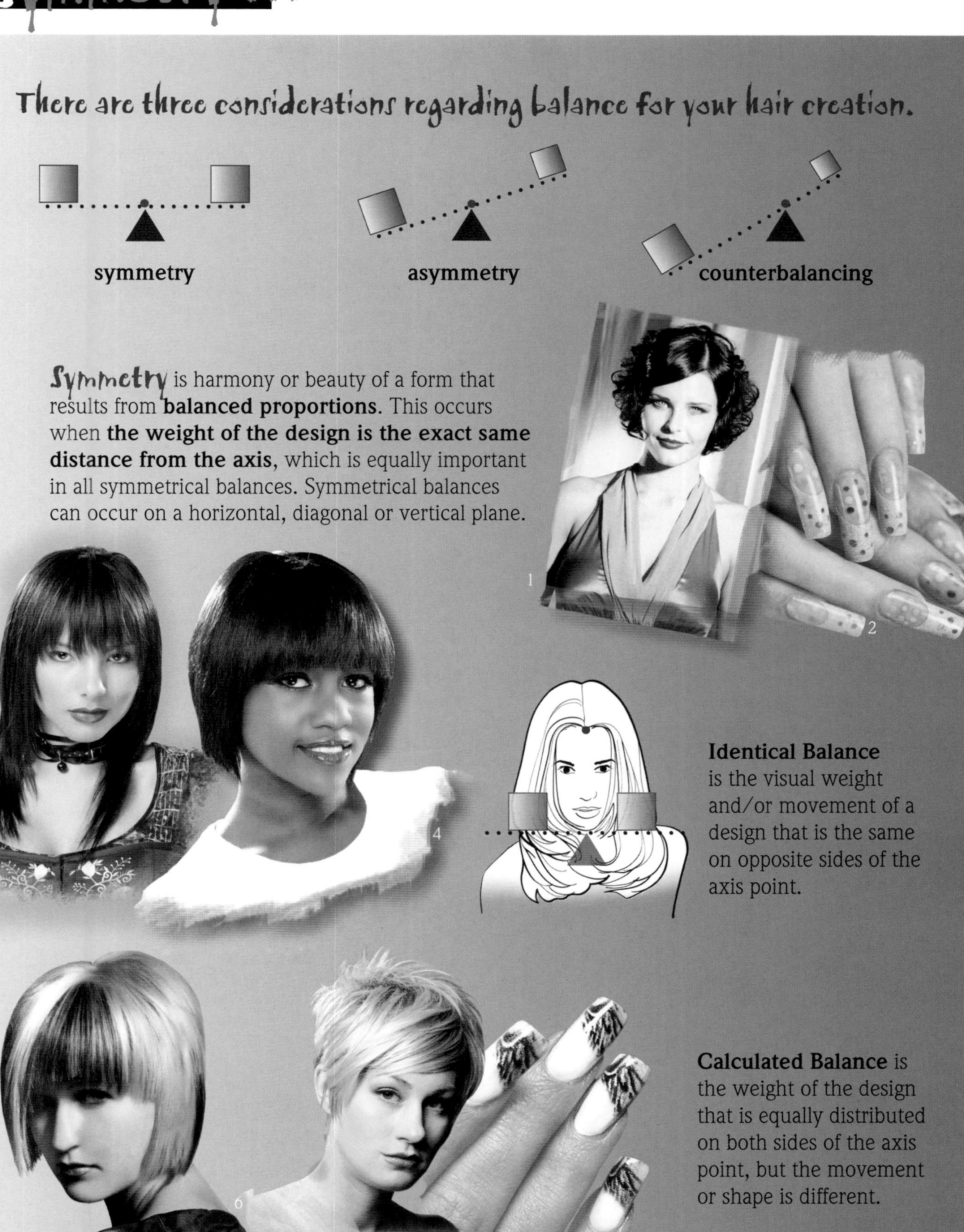


**Symmetry** is harmony or beauty of a form that results from **balanced proportions**. This occurs when **the weight of the design is the exact same distance from the axis**, which is equally important in all symmetrical balances. Symmetrical balances can occur on a horizontal, diagonal or vertical plane.

**Identical Balance** is the visual weight and/or movement of a design that is the same on opposite sides of the axis point.

**Calculated Balance** is the weight of the design that is equally distributed on both sides of the axis point, but the movement or shape is different.

# Asymmetry . . .

**Asymmetry** is **unbalanced, irregularly arranged** on opposite sides of a line or around a central point. This occurs when the **visual weights in the hairdesign are unequal** and/or placed at different distances from the axis' central point of reference showing a 45-degree angle.

The **heavier visual weight**, fullness or attraction should be placed **closer** to the axis and the **lighter visual weight**, fullness or attraction is placed **farther away** from the axis.

As the **heavier weight moves away** from the axis point, the **lighter weight will move closer** to the axis to counterbalance the hairdesign.

The weight should remain on the same design line, whether horizontal or diagonal, and maintain proportion (3:2, 2:3). Positioning the weight correctly will produce eye-pleasing designs, whether symmetrical or asymmetrical.

# Counterbalance . . .

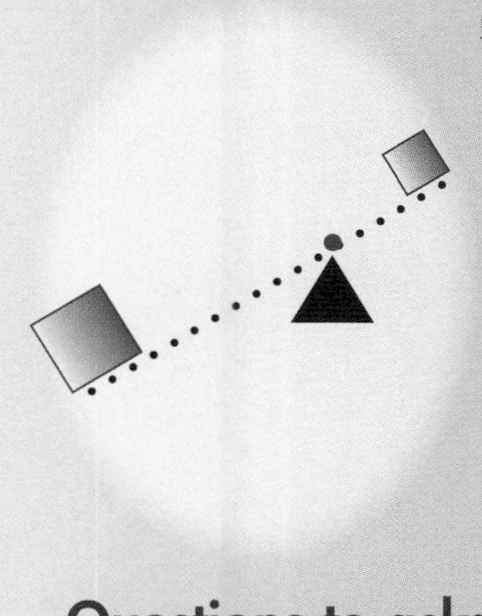

**Counterbalance** is making something balanced by distributing weight or size to **offset unbalanced proportions** and create a harmonious, flowing design. This occurs with the use of elements having **different weights and lengths in opposite areas that offset each other** to create a balanced overall form.

Planning for counterbalance begins with an evaluation of the overall body shape and size. Analyze the curves and features of the face, head, neck, shoulders and body to determine:

- Where to create either closeness or fullness
- The optimal length of the hair
- The direction or movement within the design

**Questions to ask:**
Is the style easy to manage? Does it fit his or her lifestyle?

After analyzing the body, evaluate your client's facial features and proportions. Consider each feature both individually and also as part of the entire body. A good design plan will counterbalance facial and body irregularities to create symmetry and also fit your client's lifestyle and personality.

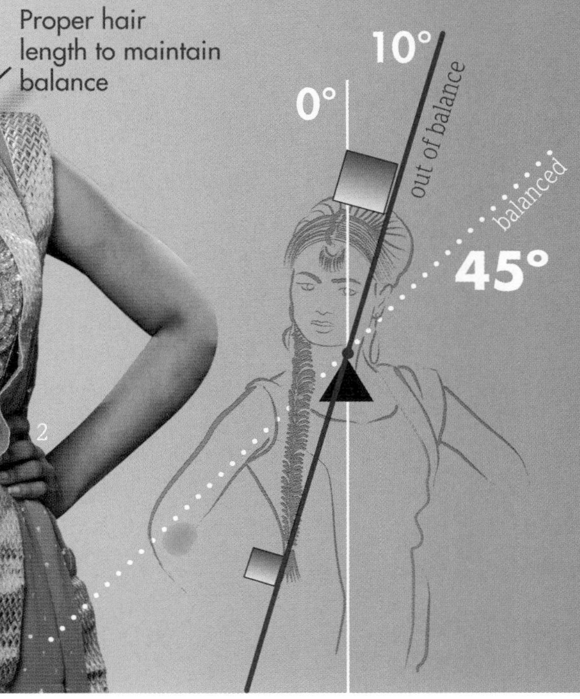

Out of balance

Proper hair length to maintain balance

10°
0°
out of balance
balanced
45°

1

2

To counterbalance weights in a hairdesign, draw an imaginary line. If the counterbalance is more than 45-degree angle from point to point, the hairstyle is **out of balance.**

6

# Emphasis . . .

**Emphasis** *is the main excitement, attraction or action of your work of art, hair, nail or makeup design. It is the* ***focal point or the heart of interest*** *that draws the viewer to gaze at the subject.*

The artist will **create a point of interest** starting with a form or shape, which is then accentuated throughout the design by using color, texture, contrast or framing. By placing the focal point or emphasis in the proper division or zone, you **counterbalance undesirable features** such as wide-set eyes, large forehead or pointy chin.

In order to understand placement of focal points, a person's **facial features** are taken into account. The **facial features are mentally categorized into three zones** in order to determine how the hair will be designed.

## Zone 1

The **first zone** is between the hairline and eyebrow line.

## Zone 2

The **second zone** is between the eyebrow line and the tip of nose.

## Zone 3

The **third zone** is between the tip of nose and the chin line.

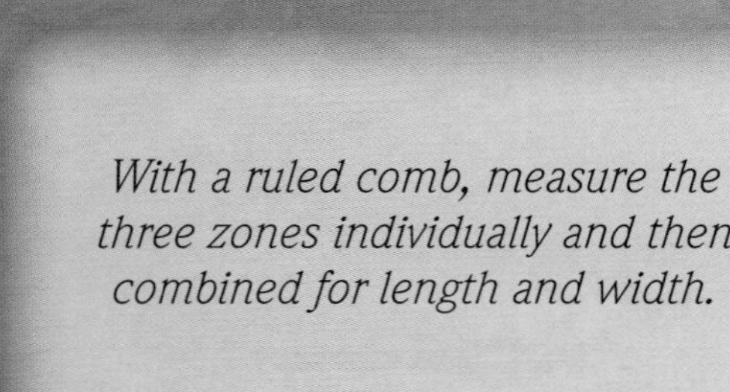

*With a ruled comb, measure the three zones individually and then combined for length and width.*

6

# Facial Zones . . .

## Zone One:

The **forehead** will vary in length and width depending on each individual. Consider this zone when determining whether a fringe should be added to a hairdesign and/or the placement of that fringe.

1

## Zone Two:

- The **eyes** are the **most expressive facial feature** and often the focal point of the overall design. However, there are times when the client needs to correct either close- or wide-set eyes. The effects of aging around the eyes may also be diminished with a well-designed hairstyle.

- The **nose** is often considered the **most prominent facial feature** because of its size and its location at the center of the face. The nose shape can either strongly influence or be influenced by the chosen hairstyle.

2

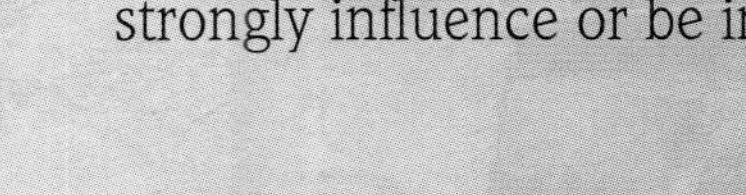

## Zone Three:

The **mouth, chin and jaw** are perhaps the **most important area** to consider in the design of a complementary hairstyle.

- The **mouth** with its size, shape and balance should all be taken into account when planning the hairstyle.
- The **chin** is viewed from the front and side for shape and size.
- The **jaw** shape influences the length, width and angularity of a style.

3

Another important area not to be overlooked is the **Neck and Shoulders**, which are **"gateways" to the body**. This area helps to properly proportion the style to the body.

# Facial Zones . . .

**The following** *examples show how focal points either* ***emphasize or divert interest*** *from/or to different facial zones or cranial divisions. The use of an imaginary line placed at each zone's focal area will divert the attention of the viewer away from the undesirable feature or will direct the viewer to emphasize the feature.*

### Zone 1

Envision an imaginary line through the widest point on or around the forehead, which will direct the eye upward to help minimize a pointy chin.

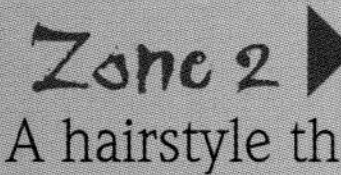

### Zone 2

A hairstyle that emphasizes width across the bridge of the nose area will also provide the illusion of width across the cheekbone area. This design is effective for a long, narrow face shape.

### Zone 3

The widest portion of the hairdesign emphasizes the mouth. This helps camouflage the wide forehead of an inverted triangle (heart) shaped face.

### Neck and Shoulders

Placing the widest portion of the hairstyle within the **neck and shoulders** can provide the illusion of shortening an elongated face while narrowing and lengthening a short neck.

# Divisions . . .

## The Cranial Divisions

Just as every person's face has a different shape, the **skull can have different shapes** too. **Hairdesigns should create the illusion of an evenly shaped head**. The cranial divisions help hairdesigners to quickly spot the shape of a client's skull. All three divisions can be viewed by examining the **profile or side view of a person's head**. Every angle, including the client's profile view, is important in planning a balanced hairdesign.

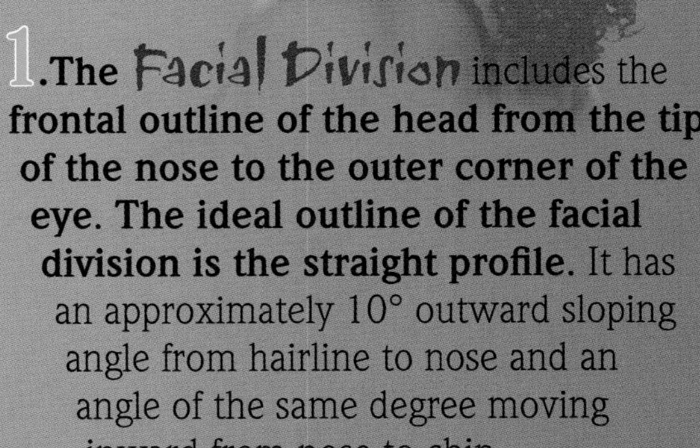

1. The **Facial Division** includes the **frontal outline of the head from the tip of the nose to the outer corner of the eye. The ideal outline of the facial division is the straight profile.** It has an approximately 10° outward sloping angle from hairline to nose and an angle of the same degree moving inward from nose to chin.

2. The **Parietal Division** is defined by the **outer corner of the eye to the back of the ear**. This area may vary from person to person depending on the position of the ears in relation to the eyes. Ideally, the upper tip of the ear should align with the corner of the eye, and the lower tip of the ear should align with the lip line (middle of the lips).

3. The **Occipital Division** includes the area from the **back of the ear to the occipital bone** (the back of the skull). Like the parietal division, the size and shape of the occipital bone varies from person to person. The ideal bone shape is evenly rounded from the top of the skull to the neck.

6

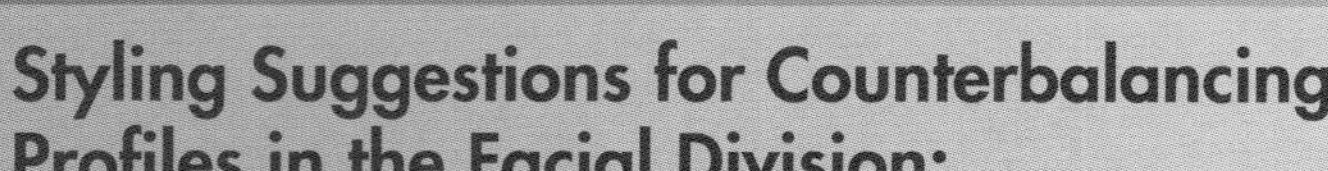

## Styling Suggestions for Counterbalancing Profiles in the Facial Division:

**Concave Profile** has a **protruding chin and forehead**, which gives the impression of a receding nose. Counterbalance these prominent features by adding soft, upward movement at the nape and hair moving gently away from the forehead and chin area.

convex

2

3

corrective

Adding volume toward the forehead and jawline corrects a convex profile.

**Convex Profile** is recognized by a **receding chin and high hairline**, which makes the nose area protrude. To minimize this rounded profile, style hair with fullness moving toward the forehead and jawline, adding volume if necessary to counterbalance a flatter crown area. A male client can mask a recessed chin line by growing a full beard.

6

## Styling Suggestions for Counterbalancing the Occipital Divisions:

### Flat Occipital Bone

add volume in the occipital division or crown area.

### Prominent Occipital Bone

add volume below the occipital bone to soften the appearance of a pointed head.

# Ornamentation . . .

**Ornamentation** in hairdesign and fashion adds to the visual experience of a client's hair or outfit. It can either **embellish or become the main focal point. Hair ornamentation** may include decorative hairpins, barrettes, hair bands or other material to attract the eye and establish a "theme" or a main emphasis of the design. The size and amount of the ornamentation must be **practical in order to create interest** in the design without overpowering it.

**Fashion ornamentation** consists of jewelry, colorful pins or other accessories that embellish or become the focal point of a client's outfit. Hairdesign and fashion ornamentation **should collaborate** to complete your client's overall appearance.

**NOTE: Rule of 13** is to never wear more than thirteen pieces of ornamental attire. Add up all flowers, bows or hair accessories, belt buckles, jewelry, shiny buttons and metal décor on shoes. Remember less is more!

6

# Motion . . .

**Motion** involves **movement, direction or force**. Design is created by the basic art principles with the scientific influences to help control the physical properties of the hair.

**The three scientific influences in hair are Energy, Mass and Tempo.**

GRAVITATIONAL FORCE

1

Energy influences gravity. **Gravity holds the hair and all objects in place.** The force of gravity on the hair keeps it from rising upward. When the hair falls downward, we refer to this gravitational energy as the natural directional motion of the hair or the "natural fall."

MASS

Mass is the amount of space matter takes up. **Hair takes up space**; therefore the size, bulk or magnitude of a hairdesign will determine the amount of mass created. Mass can be deceptive, like an optical illusion. A full or wide hairstyle with space within its design may appear to be greater in mass than a solid design that takes up less space but creates more of the total mass.

2

Tempo refers to design movement. The rate of motion or speed in the hair will produce a **decelerated (slow), moderate (medium), or accelerated (fast) tempo**, or any combination of tempo rates.

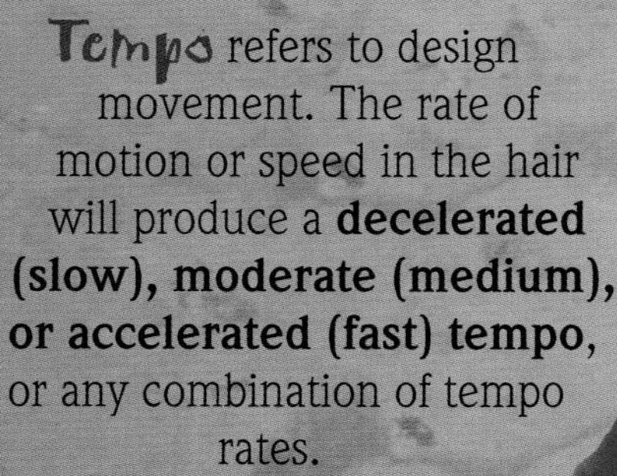

FAST

MEDIUM

SLOW

# Laws of Motion . . .

Sir Isaac Newton
1642-1727

As stated in the CLiC Hairdesigning book, Sir Isaac Newton was responsible for developing the three laws of motion. Let us review each law.

**Law One** states that an **object (hair) remains in motion** until a force is applied to stop it (hairspray) or to divert its direction.

**Law Two** shows a direct relationship between mass (size), speed (acceleration) and force (energy). This law simply says that the **larger an object is the more force and speed it takes to move it**. Therefore, when working with large amounts of hair, more speed and force are needed.

**Law Three** states that in **every movement there is a second opposite movement**. This law applies in making a wave or curved motion (arc) in hairdesign; when one arc goes forward, the second arc must travel backward.

## Interruption of Motion

**Diversion or Interruption of Motion** creates a **visual break in the continuity of a design** by changing the direction of a line or movement after it traveled too far in one direction.

The **theory of diversion or the interruption of motion** is present when the emphasis of motion **directs the attention away from a repetitive movement** and shifts it to a more stimulating area of the finished design. The eye will focus on the emphasized part of the design, distracting it from the recurring area.

# Rhythm . . .

**Along with the principle of Motion is Rhythm** ... the two operate simultaneously to blend elements or create harmony in a design.

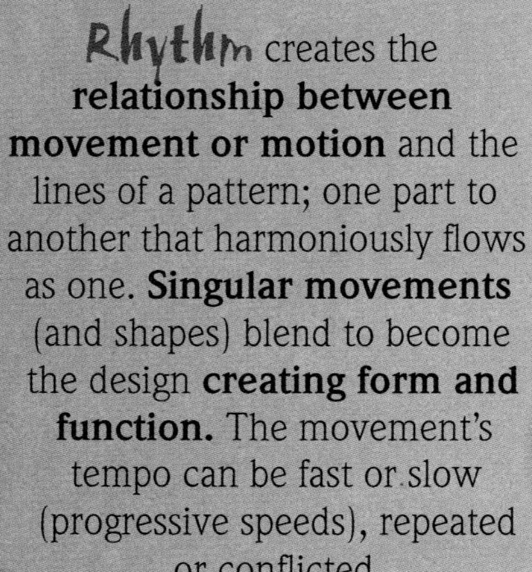

Rhythm creates the **relationship between movement or motion** and the lines of a pattern; one part to another that harmoniously flows as one. **Singular movements** (and shapes) blend to become the design **creating form and function.** The movement's tempo can be fast or slow (progressive speeds), repeated or conflicted.

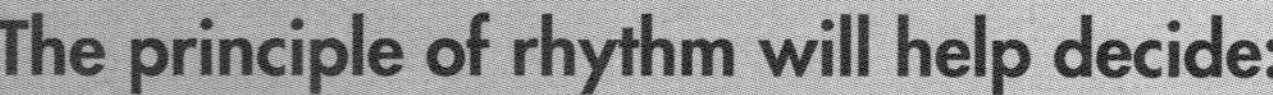

## The principle of rhythm will help decide:

- How often shapes, textures or colors are repeated within the design
- The size of the elements or components
- The interruption of motion within the design
- The rhythm of texture (tempo) as accelerating (increasing), staying the same or decelerating (decreasing) throughout the hairdesign

# Types of Rhythm . . .

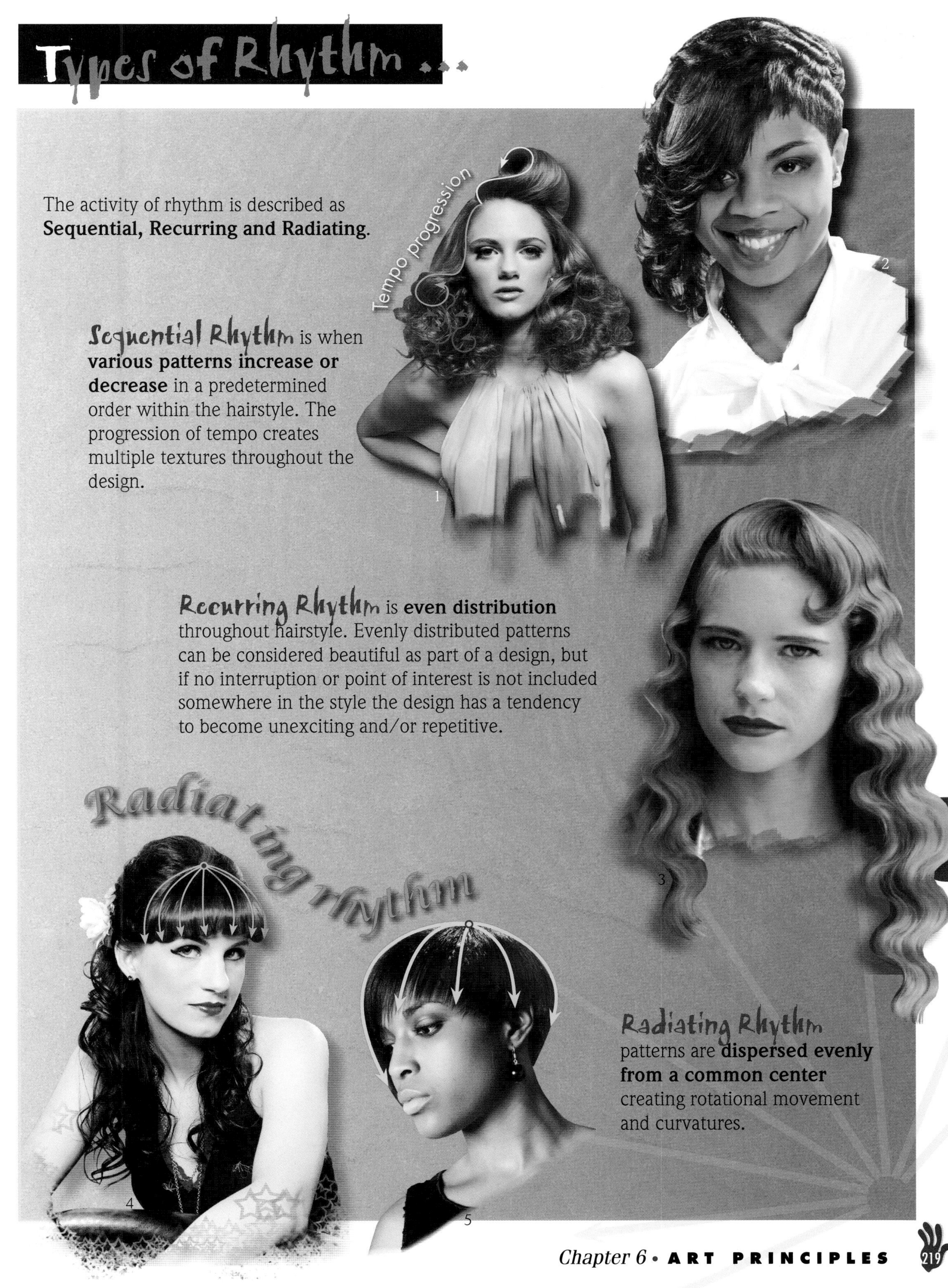


The activity of rhythm is described as **Sequential, Recurring and Radiating.**

**Sequential Rhythm** is when **various patterns increase or decrease** in a predetermined order within the hairstyle. The progression of tempo creates multiple textures throughout the design.

**Recurring Rhythm** is **even distribution** throughout hairstyle. Evenly distributed patterns can be considered beautiful as part of a design, but if no interruption or point of interest is not included somewhere in the style the design has a tendency to become unexciting and/or repetitive.

**Radiating Rhythm** patterns are **dispersed evenly from a common center** creating rotational movement and curvatures.

# Rotation ...

## The Theory of Rotation

**Rotation** is the act of turning a solid body on an axis. An **axis** is a fixed point of reference from which a body or geometric shape rotates or turns.

Hairdesigners comb hair on an axis to create different appearances. One axis that may be used is **a base**, which is located on the head. A **base** is the **stationary area of the hair strands** located on and attached to the scalp. Growing from the base, the stem or hair shaft acts as the directional controls from which hair rotates.

## Rotational Direction

**Direction** is the path in which the hair flows. The **directional movement or motion** of the hair within a design is created by the joining of straight or curved lines.

When designing hair, we use the terms **clockwise and counter-clockwise** to describe curved directional movements.

The term **clockwise** describes curls which are formed in the **same direction (to the right) as the hands move** on an analog-type clock or timepiece.

The term **counter-clockwise** describes curls formed in the **opposite direction (to the left)** from which the hands of the clock move. The directions are constant; however, the line on which they sit can change.

# Rotational Force . . .

How far the hair must travel and the momentum that it takes to get there is **force**.

The hair will react to **gravitational force by falling downward**. In order to get the hair to react **against gravity when styling**, an external force must be applied. From a point of reference – the axis – the hair moves in a specific curved direction (clockwise or counter-clockwise). The **placement of the axis in combination with the amount of gravitational force applied** will determine the amount of movement (lift or fall) the hairdesign pattern will have.

## Applying Rotational Force



**In making design decisions**, you must account for the force needed to move the hair into the desired style.

When rotating a circle you need **more force to close the outer loop at the same time as you close the inner loop.** For example, when runners in a line begin to rotate, the first (inner) runner in line barely changes her/his position while the last (outer) runner uses all of her/his strength and force to get into the line.

In hairdesign, **concentric shapes** have a common axis or starting point and repeat in different sizes from **smaller to larger** of the same shape.

## Axis Locations

### Front View

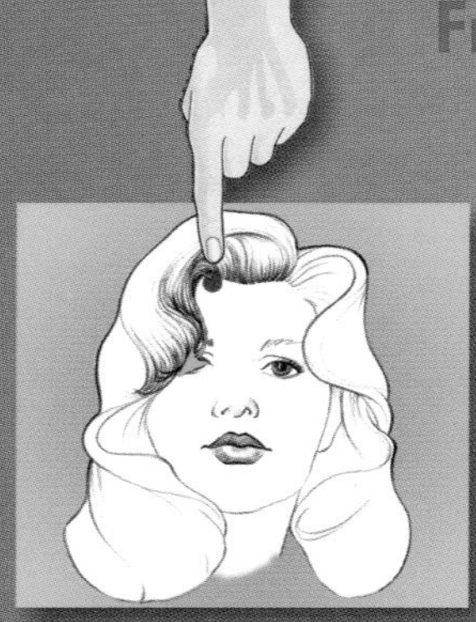

**One-Quarter Fringe –**
To place a **minimal amount of hair** falling into the fringe area and expose most of the forehead, create the axis point on the client's right side of hairline, using the client's right eyebrow as a reference area.

**One-Half Fringe –**
To place a **moderate amount of hair** falling into the fringe area, create the axis point at the center hairline, directly above the nose.

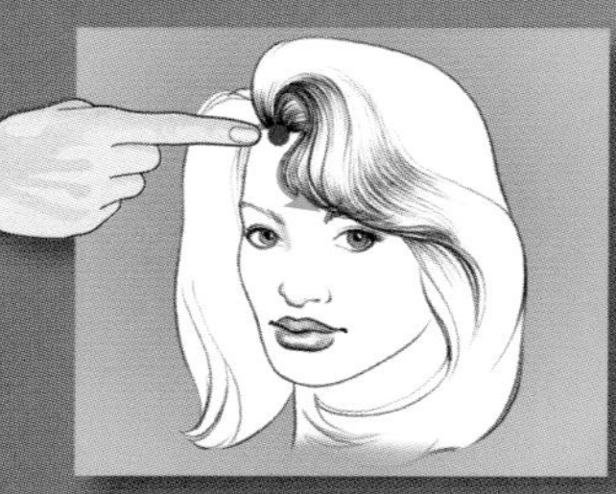

**Three-Quarter Fringe –**
To place a **maximum amount of hair** into the front hairline's fringe area and cover most of the forehead, place the axis point on the client's left side of hairline, using the client's left eyebrow as a reference area.

### Side View

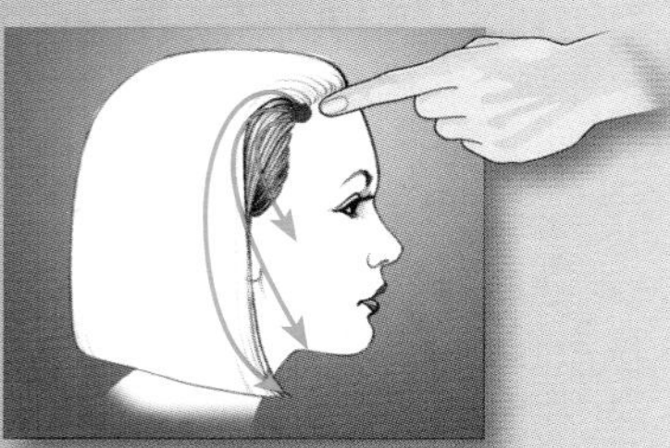

**For less lift/more fall,** place the axis point at the upper portion of side hairline.

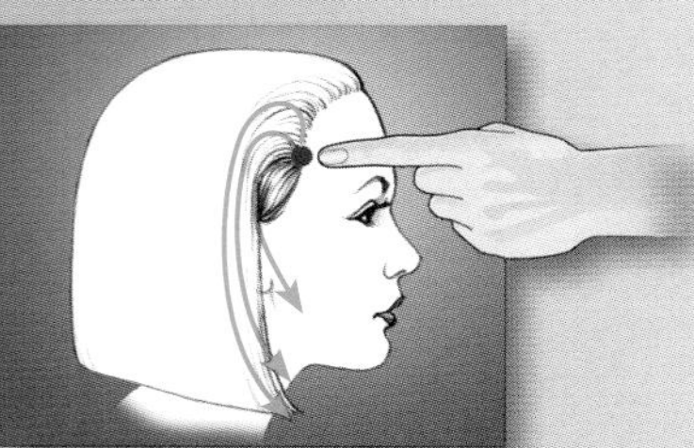

**For moderate lift/fall,** place the axis point at center of the side hairline.

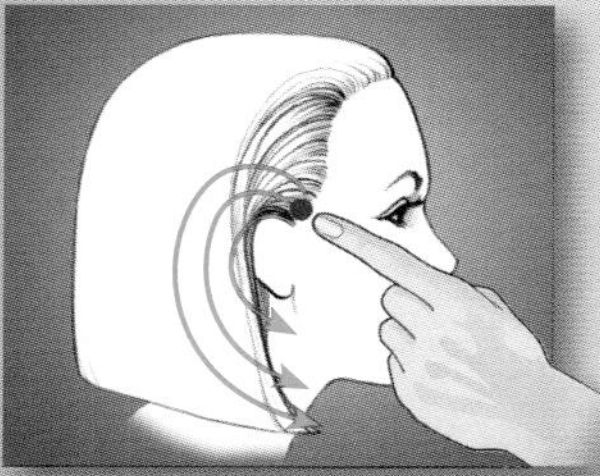

**For more lift/less fall,** place the axis point at lower portion of the side hairline.

## EXERCISE

### Finding the Axis of Rotation

Practice placing the axis point at various areas along the hairline and mold the hair into the rotational force.

1. Use your index finger to place the axis at the desired area for lift or fall in the design's hair flow.
2. All hair to the one side of the axis placement will have lift and all hair to the other side will fall into the fringe.

# Rotational Tempo . . .

Now that you understand and have practiced the rotational force, the next area of study is the rotational tempo or speed.

**Rotational tempo** is the pace or **speed of the hair through gravitational** force to create and complete a design.

Previously, we showed how the outer circle must travel faster than the inner circle. However, the inner circle will make more rotations than the outer circle, creating a more accelerated tempo. Therefore, pin curls, rollers or iron curls with a small diameter will produce tighter wave or curl formations with a more accelerated tempo than those with a larger diameter.

## Examples:

A **pin curl with no stem** produces a curl with an **accelerated tempo** or wave pattern with the least amount of movement. A **half stem pin curl** allows moderate movement or tempo. A **full stem pin curl** will produce a **decelerated tempo**, but the greatest amount of movement from the base.

An **on-base roller placement** using a small diameter roller creates **more lift and an accelerated tempo** compared to a large under-directed roller's closeness to the scalp and decelerated wave pattern.

**Ovaloid patterns** in finger waving produce a tempo that starts in the narrow open end as accelerated and travels toward the wide closed end, becoming more decelerated. By alternating the ovaloids, you can produce balanced wave formations. A **concentric shape** has a common axis or starting point and repeats different sizes from either **small to large, or large to small.**

# Combing Concepts ...

*Perfecting the skills necessary to give **hair lift, direction, and form** requires practice, attention to detail and knowledge of the following international combing concepts.*

**French Lacing Techniques** are also referred to as cushioning, interlocking, backbrushing or backcombing. **Lacing** means to compress hair together with a comb or brush for height and control.

## International Combing Concepts

**Compact Lacing** is used to create the most volume (convexity) in a hairdesign.

Hold a smoothed subsection of hair firmly between your middle and index fingers at 90-degree angle from the scalp.

Compact the hair by inserting a comb 1-2 inches (2.5-5 cm) from the scalp and push the hair down to the scalp. Repeat this step by gradually building a firm cushion of hair.

Smooth the surface of the cushioned hair while retaining the lift into the design's form.

6

# Combing Concepts ...

**Directional Lacing** is used to follow a particular line in a set or to create moderate volume (convexity) in a hairstyle. Use larger subsections of hair than what was used for the compact lacing technique.

The hair is held at less than 90-degree angle to achieve the desired amount of lift and direction.

Always lace in the direction the hair will travel. Lacing the underside of the hair strand produces volume; lacing on top of the hair creates closeness.

Smooth the surface of the cushioned hair while maintaining the direction established during the lacing technique.

**Interlocked Lacing** is used to create little to no volume (convexity) in the hair. This technique joins hair from a previous subsection into the next, creating a fluid movement or design.

Divide the hair into subsections and lace each one separately.

Picking up two subsections, lace subsections together.

Smooth the hair surface of the joined subsections to finish the style.

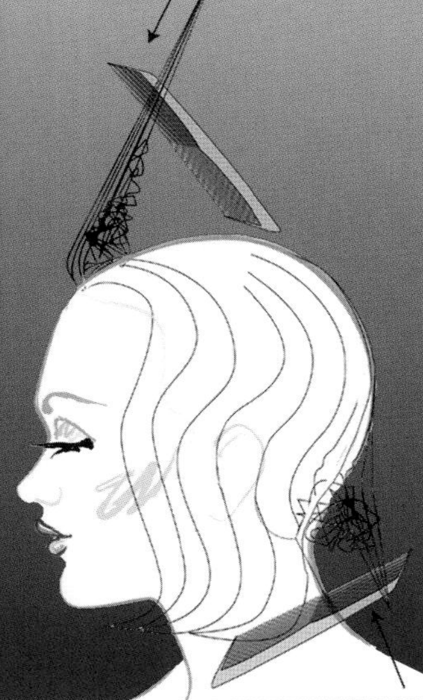

6

# The three memories of hair formation:

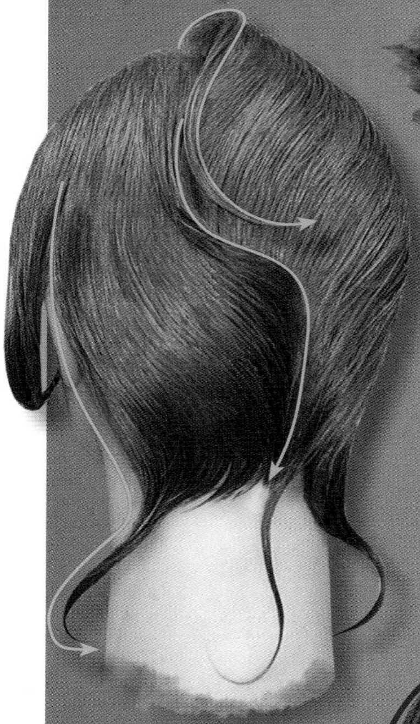

**Wet Memory** is achieved when the hair has been formed onto rollers, set in pin curls or molded into a specific design and then is ready to be dried.

HEAT

**Dry Memory** is achieved when heat has been applied to a wet style. This can be accomplished by using a hood dryer or airformer. A curling iron, flat iron or hot rollers may also be used once the hair has been dried.

**Directional Memory** is achieved when you relax the dry form with a brush and comb into a finished design.

## Combing Concepts ...

### Applying Directional Memory

DIRECTIONAL MEMORY

1. When the hair has been dried and cooled thoroughly, remove all setting tools. Relax the set by brushing, starting at the ends of the hair and working toward the scalp. Follow the brush with the palm of your hand to ensure the hair is smooth.

2. Place the palm of your hand on the client's head and gently push the hair forward. This will direct the hair into the general style in which it was set. Apply the desired lacing (backcombing) technique. Always follow the direction in which the style was set.

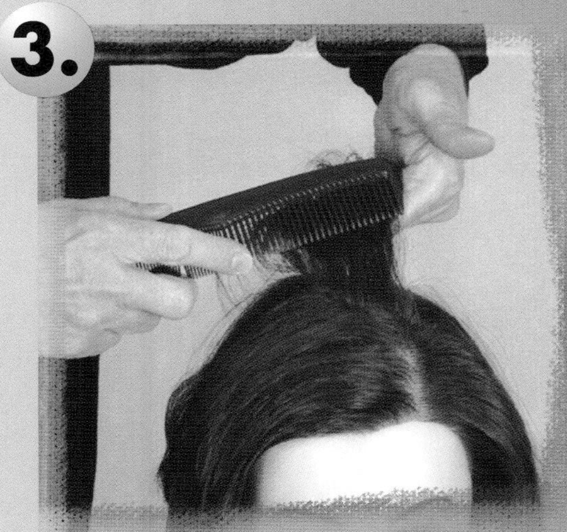

3. Surface-comb or brush the hair and smooth into the desired form. Be careful not to penetrate the teeth of the comb or brush too deeply into the hair thus removing the cushioning/lacing.

4. Use the end of a rattail comb or a hair pin to lift areas of your design where necessary and smooth with your palm to detail the form and complete the finished hairstyle.

### EXERCISE

Practice the three memories of hair formation using all three lacing techniques to finish the hairdesign.

# Repetition ...

**Repetition** *is how often the lines, angles, colors, textures or patterns are repeated in sequence within a design.*

The theory of repetition is the act of repeating patterns, colors, shapes, textures and other designs. Repetition can be created in vertical, horizontal or diagonal directions in clothing, makeup and hairdesign, either individually or combined.

Repetition creates the unity within the design by linking common features together. However, hairdesigns can become boring if elements or components are repeated too often. When considering odd and even patterns in design, think in terms of repetition versus randomness.

1

## The principle of repetition is used within hairdesigns to:

- Help create the outer silhouette or form
- Emphasize a shape or other component by repeating it
- Relate the other elements of a total look to the hairstyle, such as clothing and makeup choices

Repetition in color pattern

6

2

## REPETITION IN WAVE PATTERN

**Ovaloid** spacing between finger wave ridges (where the open end is smaller than the closed end) is considered random or odd, producing a more varied and stimulating visual pattern.

The hollow between ridges in this finger wave pattern is repetitively spaced or uniform and therefore considered even-looking and predictable.

# Repetition ...

*In art, as in nature,* creations are artistically arranged in **uneven numbers or sizes.** The common factor is that all things in nature are not equally balanced or proportioned. Each is designed by nature to attract and keep your interest through odd proportions in design elements.

**The human brain tries to find order in chaos.** Examine what happens when people attempt to insert the perfect shape into nature's art. The shape may become too evenly organized in its proportioned elements, creating a design that is repetitious and uninteresting to our brain.

When you take the time to examine a tree, a mountain range or a field of flowers, notice that the **odd proportions and numbers** appearing everywhere in nature are what make them so interesting.

**Odd numbers** and sizes create contrast and excitement, capturing and holding our interest.

**Even numbers** create repetition. Our brain quickly learns what to expect next and loses interest.

1

2

# Harmony . . .

**Harmony** *is the* ***aesthetic placement of shapes and lines.*** *It creates a flow or sense of consistency throughout the entire hairdesign.*

**The theory of harmony** is when **one or more components are synchronized.** Harmony exists if the design is **pleasing to the eye**. The makeup, hair and clothing all complement the client's personality, lifestyle and features.

**The principle of harmony** is used to create a predictable pattern either within a hairdesign or on its surface. The design can be either contrasting or similar. Abrupt changes in rhythm will disrupt the harmony.

1 2 3 4 5 6

6

## Total Look...

**When competing in a "total look" competition, the nail, makeup and hairdesign, along with fashion and body image must all coordinate.**

Examine the designs below, looking for the multiple design patterns, colors, textures and ornamentation that are all working together **harmoniously**. The hair, choice of clothing, makeup, nails and accessories all coordinate to produce an award-winning design.

1

2

### Exercise

Pick a design and list the principles and elements that are utilized to produce harmony in the finished style.

3

4

# Art Principles REVIEW QUESTIONS

## MULTIPLE CHOICE

1. What rate of tempo is caused by a slow rate of motion or speed?
   **A.** decelerated **B.** moderate **C.** accelerated
2. What do blue-based colors invoke?
   **A.** warmth **B.** brightness **C.** coolness
3. Which line extends from opposite corners on a slant providing a feeling of dimension?
   **A.** vertical **B.** horizontal **C.** diagonal
4. How is the face divided using the "Golden Ratio" and graceful proportion?
   **A.** ¼-quarters **B.** ⅓-thirds **C.** ½-halves
5. Which lacing technique uses large subsections of hair that are held at less than a 90° angle?
   **A.** compact **B.** directional **C.** interlocked
6. What three areas are the cranial divisions; the facial, parietal and?
   **A.** occipital **B.** cervical vertebrae **C.** temporal
7. What does facial feature zone one consist of?
   **A.** forehead **B.** eyes and nose **C.** neck and shoulders
8. What is created when dimension is added to a design?
   **A.** spaciousness **B.** flatness **C.** texture
9. Which law of motion states that in every movement there is a second opposite movement?
   **A.** Law One **B.** Law Two **C.** Law Three
10. Which straight shape has three equal sides and angles?
    **A.** triangle **B.** diamond **C.** kite
11. What is the medium used by the hairdesigner to express his or her art?
    **A.** canvas **B.** corkboard **C.** hair
12. When a design is unbalanced and irregularly arranged, it is considered?
    **A.** symmetrical **B.** asymmetrical **C.** harmony
13. Which profile has a receding chin and high hairline?
    **A.** concave **B.** convex **C.** counterbalance
14. What art principle creates excitement and attraction to your work of art?
    **A.** proportion **B.** motion **C.** emphasis
15. Which shape has length, width and depth?
    **A.** one-dimensional **B.** two-dimensional **C.** three-dimensional
16. The four stages of the principles of hairdesign are sketch, scale, set and?
    **A.** sculpt **B.** mold **C.** draw
17. Which hair formation memory is created on a relaxed dry form?
    **A.** wet **B.** dry **C.** directional
18. Which face shape is ideally balanced?
    **A.** square **B.** oval **C.** diamond
19. How many zones are the facial features divided into?
    **A.** three **B.** two **C.** one
20. The two directional movements in hairdesigning are clockwise and?
    **A.** horizontal **B.** counter-clockwise **C.** vertical

STUDENT'S NAME DATE GRADE

brushes consultation

filtration pH

safety

shampoo

treatments

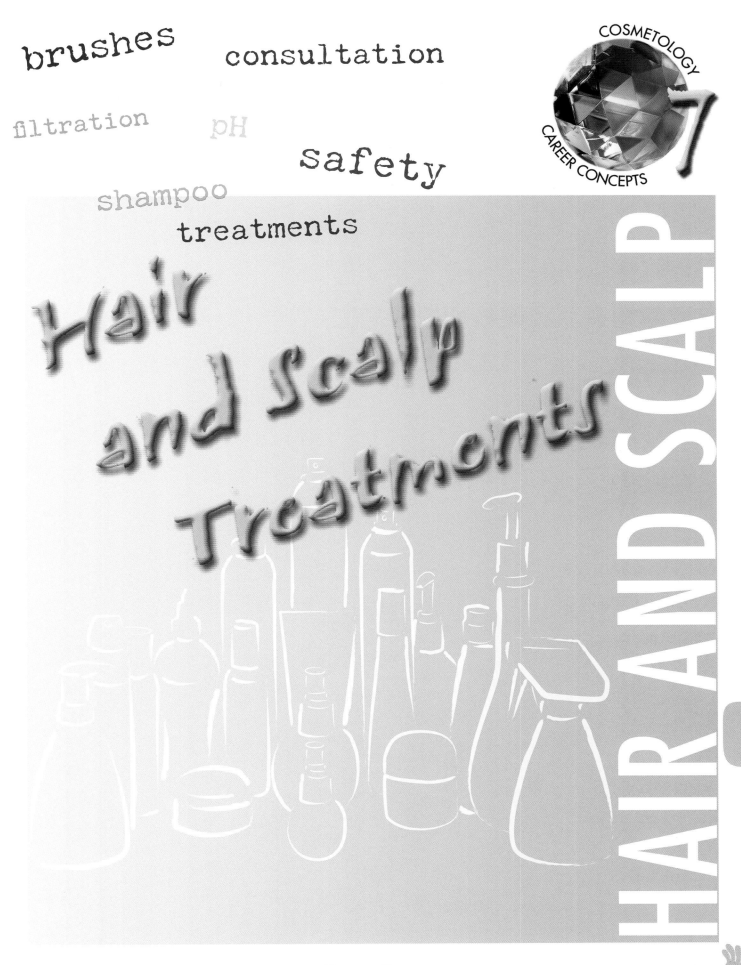

# Hair and Scalp Treatments

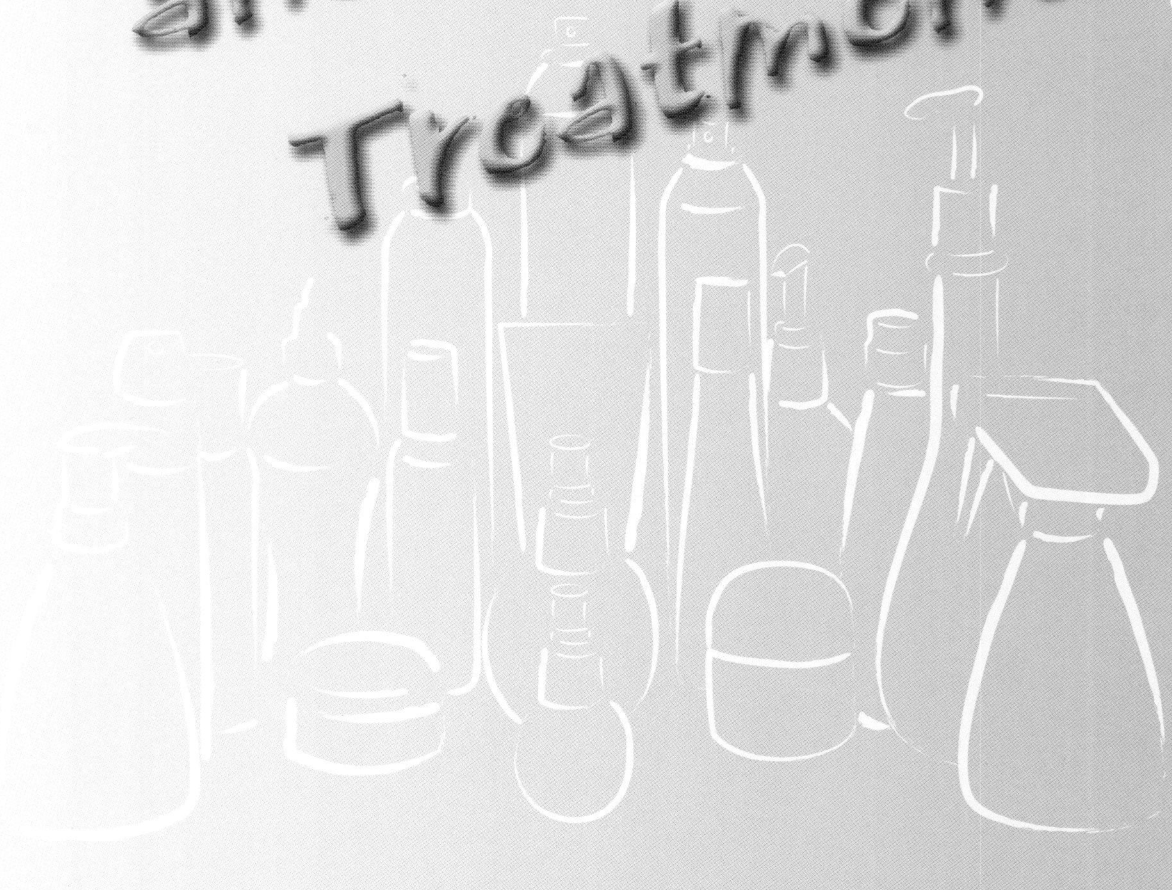

HAIR AND SCALP

7

# Terminology...

*A list of vocabulary words is provided to better acquaint you with this chapter and some of the terms used within this industry.*

ACID

ALKALINE

7 8 9 10 11 12 13 14

**Alkaline** is measurement of 7.1 to 14 on the pH scale.

**Draping** is protecting the client by applying a cape, neck strip and towel.

CLIC INTERNATIONAL

**Humectant** is a moisture retentive ingredient found in conditioners.

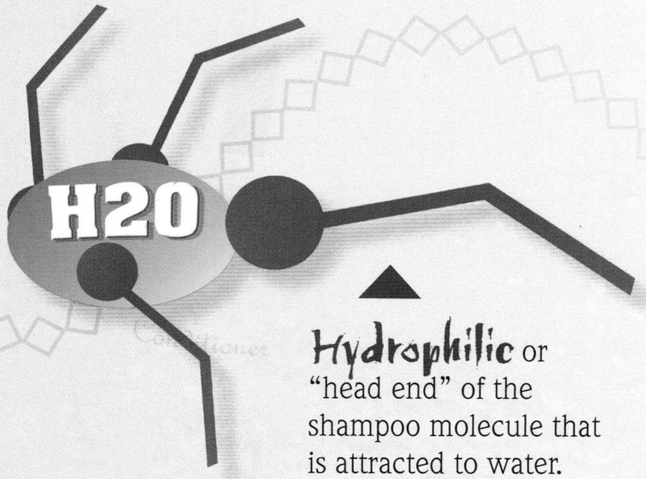

Conditioner

H20

**Hydrophilic** or "head end" of the shampoo molecule that is attracted to water.

**Hygroscopy** is the ability to easily absorb and retain moisture from the environment.

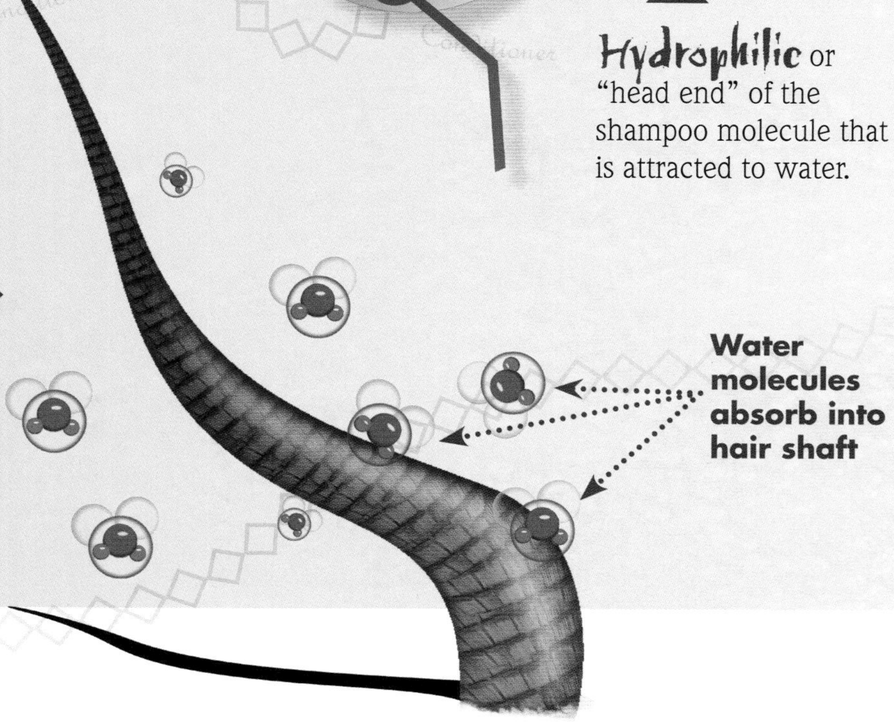

**Water molecules absorb into hair shaft**

7

# Terminology . . .

**Mannequin** is a fabricated head form used for practice and on which to apply practical services during your cosmetology career.

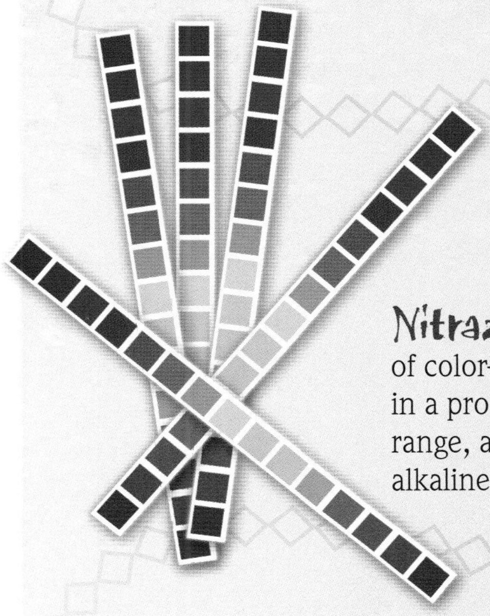

**Nitrazine Paper** is a small strip of color-coded paper that is immersed in a product to determine the pH range, and whether the product is alkaline or acid.

**Shampooing** is the act of cleansing the hair and scalp using a shampoo product.

**Surfactant** is the wetting agent in shampoo that removes dirt from surfaces such as hair.

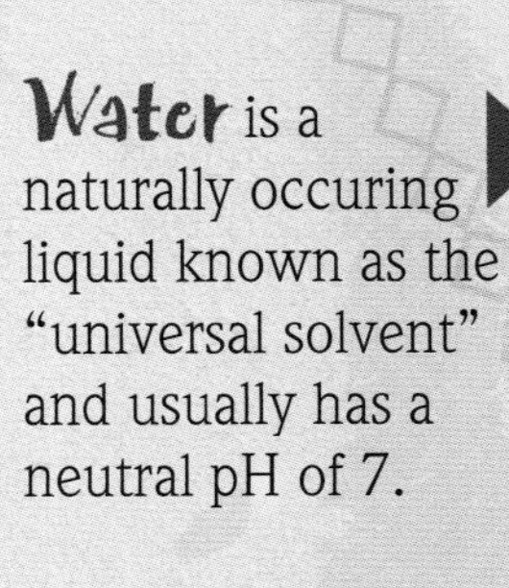

**Water** is a naturally occuring liquid known as the "universal solvent" and usually has a neutral pH of 7.

7

# Safety and Protection . . .

***As part** of your responsibility, safety must come first when servicing your clients to protect them from potential exposure to hair and scalp diseases and/or harm to skin or clothing. Therefore, it is important to provide protective clothing and follow salon sanitation and disinfection guidelines for the health and safety of everyone involved.*

**Capes** are used to cover clients' clothing to protect from damage during hair services. Capes are available in different materials, lengths, widths and colors, and have a variety of closures including Velcro®, hooks, ties and snaps. Most capes are machine washable, but not all are dryer safe. Read manufacturer's instructions prior to use.

**Neck Strips** or towels are wrapped around the client's neck to **prevent skin-to-cape contact.** They also help to catch water or chemical liquids that may possibly escape during service. Neck strips are available in paper or cloth and come in different widths and lengths.

7

"Protecting the client by applying a cape, neck strip, and towel is also referred to as "draping."

# Safety and Protection . . .

**NOTE:** Check with the regulatory agency for required draping in your area.

**1.** Draping for Regular Services (shampooing, haircutting, designing):

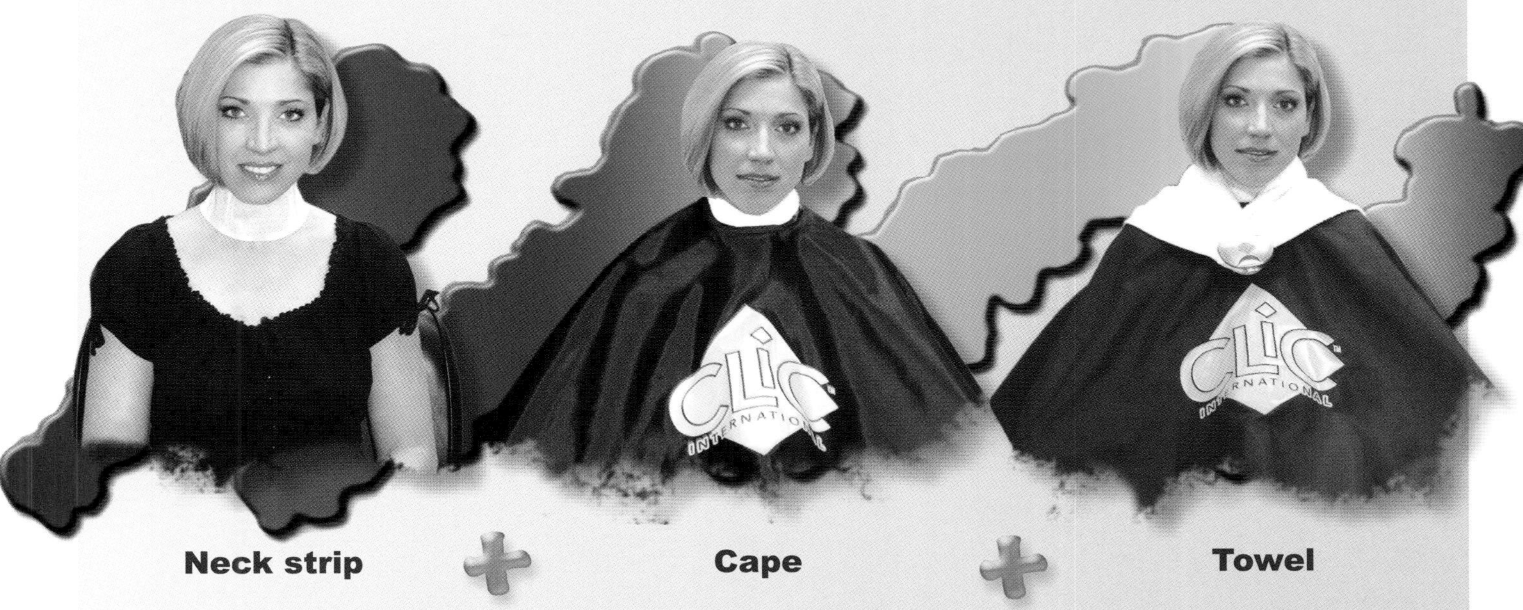


**Neck strip** + **Cape** + **Towel**

**2.** Draping for Chemical Services (permanent waving, chemical relaxing, haircoloring):

**Neck strip** + **Towel** + **Cape** + **Towel**

7

# Safety and Protection . . .

**Cloth Towels** are made from an absorbent washable material and will **prevent skin-to-cape and/or skin-to-skin contact** with service tools or liquid products. Towels are used to remove moisture from hair and dry hands after washing.

**Disposable Towels** made from non-woven fabric provide a **lint-free surface** for placement of tools during service. These towels eliminate the need for laundering and are used as an alternative to the cloth towel. They ensure each client a clean and sanitary service area.

**WARNING**: Some people have allergies or sensitivities to latex. Be sure to ask your clients about this prior to wearing latex gloves before any service.

**Gloves** are manufactured from latex, vinyl or synthetic materials to **protect hands** from stains and chemical sensitivity, and to **ensure client safety.**Gloves are required to be worn for all cosmetology services in many areas.

# Safety and Protection . . .

1

**Robes** are made of a washable material, used for nail and facial services. They provide comfort and allow easy access to the face and neck during massage and makeup application. Sometimes robes are used during chemical services such as color or permanent waving in preventing possible chemical staining of client's clothing.

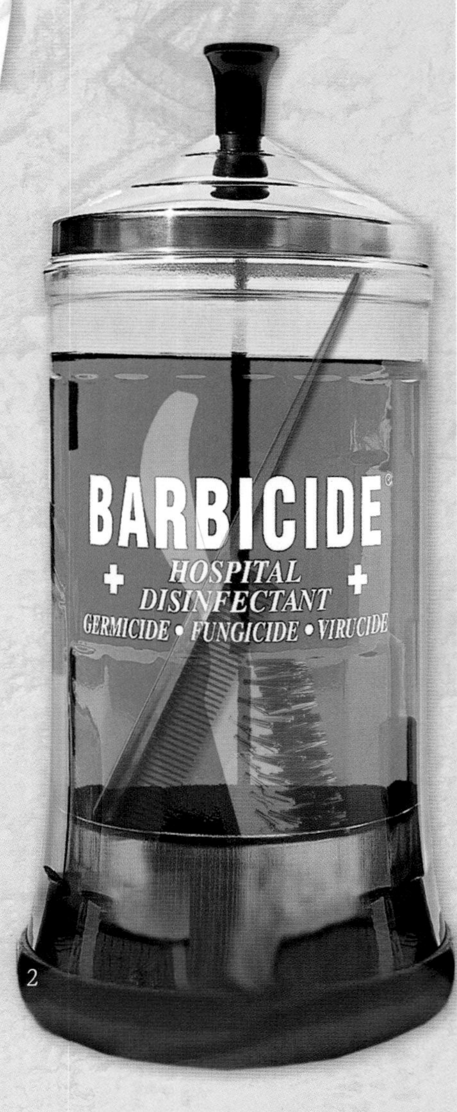

2

**Wet Disinfection System** is a sanitizer used for implements that are exposed to clients' skin or scalp. Tools are **completely immersed** in jars or special containers filled with a disinfectant solution for the allotted time determined by manufacturer's directions. Implements must be cleaned before immersion by removing all hair and using a cleaning solution of soap and water.

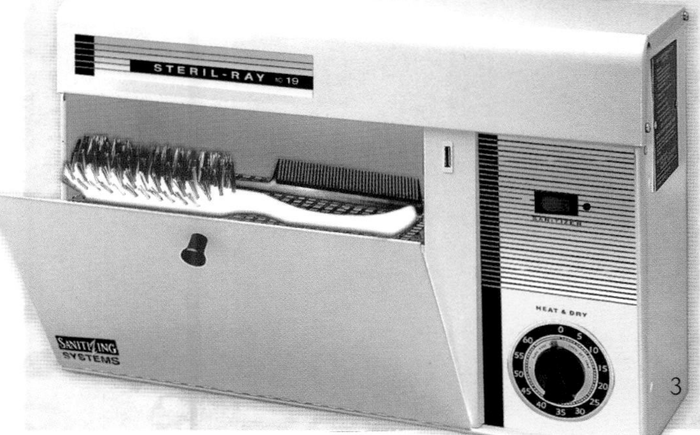

3

**Dry Disinfection System** is a sanitizer cabinet that employs an ultraviolet light where tools are **placed after being cleansed and disinfected** with a commercial solution. This keeps the disinfected combs and brushes sanitary until needed for next service.

# Water . . .

**W**ater is a naturally occuring liquid that is known as the most ***"universal solvent."*** *Water is essential to the existence of a human being. It also plays a* ***very important role*** *in servicing the client in the salon. We use water to shampoo the hair, rinse chemicals from hair such as permanent wave solution, relaxer or color. It is also used for the immersion of hands for a manicure, the feet for a pedicure and we use it to launder our towels.*

**There are two different types of water:**

1. **Hard** water remains unaltered and contains an amount of dissolved minerals such as calcium and magnesium.

2. **Soft** water is treated by removing the dissolved mineral content.

**NOTE:** The term **"impurity"** is used in reference to contaminants (chemicals) or mineral content found within water.

**There are two methods of removing impurities from the water.**

## FILTRATION

is separating water from its mineral substances, such as magnesium, iron, calcium or organic matter. Water passes through a "filter-type trap," encasing **some** minerals or particles therefore producing less contaminated water.

## Softening

is removing the "unfiltered" or dissolved mineral particles that are not eliminated through filtration. This process requires sodium resin beads to replace the calcium and magnesium minerals which are highly responsible for creating the hardness in water; this process is referred to as an **exchange**.

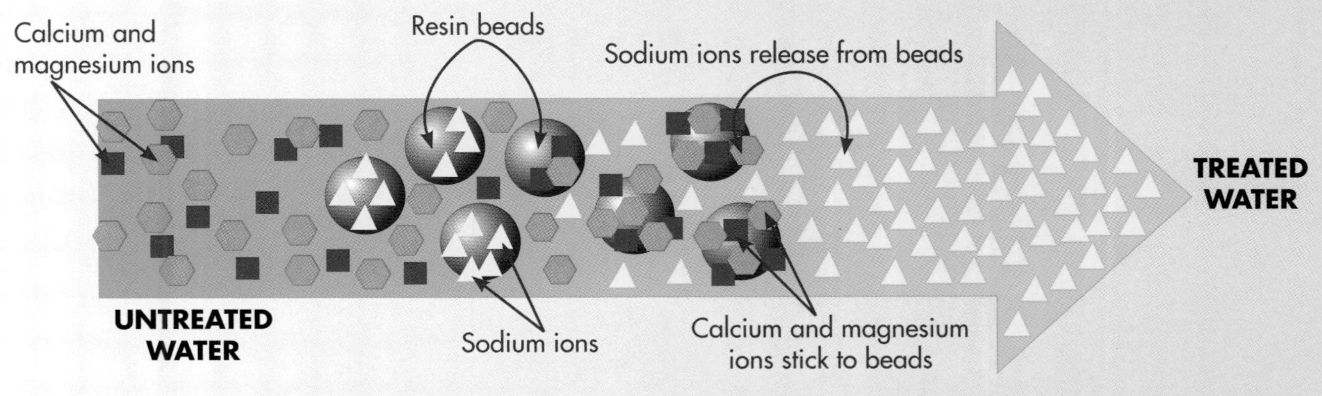

"Most water softening systems consist of a combination of filtration and softening processes to obtain optimum results."

7

**There** are various kinds of large water softening and filtering units designed to service an entire house or business, as well as smaller devices that attach to a faucet at the sink. The extent of mineral content or hardness of water, as well as other impurities will determine which method of water treatment to be installed.

## Some filtration or softening processes are:

**Carbon filters** allow water to pass through a carbon substance absorbing a broad variety of contaminants. This system is compatible with other softening processes.

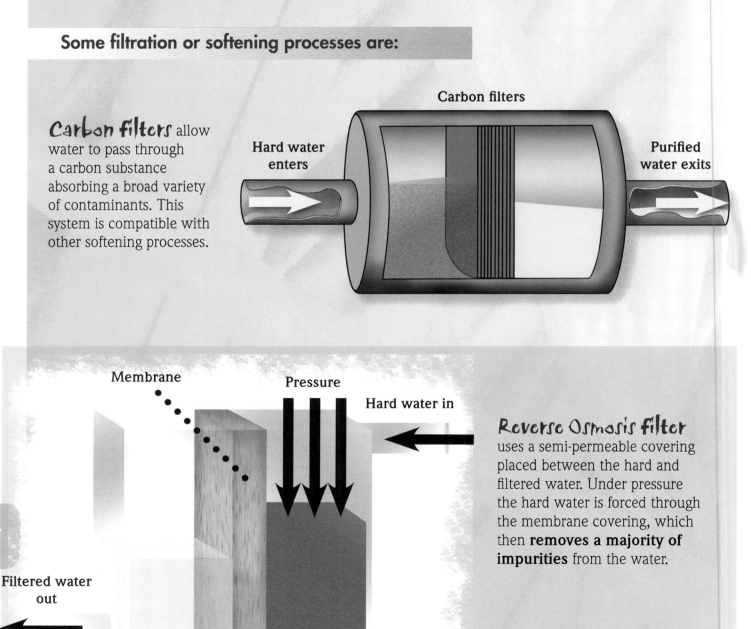

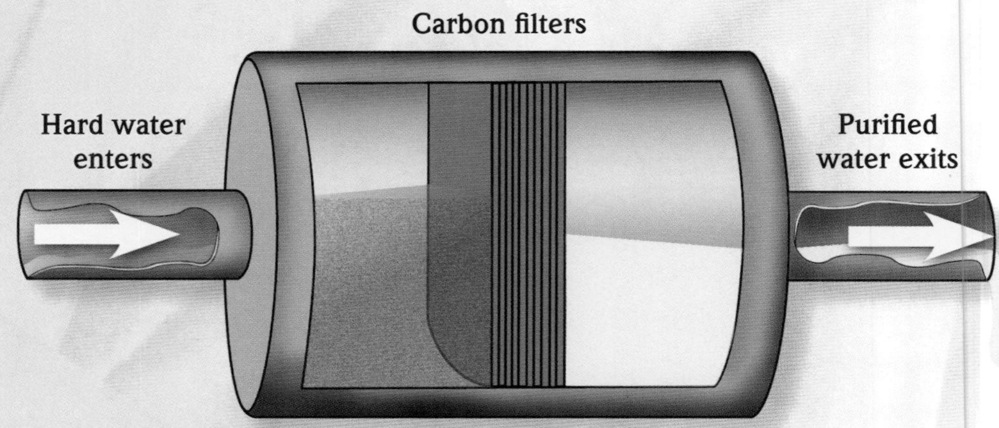


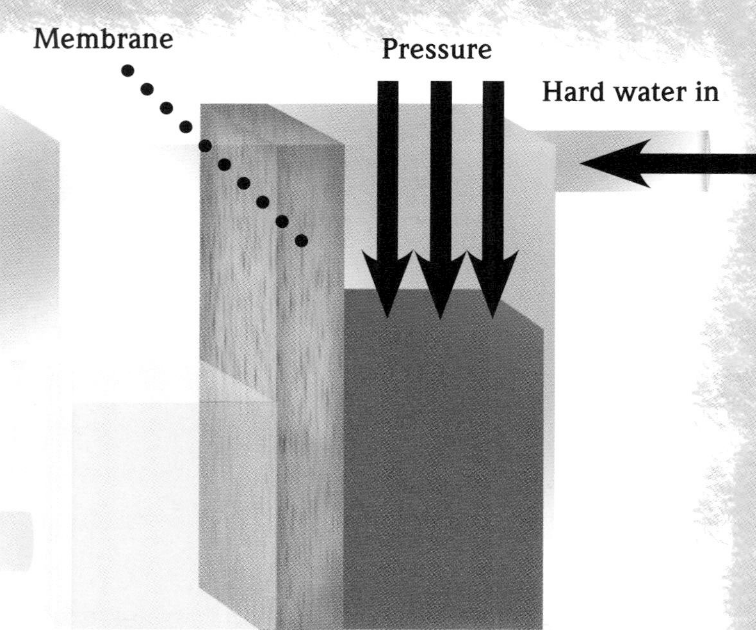


**Reverse Osmosis filter** uses a semi-permeable covering placed between the hard and filtered water. Under pressure the hard water is forced through the membrane covering, which then **removes a majority of impurities** from the water.

7

# Water . . .

**Ion Exchange softening** is infiltrating water through a layer of sodium-covered resin beads. When the water passes through, ions in the water exchange for ions on the beads. Usually this system is used in conjunction with carbon filtration and reverse osmosis.

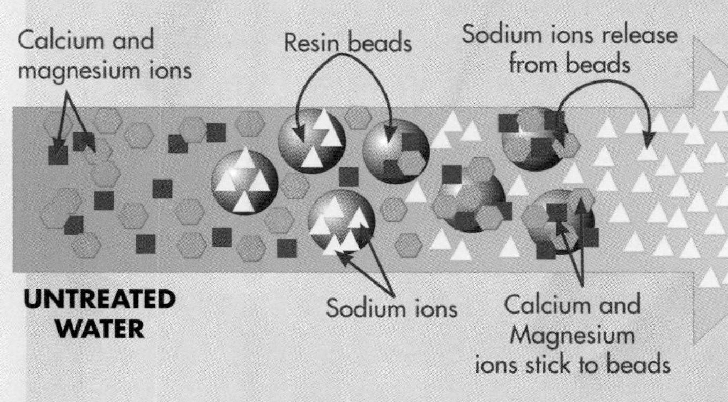


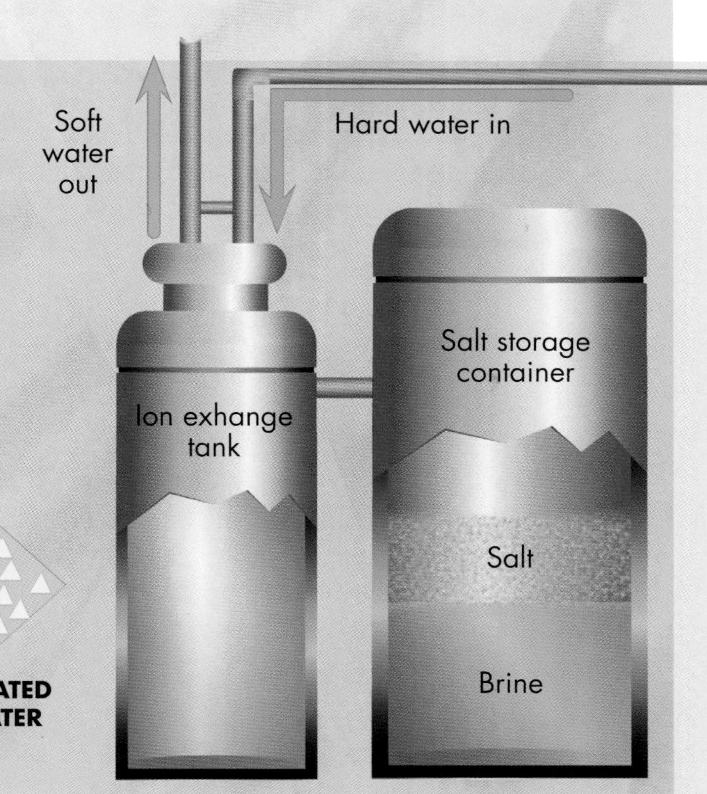


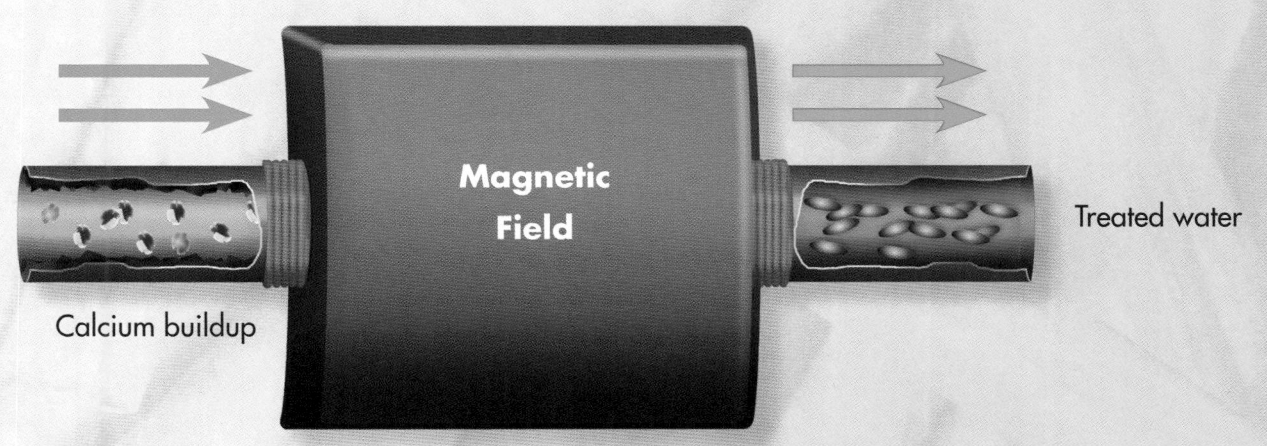


**Electromagnetic water softener** is passing water through a magnetic field, which alters the tendency for the calcium and magnesium in the water to build up on water pipes. This process is a relatively new type of water treatment; always check with manufacturer for best treatment options.

# Shampoo ...

*The main reason for a shampoo service is to* ***cleanse hair and scalp*** *by removing all oils, dirt and product buildup. This experience should be* ***enjoyable and relaxing*** *to the client. The cosmetologist will need to have knowledge in a variety of shampoos available in order to choose the one that will best meet the client's hair-care needs. To understand the many types of shampoos available to us, let us explain the main components of a shampoo.*

Generally to us when shampoo lathers or foams, it indicates that our hair and scalp is being totally cleansed. Actually, we are using an excess of shampoo ... a small amount of lather is all that is needed to ensure accurate coverage of hair and scalp for a thorough cleaning. A concentration of small bubbles in lather will clean better than large bubbles, due to the action of the foam consistency.

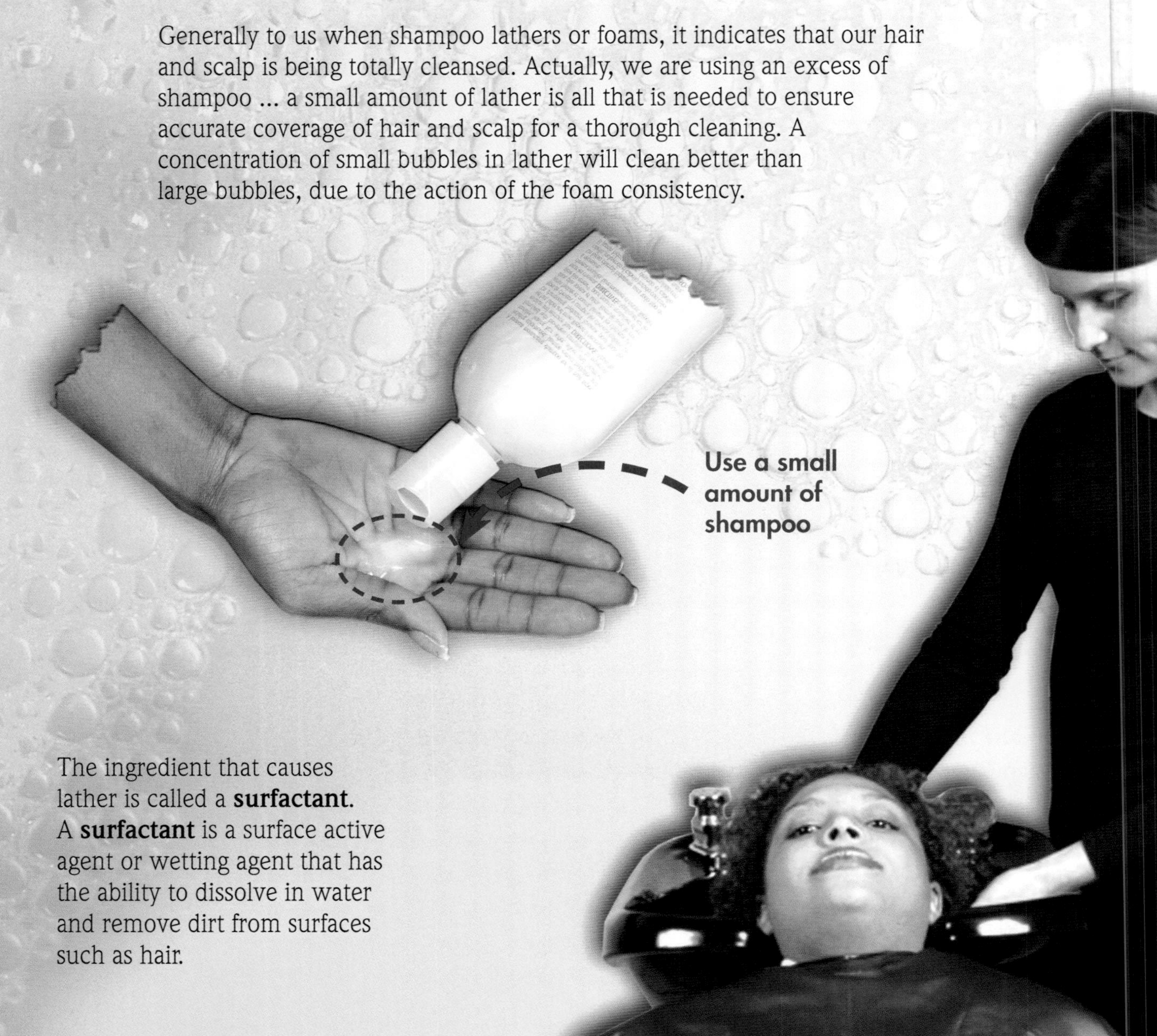
Use a small amount of shampoo

The ingredient that causes lather is called a **surfactant.** A **surfactant** is a surface active agent or wetting agent that has the ability to dissolve in water and remove dirt from surfaces such as hair.

# shampoo . . .

**The four types of surfactants are:**

1. **Anionic** (an-i-on-ik) has a detergent base that is inexpensive, but has excellent deep cleansing abilities and is easily rinsed from the hair.

2. **Cationic** (cat-i-on-ik) removes dirt from the hair shaft, in addition to providing softness and moisture.

3. **Nonionic** (non-i-on-ik) is excellent for deep cleansing and oil removal from scalp.

4. **Amphoteric** (am-fo-terr-ik) surfactants are very mild and compatible with all other surfactants.

Manufacturers formulate using one or a combination of these surfactants along with water to design an endless variety of cleansing products. This allows us to market the best hair-care products according to clients' hair condition and needs.

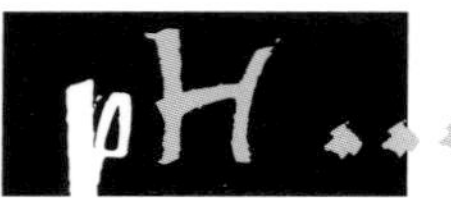


*Awareness about pH of a product will increase your knowledge on cosmetic selection and the importance of using safe professional products that pose no risk to your client's health.*

**Potential Hydrogen** (pH) is the potential amount of hydrogen ions in a solution containing water. **Acidic** solutions contain more hydrogen ions and **alkaline** solutions contain less hydrogen ions. **Acidic products contract and harden hair, and have a sour taste. Alkaline products soften and swell hair, and have a bitter taste.** A solution tested using the **pH scale** will show a range from **0 to 14.** The scale is designed logarithmically, meaning each number on the scale will increase by a multiple of 10.

This scale shows the dramatic increase in acidity or alkalinity when moving from one end of the pH scale to the other. Each number on the pH scale represents an **increase in multiples of 10**; therefore, each number is 10 times more alkaline or acidic than the next number in the sequence ... from **neutral 7 up for alkalinity** and from **neutral 7 down for acidity.**

*When you understand how to maintain proper hair, skin and nail pH levels, you will be able to market the most suitable and safe professional products to the customer for use as home maintenance treatments.*

## pH Color Chart

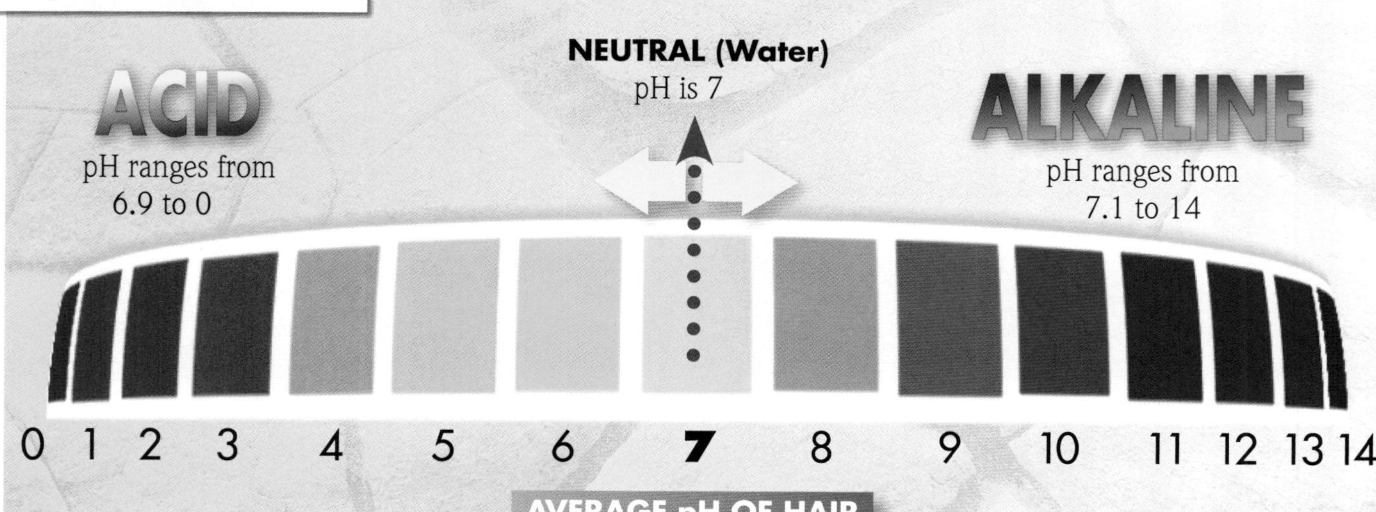


AVERAGE pH OF HAIR & NAILS (4.5-5.5)

# 4.5–5.5

The **natural pH level of hair, skin and nails** range from **pH 4.5 to 5.5**; therefore, the hair and cosmetic products you use should be **designed within the same pH range** for client safety, comfort and reliability. To determine if a product is within this range or low in acidity or high in alkalinity, test with small strips of color-coded **litmus** or **nitrazine paper.** Other pH testing methods are, the pH pencil and pH meter.

## Product Testing:

### Litmus pH paper

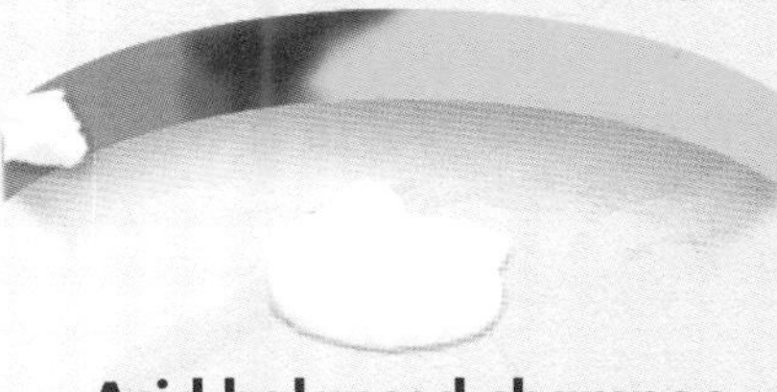

Acid balanced shampoo

**Litmus pH paper** – immerse paper into product. If paper turns blue, product is alkaline; if paper turns red, product is acid.

**Nitrazine pH paper** – immerse paper into product, wait 30 seconds. Color of paper can range from orange to dark purple. Using the color chart provided, compare the tested paper against the color on the chart to determine the pH of product.

### Nitrazine pH paper

Relaxer

**NOTE:** pH will fluctuate depending on the manufacturer and the various types of ingredients added to the products.

## The following examples indicate the pH ranges of hair service products:

- **Hydrogen peroxide** – pH 2.5 to 4.5
- **Hair conditioner** – pH 3.5 to 6.0
- **Acid balanced shampoo** – pH 4.5 to 5.5
- **Permanent wave** – pH 7.5 to 8.5
- **Powder lightener** – 10.5
- **Relaxer** – pH 13

"Always test products to determine the pH. It is important to your customer's hair condition and safety."

# Types of Shampoo . . .

*Shampooing is the act of cleansing the hair and scalp using a shampoo product. The amount of times or how often you shampoo is dependent upon how quickly your hair and scalp get dirty. The influx of cosmetic marketing along with the competitive professional image has created shampoos to be the* ***highest dollar expenditure*** *in hair-care products. There are thousands of shampoos to choose from; the* ***consumer is relying*** *on the cosmetologist to* ***recommend*** *the best shampoo for his or her hair and scalp. Below is a list of the main types of shampoos according to hair type and condition.*

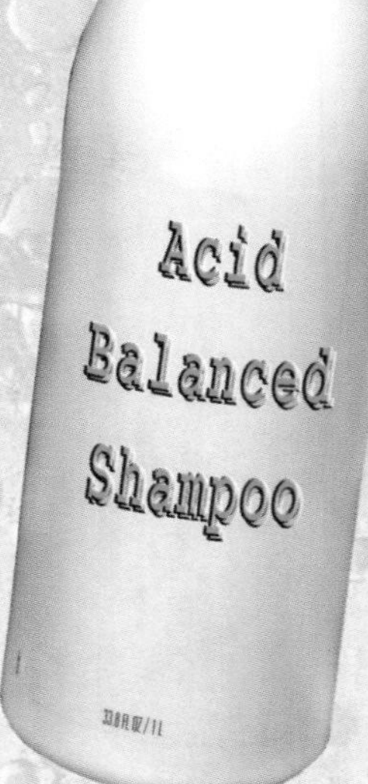


**Clarifying shampoos** are **deep cleansing** to break down product buildup. They are used either once a week or once every two weeks depending on the amount of products used daily on the hair and the hair strands' porosity.

**Acid Balanced shampoos** are generally formulated to maintain **a healthy pH of 4.5 to 5.5** for hair and skin. This shampoo prevents moisture loss from hair and assists in closing the cuticle.

**Medicated shampoos** usually contain an **anti-microbic ingredient** such as zinc or selenium sulphide to remedy dandruff or other scalp condition. These shampoos can be medically prescribed, retailed or recommended by a cosmetologist depending on severity of scalp condition. Medicated shampoos are **stronger** and may be alternated with an acid balanced or conditioning shampoo to prevent hair dryness. Refer to a medical care professional for any long-term scalp conditions.

# Types of Shampoo ...

**Conditioning shampoos** contain moisture and protein agents, which help restore elasticity and strength to hair and provide volume.

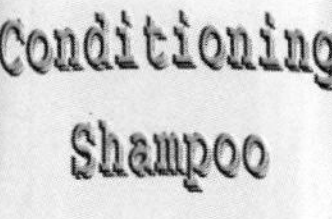

**Color shampoos** refresh, brighten or add a slight color change to the hair. They contain a surfactant with some basic color ingredients.

**Dry shampoos** are used for the clients with a head injury or illness that requires them to be bedridden. Sometimes the elderly require a dry shampoo if they are physically unable to rest their head in a shampoo bowl. This shampoo is either manufactured in a spray or powder form and applied on hair, then brushed through.

***The hair-care products used during a salon visit should be marketed for a home maintenance program. Suggestion: Offer a free "trial size" conditioner with the purchase of a shampoo.***

# How Shampoo Works . . .

## How do the hair and scalp get clean?

**Water** is usually listed as the **first ingredient** with a **surfactant being second** on the list. This means that the product contains more water with second highest being the cleansing agent.

The surfactant contains molecules composed of a **head end** called **hydrophilic** (hi-drah-fil-ik) or **"water-loving"** and **tail end** called **lipophilic** (li-puh-fil-ik) or **"dirt-loving."**

# How Shampoo Works . . .

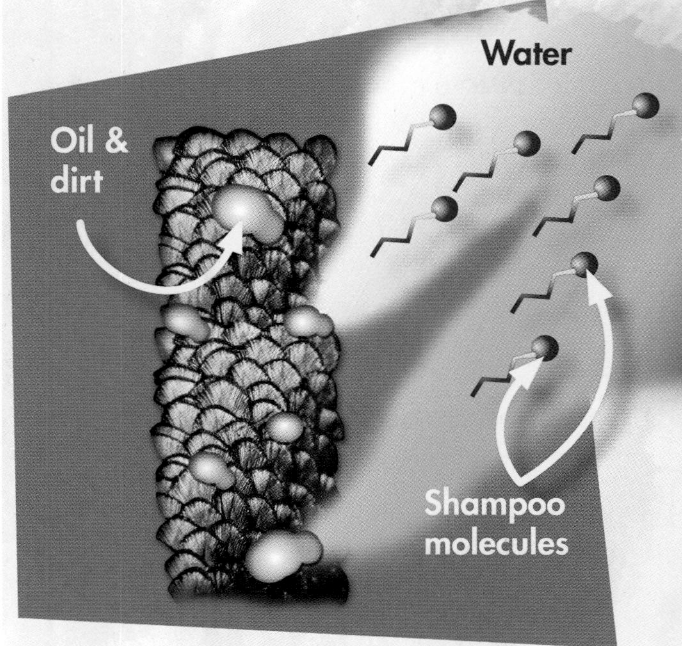


Apply shampoo to wet hair and **massage into hair and scalp.**

When this massage movement is enforced, the **tail end of the molecule attaches to the dirt, oil or product buildup.**

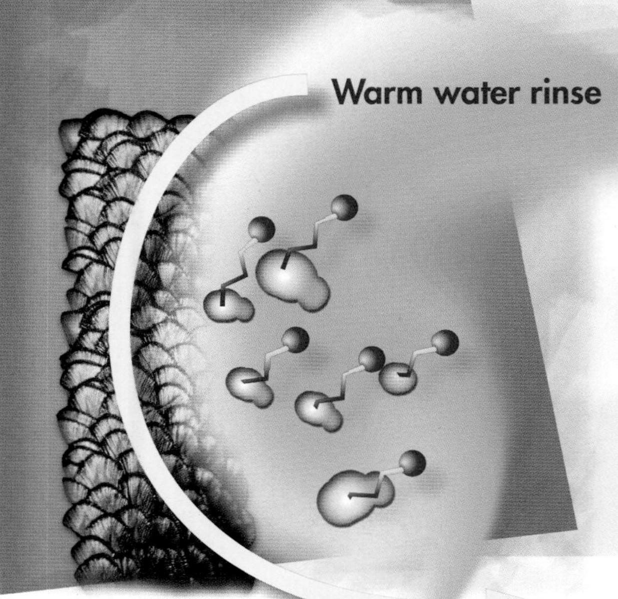


Upon rinsing shampoo out of hair, the tail end of the **molecule's head end attaches to water**, thereby forcing the shampoo out of the hair and pulling the dirt along with it down the drain.

# Conditioners . . .

*At the completion of a hair and scalp cleansing, a **conditioner** is usually applied to assist in **manageability, restore moisture or protein and/or close the cuticle of the hair.** Some types of conditioners put a temporary coating over the cuticle, while others provide deep penetration of moisture or protein to assist in hair renewal. Conditioners enhance strength and shine, and minimize damage to hair shaft.*

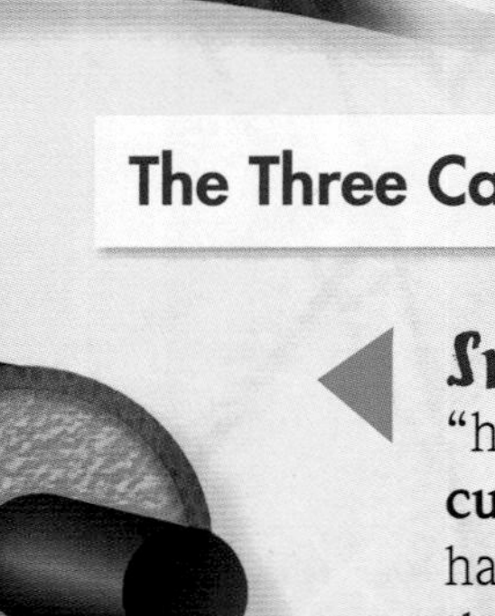

## The Three Categories of Conditioners are:

**Surface conditioners**, sometimes referred to as "hair rinses" **eliminate friction and help to flatten the cuticle.** This type of conditioner is combed through the hair after the shampoo to ensure complete coverage. It is then immediately rinsed, leaving a light coating over the hair shaft providing ease in detangling hair.

**Moisturizers** are conditioners containing the **moisture retention ingredient, humectant** (hu-meck-tent). A humectant has **hygroscopic** properties of absorbing and retaining moisture. These heavy, cream conditioners stay on the hair longer (10 to 20 minutes) for improved penetration into the cuticle. Disinfectants such as quaternary ammonium compounds (quats) may also be among the ingredients in a moisturizing conditioner to assist in providing hair shaft protection.

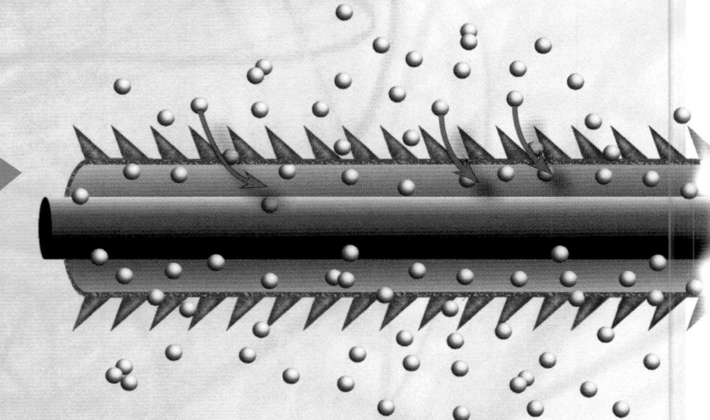

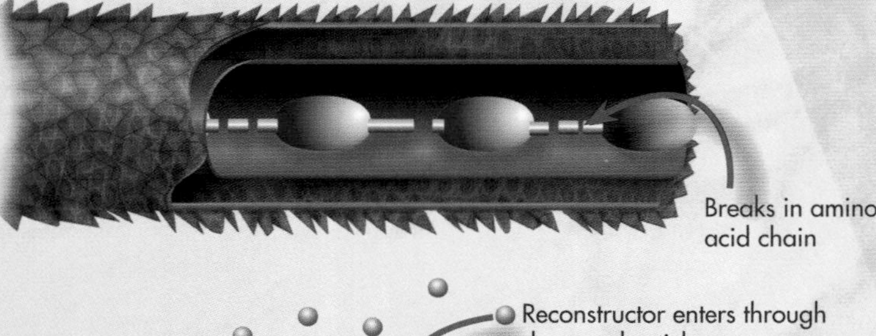
Breaks in amino acid chain

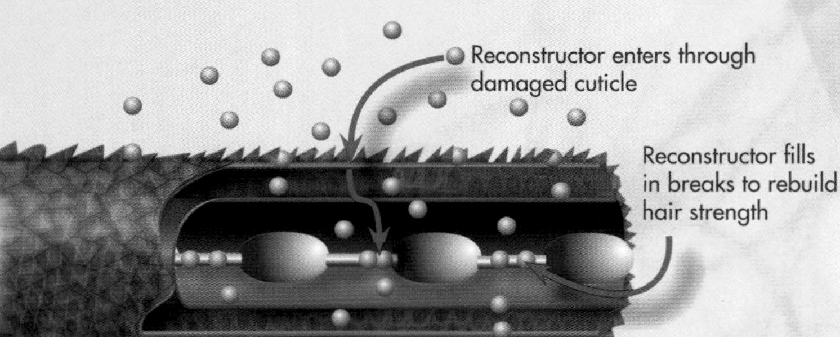
Reconstructor enters through damaged cuticle
Reconstructor fills in breaks to rebuild hair strength

**Reconstructors** (re-con-struct-ors) are **deep penetrating** conditioners incorporating technological advances that enable **rebuilding the amino acid structure** within the hair. Because amino acids are molecular and so small in size, this product is able to penetrate in the cortex. Reconstructors are left on the hair for an average of 10 to 20 minutes depending on the manufacturer's instructions.

# Conditioners . . .

New products are continuously being produced to accommodate every possible hair-care need – whether it is restoring hair to a normal pH after receiving a chemical service or creating shine to the hair by closing the cuticle. **Listed below are other types of conditioners.**

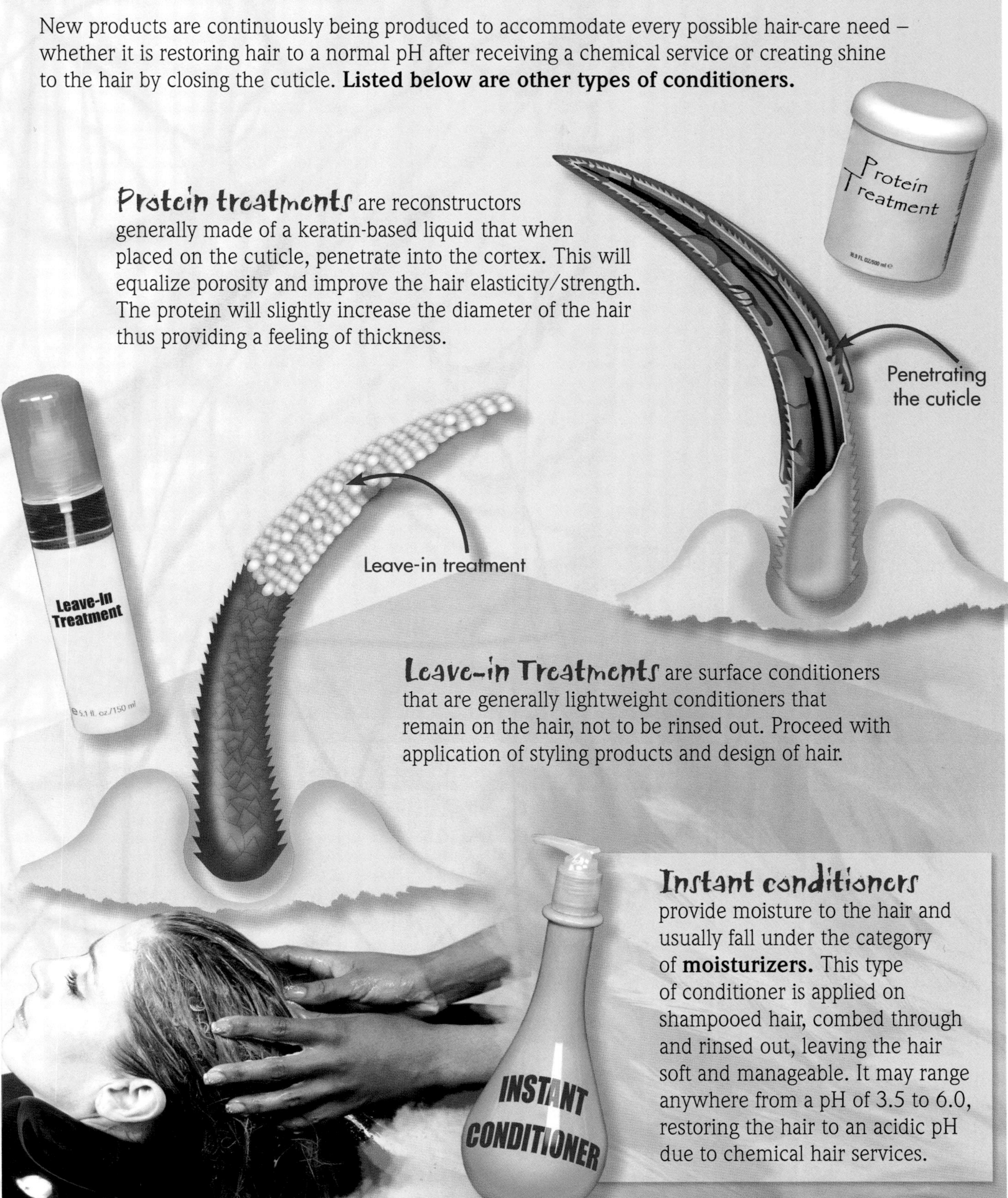


**Protein treatments** are reconstructors generally made of a keratin-based liquid that when placed on the cuticle, penetrate into the cortex. This will equalize porosity and improve the hair elasticity/strength. The protein will slightly increase the diameter of the hair thus providing a feeling of thickness.

**Leave-in Treatments** are surface conditioners that are generally lightweight conditioners that remain on the hair, not to be rinsed out. Proceed with application of styling products and design of hair.

**Instant conditioners** provide moisture to the hair and usually fall under the category of **moisturizers.** This type of conditioner is applied on shampooed hair, combed through and rinsed out, leaving the hair soft and manageable. It may range anywhere from a pH of 3.5 to 6.0, restoring the hair to an acidic pH due to chemical hair services.

# Basic Work Station . . .

*In preparing for a hair service, a proper work station setup is essential in providing an organized and detailed procedure, which will ensure a superior hair service delivery. Every tool will be at arm's reach for each step of the procedure.*

Prior to setup of the hair service tools, always disinfect the surface of your station. A clean and sanitary work station is a reflection of you. As a professional you are establishing that first impression of concern for the client's safety, health and well-being.

RA

***Follow guidelines for sanitation and disinfection set up by the regulatory agency.***

# Basic Work Station ...

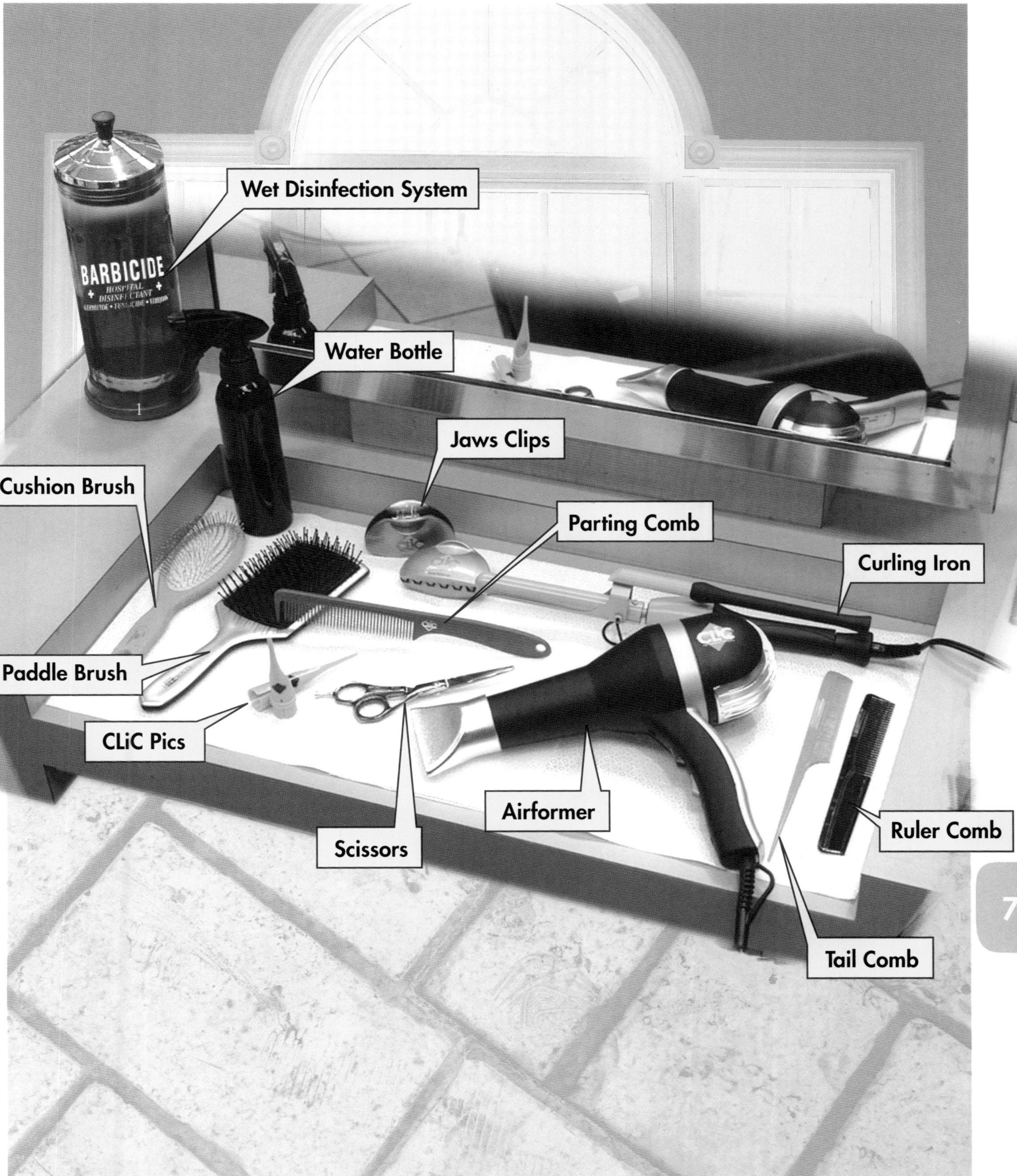

Wet Disinfection System
Water Bottle
Jaws Clips
Cushion Brush
Parting Comb
Curling Iron
Paddle Brush
CLiC Pics
Airformer
Scissors
Ruler Comb
Tail Comb

# Tail Comb Usage . . .

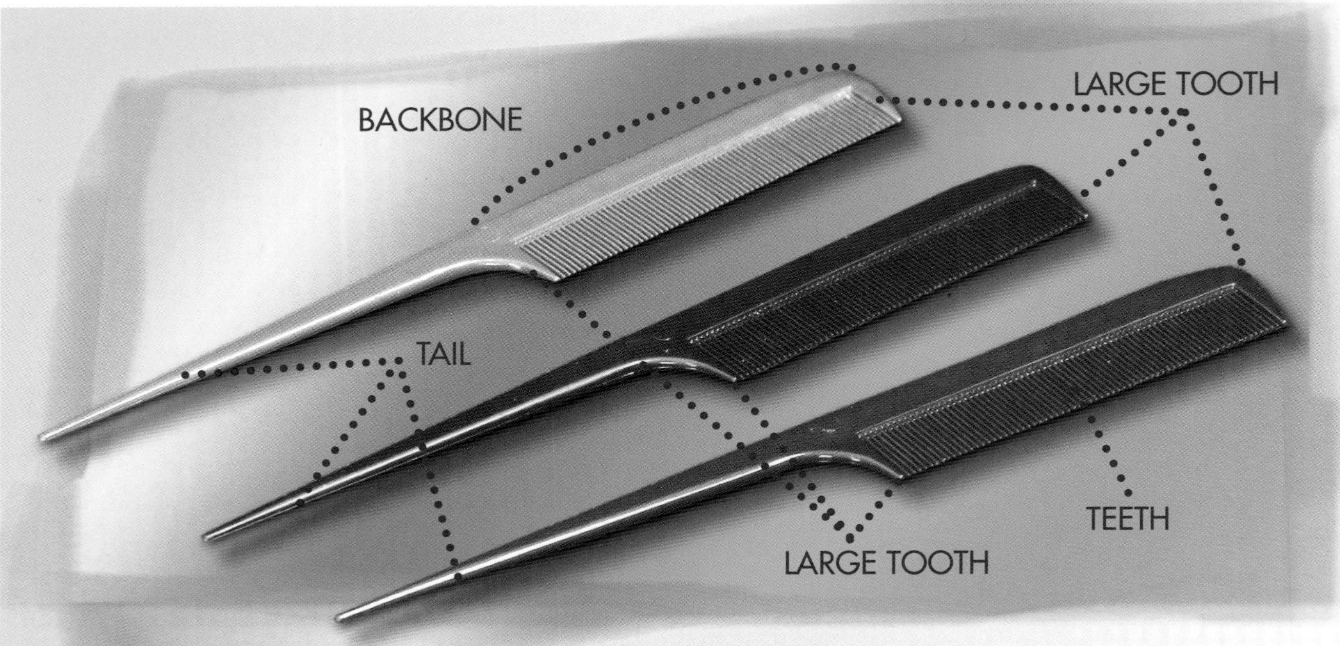


***The tail comb** is sometimes referred to as a **rattail comb** and is a very useful tool for the cosmetologist. It is used to part through hair when dividing into sections, subsectioning hair for scalp treatment brushing or for placement of perm rods in a permanent wave procedure. A tail comb varies in design according to each manufacturer and is available in different sizes and teeth configurations.*

**Placement: Comb stays in hand at all times.** Place between thumb and tips of index and middle fingers when in use. When not using comb, place in webbing of thumb.

**Control:** Practice holding comb while manipulating with different service tools such as, water bottle, perm rods, end papers or coloring brush.



### Key Elements:

 Tail combs make clean, precise partings

 Lightweight and durable

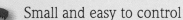

Small and easy to control

"The tail comb is an overall important tool used within the industry due to its precision in parting and controlling the hair."

# Tail Comb Dynamics ...

## SECTIONING

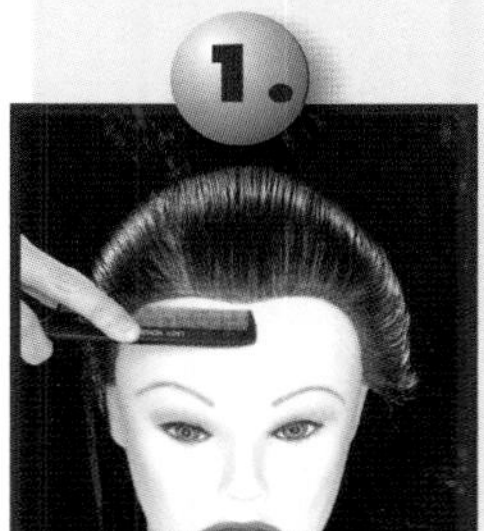
1. Center comb at front hairline.

2. Slide comb straight back.

3. Separate hair at parting and comb hair down over sides of head.

4. Center parting.

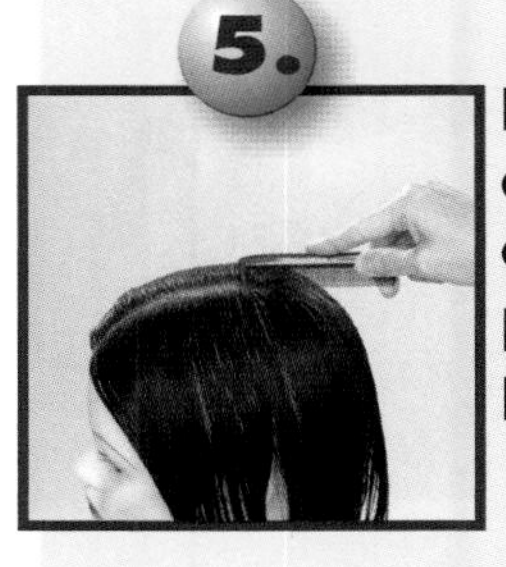
5. Place comb at control point of parting.

6. Slide comb down to high point of ear.

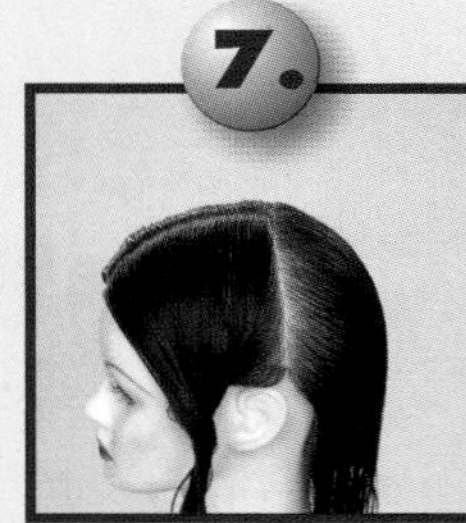
7. Completed side section; repeat on opposite side of head.

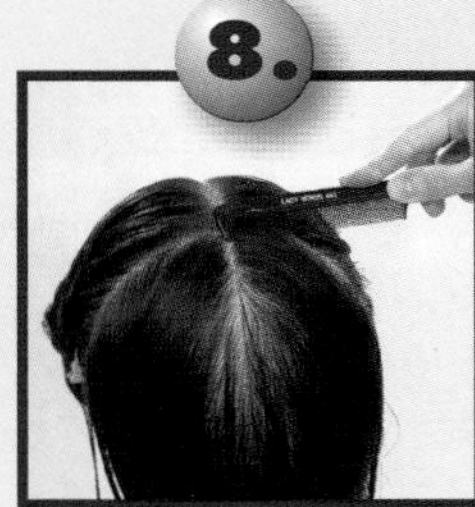
8. Place comb at control point of parting.

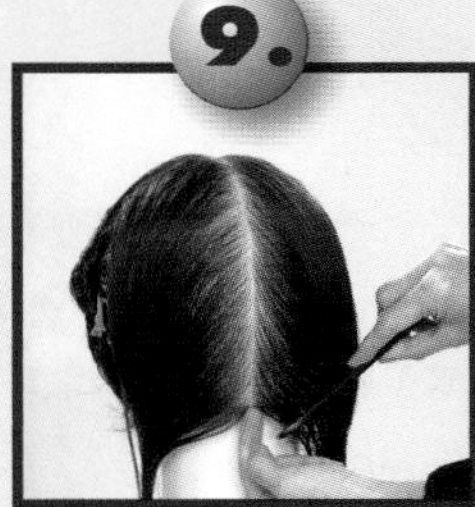
9. Slide comb down to center of nape creating the two back sections.

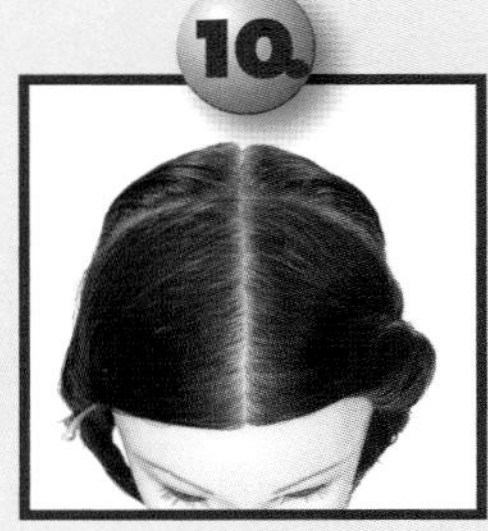
10. Completed four sections.

## SUBSECTIONING

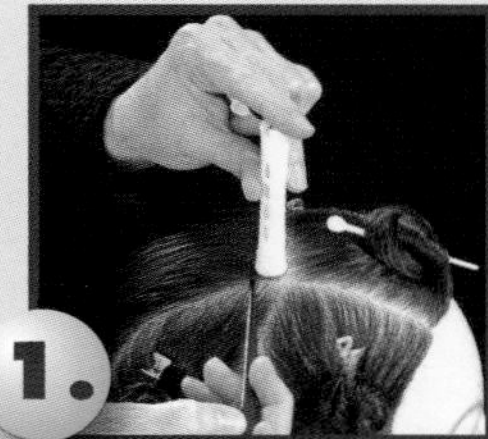
1. Diameter of tool (perm rod, roller, curling iron, etc) rests along vertical parting of section with placement tail of comb at bottom side of tool.

2. Slide comb underneath hair to opposite side of section.

3. Lift and draw comb away from scalp underneath hair.

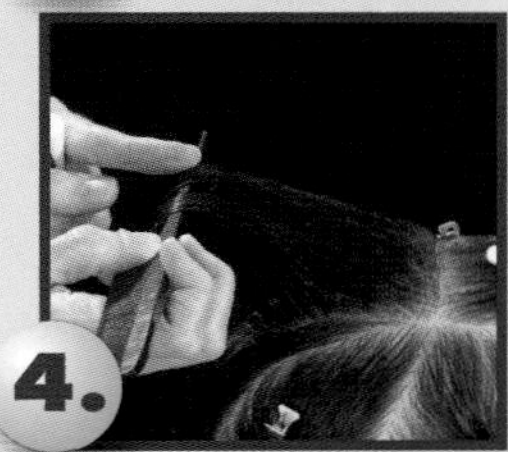
4. Slide fingers along top of comb to gather hair.

5. Gather and hold subsection of hair.

6. Separate hair subsection from comb by elevating the hair with fingers.

7. Completed subsection of hair.

7

# Brush Usage . . .

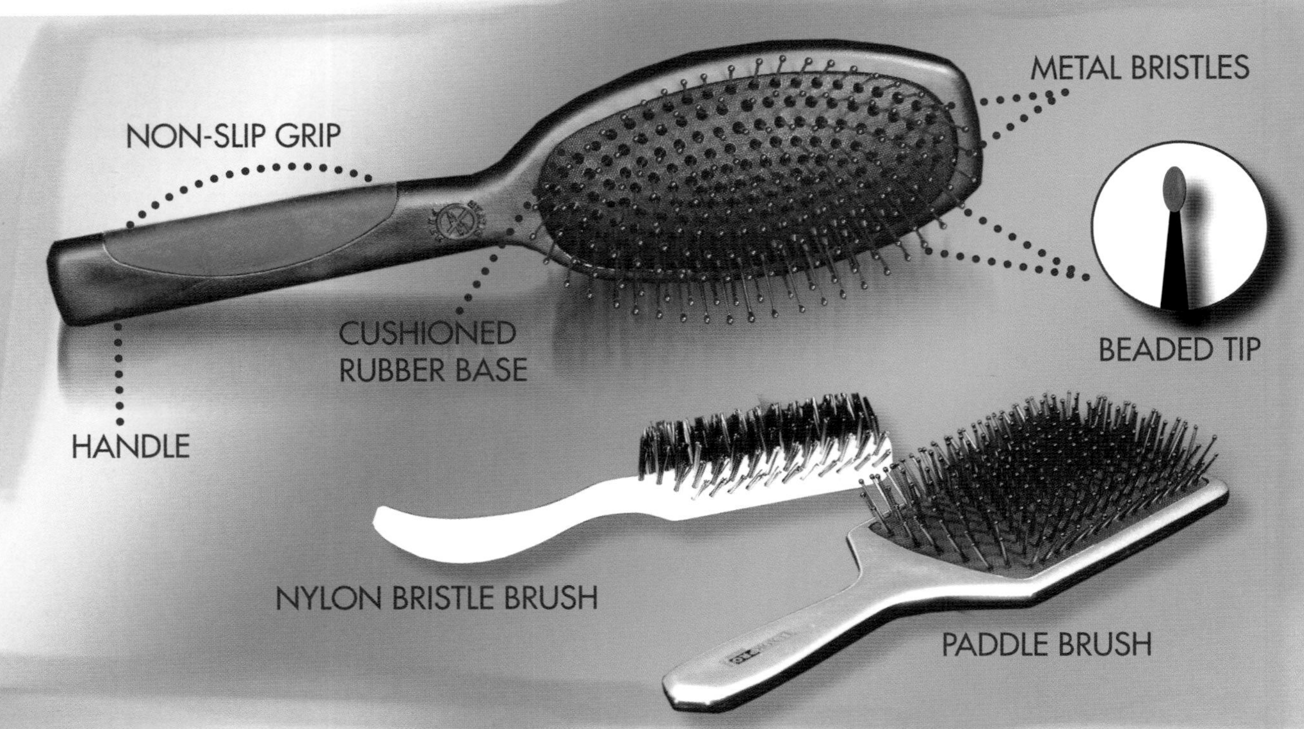


***Brushes** are highly versatile and are manufactured in various sizes. The bristles may come in nylon, boar, metal or a combination.* ***Nylon or boar bristles*** *may be used during a consultation/hair and scalp analysis to help relax the old hairdesign, loosening dirt or debris from hair or scalp prior to shampooing. The* ***metal bristles*** *will help to detangle hair after shampooing and eliminate static electricity when brushing dry hair.*

**CAUTION:** DO NOT BRUSH prior to a chemical service or if scalp is irritated due to scalp sensitivity; comb through hair to perform your analysis.

**Placement:** Insert bristles of brush at hair base using a 135-degree angle with bristles facing you. Roll brush allowing all bristles to smooth through hair. Brush entire hair shaft from base to ends.

**Control:** Hold the brush firmly in your dominant hand. Rotate your wrist slightly as you brush the hair. Hold subsection of hair at a 135-degree angle with your free hand.

7

## Key Elements:

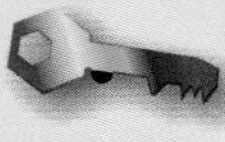

Cushion brushes act like shock absorbers. They are gentle on hair by avoiding friction thus hair breakage

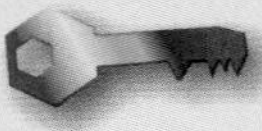

Boar or nylon bristles are best when used to prepare hair for analysis, detangling and shampooing

Brushes range in varying sizes and designs

# Brush Dynamics . . .

## ANALYSIS (relaxing design)

**1.** Place brush at outer perimeter of design.

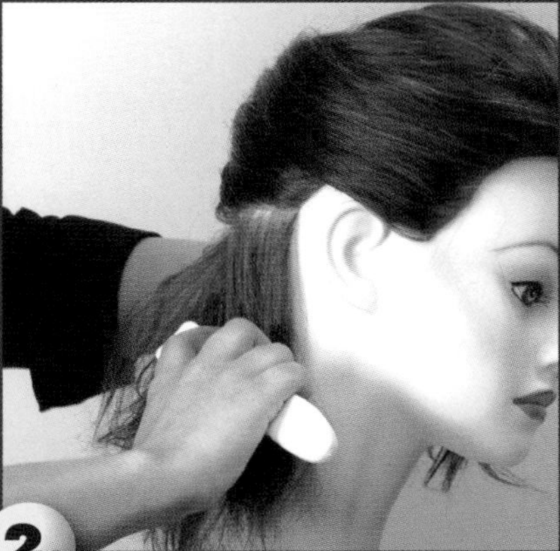

**2.** Brush through design.

**3.** Move up toward top of design.

## SUBSECTION BRUSHING (scalp treatments)

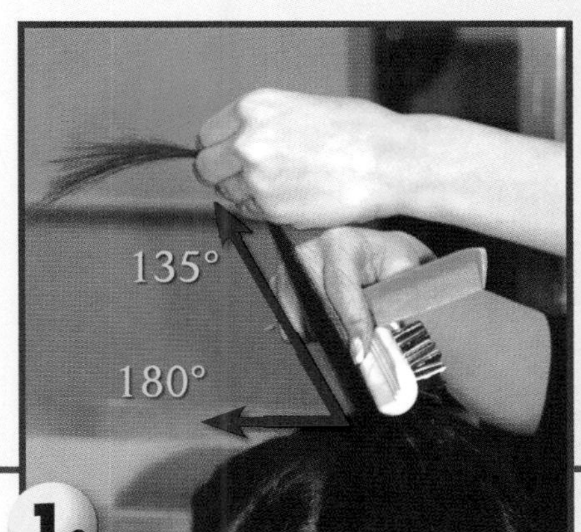


**1.** Hold subsection of hair at a 135-degree angle; insert brush on underside of subsection with bristles facing you.

**2.** Rotate brush until bristles are facing outward.

**3.** Continue to smooth through hair toward the ends.

## DETANGLING (after shampoo)

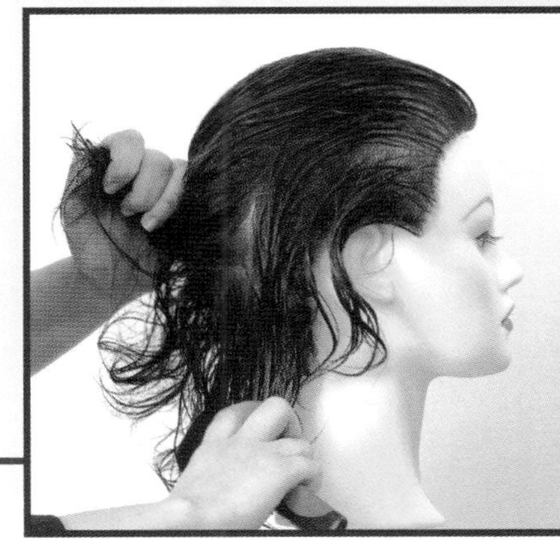

Place brush at hair ends.

Lightly tap brush through hair ends (no pulling), moving up hair shaft towards scalp.

7

# CLiC Mannequin...

*Most of the practical work performed during your cosmetology education will be on a **fabricated head form – a mannequin.** Mannequins do not complain, they do not talk back, they are patient, long suffering and they provide you with endless opportunity for practice and self improvement.*

## Your CLiC mannequin is your first client!

The mannequin head may be small, medium or large size. Medium size heads are the best for practicing most hairdressing skills. The solid portion of the mannequin may be plaster, rubber, plastic or various synthetic materials. It may have a heavy solid base, or it may terminate at the neck and fit on a metal or plastic swivel holder. Your CLiC mannequin has the finest 100 percent human hair. Once the hair is damaged, broken off or cut, it will never replace itself.

Because a CLiC mannequin is a valuable purchase, give your mannequin the best of care every time you use it. In fact, **"Treat it like a client."** As with all clients, you would not scald them with hot water, splash water over their face, or pull their hair unnecessarily. Nor would you flood them with styling aids, let your clients sit under the dryer for long periods of time, or over bleach their hair. You would not give an overprocessed permanent wave, lay them down on their nose, write or draw all over their neck/face, or carelessly drop them. As with all good clients, they **deserve the best treatment** you can give.

**Do not work on a cold mannequin**. The hair may become somewhat dry and brittle. The cold will cause the hair to break easily if it is brushed or combed roughly (especially curly hair). Room temperature is ideal.

If the hair becomes tangled or snarled, remove the tangles by combing the hair gently with a large tooth shampoo comb or a cushioned wire brush. **Start at the nape** and **gently comb through the hair** using thin sections. Remove tangles carefully as you work towards the top of head, combing or brushing the hair straight and smooth.

"CLiC mannequins are made with the highest quality 100 percent human hair."

7

# Care of Mannequin . . .

The mannequin must be shampooed whenever the hair becomes soiled. Usually two (2) students work together; one shampoos the mannequin and one student holds mannequin.

1. Remove any tangles by combing or brushing carefully.
2. Place the CLiC mannequin face up in the groove of the shampoo bowl while holding her in place with the left hand. Optional: another student holds mannequin.
3. Adjust the water pressure and temperature while holding the hose nozzle down in the sink. **Never use hot water** as this may cause the hair to tangle. Only use water at a lukewarm temperature.
4. Manipulate the hose with the right hand (if left handed, use left hand), and saturate the hair thoroughly with lukewarm water.
5. Apply a small amount of acid balanced shampoo into the palm of your hand.
6. Distribute the shampoo through the hair from the hairline down to the scalp and out through the hair ends. **Do not manipulate the hair in a back-and-forth motion.** This may cause the hair to tangle.
7. Rinse the hair **thoroughly** with lukewarm water to remove all traces of the shampoo.
8. Apply conditioner to the hair and work it through the hair in the same manner as you did the shampoo. Gently distribute the conditioner through the hair using a large-tooth comb. Allow the conditioner to remain on the hair for at least three minutes and then rinse again with slightly **cooler** water.
9. Squeeze the excess water from the hair and towel blot. To prevent tangling, **do not rub the hair.** Take the damp towel and clean the face and neck of the mannequin.
10. Wrap a clean towel around the CLiC mannequin and return to your work station. Do not allow water to drip onto the floor or over your work area. To prevent a slippery floor, place a towel on the floor beneath where you are working.
11. Detangle the mannequin's hair and comb it straight down in preparation for any practical service.

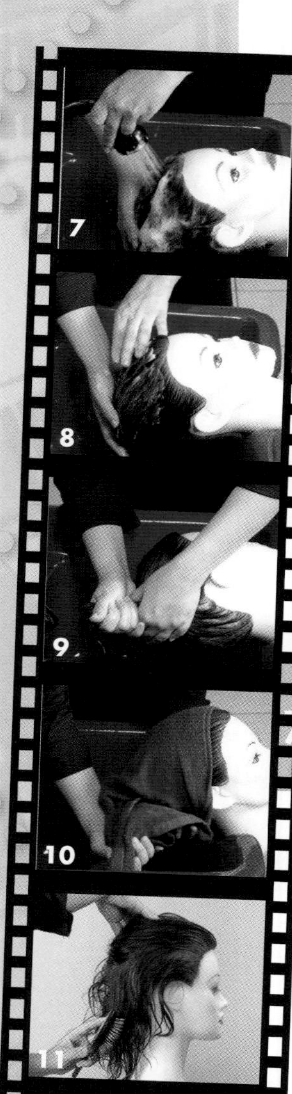

# Mannequin Stand Usage ...

**To safely** ensure longevity, reliability and performance from the CLiC adjustable tabletop mannequin stand, please follow the instructions listed below.

## Proper removal will not damage the table surface or the CLiC mannequin stand.

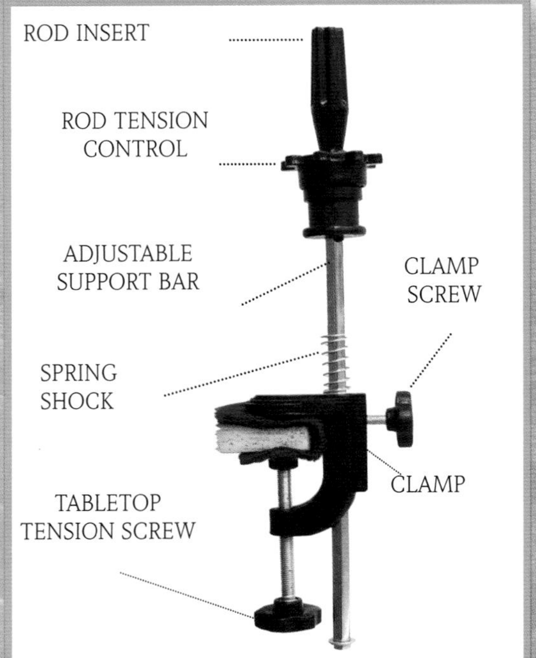

**Step 1:**
Firmly grasp the mannequin at neck with both hands. **<u>Gently</u> use a twisting motion, moving mannequin from left to right while pulling upward.** This will release the vacuum suction between the mannequin and clamp.

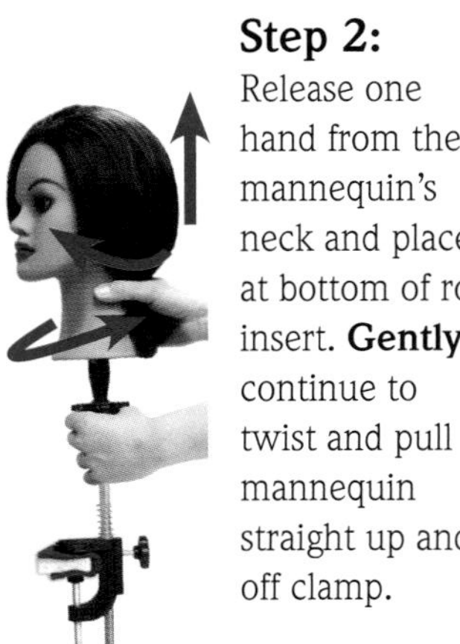

**Step 2:**
Release one hand from the mannequin's neck and place at bottom of rod insert. **Gently** continue to twist and pull mannequin straight up and off clamp.

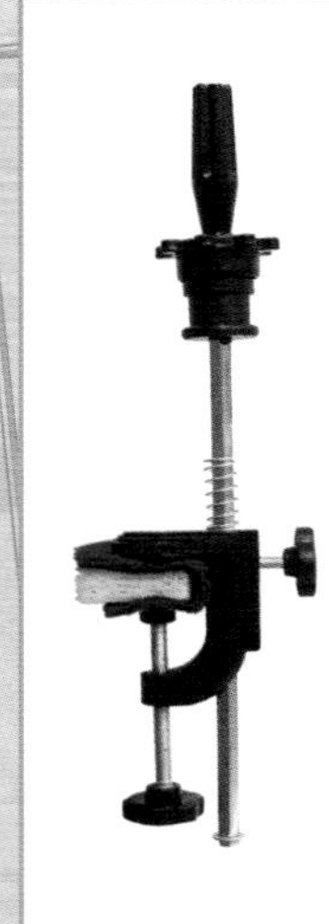

**Step 3:**
To completely separate the clamp from the table, **loosen the clamp screw first. Do not pull** clamp off the table without first loosening clamp screw. This will prevent damage to clamp and table surface.

7

**WARNING:** Aggressive pushing or pulling of the mannequin's head may break the stand and/or tabletop area.

# Mannequin Usage . . .

**When you begin working on the CLiC mannequin, prepare the hair as you would if styling a client's hair.**

Place a towel around the neck of the mannequin and secure it with a clip.

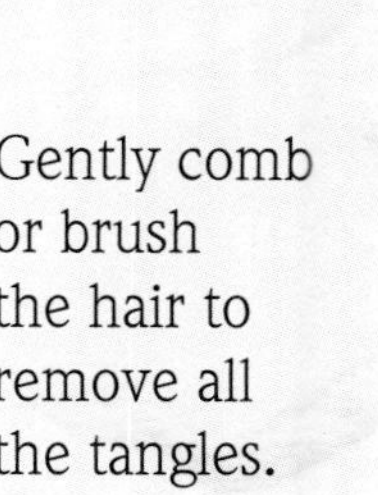

Gently comb or brush the hair to remove all the tangles.

Wet the hair thoroughly and apply the appropriate styling aid.

Style the hair according to design plan.

**The following may be performed on your CLiC mannequin.**

## A Haircutting/shaping

Ladies and gentlemen

## B Hairstyling

Pin curls
Finger waves
All types of roller sets
Wrap and molding
Airforming (blow drying)
Thermal hairstyling

## C Finishing techniques

Comb outs
Backcombing
Long hairdesigns
Braiding and hair extensions

## D Permanent waving

Sectioning/blocking
Wrapping
Chemical processes

## E Haircoloring (practice applications)

Bleach (decolorize)
Rinses, tints and toners
Highlight/lowlight techniques
Special effects

# Curly Hair Mannequin Care . . .

**The following list is a set of instructions for working on sensitive hair types.**

Prior to working on your mannequin, follow these instructions

1. Wet hair with lukewarm water before combing to avoid hair loss.

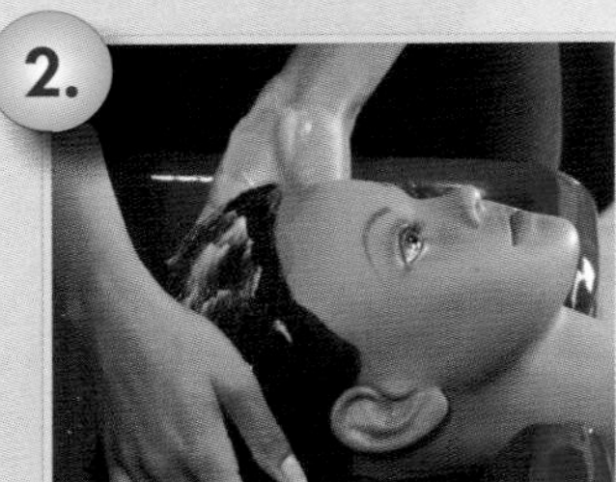

2. Apply a moisturizing balsam cream conditioner to the hair and distribute throughout.

3. While conditioner is still in the hair, use a cushioned wire brush or a large-tooth shampoo comb to gently comb through the hair. Begin by removing tangles in the nape area, working to the top of the head.

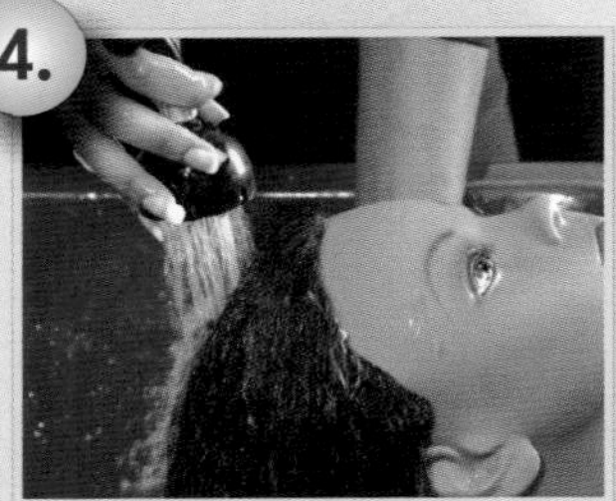

4. Rinse the conditioner from the hair using tepid water and **keep the hair as straight as possible while rinsing.**

5. Lightly shampoo (if needed) and remember to run fingers down through the hair to keep it straight. Rinse with lukewarm water.

6. Re-apply conditioner (if needed).

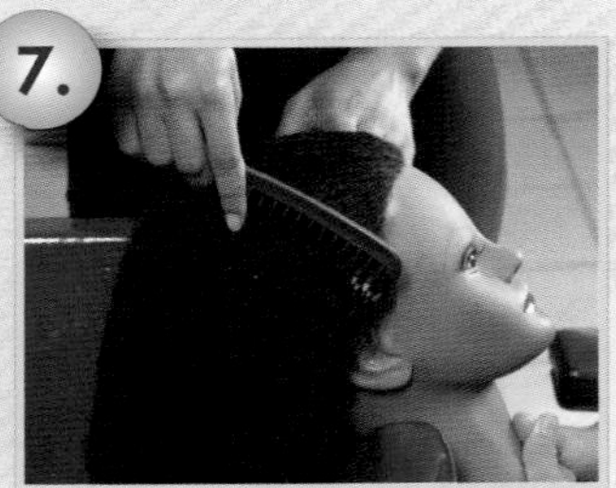

7. Comb through hair to detangle and then divide hair into four sections. While hair is wet, braid each section.

8. **Optional:** Allow hair to dry approximately 80 percent. Unbraid and let hair dry completely.

"Remember, treat your mannequin as you would a client."

## SUGGESTED GUIDELINES:

**50 - 80% dry**

airforming, razor and scissor cutting

**80 - 100% dry**

chemical services and scissor cutting

**100% dry**

thermal services and clipper cutting

# Curly Hair Mannequin Care . . .

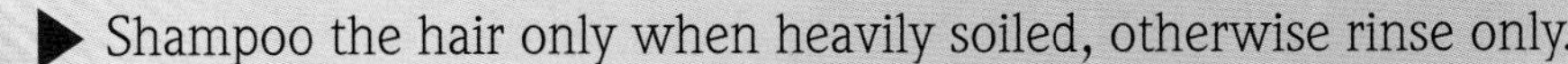

- Shampoo the hair only when heavily soiled, otherwise rinse only.
- Use **ONLY** acid balanced or moisturizing shampoo on the hair.
- Do not excessively backcomb the hair.
- Do not overuse hair spray or oil sheen.
- Test thermal tools before using on the hair (this is sensitive type hair and does not grow back).
- Do not put mannequin under a hot hooded hair dryer, wig dryer or use a hot airformer or curling iron setting, use **ONLY medium settings.**
- When airforming the hair, use a vent or Denman-type pin brush, or place a comb attachment on the end of the airformer. **Do not use excess tension.**

WARNING: **Never use sodium hydroxide relaxer on the mannequin** (if straightening the hair is desired, we recommend **ammonium thioglycolate relaxer).**

When you are finished working with your mannequin, comb the hair flat to the head and cover with a towel. Let it rest comfortably and neatly until you are ready to use again.

Take good care of your mannequin and it will assist you in becoming a better hair stylist.

Your mannequin is your first client, so service her properly.

7

# Client Consultation . . .

**Before** *any service, the cosmetologist needs to* ***communicate with the client*** *on his or her hair-care needs.* ***Hair and scalp analysis*** *is an integral part of any service to avoid any disease contamination throughout the salon. The analysis also provides the* ***necessary information*** *on client's health and hair/scalp condition. This determines whether the requested service can be performed or if an alternative is recommended.*

| DATE | SERVICE/TREATMENT | REMARKS/CHANGES |
|---|---|---|
| | | |

☑ Medical Al...

## Client Profile Card/File

Name ______ Date ______

Address ______

Occupation ______ Hobby ______

Birthdate ______

First Visit Date ______

Pregnant? ❑ Medications ❑ Allergies ❑

Health Problems ❑

Cosmo Tech ______ Lic # ______

**Hair Condition:** Normal ❑ Dry ❑ Oily ❑

**Scalp Condition:** Normal ❑ Dry ❑ Oily ❑

**Texture:** Fine ❑ Medium ❑ Coarse ❑

**Type of Hair:** Straight ❑ Wavy ❑ Curly ❑

**Density:** Thick ❑ Medium ❑ Thin ❑

**Porosity:** Resistant ❑ Normal ❑ Severe ❑ Irregular ❑

**Elasticity:** Average ❑ Low ❑

What attracted you to our salon? Friend ❑ Location ❑ Advertisement ❑ Other______

Personal Hair Treatment & Product: Shampoo ❑ Conditioner ❑ Hair Spray ❑ Gels ❑ Other ❑

I Do The Following To My Hair: Cut ❑ Color ❑ Perm ❑ Bleach ❑ Rinse ❑ Conditions ❑ Other ❑

REMARKS ______

# Scalp Treatments . . .

**Scalp treatments** *are* ***added services*** *that maintain the health and beauty of scalp and hair. As a* ***relaxing and enjoyable experience,*** *these treatments include extensive hair brushing, scalp massaging and an application of a deep conditioning treatment. The brushing and massage will help to increase blood circulation, promoting healthy hair and scalp. The types of professional products used are dependent upon your* ***client's hair and scalp condition.***

**Regular hair and scalp treatment**s provide care that will preserve a healthy scalp and luxurious hair.

**Dry hair and scalp treatments** involve the application of moisturizing products along with the use of heat for deep penetration and stimulation of sebaceous gland inactivity.

**Oily hair and scalp treatments** try to control the over-activate sebaceous glands by using deep cleansing products.

**Dandruff treatments** require the application of anti-fungal products, massage to increase blood circulation or the use of electrotherapy (refer to Chapter 11) to normalize the skin's shedding process.

"DO NOT perform a scalp treatment prior to giving a chemical service."

7

## SIMPLE LAB PROJECT

# Cleansing and Conditioning

*back bowl technique*

### OBJECTIVE

To provide a thorough cleansing and conditioning of hair and scalp. This experience should be relaxing and enjoyable. **NOTE:** This procedure shows the cosmetologist standing **behind the shampoo bowl.**

## TOOLS & MATERIALS

- Neck strip and cape/robe
- Towels
- Gloves (optional)
- Cleansing products
- Conditioning products
- Combs
- Brushes
- Client record card/file

## PROCEDURE

**"The client consultation is an important part of your professional service. Be sure to complete this step prior to each client service you provide. Your successful retail sales and customer satisfaction rates depend upon it!"**

RETAIL • RE-BOOK • REFERRAL

1. Cosmetologist sanitizes hands and station.
2. Set out service tools and materials.
3. Drape the client in preparation for service.
4. Perform a hair analysis.
5. Follow procedure as shown.
6. Follow standard cleanup procedure.
7. Document client record card/file.

**A** Starting at outer perimeter of design, brush hair ends moving up toward top of head and complete brushing over entire head. Check scalp and hair condition (texture, density, elasticity and porosity).

**B** Sanitize entire rim of bowl, hose nozzle, drain dish and water handle.

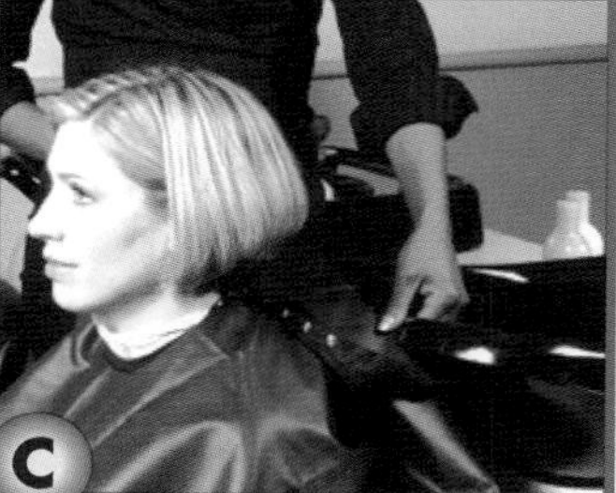

**C** Place client at shampoo bowl with back of cape draped behind chair. (if water escapes, goes on floor, not client)

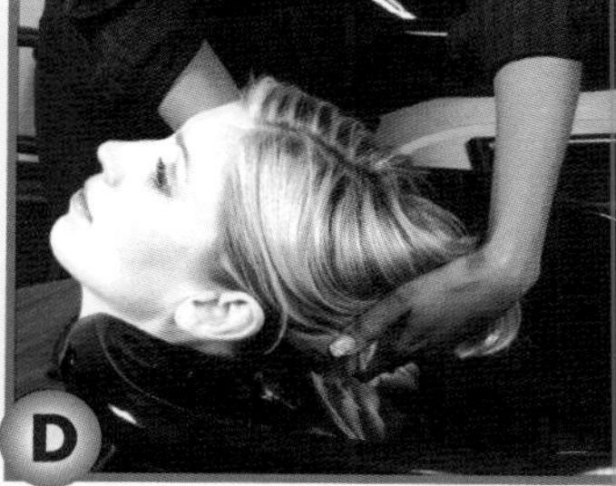

**D** **Gently** lower client's head into bowl, ensuring client's back and neck are not uncomfortable.

**E** Check that all hair is lying inside the bowl.

**F** Turn water on with nozzle facing down into sink; test water temperature on hand. **WARNING:** The higher up the water handle is pulled, the more the water pressure and amount increase.

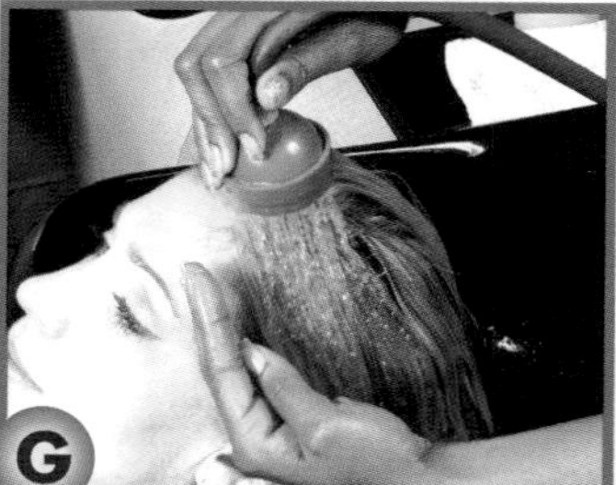

**G** Apply water to hairline moving along top and perimeter of head. Use a cupping action with your hands around hairline to prevent water from splashing onto face and ears.

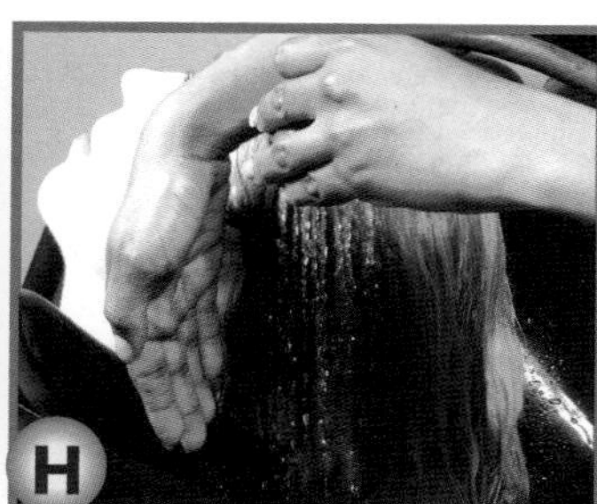

**H** With opposite hand, **lightly** push ear forward to glide nozzle along back of head. To control this movement, **CUSTOMER DOES NOT** lift head.

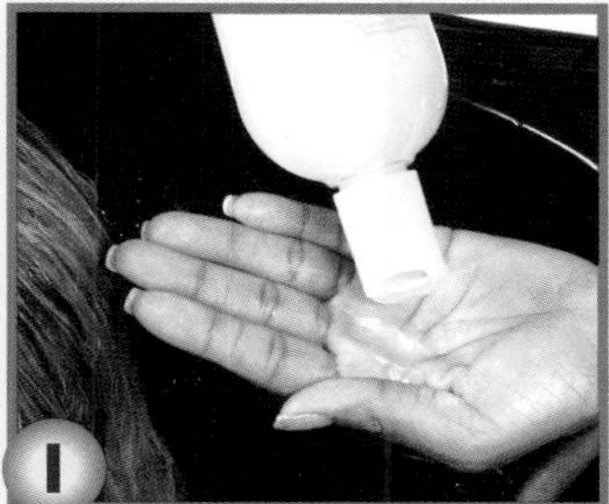
I

After hair is wet; place shampoo into your hands. This warms the shampoo before touching scalp.

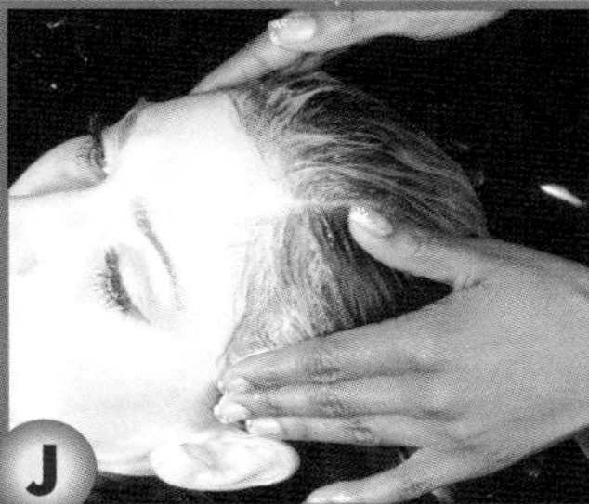
J

Apply shampoo to hair starting at hairline, working along top to back of head. Shampoo should penetrate down through hair onto scalp.

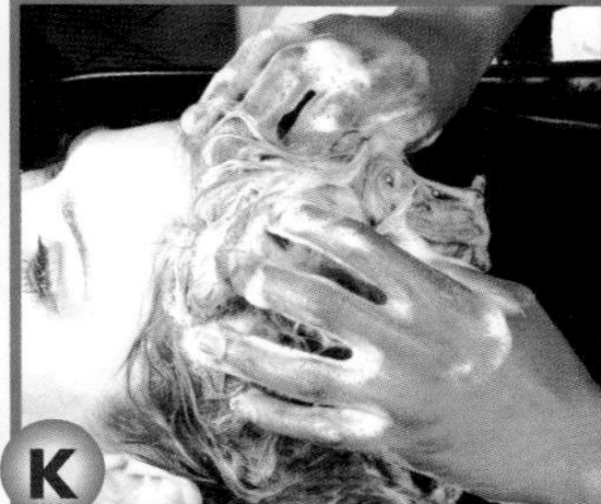
K

When sufficient lather is obtained, use cushions of fingertips and move in a **circular** rotation along frontal hairline.

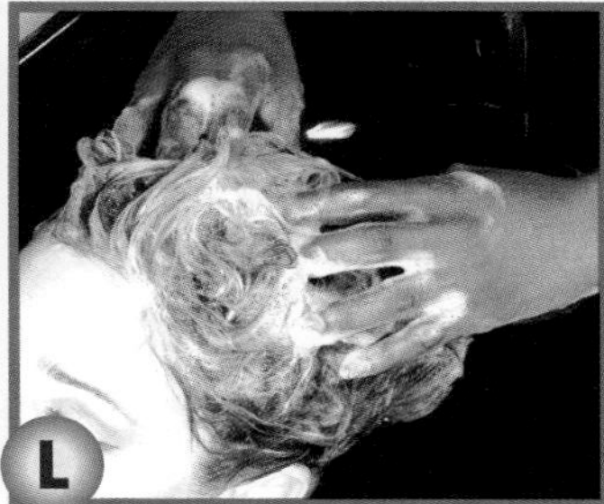
L

Continue **circular** rotation along top of head. Fingertips are rotating the scalp, not hair.

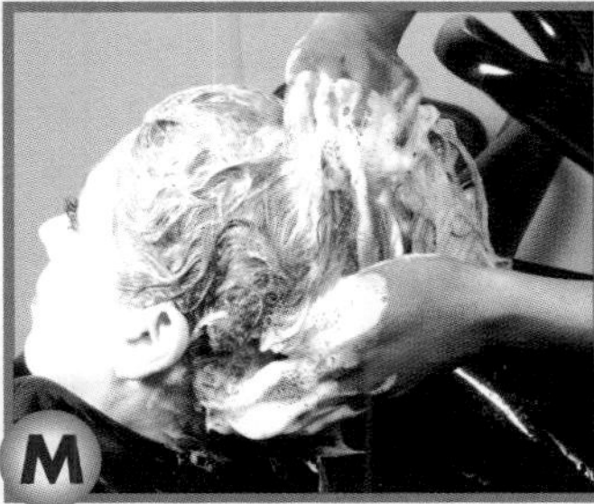
M

**Slightly** lift head and rotate fingers along back of head and hairline. **DO NOT** forget this step to ensure a thorough cleansing.

N

Continue cleansing the nape area; complete by squeezing excess shampoo from the hair.

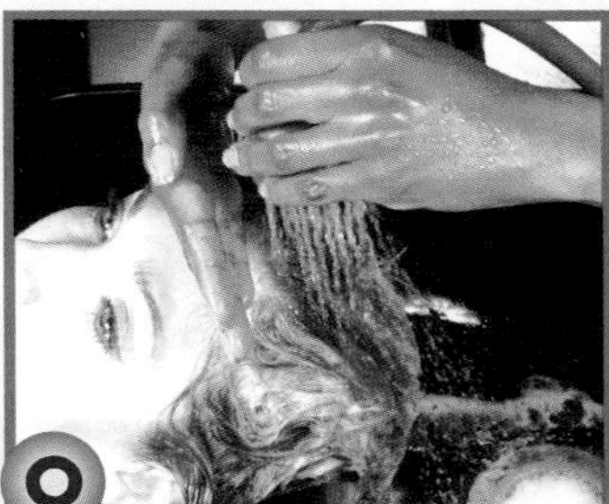
O

**Repeat Steps F thru H to rinse shampoo from hair.** Check to make sure hair is completely free from all shampoo.

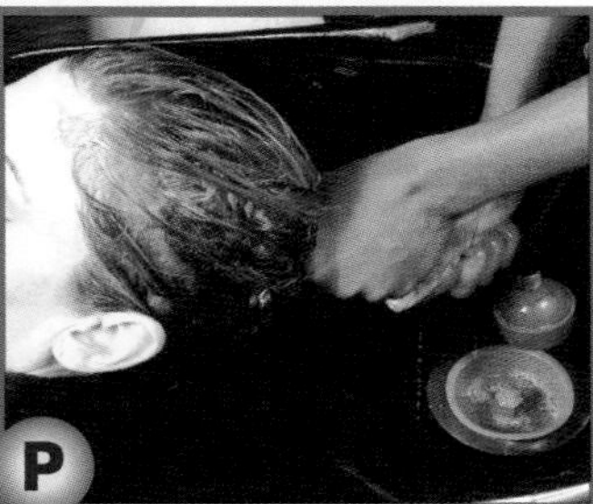
P

Squeeze excess water from hair and apply conditioner in the same manner as shampoo, **following Step J.**

Q

Comb conditioner through hair using a large tooth comb to ensure accurate coverage of product. Follow manufacturer's instructions on time allotted for conditioner to remain on hair.

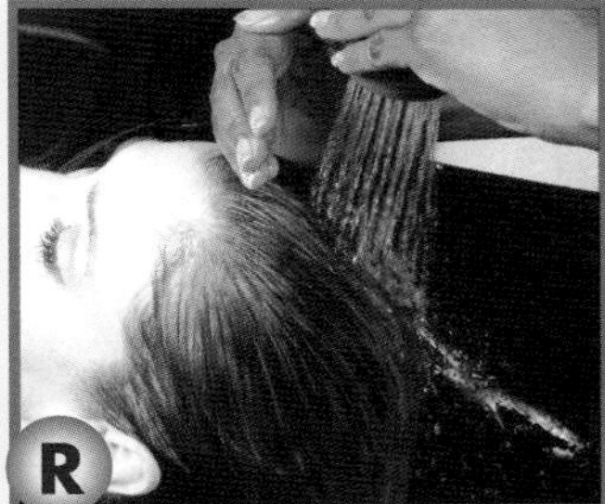
R

Rinse conditioner from hair. Squeeze excess water from hair with hands.

S

Wrap a cloth towel around hairline, blot hair and **slowly** lift head from bowl.

T

Detangle by combing through hair to prepare for next service.

"When sanitizing the shampoo bowl, be sure to clean the drain dish to remove any hair that might have fallen out during cleansing."

**EVALUATION** ______________________________

______ GRADE ______ STUDENT'S NAME ______ ID#

7

# Variation

Cosmetologist standing **beside the shampoo bowl cleansing curly hair.**

*When shampooing curly hair, follow shampooing and conditioning procedure with a few minor exceptions, which are listed below.*

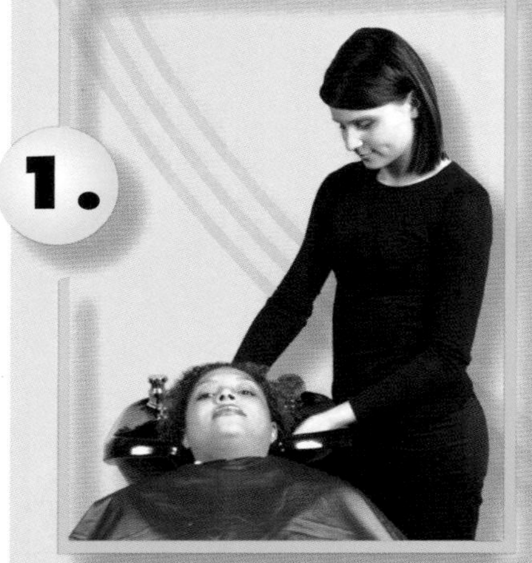

**1.** Cosmetologist standing beside shampoo bowl making sure all **hair is lying in the sink.**

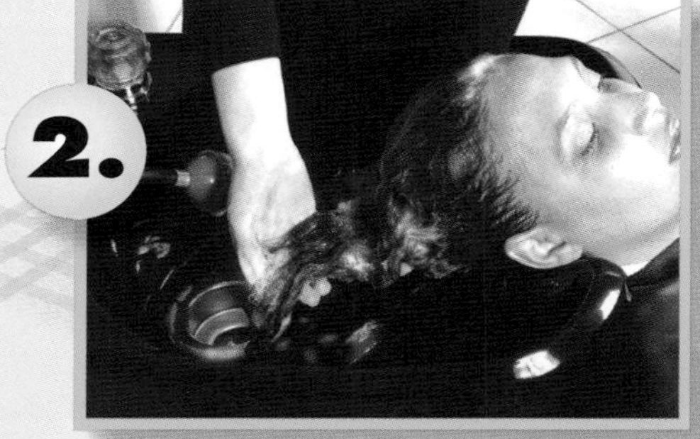

**2.** **Do not** over-manipulate the hair with excess shampoo; allow hair to fall freely within bowl.

**3.** Begin to comb or detangle starting at **ends of hair** moving towards scalp area.

**Do not start combing wet hair at scalp; this will pull and possibly cause breakage.**

7

# Variation

Cosmetologist standing **behind the shampoo bowl cleansing long hair.**

*When shampooing long hair, follow shampooing and conditioning procedure with a few minor exceptions, which are listed below.*

1. Be sure to **hold entire length of hair** when client's head is lowered into bowl. Place your hand under head and **gently guide** client into bowl.

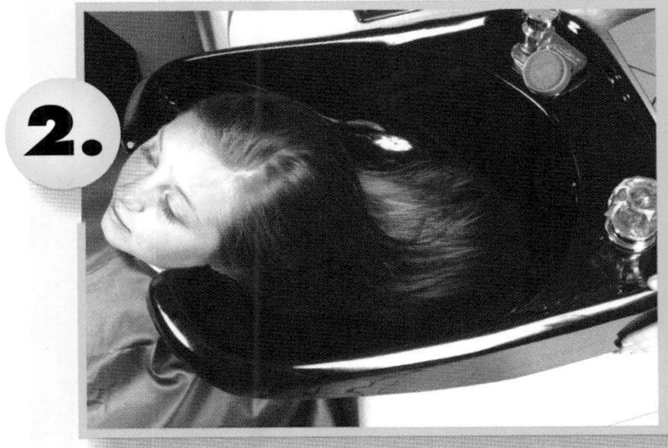

2. All hair needs to **flow freely** in the shampoo bowl.

3. Do not over-manipulate the hair with excess shampoo; **lift the hair ends** to cleanse and avoid tangling of hair.

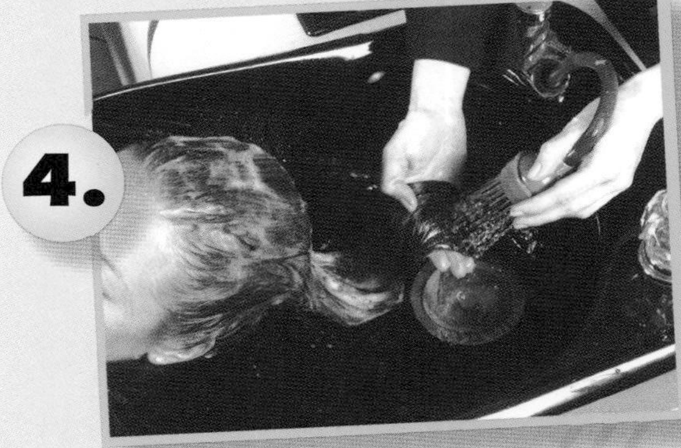

4. Rinse shampoo from hair by **lifting the hair ends.** This will prevent hair from clogging the drain and allows **water to flow over hair** to remove lather.

***Recommend client purchase a professional shampoo and conditioner for home maintenance use.***

SIMPLE LAB PROJECT

# Basic Scalp Treatment

## OBJECTIVE

To provide treatment in maintaining the health and beauty of hair and scalp.

## TOOLS & MATERIALS

- Neck strip and cape/robe
- Towels
- Gloves (optional)
- Scalp astringent/lotion
- Applicator brush
- Cleansing product
- Conditioning product
- Combs
- Hair cap and/or hood dryer
- Brushes
- Client record card/file
- Sectioning clips
- Cotton

## PROCEDURE

**"The client consultation is an important part of your professional service. Be sure to complete this step prior to each client service you provide. Your successful retail sales and customer satisfaction rates depend upon it!"**

RETAIL • RE-BOOK • REFERRAL

1. Cosmetologist sanitizes hands and station.
2. Set out service tools and materials.
3. Drape the client in preparation for service.
4. Perform a hair analysis.
5. Follow procedure as shown.
6. Follow standard cleanup procedure.
7. Document client record card/file.

A — Starting at outer perimeter of design, brush hair ends moving upward to top of head. Complete brushing over entire head. Check scalp and hair condition to determine which type of treatment is recommended.

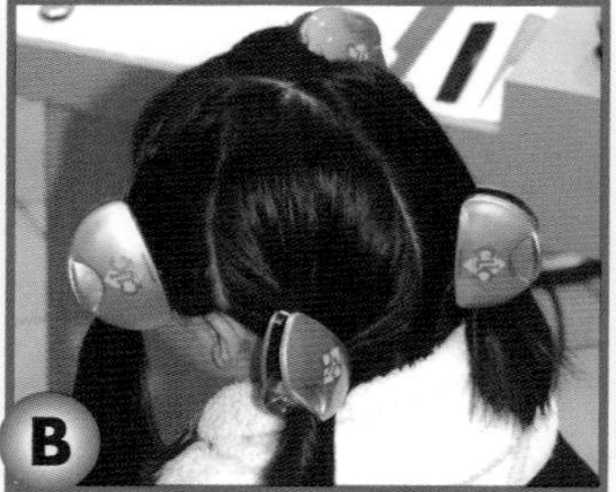

B — Divide dry hair into four sections.

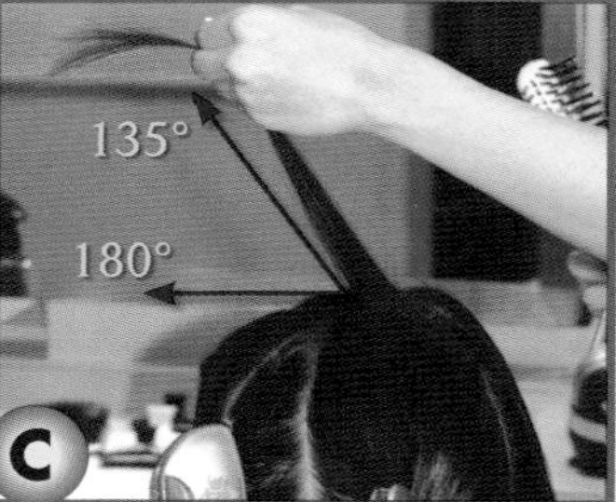


C — Starting at top right back section; take **½ inch (1.25 cm) subsection** and hold hair at a **135-degree angle above subsection.**

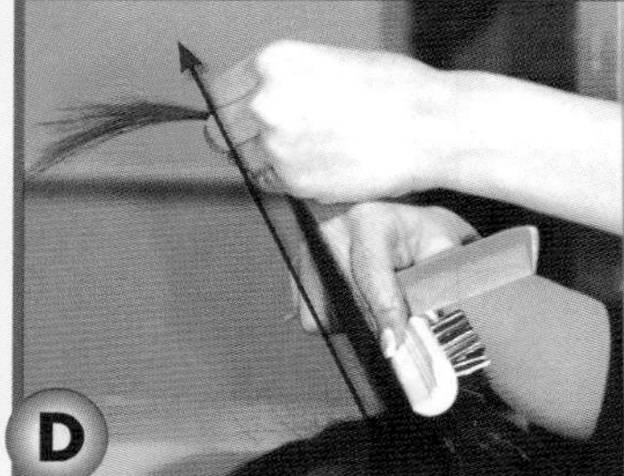

D — Place brush on underside of subsection at hair base with bristles facing you.

E — Rotate brush by turning outward as it moves up hair shaft.

F — Continue to rotate brush until bristles are facing outward, allowing bristles to smooth through hair to ends. **Repeat this step three times.**

G — Continue parting and brushing hair working down section.

H — **Repeat Steps D thru F for all sections.**

## Basic Scalp Treatment

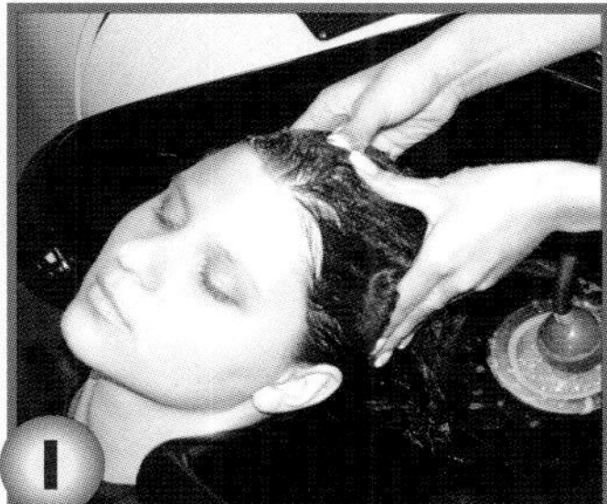

**I** When all sections are completed, **ONLY** shampoo hair. (Refer to procedure in this chapter.)

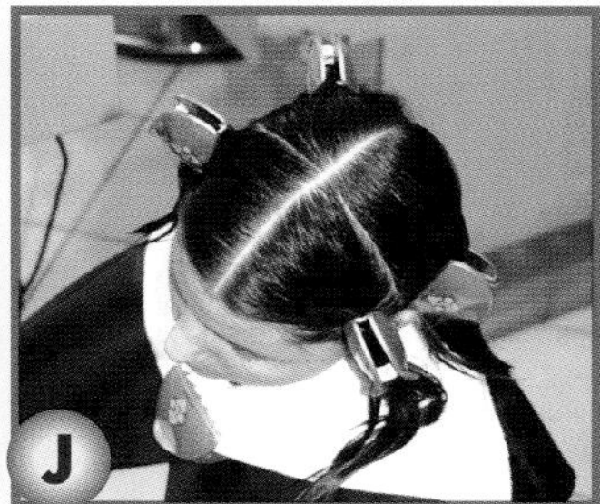

**J** Towel blot hair and re-section into four.

**K** At top of back section, take **½ inch (1.25 cm) subsections** and apply a conditioning product to area at scalp using your fingers or applicator brush.

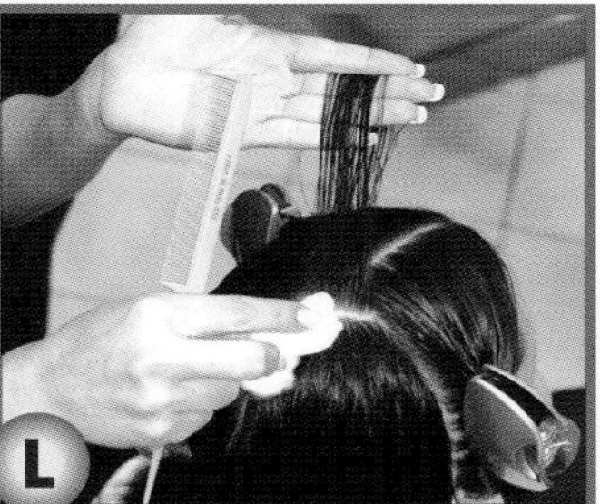

**L** **For an oily or dandruff condition,** apply a scalp astringent/lotion with a cotton ball. Dip cotton ball into product and smooth along hair parting touching scalp.

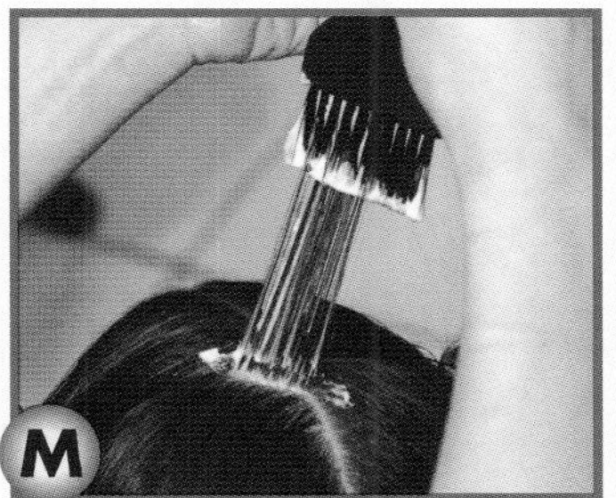

**M** Apply conditioning product to hair shaft with applicator brush.

**N** Complete all four sections repeating **Steps K and M for normal treatment or Steps L and M for oily or dandruff treatment.**

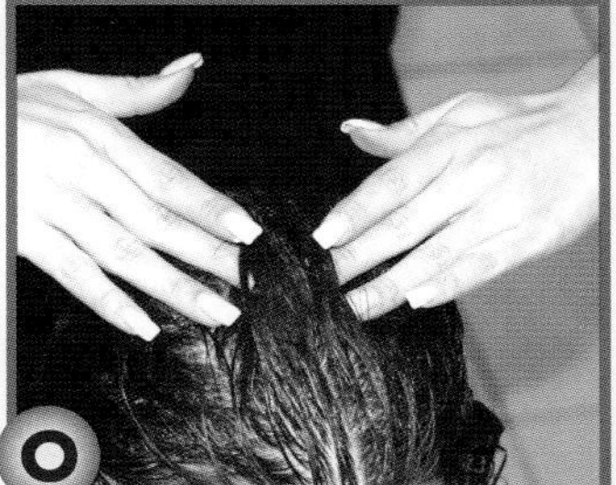

**O** Perform scalp manipulations on **normal to dry hair and scalp.** Perform electrotherapy on **oily to dandruff scalp.** (Refer to Chapter 11.)

**P** At completion of **Step O**, a hair cap is applied and client is either placed under a hood dryer or remains at room temperature. Application of heat slightly opens cuticle, allowing penetration of conditioning product. Time is determined by manufacturer's directions.

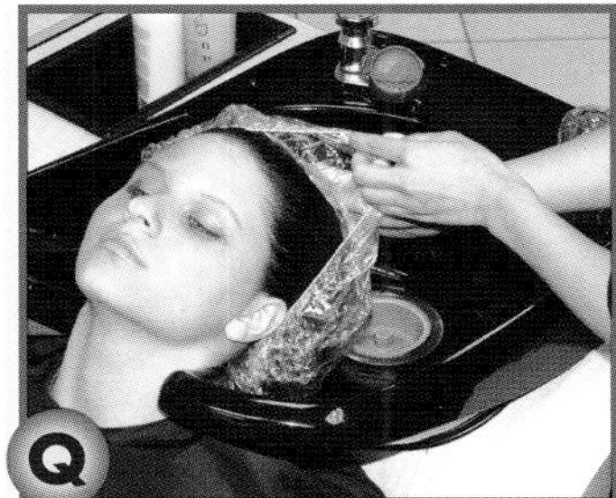

**Q** Remove hair cap, rinse hair and/or shampoo if hair is a fine texture.

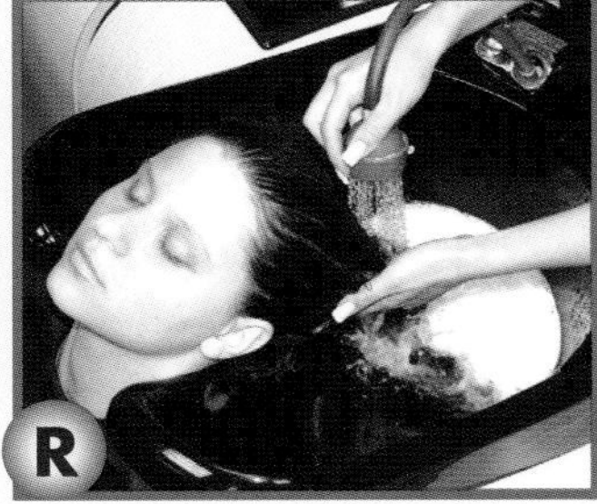

**R** Thoroughly rinse conditioner from hair to prevent a heavy, dull appearance. Towel dry and comb hair in preparation for next service.

***Recommend receiving scalp treatments one to two times a month to maintain healthy hair and scalp.***

**EVALUATION**

**GRADE** STUDENT'S NAME ID#

## SIMPLE LAB PROJECT

# Basic Scalp Massage

### OBJECTIVE

To provide a relaxing and therapeutic basic scalp massage treatment.

### TOOLS & MATERIALS

- Neck strip and cape/robe
- Towels
- Gloves (optional)
- Applicator brush
- Cleansing product
- Conditioning product
- Combs
- Brushes
- Client record card/file
- Sectioning clips

### PROCEDURE

**"The client consultation is an important part of your professional service. Be sure to complete this step prior to each client service you provide. Your successful retail sales and customer satisfaction rates depend upon it!"**

RETAIL • RE-BOOK • REFERRAL

1. Cosmetologist sanitizes hands and station.
2. Set out service tools and materials.
3. Drape the client in preparation for service.
4. Perform a hair analysis.
5. Follow procedure as shown.
6. Follow standard cleanup procedure.
7. Document client record card/file.

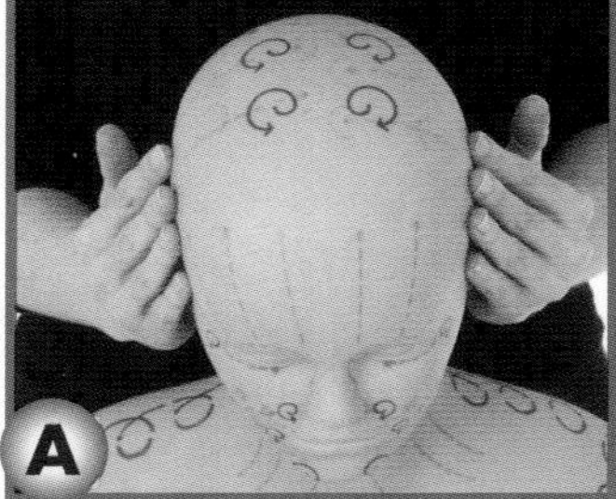

A — **Effleurage:** Place all fingers on temporalis muscles.

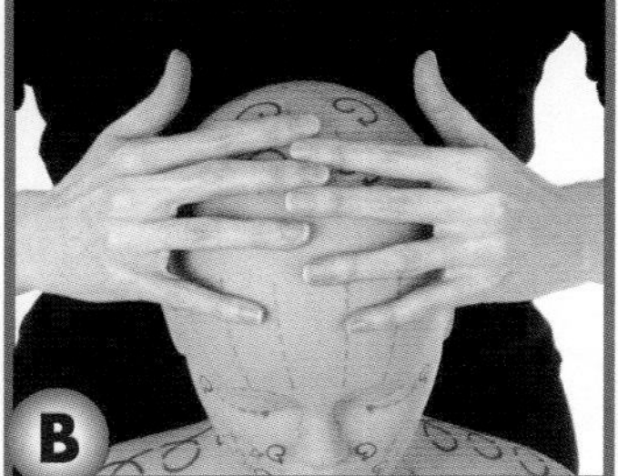

B — While applying firm pressure, simultaneously **glide** fingers up toward top of head (frontalis muscle) and interlock. **Repeat Steps A and B two times.**

C — **Effleurage:** Start by placing all fingers on occipitalis muscle.

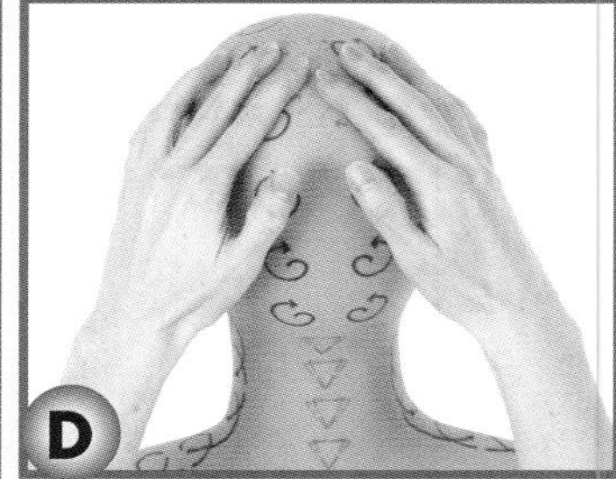

D — While applying firm pressure, simultaneously **rotate** fingers up toward top of head to frontalis musacle. **Repeat Steps C and D two times.**

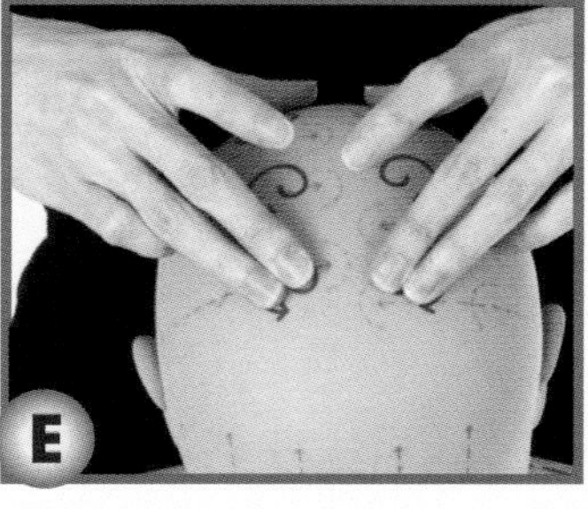

E — **Friction:** Start by placing ring and middle fingers of both hands at front hairline. Apply a firm pressure; **rotate** fingers simultaneously in a **circular movement.**

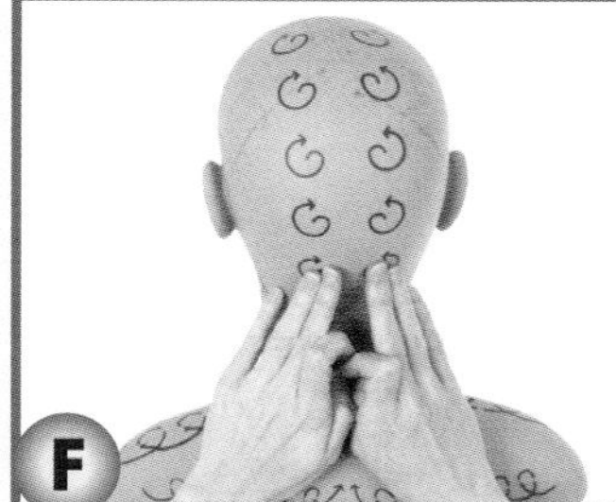

F — Continue rotating moving back to occipitalis and top of cervical vertebrae. **Repeat Steps E and F two times.**

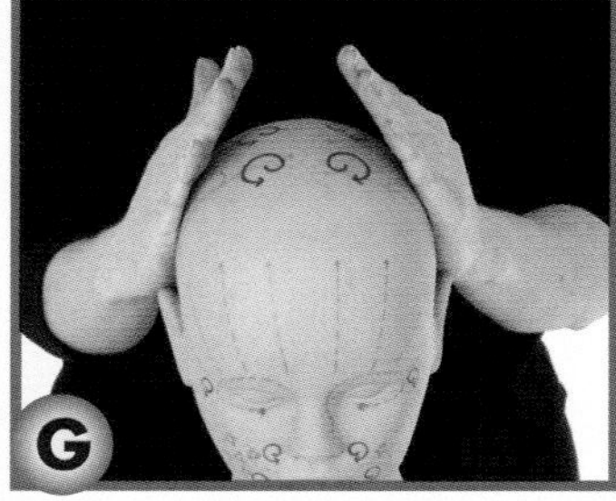

G — **Friction:** Start by placing palms of both hands at temporalis (directly above ears). Apply a firm pressure and **rotate** simultaneously in a **circular movement.**

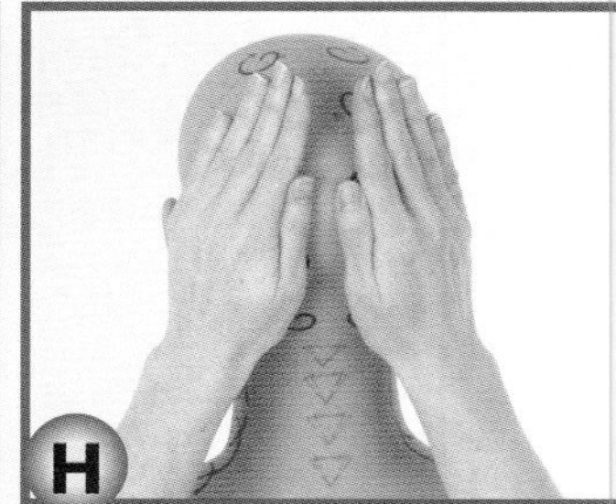

H — Place palms of both hands on lower part of occipitalis; apply a firm pressure and **rotate** in a **circular movement.**

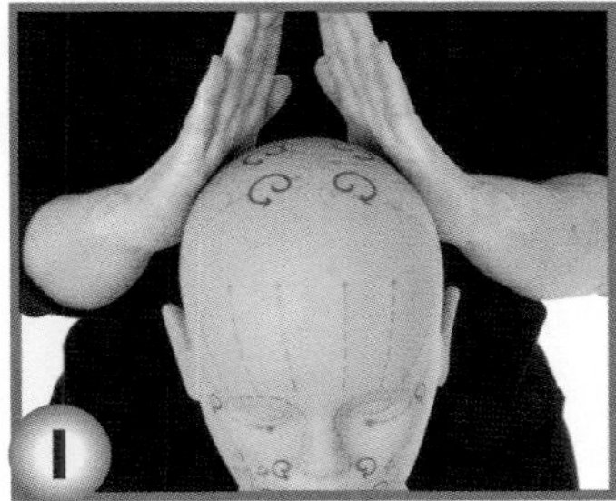


Continue by placing palms of both hands on lower part of occipitalis; apply a firm pressure and **rotate** in a **circular movement. Repeat Steps G thru I two times.**

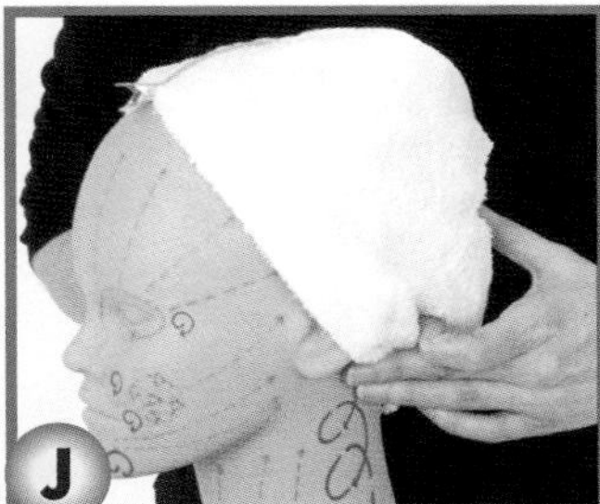


**Friction:** Start by placing ring and middle fingers of both hands at the sternocleidomastoideus (below the ears).

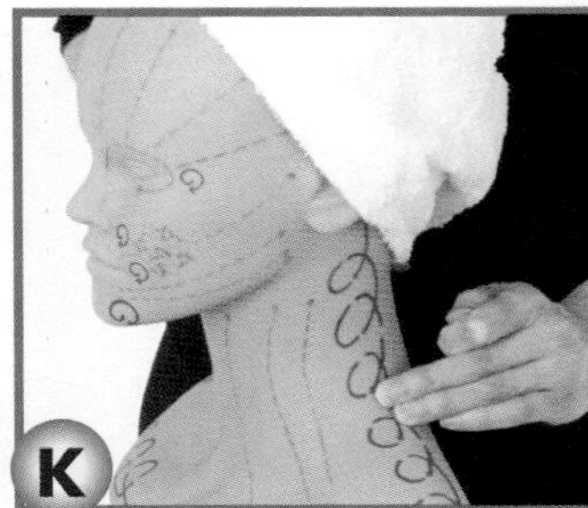


Apply a slight firm pressure and **rotate** fingers simultaneously in a **circular movement** down to base of neck.

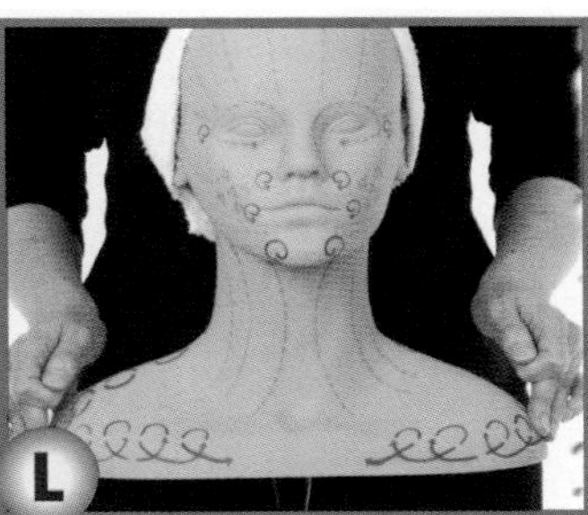


Continue to rotate out over platysma muscle (shoulder).

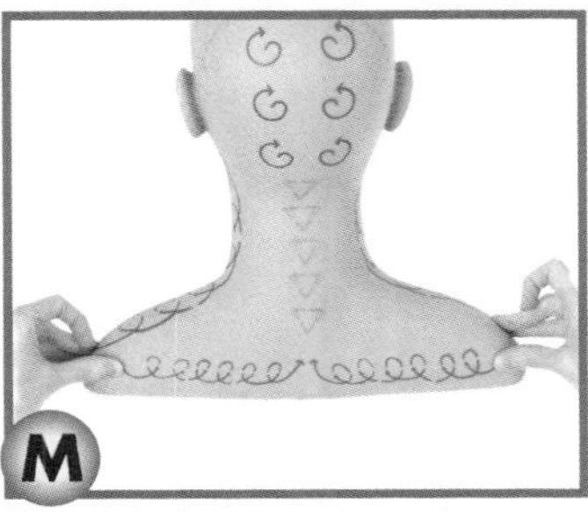


Place thumbs on trapezius muscle (back of shoulder).

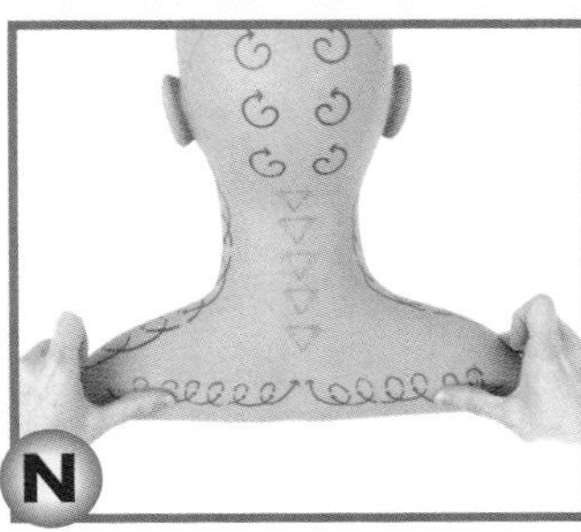


Continue to **rotate** using **circular movements** along the back.

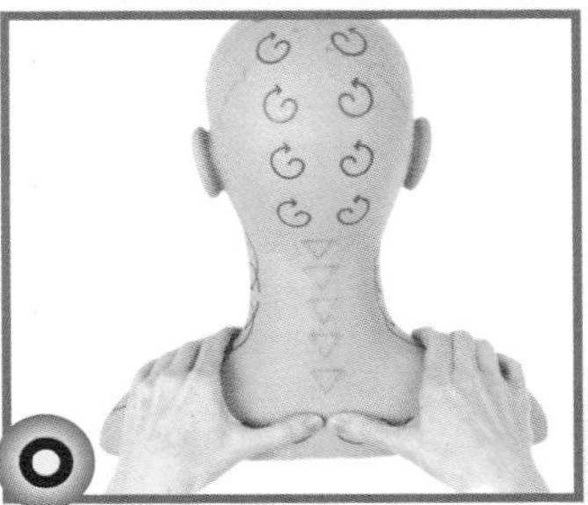


Continue rotating to center of back or seventh cervical vertebrae. **Repeat Steps J thru O two times.**

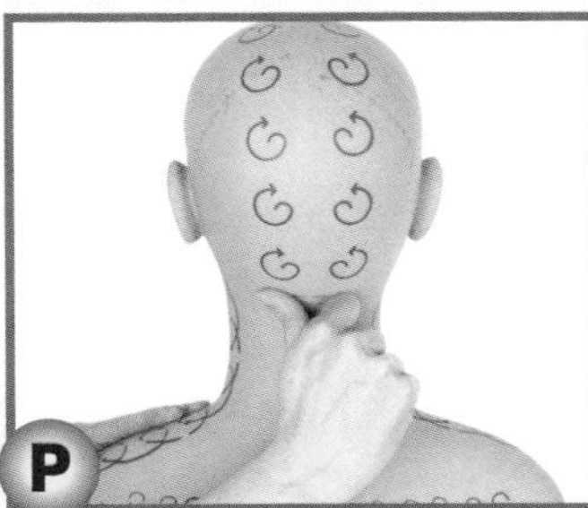


**Petrissage:** Start by placing index finger (bent) and thumb below occipitalis muscle.

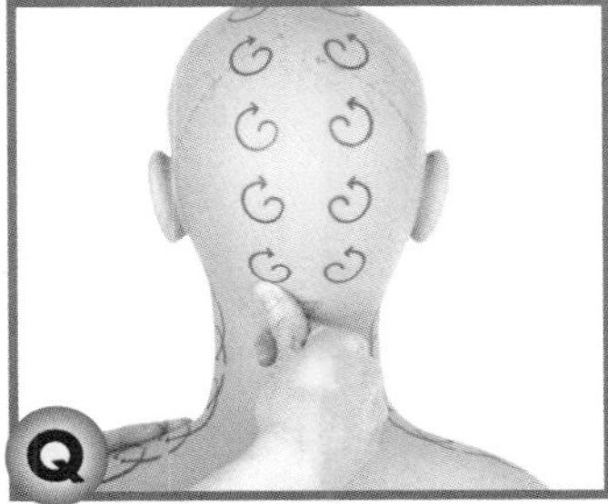


Apply a firm pressure, **grasp skin and turn finger and thumb.**

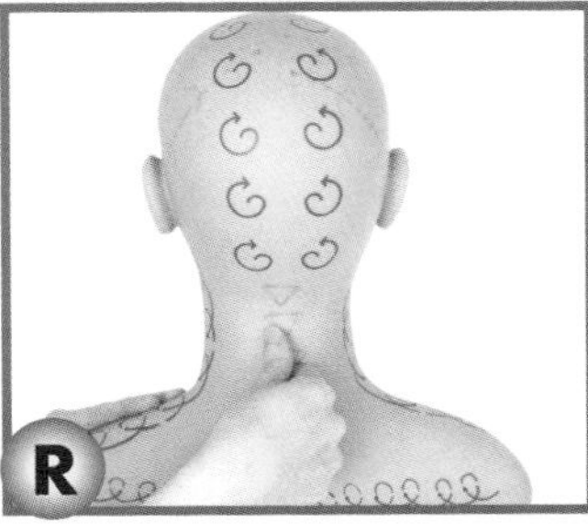


Continue moving down the cervical vertebrae by grasping skin and twisting.

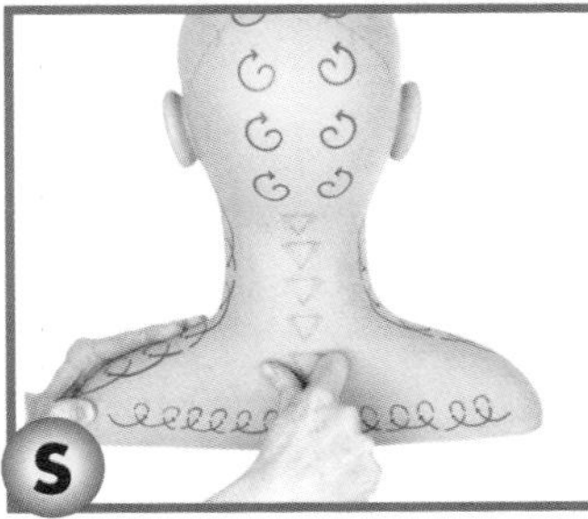


Continue movement down to seventh cervical vertebrae.

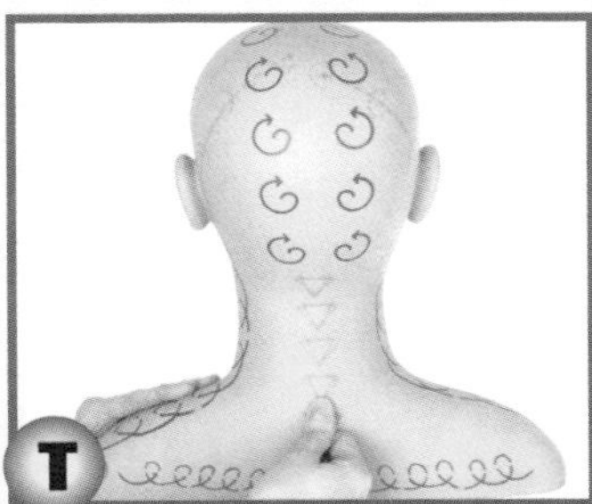


**Grasp skin** and **twist** on seventh cervical vertebrae. **Repeat Steps P thru T two times.**

"The CLiC massage mannequin makes learning massage techniques easy."

EVALUATION

GRADE | STUDENT'S NAME | ID#

# Hair + Scalp Treatments REVIEW QUESTIONS

## FILL-IN-THE-BLANKS

A. Acid
B. Anionic
C. Capes
D. Consultation
E. Cushion (Boar) Brushes
F. Disposable Towels
G. Dry Shampoo
H. Hard Water
I. Ion Exchange
J. Leave-in Treatments
K. Lipophilic
L. Litmus Paper
M. Mannequin
N. Medicated Shampoo
O. Neck Strips
P. pH
Q. Reconstructors
R. Scalp Treatment
S. Tail Comb
T. Wet Disinfectant System

1. ________ wrap around neck to prevent skin-to-cape contact.
2. ________ remains unaltered, containing dissolved minerals.
3. ________ is the potential amount of hydrogen ions in a solution containing water.
4. ________ usually contains an anti-microbic ingredient to remedy dandruff or other scalp condition.
5. ________ or "tail end" of shampoo molecule attaching to dirt.
6. ________ makes clean, precise partings.
7. ________ is your very first client.
8. ________ is the communication between cosmetologist and client on his or her hair-care needs.
9. ________ maintains the health and beauty of hair and scalp.
10. ________ eliminate the need for laundering.
11. ________ softens water by infiltrating it through a layer of sodium covered resin beads.
12. ________ is a surfactant that is inexpensive, but has great deep cleansing abilities.
13. ________ has a pH measurement of 6.9 to 0.
14. ________ are generally lightweight conditioners that are left on the hair.
15. ________ are used to prepare hair for analysis, detangling and shampooing.
16. ________ cover clients' clothing to protect from damage during hair services.
17. ________ turns blue if product is alkaline and red if product is acid.
18. ________ is used for clients with head injury or illness that requires them to be bedridden.
19. ________ are deep penetrating conditioners left on hair for an average of 10 to 20 minutes.
20. ________ is a jar sanitizer where tools are completely immersed.

7

STUDENT'S NAME DATE GRADE

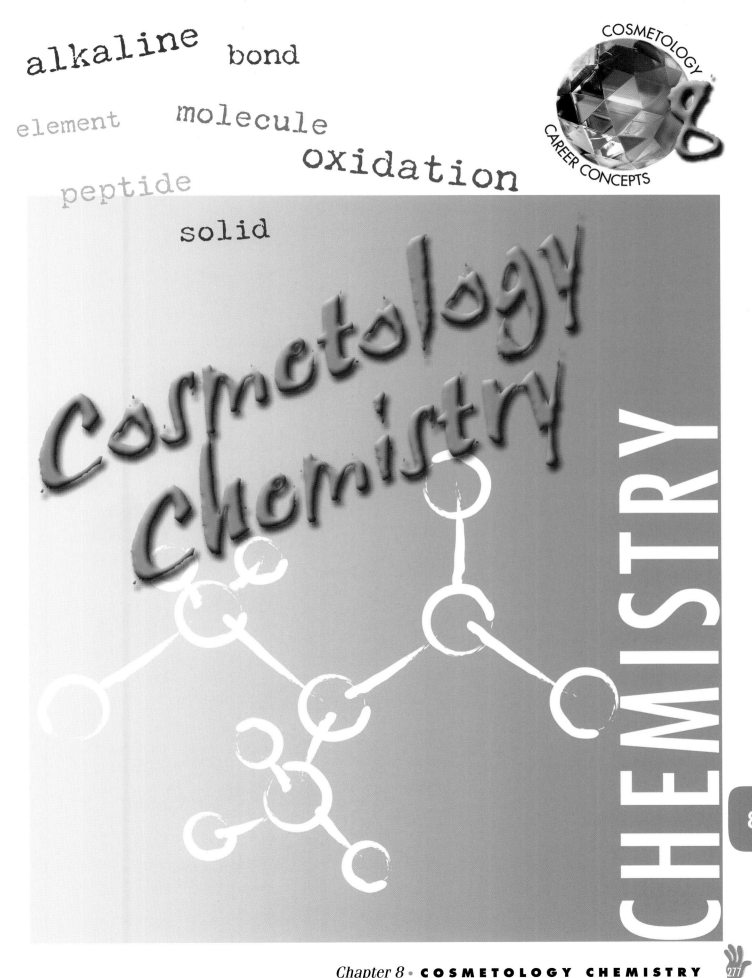

alkaline bond

element molecule

oxidation

peptide

solid

# Cosmetology Chemistry

CHEMISTRY

8

# Terminology . . .

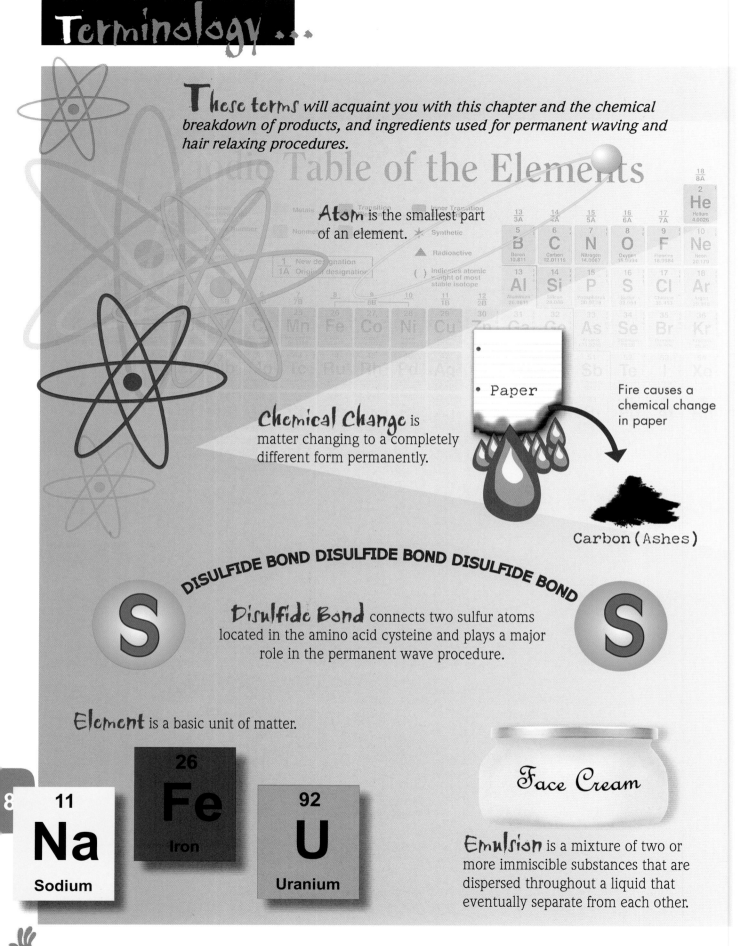

*These terms will acquaint you with this chapter and the chemical breakdown of products, and ingredients used for permanent waving and hair relaxing procedures.*

**Atom** is the smallest part of an element.

**Chemical Change** is matter changing to a completely different form permanently.

Paper

Fire causes a chemical change in paper

Carbon (Ashes)

DISULFIDE BOND DISULFIDE BOND DISULFIDE BOND

S S

**Disulfide Bond** connects two sulfur atoms located in the amino acid cysteine and plays a major role in the permanent wave procedure.

**Element** is a basic unit of matter.

11 Na Sodium

Face Cream

**Emulsion** is a mixture of two or more immiscible substances that are dispersed throughout a liquid that eventually separate from each other.

# Terminology . . .

**Hair Relaxing** is chemically altering wavy or curly hair into a straight form.

**Matter** is a substance that has mass and occupies space.

**Neutralizer** is a solution that reforms the disulfide bonds into their new curled position in a permanent wave.

**Polypeptide Chain** is a spiraling chain made up of amino acids.

**Soft Curl Reformation** is taking overly curly hair and chemically reforming the curls to larger more manageable curls or waves.

8

# Principles of Chemistry ...

*Cosmetologists need to be aware of how hair products are designed, as well as their composition, in order to produce the desired effects for their clients. By learning some basics of science and chemistry, you will gain a better understanding of the products' purpose and performance.*

## What are Science and Chemistry?

**Science** is conclusion based on careful **observation and experimentation.**

**Chemistry** is a branch of science that studies matter (anything that has mass, such as air, water and humankind) and its **transformations/changes.** It is also the study of connections between molecular and macroscopic (visible to the naked eye) events. This study is approached through the scientific method, which is a systematic procedure for solving problems and exploring nature.

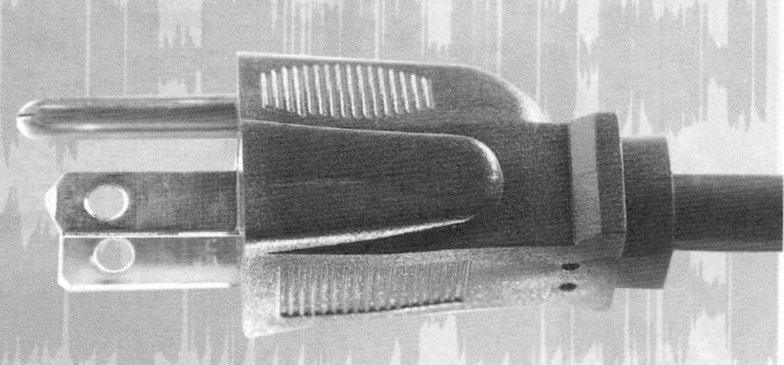

## What is a Chemical?

It is a substance used in, or produced by, the processes of chemistry.
**Everything is a chemical, except light, electricity and sound!**

"We need chemicals to survive ... from the basic water ($H_2O$ – two parts hydrogen and one part oxygen), to more complex ingredients in meeting our beauty needs such as thioglycolate acid ($C_2H_4O_2S$), which is used in permanent wave solutions!"

8

# Principles of Chemistry . . .

## Chemistry is divided into two classifications:

1. **Organic chemistry** studies matter that **contains carbon and is living or at one time was alive.** Almost all living things, whether plant or animal, usually will contain the element **"carbon."** Even though substances such as pesticides, fertilizers, gasoline or plastics are not considered alive, they contain carbon. You could say gasoline or motor oil, for example, was alive at one time because it is derived from the remains of plants and animals that lived millions of years ago. A lot of hair-care products that are manufactured naturally or synthetically are considered organic such as shampoos, conditioners and styling aids.

2. **Inorganic chemistry** involves substances that **do not contain carbon and are not living or alive.** Examples of inorganic chemistry include pure water, minerals, metals and clean air.

**NOTE:** Organic substances will burn whereas inorganic substances will not burn.

**Matter** is a **substance** of the universe that has mass and **occupies space.** It has physical and chemical properties and exists either as a solid, liquid or gas.

8

# Principles of Chemistry . . .

## The Four Main Components of Chemistry:

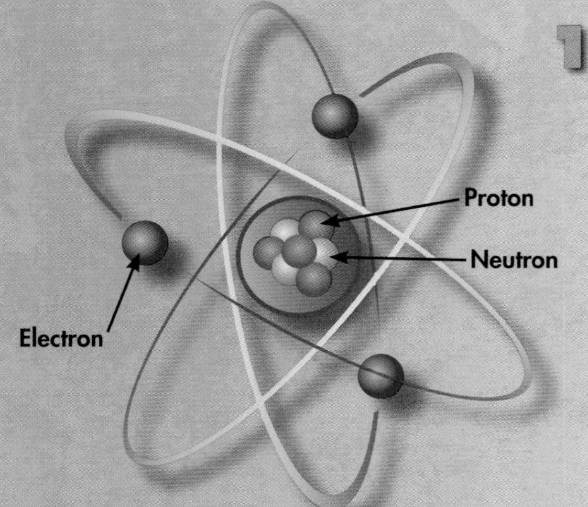

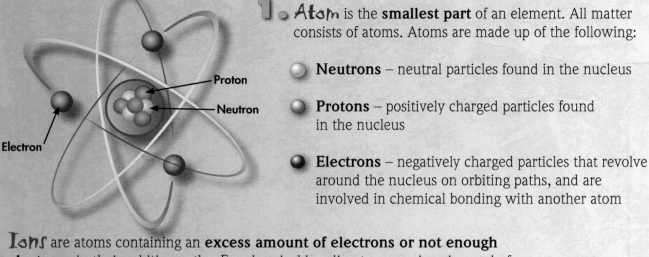

**1. Atom** is the **smallest part** of an element. All matter consists of atoms. Atoms are made up of the following:

- **Neutrons** – neutral particles found in the nucleus
- **Protons** – positively charged particles found in the nucleus
- **Electrons** – negatively charged particles that revolve around the nucleus on orbiting paths, and are involved in chemical bonding with another atom

**Ions** are atoms containing an **excess amount of electrons or not enough electrons** in their orbiting paths. For chemical bonding to occur, ions in need of stability seek out other ions and connect to form a **compound**.

**2. Element** is any substance made of one type of atom and **cannot be broken down** into a simpler one chemically; it is a **basic unit of matter.** An element chart is used to identify each element with its symbol.

| 21 Sc Scandium 44.956 | 22 Ti Titanium 47.88 | 23 V Vanadium 50.942 | 24 Cr Chromium 51.996 | 25 Mn Manganese 54.9380 | 26 Fe Iron 55.847 | 27 Co Cobalt 58.9332 | 28 Ni Nickel 58.69 | 29 Cu Copper 63.54 | 30 Zn Zinc 65.37 |
|---|---|---|---|---|---|---|---|---|---|
| 39 Y Yttrium 88.905 | 40 Zr Zirconium 91.22 | 41 Nb Niobium 92.906 | 42 Mo Molybdenum 95.94 | 43 Tc Technetium (98) | 44 Ru Ruthenium 101.07 | 45 Rh Rhodium 102.905 | 46 Pd Palladium 106.4 | 47 Ag Silver 107.868 | 48 Cd Cadmium 112.40 |
| | 72 Hf Hafnium 178.49 | 73 Ta Tantalum 180.948 | 74 W Tungsten 183.85 | 75 Re Rhenium 186.2 | 76 Os Osmium 190.2 | 77 Ir Iridium 192.2 | 78 Pt Platinum 195.09 | 79 Au Gold 196.967 | 80 Hg Mercury 200.59 |
| | 104 Rf Rutherfordium (261) | 105 Db Dubnium (262) | 106 Sg Seaborgium (263) | 107 Bh Bohrium (262) | 108 Hs Hassium (265) | 109 Mt Meitnerium (266) | 110 Uun Ununnilium (269) | 111 Uuu Unununium (272) | 112 Uub Ununbium (277) |

**NOTE:** If a substance consists of only one element then it is referred to as **elemental molecule.** Example: aluminum foil compromises only the element aluminum.

**3. Molecule** (mol-e-cule) is created when one or more atoms combine and retain their chemical and physical properties to **form matter.** Example: a molecule of water consists of two hydrogen atoms and one oxygen atom or an oxygen molecule consists of two oxygen atoms.

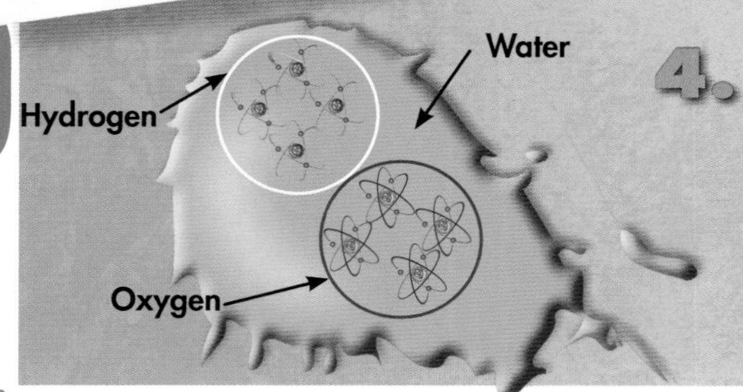


**4. Compound,** also known as **chemical compound,** is a chemical substance consisting of atoms or ions of two or more elements in definite proportions, which **cannot be separated by physical means.** Example: molecules of water are considered chemical compounds because they consist of two different atoms, hydrogen and oxygen.

## The Three Forms of Matter:

- Gas
- Liquid
- Solid

**NOTE:** Gases and vapors **are not** the same. Vapors develop when liquid evaporates. (Examples: water, acetone and alcohol.) Gases occur when a liquid is placed under extremely high or low temperatures. (Example: air we breathe is a combination of gases, consisting mostly of nitrogen and oxygen.)

**The difference is how the molecules are placed within the form they occupy!**

**Gas** consists of molecules that are **very far apart.**

**Vapor** (a component of gas) consists of molecules that are **close together.**

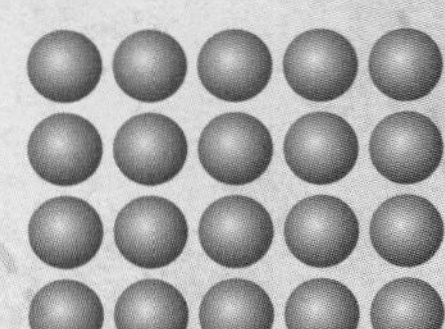

**Liquid** consists of molecules that are **very close together.**

**Solid** consists of molecules that are the **closest together.**

# Matter . . .

**Each area** of matter is distinguished by its very own property and whether there is or is not a chemical alteration.

## The two properties of matter:

**Physical properties** occur **without a chemical reaction or change** to the matter. Some **physical identities are hardness, color, weight, odor and boiling point.** Example: application of facial makeup to skin, eyelashes or eyebrows, which are all forms of matter, provides a temporary color. Cleanse the face to remove color and all forms of matter (skin, eyelashes or eyebrows) are back to original color.

**Chemical properties** cause a **chemical reaction** and change to the matter. Example: neutralization phase of the permanent wave with the chemical reaction being "oxidation." This causes the disulfide bonds in the hair (matter) to reform into a new curled position.

**Matter's form** can be altered in various ways depending on the influence of the physical forces or chemical reactions.

## Matter can go through two types of changes:

**Physical change** is matter altered to a different shape **temporarily**, but returning to its original shape. Example: water (matter) freezes, becomes a solid (ice), melts and becomes a liquid (water).

**Chemical change** is matter altered to a **completely different form permanently** (does not return to original shape when shampooed). Example: chemically altering straight hair (matter) into a wavy or curly form with the application of permanent wave lotion.

# Physical Mixture...

***Physical mixtures** consist of two or more types of matter that are **blended together, but not chemically altered.** Each part in the mixture maintains its own properties. Most everything is a mixture such as alcohol, hydrogen peroxide and water. A mixture can be separated physically or mechanically.*

The following are all physical mixtures of matter. Understanding the different types of mixtures will heighten your awareness of the science behind the products you use and methods of application.

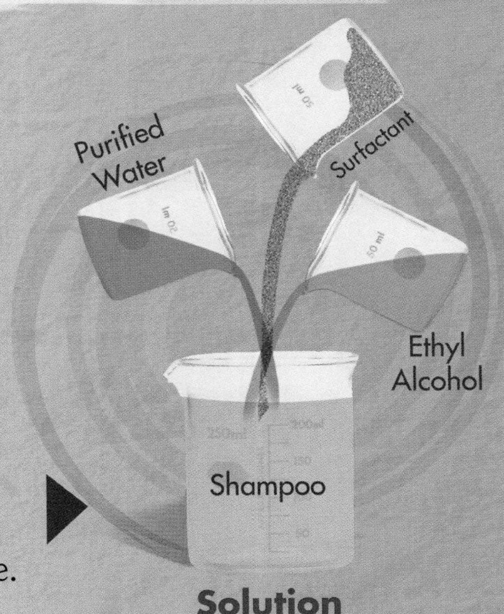


## Three types of miscible (without separation) mixtures:

**Miscible** is when a substance is able to be mixed with another substance. Example: alcohol and water.

1. **Solution** is a mixture that blends two or more small particles of gases, liquids or solids that do not separate.

A **solute** is the substance that is dissolved in the solution.

Shampoo

Solute (Surfactant, wetting agent)

A **solvent** dissolves other substances to form a **solution** with no chemical change. Example: ethyl alcohol used in many cosmetics, such as hairspray, shampoo, skin lotion or facial packs.

Solvent

Solute (Surfactant, wetting agent)

"Water is considered the "Universal Solvent," because it dissolves many substances."

# Physical Mixture ...

**2. Suspension** is a mixture that **blends large particles together without dissolving** into a liquid or solid. The particles **do not stay mixed**; they **separate back to their original state.** Suspensions must be mixed or shaken before use. Example: powder into oil or water (solid into liquid), such as certain foundation makeup for skin or nail polish.

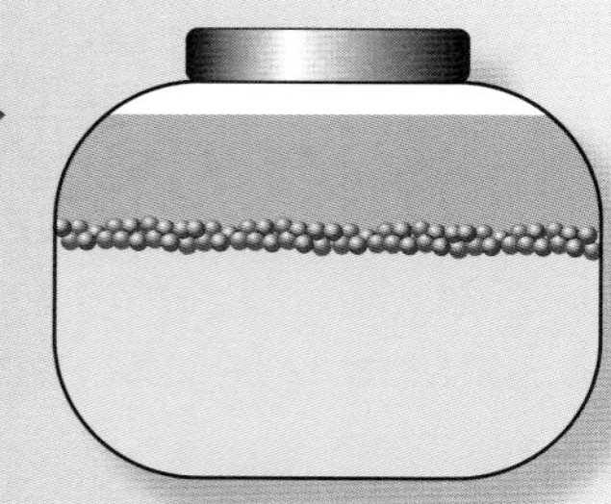

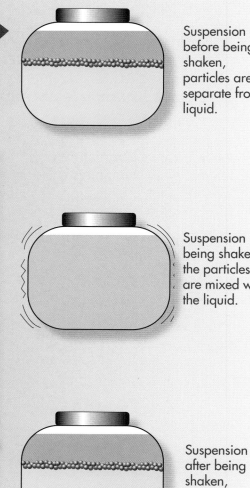

Suspension before being shaken, particles are separate from liquid.

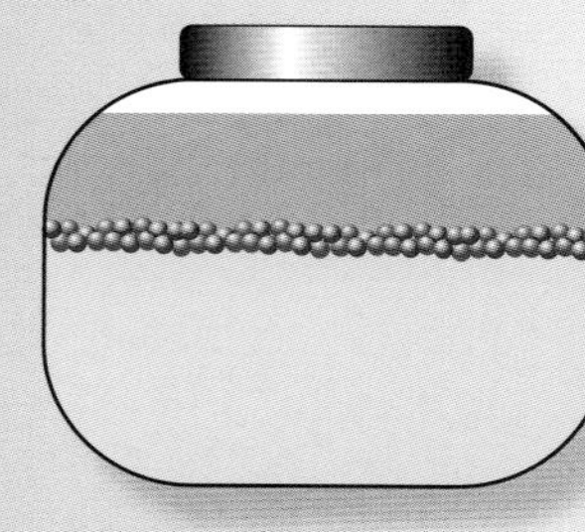

Suspension being shaken, the particles are mixed with the liquid.

Suspension after being shaken, particles reappear in the liquid after a period of time.

**3. Colloid** is a mixture composed of **tiny particles dispersed in a liquid, gas or solid.** Examples: aerosol, hand cream, pumice powder, paint.

## Immiscible (with separation) mixture:

**Oil-in-water**

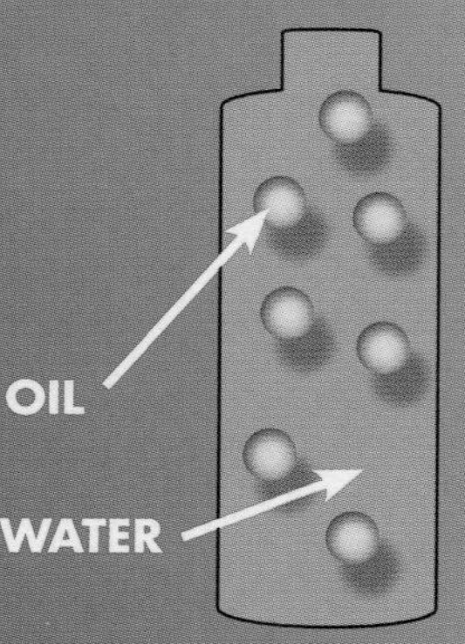


**Water-in-oil**

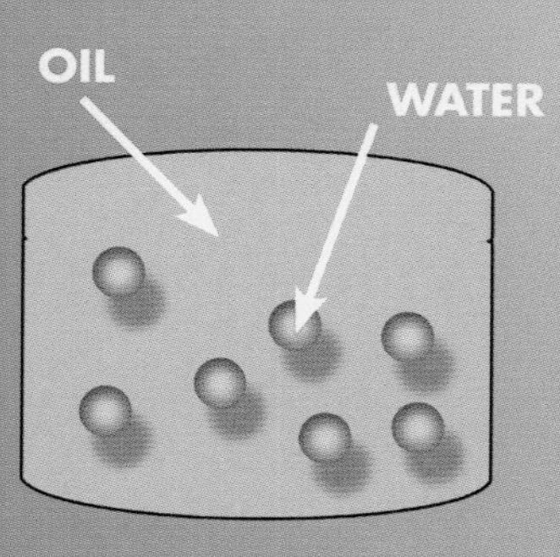


**Immiscible** is when a substance is not able to mix with another substance.

**Emulsion** is a mixture of two or more **immiscible substances that are dispersed throughout a liquid** that **eventually separate** from each other. Example: **oil dispersed into water,** such as shampoos, conditioners and haircoloring or **water dispersed into oil,** such as facial creams.

# Permanent Waving ...

**By reviewing** *what we learned in chapter 5, we know that hair is constructed of* ***amino acids,*** *which are* ***protein building blocks or units.*** *There are different kinds of amino acids that make up various types of protein ... the construction of an amino acid will determine the type of protein. The cosmetologist is most concerned with the protein* ***keratin,*** *which is a major protein in hair, skin and nails. Amino acids are chemical compounds that are made up of* ***hydrogen, oxygen, nitrogen, carbon and sulfur elements.***

## Chemical Bonding

Hydrogen—Oxygen—Nitrogen—Carbon—Sulfer

Amino acids need to come together to form the structure of hair (cortical layer). This occurs first through **bonding or linking** of the amino acids **end to end with a peptide** (pep-tide) **bond.** The **peptide bond or end bond** is **very strong** and it creates a **spiral chain effect,** which is referred to as the **polypeptide chain.** Numerous polypeptide chains are needed to form just one strand of hair.

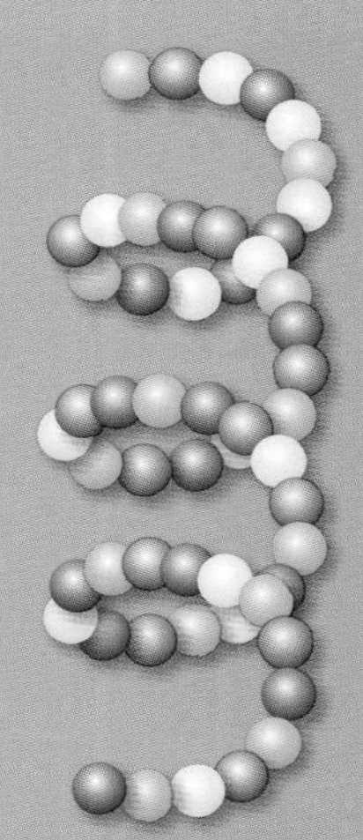
Polypeptide chain

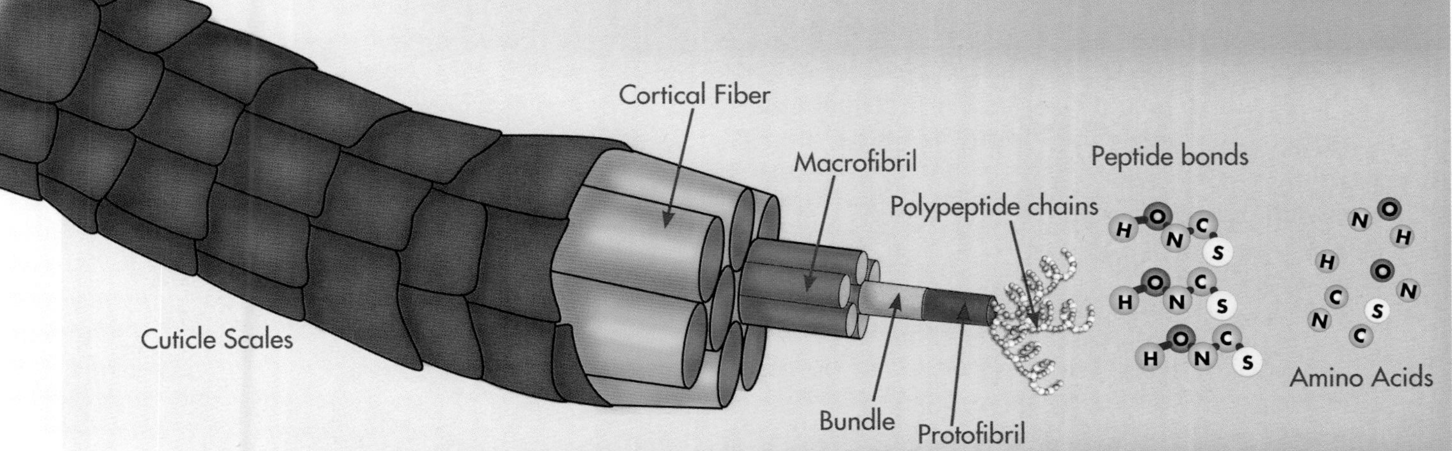


As a cosmetologist, we need to understand the details of each chemical procedure so as not to **overprocess** hair, causing damage or breakage. Overprocessing hair occurs when the **chemical actually weakens the amino acid's bonding,** which is its backbone and support.

"Poly meaning 'many' and peptide meaning the 'end bond' connection."

8

# Permanent Waving ...

**In continuing** to build the structure of hair, the polypeptide chains are connected side-by-side with three types of **cross bonds or side bonds.**

## Three Main Types of Cross Bonds

**Hydrogen bonds** are **weak, but abundant** and therefore account for approximately **33 percent of hair strength.** This bond operates on the principle of **opposite electrical charge attraction,** whereas a molecule seeks out another molecule with an excess amount of negative electrons (ion). Hydrogen bonds are **easily broken by water or heat,** but **replaced or reformed** quickly as soon as hair cools or dries.

**Salt bonds** are also **weak, but abundant** and account for approximately **33 percent of hair strength**. This bond operates on the same principle as the hydrogen bond: **opposite electrical charge attraction.** Salt bonds are **influenced by the pH of hair** such as with the alkalinity of permanent waving or hair relaxing ... once hair is restored to its normal pH, bonds are reformed.

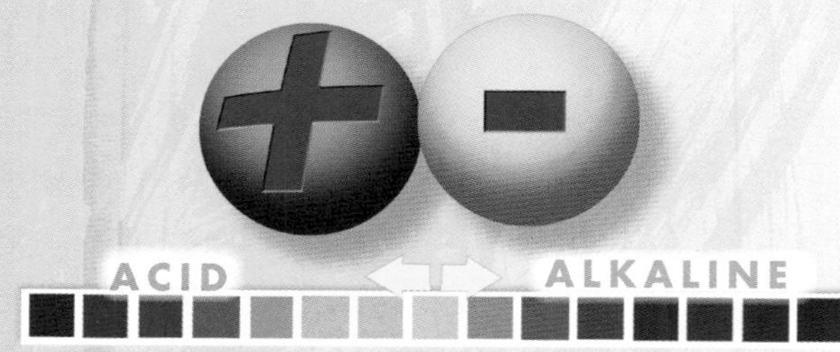


**Disulfide** (di-sul-fide) **bonds or sulfur bonds** connect **two sulfur atoms** located in the amino acid called **cysteine** (sis-tuh-een). A sulfur atom contained in the cysteine amino acid from one polypeptide chain will link up by way of the disulfide bond to a neighboring sulfur atom contained in a cysteine from another polypeptide chain. There are fewer disulfide bonds than hydrogen or salt bonds, but they are **stronger** and account for another **33 percent of the hair strength.** These bonds **ARE NOT broken by water or heat,** but are **only broken by chemical solutions,** and therefore play a major role in permanent waving and hair relaxing processes.

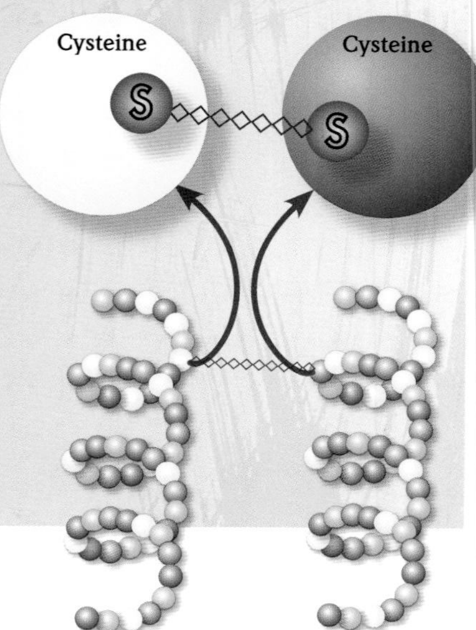

8

# Permanent Waving...

Let us take a look at what happens chemically when altering straight hair into a wavy or curly form temporarily. Hair is shampooed and conditioned (wet), which causes the **hydrogen and salt bonds to detach** and allow for hair flexibility, manageability and stretch when applying tension to wrap around a perm rod. To **temporarily (physical change)** obtain curl, allow hair to **dry and cool** and then remove rods/rollers. Once hair is dried and cooled, the hydrogen and salt bonds reconnect into a temporary wave or curl position.

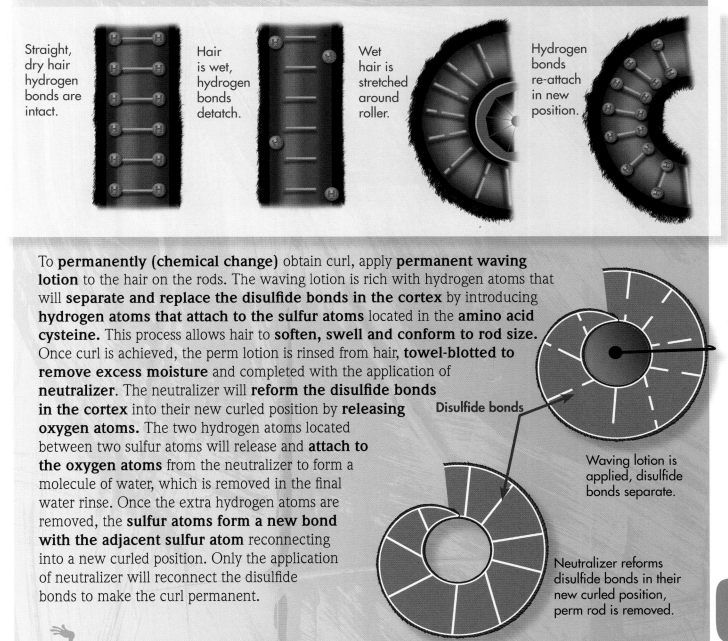

Straight, dry hair hydrogen bonds are intact.

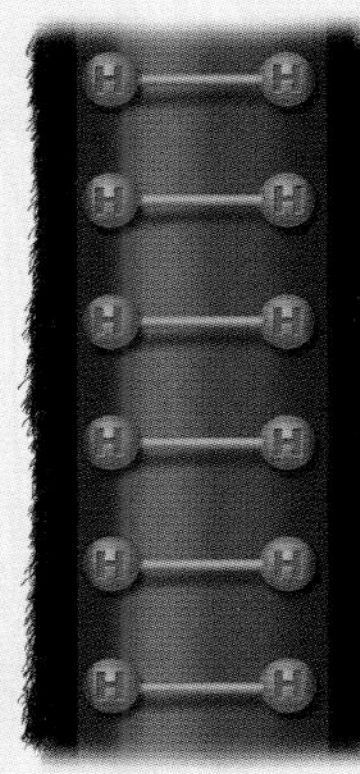

Hair is wet, hydrogen bonds detatch.

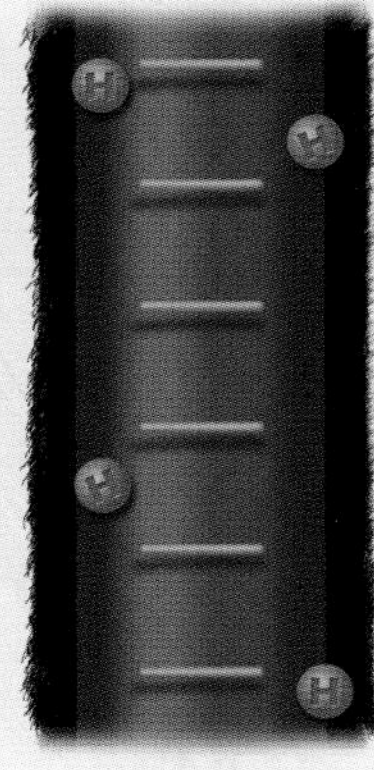

Wet hair is stretched around roller.

Hydrogen bonds re-attach in new position.

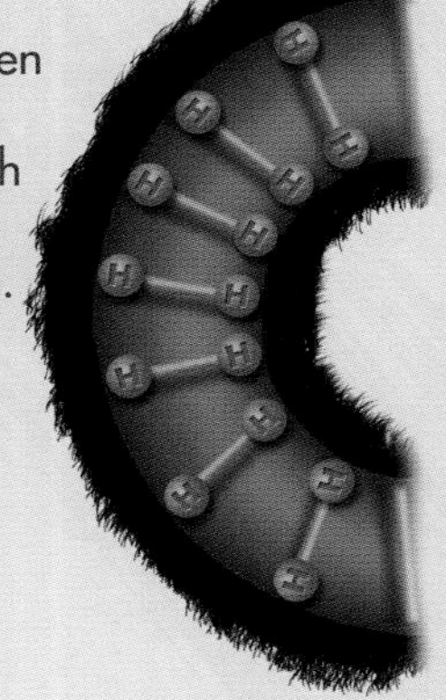

To **permanently (chemical change)** obtain curl, apply **permanent waving lotion** to the hair on the rods. The waving lotion is rich with hydrogen atoms that will **separate and replace the disulfide bonds in the cortex** by introducing **hydrogen atoms that attach to the sulfur atoms** located in the **amino acid cysteine.** This process allows hair to **soften, swell and conform to rod size.** Once curl is achieved, the perm lotion is rinsed from hair, **towel-blotted to remove excess moisture** and completed with the application of **neutralizer**. The neutralizer will **reform the disulfide bonds in the cortex** into their new curled position by **releasing oxygen atoms.** The two hydrogen atoms located between two sulfur atoms will release and **attach to the oxygen atoms** from the neutralizer to form a molecule of water, which is removed in the final water rinse. Once the extra hydrogen atoms are removed, the **sulfur atoms form a new bond with the adjacent sulfur atom** reconnecting into a new curled position. Only the application of neutralizer will reconnect the disulfide bonds to make the curl permanent.

**Disulfide bonds**

Waving lotion is applied, disulfide bonds separate.

Neutralizer reforms disulfide bonds in their new curled position, perm rod is removed.

8

"Air can neutralize the disulfide bonds back into their new curled position, but it would take 72 hours, which is not a practical suggestion for in the salon."

# Permanent Waving...

**NOTE:** The words lotion, solution or reducing agents are interchanged throughout text for the liquid used in permanent waving.

**Types** of permanent wave solutions vary according to texture and condition of hair and desired end result. The type of perm solution used is determined through **consultation with client and analysis** of his or her scalp and hair.

## The two main categories of permanent wave lotion are:

ALKALINE 

2. COVER PERM RODS

**ALKALINE permanent waves or cold waves** are processed **without heat** and usually vary in pH from an 8.5 to 9.5.

 The main ingredient in an alkaline wave is **thioglycolate** (thi-o-gly-co-late) **acid** ($C_2H_40_2S$), which is an **organic compound** of clear liquid with a strong unpleasant smell and mixes with alcohol and water. An additive of ammonia is used in permanent wave solutions.

 **Ammonia** (a-mo-nee-a) is an **inorganic compound** of colorless liquid composed of one part nitrogen and three parts hydrogen ($NH_3$). It has a pungent odor and is an alkaline substance used in the manufacture of permanent wave solutions and hair lighteners to aid in opening the cuticle layer.

 **Sodium** (Na) is a highly soluble chemical element and is an alkaline substance used in the manufacture of permanent wave lotions and chemical hair relaxers.

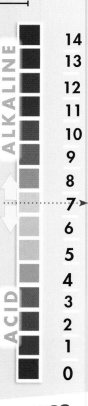

ALKALINE 14 13 12 11 10 9 8 NUETRAL 7 6 5 4 ACID 3 2 1 0

**ACID permanent waves or heat waves** are processed with the **application of heat** and usually vary in pH from a 4.5 to 7.

 The main ingredient in an acid wave is **glyceryl** (glyc-er-yl) **monothioglycolate** (ma-no-thi-o-gly-co-late), ($C_5H_{1}0O_4S$) which consists of thioglycolate acid and glycerin. (Glycerin replaces the ammonia).

 **Glyceryl** (glyc-er-yl), **derived from glycerin** (glyc-er-in) ($C_3H_5OH_3$), which is an odorless, colorless liquid and is miscible in water. Glycerin is another ingredient used in the permanent waving lotion to help lower the pH due to its moisturizing properties.

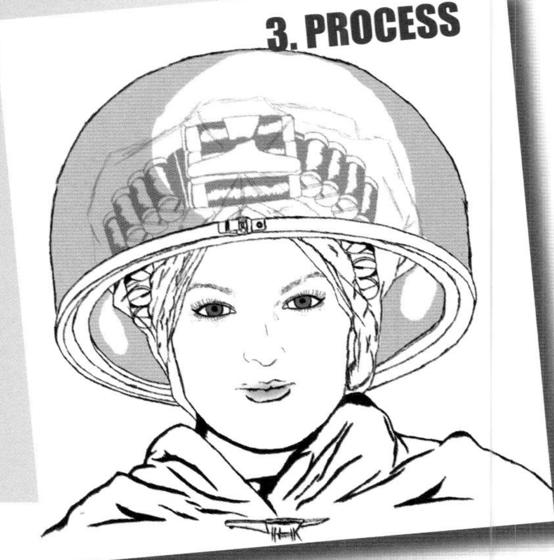

# Permanent Waving...

To complete the permanent wave procedure, the solution is rinsed from the hair to stop the chemical action. The hair is then towel-blotted thoroughly to remove excess moisture and prevent dilution of the neutralizer. **Neutralization** is the last chemical process in ensuring thorough removal of permanent wave lotion and reformation of disulfide bonds.

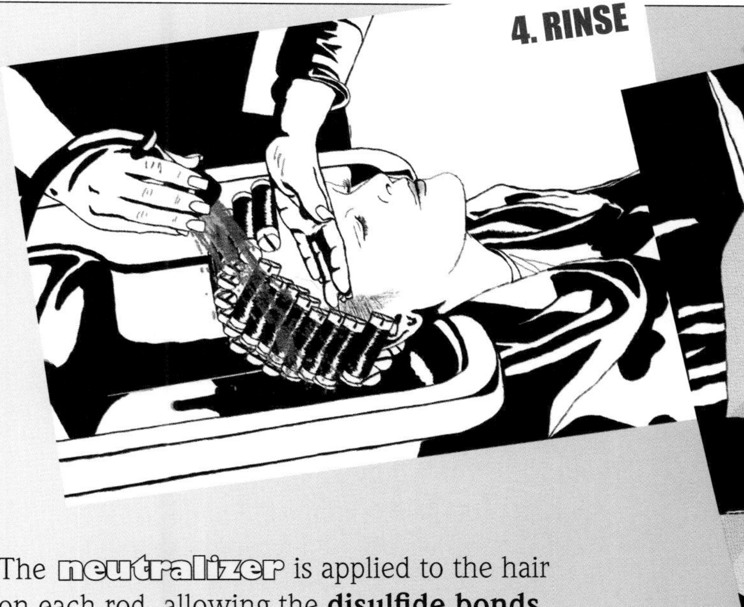


The **neutralizer** is applied to the hair on each rod, allowing the **disulfide bonds to reform in their new curled position.** Neutralizers usually range from a pH of 3.0 to 7.0.

The main ingredient in a neutralizer is **hydrogen peroxide** ($H_2O_2$), which is a clear liquid compound with a slight odor. Hydrogen peroxide is a strong **oxidizing agent** (releases oxygen) and is available in **varying strengths** with a chosen strength dependent upon type of hair service, but generally a **2 to 3 percent solution is used** in some neutralizers.

**NOTE: Oxidation** is the chemical reaction that occurs when a **substance is combined** with another **ingredient that contains oxygen. Reduction** is the chemical reaction that occurs when **oxygen is released** from a substance.

**Sodium bromate** ($NaBrO_3$) comprises of inorganic colorless, odorless crystals that release oxygen and may be used as an alternative ingredient in neutralizers.

"A slight lightening action may occur on the hair when receiving a permanent wave due to some neutralizers containing the ingredient hydrogen peroxide."

neutralizer

# Chemical Hair Relaxing ...

*Taking wavy to curly hair and chemically altering it to a straight form is referred to as **hair relaxing.** Quite simply, we are **performing the opposite of the permanent wave procedure ...** instead of reforming straight hair into waves or curls, we are rearranging curly hair into various degrees of straightness!*

**The two main categories of chemical hair relaxers are:**

1. **Metal hydroxide** (hy-drox-ide) **relaxers** are compounds formed by a metal such as **sodium, potassium and lithium** and combined with hydrogen and oxygen. They are considered **"no-mix lye relaxers."** The pH of hydroxide relaxers are usually 13 and up due to the extremely high alkaline content.

- **Sodium hydroxide** (NaOH) is a colorless, odorless, white solid inorganic compound commonly known as **lye**. It has a **high alkaline content** with a pH range of 12.5 to14 and is considered to be the **strongest** ingredient used in chemical relaxing.
- **Potassium** (po-tas-si-um) **hydroxide** (KOH) is a white, solid chemical compound with a very strong alkaline content and pH of 12 to 13.5.
- **Lithium** (lith-i-um) **hydroxide** (LiOH) is an odorless, granular powder with a strong alkaline content and a pH of 12 to 13.5.

"Depilatories or hair removal creams usually contain the active ingredient sodium hydroxide."

8

# Chemical Hair Relaxing . . .

**NOTE:** Guanidine relaxer is usually packaged with a procedure requesting the mixing of two products.

## Hydroxide relaxer that is a non-metal:

- **Guanidine** (gua-ni-dine) **hydroxide** is a combination of calcium hydroxide cream and guanidine carbonate with a pH ranging from 10 to 13. **Calcium hydroxide** (CaOH) is a highly alkaline substance that is never used by itself, but is usually mixed with other relaxer ingredients. **Guanidine carbonates** (car-bon-ates) are water-absorbing crystals that are high in alkalinity and help to provide moisture.

Disulfide bonds intact before thioglycolate is added.

**2.** **Ammonium thioglycolate** ($C_2H_4O_2$-$SH_3$-N) **relaxer** is a **"no lye"** relaxer with a pH over 10. The **chemical breakdown** is the same as the permanent wave procedure with the exception that the thioglycolate is produced in a **higher concentrated form of a cream or gel.** The disulfide bonds located in the cortex between the two sulfur atoms are broken while **hair is manipulated into a straight form.** Once desired straightness is achieved, the ammonium thioglycolate is rinsed from the hair and **neutralizer** is applied to **restore the disulfide bonds into their newly reformed position** (same neutralizer used in the permanent wave process).

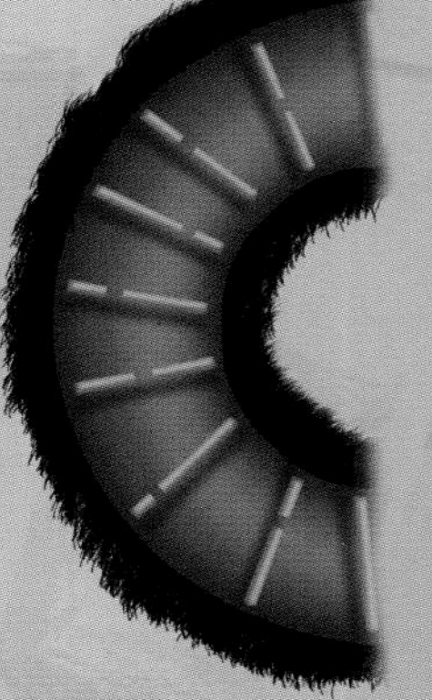

Disulfide bonds break as hair is straightened.

**NOTE:** Ammonium thioglycolate type of relaxer may be used in conjunction with the soft curl permanent wave.

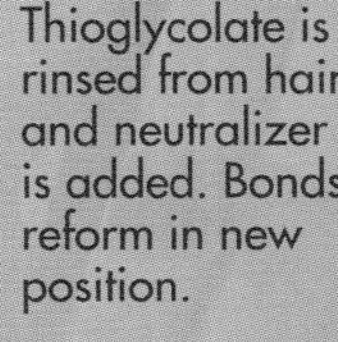

Thioglycolate is rinsed from hair and neutralizer is added. Bonds reform in new position.

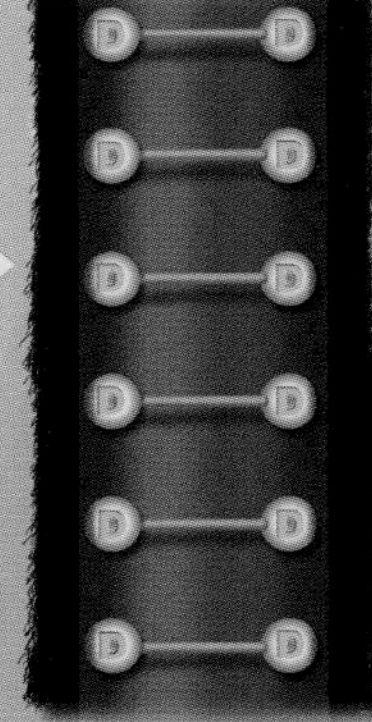

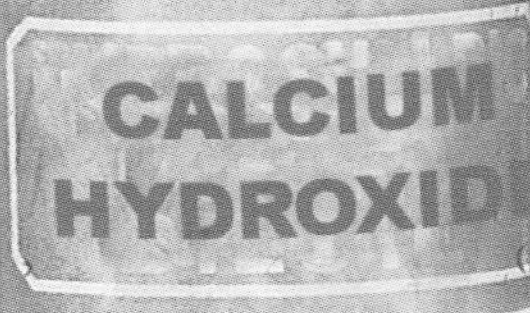


- **Ammonium bisulfite** (bi-sul-fite) or **ammonium sulfite** is a colorless, odorless solid crystal ($NH_4HSO_3$); considered a mild, **"no lye"** relaxer with a pH ranging from 6.5 to 8.

# Chemical Hair Relaxing . . .

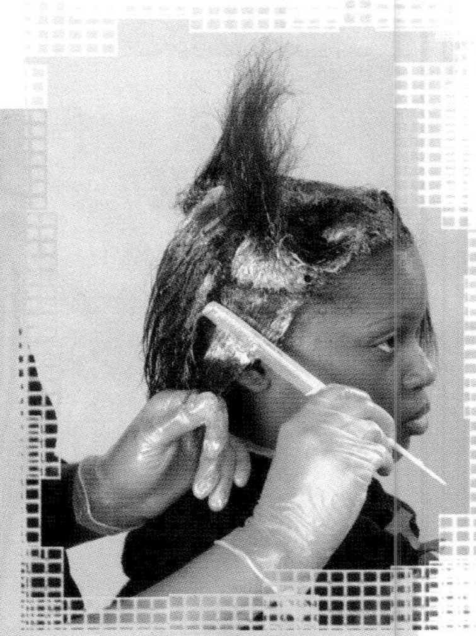

Both ammonium thioglycolate and bisulfite relaxers break down the disulfide bonds, but the hydroxide relaxers have a different and irreversible reaction.

The chemical breakdown for hydroxide relaxers is slightly different due to the **removal of only one sulfur atom.** (Remember, disulfide bonds connect by two sulfur atoms.) The **disulfide bond is then replaced** by a **lanthionine** (lan-thee-o-nine) **bond.** This process is referred to as **lanthionization** (lan-thee-o-ni-za-tion). Once the disulfide bond is broken and replaced with the new lanthionine bond; it is permanent and cannot be reformed back to a disulfide bond.

**CAUTION:** Hair chemically processed with a hydroxide relaxer **cannot** be treated with a thioglycolate relaxer or vice versa. **Extreme hair damage and breakage may occur.**

"Hair usually requires three or more shampoo treatments for thorough neutralization."

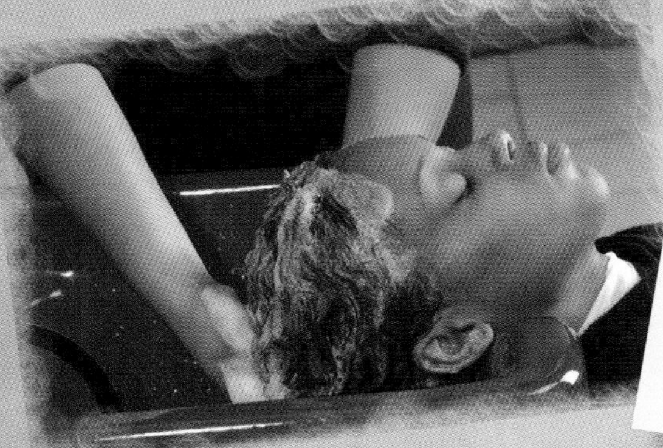

**NOTE:** Some manufacturers include in their neutralizing shampoo a pH indicator, which changes the shampoo's lather to a certain color when hair is completely rinsed clear of relaxer and returned to a normal acidic pH.

**NO oxidation** occurs in the hydroxide relaxer neutralization step as it does in the ammonium thioglycolate neutralizing. The hydroxide relaxer is rinsed from the hair, but that alone does not lower the pH; **an acid balanced shampoo is applied to restore the hair to a normal pH** and complete the neutralization.

# Soft Curl Reformation ...

A ***soft curl permanent or reformation*** *is taking overly curly hair and* ***chemically reforming*** *the hair into larger more manageable curls or waves.* ***Soft curl reformation*** *products are designed to provide two services:* ***chemically straighten the hair*** *and* ***chemically reform the hair*** *into large curls or waves.*

## Step One:

To chemically straighten the hair with an ammonium thioglycolate relaxer ... the hair is shampooed; the relaxer is applied having the same chemical breakdown as mentioned on previous page. Once hair is sufficiently relaxed and rinsed, proceed to step two, apply the permanent wave. **NEUTRALIZATION IS NOT PROVIDED IN STEP ONE!**

## Step Two:

To perform an ammonium thioglycolate permanent wave, use large diameter rods and solution-wrap the relaxed hair. The perm rods are placed in the hair following a design pattern, and hair is processed, rinsed and towel-blotted. The neutralizer is applied to hair on the rods following manufacturer's directions.

# Problem Solving...

**The Scientific Method of Problem Solving** *is a standard procedure used to evaluate criteria and develop accurate theories to explain and predict future events. Any existing perceptions or beliefs are replaced by tested and proven theories when following the four steps to the* ***scientific method.***

## The following are the four steps of the scientific method:

**1. Identify the Problem.**
Observe and describe an incident or event. A question is identified upon the description of the incident or event.

**2. Develop the Explanation.**
Develop a hypothesis to explain the incident or event. The hypothesis is a tentative assumption or reason as to what is causing the incident or event to occur.

"The Scientific Method is a valuable tool for problem solving in everyday life, not just in the science lab."

**3. Predict Future Events.**
Use the hypothesis to predict other incidents or events. If the assumption is correct, then future incidents or events would be avoided or prevented.

**4. Test Predictions.**
Perform experimental tests of the predictions. If the tests prove the predictions are true, then the hypothesis is accepted as a theory or law of nature. If the tests do not prove the predictions, then steps two through four must be modified and repeated until proven accurate.

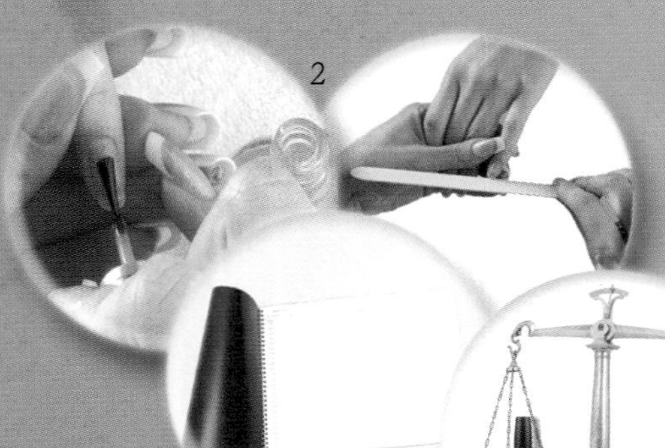

# Problem Solving...

**Example:** Let us examine the use of the Scientific Method of problem solving for a typical occurrence in the hair salon. After reviewing this problem, create another theoretical occurrence, and then work through the four steps to provide the solution to this problem.

1. **Identify the Problem:**
During the hair service consultation, the client states she would like her hairstyle to maintain its look throughout the day. The client washes her hair every day and uses a curling iron and styling products to help maintain design, but by end of day, hair is flat and straight.

2. **Develop an Explanation:**
The completion of a hair analysis determines the following: texture is fine, elasticity is low, porosity is irregular and density is medium. Fine hair with a low elasticity presents a challenge in maintaining a design throughout the day. Suggest to the client a protein penetrating conditioner prior to receiving a permanent wave.

3. **Predict Future Events:**
Explain that the protein in the conditioner will help strengthen her hair, even out the porosity and provide durability in maintaining design. The permanent wave will provide her with long lasting curls or waves, fullness and design hold. The use of a curling iron should be minimal or no longer needed; therefore less time will be spent on hair and damage to the hair will be reduced.

4. **Test Predictions:**
Apply a protein penetrating conditioner to show how strength of hair provides a longer design hold. Perform a permanent wave producing curls or waves according to hairdesign. Upon reviewing the finished results, the hairdesign will have fullness and longer lasting curls or waves. Market the protein conditioner for home maintenance and suggest four- to six-week salon visits for permanent wave maintenance that includes haircuts.

RETAIL · RE-BOOK · REFERRAL

By solving your client's problems, you help create a satisfied customer who will re-book, refer and retail professional products.

# Cosmetology Chemistry REVIEW QUESTIONS

## FILL-IN-THE-BLANKS

| | |
|---|---|
| A. | Amino Acids |
| B. | Ammonium Bisulfite |
| C. | Cysteine |
| D. | Disulfide Bonds |
| E. | Emulsion |
| F. | Glycerol Monothioglycolate |
| G. | $H_2O$ |
| H. | $H_2O_2$ |
| I. | Hydrogen Bonds |
| J. | Inorganic Chemistry |
| K. | Ions |
| L. | Lanthionine Bond |
| M. | Mixture |
| N. | Neutrons |
| O. | Peptide Bond |
| P. | Polypeptide |
| Q. | Salt Bonds |
| R. | Sodium Hydroxide |
| S. | Soft Curl Permanent |
| T. | Thioglycolate Acid |

1. ________ involves substances that do not contain carbon.
2. ________ are protein building blocks or units.
3. ________ is the strongest ingredient used in chemical relaxing.
4. ________ are the strongest and can **only** be broken by chemical solutions.
5. ________ is a spiral chain formed by the connection of amino acids.
6. ________ consists of two or more types of matter blended together with no chemical altering.
7. ________ are atoms with an excess amount of electrons in their orbiting paths.
8. ________ is a mixture of two or more immiscible substances that are dispersed throughout a liquid.
9. ________ or end bond, connects amino acids together.
10. ________ are the neutral particles found in the nucleus of the atom.
11. ________ are weak, but abundant and easily broken by water or heat.
12. ________ is a molecule of water consisting of two hydrogen atoms and one oxygen atom.
13. ________ is the main ingredient in an alkaline permanent wave.
14. ________ are influenced by the pH of hair such as in the alkalinity of permanent waving.
15. ________ is hydrogen peroxide, which is the main ingredient in the neutralizer for permanent waving.
16. ________ is an amino acid containing the sulfur atoms affected in the permanent wave procedure.
17. ________ is the main ingredient in an acid permanent wave.
18. ________ is considered a mild, "no lye" relaxer.
19. ________ replaces the disulfide bonds in the hydroxide relaxer application.
20. ________ requires hair to be straightened and receive a permanent wave in two separate procedures.

STUDENT'S NAME DATE GRADE

end papers exothermic

neutralization porosity

spiral

processing

wrapping

# Permanent Wave

PERMANENT WAVE

9

# Terminology ...

*The following few terms will acquaint you with the various methods and tools used within the permanent wave service. As you study this chapter, you will discover techniques of the past as well as today's new skills in perm wrapping to create a multitude of hair textures.*

**Concave Rods** are tools used to produce a slightly uneven curl or wave pattern within a subsection of hair.

**Croquignole** is a method of wrapping hair from ends to scalp.

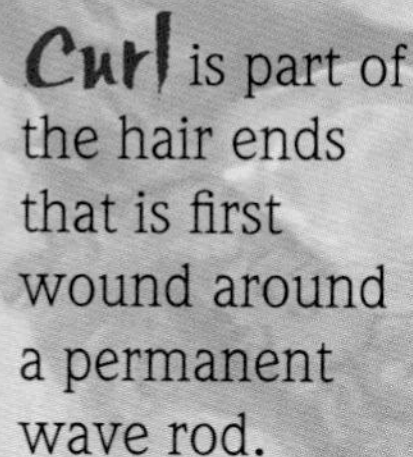

**Curl** is part of the hair ends that is first wound around a permanent wave rod.

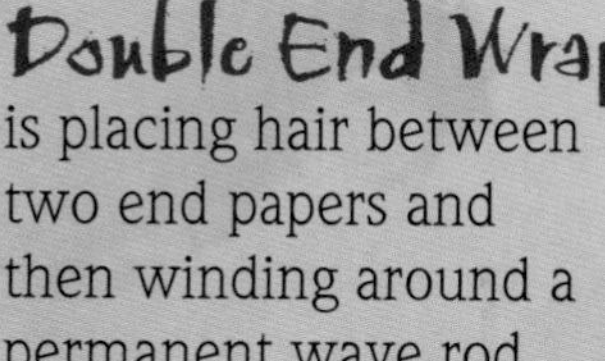

**Double End Wrap** is placing hair between two end papers and then winding around a permanent wave rod.

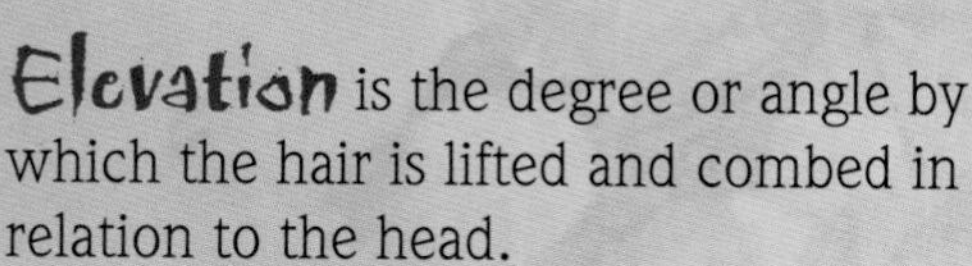

**Elevation** is the degree or angle by which the hair is lifted and combed in relation to the head.

# Terminology . . .

**Endothermic** is an acid wave processed by the application of chemical and heat.

**Sections** are manageable amounts of hair used for perm rod placement.

**Spiral** is a method of vertically wrapping long hair on perm rods or spiral-designed rods from "scalp to ends" or "ends to scalp."

**Subsection** is an amount of hair selected for the placement of each perm rod.

**Test Curl** is hair that is unwound from the perm rod during processing to determine if desired curl is achieved.

# Permanent Waving . . .

*To chemically rearrange straight hair into a newly curled or wavy form is referred to as* ***permanent waving.*** *It gives the client not born with natural curl or waves an opportunity to experience a new type of texture or appearance. The perm gives the* ***freedom of creativity*** *to a hairdesign whether wearing just a "curly look" or styling a particular design.*

The industry of permanent waving has come a long way in the development of processing hair to coincide with each era. The popularity of the perm varies with each generation bringing forth new styles and different hair textures.

**NOTE:** Permanent waving is sometimes referred to as **chemical texturizing** because the texture of the hair is changed from a smooth straight appearance to a curly or wavy appearance.

1

2

3

4

# Permanent Waving . . .

Perm Press

A German hairdresser named **Karl Nessler** (1872-1951) started working on an idea to create permanent curls in the hair in 1896. He finally succeeded in **1906** with a device called **the electric permanent wave machine.** Long hair was **spiral wrapped from scalp to ends** around metal rods that were connected by electric cords to an overhead device. A sodium hydroxide solution was applied to the hair along with heat in a procedure that took six hours to complete.

In **1924**, a Czech hairstylist **Josef Mayer** introduced the **croquignole** wrapping method for medium to short lengths of hair. This method allowed hair to be wrapped from ends to scalp and quickly became the new way for perming hair. The **"overnight wave"** also was invented around this time to produce curls or waves without the use of heat. A strong alkaline solution was applied to pre-wrapped hair and processed overnight; clients would return to salon next day to have perm completed.

In **1938**, the **cold wave** was invented by **Arnold F. Willatt** which needed no heat or machines for processing. This procedure required the use of chemicals along with body heat and room temperature to process the curl or wave, but still took six to eight hours to complete.

By the **1940s** new **improved** permanent wave formulas were discovered with a faster processing time therefore creating less damage to hair.

As fashions and hairstyles evolved, so did the permanent wave. In the **1970s**, the **acid perm** was invented. This **soft and gentle wave** contained chemical ingredients with a low pH, along with the application of an outside heat source to obtain processing. The acid wave allows for freedom of hairdesign; whether choosing to wear the "curly" look or style hair to a particular design.

# Permanent Wave Rod Usage...

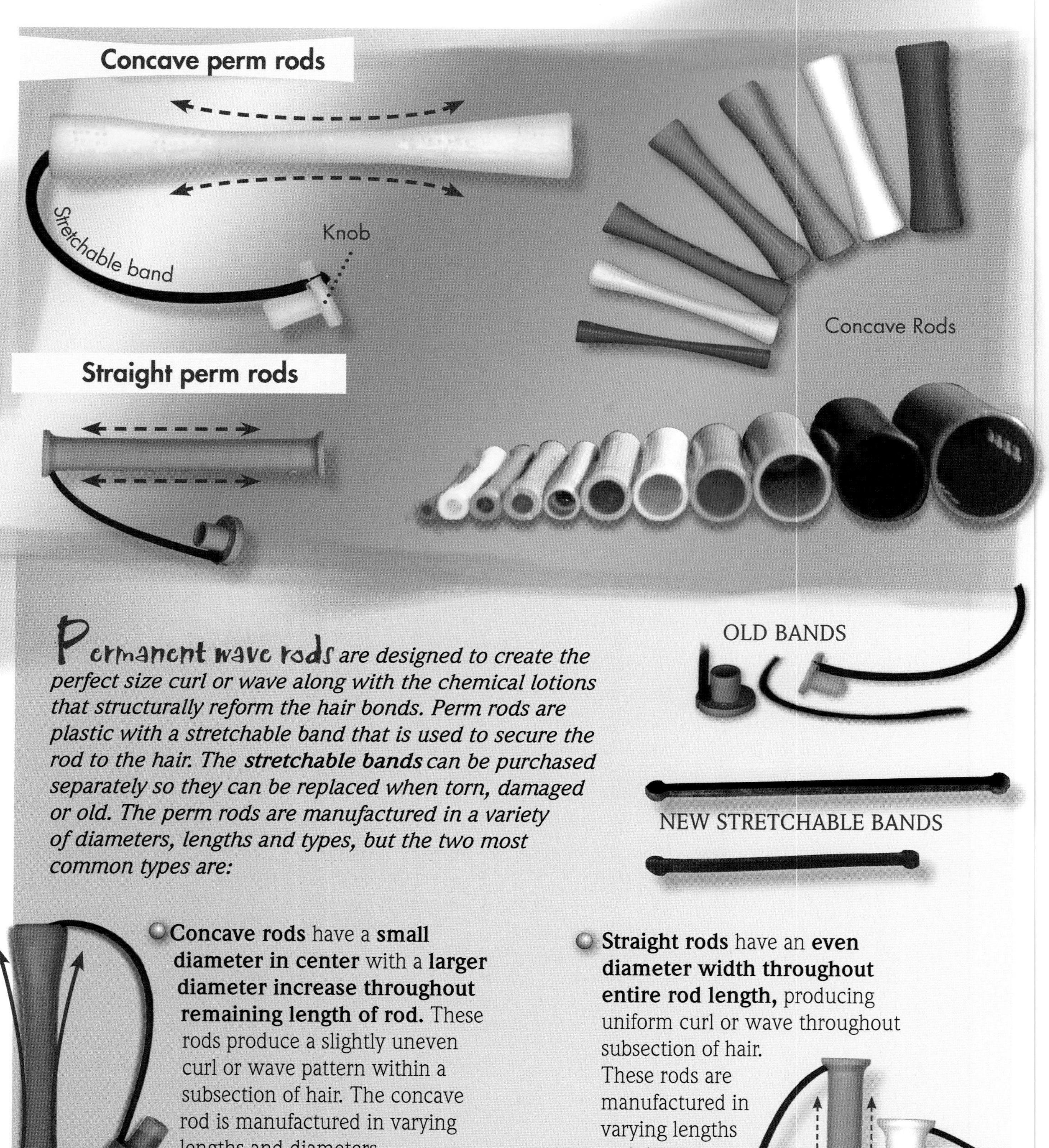

***Permanent wave rods** are designed to create the perfect size curl or wave along with the chemical lotions that structurally reform the hair bonds. Perm rods are plastic with a stretchable band that is used to secure the rod to the hair. The **stretchable bands** can be purchased separately so they can be replaced when torn, damaged or old. The perm rods are manufactured in a variety of diameters, lengths and types, but the two most common types are:*

- **Concave rods** have a **small diameter in center** with a **larger diameter increase throughout remaining length of rod.** These rods produce a slightly uneven curl or wave pattern within a subsection of hair. The concave rod is manufactured in varying lengths and diameters.

- **Straight rods** have an **even diameter width throughout entire rod length,** producing uniform curl or wave throughout subsection of hair. These rods are manufactured in varying lengths and diameters.

# Permanent Wave Rod Usage ...

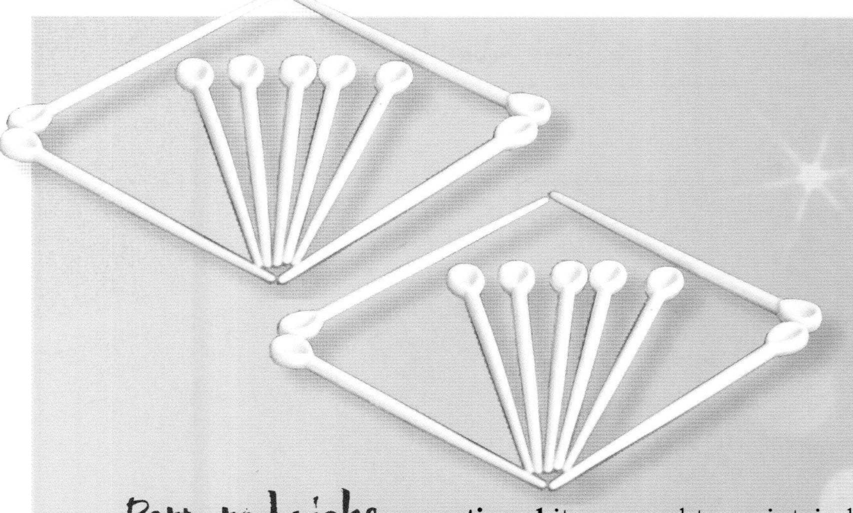

**Perm rod picks** are **optional** items used to maintain balance and eliminate pressure by lifting the bands off the hair. The picks may be used throughout the entire head or partially on top sections. **Caution:** These picks can not be used in conjunction with an alkaline permanent wave due to the great amount of tension being placed on the hair when pick is inserted under the band.

**Placement:** Perm rods are placed within sectioned patterns of wet hair. Direction of perm rod placement is determined by hairdesign. The type of rod placement determines the degree of volume that is desired for the hairdesign.

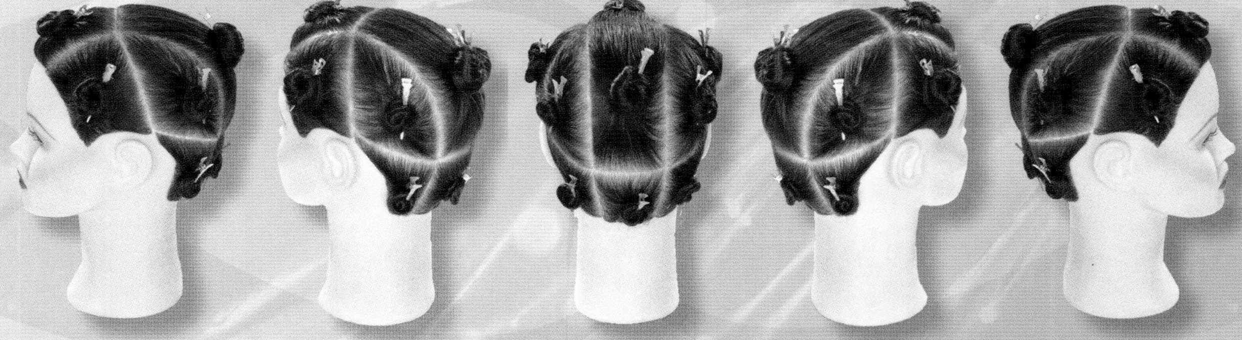

**Control:** The thumb, middle and index fingers wind the rod around the hair. Generally the rod is secured in the hair by a stretchable band with plastic knob that is locked into end of perm rod.

## Key Elements:

 Diameter or width of perm rod determines size of curl or wave

 Different types of perm rods create various curl patterns

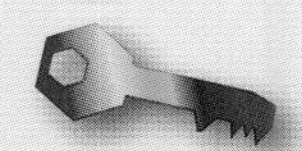 Manufactured in short or long lengths to accommodate any head size

## CONCAVE ROD APPLICATION

Select subsection of hair according to diameter of rod.

Comb hair at angle according to desired rod placement.

Place end paper wrap on hair.

Place perm rod parallel against paper; start winding paper without hair around perm rod to avoid fish hooks. Wind perm rod parallel down subsection. Apply moderate tension to keep hair and end paper smooth.

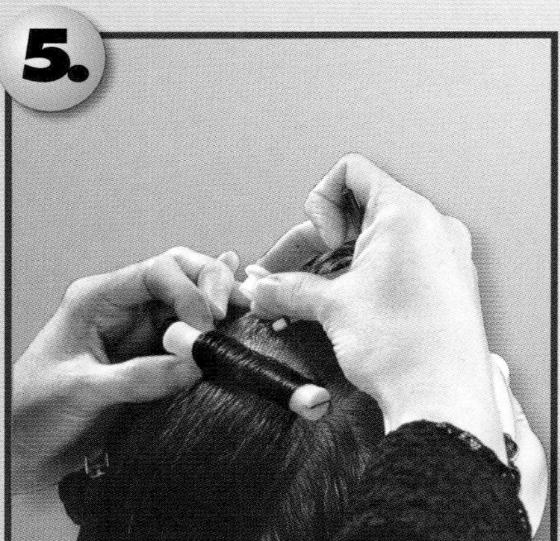


Secure rod by inserting the knob and placing stretchable band across top of rod closest to scalp, but not touching scalp.

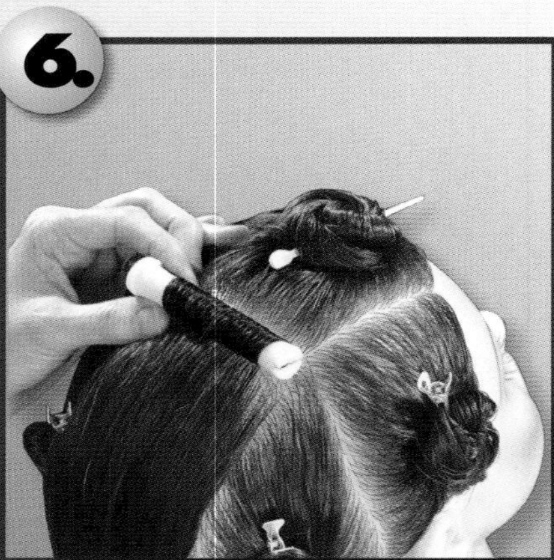


Concave rod secured and placed at scalp.

# Permanent Wave Rod Dynamics . . .

## STRAIGHT ROD APPLICATION

Select subsection of hair according to diameter of rod.

Subsection of hair to be placed around perm rod.

Comb hair at desired angle and place end paper wrap on hair.

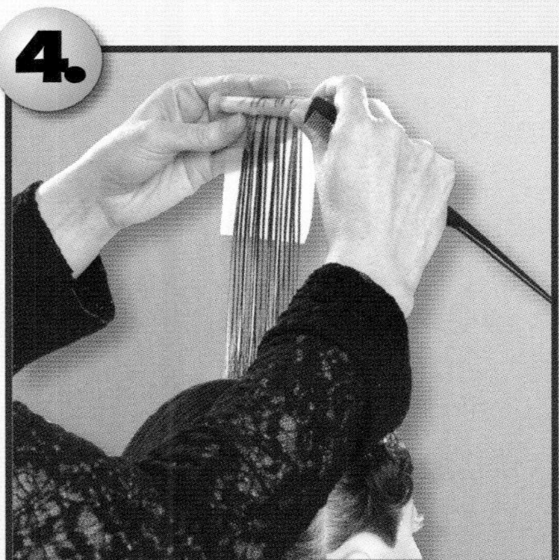


Place perm rod parallel against paper; start winding paper without hair around perm rod to avoid fish hooks.

Wind perm rod parallel down subsection. Apply moderate tension to keep hair and end paper smooth.

Secure perm rod at scalp by inserting knob and placing stretchable band parallel to top of rod closest to scalp without touching scalp. Straight rod secured and placed at scalp.

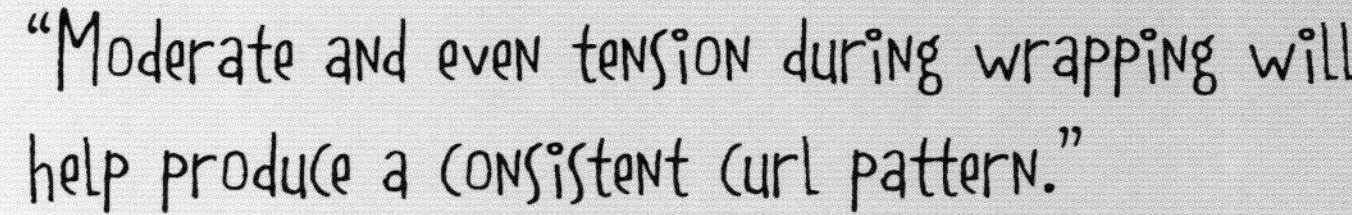

"Moderate and even tension during wrapping will
help produce a consistent curl pattern."


9

# End Paper Wrap Usage...

Fish hook end

**End papers** *are* **absorbent** *(porous) pieces of thin tissue-type paper that* ***control and protect the hair ends*** *or any* ***texturized lengths*** *of hair within a subsection. The end papers will generally cover a majority of the subsection and extend slightly beyond the hair ends. This will allow the hair to be wrapped smoothly around the perm rod and prevent "fish hook" ends.* ***Fish hook*** *ends are the result of hair ends* ***not wrapped*** *around perm rod smoothly, causing the ends to bend or crimp. End wrap papers come in various sizes and can be used on any length of hair. There are also non-absorbent (non-porous)* ***papers*** *to protect hair that is not being chemically altered as in a root permanent wave. As an option, a* ***dispenser*** *may be used for easy access to papers; another paper pops out after previous paper is pulled.*

## Placement:

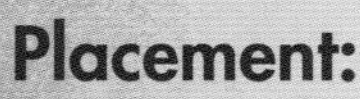

**Double end wrap** requires hair to be placed between **two end papers.** The technique allows hair to be evenly distributed within the papers. This type of wrap is excellent for long, layered or texturized hair.

# End Paper Wrap Usage . . .

**Book end wrap** requires only **one paper which is folded in half** much like a "book." Hair ends are to be combed close together and placed within the folded paper. This wrap is recommended for short hair.

**NOTE:** Avoid placing the hair into the "creased" portion of the end paper.

**Single end wrap** requires only **one paper used in conjunction with either the double end or book end wraps.** The double end or book end is placed on the hair ends followed by the single end wrap placed on top of remaining exposed hair. To ensure all texturized or uneven lengths of hair are wrapped smoothly around rod, apply as many single end paper wraps as necessary.

**Control:** The papers are placed on the hair using the thumb, index and middle fingers. Water is sprayed on the end paper allowing the paper to cling to the hair and help maintain control while wrapping.

## Key Elements:

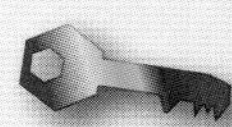

Controls hair ends to prevent fish hooks

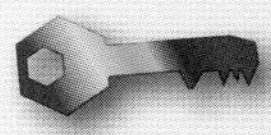

Smoothes hair to be wound around rod evenly

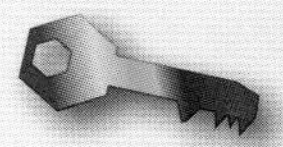

Provides an added protection to the hair from the chemicals

### DOUBLE END WRAP PLACEMENT

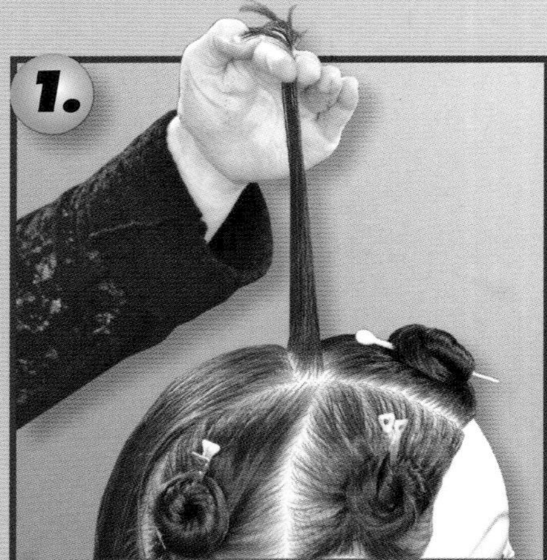

1. Comb subsection of hair at angle according to desired rod placement.

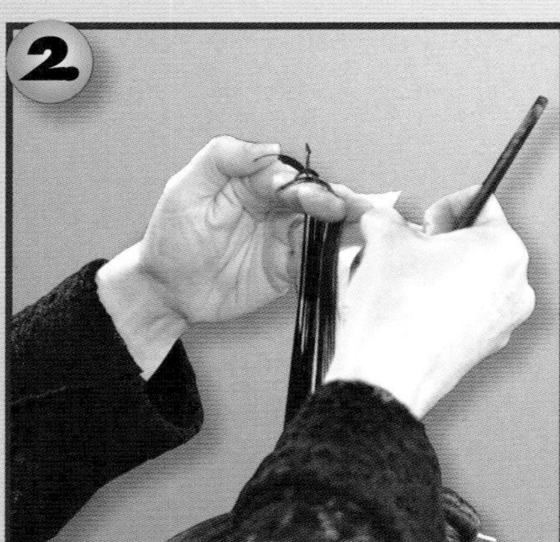

2. Place one end paper on topside of hair subsection.

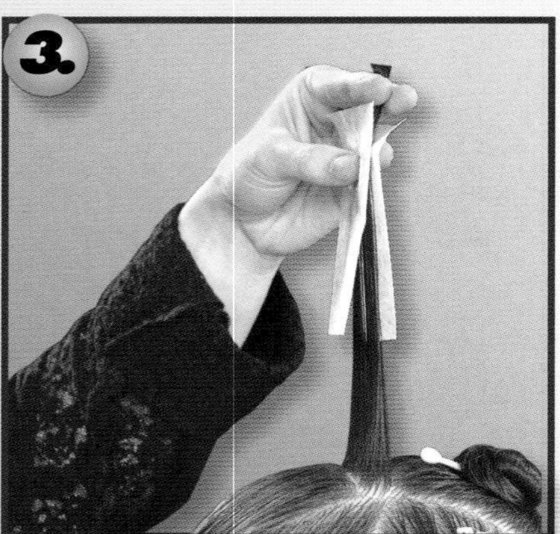

3. Place second end paper on underside of hair subsection.

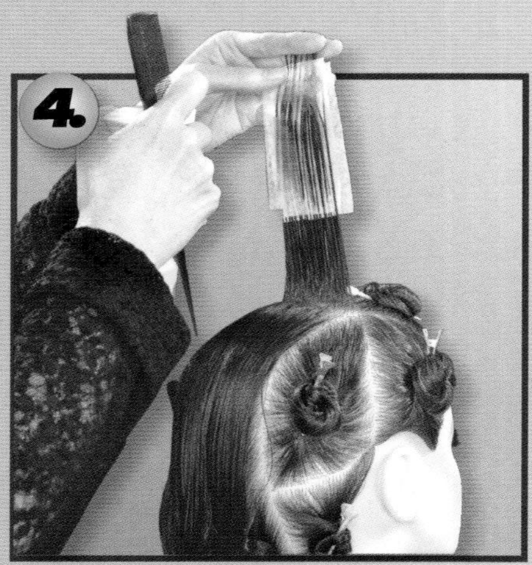

4. Lightly wet papers using water bottle; allows end papers to cling to hair.

5. Double end wrap placement.

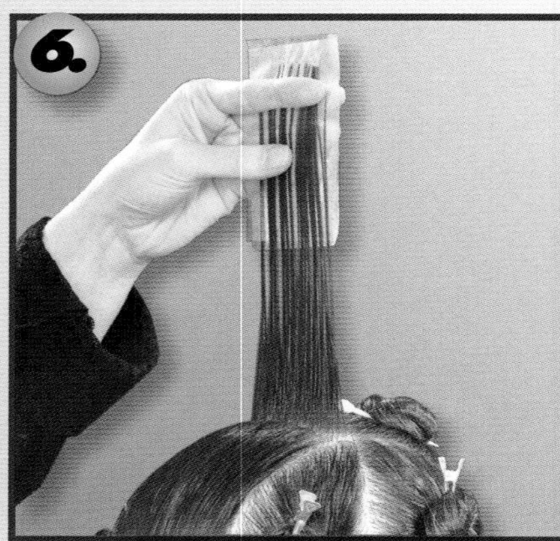

6. Slide end papers beyond hair ends to avoid fish hooks.

# End Paper Wrap Dynamics ...

## BOOK END WRAP PLACEMENT

1. Comb subsection of hair at angle according to desired rod placement.

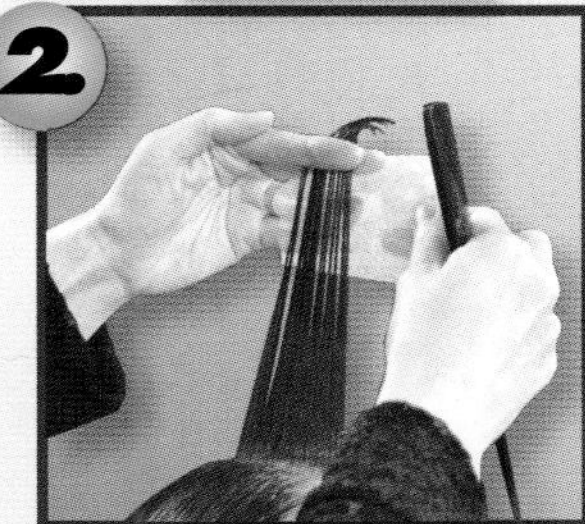

2. Place half of one end paper on topside of hair subsection.

3. Take other half of end paper and fold over the underside of hair subsection.

4. Wet paper using water bottle; allows end paper to cling to hair.

5. Book end wrap placement.

6. Slide end papers beyond hair ends to avoid fish hooks.

## SINGLE END WRAP PLACEMENT

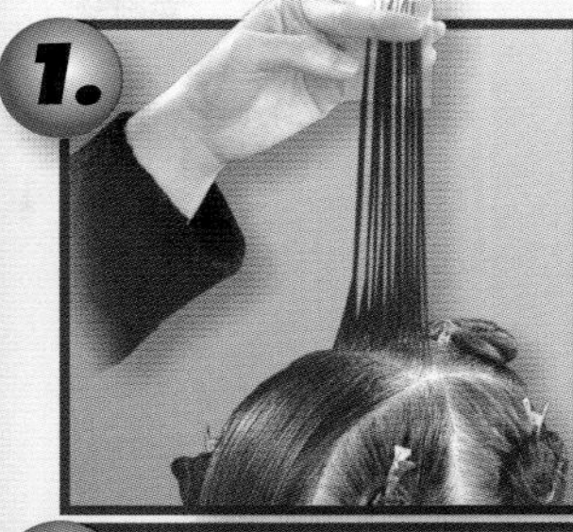

1. Apply either a double end or book end wrap to hair subsection.

2. Roll rod down subsection to end of paper wrap.

3. Place one end paper on topside of subsection.

4. Roll beginning part of single end wrap around perm rod.

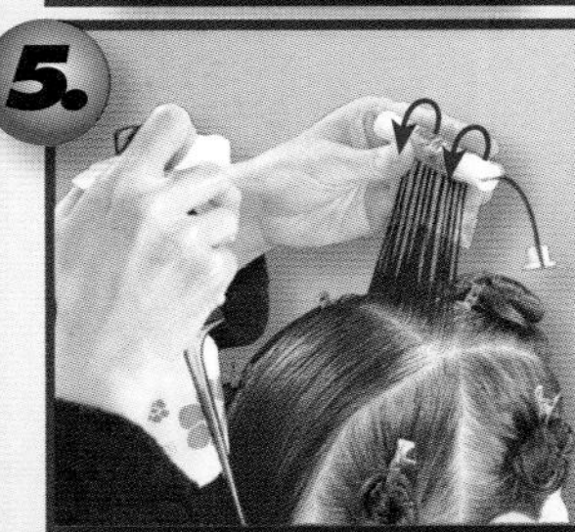

5. Wet end paper using water bottle; allows end paper to cling to hair.

6. Continue to wind perm rod down to scalp.

# Sectioning...

**Sections** consist of hair arranged in geometric shapings on various areas of the head to accomplish the total design plan. The sections are divided into **manageable amounts** of hair for control The **length of the perm rod determines the width of the hair sections.** Short length perm rods are placed in areas of sections that narrow due to conformity of different head sizes and hairlines.

**Partings** consist of the **lines used in dividing** sections or subsections. The **lines are partings** in the hair which create a subsection. The hair at the scalp is considered the base area.

**Subsections** are used to divide the sections or geometric shapes. In permanent waving, the **amount of hair determined for each subsection is created by using the diameter (width) of the perm rod.** The subsection also creates the base area, upon which the perm rod rests upon.

# Elevation . . .

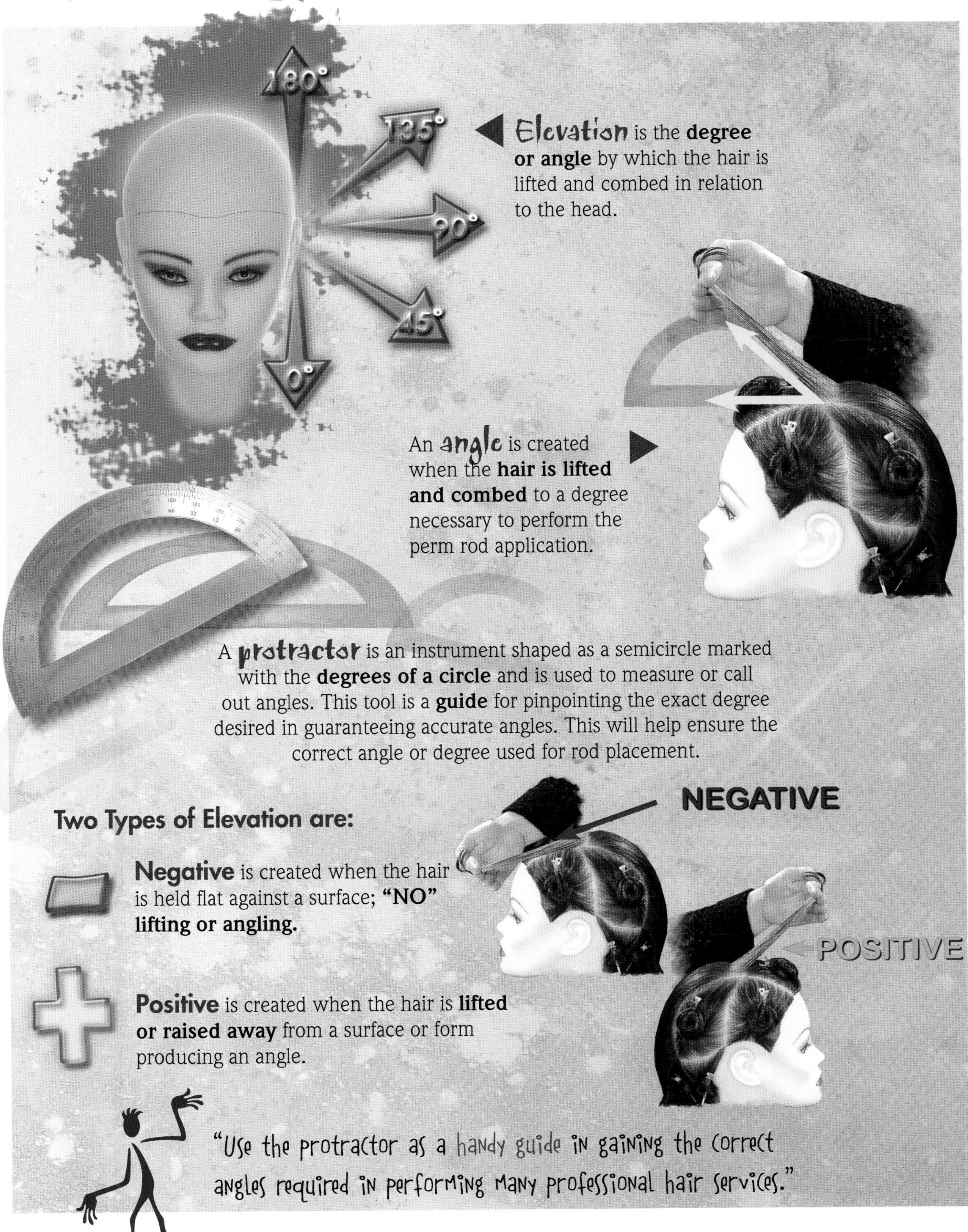


**Elevation** is the **degree or angle** by which the hair is lifted and combed in relation to the head.

An **angle** is created when the **hair is lifted and combed** to a degree necessary to perform the perm rod application.

A **protractor** is an instrument shaped as a semicircle marked with the **degrees of a circle** and is used to measure or call out angles. This tool is a **guide** for pinpointing the exact degree desired in guaranteeing accurate angles. This will help ensure the correct angle or degree used for rod placement.

## Two Types of Elevation are:

**Negative** is created when the hair is held flat against a surface; **"NO" lifting or angling.**

**Positive** is created when the hair is **lifted or raised away** from a surface or form producing an angle.

"Use the protractor as a handy guide in gaining the correct angles required in performing many professional hair services."

# Perm Rod Application . . .

***To understand** how perm rods are placed within the section of hair, we need to become better acquainted with the parts of each curl or wave. This knowledge will help clarify how rod placement contributes to the overall hairdesign.*

### The Parts of the Perm Curl or Wave are:

- **Base** is the area of hair that is attached to the scalp. When making the base selection, use the **diameter and length of the rod** as a measuring device. The end result of the permanent wave will be influenced by the length of hair, diameter of rod and rod placement.

- The **stem** is the area of hair between the base and the first turn of the hair around the perm rod. Stems are the part of the hair combed and held at an angle as the hair is wrapped around the perm rod. It is the **stem that determines the perm rod placements** as either on base, half under-directed or full under-directed.

- The **curl or circle** is the end of the hair that is first **wrapped completely around the perm rod.** The size of the circle along with the length of the hair determines the amount of curl produced from the permanent wave. A subsection of hair needs to be **wrapped around the perm rod at least two and half times** in order to create a complete curl formation.

# Perm Rod Application . . .

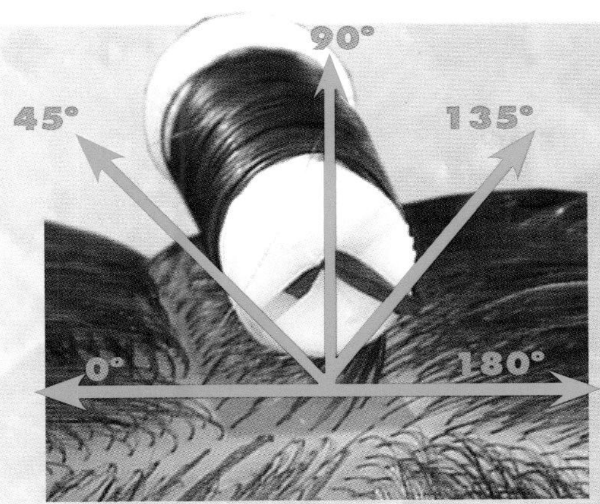


**Rod placement** is when the **perm rod rests on an area of the base** within the subsection (base section). The hair is combed at a certain degree or angle; rod is applied and wound down to scalp and rests on a certain part of the base.

## Three Types of Perm Rod Placements:

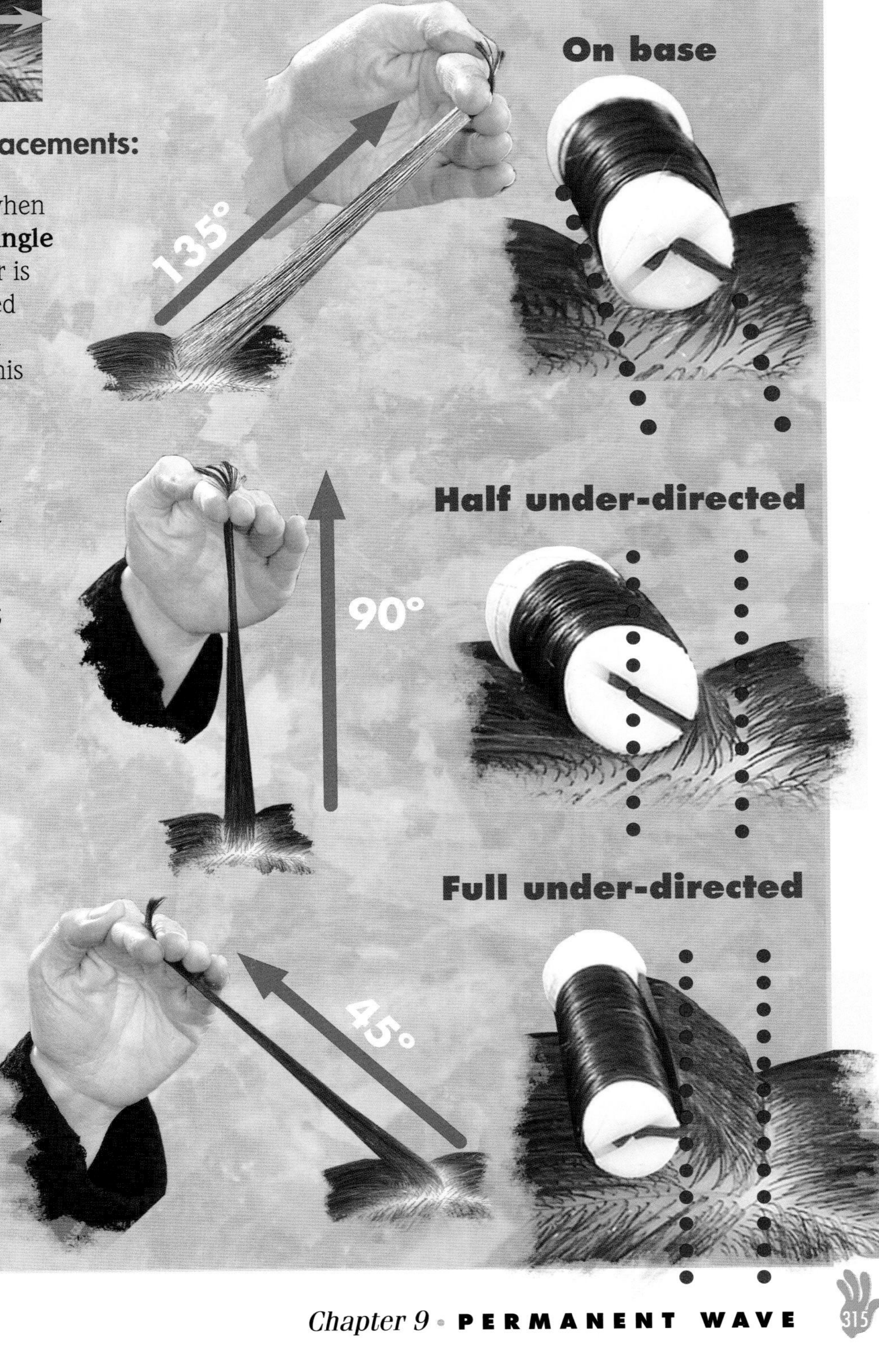

**On base placement** is created when hair is combed at a **135-degree angle above** the subsection parting; hair is wound around perm rod and rolled down to scalp. **Perm rod will sit directly on top of base area.** This placement creates a **maximum** amount of volume.

135°

**On base**

**Half under-directed placement** (or half-base) is created when the hair is combed at a **90-degree angle from center** of subsection; hair is wound around perm rod and rolled down to scalp. **Perm rod will sit directly on bottom parting of subsection.** This placement creates a **moderate** amount of volume.

90°

**Half under-directed**

**Full under-directed placement** (or off-base) is created when the hair is combed at a **45-degree angle below** the subsection; hair is wound around perm rod and rolled down to scalp. **Perm rod will sit directly below subsection or base area.** This placement creates a **minimal** amount of volume.

45°

**Full under-directed**

# Perm Wrapping Patterns . . .

**NOTE:** Hair is wound around a perm rod a maximum of **seven revolutions** to allow for thorough absorption of a chemical solution. If hair winds around rod more than seven revolutions, a long hair wrapping pattern is recommended.

*There are various methods of wrapping patterns depending on length of hair and hairdesign. The perm rods are placed within manageable sections of hair, which enables control and styling options.*

**The following are some of the common wrapping patterns:**

The **basic, nine block or straight wrap** is controlled sections of hair in which perm rods are placed in **rectangular shaped** subsections. This wrap is ideal for the client receiving roller or thermal design sets.

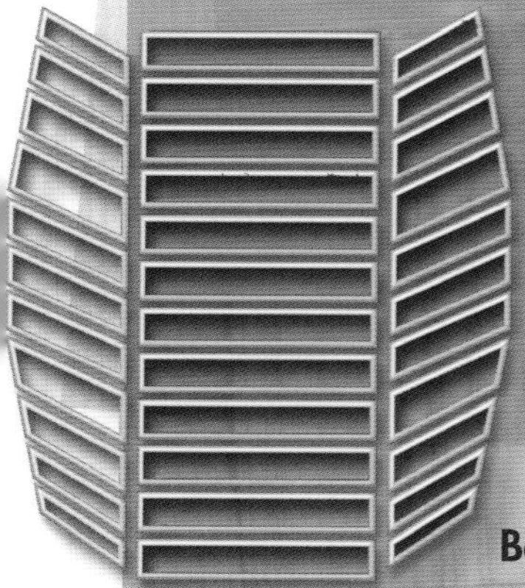

RA

Basic wrap

Curvature wrap

The **design or curvature wrap** is divided sections of hair with perm rods placed according to **client's hairdesign.** This wrap can be used in conjunction with other wrapping patterns such as a partial wrap, which may have perm rods placed following direction of hairstyle.

9

# Perm Wrapping Patterns . . .

The **bricklay wrap** has **NO** exact sections of hair; instead the perm rods are placed within a **staggered pattern of subsections.** The partings used in each subsection are **not consistent** with previous subsections due to staggered perm rod placement. This avoids splitting of hair at base area as can sometimes occur in other types of wrapping patterns.

The **weave wrap** consists of controlled sections of hair. The straight parting of hair taken for each subsection is replaced with a **"zigzag" parting,** which offers an excellent **blending of hair** within a design. This wrap is a **great transition wrap for blending hair** in a partial permanent wave.

**Partial wrap** requires permed hair to be separated from non-permed hair. A combination of a **design wrap with a weave wrap** will complement the hairstyle and allow sufficient **blending** of permed hair into non-permed hair. Always protect the hair not being permed with cream, conditioner and/or cotton.

# Perm Wrapping Patterns . . .

Long hair perm wrapping patterns offer the opportunity for the client with long hair to have a manageable and trendy design.

The **spiral wrap** is applied on hair longer than eight inches to **provide uniform curl or wave** from scalp to ends. Perm rod placement begins in nape area by dividing a horizontal parting of hair into small vertical subsections. The size of the vertical subsection is determined by diameter of rod.

Concave or straight perm rods can be used as well as rods designed specifically for spiral wrapping. If applying actual rods designed for spiral wraps such as long bendable or flexible rods, sections and subsections might be different (always follow manufacturer's directions). Hair may be wound **"ends to scalp" or "scalp to ends"** depending on perm rod used. **Overlapping of perm rods** will occur as wrap progresses toward top of head.

"Remember, a contributing factor for the intensity of curl or wave produced is the length of hair as well as the diameter of perm rod used."

# Perm Wrapping Patterns . . .

**Piggyback wrap** is used with hair longer than 10 to 12 inches (25.4 to 30.5 cm) and **provides uniform curl or wave** from scalp to ends. Hair may consist of divided sections followed by rectangular subsections created from length and diameter of perm rod. To create a piggyback rod placement, a **long length rod is rolled from mid-strand** down to scalp with remaining **ends of hair wound around a short length rod.** The short length rod will rest on top of the long length perm rod, hence the term "piggyback." This wrap may use different rod lengths or diameters, subsection directions and/or wrapping patterns.

## PIGGYBACK WRAP

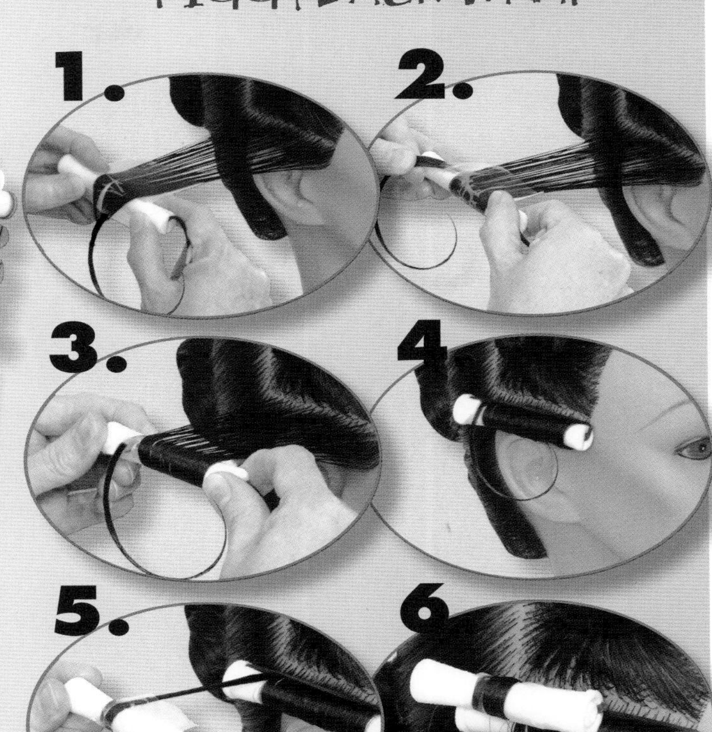


## DOUBLE ROD WRAP

**Double rod wrap** is another alternative wrap for hair longer than 10 to 12 inches (25.4 to 30.5 cm). This wrap uses **two of the same length rod** and produces a tight curl or wave pattern on the ends, progressing to a larger curl or wave toward scalp. A double rod wrap begins by winding a long length rod around the hair ends. After completing a full rotation of the rod, a long length rod is added on top of existing rod. Wrap is completed by winding both rods to the scalp.

# Perm Wrapping Patterns ...

**Ponytail wrap** consists of a **series of ponytail sections** throughout the head. Each **ponytail section is wrapped** with a series of **five to seven rods.** The section of hair at the forehead is wrapped according to hair length and style preference. This type of wrap produces curl or wave on the hair ends with minimal curl or wave towards scalp. The hair at the base is not included in the perm rod, therefore does not receive a permanent wave.

# Perm Rod Selection Guide . . .

Below is a list of common perm rods color-coded with curl and/or wave results. Diameter or width of rod determines degree of curl or wave produced in the hair. Length of hair is also a contributing factor to be considered for intensity of curl or wave.

**NOTE:** This is just a reference guide. If uncertain, always perform a preliminary test curl to obtain actual results. Remember, some manufacturers might color-code perm rods differently to identify a perm rod's diameter.

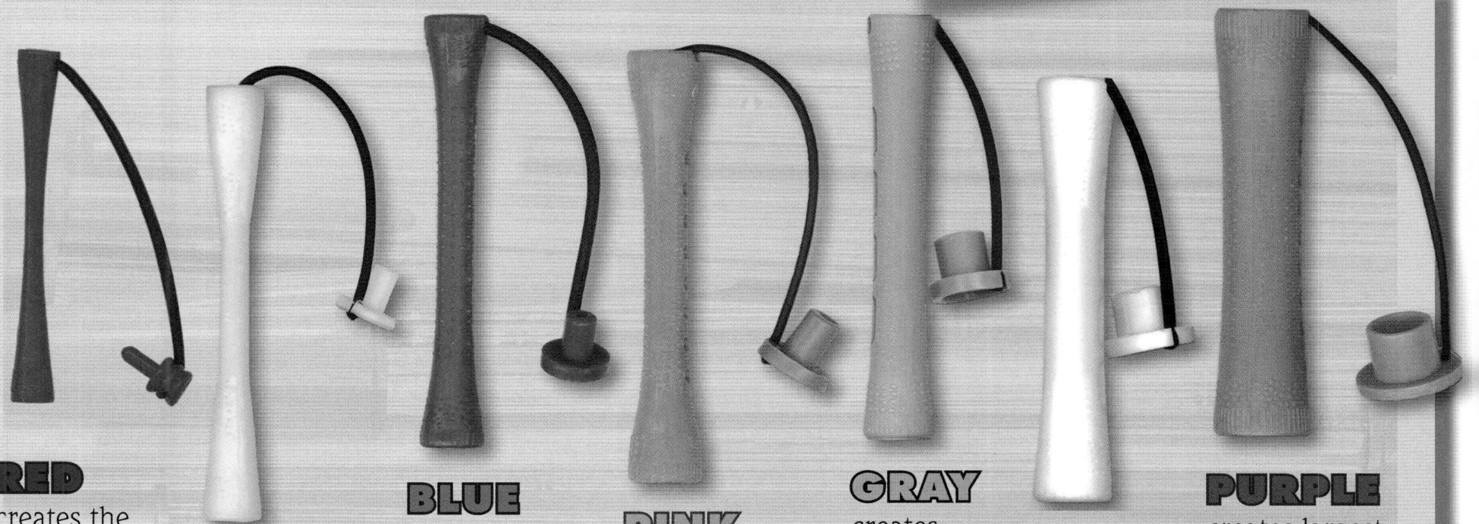

**RED**
creates the tightest curl

**YELLOW**
creates tight to small curl

**BLUE**
creates small curl

**PINK**
creates small to medium curl

**GRAY**
creates medium curl

**WHITE**
creates medium curl to large curl

**PURPLE**
creates largest curl to tight wave

**PEACH**
creates medium wave to large waves

**ORANGE**
creates large wave

**TEAL**
creates largest wave to body wave

**BLACK**
creates body with minimal wave

**BROWN**
creates just body (volume)

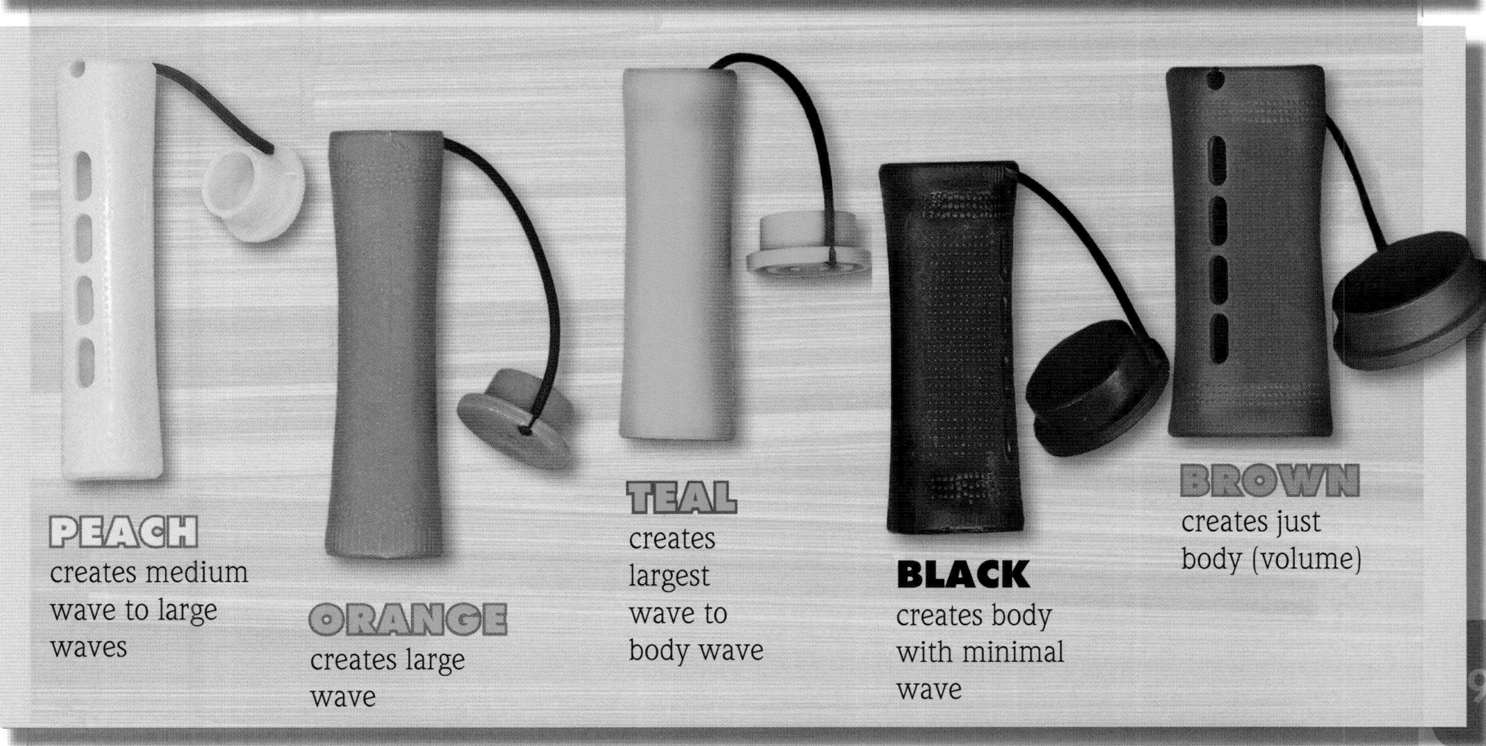

# Permanent Wave Liquid Tools . . .

*There are a variety of permanent waves to choose from to meet the styling needs of the client. A permanent wave is chosen upon careful consultation and analysis of scalp and hair. The type and condition of hair are major factors in selecting the type of perm to be used.*

## There are two major categories of permanent waves:

### 1. COLD PERMANENT WAVES (ammonium thioglycolate)

**Cold or alkaline waves** are processed at room temperature with **NO** application of heat. The only heat source is the client's body heat (naturally generated from the body). The pH of alkaline waves generally range from 8.5 to 9.5 due to ammonia as one of the chemical ingredients. The ammonia will **soften and swell the cuticle** to allow penetration of chemical into the cortex. Depending on the type of permanent wave selected, **tension or pull** of hair is required as it is being combed and wound around the perm rod. This will assist in producing the desired curl or wave. **DO NOT use tension when** wrapping perm rods into hair for cold waving due to the perm solution expanding the cuticle and possibly causing multiple hair breakage.

Once cold wave solution is applied to hair, the chemical breakdown begins **within the first five minutes;** it has a **faster processing time** than acid waves.

The cold wave is the **strongest perm solution** and is best used on hair that is classified as resistant. **Resistant hair** is when the cuticle scales are lying flat or compact, which hinders the chemical from penetrating into cortex.

Some types of perms create heat during processing due to an additive ingredient that activates a thermal reaction within the perm lotion—therefore an outside heat source is not needed. This is referred to as an **exothermic** (ex-o-ther-mic) **wave** with a pH ranging from 8.5 to 9.5.

# Permanent Wave Liquid Tools ...

## 2. ACID PERMANENT WAVES (glyceryl monothioglycolate)

**Acid or endothermic** (en-do-ther-mic) **waves** are processed by the application of chemical and heat. Another heat source such as a thermal heat replaces ammonia as an ingredient to assist in opening the cuticle for chemical penetration. The pH of acid waves generally range from 6.5 to 7.5. Because this is a mild wave, a longer processing time is usually required.

**Tension is applied** when wrapping acid waves to assist in the processing. Acid waves generally have a **slow processing time.** Once the heat is applied along with the chemical solution, the chemical breakdown begins. Acid waves are recommended for porous or chemically treated hair due to the cuticle being slightly open.

"Always read manufacturer's instructions of the permanent wave before application of perm rods. Sometimes application of a special shampoo or pre-wrap solution is required."

# Client Consultation . . .

*Before a permanent wave, the cosmetologist needs to **communicate with the client** on his or her hair-care needs and the hair service requested. It is important to analyze the client's hair and scalp as part of your consultation. Compile answers on **client profile cards**, which are questionnaires containing useful client health and hair-care information. The results will decide the type of permanent wave, perm rods and wrapping pattern used in delivering a competent chemical service.*

| DATE | SERVICE/TREATMENT-Formula/Product, ounces, time, rod size | REMARKS/CHANGES |
|---|---|---|

☑ Medical Ale

**Client Profile Card/File**

Name ____ Date ____

Address ____

____

Occupation ____ Hobby ____

Birthdate ____

First Visit Date ____

Oral Contraceptives? ❑ Pregnant? ❑ Trying to be? ❑

Medications ❑ Allergies ❑

Health Problems ❑

**Professional Haircoloring:** Temporary ❑

Semi-Permanent ❑ Demi-Permanent ❑ Permanent ❑ Home Haircolor ❑

Cosmetologist ____ Lic # ____

**Hair Condition:** Normal ❑ Dry ❑ Oily ❑

**Scalp Condition:** Normal ❑ Dry ❑ Oily ❑

**Texture:** Fine ❑ Medium ❑ Coarse ❑

**Type of Hair:** Straight ❑ Wavy ❑ Curly ❑

**Density:** Thick ❑ Medium ❑ Thin ❑

**Porosity:** Resistant ❑ Normal ❑ Severe ❑ Irregular ❑

**Elasticity:** Average ❑ Low ❑

**Length:** 1 to 6 inches ❑ 7 inches or longer ❑

What attracted you to our salon? Friend ❑ Location ❑

Personal Hair Treatment & Product: Shampoo ❑ Conditioner ❑ Hair Spray ❑ Gels ❑ Other ❑

I Do The Following To My Hair: Cut ❑ Color ❑ Perm ❑ Bleach ❑ Rinse ❑ Conditions ❑ Other ❑

REMARKS ____

____

9

# Hair and Scalp Analysis . . .

1

**The following seven areas are to be analyzed before receiving a chemical service:**

## 1. Scalp Condition

The scalp needs to be free from open sores or abrasions to proceed with any chemical service. If there are any signs of sores or scalp disease, **DO NOT** perform a permanent wave; refer to medical care professional.

## 2. Texture

is referring to the **diameter** or width of a single hair strand. The texture of hair might affect processing times due to varied thicknesses of each hair type. **Coarse** hair, having a large diameter, might require a **longer** processing time. **Medium** hair, having an average diameter, generally **does not cause problems** when perming. **Fine** hair, having the smallest diameter, usually will process the **quickest**. Condition of cuticle will also play a major role in speed of processing.

2

3

4

"Refer to chapter 5 for more information on hair and scalp analysis."

# Hair and Scalp Analysis ...

**NOTE:** A **pre-wrap solution** is recommended to help equalize porosity along the hair strand.

## 3. Porosity

describes the amount of water the hair absorbs within a relative amount of time. When hair is porous (cuticle scales are lifted), liquid will absorb quicker as opposed to hair with scales lying flat. In **non-porous** or **resistant hair**, liquid will penetrate slower. This is a major factor to consider when deciding on the type of permanent wave to be used.

Hair of **normal porosity** has an average amount of absorption. Hair of **severe** porosity will have a quicker liquid absorption, and will therefore be susceptible to overprocessing. **Irregular porosity** creates an uneven absorption of liquid, which can result in overprocessing or underprocessing of permanent wave and irregular curl or wave patterns.

## 4. Elasticity

is the capability of the hair strand to stretch and return to its previous form without breaking. The stretch of the hair determines if it is strong enough to receive a perm and also have the ability to retain curl or wave. **Average elasticity** generally presents no problems when perming. **Low elasticity** may not retain curl or is susceptible to damage.

## 5. Density

is the number of hair strands per square inch (2.5 cm) on the scalp. This will determine the amount of perm rods to be placed in the hair plus the amount of chemical product used. **Thick hair** will require a larger number of perm rods with an increase of chemical solution. **Thin hair** will require fewer perm rods with less chemical solution.

# Hair and Scalp Analysis ...

**6.** **Length** of hair determines the type of wrapping pattern and perm rods used. Generally, if hair is longer than 8-inches (20.32 cm), a long hair wrapping pattern is used. The amount of chemical products used is increased for the long hair permanent wave.

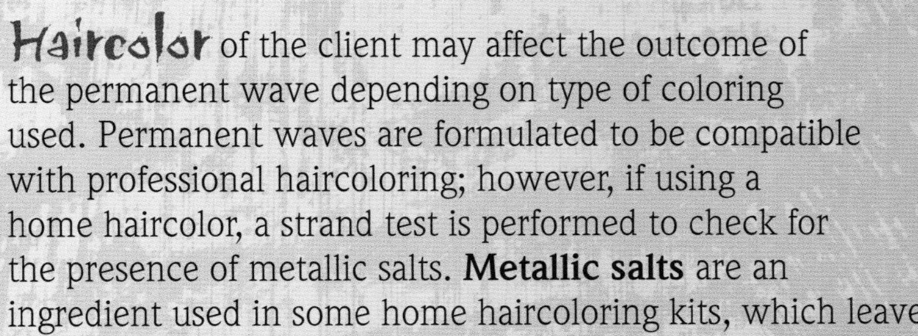

**7.** **Haircolor** of the client may affect the outcome of the permanent wave depending on type of coloring used. Permanent waves are formulated to be compatible with professional haircoloring; however, if using a home haircolor, a strand test is performed to check for the presence of metallic salts. **Metallic salts** are an ingredient used in some home haircoloring kits, which leave a **metal coating on the hair** effecting the proper penetration of the permanent wave solution. The type of metal used determines the color outcome such as a copper metal will produce a red color or a lead creates a brown to black color. This can result in hair discoloration, severe hair breakage or irregular curl patterns when another chemical is applied.

## Test for Metallic Salts on the Hair:

- Mix one ounce of 20 volume hydrogen peroxide with 20 drops of 28 percent ammonia in glass container.
- Place approximately 20 strands of hair into container and soak for 30 minutes.
- **No metallic salts present**, hair will lighten slightly. Hair **may receive permanent wave.**
- Hair with a **lead coating** will lighten quickly.
- Hair with a **silver coating** has no reaction within the 30 minutes.
- Hair with a **copper coating** will break apart; the solution will boil and produce an unpleasant odor.

**CAUTION:** Hair with a lead, silver or copper coating **CANNOT** receive any chemical services. The hair affected by the metals must either be cut off or some manufacturers will offer a prepared solution to remove the metals from the hair. Check with the local beauty distributor.

***If client is unable to receive a permanent wave service, recommend reconstructor treatments to help restore hair back to a healthy state.***

# Permanent Wave Processing...

## There are two major chemical phases of permanent waving:

### 1. PROCESSING

Processing is applying a chemical to perform a series of steps necessary to produce a new hair structure. As previously learned in the chemistry chapter, we know that **permanent wave solution or reducing agent** softens and swells the hair cuticle. This allows the lotion to **penetrate into the cortex**, breaking an average 50 percent of the disulfide bonds. These bonds will reposition themselves to conform to the diameter of the perm rod.

**NOTE:** Any saturated cotton will need to be replaced for the prevention of chemical burning.

Before using any chemical, a **protective cream is applied around the hairline and ears** to prevent the chemical product from resting on the skin. **Cotton is placed over the protective cream** to assist in absorbing excess chemical and also preventing the chemical from sitting on the skin.

Processing is complete once hair has been test curled to determine if hair has formed the diameter size of perm rod.

### 2. NEUTRALIZING

Neutralizing is applying a chemical that reconnects or reforms the bonds into their new curled position. At this time, **perm solution is thoroughly rinsed** from the hair for five minutes or following manufacturer's directions.

**Hair is towel-blotted** to assure complete absorption of moisture and to prevent dilution of neutralizer. Use a cloth towel to absorb moisture and paper towels for the final blot check.

The **neutralizer or rebonding agent** is applied to eliminate any remaining perm lotion from the hair and hold the disulfide bonds into their new curled position. Follow manufacturer's directions for duration of time neutralizer remains on hair and procedure in removing perm rods.

# Test Curling ...

During the permanent wave process a **test curl** is taken to determine if desired curl has been achieved. The perm rod is **unwrapped one and half times** to allow an **"S" shape** formation to appear ... looking within the shape for the diameter of the rod.

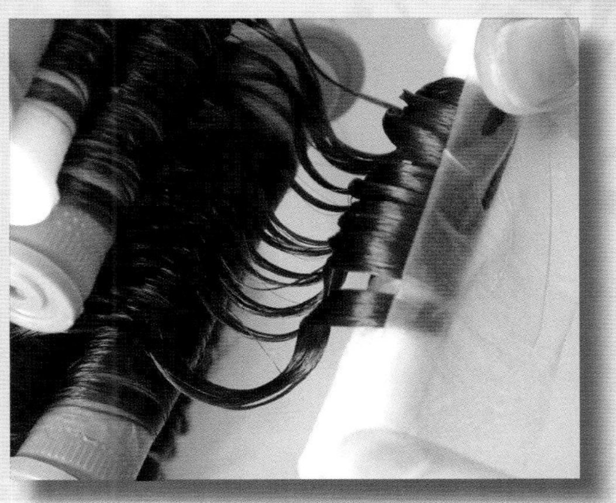

An alternate method of test curling is removing the entire rod and checking the hair ends for diameter of rod and "flip-up" effect.

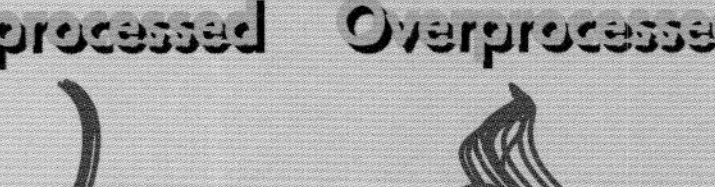

**Overprocessed hair** is when permanent wave lotion remains on the hair **beyond recommended processing time** producing dry and damaged hair. This causes increased broken disulfide bonds with further breakdown of hair structure.

**Underprocessed hair** is when the permanent wave lotion does not remain on hair long enough to produce the desired curl pattern. This may occur either through improper test curling or an insufficient amount of broken disulfide bonds and/or inadequate saturation of hair with perm lotion.

**Preliminary test curling** is an optional method **performed as part of a client consultation** to ensure the correct wave pattern and perm rod choice. Take a subsection of hair located at back area of head, wrap in perm rod, and apply permanent wave lotion, process following manufacturer's instructions and check results.

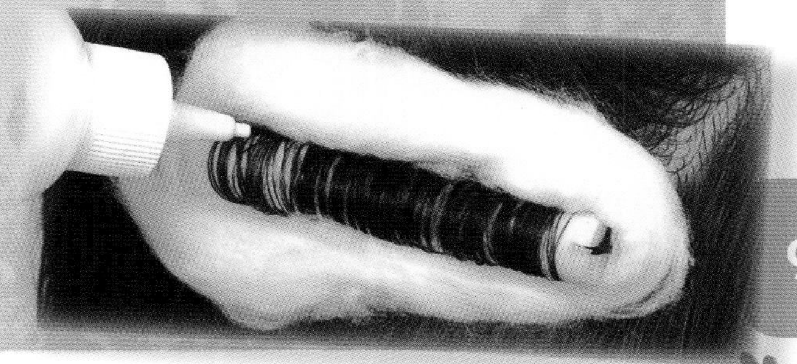

SIMPLE LAB PROJECT

# Basic or Nine Block Sectioning

Front

Side

Back

## OBJECTIVE

To perform a basic or nine block sectioning for neat, orderly panels of hair in which to place perm rods for a permanent wave.

## TOOLS & MATERIALS

- Neck strip and cape/robe
- Cloth and disposable towels
- Water bottle
- Cleansing product
- Conditioning product
- Combs
- Perm rods (long length)
- Sectioning Clips

## PROCEDURE

**"The client consultation is an important part of your professional service. Be sure to complete this step prior to each client service you provide. Your successful retail sales and customer satisfaction rates depend upon it!"**

RETAIL • RE-BOOK • REFERRAL

1. Cosmetologist sanitizes hands and station.
2. Set out service tools and materials.
3. Drape the client in preparation for a chemical service.
4. Lightly cleanse hair & scalp.
5. Follow procedure as shown.
6. Follow standard cleanup procedure.

A Center a **long length** perm rod using tip of nose as guide; **any perm rod diameter may be used.**

B Place perm rod at center hairline.

C **Place comb ¼ inch (0.6 cm) in from end of perm rod,** using as a guide to get accurate measurement of section.

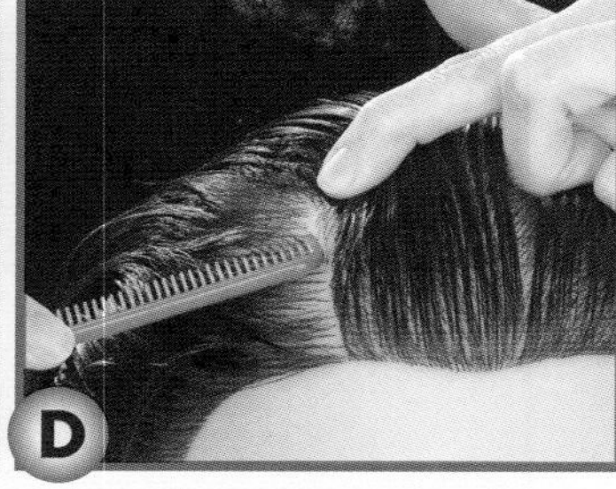

D Part hair straight back from hairline using comb.

E Continue parting hair to crown area and separate from side hair.

F **Repeat steps B thru E on opposite side.**

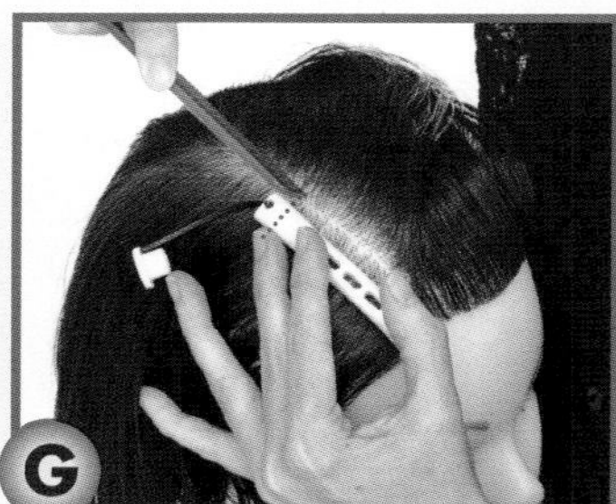

G Place perm rod along parting on either side of section and align comb ¼ inch (0.6 cm) in from end of perm rod.

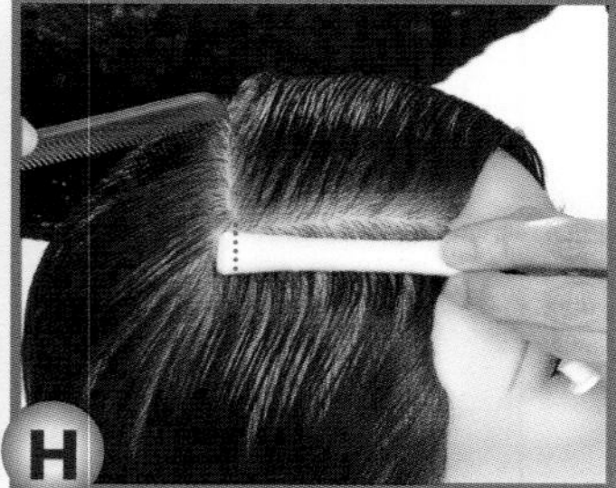

H Part straight across to opposite side of section.

# Basic or Nine Block Sectioning

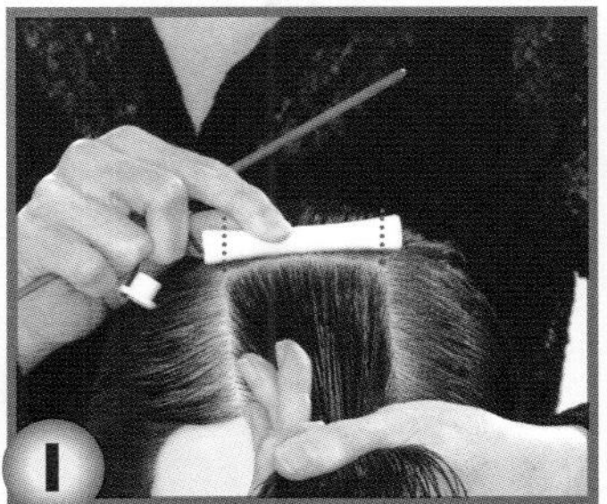

I. Check width of section using length of perm rod, ¼ inch (0.6 cm) in from both ends.

J. Completed top section; **check all four sides to be equivalent to length of long perm rod ¼ inch (0.6 cm) in from both ends.**

K. Side sections are measured throughout using the length of long perm rod ¼ inch (0.6 cm) in from both ends.

L. Side parting will generally curve, compensating for receding areas of hairline.

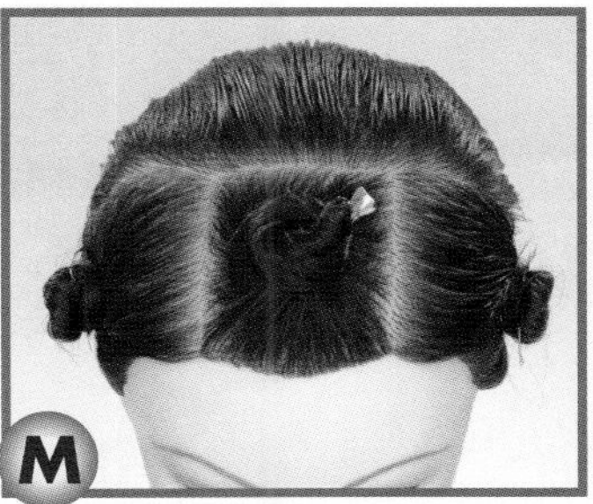

M. **Repeat steps K and L to side section on opposite side of head.**

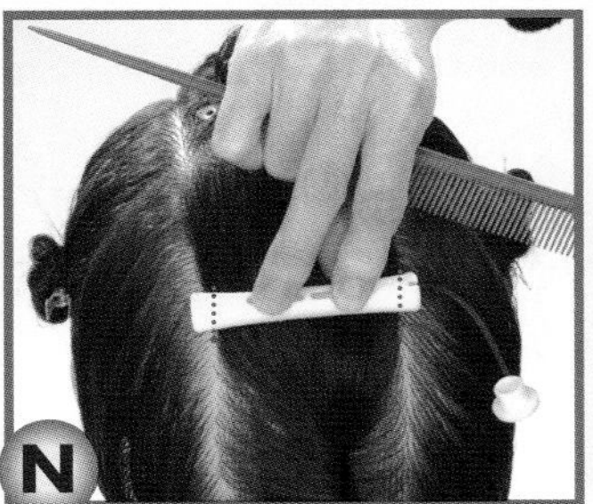

N. Center back panel measurement is **equal to long length perm rod, ¼ inch (0.6 cm) in from both ends.**

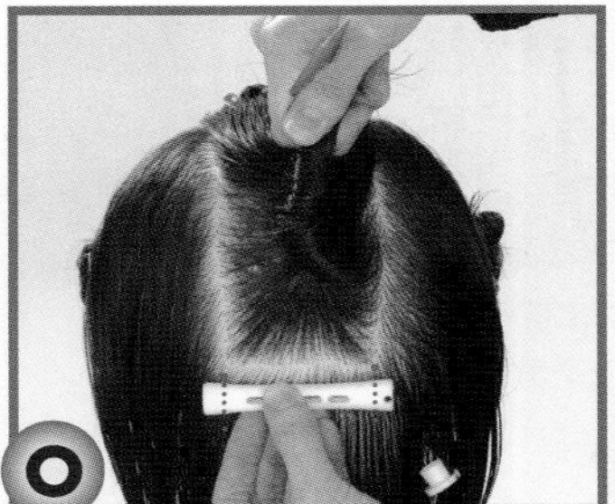

O. **Center back section is completed ½ inch (1.25 cm) below high point of ear.** Section width is equivalent to long length of perm rod, ¼ inch (0.6 cm) in from both ends.

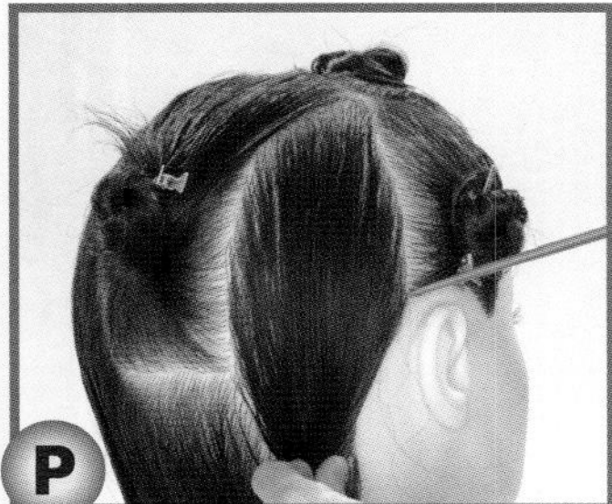

P. Side back panels are measured by parting from corner of front side section to corner of center back section.

Q. Completed side back panel; repeat on opposite side. **These sections are not equivalent to length of perm rod.**

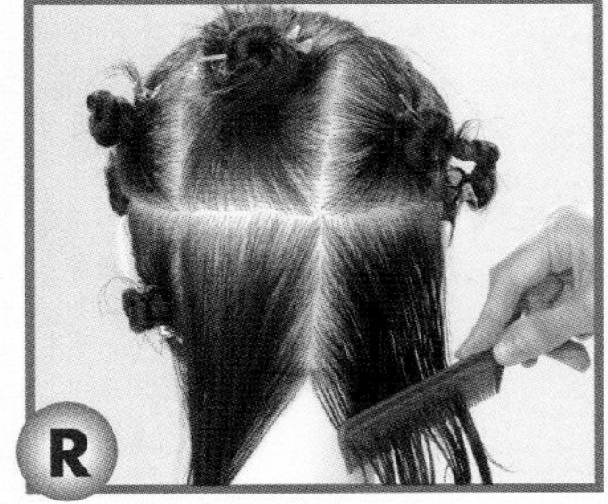

R. Bottom sections are obtained by continuing center back panel partings down to nape hairline.

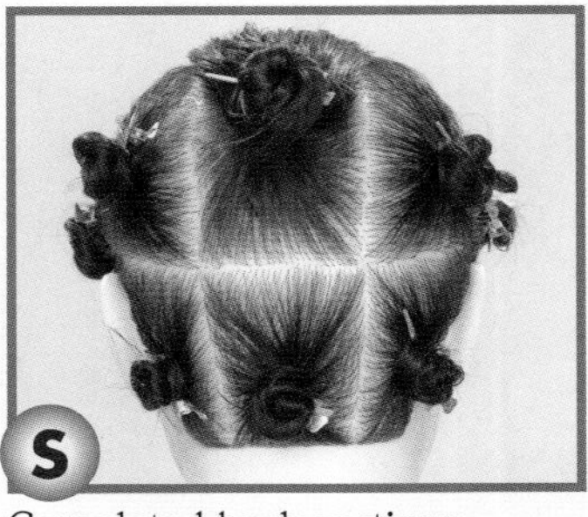

S. Completed back sections.

T. Completed nine block sectioning.

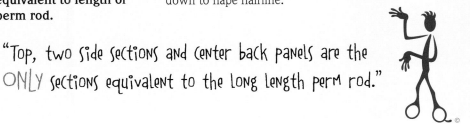

"Top, two side sections and center back panels are the ONLY sections equivalent to the long length perm rod."

**EVALUATION** ______________________________

______________________________

GRADE ____________ STUDENT'S NAME ____________ ID# ____________

## SIMPLE LAB PROJECT

# Permanent Waving on Mannequin

### OBJECTIVE

To learn how to chemically alter straight hair to a curly or wavy form by applying a permanent wave on a mannequin.

Before

After

## TOOLS & MATERIALS

- Neck strip and cape/robe
- Cloth and disposable towels
- Gloves
- End papers
- Neutralizer
- Timer
- Cleansing product
- Conditioning product
- Combs
- Cotton
- Protective cream
- Liquid styling tools
- Perm rods
- Client record card/file
- Sectioning clips
- Permanent wave lotion
- Plastic cap
- Water bottle

## PROCEDURE

**"The client consultation is an important part of your professional service. Be sure to complete this step prior to each client service you provide. Your successful retail sales and customer satisfaction rates depend upon it!"**

RETAIL • RE-BOOK • REFERRAL

1. Cosmetologist sanitizes hands and station.
2. Set out service tools and materials.
3. Drape the mannequin in preparation for a chemical service.
4. Perform a hair analysis.
5. Follow procedure as shown and manufactures instructions.
6. Follow standard cleanup procedure.
7. Document client record card/file.

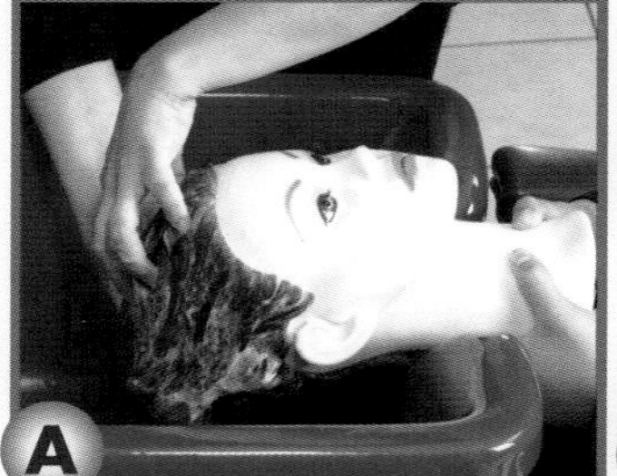

A — Lightly cleanse hair and scalp.

B — Section hair into a basic wrap.

C — Apply selected permanent wave rods.

D — Apply **protective cream and cotton** around hairline and ears. **Optional:** Cosmetologist wear gloves.

E — Pierce tip of nozzle of permanent wave bottle with a pin to eliminate overuse of solution. **Apply lotion** to top and bottom of rods, along **full length of rods.**

F — Apply lotion to middle of perm rods.

G — **Check cotton.** If saturated, replace with fresh cotton.

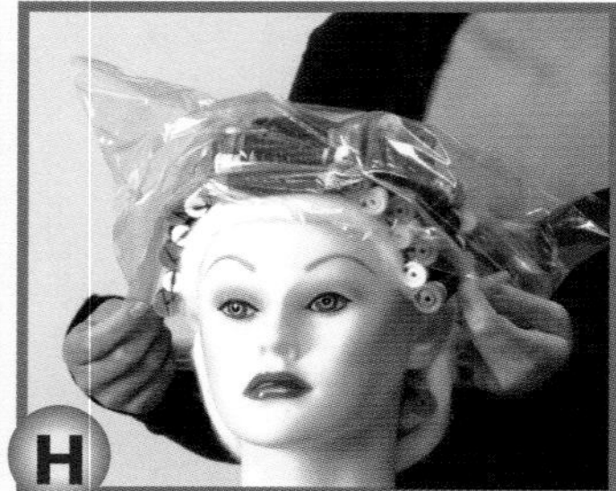

H — Apply plastic cap following manufacturer's instructions.

# Permanent Waving on Mannequin

I

Follow manufacturer's instructions for processing times. **NOTE:** Remember there is no body heat when using mannequin; therefore **processing may take longer.**

J

**Test curl** check for diameter of rod within "S" shaping. **If processing is complete, proceed to next step of procedure. If not, continue test curling until desired curl is achieved.**

K

Remove plastic cap and cotton.

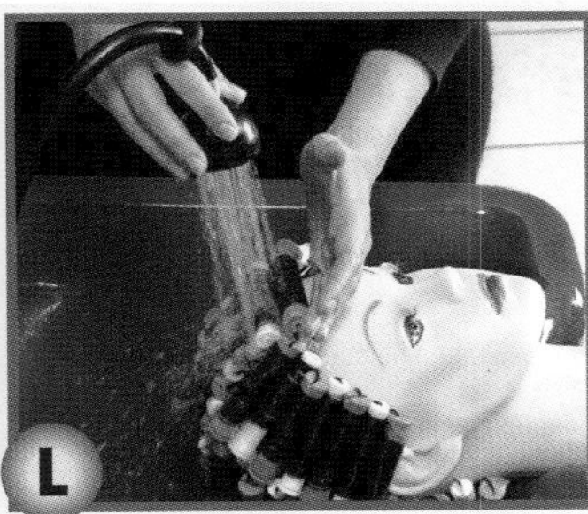
L

Rinse hair thoroughly for a minimum of five minutes leaving perm rods in hair or follow manufacturer's instructions.

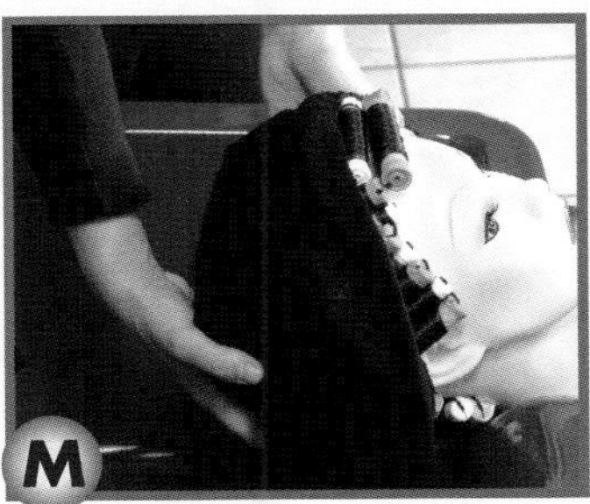
M

**Blot hair** with cloth towel to remove moisture.

N

Continue blotting hair with disposable towels to assure accurate moisture absorption.

O

Reapply fresh cotton around hairline and ears.

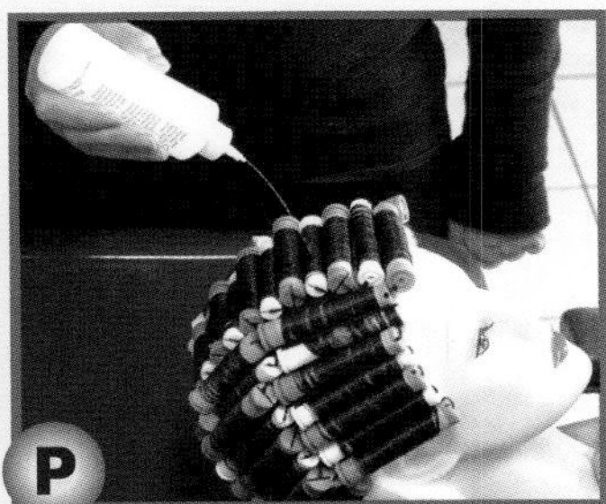
P

**Apply neutralizer** in the same manner as the permanent wave lotion. Process follow manufacturer's instructions.

Q

**Rinse neutralizer or proceed to step S,** following manufacturer's instructions.

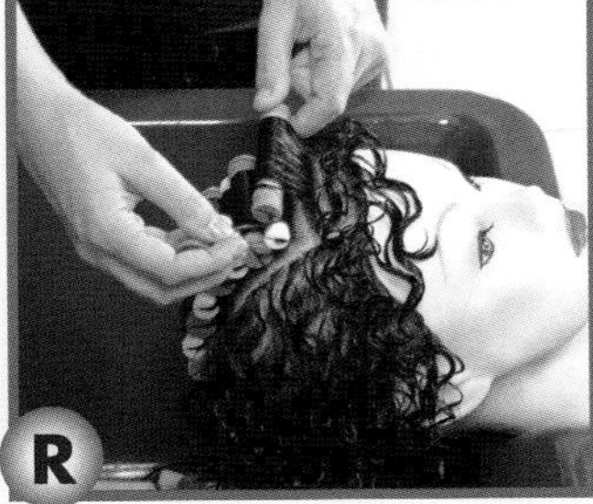
R

Gently remove perm rods without tension and work remaining neutralizer through hair; complete by rinsing chemical from hair.

S

Finish with application of light conditioner and/or styling product. Design hair or leave in a "wash-and-wear" style.

**EVALUATION** ______________________

GRADE ______ STUDENT'S NAME ______ ID# ______

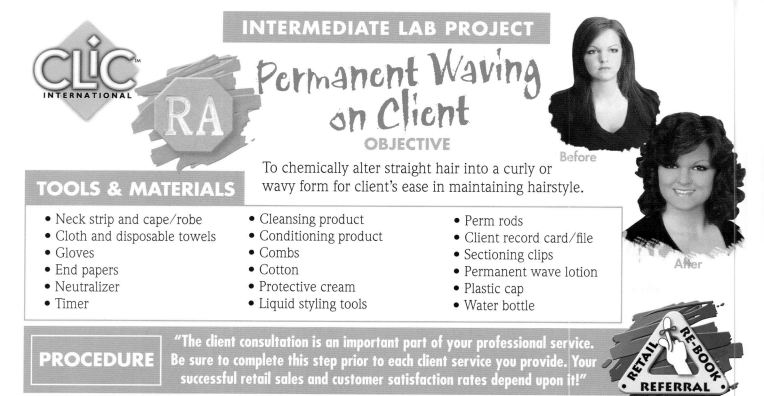

CLiC INTERNATIONAL

RA

# Permanent Waving on Client

Before

After

## OBJECTIVE

To chemically alter straight hair into a curly or wavy form for client's ease in maintaining hairstyle.

## TOOLS & MATERIALS

- Neck strip and cape/robe
- Cloth and disposable towels
- Gloves
- End papers
- Neutralizer
- Timer
- Cleansing product
- Conditioning product
- Combs
- Cotton
- Protective cream
- Liquid styling tools
- Perm rods
- Client record card/file
- Sectioning clips
- Permanent wave lotion
- Plastic cap
- Water bottle

## PROCEDURE

"The client consultation is an important part of your professional service. Be sure to complete this step prior to each client service you provide. Your successful retail sales and customer satisfaction rates depend upon it!"

RETAIL RE-BOOK REFERRAL

1. Cosmetologist sanitizes hands and station.
2. Set out service tools and materials.
3. Drape the client in preparation for a chemical service.
4. Perform a scalp and hair analysis.
5. Follow procedure as shown and manufacture's instructions.
6. Follow standard cleanup procedure.
7. Document client record card/file.

A

Lightly cleanse hair and scalp. **DO NOT** apply manipulations to avoid scalp sensitivity.

B

Section hair into a basic or design wrap and apply permanent wave rods.

C

Apply **protective cream** around hairline and ears.

D

Apply **cotton** around hairline and ears. **Optional: Cosmetologist wears gloves.**

E

**Apply permanent wave lotion** to top and bottom of rods, along **full length of rods.** A piece of cotton is held below each rod to absorb excess solution.

F

Apply lotion to middle of perm rods.

G

**Check cotton.** If saturated, replace with fresh cotton.

H

Apply plastic cap following manufacturer's instructions.

**I** Follow manufacturer's instructions for processing times and heat settings.

**J** **Test curl** check for diameter of rod, within "S" shaping. **If processing is complete, proceed to next step of procedure. If not, continue test curling until desired curl is achieved.**

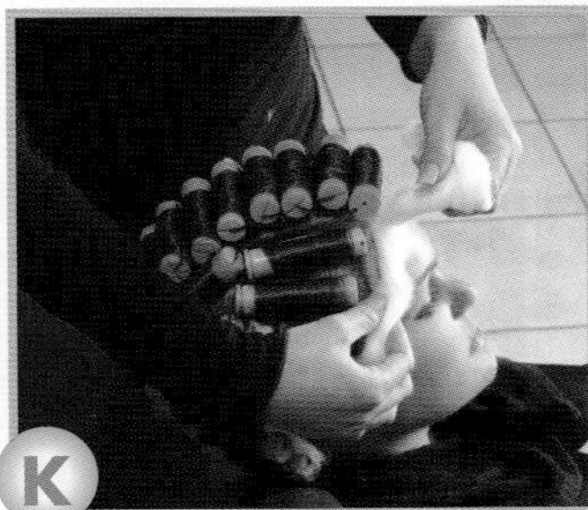

**K** Remove plastic cap and cotton.

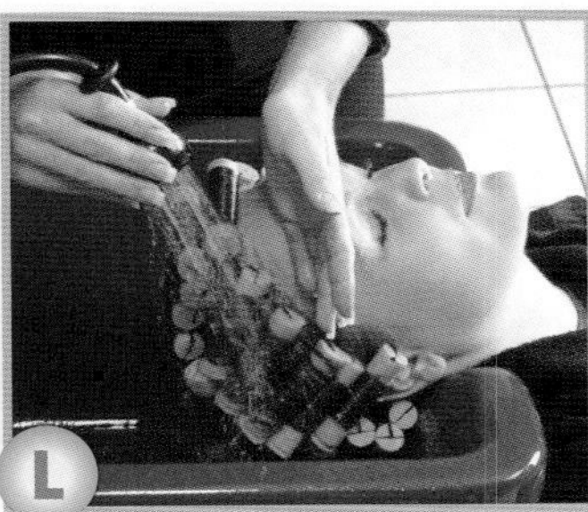

**L** Rinse hair thoroughly for a minimum of five minutes leaving perm rods in hair or follow manufacturer's instructions.

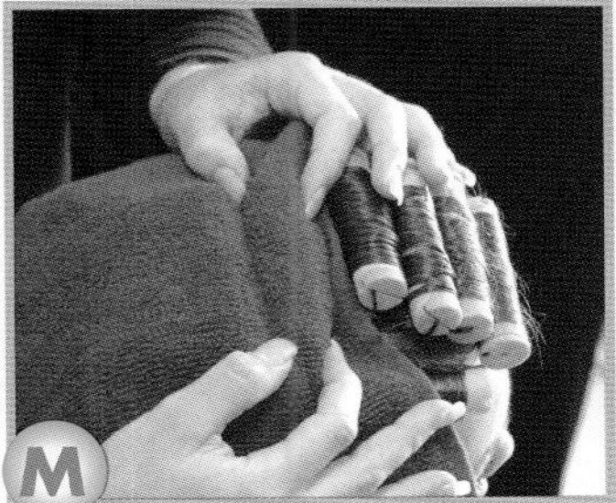

**M** **Blot hair** with cloth towel to remove moisture.

**N** Continue blotting hair with disposable towels to assure moisture absorption.

**O** **Reapply fresh cotton around hairline and ears.**

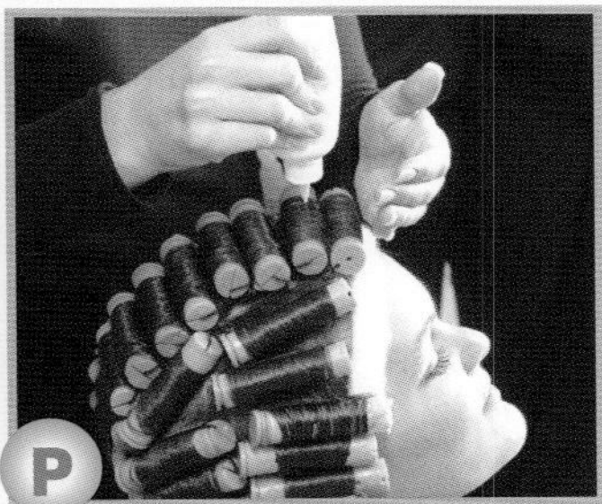

**P** **Apply neutralizer** in the same manner as permanent wave lotion.

**Q** Process following manufacturer's instructions. Gently remove perm rods without tension.

**R** Apply remaining neutralizer to the hair.

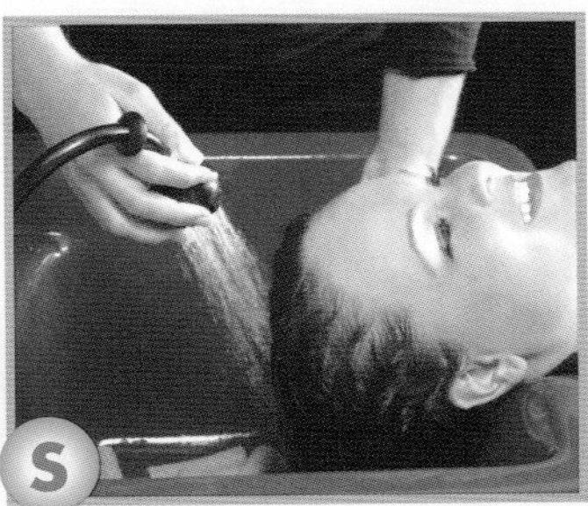

**S** Complete by rinsing neutralizer from the hair.

1

**T** **Permed hair**

Finish with application of light conditioner and/or styling product. Design hair or leave in a "wash-and-wear" style.

**NOTE:** The allowable time to wait after a permanent wave before shampooing and/or coloring the hair depends on the manufacturer of the chemical used. Always read the permanent wave instructions for after-perm care.

GRADE

STUDENT'S NAME

ID#

COMPLEX LAB PROJECT

# Permanent Spiral Wave

## OBJECTIVE

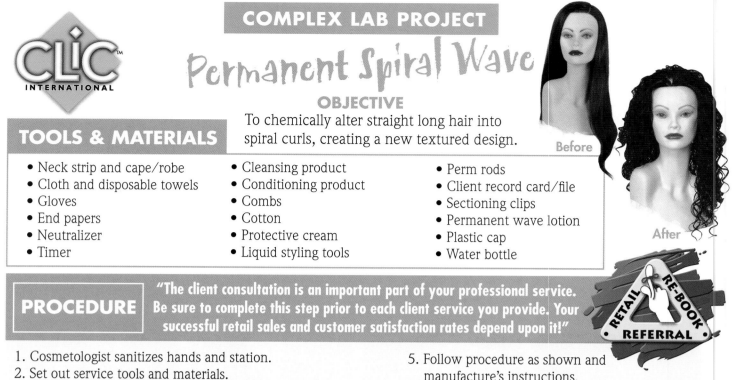

To chemically alter straight long hair into spiral curls, creating a new textured design.

Before

After

- Neck strip and cape/robe
- Cloth and disposable towels
- Gloves
- End papers
- Neutralizer
- Timer
- Cleansing product
- Conditioning product
- Combs
- Cotton
- Protective cream
- Liquid styling tools
- Perm rods
- Client record card/file
- Sectioning clips
- Permanent wave lotion
- Plastic cap
- Water bottle

## PROCEDURE

**"The client consultation is an important part of your professional service. Be sure to complete this step prior to each client service you provide. Your successful retail sales and customer satisfaction rates depend upon it!"**

RETAIL • RE-BOOK • REFERRAL

1. Cosmetologist sanitizes hands and station.
2. Set out service tools and materials.
3. Drape the client in preparation for a chemical service.
4. Perform a scalp and hair analysis. Lightly cleanse hair and scalp.
5. Follow procedure as shown and manufacture's instructions.
6. Follow standard cleanup procedure.
7. Document client record card/file.

A — Section long hair and apply rods or spiral-type rods. Rods will overlap due to excess amount of rods.

B — **Apply protective cream and cotton around hairline and ears.** Optional: Cosmetologist wears gloves.

C — **Apply permanent wave lotion** to perm rods ensuring a complete coverage of **ALL** rods. **Suggestion:** Place perm lotion in a spray bottle to ensure all rods are **evenly saturated** with solution.

D — Continue applying wave lotion.

E — **Replace saturated cotton** with fresh cotton.

F — Apply plastic cap following manufacturer's instructions. **NOTE:** A large cap will be needed to cover client's head plus rods. Also, client is unable to fit under a hood dryer for processing.

G — Follow manufacturer's instructions for processing times.

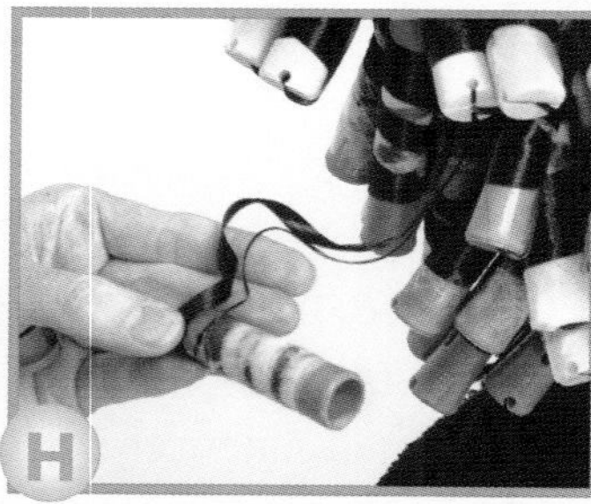

H — **Test curl** check for diameter of rod within "S" shaping. **If processing is complete, proceed to next step of procedure. If not, continue test curling until desired curl is achieved.**

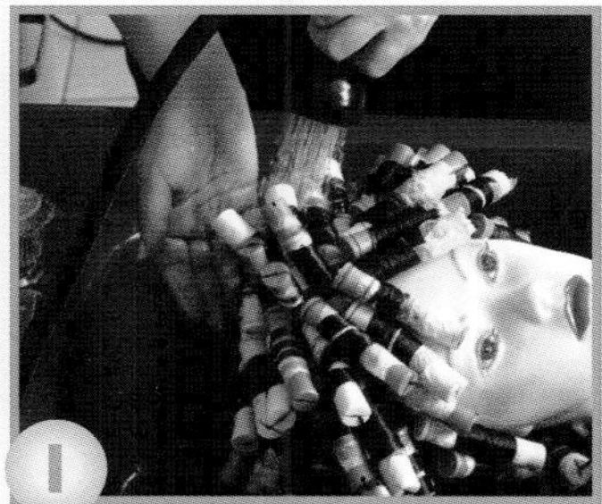

Remove plastic cap and cotton. Rinse hair thoroughly for a minimum of five minutes (leave perm rods in hair), follow manufacturer's instructions.

**Blot hair** with cloth towel to remove moisture.

Continue blotting hair with disposable towels to assure accurate moisture absorption.

Reapply fresh cotton around hairline and ears.

**Apply neutralizer** in the same manner as permanent wave lotion.

Process following manufacturer's instructions.

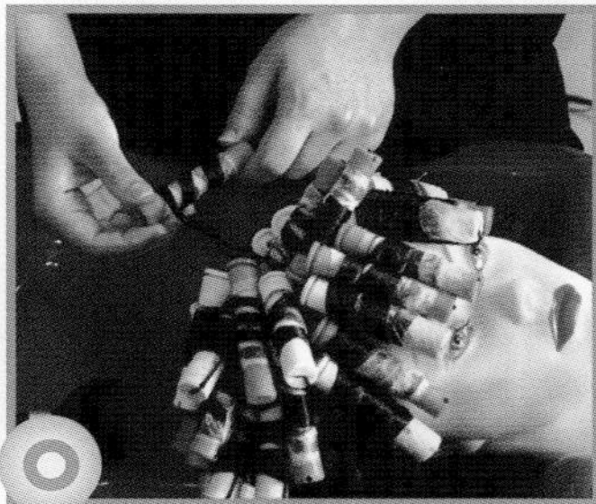

**Rinse neutralizer or proceed to step P,** following manufacturer's instructions.

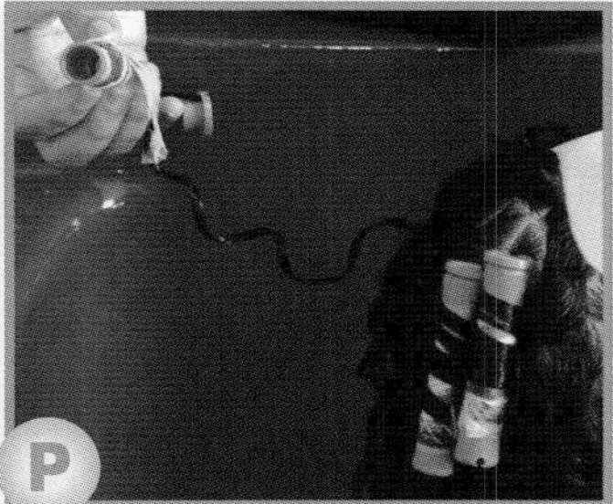

Gently remove perm rods without tension and work remaining neutralizer through hair.

Complete by rinsing chemical from hair.

Finish with application of light conditioner and/or styling product. Design hair or leave in a "wash-and-wear" style.

"A spiral wave will take an increased amount of chemical products, materials and time; therefore, a higher service cost is necessary."

GRADE STUDENT'S NAME ID#

# Partial Permanent Wave

### OBJECTIVE

To provide curl or wave to a certain area of head, creating a natural blending of permed hair into non-permed hair.

Before

After

## TOOLS & MATERIALS

- Neck strip and cape/robe
- Cloth and disposable towels
- Gloves
- End papers
- Neutralizer
- Timer
- Cleansing product
- Conditioning product
- Combs
- Cotton
- Protective cream
- Liquid styling tools
- Perm rods
- Client record card/file
- Sectioning clips
- Permanent wave lotion
- Plastic cap
- Water bottle

## PROCEDURE

"The client consultation is an important part of your professional service. Be sure to complete this step prior to each client service you provide. Your successful retail sales and customer satisfaction rates depend upon it!"

RETAIL · RE-BOOK · REFERRAL

1. Cosmetologist sanitizes hands and station.
2. Set out service tools and materials.
3. Drape the client in preparation for a chemical service.
4. Perform a scalp and hair analysis.
5. Follow procedure as shown and manufacturer's instructions.
6. Follow standard cleanup procedure.
7. Document client record card/file.

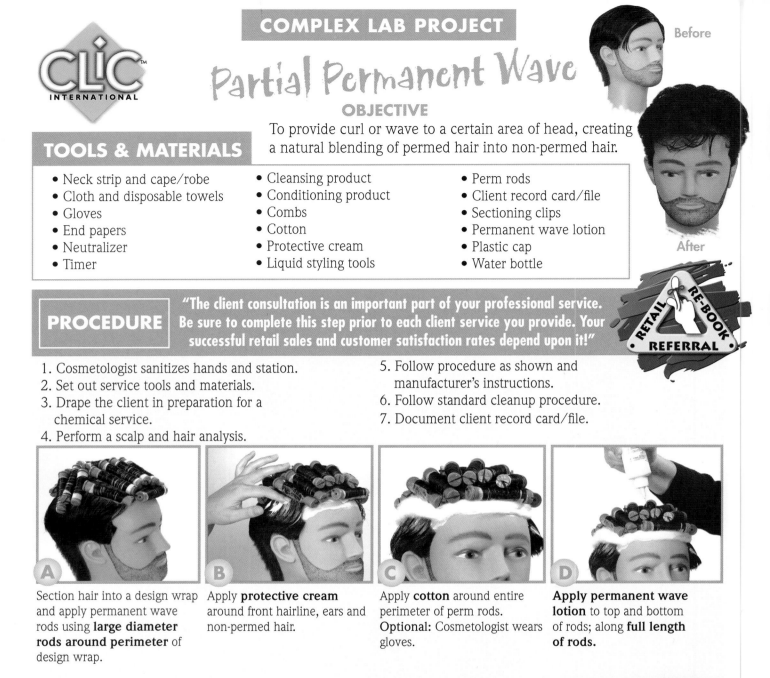

A Section hair into a design wrap and apply permanent wave rods using **large diameter rods around perimeter** of design wrap.

B Apply **protective cream** around front hairline, ears and non-permed hair.

C Apply **cotton** around entire perimeter of perm rods. **Optional:** Cosmetologist wears gloves.

D **Apply permanent wave lotion** to top and bottom of rods; along **full length of rods.**

E **Check cotton.** If saturated, replace with fresh cotton.

F Apply plastic cap following manufacturer's instructions.

G Follow manufacturer's instructions for processing times. **NOTE:** Remember **no body heat** when using a mannequin.

H **Test curl** check for diameter of rod within "S" shaping. **If processing is complete, proceed to next step of procedure. If not, continue test curling until desired curl is achieved.**

# Partial Permanent Wave

I Remove plastic cap and cotton.

J Rinse hair thoroughly for a minimum of three minutes following manufacturer's instructions.

K **Blot hair** with cloth towel to remove moisture.

L Continue blotting hair with disposable towels to assure accurate moisture absorption.

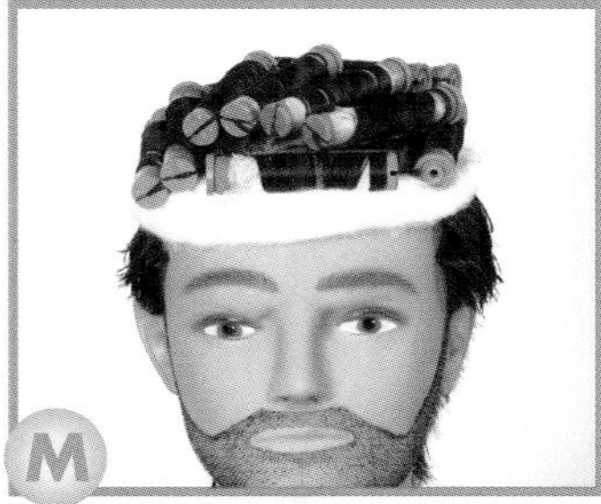

M Reapply fresh cotton around perimeter of rods.

N **Apply neutralizer** in the same manner as permanent wave lotion. Process following manufacturer's instructions.

O **Optional:** Remaining minute of processing time gently remove last row of perm rods.

P Flatten the permed hair to facilitate the blending of permed hair into non-permed hair.

Q Following manufacturer's instructions, **either rinse neutralizer or proceed to step R.**

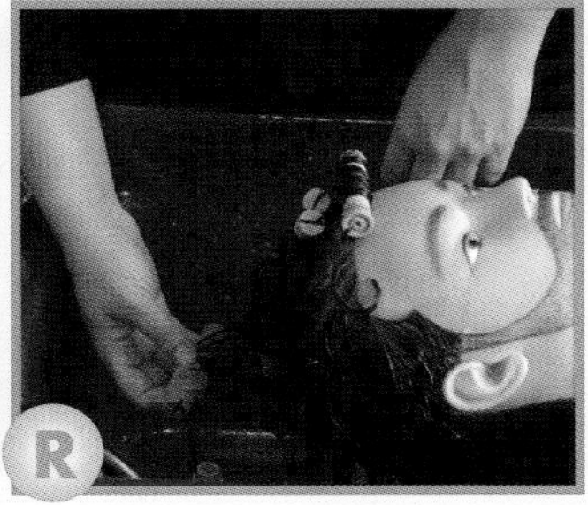

R Gently remove perm rods without tension and work remaining neutralizer through hair; complete by rinsing hair.

S Finish with application of light conditioner and/or styling product and design hair.

GRADE

STUDENT'S NAME

ID#

# Permanent Waving REVIEW QUESTIONS

## FILL-IN THE BLANKS

A. Alkaline Wave
B. Angle
C. Arnold F. Willatt
D. Base
E. Book End Wrap
F. Concave Rods
G. Design Wrap
H. End Papers
I. Fish Hook
J. Irregular Porosity
K. Partings
L. Permanent Waving
M. Piggyback Wrap
N. Resistant Hair
O. Rod Placement
P. Sections
Q. Straight Rods
R. Tension
S. Test Curls
T. Texture

1. ________ consists of manageable sections of hair that follow the direction of client's hair design.
2. ________ uses two rods with one rod sitting on top of other rod, providing a uniformed curl or wave pattern.
3. ________ or cold wave is processed at room temperature with **NO** application of heat.
4. ________ or pull of the hair created as it is being combed and wound around a perm rod.
5. ________ refers to diameter or width of a single hair strand.
6. ________ creates an uneven absorption of liquid, which can result in an irregular curl or wave pattern.
7. ________ are taken to determine if the desired curl is achieved and processing of the permanent wave is complete.
8. ________ is when the cuticle scales are lying flat, which hinders liquid absorption.
9. ________ are absorbent pieces of thin tissue-type paper that control and protect the hair.
10. ________ consist of lines used in dividing sections or subsections.
11. ________ is chemically rearranging straight hair into a new curled or wavy form.
12. ________ invented the cold wave, which needed no heat or machines for processing.
13. ________ produce **uneven** curl or wave patterns.
14. ________ produce **uniform** curl or wave patterns.
15. ________ requires only one paper in which hair ends are combed together and placed within the folded paper.
16. ________ is the result when hair ends do not wrap around the perm rod smoothly causing hair to bend.
17. ________ consist of geometric shapings arranged on various areas of the head.
18. ________ is created when the hair is lifted and combed at a certain degree for perm rod application.
19. ________ is an area selected at the scalp that is determined by diameter and length of perm rod.
20. ________ is the base area within the subsection of hair where the perm rod rests.

STUDENT'S NAME DATE GRADE

base

curly

lanthionine

lye

stabilizer

reduction

texture

# Chemical Relaxation

COSMETOLOGY CAREER CONCEPTS 10

10

CHEMICAL RELAXATION

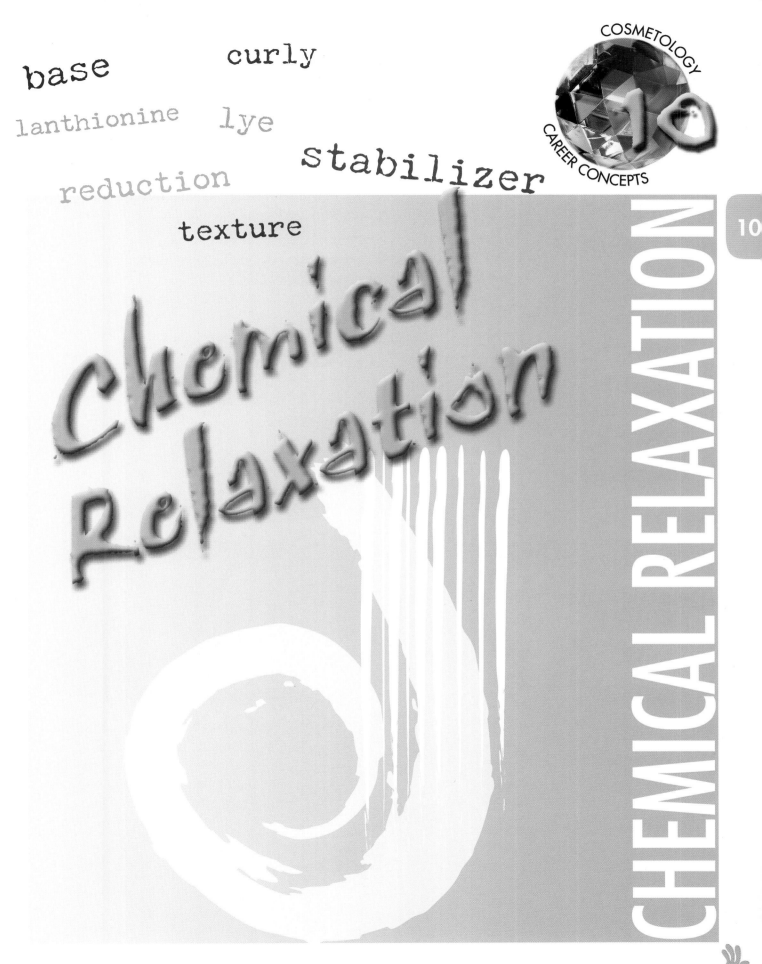

# Terminology ...

The following are some terms that will continuously be used when servicing clients in need of curl reduction services. These terms represent the knowledge needed in order to successfully perform a chemical hair treatment.

**Base** is the protective cream applied to hairline and scalp prior to the chemical relaxing treatment.

**Curl Reduction** is the determined amount of curl removed from curly hair.

**Curly Hair** is hair consisting of a series of twists/turns throughout the strand creating a coiling effect.

**Neutralizing** is applying a chemical that reconnects the disulfide bonds (thioglycolate relaxers) or reforms into lanthionine bonds (hydroxide relaxers) to the newly reformed position.

**Neutralizing Shampoo** is a lathering form of neutralizer used in conjunction with chemical relaxers to keep hair in the new reconstructed position.

# Terminology . . .

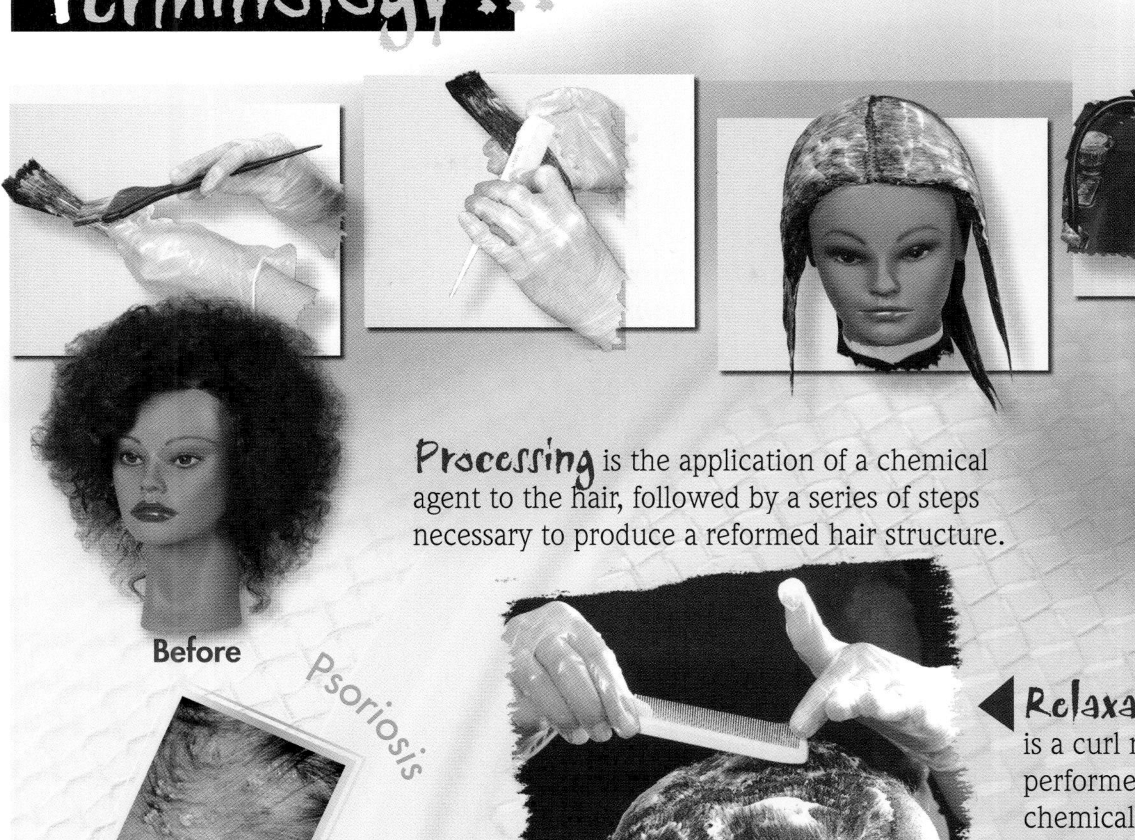

**Processing** is the application of a chemical agent to the hair, followed by a series of steps necessary to produce a reformed hair structure.

**Relaxation Test** is a curl reduction test performed during a chemical service. It consists of smoothing an area of hair with the spine of a tail comb to determine if hair is sufficiently relaxed.

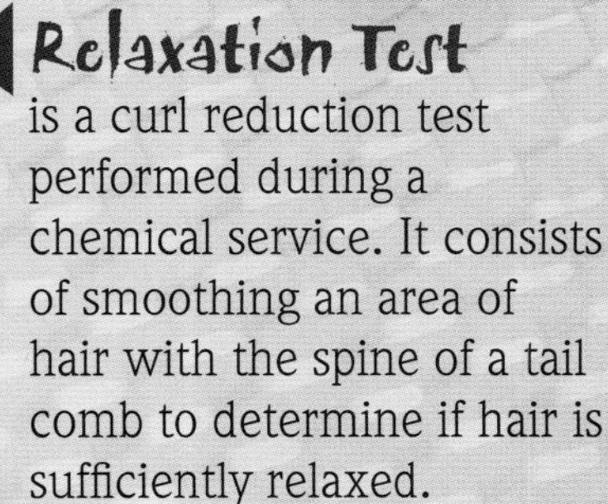

Psoriasis

1

**Scalp Condition** is part of the client consultation. The surface of the scalp is checked for sores, irritations or disease.

Strong curl pattern

**Sodium Hydroxide** is the strongest type of relaxer containing the chemical compound hydroxide and is best suited for hair with a strong curl pattern.

**Thioglycolate Relaxers** are chemical compounds with the additive ingredient **ammonia.** These are the mildest form of relaxers used to remove curl from the hair, and are compatible with a soft curl permanent.

2

10

*To **chemically alter** naturally curly or wavy hair into a straighter form is referred to as **chemical relaxing...** quite simply, it is the opposite of permanent waving. Instead of creating curl, we are **relaxing or removing curl**. This process is considered permanent until re-growth of hair occurs. Usually, the new hair will have the curly texture. Relaxing the curl in hair **is not necessarily removing the full curl amount** with the end result being straight hair; some curl may remain in the hair. This process allows better management of the hairstyle and is referred to as **reduction of curl**.*

## What exactly is curly hair?

It is hair consisting of a series of twists/turns throughout the strand creating a coiling effect. Depending on depth and amount of curl, maintaining a hairstyle may be difficult. This type of hair usually **lacks a sufficient amount of moisture** and is prone to breakage. Extremely curly hair may either have fine, medium or coarse textures, and also may vary in diameter along the strand due to **each "turn or twist" in the curl.** Each twist poses a weakness due to the diameter change.

Before

After

**Chemically relaxing the hair** provides the client with the ability to have **straight hair** or for some clients, **manageable curls,** when creating a hairstyle. As with any chemical service, condition of hair may be compromised. However, with the necessary preparatory steps, knowledge of procedure and chemicals used, along with proper home maintenance treatments, the hair can be restored back to a healthy state.

1

# Chemical Relaxing . . .

During the times of slavery, the African-Americans were forbidden to use any beautifying hair-care techniques. **At this time in history the most basic hair-care hygiene was overlooked**; instead the head was wrapped in a rag to keep hair covered and protected from the outside elements. Once colonization took place, focus was brought back on beauty as well as the scalp and hair-care needs. Once people could deal with the concentration of curl in the hair; **several entrepreneurs came on the scene in the early 1900's**, who had invented cosmetic preparations to control and maintain the curly texture.

## Sarah Breedlove (1867 – 1919)

commonly referred to as **Madam C.J. Walker,** was the inventor of the **"Wonderful Hair Grower,"** an ointment that nourished the hair and scalp. Mrs. Walker lived in an era when hair was not washed regularly and maintained; it was therefore prone to scalp disease and baldness. Ms. Walker was a woman of strength and endurance, and was determined to educate and provide women with the best cosmetic preparations for their unruly and curly hair. For more information, go to www.madamcjwalker.com

## Garrett A. Morgan (1877 – 1963)

was an inventor, and when working as a sewing machine repairman, he accidentally came across an ointment that, when rubbed on a piece of textured cloth, resulted in a smooth appearance. Mr. Morgan further experimented by placing this ointment on his own hair. The same results occurred; thus the hair preparation called **"Hair Refiner"** was invented. For more information, go to http://www.ric.edu/rpotter/morgan.html

## Annie Turnbo Pope Malone (1869 – 1957)

was also an inventor of hair-care products for the individual with curly hair. Mrs. Malone gained a fortune through selling and educating people with her **"Poro" system** of hair preparations for smoothing and straightening the hair. For more information, go to http://www.csupomona.edu/~plin/inventors/malone.html

# Relaxer Liquid Tools...

**Chemical Relaxing products** *are needed in order to permanently straighten curly hair.* ***Relaxers*** *are* ***strong chemicals*** *with a* ***high pH*** *and are generally manufactured in a* ***cream form*** *having a* ***thick viscosity.*** *This allows the product to remain on the hair while being manipulated to assist in straightening the curl. There are many different types and strengths of relaxers due to the wide range of product ingredients.*

**The two common types of relaxers are Hydroxide and Thioglycolate.**

**Hydroxide (hy-drox-ide) relaxers** contain the chemical compound hydroxide (OH), which comes in various other types, such as **sodium, potassium, lithium and guanidine.**

This is the **strongest relaxer** with an alkaline pH higher than 12 and can swell the hair more than twice its diameter size; therefore, careful consideration is needed when deciding on which type relaxer to apply to the hair. (Refer to Chapter 8 Cosmetology Chemistry for more information on relaxer ingredients).

**CAUTION: Do not shampoo** hair prior to the application of a hydroxide relaxer due to its high alkaline content.

**Hydroxide Relaxer**

| 7 | 8 | 9 | 10 | 11 | 12 | 13 | 14 |
|---|---|---|---|---|---|---|---|

**ALKALINE**

# Relaxer Liquid Tools . . .

**Hydroxide relaxers** may come in **"base"** or **"no-base"** forms depending on which type of hydroxide is being used.

**Base form** (or lye) relaxers **require a protective cream applied to the hairline and scalp.**

The protective cream usually consists of a **petroleum** ingredient that is lightweight and will spread easily (through body heat) over the scalp. When a relaxer is labeled, "base relaxer," it means the relaxer is too strong to be applied **without** the application of a base or protective cream.

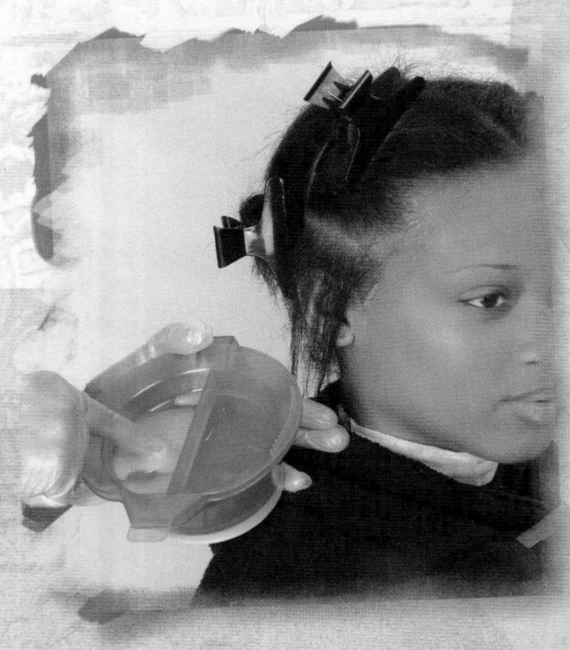

**NOTE:** If client has a sensitive scalp, it is recommended to still apply a base as a precaution.

**No-base form** (or no-lye) relaxers **do not require a protective cream** applied to the skin or scalp. This type of relaxer usually will have a slightly lower pH, and is therefore not as harsh on the scalp.

"Base is the term used for the protective cream applied to hairline and scalp prior to a chemical service."

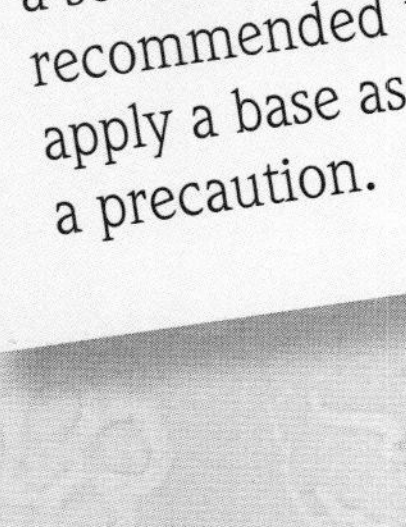

10

# Relaxer Liquid Tools . . .

"Always follow manufacturer's instructions in determining which relaxer is best used to benefit the client's hair-care needs and end results."

10

## The Categories of Hydroxide Relaxers:

| Type of Relaxer | pH | Results | Concerns |
|---|---|---|---|
| **Sodium (or lye)** | 12.5 to 14 | Quickest processing time; best used on curly, resistant, coarse texture and/or for maximum relaxation | Susceptible to scalp irritations and hair loss or breakage |
| **Potassium** | 12 to 13.5 | Quick processing time; best used on medium texture, less resistant hair and/or for optimum relaxation | Susceptible to scalp irritations and hair breakage |
| **Lithium** | 12 to 13.5 | Best used on less resistant, medium texture and/or for optimum to average relaxation | Slightly slower processing time; susceptible to scalp irritations and hair breakage |
| **Guanidine/ calcium** | 10 to 13 | Best used on less resistant, medium texture and/or for average to moderate relaxation. | Slightly slower processing time; less irritation to scalp with little to no hair breakage |

# Relaxer Liquid Tools . . .

## Thioglycolate (thi-o-gly-co-late) relaxers

are chemical compounds with the additive ingredient **ammonia** – which process the hair in the same manner as a permanent wave. This relaxer containing the ingredient ammonium thioglycolate has a low pH making it **suitable for a soft curl permanent**. The **ingredient ammonia increases the alkalinity** of the relaxer, but also assists in softening and swelling the cuticle. **Thioglycolate** is manufactured in a cream form with a thick viscosity to aid in the application of the relaxer on the hair. The hair may be shampooed prior to application of an ammonia thioglycolate relaxer — follow the manufacturer's instructions.

| Type of Relaxer | pH | Results | Concerns |
|---|---|---|---|
| Ammonium Thioglycolate | over 10 | Best used on less resistant, fine to medium texture and/or for optimum to average relaxation; **compatible with a soft curl permanent** | Slower processing time; not recommended for a strong curl pattern or resistant hair; less irritating to scalp and little to no hair breakage; strong ammonia odor |
| Ammonium Bisulfite | 6.5 to 8 | Best used for average to moderate relaxation and/or fine texture or tinted hair; also known as the **mildest** relaxer | Slower processing time; not recommended for a strong curl pattern or resistant hair; less irritating to scalp and little to no hair breakage; strong ammonia odor |

**CAUTION:** Hydroxide and Thioglycolate relaxers are "lethal enemies." Breakage can occur if one is applied to hair previously treated with the other. Always strand test prior to application when in doubt.

**The neutralizer**, *also referred to as a stabilizer, normalizer or fixative, reforms the disulfide bonds broken during the processing and keeps the hair in the new reconstructed position. Neutralizers also restore pH, assist in closing the cuticle and will generally have a pH range from 3 to 7.*

The type of relaxer used determines the form of neutralization – a **lathering form or non-lathering form**. Generally, **lathering or neutralizing shampoos** are used in conjunction with **hydroxide relaxers** due to the different chemical breakdown. As discussed in the chemistry chapter, only one sulfur atom is removed, replacing the disulfide bond with a lanthionine bond, which is referred to as lanthionization. **Remember this breakdown is irreversible; therefore hydroxide relaxers are not compatible with thioglycolate relaxers.** Neutralizing shampoos also help to remove any remaining chemical left in the hair and restore hair to normal acidic pH. Some product manufacturers have an additive in the neutralizer, which allows the lather to turn pink once in contact with relaxer. Upon complete removal of relaxer from hair, lather will return to a white color.

LATHERING FORM OF NEUTRALIZER

A **non-lathering neutralizer is used in conjunction with thioglycolate relaxers** due to the removal of two sulfur atoms, which are then replaced by the disulfide bond. This process is called oxidation and is done as the final step of the soft curl permanent.

NON-LATHERING FORM OF NEUTRALIZER

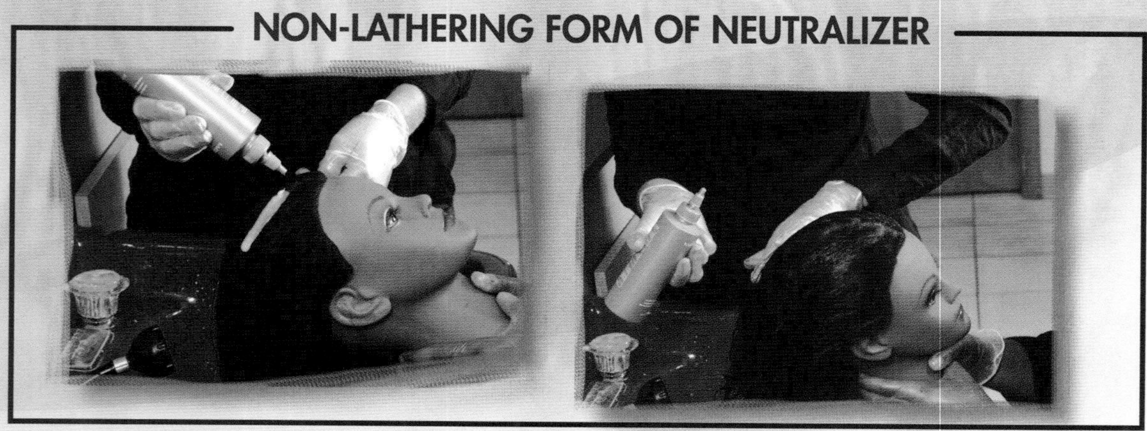

# Strength of Relaxers ...

*A* ***relaxer*** *will vary in strength according to the amount of conditioning buffers added with the main active ingredients remaining unaltered. The* ***strength of relaxer*** *used is determined during the hair and scalp analysis performed at the consultation. Remember, condition of cuticle influences the relaxer choice. The desired hairdesign will also be a factor in deciding the amount of curl reduction needed to produce the end result.*



## The three relaxer strengths:

**TYPE 1**

**Mild relaxer** is best used on hair with a **fine texture**, severe porosity, has been color treated and requires moderate relaxation

FINE

**TYPE 2**

**Regular relaxer** is typically used on hair with a **medium texture**, normal porosity and requires average to optimum relaxation

MEDIUM

**TYPE 3**

**Super relaxer** is best used on hair with a **coarse texture**, resistant porosity and requires maximum relaxation, but should be applied quickly and accurately.

COARSE

**CAUTION:** Haircoloring or lightening services should not be performed the same day as the relaxing service. Haircolor should be applied one to two weeks AFTER a chemical relaxer treatment because the cuticle is re-opened during the coloring process and, fading of the color can occur.

Hair Relaxing

Haircolor

# Curl Reduction ...

The **amount of curl removed** or degree of relaxation is referred to as **curl reduction**. Use the following guide to determine the percentage of curl relaxation. The **reduction of curl** is chosen through careful hair analysis and desired hairdesign.

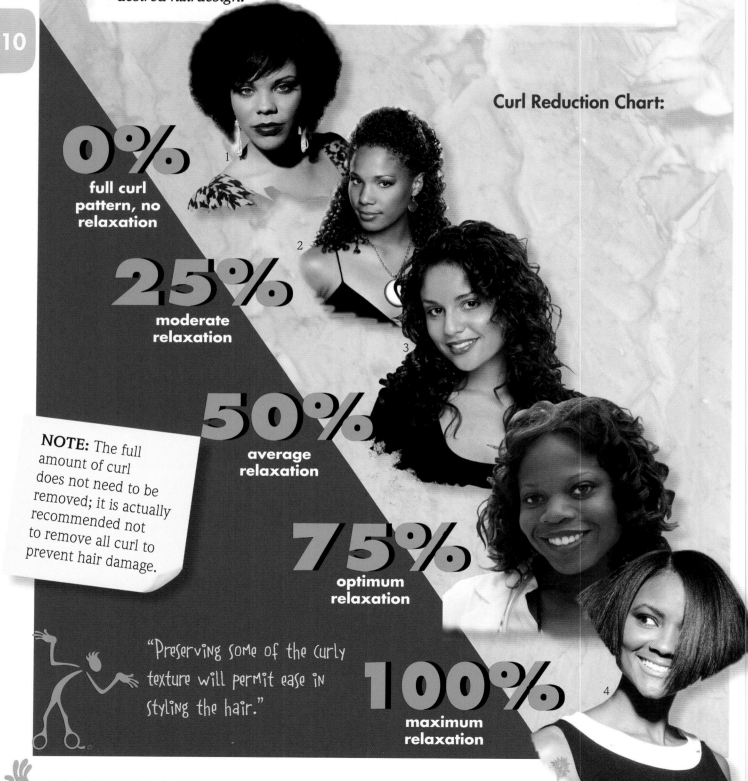

10

**Curl Reduction Chart:**

**0%** full curl pattern, no relaxation

1

**25%** moderate relaxation

2

**50%** average relaxation

3

**NOTE:** The full amount of curl does not need to be removed; it is actually recommended not to remove all curl to prevent hair damage.

**75%** optimum relaxation

**100%** maximum relaxation

4

"Preserving some of the curly texture will permit ease in styling the hair."

# Relaxer Application ...

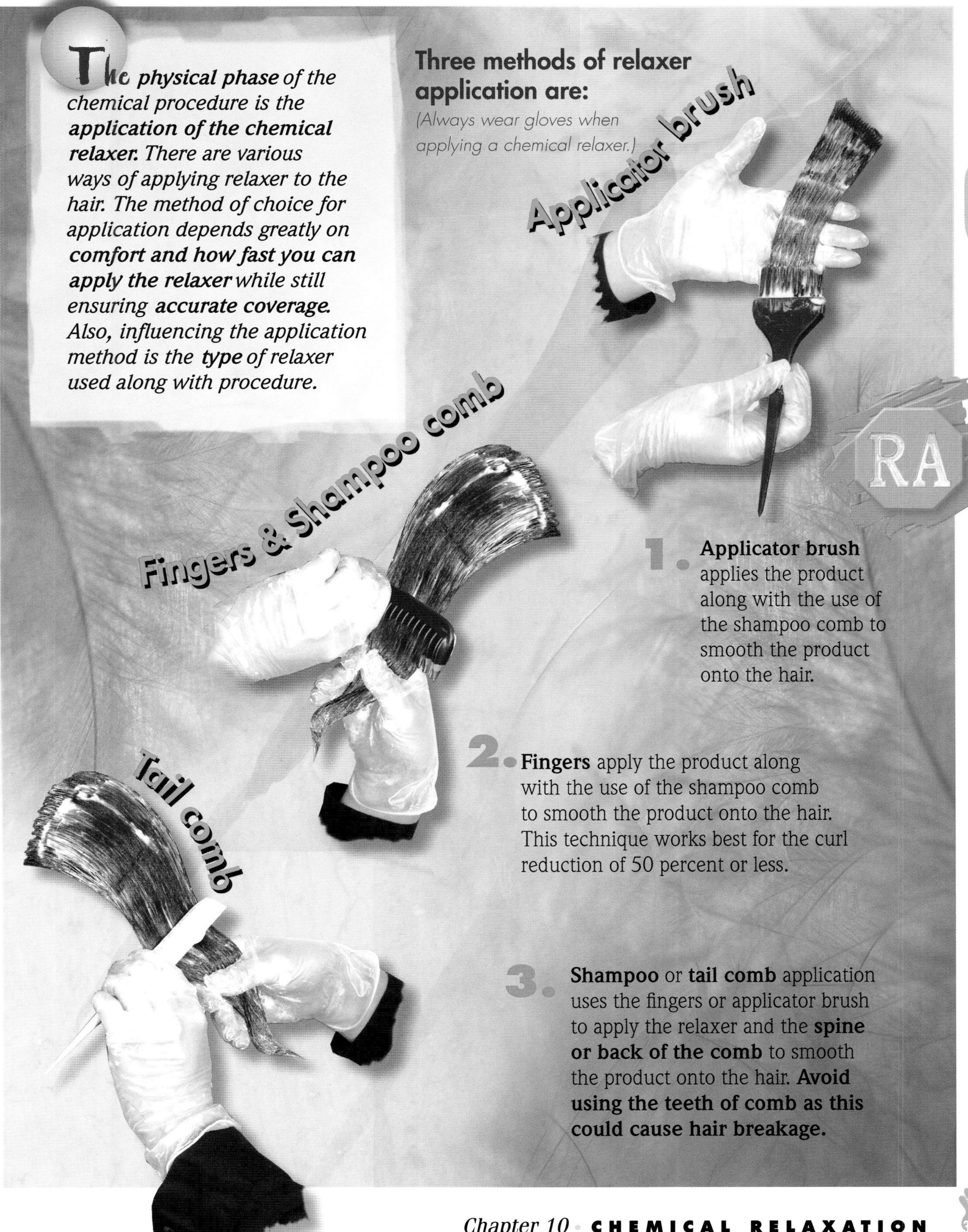


*The **physical phase** of the chemical procedure is the **application of the chemical relaxer.** There are various ways of applying relaxer to the hair. The method of choice for application depends greatly on **comfort and how fast you can apply the relaxer** while still ensuring **accurate coverage.** Also, influencing the application method is the **type** of relaxer used along with procedure.*

**Three methods of relaxer application are:**

*(Always wear gloves when applying a chemical relaxer.)*

1. **Applicator brush** applies the product along with the use of the shampoo comb to smooth the product onto the hair.

2. **Fingers** apply the product along with the use of the shampoo comb to smooth the product onto the hair. This technique works best for the curl reduction of 50 percent or less.

3. **Shampoo** or **tail comb** application uses the fingers or applicator brush to apply the relaxer and the **spine or back of the comb** to smooth the product onto the hair. **Avoid using the teeth of comb as this could cause hair breakage.**

# Strand Testing...

*Recommend a series of reconstructor treatments to restore healthy hair back to a healthy state in order to receive chemical hair services.*

*In order to accomplish a successful chemical relaxation treatment it is necessary to perform strand testing prior to and during the procedure.*

10

## Two types of strand testing performed are:

**Preliminary strand testing (relaxer test)** is performed **prior** to receiving a chemical relaxer. This strand test will determine **if the hair is capable of receiving a chemical** and if so, what relaxer would produce accurate results. **To perform this test**, use a small subsection of hair from an inconspicuous area of the head. Place a barrier of foil or paper towel underneath subsection of hair being processed. Relaxer is then applied, keeping it away from scalp to avoid body heat, which can accelerate processing. Also, keep relaxer away from hair ends, which are generally porous to avoid overprocessing. Follow manufacturer's instructions, complete full procedure and check end results.

Spine of tail comb smoothing hair

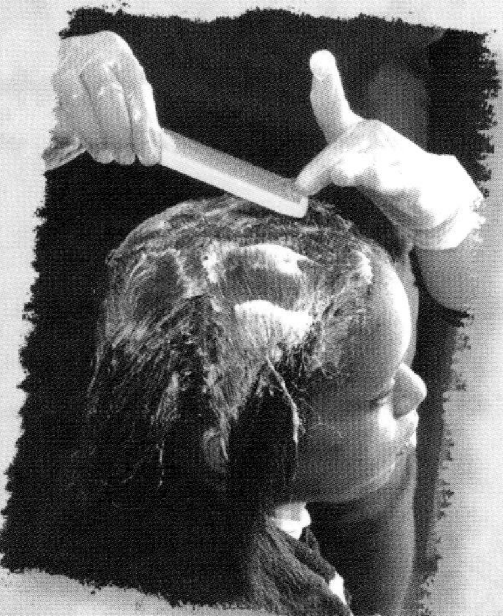

**Curl reduction testing (relaxation test)** is performed **during** the chemical treatment to determine **if hair is sufficiently processed** or completed. **To perform this test**, select a subsection of hair that may be most resistant to relaxing. Smooth hair with either a large-tooth comb or spine of tail comb to see if hair remains straight or resumes a natural curl position. Proceed to next step of procedure if hair has reached desired curl reduction. If not, reapply relaxer to that subsection and continue to process.

End result showing hair has reached desired curl reduction

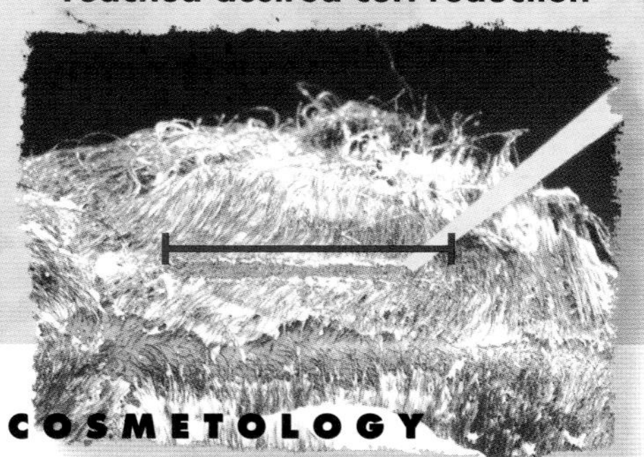

# Hair and Scalp Analysis . . .

*A client consultation is necessary before delivering any chemical service in determining if the client is able to receive the relaxer treatment. The hair and scalp are analyzed for* ***condition, texture, porosity, elasticity and density.*** *As learned in previous chapters, these areas will provide the results in deciding on type and strength of relaxer as well as the method of application to be used. Other areas that can affect the relaxers' end result would be* ***length of client's hair*** *and if the client has had* ***artificial haircoloring.*** *Compile answers on a* ***client profile card,*** *which are questionnaires containing useful client health and hair-care information.*

HAIR & SCALP EQUILIZER
DEEP CONDITIONER
HAIR CLEANSER
INTENSIVE RECONSTRUCTOR
ELASTICITY RE-BUILDER

1

| DATE | SERVICE/TREATMENT-Formula/Product, ounces, time, rod size | REMARKS/CHANGES |
|---|---|---|
| | | |

☑ Medical Ale

## Client Profile Card/File

Name ______________ Date ________
Address ______________
______________
Occupation ________ Hobby ________
Birthdate ______________
First Visit Date ______________
Oral Contraceptives? ❑ Pregnant? ❑ Trying to be? ❑
Medications ❑ Allergies ❑
Health Problems ❑
**Professional Haircoloring:** Temporary ❑
Semi-Permanent ❑ Demi-Permanent ❑ Permanent ❑ Home Haircolor ❑

Cosmetologist ________ Lic # ________
**Hair Condition:** Normal ❑ Dry ❑ Oily ❑
**Scalp Condition:** Normal ❑ Dry ❑ Oily ❑
**Texture:** Fine ❑ Medium ❑ Coarse ❑
**Type of Hair:** Straight ❑ Wavy ❑ Curly ❑
**Density:** Thick ❑ Medium ❑ Thin ❑
**Porosity:** Resistant ❑ Normal ❑ Severe ❑ Irregular ❑
**Elasticity:** Average ❑ Low ❑
**Length:** 1 to 6 inches ❑ 7 inches or longer ❑
What attracted you to our salon? Friend ❑ Location ❑

Personal Hair Treatment & Product: Shampoo ❑ Conditioner ❑ Hair Spray ❑ Gels ❑ Other ❑
I Do The Following To My Hair: Cut ❑ Color ❑ Perm ❑ Bleach ❑ Rinse ❑ Conditions ❑ Other ❑
REMARKS ______________
______________

10

# Hair and Scalp Analysis . . .

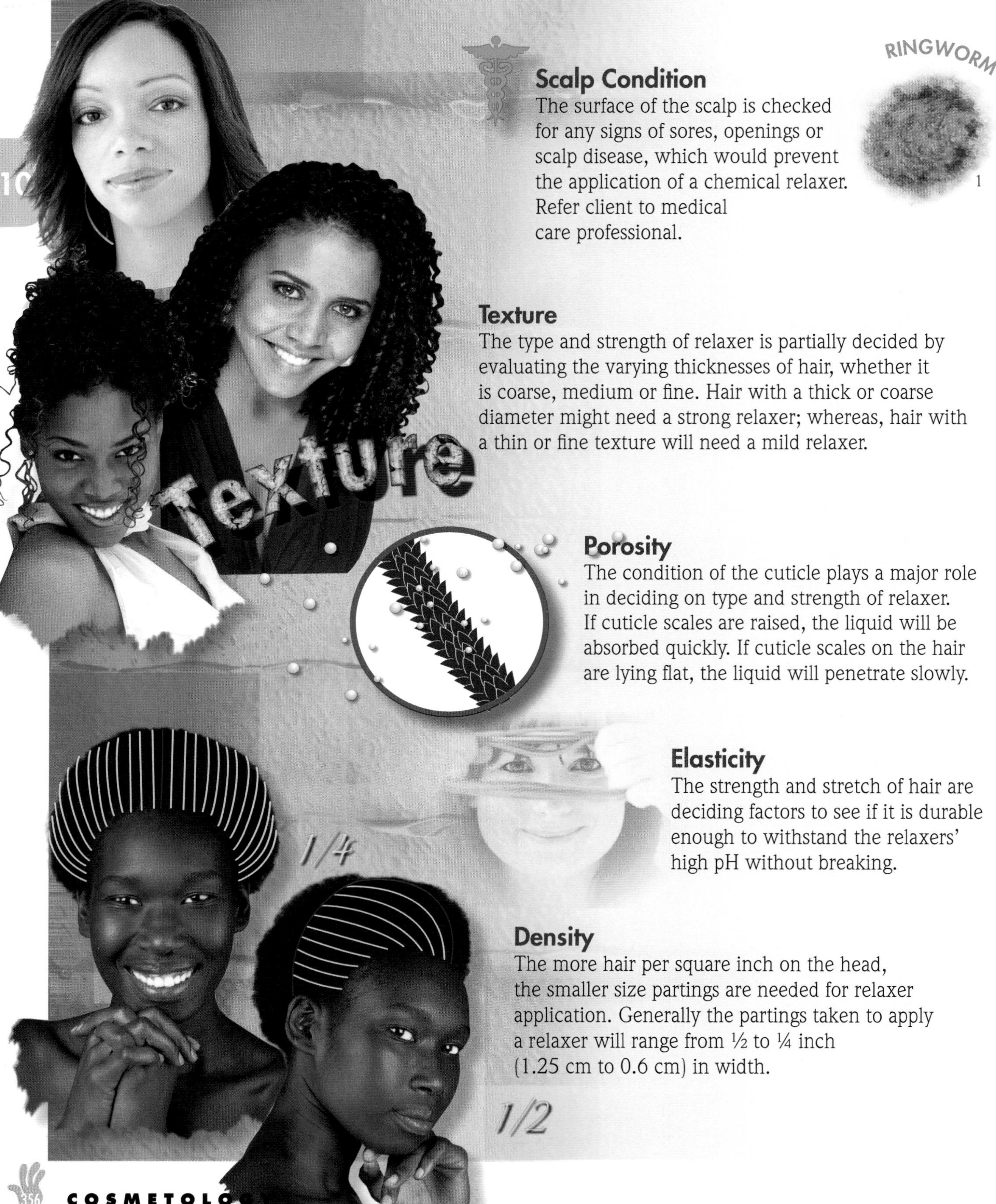


## Scalp Condition

The surface of the scalp is checked for any signs of sores, openings or scalp disease, which would prevent the application of a chemical relaxer. Refer client to medical care professional.

## Texture

The type and strength of relaxer is partially decided by evaluating the varying thicknesses of hair, whether it is coarse, medium or fine. Hair with a thick or coarse diameter might need a strong relaxer; whereas, hair with a thin or fine texture will need a mild relaxer.

## Porosity

The condition of the cuticle plays a major role in deciding on type and strength of relaxer. If cuticle scales are raised, the liquid will be absorbed quickly. If cuticle scales on the hair are lying flat, the liquid will penetrate slowly.

## Elasticity

The strength and stretch of hair are deciding factors to see if it is durable enough to withstand the relaxers' high pH without breaking.

## Density

The more hair per square inch on the head, the smaller size partings are needed for relaxer application. Generally the partings taken to apply a relaxer will range from ½ to ¼ inch (1.25 cm to 0.6 cm) in width.

**Length** of hair determines the type of wrapping pattern and perm rods used. Generally, if hair is longer than six inches (15.2 cm), a long hair wrapping pattern is used. The amount of chemical products used is increased for the long hair permanent wave.



**Haircolor** of the client may affect the outcome of the chemical procedure depending on type of coloring used. Some chemical relaxers are formulated to be compatible with professional haircoloring; however, if using a home haircolor, a strand test is performed to check for the presence of metallic salts. **Metallic salts** are ingredients used in some home haircoloring kits. They leave a **metal coating on the hair** that effects the proper penetration of a chemical product. The type of metal used determines the color outcome (for example, a copper metal will produce a red color or a lead creates a brown to black color). This can result in hair discoloration, severe hair breakage or irregular straightening or curling patterns when another chemical is applied.

### Test for Metallic Salts on the Hair:

- Mix one ounce of 20 volume hydrogen peroxide with 20 drops of 28 percent ammonia in glass container.
- Place approximately 20 strands of hair into container and soak for 30 minutes.
- **No metallic salts present**, hair will lighten slightly. Hair **may receive permanent wave.**
- Hair with a **lead coating** will lighten quickly.
- Hair with a **silver coating** has no reaction within the 30 minutes.
- Hair with a **copper coating** will break apart; the solution will boil and produce an unpleasant odor.

**CAUTION:** Hair with a lead, silver or copper coating **cannot** receive any chemical services. The hair affected by the metals must either be cut off or some manufacturers will offer a prepared solution to remove the metals from the hair. Check with the local beauty distributor.

2

## There are two major chemical phases of chemical relaxing:

## Phase 1

### Processing

**Processing** is the application of a chemical agent to the hair, followed by a series of steps necessary to produce a reformed hair structure.

**NOTE:** If any scalp abrasions were discovered during the hair and scalp analysis, do not proceed with the chemical service.

To chemically change the curly structure of hair, a **relaxer cream or lotion is applied and smoothed onto the hair**. A slight firm pressure is used on the hair during the smoothing process to accelerate relaxer absorption and assist in the curl reduction. **Visually the curl will lessen** as the smoothing process continues; a relaxation strand test is applied to determine if process is completed.

An **integral part of the relaxer procedure is to ensure client comfort and safety**. Besides covering up clothing, we must also **protect the hairline and scalp**. As discussed earlier, the chemicals used to straighten curly hair are of the highest alkaline content, and therefore may be irritating to the human skin or scalp. Application of a **"base" or protective cream is an essential step** before beginning any chemical process.

During the chemical process if client feels any burning or irritation, apply a piece of cotton saturated with neutralizer to sensitive area to stop the chemical action. If irritation persists, remove chemical relaxer immediately to prevent chemical burns. Complete procedure with the neutralization process following manufacturer's directions.

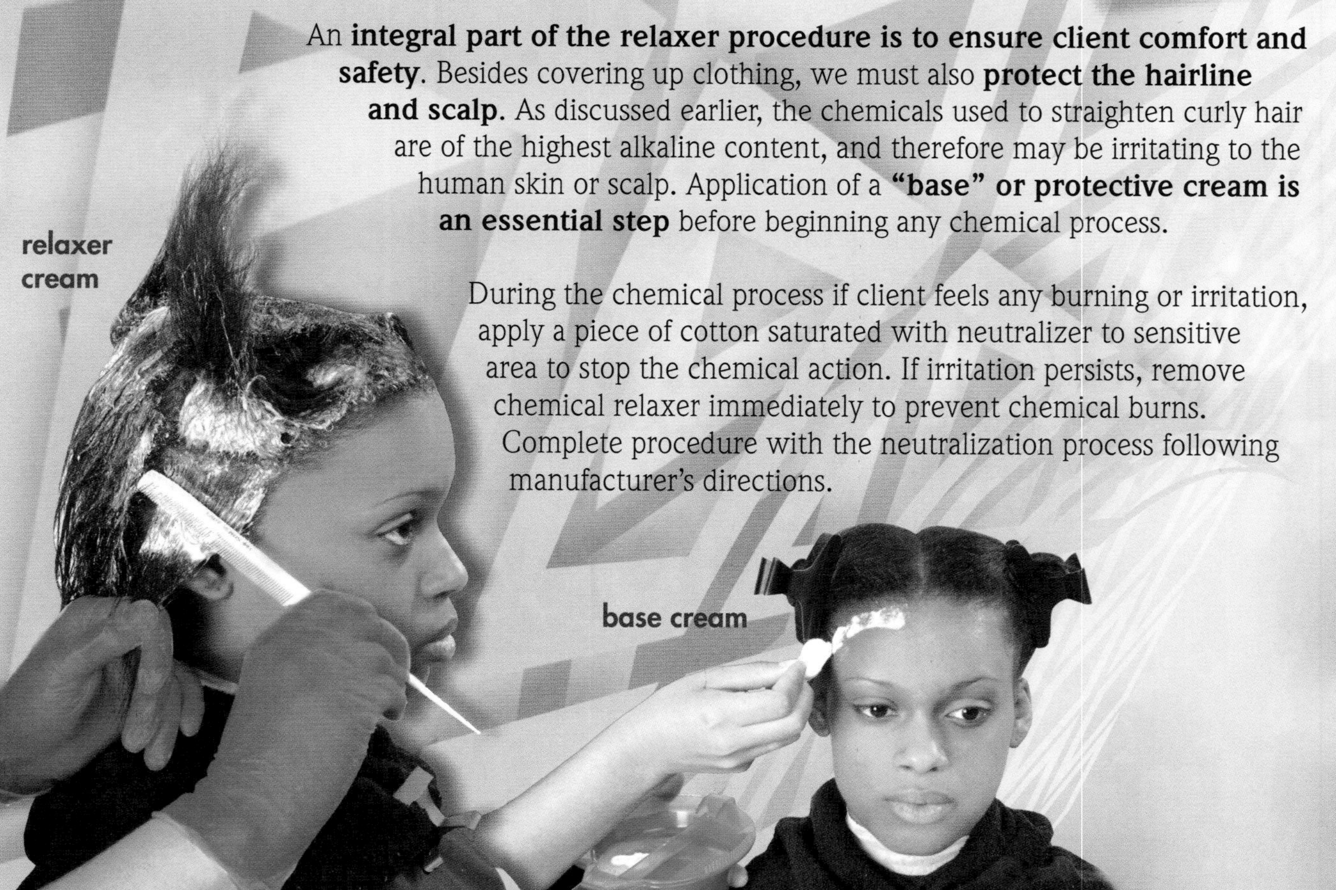

# Relaxer Procedure ...

## Phase 2

### Neutralizing

**Neutralizing** is applying a chemical that reconnects the disulfide bonds for thioglycolate relaxers or restores the hair back to a normal acidic pH when using hydroxide relaxers.

### RINSE

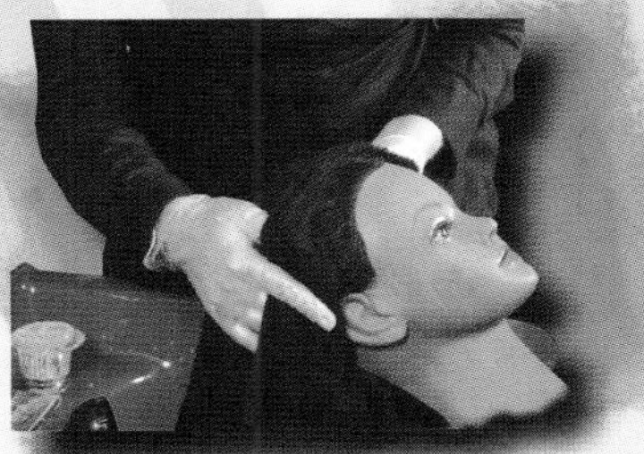

At the time of neutralization, **the relaxer is thoroughly rinsed** from the hair following the manufacturer's directions.

### NEUTRALIZE

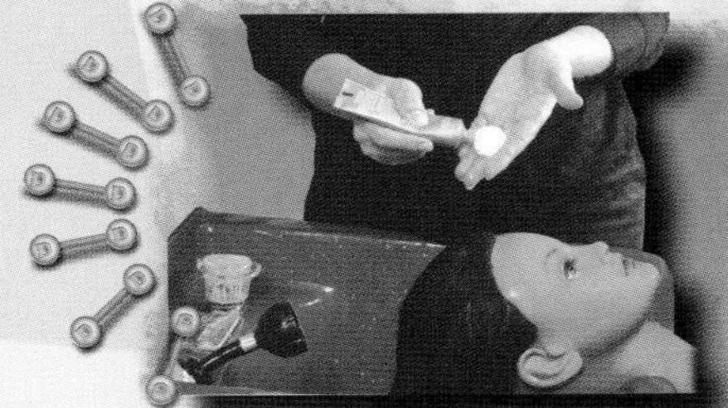

The **neutralizer or rebonding agent** is applied to eliminate any remaining relaxer product from the hair and to hold the bonds into their new straight position. Follow the manufacturer's directions for repeated applications of the lathering neutralizer and duration of time needed for non-lathering neutralizer.

### CONDITION

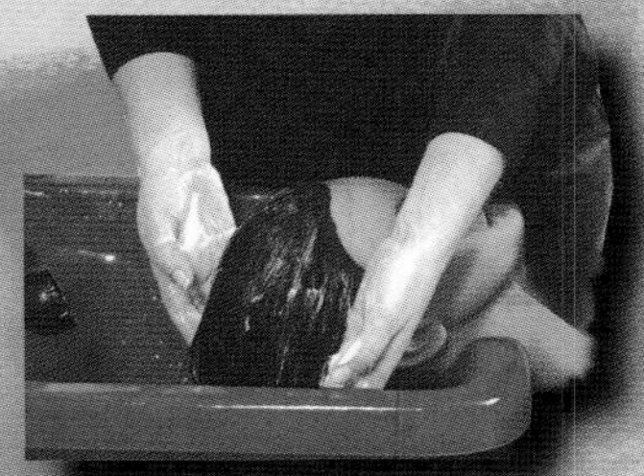

A **conditioning product** is applied once neutralization is complete to help lower pH and restore hair to a normal healthy state.

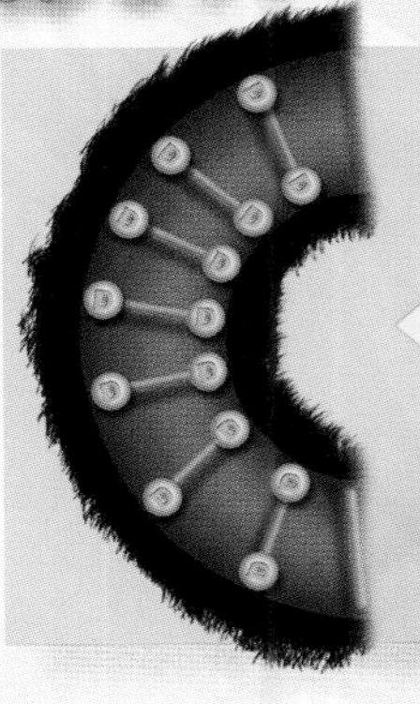

Disulfide bonds intact before thioglycolate is added

Disulfide bonds break as hair is straightened

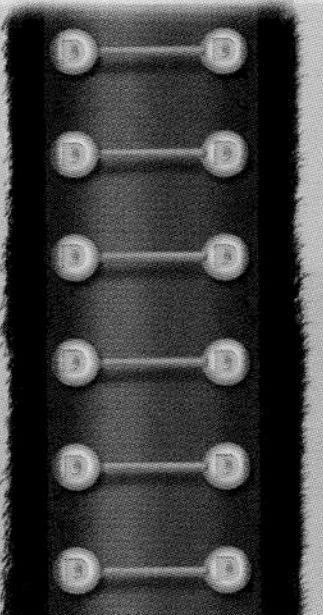

Thioglycolate is rinsed from hair and neutralizer is added. Bonds reform in new position

**NOTE:** Some manufacturers request that the hair be conditioned after processing, prior to the neutralizing step.

### Client Home Care Maintenance

Now that you have completed your chemical service, excellent customer care dictates a home maintenance program for customers to use between salon visits. Market professional retail products to assist in restoring the hair back to a healthy state and reschedule client for a follow-up appointment.

When styling hair, avoid using high-heated implements after a chemical service due to the hair's vulnerability to breakage.

Recommend that the client avoid any professional haircoloring services for one to two weeks after chemical procedure.

CLiC INTERNATIONAL

RA

## SIMPLE LAB PROJECT

# Chemical Relaxer (Ammonium Thioglycolate) on Mannequin

### OBJECTIVE

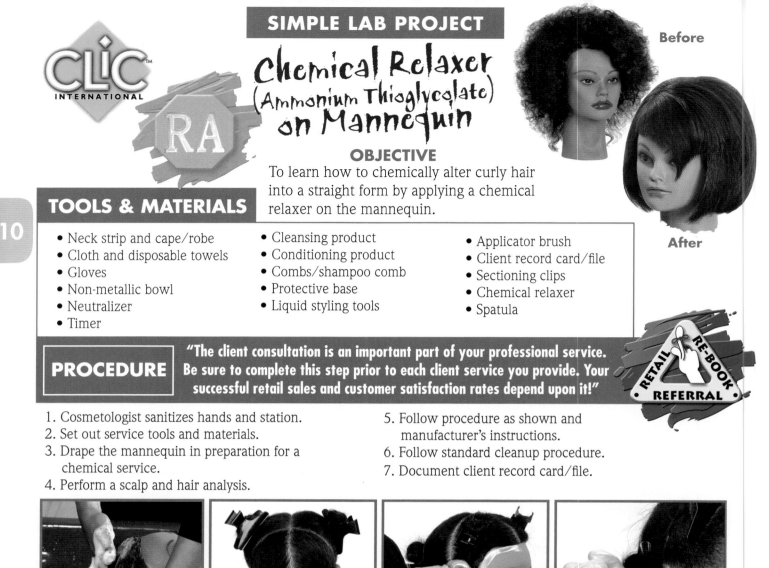

To learn how to chemically alter curly hair into a straight form by applying a chemical relaxer on the mannequin.

10

## TOOLS & MATERIALS

- Neck strip and cape/robe
- Cloth and disposable towels
- Gloves
- Non-metallic bowl
- Neutralizer
- Timer
- Cleansing product
- Conditioning product
- Combs/shampoo comb
- Protective base
- Liquid styling tools
- Applicator brush
- Client record card/file
- Sectioning clips
- Chemical relaxer
- Spatula

## PROCEDURE

**"The client consultation is an important part of your professional service. Be sure to complete this step prior to each client service you provide. Your successful retail sales and customer satisfaction rates depend upon it!"**

RETAIL • RE-BOOK • REFERRAL

1. Cosmetologist sanitizes hands and station.
2. Set out service tools and materials.
3. Drape the mannequin in preparation for a chemical service.
4. Perform a scalp and hair analysis.
5. Follow procedure as shown and manufacturer's instructions.
6. Follow standard cleanup procedure.
7. Document client record card/file.

Lightly cleanse hair and scalp to avoid irritation.

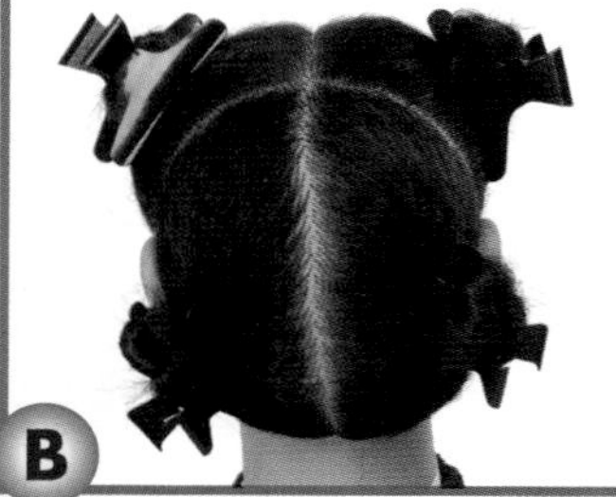


Divide hair into four sections.

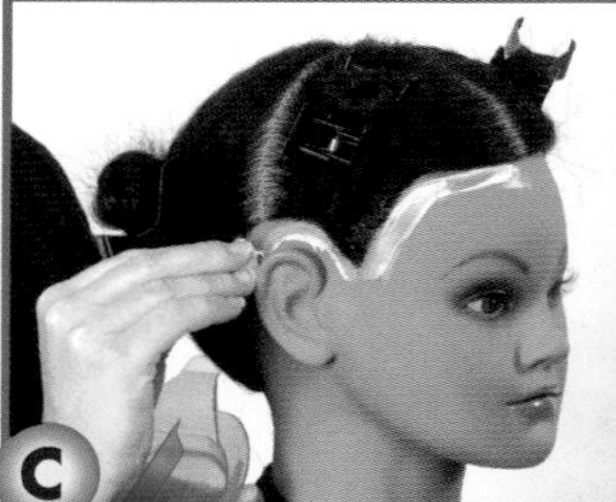


Apply protective cream (base) around hairline and ears.

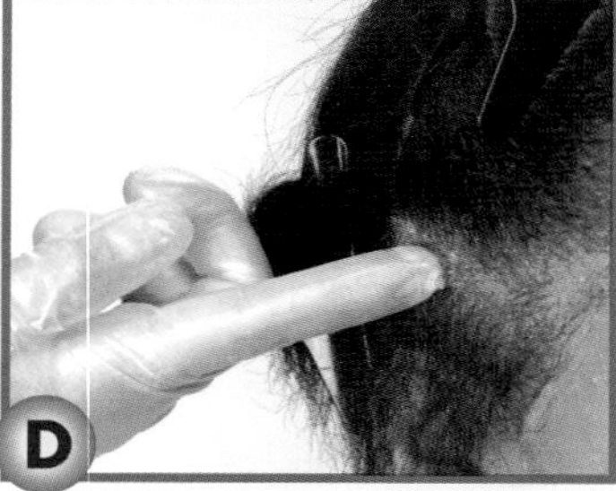


Part hair into ½ **inch (1.25 cm) subsections,** apply base to scalp area along partings. **NOTE:** No body heat to help liquify base for even coverage.

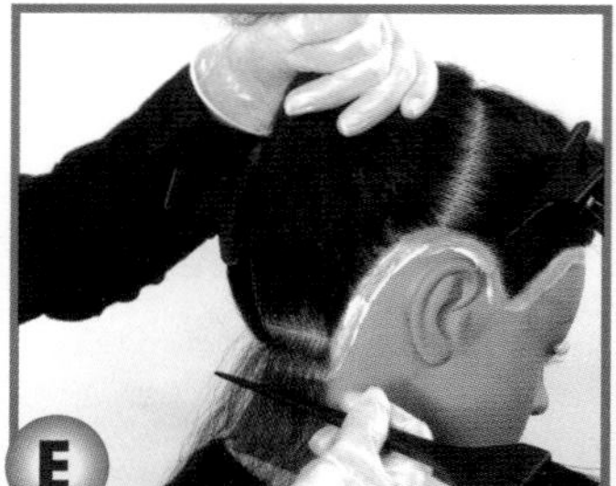


Starting at nape area of right back section, **part hair into ¼ inch (0.6 cm) subsections.**

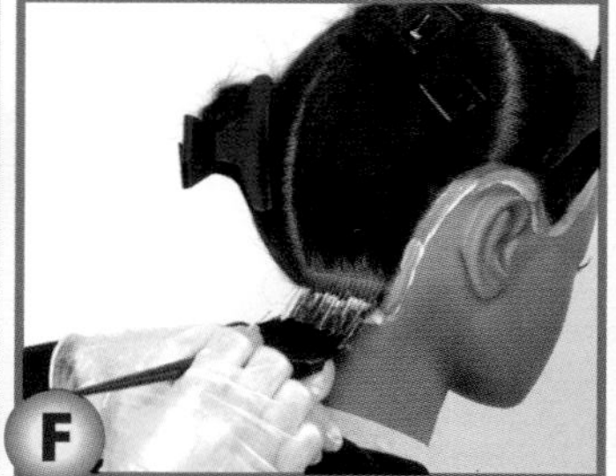


With gloves on, use an applicator brush to apply relaxer to most resistant area on head, keeping **½ inch (1.25 cm) away from scalp.**

Continue applying relaxer using **¼ inch (0.6 cm) subsections,** keeping **1 inch (2.5 cm) away from ends,** covering both sides of subsection.

Apply to all sections in the same manner.

# Chemical Relaxer on Mannequin

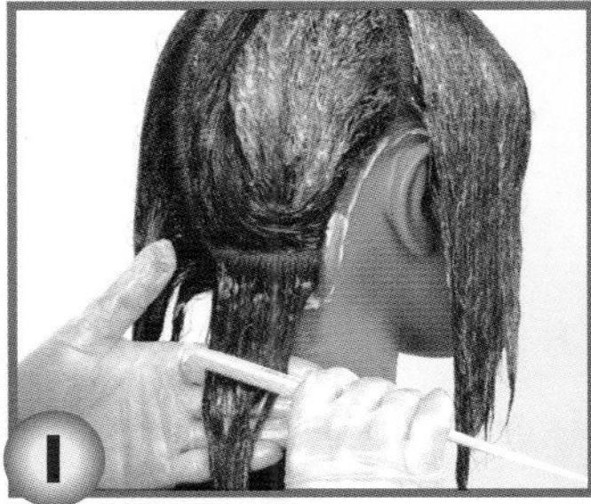

I — Start at nape area of right back section; part hair into **one inch (2.5 cm) subsections.**

J — Use tail comb or spine (back) of tail comb to smooth hair. Apply a slight firm pressure.

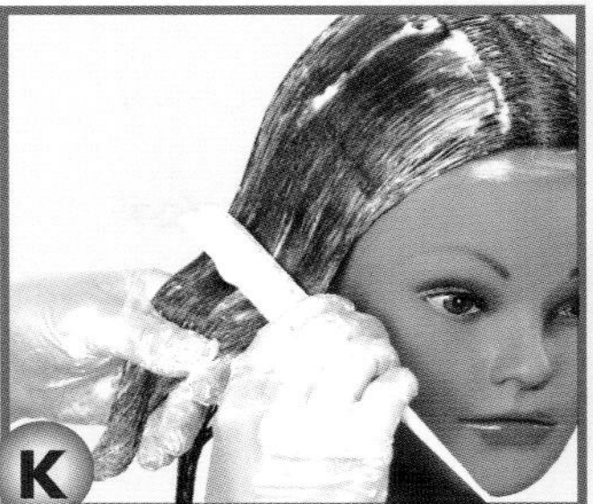

K — Continue to smooth all sections.

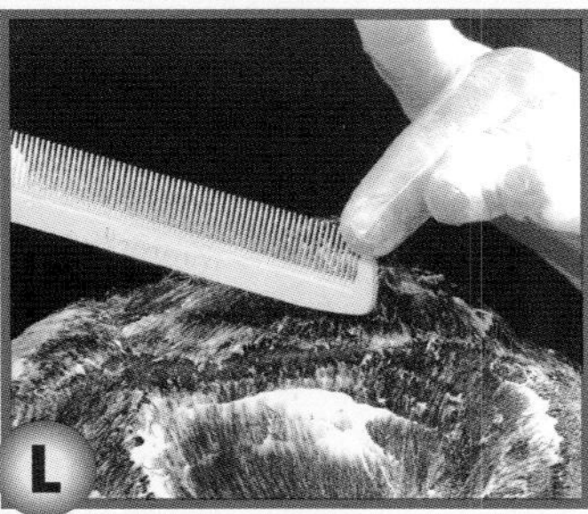

L — Perform relaxation test using spine of tail comb and smooth an area of hair to check for desired curl reduction.

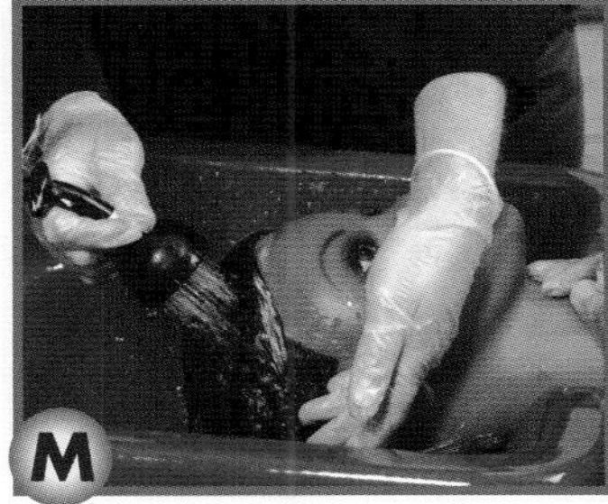

M — If hair is sufficiently relaxed, thoroughly **rinse relaxer** from hair.

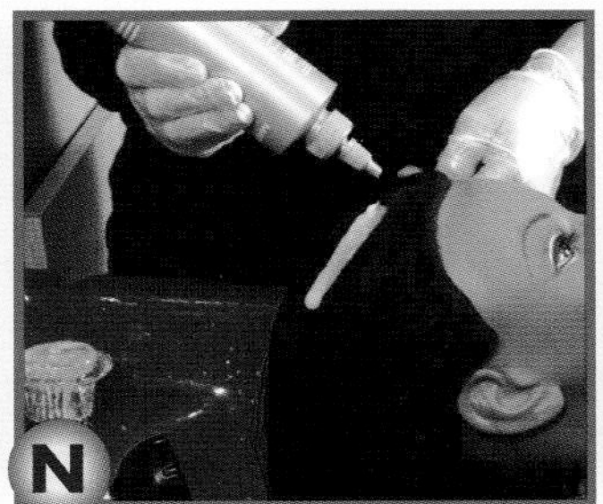

N — Towel-**blot hair** and apply neutralizing product.

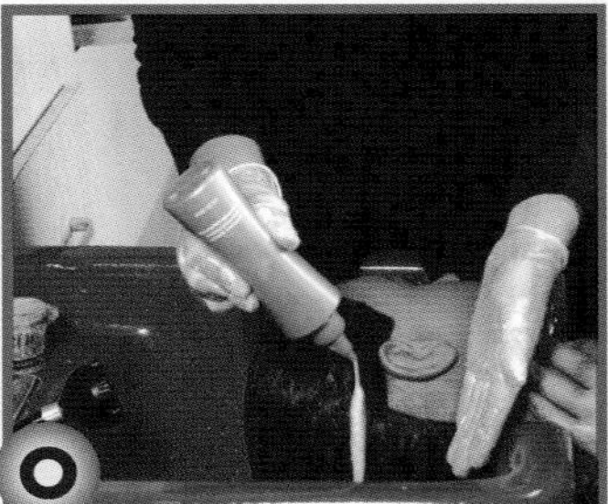

O — **Apply neutralizer** and work through hair to ensure complete coverage.

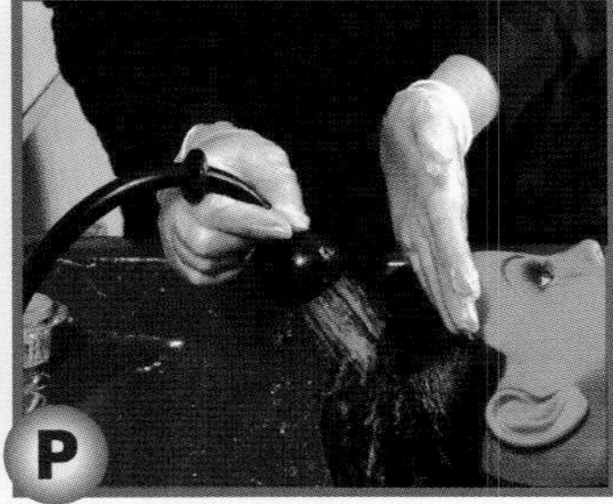

P — Process following manufacturer's instructions and rinse.

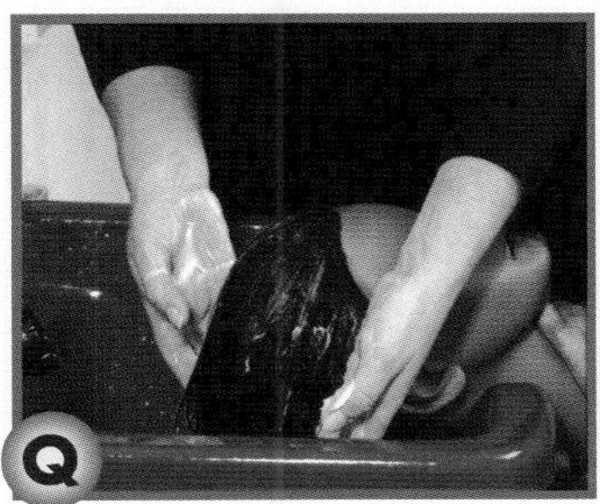

Q — Apply a conditioner product to hair.

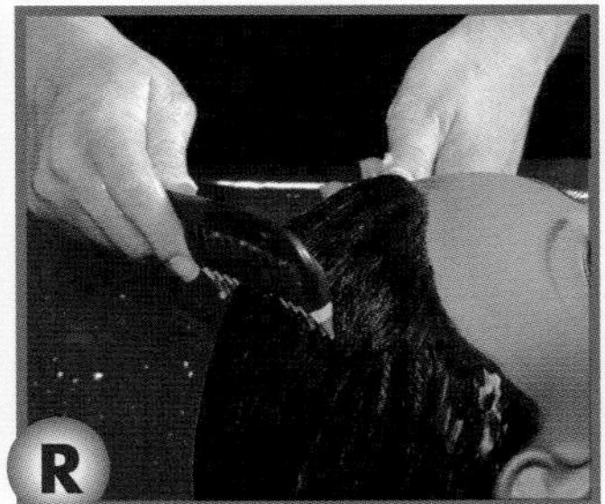

R — Comb through hair to ensure complete coverage.

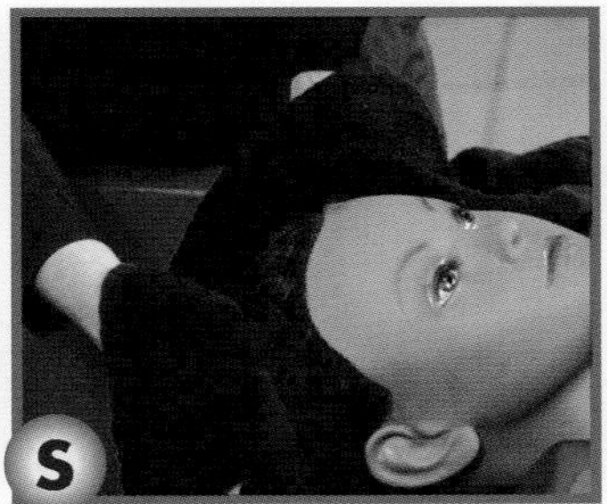

S — Rinse conditioner from hair and towel-blot.

1

T — Apply styling aids; completed chemical relaxer on mannequin.

"Use a spatula to remove enough relaxer for procedure and place in a non-metallic bowl. Never return unused product to the original container as this would contaminate the remaining product."

EVALUATION

GRADE — STUDENT'S NAME — ID#

CLiC INTERNATIONAL

INTERMEDIATE LAB PROJECT

# Hydroxide Relaxer Retouch

## OBJECTIVE

To chemically reduce the curl amount in the regrowth of curly hair for client's ease in maintaining hairdesign.

## TOOLS & MATERIALS

- Neck strip and cape/robe
- Cloth and disposable towels
- Gloves
- Non-metallic bowl
- Neutralizer
- Timer
- Cleansing product
- Conditioning product
- Combs/shampoo comb
- Protective base
- Liquid styling tools
- Applicator brush
- Client record card/file
- Sectioning clips
- Chemical relaxer
- Spatula

## PROCEDURE

"The client consultation is an important part of your professional service. Be sure to complete this step prior to each client service you provide. Your successful retail sales and customer satisfaction rates depend upon it!"

RETAIL RE-BOOK REFERRAL

1. Cosmetologist sanitizes hands and station.
2. Set out service tools and materials.
3. Drape the client in preparation for a chemical service.
4. Perform a scalp and hair analysis.
5. Follow procedure as shown and manufacturer's instructions.
6. Follow standard cleanup procedure.
7. Document client record card/file.

A Divide hair into four sections. **NOTE:** Do not shampoo prior to sodium hydroxide relaxer.

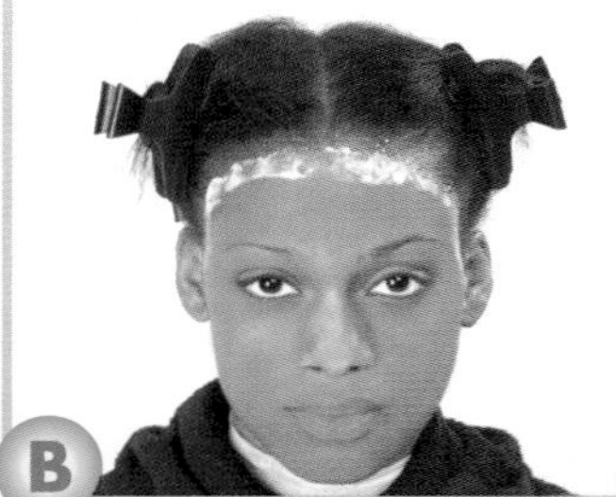

B Apply protective cream (base) around hairline and ears.

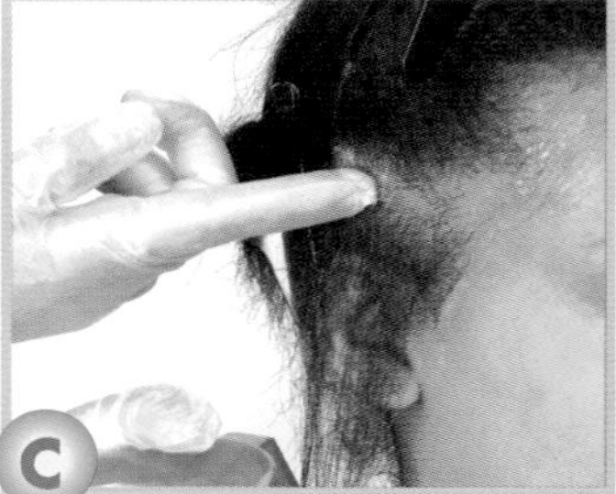

C Part hair into **½ inch (1.25 cm) subsections**, apply base to scalp area along partings. Body heat will liquify cream allowing for even coverage.

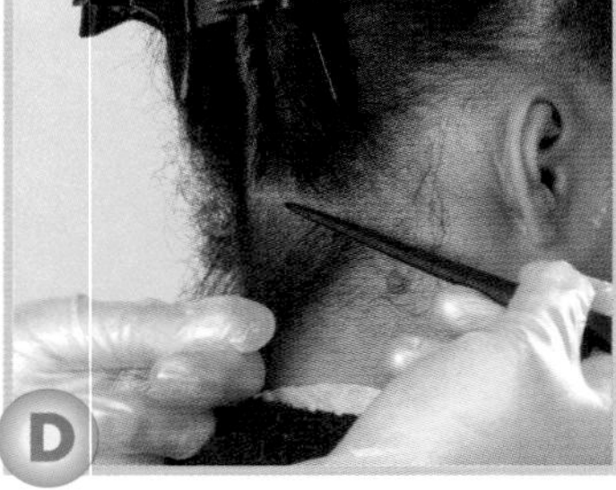

D Start at most resistant area, part hair into **¼ inch (0.6 cm) subsections.**

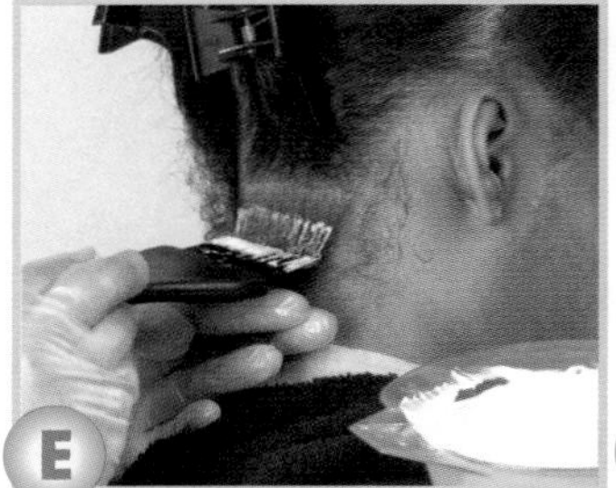

E With gloves on, use an applicator brush to apply relaxer to **regrowth area ONLY,** keeping **¼ inch (0.6 cm) away from scalp** (body heat).

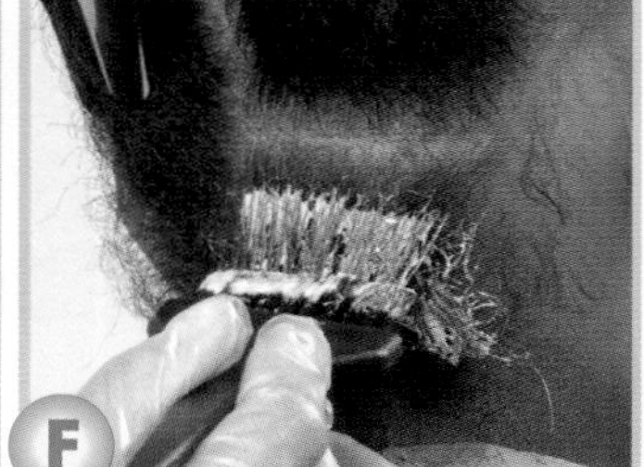

F Continue applying relaxer to **regrowth area**, covering both sides of subsection. **NOTE:** Refer to RA icon if using this procedure for regulatory testing.

G Apply to all sections in the same manner.

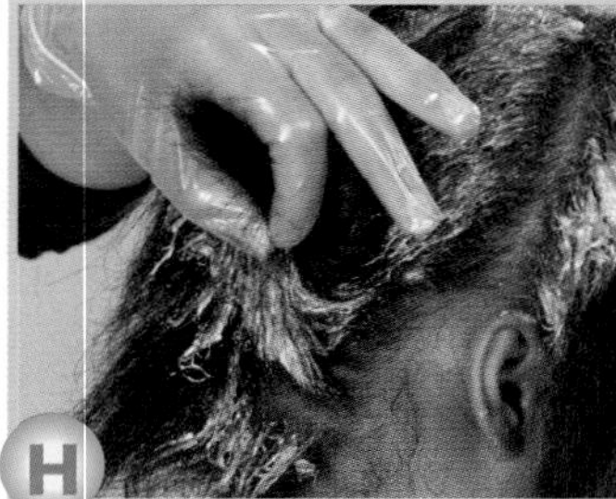

H Part hair into **one inch (2.5 cm) subsections.**

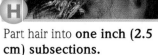

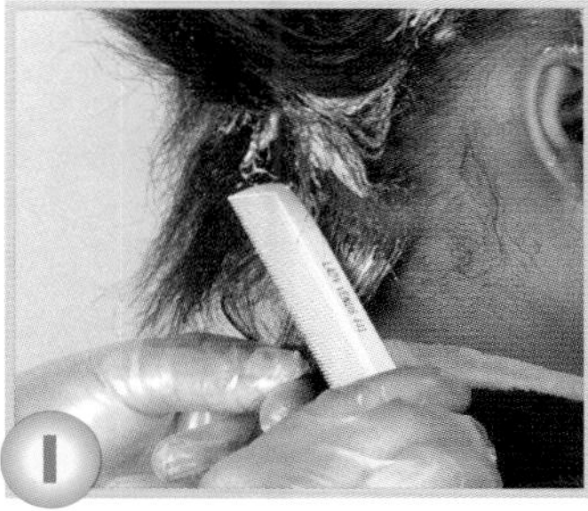
I
Use spine (back) of tail comb or large tooth comb to smooth **regrowth of hair ONLY.** Apply a slight firm pressure.

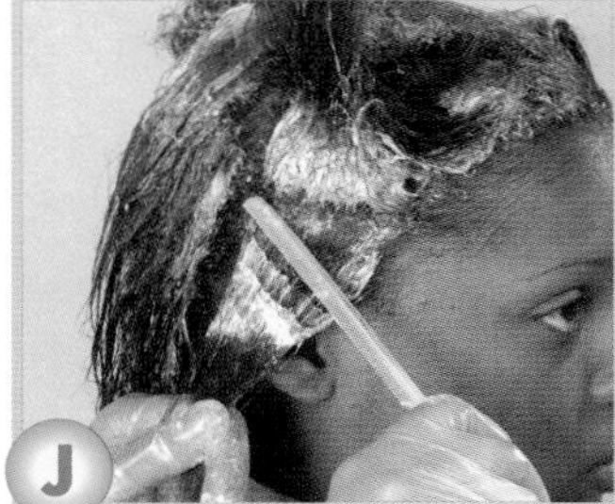
J
Continue to smooth all sections.

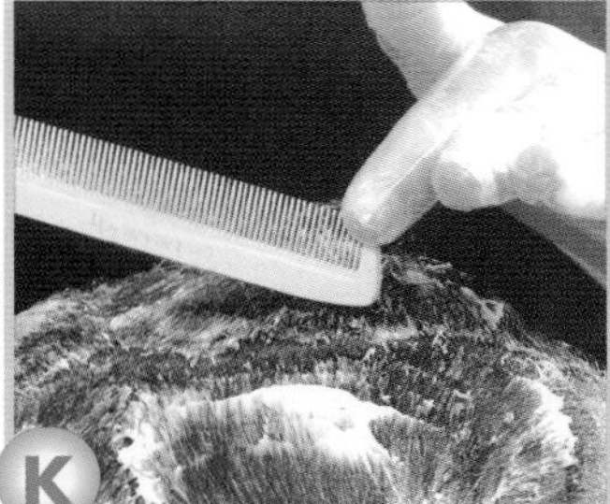
K
Perform relaxation test using spine of tail comb and smooth an area of hair to check for desired curl reduction.

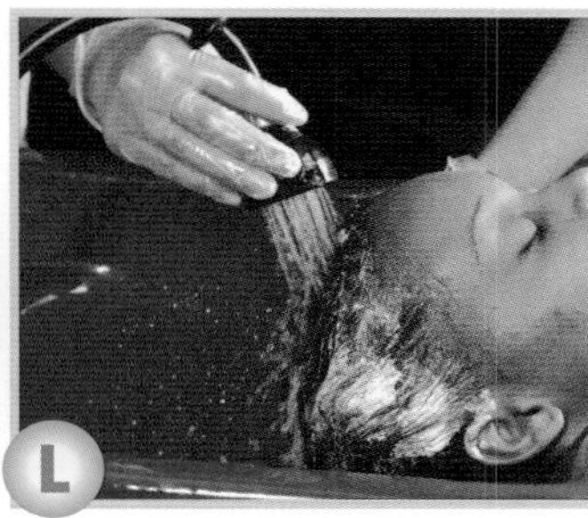
L
If hair is sufficiently relaxed, thoroughly rinse relaxer from hair.



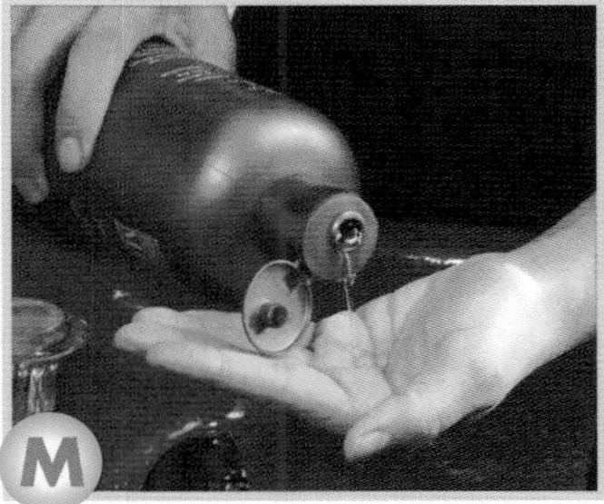
M
Apply a small amount of **neutralizing shampoo** into palm of hand and place onto hair.

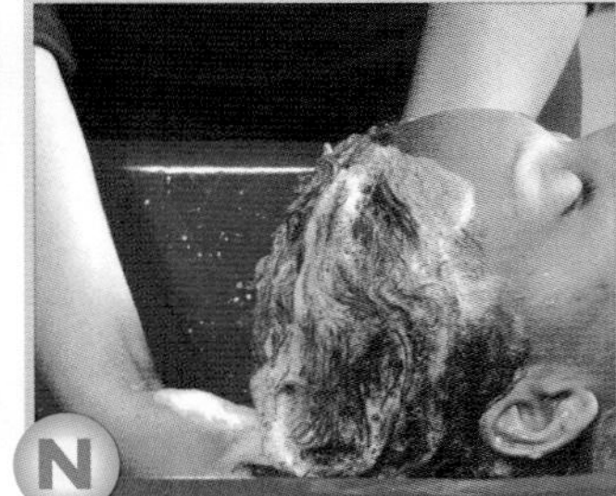
N
Shampoo hair; create a full amount of lather for complete coverage of head.

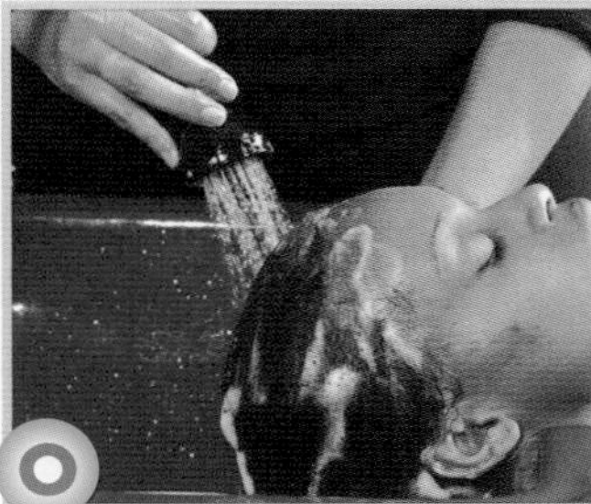
O
Rinse and **repeat steps M and N** as many times as necessary according to manufacturer's instructions.

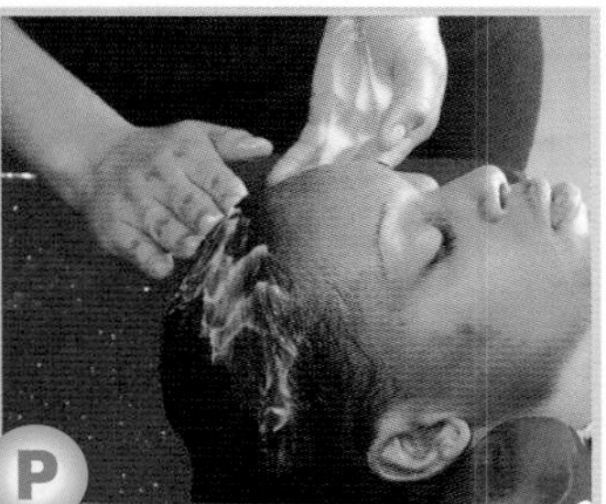
P
Apply conditioning product.

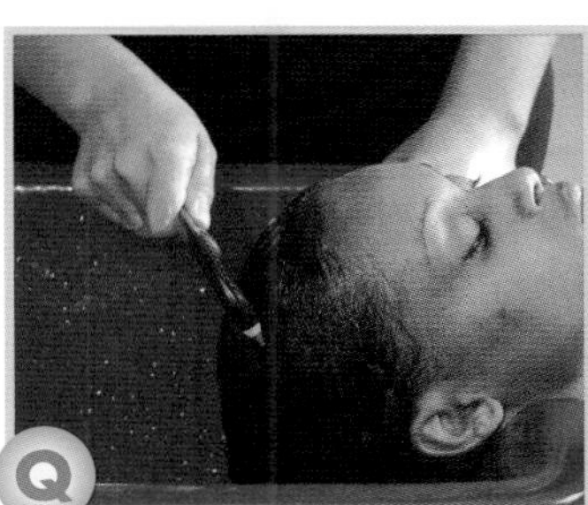
Q
Comb through to ensure complete coverage.

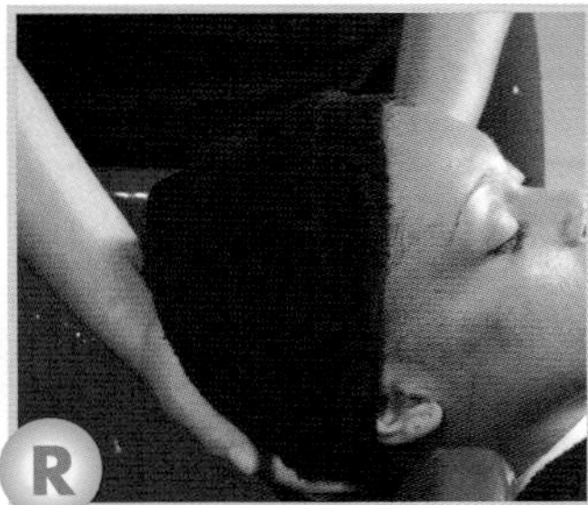
R
Rinse conditioner from hair and towel-blot.

S
Apply styling aids; completed chemical relaxer retouch.

***Apply relaxer to cover two inches of retouch area (mock). Check with your local regulatory agency for the exact amount of retouch coverage.***

**EVALUATION** ______________________________

______ GRADE ______ STUDENT'S NAME ______ ID#

CLiC INTERNATIONAL™

## COMPLEX LAB PROJECT

# Soft Curl Permanent (Ammonium Thioglycolate)

### OBJECTIVE

To chemically alter curly hair texture into manageable curls or waves.

### TOOLS & MATERIALS

- Neck strip and cape/robe
- Cloth and disposable towels
- Gloves
- End papers
- Neutralizer
- Timer
- Chemical relaxer
- Cleansing product
- Conditioning product
- Combs/shampoo comb
- Applicator brush
- Protective base
- Liquid styling tools
- Non-metallic bowl and spatula
- Perm rods
- Client record card/file
- Sectioning clips
- Permanent wave lotion
- Plastic cap
- Water bottle
- Cotton

### PROCEDURE

**"The client consultation is an important part of your professional service. Be sure to complete this step prior to each client service you provide. Your successful retail sales and customer satisfaction rates depend upon it!"**

RETAIL • RE-BOOK • REFERRAL

1. Cosmetologist sanitizes hands and station.
2. Set out service tools and materials.
3. Drape the client in preparation for a chemical service.
4. Perform a scalp and hair analysis.
5. Follow procedure as shown and manufacturer's instructions.
6. Follow standard cleanup procedure.
7. Document client record card/file.

A — Lightly cleanse hair and scalp to avoid scalp irritation.

B — Divide hair into four sections.

C — Apply protective cream (base) around hairline and ears.

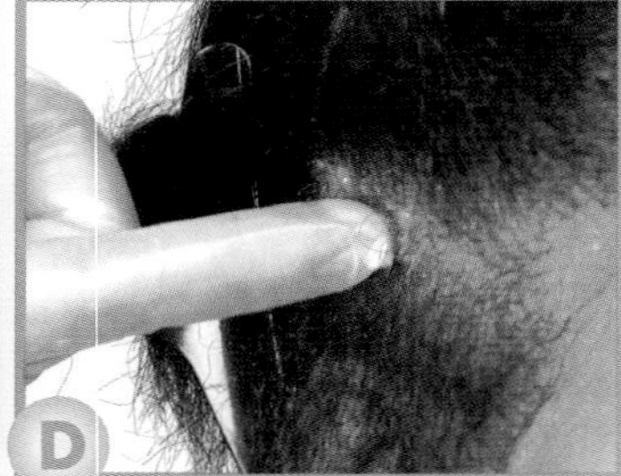

D — Part hair into ½ **inch (1.25 cm) subsections**, apply base to scalp area along partings. Body heat will liquify cream allowing for even coverage.

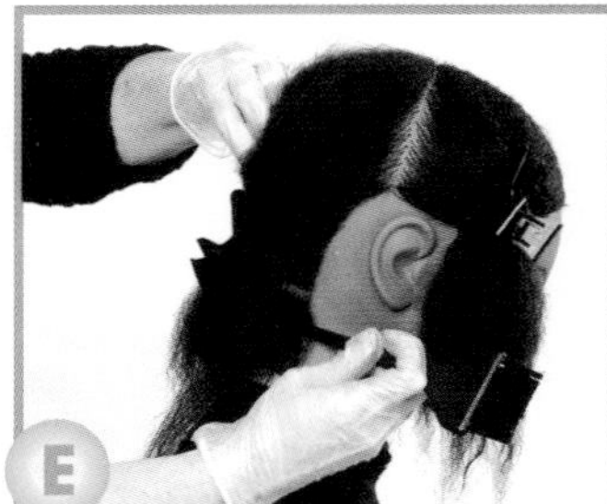

E — Start at most resistant area, using ¼ **inch (0.6 cm) subsections.**

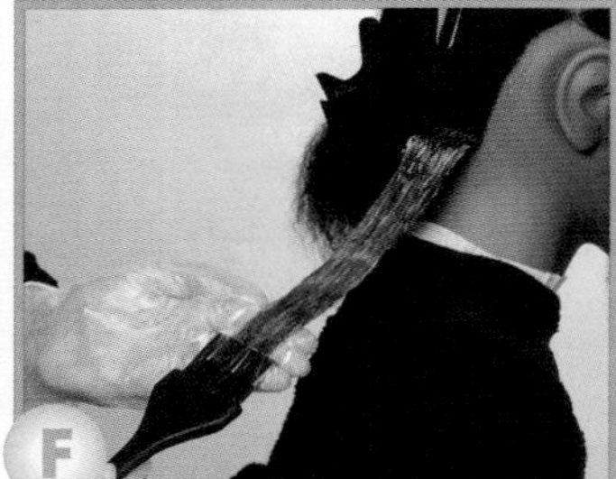

F — With gloves on, use an applicator brush to apply relaxer, keeping ¼ **inch (0.6 cm) away from scalp** (body heat) **and hair ends** (porous).

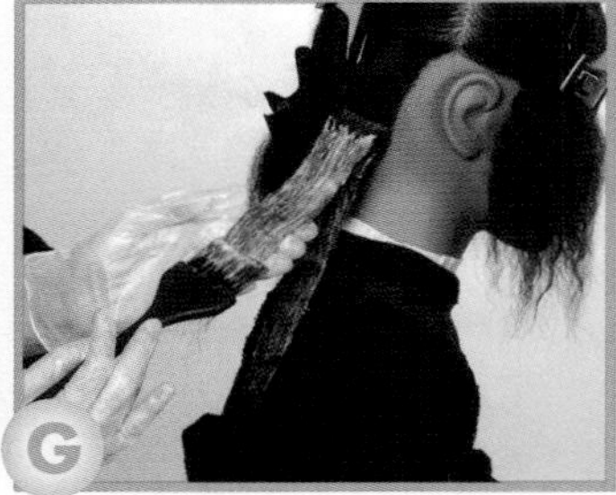

G — Continue applying relaxer using ¼ **inch (0.6 cm) subsections**, covering both sides of subsection. Apply to all sections in the same manner.

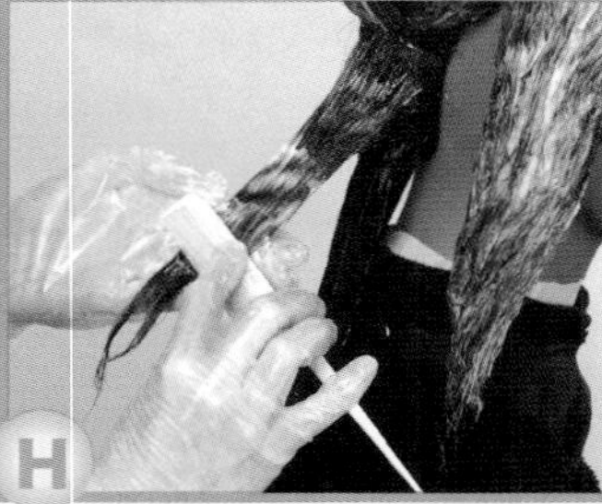

H — Start smoothing the hair using **one inch (2.5 cm) subsections** with a large tooth comb or spine of tail comb.

I
Continue to smooth sections until sufficient relaxation is reached; perform relaxation test. Hair must be smooth enough to lay flat on a perm rod.

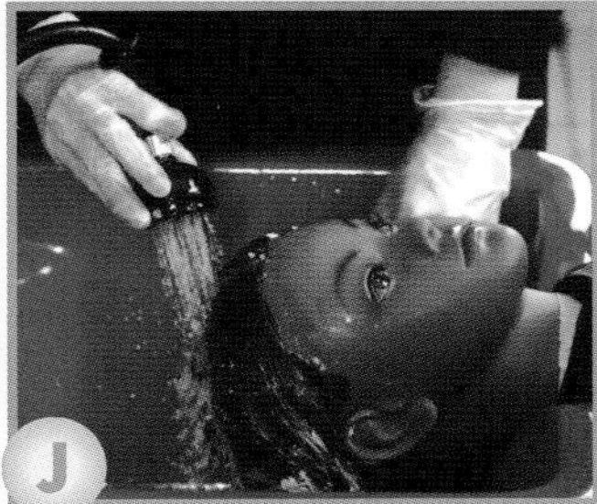
J
Thoroughly rinse relaxer from hair. **NOTE:** No neutralizer is applied at this time.

K
Section hair for application of perm rods.

L
Apply perm rods. **NOTE:** Wear gloves and follow manufacturer's directions if hair is wrapped with perm lotion.

M
Apply **protective cream and cotton** around hairline and ears. Apply permanent wave lotion to top and bottom of rods, full length of rods.

N
**Check cotton.** If saturated, replace with fresh cotton. Apply plastic cap and process following manufacturer's instructions.

O
**Test curl** check for diameter of rod within "S" shaping.

P
Remove plastic cap and cotton. Rinse hair for a minimum of 5 minutes leaving perm rods in hair.

Q
**Blot hair** with cloth towel to remove moisture. Complete blotting with disposable towels to assure accurate moisture absorption.

R
Reapply cotton around hairline and ears. **Apply neutralizer** in the same manner as permanent wave lotion. Process for 5 minutes or follow manufacturer's instructions.

S
Rinse neutralizer or gently remove perm rods; follow manufacturer's instructions. Gently comb through hair with a shampoo comb.

T
Finish with application of light conditioner and/or styling product. Design hair or leave in a "wash-and-wear" style.

**EVALUATION** ______________________________

______________________________

GRADE ______ STUDENT'S NAME ______ ID# ______

# REVIEW QUESTIONS

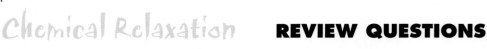

## MULTIPLE CHOICE

**1.** What product is applied on the scalp to protect from strong chemicals?
A. relaxer B. neutralizer C. base cream

**2.** What percentage of curl is removed for an average curl relaxation?
A. 25% B. 50% C. 75%

**3.** Which relaxer is the strongest and processes the quickest?
A. lithium B. potassium C. sodium

**4.** Which strength relaxer is best suited for fine textured hair?
A. mild B. regular C. super

**5.** Which strand test is performed **during** the relaxing process?
A. curl reduction B. preliminary C. porosity

**6.** The three methods of relaxer application are tint brush, shampoo/tail comb and?
A. fingers B. applicator bottle C. cotton

**7.** What occurs in the neutralization step of the relaxing process?
A. bonds separate B. bonds reform C. bonds dissolve

**8.** The five areas of analysis performed during the consultation are scalp condition, density, elasticity, texture and?
A. product usage B. hairdesign C. porosity

**9.** What part of the shampoo comb is used to smooth the hair?
A. spine B. tip C. handle

**10.** The two forms of neutralizers are non-lathering and?
A. lathering B. fixative C. stablizer

**11.** Who invented the "Wonderful Hair Grower"?
A. Annie Turnbo Malone B. Garrett Morgan C. Madam C.J. Walker

**12.** What is applied at the scalp for a **"base-type"** relaxer?
A. shampoo B. relaxer C. protective cream

**13.** Which hydroxide relaxer has the lowest pH and can be used on less resistant hair?
A. potassium B. guanidine C. lithium

**14.** What type of curl pattern does very curly hair have?
A. tight curl B. wavy C. loose curl

**15.** Which relaxer is compatible with a soft curl permanent?
A. sodium hydroxide B. ammonium thioglycolate C. calcium hydroxide

**16.** What percentage of curl is removed for maximum relaxation?
A. 100% B. 50% C. 0%

**17.** Which strength relaxer is best used on resistant and coarse hair?
A. mild B. regular C. super

**18.** What part of the relaxing procedure accelerates curl reduction?
A. rinsing B. smoothing C. neutralizing

**19.** When is a preliminary strand test performed for a relaxation procedure?
A. during B. before C. after

**20.** What size partings are used for the application of the relaxer product?
A. ¼ inch (0.6 cm) B. 1 inch (2.5 cm) C. 2 inch (5 cm)

STUDENT'S NAME DATE GRADE

current

electrode

faradic

infared

tesla

volt

11

Cosmetology Electricity

# ELECTRICITY

# Terminology . . .

*These terms are but a few to get you acquainted with this chapter on the use of electricity and light therapy within the cosmetology industry.*

11

**Alternating Current (AC)** is an electrical flow that switches direction, moving in one direction then changing to the opposite direction.

**Ampere** (amp) is measurement of how much electrical power is used.

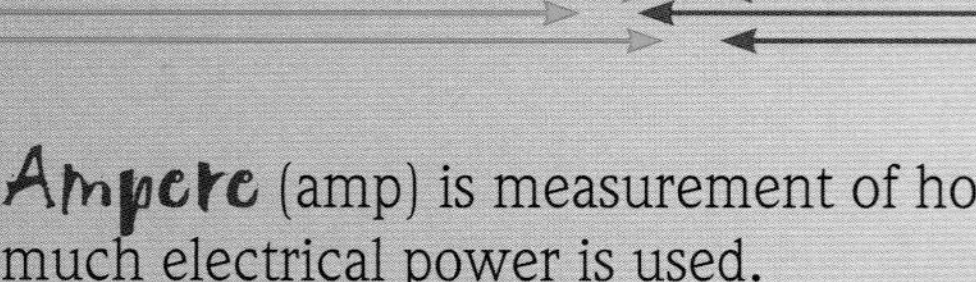

**Circuit Breaker** is a box containing small levers that will automatically shut off with an electrical overload.

**Conductor** is any material that allows and supports the flow of electric current such as a wire.

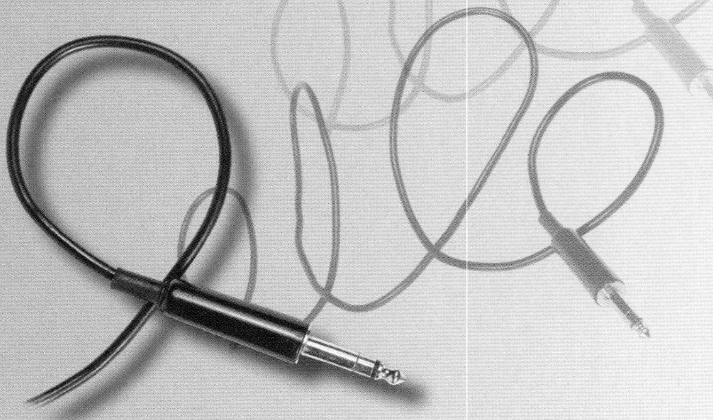

**Direct Current (DC)** is when the electrical current flows in **ONLY** one direction.

# Terminology . . .

DC Current
SOURCE
AC Current
SOURCE

**Electric Current** is the movement of electrons within a complete electrical circuit contained within a material referred to as a conductor.

**Electrotherapy** is the application of an electrical apparatus on the skin or scalp.

**Incandescent** is a type of lighting produced by a regular tungsten light bulb.

**Insulator** is a substance that prevents the flow of electricity such as rubber or wood.

**Wavelength** is the distance between each repeated crest in a wave of light.

# Electricity ...

**C**osmetologists *need to have a* ***basic knowledge of electricity*** *and the role it plays in applications on the skin and scalp during certain beauty treatments. By learning the fundamentals of electricity, you will gain a better understanding of the function and performance of the equipment these treatments utilize as well as its proper safety and handling.*

11

## What is Electricity?

**Electricity** (e-lec-tric-i-ty) is the **flow of electrical current** or charge. The reaction between a proton, a positive charge and an electron, a negative charge causes an electric current. Electricity is a secondary energy source, which means that we get it from the conversion of other sources of energy. Those energy sources might be coal, natural gas, oil, nuclear power and other natural sources, which are referred to as primary sources.

**Circuit or path of electricity** is when the electric flows through a complete route through conductors and ends where the electric began.

# Discovery of Electricity . . .

The **discovery of electricity** has been traced to an experiment conducted by a scientist that involved a kite and a key during a lightning storm. Although there have been many people who have contributed to the discovery of electricity throughout the years, the three men below have had the greatest impact on its development.

**Benjamin Franklin** (1706-1790) was a printer by trade, but also focused on science experiments and inventions. During his studies of electricity, he experimented with flying a kite during a thunderstorm with a metal key attached to its string. When the kite was struck by lightning, it could actually transmit an electrical current. This man's accomplishments set the stage for most of the innovative electrical fixtures used today. Refer to http://www.ushistory.org/franklin/info/index.htm for more information.

**Dr. Nikola Tesla** (1856-1943) established the generation, transmission and use of AC electricity. This electrical current could be transmitted over much greater distances than DC electricity. This was the future for electrical current and its use in lighting the world. Refer to http://www.teslasociety.com/biography.htm for more information.

**Thomas Edison** (1847-1931) was an inventor and innovator and introduced the first incandescent light bulb, which led to the creation of a system that centrally produced and distributed electric light, power and heat through a direct current. Refer to http://www.thomasedison.com/biography.html for more information.

# Principles of Electricity . . .

**Electricity** is a **form of energy** used to produce heat, light and power, for instance to run electrical tools. We can convert coal, gas, nuclear energy and other natural resources into electricity. For example, through water power, Niagara Falls (water power) provides the electricity for the upper New York State.

## Forms of Electrical Current:

**Alternating Current (AC)** is an **electrical flow that switches direction,** moving in one direction then changing to the opposite direction. Electrical tools used in the cosmetology industry that use AC are airformers, curling irons and flat irons.

- **Rectifier** is a device that switches AC to DC.

**Direct Current (DC)** is an **electric current that flows in only one direction.** Examples of DC tools used in cosmetology are electric files, clippers or batteries.

- **Converter** is a device that switches DC to AC.

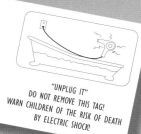

KEEP AWAY FROM WATER
DANGER-
AS WITH MOST ELECTRICAL APPLIANCES, ELECTRICAL PARTS IN THIS DRYER ARE ELECTRICALLY LIVE EVEN WHEN SWITCH IS OFF:
TO REDUCE RICK OF DEATH BY ELECTRIC SHOCK:
1. ALWAYS "UNPLUG IT" AFTER USE.
2. DO NOT PLACE OR STORE WHERE DRYER CAN FALL OR BE PULLED INTO TUB, TOILET, OR SINK.
3. DO NOT USE WHILE BATHING.
4. DO NOT USE NEAR OR PLACE IN WATER.
5. IF DRYER FALLS INTO WATER, UNPLUG IT IMMEDIATELY. DO NOT REACH INTO WATER.
FOR PROFESSIONAL USE ONLY

"UNPLUG IT"
DO NOT REMOVE THIS TAG!
WARN CHILDREN OF THE RISK OF DEATH BY ELECTRIC SHOCK!

## Various forms of Electrical Transmission:

**Conductor** is **any material** that allows or **supports the flow of electric current.** For example, metal, copper and water are excellent conductors of electricity. Notice there is always a tag on airformers cautioning not to use the device near bathtubs or sinks. If an electrical appliance is plugged in and falls into water, the water will be electrically charged and can cause electrocution.

**Insulator or nonconductor** is a substance that **prevents the flow of electricity.** Examples are cement, glass, and rubber, silk and wood. The covering on the electrical wires insulates the electrical current to prevent electrical shock and/or electrocution.

Wood insulates and prevents the flow of electric current

## How do we measure electricity?

### Measurements of Electricity

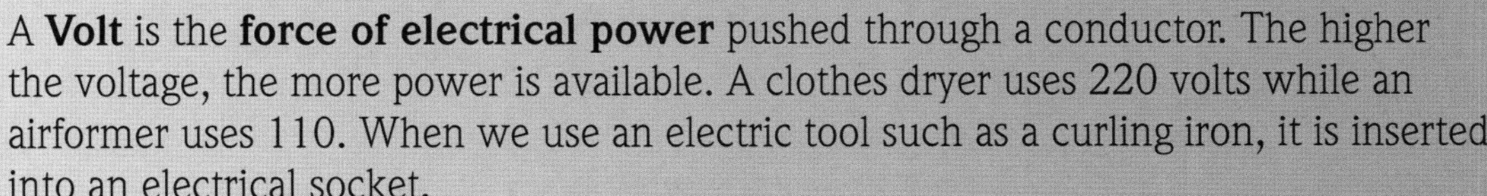

A **Volt** is the **force of electrical power** pushed through a conductor. The higher the voltage, the more power is available. A clothes dryer uses 220 volts while an airformer uses 110. When we use an electric tool such as a curling iron, it is inserted into an electrical socket.

An **electrical wall socket** is **set into the wall** and provides the "active" electrical current to power tools and/or appliances through a two- or three-prong connection. The electricity will flow from these wall sockets or outlets to the main fuse box located in another area of the salon, house or other building. There are two principal ways electricity can flow from the wall socket to the appliance or tool.



### Two Types of Electrical Connection:

**Two-Prong** is an electrical plug with **two rectangular type prongs** attached to a rubber-type material. The wider prong is considered to be neutral and helps to assist in grounding the current, which will prevent electrical shock when inserted into the wall socket.

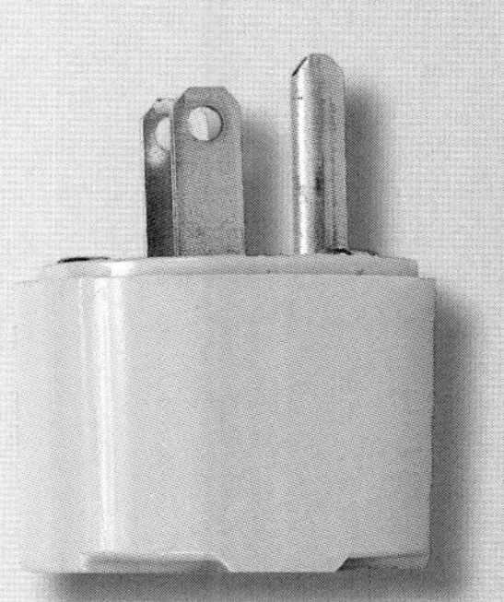

**Three-Prong** is an electrical plug with **two same size rectangular prongs** and one additional **round prong** attached to a rubber-type material. The round prong enforces the additional grounding. This will provide guaranteed safety in preventing electrical shock when plugging an appliance into a wall socket.

**There are various standards of electric current used throughout the world. Different standards require different electrical plugs.**

Belgium, Brazil, Egypt, Iran, Israel, Peru, Romania, Russia, Spain, Turkey

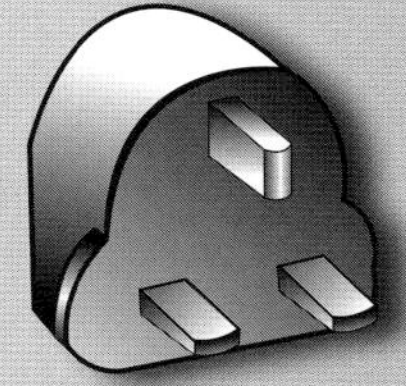

Bangladesh, El Salvador, Guatemala, Iraq, Ireland, St. Lucia, United Kingdom

Australia, China, New Zealand, Panama, Uruguay

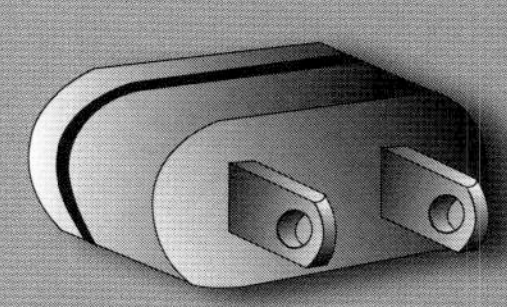

Bahamas, Canada, Japan, Peru, United States

# Principles of Electricity . . .

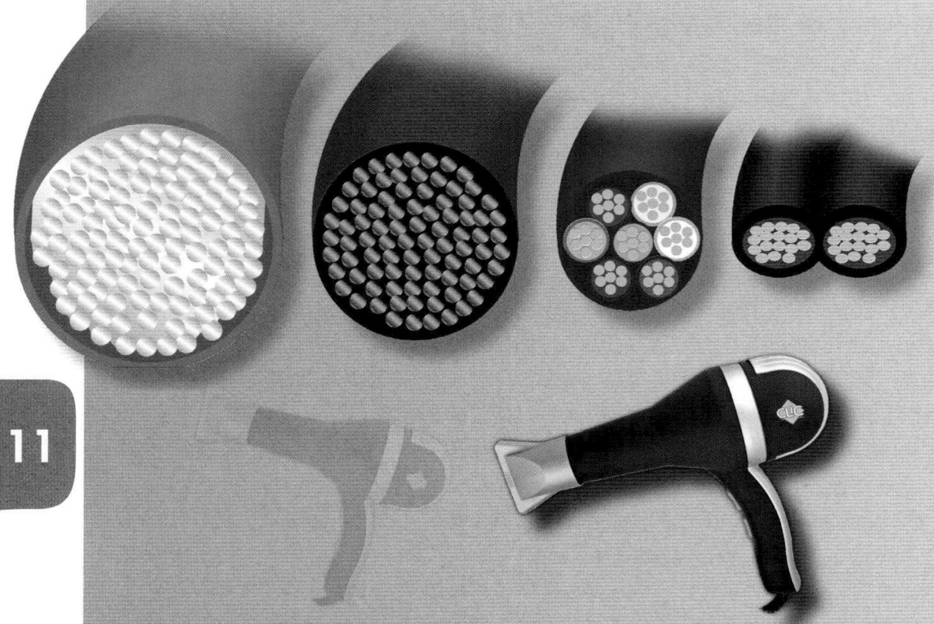

**Ampere** (am-peer) **or amp** is the measurement of how much **electrical power or current** is used. A professional airformer of 1,500 watts uses more amps than a 100-watt light bulb. A good indicator of power used is the diameter of the power cord, which is determined through a wire gauge. A **wire gauge** uses a number system to denote the bare wire size. If the gauge number is high, the cord diameter is small; therefore wires are thin, allowing only low watt usage. Example: Standard light fixtures have a wire gauge of 14 to 16, which indicates 15 to 13 amperes.

| Wire Use | Rated Amperage | Wire Gauge |
|---|---|---|
| Extension Cords | 13 Amps | 16 Gauge |
| Light and Lamp Fixtures, Curling Irons, Airformers, Flat Irons, etc. | 15 Amps | 14 Gauge |
| Receptacles, 110-Volt Air Conditioners, Hooded Dryers | 20 Amps | 12 Gauge |
| Electric Clothes Dryer and Water Heaters | 30 Amps | 10 Gauge |
| Microwaves | 45 Amps | 8 Gauge |
| Electric Furnaces, Large Electric Heaters | 60 Amps | 6 Gauge |

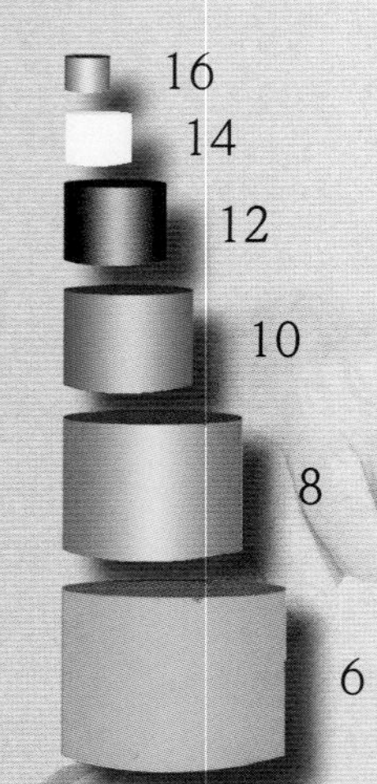


**CAUTION:** If an incorrect wire gauge is used, the following could result:

- Overheating and melting the extension cord, which may result in a fire
- Overloading the circuit where the cord is plugged into; resulting in disconnection of power flow
- Damage to the item plugged into the extension cord

**Milliampere** (mill-ee-am-peer) is less (1/1000) of an ampere. Electrical equipment used for facial treatments have controls that allow the current to be reduced to **1/1000 of an amp.** This adjustment will prevent damage to the delicate skin and muscle tissue of the client's face.

# Principles of Electricity ...

**Ohm** (oh-m) measures the **electric flow resistance** being produced. Ohm's Law relates to voltage (V), current (I) and resistance (R). Electrical current will not flow unless the volt of electric, also known as the push, is more powerful than the resistance.

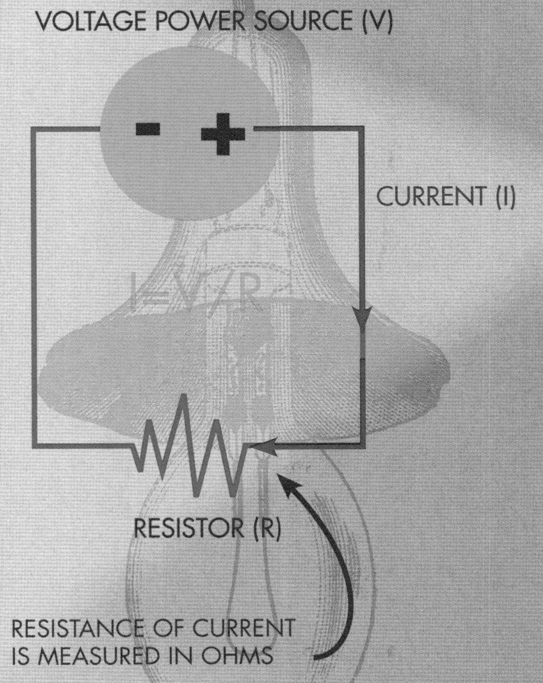

**Watt** (wot) measures the **amount of electrical power used** by an apparatus within one second. The strength of a light bulb is measured in watts. A lamp will indicate the safe wattage of the light bulb to be used. If the wattage used is higher ... the lamp could overheat.

**Kilowatt** (kil-o-wot) measures **one thousand watts of electrical power** used by an apparatus within **one second.**

"The more kilowatts of electrical power you use, the higher your electric bill."

Electricity meter measures home use in killowatts

In our homes and businesses, electrical use is measured in kilowatts or one thousand watts used per second. A 65-watt light bulb indicates how much power is consumed per second ... 65 watts of energy.

11

# Safety in Electricity ...

***In the beauty industry** most of the equipment used on a daily basis requires the power of electricity. When **designing a salon,** consideration must be taken on how many stations would be installed and used at the same time. Curling irons, flat irons, Marcel stoves and airformers all require a lot of power. When too many electrical tools are plugged into a **circuit** (a completed route of electric) the wires could overheat and cause an electrical fire.*

11

To prevent an electrical overload, a **fuse box or circuit panel** is installed in homes and other buildings. When the electrical power is hooked up to a building, the wires are channeled to either a fuse box or a circuit breaker.

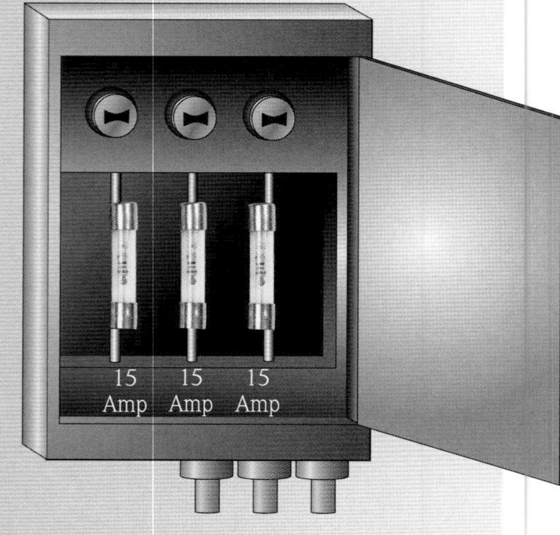


A **fuse** (fuooz) **box** contains **small devices with metal wires** that link to the main source of electricity for the entire building. These individual wires travel from the fuse through the walls into the wall socket where electrical power is obtained to run the equipment or tool. The fuse is designed to **prevent an excessive amount of electrical current from passing through the circuit.** If an overload would occur, the **fuse would either shut down or melt** and the fuse would need to be replaced.

"If too much current is being drawn at any given time, a safety feature on both the fuse box and circuit breaker box will disconnect the power source to the originating outlet thus, preventing a possible fire."

A **circuit** (cir-kit) **breaker box or panel** is a **metal container with switches that automatically disconnect or shut down** at the implication of an overload or electrical short. The advantage of a circuit breaker is that it can be **repeatedly reset.** Always disconnect electrical apparatus to check the electric connection before resetting the breaker switch.

The standard circuit is 110 volts and is used to provide power to standard appliances and tools. Electric clothes dryers, air conditioners or other large pieces of equipment may require double the amount of current, usually 220 volts. An electrician will provide the necessary amount of electrical outlets to supply an efficient amount of electricity for all the equipment being used.

# Safety in Electricity . . .

**Certified electrical** tools and equipment will help ensure the safety of the electrical tool or appliance you use. It is important that we never overload an outlet. The use of **UL or Underwriters Laboratories** guarantees that an **appliance meets or exceeds safety standards.** If additional electrical tools are needed, the use of a **surge protector** will **prevent a sudden spike of electricity,** which could cause damage. If too much power is drawn or there is a sudden spike in power, the surge protector will automatically disconnect itself from the wall outlet and break the electrical path. It is important to select a surge protector that is designed for the current being used.

UL®
Underwriters Laboratories

11

CAUTION: For safety purposes, plug only one electrical unit in a wall outlet at a time, unless you are using a power strip, which allows multiple devices to be plugged into the same outlet.

**Ground fault interrupter**

**Grounding** is a term used to **promote electrical safety,** which means the electrical current is safely carried away from you to the ground. Grounding electrical equipment will **prevent electrical shock.** When a circuit is complete, the ground wire causes the electricity to return to the ground and not through the person operating the electrical appliance. A **ground fault interrupter or GFI** is a circuit breaker device that interrupts the electrical flow to lower the pull of power. The GFI will protect against accidental electrocution if working around water or high humidity areas.

## Electricity Safety:

- Always follow manufacturers' instructions for safety, proper handling and usage of electrical equipment and tools.
- Inspect cords for insulation wear and/or damage.
- Avoid overload of plugs on one wall outlet.
- Keep electrical equipment from coming in contact with water while in use.
- Never leave your client unattended while electrical equipment is in use.
- Avoid dangling electric cords that could tangle and cause someone to fall.
- Disconnect electrical appliance by holding and pulling plug, not cord.

"Use of extension cords can pose a safety hazard if not properly installed to avoid overload."

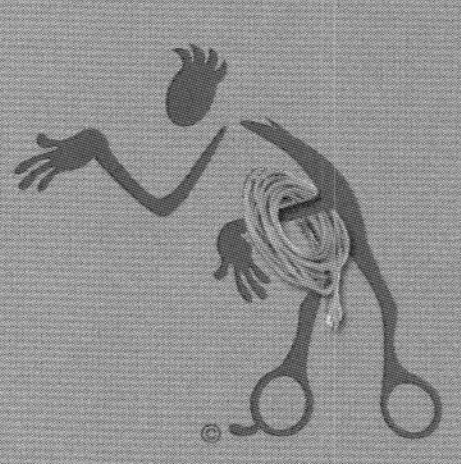

# Actions of Electrotherapy Current . . .

*In the salon/spa industry, many services are offered that require the use of electrical tools and equipment. These tools offer various results depending on the service and apparatus being used.*

**The three actions of electrotherapy current used in the beauty industry are Heating, Magnetic and Electrochemical.**

11

Heating occurs when the **electric flows through a heating element** located within a conductor causing a **temperature change** according to the control setting. If the control setting is low, the electric flow is slowed down therefore decreasing the temperature. Curling and flat irons, blow dryers and processing machines all generate heat to aid in either hairdesigning or accelerating chemical processes. Infrared lamps and tesla current, explained further on in this chapter, are used in skin and scalp treatments producing relaxing results.

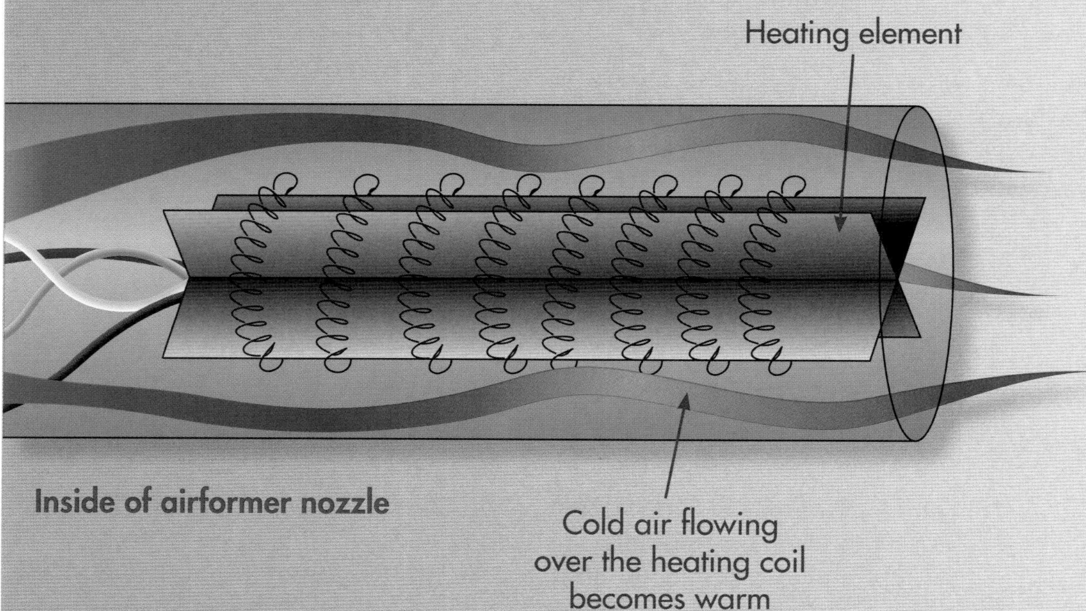
Heating element
Cold air flowing over the heating coil becomes warm

Inside of airformer nozzle

"An airformer typically will have a cold temperature setting. In this case, the electric current continues to flow, but bypasses the heating element."

Magnetic motor

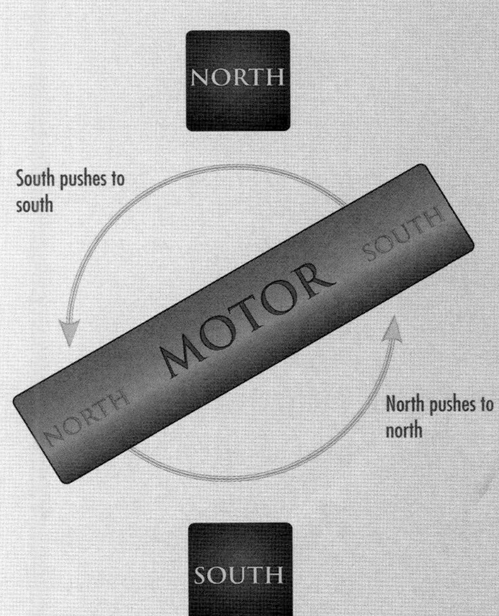


**Magnetic current,** sometimes referred to as **mechanical**, occurs when electrical **motors are manufactured with a magnetic field** using positive and negative poles that create a **push-pull, or alternating effect.** The electric current flows through the conductor and into the magnetic motor initiating the push-pull result, which causes the motor to turn. Examples would be hair clippers and trimmers. Faradic/sinusoidal currents, explained later in the chapter, with metal/glass electrodes are designed with an alternating current to produce stimulating results.

Electrochemical Galvanic Cell

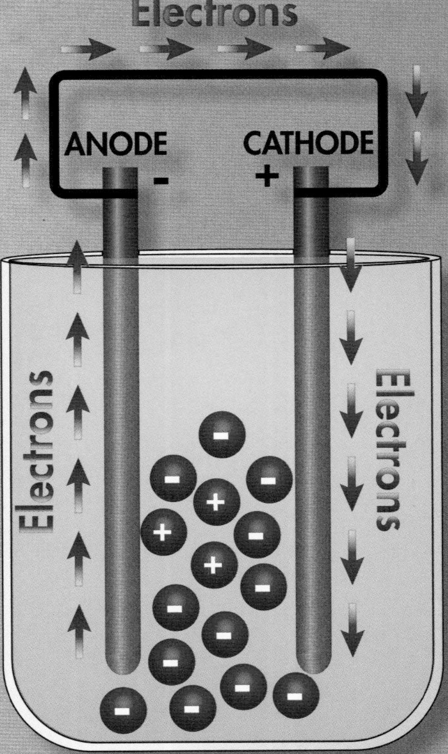


**Electrochemical** (e-lec-tro-chem-i-cal) occurs when the electric current safely **passes through a liquid solution.** The liquid becomes ionized, meaning it has unequal amount of negative and positive molecules, giving it properties that allow transmission of electric current. Galvanic current, used in facial treatments, is passed through either an alkaline or acidic liquid to aid in the repairing of skin tissue.

# Electrotherapy . . .

**Electrotherapy** *(e-lec-tro-ther-a-py) utilizes other* ***types of electrical currents and electrodes placed on the skin or scalp*** *during facial and scalp treatments. Each electric current has varying beneficial effects on the skin and underlying tissues depending on application of the current. The use of these currents will vary according to technician, client and skin condition being treated, and the service rendered. An understanding of how each electrical current works will assist in assuring and providing the best results to the client without causing injury.*

11

**The four types of electrotherapy currents are Tesla High-Frequency, Faradic, Sinusoidal and Galvanic.**

This chapter will provide **basic information for each electrotherapy current**, but always read the manufacturer's instructions when purchasing any electrical unit. Read safety and handling of apparatus to prevent electric shock and client injury.

"The most common electrotherapy currents used within the salon/spa of today are the Tesla and Galvanic."

**NOTE: Modality** (mo-dal-i-ty) is the application of a therapeutic agent, and may be another term used for the treatment of a skin condition through electric current.

# Tesla High-Frequency Current . . .

**Tesla** (tes-la) **High-Frequency current** uses alternating current (AC) that **produces heat** and provides **stimulation and/or relaxation to the skin and scalp.** The tesla current or violet ray is applied or transmitted to the skin or scalp by using an **electrode**. Depending on type of electrode used, method of application and area electrode is placed, various benefits will result.

11

**Beneficial effects of tesla high-frequency current are:**

- Promotes skin tissue healing
- Increases blood circulation
- Enhances removal of toxins
- Aids in absorption of products
- Increases glandular activity
- Promotes relaxation
- Provides a germicidal action
- Reduces congestion

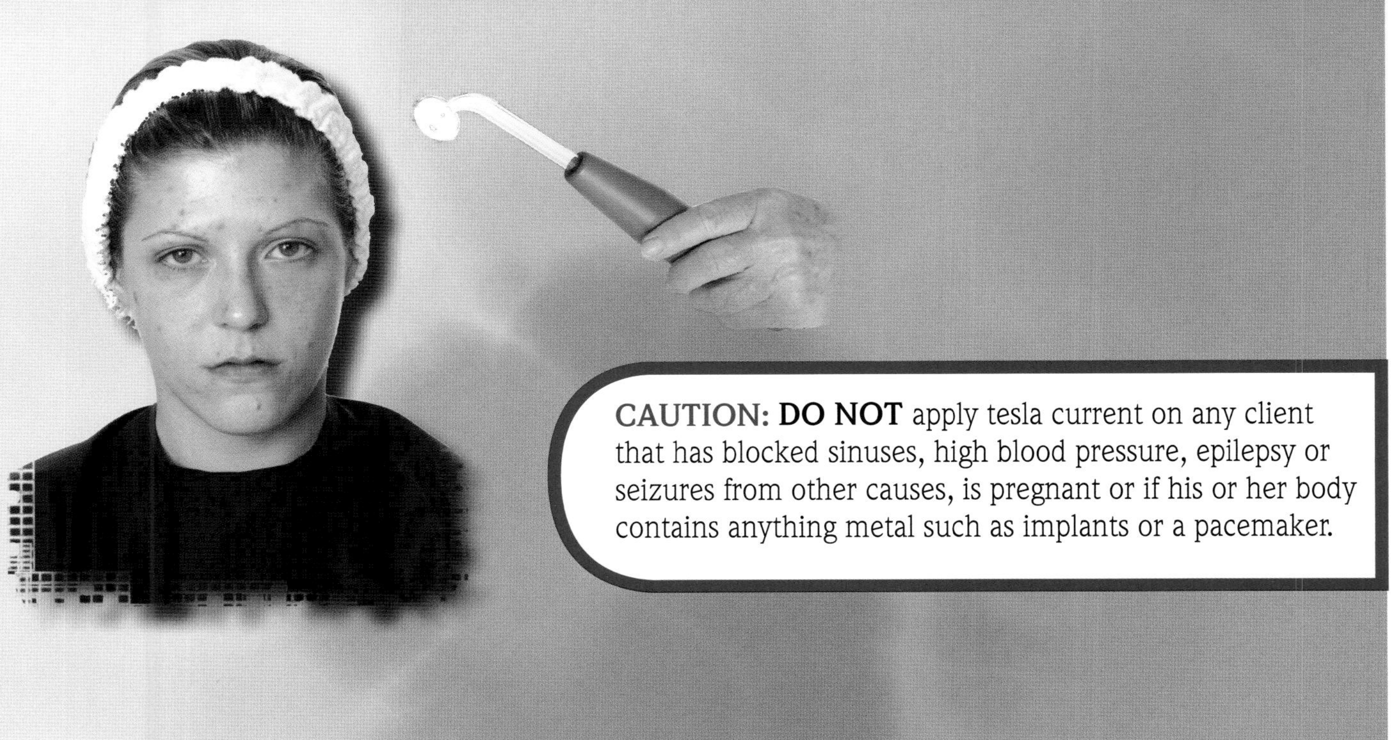

CAUTION: **DO NOT** apply tesla current on any client that has blocked sinuses, high blood pressure, epilepsy or seizures from other causes, is pregnant or if his or her body contains anything metal such as implants or a pacemaker.

# Electrotherapy Application . . .

**An electrode** is a hand-held applicator that **carries the electric current from the unit to the client's skin.** The electrodes are made of **glass, carbon or metal** and are shaped into a **comb-rake, rod, mushroom or roller-type device.** When using a glass electrode during a high-frequency current application, a violet color will appear. Increase the current – a darker violet color is shown; decrease the current – a lighter violet color appears.

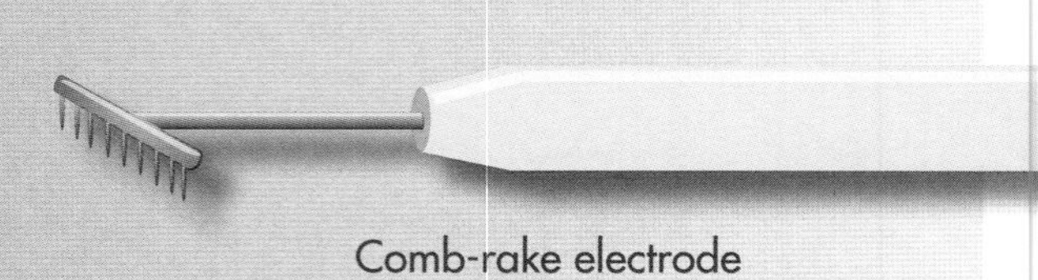
Comb-rake electrode

Mushroom electrode



What electrode is used depends on area of skin and condition being treated.

- **Comb-rake electrode** is generally used for scalp treatments.
- **Rod electrode** may be used for either facial or scalp treatments.
- **Mushroom electrode** is usually placed on the face during a facial treatment.
- **Metal discs or a roller-type device** may be used for either skin service.

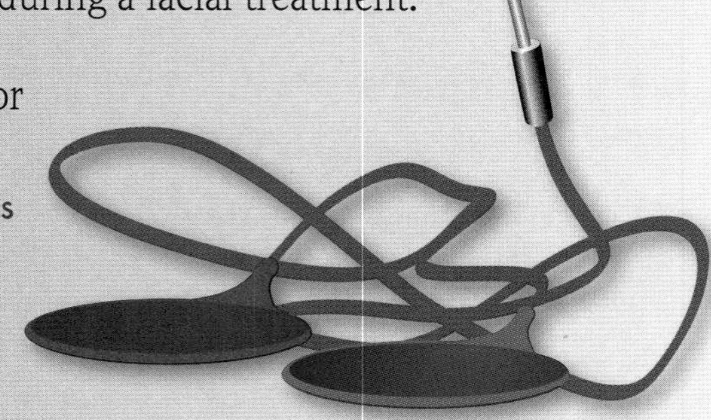
Metal discs

There are three methods in which the electrodes may be utilized during a treatment. This is determined during client consultation and skin analysis.

## Methods of Electrotherapy Application:

**Indirect method** is when the **client holds the electrode while the cosmetologist manually touches the area** and continues the treatment. **DO NOT** start the unit until the client is holding the electrode to prevent electrical shock. Turn current off before obtaining the electrode from client.

**Direct method** is when the **cosmetologist places the electrode directly on the skin or scalp.** The client holds or touches nothing.

**General application** is when **ONLY** the **client holds the electrode** and the cosmetologist starts the electric current, but **DOES NOT** touch the client. Depending on client sensitivity, use the control setting to adjust the tesla current power.

# Faradic and Sinusoidal Currents …

**Faradic** (fa-rad-ic) **current** uses alternating current and **produces muscle contraction and nerve stimulation.** To obtain the most beneficial effects from the faradic current, the **indirect method of application** is commonly used. The cosmetologist wears a wrist device with a moistened electrode attached to the underside. Another electrode is encased with moistened cotton and either hand-held by client or placed on the client's back at middle of shoulders. The professional touches either the face or scalp depending on treatment and then activates the current … this is to prevent electric shock. As the professional massages, he or she focuses attention on the motor nerve points of either face or scalp.

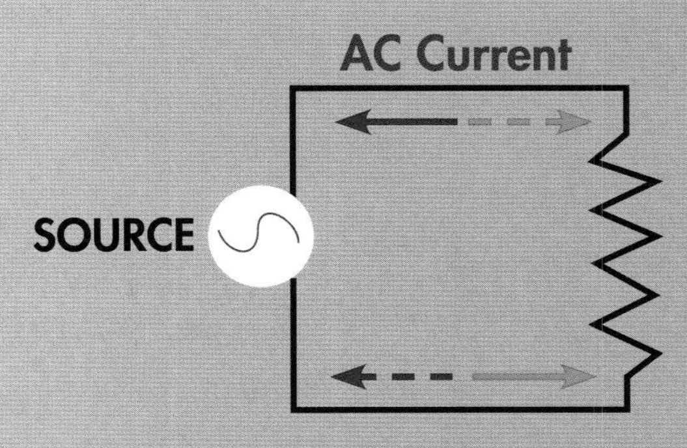


**NOTE:** When starting the faradic current along with placement on the skin, always use a low control setting and gradually increase. At end of treatment, gradually decrease the control setting before removing the faradic current from skin or scalp.

A major benefit of the faradic current is **muscle contraction and toning.** Other results are increased blood circulation, glandular activity and stimulated hair growth.

A **direct method of application** with both electrodes placed on client's skin may be used, but is not as popular as the other methods.

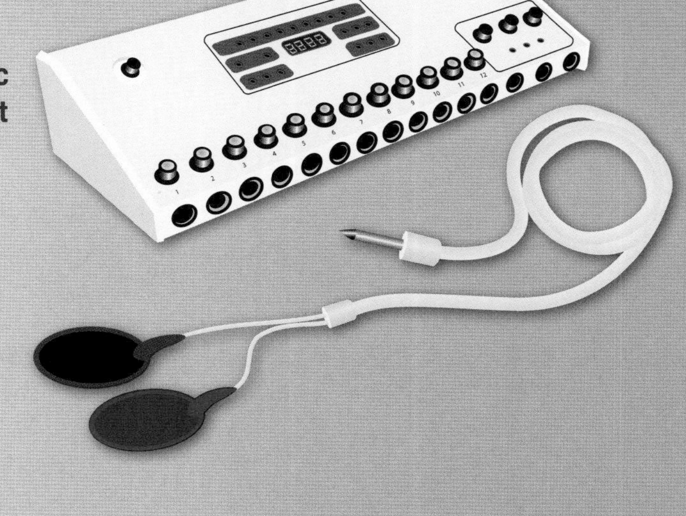

Faradic current

**CAUTION:** Electrodes may not come in contact with each other.

**Sinusoidal** (si-nu-soi-dal) **current,** based on the sine wave or sinusoid, is a light wave pattern resembling ocean waves. It also uses alternating current and **produces muscle contractions.** Like faradic, the best application is the indirect method to produce the greatest results. Both faradic and sinusoidal currents have the same beneficial results with some professionals believing that sinusoidal current has deeper penetrating power.

*Check with local regulatory agency for legal use of sinusoidal current in your area.*

# Galvanic Currents . . .

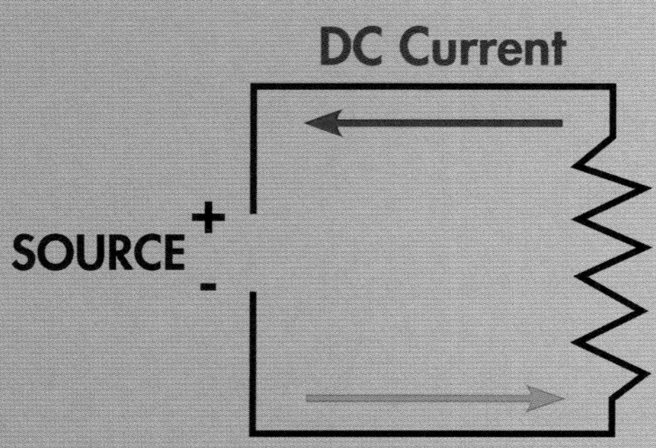


**Galvanic** (gal-van-ic) **current** uses direct current producing **electrochemical effects through the introduction of chemicals into the skin.** All types of electrotherapy current applicators have both a negative-charged pole and a positive-charged pole.

11

**Polarity** (po-lar-i-ty) means the use of positive and negative poles with an electric charge or magnetic qualities.

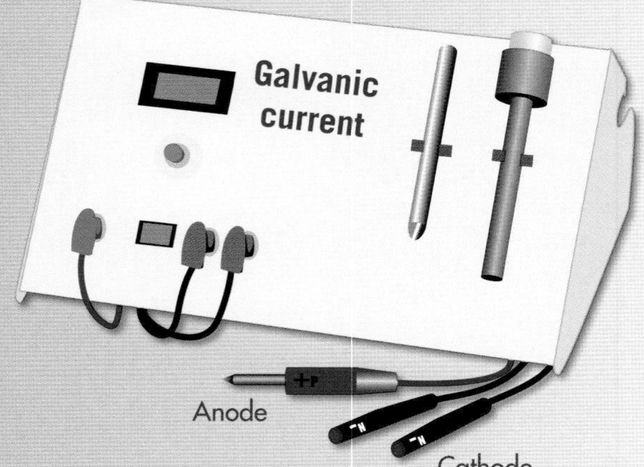


**Negative or cathode** (cath-ode) **pole** is typically designed to be **black** or marked with "N" or a minus sign (-). The negative pole has the following effects:

- Increases blood flow/circulation
- Softens skin tissue
- Provides an alkaline reaction
- Penetrates alkaline solutions into the skin
- Stimulates the nerves

**Positive or anode** (an-ode) **pole** is typically designed to be **red** or marked with a "P" or a plus sign (+). The positive pole has the following effects:

- Decreases blood flow/circulation
- Reduces redness or inflammation
- Hardens skin tissue/closes pores
- Provides an acidic reaction
- Penetrates acidic solution into the skin
- Soothes the nerves

**NOTE:** The use of a converter might be needed to use the galvanic current if salon/spa operates on an alternating current.

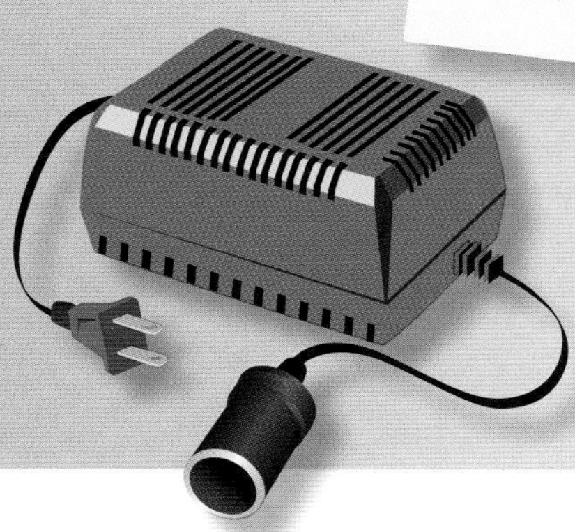

# Galvanic Current Processes . . .

***The galvanic current** process of forcing a **water-based soluble solution** into the skin is called **iontophoresis** (i-on-to-fo-ree-sis). The process using the **negative pole, which forces alkaline solutions** to penetrate the skin, is called **anaphoresis** (a-naph-o-re-sis). The process that uses the **positive pole causing acidic solutions to penetrate the skin** is referred to as **cataphoresis** (cat-a-pho-re-sis).*

## CATAPHORESIS

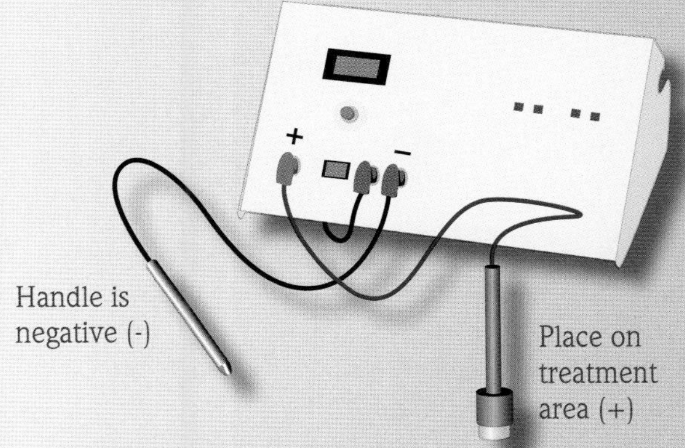


**Cataphoresis** uses the **positive pole** to produce **temporary effects** on the area being treated. The positive pole is the active electrode that is controlled by the professional; the opposite or negative (inactive) pole is held by the client. Both the positive and negative poles are wrapped with moist cotton or wipes.

How to decide which course of treatment will be beneficial to client's skin or scalp condition ... **through client consultation and skin analysis.**

## ANAPHORESIS

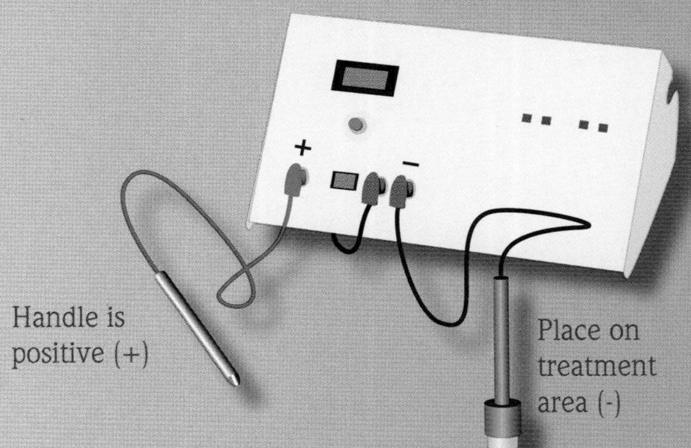


**Anaphoresis** uses the **negative pole** to produce **temporary effects** on the area being treated. The negative pole is the active electrode that is controlled by the professional; the opposite or positive (inactive pole) is held by the client. Both the negative and positive poles are wrapped with moist cotton or wipes.

**Desincrustation** (des-in-crus-ta-tion) uses the **anaphoresis process on oily or acne prone skin.** The alkaline solution along with the electric current will **liquefy the sebum/ oily substance deposits and dirt** to aid in removal. This treatment provides a deep tissue cleansing by helping to break up the dirt and hardened sebum located in the pores or hair follicles, which can create acne.

# Electrotherapy Safety . . .

**To ensure professional and client safety, consider the following areas:**
As with any medical condition, refer client to medical care professional.

## Electrotherapy treatment is NOT applied when witnessing the following skin conditions:

11

- Broken skin such as cuts, abrasions or open sores
- Infected skin/injury with pus or any severe acne conditions, such as pustules
- Inflammation of the skin
- Broken capillaries
- Contagious skin diseases

## Other areas of caution:

- All electrotherapy units are **power altered by a control setting.** At start of treatment always begin with **low power and gradually increase** until adjusted to client's satisfaction. The same rule applies at end of procedure; gradually decrease power at end of treatment.
- Electric current is shut off before removing electrode from skin.
- Electrodes **DO NOT** touch each other once electric current is operating.
- Electrodes are wrapped in moist cotton or wipe to prevent skin burns.
- **DO NOT** start any electric current before skin contact with client or professional.

"It is recommended to get additional and continued education prior to operating all electrotherapy units."

11

# What is Light Therapy?

**Light therapy** is using light rays/waves or electromagnetic radiation for the treatment of hair, skin and scalp. **Electromagnetic radiation** (e-lec-tro-mag-net-ic ra-di-a-tion) is also referred to as radiant energy that emits or radiates energy in varying degrees of wavelengths. The variety of all the wavelengths is categorized within the **electromagnetic spectrum.**

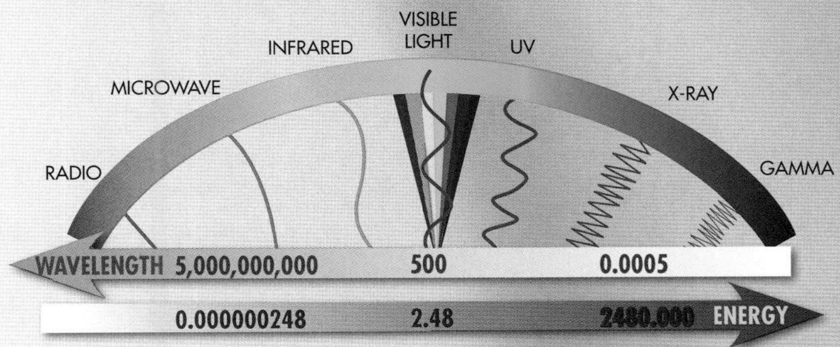


A **wavelength** is the distance between each repeated wave's crest. The length of each light wave determines the amount of energy and therefore the effect it has on area being treated. When a wavelength is short, it has more energy, but less heat. When the wavelength is long, it has less energy, but more heat.

Within the electromagnetic spectrum there are three types of light sources that are mainly used by the cosmetologist. They are **visible light, infrared and ultraviolet** with each one having different beneficial effects on the area being treated. Visible light can be viewed by the human eye, while infrared and ultraviolet light is invisible to the human eye.

**CAUTION:** When performing light therapy treatments, the client's eyes should be covered with moist eye pads. When using ultraviolet light therapy, protect client's and professional's eyes with safety goggles.

# Visable Light . . .

**V**isible light has varying degrees of wavelengths in the electromagnetic spectrum that are visible to the human eye. ***Thirty-five percent of visible light rays account for natural sunlight.*** When visible light is produced as white light, such as sunlight or the light generated from a light bulb and it strikes an object such as a prism, the white light will reflect the spectrum of colors for us to see.



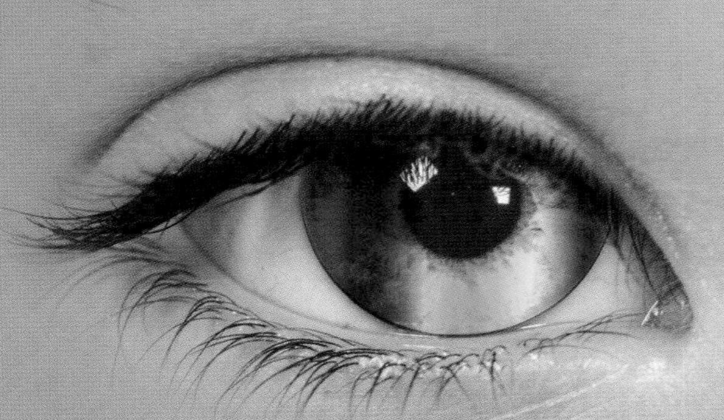

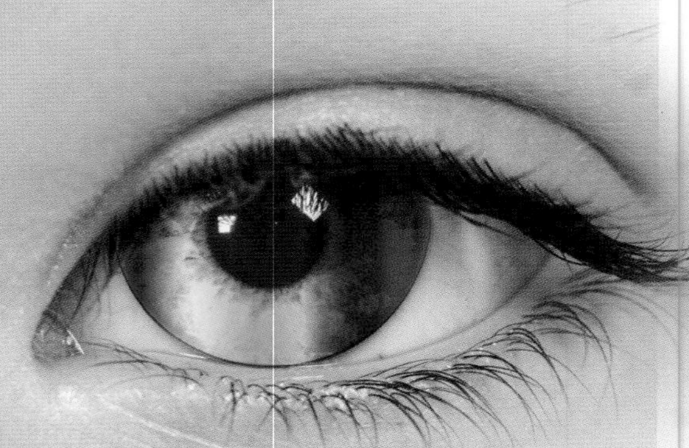

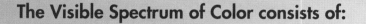

## The Visible Spectrum of Color consists of:

- **Red**
- **Orange**
- **Yellow**
- **Green**
- **Blue**
- **Indigo**
- **Violet**

If these visible colors are redirected or absorbed back into another prism, a white light is then reflected back to us.

On the electromagnetic spectrum, the color **red has the longest wavelength** and is associated with producing heat. The **color violet has the shortest wavelength** and is known for its germicidal effect.

"An easy way to remember all the spectrum colors is with our good friend, ROY G. BIV, an acronym for all visible colors."

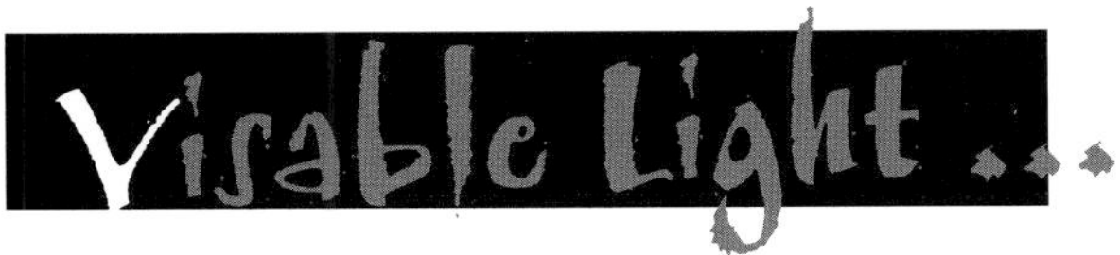


**Visible light** can be reproduced artificially as white, red or blue light with each color having a specific effect on the skin and hair.

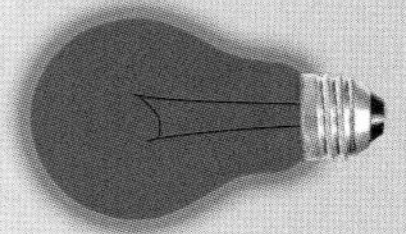

**Red Light** penetrates deeply and produces more heat. This light is best used on dry skin with application of creams or oils.

**Blue Light** has a germicidal and chemical effect, creating less heat. This light is best used on oily and acne skin to combat bacteria and reduce oil production.

**White Light** can be manufactured as either incandescent, halogen or fluorescent lighting.

Light and color affect our daily lives in many ways. The type of lighting in a beauty salon and the colors used to decorate the salon affect the environment and therefore may influence you and/or the client's mood. When viewing completed hair and skin services, certain light sources have a negative impact by producing unflattering results.

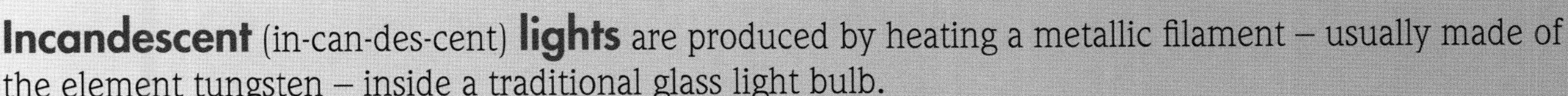

**Incandescent** (in-can-des-cent) **lights** are produced by heating a metallic filament – usually made of the element tungsten – inside a traditional glass light bulb.

- Provides soft effect that is suitable to face and hair
- Provides more heat than light
- Produces red to warm tones
- Is an expensive light source for use in operating a salon/spa

# Visible Light . . .

**Halogen** (hal-o-gen) **lights** are more efficient versions of the incandescent bulb and they last longer.

- Produce crisp, bright, white light that is slightly warmer in color than incandescent
- Maintain a long lasting light without fading
- Are popular with use in salon/spa

**Fluorescent** (fluo-res-cent) **lights** are phosphor-coated glass tubes filled with inert gas and mercury.

- Produce "cool" to "drab" tones to skin and hair, sometimes appearing a green color
- Are least expensive light sources for salon/spa
- Are improved and come in variety of colors, types and sizes

# Infrared ...

**Infrared** (in-fra-red) **light** has **long wavelengths** and consists of the invisible portion of the electromagnetic spectrum. **Sixty percent of the natural sunlight consists of infrared rays.** Since infrared rays are thermal, they are something we experience in every day occurrences. The heat that we feel naturally from sunlight, a bonfire, a radiator or even a warm sidewalk is all from infrared rays. The temperature-sensitive nerve endings in our skin can detect the difference between inside body temperature and outside skin temperature.

In a salon/spa, **infrared or heat lamps** are used either during a scalp or facial treatment. Infrared bulbs may also be used to accelerate the chemical processing of haircolor or permanent waving. **When using infrared, always cover client's eyes with safety goggles or moist eye pads and check with client on comfort level of heat.**

**CAUTION:** Average operating distance for an infrared lamp is 30 inches from the skin and maximum exposure time is five minutes.

## Infrared light is used to:

- Improve blood circulation
- Relax muscle tension
- Increase glandular activity
- Activate tissue and cell repair

# Light Therapy ...

**Ultraviolet light** (UV) is part of the invisible rays of the electromagnetic spectrum and account for **five percent of natural sunlight.** Ultraviolet rays, also known as **actinic or cold rays** have the **shortest wavelengths,** minimal penetration and provide the least amount of heat. Ultraviolet rays initiate the body to produce vitamin D, and have the ability to destroy bacteria, which serves as a germicidal treatment for skin infections. When placed in a cabinet, the ultraviolet bulb is used for tool sanitation and keeps sanitized tools free from contamination.

Ultraviolet light has three different wavelengths, which means the distance from the sun to the earth's surface. They are **ultraviolet-A, ultraviolet-B and ultraviolet-C.**

**CAUTION:** The application of ultraviolet light can be beneficial if done in moderation and by following specific distance guidelines depending on area and treatment. The average distance for a UV lamp is 30 to 36 inches and time exposure starts at three minutes with a gradual increase to eight minutes.

# Light Therapy ...

**Ultraviolet-A** (UVA) has the **longest wavelength** and penetrates into the dermis of the skin. These wavelengths take a long time to reach the deep layers of the skin and are considered responsible for **increased skin aging and wrinkling.** The **"aging" rays** can penetrate glass causing exposure year-round, even in the winter and on cloudy days. UVA rays cause skin tanning, damage, drying and aging.

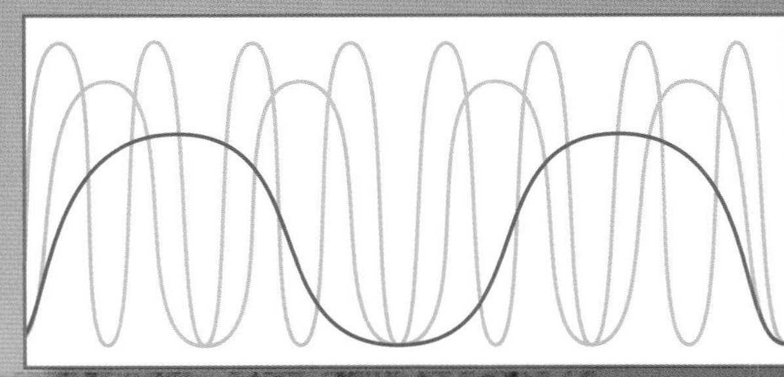

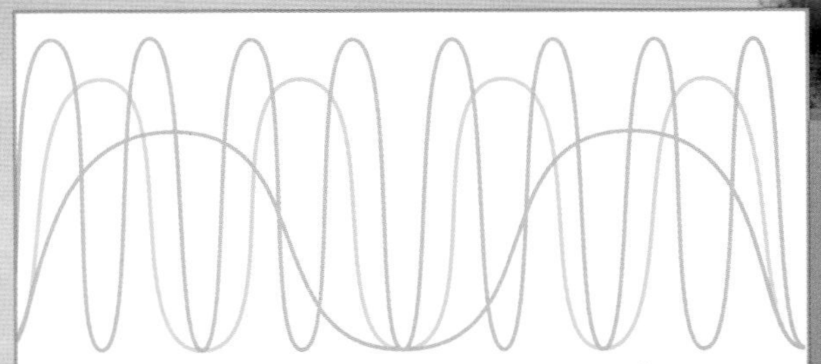

**Ultraviolet-B** (UVB) has a **medium wavelength** and is the strongest, penetrating into the epidermis. It is considered responsible for either skin "tanning" or "sunburn" depending on length of exposure time and melanin production. These rays cause the temperature to rise and are considered the **"burning rays."**

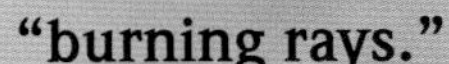

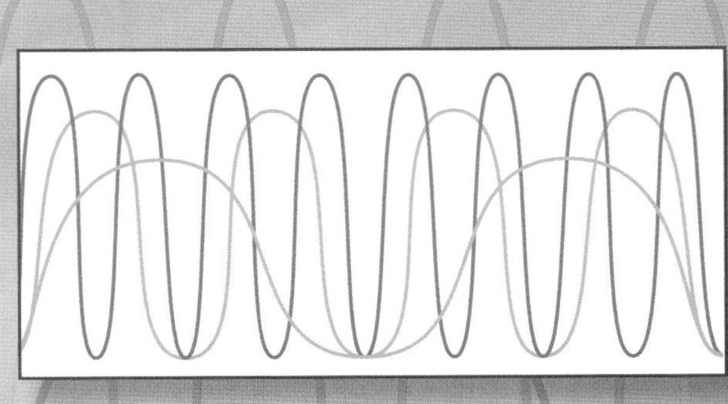

**Ultraviolet-C** (UVC) rays have the shortest wavelength and do not reach a person's skin.

Electricity **REVIEW QUESTIONS**

11

## MULTIPLE CHOICE

1. What electrical current flows in ONLY one direction?
   A. electricity B. volt C. direct current
2. The flow of electrical current or charge is?
   A. ohm B. electricity C. conductor
3. Which measures the amount of electric flow resistance?
   A. volt B. watt C. ohm
4. Which is the application of various types of electric currents that are used by way of electrodes and placed on the skin or scalp?
   A. electrotherapy B. light therapy C. massage therapy
5. A substance that prevents the flow of electricity is an?
   A. insulator B. conductor C. water
6. Examples of conductors are metal, copper and?
   A. water B. applicator bottle C. cotton
7. What is the measurement of how much electrical power or current is used?
   A. volt B. ampere C. ohm
8. The law that relates to voltage (V), current (I) and resistance (R) is?
   A. law of gravity B. OSHA C. ohms law
9. What does the acronym UL represent?
   A. Underwriters Laboratory B. Union Laws C. United Laboratory
10. When a circuit is completed, the ground wire causes the electricity to return to the?
    A. ground B. circuit box C. socket
11. Who invented the "Tesla Current?"
    A. Benjamin Franklin B. Thomas Edison C. Dr. Nikola Tesla
12. Which type of current is used by high-frequency current?
    A. volt B. direct C. alternating
13. Which form of electrical therapy uses glass electrodes?
    A. galvanic B. high-frequency C. sinusoidal
14. What effect does a negative pole have on the skin?
    A. decreases blood flow B. soothes nerves C. produces alkaline reaction
15. Which form of light therapy causes aging?
    A. UVB B. UVA C. wavelengths
16. Which type of light therapy produces the most amount of heat?
    A. visible light B. infrared rays C. ultraviolet rays
17. When all colors are redirected back into the prism, what color appears?
    A. blue light B. red light C. white light
18. Which UV ray has the longest wavelength?
    A. UVA B. UVB C. UVC
19. Incandescent lights produce?
    A. no tones B. warm tones C. cool tones
20. Visible light is produced by electromagnetic radiation, also known as?
    A. radiant energy B. UVA C. wavelengths

STUDENT'S NAME DATE GRADE

collagen dermatologist

epidermis lesions

pustules

oily

sunscreen

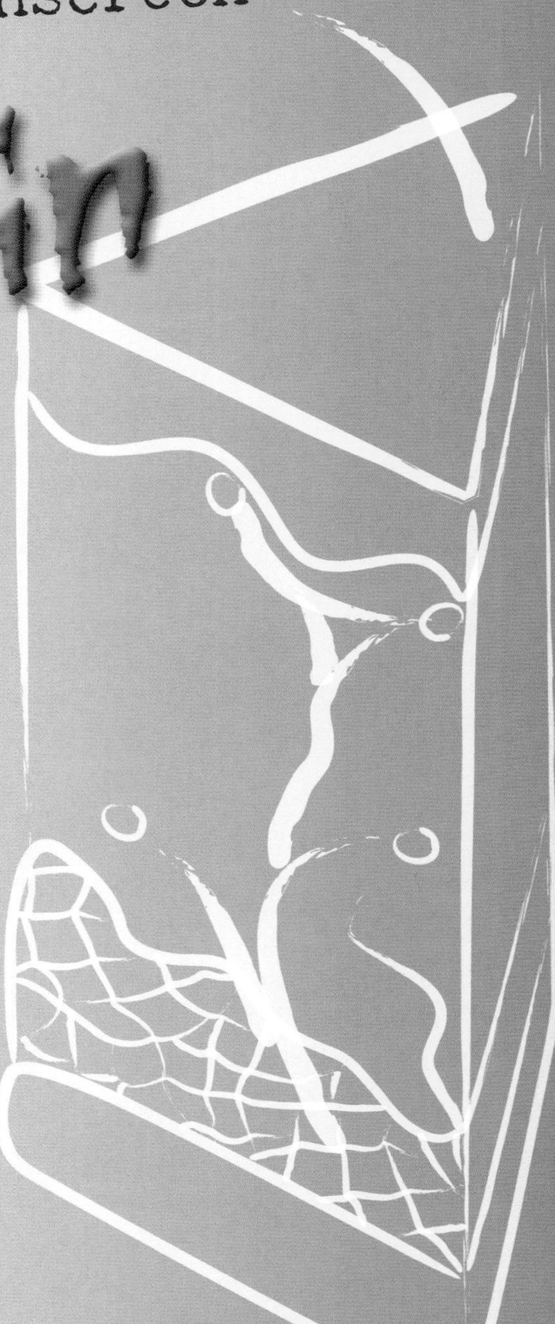

# skin

12

# SKIN

# Terminology ...

*The following vocabulary is intended to better acquaint you with terms that are frequently used within this chapter and the industry. This chapter covers* ***some of the terms*** *used for the skin and its conditions, disorders and diseases that will be of concern to the cosmetologist.*

**Aging** is a natural occurrence revealing itself in the skin appearing as **wrinkles** or **fine lines.**

**Blackheads** are open skin lesions containing hardened sebum referred to as **comedones.**

1

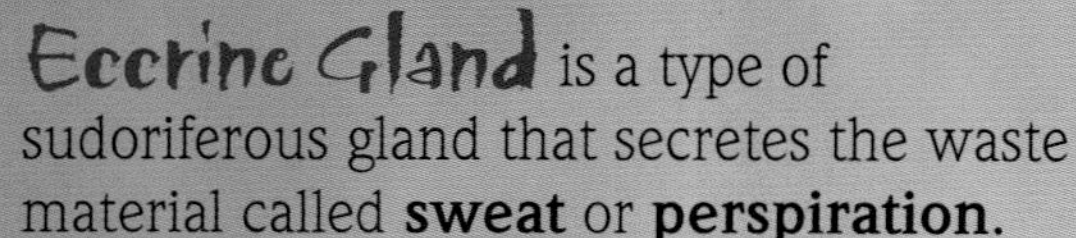

**Eccrine Gland** is a type of sudoriferous gland that secretes the waste material called **sweat** or **perspiration.**

2

**Melanin** is the **coloring matter** derived from the melanocyte cell located in the epidermis and dermis of the skin.

**Normal Skin** has a healthy glow with a **smooth, moist texture.**

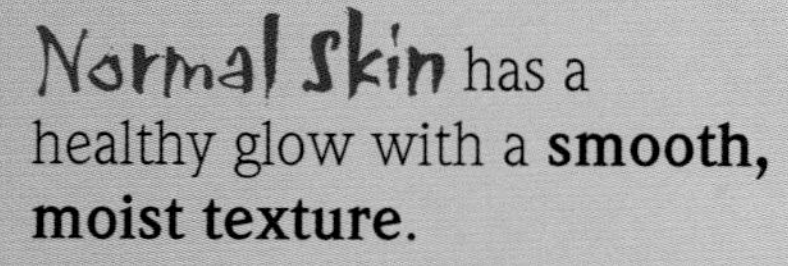

# Terminology . . .

**Sebaceous Gland** is a duct gland that secretes an oily substance called **sebum**, which lubricates the skin.

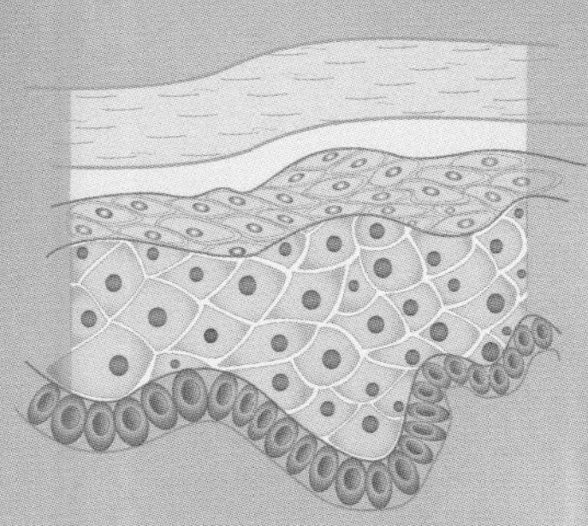

**Stratum Corneum** is the **protective layer** of the epidermis consisting of scale-like cells that are continuously shedding.

**Sun** is a brilliant **star** that emits ultraviolet radiation in three different strengths, which may produce damaging and aging effects to the skin.

**Sun Protection Factor (SPF)** is represented as a "**number**," which rates the length of time allowed for sun exposure without having adverse effects.

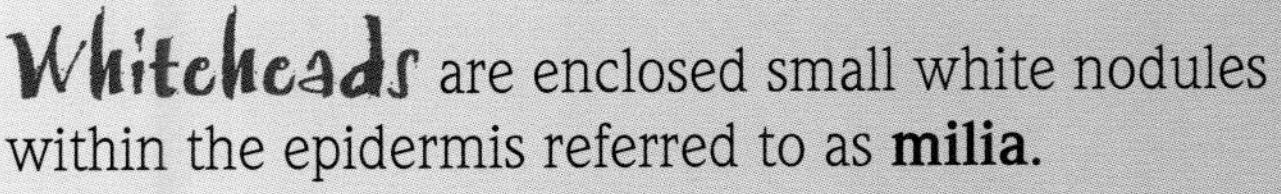

**Whiteheads** are enclosed small white nodules within the epidermis referred to as **milia**.

12

# Purpose of the Skin ...

***Skin** is a **valuable covering** on our bodies protecting the underlying systems. The skin's importance is sometimes disregarded or unappreciated, consequently being abused with chemicals, lifestyle or environment. Just like our bodily systems, skin is also an organ, the **largest organ of the body** and must be maintained to ensure a long life.*

The ideal and most desirable skin is healthy and glowing. **Healthy skin** has a **smooth, fine texture** and is somewhat acidic. It has **soft, slightly moist, elastic qualities** and is **free from blemishes, disease and disorders.** If appropriately cared for – and maintained using professional skin-care products as well as a lifestyle consisting of exercise and proper nutrition – the skin may achieve this type of appearance.

**NOTE:** Always check with a skin-care professional before purchasing any skin-care products; as what is best depends on your skin type and condition.

# Functions of the Skin . . .

*The skin is designed to naturally protect the body's underlying structures, tissues and organs. Its purpose is to provide functions that help maintain body temperature, skin sensitivity, pH and injury.*

## The six functions of the skin are:

1. **Protection** is guarding against the skin's enemies; such as UV rays, extreme weather conditions, poisonous plants and insect bites.

2. **Heat Regulation** is maintaining a body temperature of 98.6° Fahrenheit (37° Celsius) through the blood and excretion of perspiration.

3. **Absorption** allows products to penetrate the skin to keep it supple and pliable, which helps to retain the stretch or elasticity.

4. **Secretion** is when sebum, an oily substance, is delivered from the sebaceous glands to provide moisture and maintain skin's elasticity.

5. **Excretion** is accomplished when the sweat glands dispel perspiration. This maintains a healthy temperature by cooling the body.

6. **Sensation** is through touch, heat, cold, pressure and pain receptors that stimulate the nerve endings. These receptors are situated near the hair follicles within the dermis and send messages to the brain to react to the sensation.

12

# Divisions of the Skin . . .

*The skin is made up of three divisions called the* ***Epidermis, Dermis and Subcutaneous Tissue****. Each division is constructed of* ***cellular layers*** *that represent a different function and characteristic, but uniquely work together to produce the skin. Each skin division, along with the layers that construct that division will be explained starting with the epidermis. The epidermis is visually seen and exposed first to environmental elements, chemicals, UV rays and injury.*

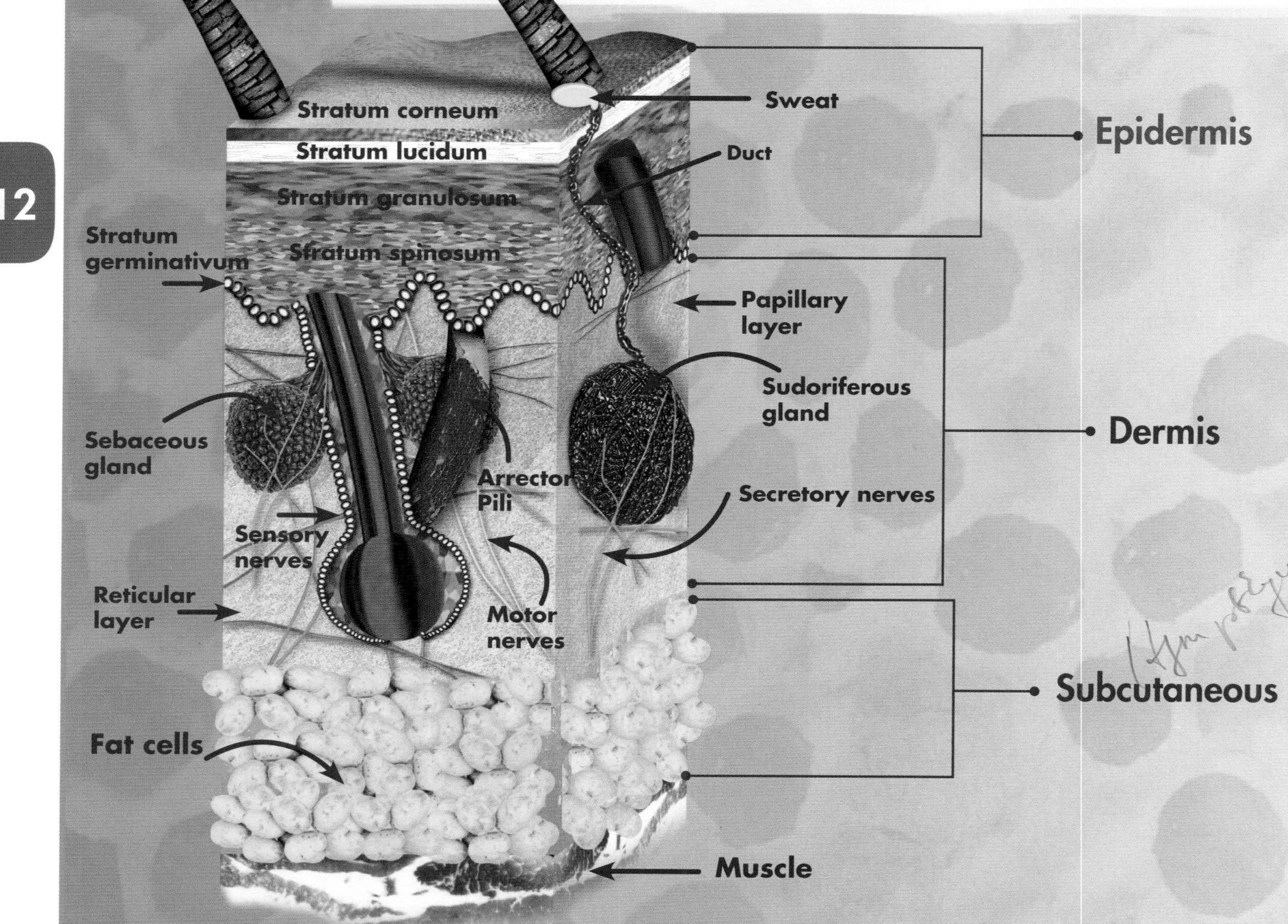

12

**Epidermis** is the top **protective division or "cuticle" portion** of the skin, containing many small nerve endings, but no blood vessels. This division consists of five layers and is developed though the reproduction cycle or regeneration of new cells. This **reproduction or cell division** is commonly referred to as **mitosis** and occurs when the cells rapidly divide producing an abundance of skin cells. As this process continues and the cells become overcrowded, they are pushed upward forming the layers of the epidermis. The cells take on a variety of shapes and then eventually shed once reaching the top layer. This division varies in thickness depending on area of body; we find the **thinnest areas on eyelids and thickest on soles of feet and palms of hands**.

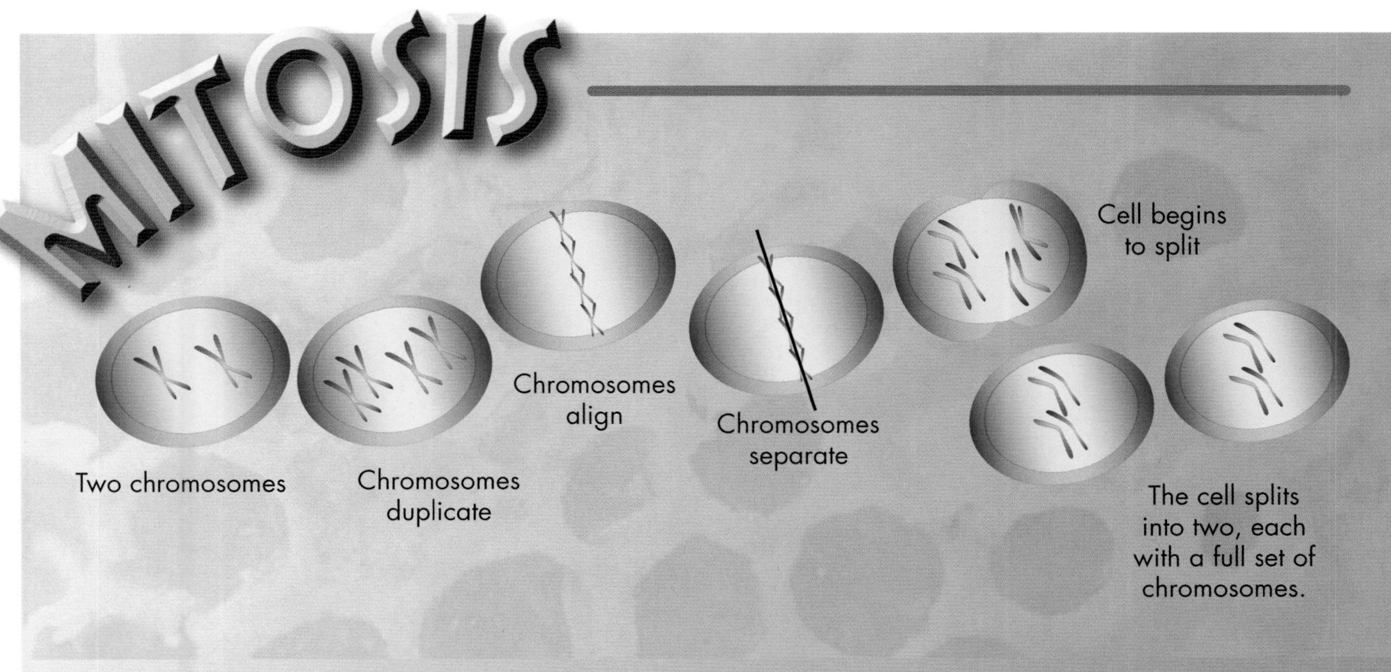




## Keratinization

A process called **keratinization** (ker-a-tin-i-za-tion) converts living skin cells into hard protein cells. **Keratinization** will occur as the excess cells are forced to move upward, pushing against each other, losing their moisture content, flattening and then hardening with a **water-proof protein called keratin** thus completing the cycle by shedding. This whole series of events takes an **average of 28 to 30 days** depending on age/health of individual and area of body.

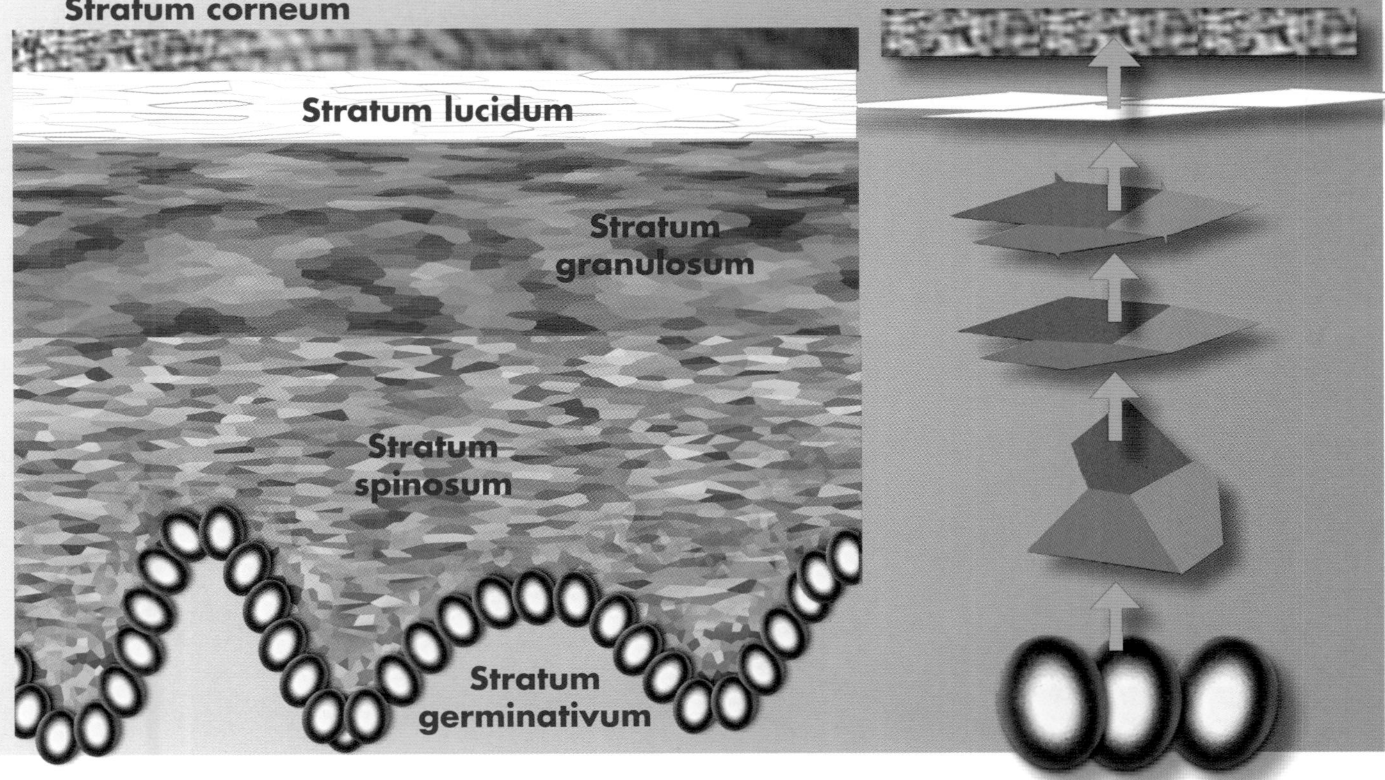

**Listed are the five layers of the epidermis and their characteristics and functions:**

***Starting from the bottom layer moving up toward top layer**

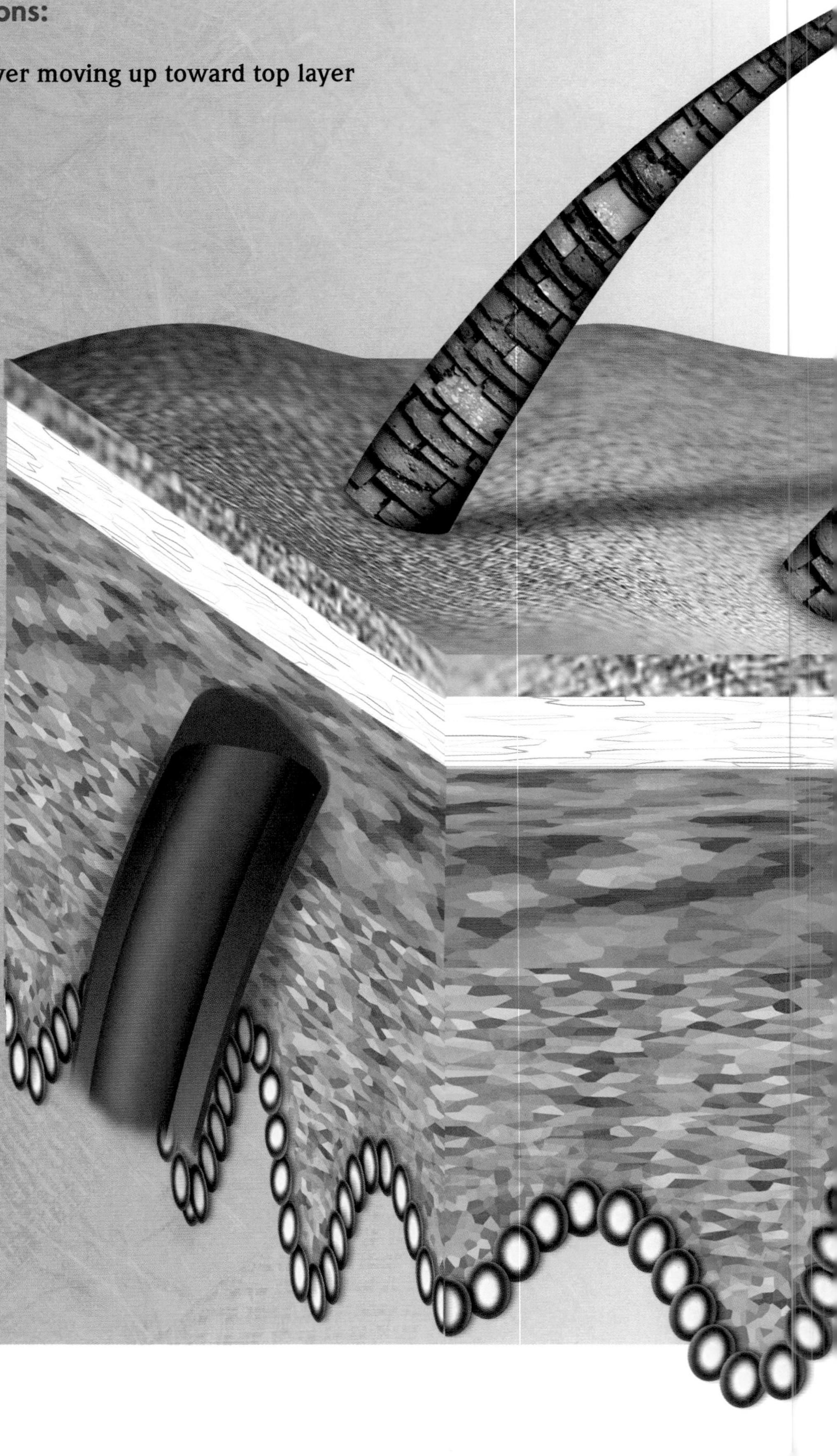

**1. Stratum Germinativum** (strat-um jur-mi-nah-tiv-um) or **basal layer** is basically known as the **birth layer of the epidermis** and it is where the epidermis begins. This bottom layer is where the skin cells are new, plump and alive. **Melanin** or **coloring matter** also is in this layer providing natural color to the skin and protecting it from exposure to ultraviolet rays from the sun or tanning beds.

12

**2. Stratum Spinosum** (strat-um spin-o-sum) or **spiny layer** is when the cells develop tiny spines that assist in **binding all cells tightly together**. In this layer, the **keratinization process begins** due to increased cell reproduction.

# Divisions of the Skin ...

**3. Stratum Granulosum** (strat-um gran-yoo-loh-sum) **layer** contains **granular-like cells**. This is where the process of **keratinization is most effective**. As the cells are forced upward, they start to flatten and become hardened due to the introduction of the **protein, keratin**. This **keratin remains soft** to allow for skin's elastic and flexible nature, unlike the keratin used in nails and hair, which is hard.

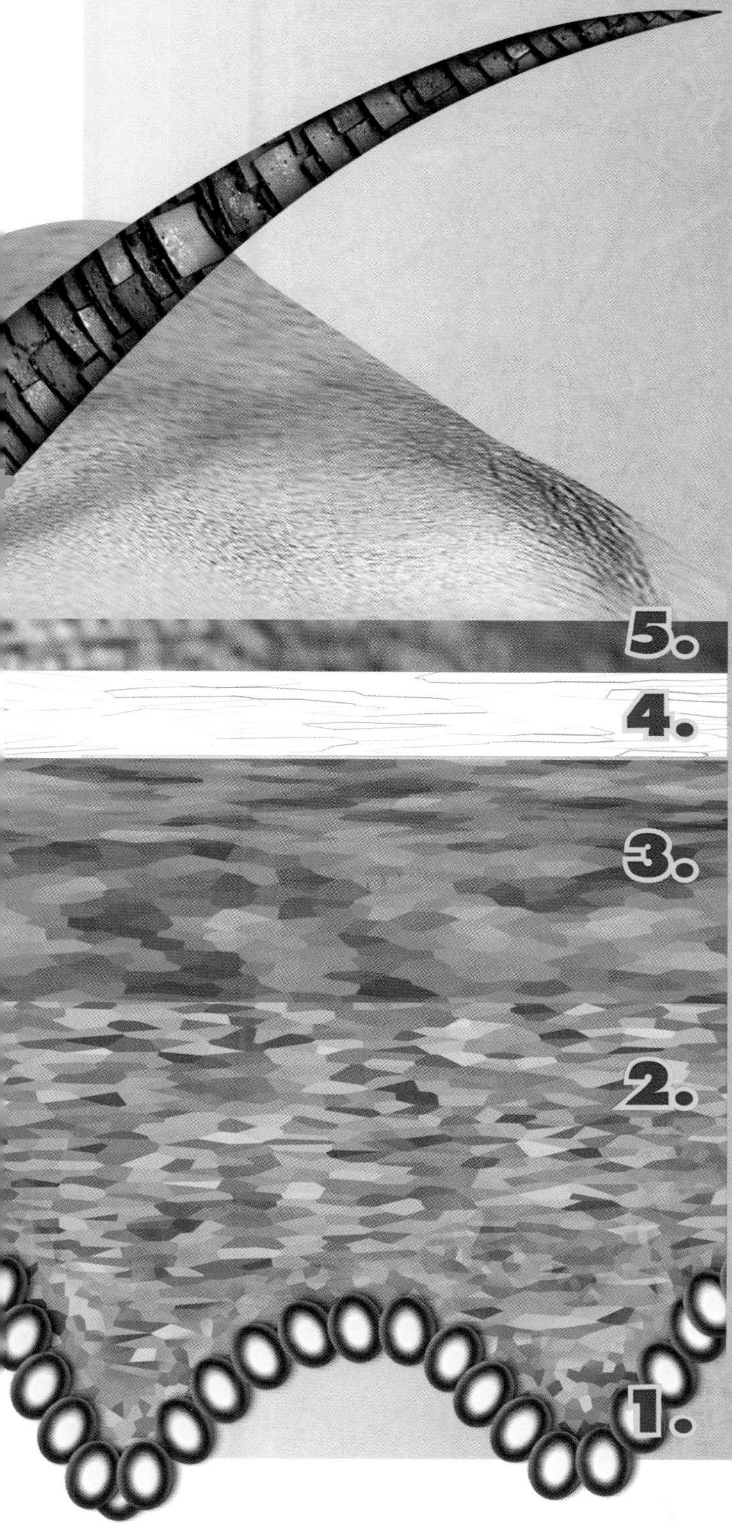

**4. Stratum Lucidum** (strat-um loo-si-dum) **layer** is made up of **clear cells**, which allow light to pass through. The cells in this layer continue to be pushed upward, flatten, becoming keratinized and transparent. This layer is mostly found on the palms of hands and soles of feet.

12

**5. Stratum Corneum** (strat-um kohr-nee-um) or **horny layer** consists of tightly-packed, **scale-like hardened cells** that are continuously being shed and replaced by new cells therefore renewing this portion of the skin on an average of every 28 to 30 days. This **protective layer** has a **natural thin film covering called the acid mantle**, which consists of a tiny amount of water (sudoriferous glands) and oil (sebaceous glands) helping to maintain the skin's **pH of 4.5 to 5.5**. This acid mantle is **not visible** to the naked eye, and can only be seen with the aid of a microscope. Products high in alkalinity can deprive the stratum corneum of this naturally occurring protective barrier.

5.
4.
3.
2.
1.

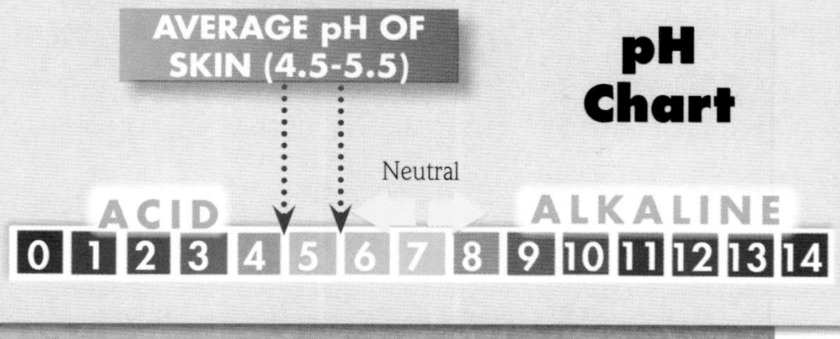

# DERMIS

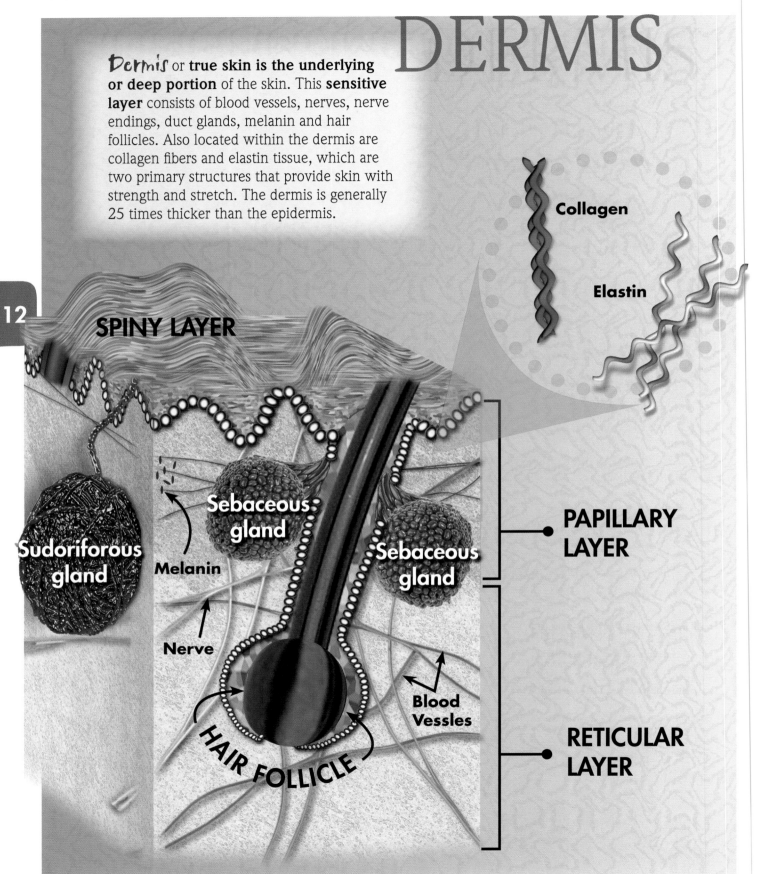

**Dermis** or **true skin is the underlying or deep portion** of the skin. This **sensitive layer** consists of blood vessels, nerves, nerve endings, duct glands, melanin and hair follicles. Also located within the dermis are collagen fibers and elastin tissue, which are two primary structures that provide skin with strength and stretch. The dermis is generally 25 times thicker than the epidermis.

# Divisions of the Skin . . .

**Below are the two layers of the dermis and their characteristics and functions:**

The papillary and reticular layers play a key role in producing the skin's natural functions.

1. **Papillary** (pa-pil-ah-ry) **layer** is situated directly underneath the epidermis and contains small blood vessels, melanin, hair follicles, oil glands and sensory nerve endings. Where the epidermis and dermis meet and interlock is referred to as the **epidermal-dermal junction.**

2. **Reticular** (re-tik-u-lar) **layer** is located below the papillary and assists in supplying the skin with nutrients and oxygen. It contains a majority of the skin's structures such as a network of nerve fibers, hair papilla, blood and lymph vessels, sweat glands and the arrector pili muscles.

## HYPODERMIS

**Hypodermis** (hy-po-der-mis) or **subcutaneous** (sub-cu-ta-ne-ous) **tissue** is the deepest portion of the skin found below the dermis and contains the fatty tissue called **adipose.** This **fatty layer** consists of the extended branches of blood vessels, nerve endings and the fats for energy, providing a protective cushion for the epidermis.

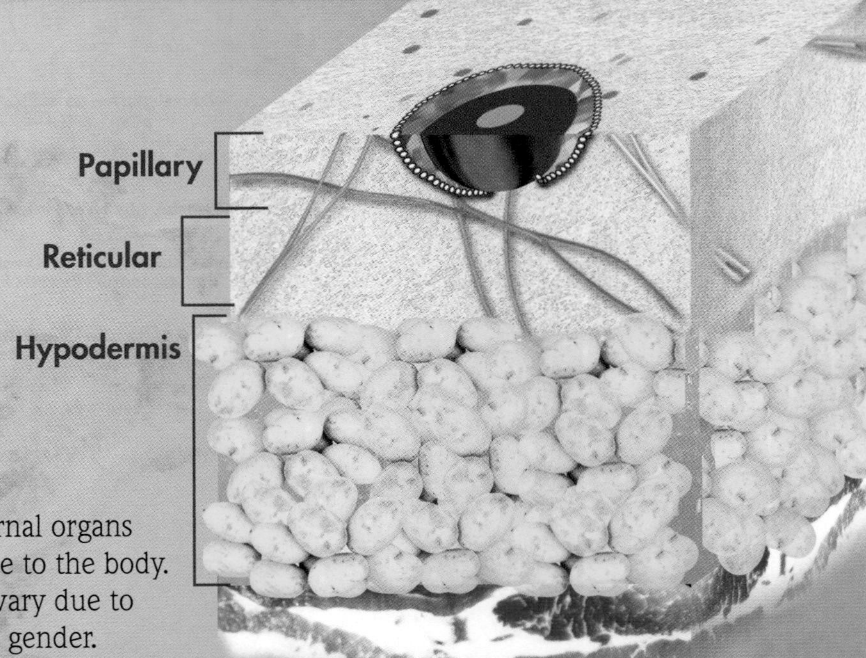


The hypodermis **protects** the internal organs and provides smoothness and shape to the body. The thickness of this division will vary due to individual's age, overall health and gender.

# Skin Glands...

*Located within the dermis are skin glands that perform many useful functions in our body. These glands are referred to as **duct glands** because they **secrete matter from the body and deposit** it on the skin's surface.*

There are **two types of duct glands** of concern to the cosmetologist. The over- or under-activity of these glands will propose a direction as to what type of treatments and products are to be used on the skin.



1. Sudoriferous
2. Sebaceous

## 1

**Sudoriferous** (su-der-if-er-us) **or sweat glands** consist of tube-like ducts that begin in the dermis and extend into the epidermis by attaching themselves to hair follicles. The base of the tube masses into a coil and is called a **fundus**. The sweat glands are supported by the nervous system.

### The two types of sudoriferous glands are Eccrine and Apocrine

**Eccrine** (ec-crine) **glands** are located throughout the body, but are numerous on the face, palms of hands and soles of feet, and are activated by heat or bodily activity. The eccrine glands secrete a waste material called **sweat or perspiration**. Sweat is a self-cleansing mechanism produced by the body to get rid of toxins. It assists in maintaining a healthy body temperature by its cooling effects through evaporation. Sweat also supplies an acidic pH to the skin due to the sweat's content of water, fat and some salt.

**Apocrine** (ap-o-crine) **glands** are located in the armpits and pubic area, and are activated by stress and/or puberty. Their glandular secretions are similar to sweat but a little thicker creating a distinct body odor.

# Skin Glands...

**Sebaceous** (si-bay-shus) **glands or oil glands** consist of sac-like structures attached to the hair follicles and encompass the full length of the dermis and epidermis. These glands are located throughout the body with the exception of the palms of hands and soles of feet. The oil glands are activated by stress, diet or adolescence (hormonal imbalance).

**The sebaceous glands** secrete an **oily substance** called **sebum**, which is a mixture of fats or lipids. **Sebum** provides moisture to the skin and hair, lubricating and preventing the possibility of the skin wrinkling and/or hair breakage.

12

It is a thin layer of **sebum and sweat** that provides a skin barrier in helping to resist dirt and germs from entering the body. This microscopic film is called the **acid mantle or hydro-lipid system** and is acidic in pH, ranging from **4.5 to 5.5**. The **acid mantle** protects and nourishes the skin creating softness and pliability.

## Problems with Duct Glands

When the sudoriferous and sebaceous glands do not function normally and are either **under- or over-active**, problems can arise. An **under- or over-active gland** can create certain **skin disorders** that will require special facial treatments or medical attention. Through client consultation and skin analysis, the cosmetologist can determine whether to proceed with a facial service or recommend medical attention.

"Generally our bodies secrete one to two pints of liquids daily depending on level of activity."

# Skin Color . . .

*The natural color of your skin is dependent upon the amount of melanin within the stratum germinativum and papillary layers of the skin.*

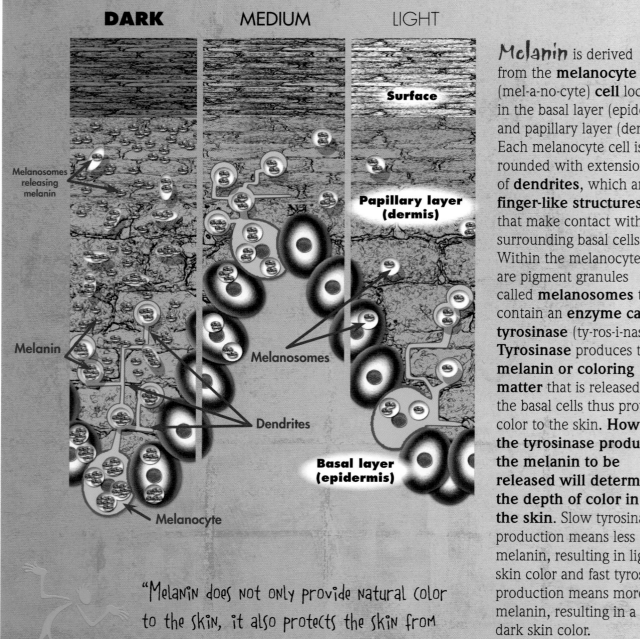

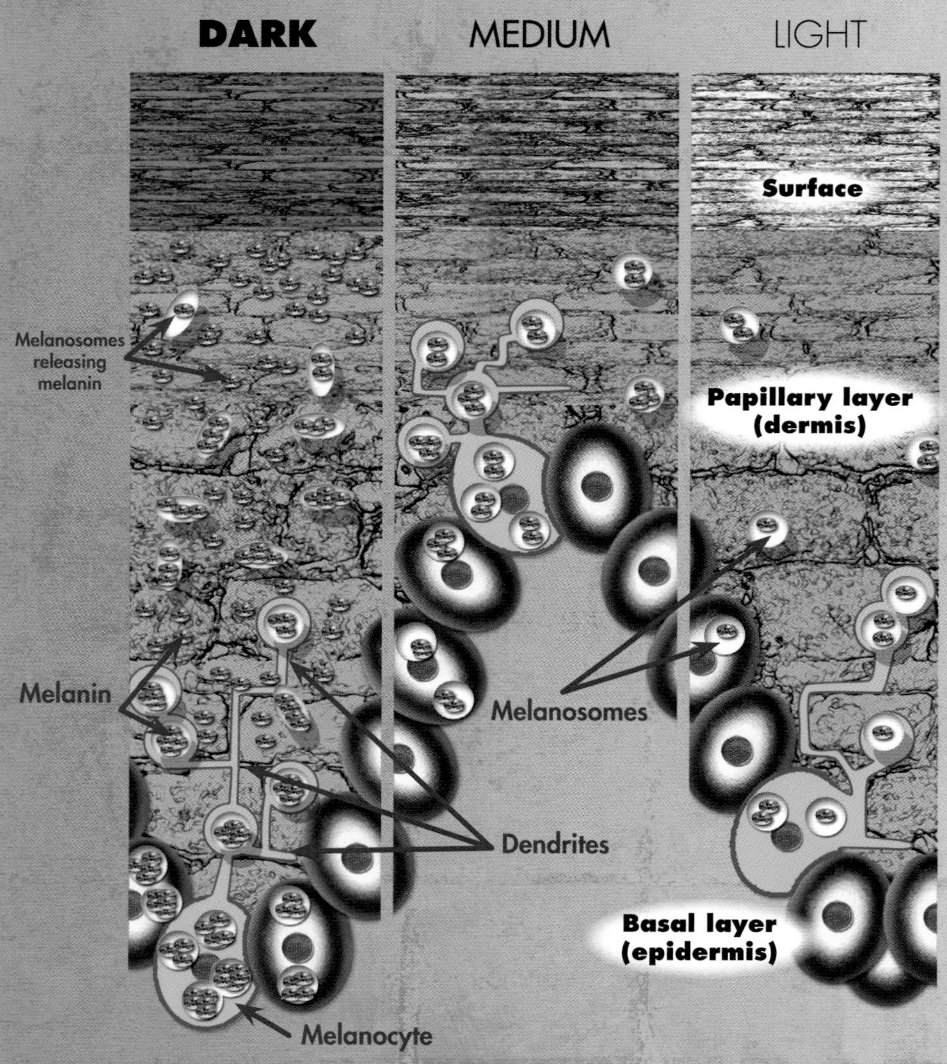


**Melanin** is derived from the **melanocyte** (mel-a-no-cyte) **cell** located in the basal layer (epidermis) and papillary layer (dermis). Each melanocyte cell is rounded with extensions of **dendrites**, which are **finger-like structures** that make contact with surrounding basal cells. Within the melanocyte are pigment granules called **melanosomes** that contain an **enzyme called tyrosinase** (ty-ros-i-nase). **Tyrosinase** produces the **melanin or coloring matter** that is released into the basal cells thus providing color to the skin. **How fast the tyrosinase produces the melanin to be released will determine the depth of color in the skin.** Slow tyrosinase production means less melanin, resulting in light skin color and fast tyrosinase production means more melanin, resulting in a dark skin color.

"Melanin does not only provide natural color to the skin, it also protects the skin from the ultraviolet rays produced from the sun."

# Nourishment of the Skin ...

*Just like our bodies need nourishment to maintain optimum health, the same is true for our skin.* ***Blood and lymph supply nutrients*** *to our skin through the* ***foods we eat and liquids we consume.*** *Taking care of ourselves through eating properly and maintaining a regular exercise program will promote the health of our skin.*

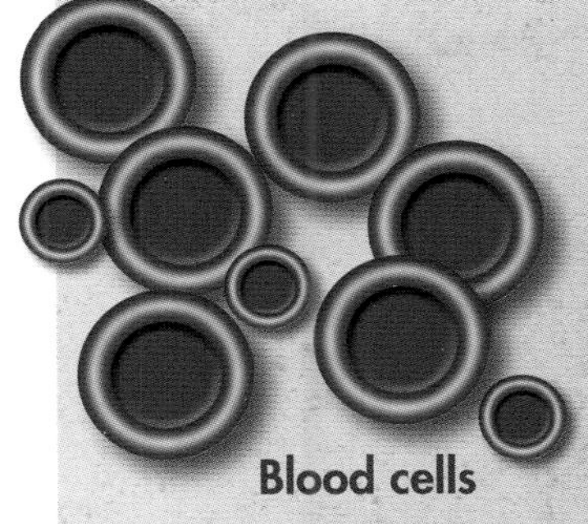
Blood cells

**Blood** is a **nourishing fluid** that supplies nutrients, carries away waste products and protects the body from pathogenic bacteria. The nutrients supplied from foods that are beneficial in skin repair and growth are **proteins, fats, carbohydrates, vitamins, minerals and water.** When skin becomes injured, blood platelets (tiny color-free particles) help in the clotting or coagulation of blood to assist in the healing process.

12

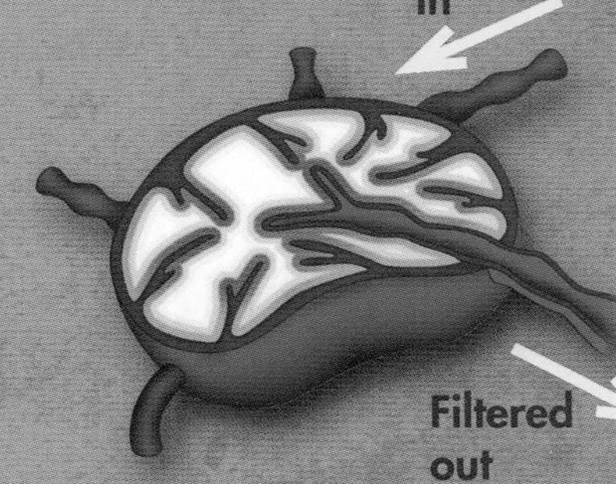


**Lymph** is a **clear, yellowish fluid** that travels through a vessel and is then filtered by a lymph node. The lymph node filters out impurities, bacteria and waste materials that help to fight against infection and protect the skin from disease.

**Water** is a very **important nutrient to the skin** to help **eliminate waste** and **regulate body temperature** as well as **hydrate the skin cells.** Body weight comprises 50 to 70 percent water. The amount of water consumed by each individual will vary depending on the person's body weight and activity level. **Follow this simple formula**: Divide your body weight by 16; the resulting number will be how many 8-ounce glasses of water you should consume daily. If performing intense exercise, you will need to add another two 8-ounce glasses of water to your daily water consumption.

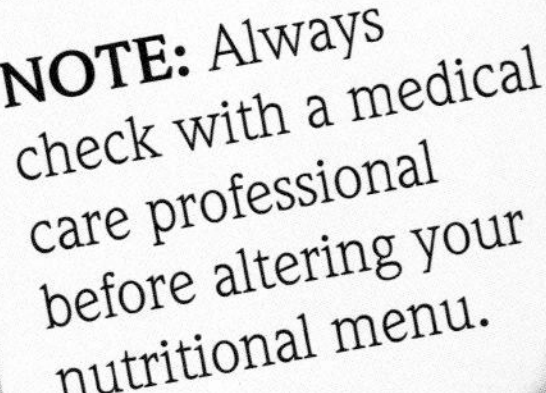

**NOTE:** Always check with a medical care professional before altering your nutritional menu.


"If your weight is 168 lbs, your average water consumption should be 10.5 8-ounce glasses a day."

# Nerve Fibers of the Skin ...

*The **nerve fibers or branches** of the skin are located within the dermis. They are responsible for **sending and receiving messages from the brain to the nerves** for the reaction of a **muscle contraction, glandular activity or to experience a sensation**. Most of the nerve endings are contained in the fingertips and soles of feet resulting in high sensitivity in these areas.*

**The three major nerve endings are Motor, Secretory and Sensation:**

12

**Motor nerve fibers** are responsible for **carrying impulses to the muscle** to create contraction of that muscle. The arrector pili muscle reacts with muscle contraction by creating a skin appearance of **"goose flesh or bumps."** This is usually caused by an impulse of cold temperatures or becoming frightened.

**Motor nerve fiber**

# Nerve Fibers of the Skin . . .

**Secretory nerve fibers** branch from the nervous system, **regulating the function of the sudoriferous and sebaceous glands.** These nerve fibers may be activated through stress, bodily activity or environmental temperatures. Any one or all of these factors can generate the **production of sweat or oil** in reaching the surface of the skin.

**Sensory nerve fibers** connect with the five nerve receptors, which are situated near the hair follicles within the dermis and respond with a signal to the brain to **react to a particular sensation**. The five sensations are **heat, cold, touch, pressure and pain** with each having its own receptor. When the pain receptor is stimulated, the **brain is signaled for the body to react** by verbalizing an "ouch" and/or moving away from what is causing the pain.

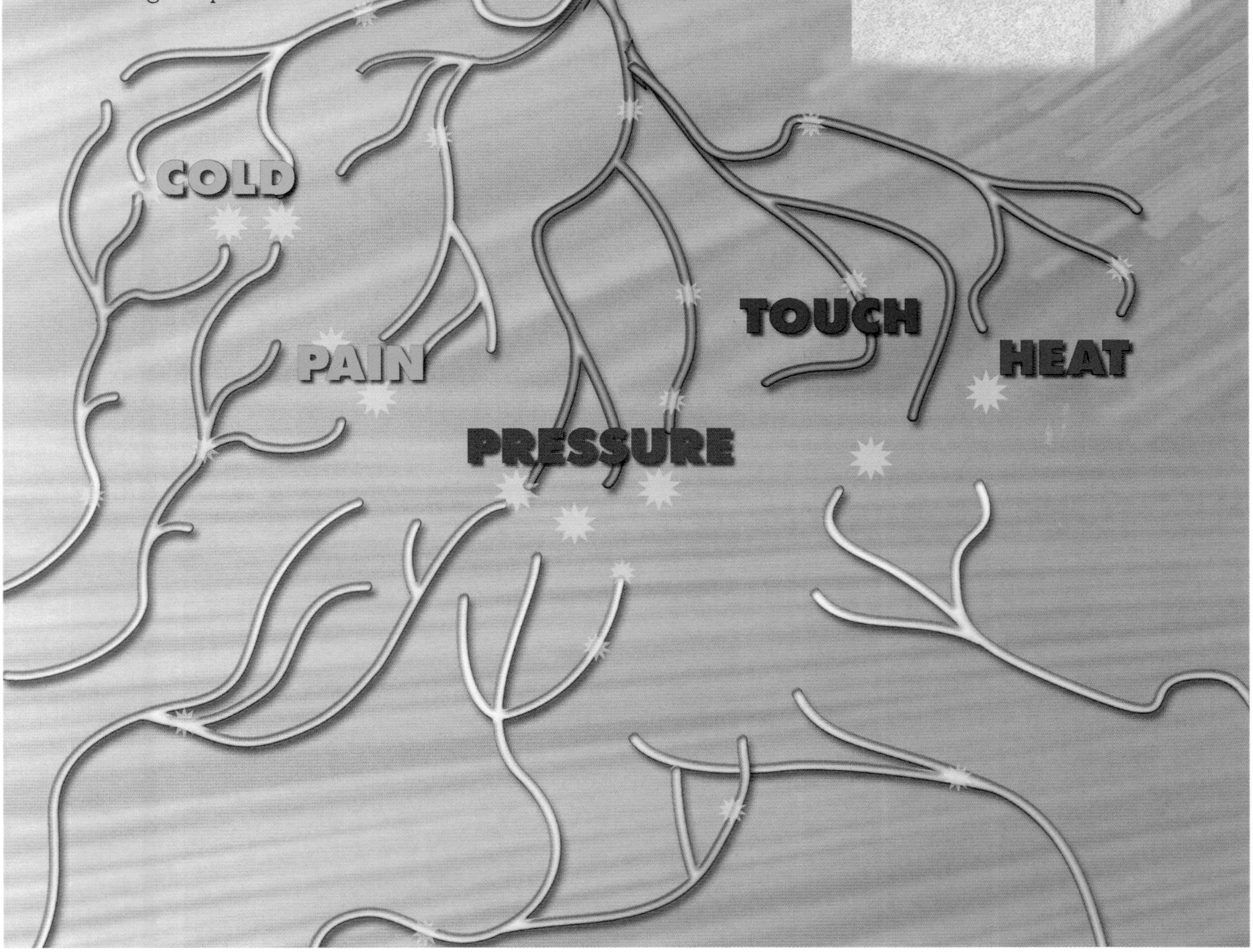

sweat

COLD

PAIN

PRESSURE

TOUCH

HEAT

12

# Flexibility of the Skin . . .

*In order for the skin to stretch and return to its original form, the **primary structures of collagen** (col-la-gen) **and elastin** (elas-tin) must be present and healthy. Due to improper skin-care, frequent weight gain or loss, environment (sun), heredity, age(hormones) or gender, these structures are worn down and slowly damaged resulting in wrinkling or sagging of the skin. Collagen and elastin fibers make up a majority of the skin, about **70 percent of the dermis.***

The **fibroblast** (fi-bro-blast) **cells** are **tissue-forming cells** located within the dermis and are responsible for the production of collagen fibers and elastin tissue. Fibroblast cells are **small and spindle shaped** helping to maintain the structural network of connective tissue and assist in the healing process of any injury to the skin.

12

**Collagen** is a **major fibrous protein** that maintains the **skin's firmness and form**. It provides structural support by holding all other tissues together within the dermis. Collagen fibers are weakened by any of the following repetitive conditions: moisture loss, excessive exposure to the sun, age and fluctuation of weight gain/loss. The fibers are eventually worn down and loss of skin tone and pliability are the result. A topical treatment of **vitamin C and its derivatives** is an important element in stimulating the production of collagen and combating the aging process. For more information, go to: http://www.smartskincare.com

"Collagen acts as a glue-producing substance."

# Flexibility of the Skin . . .

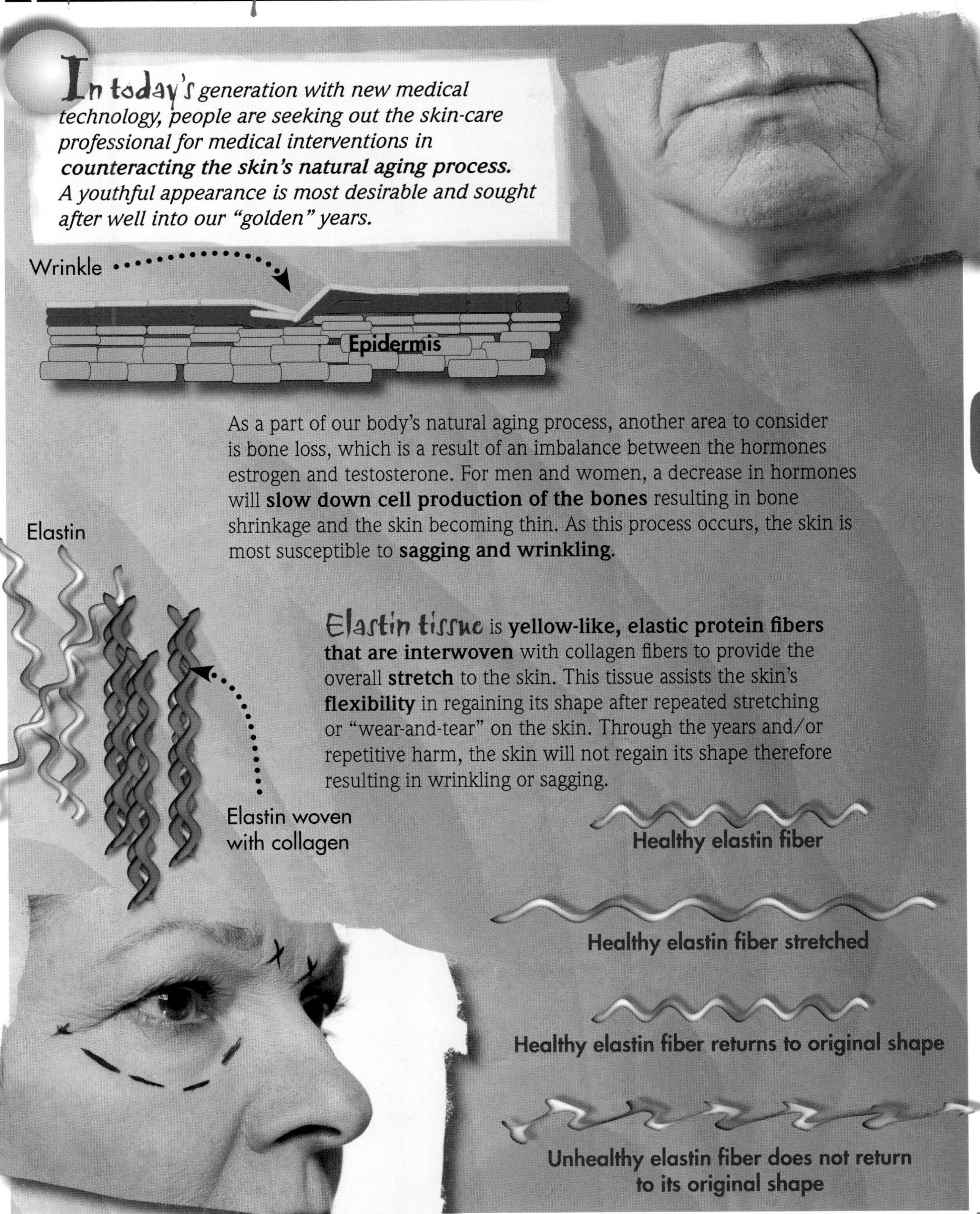


*In today's generation with new medical technology, people are seeking out the skin-care professional for medical interventions in* **counteracting the skin's natural aging process.** *A youthful appearance is most desirable and sought after well into our "golden" years.*

As a part of our body's natural aging process, another area to consider is bone loss, which is a result of an imbalance between the hormones estrogen and testosterone. For men and women, a decrease in hormones will **slow down cell production of the bones** resulting in bone shrinkage and the skin becoming thin. As this process occurs, the skin is most susceptible to **sagging and wrinkling**.

**Elastin tissue** is **yellow-like, elastic protein fibers that are interwoven** with collagen fibers to provide the overall **stretch** to the skin. This tissue assists the skin's **flexibility** in regaining its shape after repeated stretching or "wear-and-tear" on the skin. Through the years and/or repetitive harm, the skin will not regain its shape therefore resulting in wrinkling or sagging.

# Skin Aging . . .

*Aging is a natural occurrence with the human body and the skin; however, sometimes this process is accelerated through incorrect skin-care, heredity or genetics. Improper skin-care will result in the skin's tone weakening, resulting in premature wrinkling or sagging of the skin.*

**Sun exposure** is a major factor in the aging of skin. The warmth and glow of the sun acts much like a magnet, attracting people to bask in it. We flock to the beaches to absorb the rays by either relaxing on the sand and/or cooling off by the pool, exposing ourselves to the ray's reflection off the water. Year after year, this sun exposure will eventually have long-term harmful effects on the skin. Using a lotion or serum consisting of a combination of vitamins A and E may assist in combating against the damaging effects of the sun.

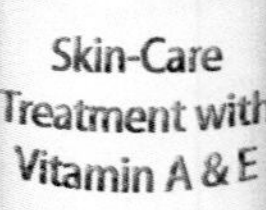


12

## Two visual effects of the sun on the skin are either sunburn or suntan.

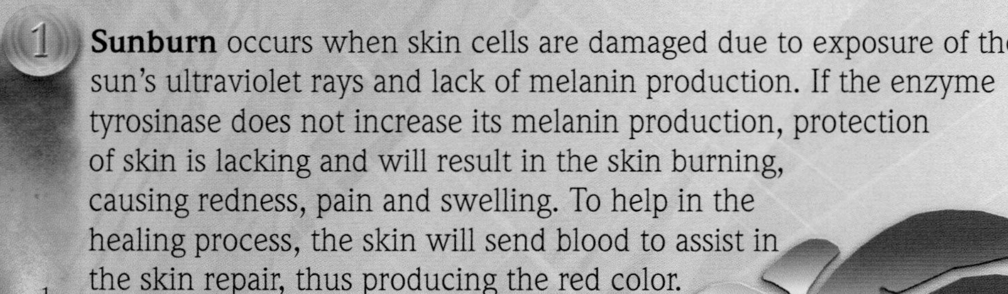

1 **Sunburn** occurs when skin cells are damaged due to exposure of the sun's ultraviolet rays and lack of melanin production. If the enzyme tyrosinase does not increase its melanin production, protection of skin is lacking and will result in the skin burning, causing redness, pain and swelling. To help in the healing process, the skin will send blood to assist in the skin repair, thus producing the red color.

2 **Suntan** is a slight browning of the skin resulting from exposure to ultraviolet rays from the sun or tanning beds. The enzyme tyrosinase, encased in the melanosome, is stimulated and produces an abundance of melanin to protect the skin. The increased amount of melanin creates a darkened effect to the skin resulting in a tan.

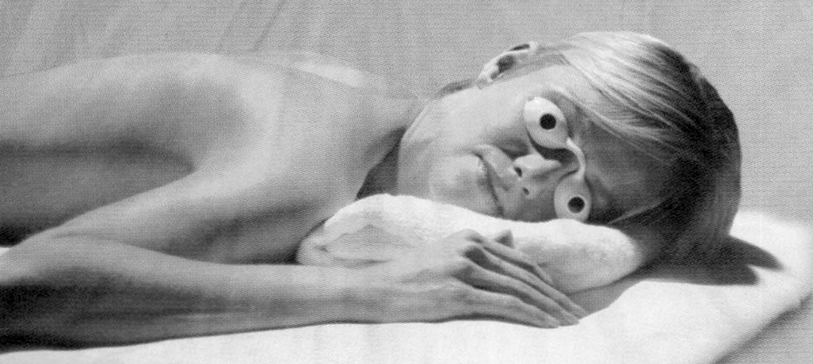

"Experts believe that 80 percent of the skin's aging is due to UVA and UVB sun rays."

# Sun Exposure . . .

***The sun** is a brilliant star in the sky emitting intense ultraviolet radiation. Ultraviolet (UV) radiation is the invisible rays of the light spectrum. The distance from the sun to the earth's surface determines the ultraviolet wavelength. Each wavelength varies in distance and its effects on the skin.*

## Sunlight comes in three different wavelengths: Ultraviolet-A, Ultraviolet-B and Ultraviolet-C.

- **Ultraviolet-A (UVA)** has the **longest wavelength** and penetrates deep into the dermis area of the skin. These wavelengths take longer to reach the deeper layers of the skin and are considered responsible for increased skin aging and wrinkling. The **"aging" rays** can penetrate glass and exposure is all year-round, even in the winter and on cloudy days.

**NOTE:** The UVA and UVB rays are used in the tanning beds or sun lamps.

- **Ultraviolet-B (UVB)** has a **medium wavelength** and is the strongest, penetrating into the epidermis. It is considered responsible for either "tanning" or "sunburning" of the skin depending on length of exposure time and melanin production. These **"burning" rays** pose the risk of causing skin damage and/or possible skin cancer.

- **Ultraviolet-C (UVC)** has the **shortest wavelength** and does not reach the earth's surface due to the ozone layer.

# Sun Exposure . . .

## Why is the sun harmful to your skin?

We understand more now than in the past about the adverse effects on the skin of long-term sun exposure or "sun-worshipping."

While the sun has some benefits for the health of skin, such as helping our body to produce vitamin D to strengthen bones and assist in preventing against disease, it also poses damaging risks if exposure is not done in moderation.

12

**Avoid the hours between 10 a.m. to 4 p.m.** unless using sunscreen protection. This is when the sun's rays are the highest and strongest.

**Skin's Natural Protection**
The body's natural reaction to sun exposure is to protect the skin. This is achieved through an increase in melanin production. The **speed of melanin production** will create a darker skin appearance thus producing a "tan." If the rate of melanin produced is slow, the skin will burn before the pigment can protect the skin from the ultraviolet rays. Light skin is more prone to the damaging effects of the sun as opposed to dark skin.

# Sun Exposure . . .

**Sunscreen** is a cosmetic product that chemically **absorbs UV rays.** It lists a **sun protection factor (SPF)**, which is a number that rates the length of time allowed for sun exposure before burning the skin. The **number represents the sun exposure time** before either going indoors or reapplying sunscreen. How often sunscreen is applied is dependent upon swimming, sweating and manufacturer's directions.

**Example:** An SPF 15 would provide 150 minutes or 2 ½ hours of sun time without reapplying sunscreen or going indoors. SPF 30 would provide 300 minutes or five hours of sun protection. Sun Protection factors range anywhere from 2 to 60.

**NOTE:** SPF of 15 or higher is the recommended protection from the Skin Cancer Foundation with a reapplication every two hours.

12

**Sunblock** is a cosmetic product that places a barrier on the skin to physically repel both the UVA and UVB rays. These products usually have a thick viscosity and are hard to spread over skin. They contain either a zinc oxide or titanium dioxide, which both consist of a white pigment that can block out UVA and UVB rays.

**Which sun protection product to use?** Area of body and/or length of sun exposure will determine the product of choice. Sunscreen and sunblock can be used in conjunction with one another. Always check with product manufacturer for best results.

Sunblock

"Generally, the lighter the skin color, the higher the recommended SPF."

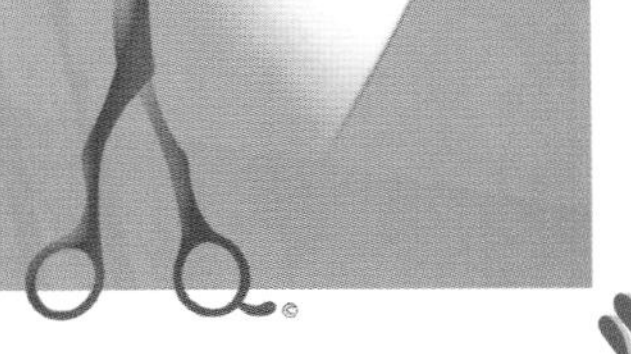

# Types of Skin ...

*During a skin analysis the client's face is viewed through a magnifying glass to determine pore size and skin type.* ***Pores*** *are openings at the hair follicles where sweat and sebum are dispersed. A person's skin type is developed either through* ***heredity, environmental factors, bodily functions or maintenance of skin.*** *The skin may either be improved or aggravated by environmental surroundings, inadequate products, or over- or under-active duct glands. The main purpose of the cosmetologist is to provide the necessary products or treatments for maintaining or improving the client's skin, as well as to complete the service with a proper home-maintenance regimen.*

12

## The Four Main Types of Skin:

**1.** **Normal Skin**
is when the texture appearance is **smooth, moist and soft** with a healthy glow. This type of skin is without blemishes, blackheads and wrinkles. Normal skin is a rarity, but the main objective is to preserve its beauty.

**2.** **Combination Skin**
consists of two types of skin; **normal to dry skin on outer perimeter** of face with an **oily condition on the "T" zone area** of face. The "T" zone or middle panel consists of the forehead, nose and chin. This area may be shiny with large pores, blackheads or pimples created by an excess of sebum. The outer perimeter consists of the cheeks and hairline, and may either have a smooth texture or a rough, scaly appearance. This type of skin requires a specialized skin-care regimen for simultaneously treating two different types of skin.

T-Zone

# Types of Skin . . .

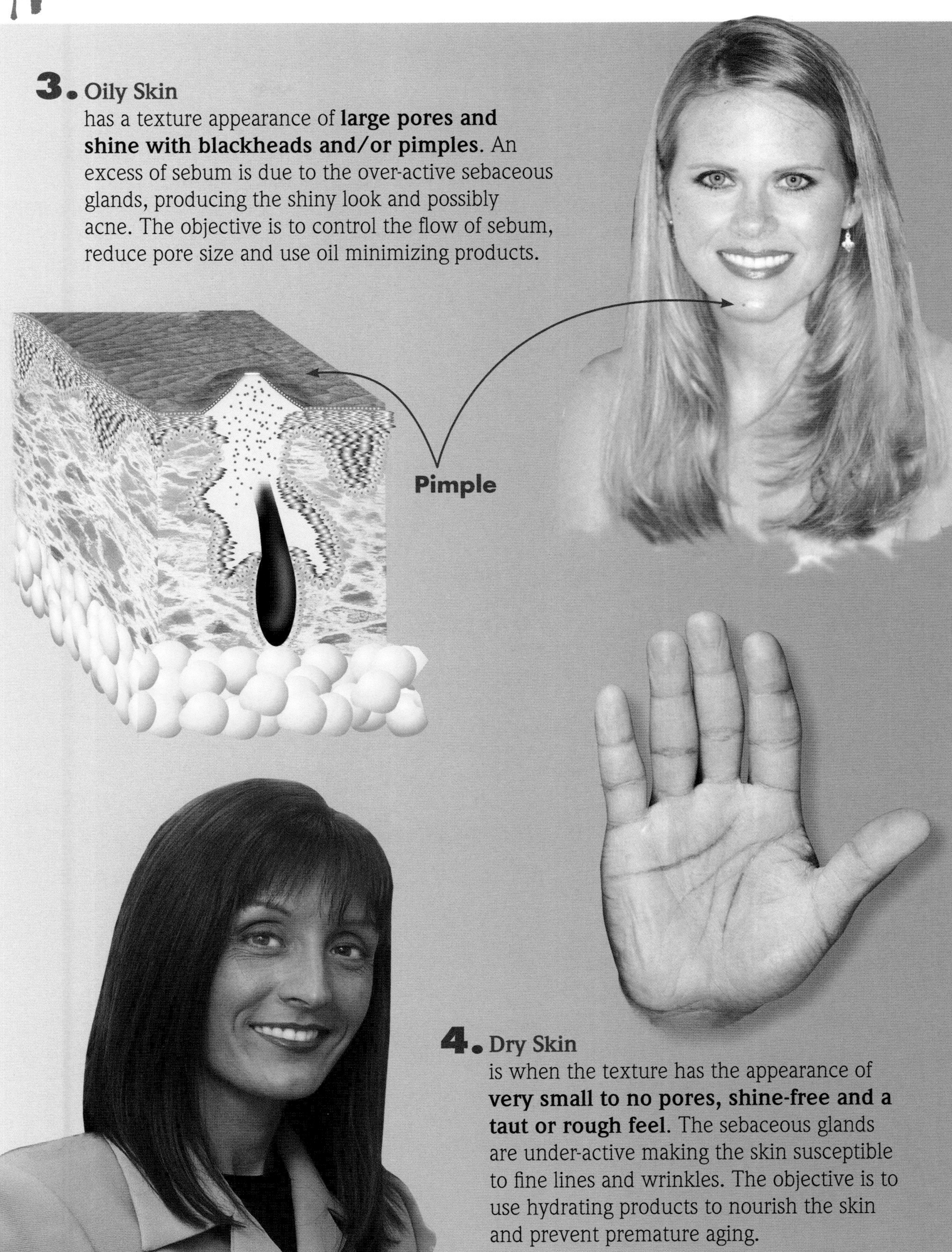


**3.** Oily Skin
has a texture appearance of **large pores and shine with blackheads and/or pimples**. An excess of sebum is due to the over-active sebaceous glands, producing the shiny look and possibly acne. The objective is to control the flow of sebum, reduce pore size and use oil minimizing products.

**4.** Dry Skin
is when the texture has the appearance of **very small to no pores, shine-free and a taut or rough feel.** The sebaceous glands are under-active making the skin susceptible to fine lines and wrinkles. The objective is to use hydrating products to nourish the skin and prevent premature aging.

# Skin Facts ...

*Here are* ***some interesting statistics*** *regarding* ***one square inch of skin.*** *Use a ruler to visually determine the size of skin we are going to study. For this to become even more apparent, take a piece of paper and draw the exact diameters of one square inch of skin. What you will find is intriquing, all the* ***cells, network of glands, blood vessels and fibers*** *contained in this small area ... it is truly astounding!*

## One Square Inch of Skin contains:

* *These facts will vary depending on cultural background, type, age and genetics of each individual.*

12

- 60 to 65 hair strands
- 1,000,000 cells
- 95 to 100 sebaceous glands
- 15 to 20 feet of blood vessels
- 600 to 650 sweat glands
- 12 feet of nerves
- 19,000 sensory nerve fibers
- 12 sensory nerve cells
- 1,250 to 1,300 pain nerve receptors
- 12 cold nerve receptors
- 155 pressure and touch nerve receptors

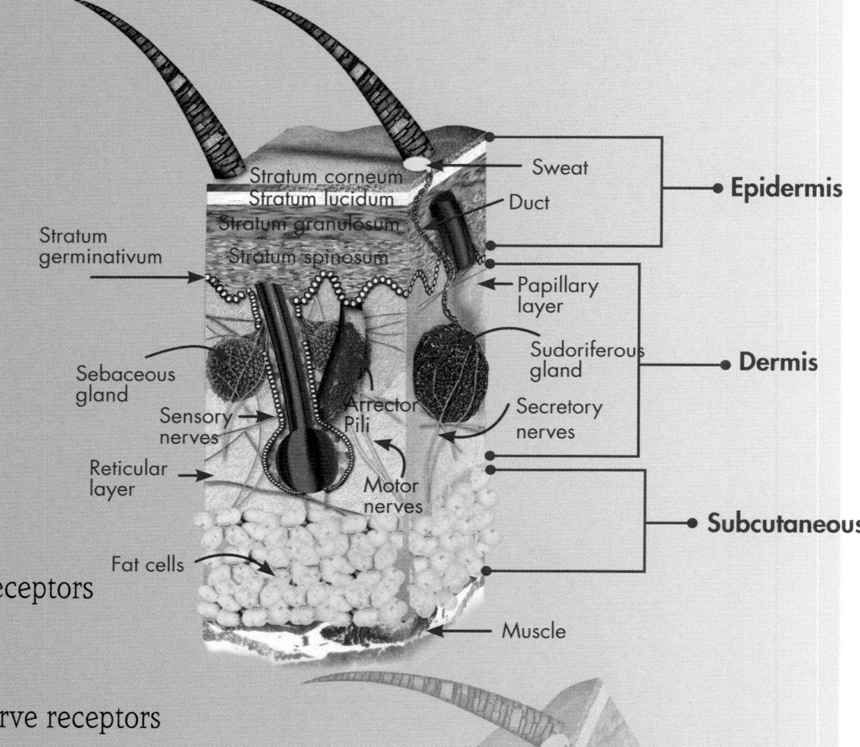


"On an average adult, the amount of skin is about 20 to 22 square feet and weighs around 7 to 10 pounds."

# Skin Differences . . .

***We already learned*** *that there is more melanin in medium to dark skin types (multi-cultural skin) – but are there any other differences we need to be aware of when servicing all the degrees of skin color?*

Yes, there are slight distinctions in the genetic composition of the skin for Caucasian, Asian, African-American and Hispanic individuals.

12

| Caucasian Skin | Asian Skin | African-American Skin | Hispanic Skin |
|---|---|---|---|
| Skin shedding cells contain **no** melanin | Skin shedding cells contain melanin | Skin shedding cells contain melanin | Skin shedding cells contain melanin |
| Skin sheds at an average rate | Skin sheds at an average rate | Skin sheds at a slower rate; more dead skin cell buildup | Skin sheds at an average rate |
| Stratum corneum layer is thinner | Stratum corneum layer is thicker | Stratum corneum layer is thicker | Stratum corneum layer is thicker |
| Skin ages faster | Skin ages slower | Skin ages slower | Skin ages slower |
| Skin burns easily, tans gradually | Skin tans, rarely burns | Skin tans easily | Skin tans well, rarely burns |
| Slower melanin production | Medium melanin production; hyper-pigmentation is common | Faster melanin production; hyper-pigmentation is common | Faster melanin production; hyper-pigmentation is common |
| Varying pore openings; common T-zone appearance | Larger pore openings | Larger pore openings | Varying pore openings; common T-zone appearance |

**Disclaimer:** ***This is a general chart based on a summarized compilation of research; a person's actual skin composition will vary depending on enviornmental conditions, health, heredity and skin-care regimen.***

Knowing the differences will assist in personalizing the skin-care service, applying and marketing the proper skin products as well as offering preservative or corrective treatments.

# Skin Specialty Terminology ...

***These terms** relate to the **medical care professionals or skin-care specialists** within the skin-care industry that dedicate their time and expertise to offer treatments for a skin disorder or disease, or to provide the relaxing effects and preventative results of a facial.*

**Dermatology** (der-ma-tol-ogy) is a **branch within the medical field** that covers the study of skin and the conditions, diseases and disorders affecting the skin.

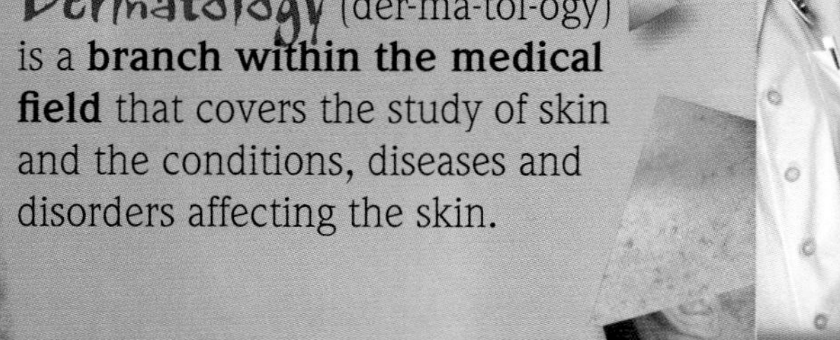

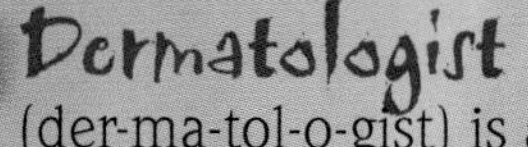

**Dermatologist** (der-ma-tol-o-gist) is a **medical care professional** that is able to diagnose and treat skin conditions, diseases and disorders.

12

**Esthetician** (es-the-ti-cian) is someone who is educated and licensed in the principles of skin and the art of skin-care, providing **facial treatments for the beautification of the skin**.

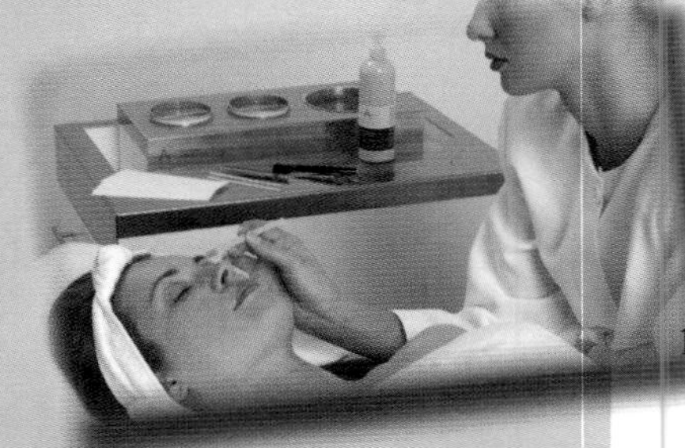
1

**The following terms are common words used within the skin-care industry to describe the duration of a skin condition, disorder or disease.**

**Chronic** (chron-ic) describes a skin disorder that is **long-lasting or recurring**. Examples are acne, rosacea or seborrhea skin conditions.

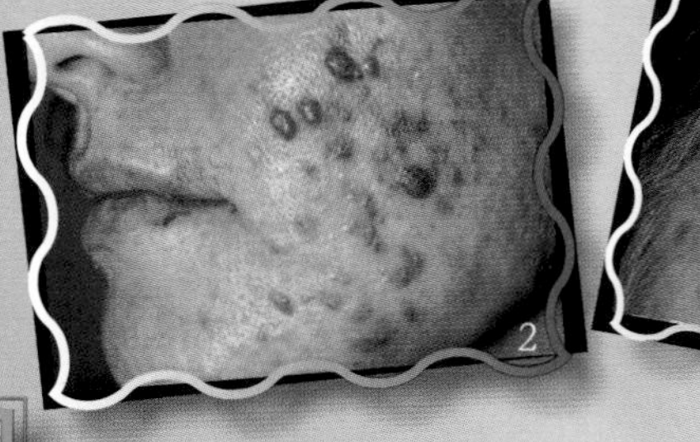
2

3

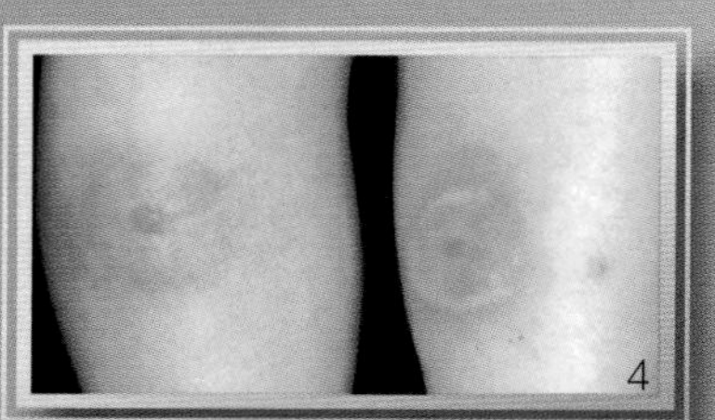
4

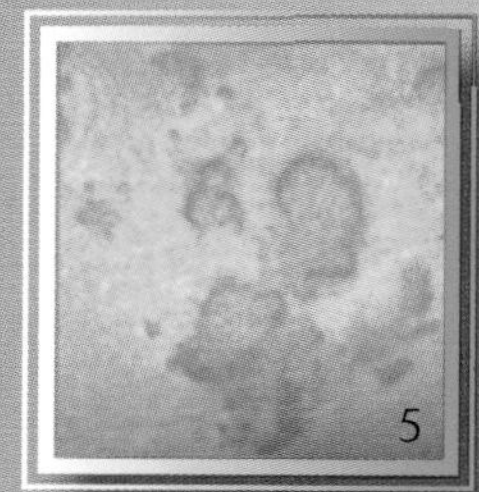
5

**Acute** (a-cute) is when a skin disorder or disease is of **short duration, but severe** and painful. Examples are wheals, herpes simplex or miliaria rubra.

# Conditions of the Skin . . .

*Along with determining the client's skin type, there are other areas of concern that may be present and need to be analyzed as well. A **skin condition** is generally a visual malformation or a deviation from the standard functions of the skin. A daily routine of using the proper skin-care regimen will keep these conditions maintained and under control.*

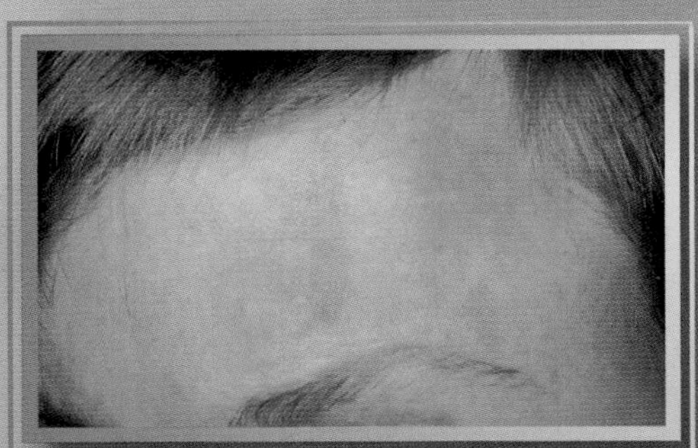

**Sensitive skin** is susceptible to **itching, burning, irritation, or inflammation.** This skin condition is prone to **allergic reactions** to certain products. A **skin product test** is required to check for sensitivity of product. Apply a small amount of product on inside of elbow; check for redness, burning or itching. Avoid products that are strong, fragranced and abrasive.

12

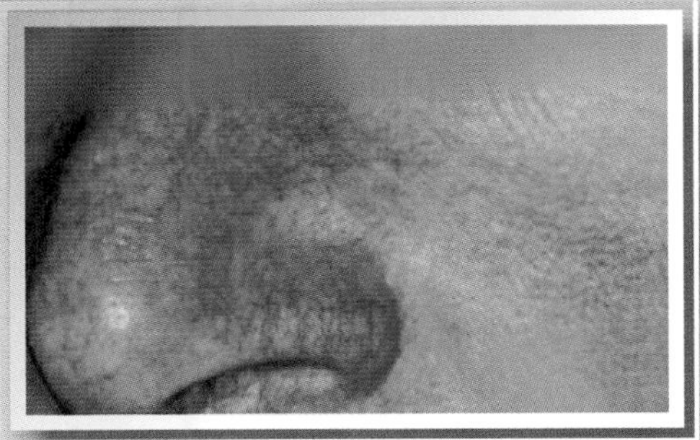

**Couperose** (cou-per-ose) **skin** is characterized by the **dilation of small blood vessels** or **telangiectasia** (tel-an-gi-ec-ta-sia) appearing at the **surface of skin**. The small blood vessels or capillaries are weakened by expanding but not contracting back to normal size therefore appearing more defined and easily seen through the skin. Avoid extreme temperature changes, spicy foods, alcohol and the sun to prevent further inflammation to the skin. Advance stages of this condition are rosacea or acne rosacea.

**Mature skin** is characterized by a **thin, loose and dry** appearance. Everything starts to **slow down with age**, as do the functions of the skin. The sebaceous glands do not produce the same amount of sebum, and collagen and elastin production are slowed, resulting in skin sagging or wrinkling. The blood circulation is slowed, affecting the regeneration of cells, which thins out the epidermal layer. Use anti-aging or hydrating skin products along with facial treatments to promote blood circulation.

**Sun-damaged** or **hyper-pigmented skin** is characterized by **patches of pigmented skin** appearing light to dark brown. Treatments usually consist of mild exfoliation or use of sunscreens to avoid further damage. Refer client to a medical care professional for other intensive skin treatments.

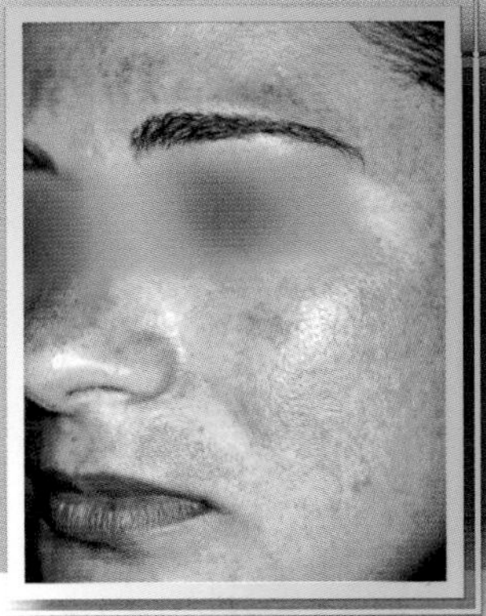

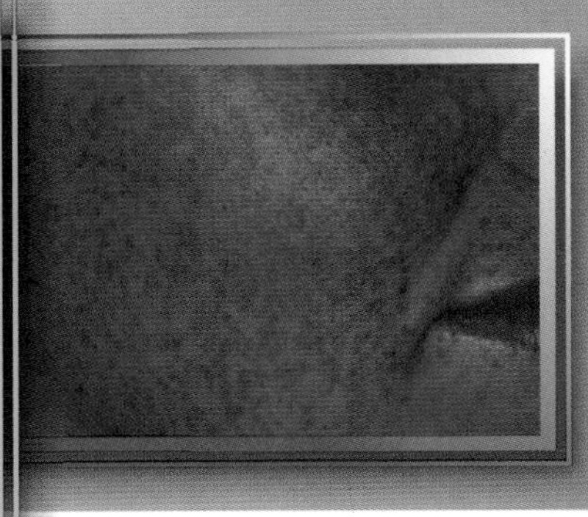

# Lesions of the Skin ...

**Skin lesions** *are* ***structural changes of the skin*** *that vary in size, shape, texture and color. Skin lesions can be caused by genetics or acquired through an allergy, or after contracting a disease.* ***Lesions are grouped into two major categories: primary and secondary.*** *A primary lesion may progress to a secondary lesion due to* ***natural progression or damage*** *to lesion through manipulation such as scratching or picking.*

**Look for this medical symbol when a client needs to be referred to a medical care professional.**

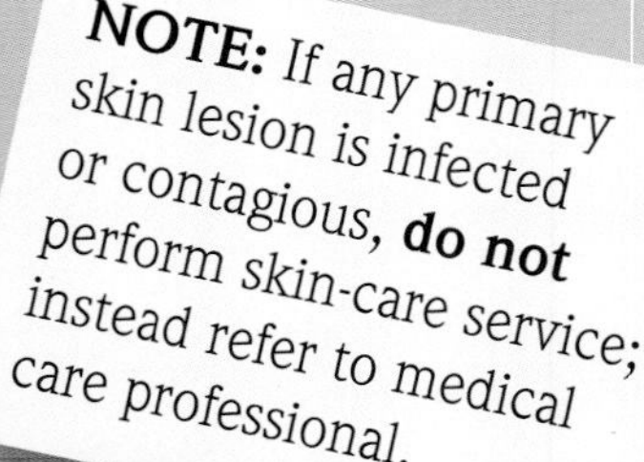
**NOTE:** If any primary skin lesion is infected or contagious, **do not** perform skin-care service; instead refer to medical care professional.

12

## Primary lesions:

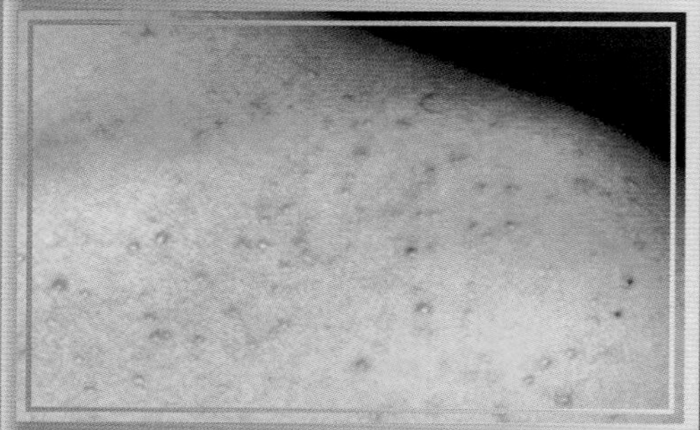

**Papule** (pap-ule) is a **small elevated pimple** usually containing **no** pus.

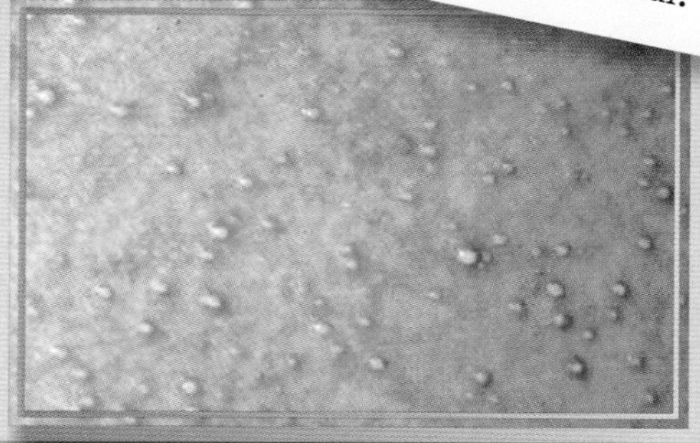

**Pustule** (pus-tule) is an **inflamed elevated pimple** that **contains** pus. The skin surrounding the pimple is red and swollen due to underlying pus which is usually a sign of infection.

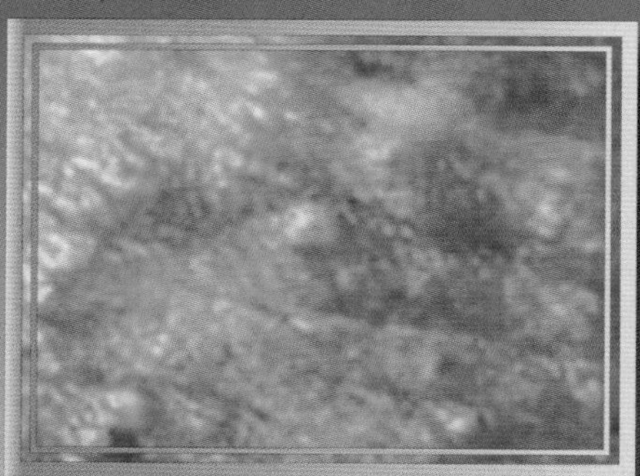

**Tubercle** (too-ber-cle) or **nodules** are **small, prominent solid lumps** enclosed within the epidermis and may extend into the dermis. Nodules generally appear having an inflamed base, which may be painful.

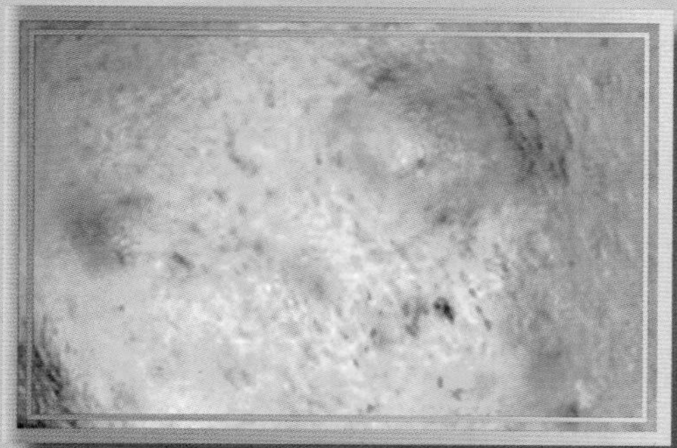

**Tumor** (tu-mor), referred to as a **cyst,** (syst) is an **enclosed sac of abnormal cell mass** consisting of a liquid or semi-solid material of bacteria, white blood cells and dead skin cells. Cysts are either located within the epidermis or penetrate into the dermis and may be benign or malignant. Refer client to a medical care professional.

# Lesions of the Skin ...

## Primary lesions:

**Macule** (mac-ule), or plural form **maculae** (mac-yu-ly) are **flat, small colored spots** appearing in various colors, shapes and sizes depending on body location; examples are freckles, moles or birthmarks.

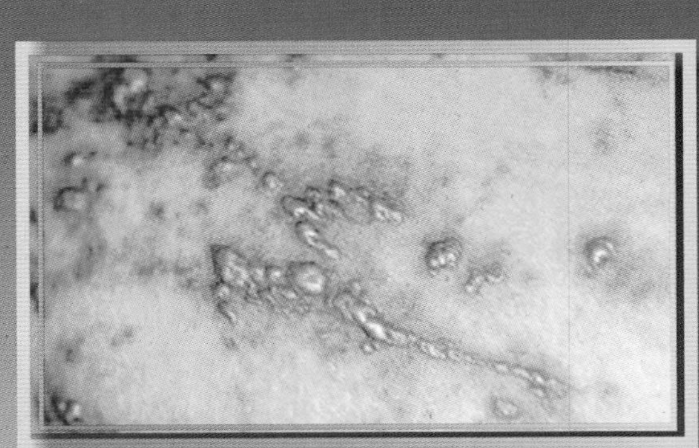

**Vesicle** (ves-i-cle) is an **elevated blister or sac** filled with a clear fluid located within or directly below the epidermis. Example: poison ivy or cold sores.

12

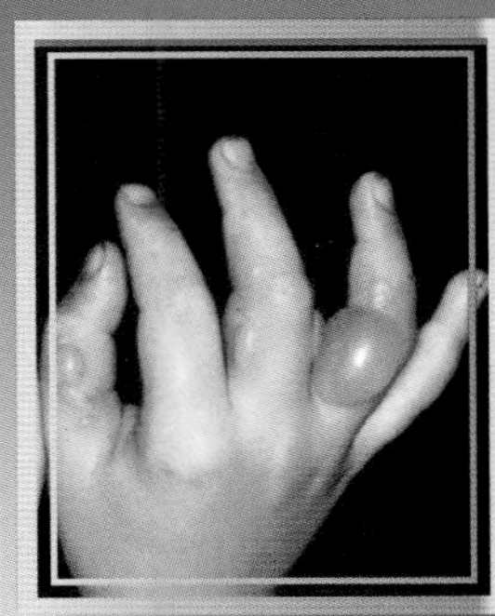

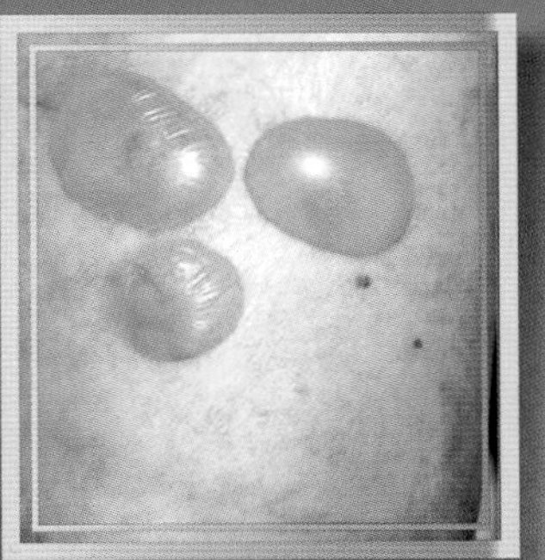

**Bulla** (bull-a), or plural form **bullae** (bull-e) are **vesicles or blisters**, but larger in size.

**Wheal** (wheel) or **hives** is an **itchy swollen mass** that occurs shortly after a mosquito bite or allergic reaction. **Urticaria** (ur-ti-car-e-uh) is the technical term for wheal.

## Some causes for primary lesions are:

**Genetic** – inherited the cells that cause the lesions. Examples: a mole, freckle or hyper-pigmentation.

**Environmental** – extreme temperatures or long-term exposure. Examples: sunburn, frostbite, chapped skin.

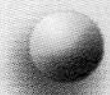

**Allergic** – skin sensitivity to products, food or insects. Examples: hives, rash or blisters.

**Lifestyle** – acquired through injury, body changes (hormonal balance) or healthy living (exercise). Examples: scar, dandruff, abrasions, cancers (tumors or cysts).

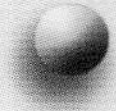

**Bacterial Invasion** – skin infections caused by parasites or viruses. Examples: ringworm, scabies, warts or acne.

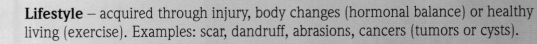

# Lesions of the Skin . . .



A **secondary lesion** exists with the progression of the primary lesion. The **primary lesion advances** into the later stages of development as a result of healing, irritation or infection.

## Secondary lesions:

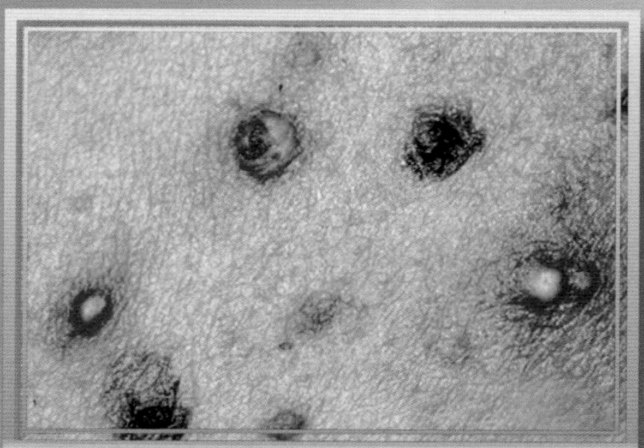

**Crust**, commonly known as a **scab** is the **dried and hardened accumulation of blood, sebum or pus** that forms over an injury to the skin. This generally occurs through the body's natural healing process. The technical term for scab is **cicatrix** (ci-ca-trix).

**Scale** is the **accumulation of hardened dead skin cells** that shed from the epidermal layer. Some common conditions that result in a scaly appearance are dandruff, psoriasis or fungal infections.

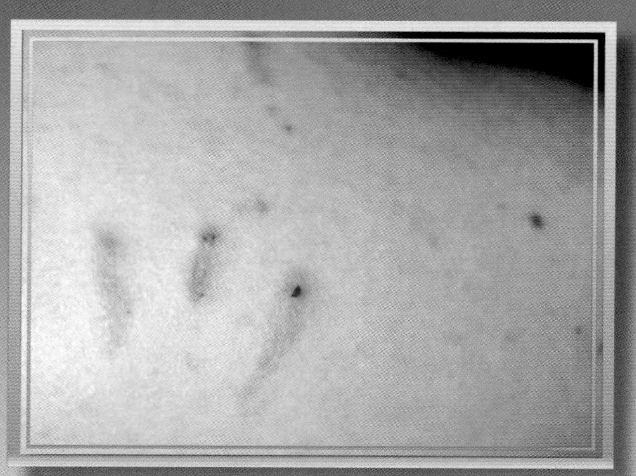

**Excoriation** (ex-co-ri-a-tion) occurs through the **scraping or scratching** of the epidermal layer or skin's surface. This can occur with an existing sore being scratched, irritating the existing injury.

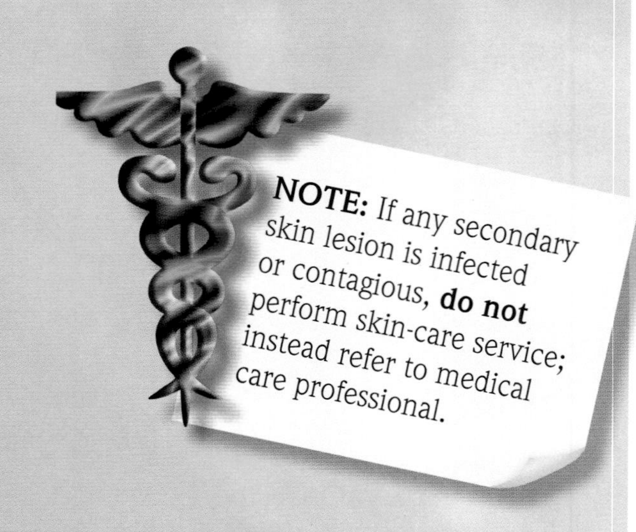

**NOTE:** If any secondary skin lesion is infected or contagious, **do not** perform skin-care service; instead refer to medical care professional.

# Lesions of the Skin . . .

## Secondary lesions:

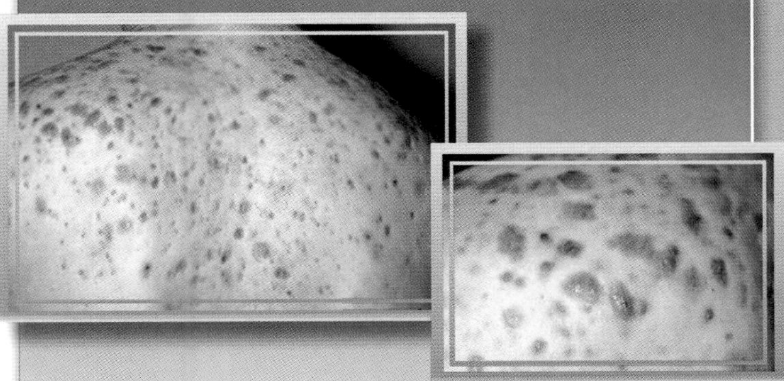

**Scar** is a **flat or raised discolored mark** on the skin that appears with the healing of an injury or disorder. Examples: acne, eczema or sebaceous cysts.

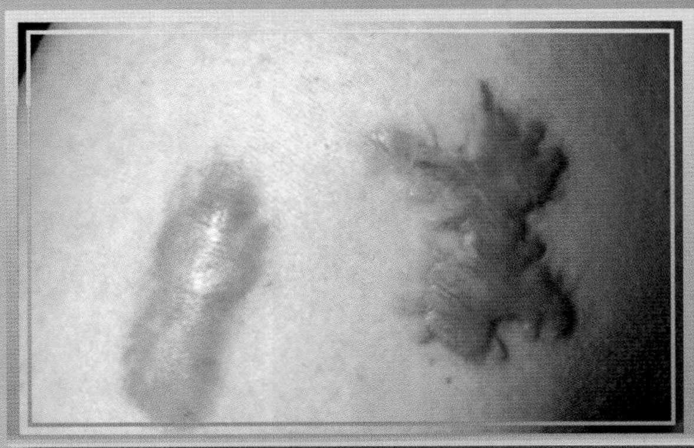

**Keloid** (ke-loid) is a **thick, slightly raised scar** resulting from excessive skin growth.

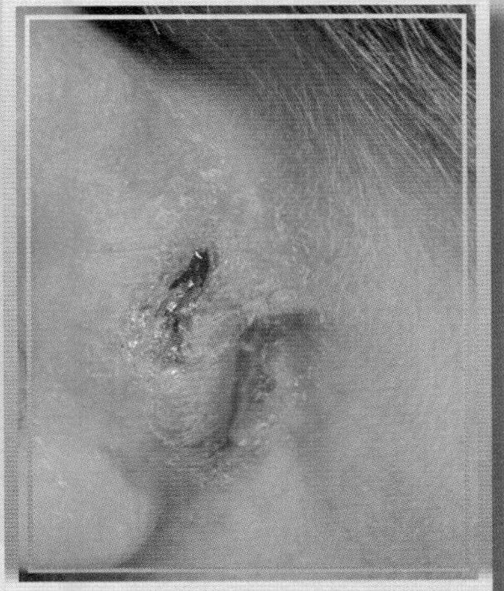

**Fissure** is an **opening or crack** in the skin that may penetrate down into the dermal layer. This typically happens through environmental over-exposures of cold, wind or water.

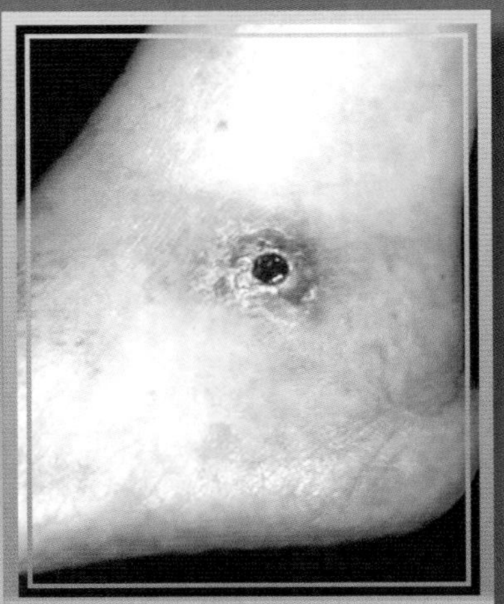

**Ulcer** (ul-cer) is a **skin opening with depth due to loss of epidermis and partial dermis;** accompanied by pus if infection occurs.

Certain skin lesions such as moles or freckles are a **normal result** of everyday life occurrences. Some of these lesions can **be treated surgically** while others simply require the **offending agent (insect) to be removed** in order to heal the lesion. Then there are the lesions caused by infection that need **medication to fight off the bacterial invasion.** Regardless of whether a lesion is preventable or not, as a cosmetologist, you will need to be able to **recognize each of these lesions** in order to offer the best possible treatments and products or refer the client to a medical care professional.

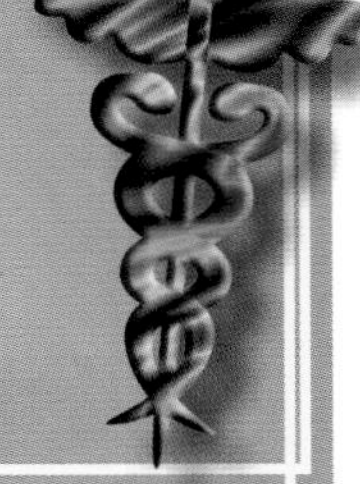

*If the function of the oil glands become either over- or under-active, certain disorders may result, causing problematic skin.*

## Sebaceous gland disorders:

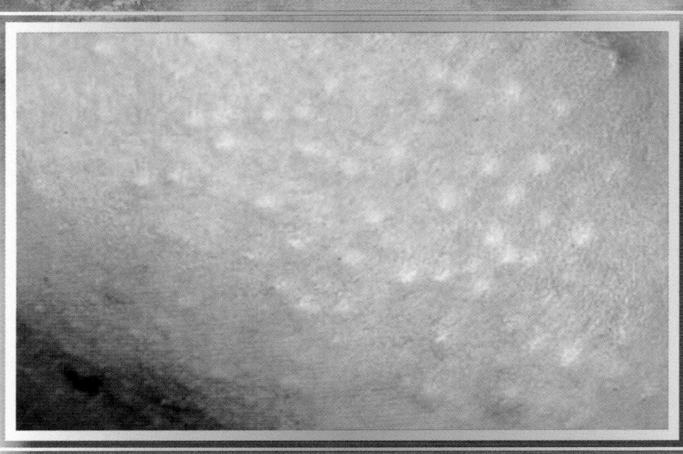

**Milia** (mil-ee-uh), or singular form **milium** (mil-e-um), referred to as **whiteheads** are small, white nodules that are **enclosed** within the epidermis. They are caused by hardened sebum and may appear on face and chest.

**Comedones** (com-a-dones) or singular form **open comedo** (com-a-do), referred to as **blackheads**, which are open skin lesions containing hardened sebum. The **open pore** appears black due to being clogged with sebum and bacteria.

# Disorders of the Skin . . .

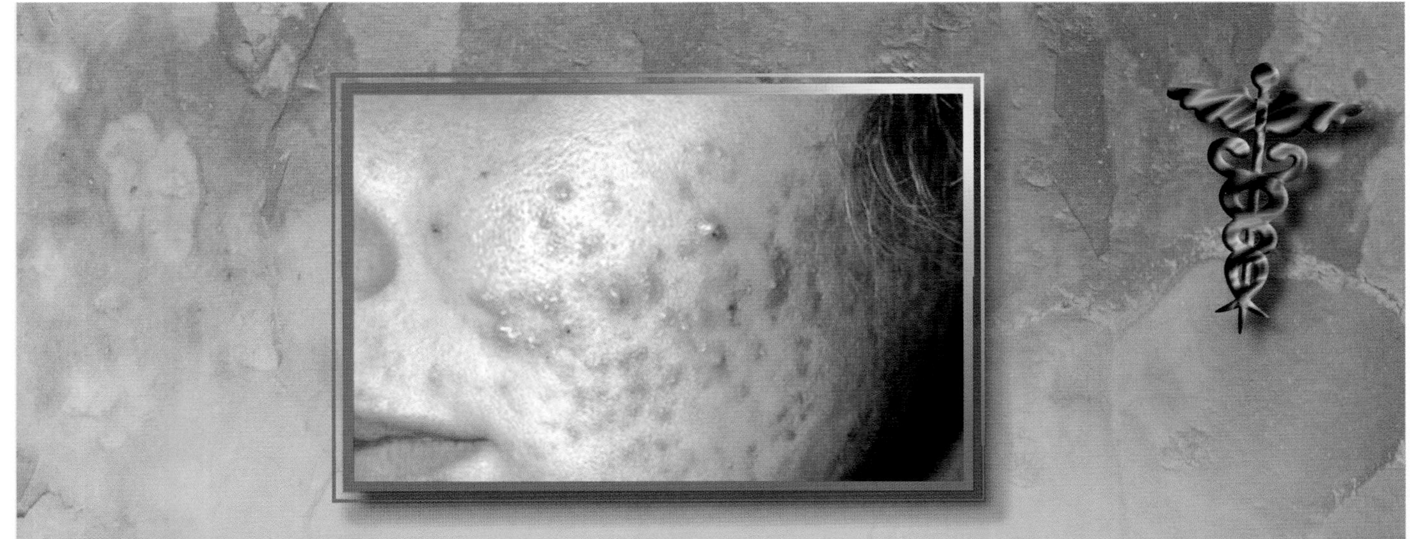

**Acne** (ac-nee) or **acne vulgaris** (vul-ga-ris) is the outcome of whiteheads, blackheads and/or papules that become irritated and lead to infection. The sebaceous glands over-produce an excess of sebum that mixes with a bacteria referred to as **propionibacterium** (pro-pi-on-i-bac-te-ri-um). This causes the opening of the hair follicles to become blocked resulting in an eruption of **pustules/ pimples** that contain pus and generally will have a red and swollen appearance. Refer client to a medical care professional. Some contributing factors for acne are: stress, hormonal changes, heredity, hygienic living or inadequate skin-care.

12

**Cystic** (cys-tic) **acne** is a type of acne that advances into **enlarged solid or semi-solid lumps** located within the hair follicle. The hair follicle expands and ruptures leaking a sebaceous matter consisting of sebum, pus, dead skin and white blood cells into the surrounding skin. This results in deep tumors or cysts causing pain and possible scarring of skin tissue. Refer client to a medical care professional.

Sebaceous gland disorders:

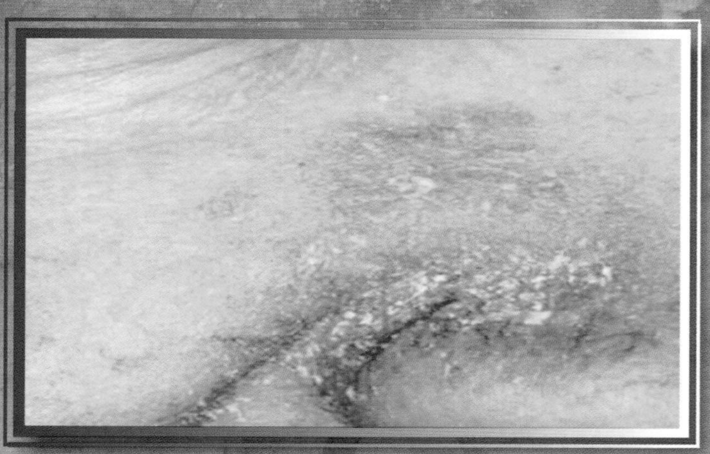

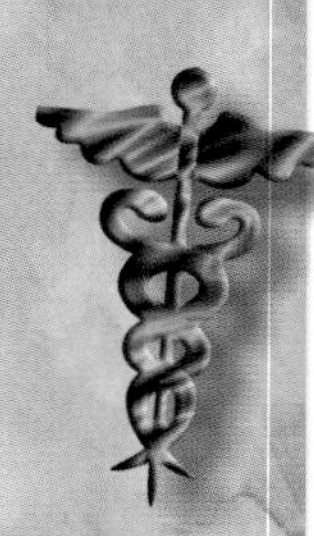

12

**Seborrhea** (seb-or-rhe-a) **Dermatitis** (der-ma-ti-tis) is associated with a chronic inflammation of the sebaceous glands producing **greasy or dry, off-white scales or patches** on the skin. The skin may appear red and feel itchy. This condition may be present on face, scalp or other areas of body. In infants, it is known as **cradle cap**. Refer client to a medical care professional.

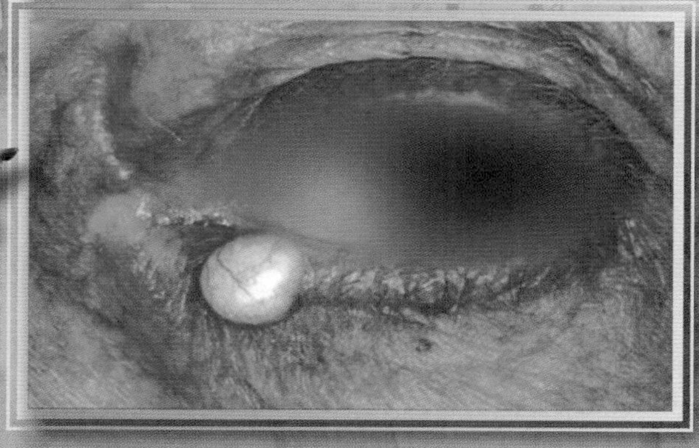

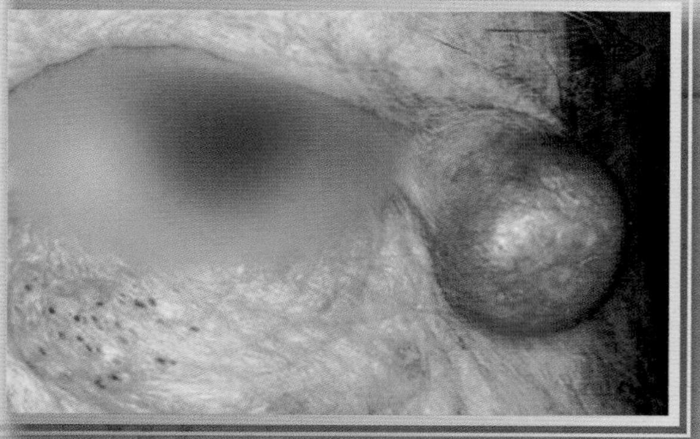

**Steatoma** (ste-a-to-ma) **or sebaceous** (se-ba-ceous) **cyst** occurs when a sebaceous gland is blocked creating a **sebum-filled sac or fatty tumor** within the skin. This may appear on any area of the face or body and varies in size from either small or large, like an orange. Refer client to a medical care professional.

**Asteatosis** (a-ste-a-to-sis) is characterized by **dry, scaly patches** on the skin due to **under-active sebaceous glands** or **long-term exposure to extreme cold temperatures**. This skin disorder is common with elderly people or clients with jobs related to the outside elements.

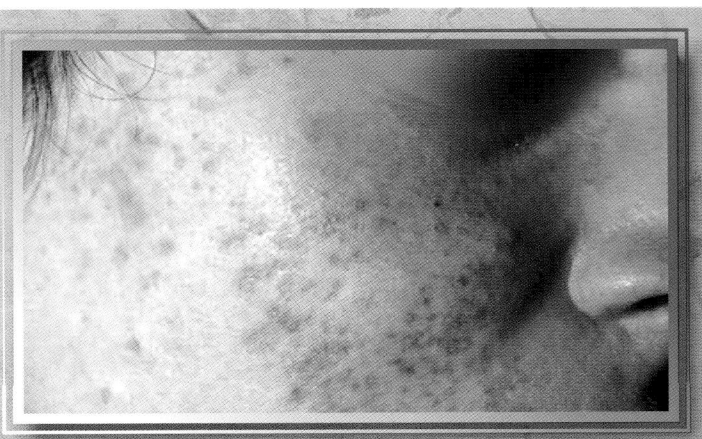

**Rosacea** (ro-za-she-a) is a chronic skin disorder with inflamed areas of the face appearing mostly on nose and cheeks. It is characterized by **telangiectasia** (tel-an-gi-ec-ta-sia) or over-dilation of the tiny blood vessels, which produces a **flushing, swollen and broken blood vessel appearance** to the face.

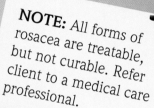

**NOTE:** All forms of rosacea are treatable, but not curable. Refer client to a medical care professional.



## Severe stages of rosacea are:

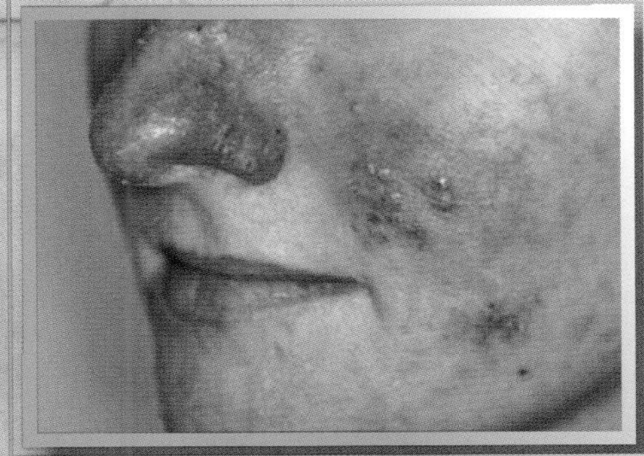

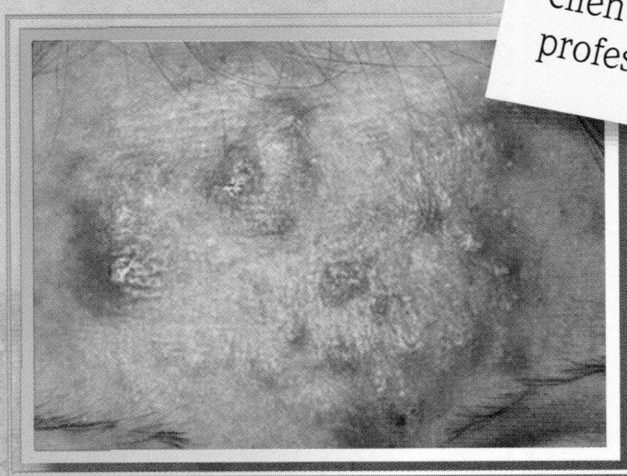

**Acne Rosacea** is an advanced condition of rosacea producing papules and pustules that may contain pus. This skin disorder is sensitive, painful (burning sensation) and may be aggravated by certain foods (spicy), extreme temperature changes, nicotine and alcoholic beverages.

**Rhinophyma** (rhy-no-fee-ma) **Rosacea** (bulbous) is the advanced stage of acne rosacea producing an enlarged nose and puffy upper cheek area. This skin disorder is most common in adult men and disfigures the face due to the enlarged bumps.

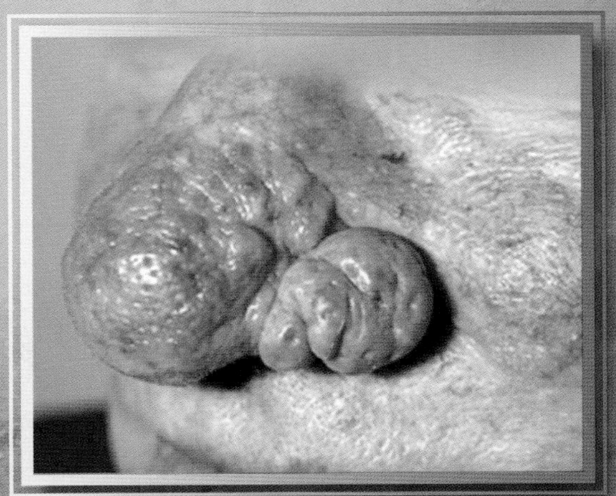

# Disorders of the Skin . . .

## Inflammations of the skin:

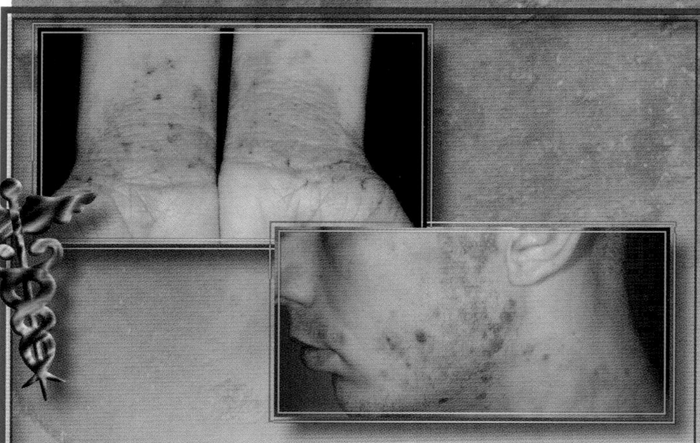

**Dermatitis Venenata** (ven-e-na-ta) or **contact dermatitis** is caused by the **skin's sensitivity to the exposure or use of a certain product** producing an **allergic reaction.** It is characterized by a rash, inflammation or blisters and is **non-contagious.** Discontinue use of product and refer client a medical care professional.

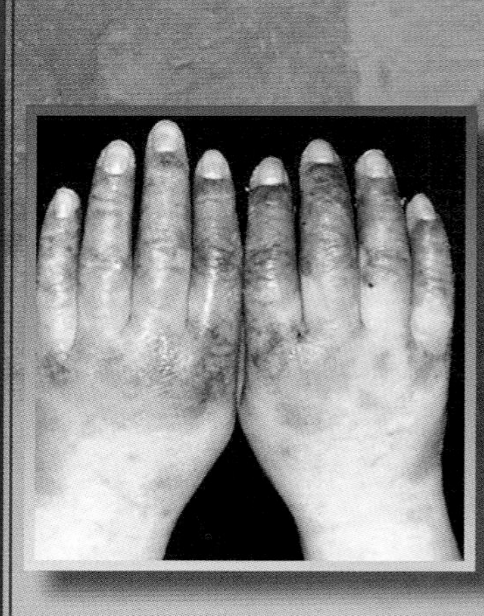

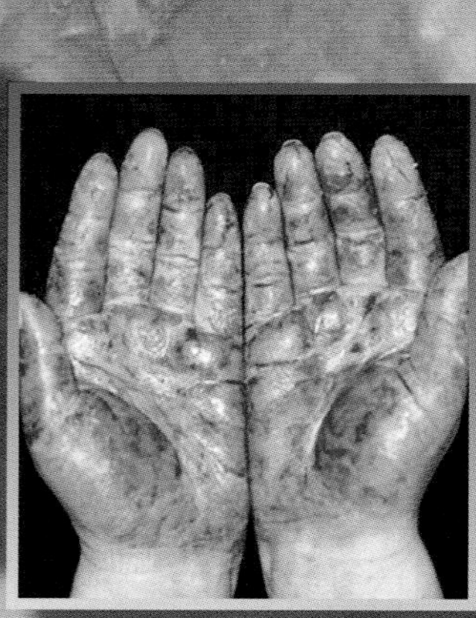

**Eczema** (ek-ze-ma) is an inflammatory **non-contagious** skin disorder with an appearance of **blisters, papules or scales.** It produces a burning and itching sensation and appears on various areas of the body. Refer client to a medical care professional.

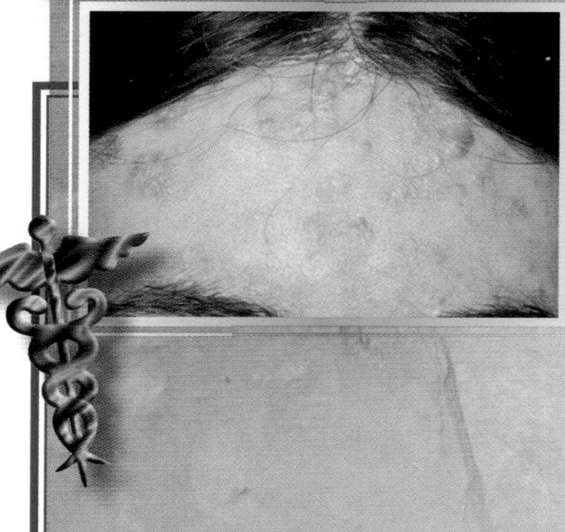

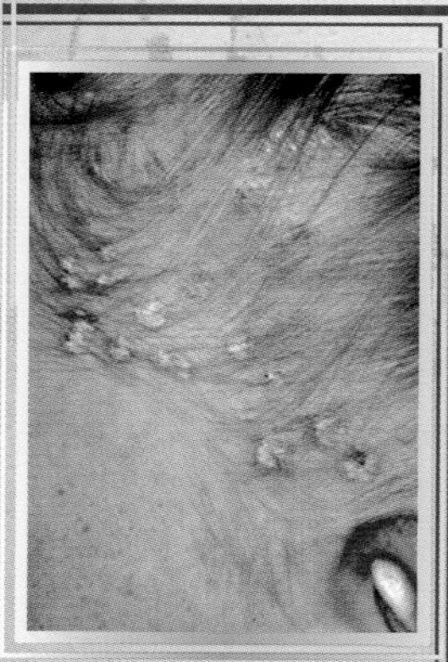

**Psoriasis** (so-ri-a-sis) is a chronic **non-contagious** skin disorder that appears as **rough, dry, red patches covered with silvery-white scales or crusts** and is caused by an over-production of the stratum corneum skin cells. It typically is found on the scalp, elbows or knees and usually is inherited. Refer client to a medical care professional.

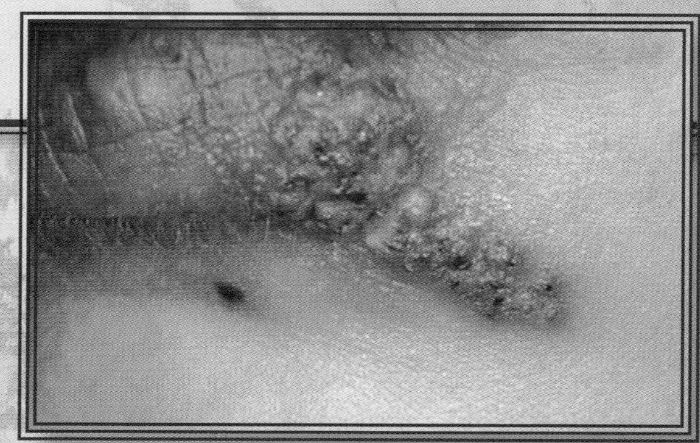

**Herpes Simplex** (her-peez sim-plex), commonly know as **fever blister or cold sores** is a **contagious** skin disorder associated with a viral infection. It is characterized as an eruption of a **vesicle or group of vesicles** situated on an inflamed base producing a painful, burning sensation. The blisters are located around the lips, nostrils or eye area. Refer client to a medical care professional.

# Disorders of the Skin . . .

*If the function of the sweat glands becomes either over- or under-active, certain disorders may result, causing problematic skin.*

## Sudoriferous gland disorders:

**Bromhidrosis** (brom-hi-dro-sis) is **foul-smelling body odor** caused from increased perspiring at underarms or feet.

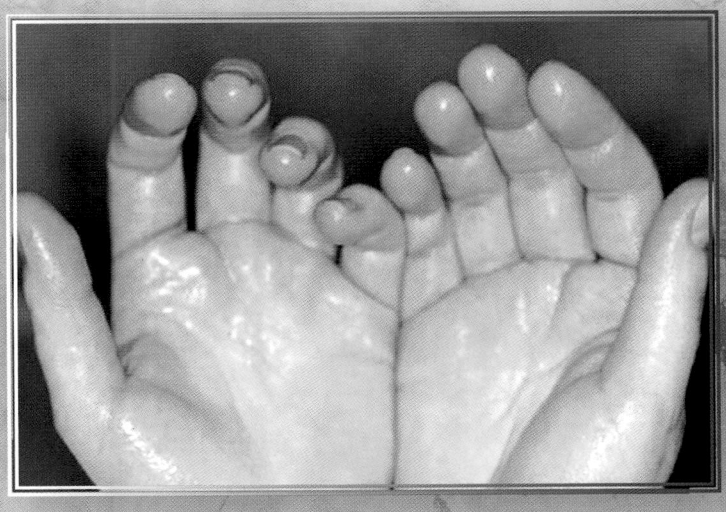

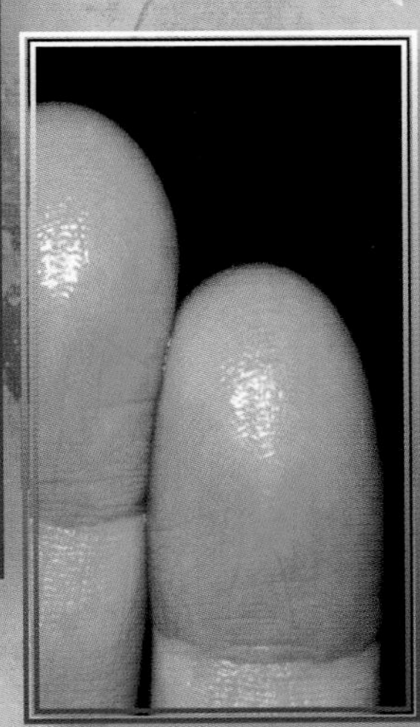

**Hyperhidrosis** (hy-per-hi-dro-sis) is excessive perspiration, an **unusual increase of sweating** occurring on any area of body. Refer to a medical care professional.

**Anhidrosis** (an-hi-dro-sis) is a condition caused by the **body's inability to perspire/sweat**. The body does not cool itself when hot, therefore is very susceptible to overheating. Refer to a medical care professional.

**Miliaria rubra** (mil-i-a-ria ru-bra), commonly known as **prickly heat** is an **acute sudoriferous gland disorder** appearing as small red papules (rash) caused by exposure to high heat or humidity.

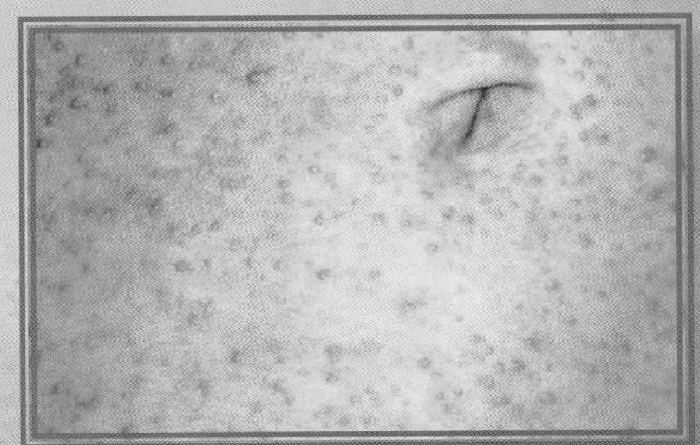

12

# Pigmentations of the Skin . . .

*Changes in skin color are partly influenced by either the* ***increase or decrease of melanin*** *or pigment production, which is greatly dependent upon physical or environmental factors. The* ***physical factors*** *are hereditary or hormonal changes and the* ***environmental factors*** *are either long-term exposure to ultraviolet rays, whether that would be the sun or tanning bed or an extreme cold temperature.*

1

**Albinism** (al-bi-niz-em) is a rare, inherited skin disorder characterized by **total or partial lack of melanin** throughout the body. The **skin and hair are white**, and the eyes are pink/red. An albino has a hypersensitivity to light and the sun and will need to protect him or herself during daylight hours.

12

**Leukoderma** (loo-ko-der-ma) occurs through either a congenital skin disorder or by frequent sun exposure producing **patches of skin that are devoid of pigment or melanin.**

## The two types of leukoderma are:

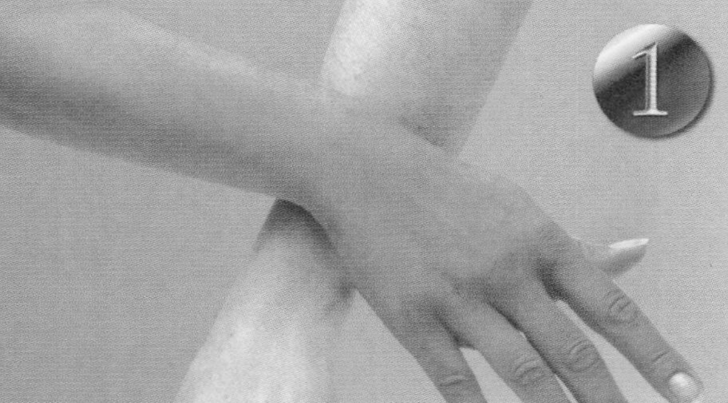

1. **Tan** is when the **pigmentation of the skin is accelerated** due to exposure of the sun's ultraviolet rays or tanning beds. The increased pigmentation creates a **browning effect on the skin** thus providing protection from the harmful effects of the sun.

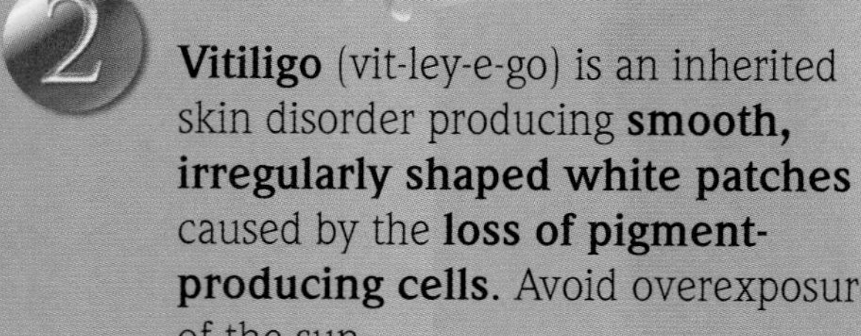

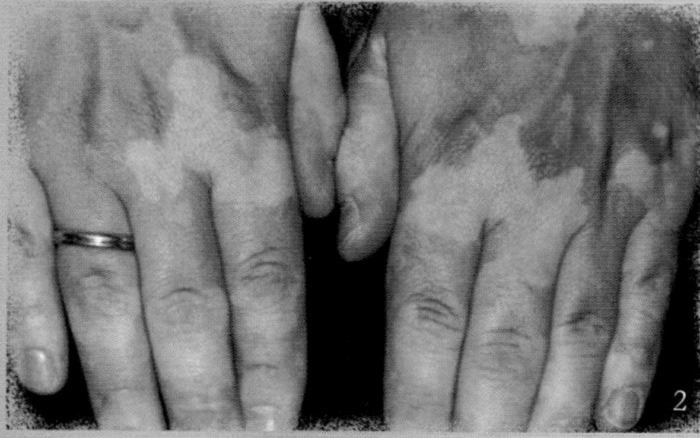

2

2. **Vitiligo** (vit-ley-e-go) is an inherited skin disorder producing **smooth, irregularly shaped white patches** caused by the **loss of pigment-producing cells.** Avoid overexposure of the sun.

# Pigmentations of the Skin ...

**Chloasma** (kloh-as-mah), commonly known as **liver spots or moth patches,** consists of **light to dark brown spots** scattered on hands, arms or face. These spots may occur through frequent sun exposure, hereditary or hormonal changes such as pregnancy.

**Lentigines** (len-tij-i-nes) is the technical term used for **freckles**, which are **flat, small colored spots** in various colors, shapes and sizes. Generally freckles will appear on the face or other parts of the body, and result from a combination of physical and environmental factors.

**Nevus** (ne-vus) or **birthmark** is characterized as either a **raised or non-raised, small or large irregularly shaped mark or stain** on the skin. It can appear in **various shades of brown or as reddish-purple** due to dilation of surface blood vessels. Birthmarks are located on any area of the body and must be constantly monitored for any changes to shape, texture, size and color. If a change occurs, advise client to see a medical care professional.

12

# Abnormal Growths of the Skin . . .

*An excessive or abnormal growth of the skin is referred to as* ***hypertrophy*** *(hy-per-tro-phy). The skin growths listed are generally benign, but must routinely be monitored for any changes in shape, texture, size and color. If a change occurs, advise client to see a medical care professional.*

12

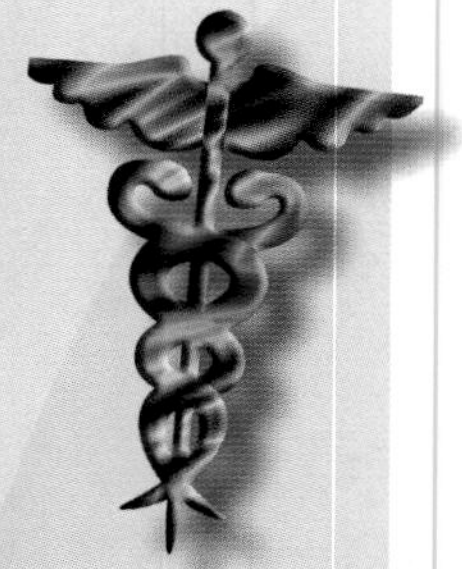

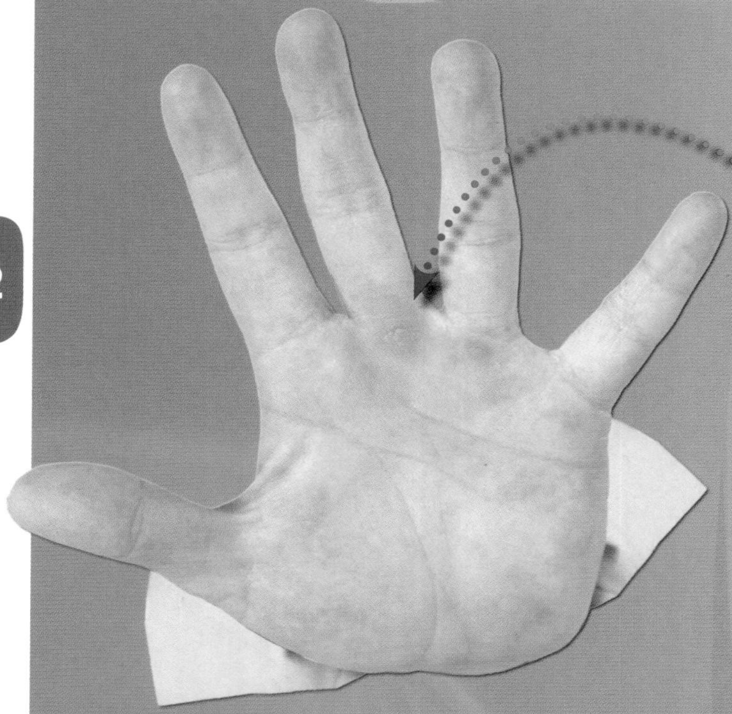

**Keratoma** (ker-a-to-ma), commonly known as a **callus or tyloma** (ty-lo-ma) is a **thickened or hardened area of skin** caused by friction, continual rubbing or pressure over the same part of skin. For callus removal, recommend the client see a medical care professional.

1

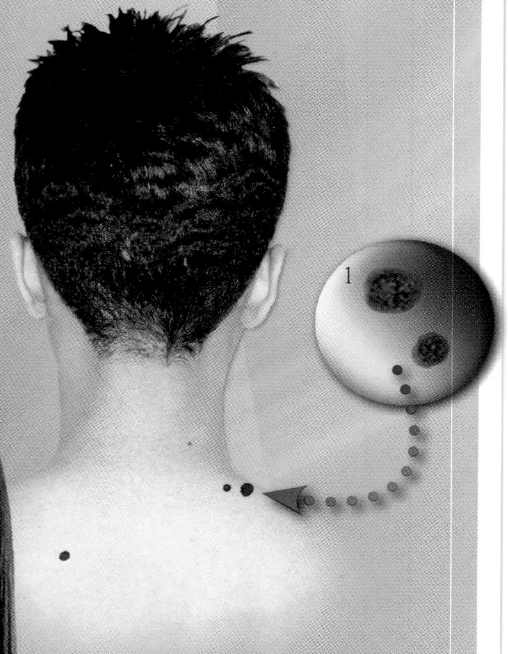

**Mole** is a **small, flat or raised pigmented spot** on the surface of the skin, ranging from light to dark brown. A mole can appear on any part of the body, but must be checked for any changes in shape, texture, size and color.

**NOTE:** If a change occurs or hair grows from the mole, **DO NOT remove**; instead see a medical care professional.

# Abnormal Growths of the Skin ...

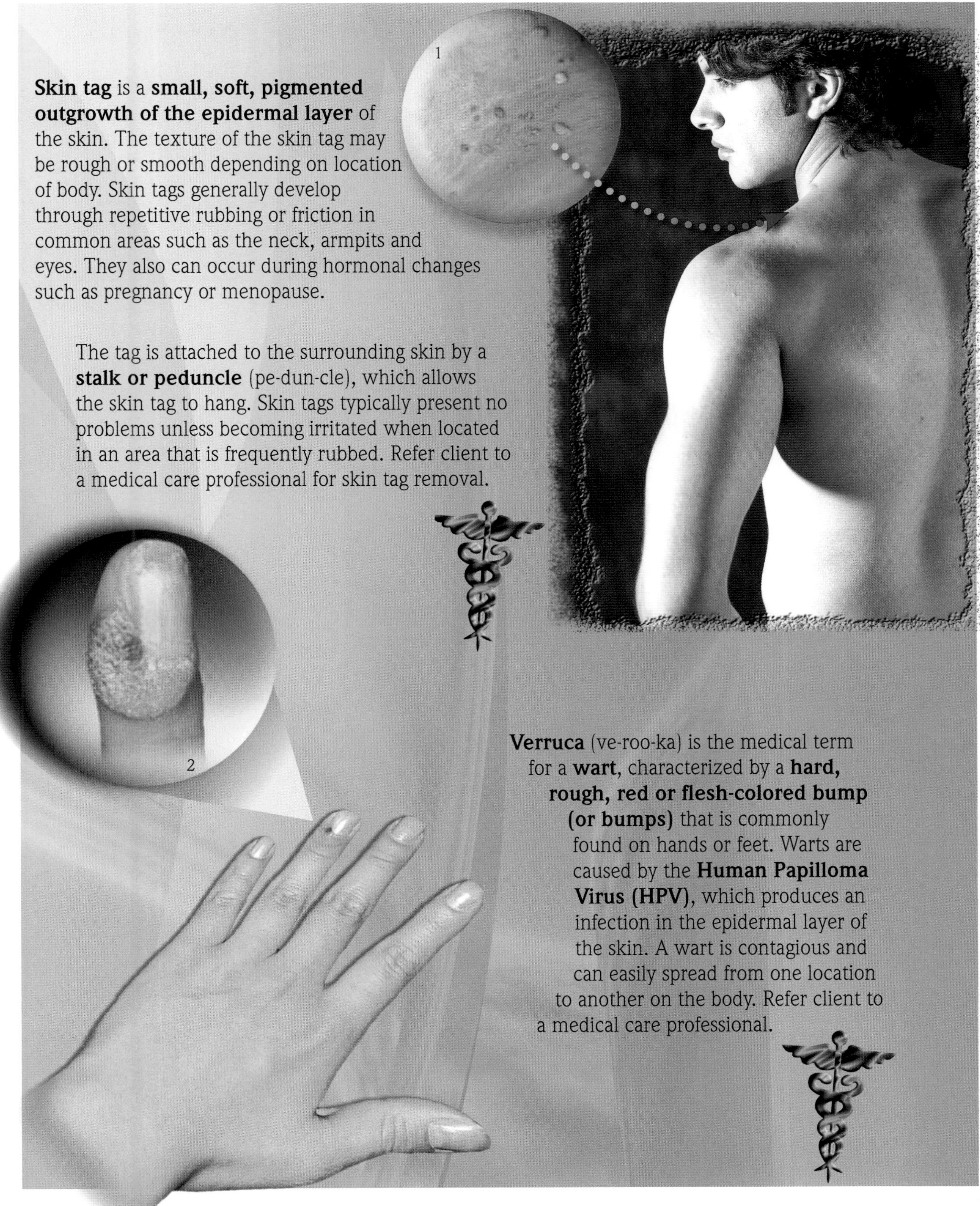

**Skin tag** is a **small, soft, pigmented outgrowth of the epidermal layer** of the skin. The texture of the skin tag may be rough or smooth depending on location of body. Skin tags generally develop through repetitive rubbing or friction in common areas such as the neck, armpits and eyes. They also can occur during hormonal changes such as pregnancy or menopause.

The tag is attached to the surrounding skin by a **stalk or peduncle** (pe-dun-cle), which allows the skin tag to hang. Skin tags typically present no problems unless becoming irritated when located in an area that is frequently rubbed. Refer client to a medical care professional for skin tag removal.

1

2

**Verruca** (ve-roo-ka) is the medical term for a **wart**, characterized by a **hard, rough, red or flesh-colored bump (or bumps)** that is commonly found on hands or feet. Warts are caused by the **Human Papilloma Virus (HPV)**, which produces an infection in the epidermal layer of the skin. A wart is contagious and can easily spread from one location to another on the body. Refer client to a medical care professional.

12

# Types of Skin Cancer . . .

**Skin cancer** *occurs with the* ***production of malignant cells*** *found in the epidermal or dermal layers of the skin. The primary reason for skin cancer is believed to be overexposure to ultraviolet light rays, whether from the sun or tanning beds. Depending on level of severity and the skin cell location, there are three* ***types of skin cancers.***

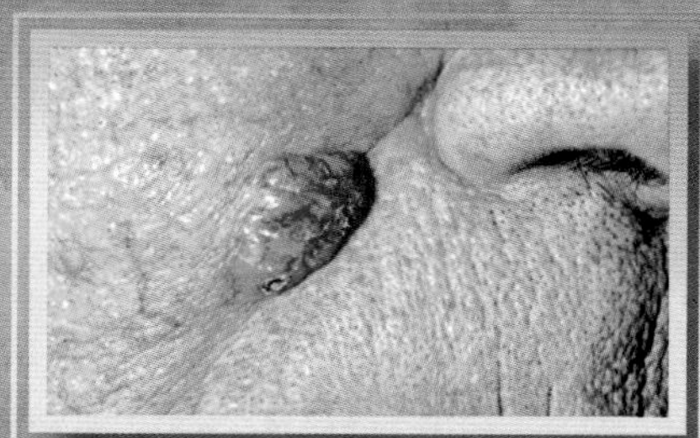
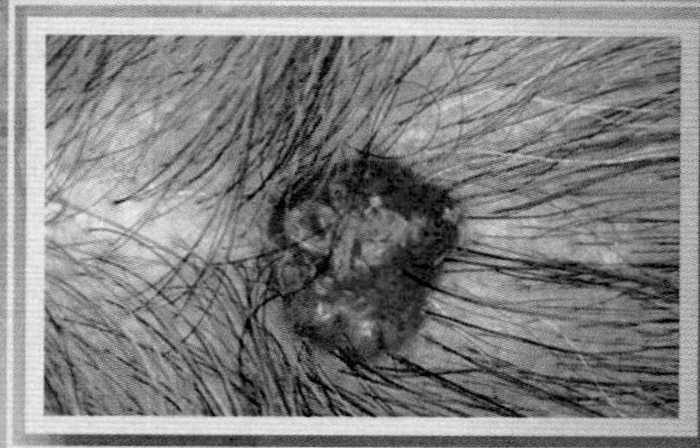
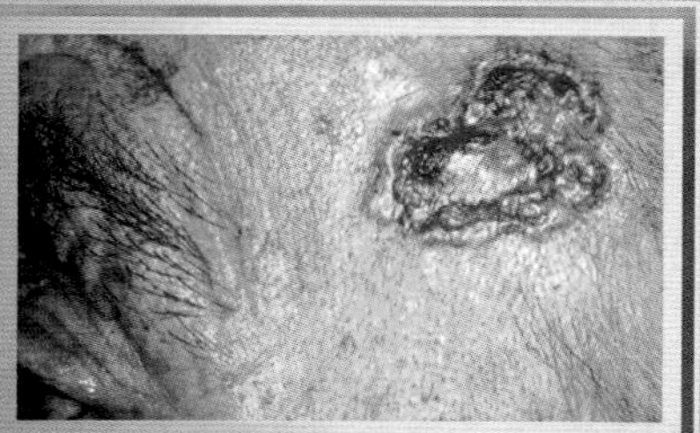

12

**Basal cell carcinoma** (car-ci-no-ma) is a non-melanoma type, the most common and mildest form, affecting the **basal (round) cells** located in the stratum germinativum layer. It is characterized either as a **small red bump with a surface appearance of blood vessels or a "pearly" nodule with a rough texture**. These cells grow slowly and therefore usually **never metastasize** (me-tas-ta-size) or spread rapidly.

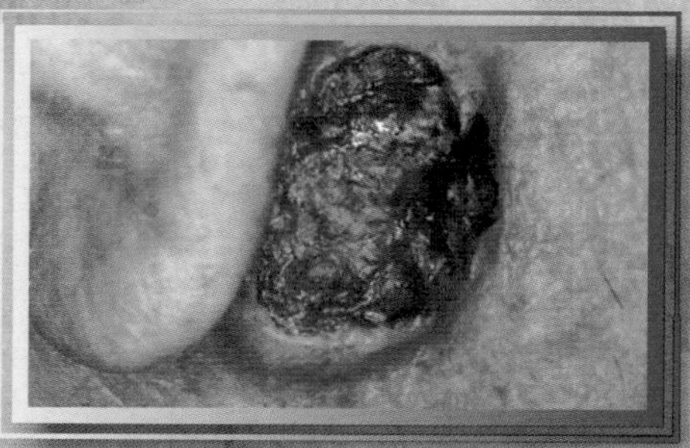
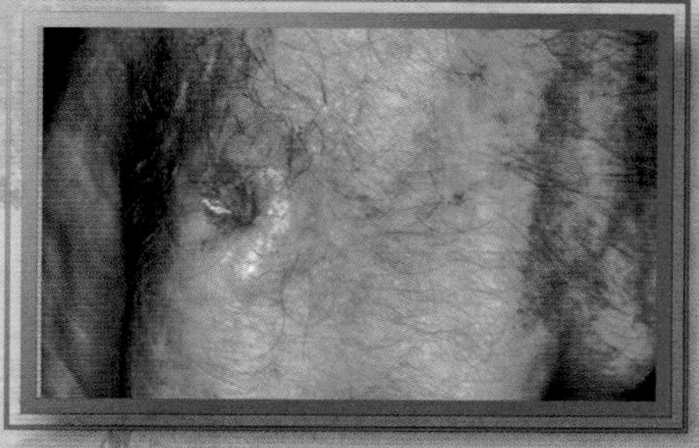

**Squamous** (squa-mous) **cell carcinoma** is also non-melanoma type and affects the **scale-like hardened cells** located in the stratum corneum layer of the epidermis. It has an appearance of **enlarged red nodules and a rough texture**. The squamous cells **metastasize quickly** therefore spreading to other areas of the body.

# Types of Skin Cancer . . .

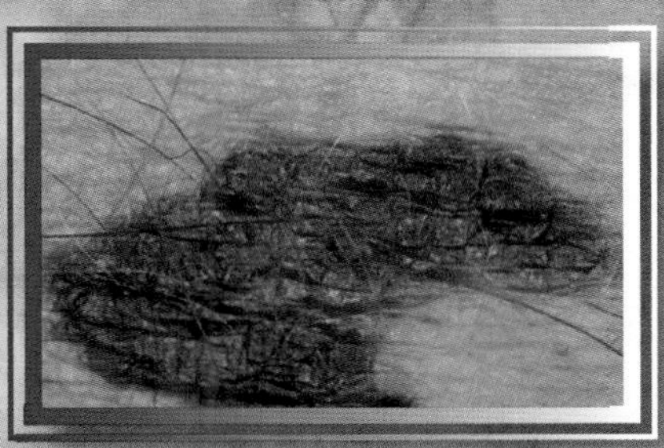

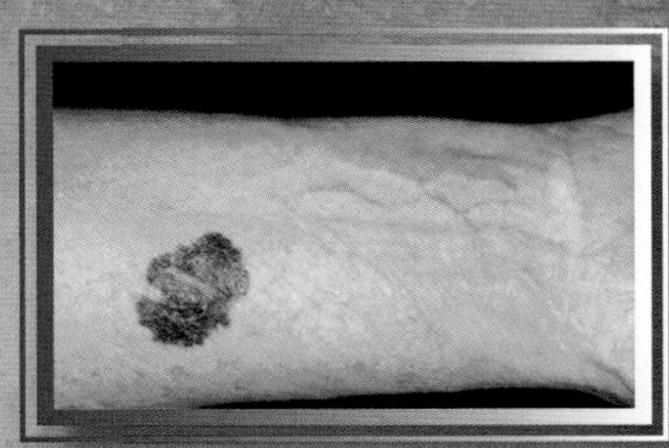

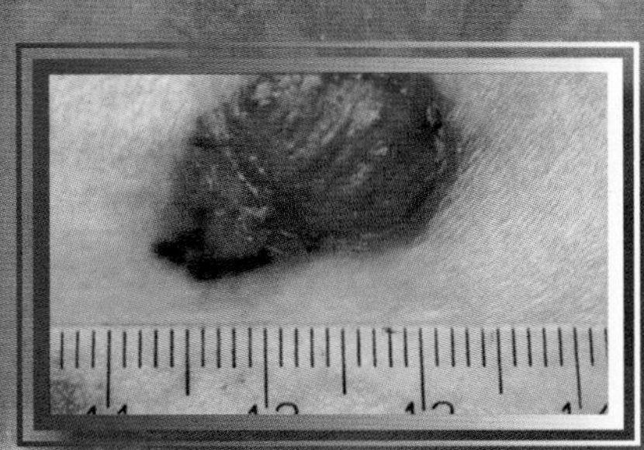

**Malignant melanoma** (ma-lig-nant mel-a-no-ma) is the most dangerous form of skin cancer appearing as **dark brown or black spots or lesions with an uneven shape and/or texture**. These cells are created by the **pigment-producing cells** located in the stratum germinativum and papillary layers of the skin. It may begin as a common skin lesion or mole, but through a change in shape and/or color becomes a concern and referral to a medical care professional.

12

Early detection is a key factor and important in finding a **faster cure** for all types of skin cancer. As a cosmetologist it is important for you to be able to recognize and look for the signs of any changes that occur in the abnormal growths of the skin.

**NOTE:** We never diagnose or treat the skin disorder or disease, but **suggest** that the client see a medical care professional.

**Follow the A, B, C, and D's of checking for changes that might occur in abnormal growths of the skin.**

**A- Asymmetry:** Does half of the skin growth look like the other half?

**B- Border:** Are the edges of the skin growth irregular, jagged or not smooth?

**C- Color:** Is the color varied throughout skin growth in shades of brown, black, red, blue or white?

**D- Diameter:** Is the circumference of the skin growth sizeable – greater than 0.24 inches (.60 cm) – and/or changes in symptoms, such as itching or bleeding?

"For more information, go to The Skin Cancer Foundation at www.skincancer.org, or American Cancer Society at www.cancer.org."

*All the skin diseases associated with plant or animal parasites are extremely contagious. **DO NOT** service client, but refer to a medical care professional.*

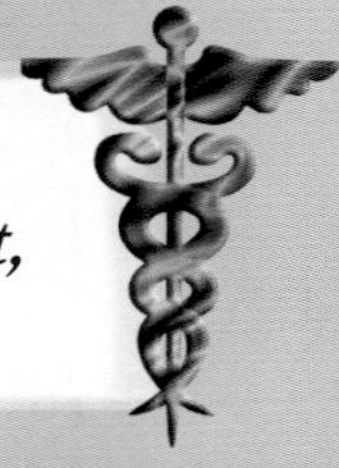

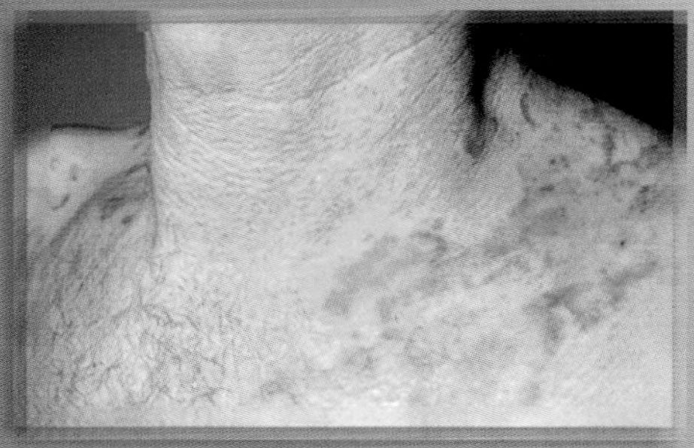

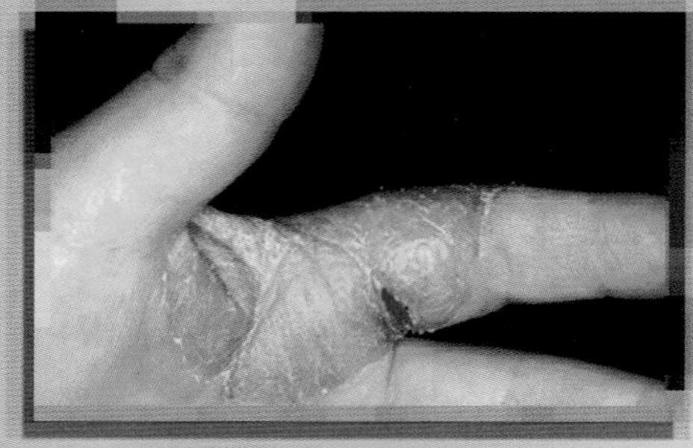

12

**Ringworm** is a contagious disease caused by a **fungus** (plant parasite). The technical term for ringworm is **tinea** (tin-ee-ah) and is characterized by a **scaly red patch or ring** that can be found on any area of the body.

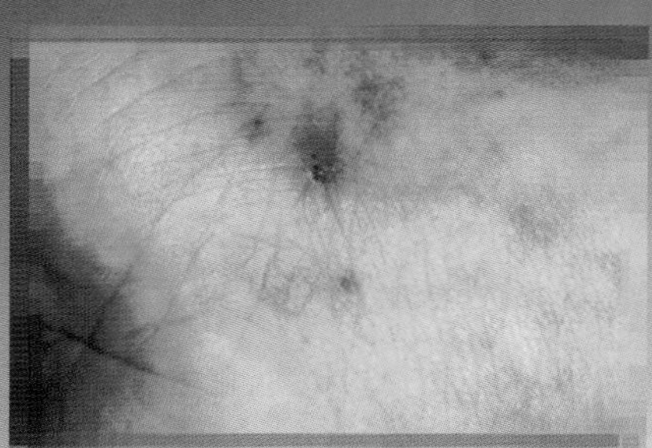

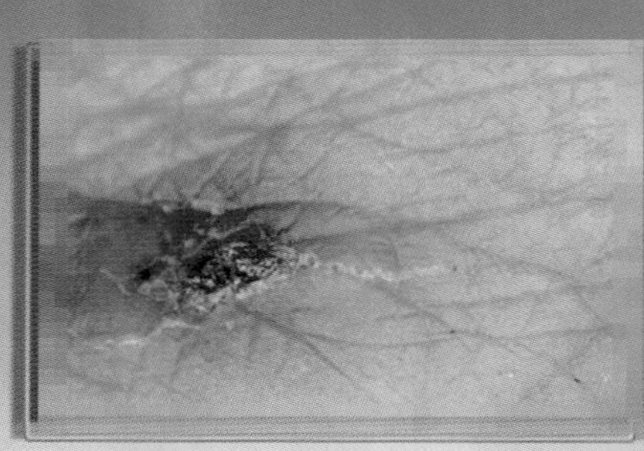

**NOTE:** Both ringworm and scabies are discussed in Chapters 3 and 5.

**Scabies** (sca-bies) is caused by the animal parasite referred to as the **"itch mite."** It burrows under the skin creating passages in which to lay its eggs. The skin has the appearance of red bumps with possible blistering due to the intense sensation to scratch the skin.

**Impetigo** (im-pe-ti-go) is a common skin disease caused by both types of streptococcus and staphylococcus bacteria. It usually begins as a **small sore**, developing into a **group of blisters filled with a yellow-brown liquid** that ooze and eventually dry to form a crust. Impetigo is **very contagious** due to the opening of the vesicles through itching and scratching; bacterial fluid is then leaked from the blisters and spread to any area of body. Refer client to medical care professional. Treatment is dependent upon severity of infection, either requiring antibiotics taken orally or a prescription antibacterial cream.

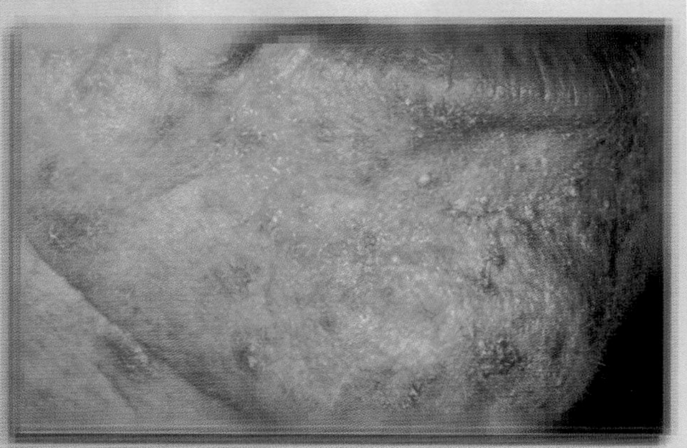

# Diseases of the Skin . . .

**Lice** (plural) or **louse** (singular) is an animal parasite ranging in size from .01 to .06 inches (.03 cm to .15 cm) living and **feeding on blood from the human body**. These **wingless** animal parasites are contagious and easily transmitted from one person to another through close contact, such as in heavily populated areas, sharing the same clothing, brushes or hats.

## The three types of lice and their bodily locations are head, body and pubic.

**Head lice** live on the scalp, attaching their eggs or nits onto the hair shaft. The lice are tan or light brown in color and the nits are yellow-white.

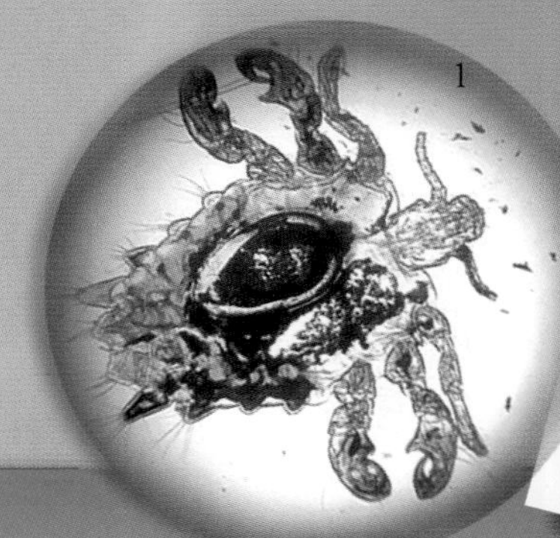


**NOTE:** For more information on head lice refer to Chapter 5.

**Body lice** are the most difficult to find because they **hide within the fold or seams of the person's clothing.** The lice come out to feed on the human blood and then return to the clothing. Wearing the same clothes day after day or sharing the same bedding constitutes some of the risks in acquiring body lice.

**Pubic lice** are commonly **located on the genital area** attaching to the pubic hair. This type of lice is also referred to as **crab lice** due to the parasite having a resemblance to a "crab." Crab lice may also be **found on facial or other body hair**. They basically survive in the same manner as head lice, laying and attaching their eggs or nits onto the hair strand. Pubic lice are difficult to find due to their small size, but they leave behind fecal (waste) matter characterized as black-brown specks that fall onto the undergarment.

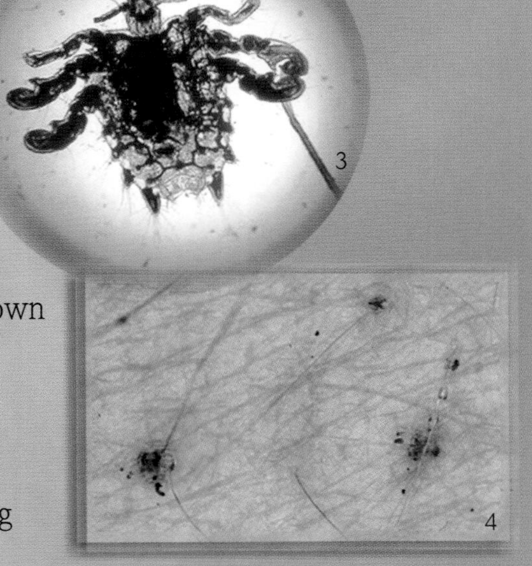


All three types of lice produce the **sensation to itch**. This occurs when the lice bite the skin or when they scurry from location to another. Infection may result if the scratching produces an opening of the skin making it susceptible to bacterial invasion.

# REVIEW QUESTIONS

| |
|---|
| A. Acute |
| B. Collagen |
| C. Crust |
| D. Dermis |
| E. Elastin Tissue |
| F. Hypodermis |
| G. Impetigo |
| H. Keratinization |
| I. Malignant Melanoma |
| J. Mitosis |
| K. Motor Nerve Fibers |
| L. Nevus |
| M. Pores |
| N. Psoriasis |
| O. Rosacea |
| P. Skin |
| Q. Stratum Germinativum |
| R. Stratum Lucidum |
| S. Sunscreen |
| T. Ultraviolet-B |

## FILL-IN-THE-BLANKS

1. ________ cause muscle contraction creating a "**goose flesh**" skin appearance.
2. ________ is a major protein that provides structural support to all other tissues within the dermis.
3. ________ converts the living skin cells into hard protein cells as they move upward changing shape within the epidermis.
4. ________ appears as red patches covered with silvery-white scales or crusts.
5. ________ is a skin disease created from bacteria producing blisters filled with yellow-brown liquid.
6. ________ has a medium wavelength and is responsible for either "tanning" or "sunburning" of the skin.
7. ________ is a valuable covering on our bodies protecting the underlying systems.
8. ________ or true skin consists of two layers, papillary and reticular.
9. ________ is when a skin disorder or disease is of short duration, but is sever and painful.
10. ________ is the most dangerous form of skin cancer appearing as unevenly shaped dark brown or black skin lesions.
11. ________ is a cosmetic product that chemically absorbs ultraviolet rays.
12. ________ is the reproduction or cell division that creates the layers within the epidermis.
13. ________ is elastic protein fibers that are interwoven with collagen fibers providing stretch to skin.
14. ________ is made up of clear cells and is mostly found on palms of hands and soles of feet.
15. ________ or birthmark is either raised or non-raised irregularly shaped mark or stain on the skin.
16. ________ or **fatty layer** provides a protective cushion for the epidermis.
17. ________ are openings at the hair follicles where sweat and sebum are dispersed.
18. ________ is a chronic skin disorder with dilation of tiny blood vessels appearing on nose and cheeks.
19. ________ is a secondary lesion known as a scab, which forms over an injury to the skin.
20. ________ or basal layer is where the epidermis is created.

STUDENT'S NAME DATE GRADE

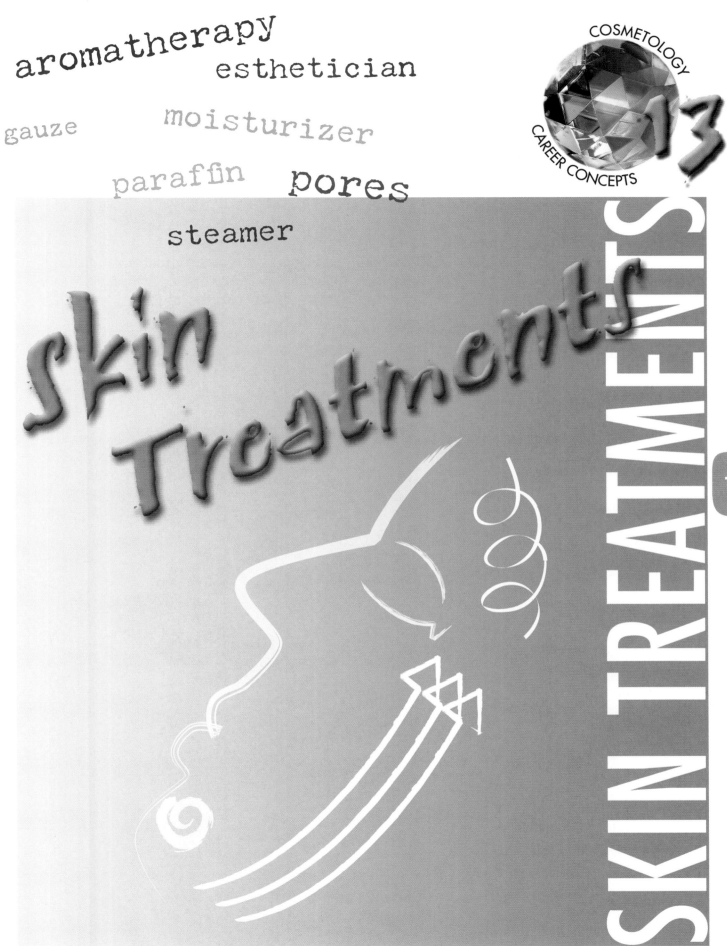

aromatherapy

esthetician

gauze

moisturizer

paraffin

pores

steamer

# Skin Treatments

SKIN TREATMENTS

13

# Terminology . . .

The terms listed are *"a handful"* of words to learn in order to perform the most beneficial and relaxing facial treatments within the skin-care industry. Review these words to continue **building your professional vocabulary.**

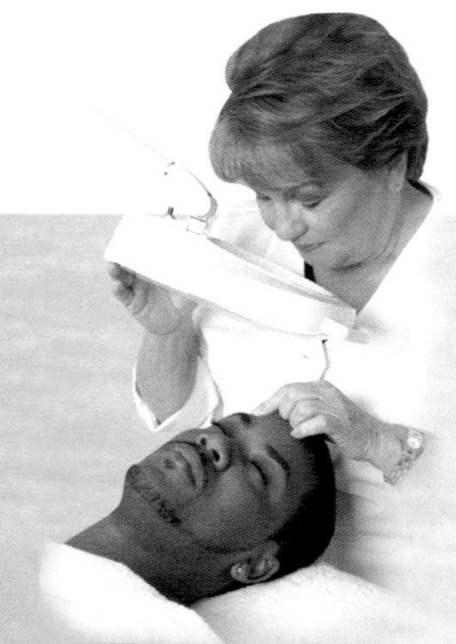

**Analysis** is an actual **"visual" examination** of the client's facial skin by cleansing and viewing the skin under a magnifying glass.

**Cleanser** is a cosmetic product used to remove dirt, oils and makeup that rest on the skin surface.

13

**Corrective** (correct) refers to rectifying a skin condition or ailment with the application of cosmetic products for treatment.

**Essential Oils** are concentrated scents derived and distilled from minute sacs in the roots, stems, bark, berries, leaves and flowers of botanical sources, including plants and trees.

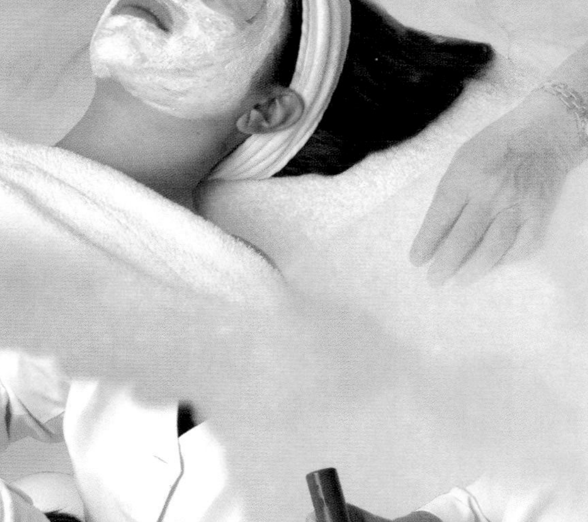

**Exfoliation** is a process that removes the dead skin cells from the stratum corneum layer of the epidermis either mechanically or chemically.

# Terminology . . .

**Facial Treatment** is a skin-care service performed by a licensed professional involving a series of deep cleansing and nourishing therapies to the skin of the face and neck.

1

2

**Mask** is a cosmetic product applied over the entire face that remains on the skin for a recommended amount of time, providing a specific benefit in skin restoration.

13

3

**Materials** are supplies used in conjunction with liquid tools to accomplish a safe and successful facial treatment.

**Organic** is a naturally developed substance that was **not forced** to grow quickly by the use of chemicals.

4

5

**Preservative** (preserve) relates to protecting the skin from environmental elements or neglect through the application of cosmetic products for skin-care maintenance.

# Skin-Care . . .

***The skin-care market** is reaching levels of growth never seen before, due to the increased demand of **proper skin-care** and **maintaining a youthful appearance**. This demand may come from the client that is in need of a **remedy for a skin condition or ailment,** or the individual that desires a **facial treatment** that balances between **relaxation** and **preserving the skin's beauty.***

Today's consumers want to achieve a healthy lifestyle and are concerned about the environment and what is placed on their skin and into their bodies. A majority of clients today also expect the use of environment – and skin-friendly products along with the benefits and effects of the facial treatments. Supporting this belief is the organization **Lifestyles of Health and Sustainability or LOHAS,** whose label can be applied to a group of people, a business or service that **promotes personal development**. LOHAS clients are committed to **taking care of themselves** and the **environment** by using earth-friendly or organic products.

**Organic** refers to a **naturally** developed substance that was **not forced** to grow quickly by the use of chemicals. The LOHAS client wishes to receive **customized therapy treatments** that naturally provide the benefits and effects of a skin-care treatment. These individuals will most likely make up a majority of your clientele and will expect the professional to respect these principles.

"For more information on LOHAS, go to: www.lohas.com."



©

# Skin-Care ...

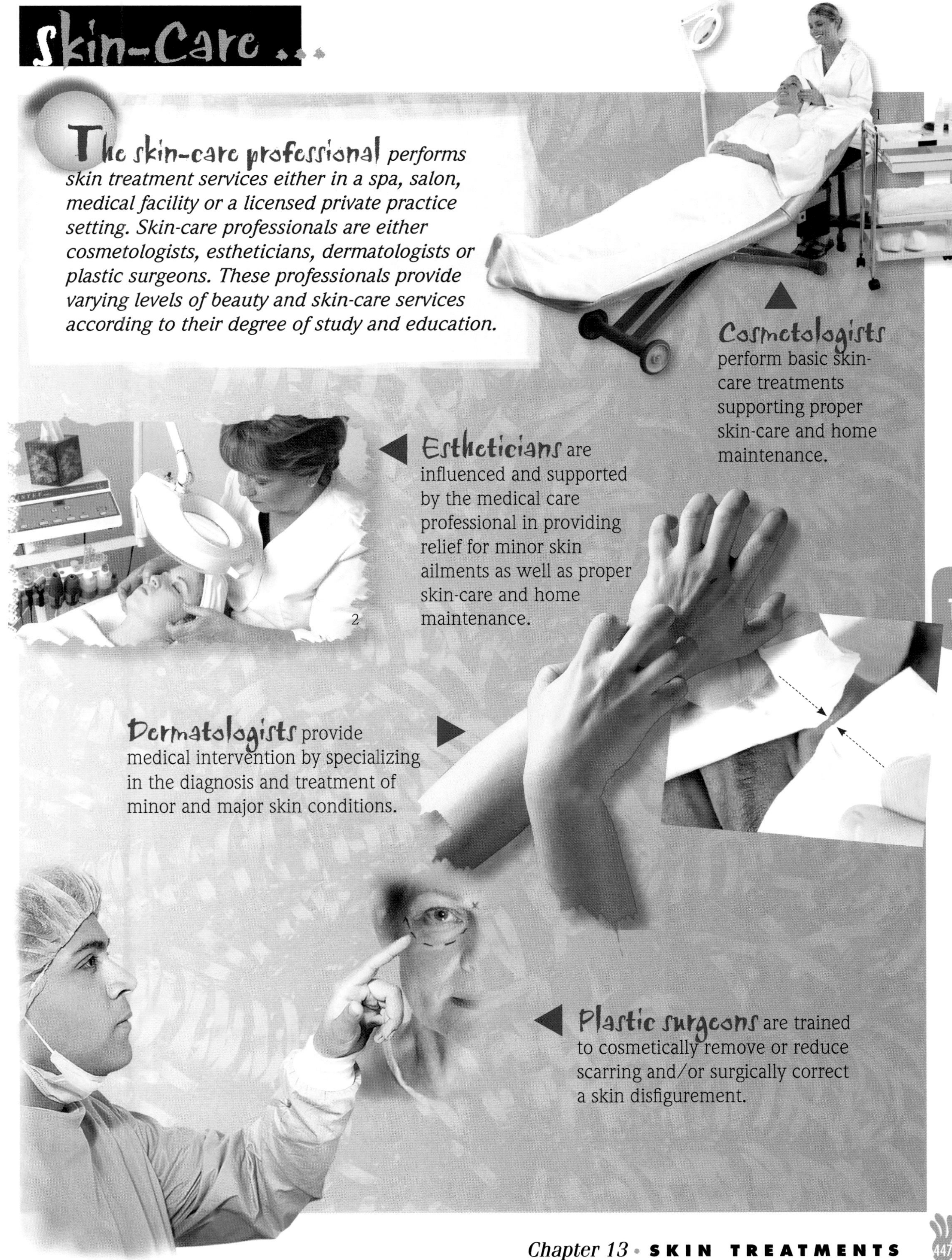


*The skin-care professional performs skin treatment services either in a spa, salon, medical facility or a licensed private practice setting. Skin-care professionals are either cosmetologists, estheticians, dermatologists or plastic surgeons. These professionals provide varying levels of beauty and skin-care services according to their degree of study and education.*

**Cosmetologists** perform basic skin-care treatments supporting proper skin-care and home maintenance.

**Estheticians** are influenced and supported by the medical care professional in providing relief for minor skin ailments as well as proper skin-care and home maintenance.

**Dermatologists** provide medical intervention by specializing in the diagnosis and treatment of minor and major skin conditions.

**Plastic surgeons** are trained to cosmetically remove or reduce scarring and/or surgically correct a skin disfigurement.

# Skin Treatment Tools . . .

**Skin treatment tools** *are the supplies used in conjunction with liquid tools to accomplish a safe and successful facial treatment. These are the* ***basic, but necessary items*** *required to ensure for client comfort and protection, along with using the proper sanitation guidelines when applying products.*

1

**Robes** are made of a washable material and are **worn by the client** during a facial service. They provide comfort and allow easy access to the face, chest and neck during massage and makeup application.

2

**NOTE:** Most of these tools are explained in Chapter 7.

13

**Cloth Towels** are made from an **absorbent washable material** and are used to **safely cover the skin** during a facial. They provide comfort and protection and may be used to assist in the removal of products from face.

3

4

**Headband or Covering** is either a thin strip of cloth-type material that **pulls hair back from the face** or is a cloth or plastic cap that **covers all the hair**. This is used during a facial to keep hair from coming in contact with face and/or product.

# Skin Treatment Tools . . .

**Protective Sheet or Blanket** is a **covering for the body** during a facial or massage treatment. It provides protection and comfort for the client while he or she enjoys the relaxing benefits of massage.

**Gauze** is a thin loosely woven fabric made of cotton, silk or wool that is pre-cut to the shape of the face. This **sheer material rests on the face** during a paraffin wax treatment to **prevent the wax from adhering to the vellus or lanugo hair** as it hardens. The gauze may also be used to **keep the mask in place**, and keep the product from dripping.

1

**Disposable Towels** are made from non-woven fabric that provides lint-free results during skin-care services. These **towels are throwaways**, eliminating the need for laundering and ensuring client safety and cleanliness.

2

# Skin Treatment Tools . . .

**Gloves** are manufactured from latex, vinyl or synthetic materials to **protect hands** in the event of product sensitivity and to promote client safety.

**CAUTION:** Some people have allergies or sensitivities to latex. Be sure to ask your clients if they have any latex sensitivity prior to wearing gloves before service.

**Spatulas** assist in the **removal of product** from a container. For sanitary purposes, never use your fingers to remove products from a jar. The spatula should **never be in contact with your client's skin** to prevent contamination of product. Therefore, there is **"no double dipping."** Spatulas come in a variety of sizes and shapes depending on manufacturer.

**Product Containers** are bowls or dishes that **hold liquid tools** during the skin-care service. Following sanitary guidelines the professional will then use a spatula or brush to dispense product from the container.

# Skin Treatment Tools . . .

**Cotton Pads or Wipes** may be used to **apply or remove cream or liquid products** to and from the skin during a facial. Cotton helps to absorb product excess and prevent overuse. **Optional:** Cotton pads, when lightly moistened (water or toner), may be applied over eye area for calming effect during a facial treatment. A covering over the eyes assists in keeping client's eyes closed.

**Circular Sponges** may be used to **remove product from the skin surface** during the skin-care treatment. Sponges are made of a porous substance and when moistened with water and glided over the skin, will assist in removing product.

**Applicator or Fan Brush** is used to **apply product evenly over the skin** during a facial treatment. The fan brush spreads a precise amount of liquid or lotion to avoid overuse of product.

13

# Skin Treatment Liquid Tools ...

***For all skin services,** the use of products is essential for the proper delivery of a facial treatment. There are numerous products available for your choosing that are designed specifically to **meet the needs** of a particular **skin type or condition**. The following basic liquid tools are separated into three categories: cleanser, toner and moisturizer.*

**Cleansers** are cosmetic products used to remove dirt, oils, dead skin cells, makeup or any other pollutants that rest on the skin surface. There are a variety of cleansers to choose from with each having a specific purpose and result.

## Types of Cleansers:

**Lathering cleanser,** which is derived from the ingredient called a **surfactant or a detergent,** produces a foam or sudsy consistency. The **surfactant** is designed to dissolve in water and remove dirt and oils from the skin. The lathering cleanser is best suited for **combination and oily skin**; however, depending on manufacturer there are lathering cleansers designed for the normal to dry skin types. The cleanser strength will vary according to the percentage of detergent plus the list of other ingredients used in the product.

**Non-Lathering cleanser** is best suited for **dry to sensitive skin types** due to its creamy consistency. This type of cleanser does not produce lather and is not rinsed from the skin with water; instead the product is removed with a dampened sponge or cotton pad. This cleanser is gentle due to the hydrating and softening effects.

For a skin cleanser to have a **maximum effect**, it should be water-soluble so it can be easily removed from the skin without leaving cleanser residue behind. Any residue from product remaining on the skin might possibly clog pores and lead into the development of other skin problems.

# Skin Treatment Liquid Tools . . .

1

**Toners** are sometimes referred to as **astringents or fresheners**. These are liquid skin products that help to close the pores after cleansing and therefore protect the skin from dirt and other pollutants.

The toner also assists in restoring the skin's pH and helps to hydrate and calm the skin. **Astringents or toners** are strong due to a high germicidal content and are usually recommended for combination or oily skin types to promote healing. **Fresheners** are milder and used for normal to dry skin types due to the hydrating effects on the skin.

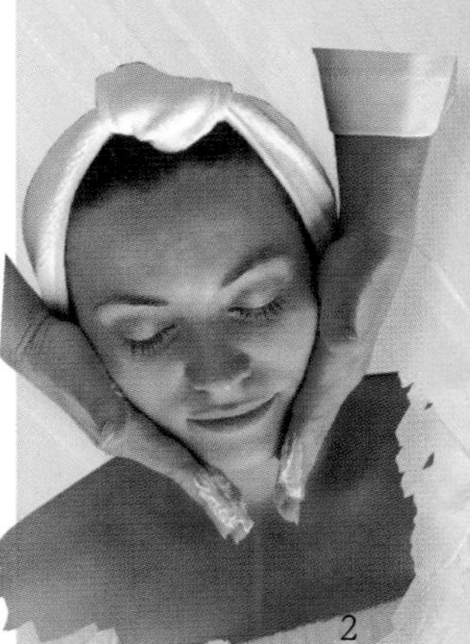
2

**Moisturizers** are skin-care products that soften the epidermal layer and restore hydration or moisture loss. The two major ingredients in the moisturizer are the emollient and humectant.

- **Emollients** act as barriers to prevent moisture from leaving the stratum corneum layer of the epidermis. They also impart lubricating qualities, providing a soft, smooth appearance.
- **Humectants** have the ability to absorb and retain moisture, assisting in the repair and prevention of a dry, scaly skin surface.

**NOTE:** Due to the harmful effects that sun exposure can have on the skin, it is recommended that moisturizers contain a broad-spectrum sunscreen, thus protecting against both UVA and UVB.

3

**Moisturizers vary according to a "water-to-oil" ratio for various skin types.**

The moisturizer used for **normal to dry skin types** is designed to impart and restore healthy levels of lubricants to the skin's surface. Heavier creams that contain extra amounts of emollients are intended to supply a rich, smooth and soft texture to the skin.

The moisturizer used for **combination to oily skin types** is designed to supply a small amount of emollients due to the body's natural supply of oils. For these skin types, a lightweight lotion protects the skin surface without producing a heavy feeling or "greasy" appearance.

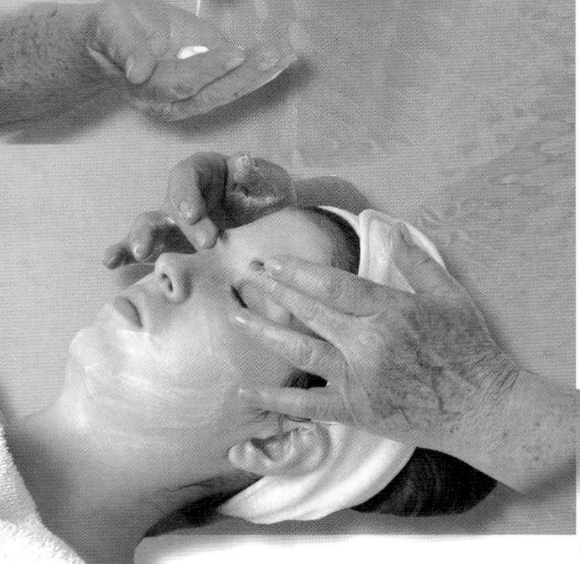

# Skin Treatment Liquid Tools . . .

***Some liquid tools** are **special therapy products** that provide additional benefits to improve the client's skin appearance. They usually assist in anti-aging protection and increase product penetration during and after a facial treatment. These liquid tools may be used to treat a certain skin type, condition or ailment. Each specialty liquid tool is listed with its **benefit and result**.*

**Masks** are cosmetic products that are applied over the entire face and remain on the skin for a recommended amount of time. A mask is designed for a specific purpose; **deep cleansing, moisturizing or sloughing off dead-surface skin cells**. Masks can be applied as often as twice a week depending on skin type and/or condition to assist in restoring healthy skin function.

**NOTE:** Because masks cover the face, always check with the client before service to see if he or she is claustrophobic.

## Types of Masks:

**NOTE:** When removing the mask, rest towel on the skin allowing the moist heat to soften the clay product; be careful not to stretch softened skin.

13

**Clay-base masks** are deep cleansing, absorbing the oils and drawing impurities from the skin's pores. This mask is ideal for **oily and combination skin types**. The clay mask contains mildly astringent qualities helping to heal and soothe inflammation, and tighten pore size. The mask will dry and harden on the skin and needs to be removed with a warm, moist cloth towel.

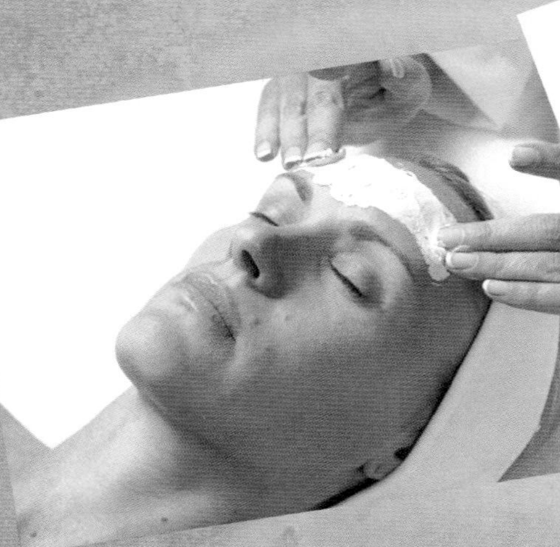

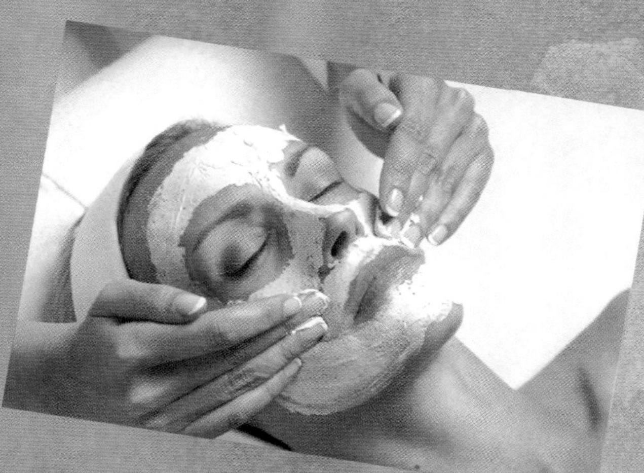

**Cream masks** are beneficial for **dry, normal or sensitive skin types** and produce moisturizing results. The cream mask does not dry on the skin and is usually removed by either gently wiping the product from the face or by using a warm, moist cloth towel. The skin should appear smooth, soft and hydrated.

# Skin Treatment Liquid Tools . . .

**Gel masks** increase the hydration of the skin by **sealing in moisture** created by the mask treatment. The gel mask solidifies, which allows the product to be peeled off the skin's surface creating a slight exfoliation of dead skin cells. This type of mask is suitable for **dry to normal skin types** providing intense moisturizing effects.

## Paraffin wax masks

work by combining a paraffin wax and a moisturizing cream to **increase product penetration** into skin. **Paraffin** is a **synthetic translucent wax** that is white or lightly colored, and has a mild greasy touch. It comes pre-packaged and is **heated** slightly above normal body temperature, **melted** and **applied over gauze**, and then placed on top of moisturizing cream. As the wax cools, it hardens into a candle-like appearance.

1

**CAUTION:** Always test temperature of wax on inside of your arm before applying to client's skin.

Paraffin has no benefits to the skin except for **supplying the heat** necessary to **open the skin's pores**, allowing the cream to penetrate. The heated paraffin **increases body temperature** causing the skin to perspire. The sweat is trapped, forcing it to re-enter the stratum corneum layer producing hydrating results. The paraffin mask is beneficial for normal to dry skin types.

*Promote paraffin facial treatments during the winter months to counteract the drying effects of cold air on the face.*

13

# Skin Treatment Liquid Tools . . .

**Exfoliation** is a process that chemically or mechanically **removes the dead skin cells** from the stratum corneum layer of the epidermis. This process **improves product penetration and skin texture** by unclogging pores, reducing fines lines, hyperpigmentation (sun spots) and wrinkles. It gives the skin a smooth, glowing appearance and assists with even makeup application. Regular exfoliation treatments accelerate cell renewal turnover, resulting in healthier and younger looking skin. Exfoliation treatments may be performed on any skin type and as often as twice a week; however, use caution on sensitive and couperose skin conditions.

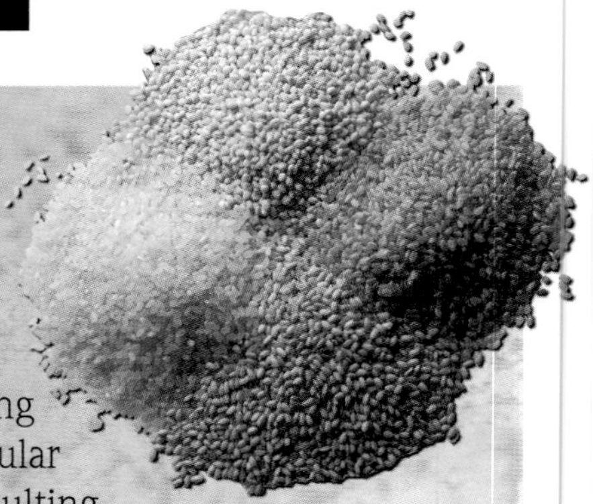

Exfoliant products are either **invasive or non-invasive** . . . the difference is that invasive exfoliation will **penetrate deeper into the dermis** whereas non-invasive exfoliation will **penetrate only the epidermal layer**. The skin-care professional uses only the non-invasive approach to removing the dead surface skin cells. A medical care professional is recommended for the deeper skin tissue conditions.

1

13

**NOTE:** Advanced education is required in order for the skin-care professional to offer non-invasive exfoliating treatments both mechanically or chemically to their clients.

## Two types of exfoliation treatments:

1. **Mechanical exfoliation** involves the use of a manual application or machines to remove the skin's dead cells. An **exfoliant product or abrasive material** is physically applied and "rolled" over the skin to create the **friction** necessary to remove dead surface cells. Exfoliants or scrubs contain **mild abrasive or coarse ingredients** such as small granules of sugar, pumice, crystals, oats or crushed seeds. By **rubbing the scrub over the skin,** dead skin cells are lifted from the surface. Also, an abrasive material such as a cloth pad or brush may be used to help in the exfoliation process, whether it is performed manually or by machine.

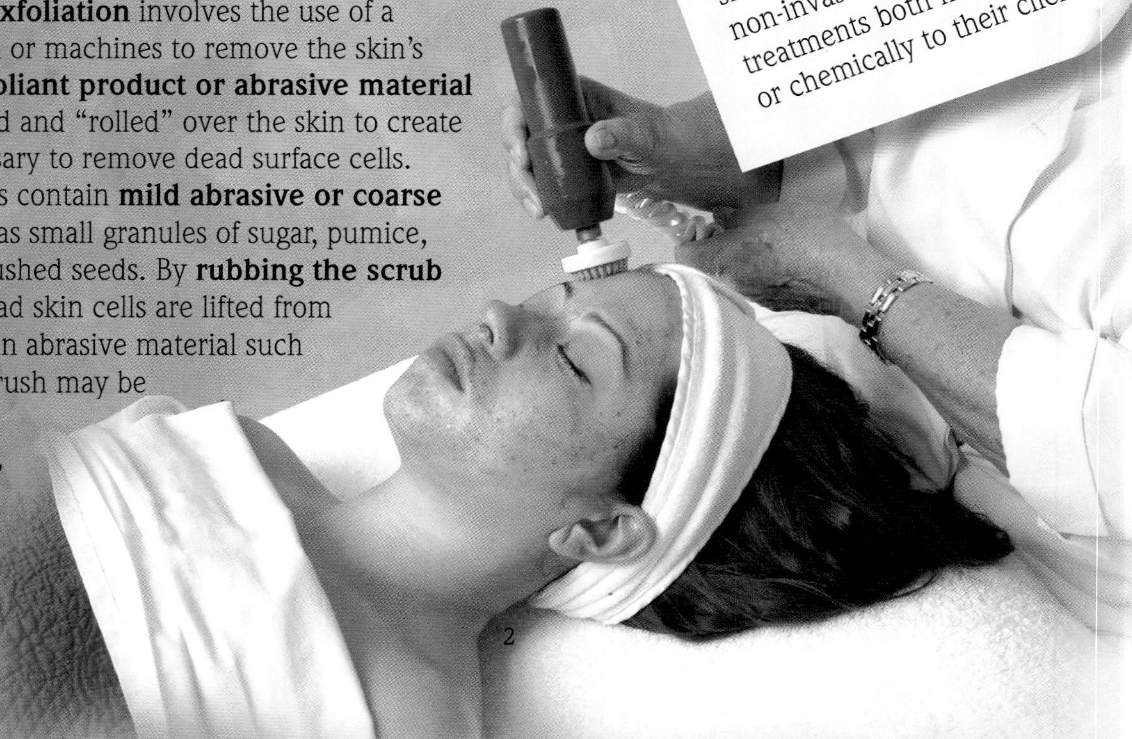

2

# Skin Treatment Liquid Tools . . .

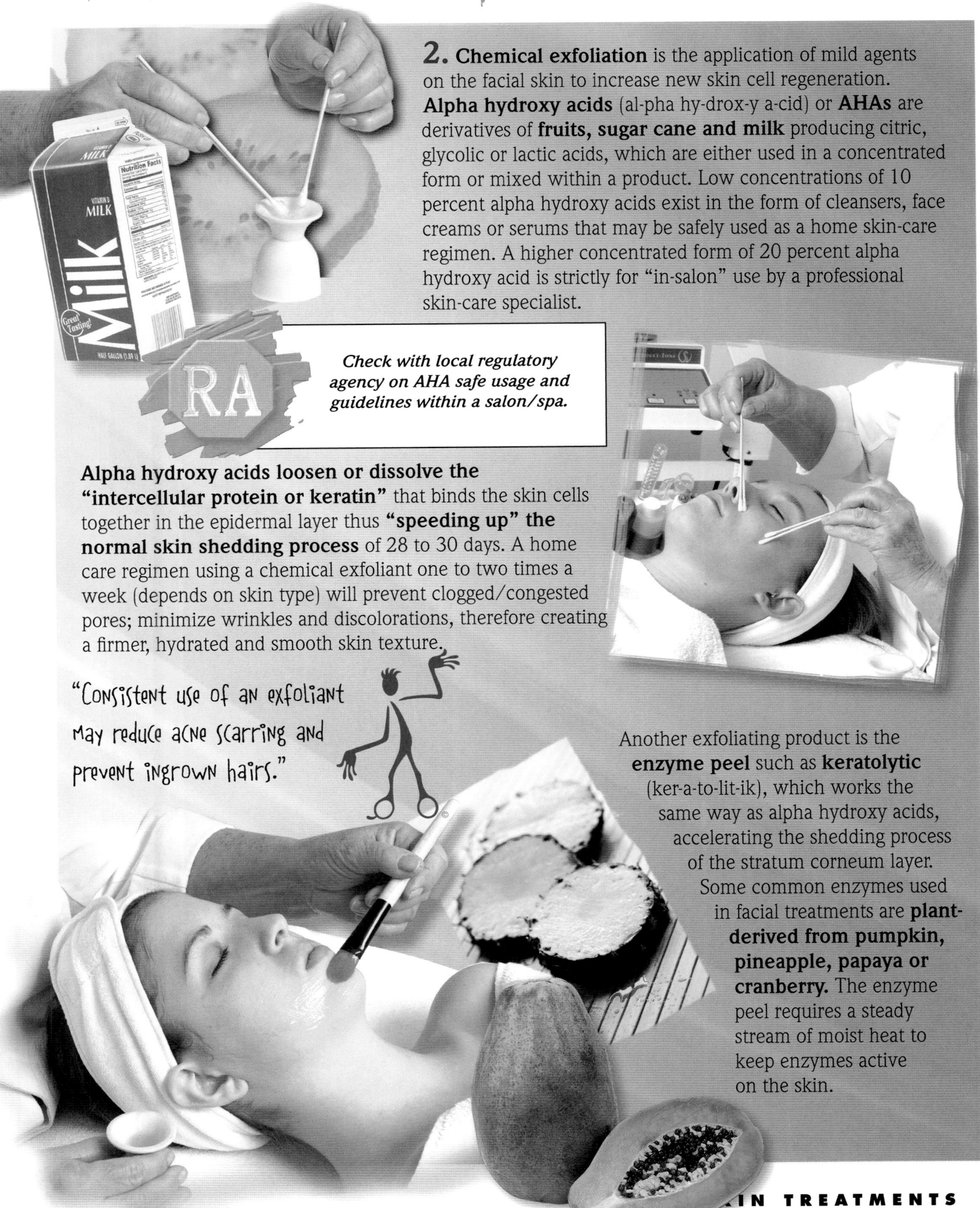


**2. Chemical exfoliation** is the application of mild agents on the facial skin to increase new skin cell regeneration. **Alpha hydroxy acids** (al-pha hy-drox-y a-cid) or **AHAs** are derivatives of **fruits, sugar cane and milk** producing citric, glycolic or lactic acids, which are either used in a concentrated form or mixed within a product. Low concentrations of 10 percent alpha hydroxy acids exist in the form of cleansers, face creams or serums that may be safely used as a home skin-care regimen. A higher concentrated form of 20 percent alpha hydroxy acid is strictly for "in-salon" use by a professional skin-care specialist.

***Check with local regulatory agency on AHA safe usage and guidelines within a salon/spa.***

**Alpha hydroxy acids loosen or dissolve the "intercellular protein or keratin"** that binds the skin cells together in the epidermal layer thus **"speeding up" the normal skin shedding process** of 28 to 30 days. A home care regimen using a chemical exfoliant one to two times a week (depends on skin type) will prevent clogged/congested pores; minimize wrinkles and discolorations, therefore creating a firmer, hydrated and smooth skin texture.

"Consistent use of an exfoliant may reduce acne scarring and prevent ingrown hairs."

Another exfoliating product is the **enzyme peel** such as **keratolytic** (ker-a-to-lit-ik), which works the same way as alpha hydroxy acids, accelerating the shedding process of the stratum corneum layer. Some common enzymes used in facial treatments are **plant-derived from pumpkin, pineapple, papaya or cranberry.** The enzyme peel requires a steady stream of moist heat to keep enzymes active on the skin.

13

# Skin Treatment Liquid Tools . . .

*The following liquid tools are specialty items for use during a skin-care treatment or home care regimen. These products provide a particular function whether to hydrate the skin, permit ease in gliding over the skin for massage or to remedy a certain skin condition.*

**Massage Cream or Oil** is a **lubricating product** applied to the skin that **permits the fingers to glide over the skin** during a facial massage treatment. A massage cream may be manufactured in various consistencies to complement each skin type and condition. Oily skin needs a lightweight lotion with a ratio of "water-to-oil" as opposed to dry skin, which requires a cream enriched formula with an "oil-to-water" ratio.

13

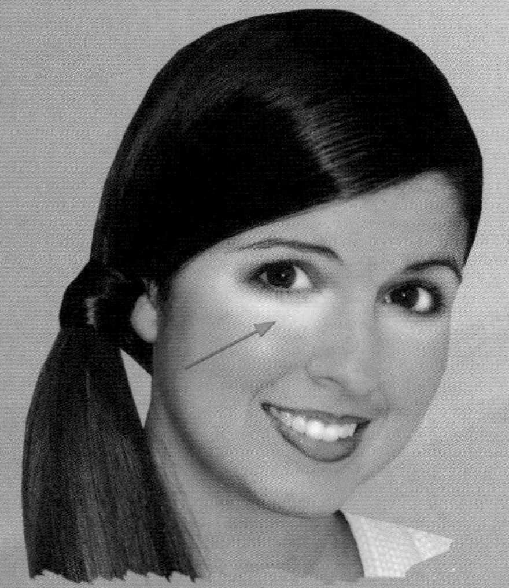

**Eye Cream** is a cosmetic product used specifically around the eyes to **increase firmness, reduce puffiness and lighten dark circles**. Eye cream is concentrated with emollients that contain no fragrances and are mild enough to use around the eye and on the eyelid.

**Night Cream** is an intensive skin-care product **used in the evenings** while the body is resting to repair any specific skin conditions. These creams are richer and more concentrated than creams used during the day and are designed for a specific purpose.

# Natural Mask Liquid Tools . . .

**Natural masks** are **inexpensive alternatives to skin care** by utilizing natural products such as eggs, oatmeal, honey, yogurt as well as fruits, herbs and plants. These treatments can be prepared in your own home providing some of the same benefits as the commercially prepared products.

## Some natural products with their benefits:

**Honey** has **moisturizing properties** and is rich in enzymes, vitamins and minerals. It can assist in the exfoliation process of removing impurities and dead surface skin cells.

**Oatmeal** has **hypoallergenic qualities** and may **alleviate dry, itchy skin.** The oats can be used to soften and exfoliate the skin, removing the dead surface skin cells.

**Peaches or plums** are excellent **deliverers of alpha hydroxy acids,** which assist in increased cell renewal promoting a healthier skin appearance. These fruits help to minimize fine lines, sun or age spots and wrinkling.

**Bananas or strawberries** are **rich in vitamin C** and are **acidic in pH,** helping to restore the skin's balance and moisture level. These fruits also help to reduce fine lines and wrinkling.

**Carrots or sweet potatoes** are **rich in retinol** (re-tin-ol), which is a small molecule that can penetrate the skin and **stimulate production of elastin and collagen.** This natural additive may result in minimizing the appearance of fine lines or wrinkles.

To formulate a naturally-made mask, the ingredients used are typically prepared by **grating, pureeing or blending the fruit or vegetable to create a paste-like substance.** Sometimes a base of yogurt or essential oils is added to enhance the benefits of the natural mask. A natural mask mixture should be stored in the refrigerator and has a shelf-life of one week.

For more information on creating your own facial mask, go to www.pioneerthinking.com/gh_facialmasks.html

"There are a multitude of mask products to choose from within the industry. As the professional, you will need to find what best suits your client's skin type or condition."

13

# Aromatherapy Tools . . .

***To deliver** an **optimal skin-care service**, the professional will utilize every aspect of the beauty industry. Any skin-care treatment can be **enhanced by the use of essential oils,** which may be incorporated into skin-care products or applied directly onto the skin during a facial treatment.*

**Aromatherapy** is the **use of fragrances of essential oils** to promote rejuvenation and health of both the mind and body. Understanding the art of aromatherapy and each essential oil's benefits and effects requires study in order to improve the delivery of the cosmetic products.



**Essential oils** are **concentrated scents** derived and distilled from minute sacs in the **roots, stems, bark, berries, leaves and flowers** of botanical sources, including plants and trees. Always refer to a reputable manufacturer within the wellness or beauty industry when purchasing essential oils. Oils are packaged in **amber or blue glass bottles** (with a lid) and should be stored in a **cool, dark location**, away from sunlight, to obtain the longest shelf-life.

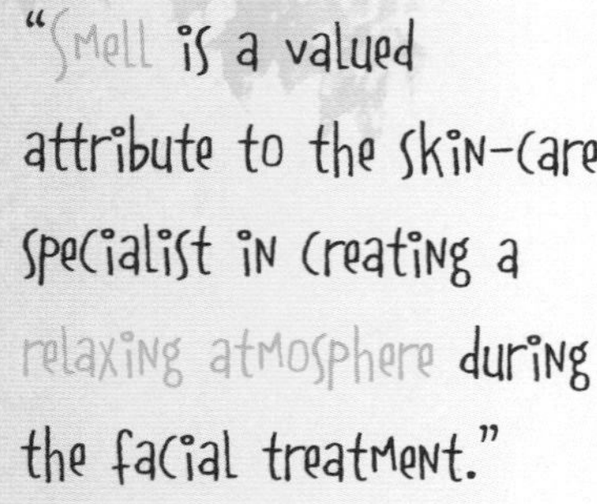

"Smell is a valued attribute to the skin-care specialist in creating a relaxing atmosphere during the facial treatment."

# Aromatherapy Tools . . .

## The Uses of Essential Oils:

**During any massage treatment** – select an essential oil that will benefit the needs of the client. For example, stimulating orange oil may be used to increase blood circulation, while the scent of lavender will produce soothing effects to induce relaxation.

Orange

Peppermint

**Skin-care treatments** – some essential oils may alleviate the symptoms of certain skin conditions. For example, chamomile, geranium and lavender help treat dermatitis. Other oils such as lemongrass may balance an oily skin condition and promote healing of acne.

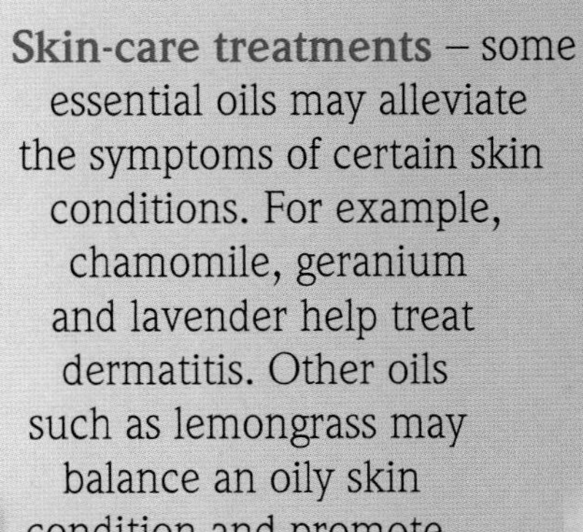

Lavender

Chamomile

**Added to cleansers, toners, skin lotions/ creams or other oils** – aromas enhance the properties of the products applied to the skin. Add peppermint to bath water or a shower to relieve sinus congestion or use rosewood essential oil for skin softening and healing.

**Released as a fragrance into the environment** – for relaxation (rose), stress-relief (chamomile oil), or guarding against viruses or bacteria (tea tree). This can be accomplished when the oils are dispersed through evaporation using a diffuser, humidifier or vaporizer.

Tea tree

13

# Aromatherapy Tools . . .

**Essential oils**
are potent and generally not used directly on the skin if undiluted. Some oils are stronger than others and may cause sensitivity to the skin, while milder oils are safe on the skin without dilution.

**NOTE:** As a precaution, always perform a patch test on a small area of the skin to check for sensitivity.

The most common methods for diluting essential oils are either through the use of distilled water or carrier oils. **Carrier oils** are inexpensive base oils that originate from **vegetables, seeds or nuts** and assist in the safe delivery of pure oils into the skin.

## Some Carrier Oils include:

**Jojoba** (ho-hoba) **oil** is pressed or extracted from the **seed of the jojoba shrub**, providing deep moisturizing and healing properties. This oil has qualities that are similar to our skin's natural oil, therefore making it beneficial to all skin types.

**Coconut oil** is derived from the **endosperm (white meat) of the coconut** and absorbs readily into the skin, leaving a smooth and silky texture.

**Wheatgerm oil** is extracted from pressing the **budding piece of the wheat grain** and is high in vitamin E. This oil is a natural antioxidant, which combats aging and cancer, and promotes skin cell regeneration and improves blood circulation.

**Sweet Almond oil** is expressed from the **sweet almond nut** and provides hydrating effects to irritated or dry skin. It leaves a slight "greasy" feeling on the skin and is high in vitamin E.

**Apricot Kernel oil** is expressed from the **seed of the apricot** and is high in vitamins A and C. This oil absorbs easily and is excellent for mature or sensitive skin types.

# Aromatherapy Tools ...

You can use essential oils for many different purposes and various responses. **Blending two or more essential oils** is an option to obtain multiple effects or benefits. By combining essential oils, you are utilizing the **wonderful healing properties of the oils** and further enhancing the facial treatment. Below is a list of some essential oils that have been categorized according to their effects:

**Oils for Relaxing Effects:**
Chamomile, Clove, Frankincense, Geranium, Lavender, Melissa, Orange, Patchouli, Rose, Spikenard, Ylang Ylang

**Oils for Germicidal Effects:**
Cinnamon, Clove, Eucalyptus, Lavender, Lemon, Myrrh, Peppermint, Rosemary, Tea Tree

**Oils for Stimulating Effects:**
Cedarwood, Jasmine, Lemon, Peppermint, Rosewood

**Suggested essential oils used during facial treatments for dry skin:**
Jasmine, Lavender, Myrrh, Orange, Patchouli, Peppermint, Rose, Rosewood, Sandalwood, Spikenard

**Suggested essential oils used during facial treatments for oily/acne skin:**
Cedarwood, Chamomile, Citronella, Clove, Eucalyptus, Geranium, Lavender, Lemongrass, Myrtle, Orange, Patchouli, Tea Tree

**CAUTION:** Many essential oils should not be used on pregnant clients. Oils such as, peppermint or geranium can trigger the body's delicate hormonal balance during pregnancy.

Rosemary 1

Cedarwood 2

Rose

Lemon

Jasmine

Clove

Geranium

# Aromatherapy Tools...

## Some of the essential oils for use:

**Cedarwood** is steam distilled from the bark of the **cedar tree** and may be used effectively as an astringent to control sebum, an oily substance produced from the sebaceous glands. It is considered to have calming and antibacterial properties.

**Chamomile** (cham-o-mil) is steam distilled from the **flower** and is used to relieve insomnia, nervous tension and remedy skin conditions such as acne, eczema and scar tissue. It has antioxidant, relaxant and anti-inflammatory properties.

**Cinnamon** (cin-na-mon) is steam distilled from the **bark of the cinnamon tree** and is useful in protecting against bacterial infections. It is highly antibacterial, antifungal and antiviral and is truly valuable in the prevention of disease.



**Eucalyptus** (yooka-lip-tus) is steam distilled from the **leaves of the plant** and is useful in clearing any respiratory ailments due to its decongestive qualities. It is helpful in treating acne and protecting against infection.

**Geranium** (ge-ray-nee-um) is steam 1
distilled from the **leaves of the flower** and is used for skin cell regeneration and healing. It has antibacterial qualities and helps to cleanse oily skin, improves blood circulation and balance mind and spirit.

**Jasmine** (jaz-min) comes from **flowers harvested in the evening** to obtain maximum fragrance, which contributes to its expense as a scent. This fragrant oil has uplifting, stimulating and antibacterial qualities. It may be used to improve eczema and mature skin conditions.

# Aromatherapy Tools . . .

**Lavender** is steam distilled using the **top of the flower** and is well known for treating and healing infections, burns and insect bites due to antiseptic, antibacterial and antiviral properties. It is also appropriate for treating headaches and stress, having a pleasant smell and relaxing effect.

**Lemon** is pressed from the **rind of the fruit**, promoting clarity and increased blood circulation. It has deep cleansing results and helps to reduce fine lines and combat acne.

**Orange** is pressed from the **rind of the fruit** and is considered to reduce insomnia and increase blood circulation. It revitalizes a dull skin complexion and decreases the appearance of fine lines.

13

**Peppermint** is steam distilled from the **leaves and stems of the flower** producing anti-inflammatory and antiseptic qualities. Due to its antibacterial qualities and the cooling effect on the skin, peppermint is ideal for relieving pain and treating skin sores. This pure oil produces a menthol smell acting as a decongestant and increasing mental alertness/energy.

1

**Rose** is steam distilled from the **flower** producing anti-inflammatory and relaxant properties. This expensive oil has been used for thousands of years, releasing an intoxicating fragrance that promotes harmony and balance. Rose oil assists in the prevention of skin conditions such as wrinkles and scarring.

2

**Tea Tree** is steam distilled from the **leaves of the tree** and is powerful in its antibacterial, antifungal and antiviral qualities. It is used to heal fungal infections and for the relief of skin sores and acne conditions.

"For more information
on ALL essential
oils, go to:
www.youngliving.com"
©

# Skin Treatment Equipment ...

**The** *use of* ***facial equipment*** *will enhance the benefits of receiving a skin-care treatment. Machines* ***increase product penetration and effectiveness,*** *providing a relaxing, competent and professional treatment.*

**NOTE:** If a steamer is not available, a warm, moist towel placed on the face may be used to soften skin and open pores.

13

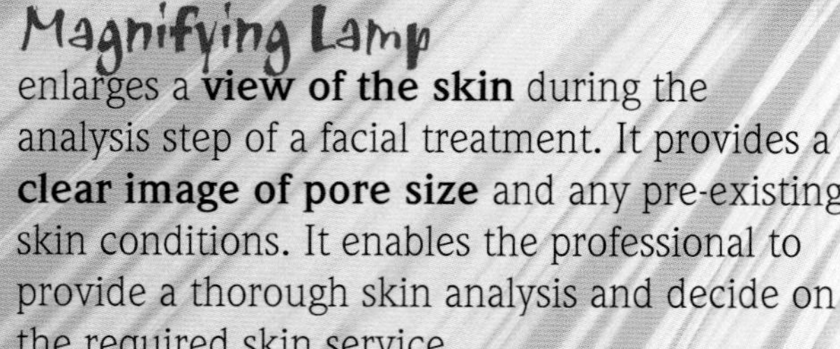

**Magnifying Lamp** enlarges a **view of the skin** during the analysis step of a facial treatment. It provides a **clear image of pore size** and any pre-existing skin conditions. It enables the professional to provide a thorough skin analysis and decide on the required skin service.

**CAUTION:** Clients with asthma or any breathing conditions might not be able to receive the steam.

**Steamer** produces a **steady warm, moist steam** over the skin of the entire face or a specific area. The warm steam **softens the skin and opens pores**, creating good product penetration and a deep cleansing. This step is crucial during the analysis and cleansing steps of the facial treatment.

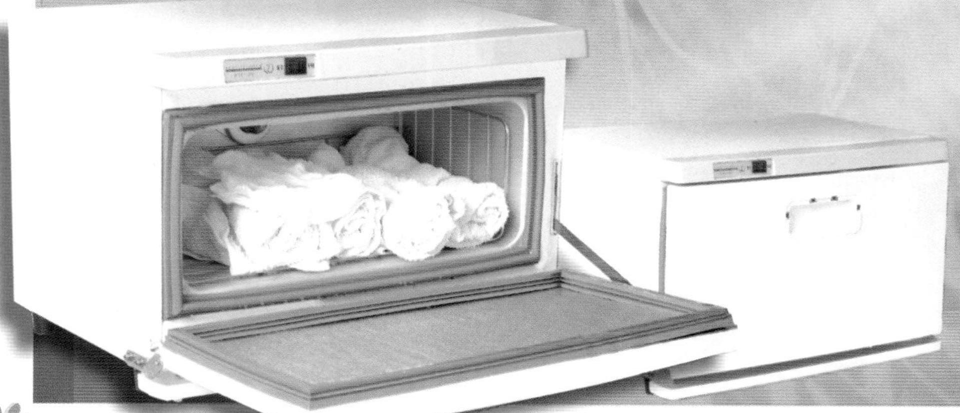

**Towel Warmer** is an enclosed **heated cabinet or compartment** containing moist cloth towels or cotton pads. The warmer **stores the towels** during the facial treatment providing the skin-care specialist with **easy access of towels** as needed.

# Skin Treatment Equipment . . .

**Suction machine** is used for **extraction of blackheads or mild pustules** from the skin's surface. A glass applicator is the electrode that is placed on the skin, gently gliding over a specific area producing a slight "pulling" action. This machine is used as an option to manually extract blackheads or pimples.

**NOTE:** Machines are an optional choice for use and require advanced study in order to learn operating instructions and benefits.

**Brushing machine** consists of **various designed brush applicators** that are attached to a rotating head. The brush applicator comes in various bristle textures and sizes depending on area of use; a small, soft brush applicator is preferable for facial treatments. This brushing technique is an **alternative form of exfoliation** to remove dead surface skin cells and produce a smooth skin surface appearance.

13

**CAUTION:** Do not use any machines on clients with high blood pressure, or open wounds, those who are pregnant, have sensitive skin types or conditions, are under the care of a medical care professional or are using any topically medicated skin lotions.

**High-Frequency Current machine** uses glass-designed electrodes that emit a violet light as they glide over the skin. There are various shaped electrodes depending on area of use, but the main **facial electrode** is **mushroom-shaped** to permit a "sliding action" across the surface of the skin. The high-frequency current **warms the skin's tissues** and **stimulates blood flow,** therefore allowing better product absorption. High-frequency current also has a **germicidal effect** and may be used after extraction of blackheads or pustules. For more detailed explanation on high-frequency current, refer to Chapter 11.

# Skin Treatment Furniture . . .

**When** deciding on the necessary furnishings for providing the utmost in skin-care services, remember to think **functional** for both you and the client. The next consideration is the **image** you wish the salon to convey to your customers. Skin-care furniture needs to **provide comfort** for the client and **ease** for you in delivering the most proficient facial treatment. While there are numerous facial tables, stools and chairs to select from, your design of choice will reflect the salon's image as well as your personality.

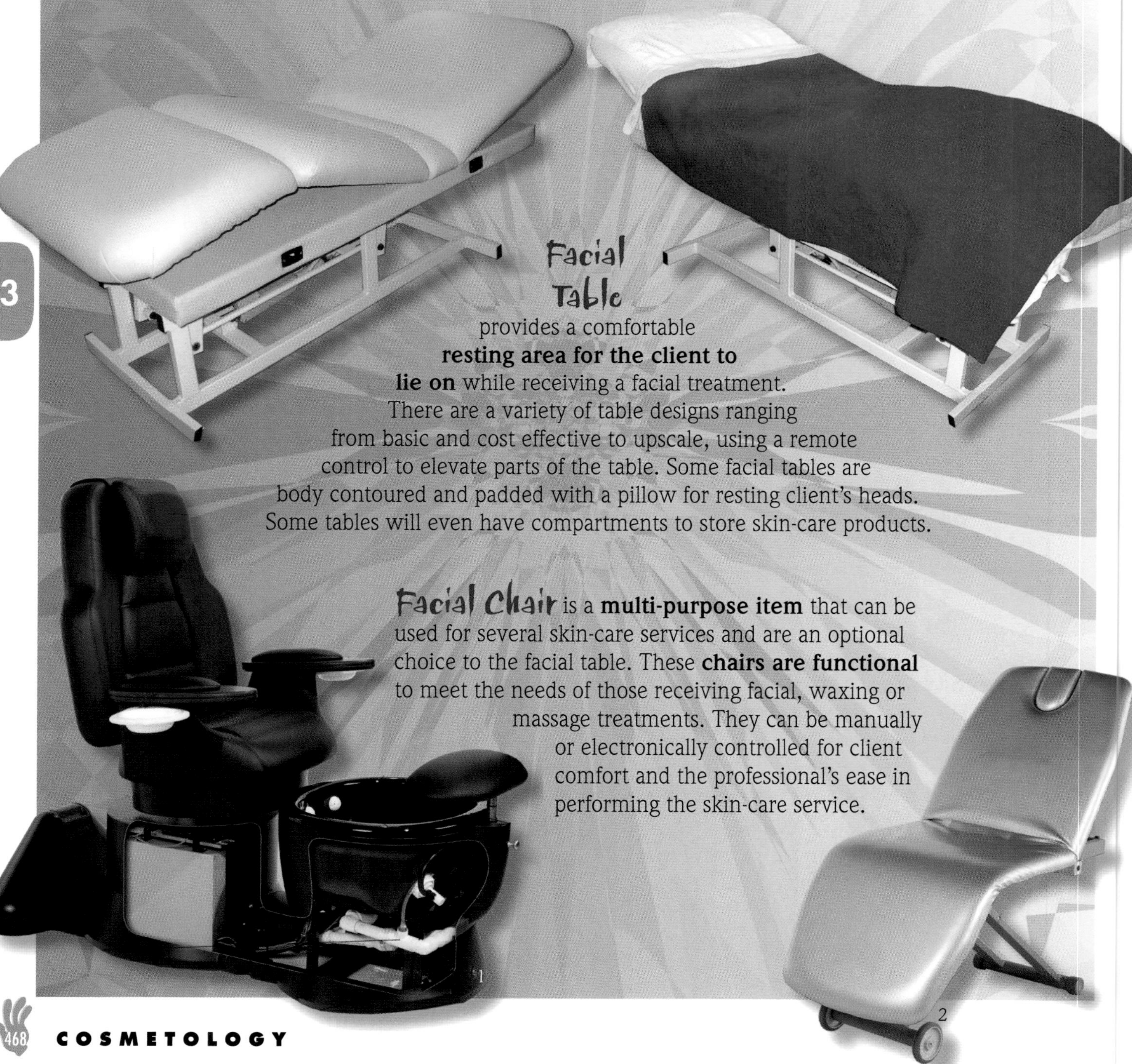

13

**Facial Table** provides a comfortable **resting area for the client to lie on** while receiving a facial treatment. There are a variety of table designs ranging from basic and cost effective to upscale, using a remote control to elevate parts of the table. Some facial tables are body contoured and padded with a pillow for resting client's heads. Some tables will even have compartments to store skin-care products.

**Facial Chair** is a **multi-purpose item** that can be used for several skin-care services and are an optional choice to the facial table. These **chairs are functional** to meet the needs of those receiving facial, waxing or massage treatments. They can be manually or electronically controlled for client comfort and the professional's ease in performing the skin-care service.

1

2

# Skin Treatment Furniture . . .

**Professional Stool or Chair** allows the technician to **move about with quick and easy movements.** The chair or stool is equipped with roller wheels to **accommodate the technician's mobility** in obtaining products and/or reaching the client. Some chairs provide a back support for the technician's comfort during service delivery. Chair designs range from basic to highly specialized and fashionable depending on the manufacturer.

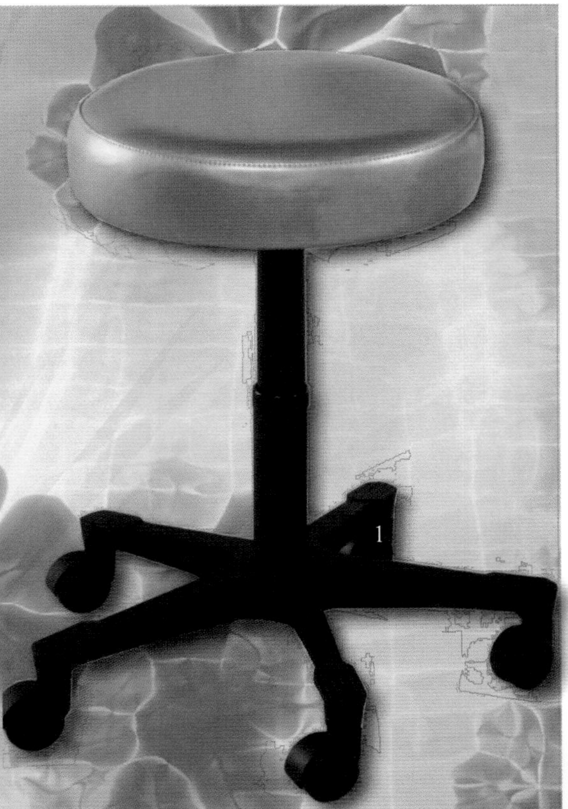

1

2

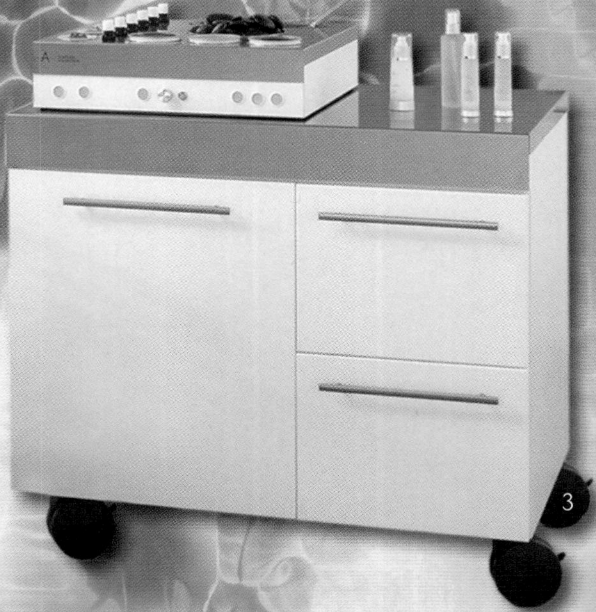

**Product Tray or Trolley** holds and stores the professional's products while in use, permitting **safe and easy access** during the skin-care services. Some product trolleys have roller wheels to accommodate mobility and ease in getting to products at any angle.

3

13

# Facial Treatments ...

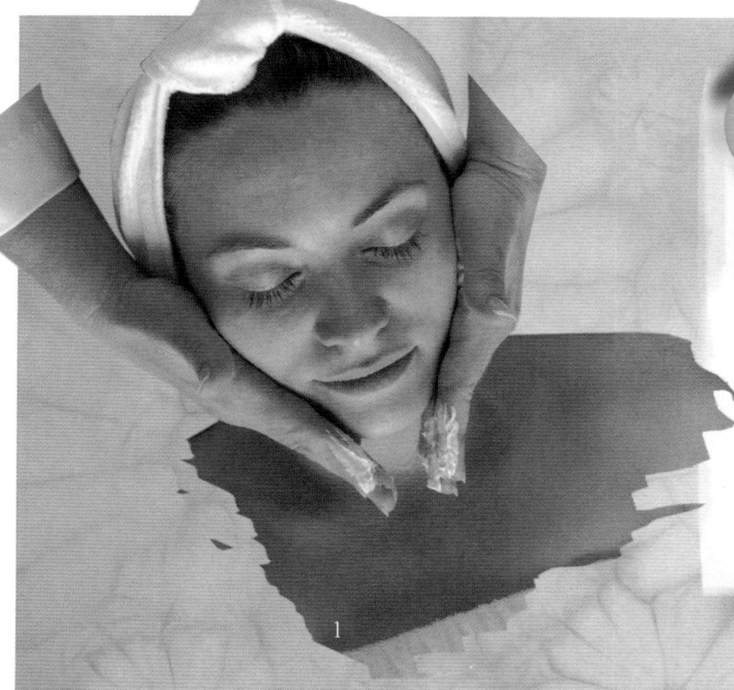
1

There are many benefits to receiving a professional facial treatment. A ***facial treatment*** is a skin-care service involving a ***series of deep cleansing and nourishing therapies*** to the skin of the face and neck. The intensity of the facial treatment is based on the skin type or condition, and if there is any pre-existing skin ailment. The use of equipment, application of massage and specific products increase the time and depth of the treatment.*

13

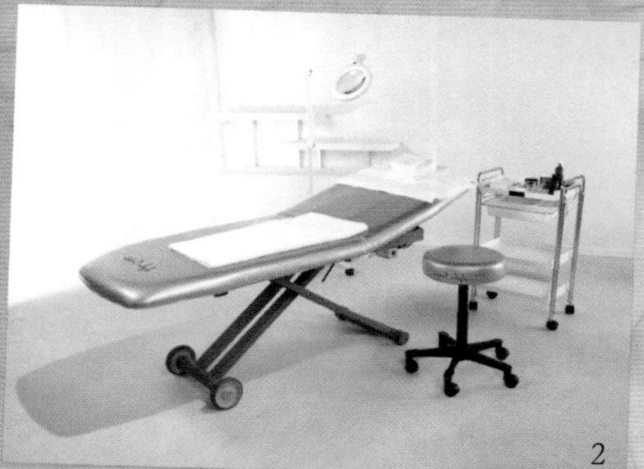
2

A facial treatment, as with all skin-care services is delivered in a **professional licensed facility** promoting a stress-free environment of relaxation and enjoyment. Today's customers are looking for an "escape" and want to unwind from the hectic demands and schedules in their lives.

**Facial treatments are categorized either as being preservative or corrective.**

**Preservative** (preserve) relates to protecting the skin by the application of cosmetic products for skin-care maintenance.

- **Preservative facial treatments** are delivered to **maintain and protect the health of the skin** and provide the added benefits of toning or tightening the skin through massage. Deep cleansing as well as increasing the blood circulation are also accomplished with this type of treatment.

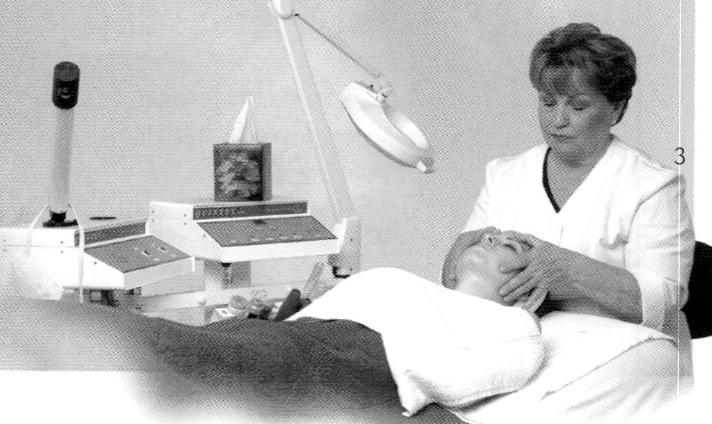
3

# Facial Treatments . . .

**Corrective** (correct) refers to rectifying a skin condition or ailment with the application of cosmetic products for treatment.

- **Corrective facial treatments** are performed to **assist in the remedy of a skin condition or ailment**. These treatments are used to manage or retard a pre-existing condition such as skin that is clogged or congested with blackheads/whiteheads or minimize fine lines or possibly remedy a dry skin condition.

1

**Benefits of receiving a facial treatment:**

- Restore normal skin function
- Cleanses skin at a deep level
- Provide relaxation
- Increase blood circulation
- Assist in skin and muscle toning
- Assist in the healing of a skin condition or ailment

## How often should a facial treatment be given?

It is recommended to schedule a facial at least **once every four to six weeks** for maintenance, provided a professional skin-care regimen is continued at home. Clients with certain skin types or conditions are advised to receive a facial treatment once a week.

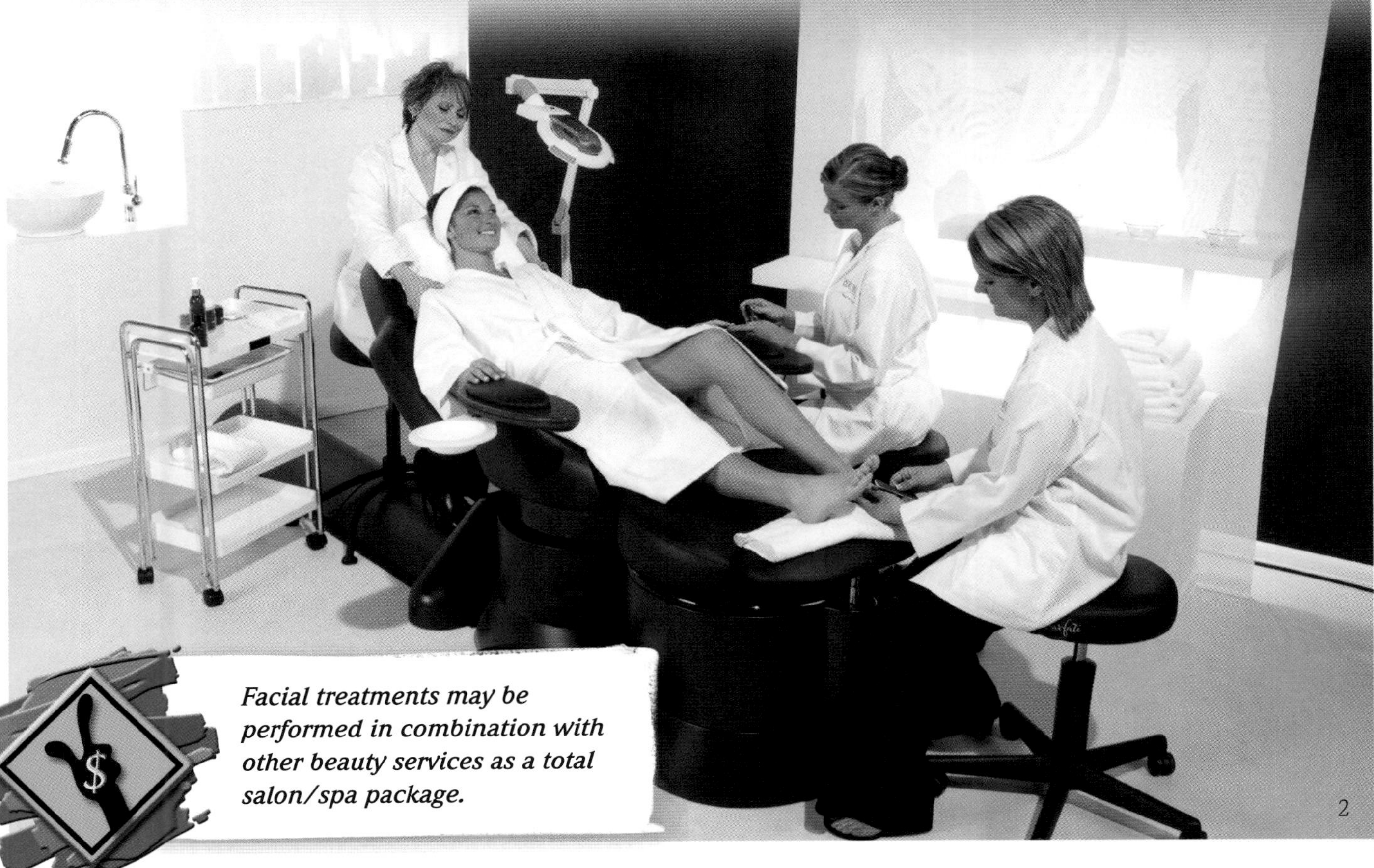

2

*Facial treatments may be performed in combination with other beauty services as a total salon/spa package.*

# Client Consultation . . .

*Prior to any skin service, the* ***cosmetologist should communicate*** *with the client on his or her* ***skin-care needs.*** *As a professional, it is necessary for you to* ***listen, ask a series of questions and document answers.*** *During consultation, the cosmetologist records all information on a client record card.*

**The following are a few questions to ask the client during a consultation:**

1) How is your general or overall health?

2) Are you currently being treated by a medical care professional? If so, why and what type of treatments and/or medications are you receiving?

3) Are you taking any daily medication?

4) What products are you currently using for skin-care and what is your skin-care regimen?

5) What is your occupation and general lifestyle?

**NOTE:** Assure client confidentiality, but stress the importance of accurate information to provide client safety and optimal results.

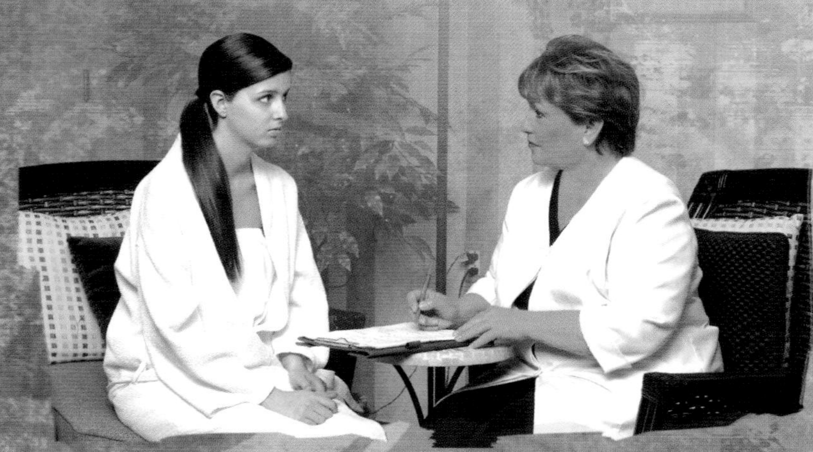

# Client Consultation . . .

DATE SERVICE/TREATMENT REMARKS/CHANGES

☑Medical Al

## Client Profile Card/File

Name ____________ Date ______

Address ____________

____________

Occupation ______ Phone ______

Birthdate ____________

Referred by ____________

Date of consultation ______ Age__ Gender__

Oral Contraceptives? ❑ Pregnant? ❑ Trying to be? ❑

Medications ❑ Allergies ❑ Health Problems ❑

Cosmetologist ______ Lic # ______

**Facial Area:**

Normal ❑

Dry ❑

Combination ❑

Mature ❑

Thin, sensitive skin ❑

Oily ❑

Open pores ❑

Comedones (blackheads) ❑

Milia (whiteheads) ❑

Acne ❑

Vulgaris ❑ Chronic ❑

Cystic ❑ Rosacea ❑

How many years? ___

Scars (acne, etc.) ❑

Wrinkles ❑

Superficial lines ❑

Deep lines ❑

Relaxed elasticity ❑

Good elasticity ❑

Couperose (capillaries) ❑

Discolorations ❑

REMARKS ____________

____________

13

# Skin Analysis . . .

*After the client consultation is completed, a skin analysis is performed to decide the skin type and which facial treatment and products are to be used. The analysis is an actual* ***"visual" examination*** *of the client's skin.*

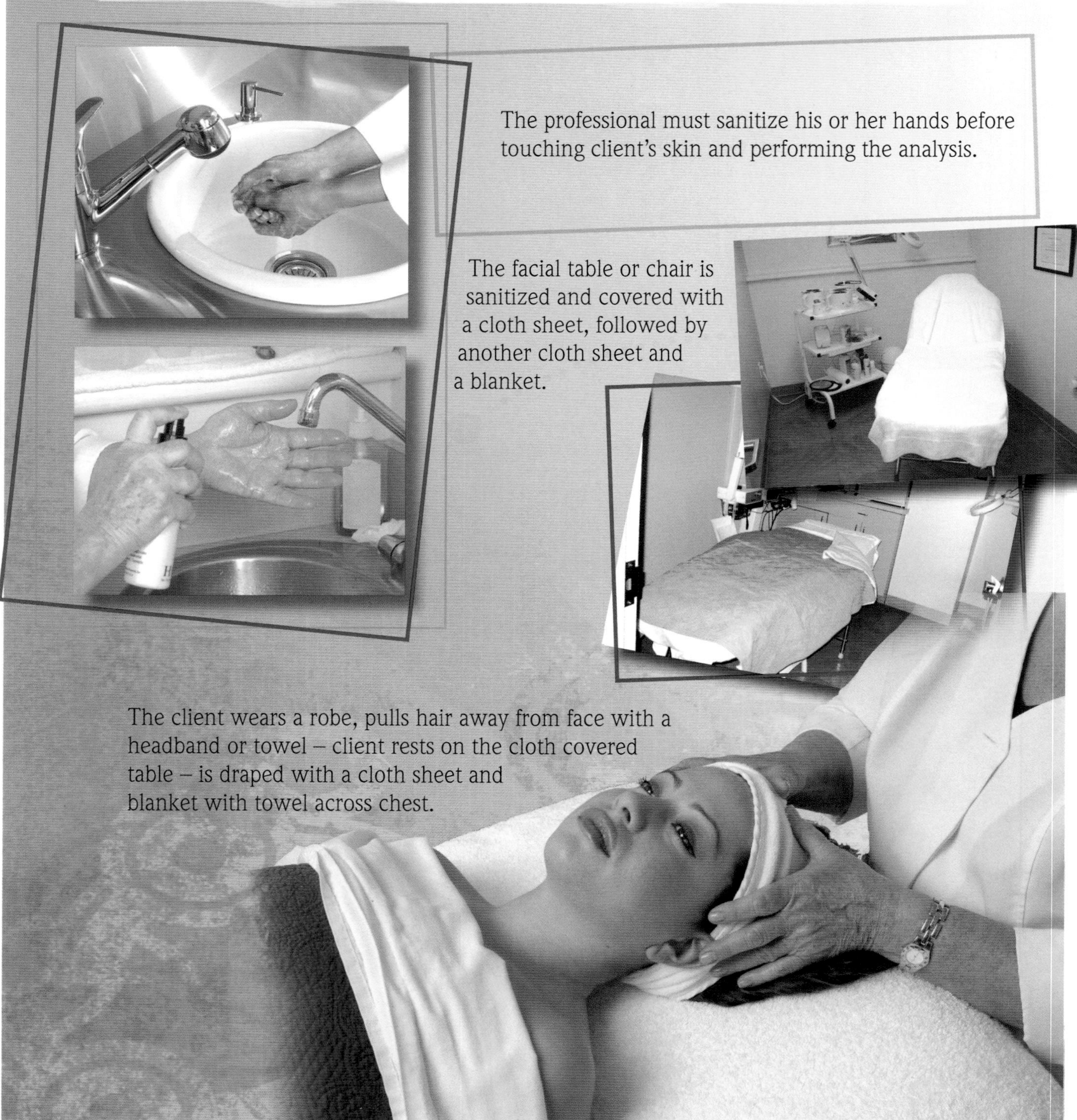

The professional must sanitize his or her hands before touching client's skin and performing the analysis.

The facial table or chair is sanitized and covered with a cloth sheet, followed by another cloth sheet and a blanket.

The client wears a robe, pulls hair away from face with a headband or towel – client rests on the cloth covered table – is draped with a cloth sheet and blanket with towel across chest.

# Skin Analysis . . .

The client's skin is cleansed and a magnifying glass is used to view the skin type, pore size and areas of concern.

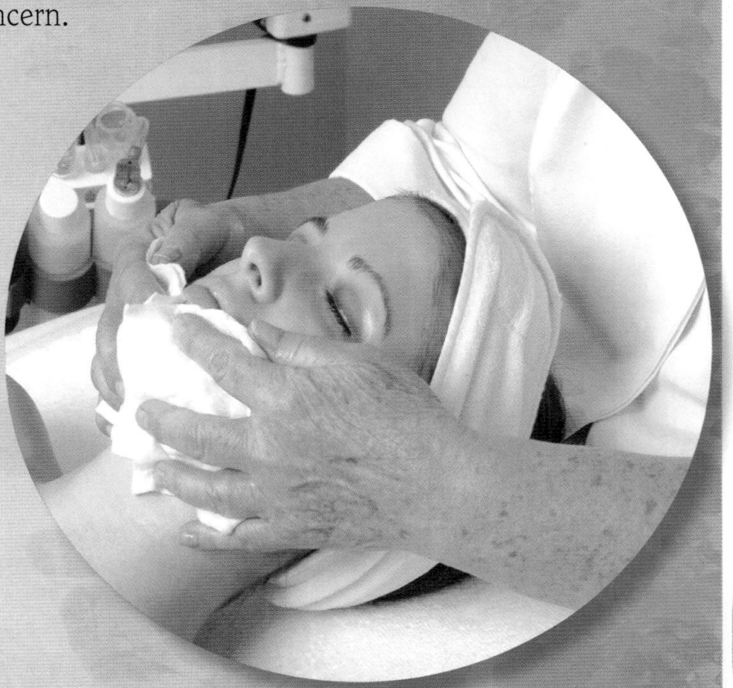

**Cleansing the skin** is necessary to accurately determine the client's skin type. **Pore size**, whether visible or absent, is the first area of importance to check. The amount of sebum secreted from the sebaceous glands, as well as location, determines pore size and whether the skin is oily, combination or dry.

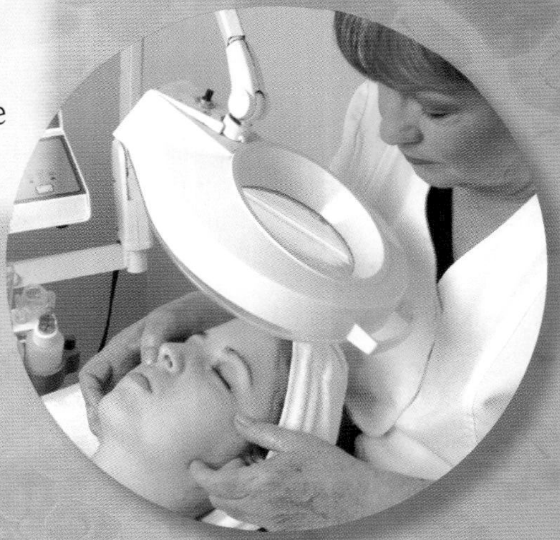

**DISCLAIMER:** *Consultation and skin analysis are standard procedures before every facial treatment; however, each skin treatment is individualized according to client's skin type, condition and need. The products used and their application will differ to accommodate each individual's skin-care maintenance.* ***The following procedures listed offer a "format" to use; or you may develop your own system of applying the products during a treatment.*** *As the professional, you must make those necessary adjustments to assure your client a proper skin-care regimen.*

CLIC INTERNATIONAL RA

SIMPLE LAB PROJECT

# Preservative Facial Treatment

Before

After without Makeup

After with Makeup

### OBJECTIVE

To maintain the health and beauty of the facial skin and promote relaxation.

## TOOLS & MATERIALS

- Robe
- Cloth & disposable towels
- Headband or cap
- Protective sheet or blanket
- Gloves (optional)
- Applicator brush
- Spatulas
- Cotton or cotton pads
- Product containers
- Cleanser
- Exfoliation product
- Essential oils (optional)
- Toner
- Moisturizer
- Massage cream or oil
- Client record card/file
- Mask product

## PROCEDURE

**"The client consultation is an important part of your professional service. Be sure to complete this step prior to each client service you provide. Your successful retail sales and customer satisfaction rates depend upon it!"**

RETAIL RE-BOOK REFERRAL

1. Cosmetologist sanitizes hands and station.
2. Set out service tools and materials.
3. Drape the client in preparation for service.
4. Follow procedure as shown and manufacturer's instructions.
5. Follow standard cleanup procedure.
6. Document client record card/file.

13

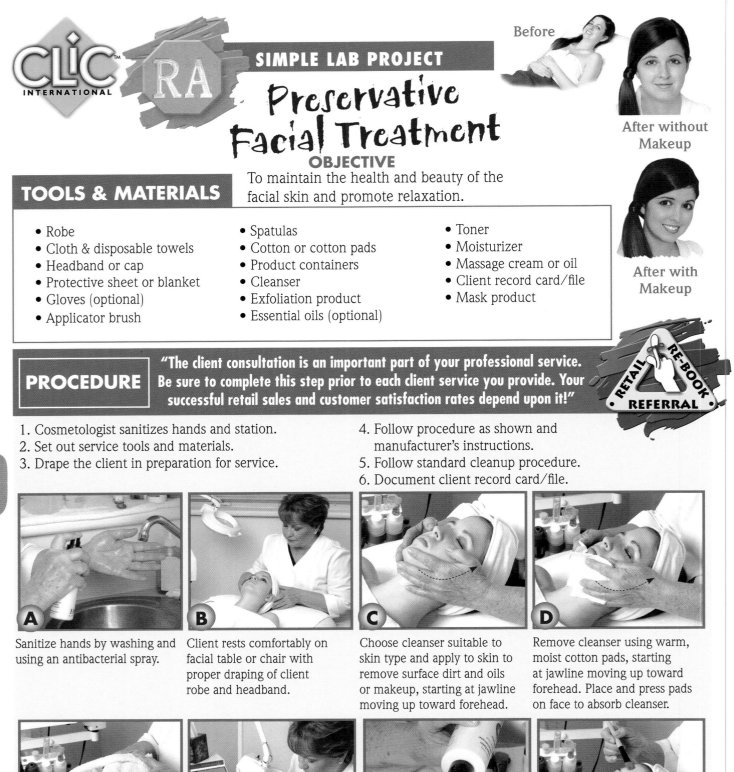

A Sanitize hands by washing and using an antibacterial spray.

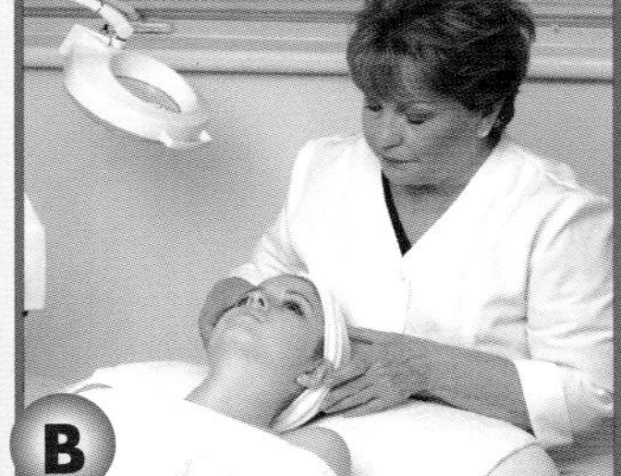

B Client rests comfortably on facial table or chair with proper draping of client robe and headband.

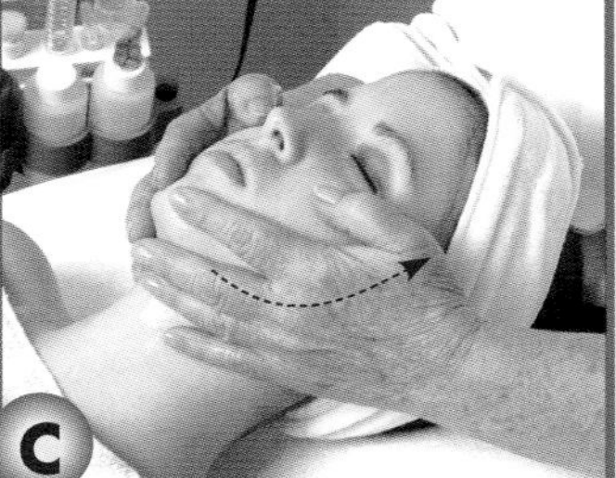

C Choose cleanser suitable to skin type and apply to skin to remove surface dirt and oils or makeup, starting at jawline moving up toward forehead.

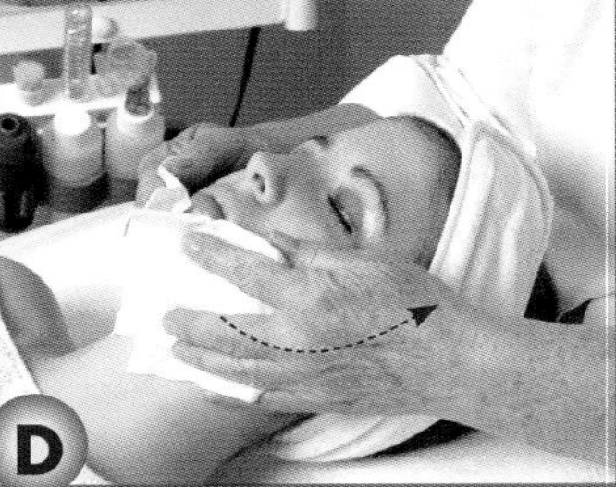

D Remove cleanser using warm, moist cotton pads, starting at jawline moving up toward forehead. Place and press pads on face to absorb cleanser.

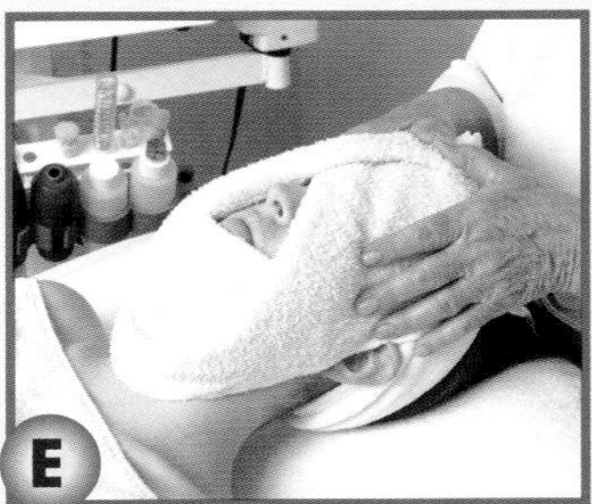

E Place and wrap a warm, moist cloth towel on face, pressing on skin to hydrate and increase perspiration.

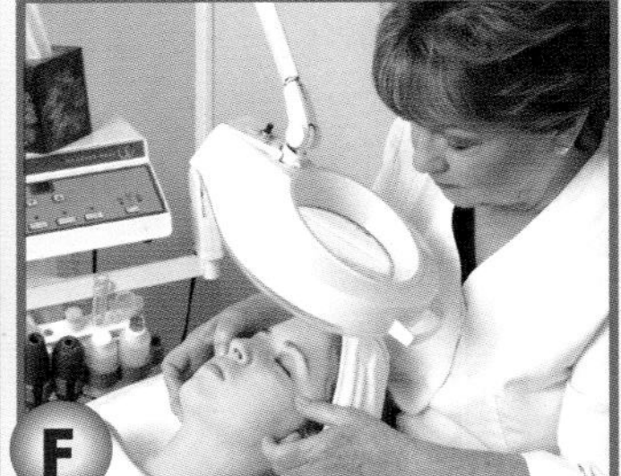

F Perform skin analysis using a magnifying lamp. Check on skin type, pore location/size and if any skin conditions exist.

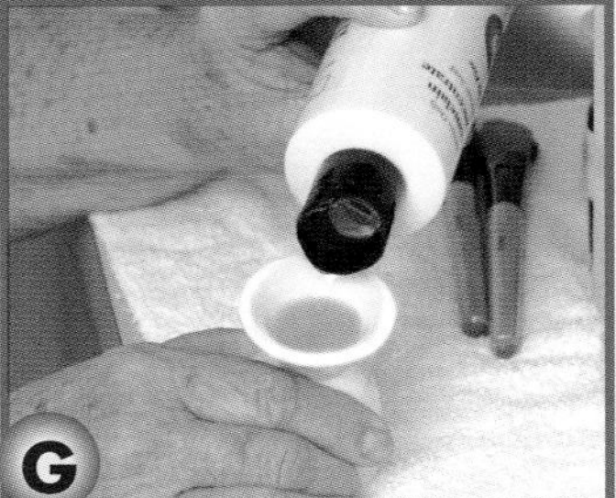

G Prepare an exfoliating treatment (AHA-enzyme peel) to assist in removal of dead surface skin cells.

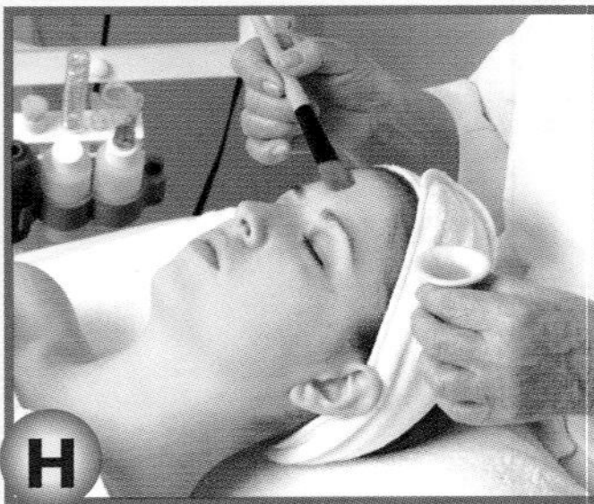

H Use an applicator brush, apply product to entire facial skin, except lips and eyelids. This treatment will produce a slight tingling feeling.

## Preservative Facial Treatment

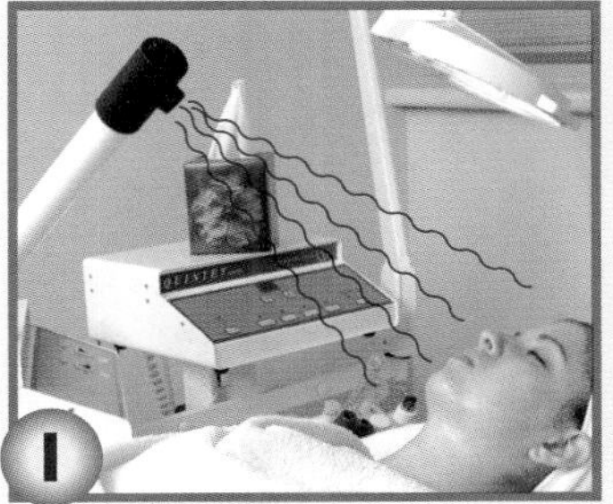

**Optional:** The use of steam over the face will assist in product penetration and will keep exfoliant moist.

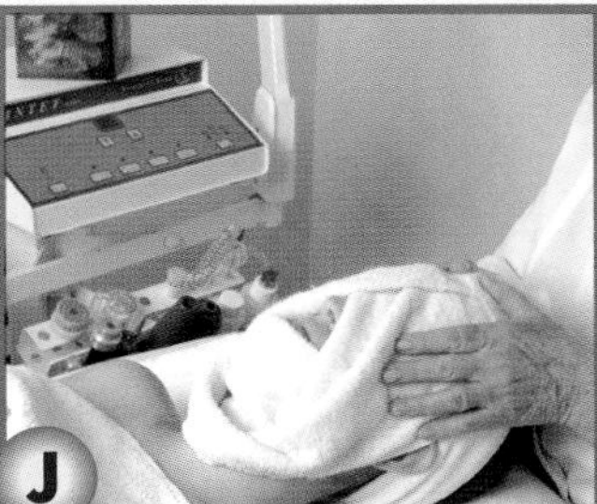

To remove the enzyme peel, use warm, moist cloth towel, lightly place and press over entire face.

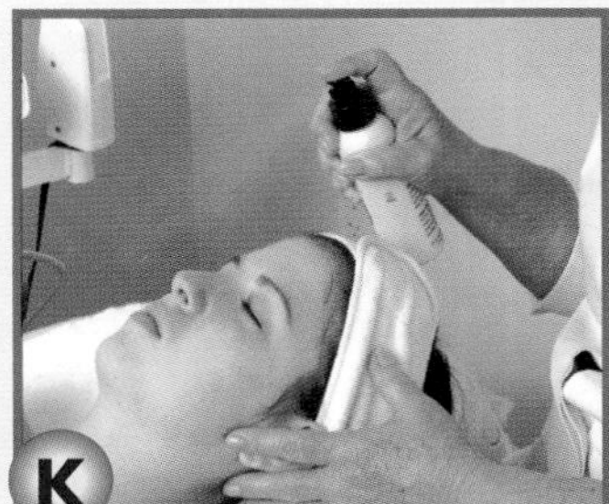

Apply a toner or astringent in either a spray or liquid form. If using spray-form, lightly mist in the air to prevent startling client.

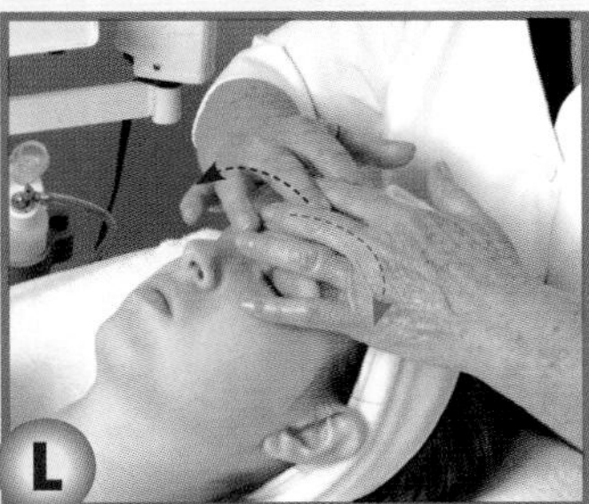

Using a massage oil or cream, perform facial manipulations, starting with an **effleurage** (stroking) movement across the forehead (frontalis). Refer to basic facial massage procedure in this chapter.

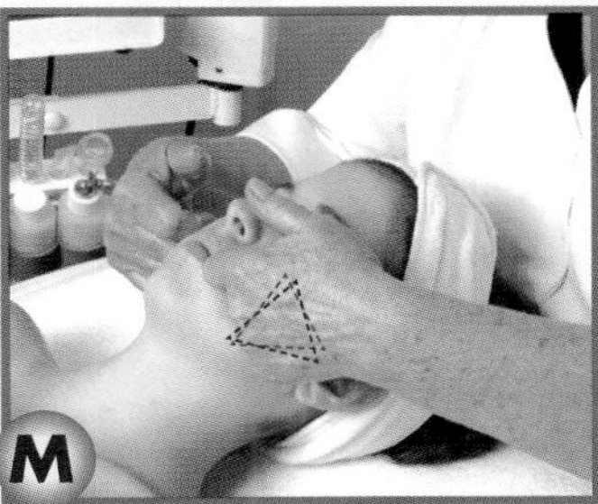

Continue massage with **petrissage** (kneading) movements over the cheek muscles (zygomaticus major and minor) and forehead area.

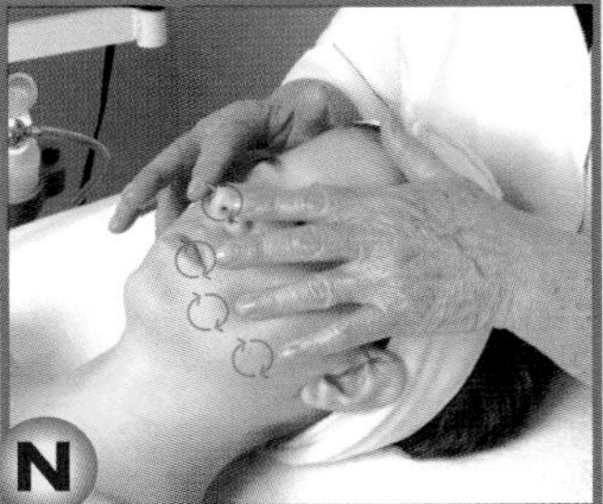

Apply **percussion** (tapping) movements across cheeks and complete with stroking down neck muscle (trapezius) to chest muscle (pectoralis).

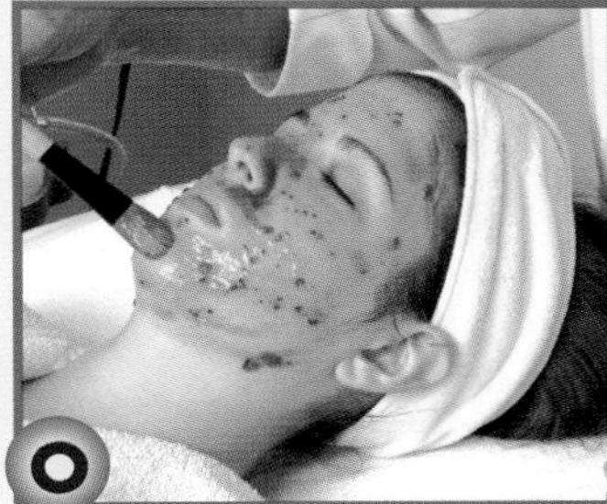

Apply a mask suitable to client's skin type over entire face using brush, except lips and eyelids.

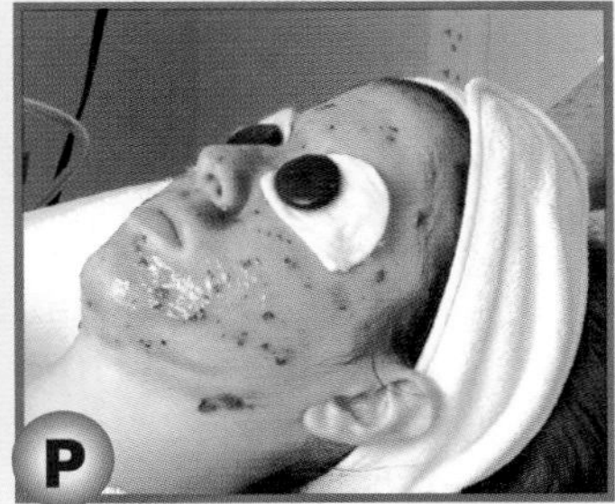

Cover eyes and allow mask to stay on skin following manufacturer instructions.

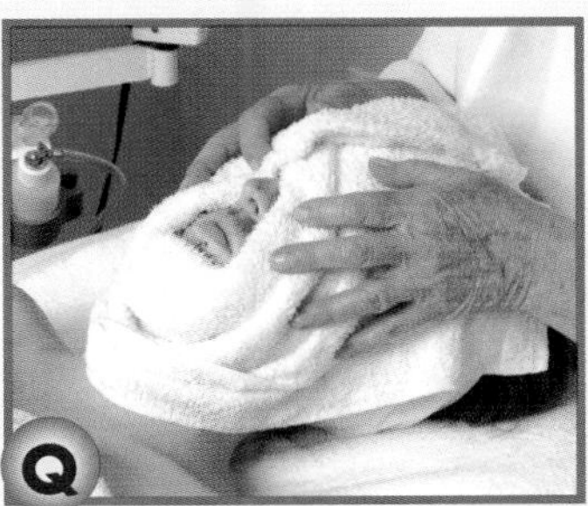

Apply and press warm, moist cloth towel to skin to remove mask.

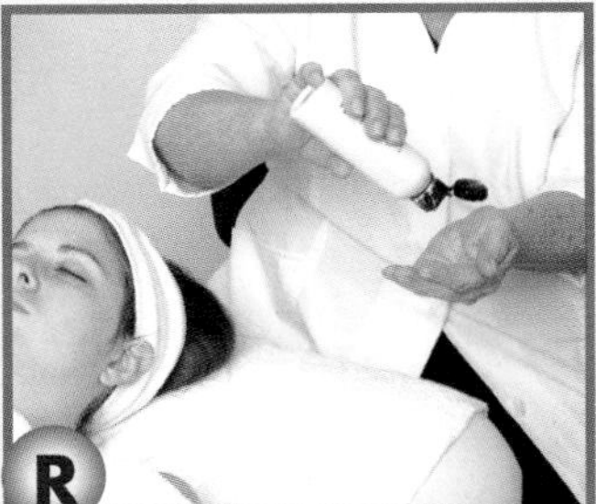

Place moisturizer with sunscreen in hand to warm product.

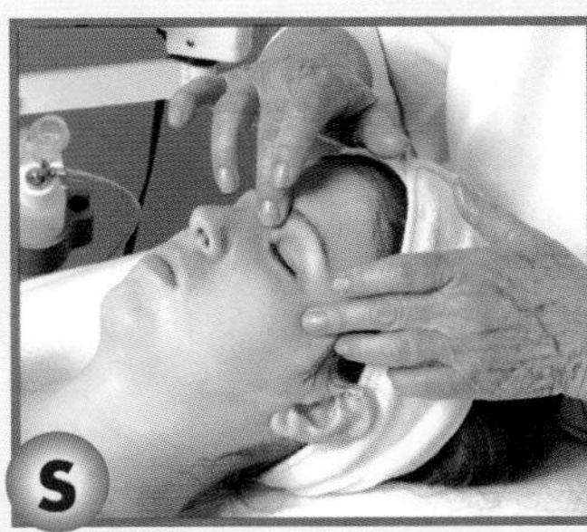

Apply moisturizer over entire face, including eyelids and lips.

**Completed preservative facial treatment.**

GRADE | STUDENT'S NAME | ID#

CLiC™ INTERNATIONAL

RA

SIMPLE LAB PROJECT

# Preservative Facial Massage

Before

After without Makeup

## OBJECTIVE

To tone and tighten facial skin, increase blood circulation and promote relaxation.

## TOOLS & MATERIALS

- Robe
- Cloth & disposable towels
- Headband or cap
- Protective sheet or blanket
- Gloves (optional)
- Spatulas
- Cotton or cotton pads
- Product containers
- Cleanser
- Applicator brush
- Essential oils (optional)
- Toner
- Moisturizer
- Massage cream or oil
- Client record card/file

## PROCEDURE

**"The client consultation is an important part of your professional service. Be sure to complete this step prior to each client service you provide. Your successful retail sales and customer satisfaction rates depend upon it!"**

RETAIL RE-BOOK REFERRAL

13

1. Cosmetologist sanitizes hands and station.
2. Set out service tools and materials.
3. Drape the client in preparation for service.
4. Follow procedure as shown and manufacturer's instructions.
5. Follow standard cleanup procedure
6. Document client record card/file.

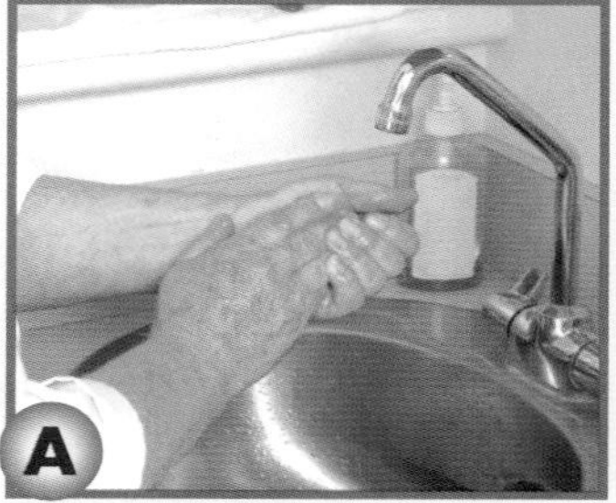

Sanitize hands by washing and using an antibacterial spray.

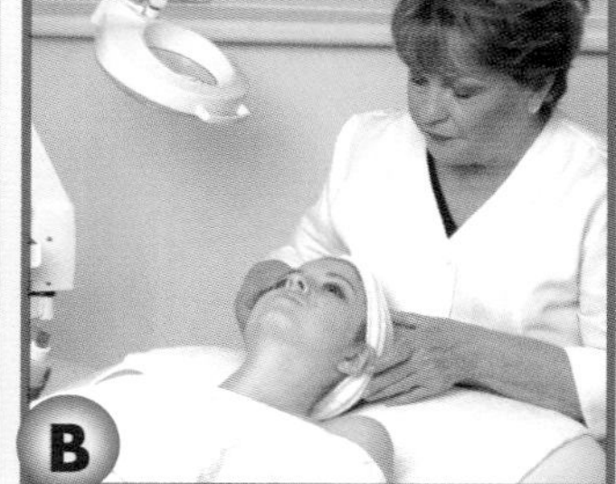

Client rests comfortably on facial table.

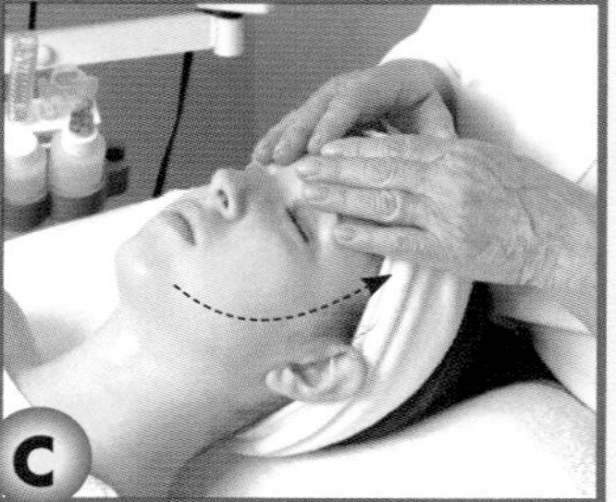

Apply cleanser suitable to skin type, starting at jawline moving up toward forehead.

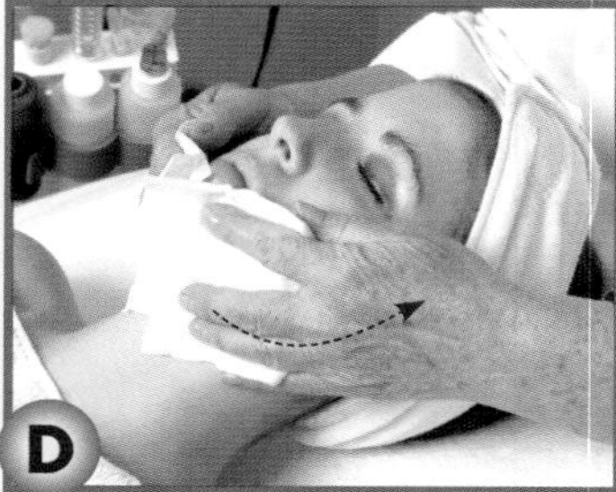

Remove cleanser using warm, moist cotton pads and cloth towel on face.

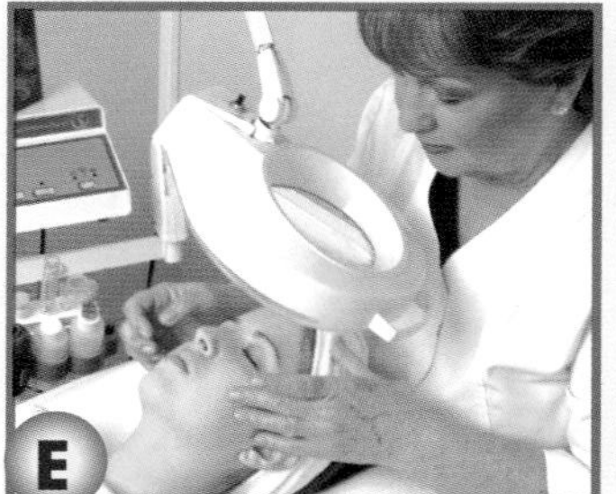

Continue with facial treatment, performing the skin analysis and exfoliation mask.

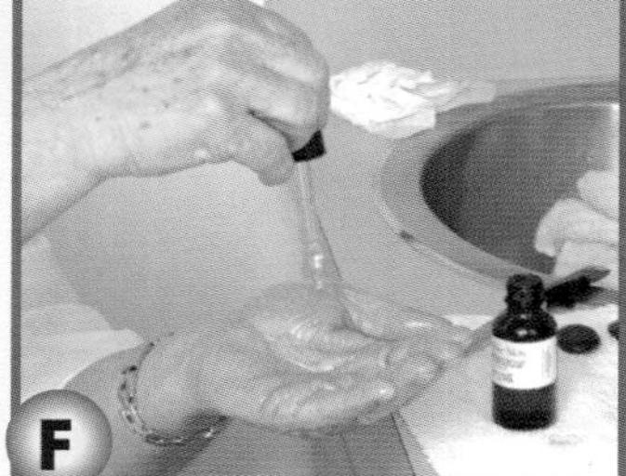

Apply massage oil or cream to the palms of hands first to warm product.

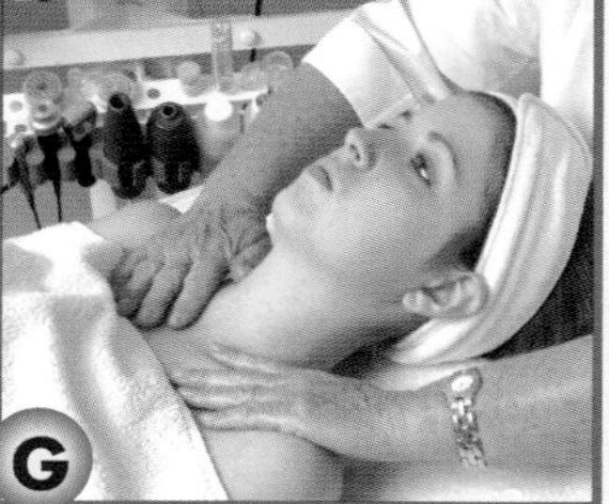

Place palms of hands on chest (pectoralis muscle) moving product over chest muscle and neck muscles (platysma and sternocleidomastoideus).

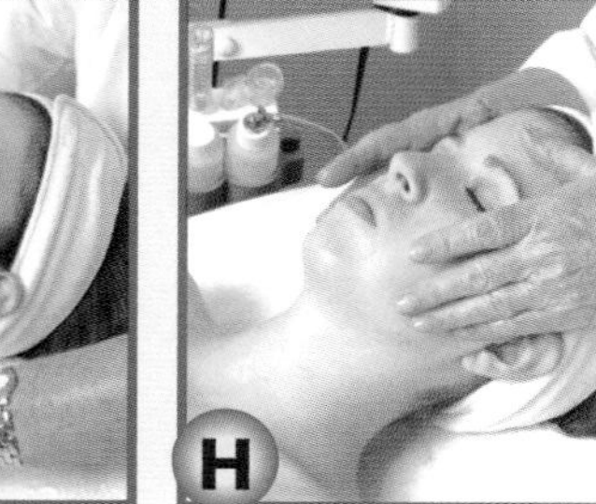

Continue spreading massage cream or oil over entire face.

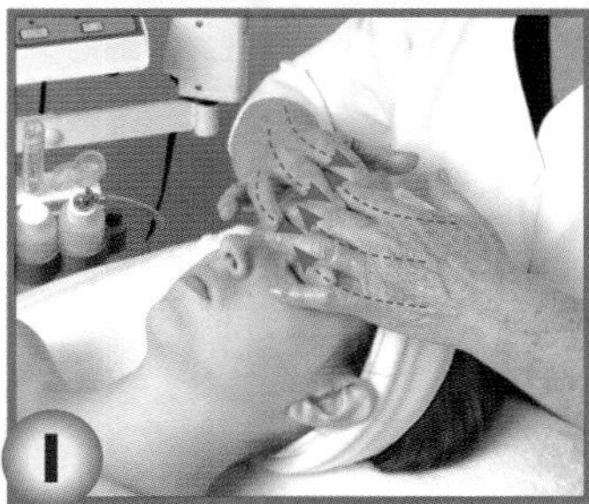
I

Perform facial manipulations, starting with the effleurage (stroking) movement of interlocking fingers across the forehead (frontalis).

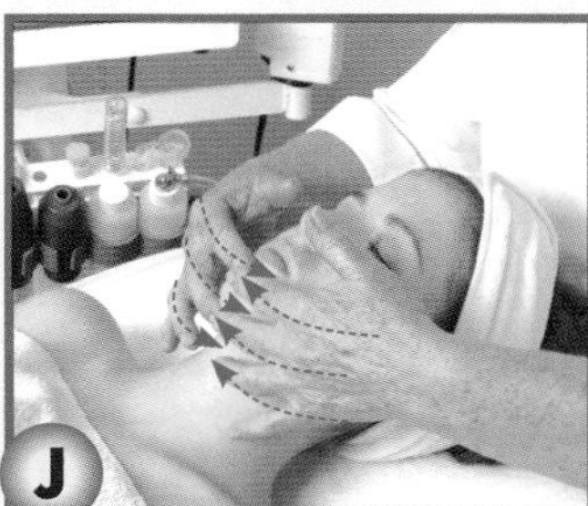
J

Continue effleurage movement of interlocking fingers over chin muscle (mentalis) and across lower part of cheeks

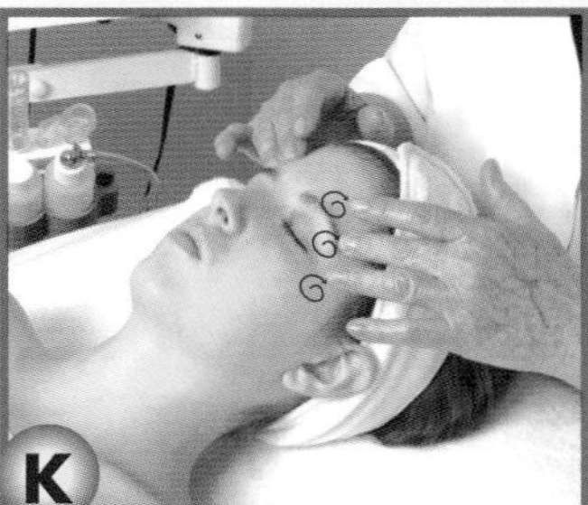
K

Apply circular movements around eye and eyebrow muscle (orbicularis oculi).

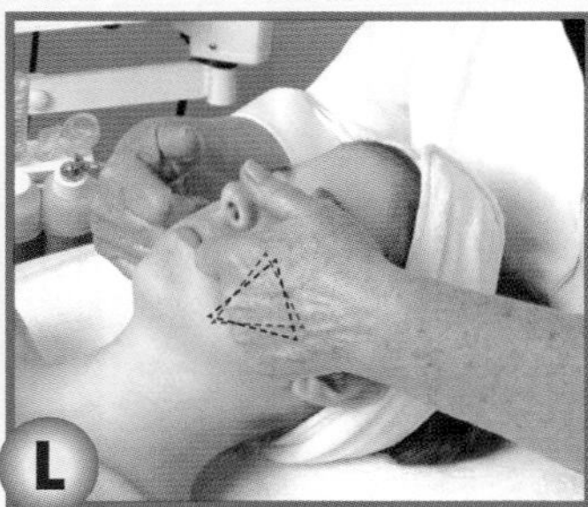
L

Continue massage with petrissage (kneading) movements over the cheeks and forehead area.

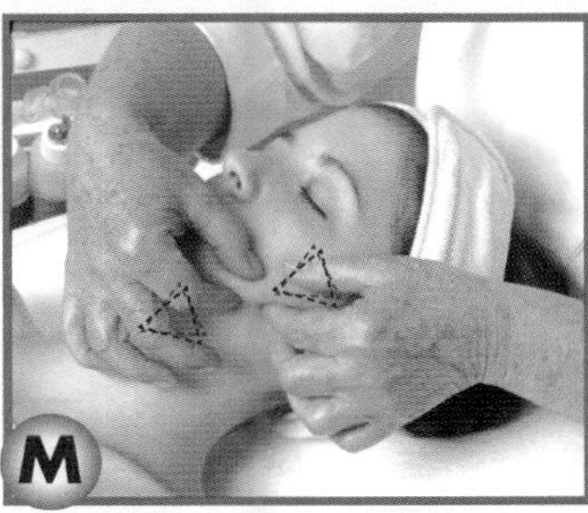
M

Apply friction (pinching) movements over cheek muscles (zygomaticus major and minor) area.

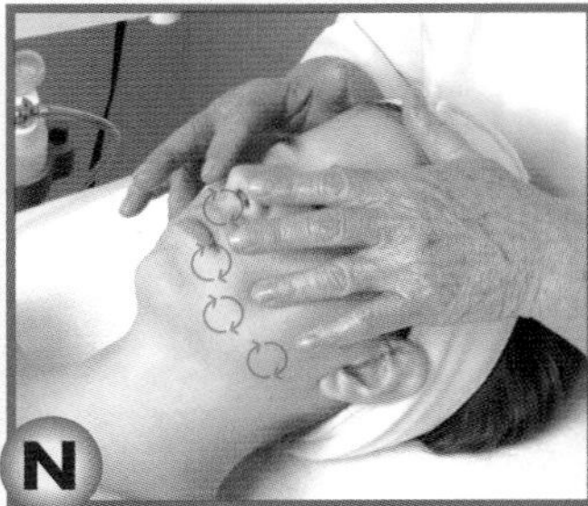
N

Apply percussion (tapping) movements over cheek area.

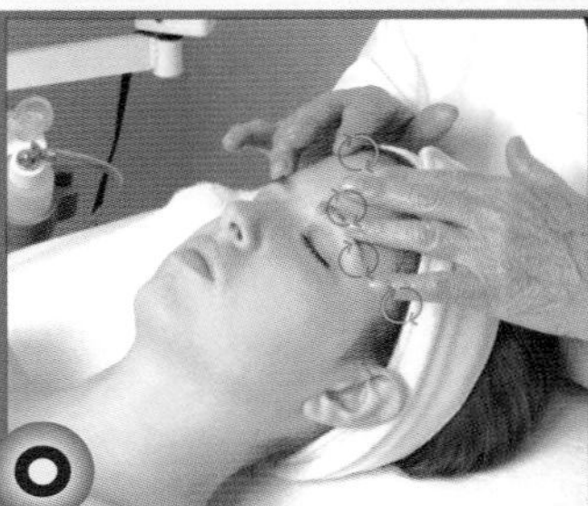
O

Continue the tapping movement across the forehead muscle.

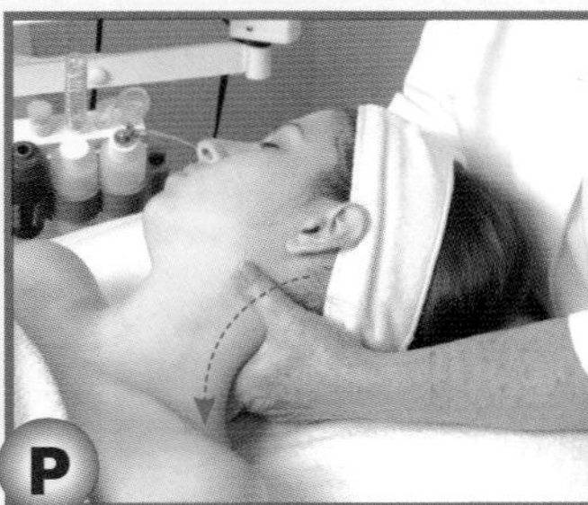
P

Perform effleurage movement of stroking down the neck muscle (trapezius).



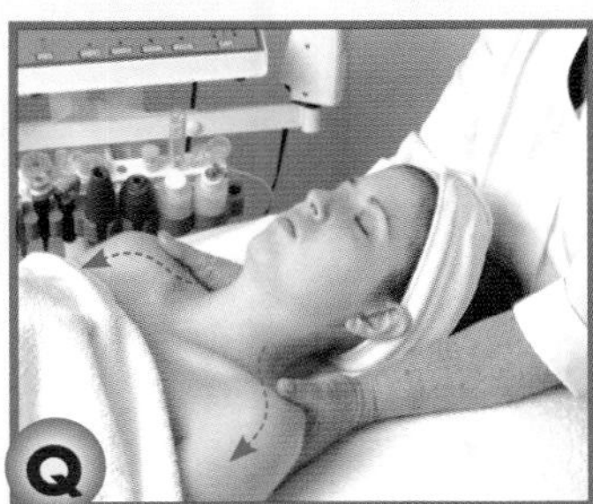
Q

Continue stroking down the back muscle (trapezius) area.

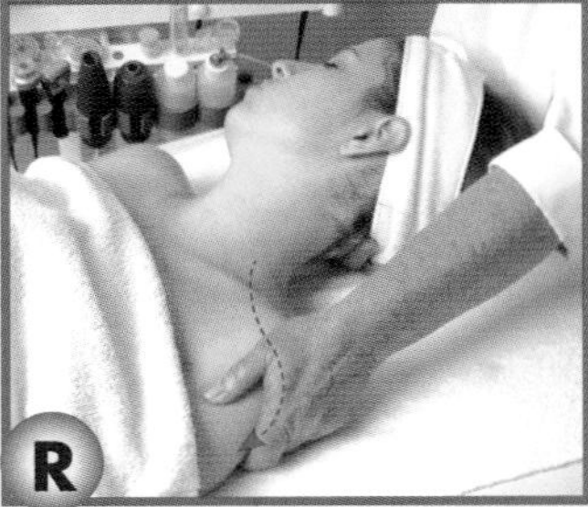
R

Complete facial massage by lightly stroking over and down the shoulder. **Optional:** application of a mask.

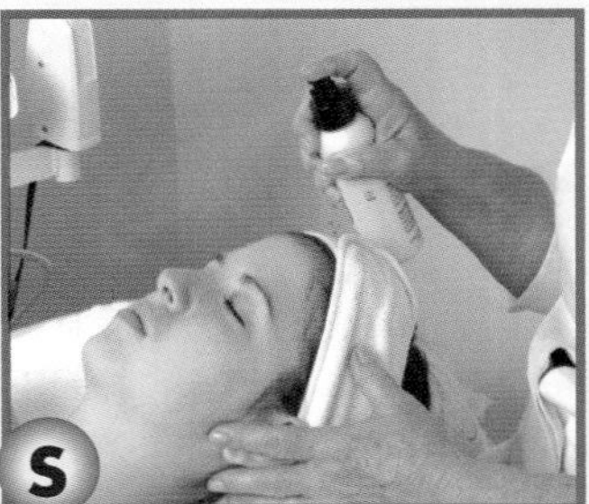
S

Apply a toner or astringent in either a spray or liquid form. Finish with application of a moisturizer and sunscreen.

T

**Completed preservative facial massage.**

## EVALUATION

GRADE    STUDENT'S NAME    ID#

CLiC™ INTERNATIONAL

**INTERMEDIATE LAB PROJECT**

# Corrective Facial Treatment for Oily Skin (Male)

## OBJECTIVE

To provide a deep cleansing and rejuvenating skin-care treatment for oily skin.

## TOOLS & MATERIALS

- Robe
- Cloth & disposable towels
- Headband or cap
- Protective sheet or blanket
- Gloves
- Mask product
- Spatulas
- Cotton or cotton pads
- Product containers
- Cleanser
- Applicator brush
- Essential oils (optional)
- Toner
- Moisturizer
- Massage cream or oil
- Client record card/file
- Exfoliation product

## PROCEDURE

**"The client consultation is an important part of your professional service. Be sure to complete this step prior to each client service you provide. Your successful retail sales and customer satisfaction rates depend upon it!"**

RETAIL RE-BOOK REFERRAL

1. Cosmetologist sanitizes hands and station.
2. Set out service tools and materials.
3. Drape the client in preparation for service.
4. Follow procedure as shown and manufacturer's instructions.
5. Follow standard cleanup procedure
6. Document client record card/file.



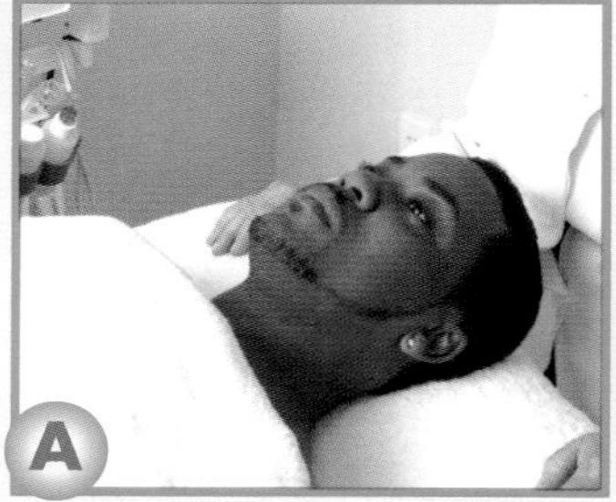

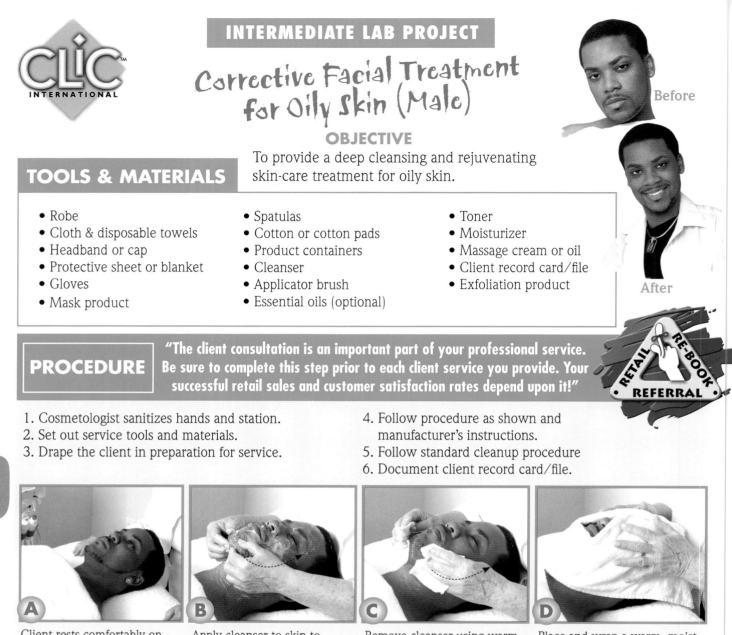

A Client rests comfortably on facial table or chair. Sanitize hands by washing and using an antibacterial spray.

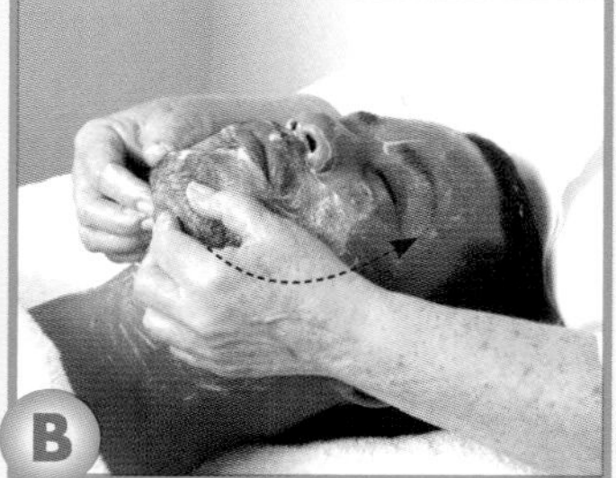

B Apply cleanser to skin to remove surface dirt and oils, start at jawline moving upward to forehead and back down face following direction of facial hair.

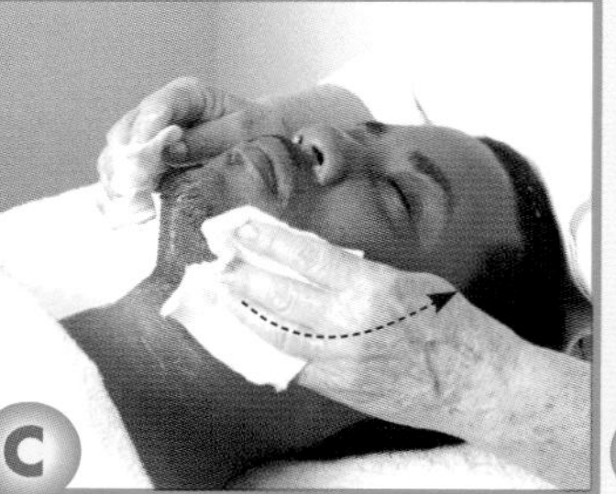

C Remove cleanser using warm, moist cotton pads, starting at jawline moving up toward forehead.

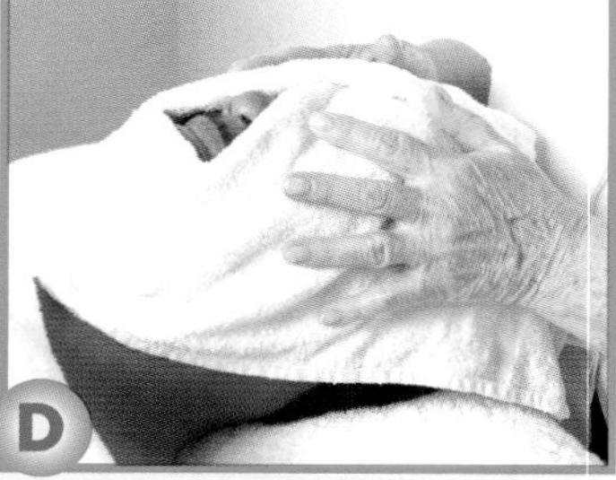

D Place and wrap a warm, moist cloth towel on face.

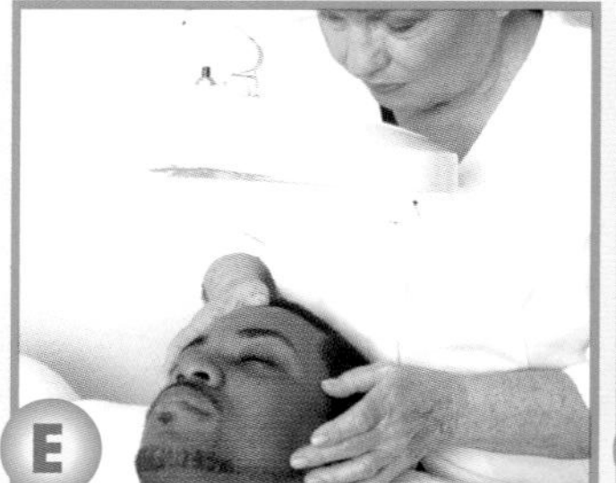

E Perform skin analysis using a magnifying lamp. Check on skin type, pore location/size and scaly or dry areas of skin.

F Prepare an exfoliating treatment (suitable to skin type) to assist in removal of dead surface skin cells.

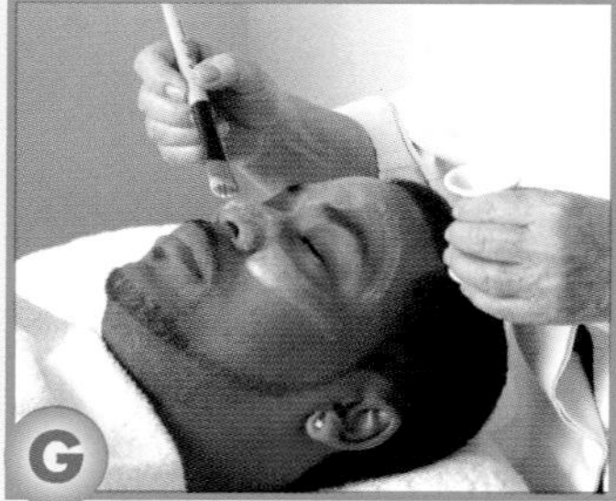

G Use an applicator brush, apply to entire facial skin, except lips and eyelids.

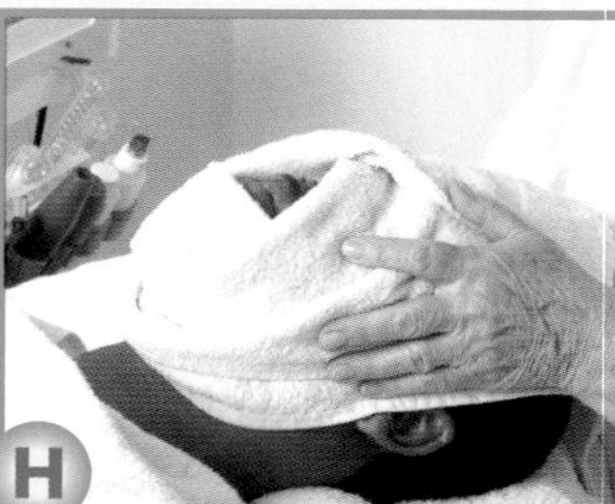

H To remove exfoliant, use warm, moist cloth towel placed and pressed over entire face

# Corrective Facial Treatment for Oily Skin (Male)

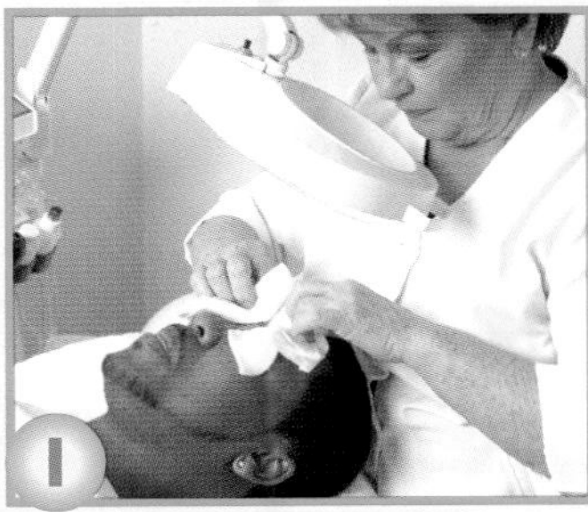
I

**Optional: Extraction of blackheads or pimples.** Apply moist cotton pads over eyes: hold a soft tissue in each hand and place at area of extraction.

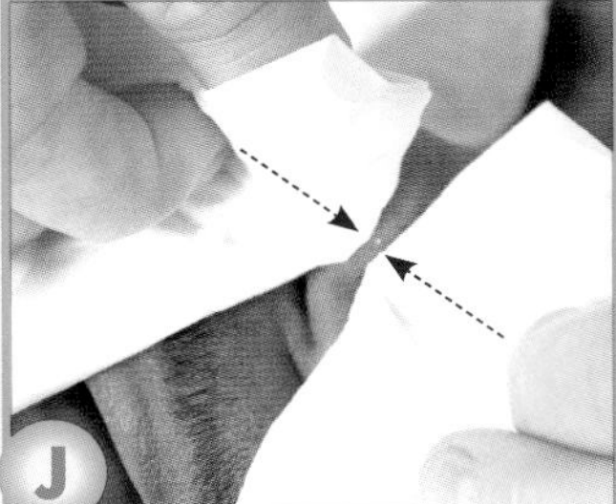
J

Recommended to wear gloves. **Gently** squeeze - press down and in - the area surrounding blackhead or pimple.

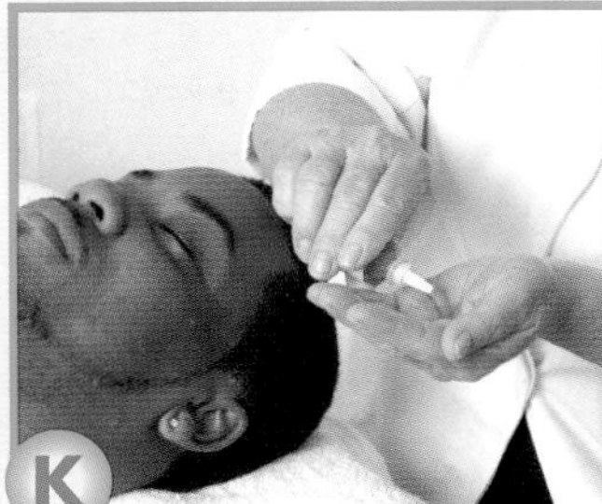
K

**Lightly** dab a serum enriched with vitamins and minerals to promote healing of skin.

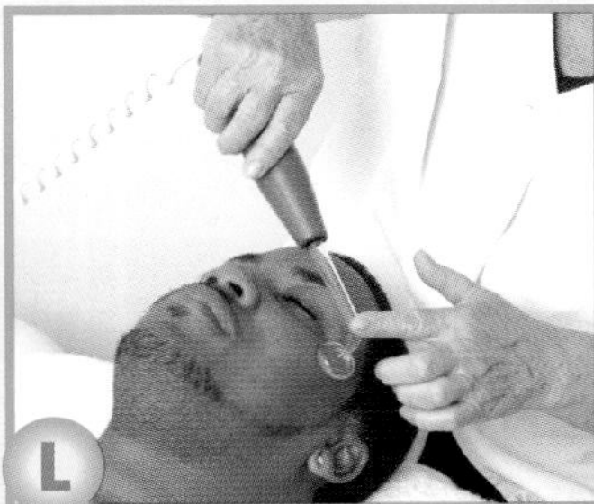
L

**Optional:** Use high-frequency current with a facial glass electrode, glide over areas of extraction to kill germs and increase healing.

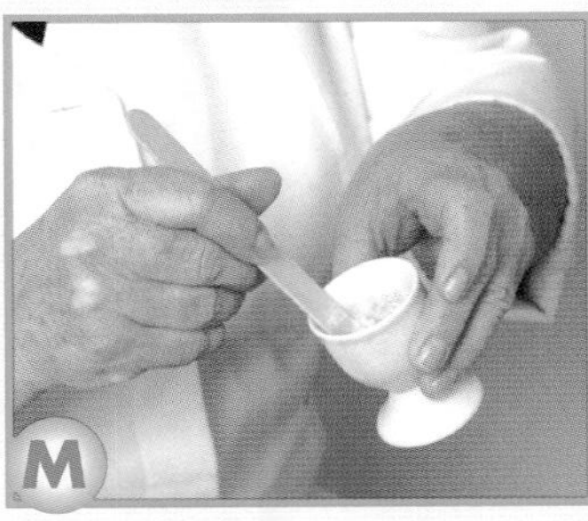
M

Prepare a clay mask to draw out sebum and impurities from the skin.

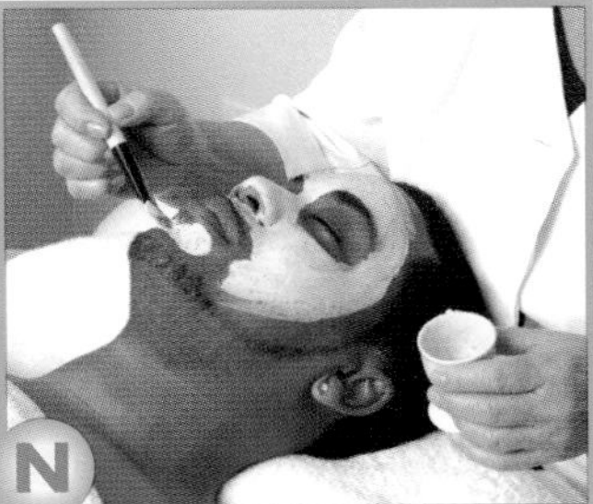
N

Apply to all areas of face with the exception of eyelids, lips and for men, any facial hair.

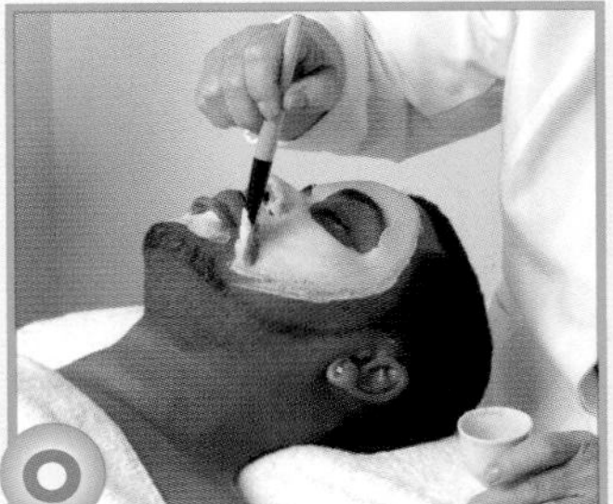
O

Allow mask to dry and remain on skin following manufacturer's instructions.

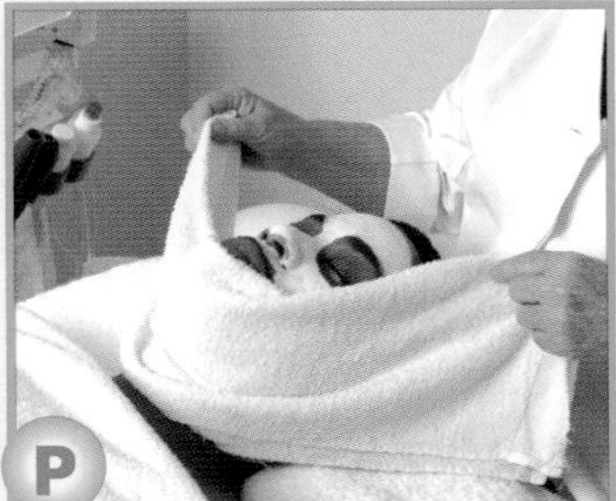
P

Place and press a warm, moist cloth towel on skin to remove mask product.

13

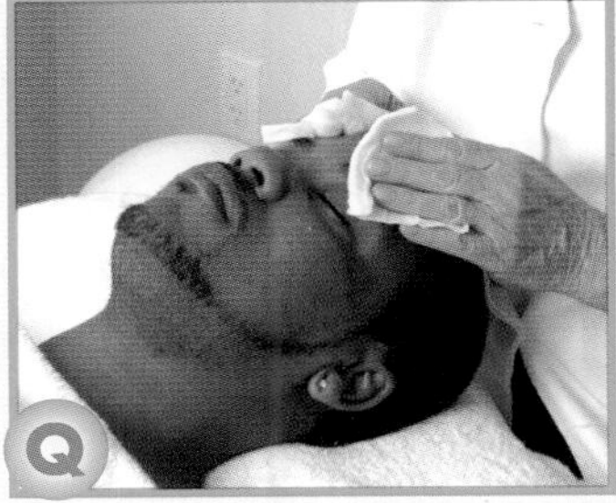
Q

Continue to remove clay mask using warm, moist cotton pads.

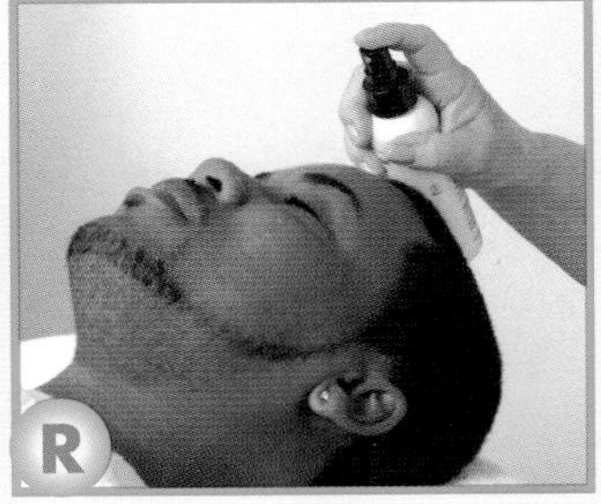
R

Apply a toner or astringent using either a spray or liquid form.

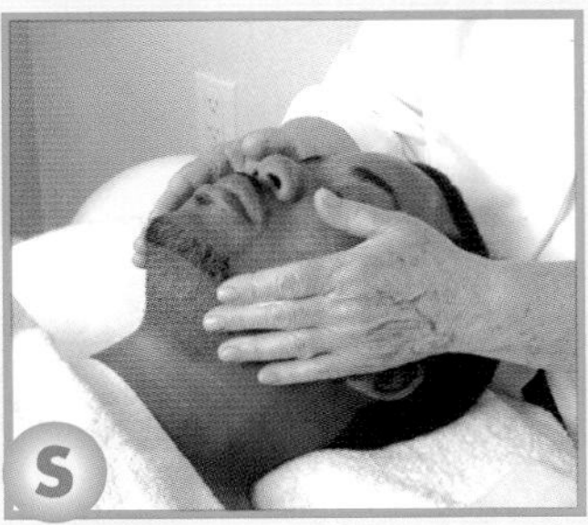
S

Apply moisturizer with sunscreen over entire face, including eyelids and lips.

T

**Completed facial treatment for oily skin.**

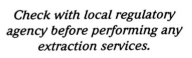

***Check with local regulatory agency before performing any extraction services.***

**EVALUATION** ______________________________

______________ ______________________________ ______________________________
**GRADE** STUDENT'S NAME ID#

INTERMEDIATE LAB PROJECT

# Corrective Facial Treatment with Chemical Peel

(AHA-Glycolic Acid)

Before

After without Makeup

After with Makeup

## OBJECTIVE

To encourage new skin cell regeneration through a series of exfoliating treatments.

## TOOLS & MATERIALS

- Robe
- Cloth & disposable towels
- Headband or cap
- Protective sheet or blanket
- Gloves (optional)
- Mask product
- Spatulas
- Cotton or cotton pads
- Product containers
- Cleanser
- Applicator brush
- Essential oils (optional)
- Toner
- Moisturizer
- Massage cream or oil
- Client record card/file
- Glycolic acid

## PROCEDURE

"The client consultation is an important part of your professional service. Be sure to complete this step prior to each client service you provide. Your successful retail sales and customer satisfaction rates depend upon it!"

RETAIL • RE-BOOK • REFERRAL

1. Cosmetologist sanitizes hands and station.
2. Set out service tools and materials.
3. Drape the client in preparation for service.
4. Follow procedure as shown and manufacturer's instructions.
5. Follow standard cleanup procedure
6. Document client record card/file.

13

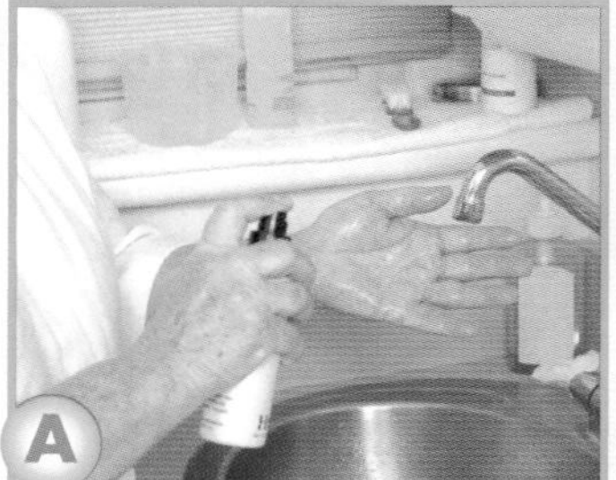
A Sanitize hands by washing and using an antibacterial spray.

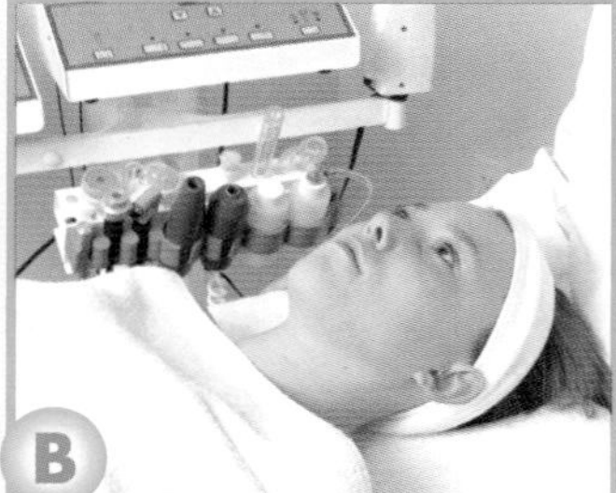
B Client rests comfortably on facial table or chair with a proper draping of client robe and headband.

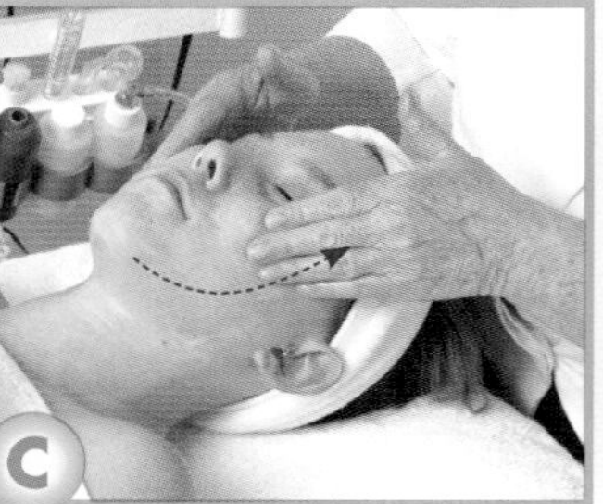
C Apply cleanser to skin to remove surface dirt and oils or makeup, starting at jawline moving up toward forehead.

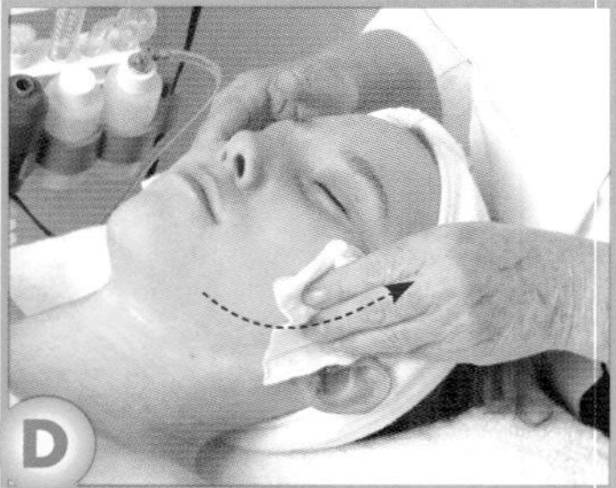
D Remove cleanser using warm, moist cotton pads, starting at jawline moving up toward forehead.

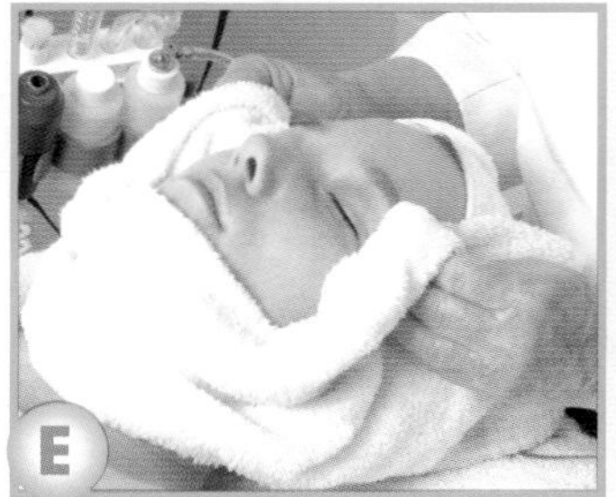
E Place and wrap a warm, moist cloth towel on face to remove any excess product and keep skin moist.

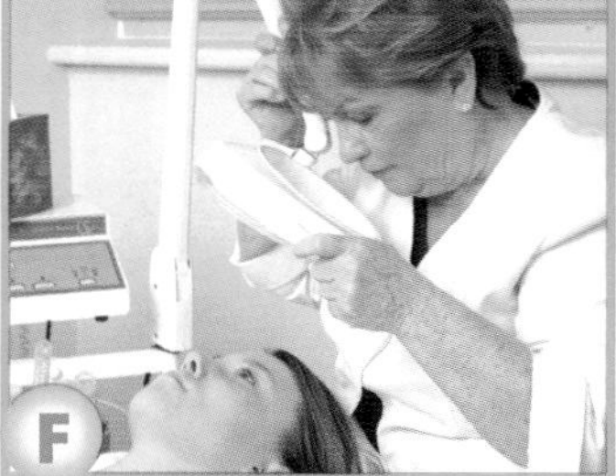
F Perform skin analysis using a magnifying lamp. Check on skin type, pore location/size and scaly or dry areas of skin.

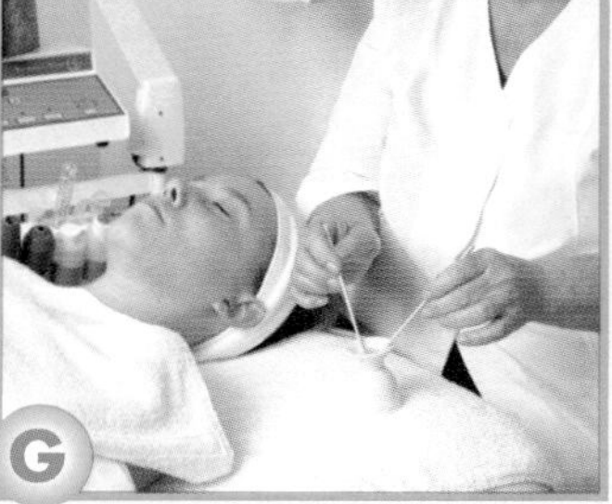
G Place glycolic acid into container and use disposable cotton-tipped applicators to glide product over skin.

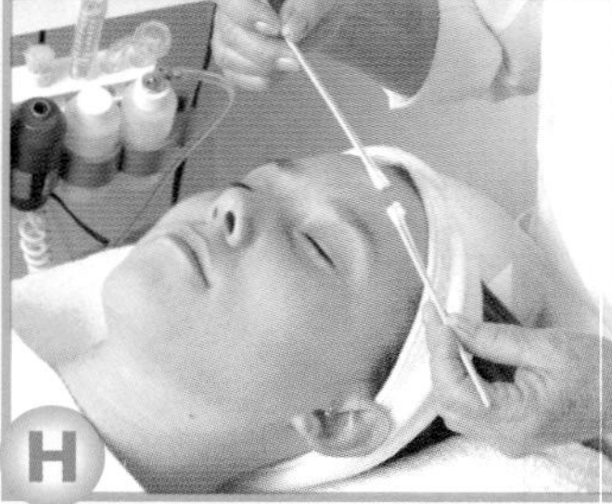
H **Gently** apply glycolic acid to the skin, starting at the forehead. **Optional:** Keep moving product over face to provide a higher degree of exfoliation.

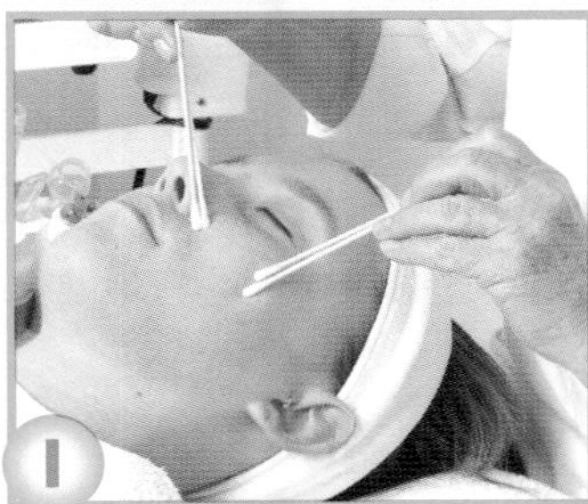
I

Continue applying product to cheeks, nose and chin areas. **CAUTION: DO NOT** apply glycolic acid to lips or eyelids.

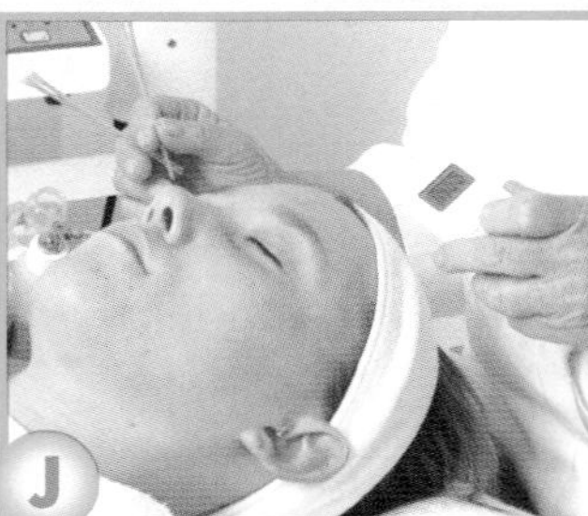
J

Glycolic acid may remain on skin 5 to 10 minutes, with a maximum of 10 minutes. This treatment will produce a slight itching and burning feeling.

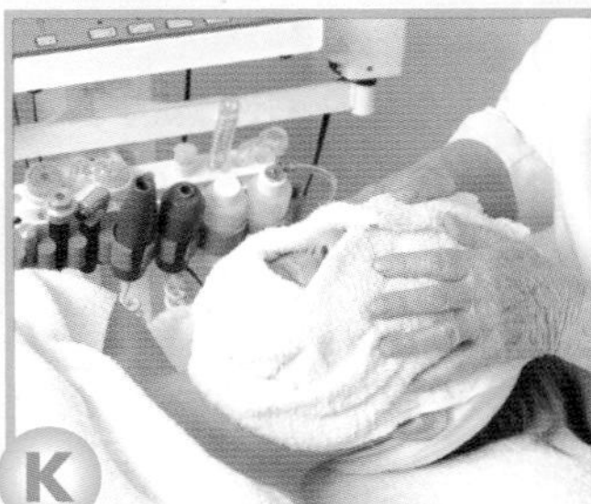
K

Remove glycolic product with warm, moist cloth towel using light pressure. Skin is sensitive to heat.

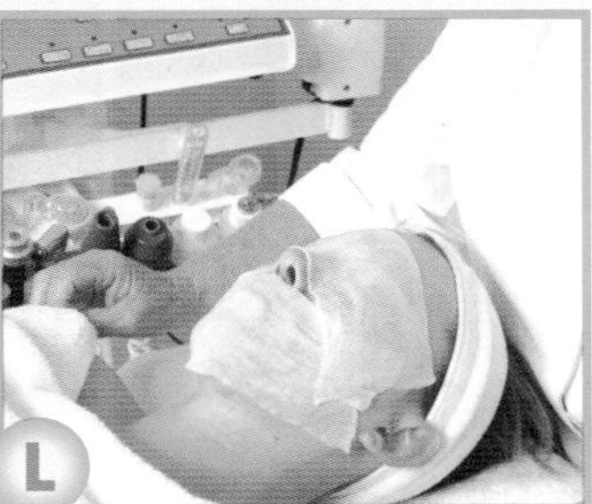
L

Apply and press cool, moist cotton pads to skin to reduce heat.

M

Place a mask enriched with vitamins into container.

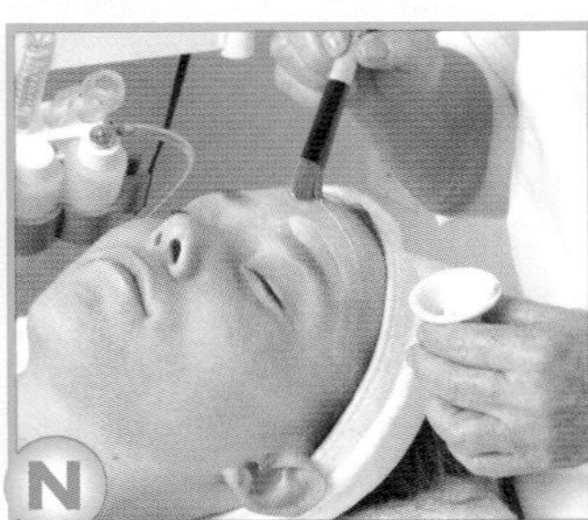
N

Apply mask to entire face using an applicator brush, starting at the forehead.

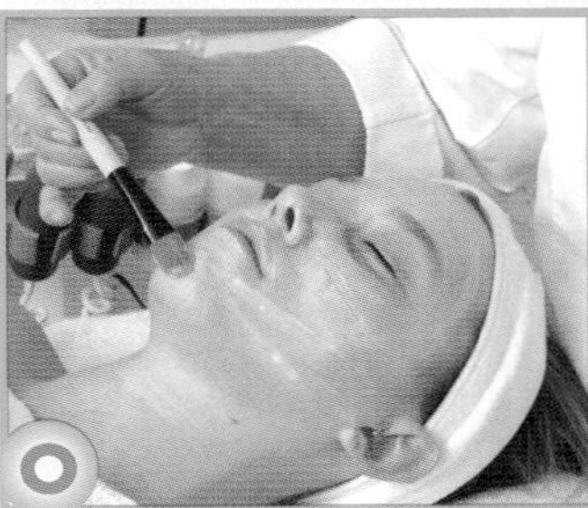
O

Continue applying mask to face with the exception of the eyelids and lips.

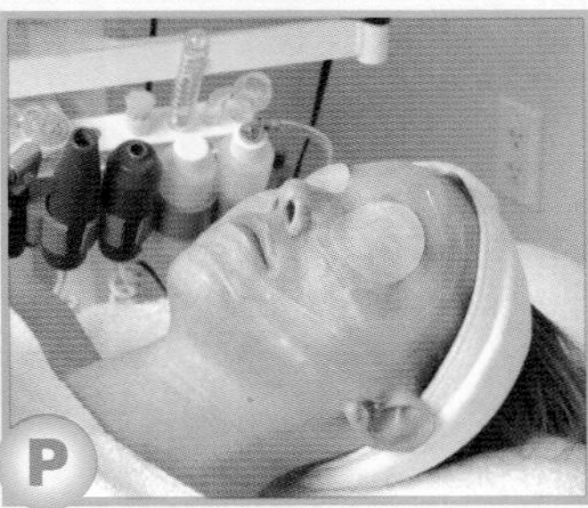
P

Place eye pads and allow mask to stay on skin for recommended time following manufacturer's instructions.

13

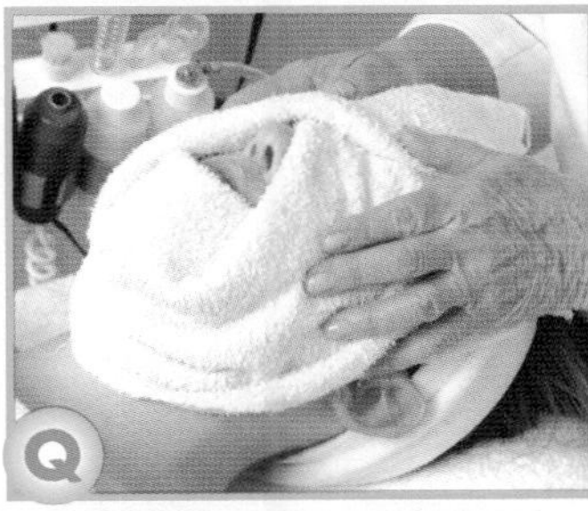
Q

Place and press a warm, moist cloth towel to skin to remove mask product.

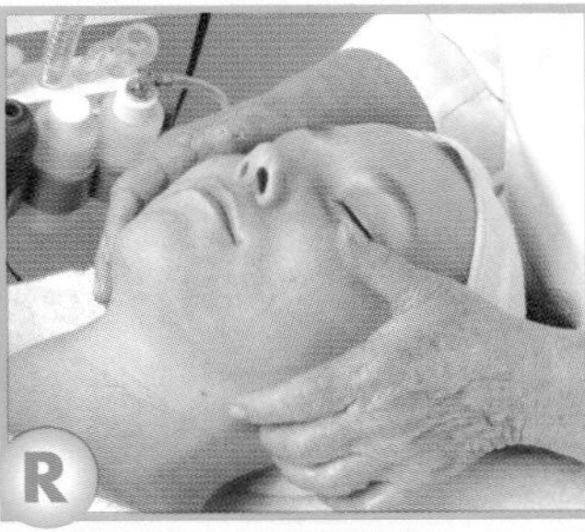
R

Apply moisturizer with sunscreen over entire face, including eyelids and lips.

S

**Completed facial treatment with glycolic acid peel.**

***Recommend four to five glycolic acid treatments, with one treatment per week due to skin regeneration occurring every 28 to 30 days.***

**EVALUATION** ______________________________

GRADE ______ STUDENT'S NAME ______________ ID# ______________

COMPLEX LAB PROJECT

# Corrective Facial Treatment using Brush Attachment

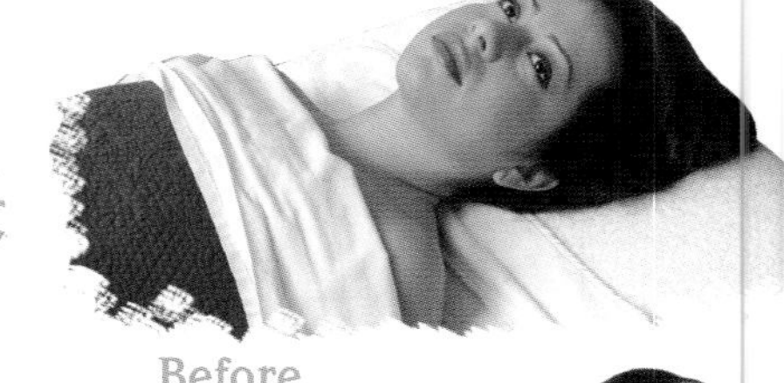
Before

After

**OBJECTIVE**

To offer a mechanical alternative for exfoliation to treat a congestive skin condition.

## TOOLS & MATERIALS

- Robe
- Cloth & disposable towels
- Headband or cap
- Protective sheet or blanket
- Gloves (optional)
- Mask product
- Spatulas
- Cotton or cotton pads
- Product containers
- Cleanser
- Applicator brush
- Essential oils (optional)
- Toner
- Moisturizer
- Massage cream or oil
- Client record card/file
- Exfoliation product

## PROCEDURE

**"The client consultation is an important part of your professional service. Be sure to complete this step prior to each client service you provide. Your successful retail sales and customer satisfaction rates depend upon it!"**

RETAIL RE-BOOK REFERRAL

13

1. Cosmetologist sanitizes hands and station.
2. Set out service tools and materials.
3. Drape the client in preparation for service.
4. Follow procedure as shown and manufacturer's instructions.
5. Follow standard cleanup procedure
6. Document client record card/file.

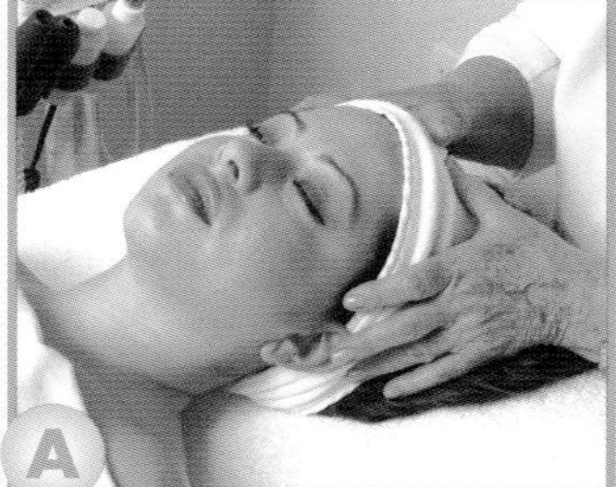
A Client rests comfortably on facial table or chair. Sanitize hands by washing and using an antibacterial spray.

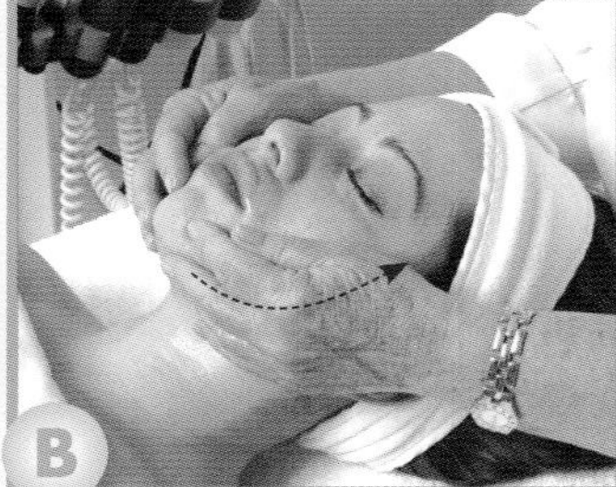
B Apply cleanser to skin to remove surface dirt and oils, starting at jawline moving up toward forehead.

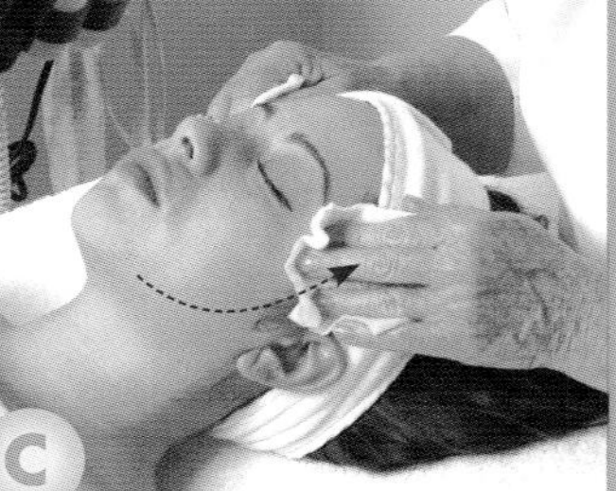
C Remove cleanser using warm, moist cotton pads, starting at jawline moving up toward forehead.

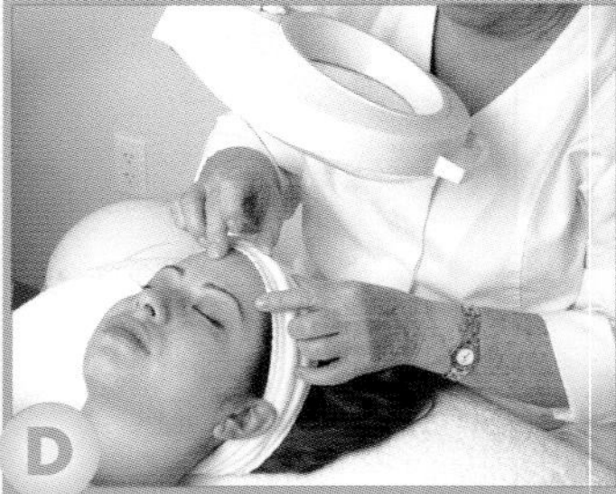
D Perform skin analysis using a magnifying lamp.

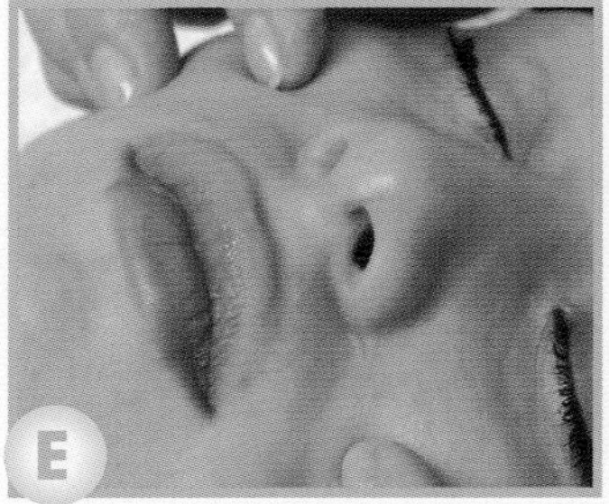
E Check on skin type, pore location/size and scaly or dry areas of skin.

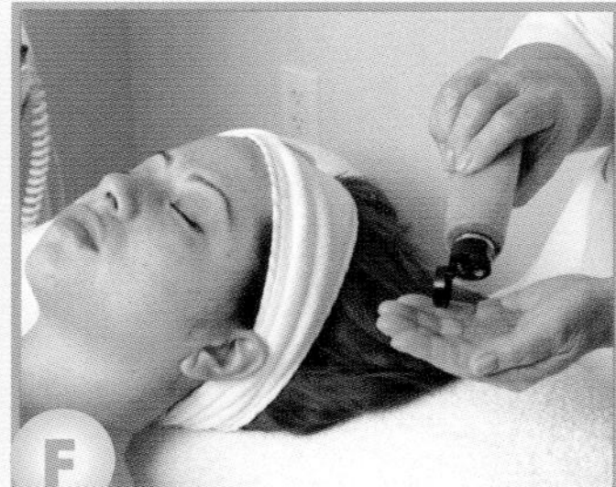
F Prepare and apply an exfoliating treatment to assist in loosening the dead surface skin cells.

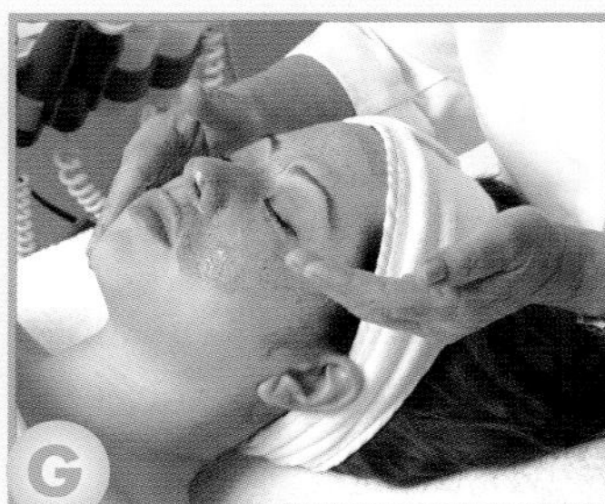
G Apply exfoliating mask to entire face except lips and eyelids.

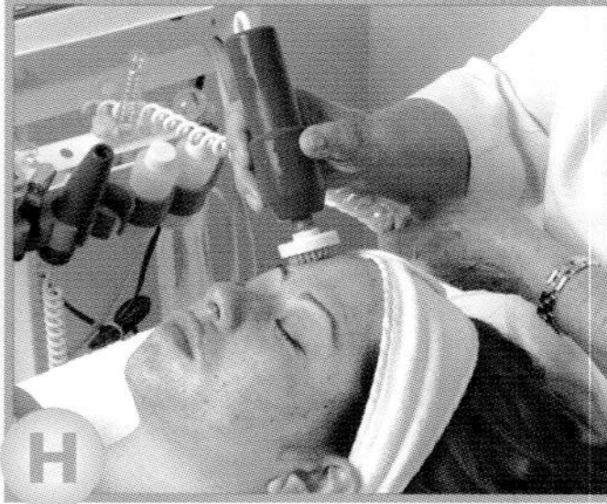
H Use a brush attachment and glide over the skin for a mild mechanical scrub.

## Corrective Facial Treatment using Brush Attachment

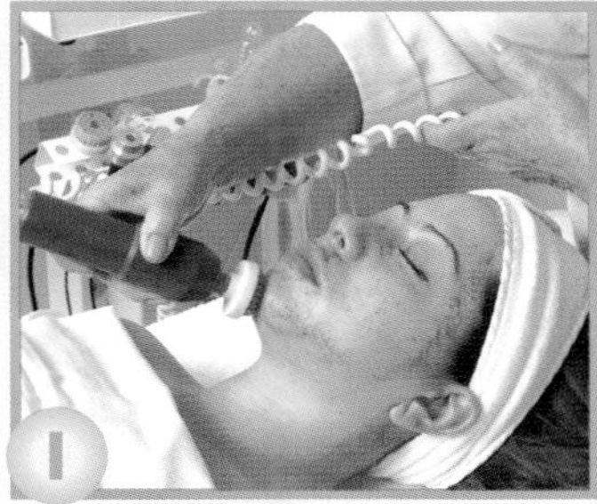
Continue **lightly** gliding the brush over face for 1 to 2 minutes. This will accelerate the exfoliating action of the dead surface skin cells.

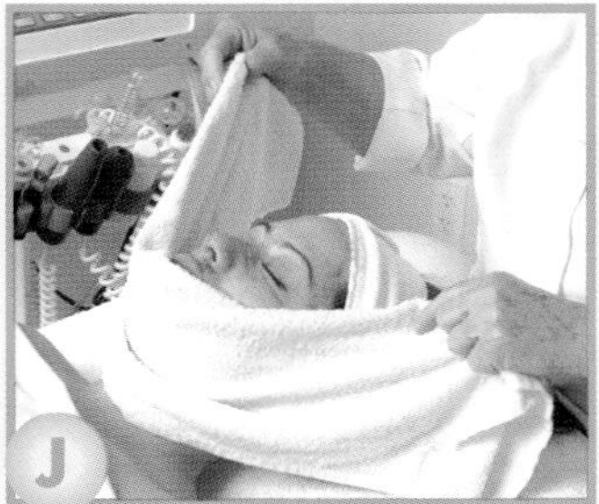
Remove the exfoliant by using a warm, moist cloth towel placed and pressed over entire face.

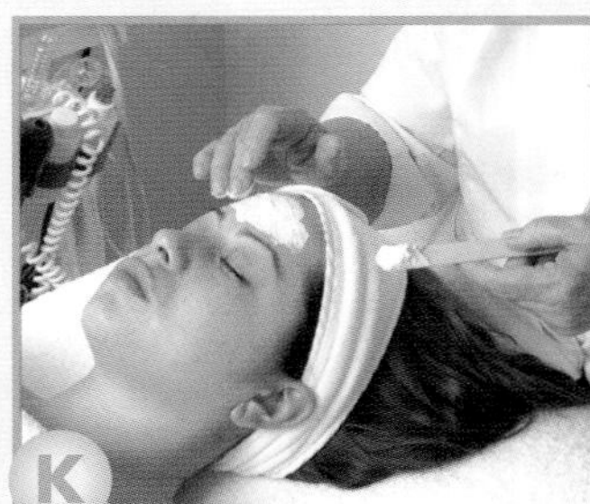
Apply a mask treatment (suitable to skin type) to skin.

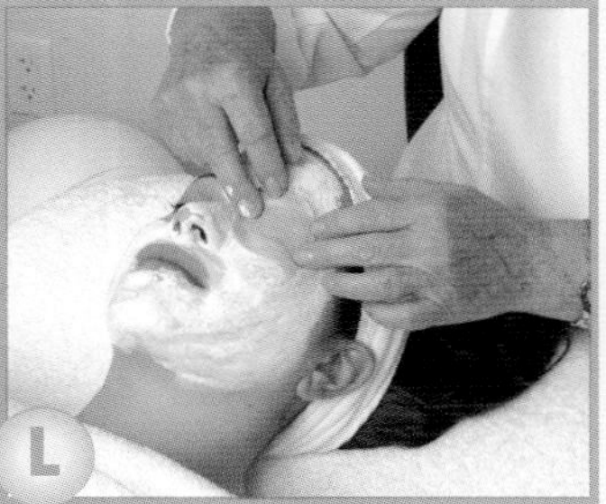
Cover entire face with mask omitting eyelids and lips. Place moist cotton pads over eyes. Allow mask to dry following manufacturer instructions.

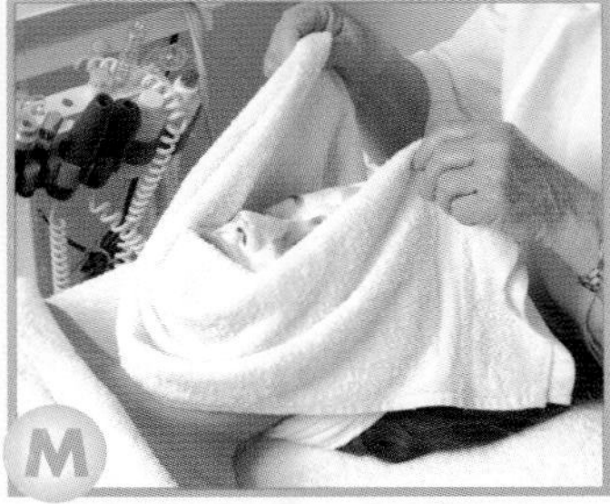
Place and press a warm, moist cloth towel to skin to remove mask product.

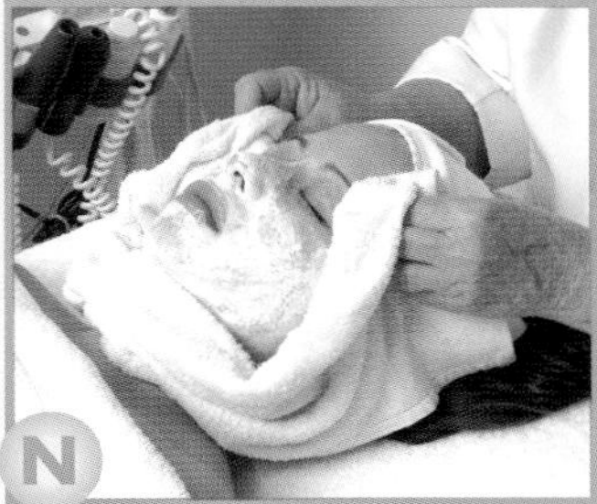
Continue removing mask using moist, cloth towel until all product is off skin.

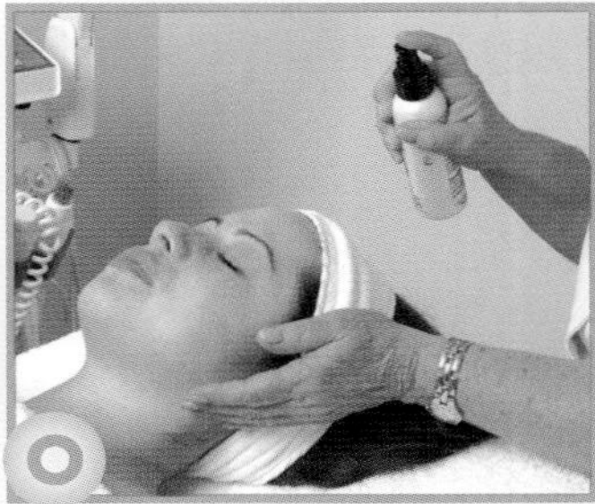
Apply a toner or astringent in either a spray or liquid form.

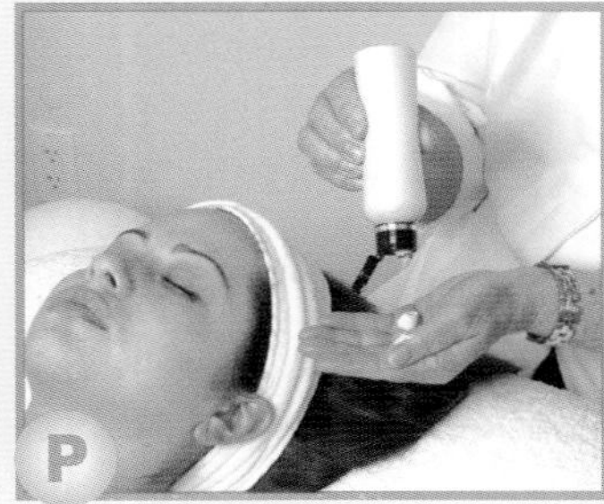
Dispense moisturizer with sunscreen in your hands.

13

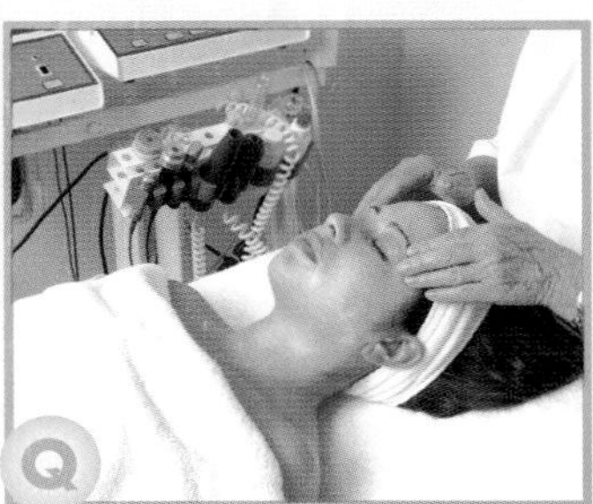
Apply moisturizer over entire face, including eyelids and lips.

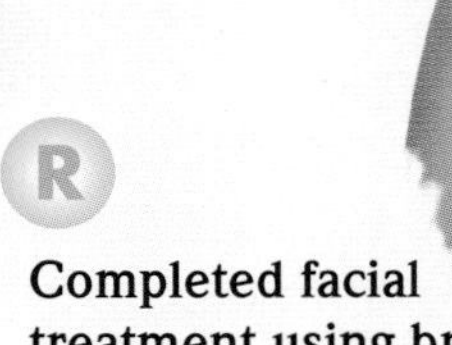
**Completed facial treatment using brush attachment.**

"Always check client's medical history before applying any facial machine due to the high stimulating effects."

EVALUATION

GRADE

STUDENT'S NAME

ID#

# Skin Treatments REVIEW QUESTIONS

## MULTIPLE CHOICE

1. Which essential oil has antibacterial, antifungal and antiviral qualities?
   A. rose B. cinnamon C. chamomile
2. Which cosmetic product removes surface oils, dirt and makeup from the facial skin?
   A. cleanser B. toner C. moisturizer
3. What does exfoliation do to the stratum corneum layer of the epidermis?
   A. remove dead skin cells B. accumulate dead skin cells C. increase melanin production
4. Which facial machine is used during the facial treatment to soften the skin and open the pores?
   A. suction B. brushing C. steamer
5. What must be done to the facial skin prior to a skin analysis?
   A. cleansed B. exfoliated C. masked
6. What natural product is rich in retinol, which stimulates elastin and collagen production?
   A. honey B. bananas C. carrots
7. What is used to accommodate the technician's mobility in reaching the client and products?
   A. product tray B. professional stool C. facial table
8. Which essential oil is used as an astringent to control over-production of sebum?
   A. cedarwood B. jasmine C. lavender
9. Paraffin wax masks are beneficial for which skin type?
   A. normal to dry B. combination to oily C. acne
10. Which of the following material is a loosely woven fabric that rests on the face prior to the application of a paraffin wax facial?
    A. cloth towels B. gauze C. head band
11. How often is it recommended for a client to receive a facial treatment?
    A. every four to six weeks B. every six months C. once a year
12. What percentage of alpha hydroxy acid is ONLY recommended for "in-salon" use?
    A. 5% B. 10% C. 20%
13. Which cosmetic product is recommended that contains a broad-spectrum sunscreen?
    A. moisturizer B. freshener C. cleanser
14. A facial treatment offers deep cleansing and nourishing therapies to the face and?
    A. back B. neck C. chest
15. Which skin-care professional diagnoses and treats minor and major skin conditions?
    A. cosmetologist B. esthetician C. dermatologist
16. Which cosmetic product softens the epidermal layer and restores hydration?
    A. cleanser B. toner C. moisturizer
17. The magnifying lamp is used during the skin analysis of the facial treatment to?
    A. open skin pores B. stimulate blood flow C. enlarge view of skin
18. Alpha hydroxy acids are natural derivatives of sugar cane, milk and?
    A. fruits B. beef C. mud
19. Eye cream will reduce puffiness and has what effect on dark circles?
    A. lightens B. darkens C. enhances
20. When is the client consultation performed for a facial treatment?
    A. during B. after C. prior

STUDENT'S NAME DATE GRADE

eyebrow folliculitis glabella hirsutism shaving tweezers waxing

# Hair Epilation

HAIR EPILATION

14

# Terminology . . .

*The following explanations will acquaint you with a few of the terms used within the hair removal industry. As you progress into this chapter and learn about hair removal methods, you will further enhance your vocabulary.*

1

**Depilatory** is a chemical agent applied directly to the skin to assist in dissolving and removing of surface hair (hair shaft).

**Epilation** is a term referring to removal of the hair shaft and root by pulling it out from the skin.

**FDA** is the Food and Drug Administration – a federal government office in the U.S. Department of Health and Human Services – that establishes laws for the safety of cosmetics and provides guidelines for effectiveness of therapeutic tools for consumer use.

14

**Flint** is a hard, fine-grained stone. Because it flakes and is easily transformed into sharp-edge tools, the stone was used in the early civilizations and eventually became a method for removing hair.

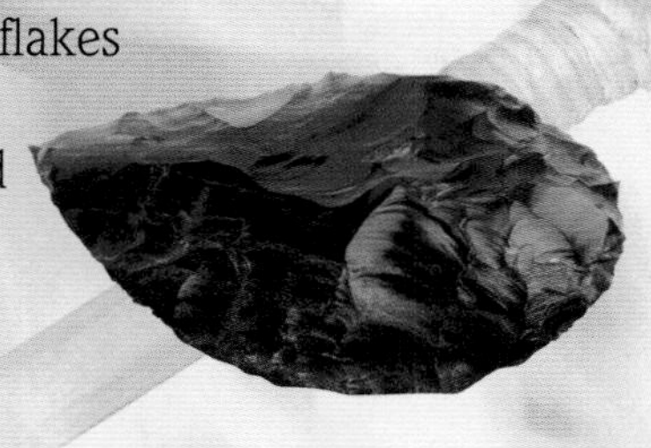

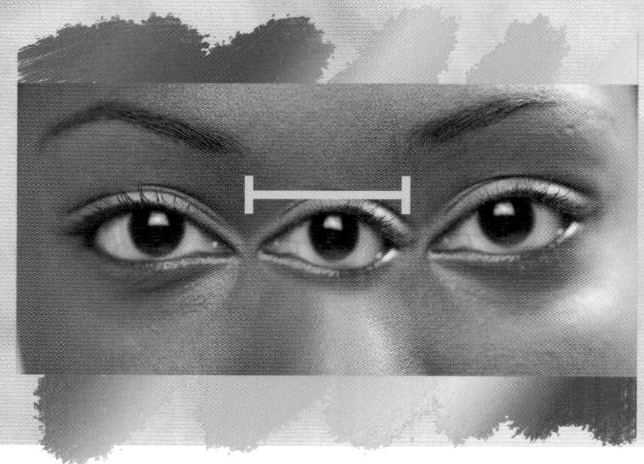

**Glabella** is the area between the two eyes, directly above the bridge of the nose. It is used for placement of a third eye (positioned between the eyes) when determining the eye-set position.

# Terminology . . .

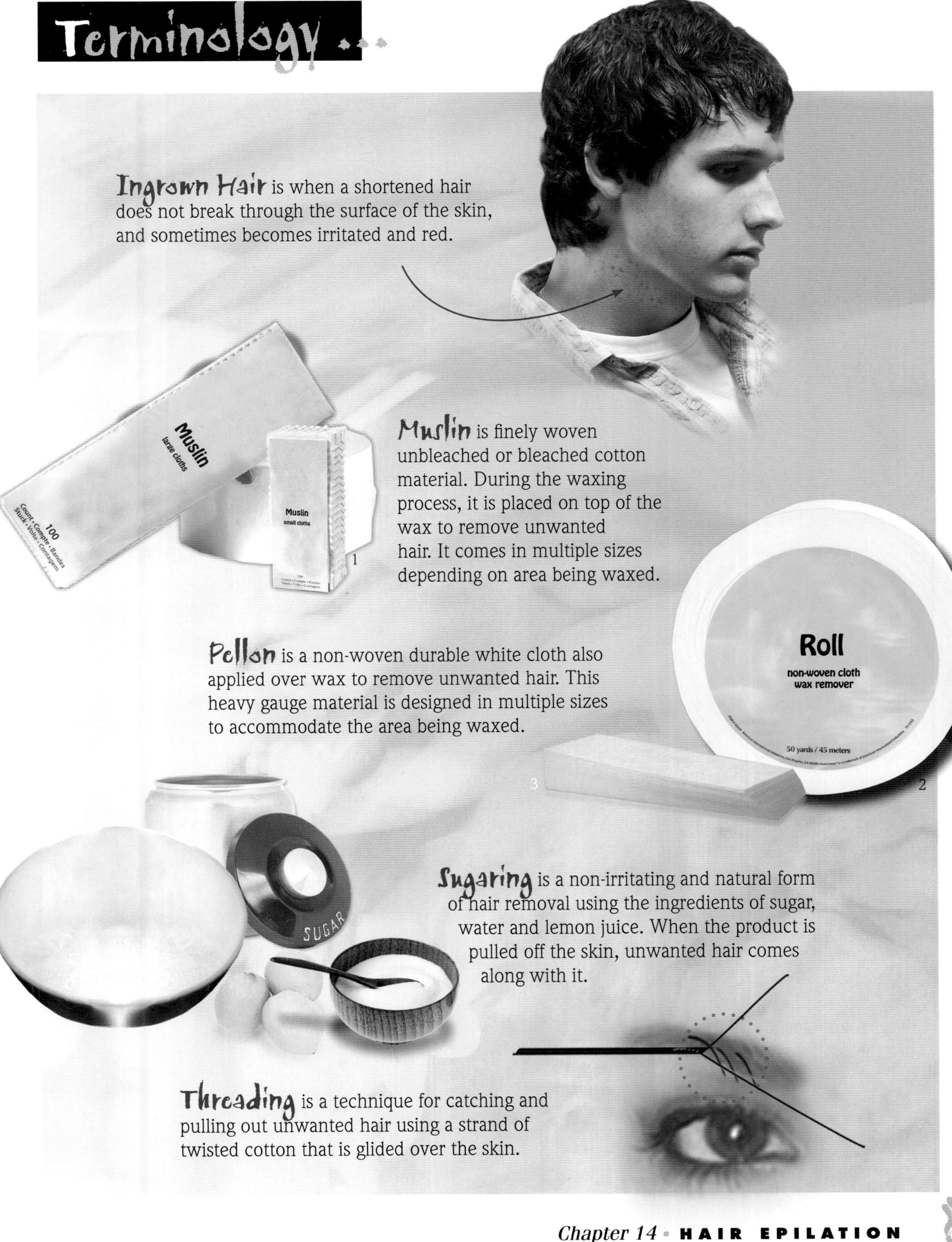


**Ingrown Hair** is when a shortened hair does not break through the surface of the skin, and sometimes becomes irritated and red.

**Muslin** is finely woven unbleached or bleached cotton material. During the waxing process, it is placed on top of the wax to remove unwanted hair. It comes in multiple sizes depending on area being waxed.

**Pellon** is a non-woven durable white cloth also applied over wax to remove unwanted hair. This heavy gauge material is designed in multiple sizes to accommodate the area being waxed.

**Sugaring** is a non-irritating and natural form of hair removal using the ingredients of sugar, water and lemon juice. When the product is pulled off the skin, unwanted hair comes along with it.

**Threading** is a technique for catching and pulling out unwanted hair using a strand of twisted cotton that is glided over the skin.

# Hair Removal History . . .

*Hair removal is the process of both temporarily or permanently eliminating body and facial hair. The art of removing hair has evolved though the centuries, and much like styling, reflects upon the culture, fashion and technology of the times.*

Flint

## According to cave paintings,

the Neanderthal people were not always depicted as having facial hair. It is believed that they held **two seashells together to pull hair out** – like tweezers – or they used **flint, a flaky rock** to make sharp-edged tools such as arrowheads. These were scraped over the skin to remove hair.

14

Thousands of years ago, a hair-free body was considered part of hygienic living or was a part of a ritual associated with religious custom.The first evidence of **waxing** was seen in the Egyptian culture when women used beeswax or a sugar-base concoction scented with oils to remove hair. Arabian women used a technique called **"threading,"** which was a piece of cotton string held in their fingers and moved briskly over the skin catching any unwanted hair and tugging it free from the follicle.

Some hair removal methods consisted of homemade concoctions or depilatory pastes made with either lime or lye depending on the century. The **razor was discovered** in the Bronze Age and, into the early 1700s, was constantly updated to provide comfort and safety.

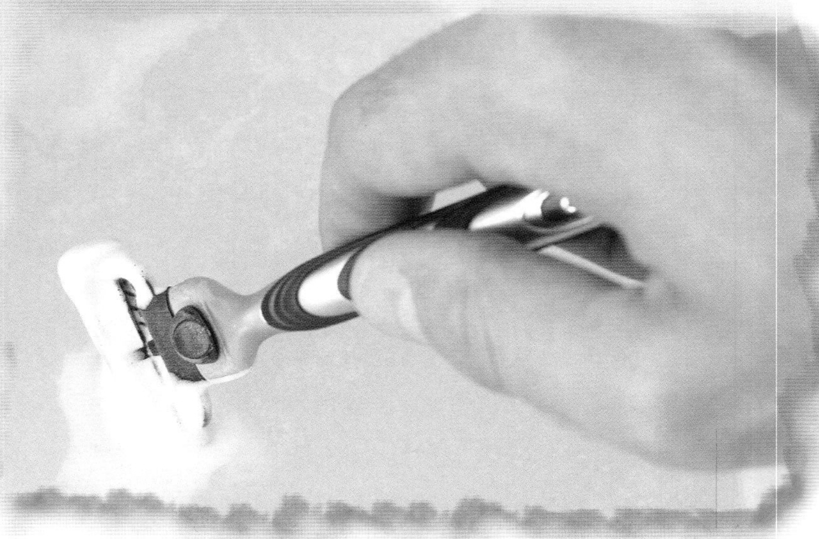

# Hair Removal History ...

brothers Fredrick, Richard and Otto Kampfe created the first Star **"safety razor,"** which was modified by **King C. Gillette** in 1901. This was the first **double-edged blade that was disposable and had to be replaced by a new blade.**

Safety Razor

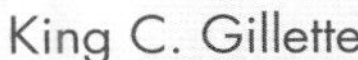


14

Dr. Charles E. Michel

**In 1875, Dr. Charles E. Michel** developed a permanent hair removal technique called **electrology,** awarding him the title **"The Father of Electrolysis."** This method involves inserting a tiny needle into a hair follicle, and destroying the papilla using an electrical current. In the late 1900s, **Dan Mahler** expanded on the electrolysis business and founded the electrolysis equipment company "Instantron," which is still in operation today.

# Hair Removal History . . .

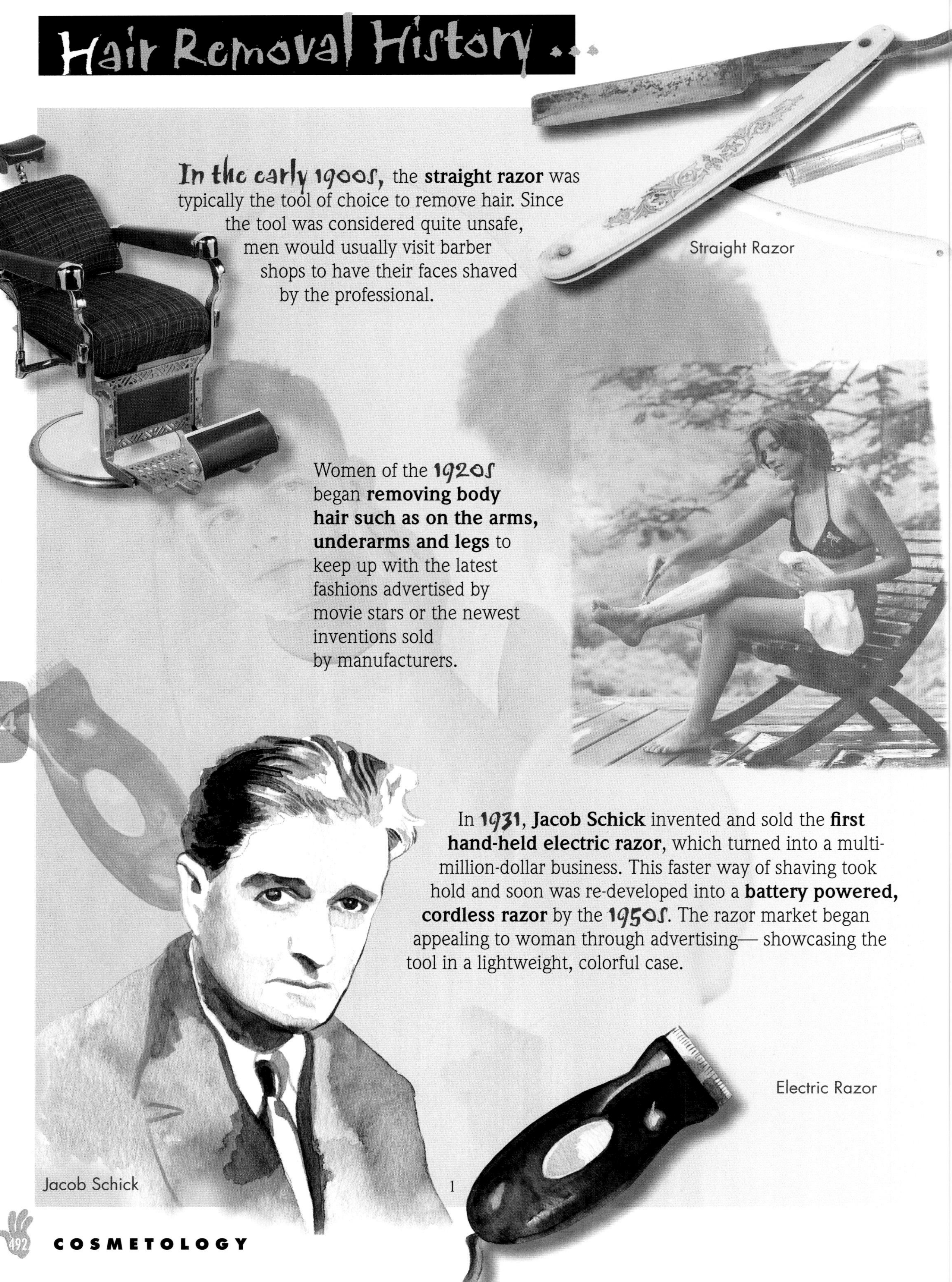

**In the early 1900s,** the **straight razor** was typically the tool of choice to remove hair. Since the tool was considered quite unsafe, men would usually visit barber shops to have their faces shaved by the professional.

Straight Razor

Women of the **1920s** began **removing body hair such as on the arms, underarms and legs** to keep up with the latest fashions advertised by movie stars or the newest inventions sold by manufacturers.

In **1931**, **Jacob Schick** invented and sold the **first hand-held electric razor**, which turned into a multi-million-dollar business. This faster way of shaving took hold and soon was re-developed into a **battery powered, cordless razor** by the **1950s**. The razor market began appealing to woman through advertising— showcasing the tool in a lightweight, colorful case.

Electric Razor

Jacob Schick

1

# Hair Removal History . . .

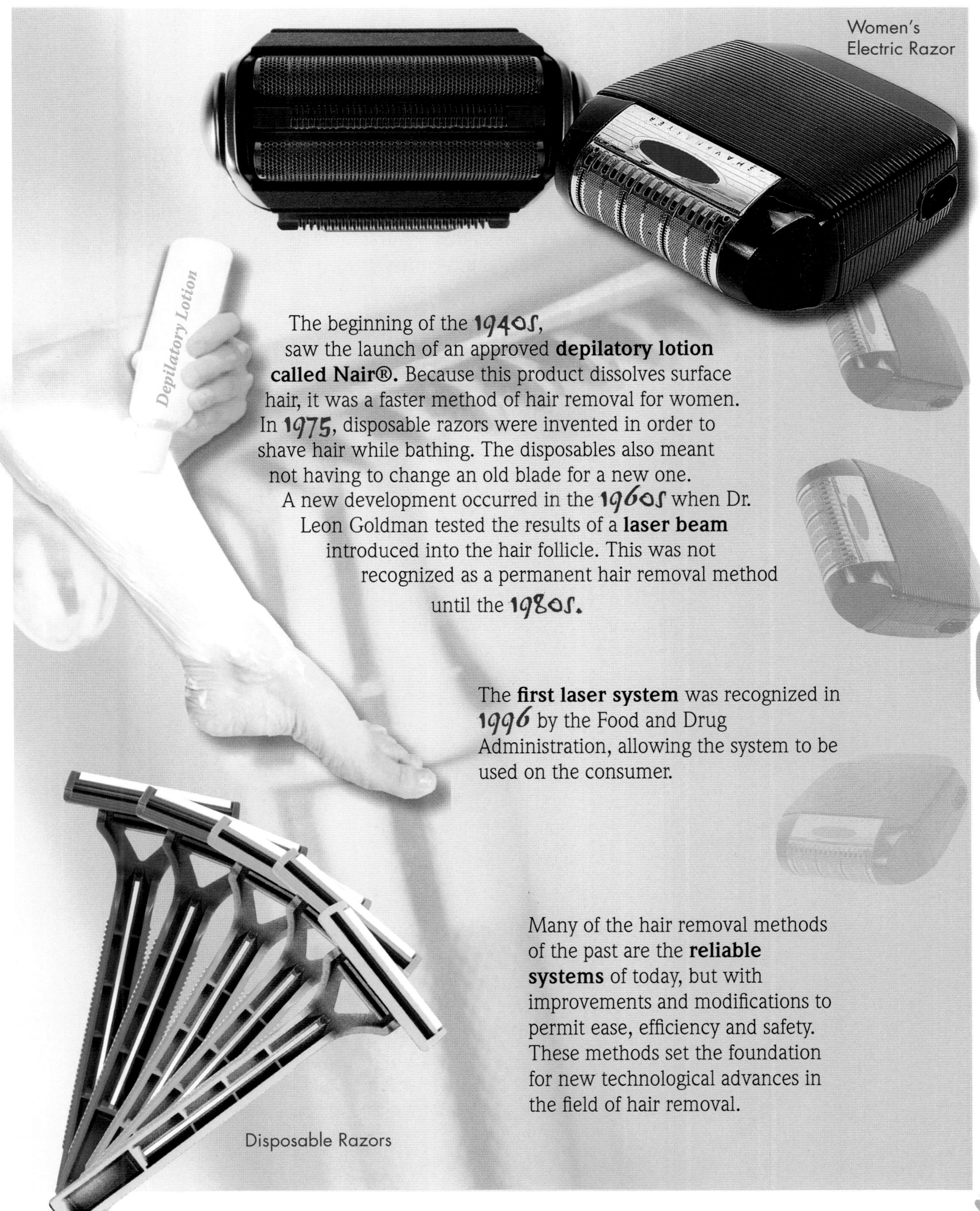


Women's Electric Razor

The beginning of the 1940s, saw the launch of an approved **depilatory lotion called Nair®.** Because this product dissolves surface hair, it was a faster method of hair removal for women. In 1975, disposable razors were invented in order to shave hair while bathing. The disposables also meant not having to change an old blade for a new one. A new development occurred in the 1960s when Dr. Leon Goldman tested the results of a **laser beam** introduced into the hair follicle. This was not recognized as a permanent hair removal method until the 1980s.

The **first laser system** was recognized in 1996 by the Food and Drug Administration, allowing the system to be used on the consumer.

Many of the hair removal methods of the past are the **reliable systems** of today, but with improvements and modifications to permit ease, efficiency and safety. These methods set the foundation for new technological advances in the field of hair removal.

Disposable Razors

# Hair Removal . . .

*Removal of unwanted hair from the body or face is accomplished either by extraction of the hair root from the skin's dermal layer or cutting off the hair shaft from the skin's surface.*

As discussed in Chapter 5, there are basically two types of hair: **Lanugo** (la-nu-go) **or vellus** is the soft, white downy hair found on any area of the body; and **terminal** is the remaining pigmented hair located on scalp, arms, underarms, legs and in the nose and ears of men and women. Lanugo hair is sometimes difficult to see and is thin and fine in texture whereas terminal hair is typically pigmented and will vary in texture and thickness. All hair acts as a protector to the skin and is a healthy body covering. What needs to be established is if it is a deterrent in obtaining the optimal beauty balance!

**Hirsutism** (her-soo-tism) **also referred to as hypertrichosis** (hy-per-tri-cho-sis) is extreme hairiness or excessive growth of hair sometimes on **uncommon areas** of the face and body. This condition may be a result of an imbalance of hormones, certain medications or genetics (heredity). Excessive hair growth typically occurs for women above the lip and/or underneath the chin or hairline extending onto the cheek or forehead.

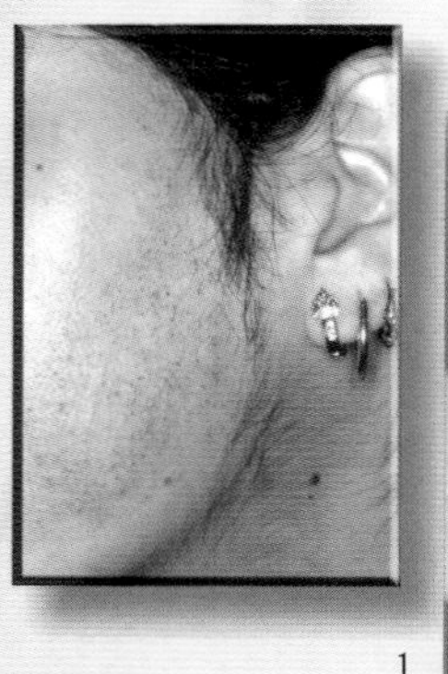

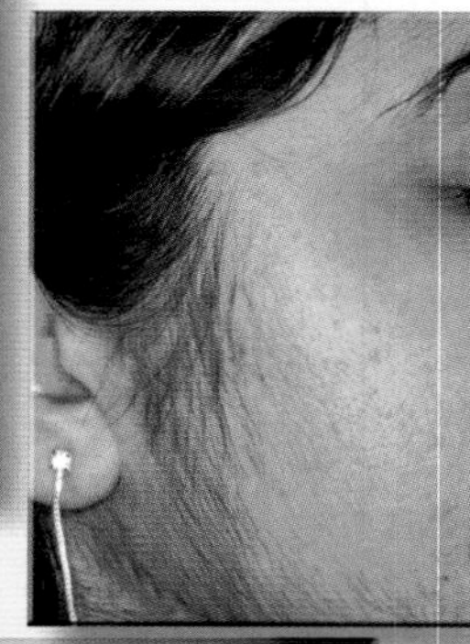

1

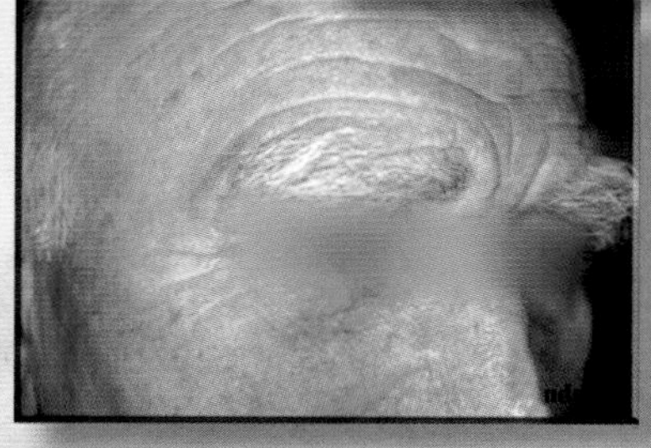

Virtually **any hair may be removed,** from the bothersome and recurring hair some women get above the lip, under the chin or on sides of the face, to the legs and underarms of the body, to the area around the abdomen and bikini region. **Men are also participating in this common practice** by getting rid of excess hair on their eyebrows, earlobes or even on the chest and back. The recommendation for those seeking a fast and safe approach in getting rid of excess unwanted hair is to speak to a professional for the appropriate hair removal method.

# Hair Removal Methods ...

**There** are **multiple methods of hair removal** to choose from, including those offering temporary and permanent results. The method of choice is dependent upon unwanted hair location, the cost of service and the end results.

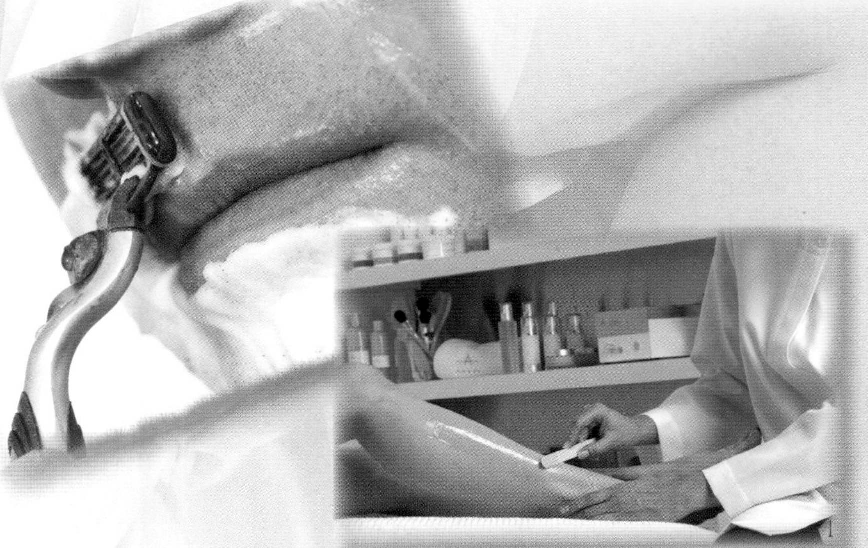

A **temporary hair removal** method **removes** the surface hair or hair shaft (non-living fiber) that rests above the skin or scalp. Some of the temporary methods also **extract or pull out** the hair root and bulb that is situated below the skin or scalp from the follicle or pocket of skin.

A **permanent hair removal** method uses either an electrical current or a light source to destroy the papilla (the papilla supplies nourishment for growth of hair) located deep within the follicle. Consult with a reputable electrologist to determine if the desired area of hair may be removed permanently. Permanent hair removal is accomplished through multiple visits and might not be conducive to the client's lifestyle.

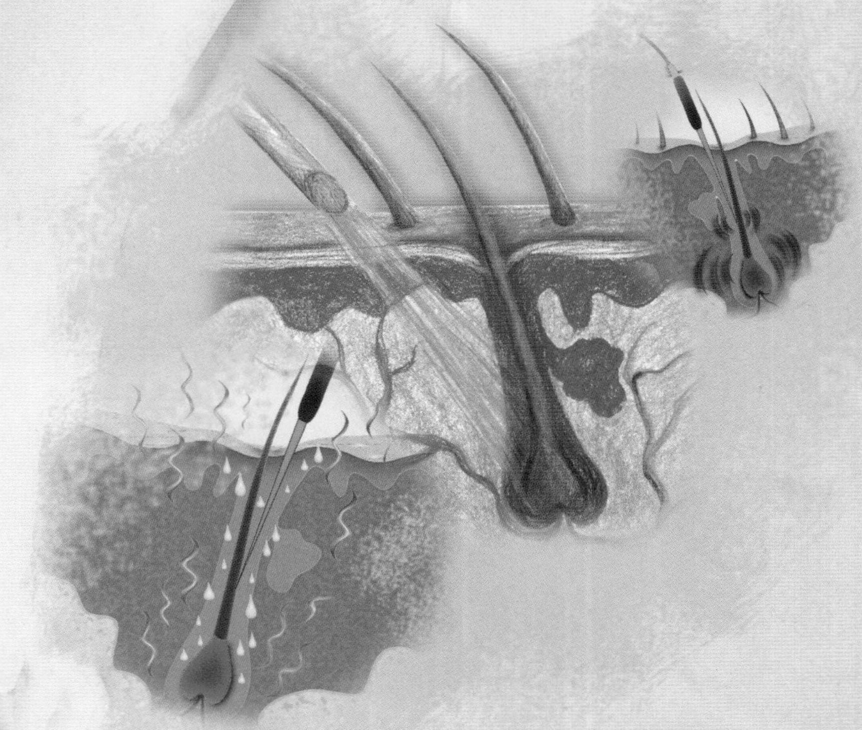

## Methods of Temporary Hair Removal are:

1. **Shaving** is gliding a manual or electric razor across the skin removing the surface hair. This is an old and reliable temporary method for **removing large amounts of hair** quickly. It lasts until hair grows back, generally one to three days depending on type and texture of hair. A mild exfoliation occurs when shaving due to the removal of dead surface skin cells from the razor's gliding action over the skin. This gliding action creates blunt hair ends resulting in the hair feeling thick when it grows again.

"To prepare the skin for shaving, clean with mild cleanser and soften skin with warm water and towel. Optional: Use a shaving cream, gel or lotion to moisturize skin and keep unwanted hair soft for easy removal."

2. **Tweezing** is a method using a tweezers to **pull individual hair** out in a small area such as the eyebrow or chin. This technique is recommended for small areas of the face or for any remaining hair left after completing other methods of hair removal. To maintain existing hair growth direction, **always pull hair out in the direction in which it grows.** Tweezing lasts longer than shaving because the underlying hair root is pulled out from skin. Time for re-growth will vary with each individual depending on speed of hair growth.

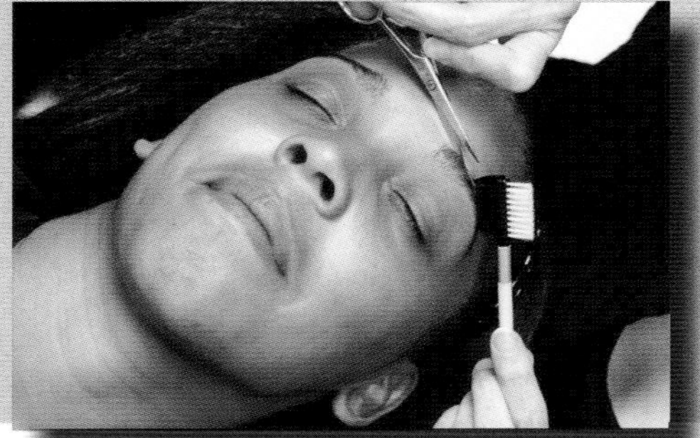

**Optional:** If eyebrow **hair is too long,** use a brow brush and small scissors, comb hair up and trim along eyebrow design.

# Hair Removal Methods ...

3. **Threading** is a technique using a piece of **twisted cotton thread** that is glided over the skin **catching and pulling out the unwanted hair.** This hair removal method was practiced centuries ago in the Middle Eastern countries. Threading (also known as "banding") is an inexpensive method and is less traumatizing to the skin than tweezing. It is most commonly performed on the eyebrows, lips or chin by a trained individual. Threading is a technique that has traditionally been handed down from one generation to the next – usually mother to daughter – and finding a skilled "threading technician" is difficult.

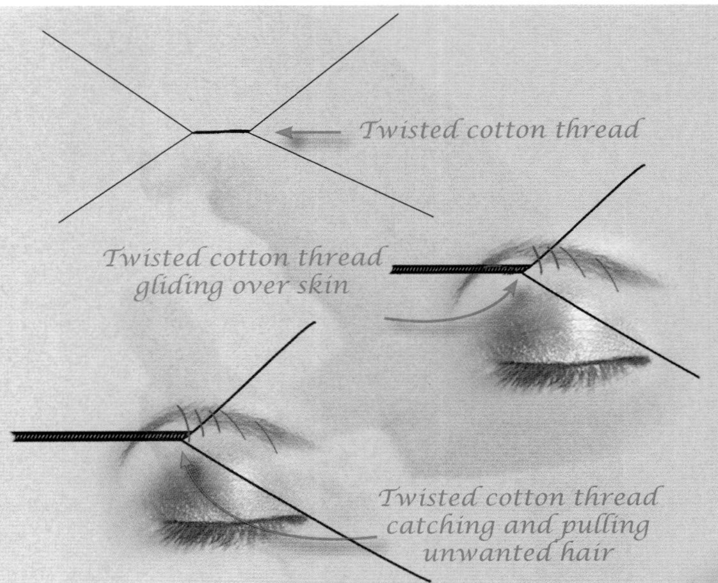


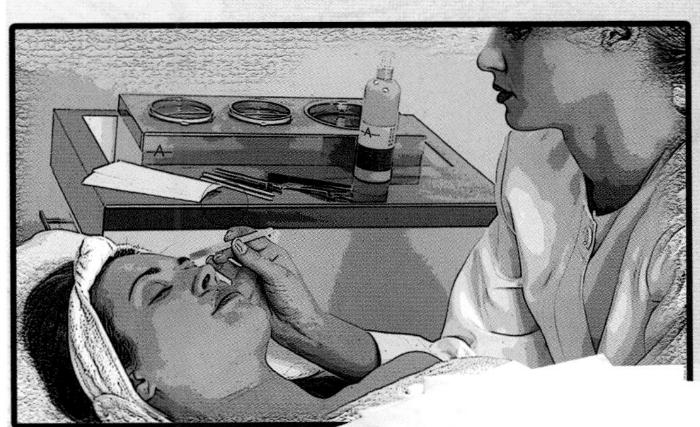
1

4. **Depilatories** (de-pil-a-to-ries) are chemical products that break down the composition of hair thus **dissolving the hair shaft only.** They are applied **directly over the skin** and removed by a cloth. A depilatory comes in many forms such as a lotion, cream, gel, spray or roll-on depending on the manufacturer. The chemicals used that assist in **breaking down the disulfide bonds** are some of the same ingredients used to chemically straighten curly hair, like sodium hydroxide, and calcium or sodium thioglycolate.

14

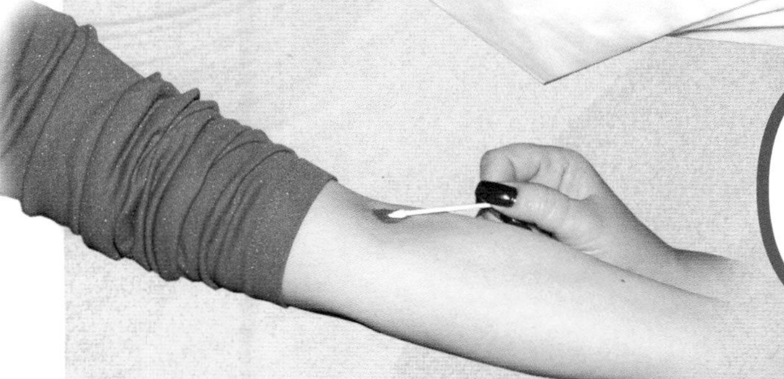

**CAUTION:** In a salon, a patch or allergy test is needed to determine if a client is sensitive or allergic to the depilatory product. Select an area of skin and apply a small amount of depilatory product, checking for allergic reaction.

Since depilatories come in varying strengths and rest on the skin as well as the hair, a mild exfoliation of the dead skin cells will occur along with possible skin irritation or sensitivity. This procedure **ONLY** removes surface hair, lasting until new hair grows beyond the epidermis. Always follow the manufacturer's instructions on how to use these products and the length of time they should be left on the skin.

2

**5. Waxing** uses a product that **adheres to the hair shaft** and when the wax is removed from the skin the hair automatically comes along with the wax. The **wax encases or envelopes the hair** and slightly attaches to the tip of the hair root, which allows the root to be pulled from the follicle. Waxing is the most popular and preferred method of choice to removing unwanted hair quickly.

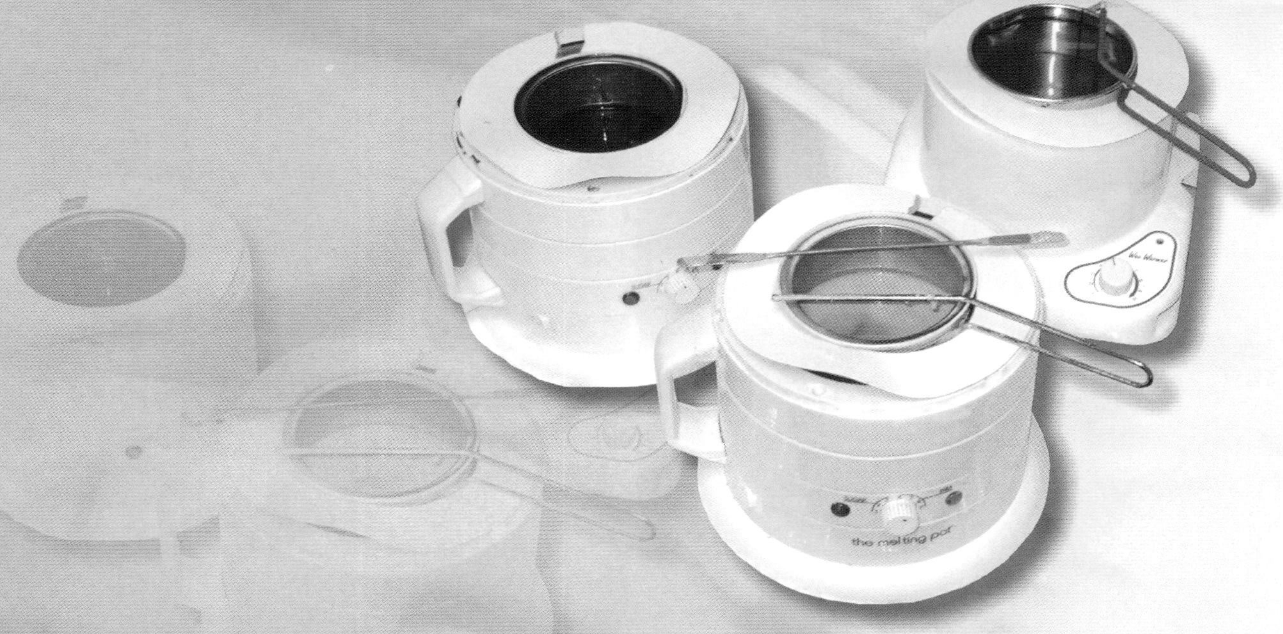




Waxing generally lasts longer than other temporary hair removal methods, and those using this method may experience a gradual reduction in hair growth altogether with repetitive wax services. Depending on growth of hair, texture and area of unwanted hair, duration between services may be four to six weeks. The wax used in this method is derived from a combination of ingredients such as beeswax, oils, fats and resin along with mild fragrances.

# Hair Removal Methods ...

NOTE: Do not overheat hard wax or allow wax to remain heated for 24 hours. This will prevent the wax from losing its hair removal abilities.

***There are two forms of wax, a hard or non-strip wax and a hot or strip wax:***

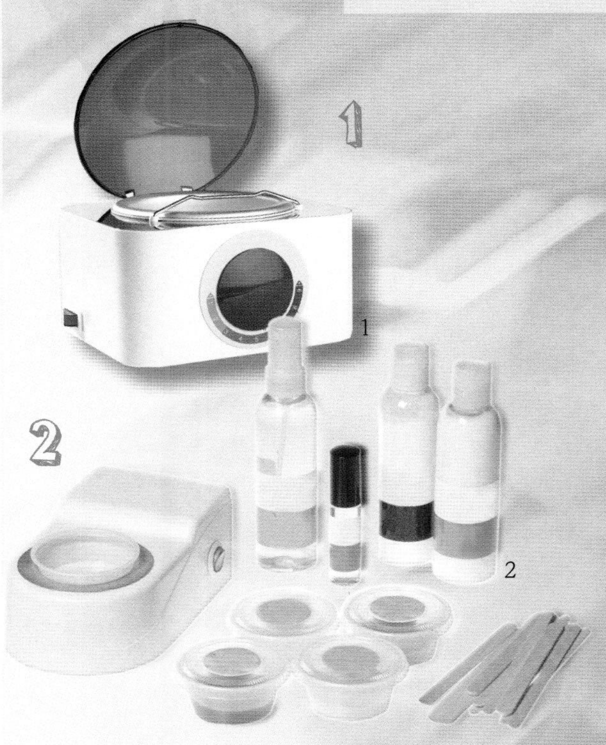

**Hard wax** is contained in a **wax pot** that is **thermostatically controlled and melted at a safe temperature** of 125°F/51.6°C to 140°F/60°C before applied to an area of the face or body. Due to the low temperature, hard wax will set and harden fast and have a thick consistency. Before application, hard wax is a golden-yellow color that is shiny and tacky, but once applied to the skin and cooled, the wax takes on a **dull and pliable texture**. Wax will become brittle if left on the skin beyond the dull appearance stage and will be physically difficult and uncomfortable to remove from the skin.

**Application and removal:** There is **no cloth used to remove hard wax**, it is recommended to test temperature of wax on **your palm of hand** before placing wax on client's skin. Once wax is temperature ready, place product over hair in the **direction of hair growth** to allow wax to properly adhere to base of hair. Follow through with another coating of wax by gliding over top of the first wax strip to obtain a solid coverage of entire hair shaft. The coating of wax needs to have a **clean, even and slightly thick edge** along the entire border for ease in removal (uneven edges break off during removal and are difficult to get off of skin). Thickness of wax is generally no more than 1/8 (0.3cm) inch on face and ¼ (0.6cm) inch on larger areas of body in a strip no longer than 12 (30.48cm) inches on the body. To remove, grasp one end of the wax with a tight hold; **removing quickly** in opposite direction of hair growth.

Spatulas

# Hair Removal Methods . . .

**Hot wax** is contained and heated much like hard wax except it needs to be **heated to a higher temperature** – up to 165°F/73.9°C. Hot wax consistency is **more liquid** than hard wax and it does not set as quickly when placed on the skin. Honey and essential oils are often added to its pre-existing ingredients. Hot wax is a transparent honey color with a smooth texture. Some hot waxes come in **colorful creamy textures** made for sensitive areas of the body and types of skin.

**Non-splintering wood spatulas, roller or disposable applicators** are used for application of soft wax. The spatulas and applicator heads vary in size to accommodate the area being waxed.

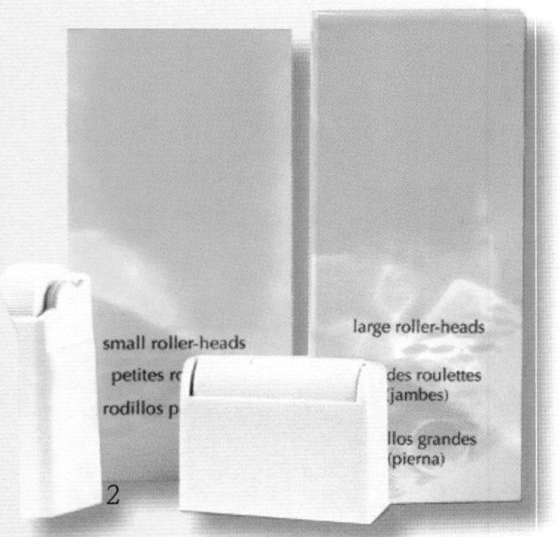


14

Wooden Spatulas

**Application and removal:** Dip the wooden spatula into the wax pot, scraping the excess wax off one side of stick along **scraping bar** (located on most wax pots). Hold spatula at a 45-degree angle. Glide spatula along skin following direction of hair growth, starting at a less dense area of unwanted hair and moving to a denser area. Place the **cloth strip** (either pellon or muslin) over the wax, keeping a small area of cloth for gripping. Smooth the cloth one to two times to encourage adhesion of wax to cloth. Pull skin taut and **remove the cloth quickly** in opposite direction of hair growth. **DO NOT reapply wax** over same area more than once; if necessary, tweeze any missed unwanted hair.

Muslin

Wax Roller

**Optional Faster Technique:**

**Speed Waxing** is when wax is applied to an **entire or large area** of unwanted hair and a cloth strip (or strips) is repeatedly used in **rapid succession to remove unwanted hair** in that area. The pellon cloth strip is recommended for speed waxing because wax will build up during this process and pellon better resists leaking of wax through material.

**Pellon**

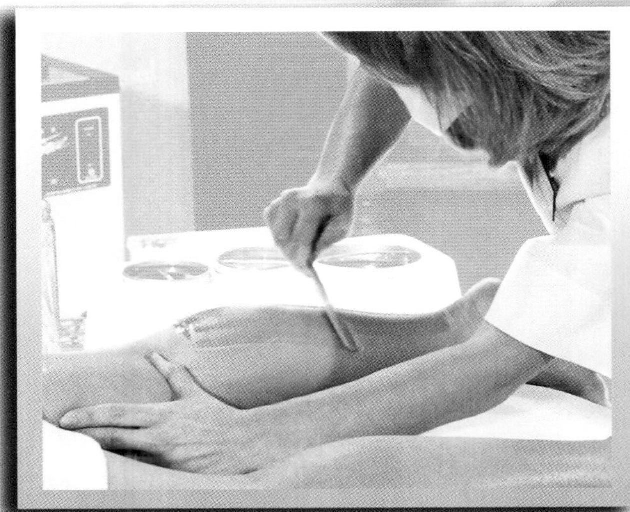

**CAUTION:** Always test the temperature of the wax by applying a small amount to palm of hand or wrist to ensure for client safety and comfort.

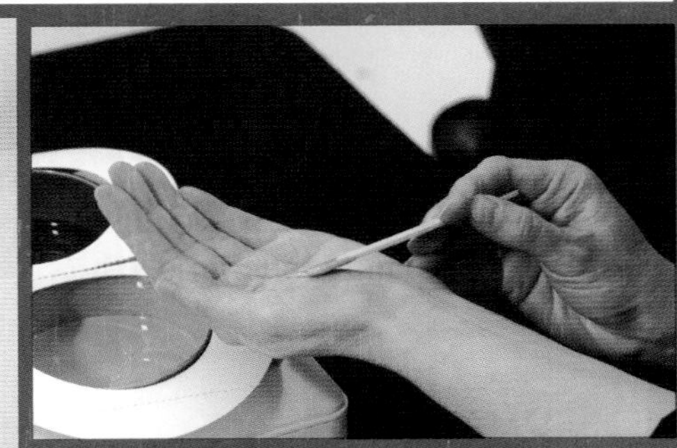

14

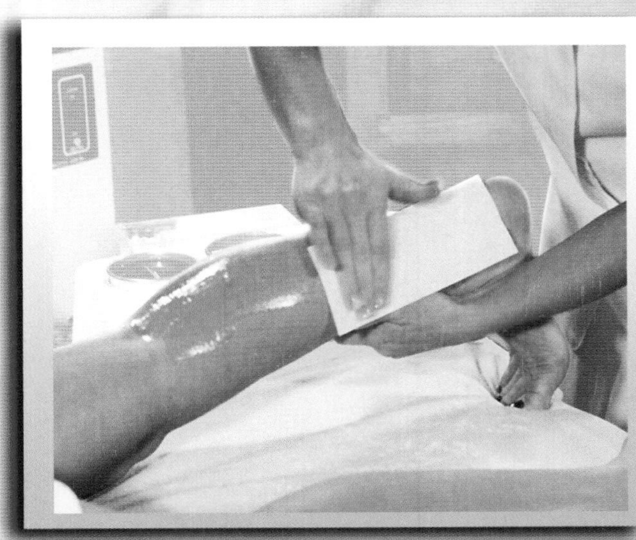

"Always follow manufacturer's directions when heating and applying wax to skin." ©

# Hair Removal Methods . . .

1

6. **Sugaring** is a **non-irritating and natural form** of hair removal borrowed from the ancient Egyptians. Its origin probably was a sugar paste that was used to treat wounds and aid in their healing process. Sugaring starts with a mixture of **sugar, water and lemon juice.** These ingredients are heated until the mixture becomes a paste. The paste is rolled into a ball, flattened onto the skin adhering to the unwanted hair, and then the paste is removed taking the hair along with it.

2

There are **two methods of application:** either with **a cloth strip** to remove the sugar paste from the skin or just **removing the sugar paste by itself.** This depends upon the manufacturer and the professional's choice.

**NOTE:** Some manufacturers add chemical ingredients such as synthetic resins (for hardening) and fragrances, thus altering the non-irritating qualities of the sugaring method. **Always check product ingredients and read the labels.**

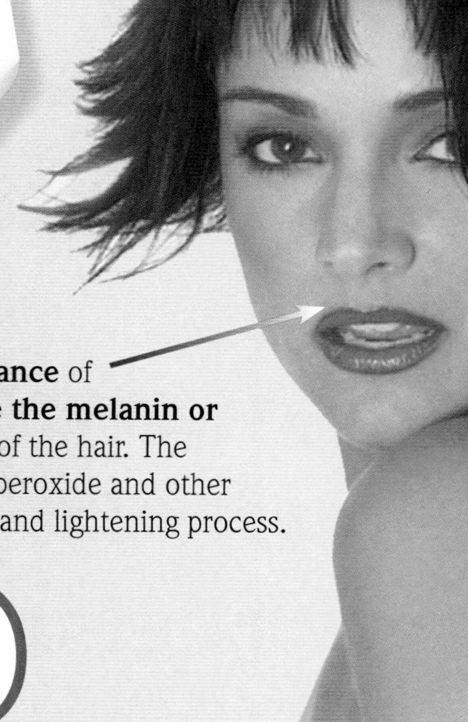

3

## Alternative Method
### (if not wanting to remove hair):

**Bleaching** is a used to **diminish the appearance** of unwanted hair. Bleach will **lighten or diffuse the melanin or pigment granules** located within the cortex of the hair. The ingredients used to lighten hair are hydrogen peroxide and other activating agents that accelerate the softening and lightening process.

CAUTION: A patch or allergy test is needed to determine if a client is sensitive or allergic to the bleach product.

## Methods of Permanant Hair Removal are:

The following explanations are brief. If interested in learning more about these services refer to the American Electrology Association at www.electrology.com and Hair Removal Journal at www.hairremovaljournal.org.

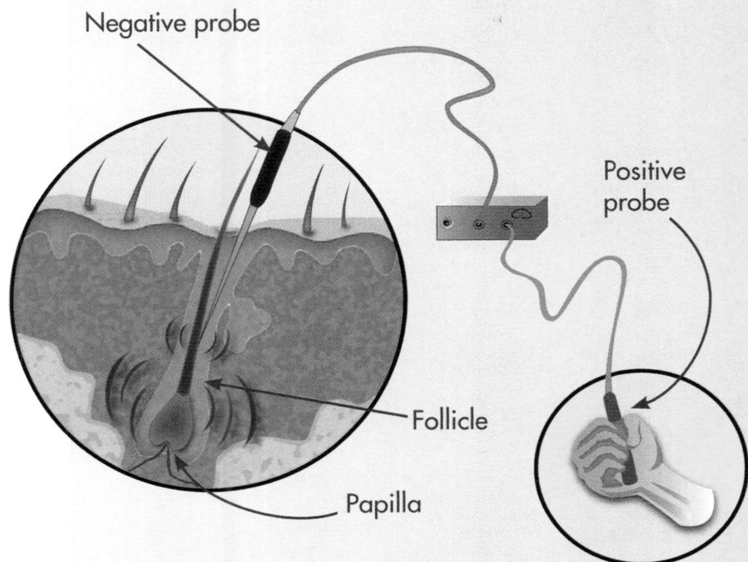


**Electrolysis** (e-lec-trol-y-sis) uses a **(DC) direct current** (flow of electrons in one even and constant direction) to produce galvanic energy. This energy is created when a person (client) holds a positive probe in his or her hand and the **negative probe is inserted into the hair follicle.** The electric current moving from negative (electrode inside hair follicle surrounded by the skin) to positive creates an action called ionization that rearranges the molecules and forms a lye substance, which **deteriorates the hair's papilla.**

**Thermolysis** (ther-mol-y-sis) uses an **(AC) alternating electrical current** (flow of electrons, one direction, then in opposite direction) to produce high-frequency waves that travel through a probe that is placed in a hair follicle. The probe is surrounded by the skin's moisture and water molecules, which start to vibrate and produce heat. The **heat damages and destroys the dermal papilla.** Because there is more moisture at the hair's root and papilla, heat in that area is increased in order to target and destroy the papilla.

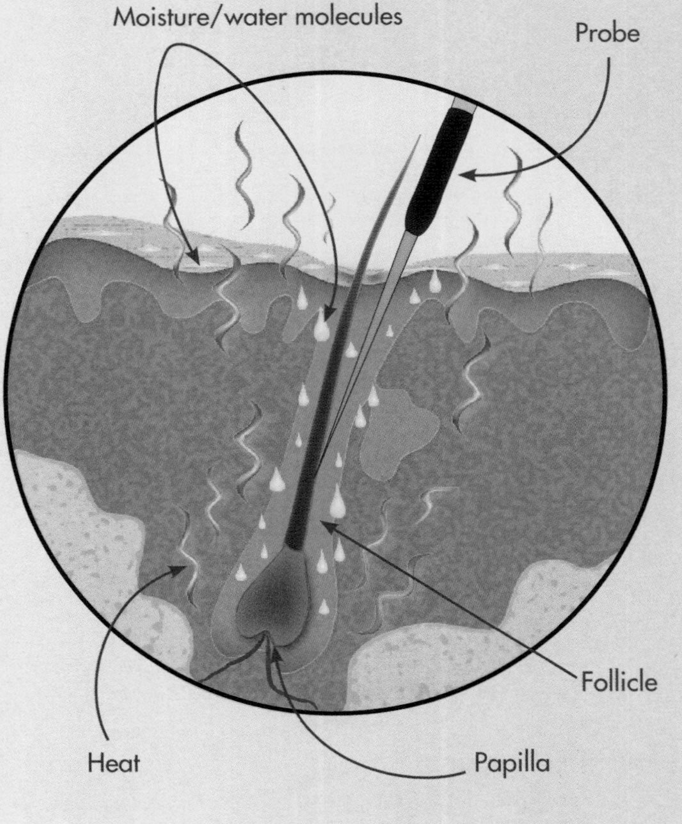


"Refer to Chapter 11 Cosmetology Electricity for detailed information on electricity."

14

**Laser hair removal** accomplished through selection of a **specific wavelength that will absorb light into the hair follicle to cause sufficient damage to the dermal papilla without touching surrounding skin**. A laser emits pulses of a light beam produced from a device containing minerals and gases. As the light beam concentrates on the dark pigment located near the papilla, the beam is absorbed, heating the pigments and destroying the papilla. Laser hair removal is **ONLY** suited for hair with dark pigment or melanin.

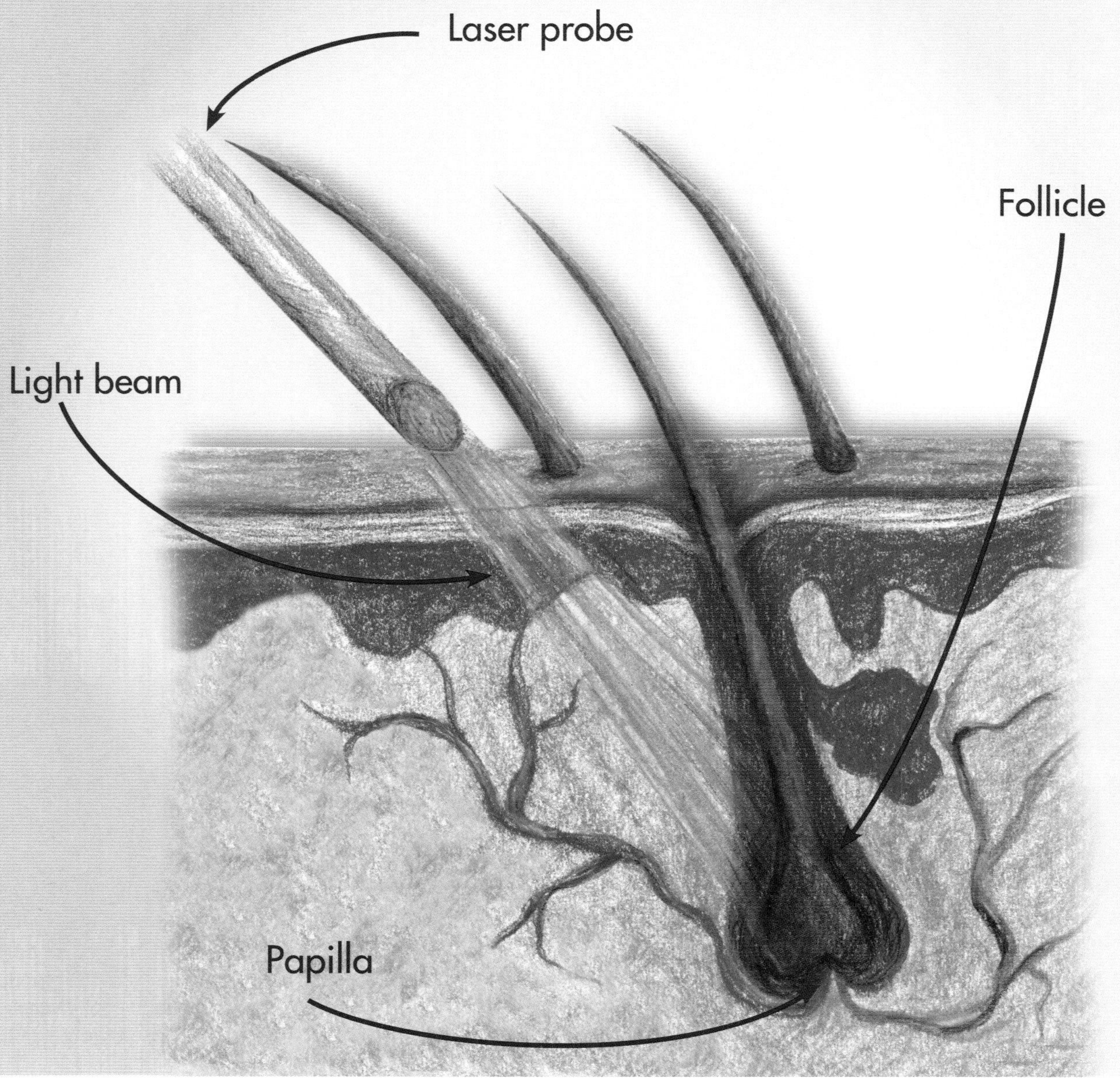

Laser probe

Follicle

Light beam

Papilla

**Alternative Method:**

**Electronic tweezing** is a technique that holds an **individual hair by electronic tweezers** and transmits a high-frequency current down the hair shaft to the hair root to destroy the papilla. The **electric current may or may not always reach the papilla** making this an unreliable source for permanent hair removal.

**NOTE:** The **FDA does not recognize** electronic tweezing as a permanent hair removal method.

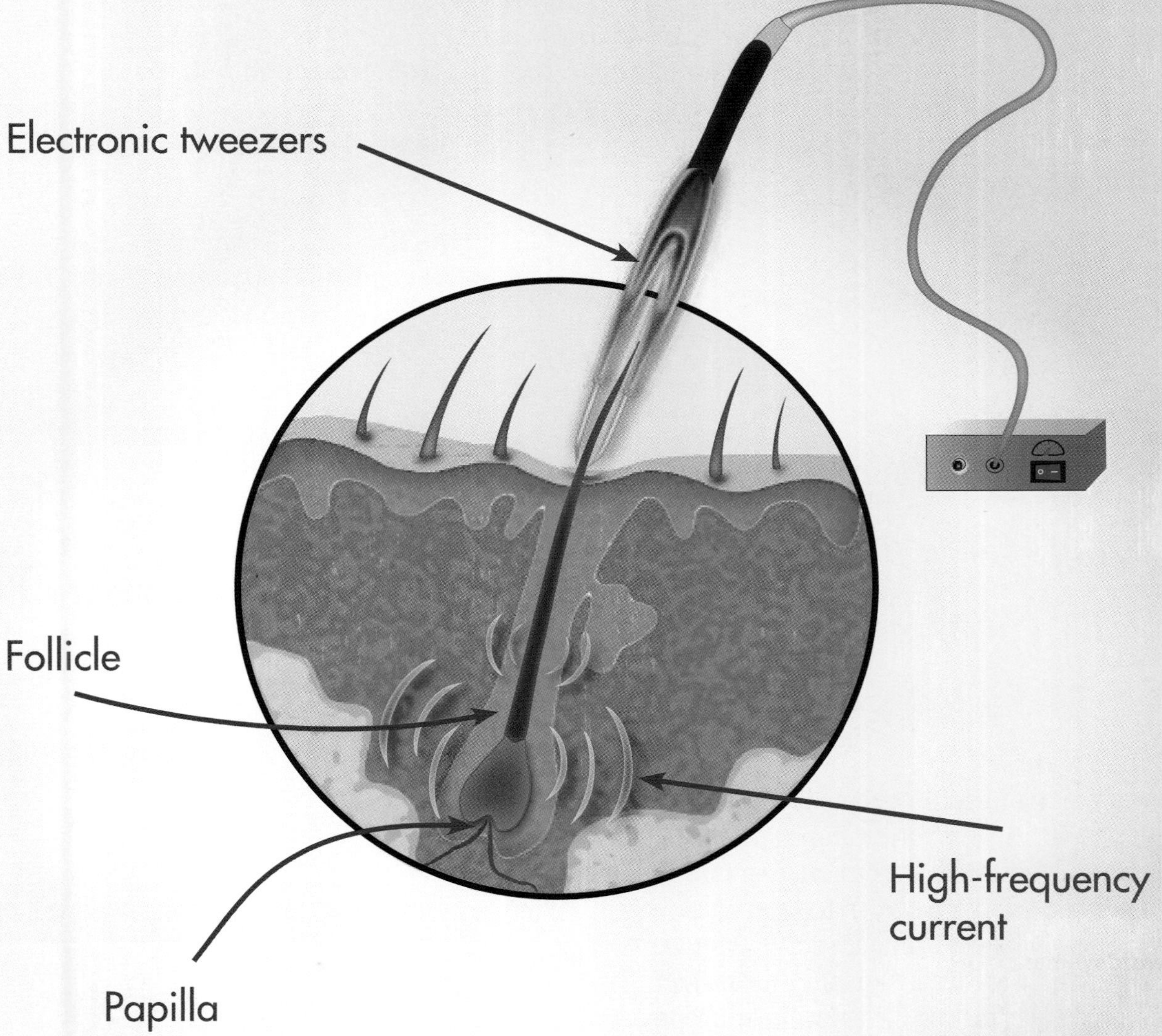

"In order to perform these treatments, advanced education and training are required."

# Hair Removal Tools . . .

**The tools** *used for hair removal are necessary in performing* ***a safe and comfortable treatment*** *for the client. These supplies, used in conjunction with liquid hair removal products, will ensure a safe and successful hair removal service. For tool sanitation, refer to Chapter 3 Salon Safety.*

**Cloth Strips** or **Epilating** (e-pi-lat-ing) **Cloths** are placed over a waxed area, **attaching to the wax and unwanted hair.** The cloth is made of either muslin or pellon and is purchased in pre-cut sizes or custom cut to accommodate any area being waxed.

1

- **Muslin** is finely-woven bleached (soft and white) or unbleached cotton material that is discarded once wax is removed from skin.
- **Pellon** is a non-woven durable white cloth that can be used on both sides to remove wax from skin before disposal.

14

**Gloves** are manufactured from latex, vinyl or synthetic materials to **protect hands** from stains and chemical sensitivity, and to **ensure client safety**. Gloves are required to be worn for certain skin services in many geographic areas. On occasion, when very coarse hair is removed and the skin is sensitive, a small amount of blood may emerge from the follicle area. Wearing gloves will eliminate skin contact to blood.

**CAUTION:** Some people have allergies or sensitivities to latex. Be sure to ask your clients about this prior to wearing latex gloves before any hair or skin service.

2

# Hair Removal Tools . . .

**Eyebrow Pencil** is a colored pencil that provides **precise eyebrow shaping** by either filling in areas void of hair or darkening existing hair to produce a detailed eyebrow design.

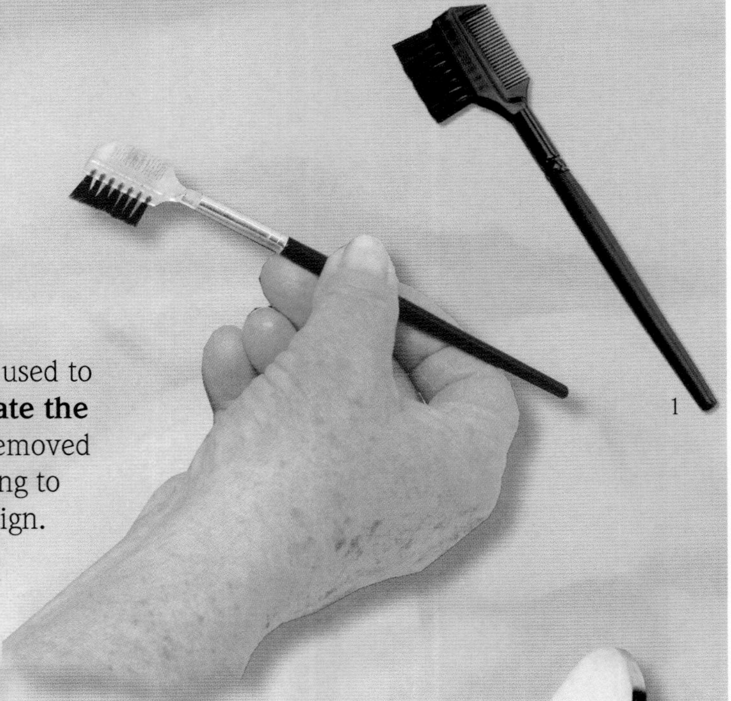

**Eyebrow Brush** is a tool used to **smooth, control and separate the eyebrow hair** that is being removed and the hair that is remaining to complete the eyebrow design.

1

14

**Tweezers** are used to **grab hold of individual hair** and pull them out of the skin. Tweezers come in a variety of designs to assist in removing very short hair or newly grown hair and all types of textured hair.

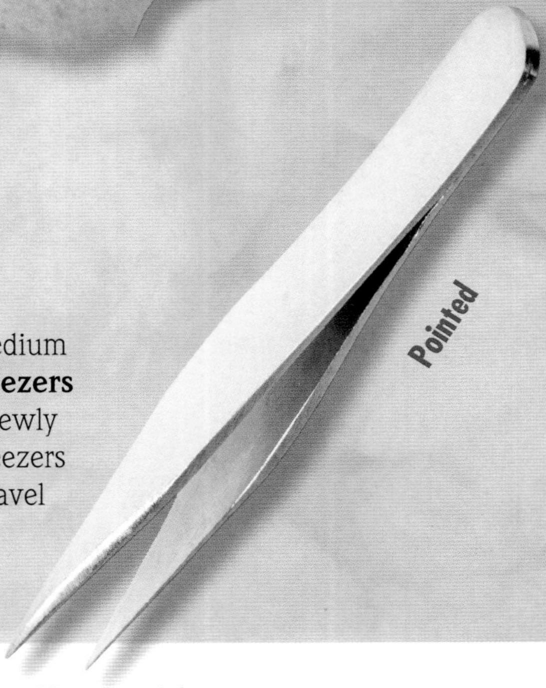

**Slanted tweezers** grip stubborn medium to coarse textured hair. **Pointed tweezers** are great for removing very short, newly grown to fine textured hair. The tweezers also come in small sizes for easy travel and convenience.

Pointed

Slanted

# Hair Removal Tools...

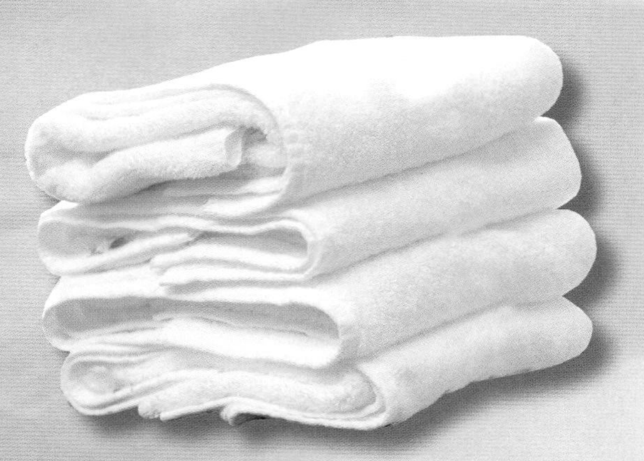

**Cloth Sheets or Towels** are made from an **absorbent washable material.** A **cloth sheet** provides a covering over the body while receiving hair removal skin services. **Cloth towels** are used to provide protection from product coming into contact with client's skin and clothing.

**Headband or Covering** is either a thin strip of cloth that **pulls hair away from the face** or is a cloth or plastic cap that **covers all the hair.** This will keep hair from coming in contact with any wax product during hair removal services performed on the face.

**Cotton** is used to **apply cream or liquid products** to the skin either before or after hair removal service. Cotton assists in absorbing excess product and discourages overuse.

# Hair Removal Tools . . .

**Spatulas** assist in the **removal of wax** from heating units and are used as **applicators in applying wax** to the skin. Spatulas come in a variety of sizes and shapes and are made of a smooth non-splintering wood. It is considered both safe and sanitary to use an applicator and to re-dip to acquire more wax. The spatula is covered with wax therefore does not directly touch the skin ... the wax makes the first contact on the skin.

*Most regulatory agencies remind us in order to maintain sanitary conditions we are to avoid "double-dipping," which is when the applicator is placed in a product, applied to the skin and then returned to obtain more product. A comfortable and effective heated pot of wax registers from 140 to165°F/60 to 75°C, which is considered a high enough temperature to destroy most microbic life.*

**Orangewood Sticks** are made from a hard wood and have multiple purposes. This disposable stick is used in hair removal as **a guide for eyebrow measurement.** The orangewood stick with its long slender design will determine the precise markings for which hair is removed and which hair must stay to complete eyebrow design.

Eyebrow Measurement

Orangewood Sticks

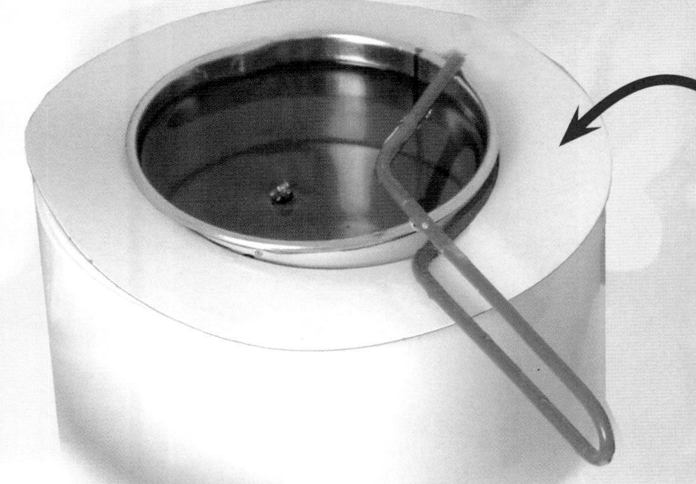

**Wax Pot Collar** is a round durable paper collar that sits along the perimeter of the wax pot opening. It is used on some wax pots to **catch excess wax** that occasionally drips from the spatula or applicator when transferring wax over to a client's skin.

# Hair Removal Liquid Tools...

*There are liquid tools that will **prepare the skin** for the hair removal process and **soothe the skin** afterwards to resolve the trauma induced by having unwanted hair shaved or pulled out. The products reviewed below are used to **assist in better adhesion** as well as **remove product residue** after service.*

**NOTE:** Avoid a cleanser with an oil base as this will hinder adhesion of wax to the skin.

## Hair Removal Pre-Treatment Steps:

1

**Skin Cleanser** is a cosmetic product designed to **remove dirt, oils, dead skin cells and makeup or any other pollutants** that rest on the skin surface. There are a variety of cleansers to choose from depending on skin type (refer to Chapter 13 Skin Treatments).

2

**Astringent,** sometimes referred to as **toner or freshener,** is a liquid skin product that protects the skin from dirt and pollutants by closing the pores and restoring the skin's natural pH after cleansing and hair removal services.

14

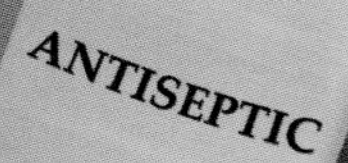


3

**Antiseptic** is an agent that **prevents or reduces infection** by eliminating or decreasing the growth of microorganisms. It can be applied **safely to the skin** prior to a hair removal service.

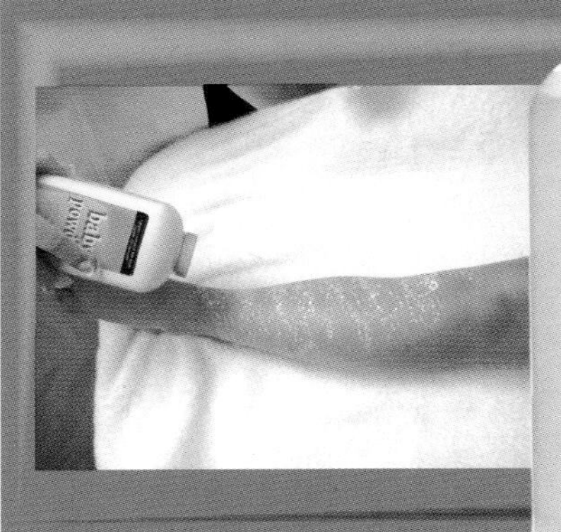

Dusting Powder

Dusting Powder

4

**Powder** is a finely grained cosmetic substance that is sprinkled over the skin to **absorb moisture,** thereby allowing the wax to adhere effectively on the skin. A recommended powder would be one that is fragrance-, talcum- and oil-free with a cornstarch base. Powder provides a **protective buffer** between the wax and skin.

# Hair Removal Liquid Tools...

## Hair Removal Post-Treatment Steps:

**Moisturizer** is a skin-care product that **softens the epidermal layer and restores hydration** or moisture loss that can occur due to use of harsh skin cleansers or exposure to the environmental elements.

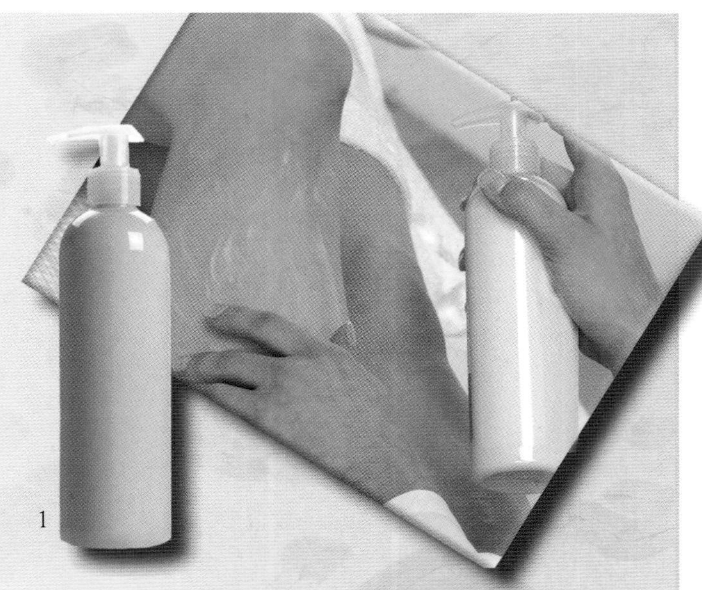

1

2

**Wax Remover** is a cosmetic product smoothed over the skin after waxing to **remove any wax residue.** It consists of oils and emollients that assist in softening the wax, allowing comfortable and easy removal. This product usually contains moisturizing ingredients to help soothe the skin.

**Soothing Cream** is a cosmetic cream, lotion, oil or gel applied over the waxed area to **calm the skin.** It helps to minimize swelling, burning, itching and redness. Natural ingredients such as chamomile or lavender – or the synthetically produced cortisone – may be used to calm the skin and relieve irritated skin symptoms.

3

**CAUTION:** Swelling or hives may occur on sensitive or fine-textured skin when waxing is complete. If this happens, use ice or an ice pack to calm the skin.

# Eyebrow Design . . .

***A properly** designed eyebrow will **complement an individual's eye and facial shape.** An arch or contour is shaped along the brow bone to create a pleasing eyebrow appearance and may create the illusion of balance. The emphasis of the eyebrow arch may either offset a full or narrow facial shape or dimminish the appearance of close- or wide-set eyes.*

## There are Three Eye-Set Positions; wide-set, close-set and balance-set.

**Eye-set position** is determined when a **third** eye is placed between a person's two eyes. The area between the two eyes is referred to as the **glabella** (gla-bel-la).

**Close-set eyes** are when a third eye is placed on the glabella and it **overlaps** onto a person's two eyes.

**Wide-set eyes** are when a third eye is placed on the glabella and there is **a gap** between the third eye and a person's two eyes.

**Balance-set eyes** are when the third eye **fits perfectly** on the glabella (from tear duct to tear duct) between a person's two eyes.

# Eyebrow Measurement...

***Unlike** with other areas of the face or body, removing **unwanted eyebrow hair requires precise markings** to determine which hair remains and which hair is removed. Once the eyebrow area is clean, an orangewood stick, eyebrow brush and pencil are used to take the measurements and place the markings.*

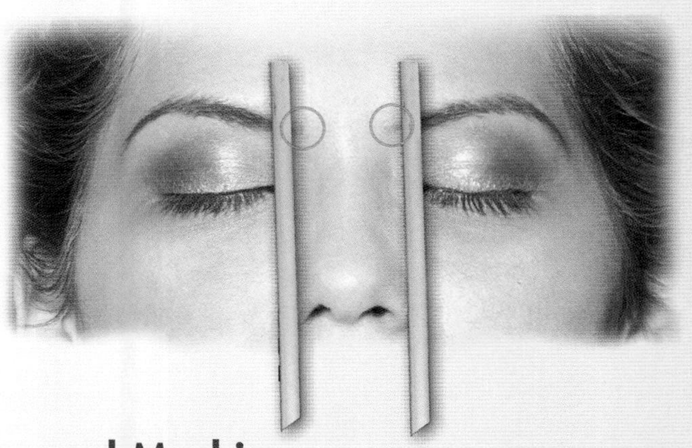

## First Marking:

Place tip of orangewood stick at corner of nose, and align stick straight up to intersect with **inside corner of eye's tear duct.** Place a small vertical line along inside corner of eyebrow. This shows the exact amount of unwanted hair to be removed to create the beginning of the eyebrow.

## Second Marking:

Place tip of orangewood stick at corner of nose, and diagonally align stick to intersect with **outside corner of eye.** Place a small vertical line along outside of eyebrow and stick. This shows the exact amount of unwanted hair to be removed to determine where the eyebrow would end.

## Third Marking:

**For close-set eyes**, have client look straight ahead, place orangewood stick **vertically** on cheekbone straight up to intersect with **outer area of iris (colored part of eye).** Draw a vertical line in pencil where stick meets the eyebrow. This marks the area where the eyebrow's arch will be.

**For wide-set eyes**, have client look straight ahead, place orangewood stick **vertically** on cheekbone straight up to intersect with **center of eye's pupil.** Draw a vertical line in pencil where the stick meets the eyebrow. This marks the area where the eyebrow's arch will be.

**For balance-set eyes**, have client look straight ahead, place tip of orangewood stick at corner of nose, **diagonally align stick to intersect with center of eye's pupil** meeting at eyebrow. Draw a vertical line where the stick meets the eyebrow. This marks the area where the eyebrow's arch will be.

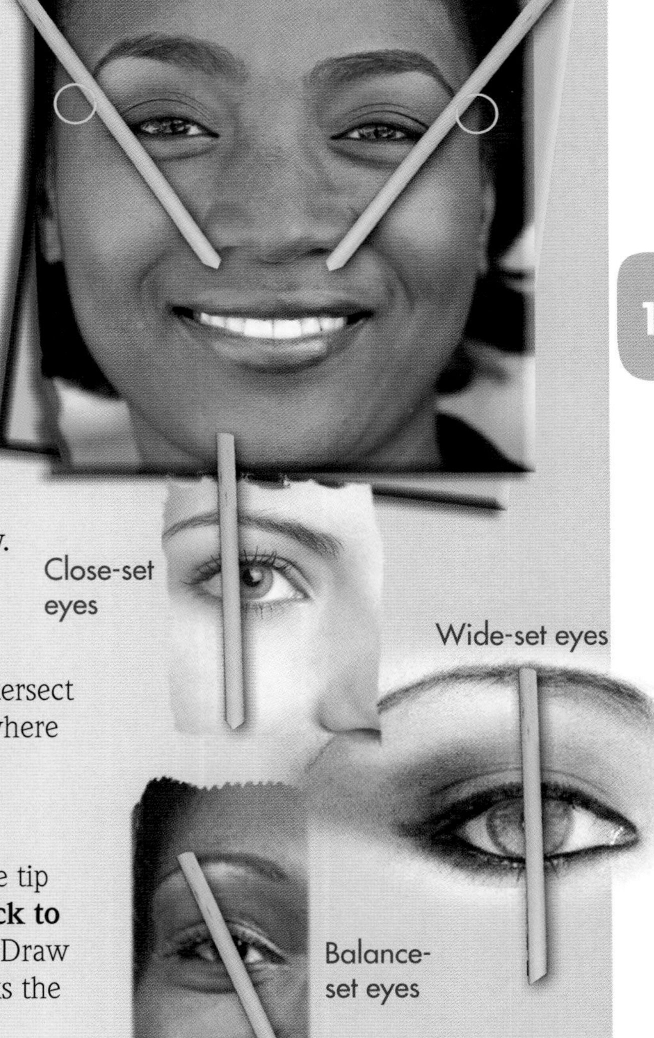

# Hair Removal Skin Conditions ...

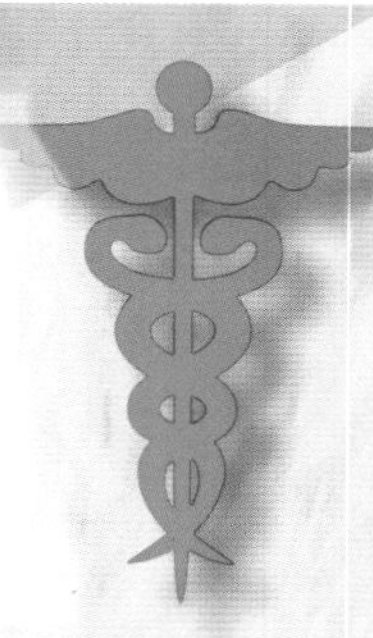

*There are certain skin conditions that can be aggravated by some hair removal methods. Using sanitary hair removal tools along with proper sanitary pre- and post-treatment applications will help to minimize the risk of skin irritation or infection. Depending on the severity of a skin condition, a client may need to consult a medical care professional.*

## A client's skin type and texture of hair may impact the following skin conditions:

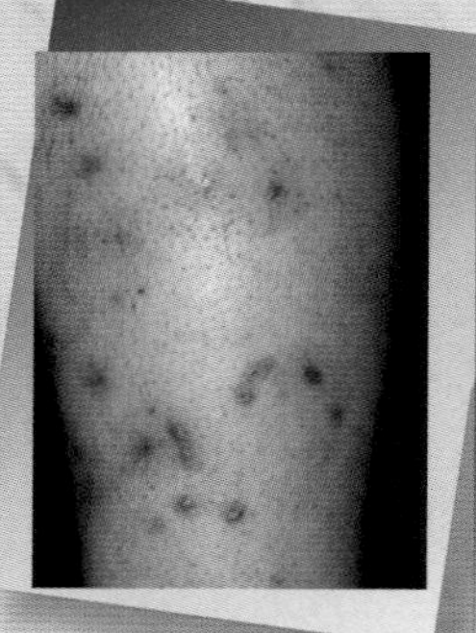

Folliculitis

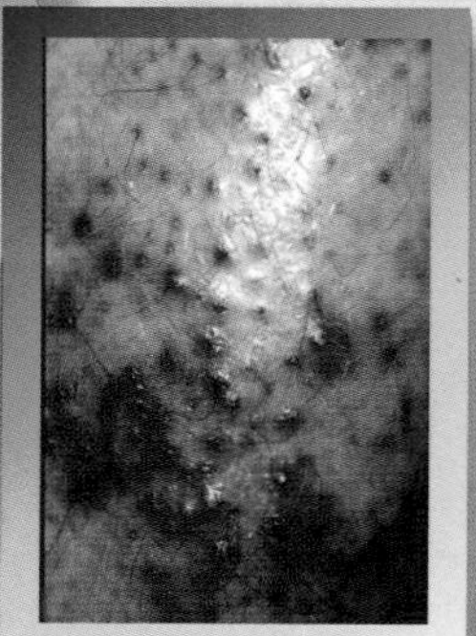

Furnuncle

Shaved skin is susceptible to **folliculitis** (fol-lic-u-li-tis) or **furuncle**, a condition that arises when bacteria get into the hair follicle through the opening of pores, resulting in swelling and inflammation. When a razor glides across the skin, a mild exfoliation is occurring; this exposes the hair follicle openings (pores), making the skin susceptible to invasion by dirt and bacteria.

14

**Pseudofolliculitis** (pseu-do-fol-lic-u-li-tis) is another condition prone to shaved skin that can result when short curly hair curves and re-enters the skin as it is growing, creating boils, abscesses and ingrown hair. If occuring on the face, along beard area, the condition is referred to as pseudofolliculitis barbae, tinea barbae or barber's itch.

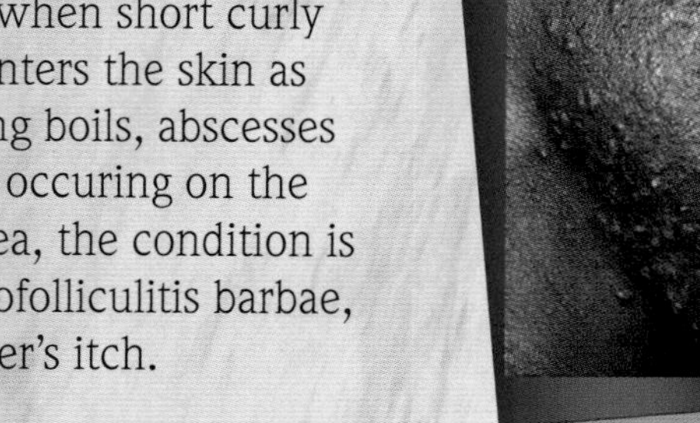

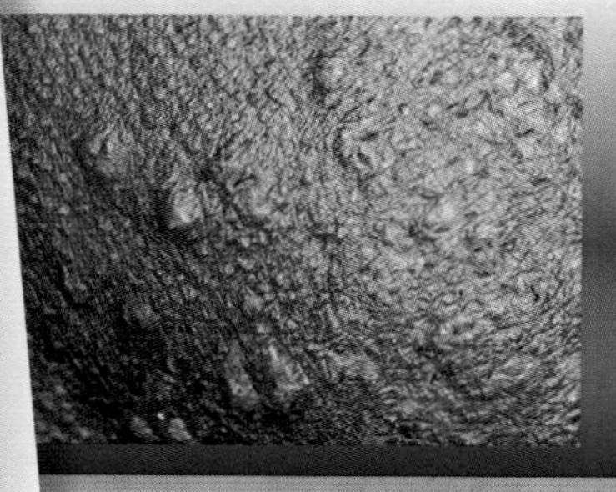

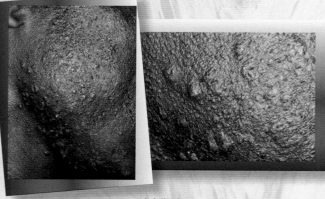

Pseudofolliculitis

Ingrown Hair

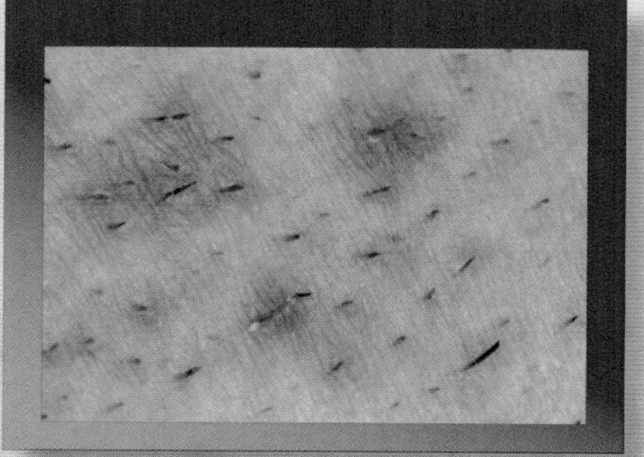

**Ingrown hair** occurs when the shortened hair has grown at an extreme angle and is unable to push through the surface of the skin. The hair is visible, but it lies in the stratum corneum layer. Ingrown hair may become irritated and red until the hair reaches through the top layer.

# Phone Client Consultation . . .

*A customer calling to schedule an appointment for hair removal will need to be made aware of certain* ***preparation criteria prior to day of treatment.*** *Once the client arrives on the day of scheduled service, the consultation will continue with the completion of a client profile card and release form.*

"Keep in mind, not every salon/spa offers ALL hair removal methods!"

*A* ***"walk-in" client*** *may be serviced depending on area of hair removal and upon completion of client consultation.*

**Phone consultation preparation criteria:**

Unwanted hair of a **fine or medium texture** needs to be **¼ inch (0.6 cm) in length.** For coarse texture hair a **½ inch (1.25 cm) in length** is required.

**Avoid tanning or sunbathing** 24 hours **before and after** hair removal service.

**Exfoliating** the skin is allowed the day before hair removal service, but **NOT** day of service.

For clients with dry skin (legs), applying moisturizer on day of hair removal service is permitted, but **not directly before service.**

Skin conditions such as varicose veins, moles, warts or skin tags may **NOT be waxed over,** just surrounding area.

14

# Client Consultation...

*Before the hair removal service, the cosmetologist needs to* ***communicate with the client*** *on his or her hair removal needs and the hair removal service requested. Compile answers on* ***client profile cards,*** *which are questionnaires containing useful client history, health and skin-care information. The results, along with additional questions, will decide the type of hair removal method to be used in delivering a competent service.*

## Additional questions to ask your client:

1. Have you received any hair removal services in the past?
2. Do you currently have ingrown hair or are you susceptible to ingrown hair?
3. Do you experience skin sensitivity to any skin-care products?

It is important to analyze the client's skin and area of unwanted hair as part of your consultation. **Drape the client** the same as you would for a facial treatment; making sure all hair is pulled away from face and clothing is protected with cloth sheet or cape. **Cleanse the face** to remove any existing makeup, dirt, oils or any other pollutants that rest on the skin surface. Clean skin will provide accurate analysis in checking for direction of hair growth, thinning areas, scarring and length of hair.

At close of the consultation, explain to the client the **detailed procedure** for the recommended hair removal service, the possible longevity of the chosen hair removal method and maintenance visits back to salon.



**Client Profile Card/File**

Name____________________ Date__________
Address____________________
Telephone Home__________ Work__________ DOB__________

Skin Disorder: ☐ Eczema ☐ Seborrhea ☐ Dermatitis ☐ Psoriasis
Sunburn Location____________________
Moles(s) Location____________________
Varicose Veins Location____________________
Rx Medicine(s)____________________
Are you pregnant?____________________
Hair Texture: ☐ Fine ☐ Medium ☐ Coarse ☐ Lanugo

**Face Waxing**
Are you currently using any skin-care products?____________________
Are you currently undergoing any specialized facial/skin treatments?____________________

Technician's notes:____________________

I understand that it is my sole responsibility to notify the waxing technician of any changes to the above information before any waxing service.
Client's Signature____________________ Date__________
Parent or Guardian (if under 18 years of age) Signature____________________
Technician's Signature____________________ Date__________

# Client Consultation . . .

**The release form** *tells the client that there are* ***certain risks involved when performing any hair removal services.*** *The cosmetologist or technician's responsibility is to always ask a new client or the returning client if there have been any* ***changes in his or her skin or skin-care regimen.*** *To complete any hair removal service, market a proper* ***home skin-care regimen*** *for the client. This will establish an ideal support for the service provided by the professional as well as maintenance to keep the client's skin healthy.*

**NOTE:** When creating the salon/spa's hair removal release form, have a legal professional review over the policy.

## Hair Removal Service Release Form

Certain risks such as bruising, redness or skin lifting may accompany a waxing service, especially on the face. These conditions may be further aggravated by the application of harsh cosmetics (non-professional), prescription medications (blood thinners, diabetic medicine or antibiotics), topical treatments (accutane, Retin-A or alpha hydroxyl acids) and creams (cortisone).

Avoid any waxing services if under the care of an esthetician or dermatologist and are receiving skin exfoliation treatments. Avoid tanning or sunbathing 24 hours before and after hair removal services. Do not wax over varicose veins, moles, warts or skin tags; may wax surrounding area.

### Client Acknowledgment

- I have read and understand the information on this release form.
- I am aware and understand there are certain risks involved if I am using or begin using any cosmetic products or pharmaceutical medications or topical treatments prior and immediately after waxing services.
- I am not under an esthetician or dermatologist's care.
- I am under an esthetician or dermatologist's care and accept full acknowledgment and responsibility of certain risks involved when receiving any type of waxing service.

Client's Signature ______________________ Date __________
Parent or Guardian (if under 18 years of age) Signature ______________________
Technician's Signature ______________________ Date __________

**Disclaimer:** *The release form shown is an example and not to be duplicated for your own personal salon use.*

14

CLIC INTERNATIONAL

SIMPLE LAB PROJECT

# Upper Lip Waxing (Cream Wax)

Before

After

## OBJECTIVE

To remove unwanted hair above the top lip quickly and effectively using a wax product.

## TOOLS & MATERIALS

- Cloth and disposable towels
- Robe
- Headband or plastic cap
- Gloves
- Client record card/file
- Powder
- Soothing cream
- Wax remover
- Cloth strips (pellon or muslin)
- Cotton
- Spatulas
- Release form
- Skin cleanser
- Wax applicators
- Tweezers
- Wax product
- Wax heater

## PROCEDURE

**"The client consultation is an important part of your professional service. Be sure to complete this step prior to each client service you provide. Your successful retail sales and customer satisfaction rates depend upon it!"**

1. Cosmetologist sanitizes hands and station.
2. Set out service tools and materials.
3. Drape the client in preparation for service.
4. Perform hair texture and skin analysis on upper lip area.
5. Follow procedure as shown and manufacturer's instructions.
6. Follow standard cleanup procedure.
7. Document client record card/file.

14

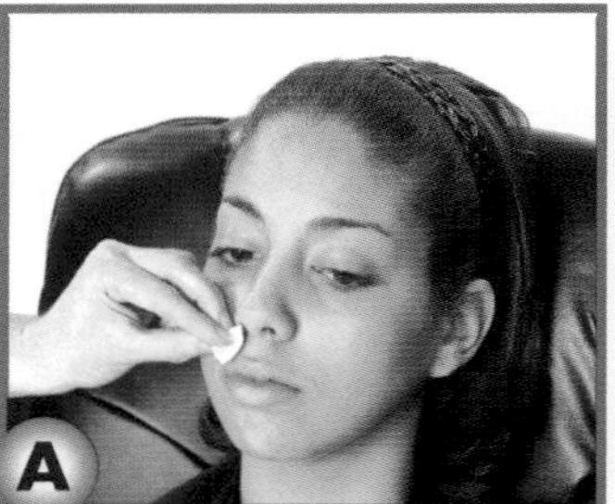

A — Clean above top lip area to remove makeup, dirt and oils. **Optional:** Apply powder over unwanted hair area for better wax adhesion to skin.

B — Using an applicator, dip into wax to check temperature and consistency.

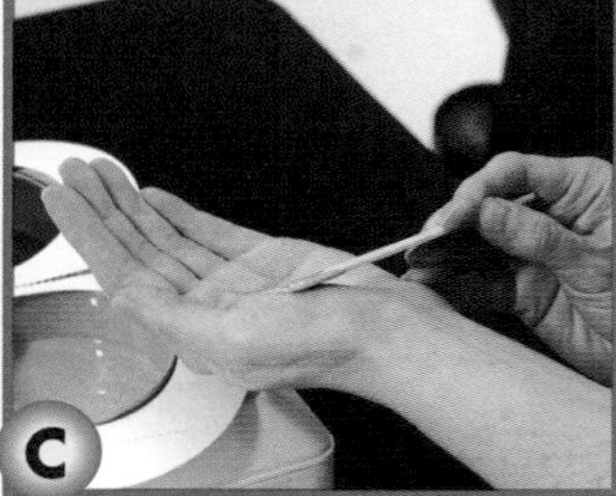

C — **Check temperature** of wax by applying a small amount to palm of hand or wrist. Remove wax and if too hot, adjust temperature and repeat test.

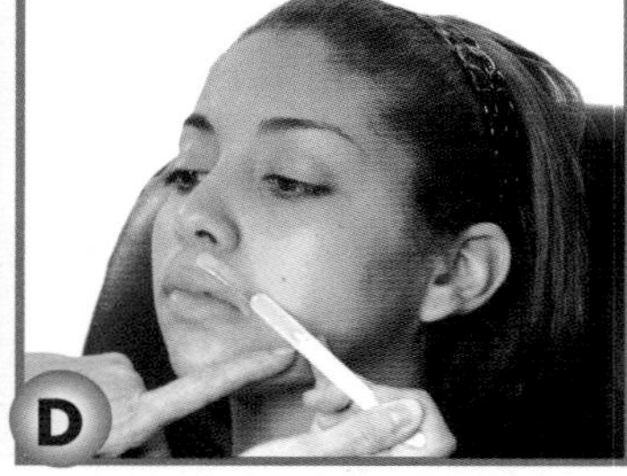

D — Start by applying wax to septum (middle area of nose that divides the nostrils) down left side of upper lip following direction of hair growth.

E — Apply and smooth cloth strip over wax for adhesion. Allow extra cloth at end of wax line.

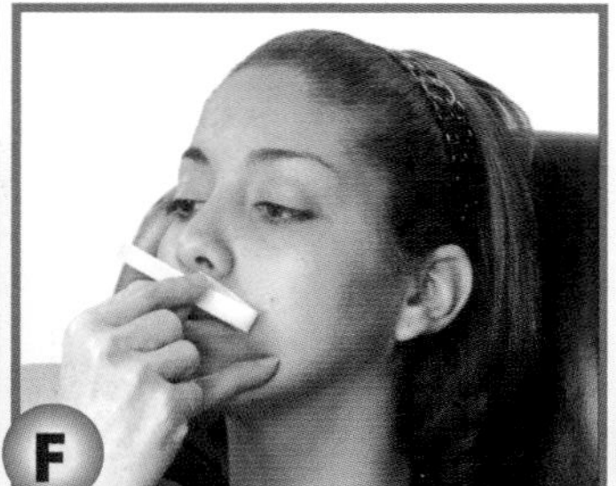

F — Pull skin taut with fingers of one hand; opposite hand will hold end of cloth

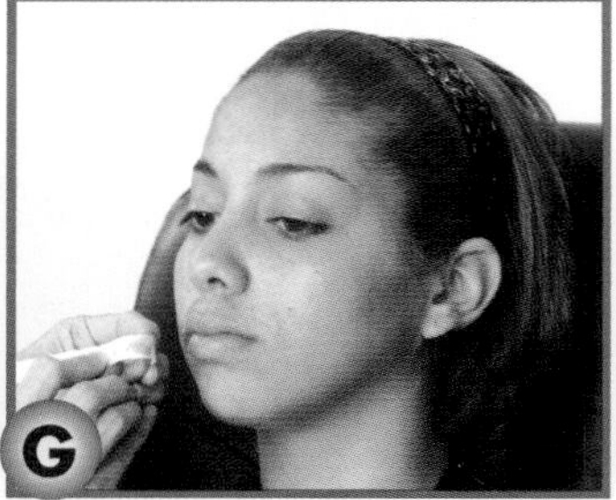

G — Pull cloth off skin in opposite direction of hair growth. Apply slight pressure to area to lessen pain.

H — Repeat on opposite side of septum and upper lip by applying wax to unwanted hair following direction of hair growth.

## Upper Lip Waxing

Place and smooth cloth over wax for adhesion.

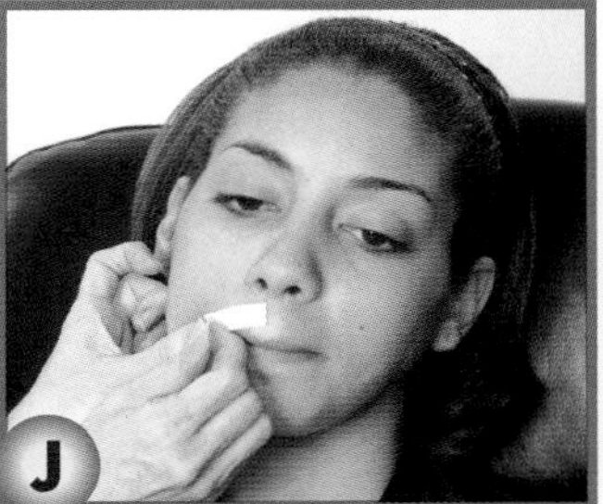

Pull skin taut with fingers of one hand; opposite hand will hold end of cloth.

Remove cloth in opposite direction of hair growth.

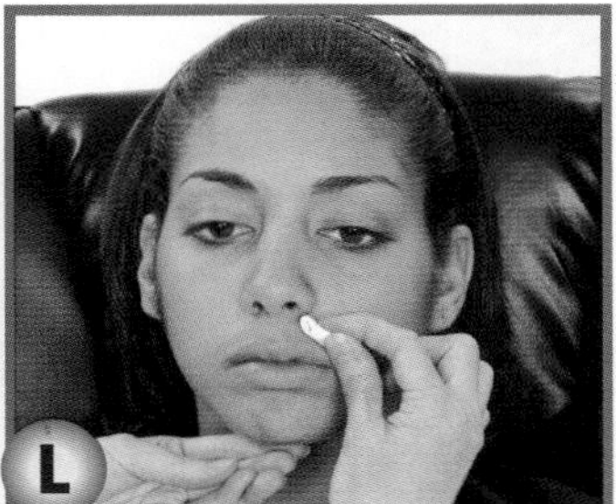

To rid the skin of any leftover wax, clean with wax remover. Apply a soothing cream to waxed area to reduce pain and skin swelling.

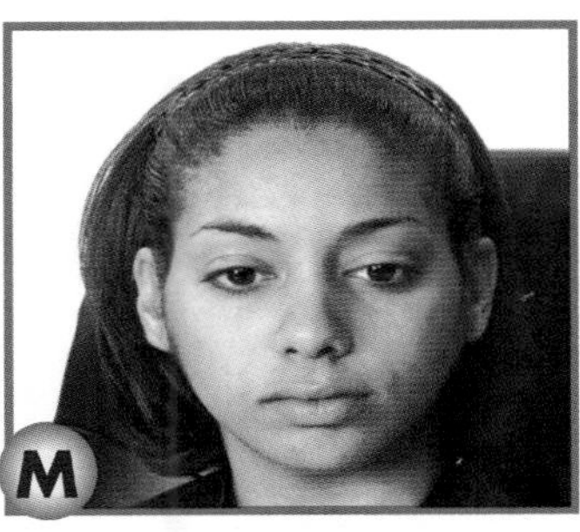

**Completed lip waxing.**

1

**NOTE:** Chin or jawline waxing may be performed in same manner as lip waxing.

*If client is receiving a makeup application, offer a complimentary eyebrow or upper lip waxing as an introduction to promote hair removal services.*

**EVALUATION** ______________________________

**GRADE** ______ STUDENT'S NAME ______ ID# ______

CLiC INTERNATIONAL

## INTERMEDIATE LAB PROJECT

# Eyebrow Waxing (Cream Wax)

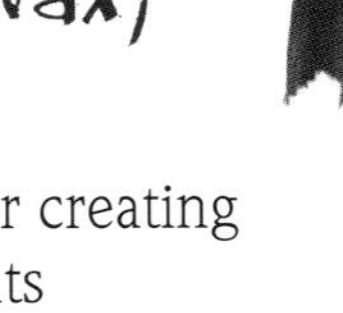
Before

After

### OBJECTIVE

To learn a fast and easy approach for creating an eyebrow design that complements the eyes and face.

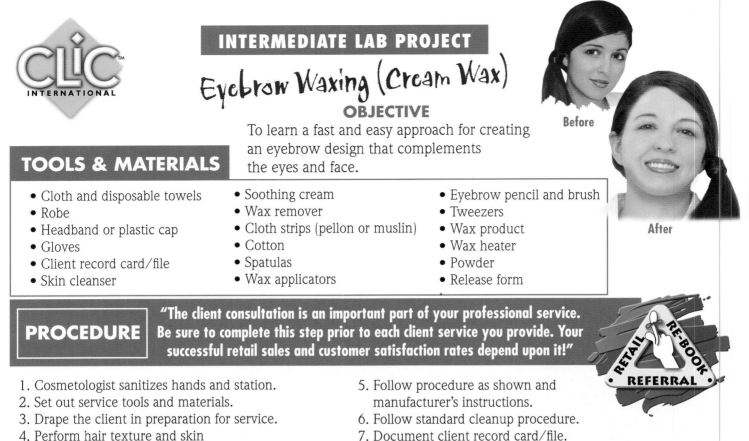

## TOOLS & MATERIALS

- Cloth and disposable towels
- Robe
- Headband or plastic cap
- Gloves
- Client record card/file
- Skin cleanser
- Soothing cream
- Wax remover
- Cloth strips (pellon or muslin)
- Cotton
- Spatulas
- Wax applicators
- Eyebrow pencil and brush
- Tweezers
- Wax product
- Wax heater
- Powder
- Release form

## PROCEDURE

**"The client consultation is an important part of your professional service. Be sure to complete this step prior to each client service you provide. Your successful retail sales and customer satisfaction rates depend upon it!"**

RETAIL · RE-BOOK · REFERRAL

1. Cosmetologist sanitizes hands and station.
2. Set out service tools and materials.
3. Drape the client in preparation for service.
4. Perform hair texture and skin analysis for eyebrow design
5. Follow procedure as shown and manufacturer's instructions.
6. Follow standard cleanup procedure.
7. Document client record card/file.

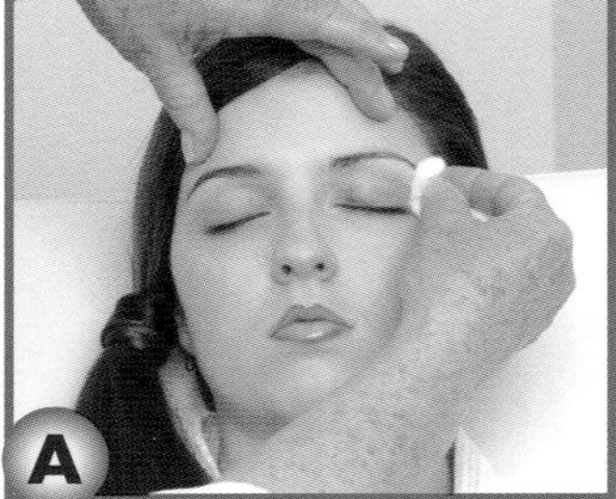
A
Using a skin cleanser and cotton, wipe eyebrow area clean to remove makeup, dirt and oils. **Optional:** Apply powder over unwanted hair area to allow for wax adhesion to skin.

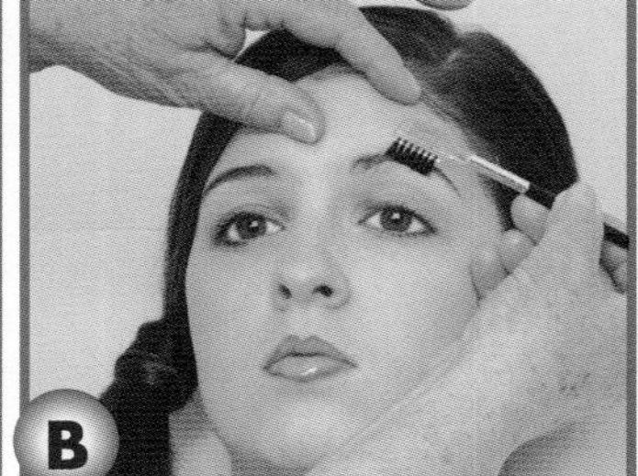
B
Brush eyebrows using an eyebrow brush to determine what hair is going to be removed. **Optional:** Place markings to identify the unwanted hair.

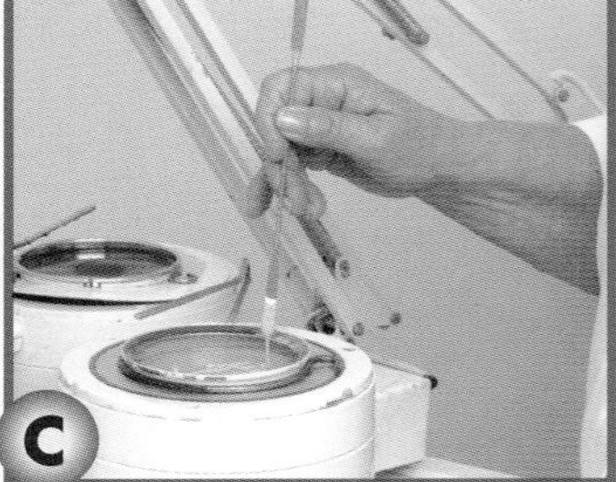
C
Using an applicator, dip into wax to check for temperature and consistency.

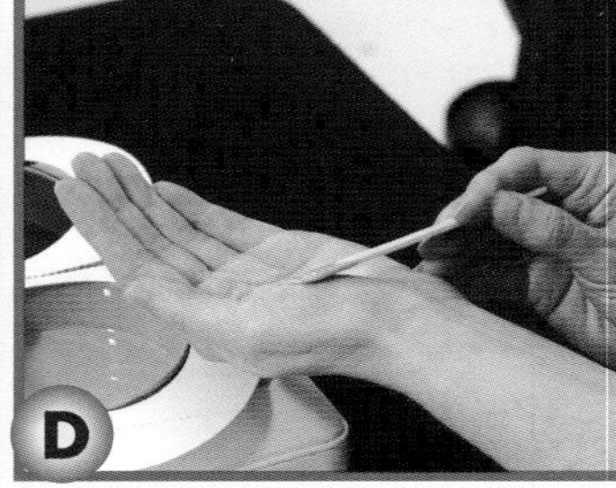
D
Check temperature of wax by applying a small amount to palm of hand or wrist. Remove wax and if too hot, adjust temperature and repeat test.

E
Start by applying wax underneath beginning of eyebrow following direction of hair growth.

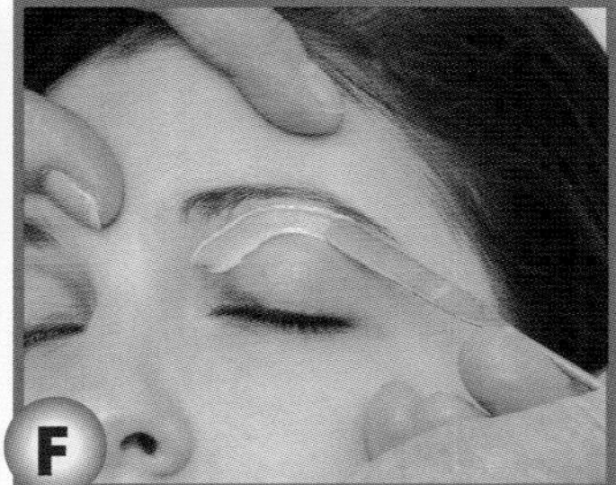
F
Continue by spreading wax across the underneath of eyebrow.

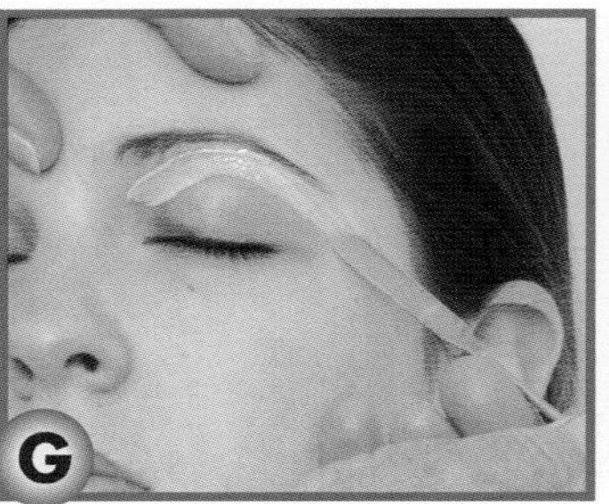
G
Spread wax to very end of eyebrow following the natural arched contour and hair growth pattern.

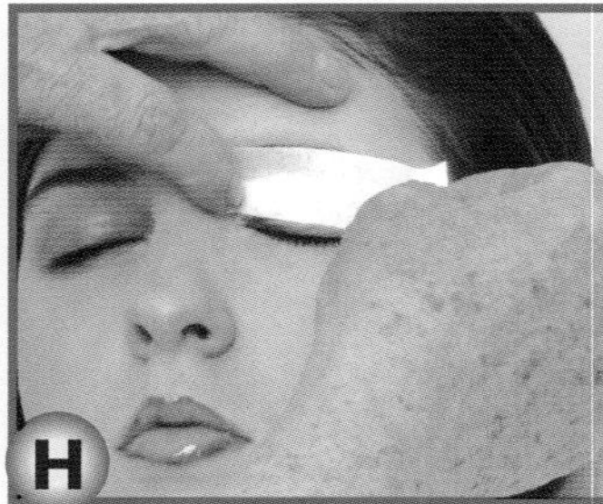
H
Apply and smooth cloth strip over wax for adhesion following direction of hair growth. Allow extra cloth at end of wax line.

## Eyebrow Waxing

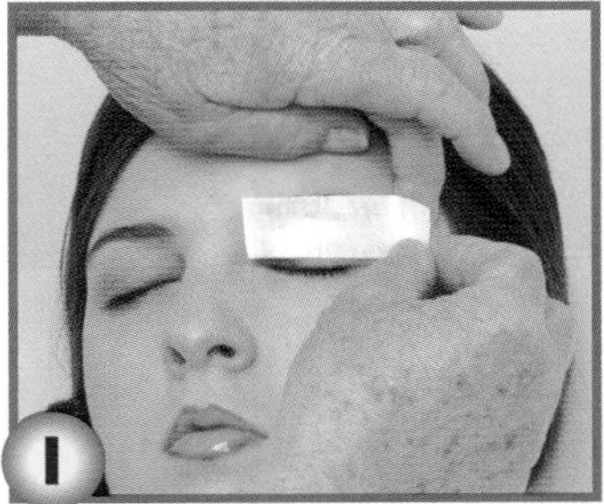


Pull skin taut with fingers of one hand; opposite hand will hold end of cloth

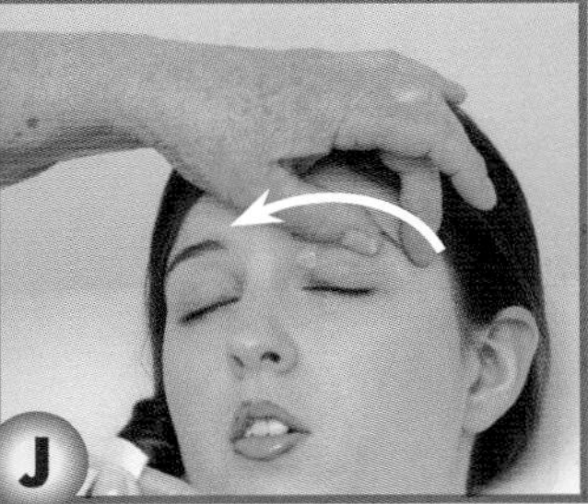


Pull cloth off skin in opposite direction of hair growth. Apply slight pressure to area to lessen pain.

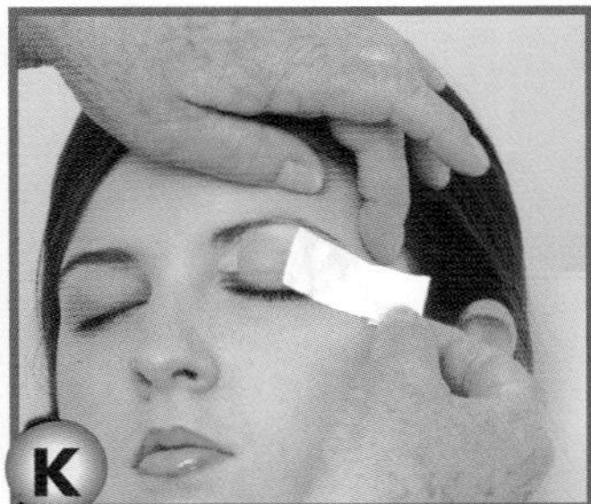


Replace cloth to continue removing unwanted hair. When removing cloth, keep close to skin area to prevent lifting and ripping of skin.

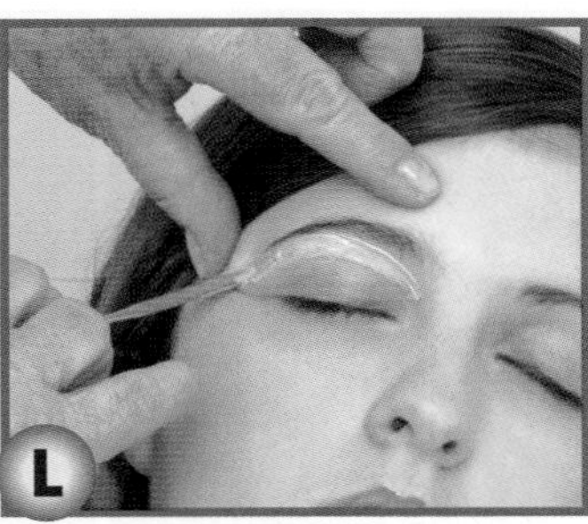


Repeat on opposite eyebrow by applying wax to unwanted hair following direction of hair growth.

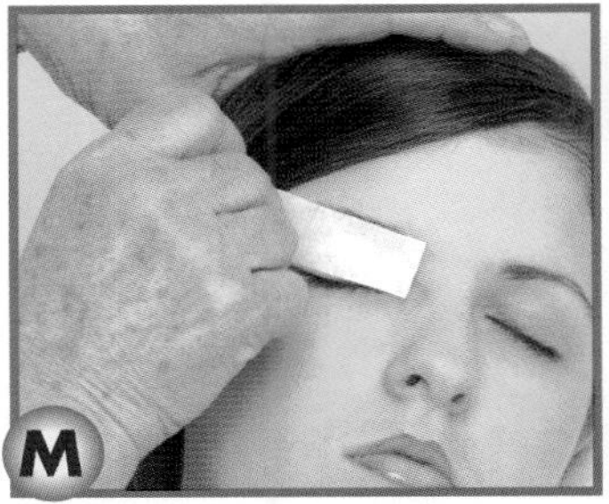


Place and smooth cloth over wax for adhesion. Remove cloth in opposite direction of hair growth.

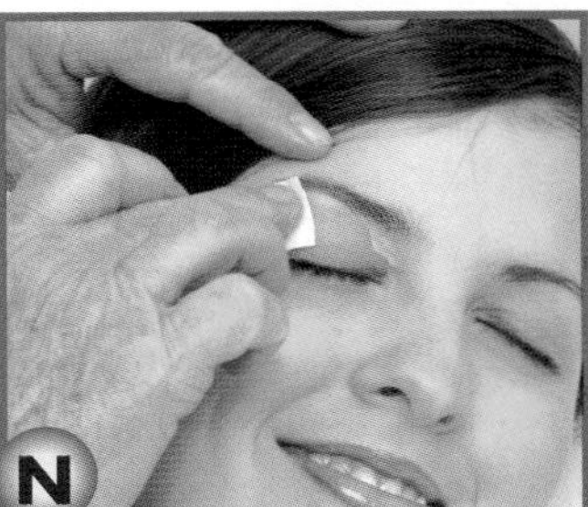


Continue to remove wax and unwanted hair.

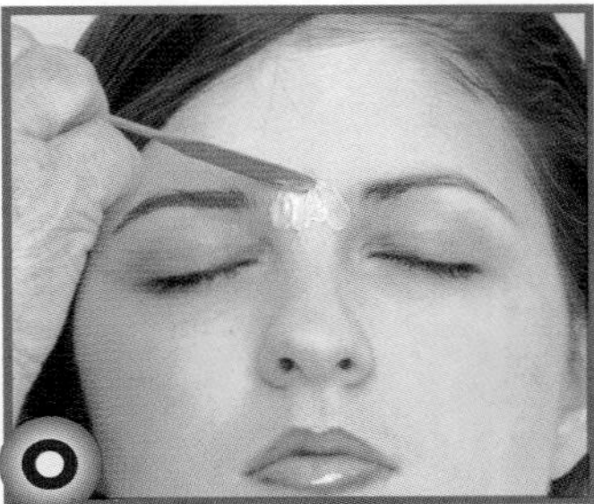


Apply wax to center of eyebrow in an upward direction to follow hair growth direction.

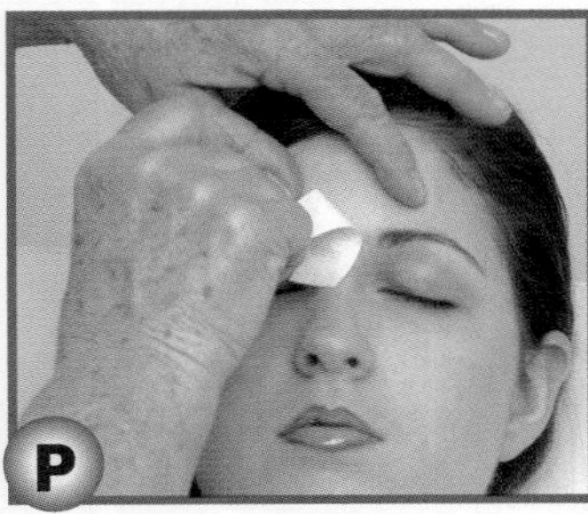


Apply cloth and remove in opposite direction.

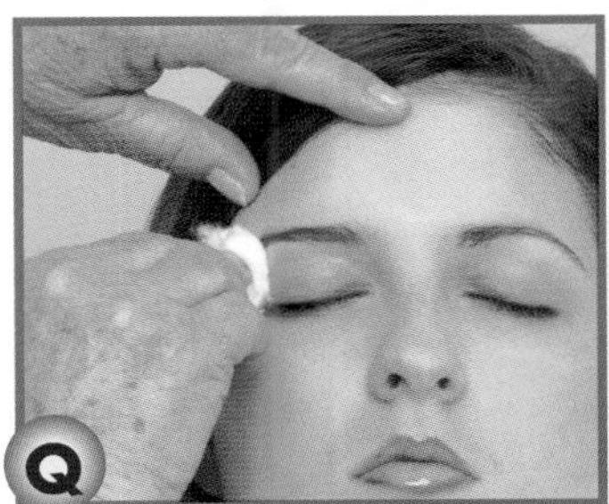


To rid the skin of any leftover wax, apply wax remover over eyebrow area.

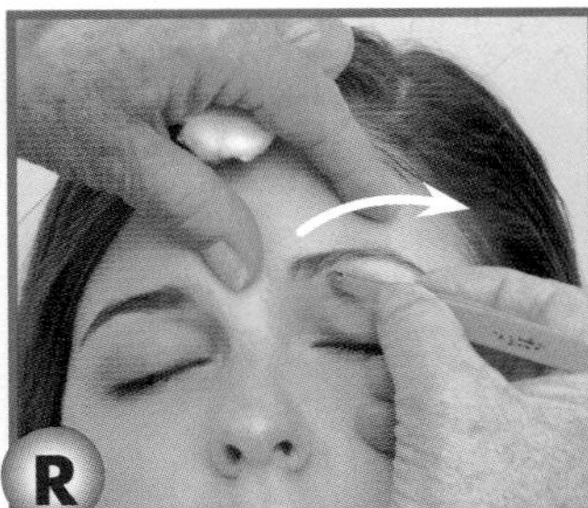


Tweeze any unwanted hair missed in the waxing process by pulling out in direction of hair growth.

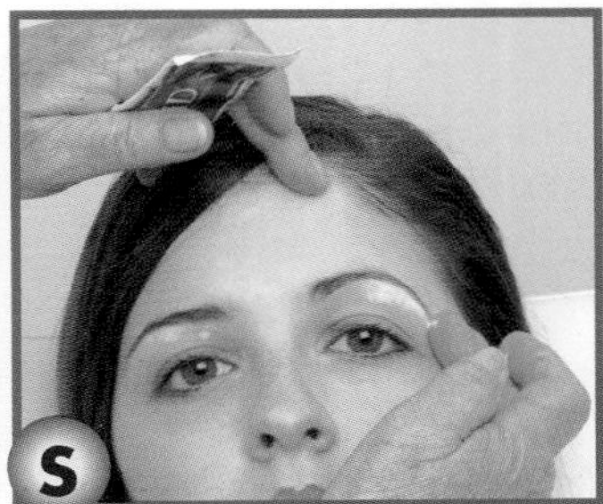


Apply a soothing cream or moisturizer to waxed area to reduce pain and skin swelling.

**Completed eyebrow**

**EVALUATION** ______________________________

**GRADE** ______ STUDENT'S NAME ______________________ ID# ______________

COMPLEX LAB PROJECT

# Leg Waxing

### OBJECTIVE

To remove unwanted leg hair safely and quickly using hot wax.

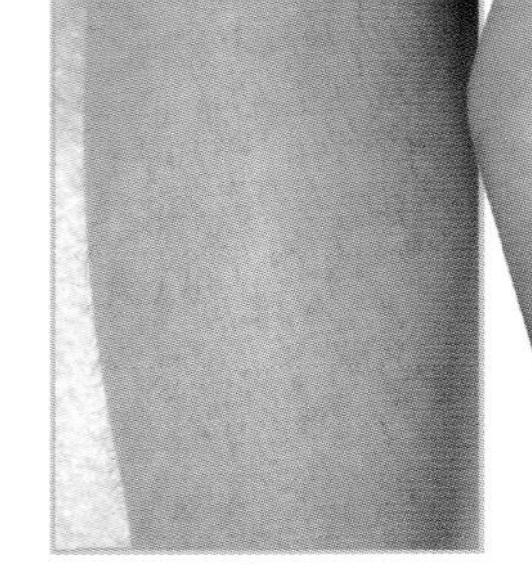

Before

After

## TOOLS & MATERIALS

- Cloth and disposable towels
- Robe
- Headband or plastic cap
- Gloves
- Client record card/file
- Release form
- Soothing cream
- Wax remover
- Cloth strips (pellon or muslin)
- Cotton
- Skin Cleanser
- Spatulas
- Wax applicators
- Wax product
- Wax heater
- Powder

## PROCEDURE

**"The client consultation is an important part of your professional service. Be sure to complete this step prior to each client service you provide. Your successful retail sales and customer satisfaction rates depend upon it!"**

RETAIL • RE-BOOK • REFERRAL

1. Cosmetologist sanitizes hands and station.
2. Set out service tools and materials.
3. Drape the client in preparation for service.
4. Perform hair texture and skin analysis on leg area.
5. Follow procedure as shown and manufacturer's instructions.
6. Follow standard cleanup procedure.
7. Document client record card/file.

14

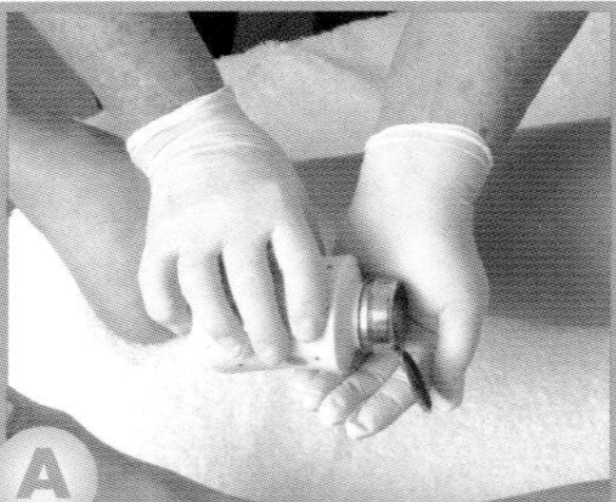

A Apply skin cleanser to palms of gloved hands.

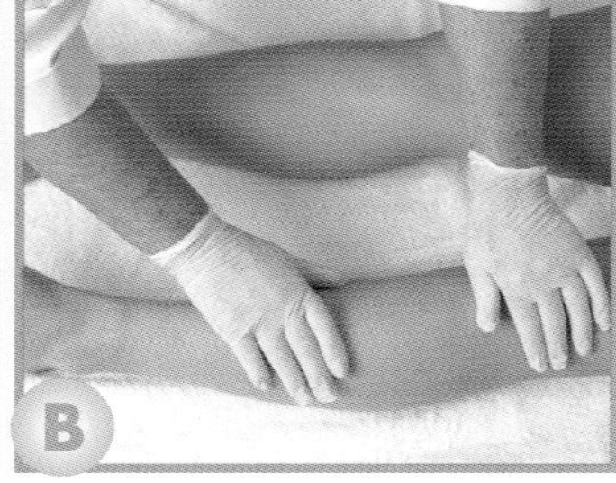

B Wipe leg area clean to remove dirt and oils. **Optional:** Apply powder over unwanted hair area to allow for wax adhesion to skin.

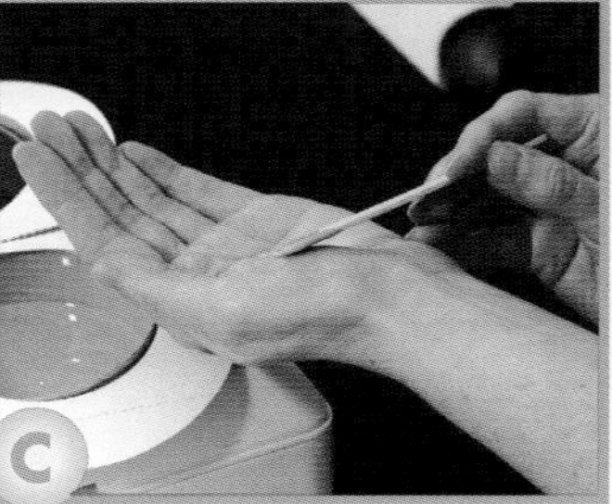

C Check temperature of wax by applying a small amount to palm of hand or wrist. Remove wax and if too hot, adjust temperature and repeat test.

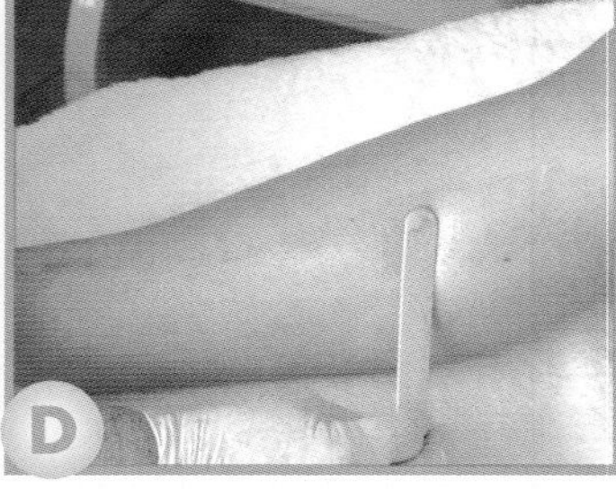

D Start by applying wax to inner side of lower leg following direction of hair growth.

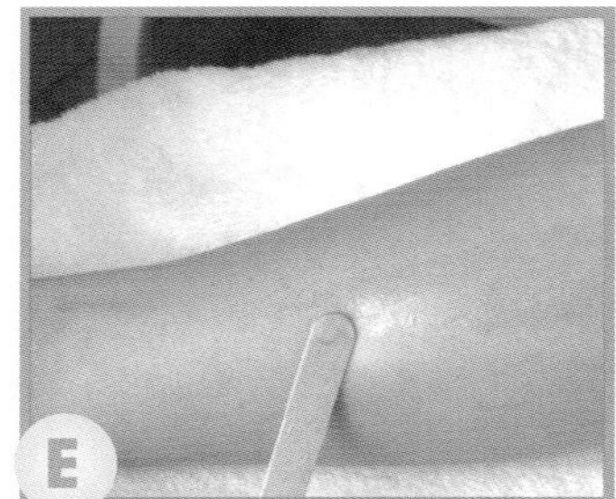

E Apply enough wax to encompass an amount of leg that will allow placement of a large cloth over waxed area.

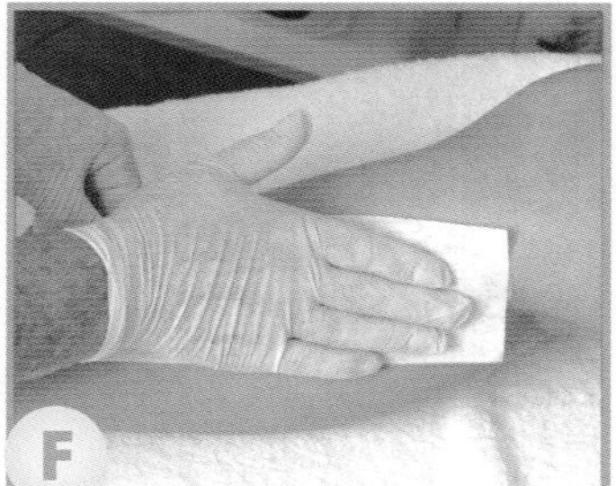

F Apply and smooth pellon strip over wax for adhesion. Allow extra cloth at end of wax line.

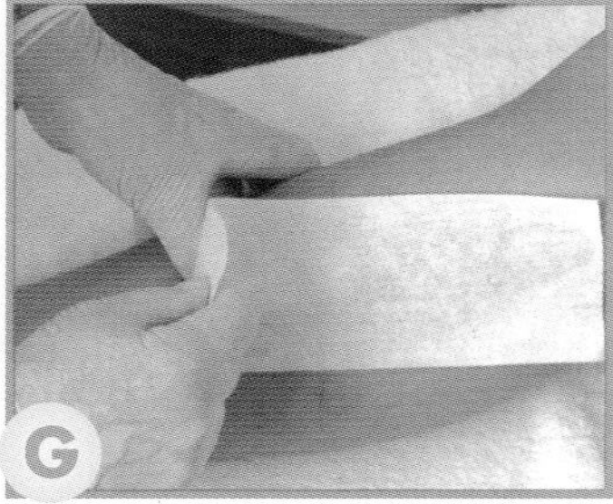

G Pull skin taut with fingers of one hand; opposite hand will hold end of cloth. Remove cloth and apply pressure over waxed skin.

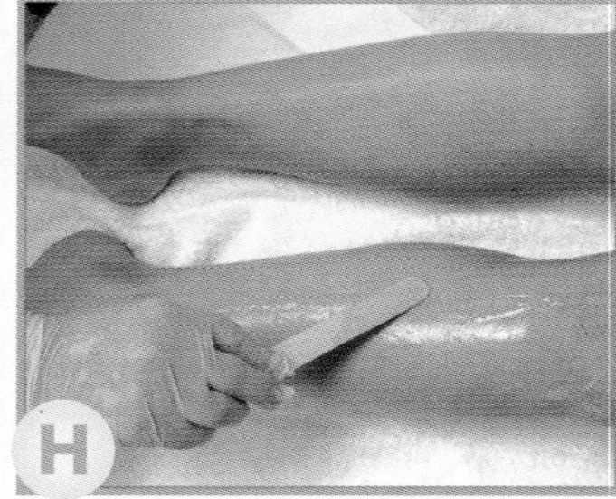

H Continue to apply wax on topside and opposite inner leg area.

## Leg Waxing

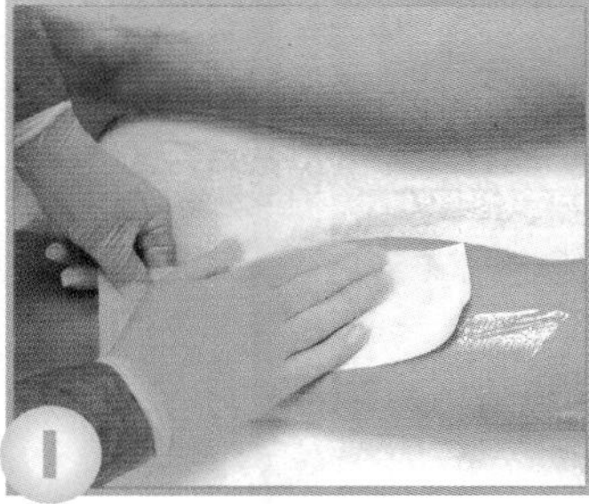

I — Apply and smooth pellon strip over wax for adhesion. Allow extra cloth at end of wax line. Remove cloth and apply pressure.

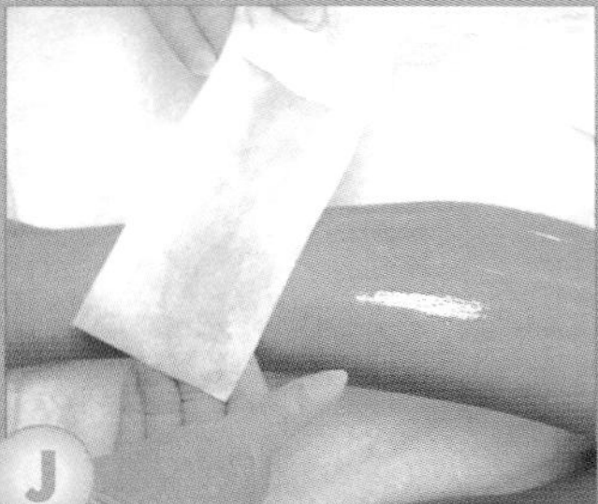

J — Repeat on topside of opposite leg; apply wax, remove cloth and apply pressure.

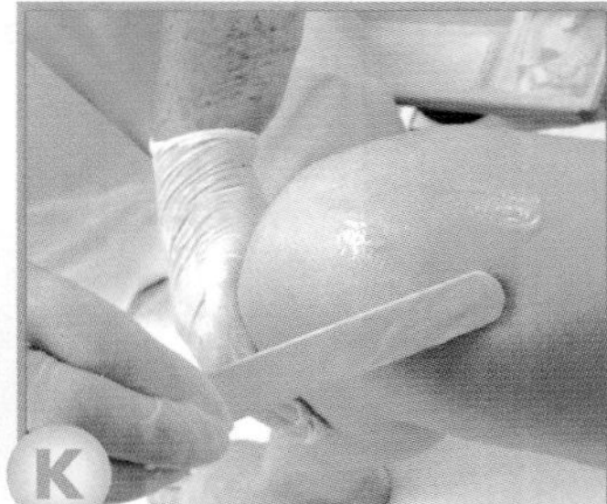

K — Apply wax to knee area having client bend her knee for skin tautness.

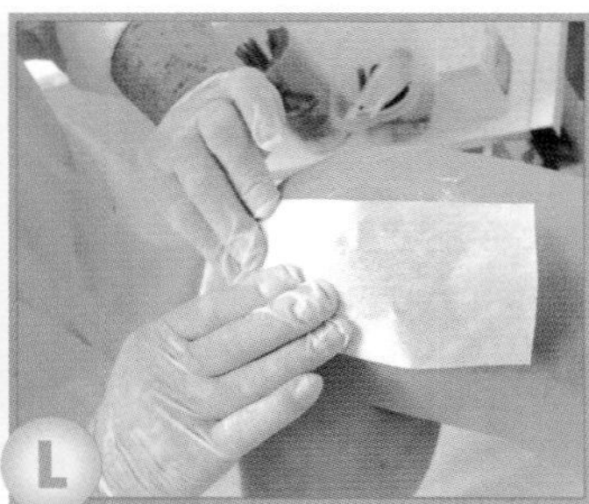

L — Apply and smooth cloth over wax.

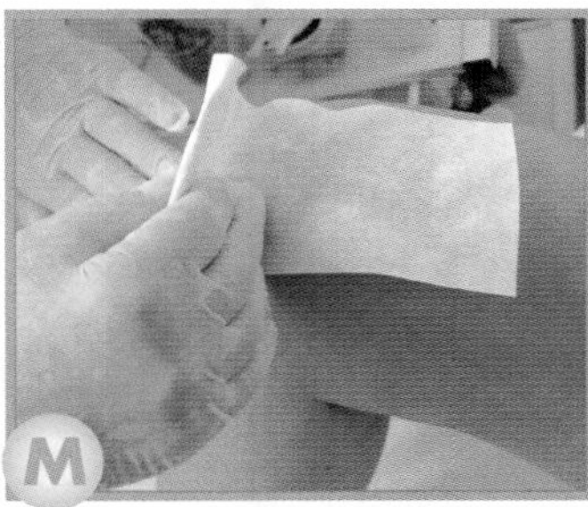

M — Remove cloth and apply pressure.

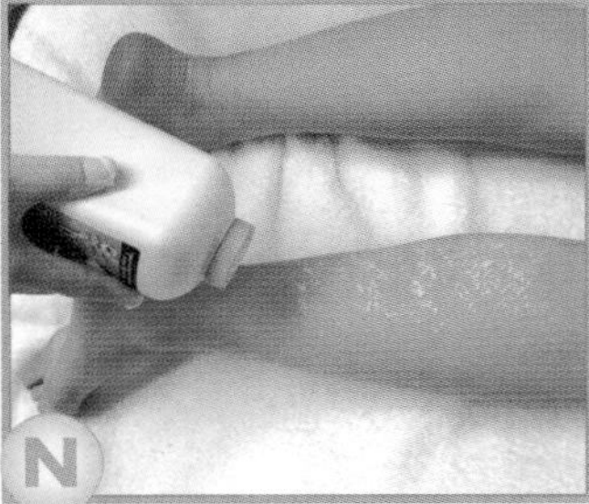

N — Re-position client and have her lie on stomach to do underside of lower legs. **Optional:** Apply powder.

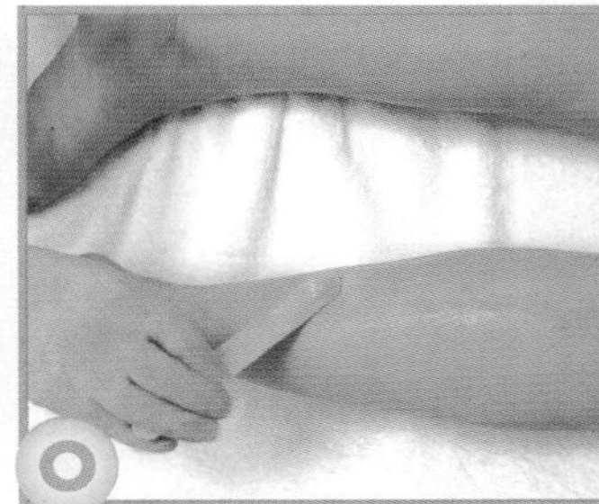

O — Apply wax to underside of lower leg following hair growth direction.

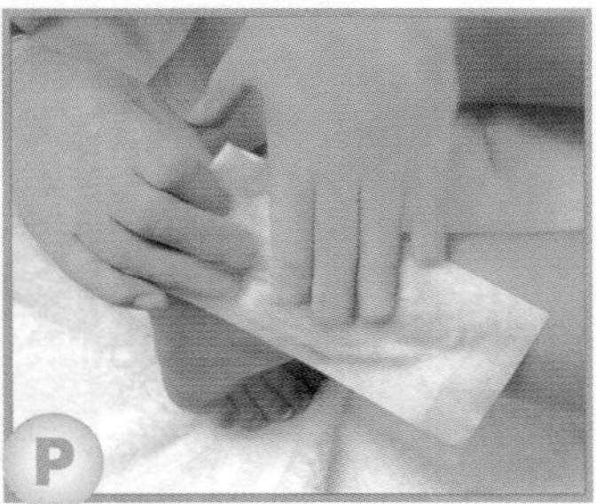

P — Apply, smooth and remove cloth.

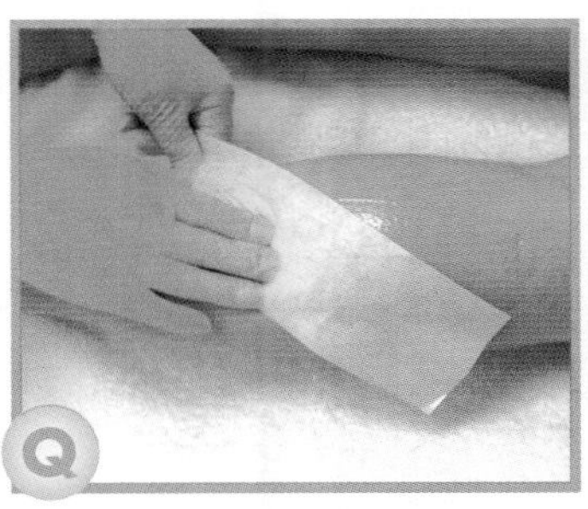

Q — Continue with application of cloth to remove wax and unwanted hair.

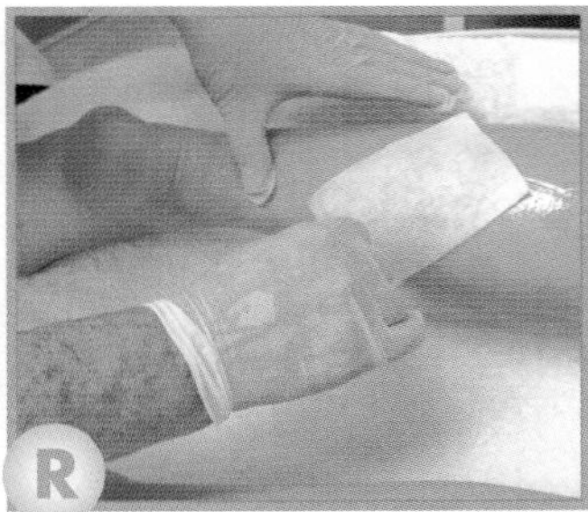

R — **Repeat Steps O thru Q on opposite leg.**

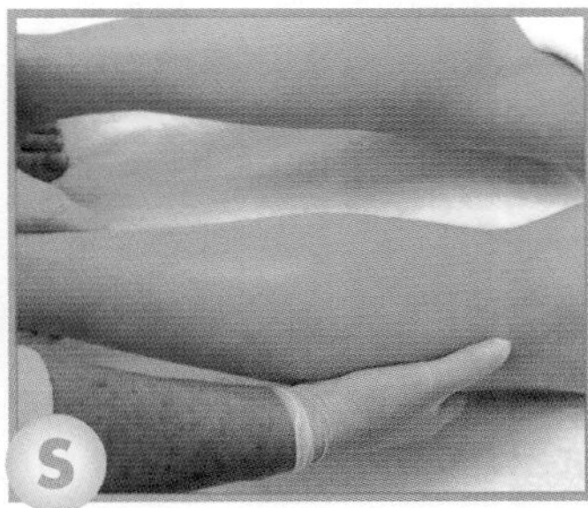

S — Apply a wax remover product to legs to clean off any excess wax residue.

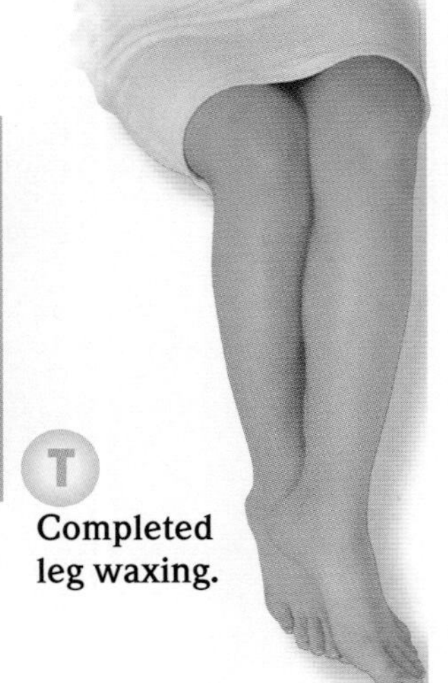

T — **Completed leg waxing.**

*Suggest the client return to the salon within one to two weeks to remove any new emerging (anagen) hair.*

"Optional, but we recommend wearing gloves for all hair removal services!"

**EVALUATION** ______________________________

GRADE ______ STUDENT'S NAME ______________ ID# ______________

# REVIEW QUESTIONS

## FILL-IN-THE-BLANKS

A. Client Profile Cards
B. Close-Set Eyes
C. Cloth Strips
D. Depilatory
E. Electrolysis
F. Eyebrow Brush
G. Hirsutism
H. Ingrown Hair
I. Jacob Schick
J. Patch Test
K. Pellon
L. Powder
M. Pseudofolliculitis
N. Release Form
O. Soothing Cream
P. Straight Razor
Q. Sugaring
R. Tweezing
S. Waxing
T. Wax Remover

1. ________ is sprinkled over skin to allow wax to effectively adhere to unwanted hair and skin.
2. ________ are when the third eye overlaps onto a person's two eyes.
3. ________ is a method to permanently remove unwanted hair using a direct electrical current.
4. ________ was a typical tool of choice used in the early 1900s to remove men's facial hair.
5. ________ is a condition when excessive hair growth occurs on uncommon areas of the face and body.
6. ________ is a cosmetic product applied over the skin to dissolve unwanted hair.
7. ________ uses a product that encases the entire hair shaft, which pulls out hair root from follicle.
8. ________ invented and sold the first hand-held electric razor in 1931.
9. ________ is a method using a tweezers to pull out individual hair in a small area.
10. ________ occurs when shortened hair is unable to push through the surface of the skin.
11. ________ are questionnaires containing useful client history, health and skin-care information.
12. ________ is a tool used to smooth, control and separate eyebrow hair.
13. ________ is a cosmetic product applied over waxed skin to calm and minimize swelling and redness.
14. ________ are placed and smoothed over wax to allow adhesion and removal of wax and unwanted hair.
15. ________ is a condition when short curly hair curves and re-enters the skin creating boils and abscesses.
16. ________ tells the client there are certain risks involved when performing any hair removal service.
17. ________ is a non-woven durable white cloth applied over wax to remove unwanted hair.
18. ________ determines if a client is sensitive or allergic to product being applied on skin.
19. ________ is a cosmetic product applied over waxed skin to remove any leftover wax residue.
20. ________ is a non-irritating and natural form of temporary hair removal.

STUDENT'S NAME DATE GRADE

# Art of Makeup

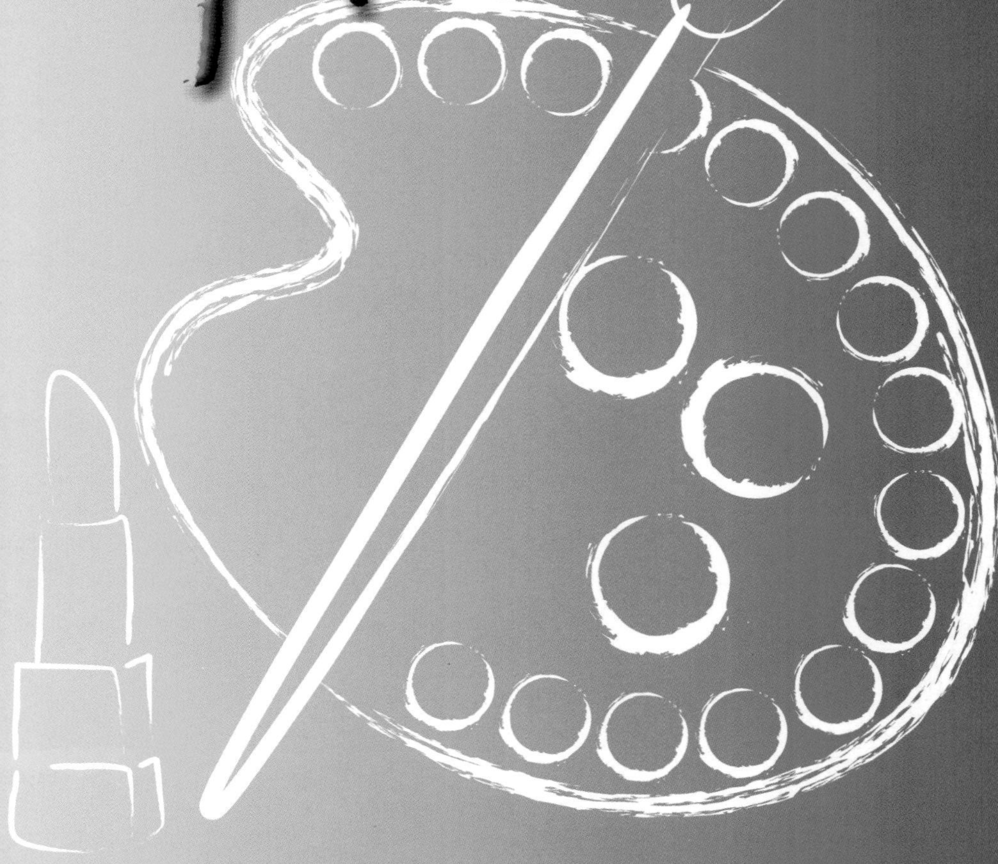

# ART OF MAKEUP

15

# Terminology ...

*The following terms are but a few to assist in learning the language you will be exposed to throughout this chapter. This visual vocabulary reveals the image of the word as well as the definition to stimulate learning.*

**Blending** is spreading and mixing colors together following a certain direction to avoid a visible line of demarcation.

**Brushes** are an assortment of non-disposable applicators designed to apply color to the skin.

1

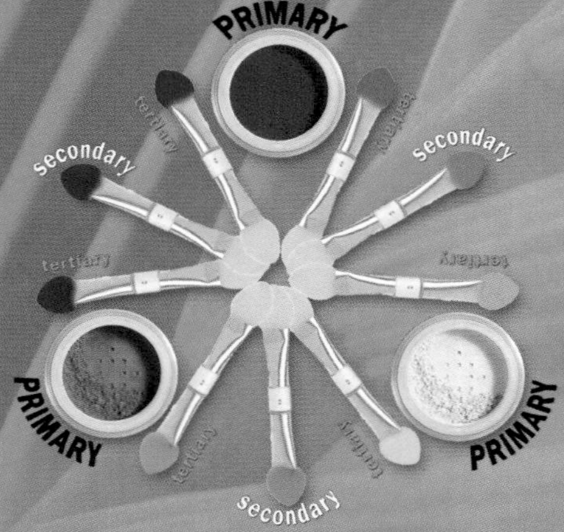

**Color Wheel** is the artist's tool showing the primary, secondary and tertiary colors and how they relate to one another.

15

**Complementary Colors** are derived from mixing a primary and a secondary color that are opposite each other on the color wheel.

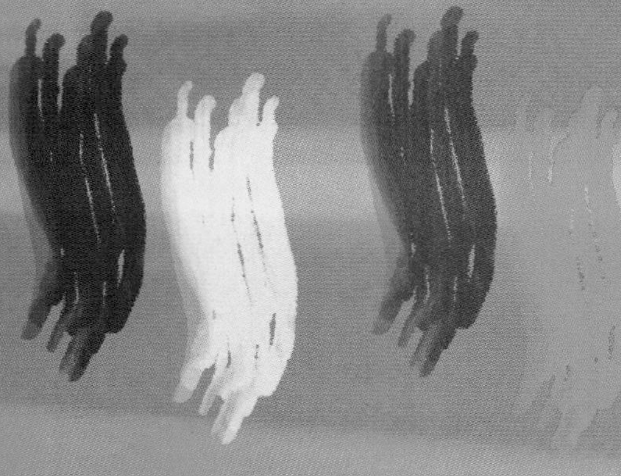

3

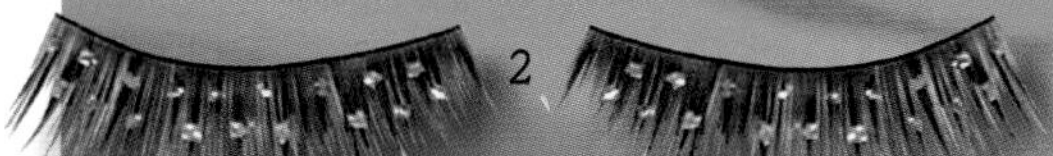

2

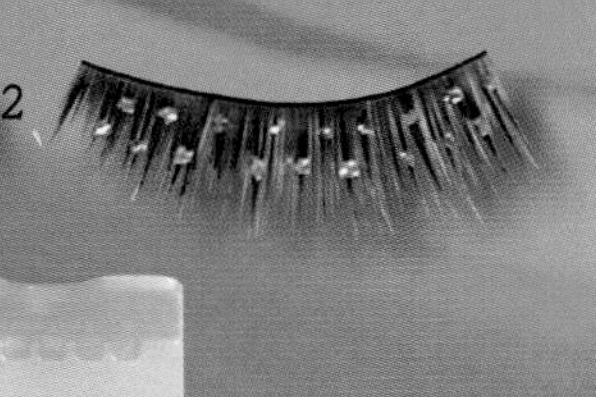

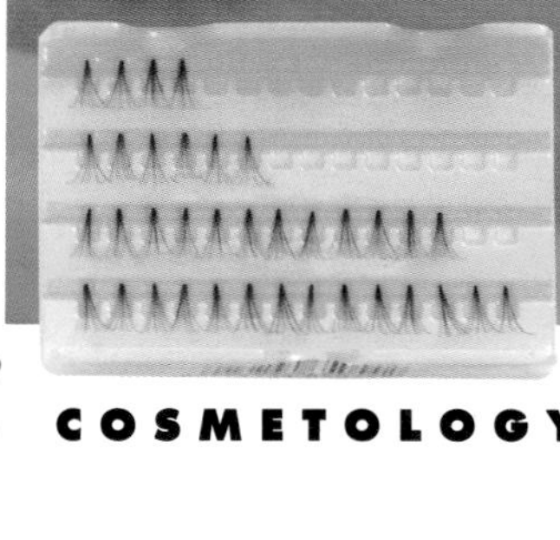

**Eyelash Extensions** are artificial lashes added to the existing lashes to create thicker, longer eyelashes, enhancing the look and shape of your eyes.

# Terminology . . .

**Foundation** is a cosmetic product that covers and/or blends uneven skin tones on the face and neck.

**Eye Makeup Remover** is a product used to remove makeup over the eye area without stretching the skin.

1

**Hue** (hyoo) is a general name for color.

2

**Highlighting** is the application of light or bright shades of color to a particular area of the face to bring attention to a certain feature.

3

4

**Shadowing or Shading** is the application of dark shades of color to a particular feature in order to minimize or detract attention from that area.

15

# History of Makeup ...

## A small summary on the history of beauty ...

The **purpose of makeup** has not changed from as long ago as 4000 BCE, 1
when the **Egyptians** were preoccupied by **cleanliness, smelling good and looking their best.** Makeup also had a spiritual meaning: it was believed that beauty was pleasing to the gods, and tending to beauty would protect them from evil.

The Egyptians always searched for new methods or ingredients to use to accommodate their beauty needs. Because of these beauty practices, they possessed the knowledge and ability to mix ingredients, thereby creating the right combinations of colors for the ideal look. For example, a dark powder was made using ash, lead, copper ores, ochre, burnt almonds and oxidized copper. This powder – called **kohl** – was applied around the eyes on both men and women. The cleansing regimen for the Egyptians consisted of cosmetic cleansers, perfumes, face creams and body oils. The ancients also used essential oils such as chamomile, rose, myrrh, lavender and peppermint along with the carrier oils of almond, olive and sesame.

## Each culture's history of beauty ...

2

In 1500 BCE, **rice powder paint** was used to color faces white in **China and Japan.** Eyebrows were shaved, and teeth were painted black or gold. **Henna dyes** were used to stain the hair and face, as well for tracing the veins on the skin.

In 1000 BCE, **Greek upper class women and men** kept their precious cosmetics in intricate boxes. To redden the cheeks **rouge** was applied, and to create a fair complexion, various **white powders** were made from white lead or chalk. Women applied **ochre** (o-chre), **clay stained red with iron,** for lipstick and painted their palms with henna to create a young appearance.

When we look at the history of makeup, we see that pale skin was a sign of wealth and held certain merit in society.

# History of Makeup . . .

**From the middle ages until the Industrial Revolution,** a majority of the people worked outside in the sun and had developed dark skin, but the wealthy remained indoors maintaining very fair complexions. As it was fashionable to have a light skin tone – anyone not from the wealthy class made their faces pale using white lead paint.

**To keep in step with fashion,** women during the sixth century would apply leeches to their skin to bleed out, which made the skin pale.

**In the 16th and 17th centuries,** the wealthy dropped **belladonna** (bel-la-don-na), a poisonous herb, into their eyes to **dilate the pupils and provide a "dreamy look."** Noblewomen drew blue veins on their neck and shoulders to emphasize their exalted status thus developed the term **"bluebloods."** Italy and France became the chief centers for manufacturing cosmetics in Europe and the pale complexion maintained its popularity.

A woman with a **high forehead** was considered beautiful during the **Elizabethan era,** and upper-class women plucked or shaved their eyebrow hairs to achieve this look. They also covered their skin with **ceruse** (ce-ruse), a lead-based makeup, which caused disfiguring or scarring that lead to the addition of more makeup.

Belladonna Plant

**During the 18th century,** **vermilion** (ver-mil-ion) **rouge,** which was derived from sulfur and mercury, achieved popularity. However some of the consequences from its use were lost teeth, gingivitis and risk to the kidneys and nervous system.

By the **late 1800s,** history shows that zinc oxide was found to be a safer alternative for creating the much desired **"pale look."** Even today zinc oxide is still a natural cosmetic ingredient that is used for base makeup as well as sun protection products.

15

# History of Makeup . . .

**The 20th century was considered the "cosmetic" century.**

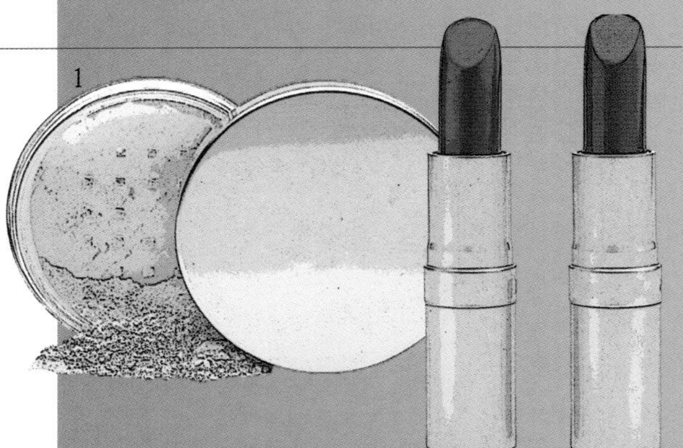

1

**During the 1900s – 1910s,** salons were opened by cosmetic manufacturers to promote and market their products. Cosmetic manufacturers worked with various chemicals to create longer-lasting formulas for extended shelf-life of products.

2

**1920s – 1930s,** Hollywood stars began influencing makeup trends by creating thin, sloping black eyebrows using tweezers and an eyebrow pencil. On the face, rouge and powder were used along with red or orange lipstick to create full lips.

4

3

**1940s – 1950s** continued with the emphasis of full lips, but eyebrows were now defined following the natural brow line. Since the television was developed, marketing for cosmetics and makeup products really took off.

5

# History of Makeup . . .

**1960s – 1970s** focused on emphasis of the eyes by using eyeliner (usually liquid) and/or applying false eyelashes for fuller, longer lashes. Another style was simply wearing no makeup for a natural appearance.

1

2

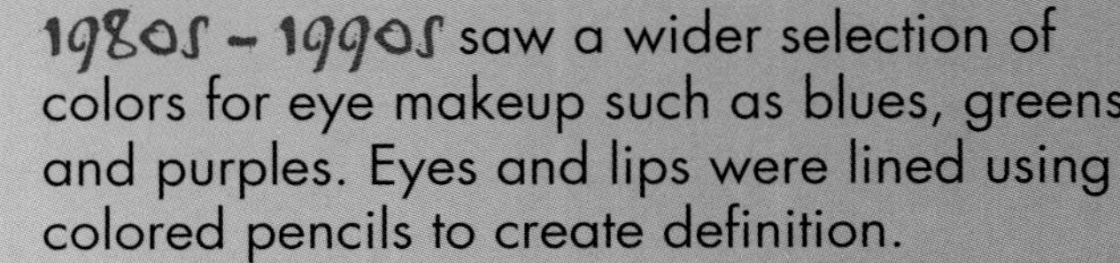

**1980s – 1990s** saw a wider selection of colors for eye makeup such as blues, greens and purples. Eyes and lips were lined using colored pencils to create definition.

**Today,**
**natural beauty** is at the forefront and is a reflection of how well we take care of ourselves. It is all about seeking the best skin-care products and treatments to prevent the signs of aging. Today's multi-billion-dollar cosmetic industry must meet strict government guidelines and follow safe manufacturing standards. Learning from the past has brought us "full circle" – back to today and the future – to manufacture and supply natural products and cosmetics to the consumer in order to look and feel beautiful.

3

4

# Art of Makeup . . .

1

**Makeup is an art,** *which requires knowledge of the face, colors and their relationship to one another, and the principles of optical illusion. The* ***art of makeup*** *is the* ***ability to enhance facial features, cover and diminish flaws or imperfections as well as create dramatic effects for special occasions.*** *If not applied correctly, makeup can have the opposite results – making the individual look "made-up" and/or allow imperfections to be more noticeable. Makeup should enhance the person's facial features by creating balance and harmony.*

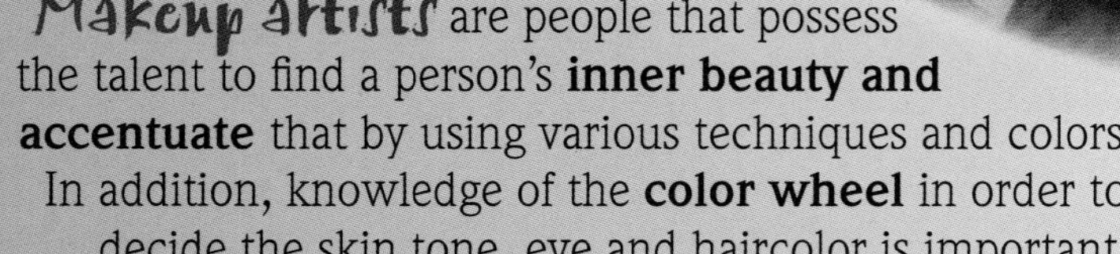

**Makeup artists** are people that possess the talent to find a person's **inner beauty and accentuate** that by using various techniques and colors. In addition, knowledge of the **color wheel** in order to decide the skin tone, eye and haircolor is important to achieving a balanced and complementary look for the client. While millions of women wear makeup every day, a skilled makeup artist can advise and guide the client in deciding the best color shades to benefit her features.

15

2

# Art of Makeup . . .

1

For the makeup artist, **various avenues in which to branch out** into the makeup field, whether you would like to be a theatrical makeup artist, or to specialize in formal applications for weddings, modeling or pageantry.

2

3

**Makeup trends change,** but the key to always looking your best is to acquire the knowledge of applying the proper products, tools and techniques. When these techniques are mastered, you will be **able to adjust any makeup application** to be fashionable yet trendy creating a most unique look.

4

5

# Makeup Tools . . .

*To accomplish **a successful makeup application,** certain tools are required to professionally apply makeup to the skin. The term **"tools"** in this chapter indicates any supply, material or accessory necessary to accomplish the task. The correct tool will ensure satisfaction in the application, helping to create a perfect finish. The type of makeup will dictate the tool or accessory used for the application.*

## There are two categories of makeup tools: disposable and non-disposable.

**Disposable tools** are thrown away after each use. (No double-dipping into cosmetics or other products. To avoid contamination, use a new applicator.)

**Non-disposable tools** are cleansed and disinfected before each use. This type of tool is discarded only when deteriorated.

## The following are disposable tools:

**Cosmetic Sponges** are made from an absorbent material, which may either be discarded or washed after each use. The sponges are ideally used to apply **creams, liquids and powder** foundations. These sanitary cosmetic sponges come in a variety of sizes and shapes and can also be used to **blend eye shadow, concealer and contour powder.**

**Spatulas** are a popular choice for the prevention of cross contamination. They are manufactured in a wide range of shapes and sizes and are used to **remove product from containers.** This will avoid dipping fingers into product, which can introduce bacteria.

# Makeup Tools . . .

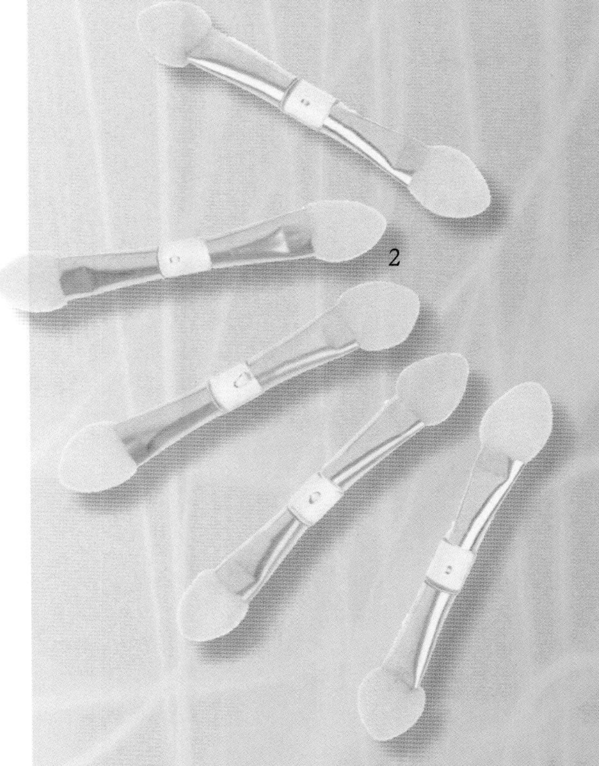

1

2

**Applicators** are small, multi-purpose and disposable, made from **sponge or cotton material.** The applicator ends are either single- or double-headed and are used to **apply, smooth and blend eye colors** over the eyelid area. The sponge-tip ends generally have a round or pointed shape; the round end is used to apply base colors and the pointed end is for blending and detailing. The applicators may be used to **correct makeup mistakes and/or retrieve creams or liquids** from containers to prevent cross-contamination.

3

4

**Mascara Wands** are disposable wands with spiral bristles that are used to **apply mascara** and test the mascara's color and consistency. To use: dip wand into mascara tube, move in a circular motion for bristles to grasp product. Avoid pumping the wand in and out of tube, which forces air into the tube and thickens the mascara.

5

**Blotting Papers** are used to **absorb excess oil from the skin** without disturbing the makeup. The papers are manufactured in various sizes and are made from either, rice, linen or flaxseed, which are known for their absorbent qualities. These materials grab and hold ONLY the oil without removing makeup.

# Makeup Tools...

**The following are non-disposable tools: (Sanitize before and after each use.)**

**Bowls or Cups** are used for **holding liquid product and/or mixing or blending** to create formulas or various colors.

**Pencil Sharpener** is an essential tool for **sharpening and sanitizing pencils** of any size in order to maintain a professional and precise application. **To use,** place pencil into opening and rotate the sharpener. Dispose excess shavings and wipe pencil tip with tissue to remove tiny bits of wood before placing at eyebrow, eyes or lips.

**Eyelash Curler** is a tool used to curl the lashes **effectively and safely.** Curlers have a rubber pad on which the lashes rest. This allows an appropriate amount of pressure to be used without damaging the lashes. **To use,** insert lashes directly in opening of curler, align the upper lashes along the rubber pad, bring the handles of the curler together, and gently close for a few seconds and release. Repeat if necessary depending on how much curve is desired.

**To complete the lashes,** add mascara to accentuate and hold lashes in curved position.

Before

After

# Makeup Tools . . .

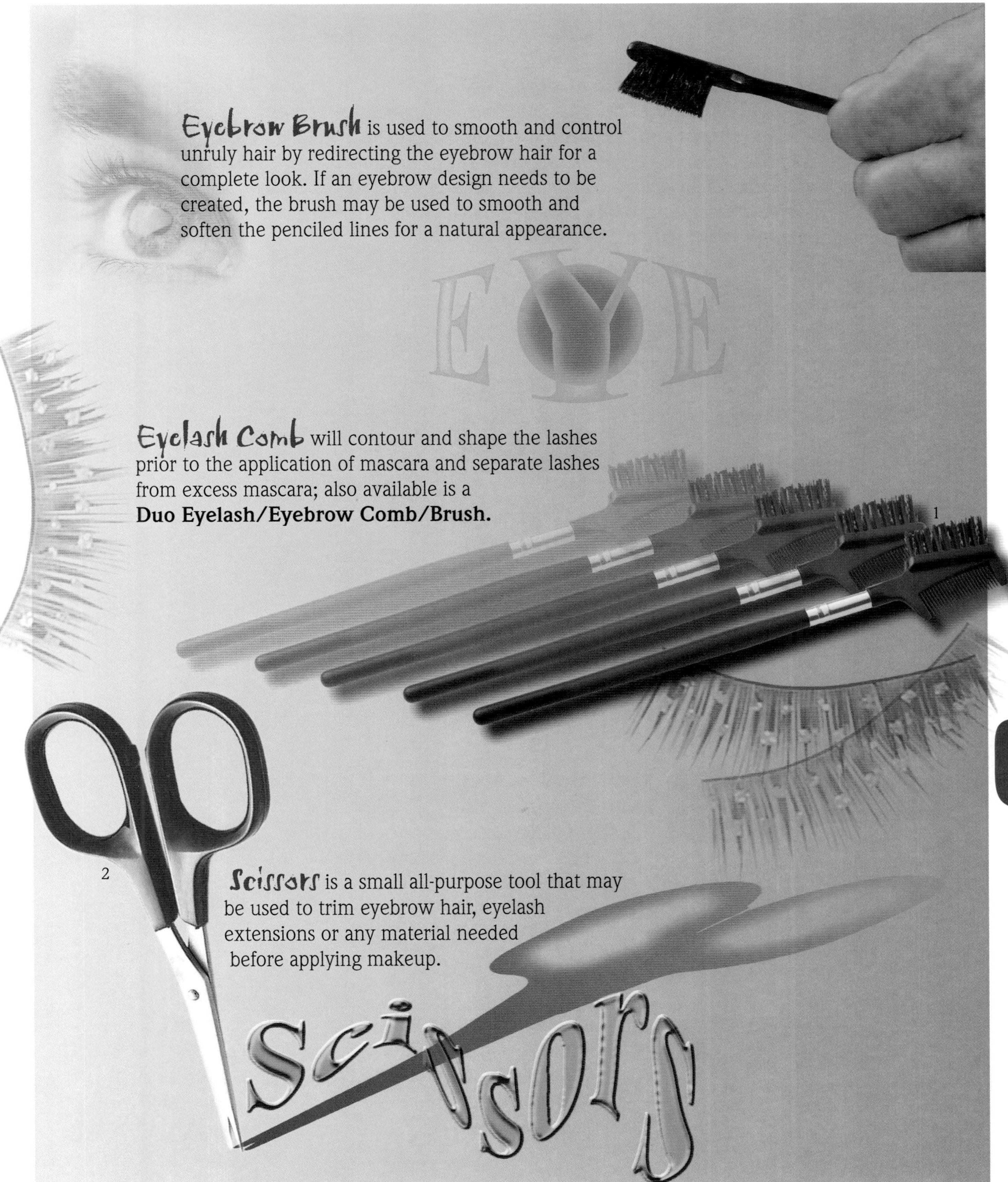


**Eyebrow Brush** is used to smooth and control unruly hair by redirecting the eyebrow hair for a complete look. If an eyebrow design needs to be created, the brush may be used to smooth and soften the penciled lines for a natural appearance.

**Eyelash Comb** will contour and shape the lashes prior to the application of mascara and separate lashes from excess mascara; also available is a **Duo Eyelash/Eyebrow Comb/Brush.**

**Scissors** is a small all-purpose tool that may be used to trim eyebrow hair, eyelash extensions or any material needed before applying makeup.

# Makeup Tools...

**Makeup brushes** *are an assortment of* ***non-disposable applicators*** *designed to apply color to the skin. Makeup brushes are manufactured in various sizes, shapes and designs for use on certain areas of the face. The bristles of the brush are either made from* ***animal (natural) or synthetic (nylon).*** *Natural hair brushes such as sable (weasel) or goat allow a gentle yet effective application. Using professional brushes will result in precision makeup application with a flawless finish.*

Makeup brushes

15

**Angled foundation brush** is an essential tool for creating a flawless finish. The distinctive tapered edges enables precision application around the eyes and nose while the flat brush shape smoothes out cream or liquid foundation.

**Foundation brush** sweeps foundation over the face for flawless coverage. With a tapered tip for precision, this brush provides an exact deposit of foundation over the pores, crevices and lines and is perfect for the application of crème or liquid foundations.

# Makeup Tools . . .

1

2

**Concealer brush** works with crème concealer to reach around the small areas of the eyes and allows you to deposit the right amount of concealer.

4

**Powder brush** works with loose, pressed or bronzing power to achieve a soft finished look without a mask appearance.

3

5

15

# Makeup Tools . . .

## EYE BRUSHES

**Eyeshadow brush** is used to apply the shadow base color, which evens out skin tone and helps the next color blend more easily.

**Angled eyeshadow brush** blends and contours shadows while the angled side sweeps color from the corners into the crease.

**Eyeshadow crease brush** fits perfectly in the crease of the eye; used to blend and soften all colors together.

**Eyeliner brush** is a wide, flat brush for bold or soft eye lining, which can be used for wet or dry base eye colors.

**Eye detailer brush** allows for a precise and even line.

**Eye smudge brush** is a round-tipped sponge brush that is shaped to create the soft, smoky eye look.

# Makeup Tools . . .

## EYEBROW BRUSH

**Angled brow definer brush** will blend after placement of eyebrow pencil or is used to apply brow color.

## CHEEK BRUSHES

**Bronzer brush** is soft and dome-shaped and used to refine color or for placement of color on the cheeks, shoulders and décolletage (de-colle-tage), which is the lower part of the neckline.

**Blush brush** is used for a smooth even application of color with a blended and natural finish.

15

## LIP BRUSH

**Lip brush** defines and fills in the lips with color. Lip brushes are also available in a retractable form to eliminate the bristles from exposure and ease of travel.

# Makeup Liquid Tools ...

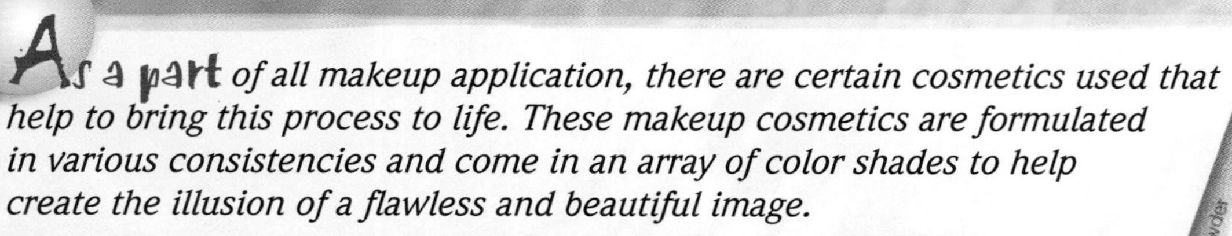

*As a part of all makeup application, there are certain cosmetics used that help to bring this process to life. These makeup cosmetics are formulated in various consistencies and come in an array of color shades to help create the illusion of a flawless and beautiful image.*

**The following is a general overview of makeup products used on the face.** Every manufacturer's cosmetic products will vary in their application, color shades and formulation. Always read the manufacturer's instructions before use.

**Foundation** is a cosmetic product that covers or blends uneven skin tones of the face and neck. Sometimes referred to as a **base makeup,** it is applied on the skin before any other cosmetic product to help conceal blemishes or any other imperfections. Do not use foundation to change skin color; these products are made to improve the complexion, not to change the color.

**NOTE:** Some artists will apply concealer to the skin first before application of the foundation.

# Foundation . . .

**Mineral makeup** offers a **natural and kinder approach** to applying makeup for the health conscious consumer. Today, we are more aware and concerned about what is being placed on our skin and are able to educate ourselves by **reading the product's ingredients and through research.** Mineral makeup is **devoid of chemicals, preservatives, fragrances and dyes** that can irritate or harm the skin. Mineral foundation is considered non-clogging, calming to the skin and protects the skin from the sun's harmful rays. **Titanium dioxide** (ti-ta-ni-um di-ox-ide) or **zinc oxide** are two main ingredients found in sunscreen products and are also found in mineral makeup products.

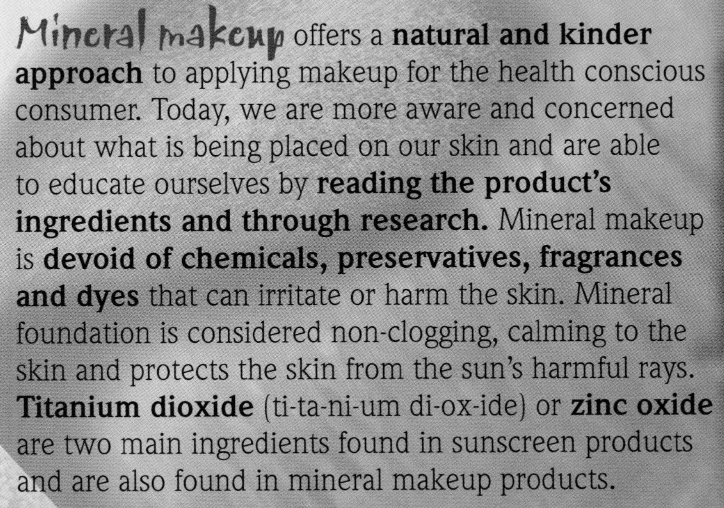

1

2

**Foundation** comes in multiple shades ranging from very light, light and medium to dark and very dark in order to complement a person's skin tone. **Pigments used to make foundation shades** are either naturally derived from minerals or produced from **coloring agents referred to as "lakes."** Lakes consist of translucent pigments in a variety of colors.

# Foundation ...

## Types of Foundation Formulations

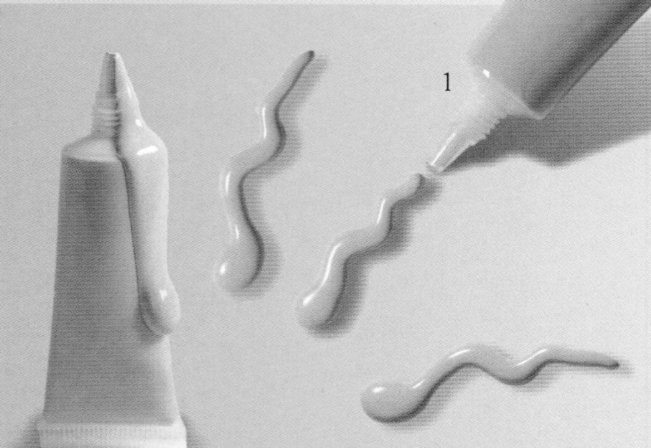

**Liquid foundation** is the most common and provides a **light to medium coverage** creating a **"matte" appearance** for normal, dry, combination and oily skin types. The liquid spreads easily over the skin helping to **minimize pore size.** This foundation is manufactured as water- or oil-base and dries quickly once applied to skin.

**Cream foundation** provides **medium to heavy coverage** and may be used as a concealer as well as a foundation due to its **minimizing effects on fine lines and wrinkles.** This foundation typically hydrates the skin and therefore is recommended for dry skin types.

**Powder foundation** is loose with added pigments, and creates a **soft natural appearance** with **sheer coverage.**

**Cake foundation** (pancake) is a heavy foundation providing **exceptional coverage** and is applied with a damp disposable sponge. This type of foundation is typically used for theater and film and to **cover pigmentation defects and scars.**

# Foundation . . .

NOTE: Some moisturizing products are tinted (color has been added), which will simultaneously condition the skin and provide minimal coverage.

**Cream to Powder** is an alternative to liquid foundation, which will create a **matte to semi-matte appearance** and a powdery finish. This foundation is best used on an oily skin type and applied with a damp cosmetic sponge.

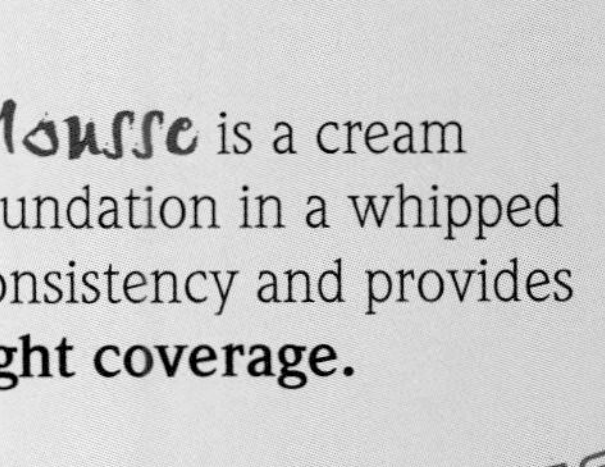

**Mousse** is a cream foundation in a whipped consistency and provides **light coverage.**

The client's skin type, preference and desired results will assist in a foundation selection.

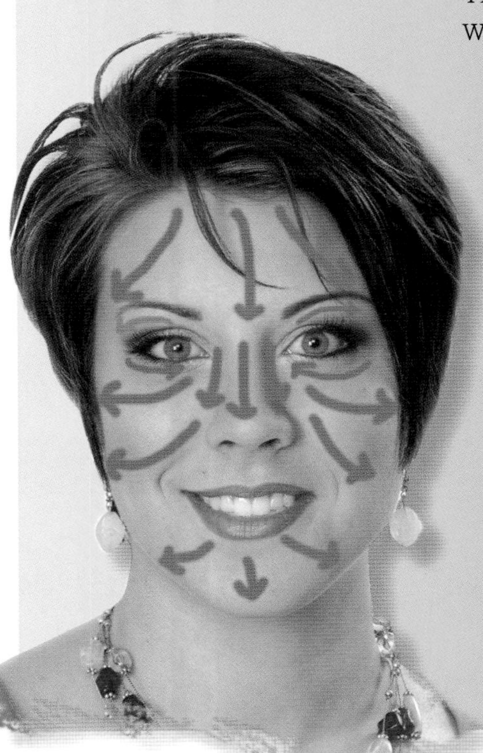

**To apply foundation correctly** and achieve a natural and blended finish, begin at center of forehead, move down over nose and blend over and under the eyes. Continue outward to the cheeks, down over the lips to the chin and along the jawline. This will keep the makeup concentrated in the area of the face where the greatest number of imperfections are typically located, as well as avoid a foundation line along the jawline.

"Place 'creams on creams' and 'powders on powders' to avoid clumping."

15

# Concealer ...

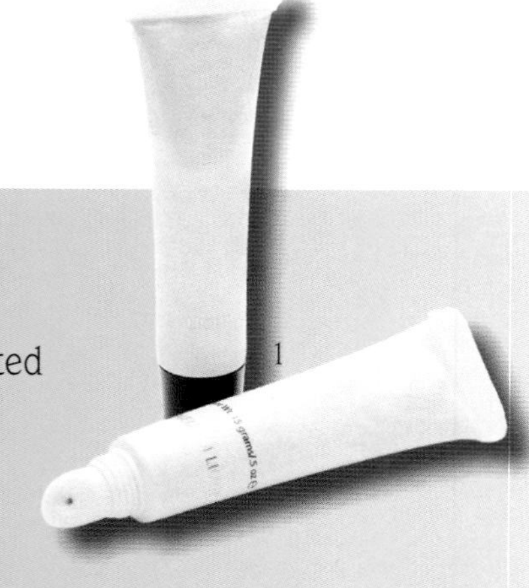

**Concealer,** referred to as **cover-up,** is used to camouflage **facial imperfections, cover dark circles or uneven skin tones** and provides the **illusion of balanced features.** Concealer is a concentrated product that can be **used in conjunction with foundation,** applied either before the foundation or after, depending on the desired result. Concealer is manufactured in a wide variety of shades and comes in small tubes with wands, jars, sponge-tip applicators in pencil form.

## Forms of Concealer

**Cover stick** is applied with a brush and blended with a sponge to create a creamy matte finish.

**Cream** is lightweight, applied with a brush or sponge to create a natural finish.

**Liquid** is great for covering dark circles under the eyes or uneven skin tones on dry skin types.

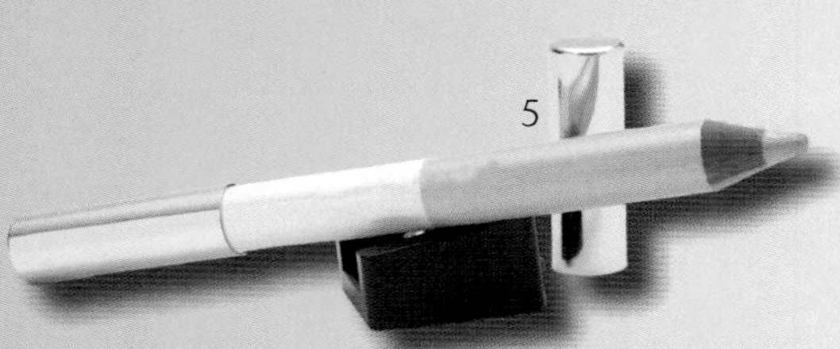

**Pencil** is used for accuracy and to focus attention on a specific area.



Concealer colors have the same range as foundation shades. When choosing concealer, look for a color that is a **full to half shade lighter than the client's complexion or skin tone.** The thicker the formula, the more concentrated the product, and the better the product's ability to hide skin imperfections. Also, there are tinted concealers that provide the following: yellow-tinted shades lighten brown discoloration and purplish or grayish scars, while green-tinted shades help neutralize redness.

**When applying concealer,** use a makeup sponge, wand or applicator and lightly **"dab" and spread product** on the area to be covered. Remember, dab, "no rubbing." This will avoid wiping away the foundation. Generally, the stick concealer has the greatest coverage, followed by the jar, tube and sponge-tip applicator depending on the manufacturer.

# Face Powder...

**Face powder** is used to **seal foundation and concealer** and **give a matte (no shine) finish.** Powder is great for **absorption of oil** and providing a smooth base for eye and cheek color application. Face powders come in either **translucent or tinted formulas.** Translucent powder is a **sheer shade** that is compatible with all skin colors and does not add color to the face. The tinted powder formula consists of **various shades** and is used to complement a person's natural skin tone.

2

## Types of Face Powder

1

**Loose powder** is a lightweight mixture of cornstarch or talc with the addition of some coloring pigments. The packaging for loose powder is generally a jar and the powder is applied with a large powder brush creating a **natural finish.**

3

**Pressed powder** contains an added ingredient that binds powder particles and pigments together to create a pressed consistency familiarly packaged in a compact. These binding agents may also clog pores and contribute to a mask-type appearance. Compact powder is great for **quick and easy touch-ups** throughout the day.

The choice of face powder to be used is determined by the professional, client's skin type and desired end result.

4

15

# THE EYES HAVE IT!

**Eyes are the most prominent feature of the face** and are a powerful asset once the overall makeup application is complete. **Eye makeup or eye shadow** can help **define and enhance the eyes** by minimizing eye imperfections. Eye makeup comes in a multitude of colors ranging from highlighter shades to very dark colors, which may be used for shadowing or contouring an area of the eyelid. When eye shadow is used sparingly, it can create a **modest look for the day** or if applied darker, will create a **dramatic evening appearance.**

1

2

3

15

Eye color is available in pencil, powder (both loose and pressed form) and cream. Eye color finishes can be frosted, matte, metallic, shimmer or moist.

4

# Eye Color ...

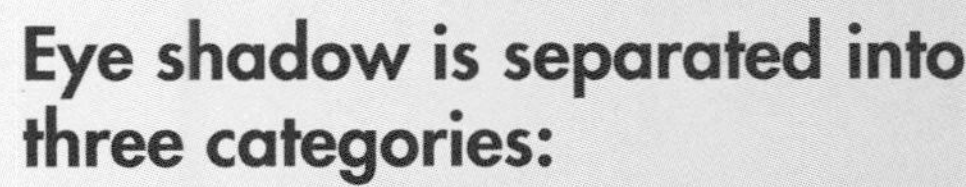

## Eye shadow is separated into three categories:

1 **Highlight** is a light color that will make an area appear larger, emphasizing the area.

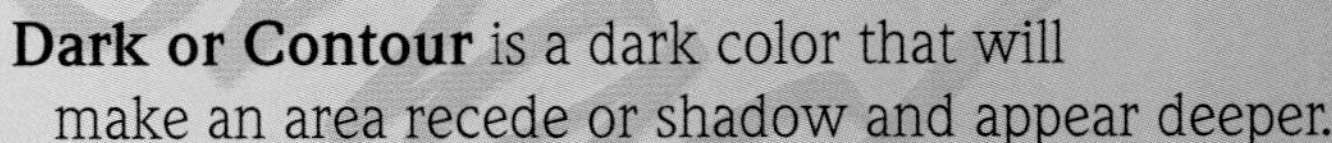

2 **Dark or Contour** is a dark color that will make an area recede or shadow and appear deeper.

3 **Base** is a medium color used to blend two or more colors or may be used as a base color.

**Lid primer** is applied to the eyelid prior to eye makeup to prevent smearing and long wear of colors.

Lid primer

**For a general (non-corrective) eye color application,** place lid primer on eyelid, use sponge-tipped applicators or eye brushes to apply highlight color below brow bone. Apply a color that is darker than skin tone to the crease of eyelid or area in need of receding. Use a medium color as a blending color to join the dark and the highlight colors together. **Optional:** The medium color may be applied to the entire lid as a base color for ease in blending other colors.

15

# Eyeliner . . .

**Eyeliner** builds emphasis on the eyes by **shaping and defining the outline of the eyes,** whether by adding a soft line or a dramatic stroke. Eyeliner is **applied after eyelid color and before mascara** to avoid muting the liner color. To create the **illusion of the eyes appearing larger than the natural eye and lashes fuller than the natural lash,** application of liner is done by drawing a line across the upper lid along the lashes, a quarter inch (0.6 cm) away from the inside corner to outside corner of eye. Draw directly along the lash line for bottom of eye, starting a quarter inch away from inner corner of eye and extending to the outer corner, avoid inside of rim.

1

2

3

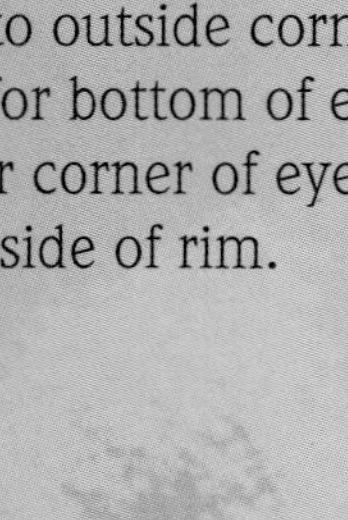

## Types of Eyeliners

**Pencil liner** is generally easy to apply, and you can use different techniques to vary the look.

- **For defined lines,** sharpen your eyeliner pencil before application.
- **For soft lines,** use a sponge-tipped applicator to gently smudge the lines after application.

4

5

15

**Liquid liner** is applied with a fine tip brush and requires a very steady hand to create a smooth line that **offers precision and drama.** This type of liner is recommended for ONLY top of eyelid due to its dramatic effect.

**Cream to Powder Liners** provide versatility through an array of colors as well as a natural, soft line to accentuate any eye color. This type of liner lasts until face is cleansed and may also be used as eye or eyebrow color.

6

RA

**CAUTION**: Do not use eyeliner on inner rim of eyes to avoid infection and permanent pigmentation of the mucous membrane. Always sharpen pencil before and after client use for sanitary purposes.

# Eyebrow Color...

**Eyebrow color** adds **shading to the sparse eyebrow, corrects brow shape** and **adds color to eyebrow area that is void of hair.** Eyebrow hair should **complement and be a shade similar to the hair on the head.**

**To apply color to the eyebrow,** draw fine, short upward strokes following the natural hair growth direction along curve of brow line.

## Types of Eyebrow Color

**Pencil** is the most common form of eyebrow coloring that adds precision and emphasis to the hair.

**CAUTION:** Always sharpen pencil before and after client use for sanitary purposes.

RA

**Powder** is a matte substance consisting of coloring agents that cling to the hair creating a dark eyebrow appearance. This form of eyebrow color is applied with an angled brush using light strokes for blending. **Optional:** eyelid color may also be used.

**Gel** is a clear or colored liquid that is used for coarse, unruly hair. Eyebrow color is applied first and sealed with the gel.

*For any makeup service, offer a free eyebrow design with tweezing or waxing.*

15

# Mascara . . .

**Mascara** is applied to **enhance the natural eyelashes** by making them **appear darker, thicker and longer.** Mascara **completes the eyes,** and can even look great by itself, without the addition of eye makeup.

The most common mascara colors are brown and black, but mascara does come in a variety of other colors depending on manufacturer. Mascara is packaged in a **tube that includes a wand applicator.** One end of the wand consists of bristles in different shapes and sizes. Mascara is available in liquid, cake or cream and is formulated for conditioning, waterproof or length enhancing.

1

**To apply mascara,** dip the wand inside the tube by rotating the wand to evenly coat the bristles. Place the wand parallel to the underside of the upper lashes – along the rim of eyelid. Move the wand back and forth to coat the base of lashes and create full lashes. Pull the wand through to the ends of the lashes and repeat until the desired effect is achieved. **For a more dramatic effect,** coat the top of the upper lashes in the same manner as the underside. Complete with an additional coat of mascara to the underside of the upper lashes to prevent drooping. Apply to lower lashes by holding the wand vertically, lightly gliding the wand down the lengths of the lashes in short, downward strokes, working from inner to outer corner of eye.

**NOTE:** Do not pump the mascara wand in and out of the tube as this will cause product dryness, promote bacterial growth, and shorten the shelf-life of the mascara.

15

### Dual-ended Mascaras

Some mascaras come with a primer on one end of the wand and a colored formula or comb attached to the opposite end of wand. The primer is either a conditioning agent or a thickener and the comb is used to separate the lashes.

2

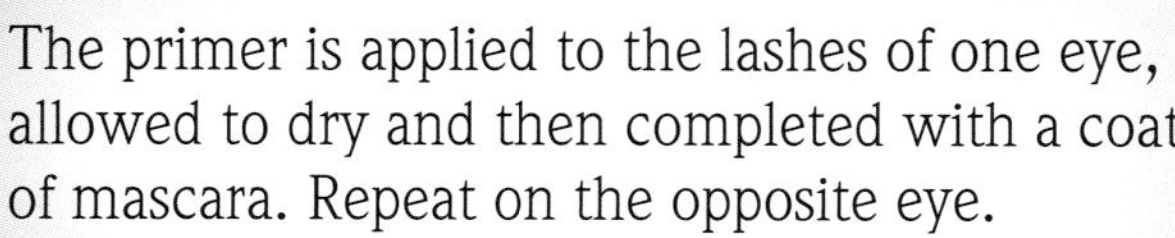

The primer is applied to the lashes of one eye, allowed to dry and then completed with a coat of mascara. Repeat on the opposite eye.

# Cheek Color . . .

**Cheek color,** referred to as **blush or rouge,** provides a **healthy glow to the skin.** Emphasis to the cheek structure should be subtle with the color blended to create a soft, natural glimmer.

## Types of Cheek Colors

1

**Powder blush** is the most common form and is packaged loose or pressed. **Loose powder** comes in a jar and is applied with a blush brush. **Pressed powder** is a solid form in a compact case and is applied with either a brush or cosmetic sponge.

**Cream blush** is applied directly after the foundation for blending purposes and is recommended for dry to normal skin types.

**Liquid and gel blush** have similar qualities as the cream cheek color with direct application after the foundation. These types of cheek colors have the potential to clog the pores; be sure to remove this makeup each evening.

**NOTE:** Some cheek colors and bronzers may also be used as eye colors.

**Bronzer** is the newest alternative in adding a **slight sun-kissed appearance** to the skin without actually soaking up the sun's rays. A bronzer shade is typically a warm-based color and is packaged loose or in compact form. Some cosmetic companies are producing a combination of warm and cool-based bronzers for the light skin types.

2

**When applying cheek color:** locate the hollow below the cheekbone, place blush at center of cheek on the hollow area. To get an approximate location to center of cheekbone, place two fingers alongside of nose. No color is placed where the fingers are resting; blush color should extend out from the fingers toward hairline. **Optional:** Some makeup artists believe starting color at hairline and moving down over the cheekbones creates a more natural appearance because the concentrated color is along the hairline.

3

**If desiring prominent cheekbones:** use a light and dark shade. Apply the dark shade to the hollow area below cheekbone and the light color directly on the cheekbone, blend where the two colors meet. The light cheek color will enhance the cheekbone, while the dark color will recess the area below the cheekbone creating the illusion of high cheekbones.

# Lip Color . . .

**Lip colors or lipsticks** are products that **add color and/or shine to the lips** and are applied using a brush or applicator. Lip colors come in a wide range of colors and are packaged in metal or plastic tubes, small jars or as sticks.

**Lip liners** are used to **define the lips and prevent color from bleeding into the skin** that surrounds the mouth. Liners are typically packaged in pencil form and can be used to color the entire lips or to layer color. To apply in layers, place liner color on lips followed by another lip color to complete the lips.

15

# Lip Color . . .

## Types of Lip Color

- **Glosses** provide minimal coverage and are sheer or tinted and add shine and/or a small amount of color.
- **Cream** is a moisturizing or hydrating lipstick that contains oils and conditioners. The coverage is medium, adding a soft and subtle appeal with a "balmy" finish to the lips. Some cream lip color is frosted adding a pearly or opalescent touch.
- **Pencils** are long-lasting due to the high pigment content, creating a matte appearance.

**CAUTION:** Always sharpen before and after client use for sanitary purposes.

RA

- **Gel** is similar to gloss with the exception of more pigment concentration. Gels add shine and coverage is not as long-lasting.

As with all makeup application, lip color choices are determined by the professional through client consultation and desired end result.

**To apply lip color or liner,** begin at outer corners of upper lip, follow natural lip line and move toward the center peaked area of lips. Repeat on bottom lip.

"When placing lipstick on a client, never apply directly from the container. Use a lip brush, applicator or spatula to avoid cross-contamination."

15

# Makeup Safety ...

***Cosmetics**, such as mascara, eyeliner and eye shadow are considered **foreign objects that could accidently enter the eyes.** The most serious problem that could result in the application of eye makeup is **injury to the cornea** (clear membrane over the iris). Any makeup applicator, mascara wand or fingernail could possibly **scratch the eye** if the person applying is not careful. Also, **allergic reactions may occur** from preservatives used in the makeup causing tearing, itching, swelling and/or redness to the eyes. Refer client to medical care professional if any of these conditions occur.*

## Summary of safety tips when applying eye makeup:

1

- Eye makeup removers are safely designed to be used near and around the eye. **Follow manufacturer's directions** to avoid any adverse effects or overuse of product.

2

- **Sharpen eyeliner pencils before and after use** of each client. This will keep the pencil sanitary thus prevent contamination.

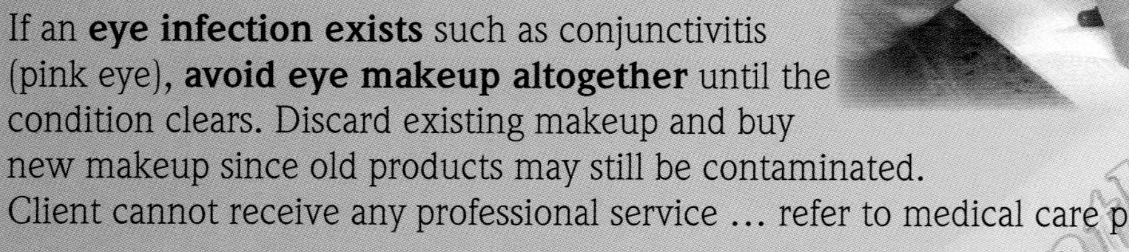

- If an **eye infection exists** such as conjunctivitis (pink eye), **avoid eye makeup altogether** until the condition clears. Discard existing makeup and buy new makeup since old products may still be contaminated. Client cannot receive any professional service ... refer to medical care professional.

- **Replace old cosmetics approximately every six months** to avoid contamination of products. Old cosmetics may contribute to eye infections.

- **Never share makeup** with another individual to prevent cross-contamination and spread of disease.

- **Avoid sampling makeup items at department store cosmetic counters,** unless they have individual color palettes, disposable applicators and wands. This will prevent the spread of infectious diseases caused by bacteria and/or viruses.

# Makeup Safety . . .

- All cosmetics are kept clean and sanitary by following the **"no double-dipping" rule;** use spatulas or applicators to remove product from containers and discard after each individual's use.

- **Always wash your hands before applying makeup** and use sanitary and disinfectant tools.

- **Cosmetics should not be stored at a temperature above 85° F.** The preservatives within the product may lose their effectiveness if they are exposed to extreme temperatures of heat or cold.

- As with any cosmetic product sold to consumers, eye cosmetics are **required to have an ingredient declaration on the label.** If they do not, they are considered misbranded and illegal. In the United States, the use of color additives is strictly regulated. Some color additives are approved for cosmetic use and some are not approved for specific areas such as near the eyes. If the product is properly labeled, you can check to see whether the color additives on the label are in the FDA's List of Color Additives Permitted for Use in Cosmetics. Research the Food and Drug Administration website: www.fda.gov and click on cosmetics.

- Brushes are **cleansed and disinfected with a brush cleaner** following the manufacturer's instructions. Follow the service tool manufacturer for the guidelines in cleansing and disinfection or refer to your local regulatory agency.

# Theory of Color ...

*Whether applying color on hair, nails or skin, a professional must have knowledge of the color wheel and the law of color must be understood in order to produce the best complementary color results.* ***Makeup application*** *is cosmetic placement of colors to the face utilizing the concept of the color wheel and law of color.*

**Color brightens our world and captivates our eyes.** It is a physical phenomenon of light or visual perception associated with the various wavelengths seen by the eye. Color has meaning; reaction to color is either logical or emotional, varying from one individual to another.

15

The **visible light color spectrum** is derived from the theory that when light passes through and into a glass or prism, it will separate into seven colors ... red, orange, yellow, green, blue, indigo and violet.

These colors are displayed in the beauty of a rainbow as the sun shines through the raindrops.

"Color is light, light is color ... proven by Sir Isaac Newton!"

# Principles of Color . . .

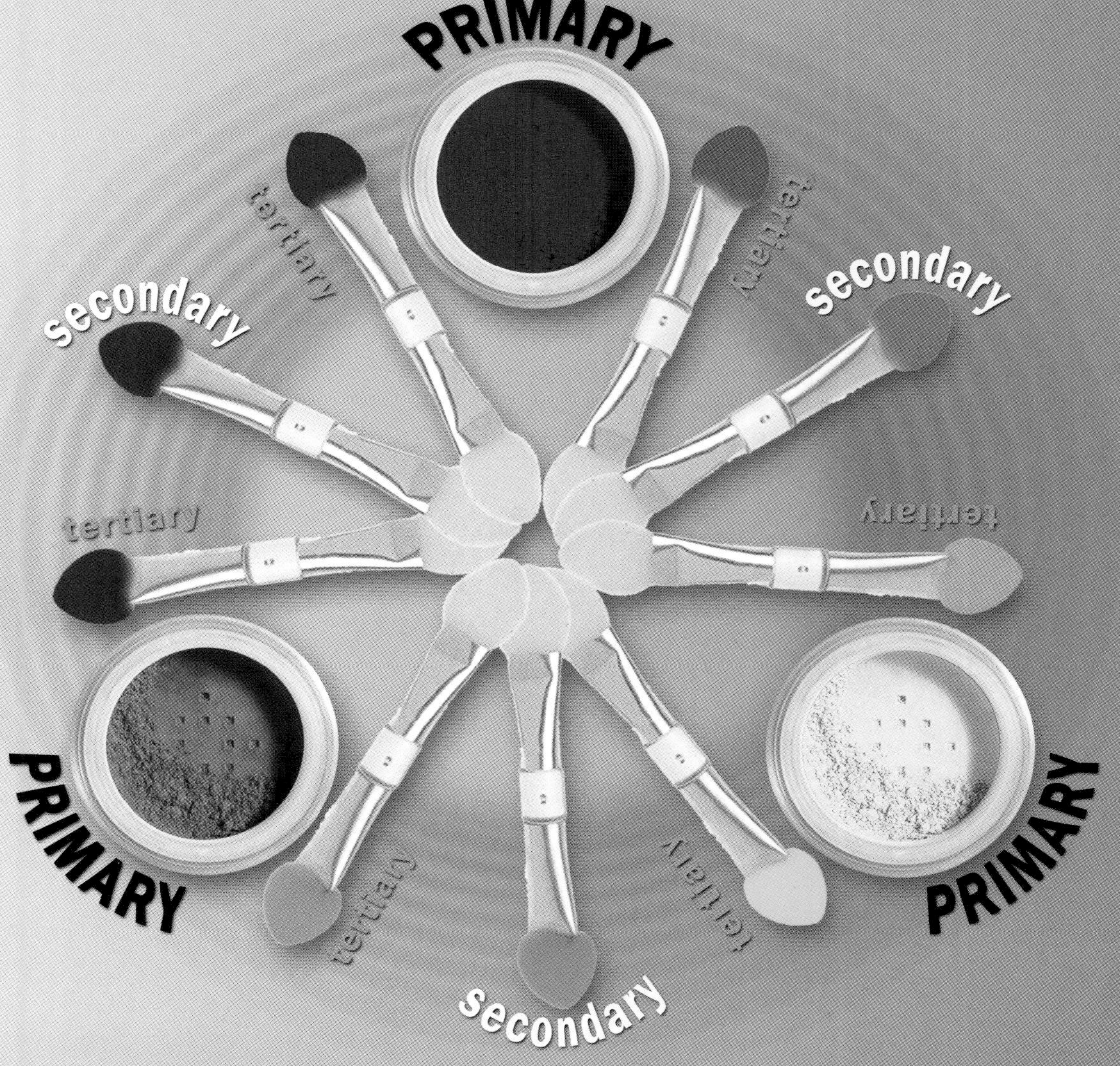

15

## The Three Main Principles of Color

**Primary colors** are the **basic colors** from which all other colors are produced. These colors are also considered the **purest** colors. They are red, yellow, and blue.

**Secondary colors** are formed when **combining two primary colors in equal proportions.** The combinations of the following primary colors will give you the secondary colors: Red + Yellow = Orange, Yellow + Blue = Green, Red + Blue = Violet

**Tertiary colors** are created by **mixing a primary color with the neighboring secondary color.** They are red-orange, red-violet, yellow-orange, yellow-green, blue-green and blue-violet. Tertiary colors always state the primary color first.

# Principles of Color ...

**Complementary colors** are derived from mixing a primary and a secondary color that are opposite each other on the color wheel. Example: Blue and Orange (Y&R), Red and Green (Y & B), Yellow and Violet (R & B).

These colors when mixed together will **cancel out the secondary color.** For example, if you want to neutralize green, add some red, which is found opposite the green on the color wheel or is the missing primary color needed to neutralize or counteract the green.

When combining complementary colors, each color must be of equal strength and value in order to achieve the desired result.

**NOTE:** When adding any secondary color to its primary, the result is a combination of all three primary colors.

Green tinted powder helps to minimize a red complexion

**Neutral colors** are not located within the visible light spectrum and contain minimal to no pigment or color. These colors are white, black and gray and exist through either the reflection or absorption of light.

- **White** occurs when **all colors are reflected** at an equal distance.
- **Black** appears when **all the colors are absorbed** equally, reflecting no color.
- **Gray** is a result of **partial color reflection.** The lightness to darkness of gray is determined by the amount of light reflection. When a greater amount of light is reflected, the result is light gray; a small amount of gray reflected results in dark gray.

# Temperature of Color ...

**Color has a temperature**
Color is classified into two temperatures or undertones: **Warm and Cool**

**Cool** is associated with the sky or water. Colors ranging from **blue** to **green and violet are considered cool.**

**Warm** is associated with fire or the sun. Colors that include red, yellow **or** orange **are classified as being warm.**

**Pure colors** can usually be classified under the seasons of the year when related to their temperature of warm or cool. **Clear/cool** palettes are especially found in the **winter** and **clear/warm** palettes are generally found in the **spring.** You will find that most **summer colors are mute/cool** and **autumn colors are mute/warm** creating a soft or dusty feeling. You obtain this effect by adding gray to a color.

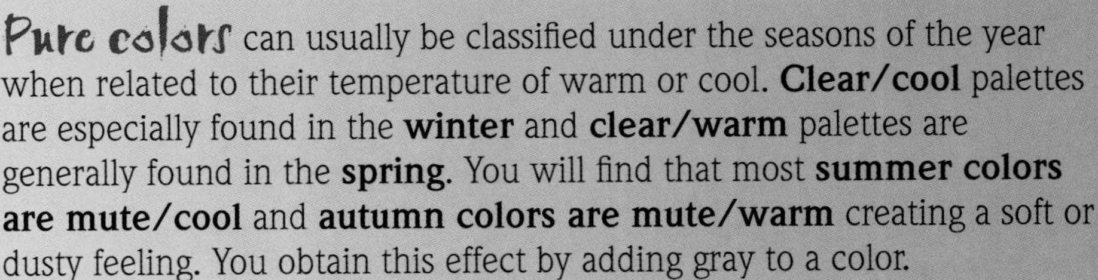

"Try to avoid intermixing warm and cool tones ... since contrasting colors result in disharmony!"

15

# Elements of Color ...

*To recognize the art behind makeup design, the artist will need to understand the* ***elements of color.*** *The artist will depend upon these elements to apply color basics, or to bring harmony to unbalanced face proportions. The elements of color are also necessary as the artist expands upon his or her creativity to create avant-garde makeup design, and to set the stage for the future makeup color trends.*

## Elements of Color are:

**Pigment, Three Dimensions of a Color, Color Harmonies and Color Reflection**

**First Element:** **Pigment** is what gives color its color. No matter what the pigment's source, whether natural, chemical or mineral, the same color theory holds true. All items of makeup contain pigment whether formed in a water-based, oil-in-water, wax-based, cream, stick, cake or mineral base.

**Second Element:** **Three dimensions of a color** are **hue, value, and intensity** which help to accurately describe color.



**Hue** is a **general name for color.** It is determined by the wavelength's range within the light spectrum or **its position on the color wheel.** Each color has subtle variations; when viewing a color, the individual will decide the color name. Primary colors are the basis by which all other colors are established.

# Elements of Color . . .

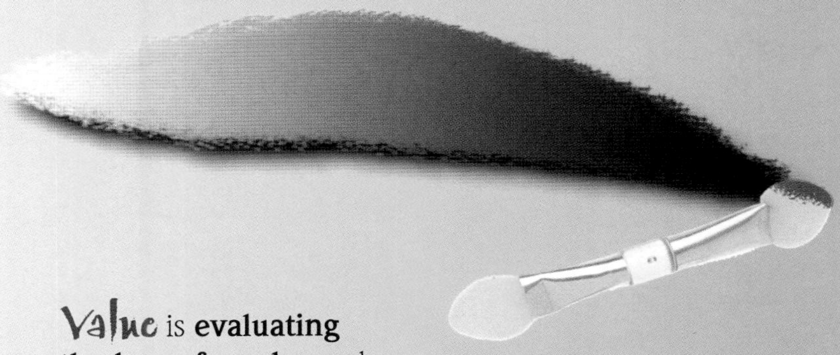

**Value** is **evaluating the hue of a color** and determining whether it is **light or dark** due to the quantity of light reflected or absorbed. When a **hue reflects varying amounts of light, the wavelength is changed therefore the color is changed.** If the amount of **light reflected is high** resulting in less absorption, or if **white is mixed with the hue, the color will appear light** (for example: **yellow**) If a **minimal amount of light is reflected** as a result of more absorption, or if **black is mixed with the hue, the color will appear darker** (for example: **blue**).

**Intensity** is the **strength of the color's appearance,** which is determined by the hue's **degree of saturation and purity of light reflection.** If there is **high clarity** in the reflection of light, **a bright, vivid color will result.** If there is **low clarity in light reflection, a dull, drab color** will appear. Mixing more then one color is another approach to altering intensity. By adding black or white to a color, it will become either darker or lighter therefore decreasing the intensity. Example: red + white = pink and red + black = dark red.

15

Red + white= pink

Red + black= dark red

**Third Element:** **Color harmonies** are the next important element in understanding color theory. **"Harmony" refers to a collection of parts that are aesthetically pleasing to the sense of sight, sound, touch, taste or smell.** In the world of color, color harmonies are a collection of colors that are pleasing to the eye and emotions. Color harmonies create a great guideline for the application of eye, cheek and lip colors.

## There are five basic color harmonies:

1. **Analogous colors** are those that are similar, usually **two colors to the left or two colors to the right of the hue on the color wheel.** These colors are harmonious and match well and are generally used for daytime and business looks.

2. **Monochromatic** color is variations in **value and intensity of a single color** for an elegant look.

3. **Complementary** colors are **opposite each other** on the color wheel and are often used for a sensuous look or for emphasizing a feature.

# Elements of Color ...

**4.** **Triad** colors are derived from a centrally placed triangle on the color wheel. These colors have a vibrant appeal with one color dominating and the other two used as accents.

**5.** **Achromatic** colors consist of black, white and gray, or any neutral color in its lightest value to its darkest value. These colors are usually located closest to the center of the color wheel and often create sophisticated looks.

**Fourth Element:** **Color Reflection** is how the color is visually seen by the viewer.

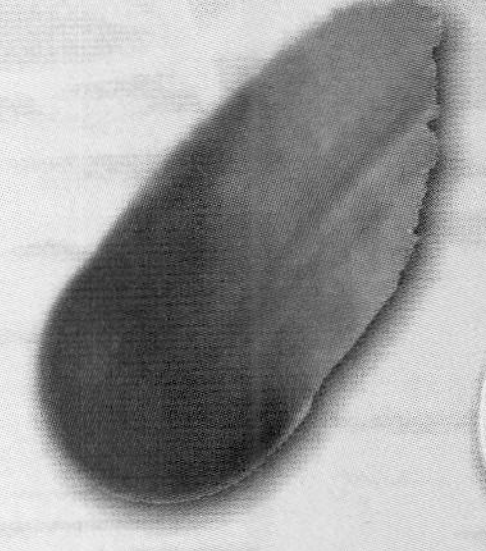
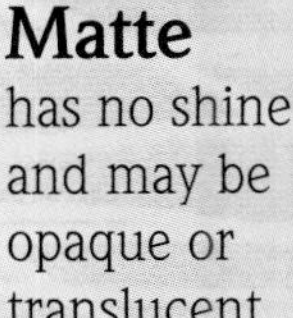
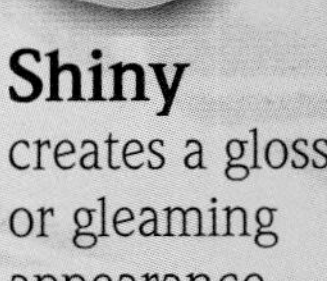

**Matte** has no shine and may be opaque or translucent

**Shiny** creates a gloss or gleaming appearance

**Metallic** is highly reflective, but not transparent and may be considered bright

**Opaque** is unclear, but not transparent

**Translucent** creates a lightly fogged appearance and is barely transparent

**Transparent** is visible or clear such as glass

15

# Color Selection...

***When deciding** what colors should be used on a person's eyes, cheeks and lips, there are certain factors to take into consideration. As an artist, you want to use colors that will **complement an individual's facial features and provide contrast to his or her natural color.** Selecting **neutral colors is always a safe approach** because they consist of both the warm and cool tones, and are compatible with any hair, skin and eye color.*

**NOTE:** In Chapter 11 (Cosmetology Electricity), we learned that incandescent lighting gives off warm tones, whereas fluorescent lights produce "cool" to "drab" tones, sometimes appearing green.

In order to select the appropriate colors to enhance a client's overall appearance, refer to the following guidelines.

1) **Analyze the client's clean skin (void of makeup) to decide skin color, level and tone.** Skin tone is the most important factor in determining the best colors to be applied. All skin types will fall under either a cool (blue or pink) base or a warm (yellow or orange) base. An olive skin tone is considered having a cool base.

2) **Decide the haircolor.** Whether a person's haircolor is natural or artificial, determine if the base color is warm or cool.

3) **Decide the eye color.** Applying a color to the eyes that matches the actual eye color is not always the wisest choice. Instead pick a complementary color, which will provide contrast to the natural eye color.

15

**NOTE:** Keep in mind this is a general approach to color selection and may be altered to provide the best choice for either client and/or the makeup artist.

1

# Skin Color . . .

**Skin color and tone** vary between individuals, regardless of cultural background and may change due to age, health, environment or inappropriate product use. Skin color tones can range from light to medium to dark, and are determined by the amount of melanin within the skin (refer to Chapter 12). Determining the skin color, plus adding in the elements of hair and eye color, along with a person's features will influence your color choices and help to personalize the makeup service. Keep in mind that the lighting in a salon, office or a home will display different skin tones, therefore creating false analysis.

## General Categories of Skin Color

### Caucasian Skin Coloring

This is the least resilient skin color and requires a proper skin-care regimen. Complexion is light with blue, pink or gold skin undertones. Depending on degree of pigmentation, sun exposure may be rapid and damaging to skin cells. Caucasian skin is susceptible to sun damage (hyper-pigmentation), dehydration, age spots and wrinkles (lack of elasticity).

### Asian Skin Coloring

This skin is versatile with a fair complexion and strong yellow undertones. The yellow undertone may cause dark shadowing under eyes. Any damage to the skin can lead to pigmentation changes where there is healing and scarring.

### African-American Skin Coloring

This is the slowest of all skin colors to show signs of aging due to a high degree of melanin. African-American skin has the widest range of undertones, which makes it difficult to choose whether the skin is cool or warm. This skin is susceptible to large pores, oily skin and breakouts.

### Hispanic Skin Coloring

This skin color is strong and contains a significant amount of melanin, making the appearance of aging take longer than other skin types. Complexion is usually olive with yellow undertones and is prone to opened pores in T-zone, breakouts and hyper-pigmentation.

**Disclaimer:** *Today, the United States' population is a melting pot of diverse heritages with each individual's skin color varying in degree of color and tone. Therefore, for the best results, it is important to determine a client's ethnic heritage and analyze his or her current pigmentation and tone prior to makeup color selection.*

# Corrective Makeup . . .

**As a skilled makeup artist,** *you will have the ability to conceal nature's imperfections. There will be clients that have facial imbalances such as eyes appearing too close together, or too far apart, the lips that are not equally proportioned or perhaps a nose that is too large or too small. Certain techniques used when applying makeup will give the illusion of balance to the face.* ***To rectify an imbalanced feature,*** *a makeup artist will utilize the* **concept of shading and highlighting.** *Dark colors will make features appear small or close together, while light colors will enhance or separate a feature.*

As learned in Chapter 6 (Art Principles), facial features are divided horizontally into **three zonal areas.** Considering these areas will determine a proportionate face as well as features that are in need of minimizing or maximizing. Use this concept during the consultation and follow through with the makeup application.

## Face divided horizontally:

**Zone 1:** Between hairline and eyebrow line

**Zone 2:** Between eyebrow line and tip of nose

**Zone 3:** Between tip of nose and chin line

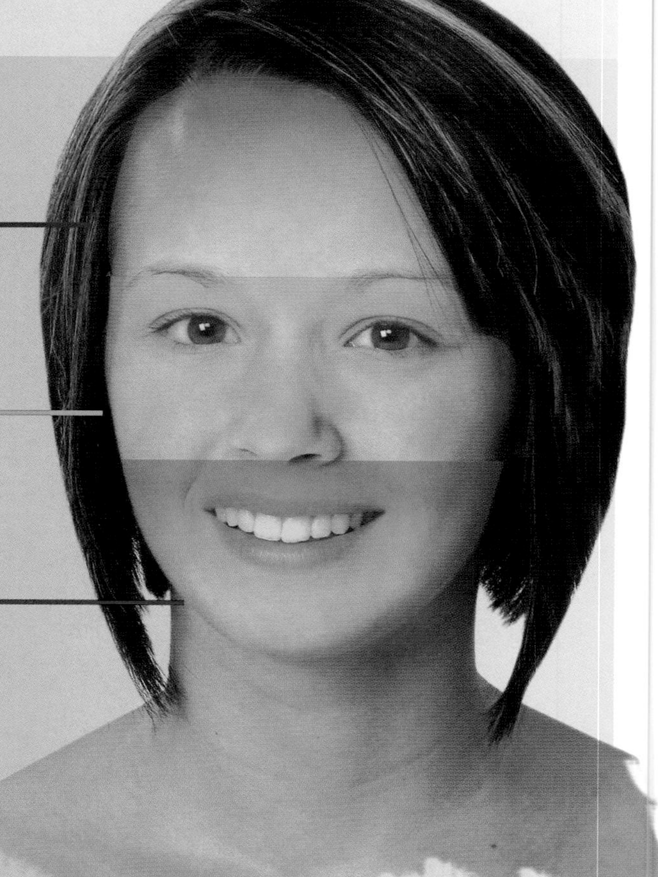

15

# Facial Shapes . . .

**Learning the face shapes** *is another area to analyze in order to apply corrective makeup skills. When all hair is pulled away from the face, a full view of the person's hairline will determine the face shape and if there is a need for correction.* ***The oval face shape is the ideal shape for overall balance,*** *thus requiring no corrective makeup. Check for other imbalanced features by viewing the facial zones. As a makeup artist, the main objective is to create the illusion of an oval face shape for all clients.*

**Face contouring** is when **light and dark colors** are positioned to counterbalance a facial feature or shape. Face contouring is applying corrective makeup to any face shape other than an oval shape. Contour colors are varying degrees of light or dark foundation and typically are applied before the main base color.

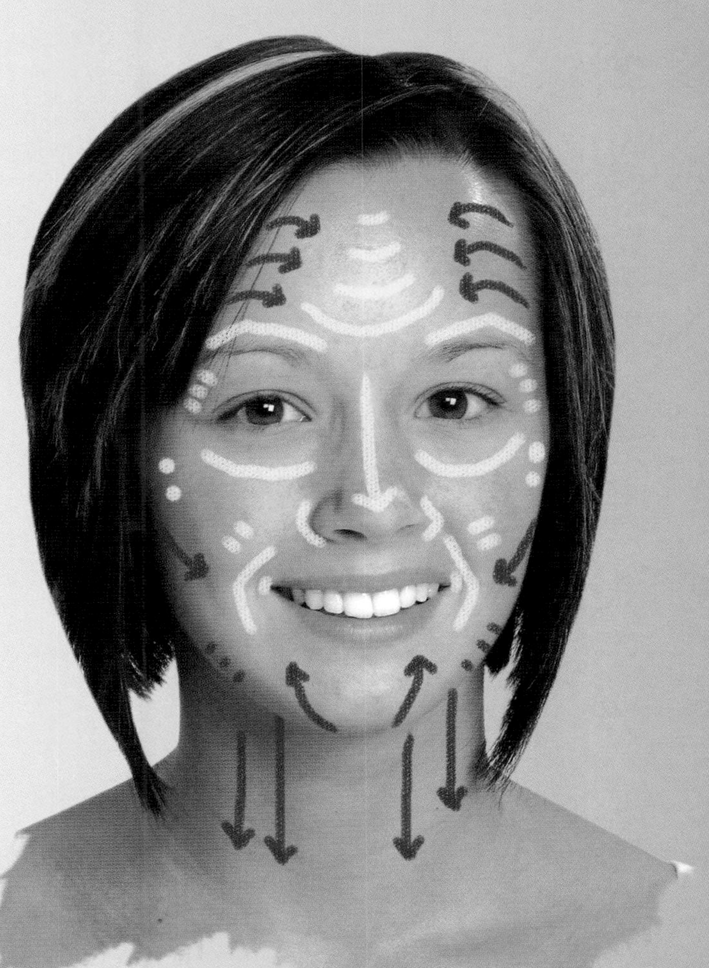

**Light or bright shades** highlight, enhance or accentuate a feature.

**Dark colors** recede imperfections, narrow or hollow an area.

**The main base** color will fall in between the selected light and dark colors, which will add to the counterbalance results.

"To recess a facial feature, apply dark shades and to bring out or highlight a feature, apply light colors."

15

# Facial Shapes...

**A round (circle) face shape** is almost as wide as it is long. This face shape needs to be slenderized by creating the illusion of length. **Darken perimeter of face along temples, cheekbones and jawline** with a foundation or concealer color. Use a light shade to highlight the middle of forehead, down through center of nose and continue to middle of chin. The light color will enhance the illusion of lengthening the face.

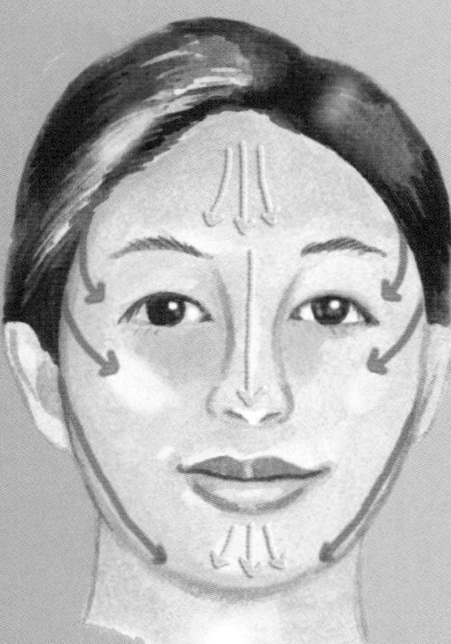

Before blending

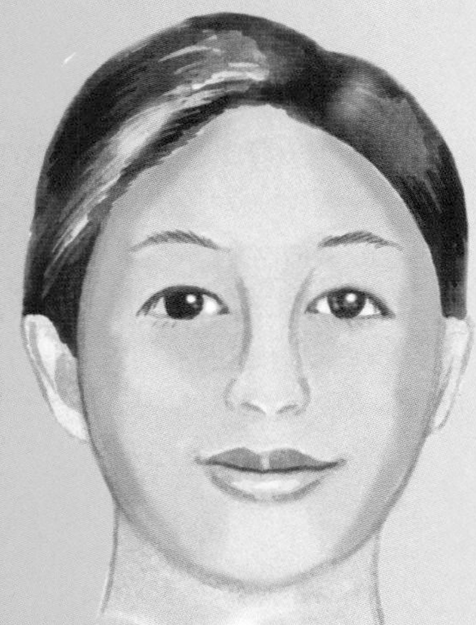

After blending

**A square face shape** is equal in width and length. The hairline is straight vertically and horizontally creating an angular structure. This face shape needs softening along the angular areas. **A dark shade of foundation is applied at corners of forehead and jawline.** A lighter shade of foundation may be placed down center of face, starting at forehead, down nose to chin.

Before blending

After blending



**A rectangle (oblong) face shape** is longer than it is wide and will typically have prominent cheekbones. To reduce the length of the face, an illusion of width is created. Blend a **dark shade of foundation across the jawline, chin and along the forehead at the hairline.**

Before blending

After blending

# Facial Shapes ...

**A triangle (pear) face shape** has a narrow forehead with fullness at jawline. An illusion is created to lengthen the face with some width added to the forehead. **Darken the outer corners of the jawline** to minimize the width to achieve a slender appearance.

Before blending After blending

**A diamond face shape** has a narrow forehead and jawline with prominent cheeks. To reduce the width in the cheek area, apply a **dark shade of foundation along the perimeter of cheekbones** at hairline. Apply a light shade on the center of chin and forehead to create an illusion of the width in those areas.

Before blending After blending

15

**An inverted (heart) face shape** is widest at the forehead and narrowest at the chin. To increase some of the width at the jawline, apply a **light shade of foundation along the sides of jawline** and to minimize the width at the forehead, apply a **dark color along hairline of forehead, temples and cheeks.**

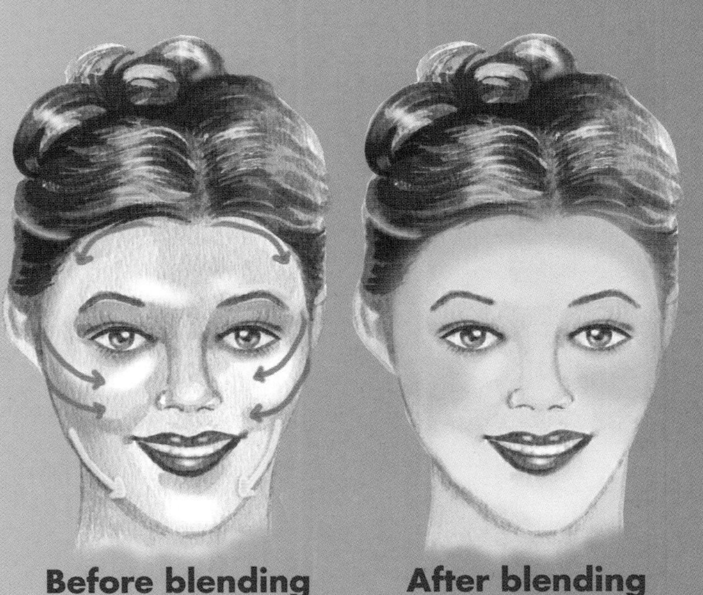

Before blending After blending

# Eye Shape Analysis ...

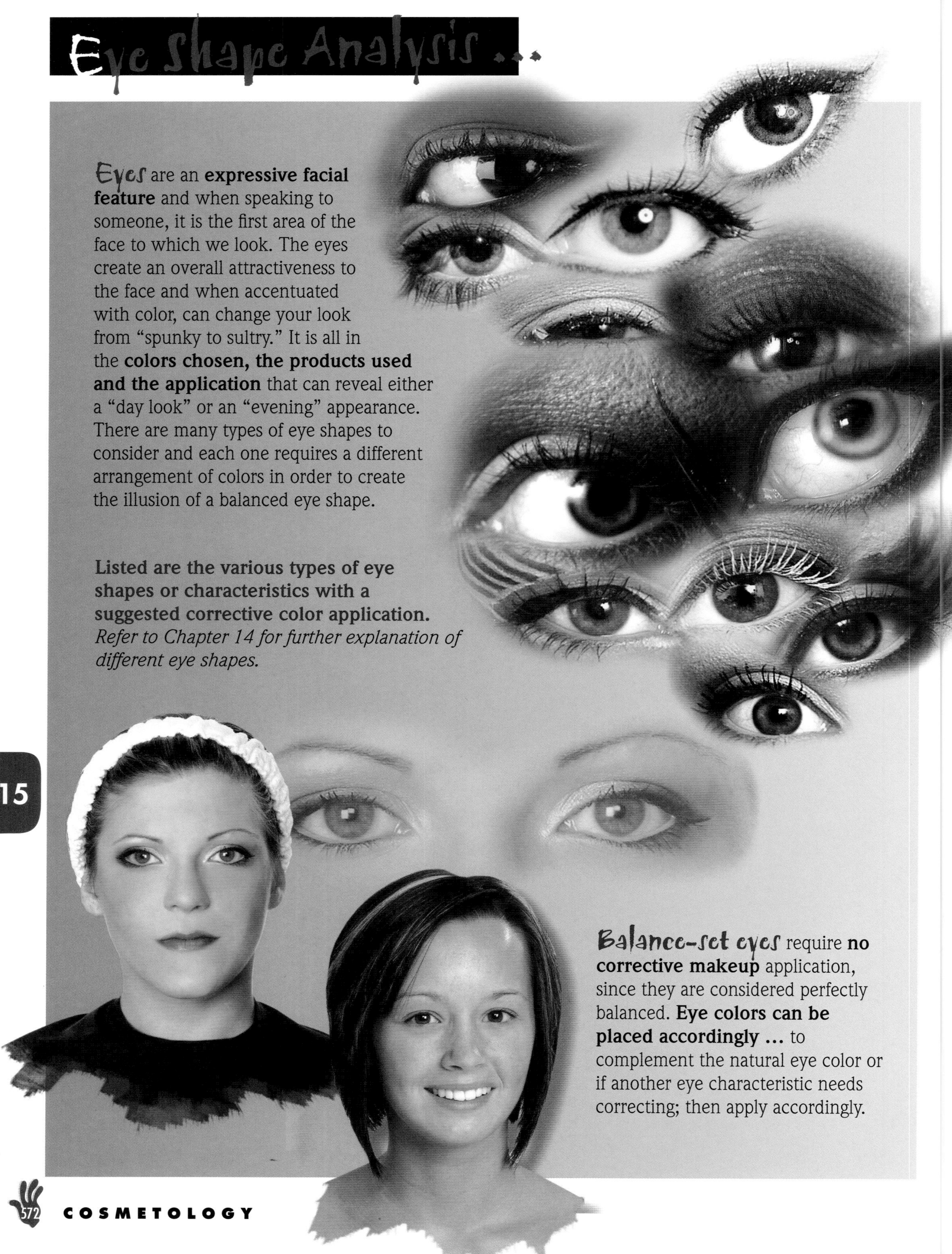

**Eyes** are an **expressive facial feature** and when speaking to someone, it is the first area of the face to which we look. The eyes create an overall attractiveness to the face and when accentuated with color, can change your look from "spunky to sultry." It is all in the **colors chosen, the products used and the application** that can reveal either a "day look" or an "evening" appearance. There are many types of eye shapes to consider and each one requires a different arrangement of colors in order to create the illusion of a balanced eye shape.

**Listed are the various types of eye shapes or characteristics with a suggested corrective color application.** *Refer to Chapter 14 for further explanation of different eye shapes.*

**Balance-set eyes** require **no corrective makeup** application, since they are considered perfectly balanced. **Eye colors can be placed accordingly ...** to complement the natural eye color or if another eye characteristic needs correcting; then apply accordingly.

15

# Eye Shape Analysis . . .

**Wide-set eyes** have a gap between the third eye and a person's two eyes. The objective is to create the illusion of balance-set eyes by applying **medium to light shades on outer portion of eye** and place **dark colors at inner area of eye** and blend colors across the lid. Line the inner portion of eye, at both upper and lower lash line, and smudge toward the outer corners using sponge-tipped applicator.

**NOTE:** For close-set eyes, tweeze or wax the eyebrow hair from the space between the eyes (glabella) to make them appear farther apart.

"Both the face and eye shape along with the eyebrow design complement each other to create overall harmony to the face."

**Close-set eyes** are when the third eye overlaps into a person's two eyes. The objective is to create the illusion of balance-set eyes by applying **light to medium shades at the inner portion of the eye,** and blending into the **dark colors placed toward outer area of eye.** Eyeliner is applied from the middle of the lid to outer corner on both top and bottom to intensify the effect and, may be softened with sponge-tipped applicator.

## Eye Shape Analysis . . .

**Disclaimer:** *The eye colors on the following images are intensified for you to see the exact placement of colors. Emphasis of eye colors is determined by client and professional during a consultation.*

**Almond-shape eyes** are literally shaped like almonds with one side rounded and the other side tapered to a point. Cover **entire lid from lashes to brow with a light color;** apply a **medium color on the middle portion of lid and a dark color on outer corner of lid.** Apply a generous layer of mascara on upper and lower lashes.

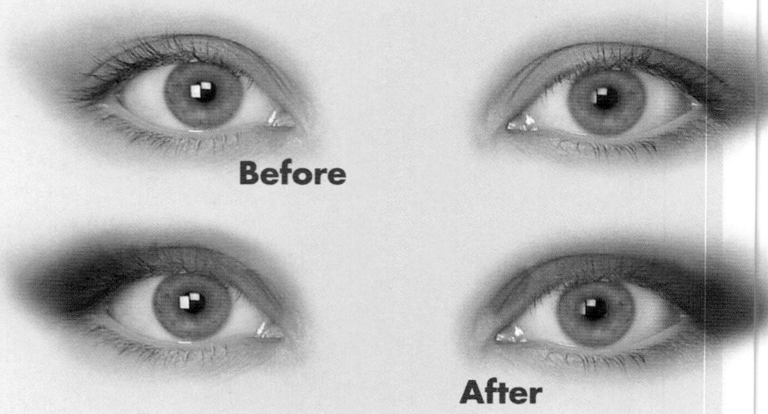


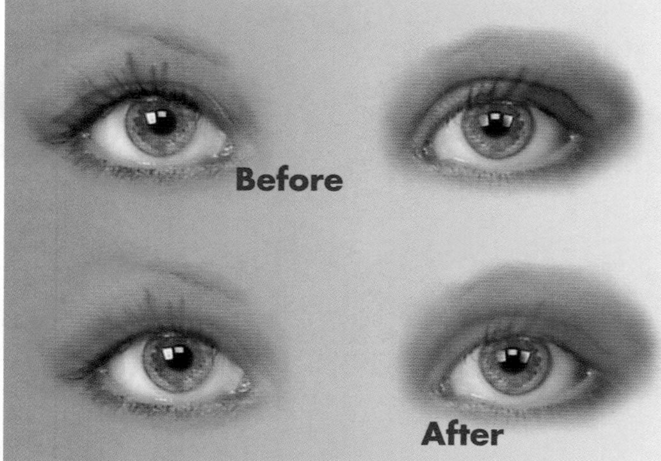


**Round-shape eyes:** Apply **light to medium colors over entire top lid and fill the crease with a dark color.** Eye line both the top and bottom lid with extension of liner out from eye slightly in an upward motion. Apply mascara generously to upper lashes and lightly on the bottom lashes.

**Deep-set eyes:** Apply **light colors to crease area of lid, a light to medium color over lid and directly on brow bone with dark colors directly above the crease area** to create depth. Eyeliner is applied to both the top and bottom of the eye, but the lines are softened with sponge-tipped applicator. Apply mascara to upper and lower lashes.

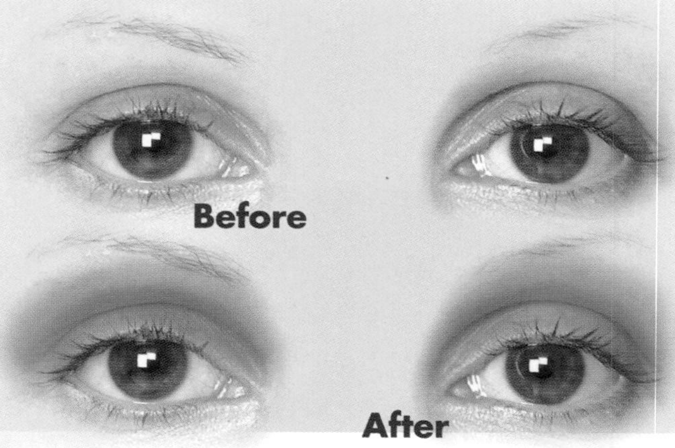


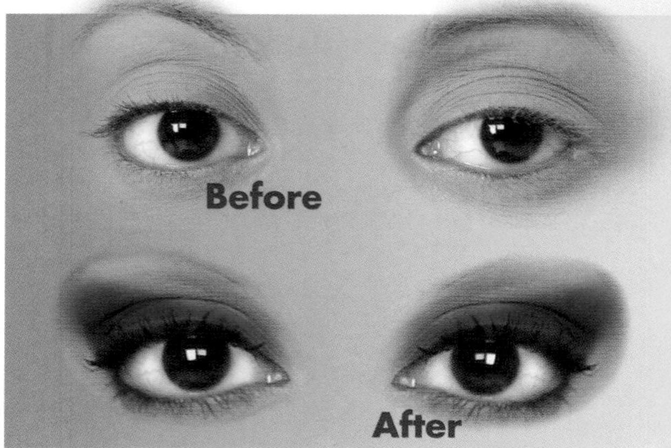


**Prominent eyes:** Apply a **medium to dark color over prominent area of eyelid and extend toward outer portion of brow.** Use a light color directly below the eyebrow. Line both the top and bottom lids with liner and soften with a sponge-tipped applicator. Apply one layer of mascara to top and bottom lashes.

# Eye Shape Analysis . . .

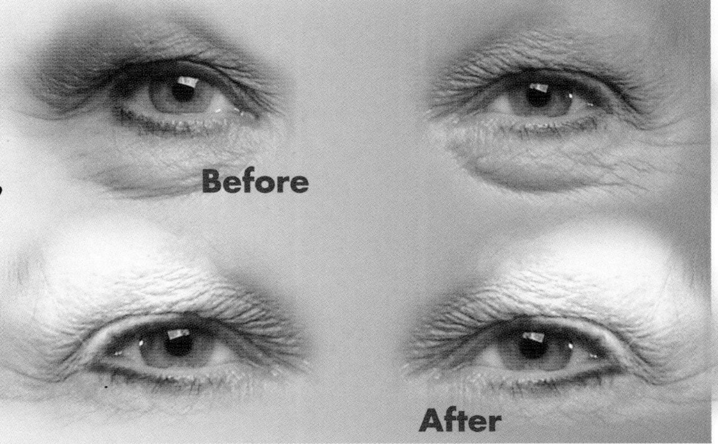


**Drooping eyes** are when the outer corners of the eye slope downward. To persuade the eyes to move upward, apply **light to medium colors directly below the brow bone into the crease, extending to outer portion of eye.** Apply a thin line using eyeliner to the lower lashes creating a slightly thicker line on outer corner of eye. Mascara is applied generously on the outer part of upper lashes and lightly on the bottom lashes.

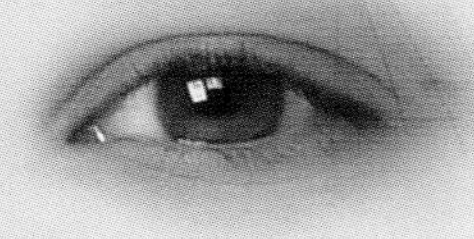

Before

**Small-shape eyes:** Use a **light color over entire lid and below the eyebrow.** Apply **medium to dark colors in the crease and over eyelid extending to outer portion of lid and slightly beyond.** Eyeliner is applied lightly from center to outer lash line to both top and bottom of eyes. Apply mascara to upper and lower lashes.

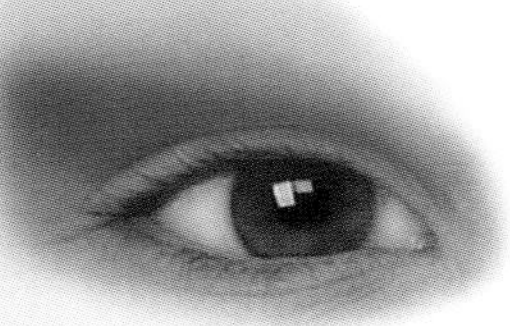

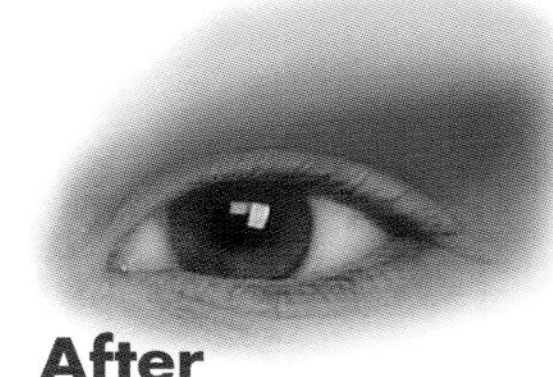

After

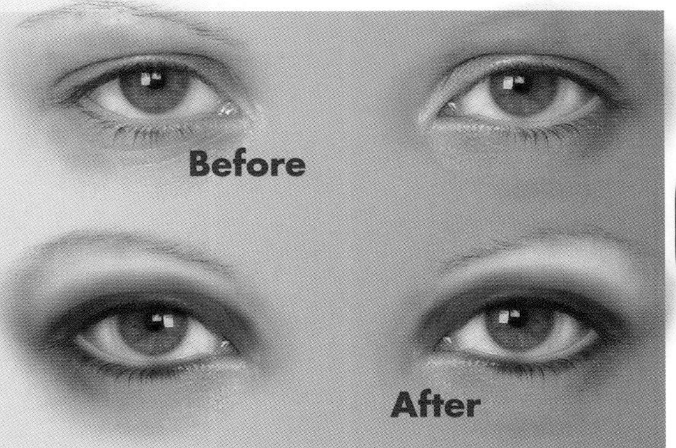


**Hooded eyes** (hidden lids): Apply a **light matte color (no frosts) to area directly below eyebrow. Use medium to dark colors over the hooded area of eyelid and blend** to color below eyebrow. Eyeliner is applied only along the lower lash line. Lightly apply a layer of mascara.

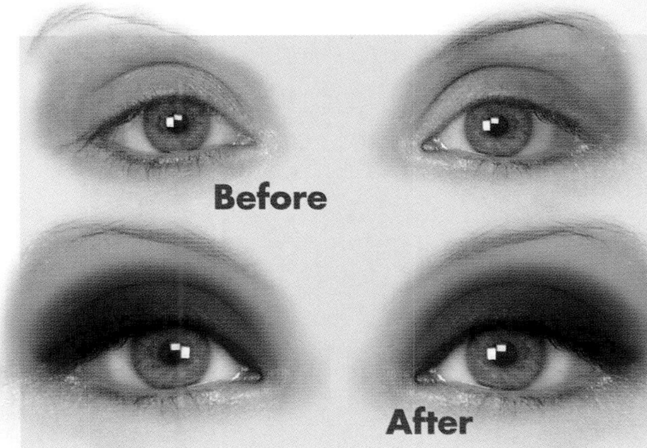


**Heavy-lidded eyes** are when the eyelids are prominent. Apply a **dark color over entire lid up to and including the crease area. Use medium to light colors above crease up to eyebrow.** Apply eyeliner to the upper lid and increase heaviness towards the outer portion of eye. Apply mascara to upper and lower lashes.

# Nose Shape Analysis . . .

## Corrective Makeup Tips for Various Nose Shapes

Before

After

**Long nose shape:** Apply a dark color to entire nose. Foundation base color needs to be lighter than color used on nose and properly blended.

Before

After

**Thin nose shape:** Apply a light color along sides of the nose. To soften a pointed nose, apply a dark color directly under tip of the nose and blend properly.

**Bump on nose:** Apply a dark color on bump and a light shade on both sides of bump and blend.

Before

After

**Crooked nose shape:** Apply a dark shade on the protruding side and a light color on the opposite side and blend.

After

Before

Before

After

**Short, flat nose shape:** Apply a light color down center to tip of nose with a dark color applied only at side of nostrils.

**Wide nose shape:** Apply a dark color along sides of nose and a thin line of light color down center of nose. Properly blend lines when foundation is applied.

Before

After

# Lip Shape Analysis...

The **lips** are the final area of the face to be analyzed along with what colors to apply to complete the look. **In well proportioned lips,** the two peaks forming the center of the **upper lip are centered with the nostrils.** The upper lip is slightly less full than the bottom lip. For corrective makeup application, the objective is to create the illusion of proportioned lips.

## Corrective Makeup Tips for Various Lip Shapes

**Large lips:** Apply foundation to lips and set with loose powder. Line lips along the inside of the natural lip line to make them appear smaller and fill in with lip color.

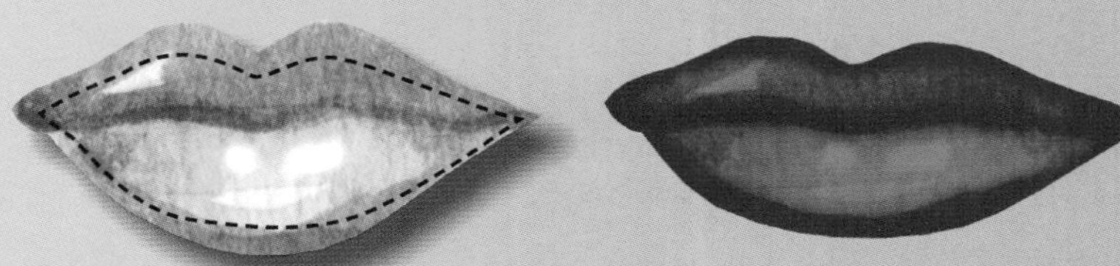

**Small lips:** Apply foundation to lips and set with loose powder. Line lips along the outside of the natural lip line to make them appear larger and fill in with lip color.

**Uneven lips:** Apply foundation to lips and set with loose powder. Line the fuller side of the lip inside the natural line and line the smaller side of the lip on the outside of the natural lip line. Apply lip color within the newly created lines.

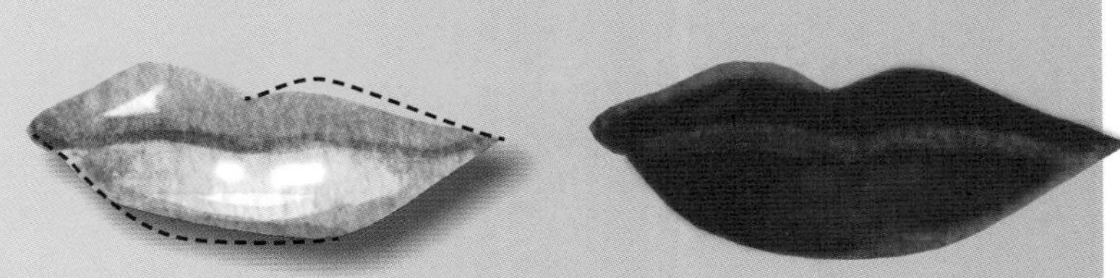



## Tips for Irresistible Lips:

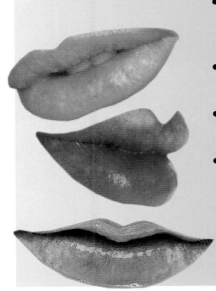

- **For long-wearing lip color:** apply lipstick, blot the lips with a tissue to set the color and remove excess. Gently apply a thin layer of loose powder, then complete the lips by reapplying lip color.
- **To increase shine of lips:** apply a thin layer of clear or colored gloss directly over the lip color or wear lip gloss all by itself.
- **To accentuate small lips:** dab a small amount of lip gloss at the center of the lips.
- **For a dazzling appearance:** apply silver, gold or iridescent lip gloss over the lip color.

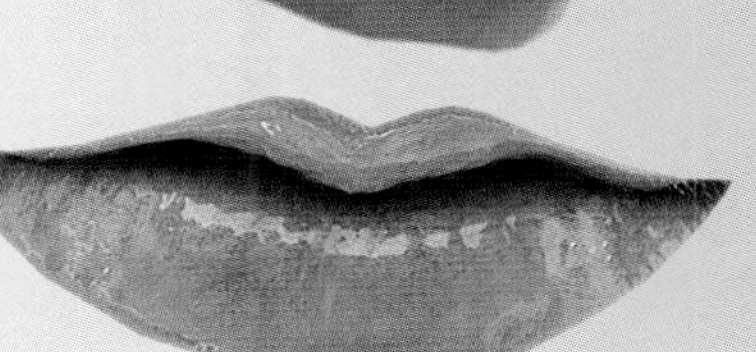

"Foundation applied over the lips first will create long-wearing lip color, as well as provide a base for correcting the lip shape."

# Eyelash Extensions ...

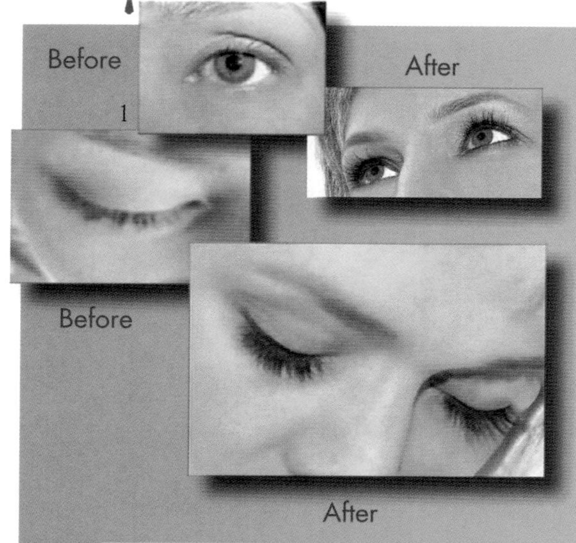


**Eyelash extensions** are artificial lashes added to the existing lashes to create thicker, longer eyelashes, enhancing the look and shape of your eyes. To create a more dramatic result, the lash extensions come in various colors and with glitter or rhinestones attached to the lash hair. The lashes are constructed with human, synthetic or animal hair and come in various designs.

**Optional:** Artificial lashes may be applied to the bottom lashes, but sometimes have a tendency to look unnatural.

RA

## Eyelash Extension Designs

Band or strip lashes

**1** **Band or strip lashes** are pre-made **eyelashes attached to a strip.** This type of extension is applied quickly, but may have a tendency to appear unnatural. This lash design has temporary durability, lasting for one day. Band lashes are the most common choice for a special occasion or event.

professional
Natural-looking, Lush Lashes
Natural Lash Kit
2

Individual lashes

**2** **Individual lashes** are the most natural-looking eyelash extensions since application involves placing **a single strand of hair one at a time** directly on the existing lashes. This lash design is long-wearing, provides length and adds volume.

Individual lashes
3

**3** **Separate flares** are artificial lashes that are more natural-looking lashes than strip lashes and tend to wear longer if properly placed and maintained. These lashes consist of **two to three small, short lashes per flare,** which separate and fan out from each other. The flares are considered an intermediate version of strip and individual lashes.

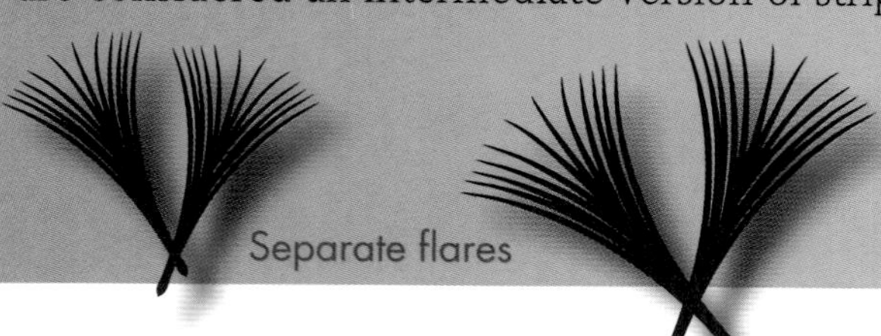

Separate flares

4
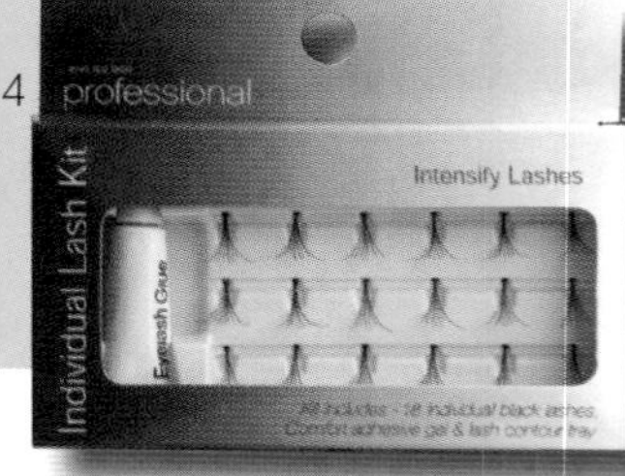


15

# Eyelash Extensions ...

## Eyelash Extension Tools

**Adhesive** is a non-irritating **bonding agent that is applied to lash extensions for adhesion** to the natural lashes. Adhesives come in either **no-fume or low-fume formulas** to accommodate the person with sensitive eyes (check with manufacturer for details). Extension adhesive is designed for durability and quick dry time to create a natural appearance and fast service.

**Adhesive remover** is a softening agent that **targets the adhesive to remove the artificial lashes** effectively and safely. The remover should be gentle and non-irritating, containing no alcohol or acetone to prevent dryness of skin and eyelashes.

**Contour eye patches** are placed directly **under the eye at the lower lash line for protection** during application of lash extensions to the upper lashes. These patches are adjustable to conform and accommodate all eye shapes. Some manufacturers offer a paper or foam tape to protect lower lashes and skin. It is the professional's preference as to what works best for a client. Both the patches and tape offer gentle removal from delicate skin.

5

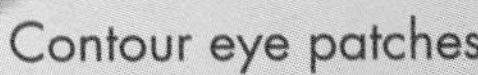

Contour eye patches

**Tweezers** are used to grip individual hair or lash extensions for application to eyelashes. Tweezers are manufactured in many sizes, shapes and styles to accommodate the professional ergonomically and creativity.

15

# Eyelash Extensions . . .

RA

**To apply artificial lashes,** first cleanse and dry the natural lashes. Use a tweezers to pick up the selected lash. Apply a small amount of adhesive and starting at center of upper lash line, place lash or lashes on top of the natural hair for adhesion to adhere to hair, **NOT SKIN.** Continue placing the lashes moving toward inner corner. Go back to center and continue to place lashes toward outer corner of lash line. To accommodate all customers, artificial lashes may specifically be designed by carefully trimming the lashes for a custom fit to the person's natural lash line.

Before

After

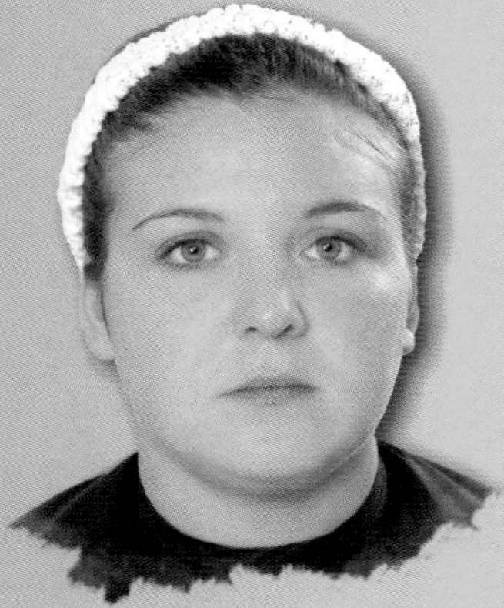

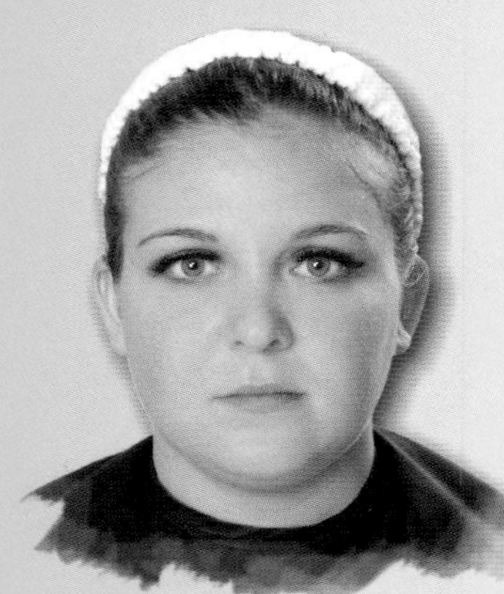

"When individual (single) lashes are applied to each individual lash hair, the procedure is referred to as eye tabbing."

**NOTE:** Mascara may or may not be used, depending on client's desired end result. If used, apply a light coat of mascara. Refer to pages 594 to 597 for detailed procedures on lash extensions.

15

## Care of Eyelash Extensions

- **Do not apply waterproof mascara** since it is difficult to remove and may break the bond of the adhesive.
- **Do not use makeup remover that contains oil** because it will weaken the adhesive.
- **Do not rub the eyes,** which could loosen lashes as well as stretch the skin around the eyes creating fine lines.
- **To carefully remove band lashes** from tray, begin at one end and roll off to other end to avoid ripping the band.
- **Do not use an excessive amount of adhesive** to avoid dripping of product onto skin and/or eyes.

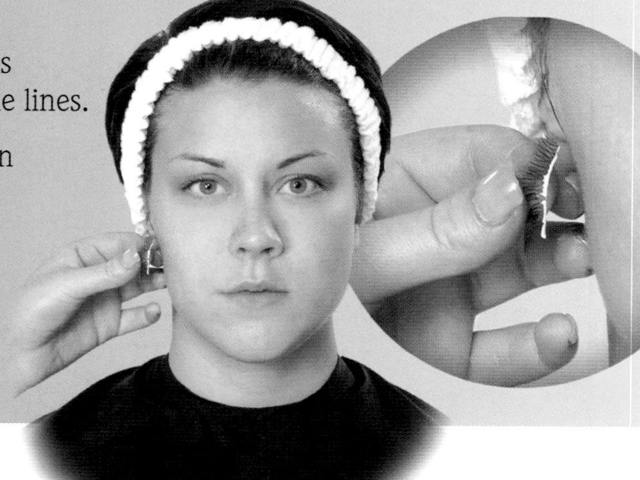

# Eyelash Extensions . . .

## Eyelash Extension Touchups

**Individual or separate flares can be replaced every two to four weeks** depending on maintenance of artificial lashes and how many lashes come out. Band lashes are removed the same day they are applied and are not to be left on overnight.

## Removal of Eyelash Extensions

**To remove eyelash extensions,** apply a small amount of adhesive or eye makeup remover on cotton-tipped applicator. Place the cotton-tipped applicator with remover on the base of the artificial lashes for a few seconds to soften and loosen the adhesive. Gently remove artificial band lashes parallel to lash line being careful not to pull on the natural lashes. Discard lashes after use.

# Client Consultation ...

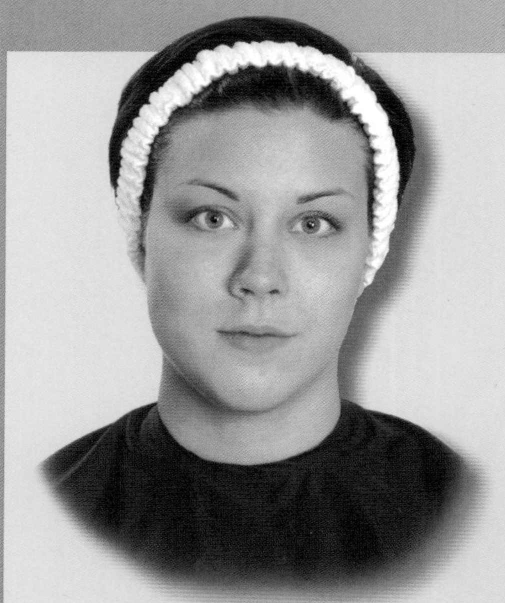

**Cape with headband**

**Before beginning any service, whether it is a part of the consultation or the actual service, the client's skin and clothing need to be protected.**

**During the client consultation,** *the professional needs to* ***communicate with the client*** *on the desired end result. Ask the following question for a better understanding of the client's needs to accomplish a successful service. Is this makeup service intended to acclimate the client to wearing makeup every day or is it for a special occasion such as a wedding or a formal occasion?* ***A crucial part of the consultation is to analyze the skin, eye and haircolor.*** *In order to get a* ***true skin color and tone analysis, the skin must be cleansed*** *to remove any existing makeup or debris.*

**Draping** protects the client's skin and clothing from any cosmetic material that may escape during makeup application. In most salons/spas, the client wears a **robe**, which provides easy access to area being serviced.

**Robes** are made of a washable material and are laundered after each client use.

1

2

A **headband** is used to pull hair back from the face or a **plastic/cloth cap** is worn to cover all the hair.

15

Once the client is properly draped the skin is **cleansed, toned and moisturized ...** this would also be performed prior to actual makeup service. As we previously learned in Chapter 13, the skin's condition will indicate the correct cleanser for the client. Follow the cleanser with a toner to bring the skin back to a proper pH and close the pores, finishing with a moisturizer.

3

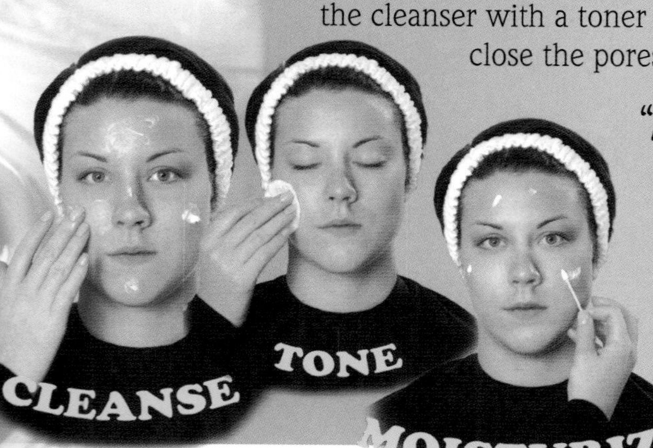


"A moisturizer with a sunscreen included will not only protect the skin from dryness and the environment, but also the harmful effects of the sun's rays."

# Skin Analysis . . .

**Client profile cards** are used for all services performed in the salon/spa. Each card is unique to the beauty service being performed. Keeping a record of the **client's skin analysis and makeup service** will not only assist you during future visits and sales, it will build client trust and loyalty. Customer service is a critical component in all areas of the business in order to build and maintain a loyal clientele base.

"When listing foundation, blush and lip colors, be sure to include the consistency of the product–whether it is powder, cream or liquid."

## Client Profile Card/File

Name____________________ Date____________________
Address____________________
Phone number__________ Work__________ Cell__________
Email____________________
Birthdate____________________

**Skin Analysis:**

| **Skin tone** (circle one) | **Skin color** (circle one) | **Skin type** (circle one) |
|---|---|---|
| Light | Caucasian | Dry |
| Medium | Asian | Oily |
| Dark | African-American | Normal |
| | Hispanic | Combination |
| | | Blemished |

**Color Analysis:**
Natural Eye Color __________ Haircolor__________

**Makeup Cosmetics:**
Cleansing Products____________________
Foundation____________________
Concealer____________________
Powder____________________
Eye Color__________ Eyeliner__________
Mascara __________ Eyebrow Color__________
Cheek Color____________________
Lip Color__________ Lip Liner__________

**Corrective Makeup:**
Face Contouring: Highlighting __________ Shadowing __________
Face Zones: One _______ Two _______ Three _______
Face Shape ______ Eye Shape _____ Nose Shape ______ Lip Shape ______

**Eyelash Extensions:**
Band Lashes _____ Individual Lashes _____ Separate Flares ______

# SIMPLE LAB PROJECT

# Full Basic Makeup

## OBJECTIVE

To learn how to professionally perform a full basic makeup application.

Before

After

## TOOLS & MATERIALS

- Robe and/or cape
- Cloth and disposable towels
- Headband or plastic/cloth cap
- Cleanser
- Toner
- Moisturizer
- Disinfectant
- Client record card/file
- Cosmetic sponges
- Applicators
- Pencil sharpener
- Eyelash curler
- Makeup brushes
- Foundation
- Concealer
- Powder
- Eye colors
- Eyeliner
- Eyebrow colors
- Mascara
- Cheek color
- Lip color and liner

## PROCEDURE

**"The client consultation is an important part of your professional service. Be sure to complete this step prior to each client service you provide. Your successful retail sales and customer satisfaction rates depend upon it!"**

RETAIL • RE-BOOK • REFERRAL

1. Cosmetologist sanitizes hands and work station.
2. Set out service tools and materials.
3. Follow procedure as shown.
4. Follow standard cleanup procedure.
5. Document client record card/file.

A — Drape the client in preparation for service.

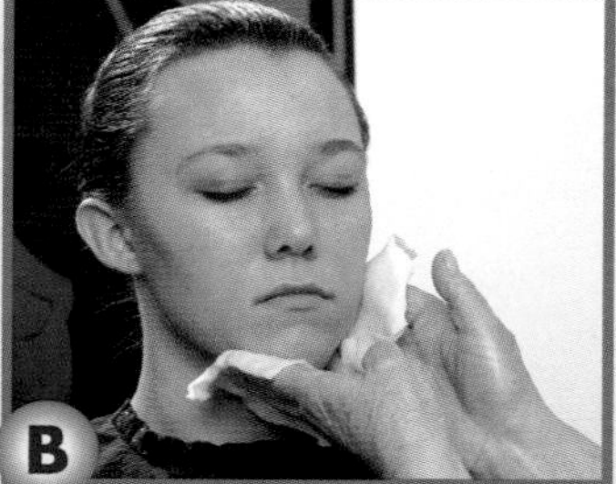
B — Cleanse, tone and moisturize face. Perform a skin analysis checking client's haircolor, eye color and skin color.

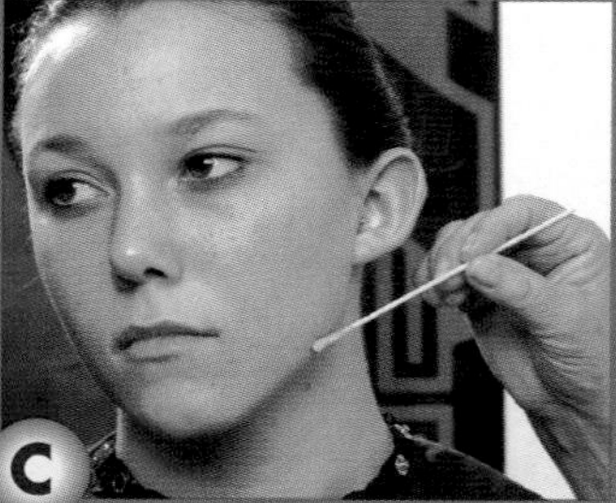
C — Test selected foundation along jawline to check if color blends with existing skin color.

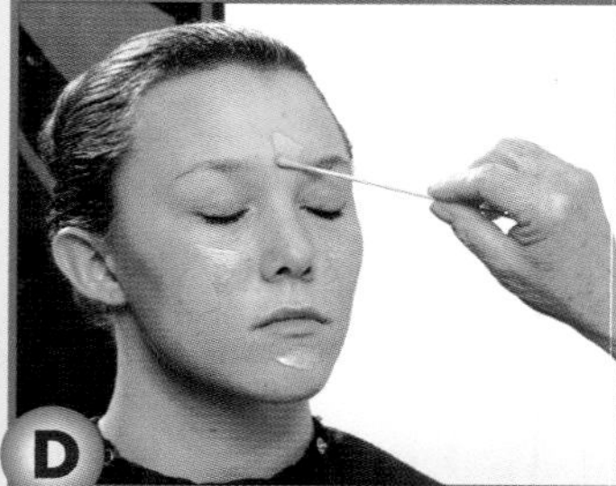
D — Apply a small amount of foundation to cheeks, chin, forehead and nose.

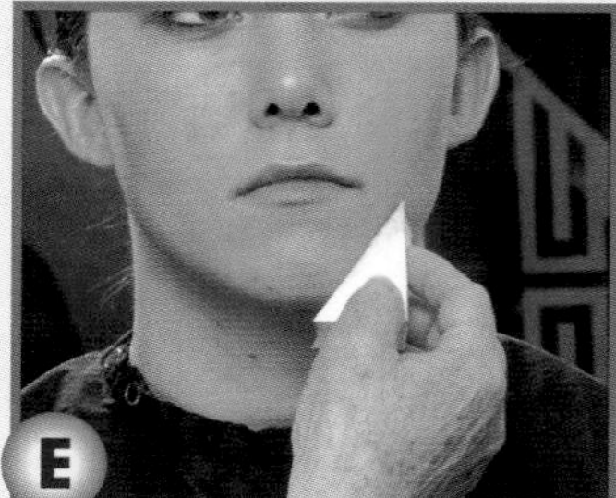
E — Use a cosmetic sponge or brush and blend foundation in a down and outward motion. Be sure to blend into hairline and below jawline to neck area.

F — Select a shade lighter than the foundation for concealer color. **Optional:** Concealer may be applied before or after foundation, depending on type of concealer used and end result.

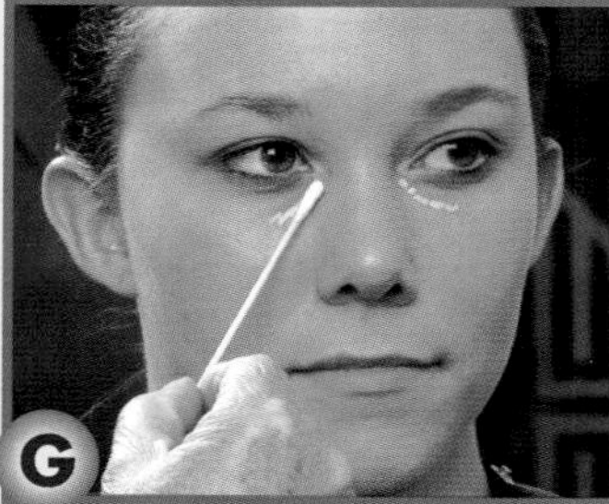
G — Apply concealer to any imperfections such as blemishes or dark circles using a sponge-tipped applicator or brush.

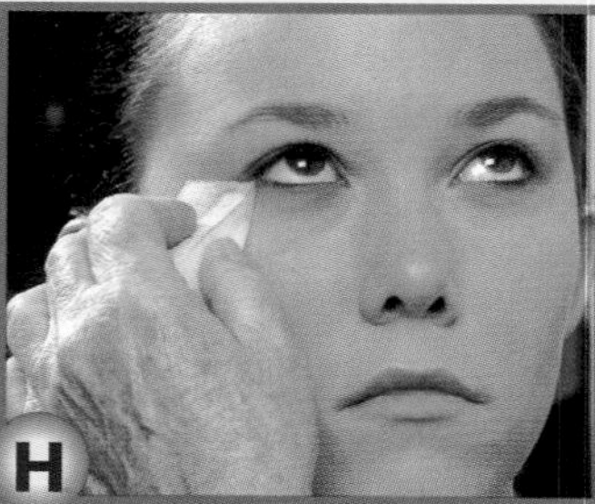
H — Gently smooth and blend concealer over the skin with a cosmetic sponge.

## Full Basic Makeup

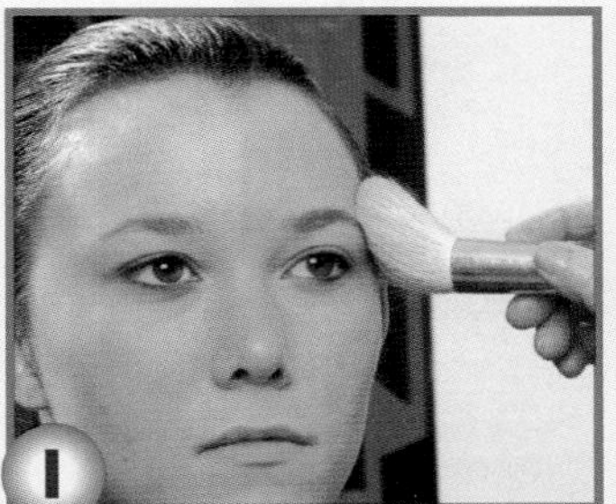
I
Apply powder using brush or cosmetic sponge to set foundation and concealer.

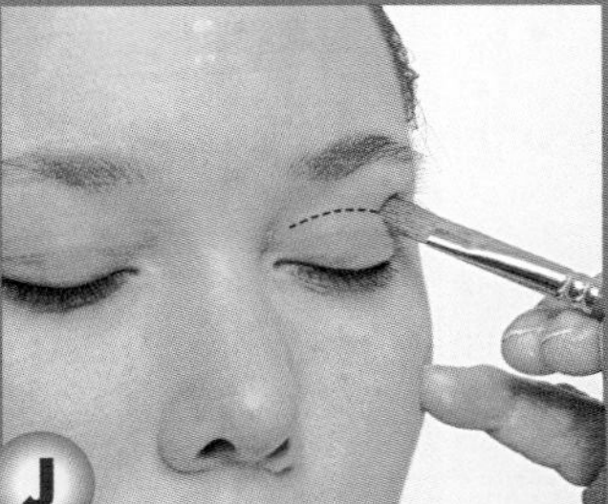
J
Apply dark eye color using a brush or sponge-tipped applicator to crease area of eyelid.

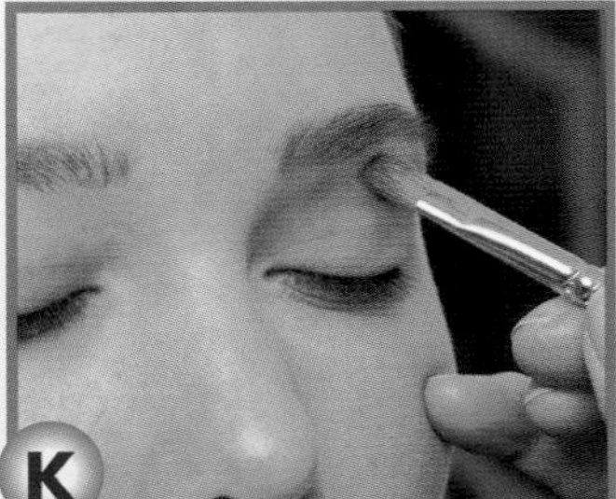
K
Apply a light eye color to area directly below the eyebrow. A medium color may be used to blend into inner portion of eyelid.

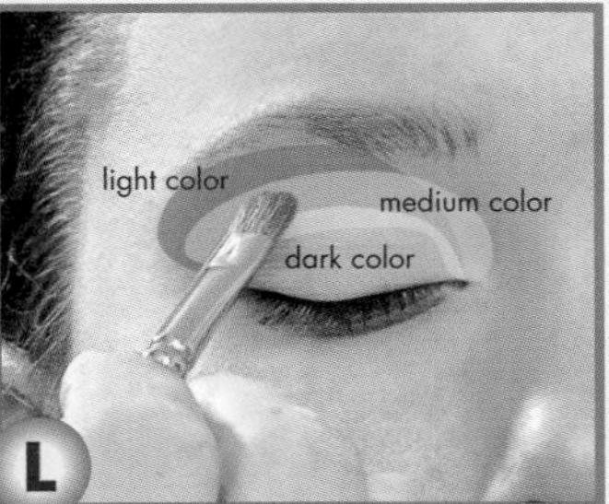

L
**Repeat eye color application to opposite eyelid.** Placement of colors is dependent upon eye shape.

M
Apply eyeliner along lashes to both bottom and top eyelids. Eye shape determines how much of eyelid is lined.

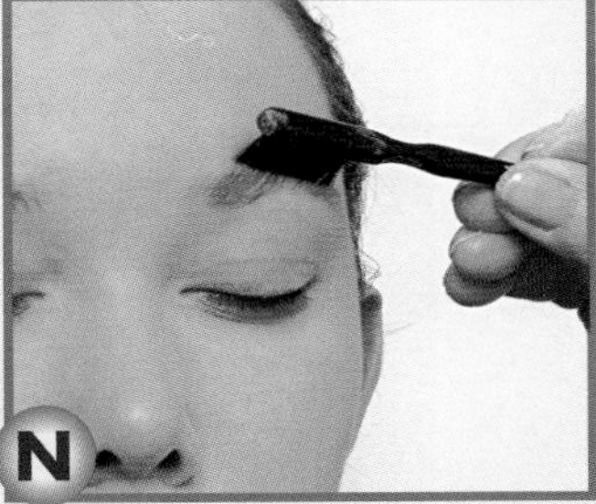
N
Brush the eyebrow hair to distribute hair in one direction. Color is applied to balance out natural color.

O
Apply eyebrow color to hair with a pencil using light feathery strokes. **Repeat on opposite side.** Sharpen pencil before and after each client use.

P
Apply mascara to bottom lashes using a disposable wand with small even strokes.

Q
Apply mascara to top lashes with a disposable wand using light even strokes.

R
Using a brush or cosmetic sponge, apply cheek color at hollow area of cheekbone and blend into hairline.

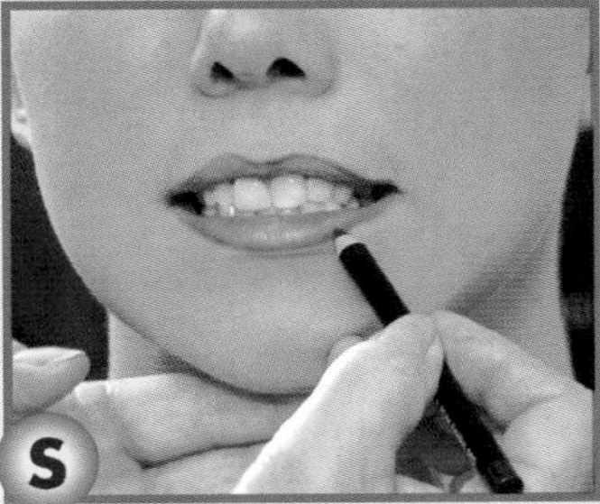
S
Using a pencil or lip brush, apply liner along natural lip line, start at outer corners moving toward center. Repeat on top and bottom lips.

T
Apply lip color within the lined lips using a brush or sponge-tipped applicator which completes the makeup application.

**Optional:** Lips may be blotted with a tissue to remove excess cosmetic.

EVALUATION ______________________

GRADE ______ STUDENT'S NAME ______ ID# ______

SIMPLE LAB PROJECT

# Corrective Makeup for Wide Forehead

Before

After

## OBJECTIVE

To learn how to create the illusion of balance to a wide forehead by applying corrective makeup.

## TOOLS & MATERIALS

- Robe and/or cape
- Cloth and disposable towels
- Headband or plastic/cloth cap
- Cleanser
- Toner
- Moisturizer
- Disinfectant
- Client record card/file
- Cosmetic sponges
- Applicators
- Pencil sharpener
- Eyelash curler
- Makeup brushes
- Foundation
- Concealer
- Powder
- Eye colors
- Eyeliner
- Eyebrow colors
- Mascara
- Cheek color
- Lip color and liner

## PROCEDURE

**"The client consultation is an important part of your professional service. Be sure to complete this step prior to each client service you provide. Your successful retail sales and customer satisfaction rates depend upon it!"**

RETAIL RE-BOOK REFERRAL

1. Cosmetologist sanitizes hands and work station.
2. Set out service tools and materials.
3. Drape the client in preparation for service.
4. Cleanse, tone and moisturize face.
5. Perform skin analysis.
6. Follow procedure as shown.
7. Follow standard cleanup procedure.
8. Document client record card/file.

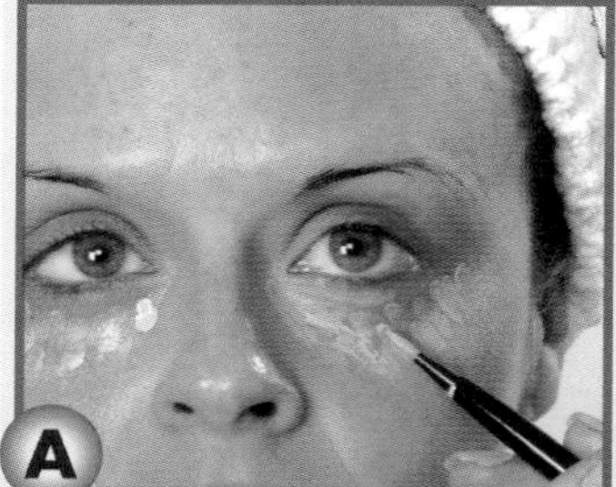

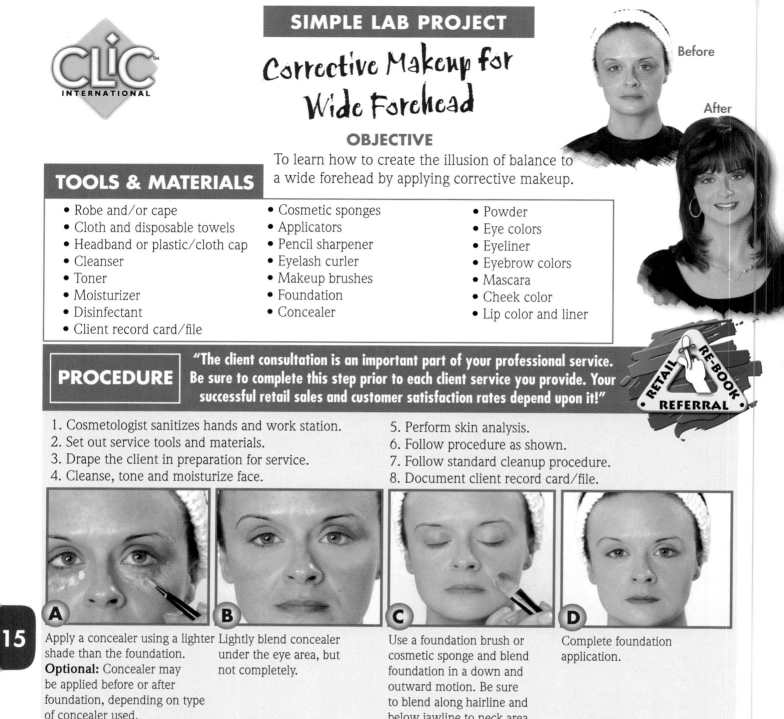

A — Apply a concealer using a lighter shade than the foundation. **Optional:** Concealer may be applied before or after foundation, depending on type of concealer used.

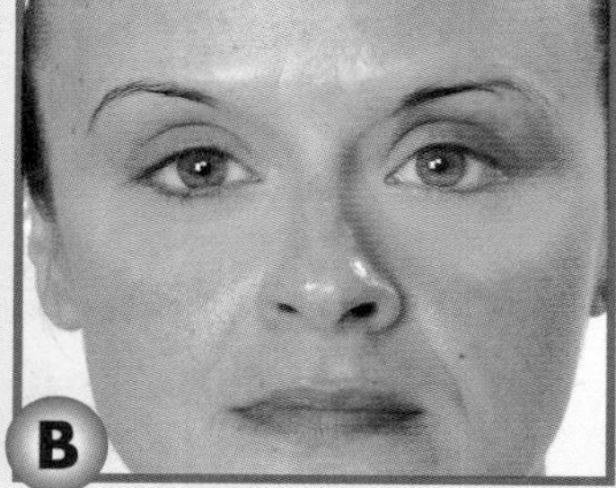

B — Lightly blend concealer under the eye area, but not completely.

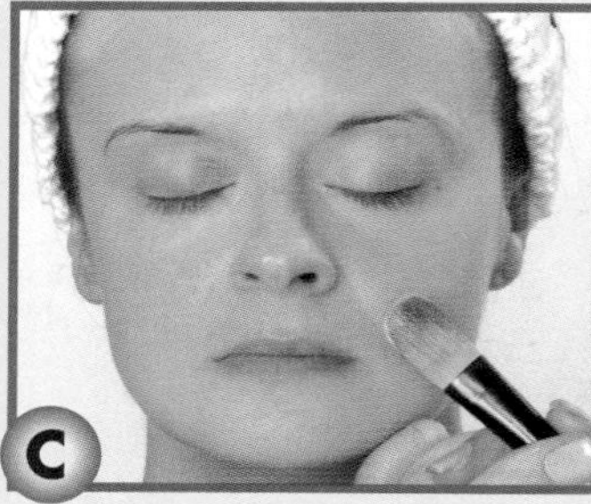

C — Use a foundation brush or cosmetic sponge and blend foundation in a down and outward motion. Be sure to blend along hairline and below jawline to neck area.

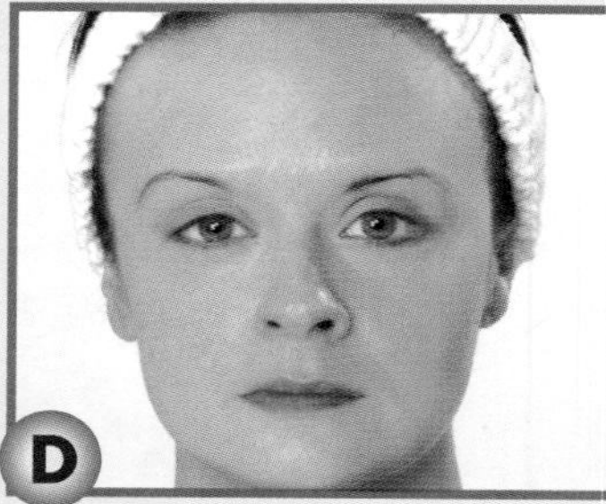

D — Complete foundation application.

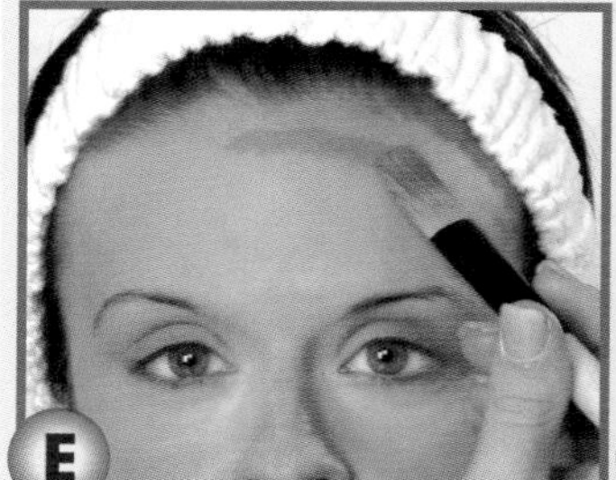

E — Use a darker color than foundation and apply to entire hairline of forehead area to minimize width.

F — Apply a light color down center of forehead to maximize balance and lightly blend.

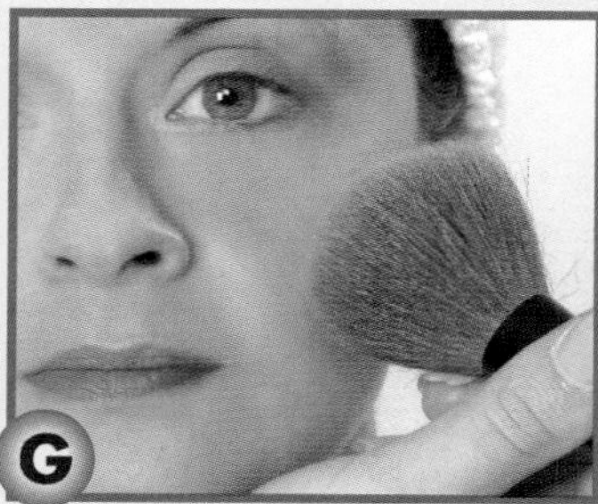

G — Apply powder using brush or cosmetic sponge to set the base color. Apply cheek color.

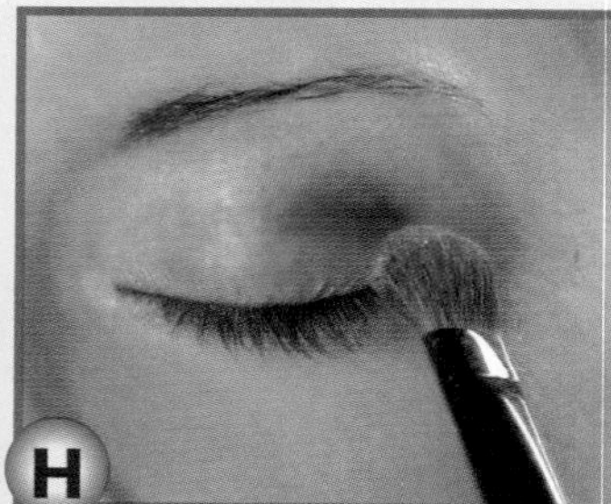

H — Apply dark eye color in crease and on half of outer portion of eyelid, with a light color on remaining eye area.

## Corrective Makeup for Wide Forehead

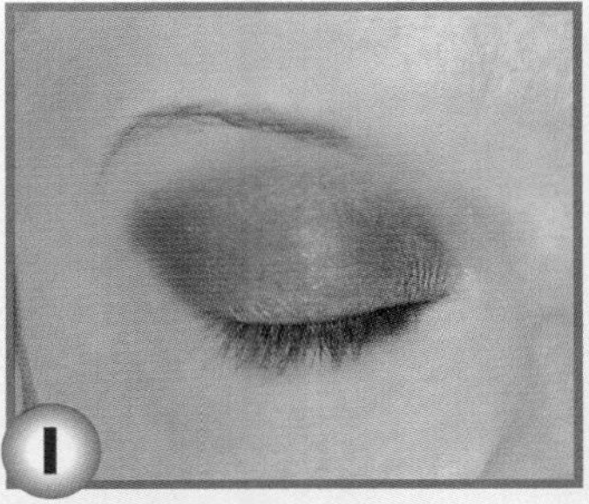

**I** **Repeat on opposite eye** with medium shade used for blending into crease and on inner portion of eyelid.

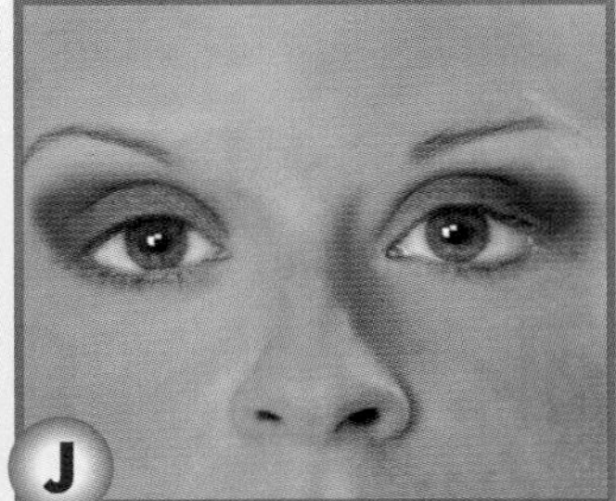

**J** Completed eye color application.

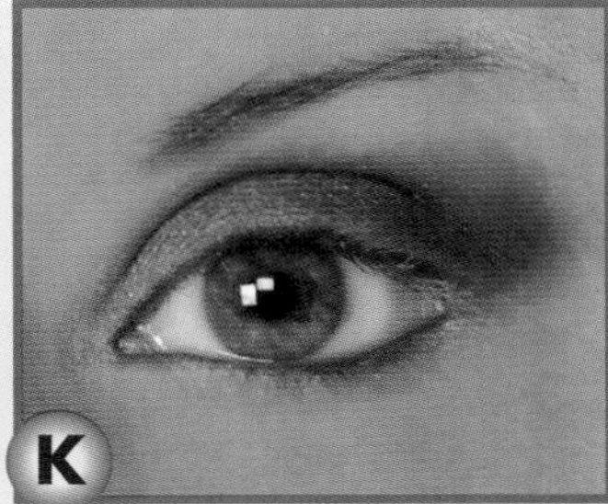

**K** **Optional:** Eyeliner is applied along lash line of top and bottom lid depending on eye shape.

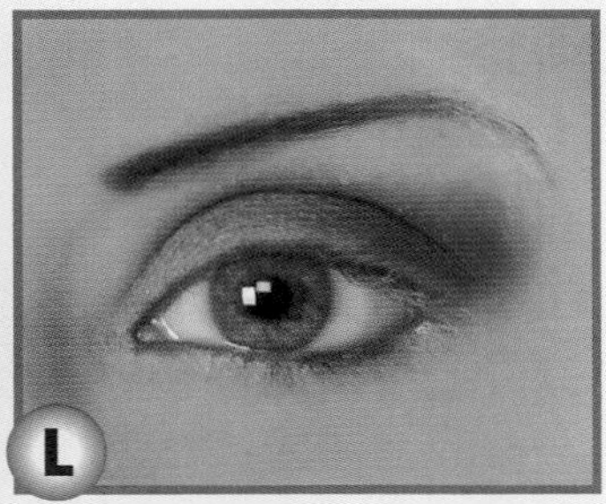

**L** Eyebrow color is applied to create an eyebrow design.

**M** Apply mascara to lower and top lashes using a disposable wand.

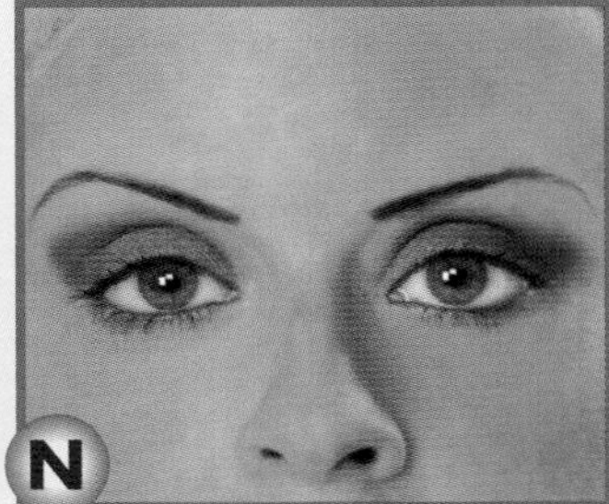

**N** Completed color application with eyes open.

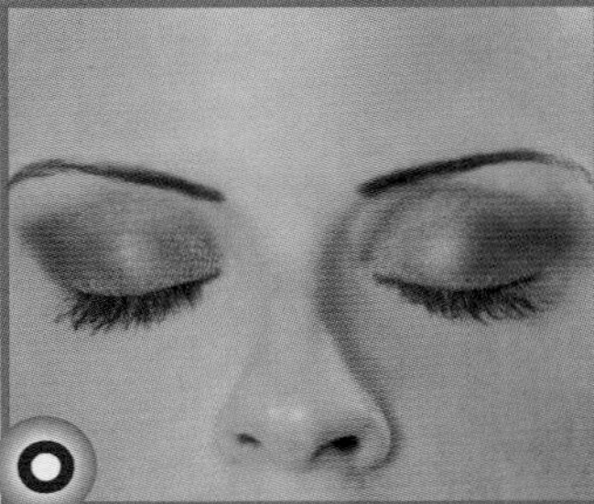

**O** Completed color application with eyes closed.

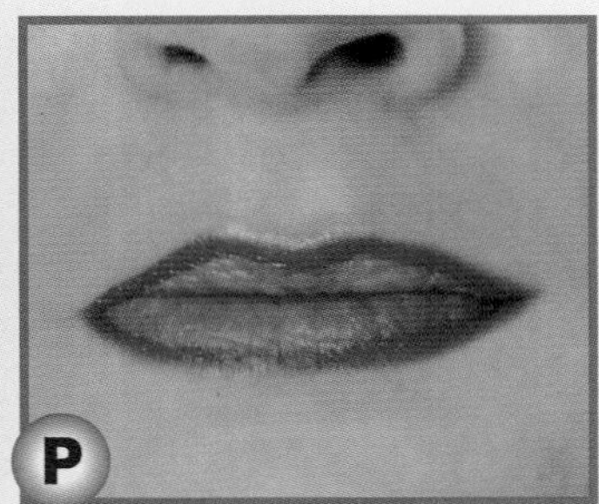

**P** Apply lip liner following the natural lip line.

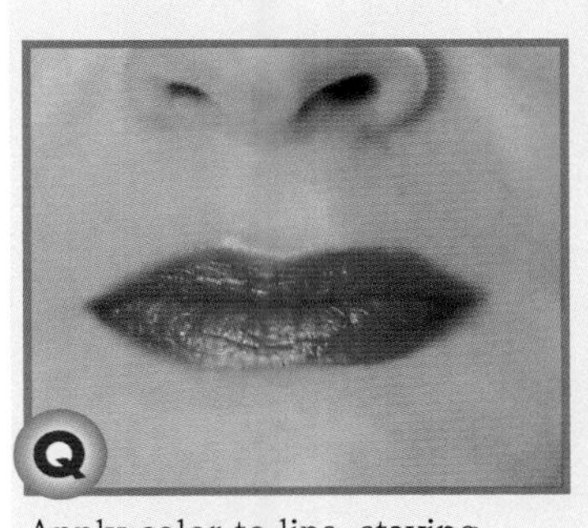

**Q** Apply color to lips, staying within the natural lined lips.

**R** Completed corrective makeup for a wide forehead.

**EVALUATION** ____________________

GRADE ____ STUDENT'S NAME ____ ID# ____

CLiC INTERNATIONAL

## INTERMEDIATE LAB PROJECT

# Corrective Makeup for Wide-Set Eyes

Before

After

### OBJECTIVE

To learn how to create the illusion of balance by applying corrective makeup to wide-set eyes.

## TOOLS & MATERIALS

- Robe and/or cape
- Cloth and disposable towels
- Headband or plastic/cloth cap
- Cleanser
- Toner
- Moisturizer
- Disinfectant
- Client record card/file
- Cosmetic sponges
- Applicators
- Pencil sharpener
- Eyelash curler
- Makeup brushes
- Foundation
- Concealer
- Powder
- Eye colors
- Eyeliner
- Eyebrow colors
- Mascara
- Cheek color
- Lip color and liner

## PROCEDURE

**"The client consultation is an important part of your professional service. Be sure to complete this step prior to each client service you provide. Your successful retail sales and customer satisfaction rates depend upon it!"**

RETAIL • RE-BOOK • REFERRAL

1. Costmetologist sanitizes hands and work station.
2. Set out service tools and materials.
3. Drape the client in preparation for service.
4. Cleanse, tone and moisturize face.
5. Perform skin analysis.
6. Follow procedure as shown.
7. Follow standard cleanup procedure.
8. Document client record card/file.

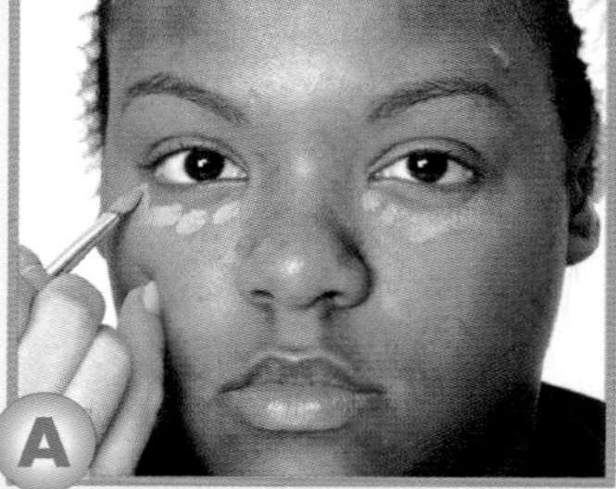
A
Apply concealer to dark circles or any imperfections using brush and lightly blend over skin.

B
Use a brush or cosmetic sponge and apply/blend foundation in a down and outward motion.

C
Apply powder using brush or cosmetic sponge to set foundation and concealer.

D
Apply cheek color.

15

E
Completed cheek color application.

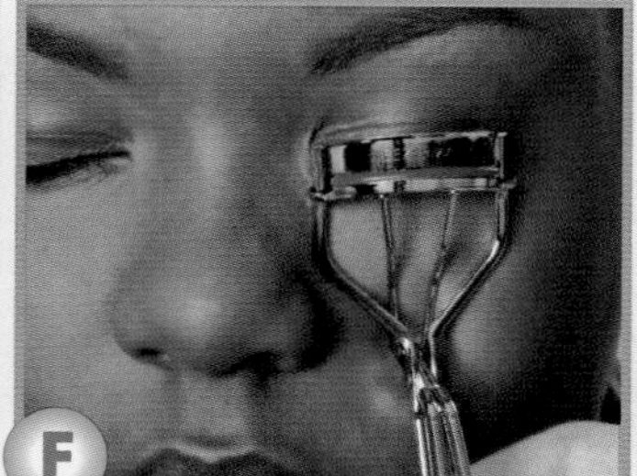
F
**Optional:** Insert opening of eyelash curl over top lashes and gently close and hold for a few seconds. **Repeat until desired curl of lash is achieved.**

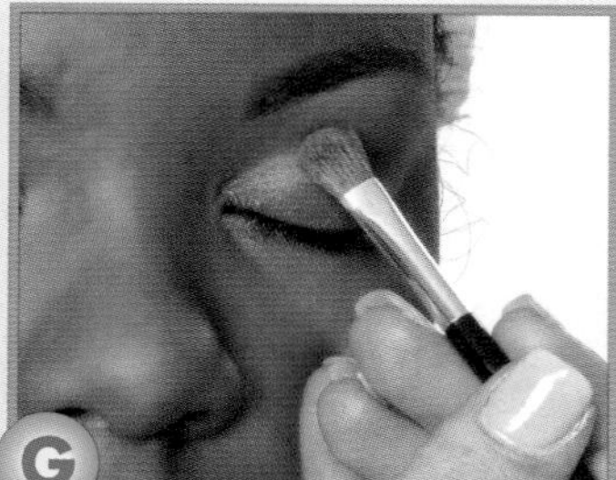
G
Place dark to medium colors on inner to center portion of eyelid.

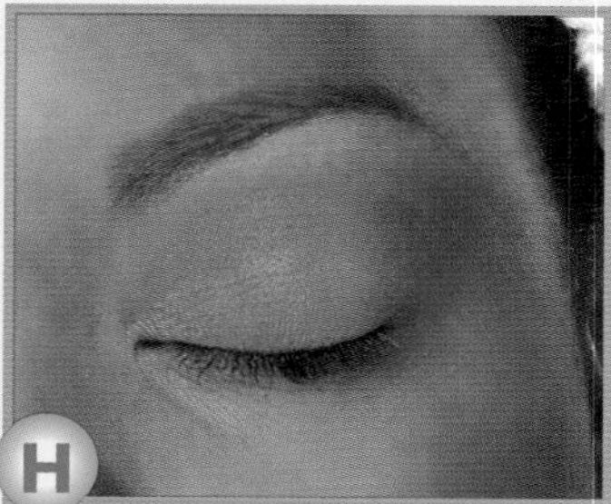
H
Place medium to light colors from middle to outer portion of eyelid.

## Corrective Makeup for Wide-Set Eyes

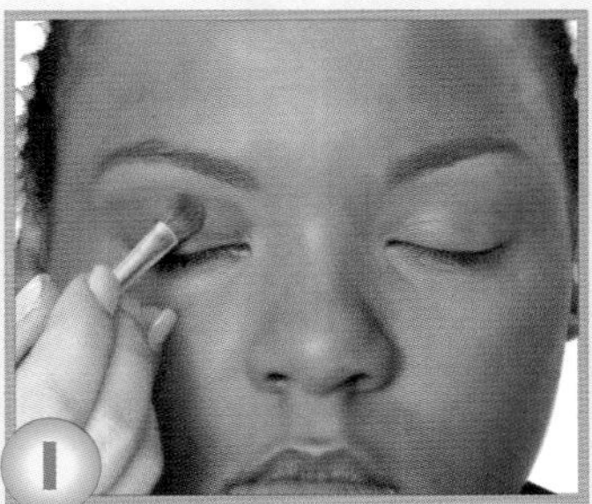

I **Repeat steps G and H on opposite eyelid.**

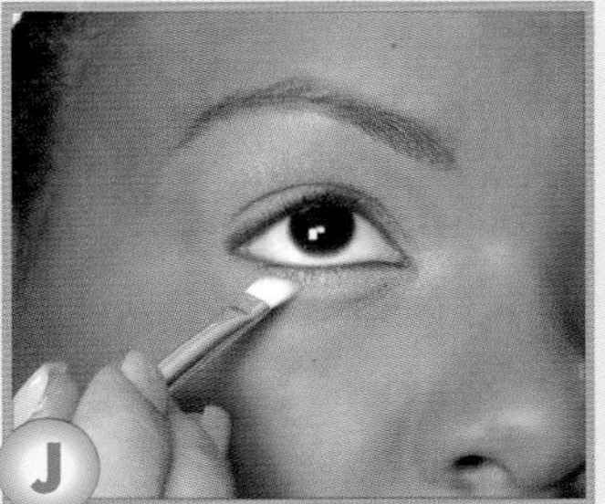

J **Optional:** Apply a small amount of dark color used on inner portion of eyelid to underneath eye.

K Client closes eyes, apply eyeliner on top eyelid along lash line.

L Client looks to the side or up, apply eyeliner to bottom eyelid along lash line.

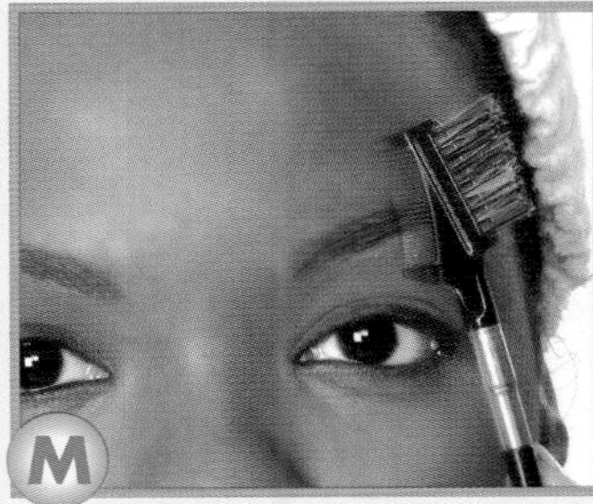

M Eyebrow is brushed and color applied **if needed.**

N Apply mascara to top and bottom lashes using disposable wand applicator.

O Completed eye color application.

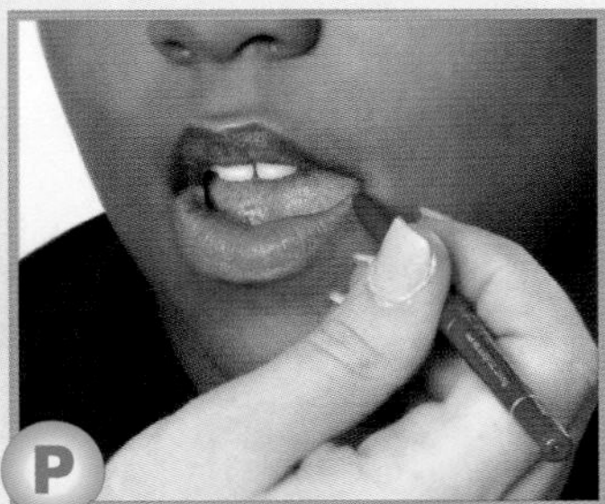

P Apply lip liner, starting at inner corner of mouth and move to center of lips.

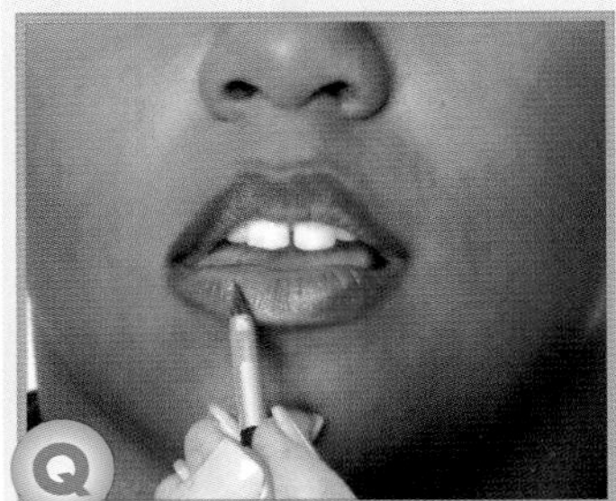

Q Fill in lips with color for balance.

R Completed corrected makeup for wide-set eyes.

**EVALUATION** ____________________

**GRADE** STUDENT'S NAME ID#

CLIC INTERNATIONAL

# INTERMEDIATE LAB PROJECT

## Corrective Makeup for Close-Set Eyes

### OBJECTIVE

To learn how to create the illusion of balance by applying corrective makeup to close-set eyes.

### TOOLS & MATERIALS

- Robe and/or cape
- Cloth and disposable towels
- Headband or plastic/cloth cap
- Cleanser
- Toner
- Moisturizer
- Disinfectant
- Client record card/file
- Cosmetic sponges
- Applicators
- Pencil sharpener
- Eyelash curler
- Makeup brushes
- Foundation
- Concealer
- Powder
- Eye colors
- Eyeliner
- Eyebrow colors
- Mascara
- Cheek color
- Lip color and liner

### PROCEDURE

**"The client consultation is an important part of your professional service. Be sure to complete this step prior to each client service you provide. Your successful retail sales and customer satisfaction rates depend upon it!"**

RETAIL • RE-BOOK • REFERRAL

1. Cosmetologist sanitizes hands and work station.
2. Set out service tools and materials.
3. Drape the client in preparation for service.
4. Cleanse, tone and moisturize face.
5. Perform skin analysis.
6. Follow procedure as shown.
7. Follow standard cleanup procedure.
8. Document client record card/file.

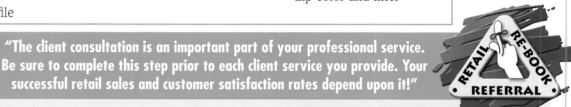

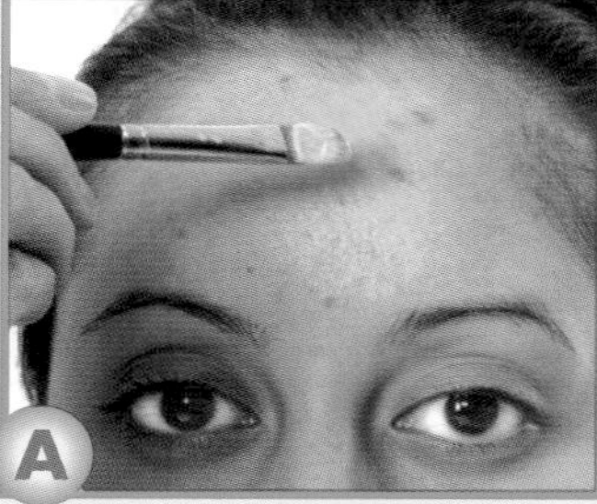
A Apply concealer to any blemished area using a brush or sponge-tipped applicator.

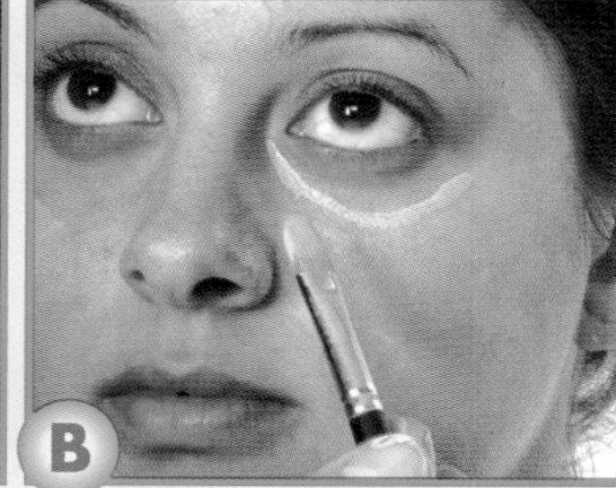
B Apply concealer to dark circles under eyes.

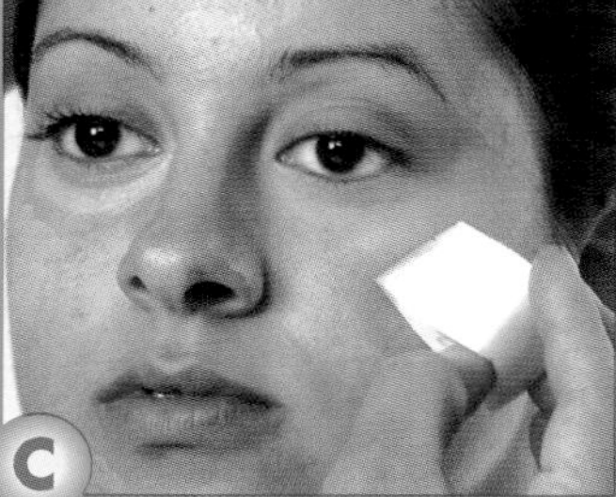
C Gently smooth and blend concealer over the skin with a cosmetic sponge

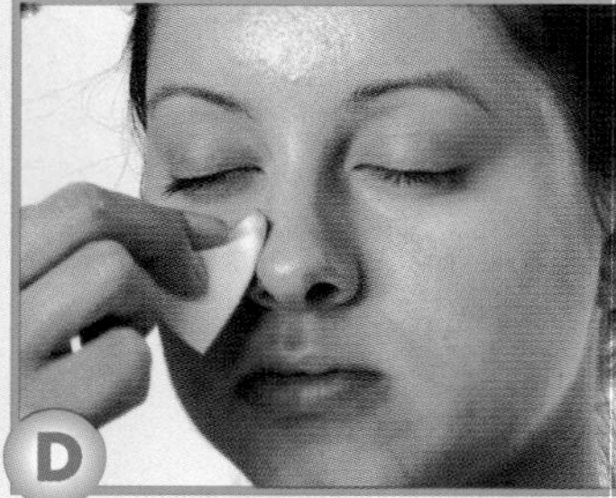
D Apply foundation using a cosmetic sponge or brush to blend foundation in a down and outward motion.

15

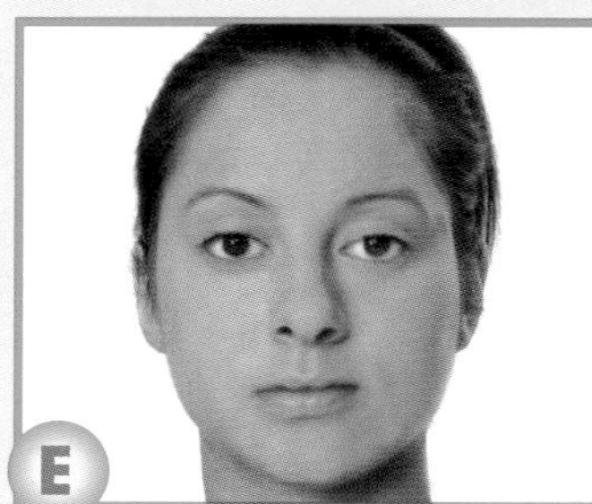
E Completed foundation application.

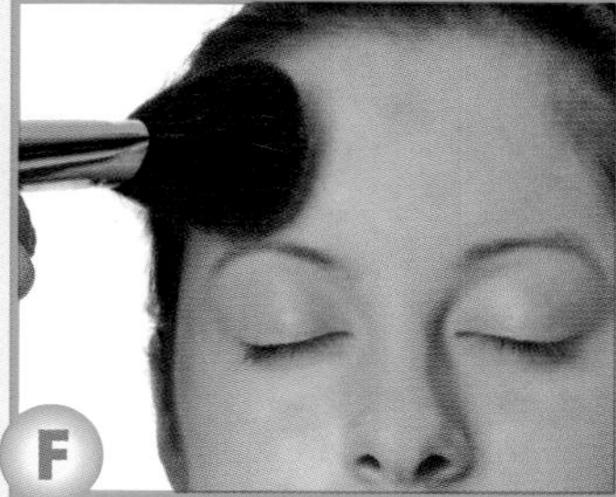
F Apply powder using brush or cosmetic sponge to set foundation and concealer.

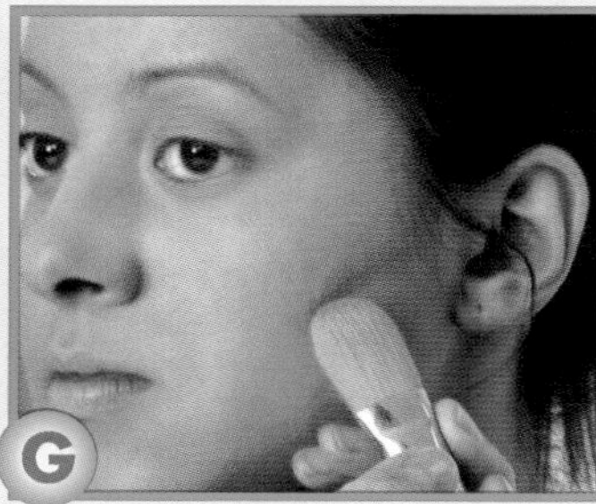
G Using a brush, place cheek color below cheekbone and blend into hairline.

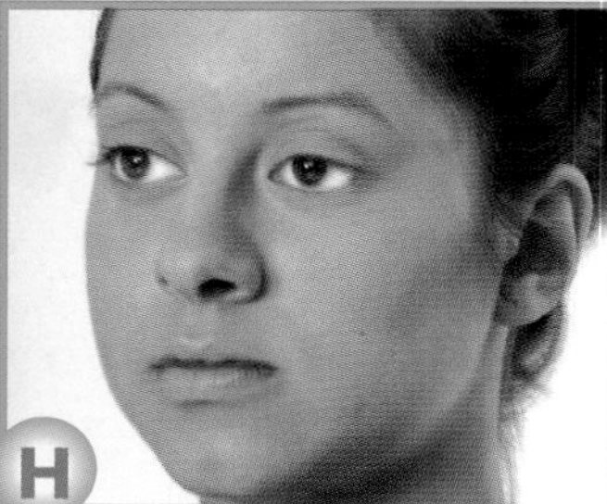
H Completed cheek color application.

# Corrective Makeup for Close-Set Eyes

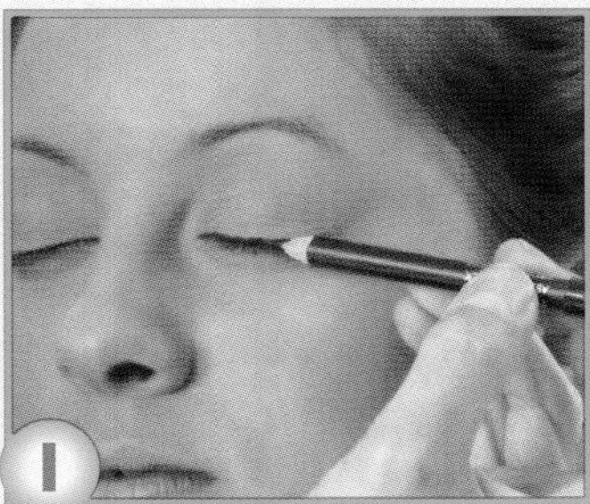
I
Eyeliner is applied along lash line of top eyelid.

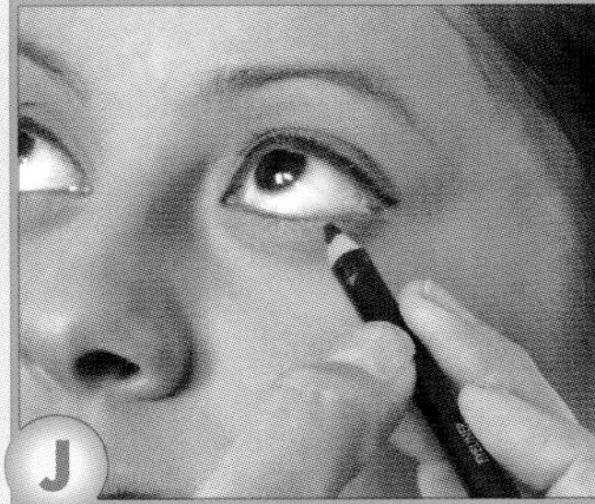
J
Eyeliner is applied along lash line of bottom eyelid. (Client may look upward to avoid seeing object coming toward her.)

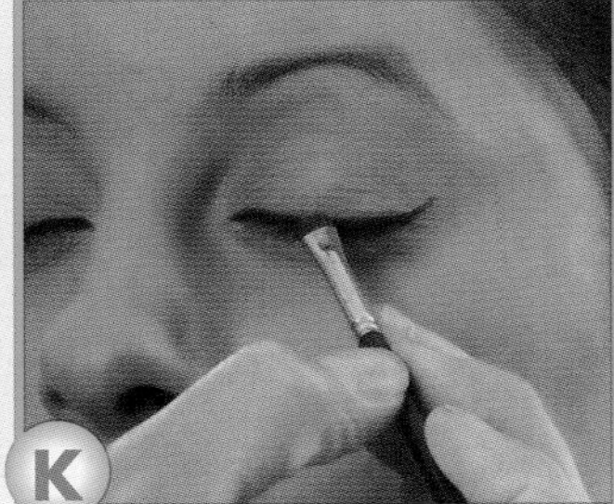
K
To lessen the harshness of a penciled line, soften with brush to smooth and blend.

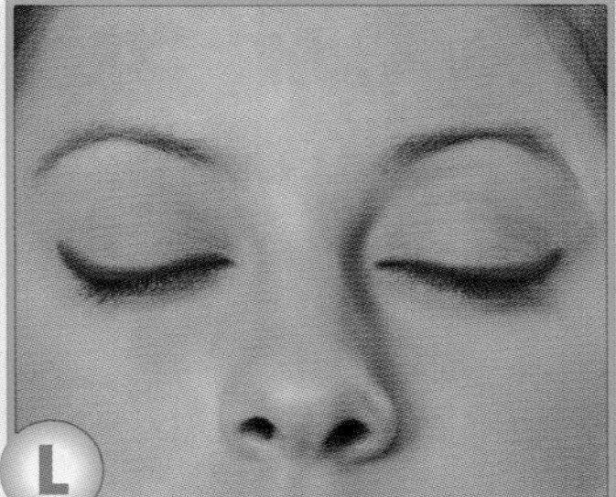
L
Completed eyeliner application.

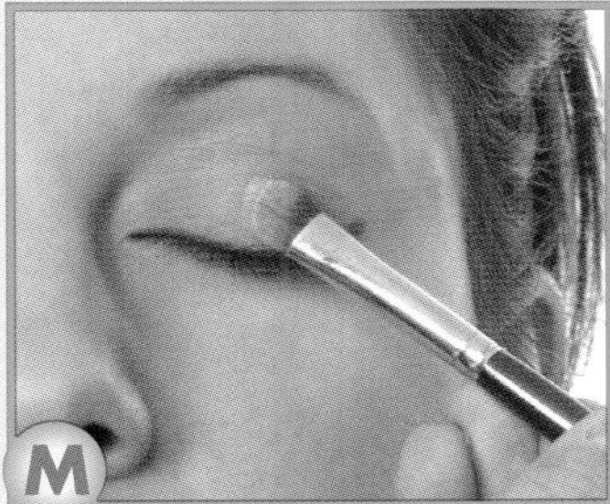
M
Apply a light color over entire eyelids of both eyes.

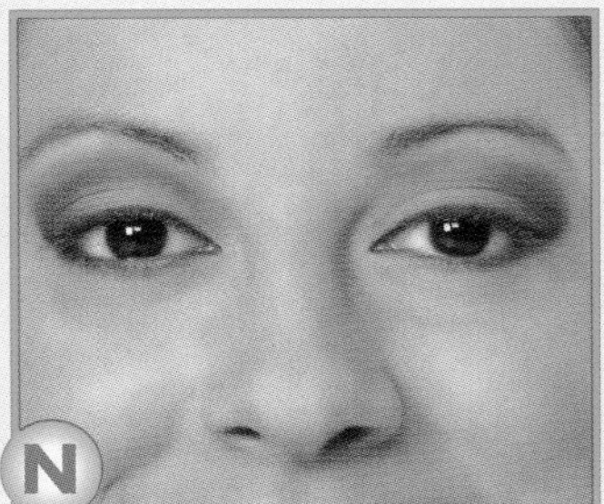
N
Use a dark eye color and place in crease area of lid extending to outer corner of eye. **Repeat on opposite eye.**

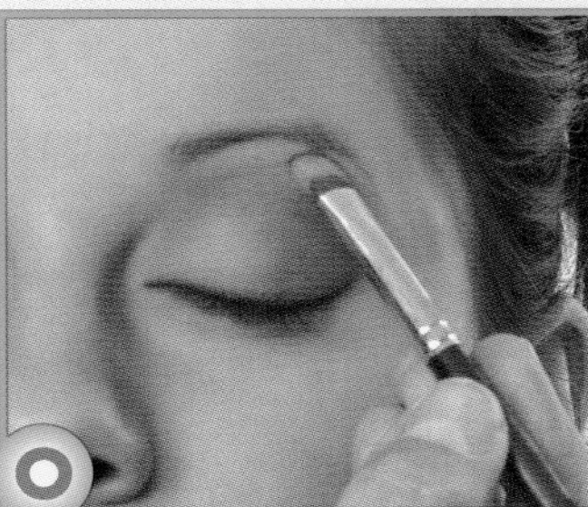
O
Highlight using a light eye color directly below the eyebrow area.

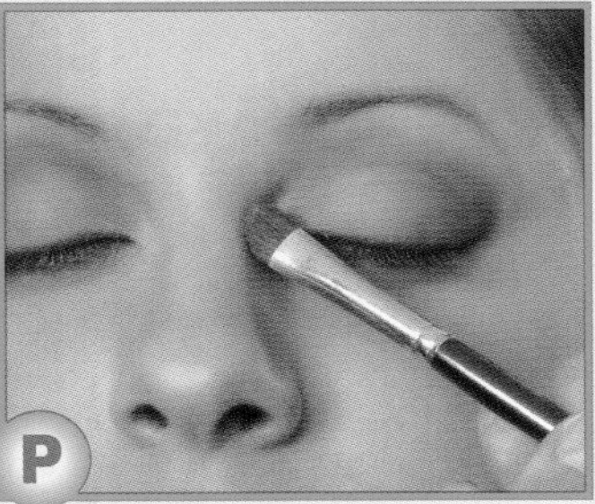
P
Use a medium eye color on inner portion of eyelid to blend all other colors.

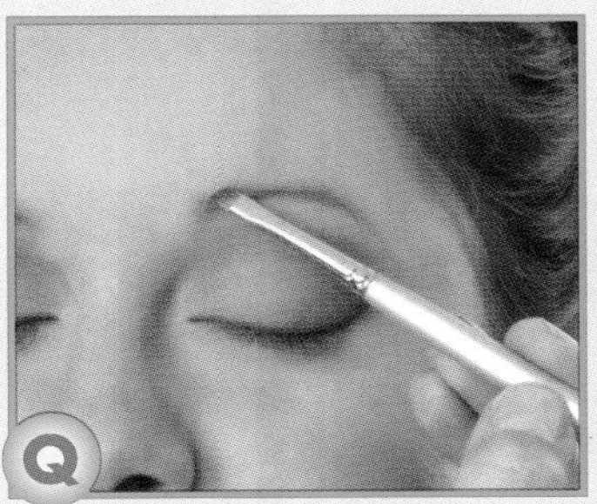
Q
Apply eyebrow color to balance natural color.

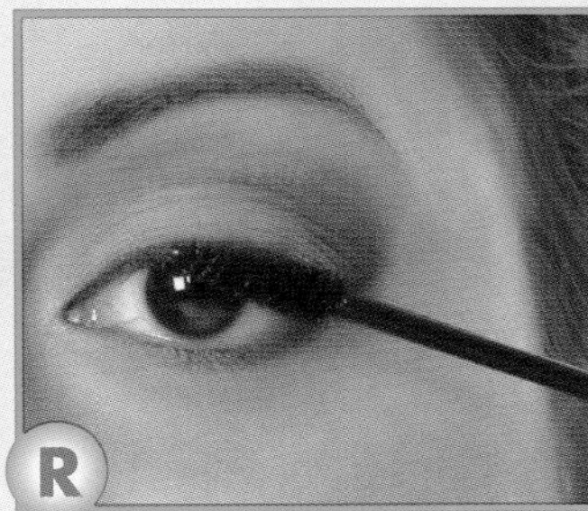
R
Apply mascara to upper and lower lashes using a disposable wand.

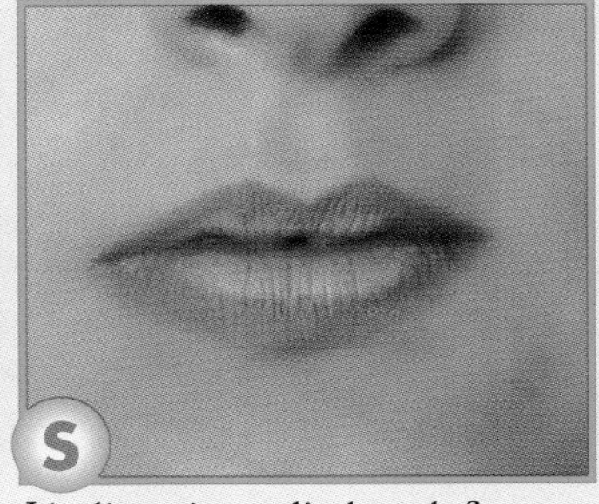
S
Lip liner is applied to define the shape of the lips.

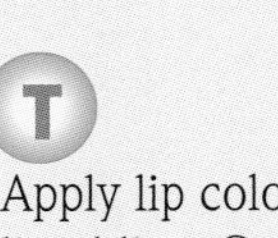
T
Apply lip color inside the lined lips. Completed corrective makeup for close-set eyes.

15

**EVALUATION** ______________________

______ **GRADE** ______ STUDENT'S NAME ______ ID#

CLIC INTERNATIONAL™

## INTERMEDIATE LAB PROJECT

# Corrective Makeup to Cover Blemishes

Before

After

### OBJECTIVE

To learn how to create the illusion of blemish-free skin by applying corrective makeup.

## TOOLS & MATERIALS

- Robe and/or cape
- Cloth and disposable towels
- Headband or plastic/cloth cap
- Cleanser
- Toner
- Moisturizer
- Disinfectant
- Client record card/file
- Cosmetic sponges
- Applicators
- Pencil sharpener
- Eyelash curler
- Makeup brushes
- Foundation
- Concealer
- Powder
- Eye colors
- Eyeliner
- Eyebrow colors
- Mascara
- Cheek color
- Lip color and liner

## PROCEDURE

***"The client consultation is an important part of your professional service. Be sure to complete this step prior to each client service you provide. Your successful retail sales and customer satisfaction rates depend upon it!"***

1. Cosmetologist sanitizes hands and work station.
2. Set out service tools and materials.
3. Drape the client in preparation for service.
4. Cleanse, tone and moisturize face.
5. Perform skin analysis.
6. Follow procedure as shown.
7. Follow standard cleanup procedure.
8. Document client record card/file.

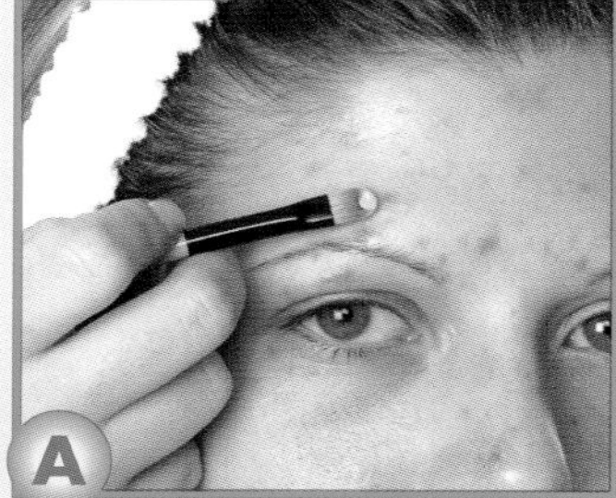

**A** Apply concealer over each blemish using brush. Select a shade lighter than the foundation for concealer color.

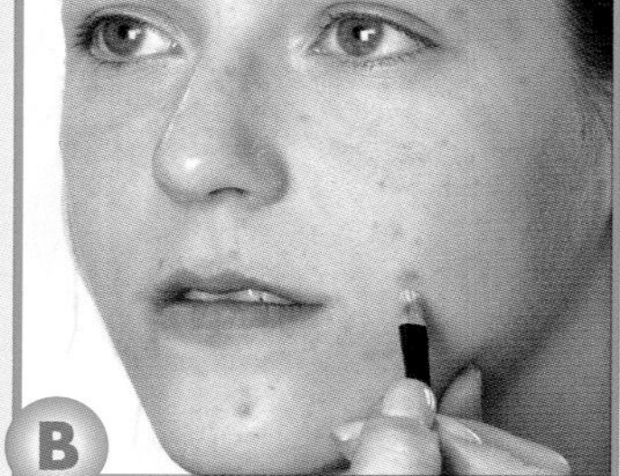

**B** Continue applying concealer, lightly blending over the skin.

**C** Dispense the selected color of foundation on a cosmetic sponge.

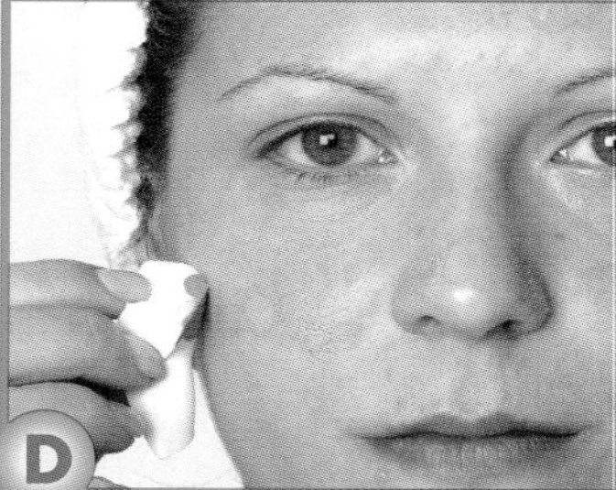

**D** Spread foundation in a down and outward motion; lightly blending over concealed areas.

**E** Apply powder using brush to set foundation and concealer.

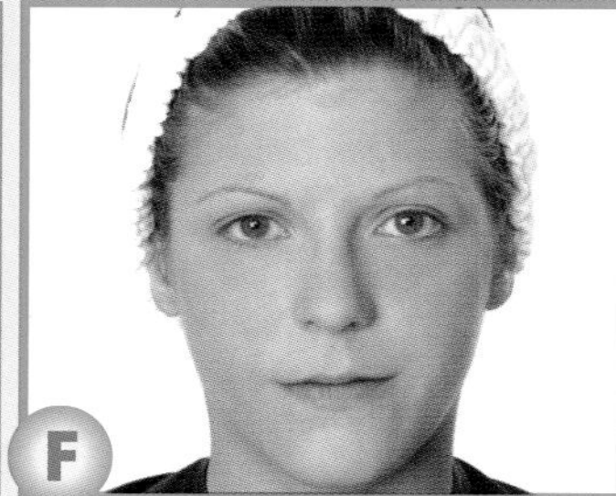

**F** Completed skin base with concealer and foundation.

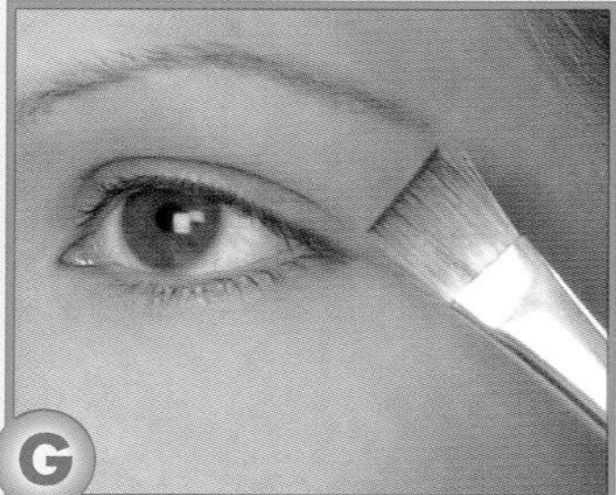

**G** Apply a light shade of eye color directly below the eyebrow.

**H** Use a color matching the natural eyebrow color and apply with brush to create a natural eyebrow balance.

## Corrective Makeup to Cover Blemishes

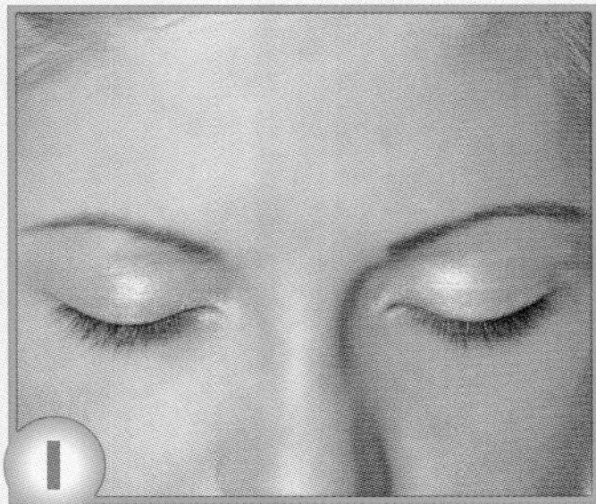
I — Apply a light color over entire lid of both eyes.

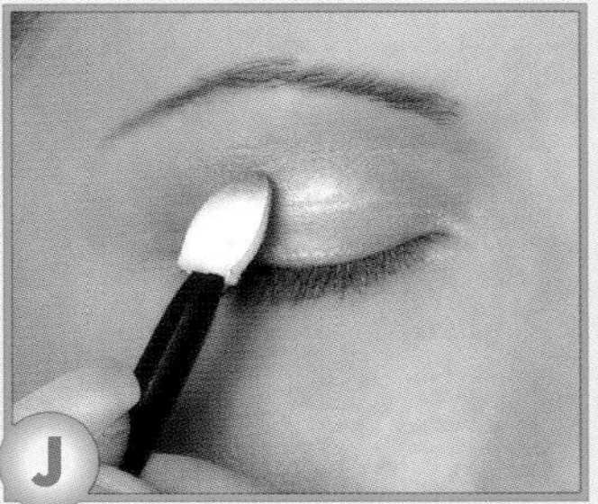
J — Apply a dark color along the crease area of eyelid.

K — Using a medium to light color, apply to inner corner of eyelid to blend colors.

L — Using a brush, apply a dark eye color to line the upper eyelid along the lashes. The line should be soft and subtle.

M — Use an eyeliner pencil to line the bottom lid along lashes.

N — Apply mascara to top and bottom lashes using disposable brush. **Repeat on opposite eye.**

O — Completed eyes with color.

P — Apply cheek color lightly over and below cheekbone.

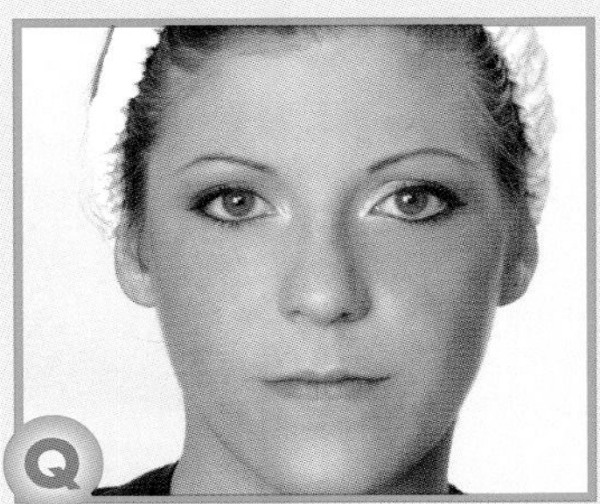
Q — Completed cheek color.

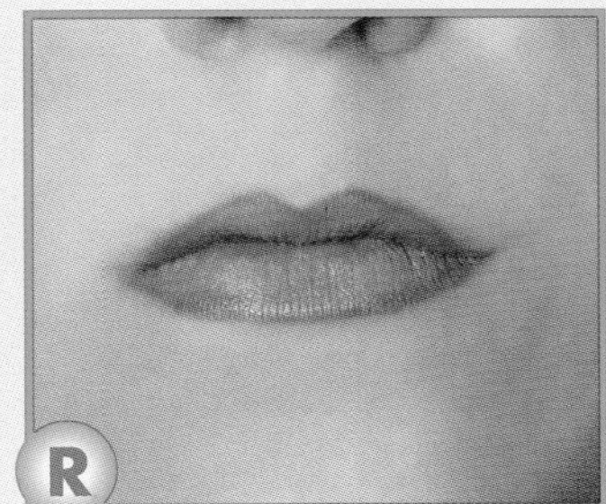
R — Apply lip liner using pencil or a lip brush with color.

S — Complete the lips by applying a matching color inside the lined lips.

T — Completed corrective makeup for covering blemishes.

"Refer client to a medical care professional if acne is especially severe."

15

**EVALUATION** ______________________________

______ GRADE ______ STUDENT'S NAME ______ ID#

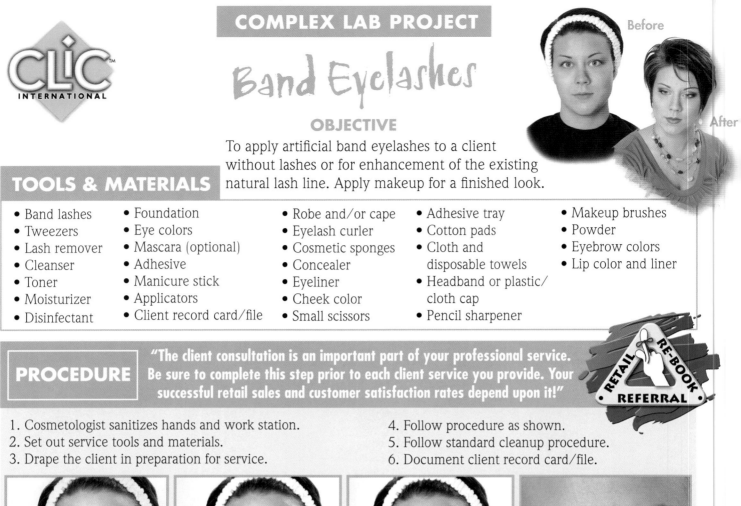

COMPLEX LAB PROJECT

CLiC INTERNATIONAL™

# Band Eyelashes

Before

After

## OBJECTIVE

To apply artificial band eyelashes to a client without lashes or for enhancement of the existing natural lash line. Apply makeup for a finished look.

## TOOLS & MATERIALS

- Band lashes
- Tweezers
- Lash remover
- Cleanser
- Toner
- Moisturizer
- Disinfectant
- Foundation
- Eye colors
- Mascara (optional)
- Adhesive
- Manicure stick
- Applicators
- Client record card/file
- Robe and/or cape
- Eyelash curler
- Cosmetic sponges
- Concealer
- Eyeliner
- Cheek color
- Small scissors
- Adhesive tray
- Cotton pads
- Cloth and disposable towels
- Headband or plastic/cloth cap
- Pencil sharpener
- Makeup brushes
- Powder
- Eyebrow colors
- Lip color and liner

## PROCEDURE

**"The client consultation is an important part of your professional service. Be sure to complete this step prior to each client service you provide. Your successful retail sales and customer satisfaction rates depend upon it!"**

RETAIL • RE-BOOK • REFERRAL

1. Cosmetologist sanitizes hands and work station.
2. Set out service tools and materials.
3. Drape the client in preparation for service.
4. Follow procedure as shown.
5. Follow standard cleanup procedure.
6. Document client record card/file.

A Gently cleanse the skin making sure to clean the eyelids.

B Apply toner to restore pH and close the pores.

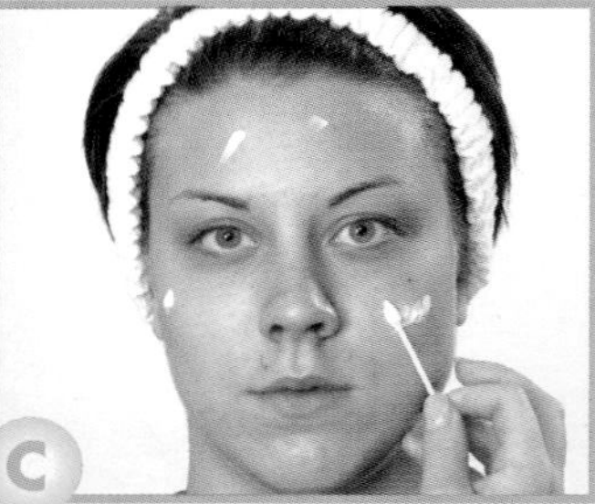

C Apply small amount of moisturizer over skin. **DO NOT** place on eyelids to ensure adhesion of false lashes.

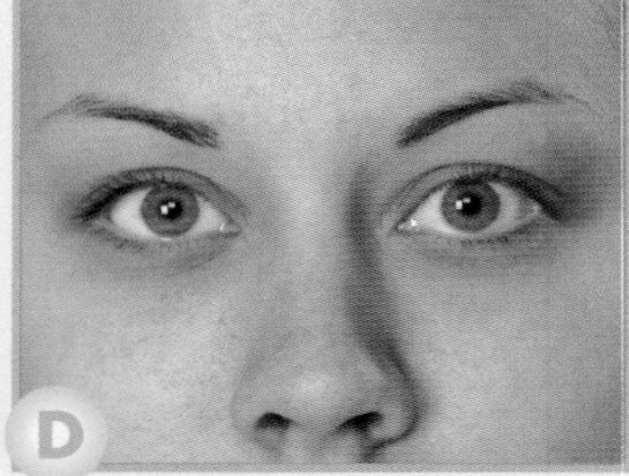

D Analyze skin and eyelashes to determine the band lashes to be used and if a custom fit is required.

15

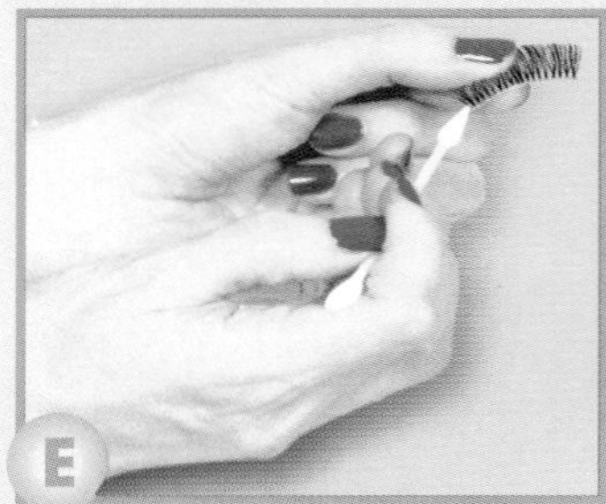

E Apply a small amount of extension adhesive to base of eyelashes using an applicator. **CAUTION:** Use minimal amount of adhesive to avoid dripping product on skin and/or eyes.

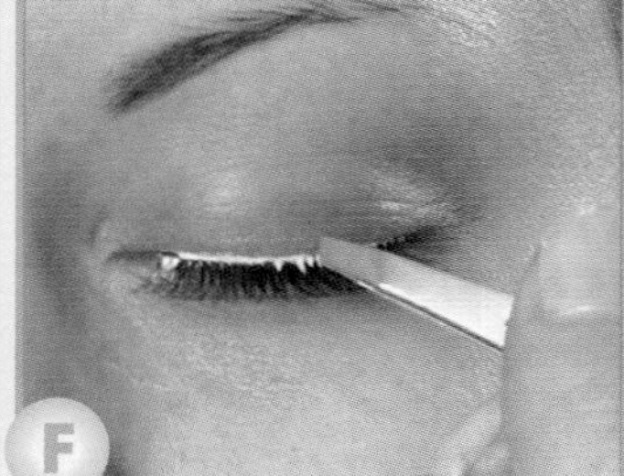

F Place artificial lashes on eyelid rim and lightly press lashes against the skin to hold in place for a few seconds to ensure proper bonding.

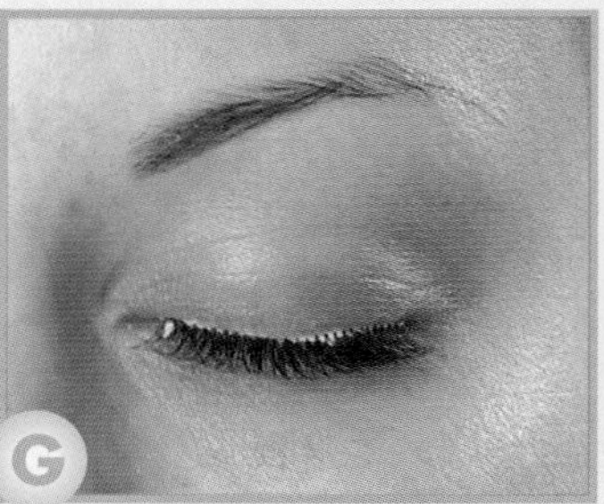

G Secured band lash, **repeat steps E and F on opposite eye.**

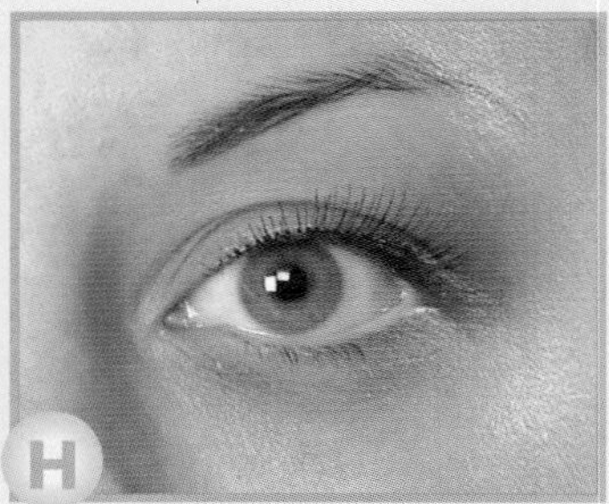

H Completed band eyelashes. Proceed with makeup application.

## Band Eyelashes

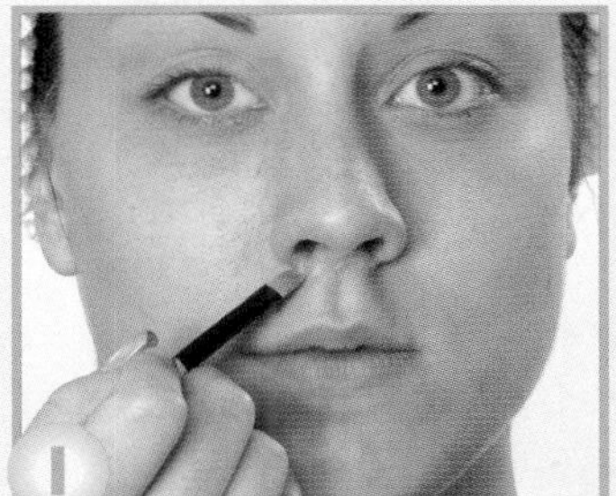
I
Apply concealer to any blemishes or darken areas of skin and lightly blend over skin.

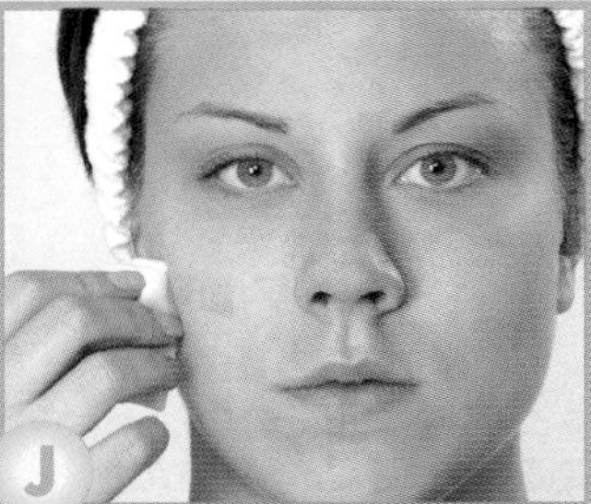
J
Apply foundation over entire facial area.

K
Use brush and apply a translucent or colored powder over skin to create a matte finish.

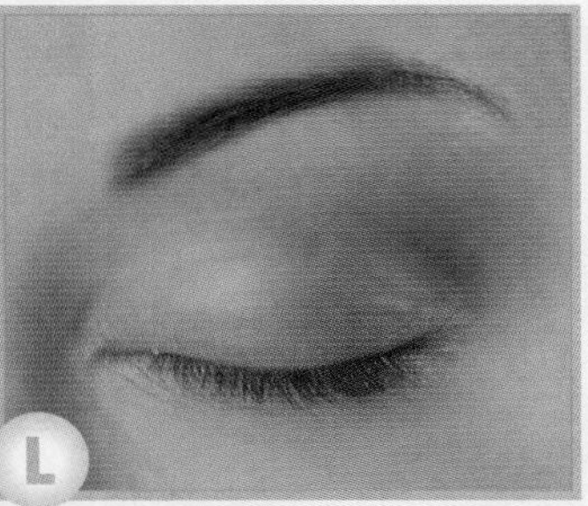
L
Apply a medium eye color over eyelid, in the crease and slightly above crease area. Apply eyebrow color for color balance.

M
Place a dark color in crease area and blend.

N
Place a light eye color on inner area of eyelid and apply eyeliner along top and bottom lash line.

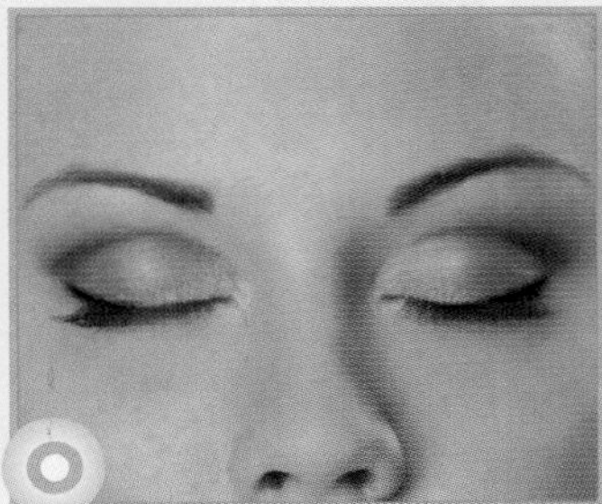
O
Completed color on eyes. **Optional:** Add mascara if needed.

P
Apply cheek color below cheekbone.

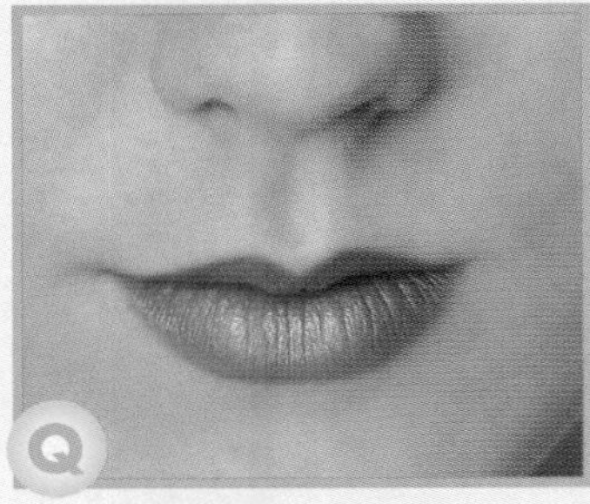
Q
Apply lip liner and lip color.

R
Completed band lashes with makeup application.

15

**EVALUATION** ______________________________

GRADE ______ STUDENT'S NAME ______ ID# ______

# COMPLEX LAB PROJECT

## Separate Flare Eyelashes

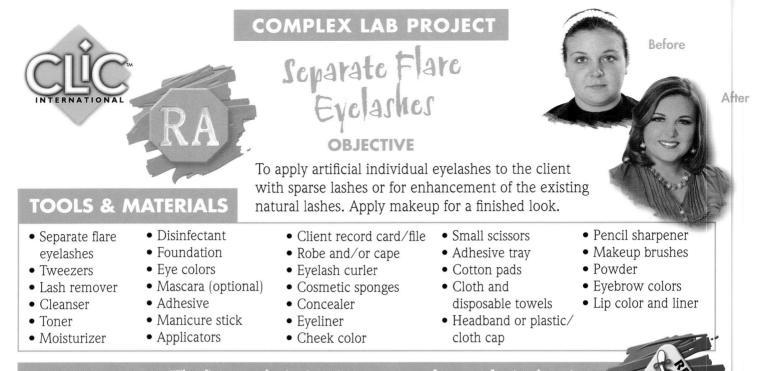

Before

After

### OBJECTIVE

To apply artificial individual eyelashes to the client with sparse lashes or for enhancement of the existing natural lashes. Apply makeup for a finished look.

### TOOLS & MATERIALS

- Separate flare eyelashes
- Tweezers
- Lash remover
- Cleanser
- Toner
- Moisturizer
- Disinfectant
- Foundation
- Eye colors
- Mascara (optional)
- Adhesive
- Manicure stick
- Applicators
- Client record card/file
- Robe and/or cape
- Eyelash curler
- Cosmetic sponges
- Concealer
- Eyeliner
- Cheek color
- Small scissors
- Adhesive tray
- Cotton pads
- Cloth and disposable towels
- Headband or plastic/cloth cap
- Pencil sharpener
- Makeup brushes
- Powder
- Eyebrow colors
- Lip color and liner

### PROCEDURE

"The client consultation is an important part of your professional service. Be sure to complete this step prior to each client service you provide. Your successful retail sales and customer satisfaction rates depend upon it!"

RETAIL • RE-BOOK • REFERRAL

1. Cosmetologist sanitizes hands and work station.
2. Set out service tools and materials.
3. Drape the client in preparation for service.
4. Follow procedure as shown.
5. Follow standard cleanup procedure.
6. Document client record card/file.

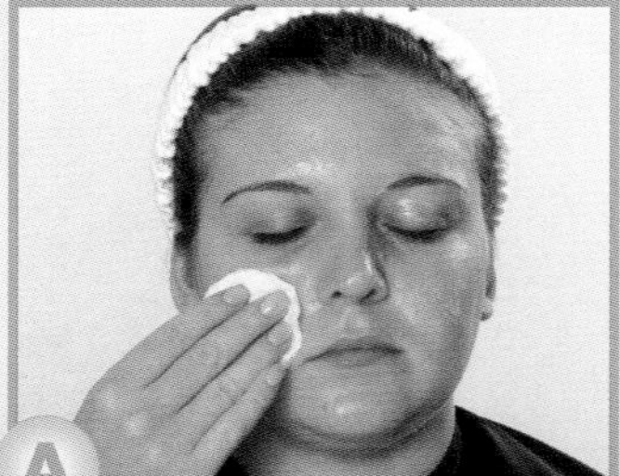

A Gently cleanse the skin making sure to clean the eyelids.

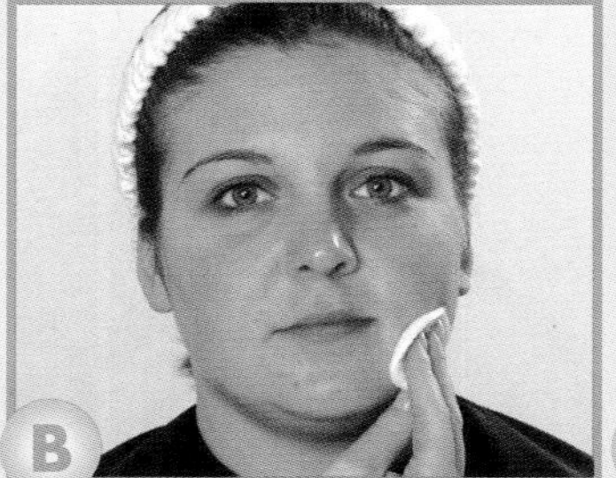

B Apply toner and a small amount of moisturizer. **DO NOT** use any oil-based product on or around eyelids.

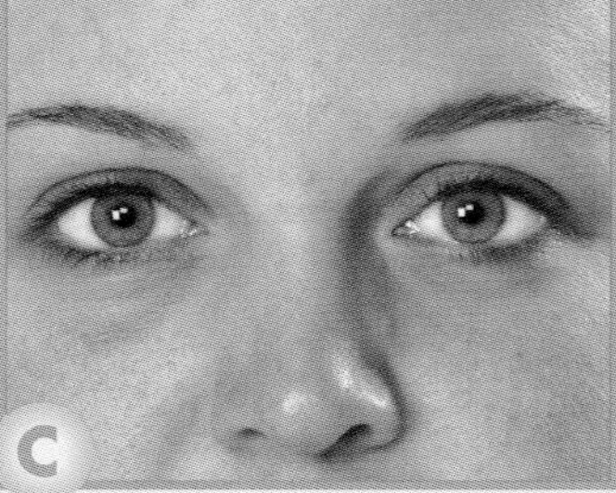

C Perform a skin and eyelash hair analysis to determine type of separate flare lashes and if custom fit is required.

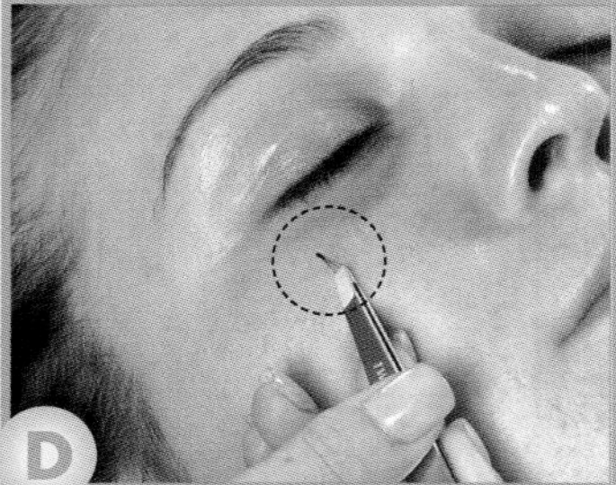

D Using a tweezers, select flare lash to be placed on natural lashes. The base of the lashes is swiped through the adhesive.

15

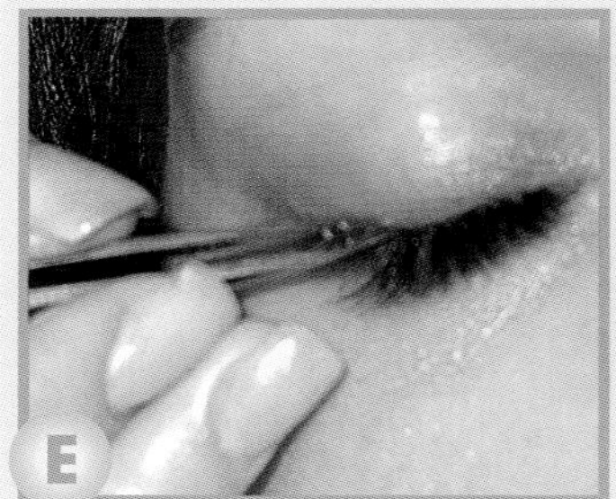

E Starting at center of eyelid, place flare lash on top of natural lashes. Artificial lash sits directly on the lash hair, **NOT** on skin.

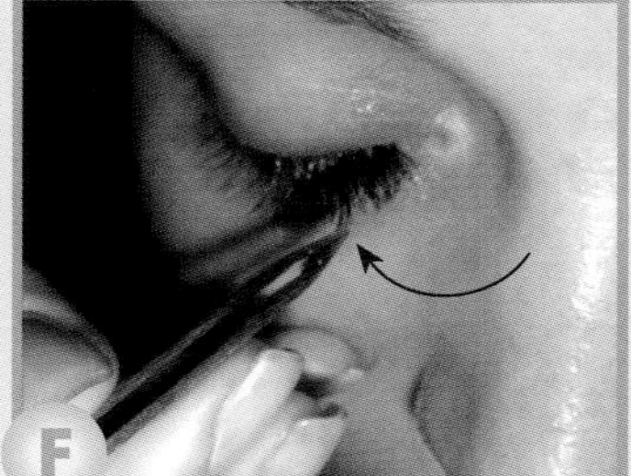

F Continue placing flare lashes on natural lashes, moving across to inner part of lash line and back to center moving to outer part of eyelid.

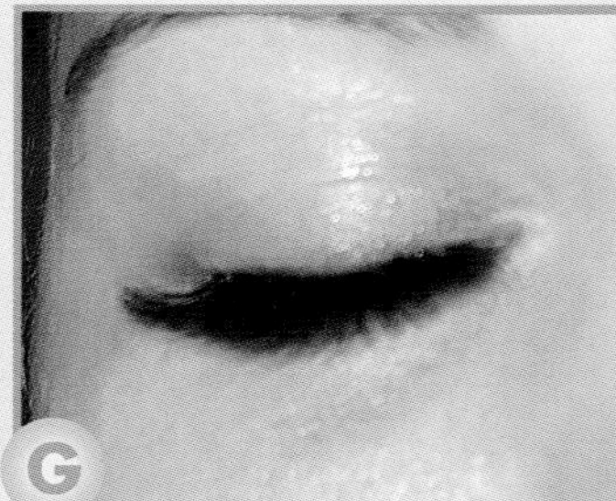

G Amount of flare lashes used depends on desired end result

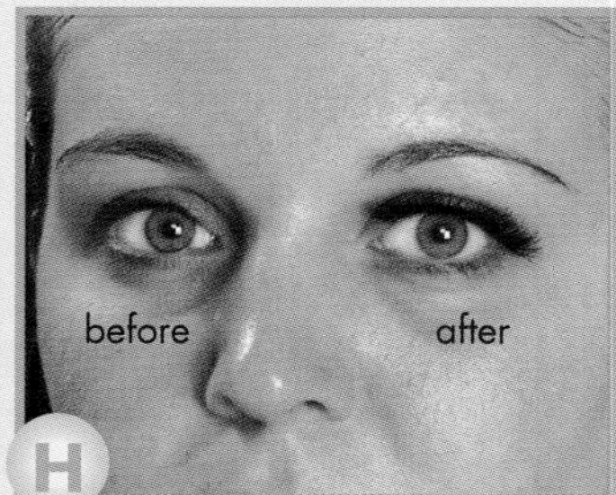

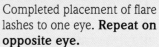

H Completed placement of flare lashes to one eye. **Repeat on opposite eye.**

## Separate Flare Eyelashes

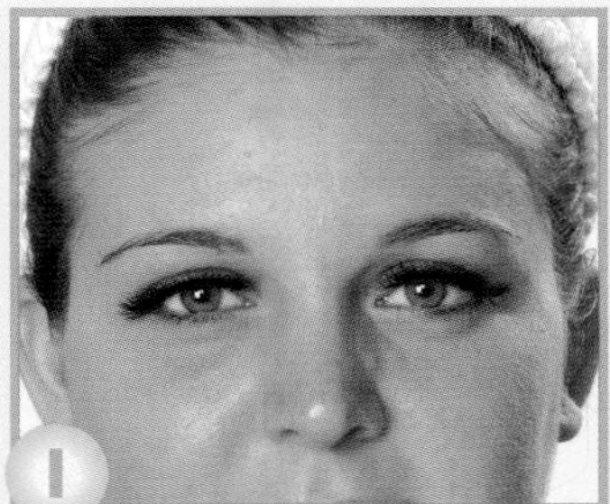

Completed flare lashes application. Proceed to makeup application.

Apply concealer and foundation over entire facial skin.

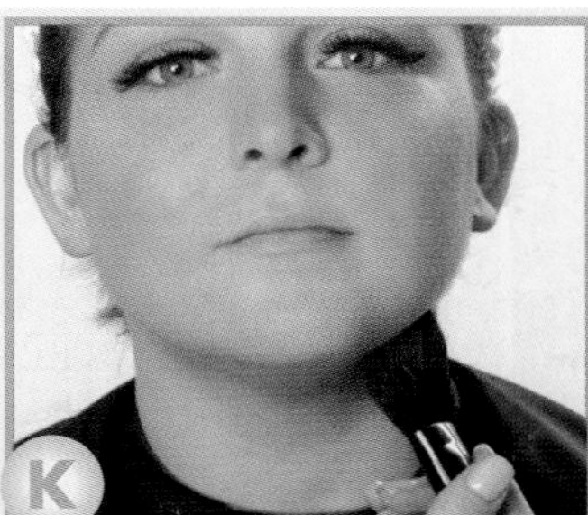

Using brush, apply powder over facial skin. Apply cheek color.

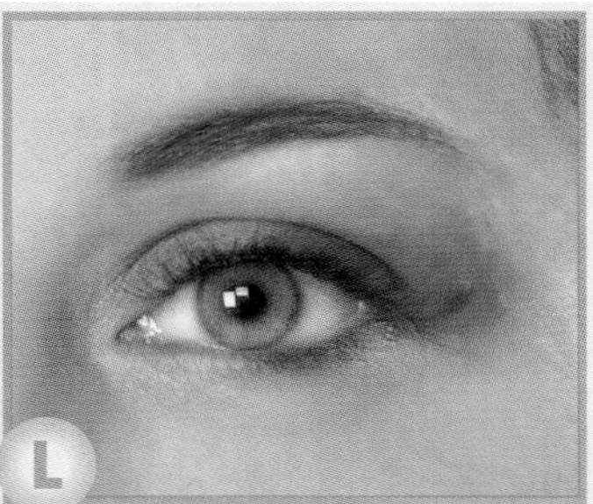

Create eyebrow design using color.

Apply medium eye color over the entire eyelids with a dark color in crease and light color directly below eyebrows.

Eyeliner is placed along bottom lash line **ONLY.** Mascara is generally not needed.

Line rim of lips with a color that matches the selected lip color.

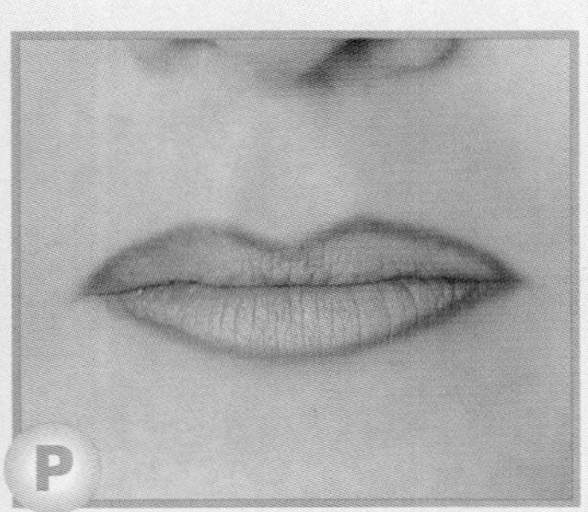

Completed lined lips.

Apply lip color within lip line.

Completed separate flare lashes with makeup application.

15

GRADE

STUDENT'S NAME

ID#

# Art of Makeup REVIEW QUESTIONS

## MULTIPLE CHOICE

1. Which tool is used to curl the eyelashes before applying mascara?
   A. applicator B. eyelash curler C. sharpener
2. What is used to sanitize the end of eye and lip liner pencils?
   A. sharpener B. cosmetic sponge C. disinfectant
3. Which principle of color combines two primary colors?
   A. primary B. secondary C. tertiary
4. Which eyelash extension design appears the most natural-looking?
   A. band/strip B. individual C. separate flares
5. Which set of eyes requires no corrective makeup?
   A. wide-set B. close-set C. balance-set
6. The three dimensions of color are hue, value and?
   A. complementary B. intensity C. temperature
7. What makeup cosmetic provides a healthy glow to the skin?
   A. powder B. eyeliner C. cheek color
8. The pigments used in foundation are produced from coloring agents referred to as?
   A. lakes B. minerals C. melanin
9. In what era was a high forehead considered beautiful?
   A. Elizabethan B. 20th Century C. Industrial Revolution
10. What is used to absorb excess oil from the skin?
    A. cosmetic sponges B. blotting papers C. brushes
11. Which face shape requires shadowing at corners of forehead and jawline to create a balanced face shape?
    A. oval B. round C. square
12. Individual lashes or separate flares are attached to the?
    A. eyebrow hair B. skin C. natural lashes
13. To create proportionate lips for someone with small lips, where is the lip line drawn?
    A. outside the natural lip line B. inside the natural lip line C. along the natural lip line
14. Which type of foundation provides exceptional coverage?
    A. liquid B. cream C. cake
15. What makeup cosmetic enhances natural eyelashes?
    A. mascara B. foundation C. lip color
16. Which face shape requires shadowing along perimeter of cheek bones to create a balanced face shape?
    A. triangle B. diamond C. rectangle
17. Which feature of the face is considered the most expressive?
    A. eyes B. lips C. nose
18. Which color is considered to have a cool temperature?
    A. blue B. yellow C. orange
19. Which tool is considered disposable and must be discarded after use?
    A. scissors B. eyelash curler C. mascara wands
20. Back in the 16th and 17th centuries, the wealthy would dilate their pupils by using belladonna, which is?
    A. henna B. an essential oil C. a poisonous herb

STUDENT'S NAME DATE GRADE

corrugations

eponychium

hangnail

matrix

onychomycosis

onyx

pterygium

# Nails

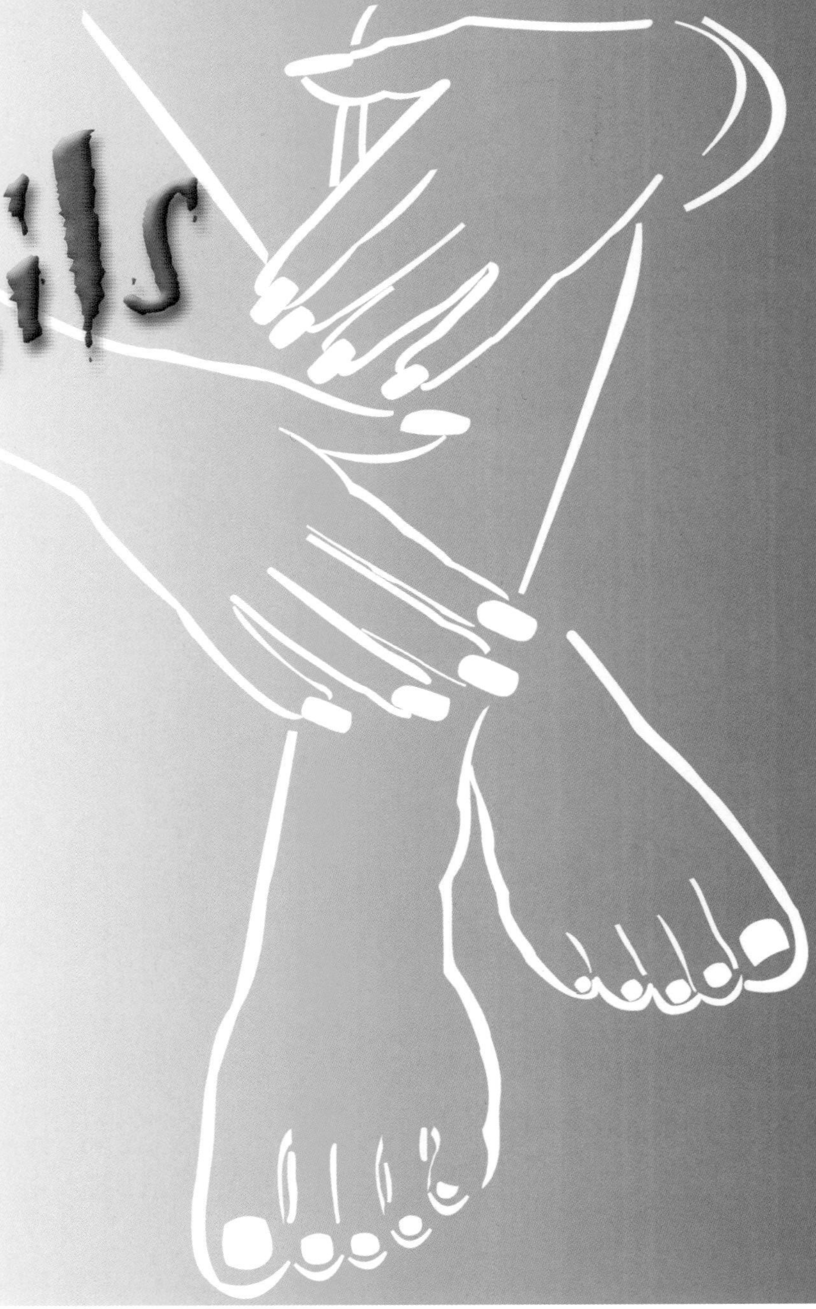

# NAILS

16

# Terminology . . .

**The term list** *comprises of just a few of the words to know when learning about the structure of the nails. There are many other important nail terms to know in order to educate you in providing the best service for your clients.*

**Allergies** occur when the immune system **overreacts** to normally harmless substances.

1

**Athlete's foot**
is called **Tinea pedis**, a fungal infection between the toes, which can spread to the toenails.

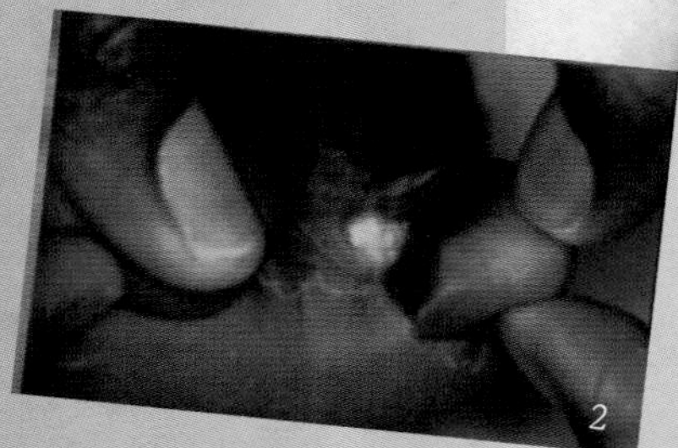
2

**Cuticle** is the small portion of **epidermis** or skin extending over and resting upon the base of the nail plate.

**Free Edge** is the part of the nail plate not attached to the skin, and can extend beyond the fingertip.

**Integumentary System** is a branch of anatomy that deals with the skin and its associated structures including the nails, hair, sweat and oil glands.

# Terminology ...

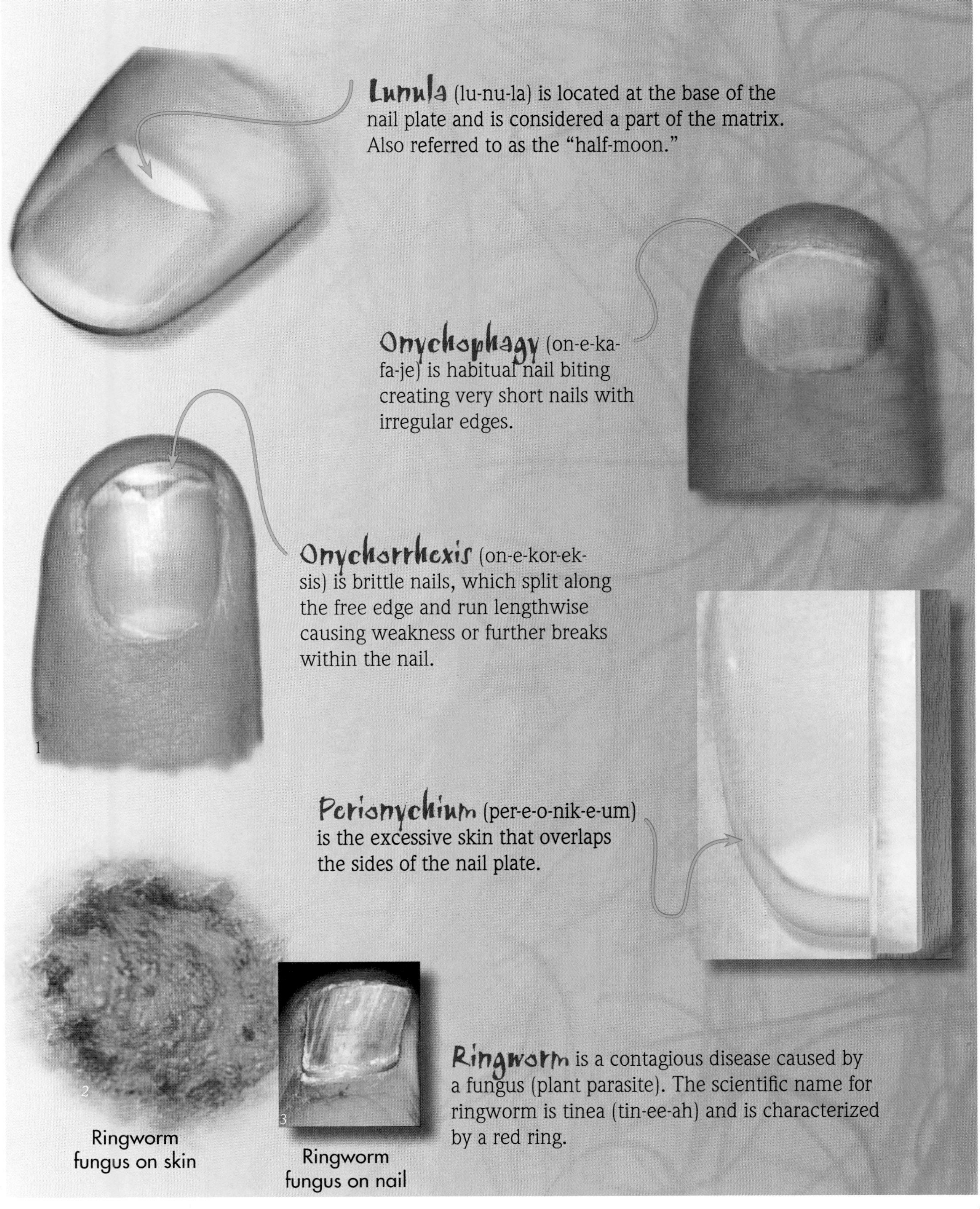

**Lunula** (lu-nu-la) is located at the base of the nail plate and is considered a part of the matrix. Also referred to as the "half-moon."

**Onychophagy** (on-e-ka-fa-je) is habitual nail biting creating very short nails with irregular edges.

**Onychorrhexis** (on-e-kor-ek-sis) is brittle nails, which split along the free edge and run lengthwise causing weakness or further breaks within the nail.

**Perionychium** (per-e-o-nik-e-um) is the excessive skin that overlaps the sides of the nail plate.

**Ringworm** is a contagious disease caused by a fungus (plant parasite). The scientific name for ringworm is tinea (tin-ee-ah) and is characterized by a red ring.

Ringworm fungus on skin

Ringworm fungus on nail

# Anatomy of the Nail . . .

***Anatomy** is the scientific study of the shape and structure of the human body and its parts. Artists, such as **Leonardo da Vinci**, have long considered the anatomy of the human body something to be respected and meticulously depicted in their compositions. These artists worked to understand as much about anatomy as possible, in order to paint the most accurate and detailed pictures of their subjects. As your understanding of the anatomy of the nail, hand and foot increases, your artistry will expand and permit you to impeccably service and care for the clients' nails.*

A **healthy nail** is translucent, slightly pink, smooth, curved, is without ridges or wavy lines, and is free from disease.

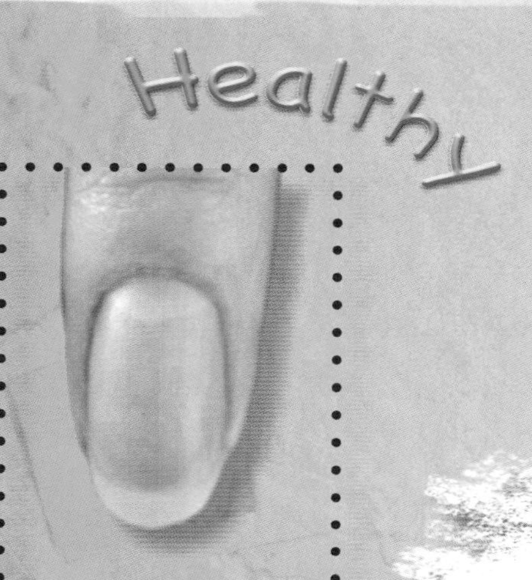


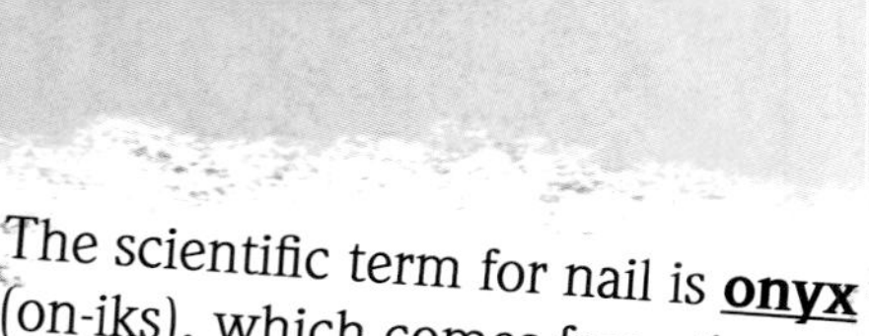


The scientific term for nail is **onyx** (on-iks), which comes from the Greek word **onyx**, meaning **nail**.

## Some Interesting Facts About the Nails

- The nails, like the hair, are composed of a fibrous protein called hard **keratin**, and become an outgrowth or appendage of the skin.
- Nails are porous and contain 15 to 30 percent water.
- It takes four to six months for a new fingernail to grow.
- The average adult growth rate is 1/10 inch (0.254 cm) per month.
- Nails tend to grow faster in warm climates and on the middle finger.
- Fingernails grow faster than toenails.
- It takes approximately 12 to 18 months to replace a toenail.
- Children's nails grow faster than adults' nails, with nail growth peaking from ages 10 to 14.

"A healthy Nail is a sign of a healthy body!"

# Anatomy of the Nail ...

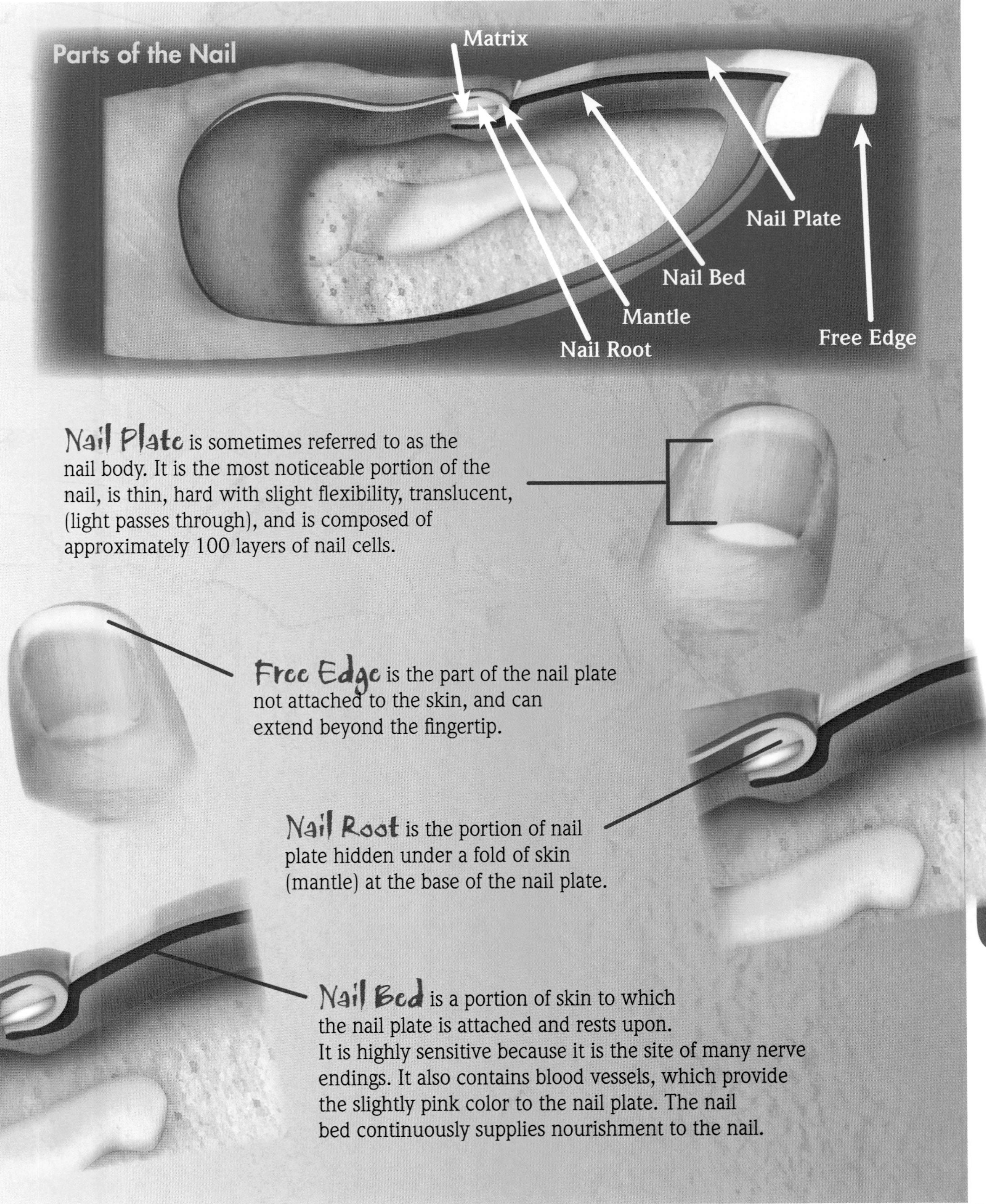


**Nail Plate** is sometimes referred to as the nail body. It is the most noticeable portion of the nail, is thin, hard with slight flexibility, translucent, (light passes through), and is composed of approximately 100 layers of nail cells.

**Free Edge** is the part of the nail plate not attached to the skin, and can extend beyond the fingertip.

**Nail Root** is the portion of nail plate hidden under a fold of skin (mantle) at the base of the nail plate.

**Nail Bed** is a portion of skin to which the nail plate is attached and rests upon. It is highly sensitive because it is the site of many nerve endings. It also contains blood vessels, which provide the slightly pink color to the nail plate. The nail bed continuously supplies nourishment to the nail.

# Anatomy of the Nail ...

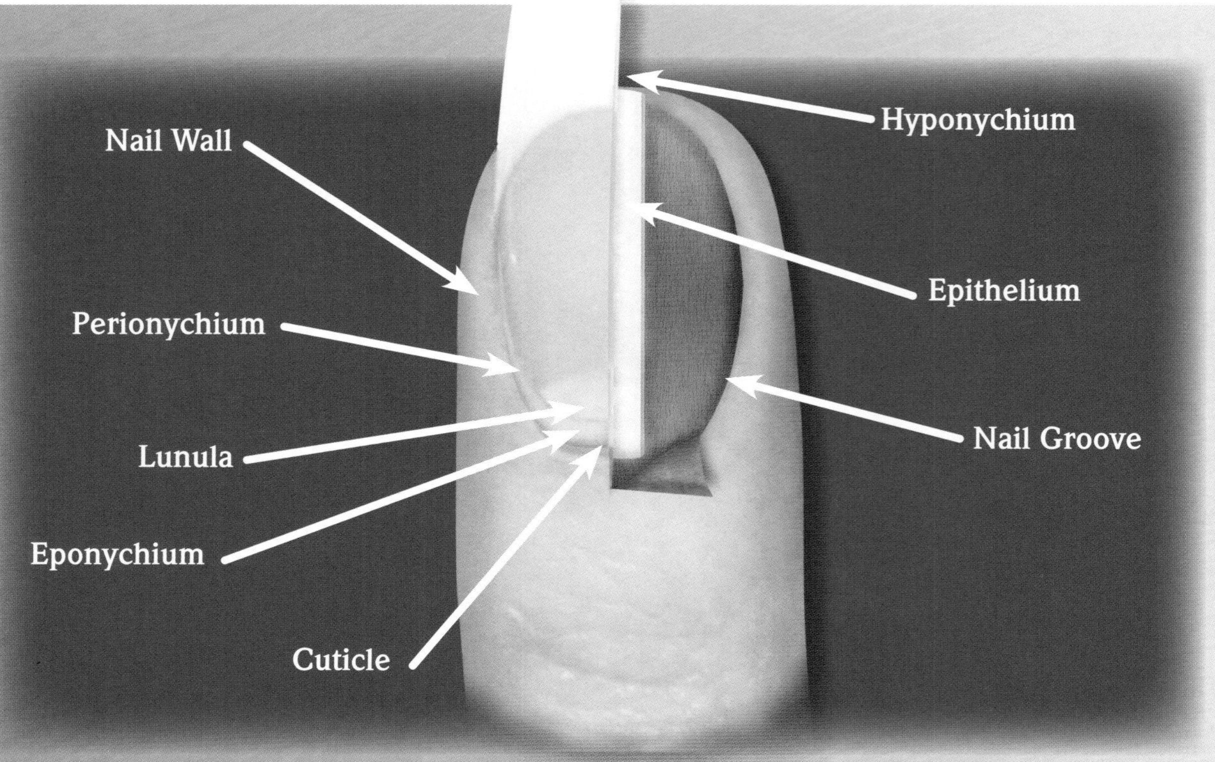

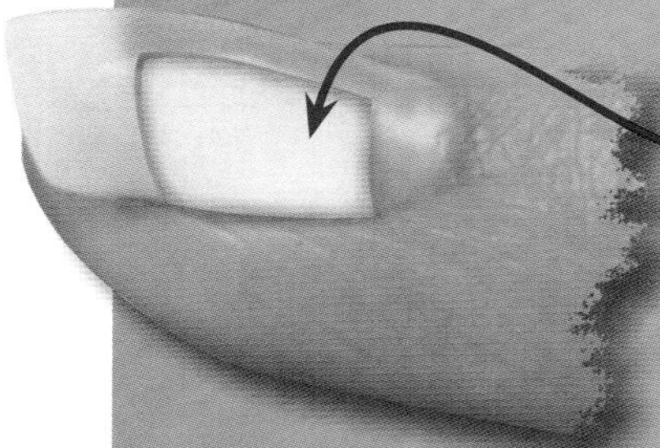

Nail Wall
Perionychium
Lunula
Eponychium
Cuticle
Hyponychium
Epithelium
Nail Groove

**Epithelium** (ep-i-the-le-um) is a thin layer of skin cells between the nail bed and the nail plate.

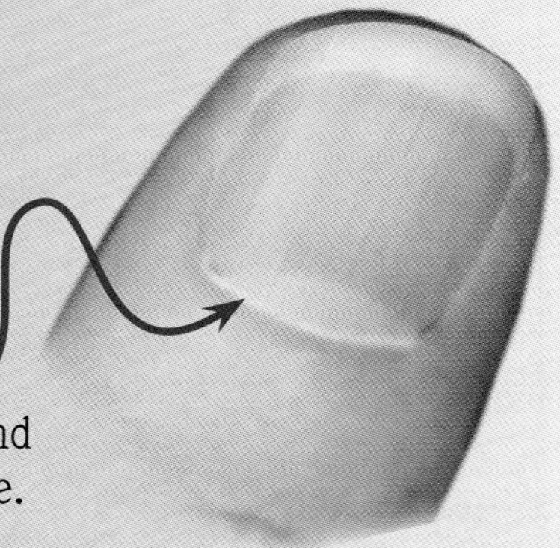

**Cuticle** is the small portion of **epidermis** or skin extending over and resting upon the base of the nail plate.

16

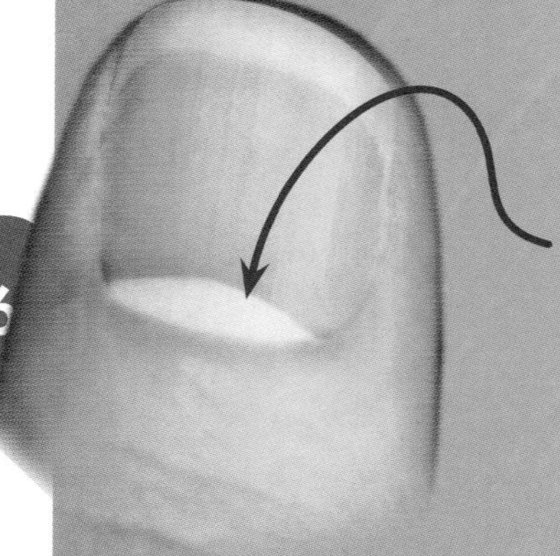

**Lunula** (lu-nu-la) is located at the base of the nail plate and is considered a part of the matrix. Also referred to as the "half-moon," the lunula is sometimes said to be the reflection of the matrix.

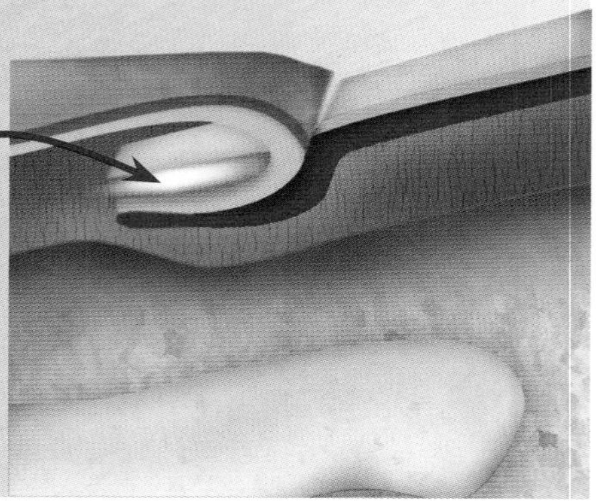

**Matrix** is the part of the nail bed that extends below the nail root and helps to produce the nail. It is made of light blue to white specialized cells. The size and shape of the matrix determines the thickness and shape of the natural nail. Ligaments hold the matrix and the nail bed onto the underlying bone.

# Anatomy of the Nail . . .

**Nail Walls** are skin folds beside the nail grooves.

**Nail Grooves** are tracks on each side of the nail plate along which the nail moves as it is growing.

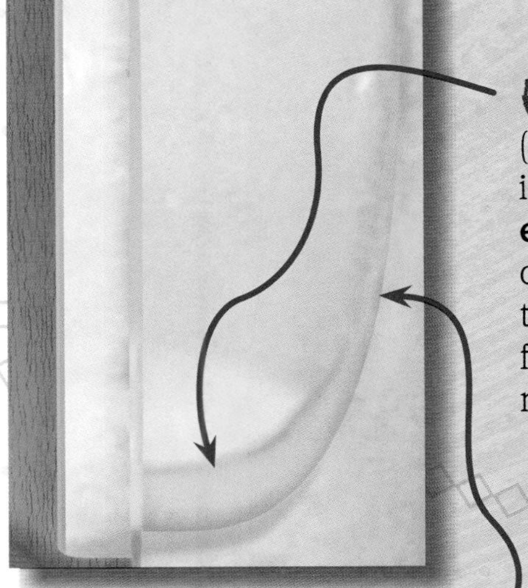

**Eponychium** (ep-o-nik-e-um) is **additional or excess** cuticle that overlaps the base of the nail and extends further up onto the nail plate.

**NOTE:** The eponychium, perionychium and hyponychium act as watertight seals. These seals provide a protective barrier on the nail plate to prevent the entrance of bacteria and dirt. Any damage to these seals could lead to infections, disorders or diseases.

**Perionychium** (per-e-o-nik-e-um) is cuticle or skin that overlaps the sides of the nail plate along the nail walls.

"When you study the nails, you are actually learning about the integumentary system which deals with the skin and its associated structures including the nails, hair, sweat and oil glands."

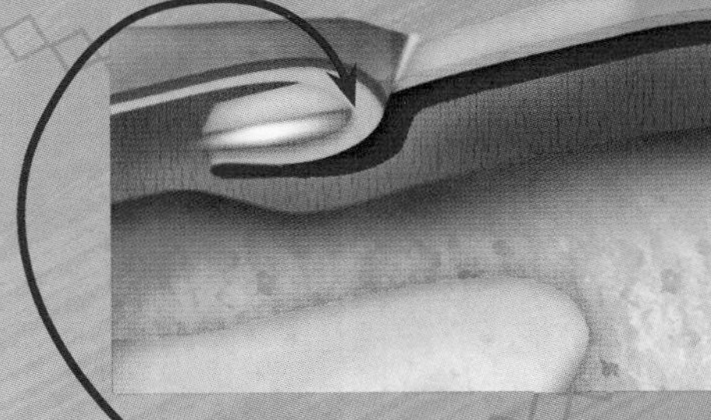

**Mantle** is a pocket-like fold of skin that holds the root and the matrix.

**Hyponychium** (hi-po-nik-e-um) is a layer of skin cells (epithelium) growing on top of the fingertips and remains attached to the underside of the free edge.

# Discoloration of the Nail . . .

*Nails are referred to as tiny mirrors of the body's health. Shiny, smooth and pink-toned nails reflect optimum health. Discoloration or pigmentation changes of the nail can indicate infection or serious medical problems and may need immediate attention.*

RA

The following chart indicates color changes possibly seen on the nail plate and the condition the color might determine whether an infection, disorder or disease is present. The cosmetologist needs to be aware of these symptoms and be able to alert customers to possible health problems.

| NAIL COLOR | INDICATES |
|---|---|
| 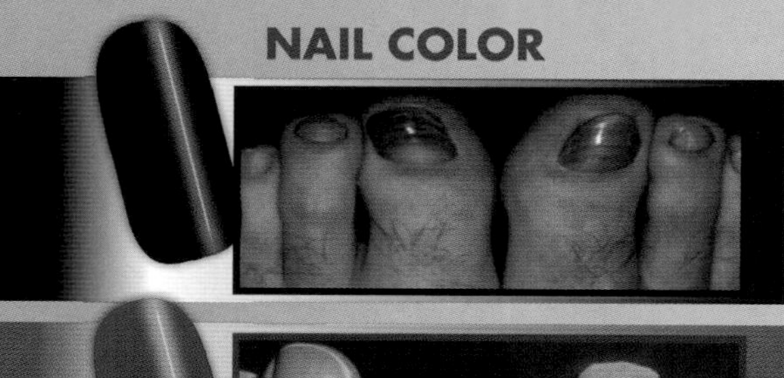 | • molds/mildew<br>• injury or bruising (bleeding under the nail) heart problems<br>• shoe pressure (runner's toe) |
| 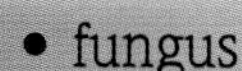 | • fungus<br>• nicotine stains<br>• injury to nail matrix<br>• certain oral medications |
|  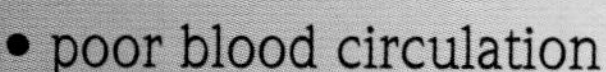 | • poor blood circulation<br>• heart condition<br>• injury or bruising (bleeding under the nail) |
| | • bacterial infection/**pseudomonas** (soo-do-monas) **aeruginosa**, found in soil and water, contaminates open wounds |
| 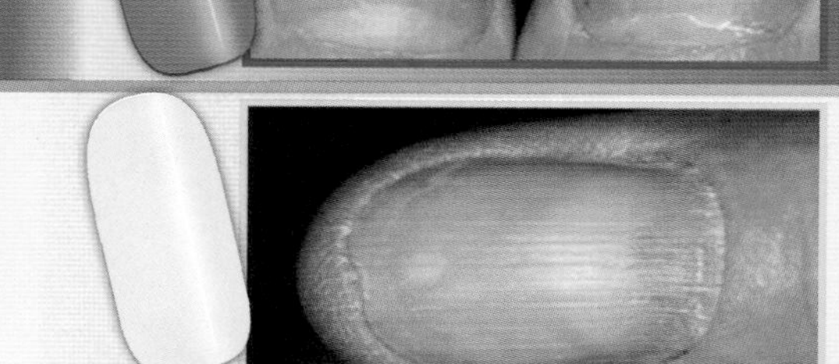 | • nicotine stains<br>• polish stains<br>• bacterial or fungal infection<br>• pus underneath nail plate |
| (whole or spots) 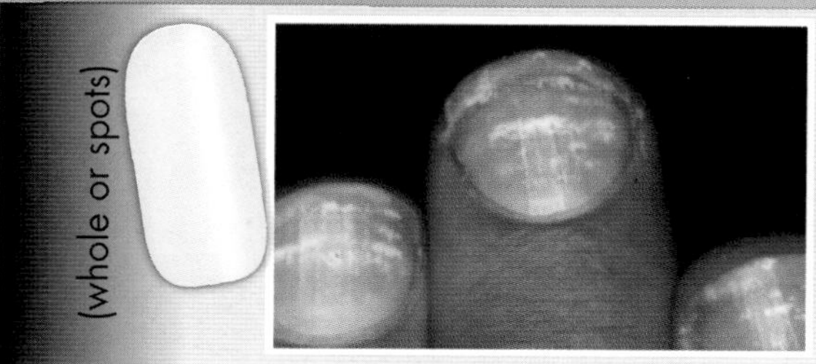 | • nail separation<br>• minor injury<br>• recovery from serious illness<br>• hormonal imbalances<br>• vitamin deficiency |

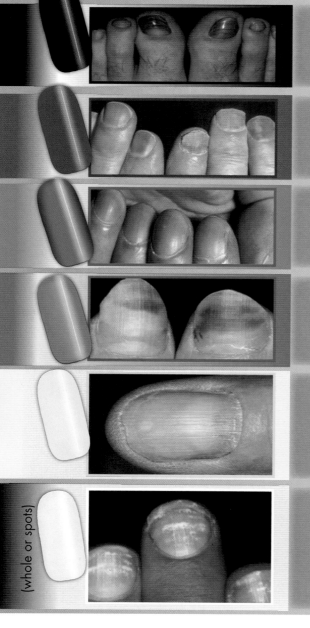

16

# Disorders of the Nail ...

***A nail disorder** can be caused by an injury, health condition or heredity. A cosmetologist must be able to recognize signs and symptoms of disorders in order to assist the client in recovery. The client might need to be referred to a medical care professional depending on the severity of the disorder. If there is no swelling, inflammation, broken skin or infection, then the cosmetologist may proceed with the nail service.*

**The following charts will indicate the disorder by symptom and sight:**

**Look for this medical symbol when medical attention is required.**

### BRUISED NAIL

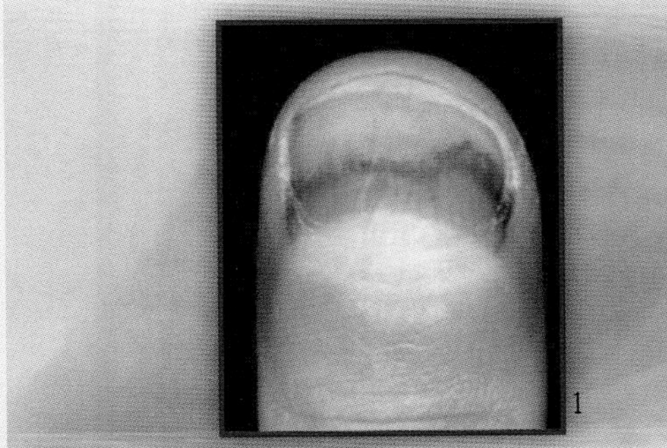

**SIGN/SYMPTOM**

blood that clots under the nail plate

**CAUSE**

injury to nail bed

**ACTION**

proceed with service, using minimal pressure over bruised area

### WART

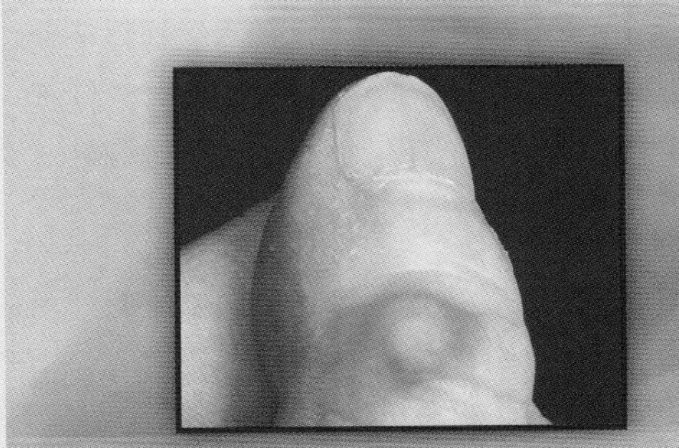

**SIGN/SYMPTOM**

a small, hard flesh-colored or red lump under or beside the nail

**CAUSE**

Human Papilloma Virus (HPV), infection in epidermal layer of skin

**ACTION**

Do not service client, recommend client to a medical care professional, HPV is considered contagious

# Disorders of the Nail . . .

## HANGNAIL or Agnail

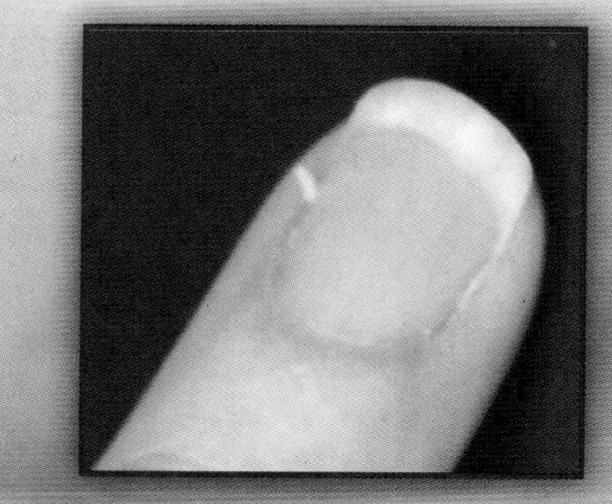

**SIGN/SYMPTOM**
a small piece of skin that has split from the cuticle

**CAUSE**
improper cuticle cutting, job related, skin dryness

**ACTION**
trim off with cuticle nippers, soften skin before cutting cuticle

## FURROWS or CORRUGATIONS

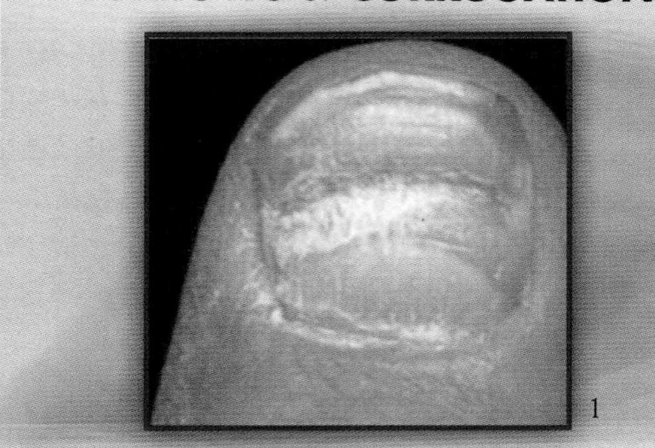
1

**SIGN/SYMPTOM**
long ridges that run horizontally or lengthwise across the nail, uneven growth

**CAUSE**
aggressive cuticle pushing, matrix injury, excessive use of cuticle and polish removers

**ACTION**
a nail service can be provided using a buffer and ridge filler, gently push around cuticle, but do not use a metal pusher

## EGGSHELL

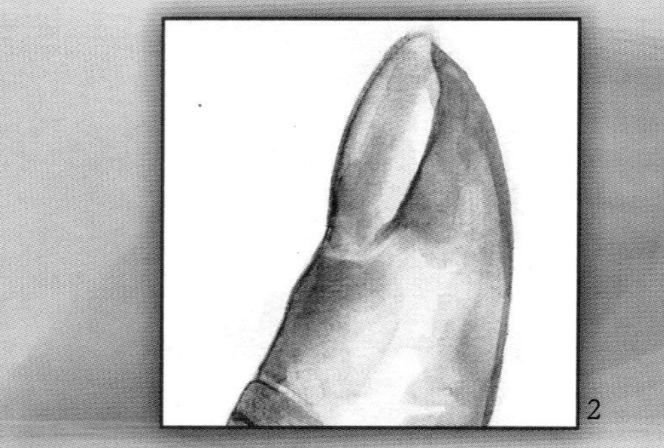
2

**SIGN/SYMPTOM**
thin, white and flexible nails, blending and conforming over fingertip

**CAUSE**
improper diet, internal disease, certain medications, nervous disorders

**ACTION**
gentle filing and no metal pusher is used to push back cuticles in nail service

## KOILONYCHIA (koy-lo-nik-e-a) or SPOON NAIL

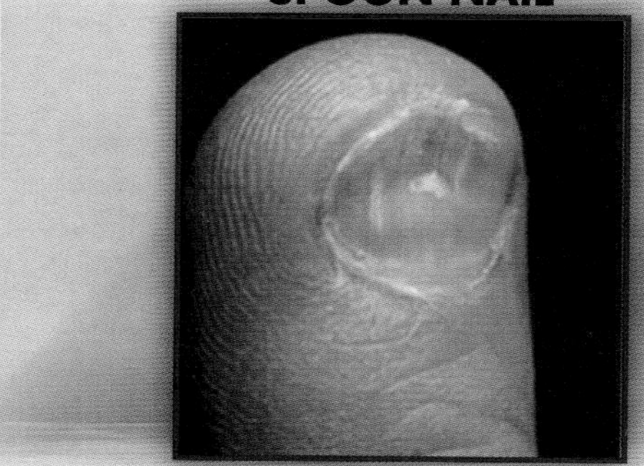
3

**SIGN/SYMPTOM**
nails that have a concave depression in the middle of the nail, nail plate edges turn up

**CAUSE**
genetic, illness, nerve disorder

**ACTION**
nail service provided using gentle filing and pressure, apply a nail strengthener, recommend client to a medical care professional

# Disorders of the Nail . . .

## MELANONYCHIA (mela-no-nik-e-a)

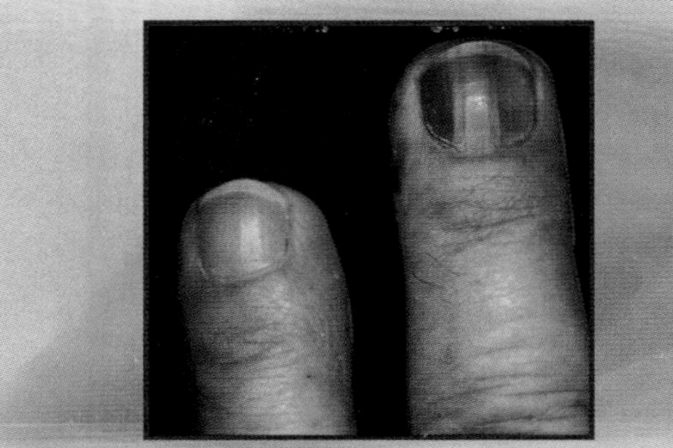

**SIGN/SYMPTOM**

dark pigment within the nail plate

**CAUSE**

excess melanin

**ACTION**

proceed with any nail service

## LEUKONYCHIA (loo-ko-nik-e-a)

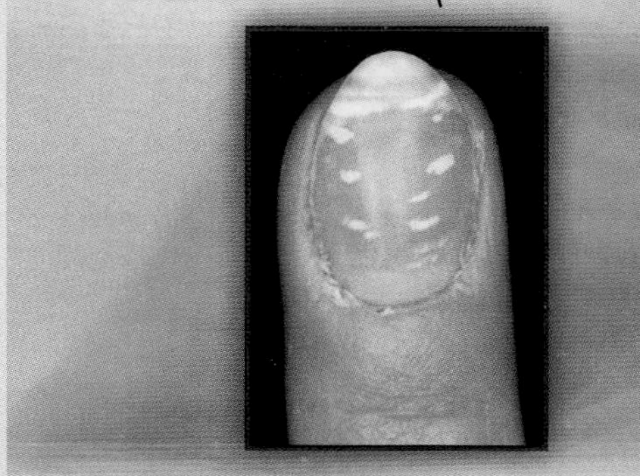

**SIGN/SYMPTOM**

white spots or streaks within the nail plate

**CAUSE**

nail injuries, hereditary

**ACTION**

proceed with any nail service

## PSORIASIS (so-ria-sis)

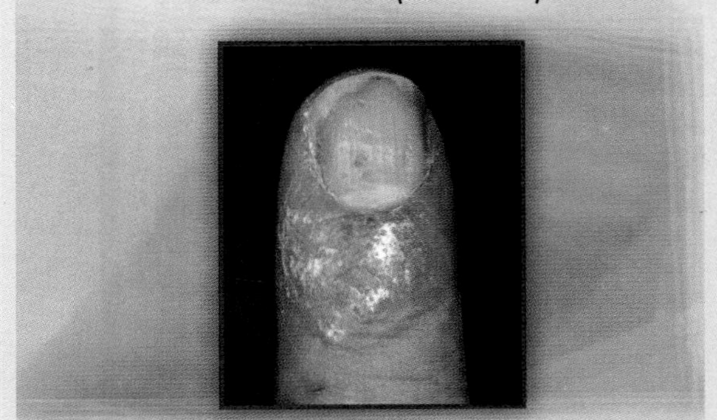

**SIGN/SYMPTOM**

nail is pitted or dimpled with brown spots

**CAUSE**

genetic

**ACTION**

recommend client to a medical care professional; not contagious

## PTERYGIUM (te-rij-e-um)

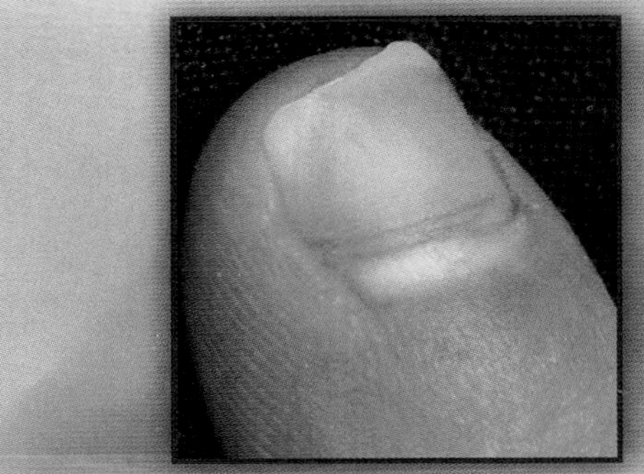

**SIGN/SYMPTOM**

excessive amount of cuticle moving forward onto the nail plate

**CAUSE**

skin disease, hereditary, trauma or injury to nail

**ACTION**

nail service provided with extra softening of skin to remove the excess cuticle; several softening treatments required

# Disorders of the Nail . . .

**ONYCHOPHAGY** (on-e-ka-fa-je) or **BITTEN NAILS**

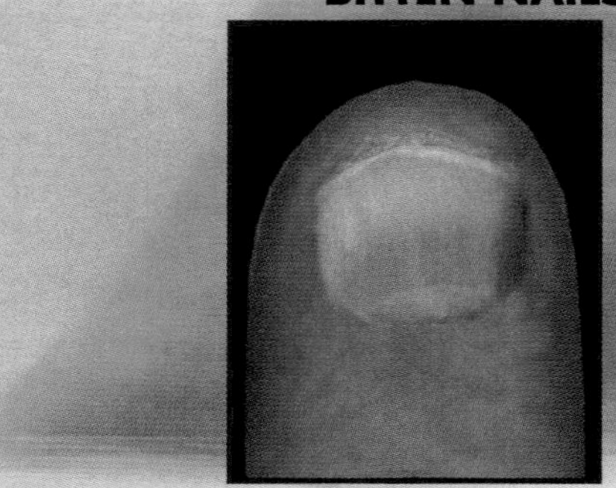

**SIGN/SYMPTOM**

very short nails with irregular edges

**CAUSE**

habitual nail biting

**ACTION**

reassure your client that the nails will grow back once they are no longer bitten. If no infection, nail service provided

**ONYCHOCRYPTOSIS** (on-e-ko-krip-tosis) or **INGROWN NAILS**

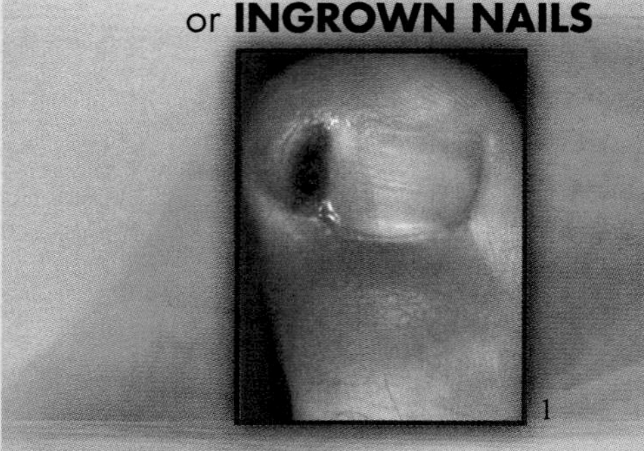

**SIGN/SYMPTOM**

nail is growing into the nail groove; inflammation can occur on one or both sides of the nail

**CAUSE**

improper filing and/or shoe fitting

**ACTION**

if no infection, nail service provided; gently round corner of nails when filing; recommend consulting a medical care professional

**ONYCHORRHEXIS** (on-e-kor-ek-sis) or **BRITTLE NAILS**

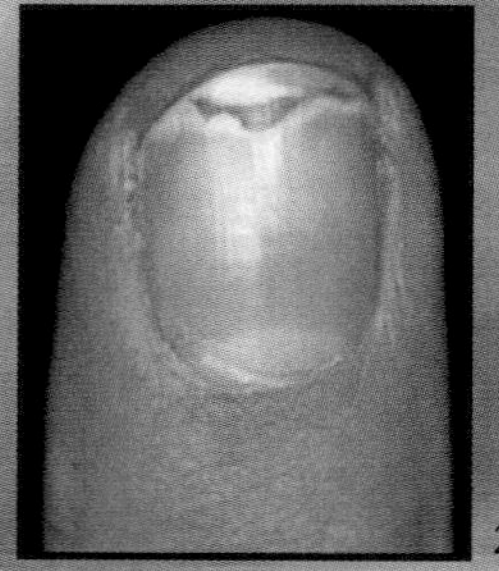

**SIGN/SYMPTOM**

splits in free edge that run lengthwise causing weakness or further breaks to the nail

**CAUSE**

excessive use of cuticle and polish removers, careless and rough filing, injury to nails

**ACTION**

nail service provided using nail strengtheners and careful filing

**ONYCHOMADESIS** (on-e-ko-ma-désis)

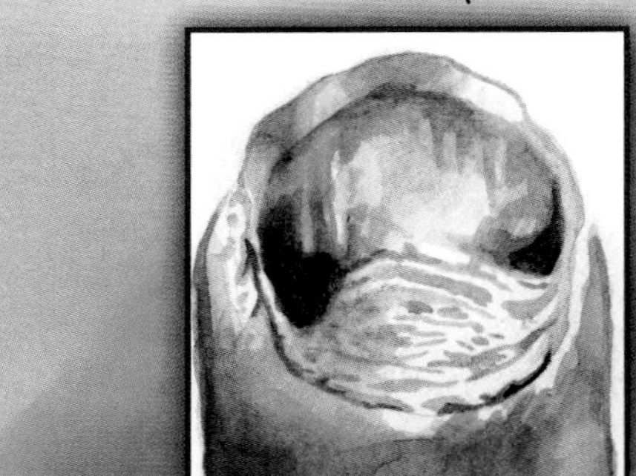

**SIGN/SYMPTOM**

complete shedding of the nail plate, starting with a groove at the base of the nail

**CAUSE**

local infection, cancer treatments, nail bed injury

**ACTION**

if no infection; nail service provided, no electric files or nail enhancements and no nail polish over affected nail

# Disorders of the Nail . . .

**ONYCHAUXIS** (on'-e-kawksis) or **HYPERTROPHY**

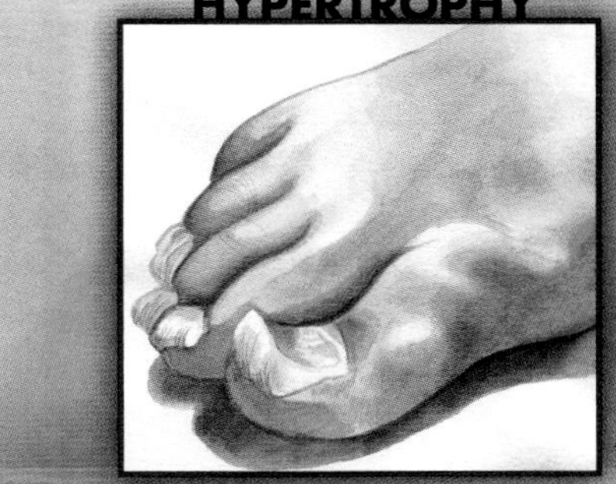

1

**SIGN/SYMPTOM**

nail plate develops an abnormal thickening in width, not length

**CAUSE**

internal imbalance, heredity, injury

**ACTION**

file nail down to a flat surface and/or buff the nail to a shine

**ONYCHATROPHIA** (on-e-ka-tro-fe-a) or **ATROPHY**

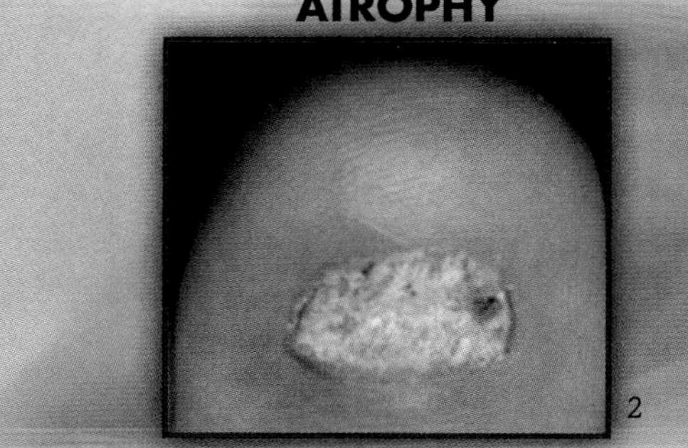

2

**SIGN/SYMPTOM**

nail slowly deteriorates, nail gets smaller and falls off

**CAUSE**

internal disease, injury to matrix

**ACTION**

nail service provided with caution, no harsh soaps, gentle filing and do not use a metal pusher

**PLICATURED** (pli-cat-ur-ed) or **FOLDED NAIL**

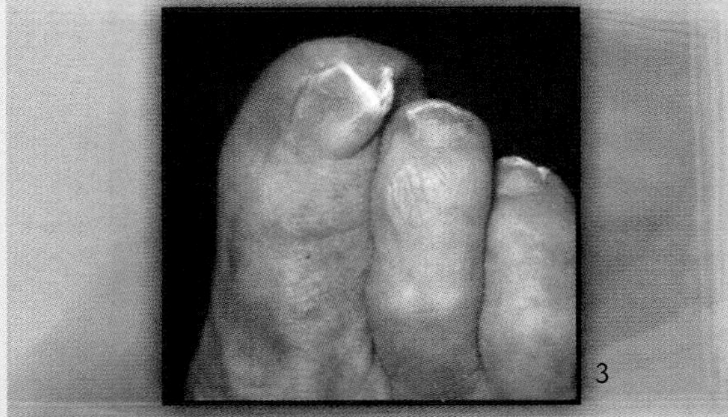

3

**SIGN/SYMPTOM**

nail plate edges fold down into the nail walls at a 90–degree angle, either on one or both sides

**CAUSE**

shoe pressure, nail bed deformity, hereditary, ingrown nails

**ACTION**

proceed with any nail service; gently round corner of nail when filing

**TRUMPET** or **PINCER NAIL**

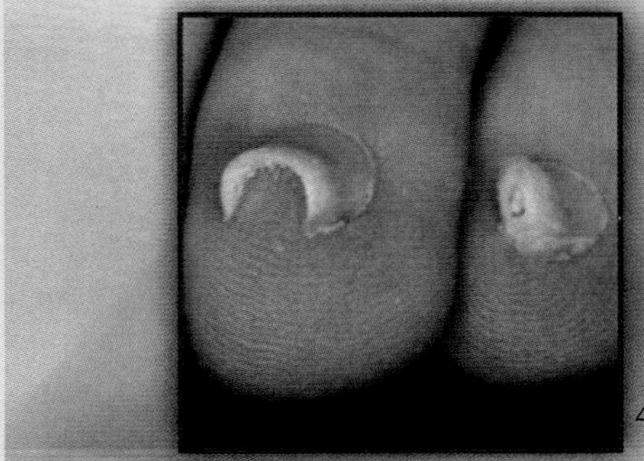

4

**SIGN/SYMPTOM**

edges of nail plate fold inward as nail grows, sometimes curling in completely, giving nail a cone shape

**CAUSE**

improper shoe fitting, hereditary, nail bed deformity

**ACTION**

carefully proceed with services; the skin under nail is attached to curled nail, refer customer to a medical care professional

# Diseases of the Nail . . .

**Onychosis** (on-e-ko-sis) is the broad, general term for any nail disease. A cosmetologist must be able to recognize the signs and symptoms of various nail diseases in order to assist the client in recovery, or determine if the client will need to be referred to a medical care professional.

**Ringworm** is a contagious disease caused by a fungus (plant parasite). The scientific name for ringworm is **tinea** (tin-ee-ah) and is characterized by a red ring. Ringworm can be found anywhere on the body, including in the beard, on the scalp and between the fingers.

Ringworm of the nails is referred to as **Tinea unguium** (un-gue-um) **or Onychomycosis** (on-e-ko-mi-ko-sis) The nails can become thick and discolored, sometimes with white, scaly patches.

1

2

RA

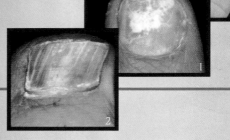

*Tinea is contagious. Do not perform nail services on a client that has ringworm or any contagious disease. Refer the client to a medical care professional. Remember to disinfect your work station and anything the customer might have touched.*

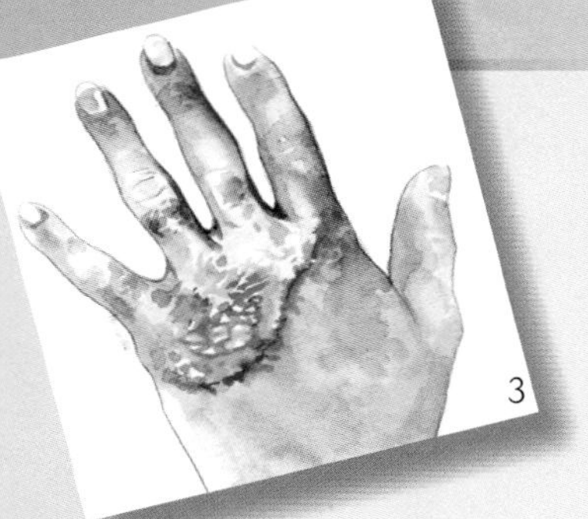

3

**Tinea manus**
is a fungal infection between the fingers and on the palms, which can eventually reach the fingernails. It emerges as circles containing small blisters that are a reddish color.

**Athlete's foot**
is called **Tinea pedis**, a fungal infection between the toes, which can spread to the toenails. The skin between the toes will be dry, scaly, inflamed and itchy, with small blisters.

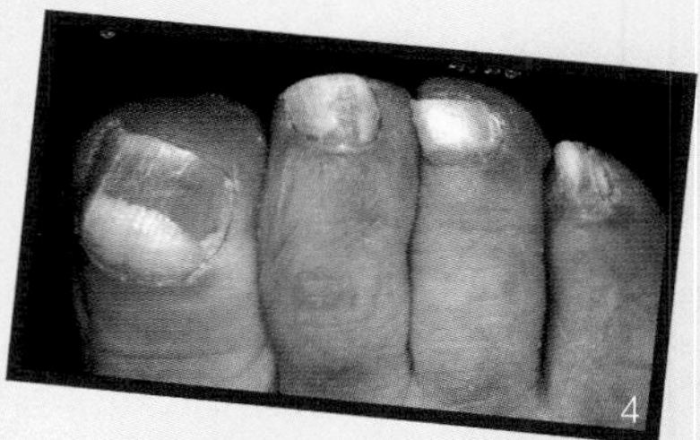

4

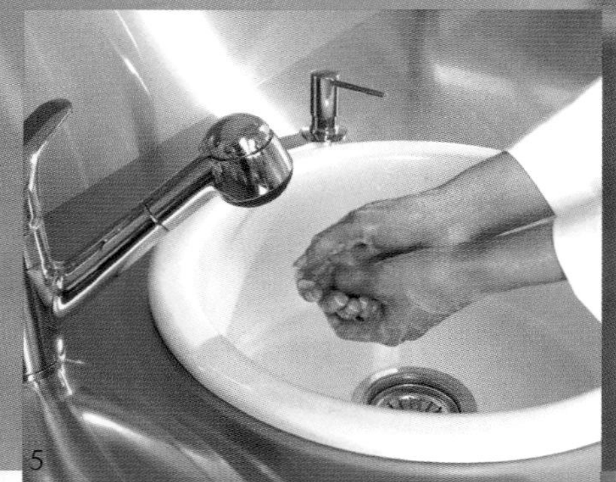

5

"What is the best way to protect yourself? Wash your hands thoroughly before and after each nail service!"

# Diseases of the Nail . . .

The following chart will indicate the disease by symptom and sight:

**PARONYCHIA** (par-o-nik-e-a)

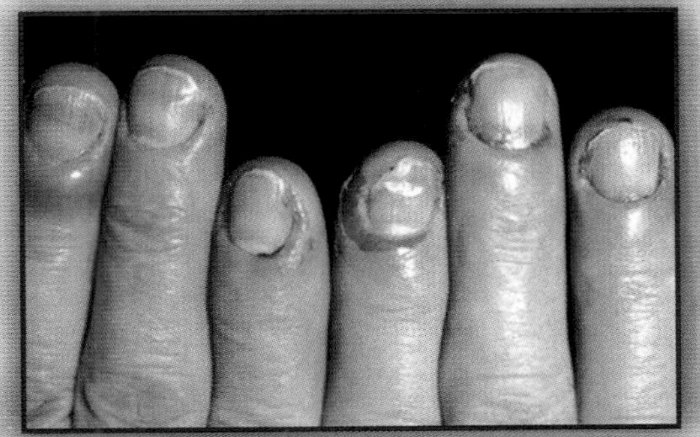

**SIGN/SYMPTOM**

inflammation of tissues surrounding or under the nail; tender, sometimes pus is present

**CAUSE**

unsanitary implements, aggressive cuticle pushing and cutting, yeast infection (fungal)

**ACTION**

contagious; recommend client to a medical care professional

**ONYCHIA** (o-nik-e-a)

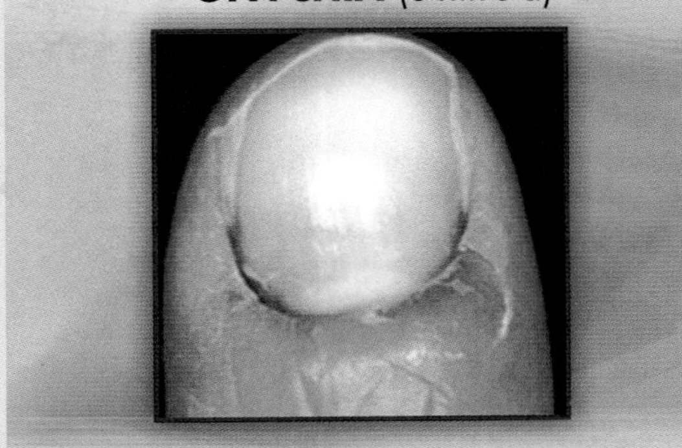

**SIGN/SYMPTOM**

inflammation of the matrix; redness, swelling around base or underneath the nail plate, sometimes pus is present

**CAUSE**

unsanitary implements is present

**ACTION**

contagious; recommend client to a medical care professional

**ONYCHOLYSIS** (on–e-kol-i-sis)

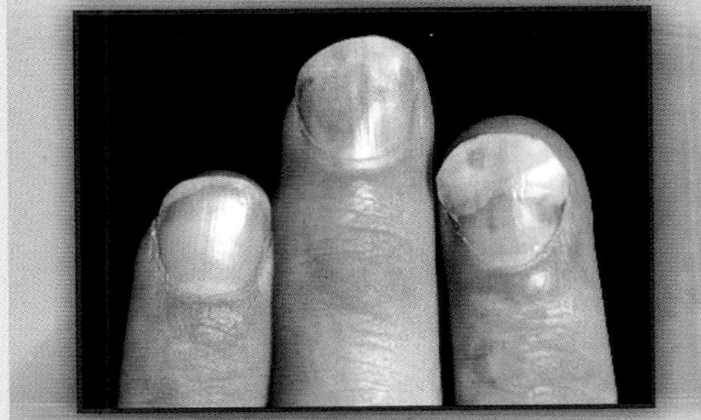

**SIGN/SYMPTOM**

nail plate separates from nail bed creating a gap, does not fall off; nail appears white; color of nail will change if infected

**CAUSE**

internal disorders, product allergies, trauma to the nail, infection

**ACTION**

recommend client to a medical care professional to prevent fungal infection

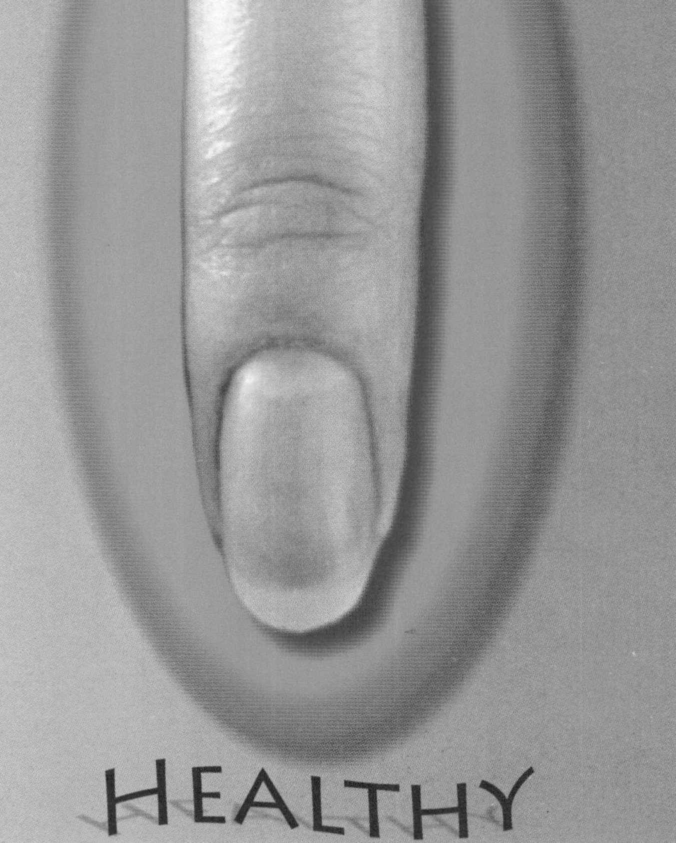

# Diseases of the Nail . . .

## PYOGENIC (pi-o-jenik) GRANULOMA (gran-yu-lo-ma)

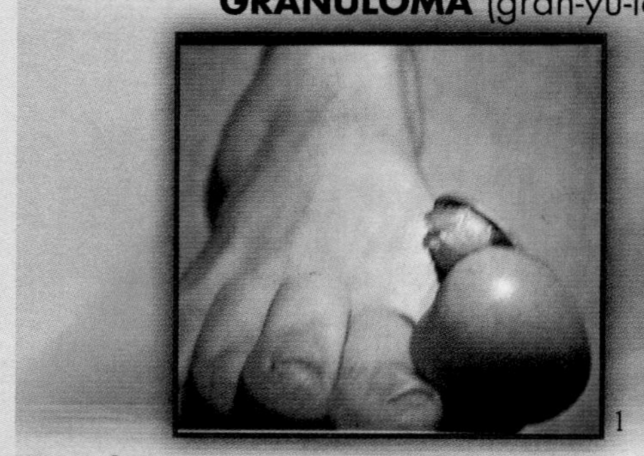

1

**SIGN/SYMPTOM**

a small rounded mass (vascular tissue) projecting from nail bed to the nail plate; inflammation

**CAUSE**

infection or injury

**ACTION**

no nail service due to inflammation; recommend client to a medical care professional

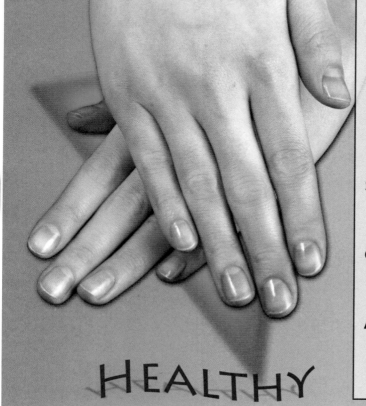

## ONYCHOPTOSIS (on-e-kop-to-sis)

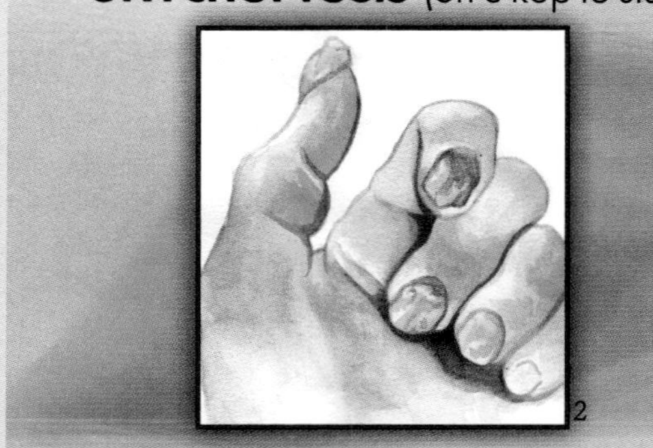

2

**SIGN/SYMPTOM**

nail detaches and falls off in whole or part

**CAUSE**

syphilis, fever, drug allergies, trauma

**ACTION**

no nail service recommended due to sensitivity of fingers; recommend client to a medical care professional

3

HEALTHY

## ONYCHOGRYPOSIS (on-e-ko-gri-po-sis)

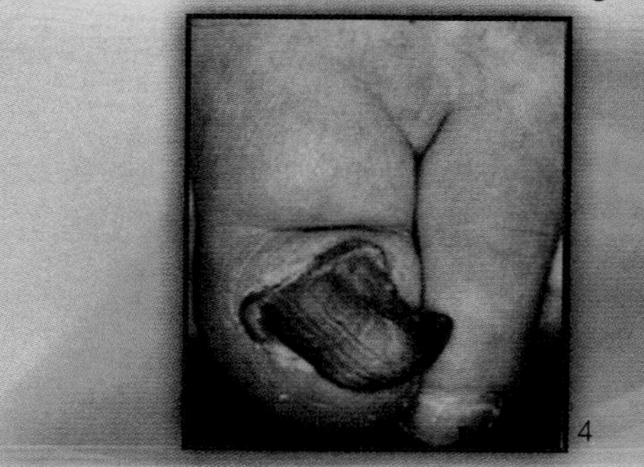

4

**SIGN/SYMPTOM**

most common on big toe; increased curve and thickness, has ridges and is difficult to cut

**CAUSE**

hereditary, injury to nail bed, improper care of nails

**ACTION**

no nail service recommended due to sensitivity of condition; recommend client to a medical care professional

# Individual Considerations ...

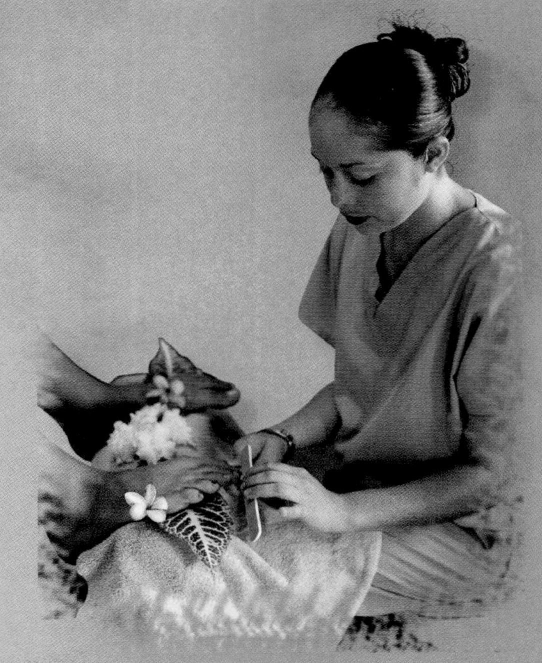

## Accommodating all clients

When conducting the client consultation, you will find that each individual has different needs or requirements. It will be your responsibility as the professional to ask how you may assist the client in providing a comfortable and successful service. Customers with special needs will generally tell you what they require. The following information will help to ensure you are prepared to accommodate the needs of all your clientele.

## Clients with Allergies

To prevent potential allergic reactions to chemicals or products, ask clients if they have any known allergies prior to beginning any service. Allergies occur when the immune system **overreacts** to normally harmless substances.

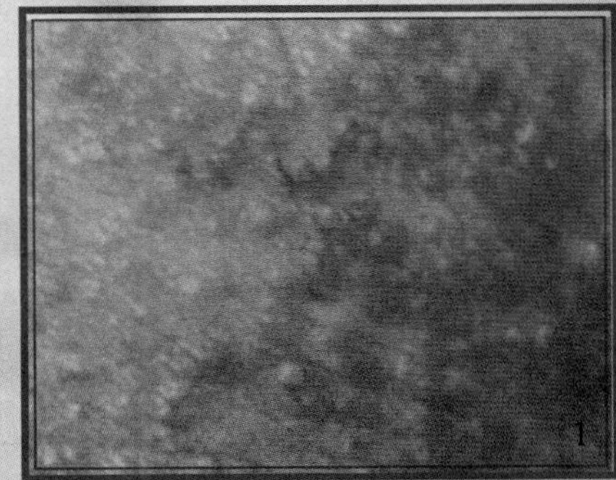

**Hypersensitivity to chemicals** affects two out of 10 people, causing mild to severe reactions during or after treatment. **Mild symptoms** include localized reactions such as rashes, itchy, watery eyes and slight congestion. **Moderate reactions** travel throughout the body, such as nausea, dizziness and weakness. **Severe reactions** include difficulty breathing or unconsciousness. Although allergic reactions may show up immediately, it generally takes sensitive clients four to six months to show symptoms of product allergy. Even though clients **may not be aware** of any allergies, pay attention to your customer's comfort and watch for symptoms.

# Individual Considerations . . .

## Visually or Hearing-Impaired Clients

Visually impaired clients may have difficulty seeing the work you are doing. Invest in a **magnifying glass** to help them choose nail colors or see the finished nail design. Be sensitive and describe what you are doing at all times. For clients without vision, offer to read the nail salon's list of services or have one printed in Braille.

To ensure that you **communicate** and **understand** the needs of a hearing-impaired client, keep a notepad and a pen at the work station. Many clients with complete hearing loss have learned to read lips, so make sure you **face them directly** when you are speaking.

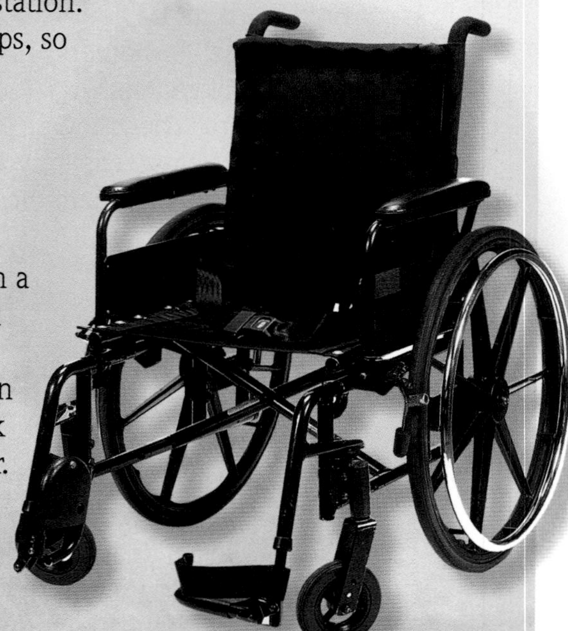

## Clients in Wheelchairs

To properly service clients who may be physically handicapped, your salon should be **accessible** to all areas, with a properly installed **ramp entrance** and **door width** that can accommodate wheelchairs easily. Inside, make certain that there is enough space at nail work stations to comfortably fit a wheelchair. You should also sit at eye level with the customer during both consultation and service.

## Pregnant Clients

Precautions must be taken in the salon to support the needs of an expectant customer. She may be **very temperature sensitive** or need **assistance moving into and out of the chair.**

The **hormones produced by pregnancy**, as well as a healthy diet and the addition of prenatal vitamins, may cause nails to grow faster, stronger and longer. However, for other women nails may become brittle, splitting or breaking more easily. The cosmetologist will have to adjust her services to the specific needs of each pregnant client, possibly seeing her more often to help maintain nail health during this time period. Use **extra caution** when using any chemicals on a pregnant client – even nail polish and nail polish remover. Have these clients consult a medical care professional before receiving any chemical treatments.

To help customers keep nails healthy while they are expecting, suggest that they wear gloves when immersing hands in water for any long periods of time and moisturize the hands and nails regularly.

## Medical History

Obtaining a brief medical history, when appropriate, can assist you **in understanding customers' nail, hand and foot health**, therefore permitting you to perform the optimal service for each client. For example, diabetic clients, who may have poor circulation in the hands and feet, may not heal quickly from wounds ... so taking extra safety measures may be required. Rheumatologic (ru-me-ta-lo-jik) conditions (a degenerative form of arthritis) can affect the feet, and hands and nails; these clients may also experience pain. The professional should be gentle when handling someone with this disease. A customer's nutrition will also affect nail health. **Communication** is the key to providing the most appropriate service for clients with medical conditions. Listen to their issues and try to understand the most helpful services to offer.

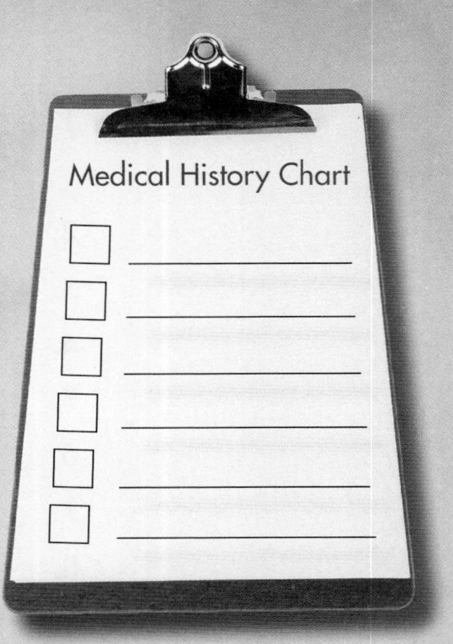

## Medications

The use of prescription medications can significantly affect nail health. Some medications may cause **positive changes** including **faster growth rate, longer or stronger nails**. Other medications can **cause weak or brittle nails**. Cancer patients undergoing chemotherapy may even experience complete nail loss. Help your clients to maintain a **positive self-image** by providing the most beautifying, soothing and rejuvenating treatments during this process.

Nails

# REVIEW QUESTIONS

## FILL-IN-THE-BLANKS

| | |
|---|---|
| A. Athlete's Foot | 1. ________ is a type of plant parasite causing a contagious disease called ringworm or tinea. |
| B. Cuticle | 2. ________ or ingrown nail; when the nail grows into nail groove. |
| C. Free Edge | 3. ________ is also called the nail body. |
| D. Fungus | 4. ________ is nail plate thickening in width not length. |
| E. Hyponychium | 5. ________ is bitten nails. |
| F. Koilonychia | 6. ________ is a scientific term for nail. |
| G. Leukonychia | 7. ________ may cause nails to become weak or brittle. |
| H. Lunula | 8. ________ is the portion of skin extending over and resting upon the base of the nail plate. |
| I. Magnifying Glass | 9. ________ is the portion of skin to which the nail plate is attached and rests upon. |
| J. Matrix | 10. ________ is part of the nail plate not attached to skin and extends beyond the fingertip. |
| K. Medications | 11. ________ is a fungal infection between fingers and on the palms of hands. |
| L. Nail Bed | 12. ________ is the part of the nail bed that extends below the nail root. |
| M. Nail Disorder | 13. ________ is caused by an injury, health condition or heredity. |
| N. Nail Plate | 14. ________ is also referred to the "half-moon." |
| O. Onychauxis | 15. ________ will help the visually impaired client to see the finished nail design. |
| P. Onychocryptosis | 16. ________ or tinea pedis is a fungal infection between the toes. |
| Q. Onychophagy | 17. ________ is the layer of skin cells under the free edge of the nail. |
| R. Onyx | 18. ________ is inflammation of skin surrounding the nail or under the nail plate. |
| S. Paronychia | 19. ________ is white spots or streaks within the nail plate. |
| T. Tinea Manus | 20. ________ is when the nail plate edges turn up creating a concave depression. |

STUDENT'S NAME DATE GRADE

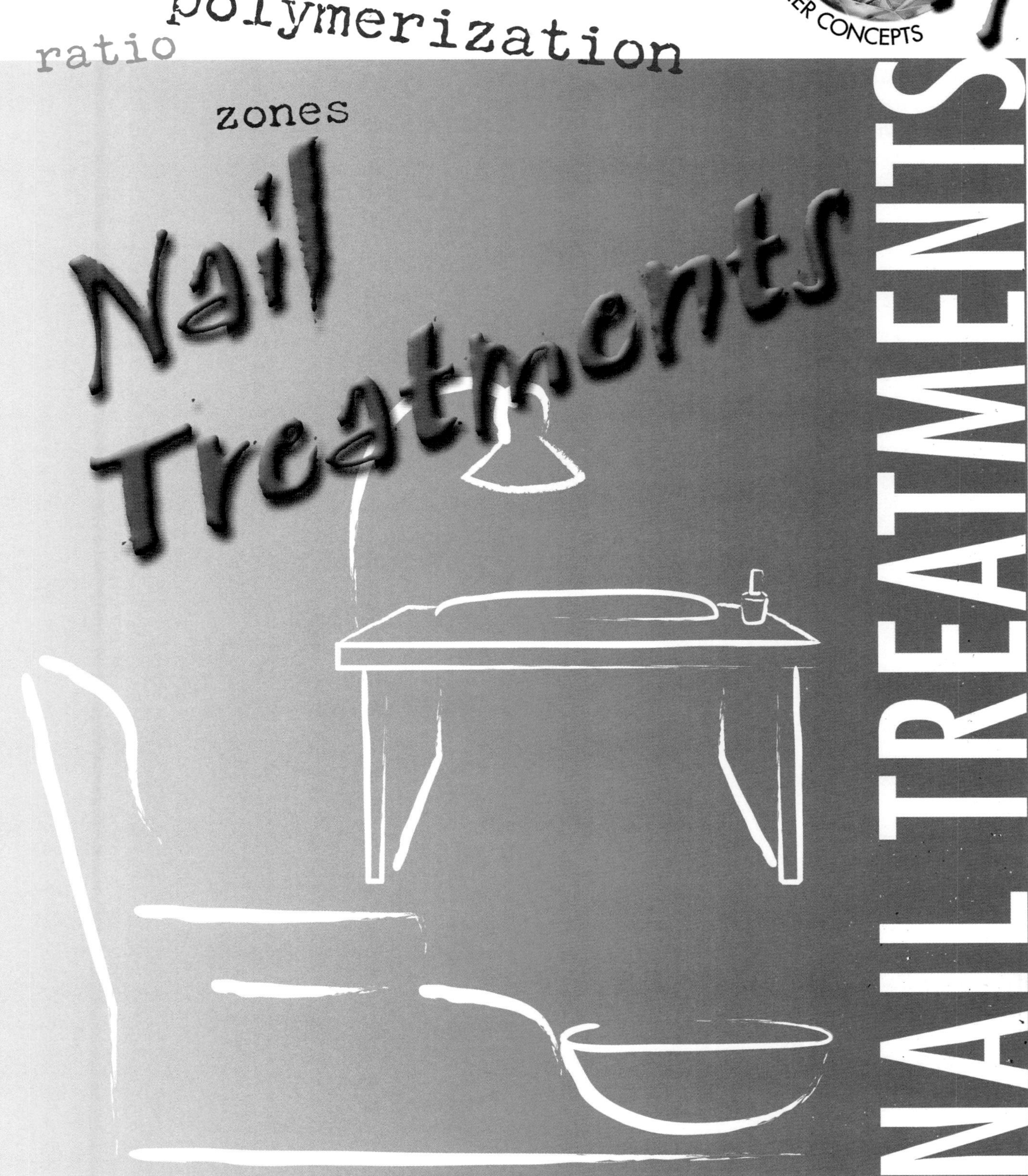
abrasive
cyanoacrylates
polish
monomer
polymerization
ratio
zones
Nail Treatments
COSMETOLOGY CAREER CONCEPTS
17
NAIL TREATMENTS
17

# Terminology ...

## In this chapter,

***we will present a visual vocabulary ... not just technical terms, but visual images that will serve as cues to assist you in learning the language you will be exposed to throughout this book.***

is the appreciation of art or beauty, a pleasing appearance.

### Artistry

is the beauty or imaginative result produced through creative ability in arrangement or execution.

1

### Ball (Bead)

is an amount of acrylic used for sculptured nails.

3

### Effleurage

is a massage technique using gliding, stroking or circular movements.

2

### Elevation

is the degree or angle by which the brush, hand or finger is raised.

2

17

# Terminology ...

**Flags**
are the hair located at the end of sculpture and nail art brushes.

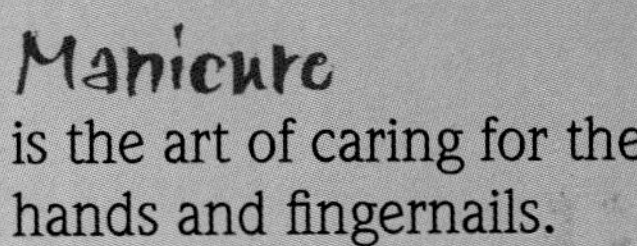

**Manicure**
is the art of caring for the hands and fingernails.

**Pedicure**
is the art of caring for the feet and toenails.

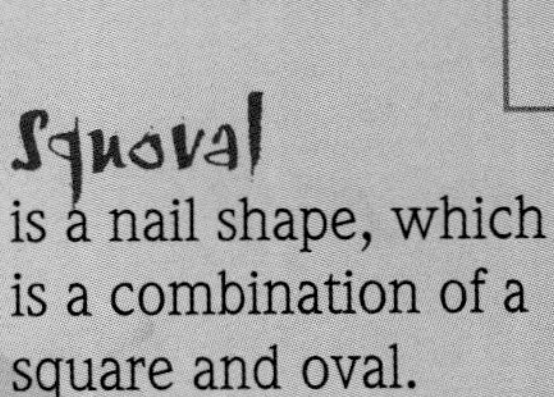

**Squoval**
is a nail shape, which is a combination of a square and oval.

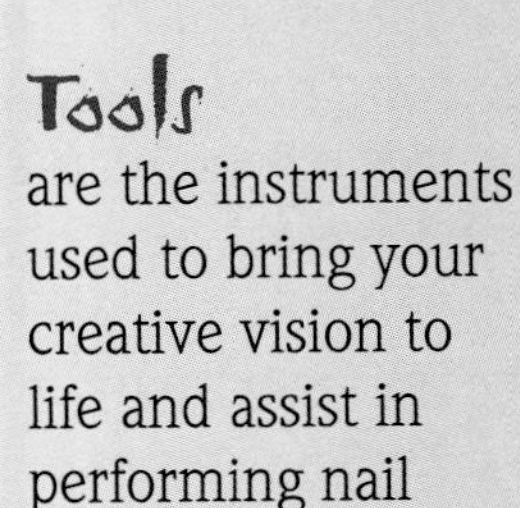

**Tools**
are the instruments used to bring your creative vision to life and assist in performing nail artistry.

# Introduction . . .

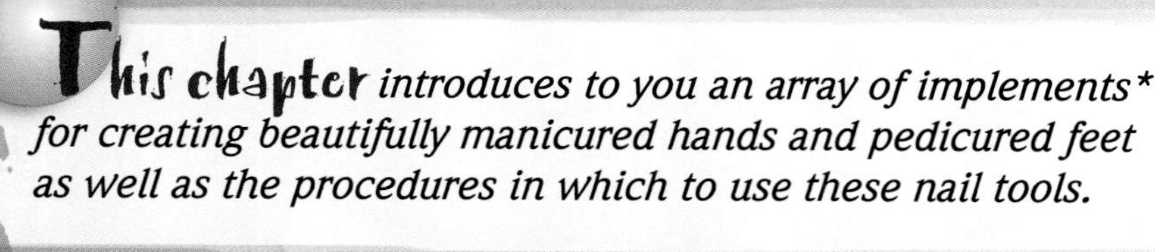

**This chapter** *introduces to you an array of implements* for creating beautifully manicured hands and pedicured feet as well as the procedures in which to use these nail tools.*

*As you master the tools, your skills will develop and open up the possibility of true success in the world of nail artistry.*

Nail artists' tools are assets to their profession; invest wisely in professional tools obtained from reputable distributors and manufacturers. Make sure the company provides outstanding service and advice on your purchase. Carefully examine the warranties and inquire about extra customer services, such as tool repair and replacement.

*While a number of the professional tools available are covered in this chapter, there may be other tools accessible, as the marketplace expands.

In this chapter, you will find an overview of the cleaning and maintenance of nail-care tools. To keep tools in their proper working order, clean and check them frequently according to the manufacturer's safety and maintenance instructions. Check with your instructor on the regulatory agency's requirements for the proper sanitation of your tools.

# Introduction . . .

Toward the end of this chapter we introduce our **competency-based learning system,** which presents some of the nail treatments that **progress from simple to complex skill levels.** You will develop professional perception, manual dexterity and tactile sensitivity by using the basic art elements and principles as you advance further into each procedure. Each treatment will be an upgrade to the previous treatment, which will give you more opportunities to meet your client's nail-care needs as they expand into other services.

First you will learn **simple skill nail treatments,** which will assist in **building a strong foundation** for all other nail procedures. The basic manicure and pedicure offer the essentials of proper nail maintenance to help create strong, healthy nails.

Next are the **intermediate skill nail treatments** that will gain you **access into the spa world** by adding masks and/or paraffin treatments along with massage to assist in the benefit of client relaxation. The additional services of nail tip application and fabric wrap procedures provide alternatives in nail strengthening and/or lengthening to fulfill the client's needs.

In **complex skill nail treatments,** we cover the procedures for **constructing a sculpted nail,** which rests upon the natural nail providing additional length, support to a weakened nail or an overall natural-looking nail. The world of nail enhancements or add-on services in the nail industry will open the door to exploring a realm of imagination, creativity and an endless array of new and exciting technological advancements in nails.

By learning these acrylic nail procedures, along with much practice, experimentation and time, you will become confident in successfully fulfilling all of your client's nail-care needs.

# Professional Protection ...

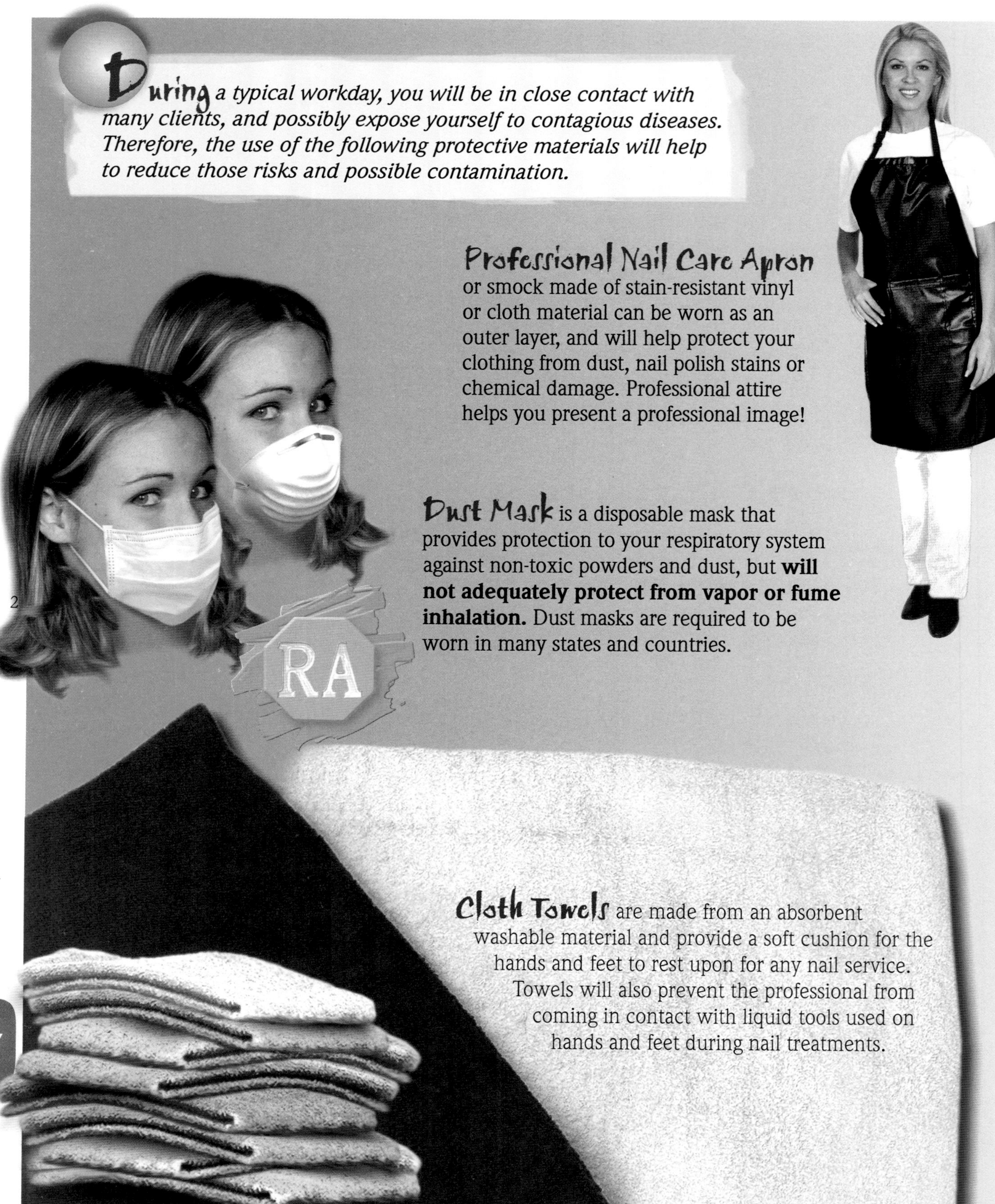

During a typical workday, you will be in close contact with many clients, and possibly expose yourself to contagious diseases. Therefore, the use of the following protective materials will help to reduce those risks and possible contamination.

**Professional Nail Care Apron** or smock made of stain-resistant vinyl or cloth material can be worn as an outer layer, and will help protect your clothing from dust, nail polish stains or chemical damage. Professional attire helps you present a professional image!

**Dust Mask** is a disposable mask that provides protection to your respiratory system against non-toxic powders and dust, but **will not adequately protect from vapor or fume inhalation.** Dust masks are required to be worn in many states and countries.



**Cloth Towels** are made from an absorbent washable material and provide a soft cushion for the hands and feet to rest upon for any nail service. Towels will also prevent the professional from coming in contact with liquid tools used on hands and feet during nail treatments.

# Professional Protection...

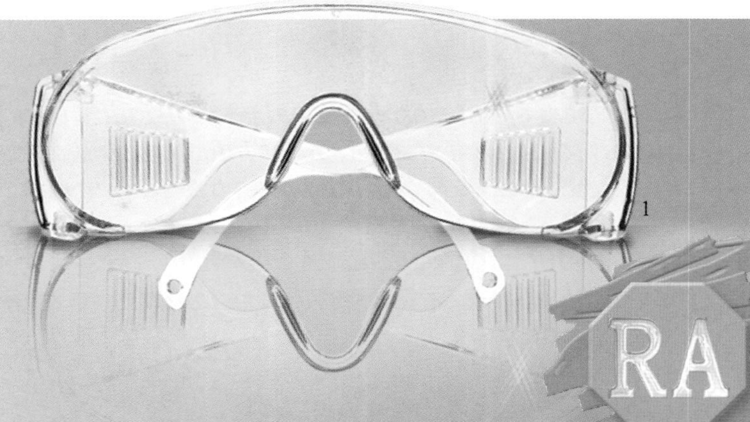

**Safety Goggles** are lightweight goggles that provide eye protection during nail filing and sculpting services. Many regulatory agencies require that safety goggles be worn.

1

**Gloves** are manufactured from latex, vinyl or synthetic materials to protect hands from stains and chemical sensitivity. Gloves are required to be worn for nail services in many areas.

2

3

**Flexible Finger Wraps** consist of breathable, waterproof tape, made of natural rubber latex. Wraps feature good abrasive resistance to protect professionals from potential abrasions, which may be created by repetitive motions such as filing. They can also be placed on top of a sterile dressing to cover existing wounds.

**CAUTION:** Some people have allergies or sensitivities to latex. Be sure to ask your clients about this, prior to wearing latex gloves or finger wraps before any nail service.

"Remember ... when it comes to protecting yourself and your client, your motto should always be 'SAFETY FIRST'!"

# Client Protection . . .

*It is part of your professional responsibility to do everything you can to prevent the spread of infection and disease from one client to the next. Providing protective clothing and following salon sanitation and disinfection guidelines are crucial for the health and safety of the salon's clients. Additionally, these actions demonstrate the excellent and caring service customers can expect to receive.*

**NOTE:** Always use washable fabrics for proper sanitation.

**Robes** are made of a washable material, used for pedicure and spa clients. They provide comfort and allow easy access to the lower legs for massage procedures.

1

**Wet Disinfectant System** is a sanitizer used for implements that are exposed to clients' skin and nails. Tools are completely immersed in jars or special containers filled with a disinfectant solution for the allotted time determined by following manufacturer's directions.

2

3

**Dry Disinfectant System** is a sanitizer that employs an ultraviolet light cabinet where tools are placed after being cleaned and disinfected with a commercial solution.

Follow your regulatory agency for proper disinfectant procedures

17

# Client Protection ...

1

**Air Purification Systems** are available to purify the air within the salon. The technology in some of today's air filtration systems is so advanced that the systems actually eliminate chemical odors caused by many artificial nail products. In addition, the air is cleansed of bacteria, fungi and virus particles that inevitably enter salons.

RA

**Dust Mask** is worn by both the professional as well as the client. It is a disposable mask that provides protection to the respiratory system against non-toxic powders and dust, but **will not adequately protect from vapor or fume inhalation.** Dust masks are required to be worn in many states and countries.

**Disposable Towels** made from non-woven fabric provide a lint-free surface for your clients' hands during services. This eliminates the need for laundering, and ensures each client has a clean and sanitary service area.

**Sterile Client Nail Kits** will keep the client's sanitized nail tools in a sterile pouch until they are ready for use. This represents another assurance of proper hygiene for the client.

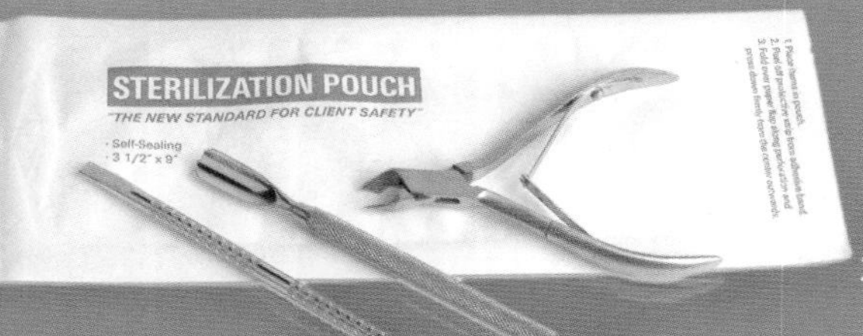

STERILIZATION POUCH
"THE NEW STANDARD FOR CLIENT SAFETY"
Self-Sealing
3 1/2" x 9"


2

# Basic Manicure Supplies ...

**When performing** *nail services, you will use some basic items to accomplish a thorough and sanitary service. The following are some of the supplies needed while performing nail treatments.*

**Manicure Bowls** are contoured with finger and palm grooves, for comfort while soaking the fingers during a manicure. They are designed to fit either hand, manufactured of plastic or ceramic and are available in assorted colors.

**Water Solution** consists of warm water with an antibacterial soap, which acts to soften the skin and provide cleansing of hands and feet. The solution is placed in a manicure bowl for hands or footbath for feet, to provide rest and relaxation.

1

**Liquid Pump Dispensers** hold and dispense liquids for use in the salon. The flip-top lid provides easy access to the product while preventing odors and evaporation when not in use. Plastic dispensers are constructed of a high-density polyethylene (pollee-ethe-leen) that can safely hold alcohol, antiseptic or polish removers.

**Spatulas** will assist in the removal of product from a container. For sanitary purposes, **never** use your fingers to remove any product from a jar. The spatula should never be in contact with your client's skin to prevent contamination of product and **"no double-dipping."**

# Basic Manicure Supplies . . .

**Cotton** is used as an applicator for hand- and foot-care treatments, and assists in the removal of nail polish from the nails. It can be applied at the end of a manicuring stick to help remove polish from the nail area around the skin, clean under the free edge of the nail and push back cuticles from the base of nails. **Nail wipes** are an alternative for removing polish from the nails.

**Container with Lid** can be made out of glass, ceramic or plastic and hold or store cotton in a sterile environment.

1

2

**Warming Lotion,** used in a manicure heater, will provide extra softening to the skin and cuticle. Clients rest their fingers in the lotion during the manicure. This process can be especially beneficial to clients with dry, rough cuticles, such as male customers or clients who have not had a recent manicure service.

3

**Disposable Plastic Cups,** used in the warming heater, contain lotion into which clients place their hands to achieve softening effects.

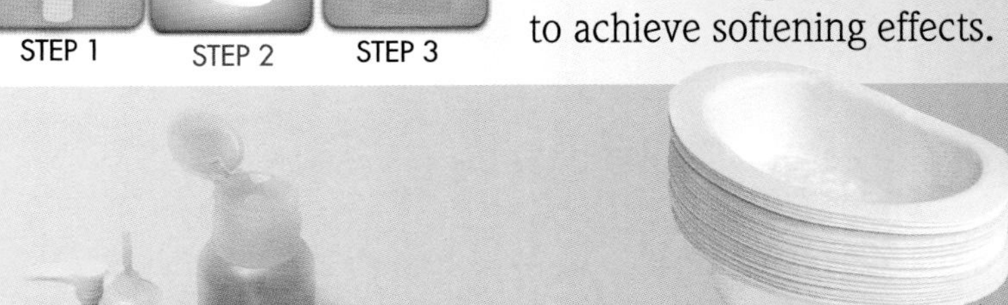

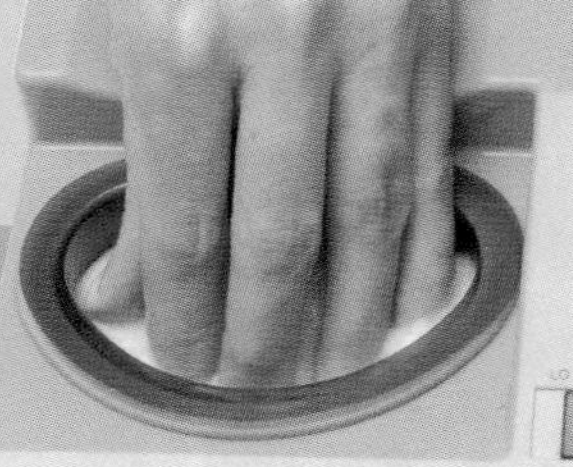

4

**Plastic Bag or Trash Receptacle** will hold any used or soiled material during the nail service. A closed container will protect customers from fumes escaping into the salon environment.

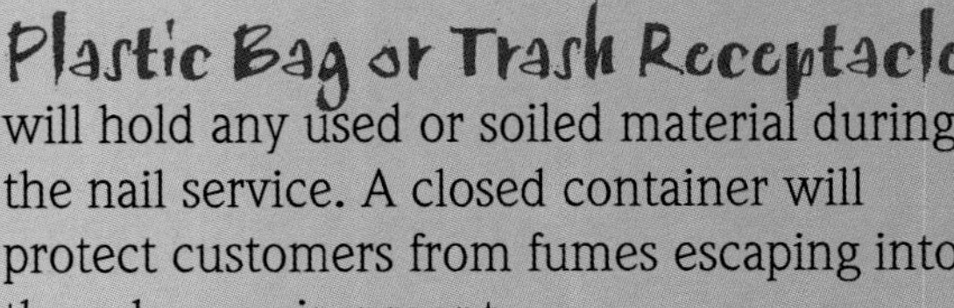

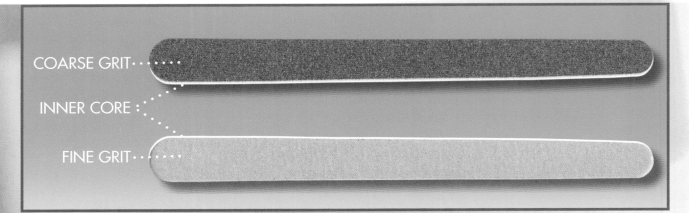

# Nail File Usage . . .

COARSE GRIT

INNER CORE

FINE GRIT

***Nail files and buffers / shiners** are used to file, shape and smooth the free edge and surface of the nail. With proper use of these tools, you can form a unique shape that accentuates the beauty of your customer's hand.*

*Nail files are made of an abrasive substance, referred to as* **"grit,"** *ranging from coarse to ultra fine. The abrasive is adhered to an inner core varying in construction from wood, cardboard, plastic or foam. These files are used for abrading, smoothing or polishing the nails. Nail files feature both natural and synthetic abrasives.*

**Placement:** The file should be held between your thumb and index, middle and ring fingers.

**Control:** The amount of pressure applied along with the grit will determine the amount of nail removal.

## Key Elements:

Nail files provide a gradual change to length of nail

Enhance the appearance of the nail by providing shine

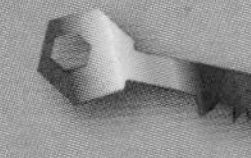
Come in a variety of colors, designs, shapes and sizes to provide an efficient nail service and create artistic expression, while being comfortable against the client's skin

17

Offer a variety in abrasive surfaces depending on nail service

The sanitation of a file is a priority in the nail-care service for your own safety and that of the client. If a file **cannot be sanitized**, then it must be discarded after use, or kept in a client's sterile individual nail kit.

# Nail File Dynamics . . .

## Shaping Dynamics for NATURAL NAILS

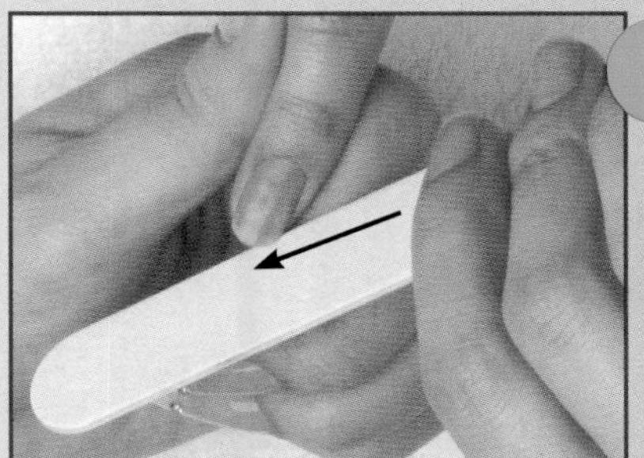

1 Place file on right corner of free edge.

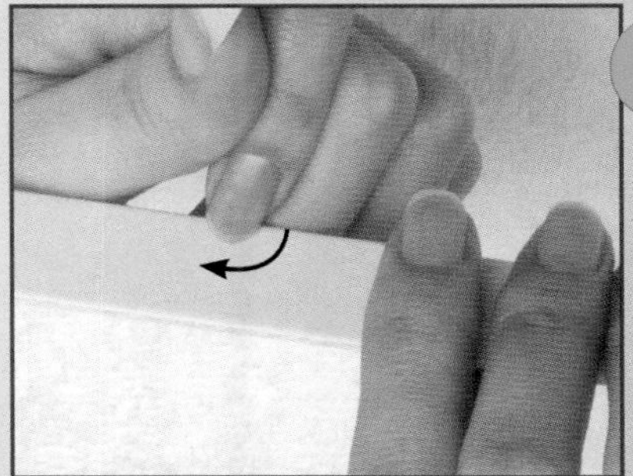

2 Slide file towards center of nail, no zigzag motion.

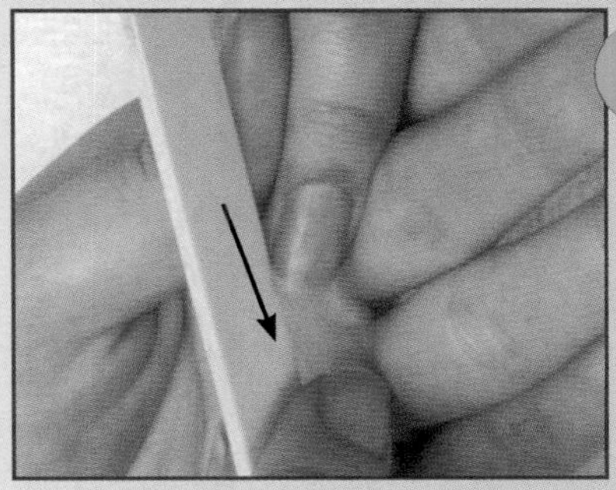

3 Place file on left corner of free edge.

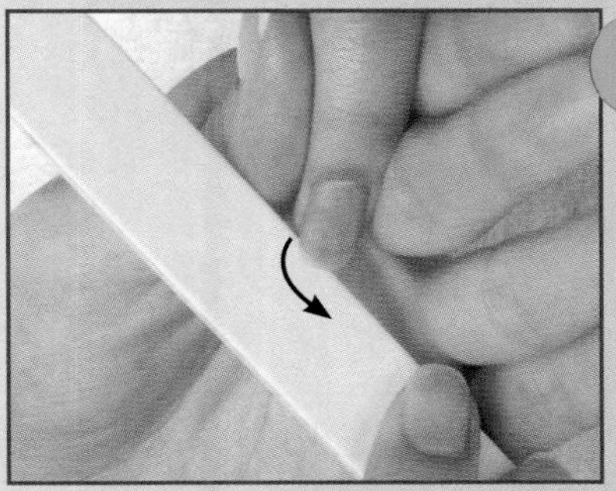

4 Slide file towards center of nail.

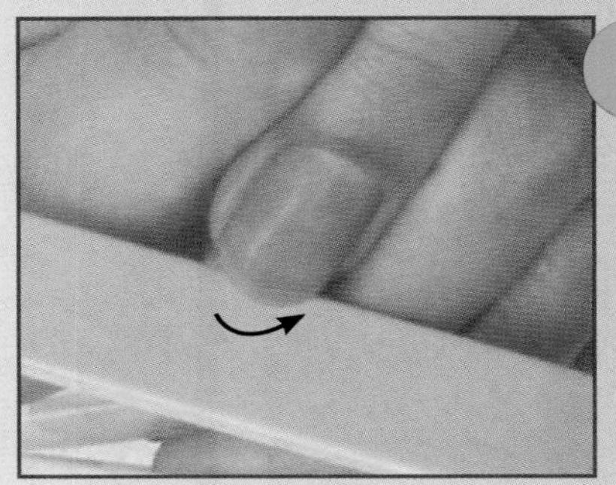

5 Continue with shaping center of free edge, no zigzag motion.

## Shaping Dynamics for SCULPTURED NAILS

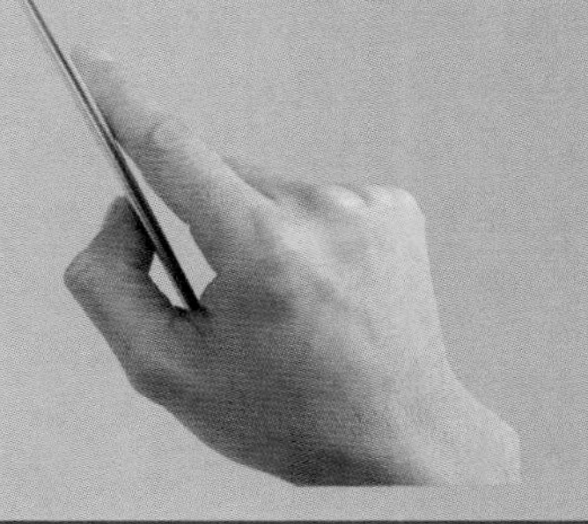

1 Hold file with index finger on top and thumb on bottom.

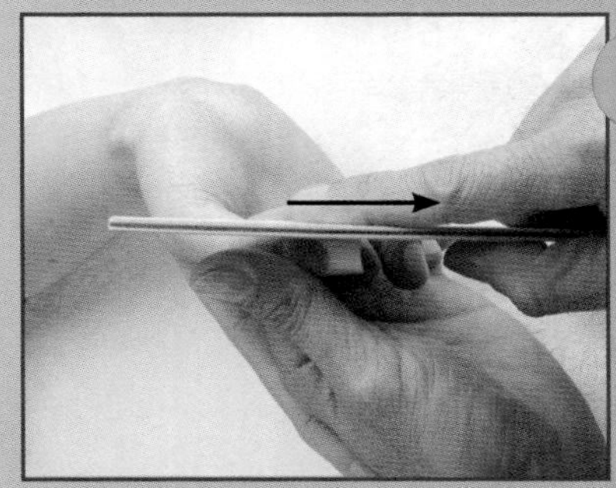

2 Place file on right side of nail and slide straight out.

3 Place file on left side of nail and slide straight out.

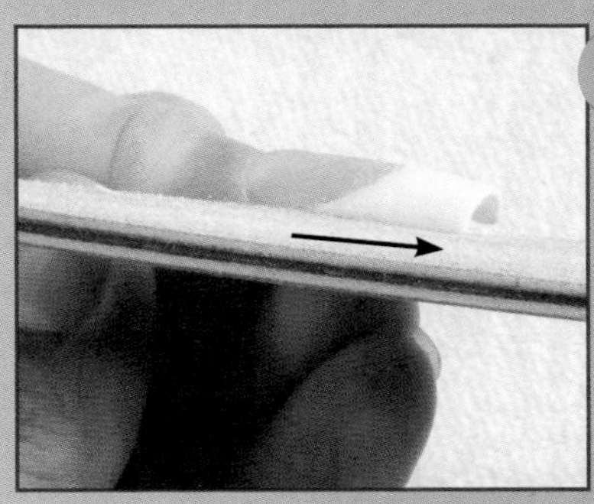

4 Slide file straight out from sidewalls to the free edge.

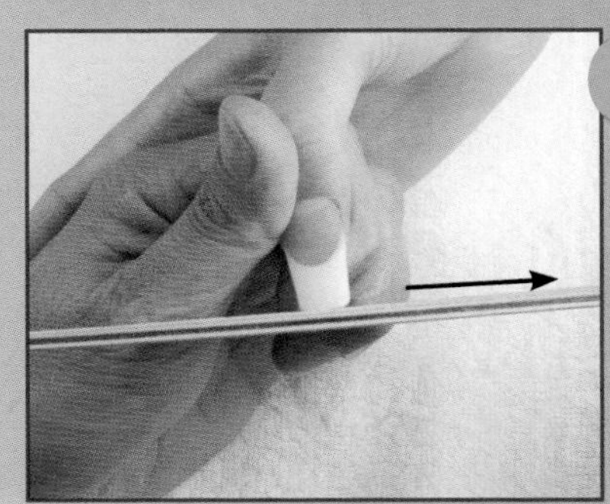

5 Place file at top of nail and slide file straight across.

# Nail File Abrasives ...

***Grit** is the abrasive surface of a nail file. The grit number indicates how many grains of abrasive substance are contained in each square inch. Grit is made from both natural and synthetic abrasives. The service you are performing, as well as the types of nails on which you are working (natural nails or nail enhancements), will be the deciding factors in what form of abrasive file you choose.*

A **grit number** determines the coarseness to fineness of a file or buffer. The higher the grit number, the less abrasive the surface; the lower the grit number, the stronger the abrasive surface. The chart below demonstrates abrasiveness and grit number, ultimately determining the function of a file.

| Abrasiveness | Grit Number | Function |
|---|---|---|
| Coarse | 100 to 149 | Shapes and reduces length of acrylic and gel nail enhancements |
| Medium | 150 to 239 | Smoothes and shapes all types of natural nails and nail enhancements |
| Fine | 240 to 399 | Smoothes artificial and natural nail surfaces; used for final filing of acrylics |
| Very Fine | 400 to 899 | Performs final filing on natural nail to remove ridges and prepares nail for buffing |
| Ultra Fine | 900 to 12000 | Buffing/finishing tool to smooth and shine the nail plate |



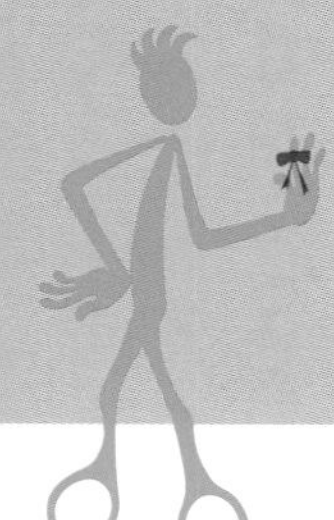

"When choosing nail files, always remember that the higher the grit number, the finer the abrasive surface."

# Files and Buffers . . .

**The shape** of each client's nails will be distinct. As you work with the nails, filing tools can bring forth a shape that is natural looking, high fashion or avant-garde. A professional will use nail files and buffers to shape and smooth the free edge and surface of the nail … artistically creating a stunning nail that was previously unseen.

Diamond File

**Diamond Files** are the hardest abrasive files and are used for shaping the free edge of sculptured nails, or to smooth and change the shape of thick natural nails. These files are reusable after being sanitized with an appropriate disinfectant.

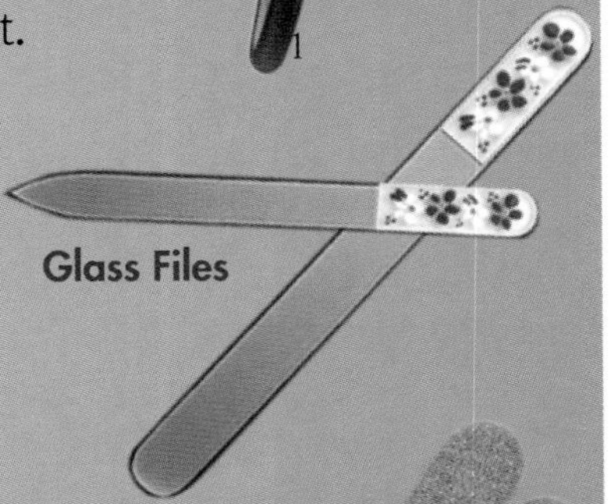

1

**Crystal or Glass Files** are also hard abrasive files and can be used to shape the free edge of any nail enhancements and the natural nails. Abrasive or grit is permanently etched into the crystal or glass. These files are reusable after proper sanitation.

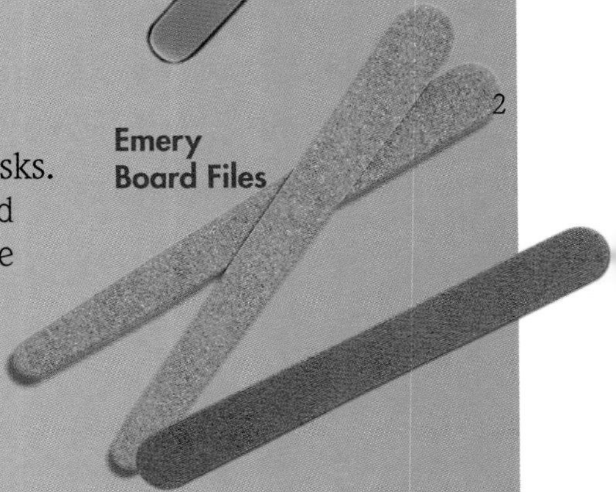

Glass Files

**Garnet and Emery Board Nail Files** are one of the most economical nail files. They consist of crushed garnet gemstone abrasive atop a wooden core, which is durable and well suited for many filing tasks. The emery board features double-sided abrasiveness – a light side coated with a fine abrasive and a dark side with a coarse abrasive. Both of these files cannot be sanitized, so they must be discarded after each use.

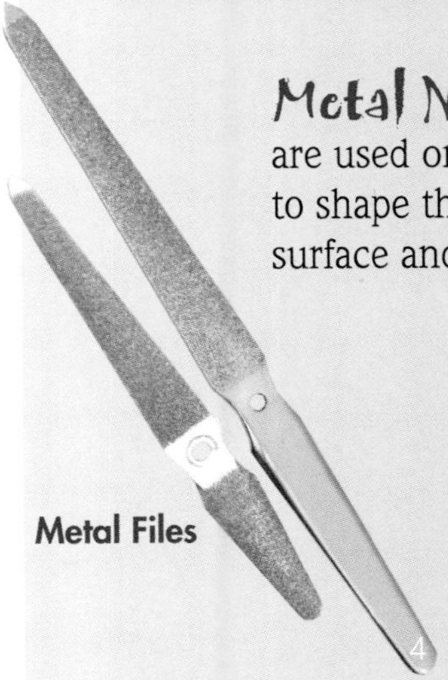

Emery Board Files

2

**Metal Nail Files or Stainless Steel Files** are used on a hard natural nail or nail enhancement to shape the free edge. These files have a non-porous surface and can be sanitized for use on multiple clients.

**Block Buffers** are used to smooth the surface of the nail and provide shine. These buffers and shiners usually can be sanitized and reused; however, buffers do wear out quickly through repeated use and should be discarded when no longer effective.

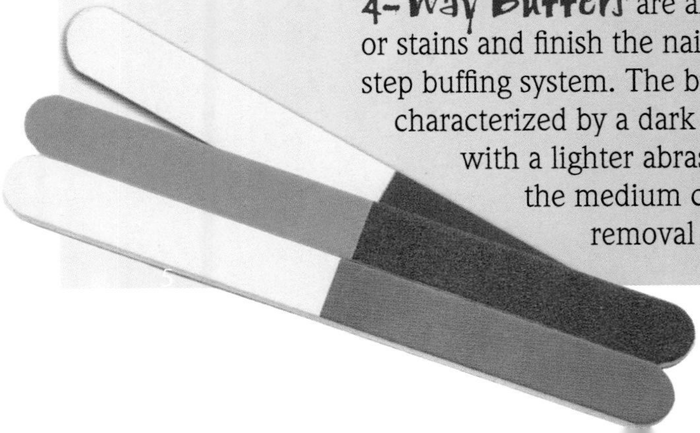

Metal Files

4

3

**4-Way Buffers** are an alternative buffing system to shape nails, remove ridges or stains and finish the nails with a shine, and are also available in a two- or three-step buffing system. The buffer will graduate from a coarse abrasive, which is characterized by a dark color, followed by a medium abrasive/color and finishes with a lighter abrasive/color. The dark color is usually designed for shaping; the medium color for removing ridges; and the lighter color for stain removal or adding shine.

17

# Cuticle Pusher Usage...

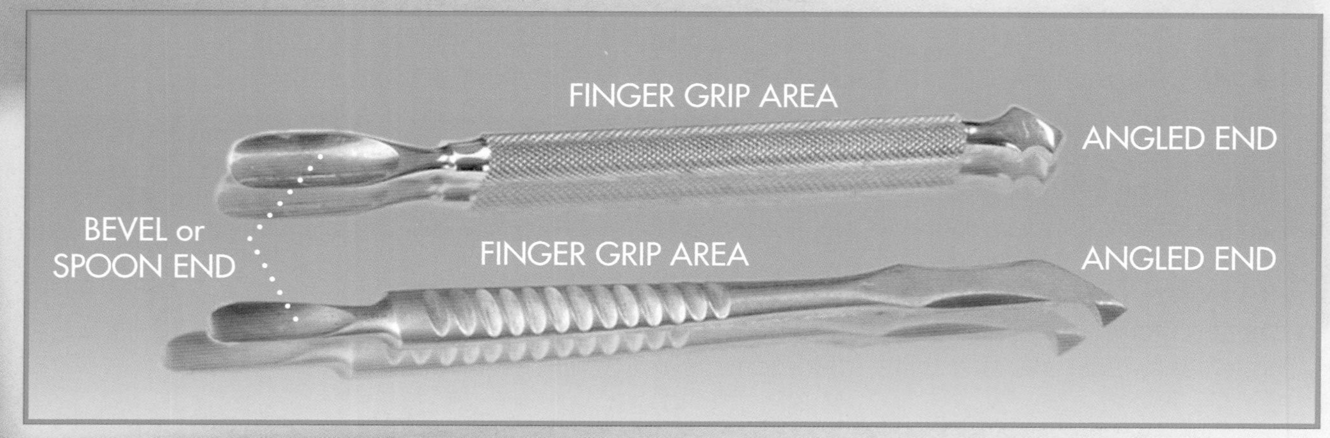


***Cuticle Pushers** gently push back loosened cuticle from the surface of the nail. These tools will help beautify the overall look of the nail. Cuticle pushers are available in plastic with a rubber tip, metal or pumice stone. They also come with various grips and designs for individual comfort preferences.* ***Optional:*** *Manicure sticks may also be used to push back cuticle.*

1

2

The cuticle pusher is sometimes referred to as a **curette** (cu-rette) because of the spoon or beveled end, which is used to lightly scoop and remove debris around the cuticle and groove areas of the nail.

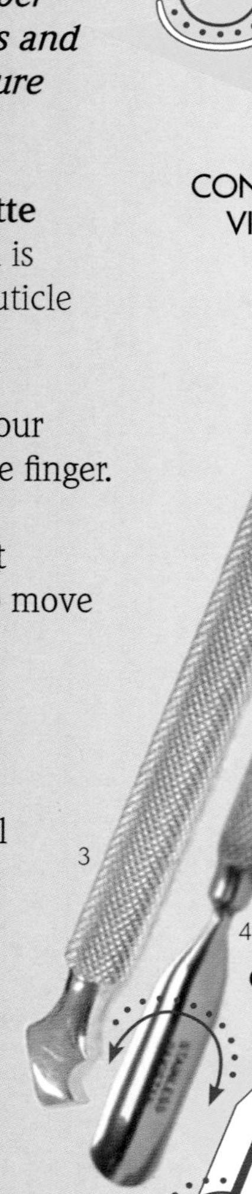


**Placement:** The cuticle pusher is held between your thumb and index finger and will rest on the middle finger.

**Control:** The thumb and index finger apply a light pressure to the pusher, which allows the pusher to move forward and lift up the cuticle.

## Key Elements:

- Cuticle pushers provide a clean appearance to the nail
- Aid in easy removal of cuticle from the nail
- Help nails appear longer because cuticle is removed, permitting additional exposure of nail surface

# Cuticle Pusher Dynamics . . .

## Metal Pusher Dynamics

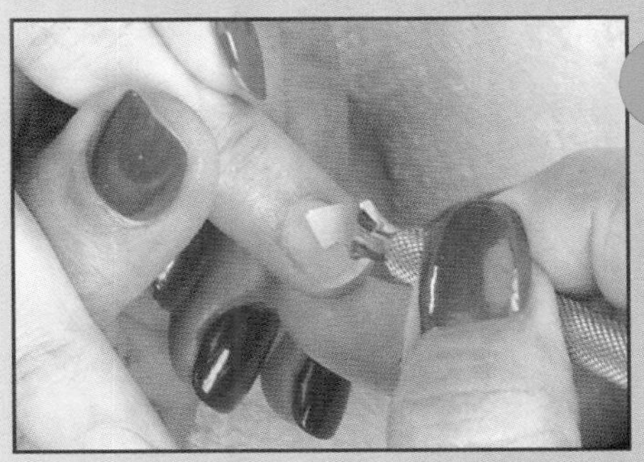

1 *Use angled end to carefully loosen cuticle.*

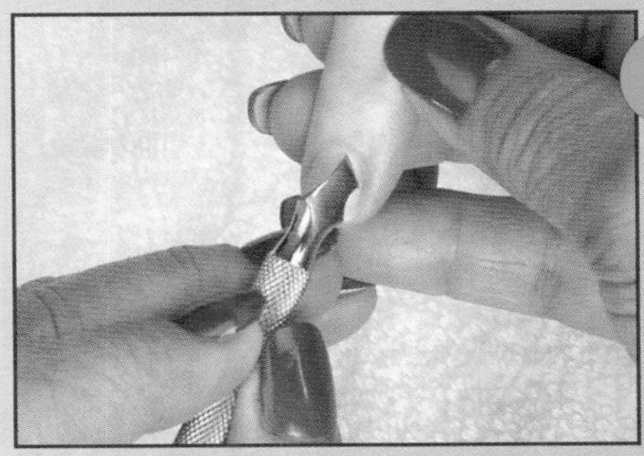

2 *Lightly slide angled end along the cuticle to help lift skin from nail plate.*

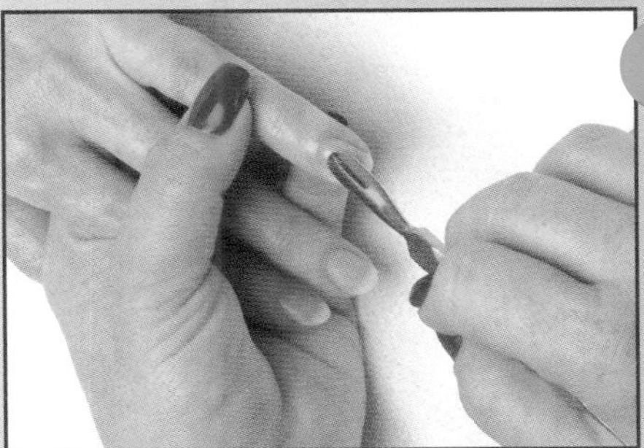

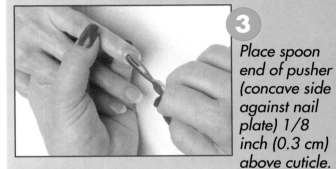

3 *Place spoon end of pusher (concave side against nail plate) 1/8 inch (0.3 cm) above cuticle.*

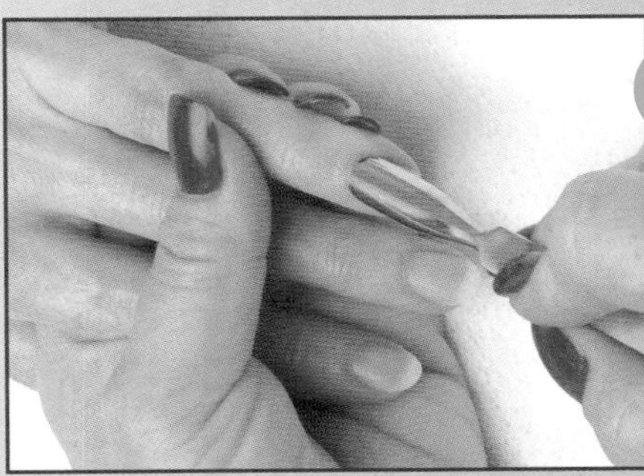

4 *Move the spoon end of pusher forward into cuticle, using slight pressure.*

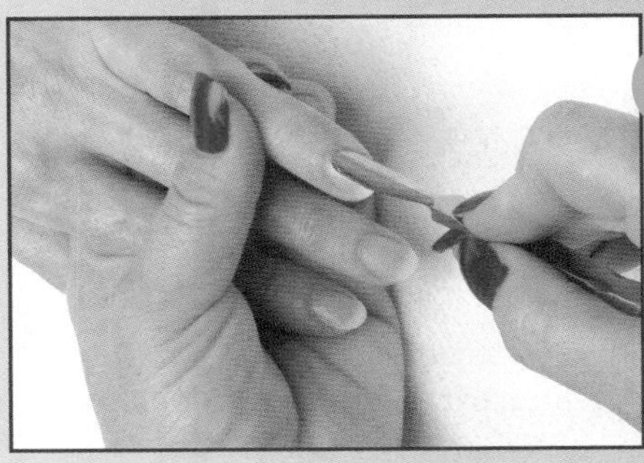

5 *Push skin away from nail grooves.*

## Manicure Stick Dynamics

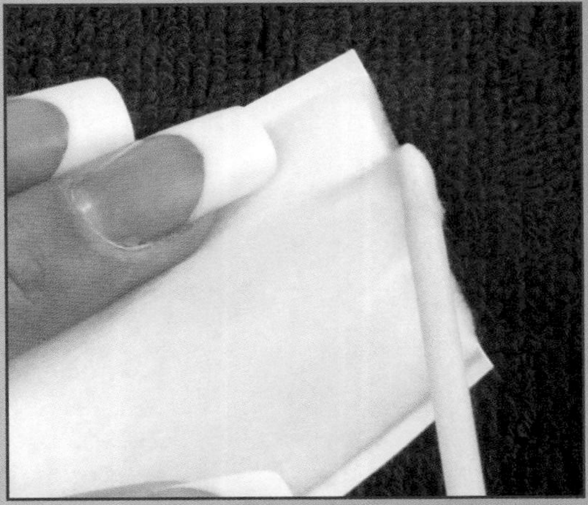

1 *Wrap cotton around end of manicure stick.*

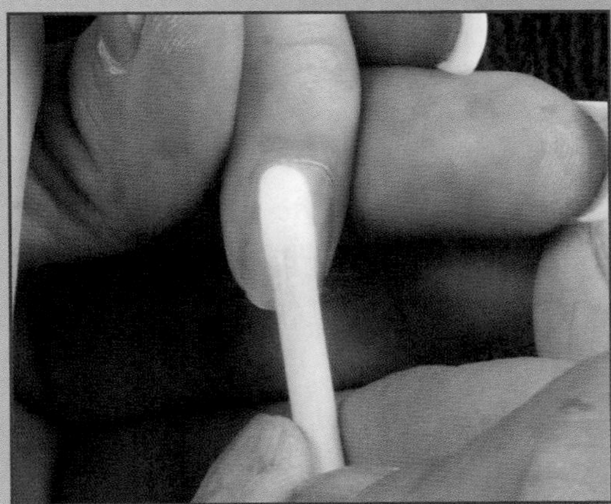

2 *Slightly push tip of cotton-wrapped manicure stick against cuticle.*

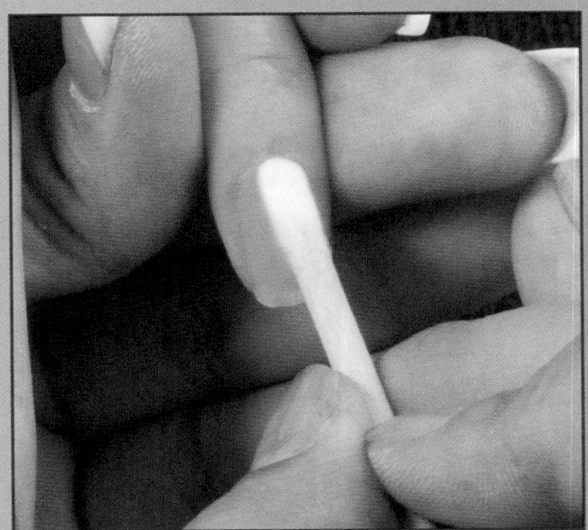

3 *Continue pushing cuticle, moving across the base of nail.*

17

# Cuticle Nipper Usage...

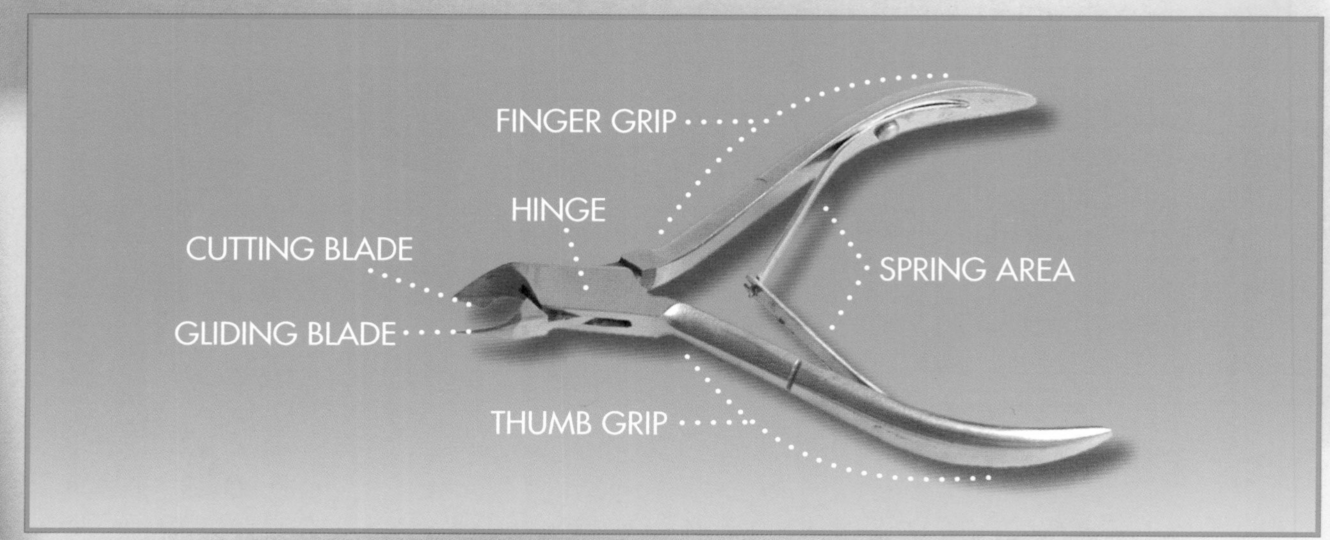


***Cuticle Nippers**, sometimes referred to as **pteryguim (te-rij-e-um) removers**, are used to remove any loose or excess skin that overlaps onto the base of the fingernail. A well-groomed cuticle keeps nails healthy and adds to the finished appearance of any nail service. Nippers are manufactured in a variety of shapes, sizes and designs available for comfort and ease of use, such as the tweezer nipper.*

**Placement:** The nipper is held in the palm of your hand with your thumb controlling the left handle and your index, middle and ring fingers controlling the right handle.

**Control:** The thumb, index finger and the ring finger control the opening and closing of the nippers.

## Key Elements:

- Cuticle nippers thoroughly remove cuticle from the nails
- Make the nail appear longer through increased visibility of the entire nail
- Provide a clean look to the nails by eliminating cuticle

17

***Check with your regulatory agency if cuticle nippers can be legally used in your area.***

## Cuticle Nipper Dynamics

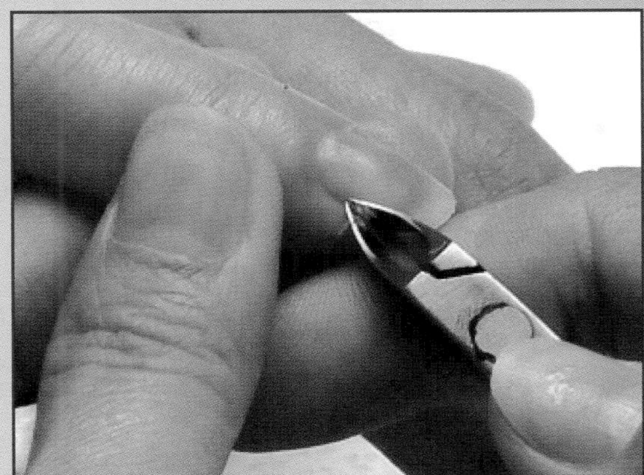

1 *Cut cuticle starting on left side of nail, along the sidewalls.* ***Optional:*** *can start on right side, using nipper blade closest to you.*

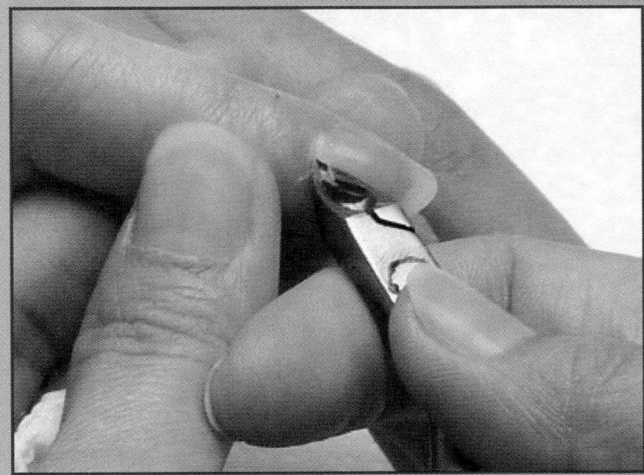

2 *Continue to cut cuticle along the base of nail.*

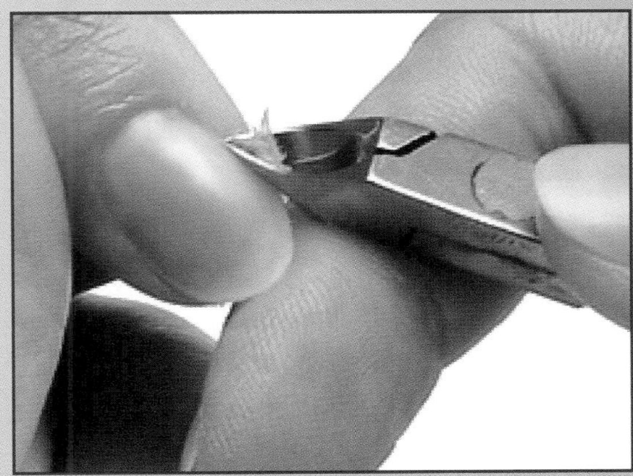

3 *Cut cuticle on right side of nail, along the sidewalls.*

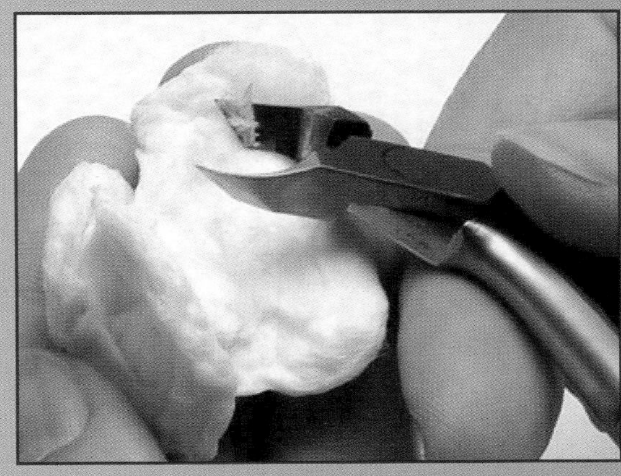

4 *Place cuticle on cotton to prevent contamination of towel.*

5 *Cut cuticle at base of nail.*

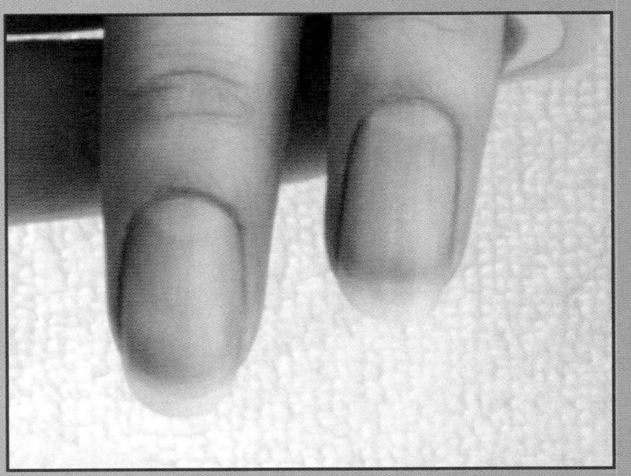

6 *Nails with cuticle removed.*

# Nail Cutting Tools...

***The nail procedures** involve tools of the trade such as cutting tools, which are designed for basic nail and skin maintenance: trimming nail length and loosening or removing cuticle skin. Nail cutting tools are also used for trimming fabric material and cutting nail tips to an appropriate length for advanced nail services.*

## Cuticle Scissor

is an alternative tool to removing loose skin.

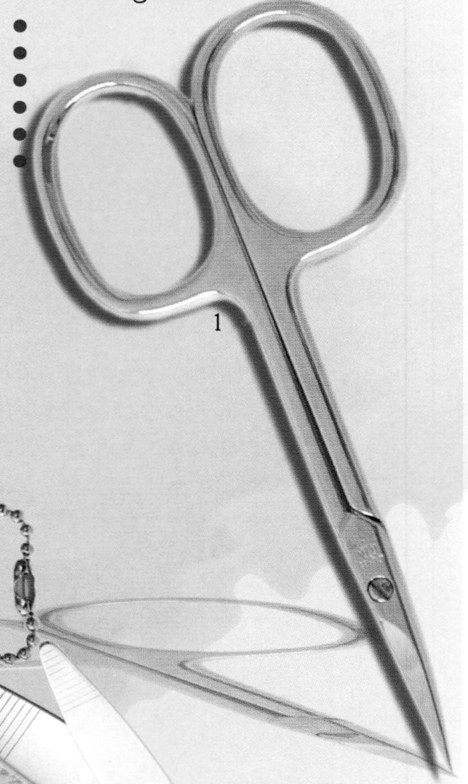

1

## Nail Clippers

shorten fingernails prior to filing and shaping.

2

## Toenail Clippers

are a stronger and larger nail clipper that will shorten the length of toenails. These clippers are manufactured with either **straight or angled jaws.** The angled jaw toenail clipper has the advantage of being able to cut highly curved toenails (plicatured or pincer nail).

3

## Nail Scissors

shorten fingernails and are an alternative to nail clippers, if desired.

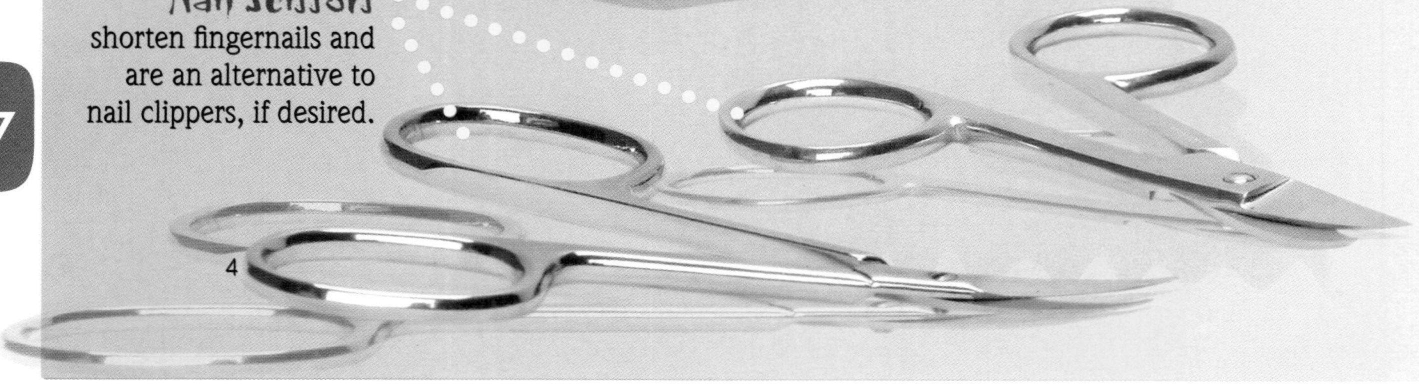

4

17

# Nail Cutting Tools ...

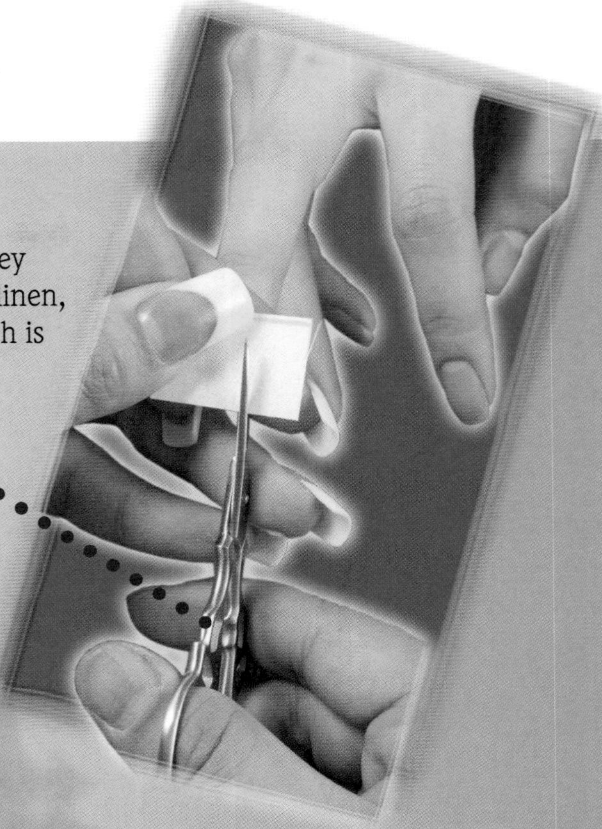

### Fabric Scissors

are all-purpose tool; however, they work especially well for cutting linen, silk and fiberglass material, which is used in a nail wrap service.

1

2

3

4

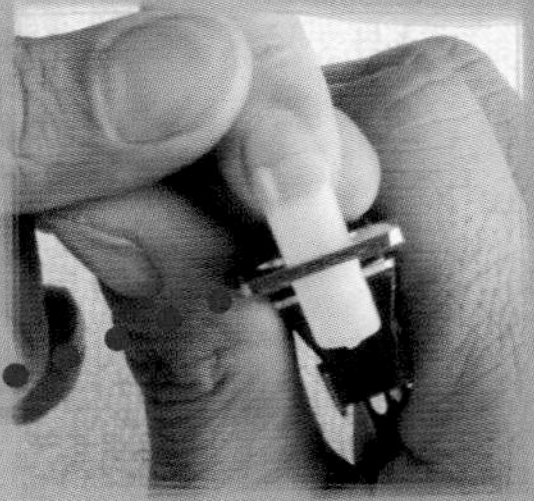

### Nail Tip Cutter

provides a quick and effective way to shorten artificial nail-tip length without cracking or shattering the product. The cutter can cut a square shape, and is a timesaving alternative compared to filing the nail.

### Acrylic Nipper

is a larger and heavier nipper used to remove nail enhancement material that has lifted away from the natural nail.

17

# Nail Polish Usage...

**Nail Polish (Lacquer or Enamel)** provides color to the nails, whether using natural shades or bold, bright colors to express a personality style. Polish is available in an assortment of high-fashion hues, ranging from the most basic colors, like red, blue and yellow, to secondary or tertiary colors, such as violet, orange or yellow-green. Today's nail chemistry lets you personalize the effects you give your clients with "fun" colors, "mood changing" colors, neon, glitter and sparkle finishes.

**Placement:** The handle of the brush is usually the lid of the polish container. The lid is placed between the thumb, index and center fingers.

**Control:** The amount of polish contained within the brush is determined by the length and width of the nail to be polished. A complete coverage of the nail generally includes two applications of colored polish.

## Key Elements:

- Nail polish can accessorize the client's fashion style by matching a lip color or other makeup, or even accenting clothing colors
- Helps cover any minor imperfections on the nails such as stains, spots or other discolorations
- Comprises chemical ingredients that make it durable and long-lasting

# Nail Polish Dynamics . . .

RA

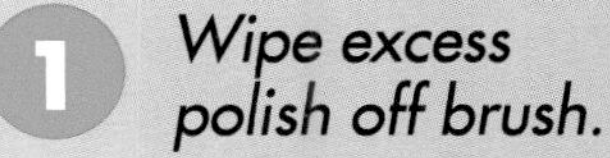

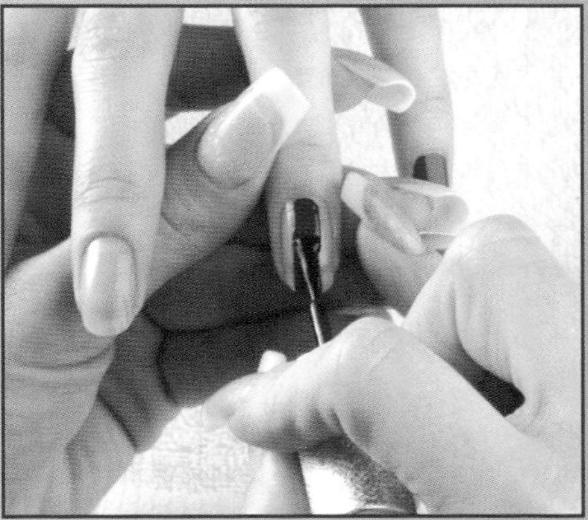

1 *Wipe excess polish off brush.*

2 *Apply brush at center of nail and move polish down toward cuticle and then stroke polish up toward free edge.*

3 *Apply polish on left side of nail.* ***Optional:*** *can start on right side if desired.*

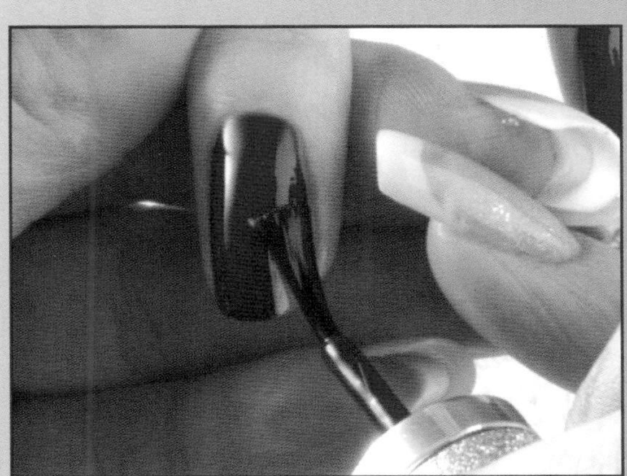

4 *Apply polish on right side of nail.*

5 *Seal end of free edge with polish (stroke across edge.)*

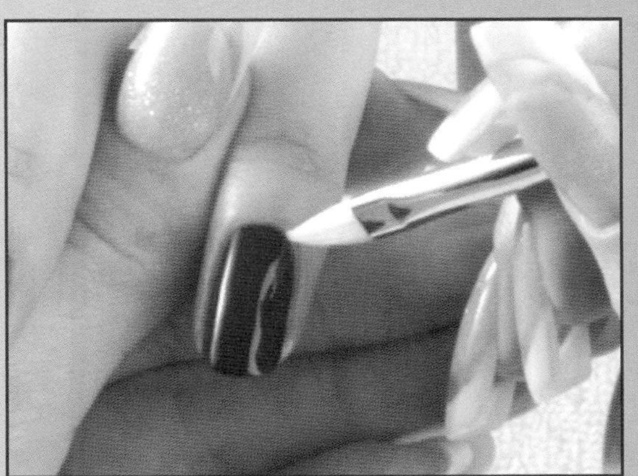

6 *Remove any polish on skin surrounding nail. Use brush or cotton-wrapped manicure stick.*

7 *Completed polish application.*

# Liquid Nail Tools . . .

*Many liquid tools are available to assist you in performing a thorough manicure. As you work with liquid tools and products, please note that most product manufacturers have a procedure or method they suggest for use with their brand. Although the directions you will find in this book represent common practices, you should carefully read all manufacturers' directions prior to usage.*

**Polish Remover** dissolves polish from the nail surface and is available in acetone and non-acetone varieties. Both are safe to use on the nail plate to remove polish. Acetone may be used to remove nail enhancements, while non-acetone is usually recommended for removing polish on artificial nails.

**Cuticle Remover** is a gentle product for softening and loosening the cuticle, making it more pliable when using the cuticle pusher or cuticle nipper. It is available in a liquid or cream form.

**Cuticle Cream or Oil** is applied after the cuticle has been removed. It provides moisture and conditioning to the skin for a soft and healthy appearance.

**Hand and Nail Conditioning Lotion** adds moisture and nourishment to the skin and nails, while also providing lubrication for the hand massage treatment.

# Liquid Nail Tools ...

**NOTE:** One application of both a base and top coat on the nails will be sufficient.

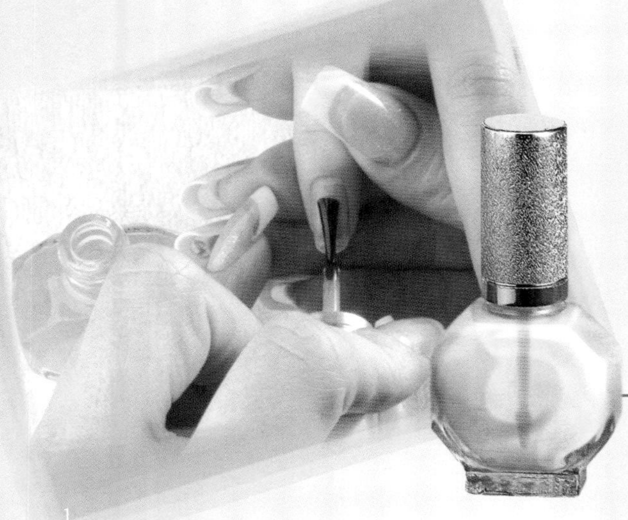

**Base Coat** provides a colorless, uniform, adherent surface. When nail polish is applied over it, the base coat protects the natural nail from stains that are sometimes caused by polish.

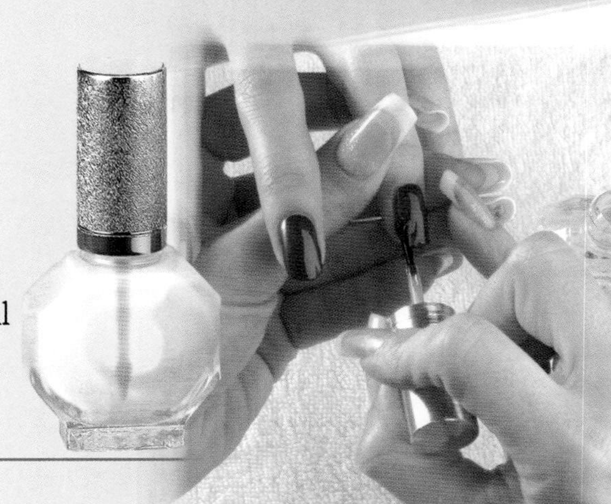

**Top Coat** is a colorless sealant applied over polish to add a shiny protective layer, which will prevent chipping, peeling and fading. Some top coats contain glitter for extra finishing effects!

**Polish Dryer** products are available in liquid or spray forms and are applied to accelerate the polish-drying process.

***Many of the professional products available in your salon may be purchased by the client. Suggest at-home maintenance, and you will be able to sell your clients the professional nail products you use!***

# Liquid Nail Tools . . .

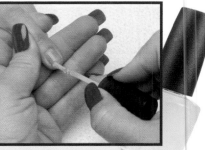

NAIL POLISH

PROTEIN STRENGTHENER

NYLON STRENGTHENER

**Nail Strengthener or Hardener** is applied to the nail plate as a base, providing a coating to help protect against splitting and peeling of the nail.

The two types of nail strengtheners are:

**Protein —** contains collagen fibers derived from animal tissue.

**Nylon —** a tough synthetic material used in a crisscross application on the natural nail.

CAUTION: **Formaldehyde,** a toxic gas, **may be found** in a nail strengthener, but has no genuine strengthening qualities; instead it is used as a preservative. It has a strong odor and the vapors can be irritating to the mucous membranes. A 2 percent formaldehyde solution legally and safely can be used in cosmetics.

NAIL POLISH

RIDGE FILLER

RIDGE

HOLLOW

**Ridge Filler** is applied under nail color, filling and sealing any wavy ridges and hollows of the nail, resulting in a smooth nail surface.

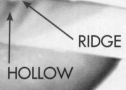

*Many products can create healthy natural nails! Recommend purchase of these products for at-home maintenance.*

17

# Nail Finishing Tools ...

*As you complete the service, stand back and admire as well as critique your work. There still may be some minor adjustments that can be made ... the finishing touches could very well turn the ordinary into the extraordinary!*

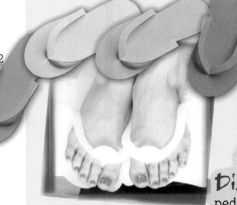

**Manicure Sticks** made from orangewood, rosewood or other hardwoods are disposable alternatives for pushing back cuticles. Manufactured with a beveled end and a pointed end, the sticks can also be used for cleaning under and around the nail edges, removing stubborn flecks of polish and for a variety of other manicuring duties. Cotton can be twisted around the tip for comfort in pushing back cuticles or for the application of nail products.

**Disposable Slippers** protect newly pedicured feet from dirt, germs, viruses and rough floor surfaces in the salon.

**Toe Separators** are worn between the toes during the application and drying of polish, keeping toes apart to prevent smudging of wet polish. They come in a variety of designs and colors for comfort and fashion appeal.

**Polishing Brushes** made from natural or synthetic bristles, create a smooth polish finish. The same brush design is used for base coat, top coat and quick-dry finish applications. Polish handles are designed for comfortable use and as a part of the artistic packaging for nail polish.

**Cleansing Brushes** help to remove filing dust and dry cuticle residue from the nails, and are used to clean under the free edge of the nail.

# Basic Manicure Table . . .

*The artist's studio is a personal space where he or she lets the imagination run wild and creativity flow. Tools and supplies are set up to be conducive to the creative process. Cosmetologists need to create similar space experiences, which allow them to create with ease and comfort.*

Now that most of the basic nail tools have been explained, the next step is to know where those tools are placed on the table.

"Prior to set up of the manicure table, always sanitize the surface!"

In preparing for the manicure service, a proper table setup is essential in providing an organized and detailed procedure, which will ensure a superior nail service. Every tool will be at hands' reach for each step of the procedure.



RA

*Personal sanitation is an important part of maintaining a clean work environment. Your hands and clothing must always be kept clean. Sanitize your hands with antibacterial liquid soap and warm water before and after every client service, as well as after bathroom visits. Waterless hand sanitizers are easy and convenient to use at your personal work stations.*

# Basic Manicure Table . . .

BARBICIDE
HOSPITAL
DISINFECTANT
GERMICIDE • FUNGICIDE • VIRUCIDE

Cuticle Pusher

Cuticle Nipper

Lamp

Wet Sanitizer with Lid and Immersed Nail Care Tools

40 Watt Bulb

Disinfectant

Container with Lid for Cotton

Hand Lotion

Hand Gel Sanitizer

Nail Brush

Cleansing Treatment

Manicure Bowl

Cotton

Cuticle Remover

Nail Polish Remover

Buffer/ Shiner

Cuticle Oil/Cream

Gloves (opt.)

Manicure Stick

Nail Files

Plastic Bag and Tape or Waste Receptacle

17

RA

*Some regulatory agencies may require the nail implements be totally immersed in disinfectant.*

# Liquid Tools for Feet . . .

*Many of today's shoe styles are highly artistic. They showcase the foot – often leaving much of it exposed. This visibility has led many women to want to pamper and beautify their feet. It is not just about using your skills to color, shape and adorn the toenails; it is also about indulging the entire foot. Cosmetologists offer their clients a broad array of pedicure services using a variety of tools to complete these services.*

*Remember that many clients ignore their feet. Professional pedicure treatments can help reduce the buildup of skin that may cause calluses, smooth rough skin and help create healthy, more attractive feet. Wide ranges of foot products are available for performing professional pedicure treatments.*

The following are some of the basic liquid products you will be using:

**Cleansing Treatments** are available for use during the initial soaking and cleansing time, such as sea bath salts, which relax and smooth the feet.

**Foot Soak Concentrate** is an antimicrobial solution to kill germs and bacteria during the initial soaking time.

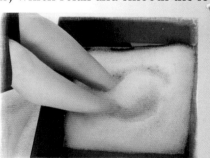

**Sloughing Lotion** can be used with a pumice stone and/or a foot file, or by itself to remove dry surface skin and calluses on the entire foot.

**Sea Salt** is made from the evaporation of sea water and used as a mild abrasive. The salts are gently spread onto the feet and lower legs for gentle exfoliation, smoothing and rejuvenating effects during the pedicure procedure.

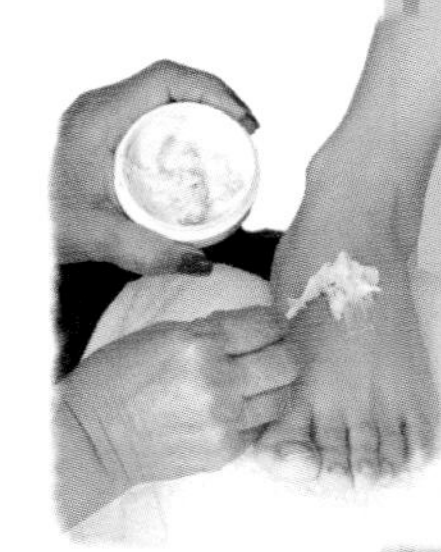

# Liquid Tools for Feet . . .

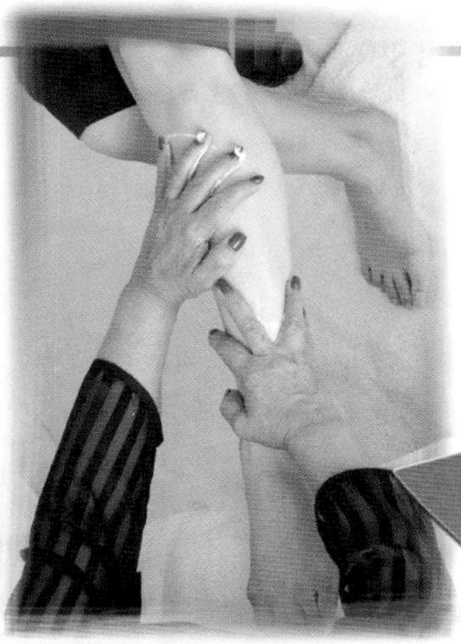

**Massage Lotion or Oil** is a non-greasy product used to provide an easy gliding motion on the skin while performing a leg and foot massage. It contains vitamins and soothing herbs to revitalize and moisturize skin during the massage process.

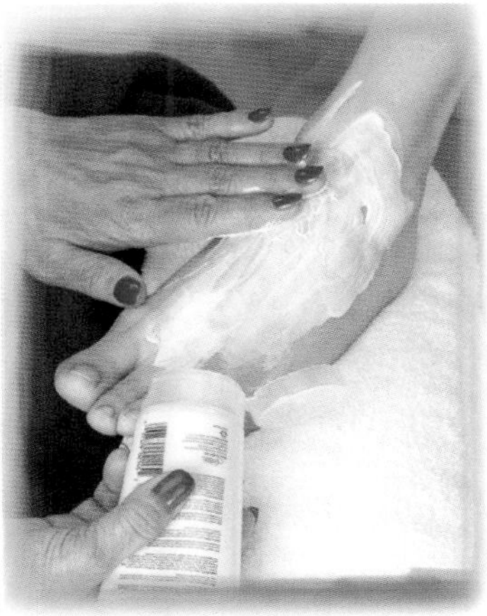

**Foot Mask** provides a refreshing and rejuvenating experience for the feet. Masks supply the skin with hydrating and smoothing effects.

**Foot and Body Lotion** will finish your pedicure treatment with a smooth finish glow and impart moisture to the skin.

**Foot Powder** helps to keep the feet dry and fresh smelling, by absorbing perspiration.

"Remind your clients to bring sandals along to wear home after their pedicure to prevent polish from smearing while damp."

Recommend an at-home maintenance program for your clients to follow between visits.

17

# Spa Service Tools . . .

*By adding a few extra steps to a basic nail service, the professional enhances the value of a salon service – making it more relaxing, rejuvenating and therapeutic. The following tools are available for spa manicure and pedicure services.*

**Paraffin Wax,** when heated, becomes a soft, warm treatment fluid for clients in which to immerse their hands and feet. This treatment is therapeutic for arthritis sufferers or clients with dry skin, and is used as an intense moisture therapy service for all clients. Paraffin is available in many scents, which help to incorporate the aromatherapy benefits.

**Paraffin Therapy Bath** is an electrical unit that heats paraffin wax to a liquid, so that clients can immerse their hands and feet in it.

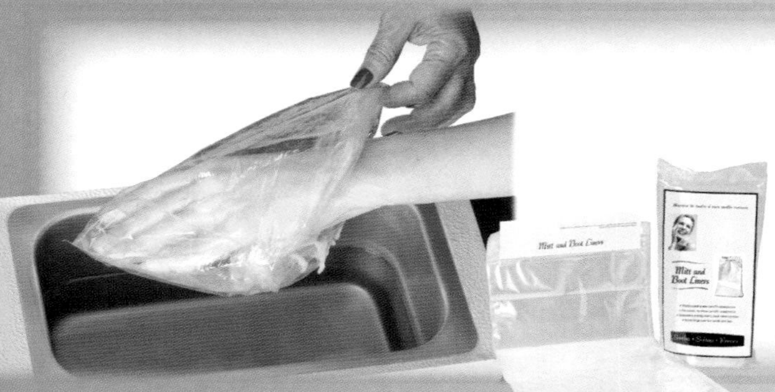

**Plastic Liners** are placed over masks or paraffin wax when applying these treatments to the hands or feet. The liners help trap the heat of the product and the body's own natural heat, permitting superb rehydration of the skin. They are also used to protect the mitts or booties from the product.

**Mitts** for the hands are applied over the plastic liners to create and maintain a naturally warm, moist environment during the paraffin therapy processing time.

# Spa Service Tools . . .

**Pumice Powder or Stone** is a mild abrasive that can be rubbed against the fingertips or bottom of feet to reduce the hardened skin referred to as a callus.

**Heated Mitts and Booties** are mechanically warmed to provide a deep conditioning treatment at a consistent temperature, allowing the paraffin or moisturizing treatment to supply continuous moisture to the hands and feet.

**Foot File or Paddle** removes dry, rough calloused skin on the bottom of feet. Files come in a form that can be sanitized or as replacement abrasive pads.

**Booties** for the feet are applied on top of the plastic liners to produce and preserve a naturally warm, moist environment during the paraffin service.

17

# Sculpting Brush Usage ...

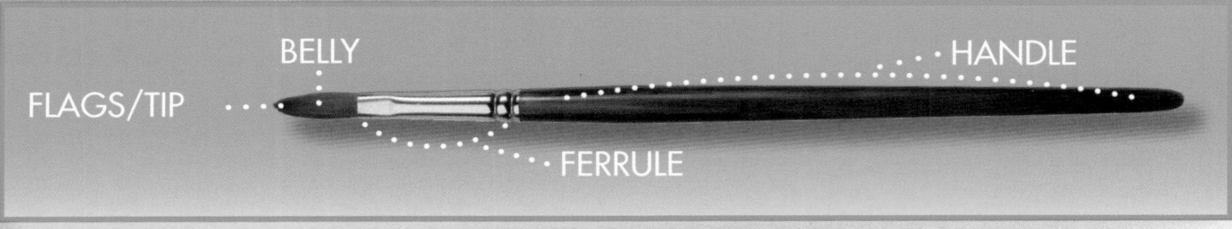


**Sculpting Brushes** are used to apply acrylic products and nail art. The brushes are manufactured using hair from a species of mink referred to as Kolinsky Sable. The Kolinsky is a member of the weasel family and lives in Siberia and northeastern China, where the cold temperature allows the Kolinsky to grow a thick, long coat. The winter tail hair from the male Kolinsky is the **ideal** hair for the construction of the brush, due to the softness and suppleness, while still providing strength and elasticity. An **alternative economical** sculpting brush is the red sable, which comes from the body of the red haired weasel. Red sable hair provides performance and durability similar to the Kolinsky brush.

The brush **handle** is made of wood, plastic, aluminum or titanium, can vary in size from long to short, and is designed for comfort and ergonomic use. A brush **ferrule** is the connecting piece between the handle at one end and the tip or flags at the other end. The ferrule is made of copper, brass or aluminum, with brass being the strongest and aluminum being the weakest and the least expensive. The **tip (or flags)** comes in many shapes ranging from round, flat or square, with the selection dependent on service being performed. Length and density of hair determines product concentration within the hair and is also a deciding factor when selecting a brush. Brushes range in price from economical to expensive, depending on the quality of hair used and the material required for the handle and ferrule. Remember, the better quality brush you use, the better the final appearance will be.

**Placement:** The brush is placed between the thumb, index and middle fingers.

**Control:** When applying the acrylic, use angles (degrees) to place the product onto the nail tip, form or natural nail, which will control the varying thickness of acrylic in certain areas of the nail.

## Key Elements:

- High-quality brushes yield high-quality results and last a long time
- Should fit the product and method of application
- Proper brushes provide ease and comfort during application

## Sculpting Brush Dynamics

1 Grasp brush between thumb, middle and index fingers of favored hand.

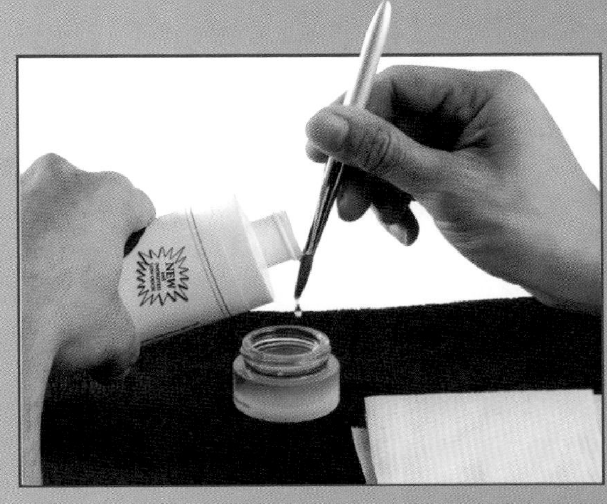

2 Pour monomer (liquid acrylic) into dappen dish using brush as a guide and to prevent spilling.

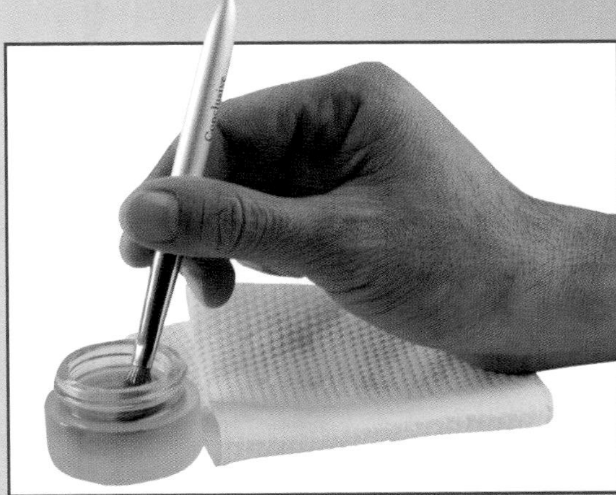

3 Dip brush into monomer for saturation of flags.

4 Remove brush from monomer and place on paper towel.

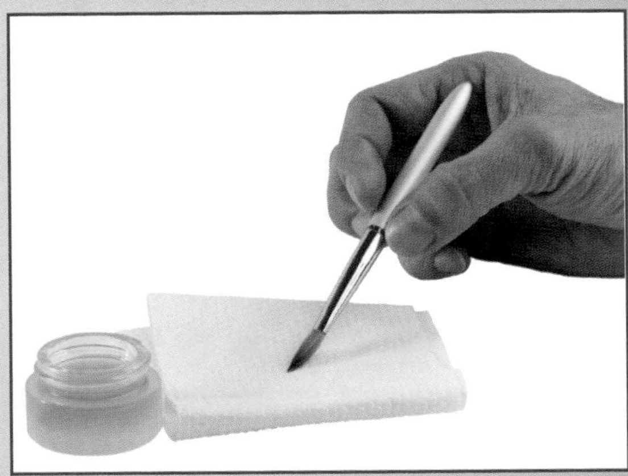

5 Wipe brush on towel to prime flags or tip.

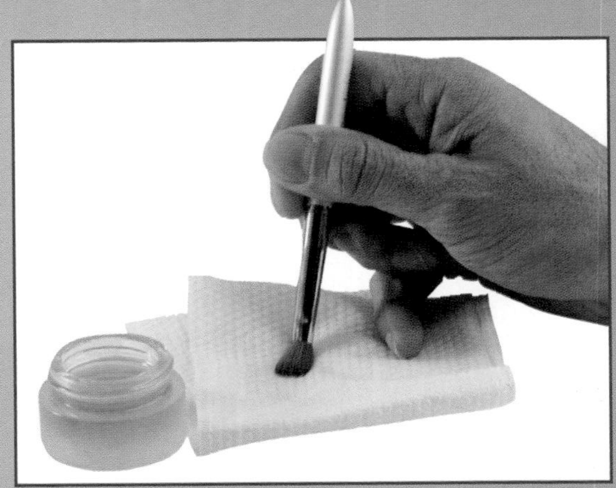

6 Press flags down onto towel to remove excess monomer.

# Nail Sculpting Tools . . .

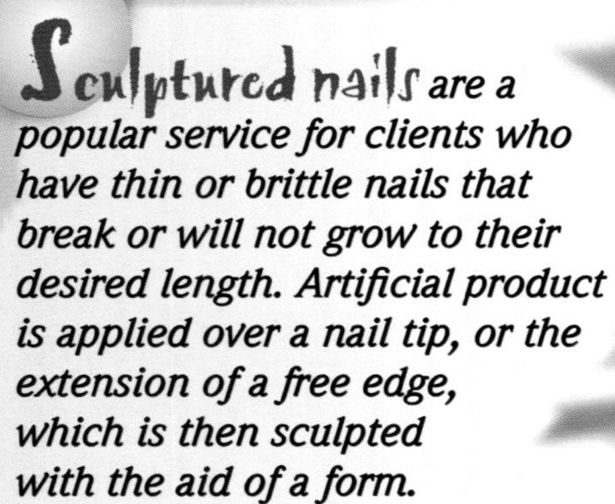

**Sculptured nails** *are a popular service for clients who have thin or brittle nails that break or will not grow to their desired length. Artificial product is applied over a nail tip, or the extension of a free edge, which is then sculpted with the aid of a form.*

1

2

3

Dappen Dish with Lid

**Dappen Dish** is a convenient size to hold either monomer or polymer for acrylic nail services, and is available in glass or plastic. A lid should accompany a dish to prevent evaporation of the product.

4

MONOMER

120 ml - 4 Fl. Oz.

**Pipettes** are used to dispense monomer safely and effectively from a bottle to the dappen dish.

**Scoop** aids in the sanitary dispensing of polymer from a jar to the dappen dish.

5

◄ **Forms** attach under the free edge of the natural nails and create nail extensions without applying nail tips. Forms are available in plastic, metal or paper (disposable) varieties.

17

# Nail Sculpting Tools . . .

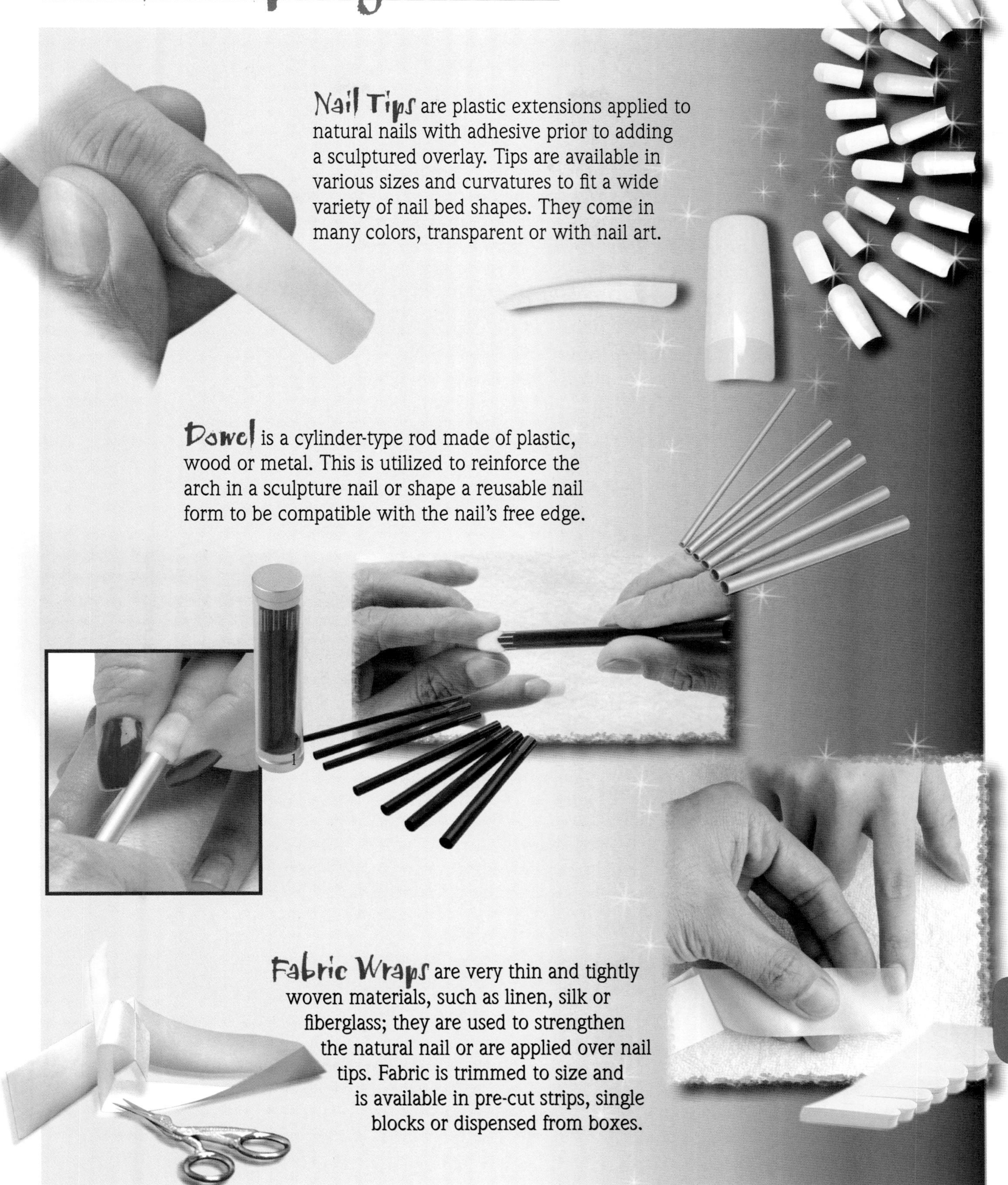

**Nail Tips** are plastic extensions applied to natural nails with adhesive prior to adding a sculptured overlay. Tips are available in various sizes and curvatures to fit a wide variety of nail bed shapes. They come in many colors, transparent or with nail art.

**Dowel** is a cylinder-type rod made of plastic, wood or metal. This is utilized to reinforce the arch in a sculpture nail or shape a reusable nail form to be compatible with the nail's free edge.

**Fabric Wraps** are very thin and tightly woven materials, such as linen, silk or fiberglass; they are used to strengthen the natural nail or are applied over nail tips. Fabric is trimmed to size and is available in pre-cut strips, single blocks or dispensed from boxes.

# Liquid Sculpting Tools . . .

*The cosmetologist must appreciate the surfaces upon which they are placing their work. A person's nails are just as valuable; you must strive for the best preparation of the nail surface, because it is vital to your creation and the client's nail health. Prior to the application of artificial nail products, it is important to prepare and protect the natural nail plate. Follow the manufacturer's instructions for the best preparatory products to use with the sculpturing products.*

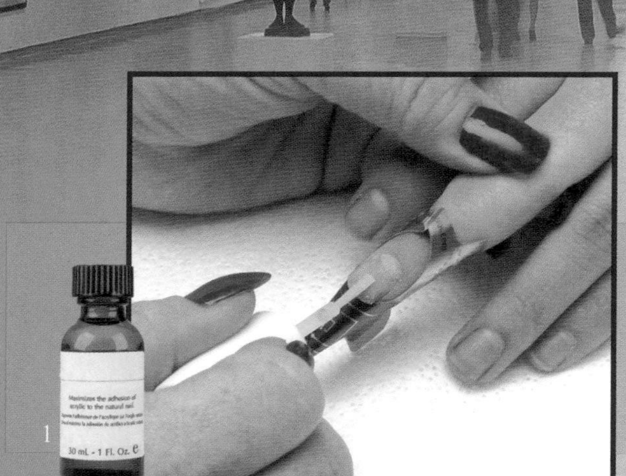

1

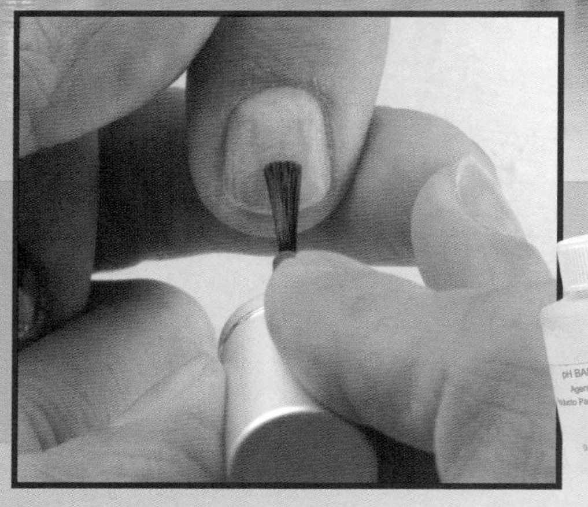

2

## Dehydrant

is a liquid solution applied first to the natural nail to help eliminate moisture, which will ensure proper adhesion.

## Primer

is a liquid solution, containing **methacrylic acid** and is applied sparingly to the natural nail plate prior to acrylic product application to assist in adhesion of the enhancement. It acts like **"double-sided"** tape and dissolves the residual oil from the natural nail, this provides durability to the enhancement. Newer to the market are **"acid-free"** primers, which contain no acid, and therefore, are not corrosive to skin and will not yellow the acrylic product.

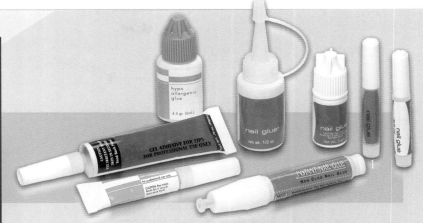

# Liquid Sculpting Tools . . .

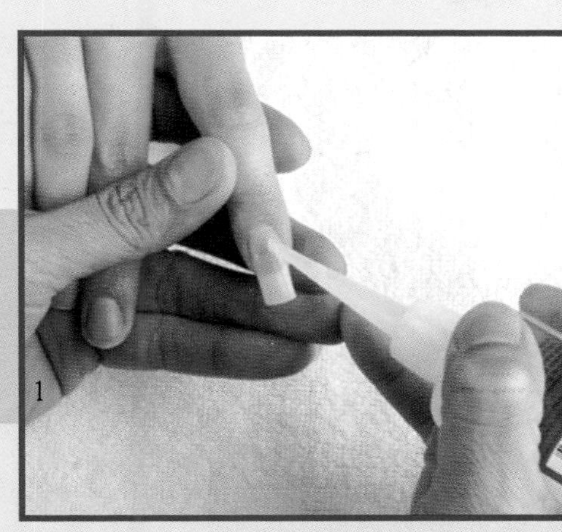

**Adhesives** are natural or sythetic substances used to bond two or more surfaces together and are manufactured in a wide array of viscosities, ranging from thick to thin. **Gel** adhesives are **thick** and provide a **strong support**, but require **long** cure times; a **thin** adhesive provides a **faster** cure time, but a slightly weaker hold. Adhesives must be stored at 60 to 85 degrees Fahrenheit (15.6 to 29.5 degrees Celsius).

"The adhesives used in the professional nail industry are not referred to as glue! Glue is actually an animal or plant by-product."

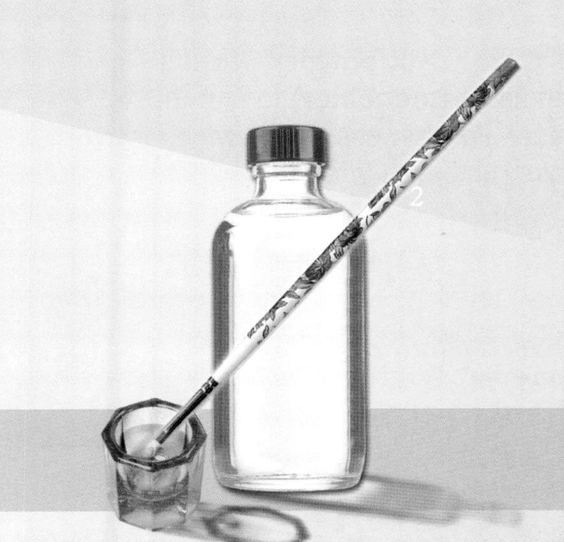

**Nail Enhancement Remover** is a solvent to dissolve artificial nails. It contains **acetonitrile** (a-ce-to-ni-trile), which is a colorless liquid with a pleasant odor.

**Brush Cleaner** is a cleaning solution that dissolves debris from the sculpting brush, which will help provide longevity to your brushes. The flags are soaked in solution following manufacturer's directions and wiped with lint-free paper towel.

# Liquid Sculpting Tools ...

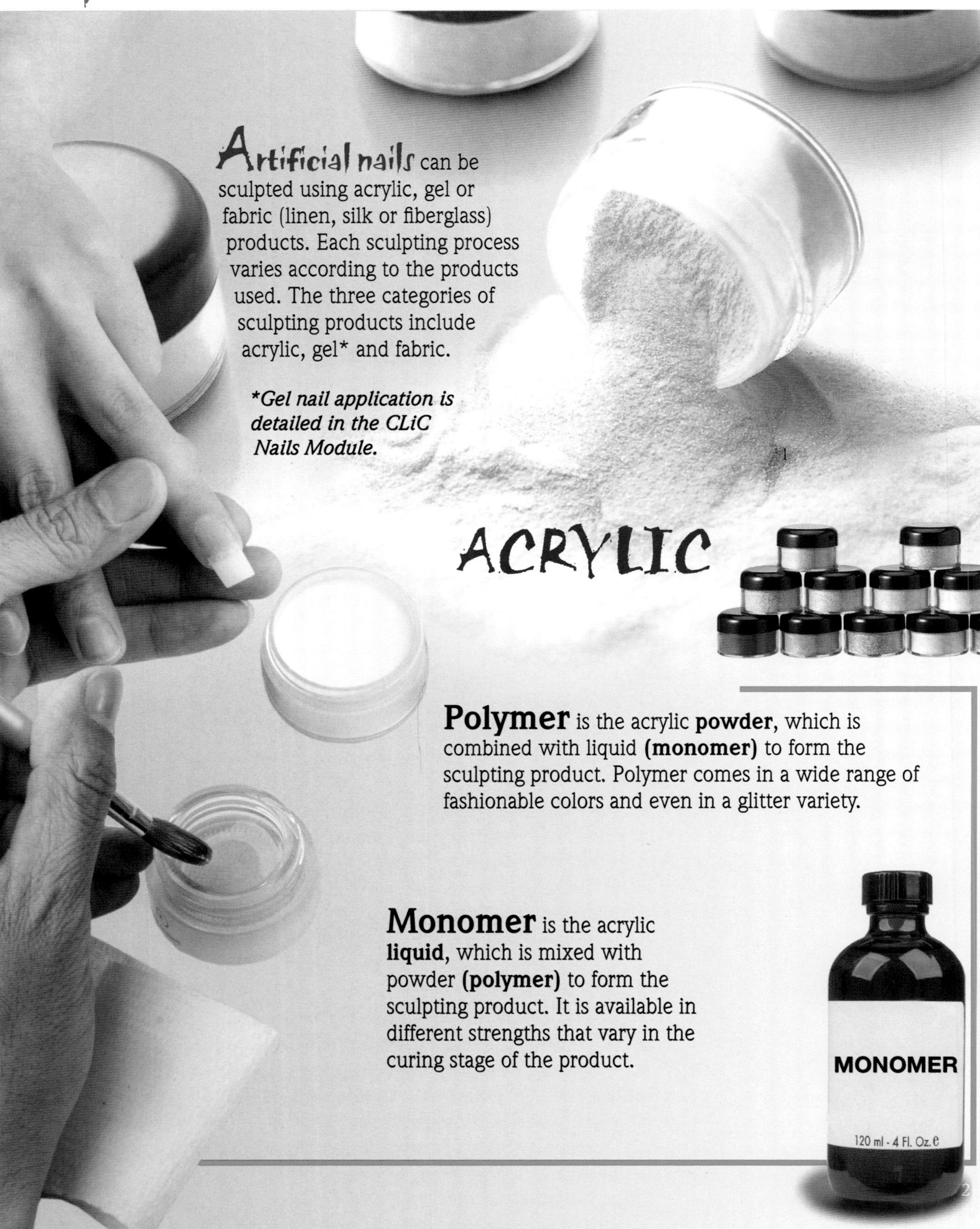


**Artificial nails** can be sculpted using acrylic, gel or fabric (linen, silk or fiberglass) products. Each sculpting process varies according to the products used. The three categories of sculpting products include acrylic, gel* and fabric.

**Gel nail application is detailed in the CLiC Nails Module.*

## ACRYLIC

**Polymer** is the acrylic **powder**, which is combined with liquid **(monomer)** to form the sculpting product. Polymer comes in a wide range of fashionable colors and even in a glitter variety.

**Monomer** is the acrylic **liquid**, which is mixed with powder **(polymer)** to form the sculpting product. It is available in different strengths that vary in the curing stage of the product.

# FABRIC NAILS

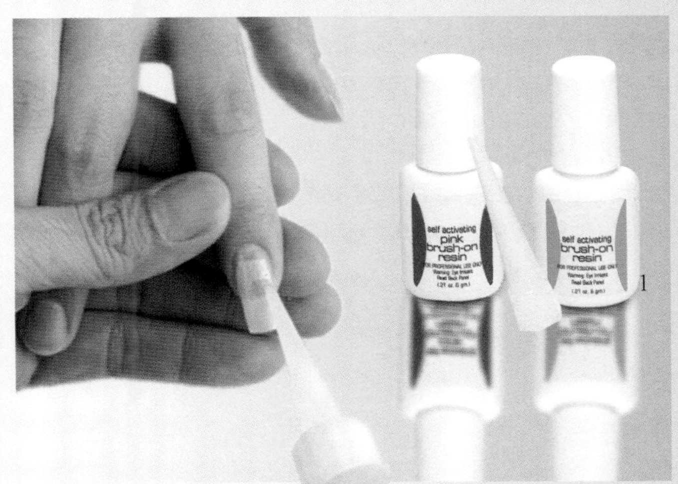


**Resin** is a **type of adhesive** applied on top of the fabric to create a hard nail surface. Resin either air-dries or comes with a spray-on **activator** for instant drying.

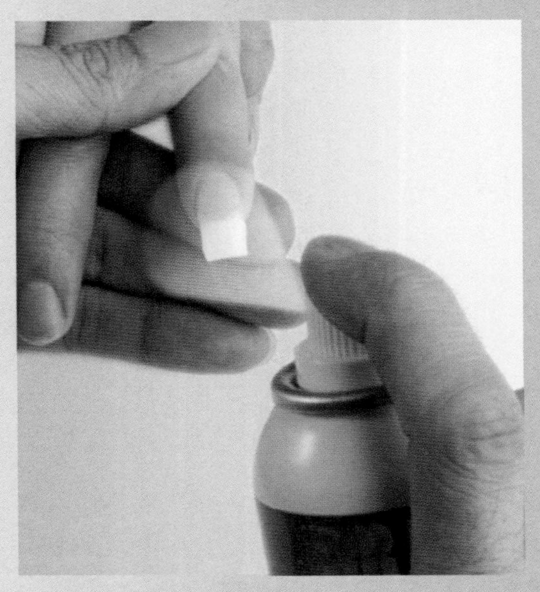

**Activator** is a **catalyst** to help quicken the drying time of the resin and comes in spray- and brush-on formulas.

"Clients like to see their fashion style carried through to their nails. Sculptured nails can be produced in unique shapes and lengths, creating a sophisticated and/or individualized look!"

17

# Nail Art Tools . . .

**Nail Art Brushes** *such as detailers, stripers, fans and other specialty brushes are designed for creating an endless variety of nail-art effects. These brushes may be manufactured much like sculpting brushes, using Kolinsky sable or red sable hair that is soft, long and strong. Synthetic brushes, such as nylon (plastic) are an economical alternative, providing good spring action and a sharp point, but may not hold the color as well within the flags or tip of the brush.*

**Paint Colors** manufactured as lacquer and water-based polish are primarily used for nail artwork.

**Marbleizing Kits** create unique and beautiful designs by using multiple colors. First, a base color is applied, and then a small damp sponge is used to blot and/or an art brush is used to swirl three coordinating colors onto the nail in a fashionable design.

**Nail Art Kits** include rhinestones, colored and metallic jewels, pearls, leaves, striping tape, confetti, foil, glitter, tweezers, sealer, bonder and adhesive. These are only a few examples of the range of nail art kits available.

# Nail Art Tools . . .

**Tweezers** are for ease in picking up small nail art items, such as rhinestones or decals, which are then placed onto the nail.

**Nail Jewelry** adds decorative flair to the nails. There are two types:

**Press-on** ornaments attach to the nail with an adhesive backing.

**Post charms** involve piercing through the nail and fastening a ring to secure the charm. The charms may come in a variety of designs such as initials or assorted other symbols.

**Colored Acrylics** provide a durable and colorful array of nail art that can be placed on top of nails in a three-dimensional art form or used as a two-dimensional design within the nail.

**Transfers** have either a self-adhesive backing or a water-release tattoo-like design, which are placed onto the nail for a fun and easily changeable style.

17

**When furnishing** a salon you have a wonderful opportunity to create an environment that is both **functional** and communicates your **image.** Foremost, your salon layout and the furnishings chosen must be useful to both you and the clients. Your next consideration is the image you wish the salon to project. The salon's image should be a reflection of your professionalism, artistry and style. All elements must work together and be consistent to create a unified design. The salon's appearance makes a bold statement about your specialties and the quality of services you provide. Each choice you make builds the image of your salon and gives it a "personality." Knowing and understanding the kind of client you wish to attract will help you make thoughtful selections.

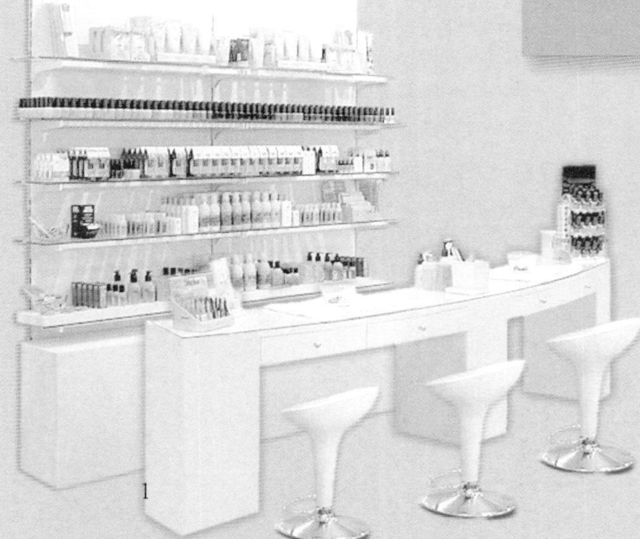

1

*"You are an image of your own work."*
***– Randy Rick***

**Nail Stations** are the most important pieces of furniture in the salon. They must provide comfort for the client and technician, sufficient working space, sanitary storage drawers and appropriate lighting to perform nail care services. Remember to focus on functionality first and stylish appearance second when selecting nail stations.

2

***Use the polish display rack as a marketing tool to encourage the purchase of the customer's favorite polish color.***

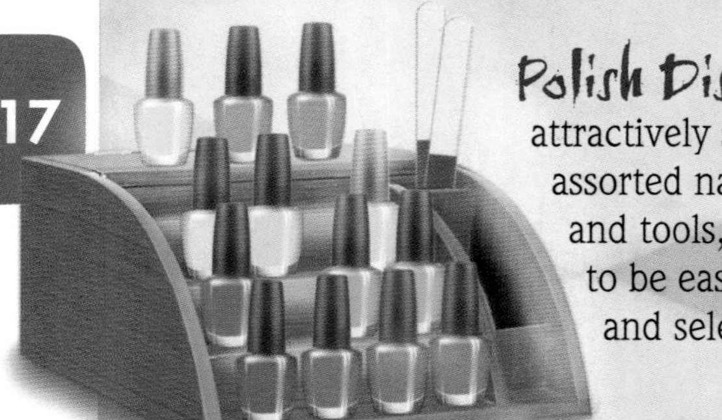

**Polish Display Rack** attractively showcases assorted nail polish colors and tools, allowing them to be easily viewed and selected.

**Client's Armrest** is a soft cushioned area placed on the client's side of the table, which creates comfort by allowing the client to rest his or her arm during a nail service. A folded towel may be used as an alternative to allow the client to maintain a relaxed position.

# Manicure Equipment and Furniture . . .

Client Chair

Technician Chair

**Chairs** for the technician are normally equipped with roller wheels for quick and easy movement. A **client's chair** is also designed with roller wheels to accommodate the client's ease of movement from the chair, so as not to disturb freshly manicured nails. Usually the client's chair will also have a back support to provide comfort during the nail service. Chair designs range from very basic to highly specialized and fashionable.

**Adjustable Lights** should use a 40-watt bulb and feature a clamp on the bottom that attaches directly to nail stations. No matter what choice you make, a well-lit space is crucial to utilizing your visual sense.

**NOTE:** A 40-watt bulb generates low heat, therefore preventing interference with the effectiveness of nail products. This wattage ensures the safety of the client and cosmetologist's skin, while providing ample working light during the service.

**Manicure Heater** will warm creams, oils or lotions and maintain them at an even temperature during the nail service. Warmed products produce greater softness and hydration during the manicure treatment.

STEP 1 STEP 2 STEP 3

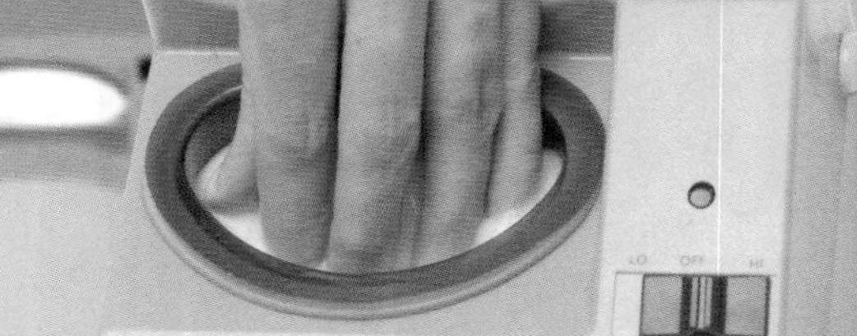

# Pedicure Equipment and Furniture ...

***Pedicure furniture** is designed in many styles, ranging from very basic and cost-effective to expensive, luxurious chairs with integrated massage units. The following are some of the basic styles, luxurious designs and components available.*

**Pedi-Cart with Foot Bath** provides a **convenient and portable stool** for the nail technician combined with an adjustable foot rest for the client's feet. Use of a pedi-cart with a stand-alone foot bath produces the comfort and relaxation needed in a pedicure, and at the same time, is a **cost-effective alternative** to the full-service chair.

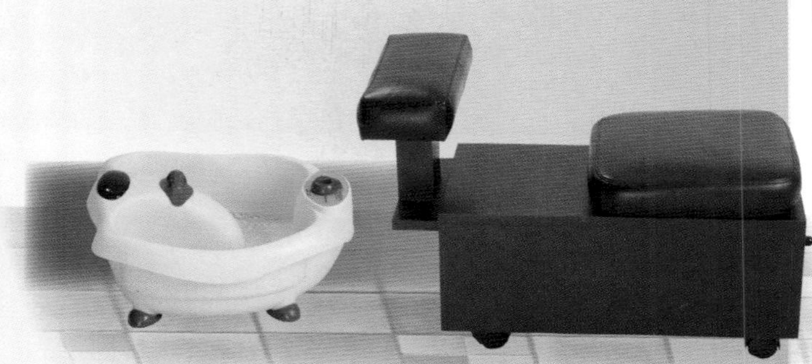

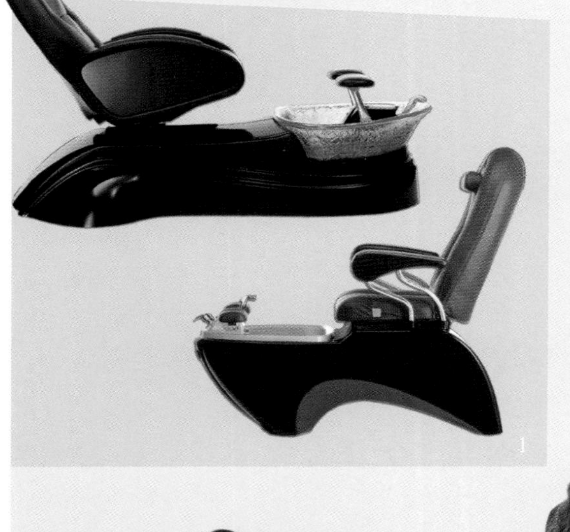

1

**Full-Service Chairs** are **luxury chairs** that incorporate the foot bath and foot rest. Standard features include running water and a drainage system, foot massage jets and a swivel chair. The deluxe **"European style" spa units** offer heat and vibrating services built into the client's chair for the ultimate experience in relaxation and comfort. With today's advanced technology, there are units with **pipe-free™ systems** to allow water to flow without the worry of concealed bacteria in pipes. These systems are easy to clean and economical to maintain.

2

# Nail shapes …

As mentioned in the art principle chapter, the design element consists of multiple traveling lines connected together … this same element applies to nail shapes. The nail shape is either formed naturally (manicure) or artificially (nail enhancement).

There are **five basic nail shapes** of natural and artificial nails.

## Square nail shape

provides great support and strength, because the width of the nail comprises the entire free edge. It is an ideal shape for clients who work with their hands, such as computer programmers, landscapers, etc.

## Rectangle/Squoval nail shape

combines the best features of both the square and oval shapes. It provides strength due to nail width, but is appealingly soft because free edge corners are slightly rounded, which hints at the oval shape. This nail is best suited for customers that work with computers or on assembly lines, due to the strength this shape provides.

## Oval nail shape

is a preferred shape for many professionals in marketing whose hands are on display. This nail is similar to the round shape, but with an increased taper along corners of free edge. The length of this nail may often exceed the fingertip.

## Round nail shape

imitates the natural nail shape, therefore making it a common choice for men or children. The nail has a milder taper then the oval shape and may extend slightly beyond the fingertip.

## Triangular/Pointed nail shape

imparts the least strength/support, therefore making it susceptible to breakage. This nail shape has a defined taper creating a pointed free edge and offers a slender appearance to the hand.

The best shape for each client is determined by:

- Structure of hands
- Length of fingers
- Evenness of nail from each sidewall
- Uniform shape of nails on all 10 fingers
- Type of client's employment/lifestyle

"Always discuss the desired nail shape with your clients prior to beginning the nail service. Provide great customer service by being a good listener and giving your clients the results they requested."

17

# Nail Enhancement Systems ...

**Long nails** *are backdrops upon which the nail artist applies his or her creativity and imagination. Around the world, the popularity of long nails continues to expand. Many women with weak or easily breakable nails are now able to achieve the length they desire through the application of artificial enhancements. A basic understanding of the products will assist you in providing a safe, comprehensive and beautifying nail service. In today's high-technology industry, new products become available to the marketplace everyday, including a variety of acrylics used for nail enhancement services!*

## Monomer and Polymer Group

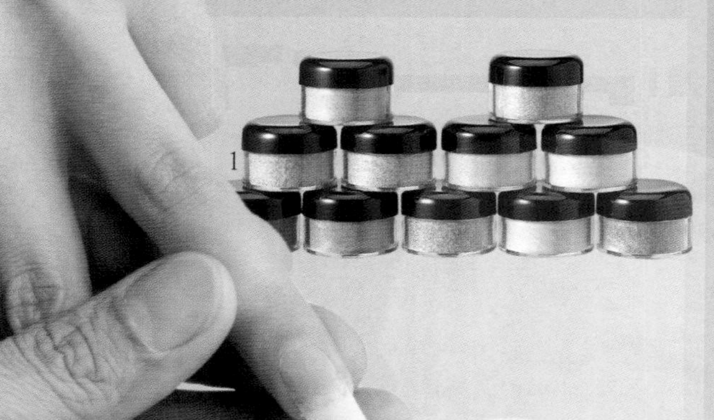

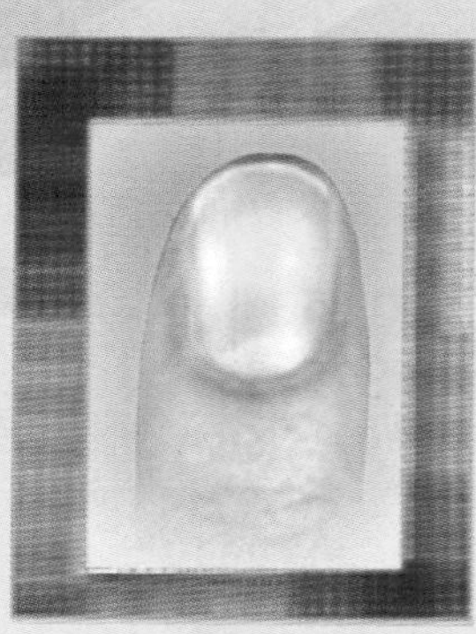

NATURAL NAIL

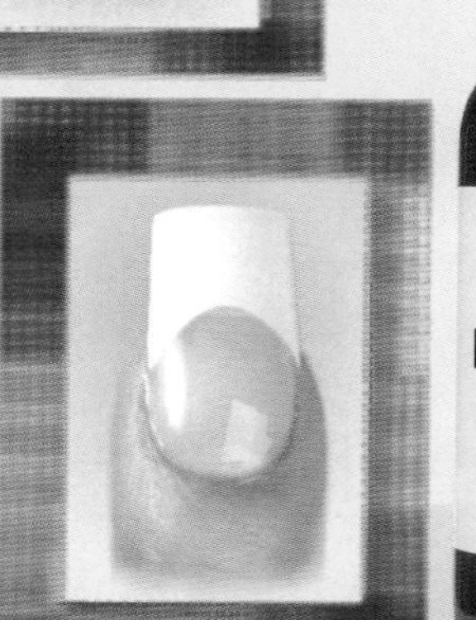

ACRYLIC ENHANCEMENT

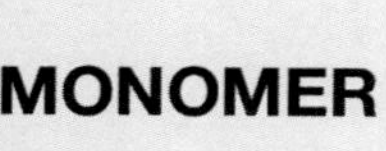

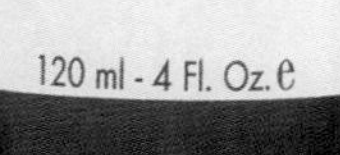



### Polymer

is the powder used for acrylic nails, which is a combination of monomers and other ingredients. A polymer is composed of many monomer molecules, linked together in groups of thousands or even millions, and along with other additives, are processed together to form a powder substance.

### Monomer

is the liquid used for acrylic nails, which is a combination of acrylic monomers, catalysts, and other key ingredients. A monomer is a molecule that can link onto other molecules to form long chains called polymers, which become the powder portion used to create a nail enhancement.

## Three Types of Monomers:

**Methyl Methacrylate (MMA)** (meth-yl meth-ac-ry-late), a type of monomer, is a colorless, volatile, flammable liquid compound ($C_5H_8O_2$) that polymerizes (meaning it cures or hardens) readily and is used especially as a monomer for acrylic resin. It has a small molecule size; therefore, it can penetrate body tissue or skin and possibly cause an allergic reaction.

**Ethyl Methacrylate (EMA)** (eth-yl meth-ac-ry-late) is a type of monomer that is a base material ($C_6H_1O_2$) used in resins, solvents, coatings and adhesives. The molecule size is slightly larger than MMA; therefore, it is not able to penetrate into the body tissue or skin, which makes it safer to use.

**Methoxy Ethoxy Ethyl Methacrylate (MEEMA)** (meth-ox-y eth-ox-y eth-yl meth-ac-ry-late) is a type of monomer used to produce nail enhancements. The molecule size is large, making it impossible to enter into body tissue or skin, thus providing client safety. This acrylic produces little to no noticeable odor because its evaporation rate is slow, which once again benefits the customer.

"Shelf-life of a monomer is generally one to two years, unless contaminated or exposed to heat or sunlight."

**CAUTION:** MMA is known to be unsafe due to reports of allergic reactions. MMA can also be extremely damaging to the natural nail because the nail enhancement becomes very difficult to remove. Regular nail enhancement removers do not work on this product!
*****FDA (Food and Drug Administration) prohibits the use of MMA in salons.***

17

## Wrap System Group

**Cyanoacrylates** (cy-a-no-ac-ry-late) are any of the several liquid acrylate monomers that readily polymerize ($C_5H_5NO_2$) by the application of water, alcohol or any weak alkaline product, **forming an adhesive**. This wrap resin monomer will quickly polymerize in water, forming long, tough chains, joining the bonded surfaces together. Cyanoacrylate monomers are **not cross-linked** (do not attach to other polymer chains), therefore are not strong, and are easily broken down by nail remover solvents.

### Nail Wrap System

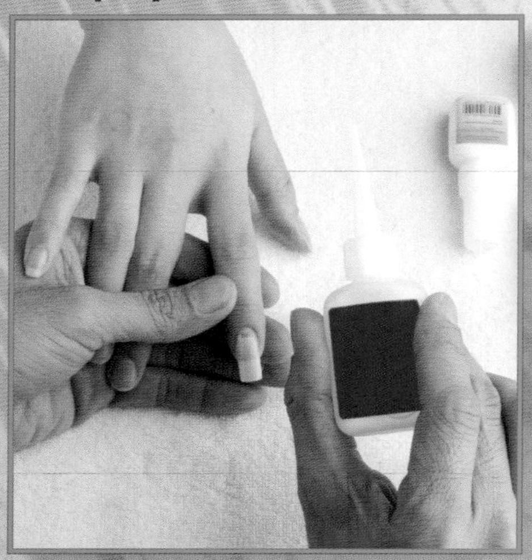

Fabric (wrap) on nail

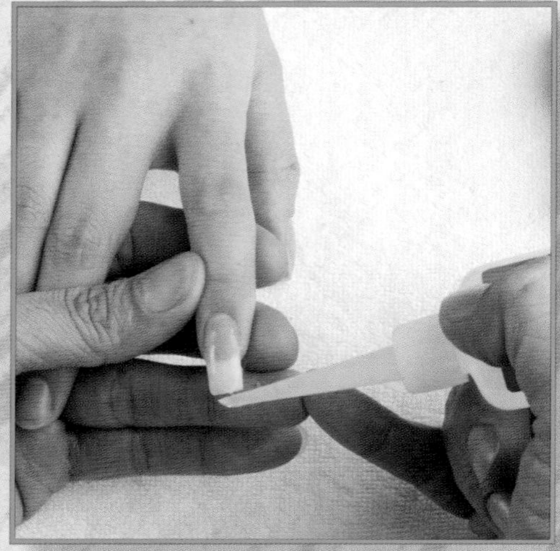

Applying wrap resin to fabric

**Additives:**

**Wrap Resin** (referred to as cyanoacrylate) is a monomer that comes from the acrylic family and may also be used in bonding an artificial nail tip to a natural nail.

**Catalyst** is an activator that helps ensure a fast cure time and generally is used in the wrap system as a spray or brush-on to cure the wrap resin.

**Fabric Wraps** consist of tightly, medium or loosely woven **fiberglass, linen or silk fabrics.** These tiny fibers are used to support and strengthen the wrap coating. The type of weave and thickness of the fabric determines the wrap's effectiveness in strengthening the natural nail. However, the cyanoacrylate liquid must be able to penetrate through the fabric to provide the reinforcement needed for the wraps.

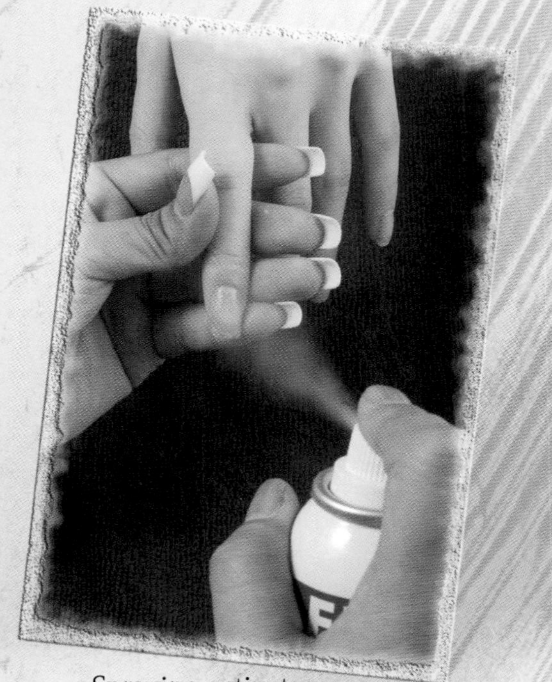

Spraying activator to fabric wrap

# Monomer and Polymer . . .

*Now that you have learned the ingredients of our acrylic groups, we will take a systematic approach to discover what happens when these ingredients combine to form the nail enhancement.*

Immerse sculpting brush into monomer

## First Step in Forming a Nail Enhancement:

**Monomers** (liquid) link with other monomers forming very long chains called **polymers**.

**Polymers** (powder) contain millions of monomer molecules or units, but in a dry form.

Place tip of brush into polymer

When combining the **monomer (liquid)** with the **polymer (powder)** a chemical reaction takes place **called polymerization** (po-lym-er-i-za-tion) **or curing**, consequently creating a hardened nail enhancement attached to the natural nail surface.

Create an acrylic ball

## Second Step in Forming a Nail Enhancement:

The combination of monomer and polymer with other additives help the polymerization to occur within a reasonable time. With the addition of a light (visible light) or heat (body or room temperature) source, the process of **hardening** the acrylic will occur at a faster rate.

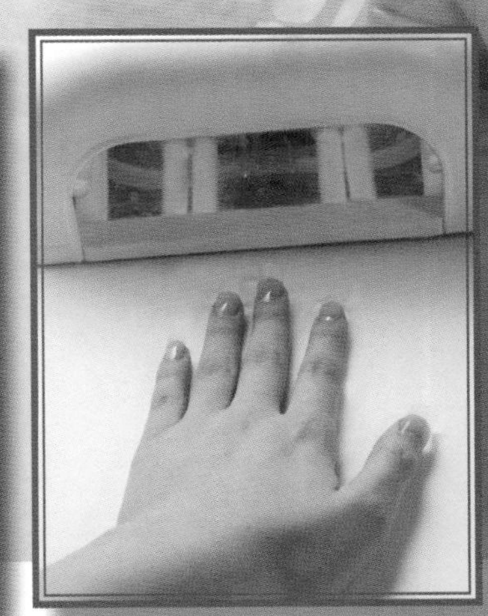

17

# Proportion . . .

*In keeping with our art principles concept, proportion is utilized in the construction of a nail enhancement and/or maintenance of any natural nail length.* ***Proportion*** *is the direct correlation of size, distance, amount and ratio between the individual characteristics when compared with the whole. Whether deciding on a length for nails or creating a nail enhancement the proper ratio will create beauty and accord.*

*When designing nail art, always try to work your art ratio from* ***small to large or large to small,*** *and* ***use odd components verses even*** *component design patterns. This will help create* ***interest to the design,*** *therefore preventing boredom.*

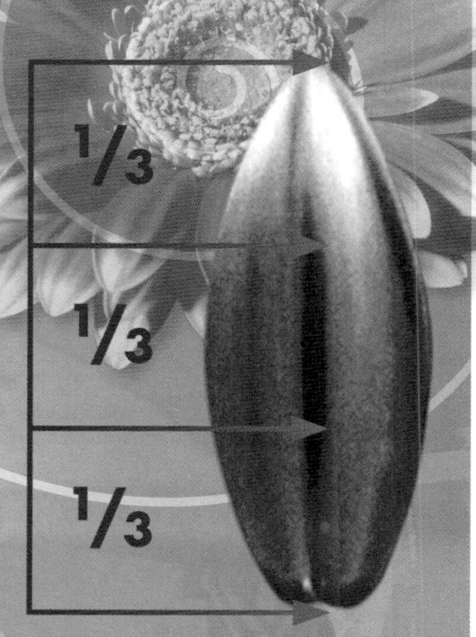


## Ratio of 2/3 for Nail Length

1/3
1/3
1/3

When choosing a nail length, it is best to think of the nail in **three segments**. The ideal proportion of the nail plate should be **2/3 of the entire nail, and the free edge should be 1/3.** This creates a balanced appearance and provides strength and durability to the nails. The professional helps to provide the customer with the proportionate nail following the "Golden Mean," whether creating artificial nails or encouraging daily treatments to initiate natural nail growth.

2/3 1/3

Length of nail is too long

"Exceptions to this rule are the clients' lifestyles, working conditions, heredity or special occasions where an extreme nail art is desired."

Ratio is a **proportional** relationship between two different numbers or quantities. Acrylic consistency is based upon the **ratio between monomer and polymer.**

For placement of a professional nail enhancement, achieving **consistency of acrylic product** requires a mastery of the accurate proportion of acrylic liquid (monomer) to powder (polymer) when forming an acrylic ball.

**NOTE:** The standard terms **ball** or **bead** may be used interchangeably throughout the nail industry for the representation of acrylic product size developed in creating artificial nails.

Unfortunately, there may not be a specific proportion or formula to follow when creating an acrylic product. However, always follow manufacturer's instructions. Creating a proper ratio is a technique discovered by **time and practice.**

The following are some basic guidelines:

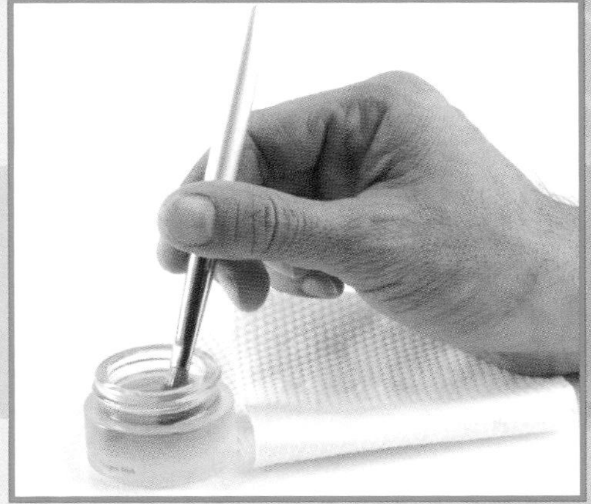

Prime the brush to be used by dipping it into the liquid monomer. Wipe brush onto the lint free table towel, holding brush at a 45-degree angle to prevent hair from fanning out.

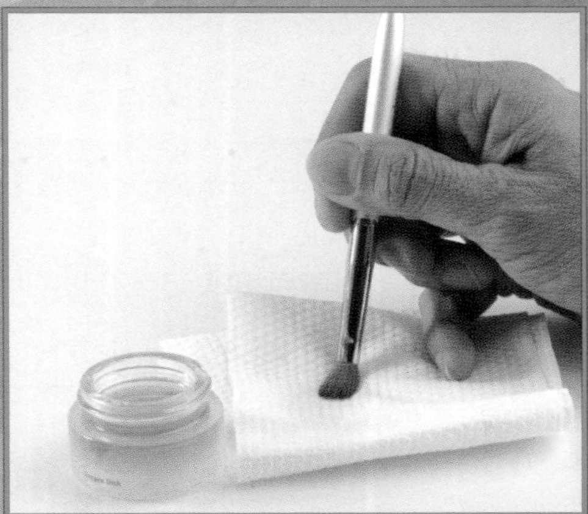

Immerse flags and belly of brush into the liquid. Amount of hair soaked will depend on ball size (follow exercise guides on next page). Lightly press hair against the inside rim of the dappen dish to eliminate excess.

# Ratio ...

Dip tip/flags of brush into powder (center of dappen dish) and lightly draw a line toward wall of dappen dish. Gather as much powder as the liquid in the hair will hold, depending on extent of polymer penetration, and form a ball of acrylic.

If acrylic consistency is **too wet/ runny,** nail enhancements are easily prone to lifting, therefore accessible to bacterial invasion.

If acrylic consistency is **too dry/ powdery**, nail enhancements will become thick, therefore prone to lifting and breakage.

"Through TIME, EXPERIMENTATION and PRACTICE, mastering the ratio of liquid to powder will help you achieve the desired product consistency."

# Acrylic Ratios . . .

## EXERCISE

On the next two pages, work with attaining the proper ratio of polymer to monomer while learning to achieve different size acrylic balls. In order to obtain optimal results, print a copy of pages 674 and 675; place a vinyl sheet over each page and begin your practice of placing small, medium and large size acrylic balls.

**Small size acrylic ball**

**Medium size acrylic ball**

**Large size acrylic ball**

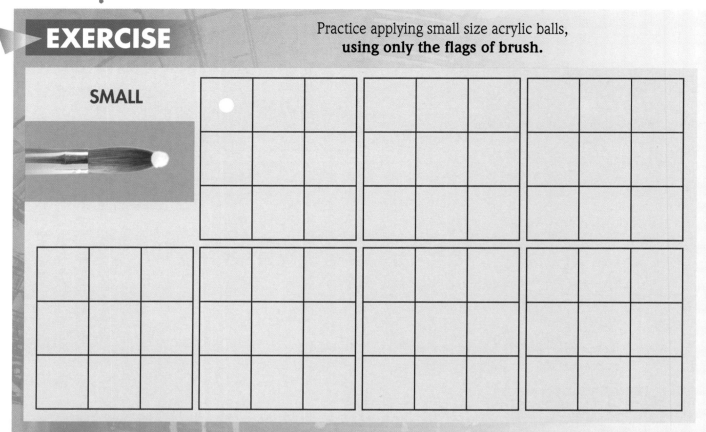

# Acrylic Ratios ...

## EXERCISE

Practice applying small size acrylic balls, **using only the flags of brush.**

SMALL

## EXERCISE

Practice applying medium size acrylic balls. **Absorb polymer into flags of brush.**

MEDIUM

17

# Acrylic Ratios . . .

**EXERCISE** Practice applying large size acrylic balls, **using full extent of flags and belly.** A large brush is generally used to obtain a bigger ball size.

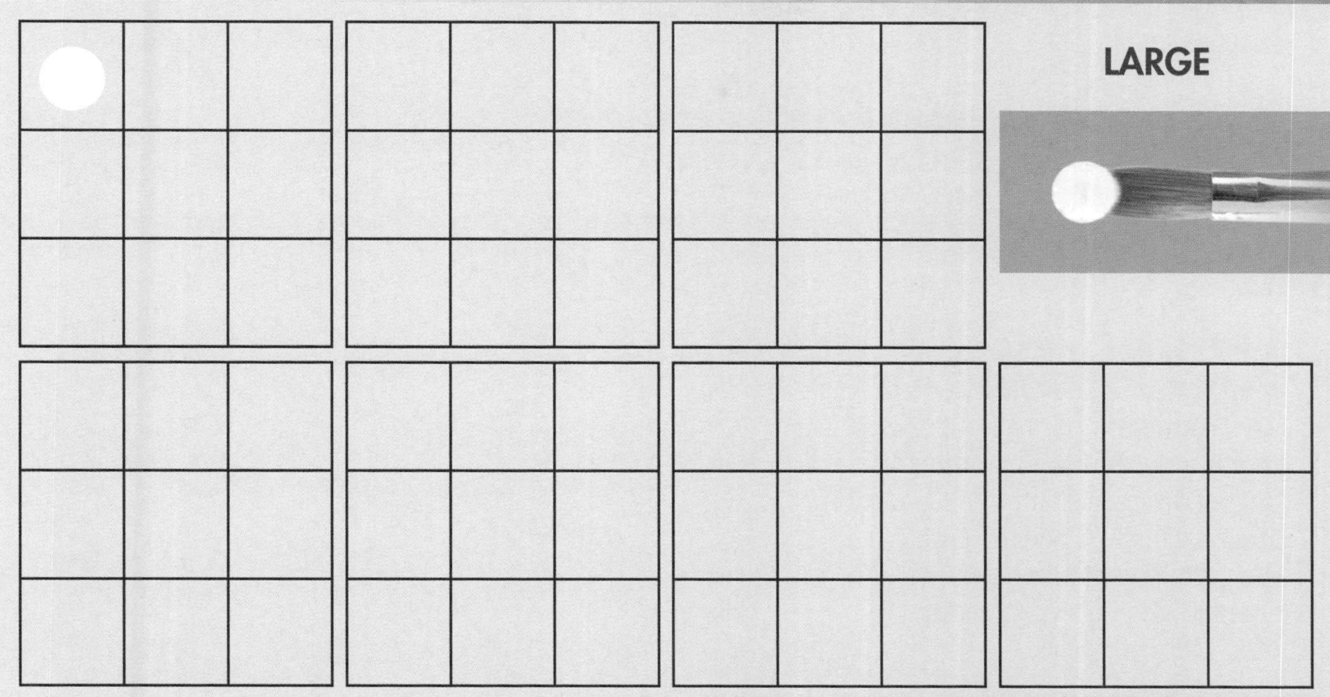


17

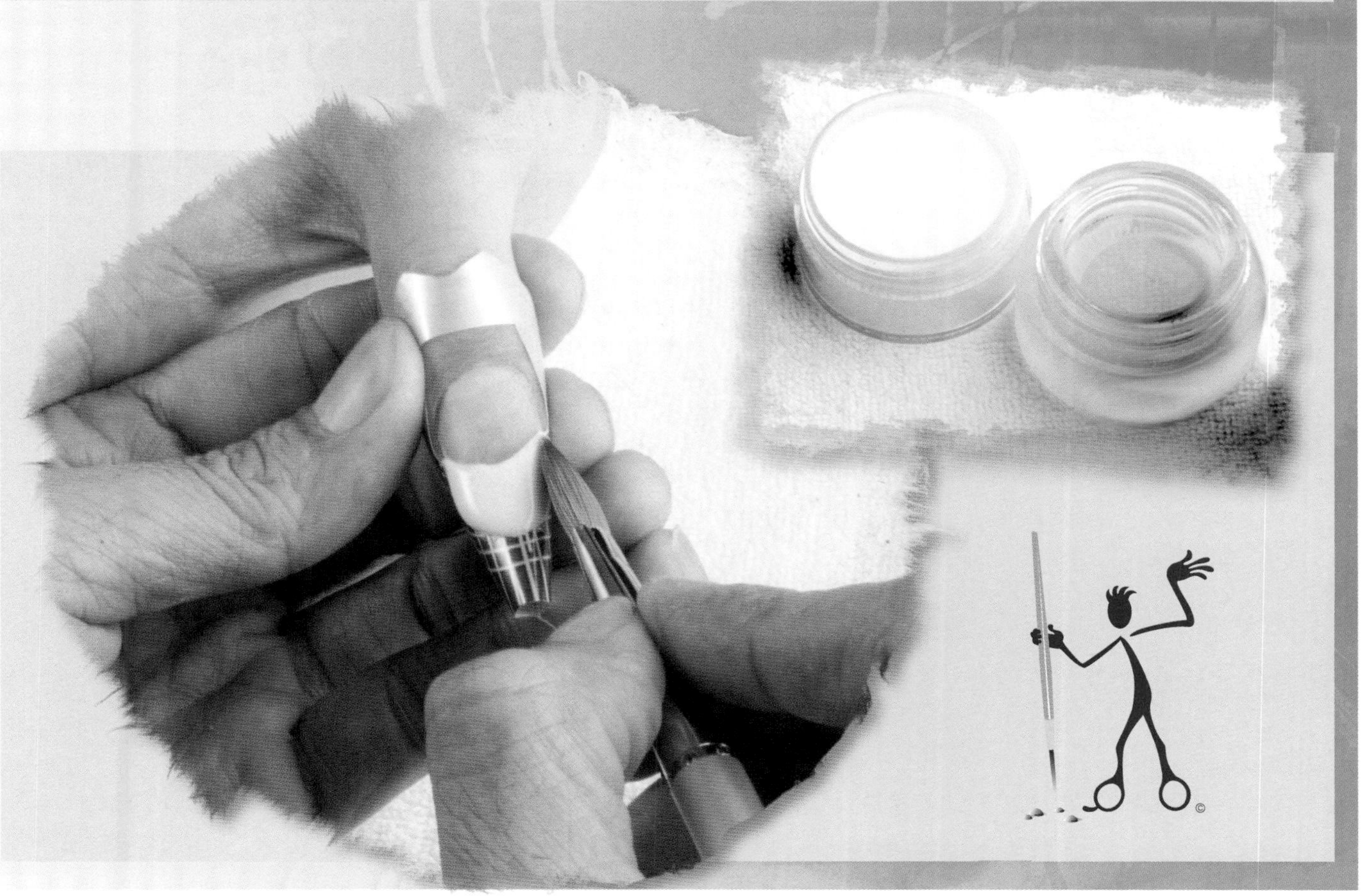

**Elevation** is the degree or angle by which the brush, hand or fingers are **raised or angled.**

An **Angle** is created when the sculpting brush or fingers are lifted to the degree necessary to perform the nail service.

A **Protractor** is an instrument shaped as a semicircle marked with the degrees of a circle, used to measure or call out angles. This tool is a **guide** for pinpointing the exact degree desired, guaranteeing accurate angles. This will help ensure that the correct angle or degree is applied when placing product onto the nail surface.

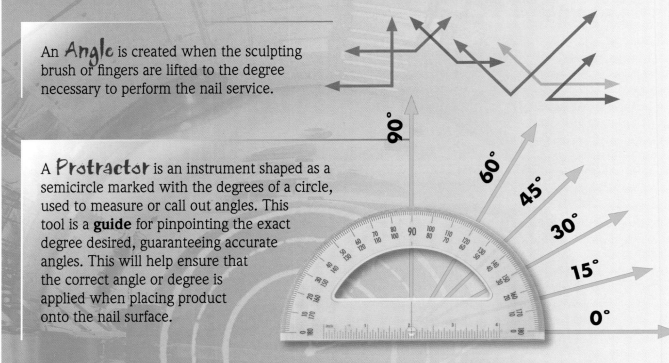

Two types of elevation are:

- **Negative**, created when the fingers or brush are held flat against a surface, with **"no"** lifting or angling.

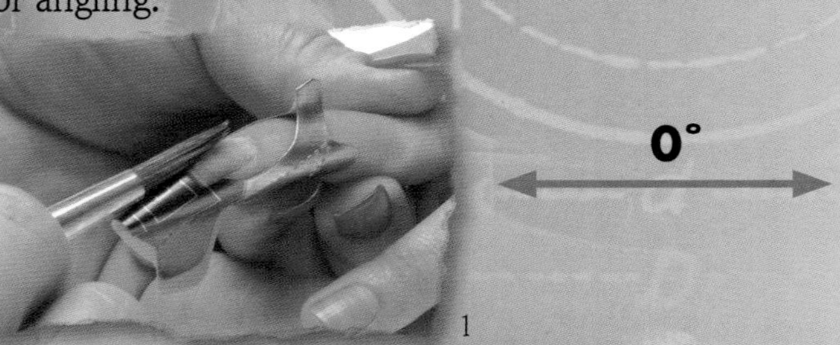

1

**The knowledge of elevation and degrees along with practice and time will achieve confidence and success in nail service performance.**

- **Positive**, created when the fingers or brush are lifted or raised away from surface producing an angle.

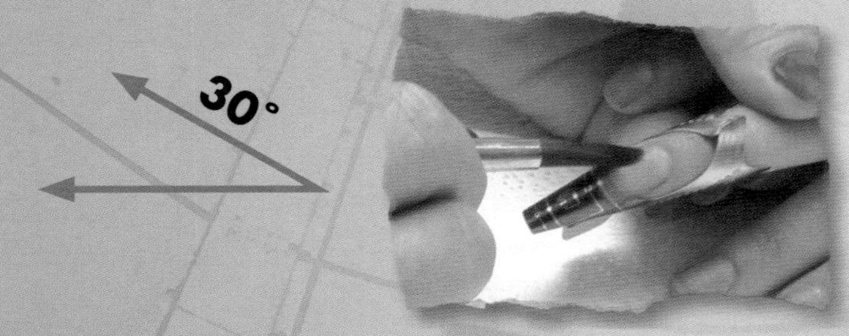

2

"Use the protractor as your guide in gaining the correct angles required in performing a professional nail service."

The **finger angle** along with **brush angles** will **ensure exact placement of acrylic** using the nail zones. Positioning a client's fingertip at an angle will allow product to conform to the natural nail without depositing extra product along nail walls or grooves. When the finger is on a slight incline, the product naturally moves down over nail due to gravity, providing a stronger support system to the stress area.

## Position of Client's Hand and Fingers:

- Arm and hand are in a relaxed position with hand placed on cushion rest or folded towel.

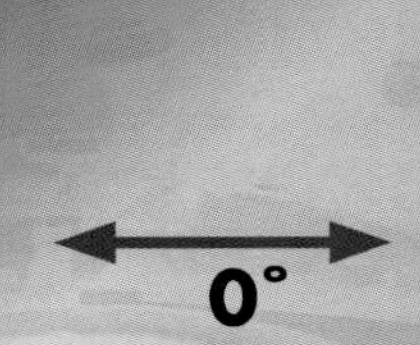


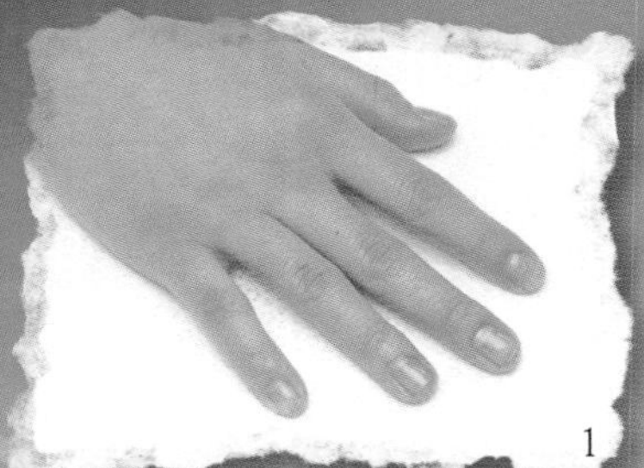
1

- The client's hand is raised with selected finger held in cosmetologist's hand at a 90-degree angle.

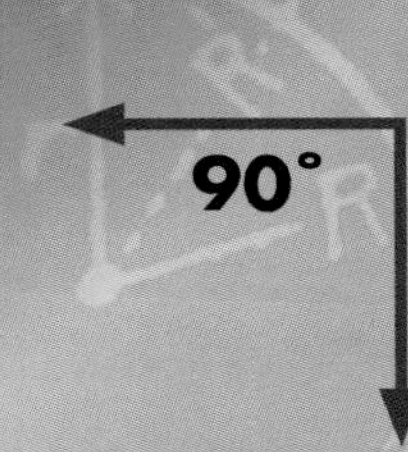


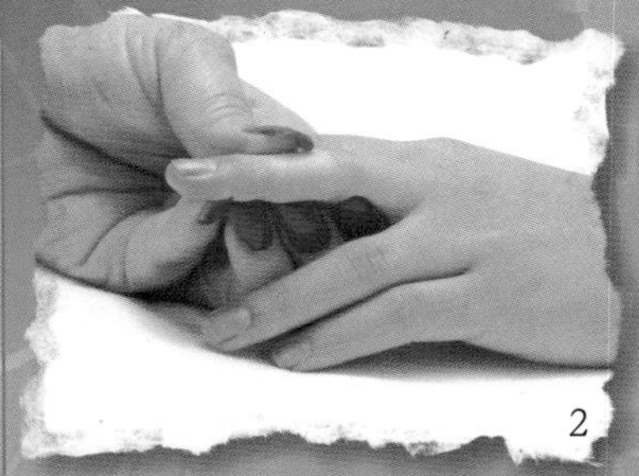
2

- The cosmetologist angles client's fingertip down at a 45-degree angle.

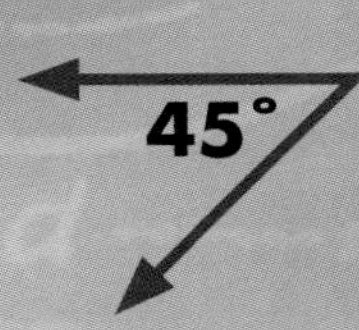


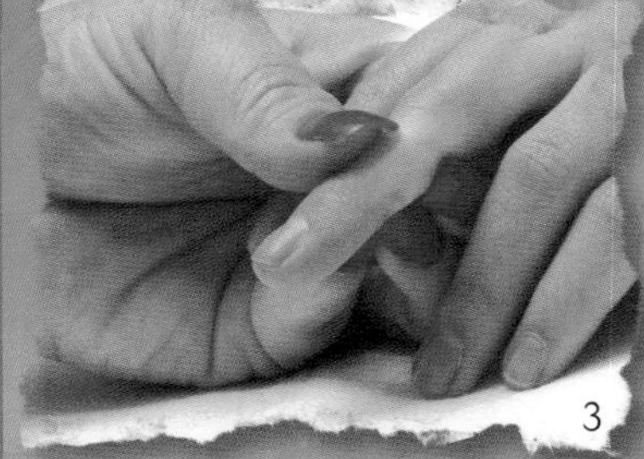
3

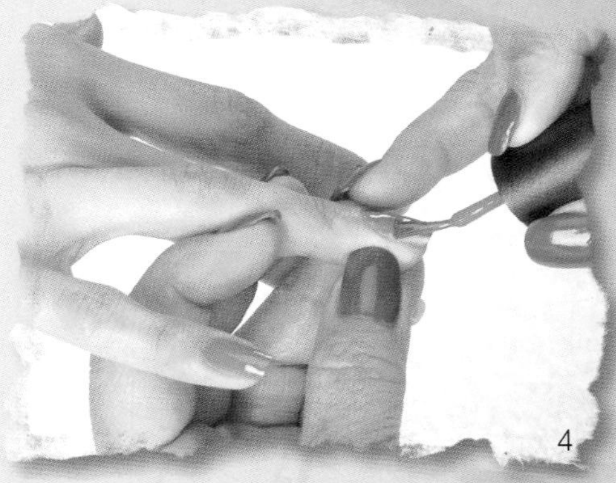
4

This same concept is used for the application of nail polish.

# Zones and Angles . . .

*Along with applying consistent product ratio and angling of brush and fingers,* ***nail zones*** *provide additional information of importance. The zones are product placement guides, which promote ease and efficiency in learning how to form an artificial nail.*

The surface of the nail is separated into **zones**, with each zone used as a guide for acrylic ball placement, which will help to eliminate any inaccuracy.

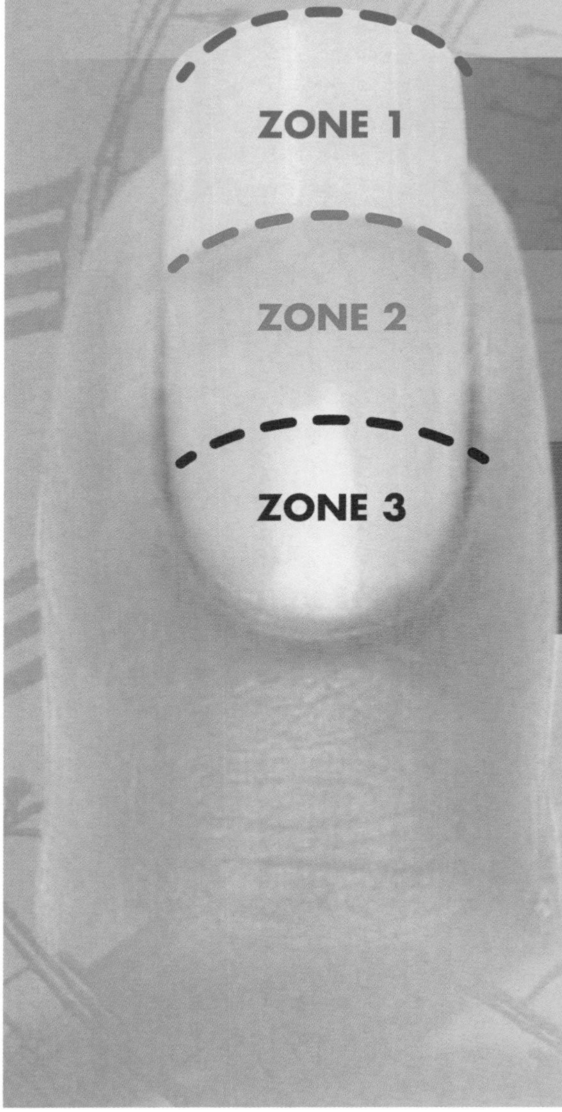

ZONE 1

ZONE 2

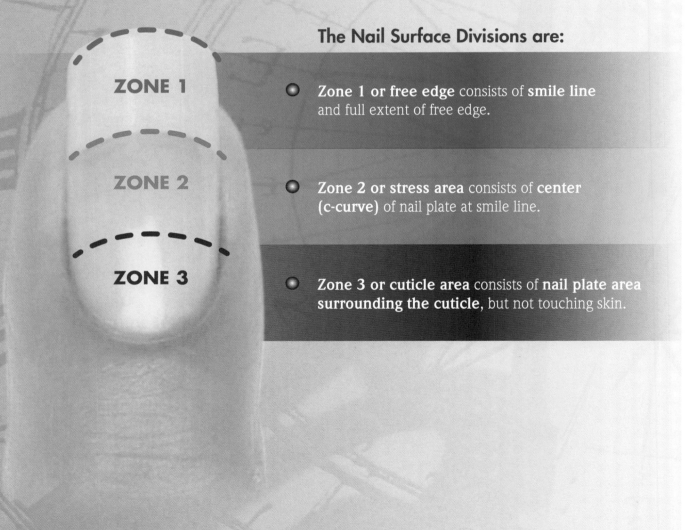

ZONE 3

## The Nail Surface Divisions are:

- **Zone 1 or free edge** consists of **smile line** and full extent of free edge.
- **Zone 2 or stress area** consists of **center (c-curve)** of nail plate at smile line.
- **Zone 3 or cuticle area** consists of **nail plate area surrounding the cuticle**, but not touching skin.

# Zones and Angles . . .

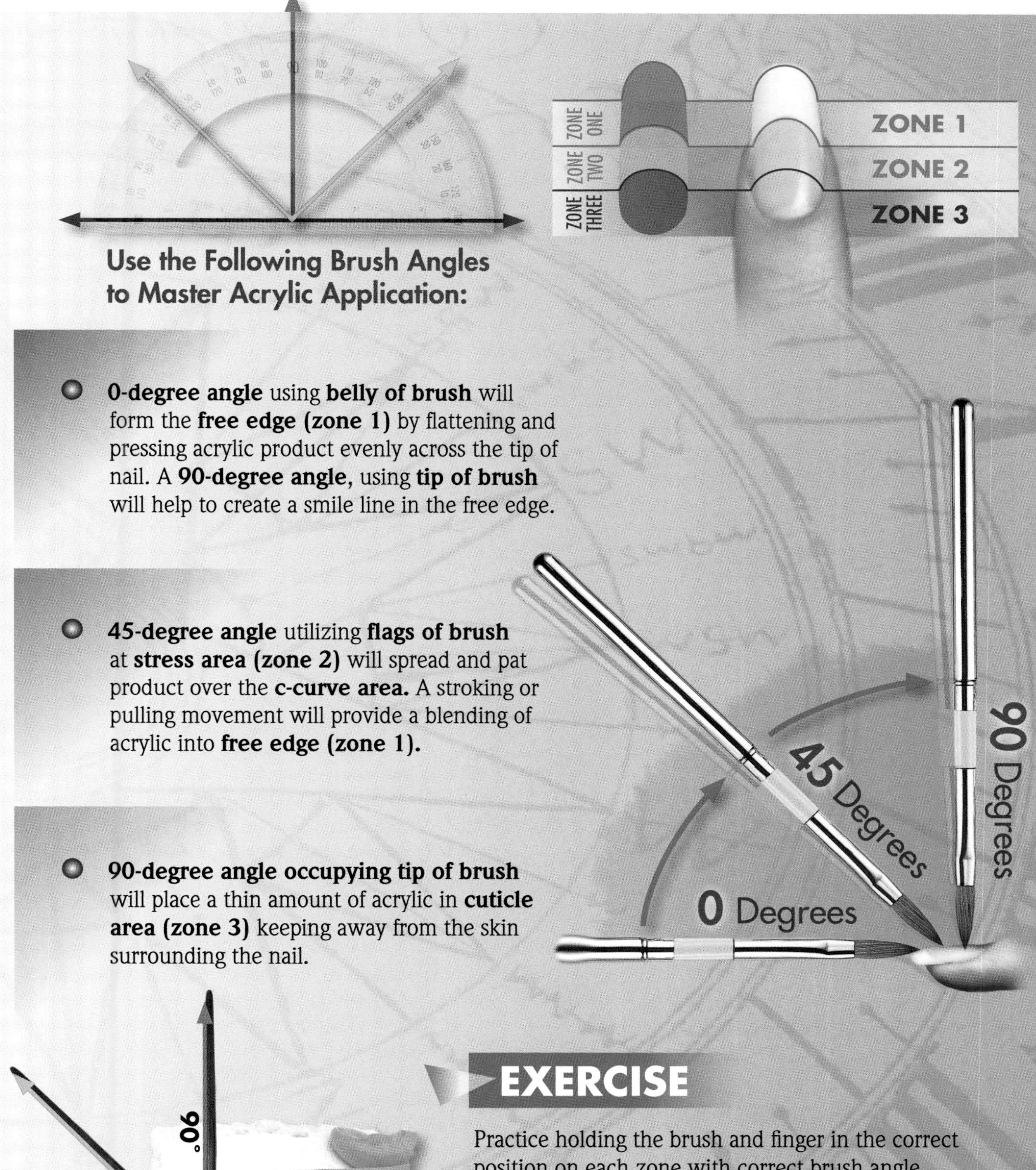

### Use the Following Brush Angles to Master Acrylic Application:

- **0-degree angle** using **belly of brush** will form the **free edge (zone 1)** by flattening and pressing acrylic product evenly across the tip of nail. A **90-degree angle**, using **tip of brush** will help to create a smile line in the free edge.

- **45-degree angle** utilizing **flags of brush** at **stress area (zone 2)** will spread and pat product over the **c-curve area.** A stroking or pulling movement will provide a blending of acrylic into **free edge (zone 1).**

- **90-degree angle occupying tip of brush** will place a thin amount of acrylic in **cuticle area (zone 3)** keeping away from the skin surrounding the nail.

## EXERCISE

Practice holding the brush and finger in the correct position on each zone with correct brush angle. **DO NOT use acrylic at this time;** this exercise is intended to convey the importance of an accurate brush and finger position.

# Zones and Angles . . .

RA

*There are three methods **of acrylic application,** each providing a level of learning for you to build upon. By starting with the three-ball method, you will exercise the development of using various size acrylic balls in obtaining a balanced nail enhancement. Each method will offer progress toward manual dexterity and efficiency in working with acrylic product. The chosen method of acrylic application is also dependent upon size of client's nail and type of nail enhancement service.*

### Three Methods of Acrylic Application:

- Three-Ball Method corresponds with the three zones of the nail.
- Two-Ball Method
- One-Ball Method

## EXERCISE

Practice applying acrylic to a nail tip by following the directions for the three-ball method application. Remember that the size of acrylic ball will vary for each zone according to natural or desired nail size.

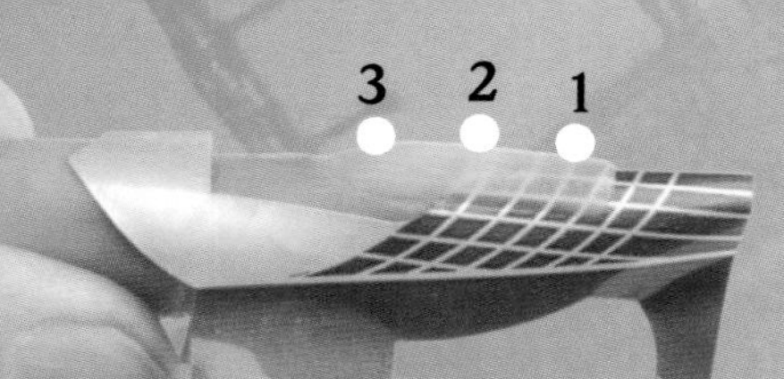


### Three-Ball Method

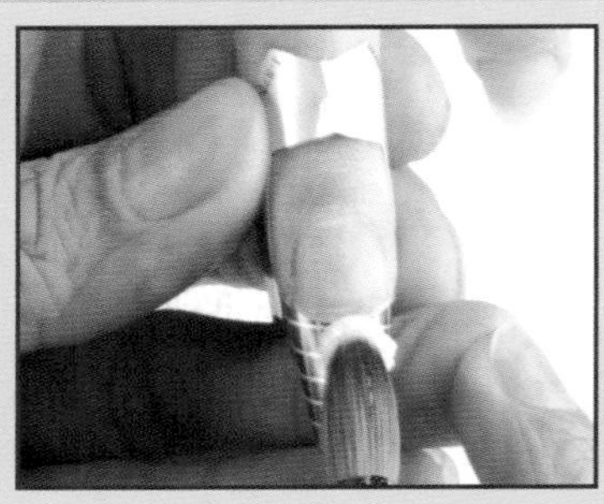
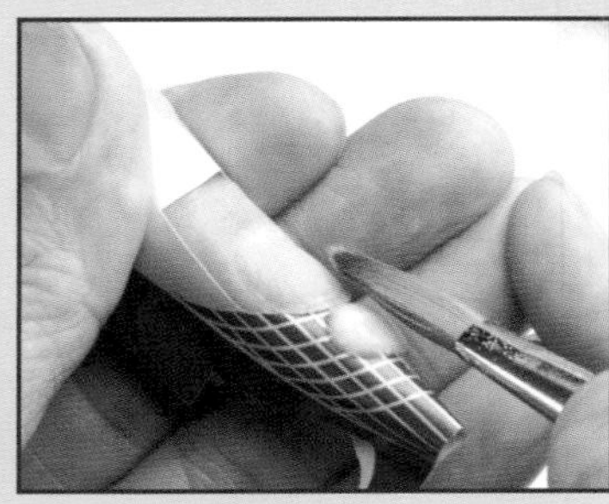

Apply Ball 1 to nail tip or form on **free edge at a 0-degree angle (zone 1)** and create the smile line.

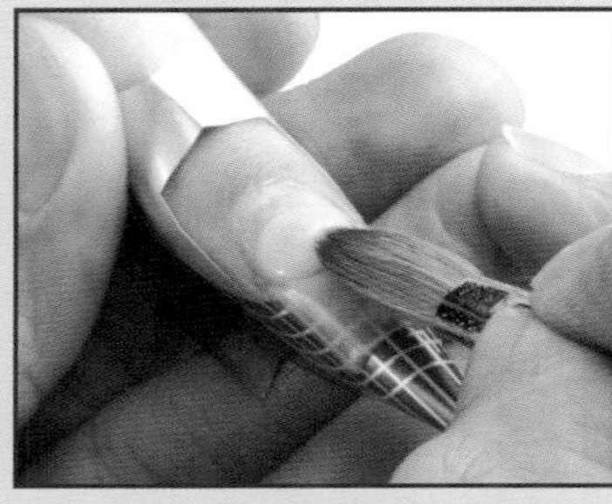

Apply Ball 2 at the **stress area at a 45-degree angle (zone 2)** to cover 2/3 of the nail plate and reinforce the extension.

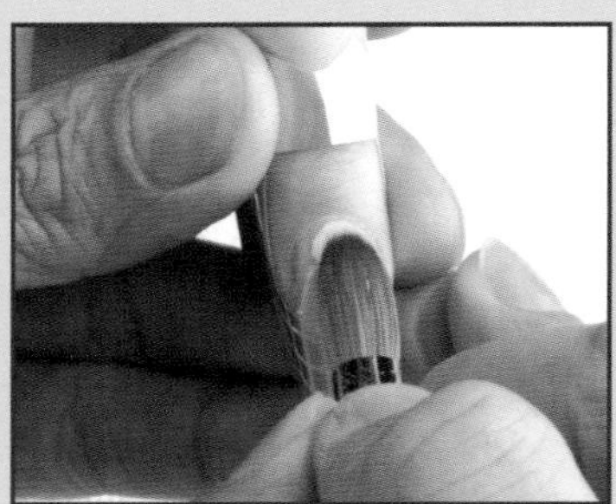
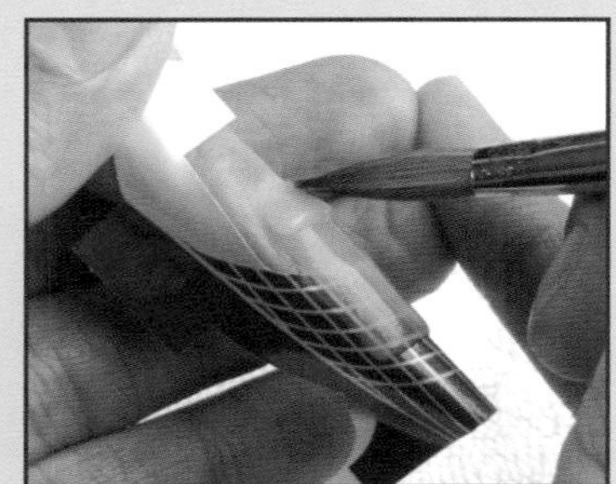

Apply Ball 3 to fill in the **cuticle area at a 90-degree angle (zone 3**) and complete the nail plate around cuticle without touching skin.

## EXERCISE

Practice applying acrylic to a nail tip by following the directions for the two-ball method application.

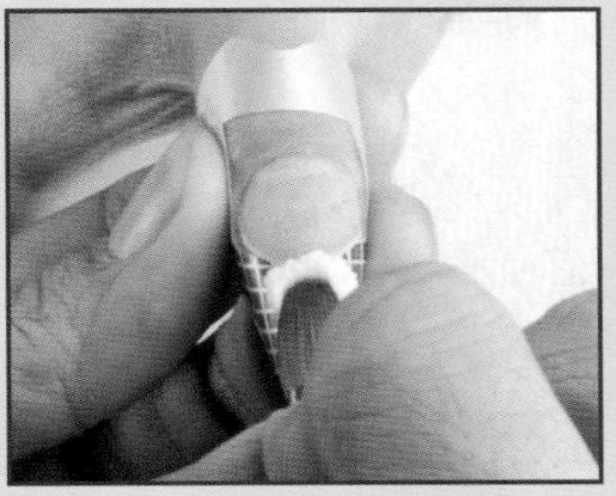

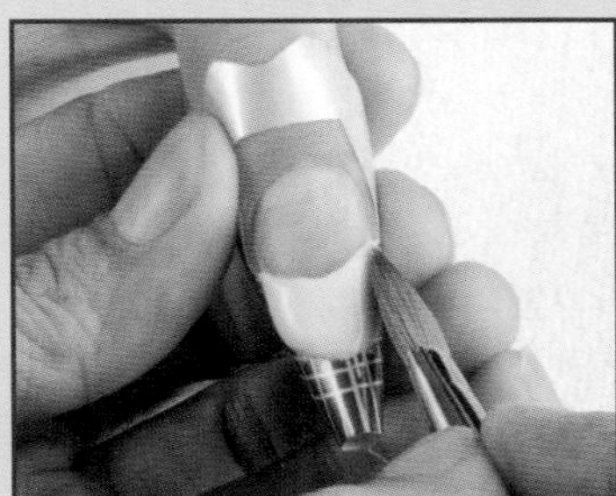

Apply Ball 1 to nail tip or form on **free edge at a 0-degree angle (zone 1)** and create the smile line.

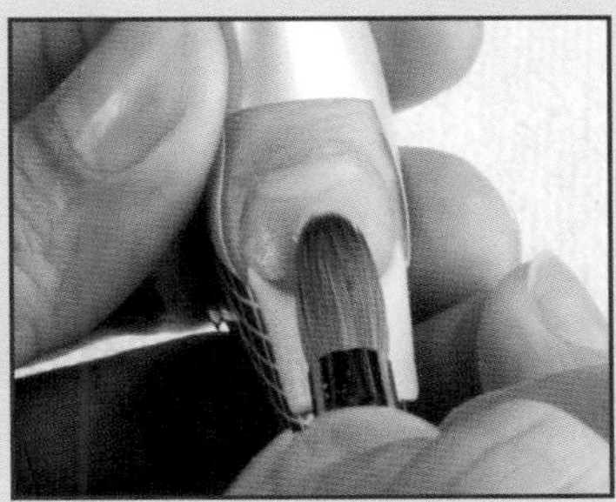

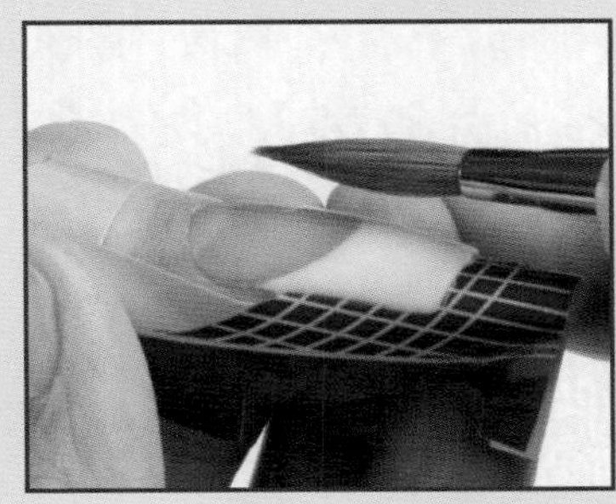

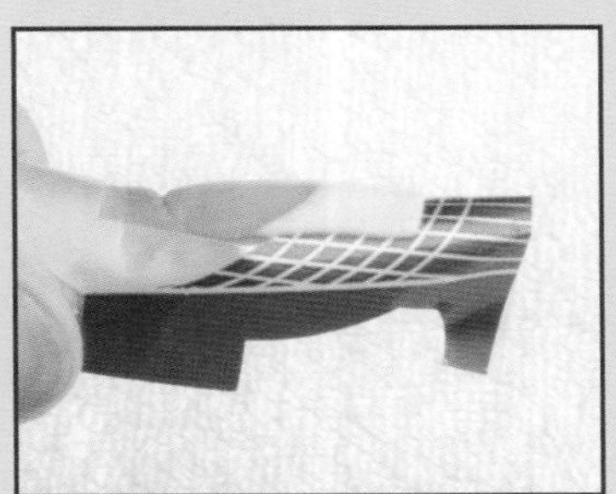

Apply Ball 2 at **stress area at a 45-degree angle (zone 2)** blending to **cuticle area at a 90-degree angle (zone 3)** and reinforcing the extension by lightly stroking product over to free edge. A large acrylic ball will be needed to cover a two-zone area.

## EXERCISE

Practice applying acrylic to a nail tip by following the directions for the one-ball method application.

One-Ball Method

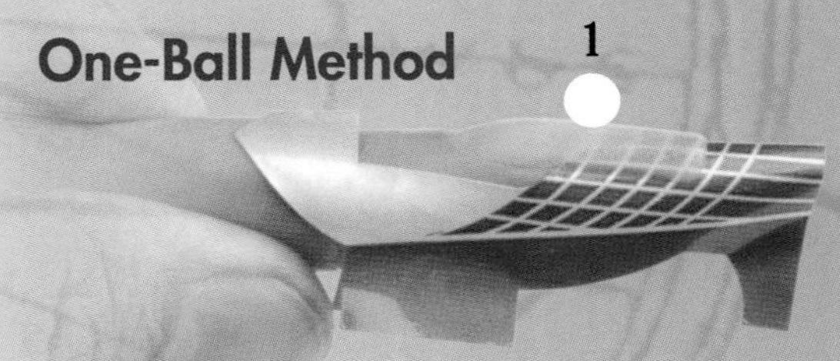


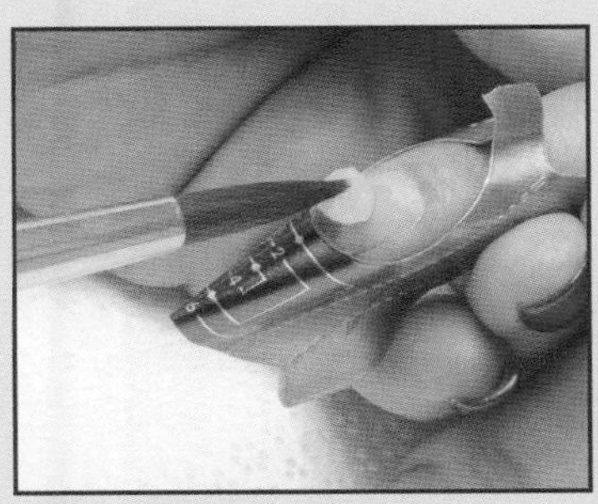

Using a large brush, apply a large ball of product at the **stress area at a 45-degree angle (zone 2)** that is big enough to cover the entire nail.

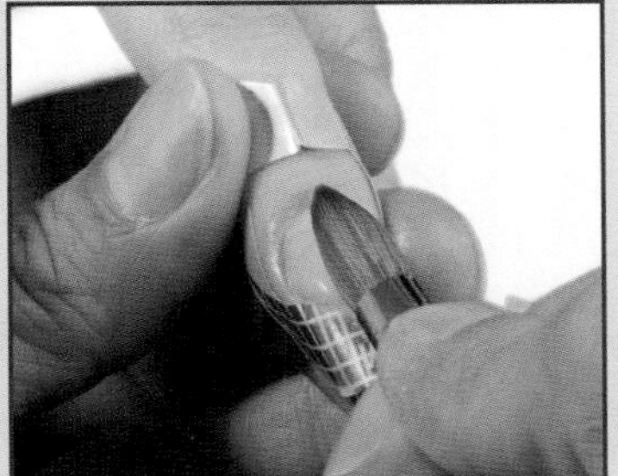

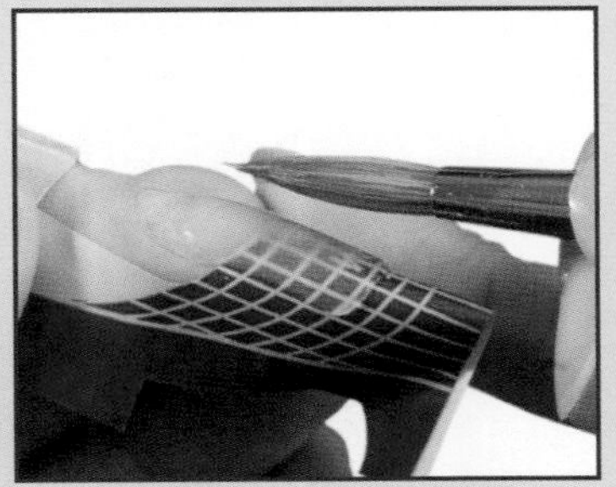

Quickly press product around **cuticle area at a 90-degree angle (zone 3)** and blend product forward to overlay the nail tip or sculpt a **free edge at a 0-degree angle (zone 1)**.

# Nail Extensions . . .

**NOTE:** If leftover ABS is recycled or reused in the manufacturing of nail tips, the quality of tip is compromised and will have a tendency to be brittle and turn yellow.

**An alternative** *for creating nail length to the natural nail is adding nail tips or extensions.* ***Nail tips*** *are made of a high-quality virgin plastic called* ***acrylonitrile butadiene styrene (ABS),*** *which is a common thermoplastic (soft and pliable when heated), used to make molded products. Tips come in many sizes – usually ranging from one being the largest and 10 being the smallest, and shapes to accommodate most every nail contour. The nail tip provides strength and endurance to support the client's daily activities.*

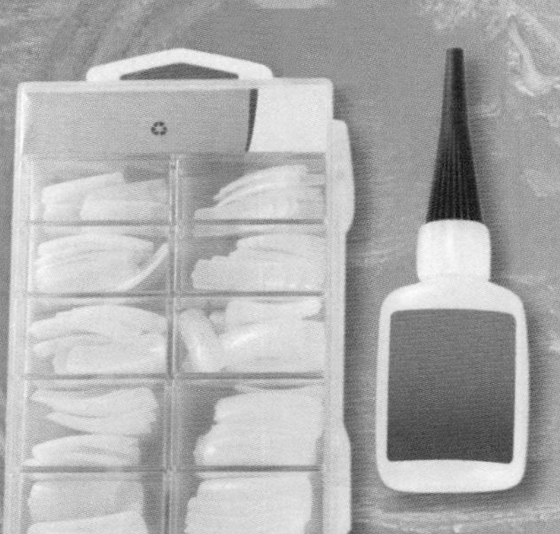

**In selecting a nail tip, consider the following parts of a tip:**

- Contact Area or Well Area
- Sidewall
- Stress Area
- C-Curve
- Arch

"Nail tips made of virgin ABS plastic are the BEST! You are only as good as the products you use."

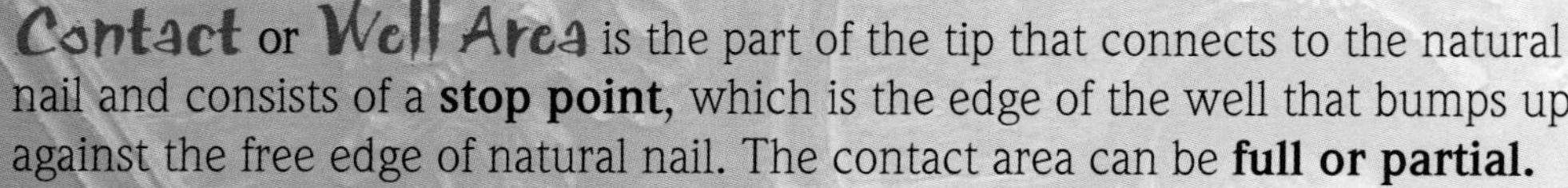

**Contact** or **Well Area** is the part of the tip that connects to the natural nail and consists of a **stop point**, which is the edge of the well that bumps up against the free edge of natural nail. The contact area can be **full or partial.**

- **Full contact** nail tip has a large well area and **must never cover more than ½ of the natural nail.** This type of tip is usually prone to air bubbles, needs more adhesive and requires more buffering.

- **Partial contact** nail tip has a small well area, usually appears as a **"French" or "white" tip** and **must never cover more than ⅓ of the natural nail.** This tip features minimum filing and adhesive, but can injure the natural nail.

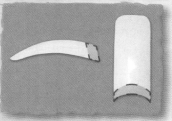

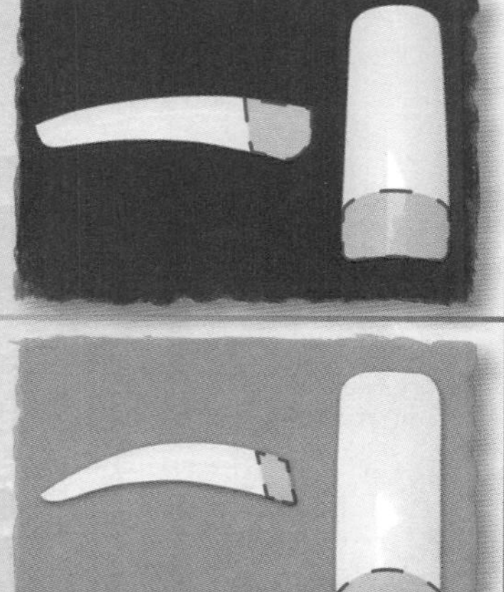

**Sidewalls** of a tip provide reinforcement and are constructed to be either **tapered or straight.** The choice of tip used depends on client's nail shape, length and amount of sidewalls. Nail tips are to balance a natural nail and **fit correctly into the nail grooves from sidewall to sidewall.**

**Stress Area** is the edge of the nail tip below contact area and is the **most vulnerable area** accepting everyday wear and tear. This area is established by proper blending of tip to natural nail and requires a thick acrylic overlay, which creates support and helps to provide a c-curve. The stress area offers strength and durability for long-length nails.

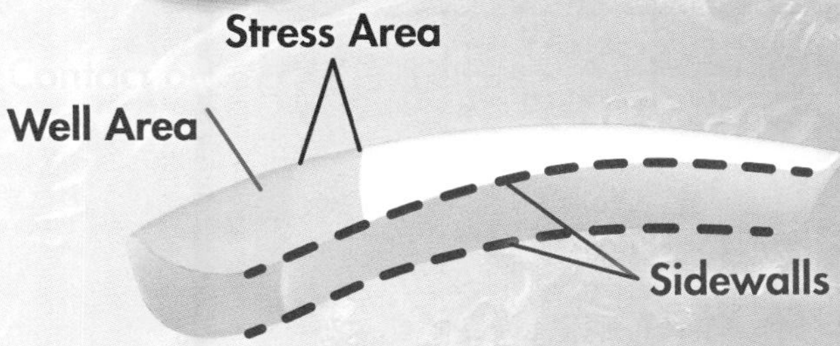


Stress Area
Contact or Well Area
Sidewalls

**C-Curve** *is part of the nail tip that forms an arc.*

The c-curve of a nail tip must match the natural nail curve to ensure a comfortable fit. Nail tips come in varying c-curve depths, ranging from 50 percent (highest arch) to 20 percent (lowest arch). The proper tip choice should complement the customer's natural nail curvature.

**Arch** is the curvature side view of a nail tip providing support to the stress area and sides of tip. Two types of arches are:

- **Elevated or high** arch, the curved or arc portion at center of tip.
- **Low arch,** located on the bottom side edges of the tip. The edges of the tip are to align with the nail grooves.

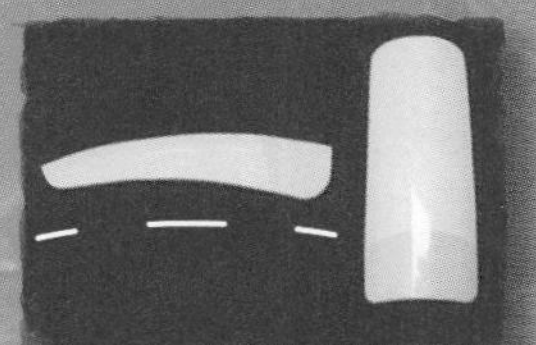

Following the same advice as the c-curve information, it is most important that the natural nail curve be considered when determining the correct nail tip.

17

# Client Consultation . . .

*Before any service can begin, the cosmetologist must communicate with the client on his or her nail-care needs. The nails of either the hand, foot or both must be analyzed to provide the necessary information on client's health, skin and nail condition. The responsibility of the professional is to avoid contaminating others within the salon. These factors determine if the client is able to be serviced or if an alternative method is recommended.*

| DATE | SERVICE/TREATMENT | REMARKS/CHANGES |
|---|---|---|
| | | |
| | | |

☑ Medical A

**Client Profile Card/File**

Name__________ Date__________

Address__________

Cosmetologist/ Technician__________

Lic #__________

E-mail address__________

Occupation__________ Hobby__________

Phone number__________

Birthdate__________

First Visit Date__________

**Nail Condition:** Normal ❑ Dry ❑ Peeling ❑ Thin/Fragile ❑

**Skin Condition:** Normal ❑ Dry ❑ Sensitive ❑

**Nail Length:** Short ❑ Medium ❑ Long ❑

**Nail Shape:** Square ❑ Squoval ❑ Oval ❑ Round ❑ Triangular ❑

Pregnant? ❑ Allergies ❑ Health Problems ❑ Medications ❑

If so, list types of medications__________

**Products used on skin or nails:**__________

**Polish colors preferred:**__________

Maintenance Frequency: 1 week ❑ 2 weeks ❑ 3 weeks ❑ 4 weeks ❑ Other ❑

I Do The Following To My Nails: Manicure ❑ Pedicure ❑ Fabric Wrap ❑ Tip Application ❑ Sculptured Nails ❑ Massage ❑ Electric File ❑ Airbrush Art ❑ Art Design ❑

REMARKS__________

17

# Nail and Skin Analysis ...

Once the client has completed a profile card and you have reviewed it, start your analysis by **observing the client's nails and skin of hands or feet** (depending on requested service) to determine if there are any contagious conditions present – view top and underneath of both hands and feet. If a disease (refer to Chapter 16) is detected, recommend the client to a medical care professional. If no disease is present, continue the analysis by asking a series of questions to determine the best treatment options. If a nail or skin condition is present, certain treatments along with home maintenance may provide a remedy to certain ailments. Offer treatment plans and/or market home maintenance treatments during in-between visits.

**Warm Oil Manicure** works well in hydrating dry cuticles or skin.

**Manicure treatment** is a great service for the nail biter or for weekly maintenance visits.

**Massage,** whether introduced with a manicure or a pedicure, offers superior relaxation for the stressful client.

5

1

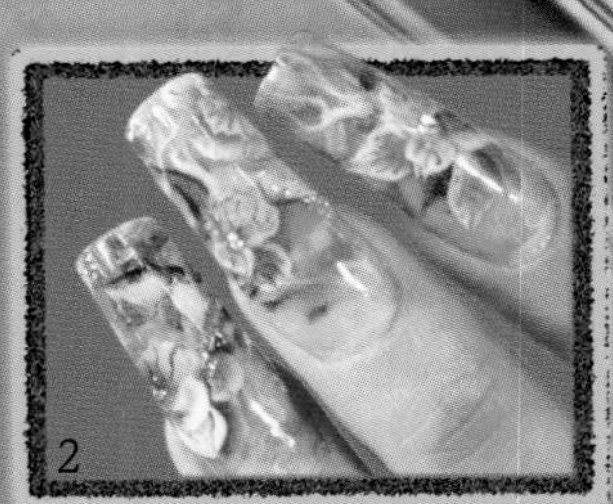

2

**Nail Design** conveys creativity, imagination and inspires artistic expression.

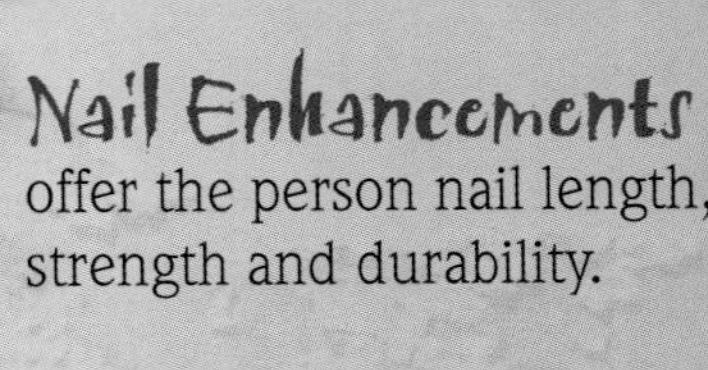

**Nail Enhancements** offer the person nail length, strength and durability.

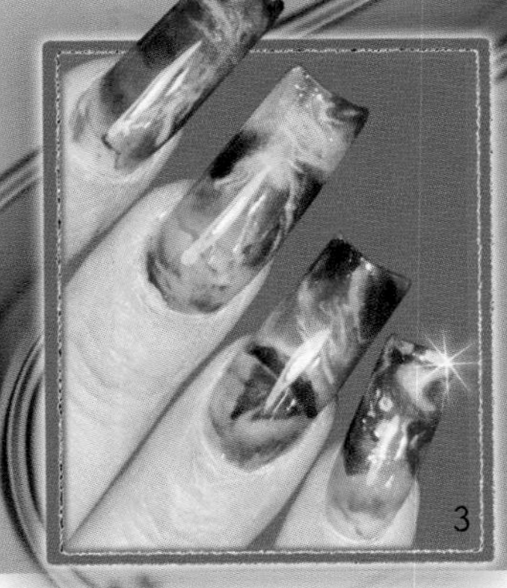

3

4

17

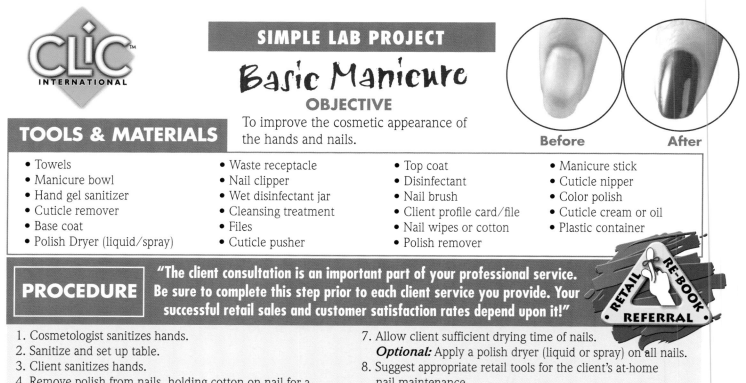

SIMPLE LAB PROJECT

# Basic Manicure

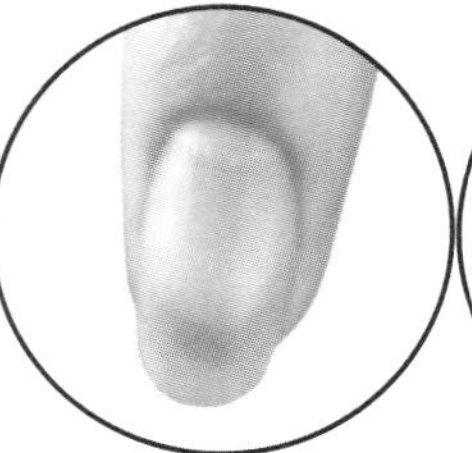
Before

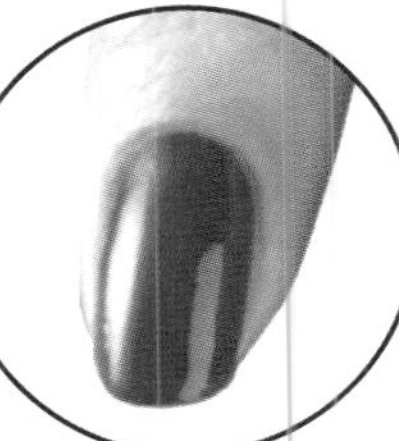
After

## OBJECTIVE

To improve the cosmetic appearance of the hands and nails.

## TOOLS & MATERIALS

- Towels
- Manicure bowl
- Hand gel sanitizer
- Cuticle remover
- Base coat
- Polish Dryer (liquid/spray)
- Waste receptacle
- Nail clipper
- Wet disinfectant jar
- Cleansing treatment
- Files
- Cuticle pusher
- Top coat
- Disinfectant
- Nail brush
- Client profile card/file
- Nail wipes or cotton
- Polish remover
- Manicure stick
- Cuticle nipper
- Color polish
- Cuticle cream or oil
- Plastic container

## PROCEDURE

**"The client consultation is an important part of your professional service. Be sure to complete this step prior to each client service you provide. Your successful retail sales and customer satisfaction rates depend upon it!"**

RETAIL • RE-BOOK • REFERRAL

1. Cosmetologist sanitizes hands.
2. Sanitize and set up table.
3. Client sanitizes hands.
4. Remove polish from nails, holding cotton on nail for a 3-second count starting on client's left side.
5. Perform a visual examination of hands and nails.
6. Follow procedure as shown.
7. Allow client sufficient drying time of nails. ***Optional:*** Apply a polish dryer (liquid or spray) on all nails.
8. Suggest appropriate retail tools for the client's at-home nail maintenance.
9. Follow standard cleanup procedures.
10. Document client profile card/file.

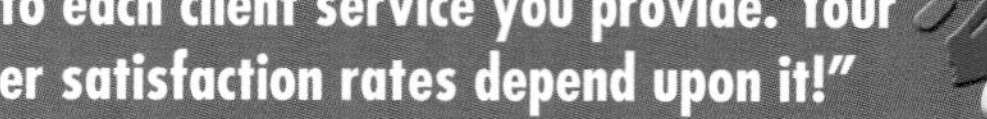

A. Cut and/or shape free edge, starting with left hand little finger. Place file at nail's corner edge and slide file to center of nail. Repeat on opposite side of nail.

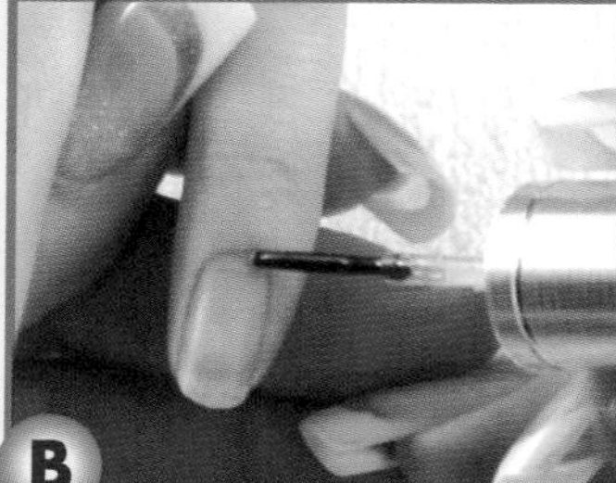
B. Apply cuticle remover to cuticle area of left hand.

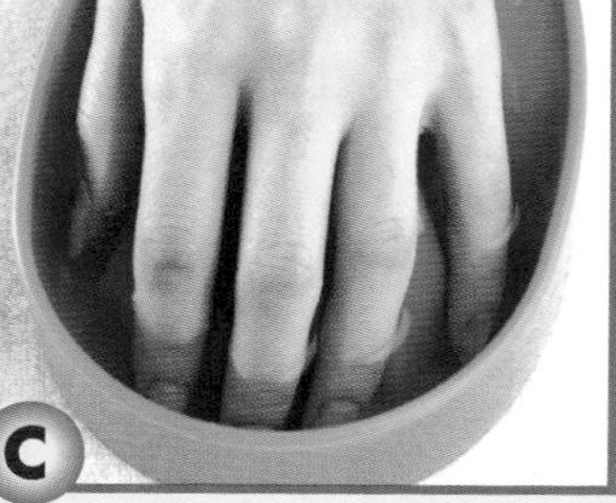
C. Soak fingers of left hand in cleansing treatment in manicure bowl. **Repeat Steps A and B to right hand.**

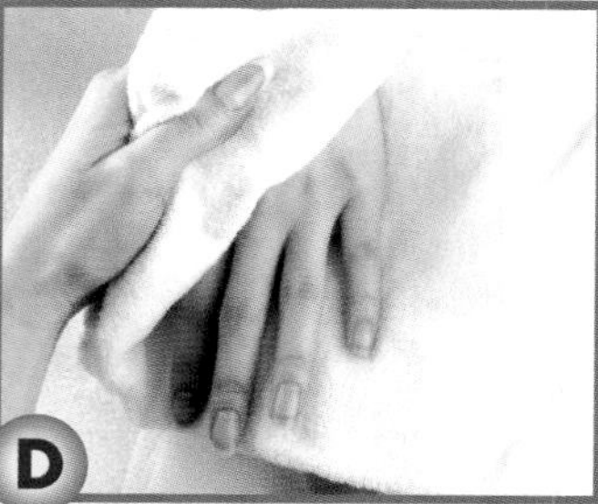
D. Remove left hand from manicure bowl, place on towel and dry fingers. **Repeat Step C to right hand.**

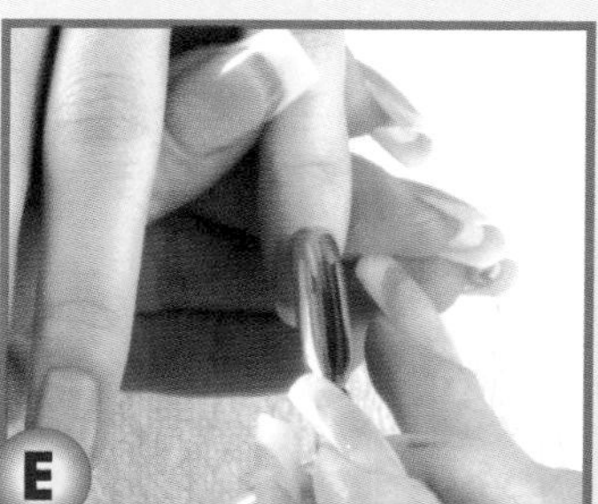
E. On left hand, **gently** push back cuticles (slightly lifting cuticle away from the nail plate), using cuticle pusher on all fingernails. **Reminder:** hold pusher at a 30-degree angle.

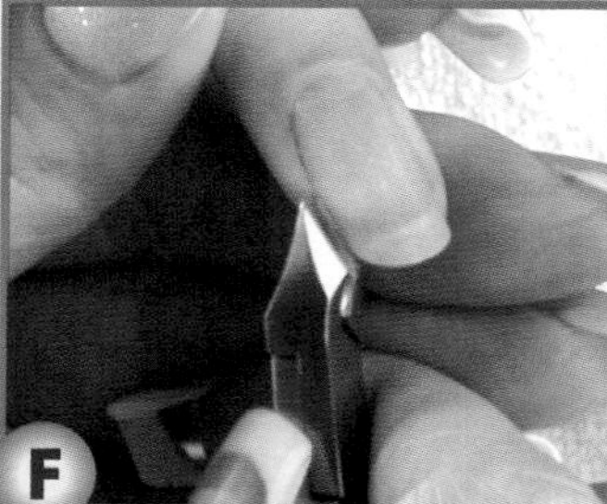
F. Cut cuticle from the nails using a cuticle nipper, **carefully** removing only cuticle.

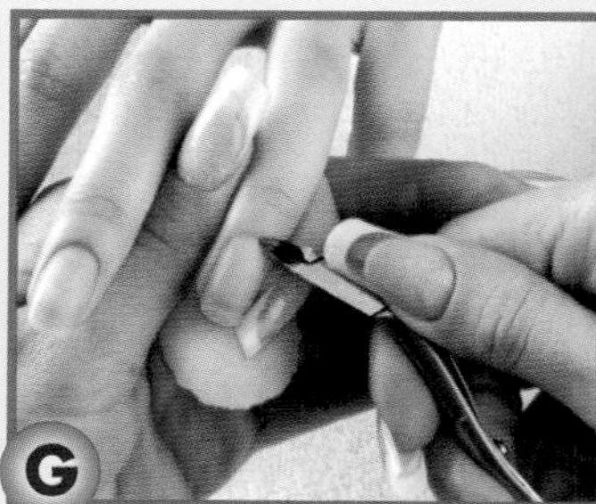
G. A moist cotton ball is placed in opposite hand for holding excess cuticle.

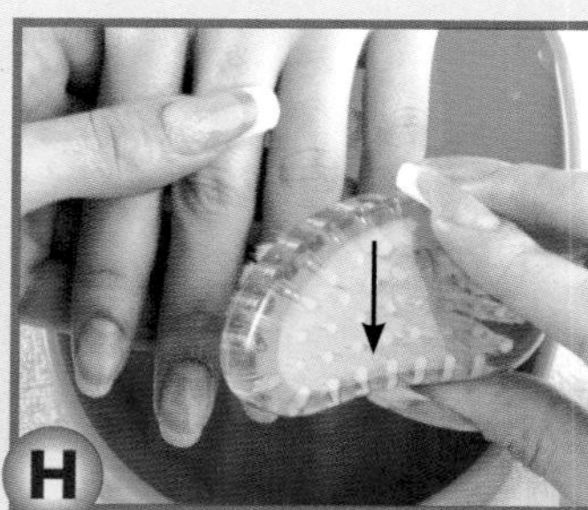
H. Using the nail brush, dip into cleansing treatment and brush the nails, from the cuticle area outward to free edge. Dry fingers and nails with towel.

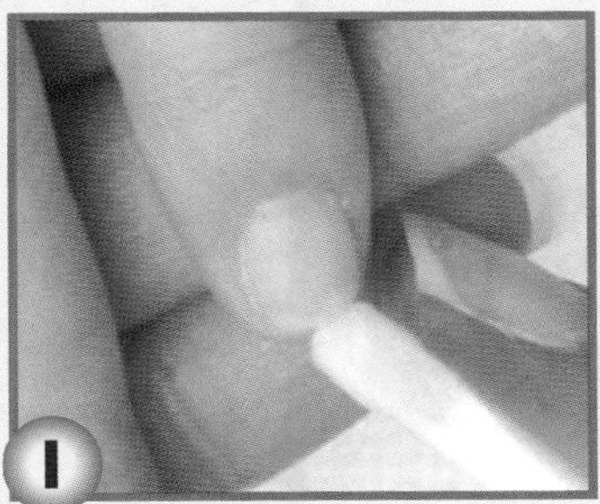

I
Clean under free edge of nail using cotton-wrapped manicure stick. **Repeat Steps D thru I on right hand.**

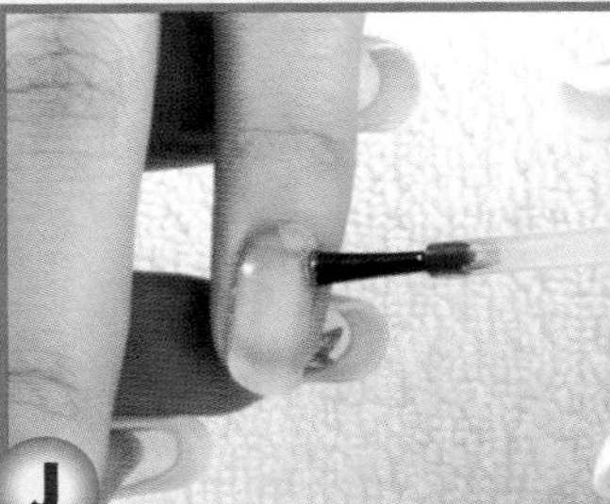

J
Apply a cuticle cream or oil at cuticle area.

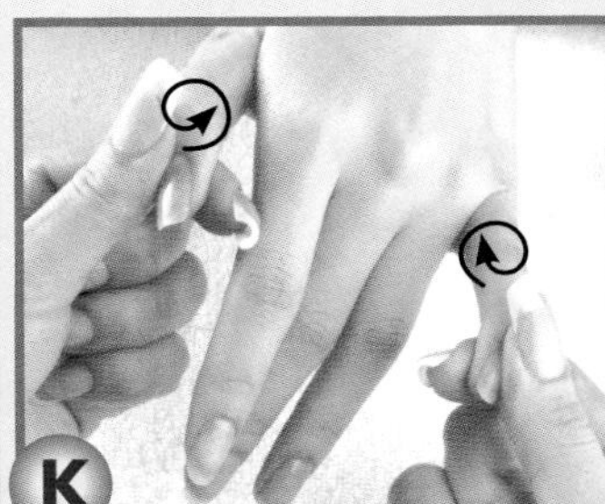

K
Starting with the little fingers, massage cuticle cream or oil into cuticle area working towards center finger.

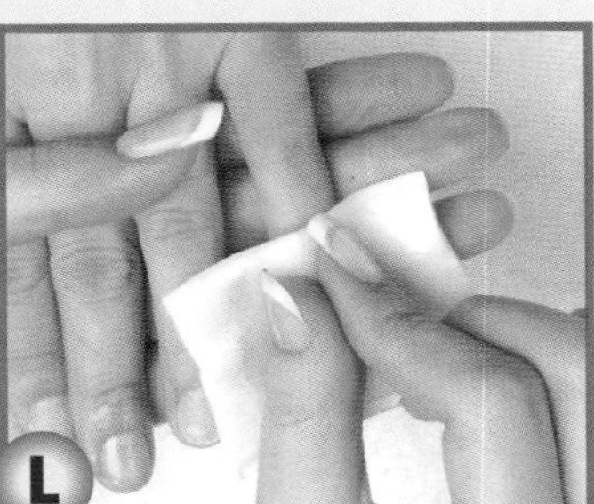

L
Remove oily residue from the nail plate with a nail wipe or cotton saturated in polish remover.

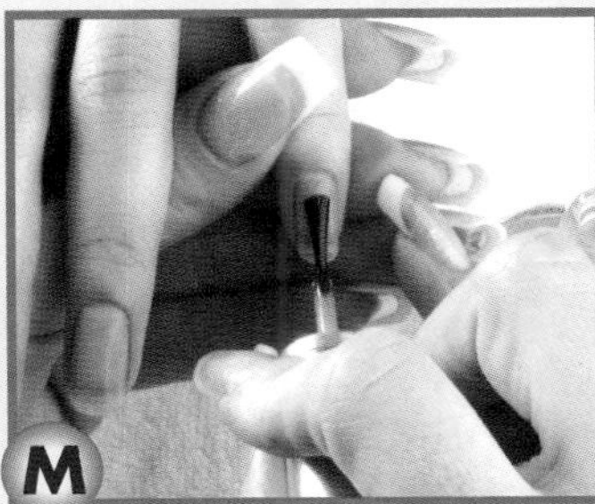

M
Apply one covering of base coat on all nails.

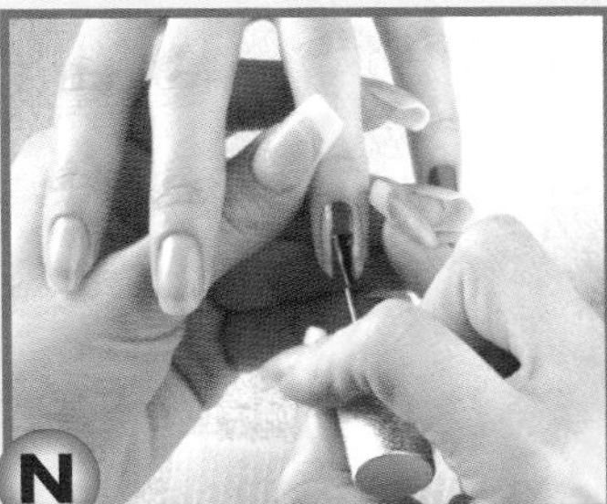

N
Apply two coats of color polish on all nails, starting with a center stroke.

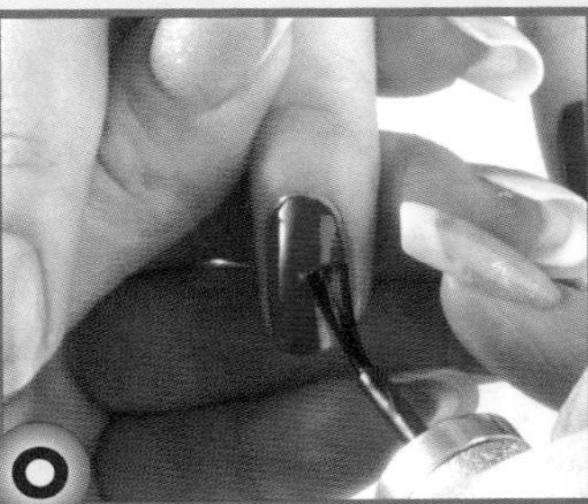

O
Continue with polish application along sides of nail.

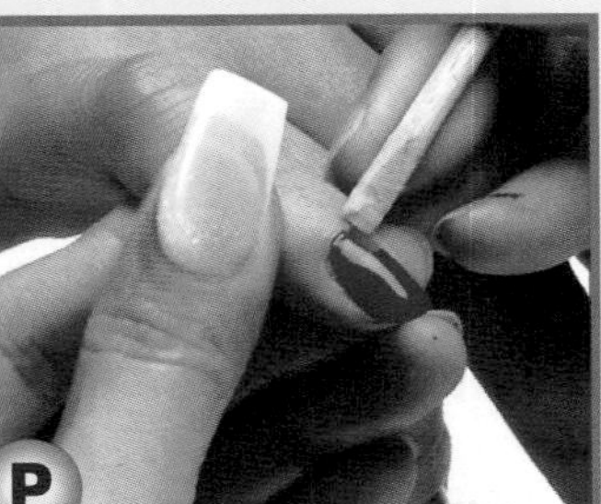

P
Clean any excess polish off skin using tip of cotton-wrapped manicure stick saturated in polish remover.

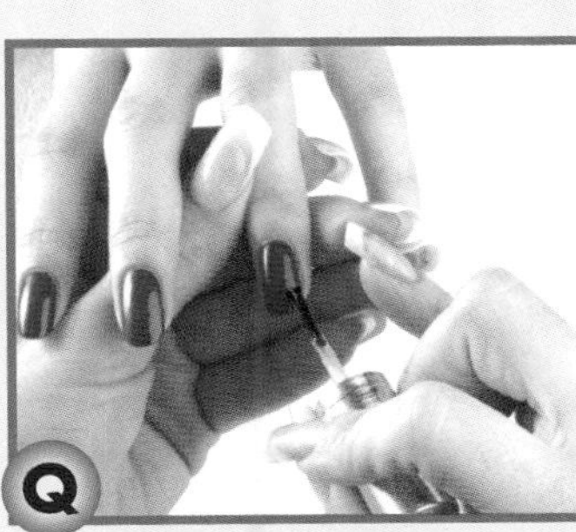

Q
Apply one covering of top coat to all nails.

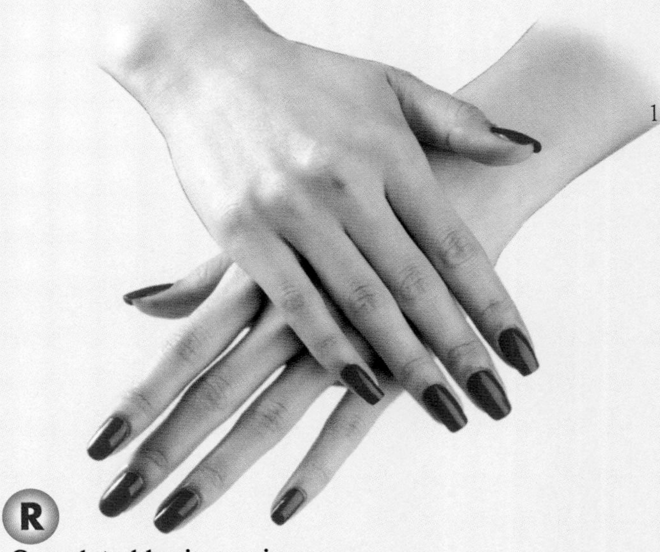

R
**Completed basic manicure.**

17

**EVALUATION**

GRADE STUDENT'S NAME ID#

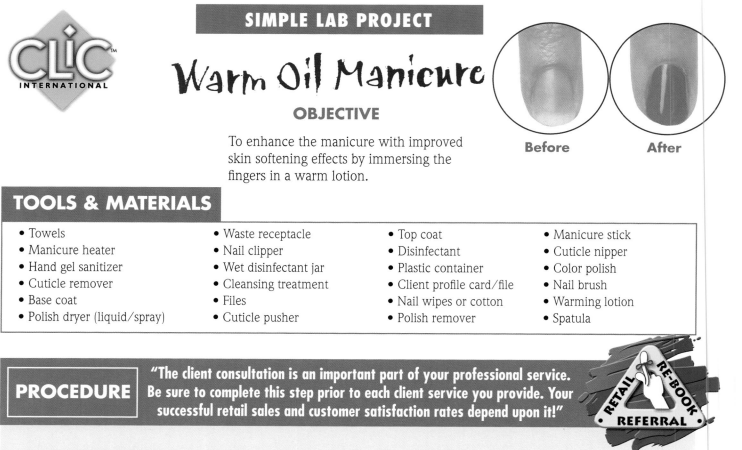

SIMPLE LAB PROJECT

# Warm Oil Manicure

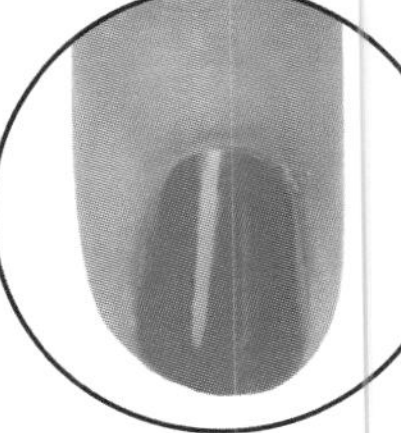

Before After

## OBJECTIVE

To enhance the manicure with improved skin softening effects by immersing the fingers in a warm lotion.

## TOOLS & MATERIALS

- Towels
- Manicure heater
- Hand gel sanitizer
- Cuticle remover
- Base coat
- Polish dryer (liquid/spray)
- Waste receptacle
- Nail clipper
- Wet disinfectant jar
- Cleansing treatment
- Files
- Cuticle pusher
- Top coat
- Disinfectant
- Plastic container
- Client profile card/file
- Nail wipes or cotton
- Polish remover
- Manicure stick
- Cuticle nipper
- Color polish
- Nail brush
- Warming lotion
- Spatula

## PROCEDURE

**"The client consultation is an important part of your professional service. Be sure to complete this step prior to each client service you provide. Your successful retail sales and customer satisfaction rates depend upon it!"**

1. Cosmetologist sanitizes hands.
2. Sanitize and set up table.
3. Client sanitizes hands.
4. Remove polish from nails.
5. Perform a visual examination of hands and nails.
6. Follow procedure as shown.
7. Allow client sufficient drying time of nails.
   ***Optional:*** Apply a polish dryer (liquid or spray) on all nails.
8. Suggest appropriate retail tools for the client's at-home nail maintenance.
9. Follow standard cleanup procedures.
10. Document client profile card/file.

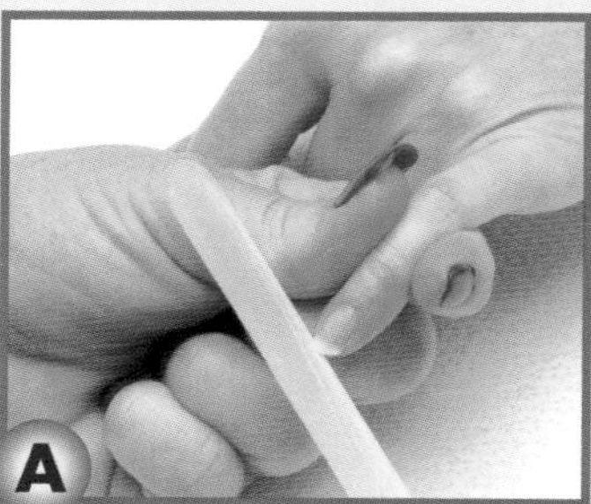

A Cut and/or shape free edge, starting with little fingernail of client's left hand.

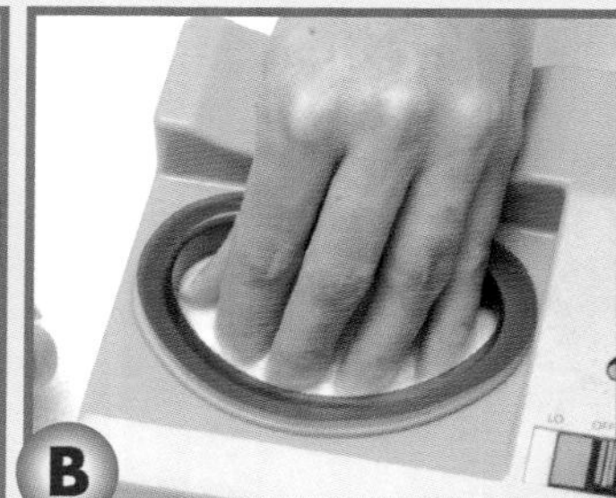

B Soak fingers of left hand in warming lotion.

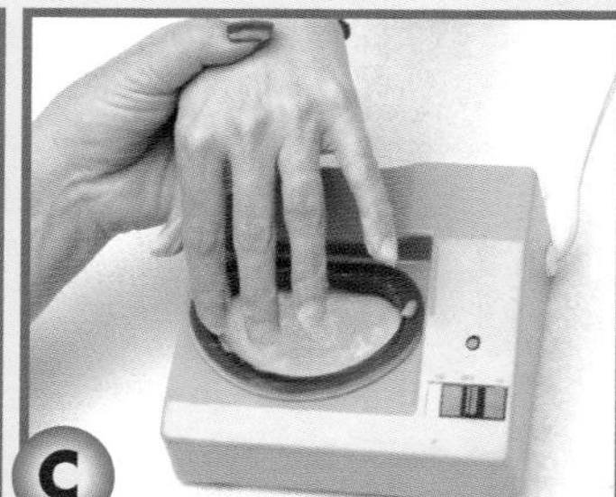

C Remove left hand from manicure heater and place on towel. **Repeat Steps A and B to right hand.**

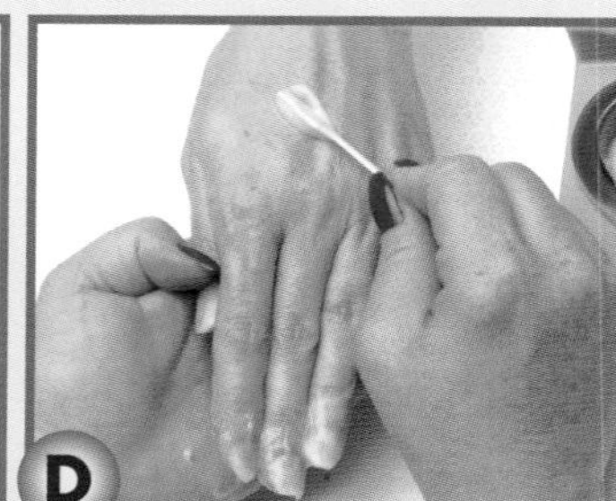

D Apply a small amount of lotion to back of hand using a spatula.

# Warm Oil Manicure

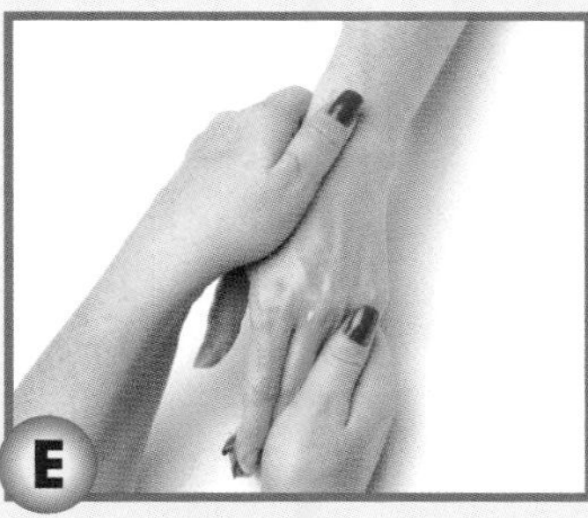

**E** Massage remaining warming lotion into hand, fingers and cuticles of left hand.

**F** On left hand, gently push back cuticles, using cuticle pusher to all fingernails.

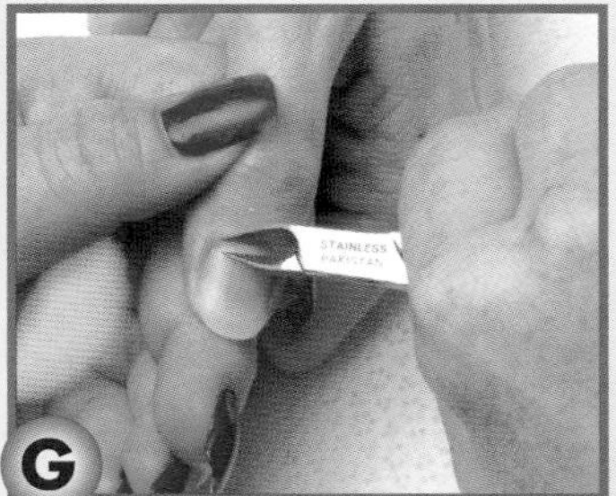

**G** Cut cuticle from the nails using a cuticle nipper, **carefully** removing only cuticle. A moist cotton ball is placed in opposite hand for holding excess cuticle.

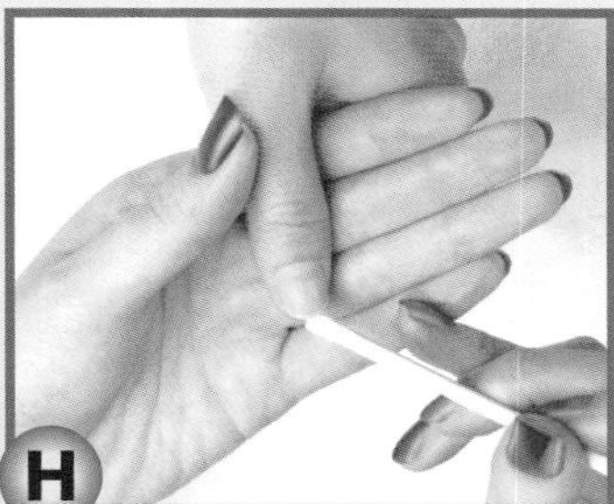

**H** Clean under free edge of nail with tip of cotton-wrapped manicure stick. **Repeaat Steps C thru H on right hand.**

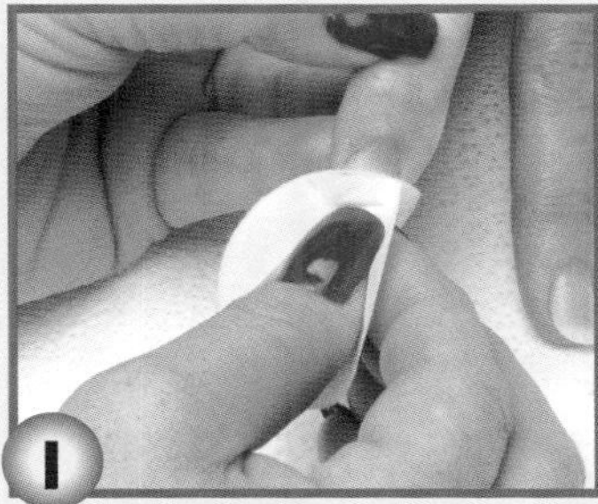

**I** Remove oily residue from the nail plate with cotton saturated in polish remover.

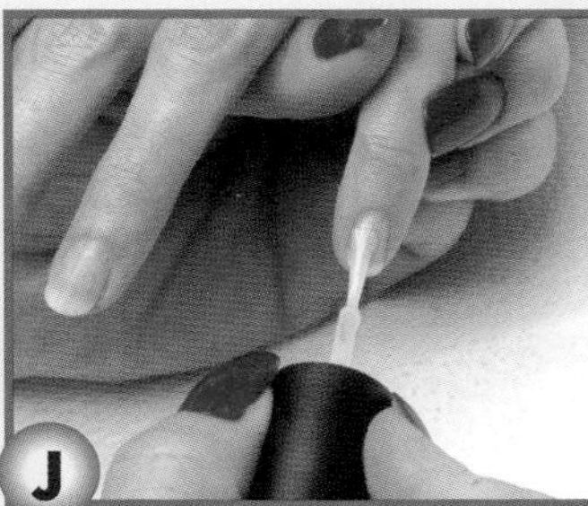

**J** Apply one covering of base coat on all nails.

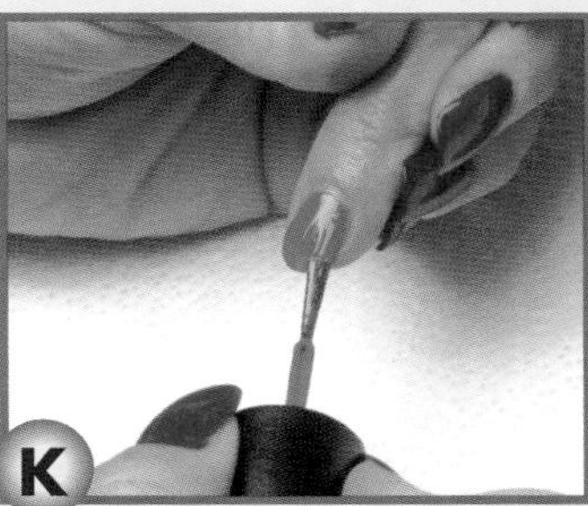

**K** Apply two coats of color polish on all nails. Clean any excess polish off skin.

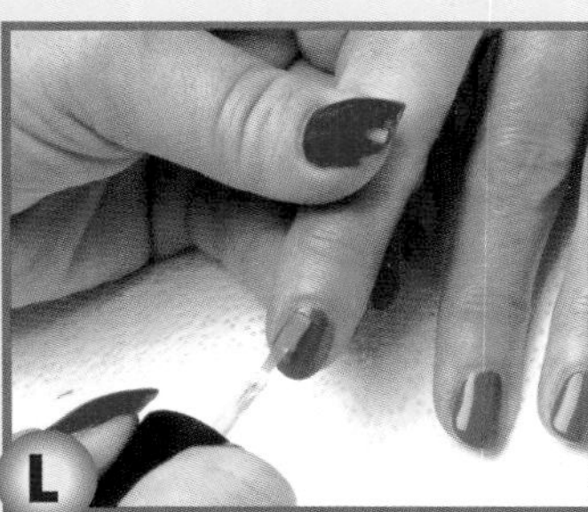

**L** Apply one covering of top coat to all nails.

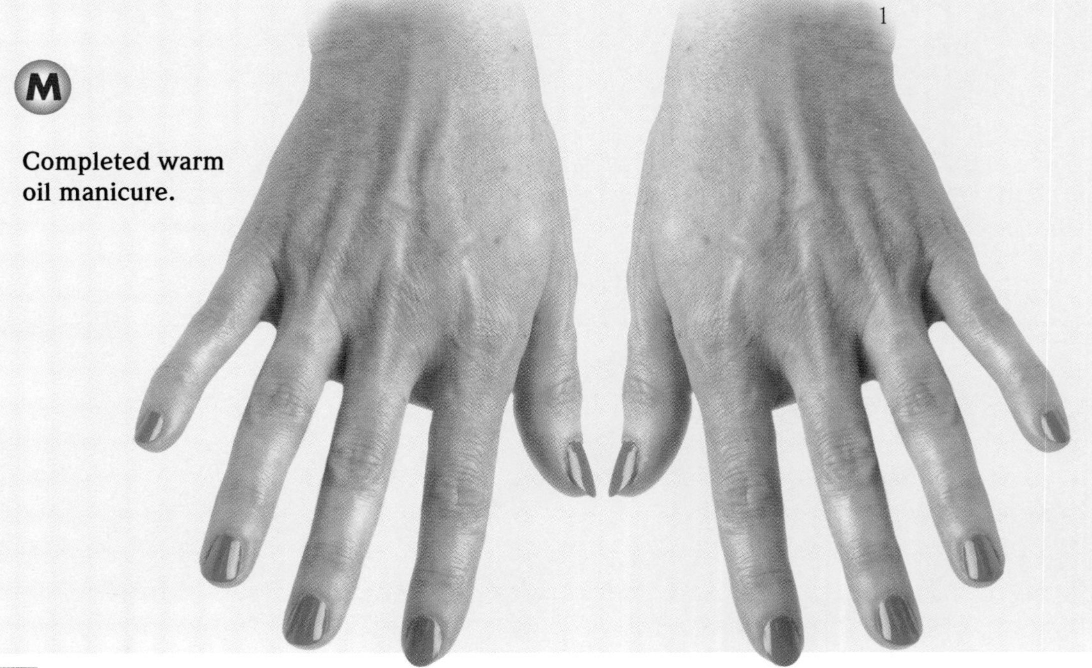

**M** **Completed warm oil manicure.**

17

**EVALUATION** ______________________________

______ GRADE ______ STUDENT'S NAME ______ ID#

## SIMPLE LAB PROJECT

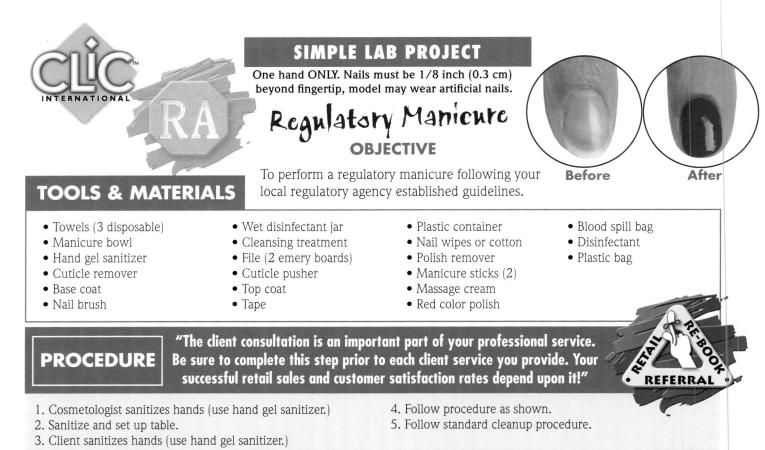

**One hand ONLY. Nails must be 1/8 inch (0.3 cm) beyond fingertip, model may wear artificial nails.**

# Regulatory Manicure

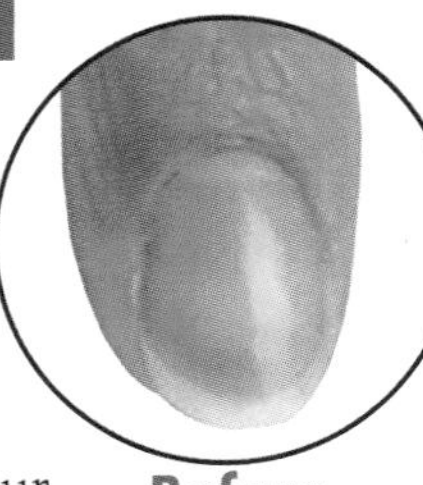

Before

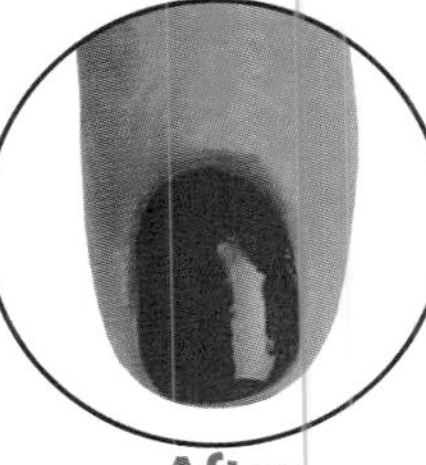

After

### OBJECTIVE

To perform a regulatory manicure following your local regulatory agency established guidelines.

## TOOLS & MATERIALS

- Towels (3 disposable)
- Manicure bowl
- Hand gel sanitizer
- Cuticle remover
- Base coat
- Nail brush
- Wet disinfectant jar
- Cleansing treatment
- File (2 emery boards)
- Cuticle pusher
- Top coat
- Tape
- Plastic container
- Nail wipes or cotton
- Polish remover
- Manicure sticks (2)
- Massage cream
- Red color polish
- Blood spill bag
- Disinfectant
- Plastic bag

## PROCEDURE

**"The client consultation is an important part of your professional service. Be sure to complete this step prior to each client service you provide. Your successful retail sales and customer satisfaction rates depend upon it!"**

RETAIL • RE-BOOK • REFERRAL

1. Cosmetologist sanitizes hands (use hand gel sanitizer.)
2. Sanitize and set up table.
3. Client sanitizes hands (use hand gel sanitizer.)
4. Follow procedure as shown.
5. Follow standard cleanup procedure.

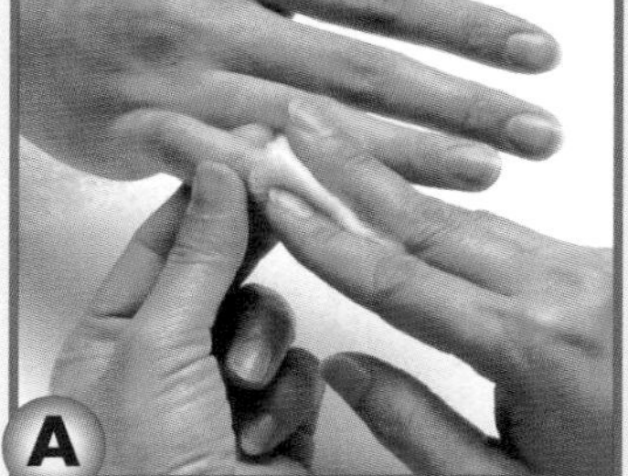

**A** Remove polish from nails, using **one of the model's hands only**. Perform a visual examination of hand and nails.

**B** Shape free edge of little finger on model's hand moving to thumb, holding at sidewalls. File outer edge corner to center, do not file on top of nail.

**C** Soak fingers in cleansing treatment in manicure bowl. Remove hand from manicure bowl and place on towel, dry fingers.

**D** For sanitary purposes, use manicure stick to acquire remover from bottle. **Do not "double-dip."**

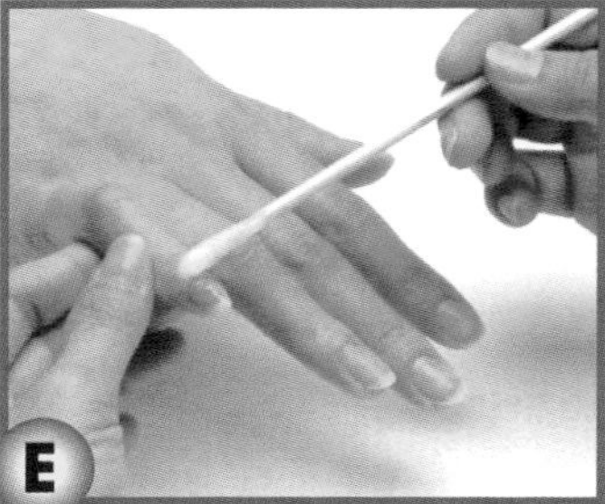

**E** Apply cuticle remover to cuticle area of nails, using cotton-wrapped manicure stick.

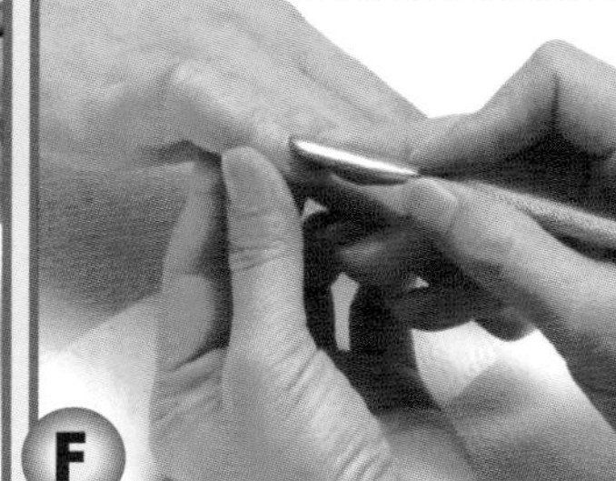

**F** **Gently** push back cuticles slightly lifting cuticle away from the nail plate. **Reminder:** hold pusher at a 30-degree angle.

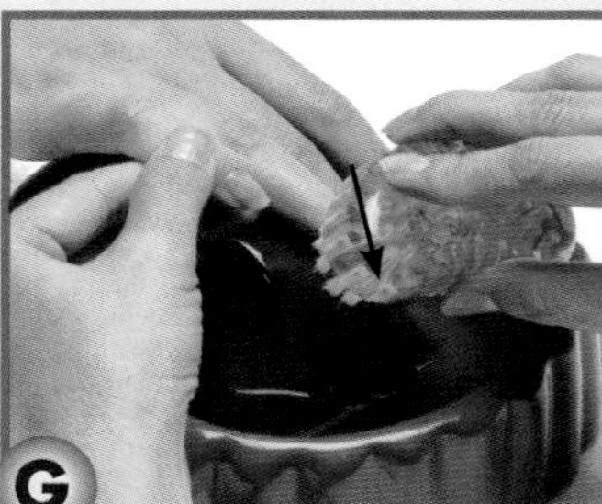

**G** Using the nail brush, dip into cleansing treatment and brush the nails, moving from the cuticle area out toward the free edge. Dry fingers and nails with towel.

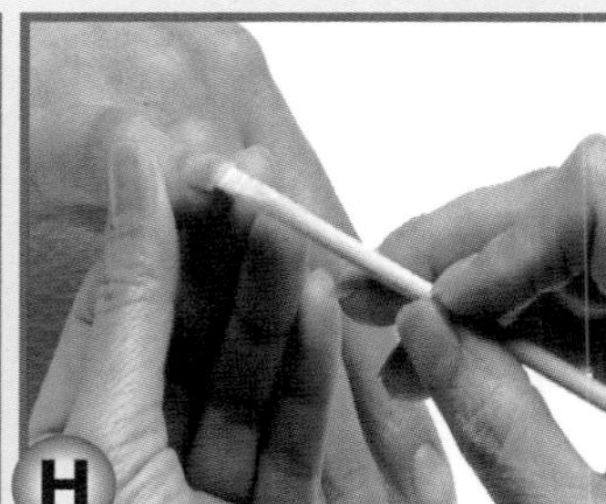

**H** Clean under free edge of nail using cotton-wrapped manicure stick. Gently buff free edge of nails.

17

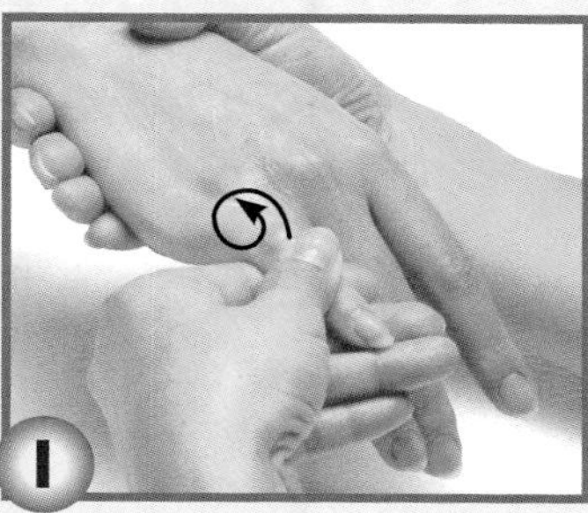
I Apply massage cream to hand and fingers, starting with little finger at fingertip.

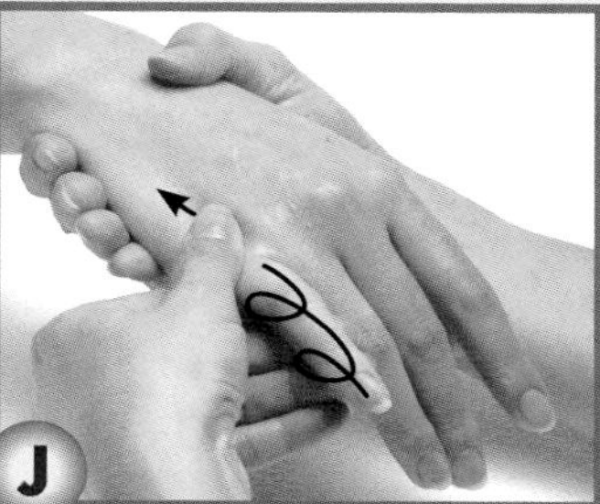
J Using a circular movement on finger, rotate up to the knuckle of the hand.

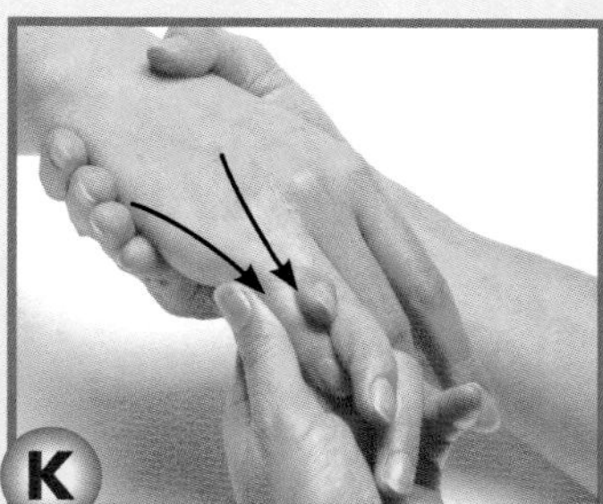
K Rotate fingers over knuckle and pull down toward fingertip.

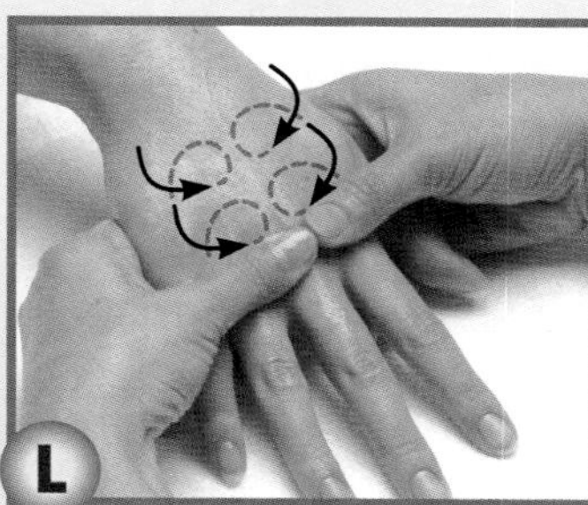
L Place your thumbs on top of model's hand with fingers on underside of hand at middle finger knuckle and perform a circular rotation up to wrist.

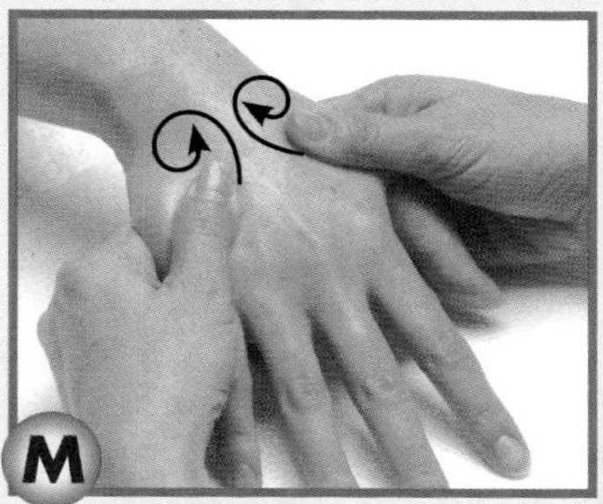
M Slide down simultaneously to index and ring knuckles, continue circular rotation to wrist, slide down to thumb and little finger knuckles and repeat to wrist.

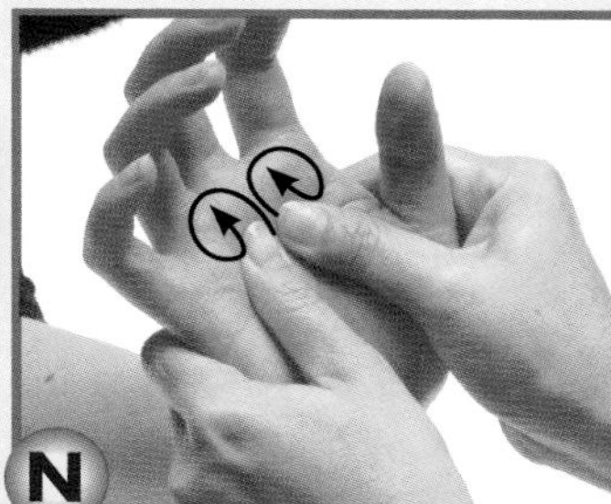
N Place your thumbs just below model's fingers in palm of hand and perform a firm circular movement.

O Rotate down to wrist, creating larger rotations to encompass entire palm area.

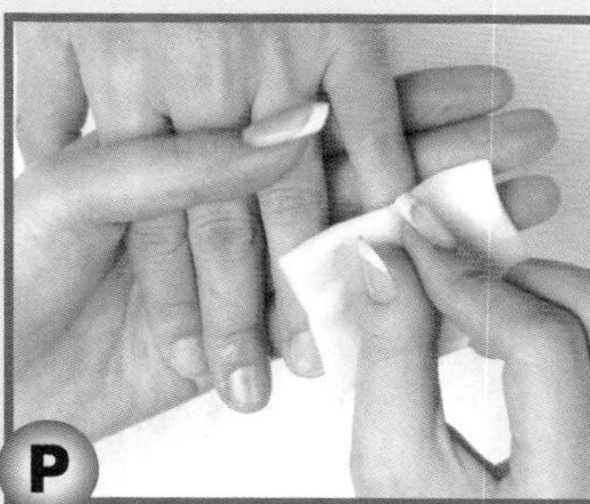
P Remove oily residue from the nail plate with cotton saturated in polish remover.

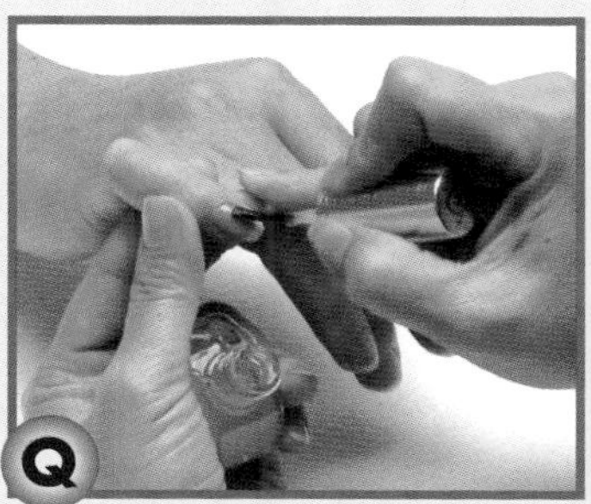
Q Apply one covering of base coat to all nails.

R Apply two coats of red color polish on all nails (applied evenly and smoothly). Clean any excess polish off skin using cotton-wrapped manicure stick saturated with polish remover.

S Apply one covering of top coat to all nails.

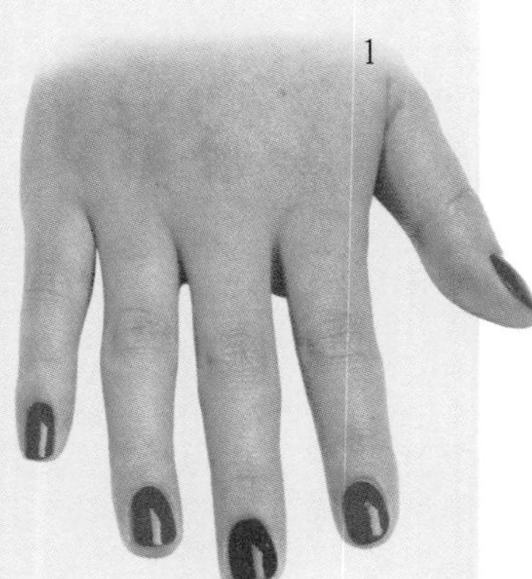
T **Completed regulatory manicure.**

17

**EVALUATION**

**GRADE** STUDENT'S NAME ID#

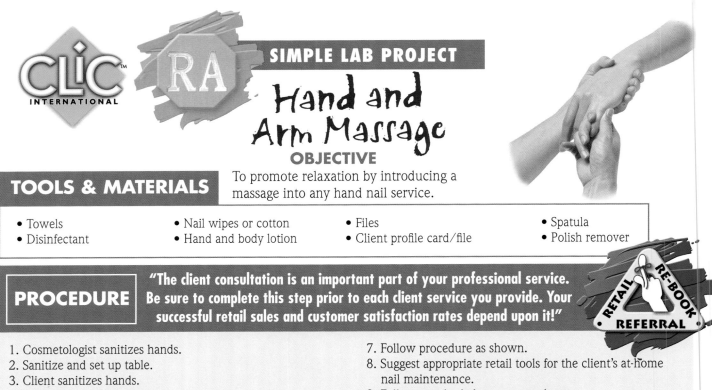

CLiC INTERNATIONAL

RA

SIMPLE LAB PROJECT

# Hand and Arm Massage

## OBJECTIVE

To promote relaxation by introducing a massage into any hand nail service.

## TOOLS & MATERIALS

- Towels
- Disinfectant
- Nail wipes or cotton
- Hand and body lotion
- Files
- Client profile card/file
- Spatula
- Polish remover

## PROCEDURE

**"The client consultation is an important part of your professional service. Be sure to complete this step prior to each client service you provide. Your successful retail sales and customer satisfaction rates depend upon it!"**

RETAIL RE-BOOK REFERRAL

1. Cosmetologist sanitizes hands.
2. Sanitize and set up table.
3. Client sanitizes hands.
4. Remove polish from nails.
5. Perform a visual examination of hands and nails.
6. Distribute hand lotion to the hand and arm.
7. Follow procedure as shown.
8. Suggest appropriate retail tools for the client's at-home nail maintenance.
9. Follow standard cleanup procedures.
10. Document client profile card/file.

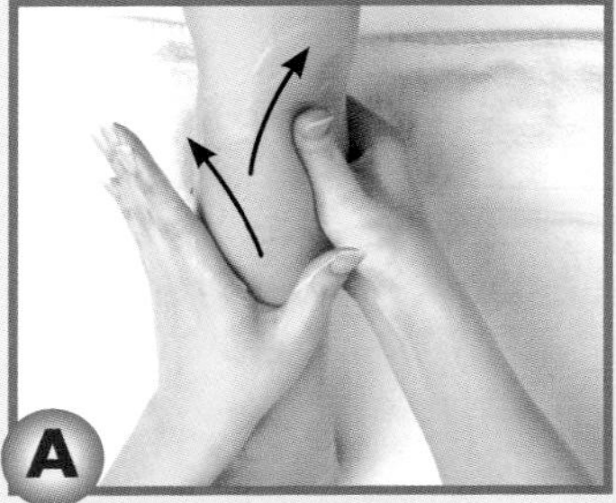

A

**Petrissage movement:** Place thumbs on top of right arm, palm down, wrap fingers around arm, slide and **twist** your hand around client's arm sliding up toward the elbow.

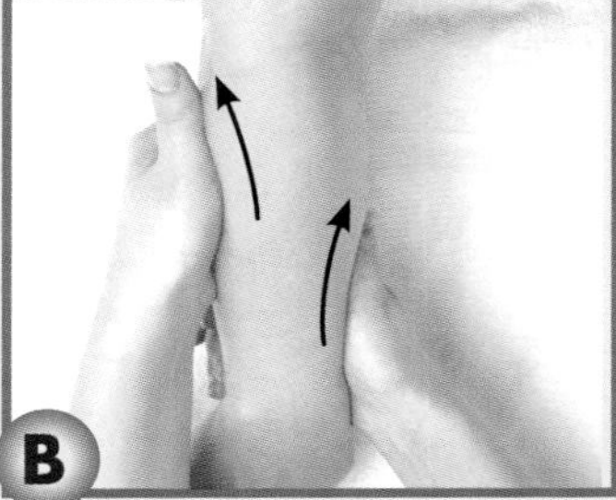

B

Palms are now on underside of arm, facing up. Slide palms down the arm to wrist; twist your hand back to beginning position. **Repeat two times** alternating between your left and right hands.

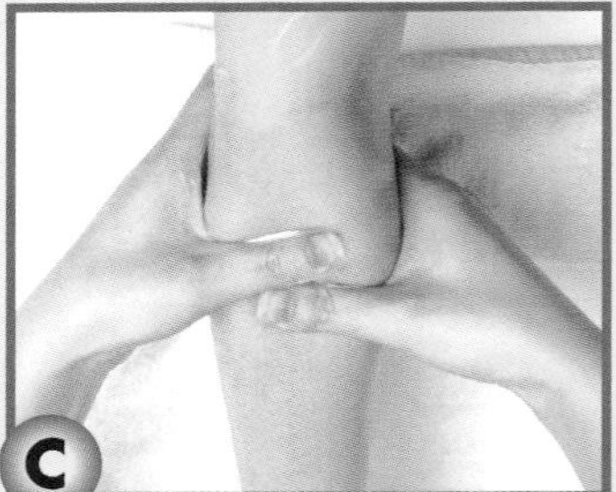

C

**Effleurage movement:** Place thumbs on top of arm with fingers underneath arm.

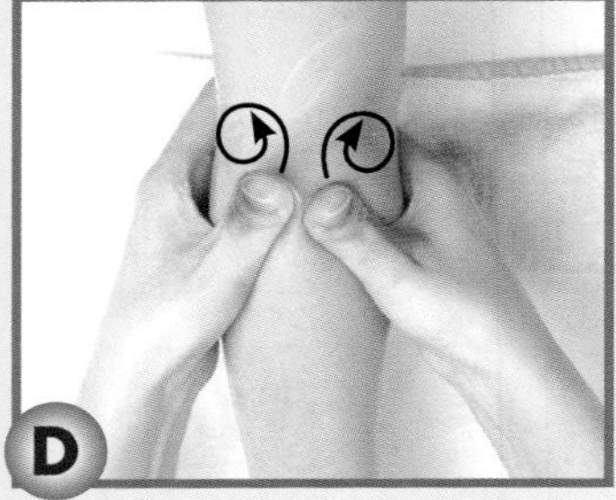

D

**Rotate** thumbs at elbow applying a medium pressure, using a circular motion.

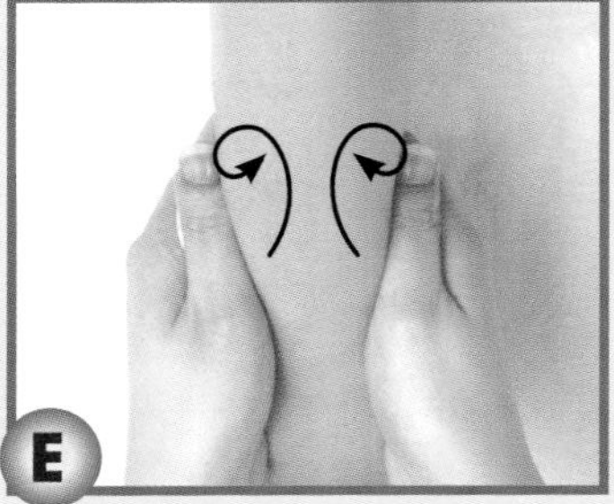

E

Use a larger circular rotation to encompass top of arm.

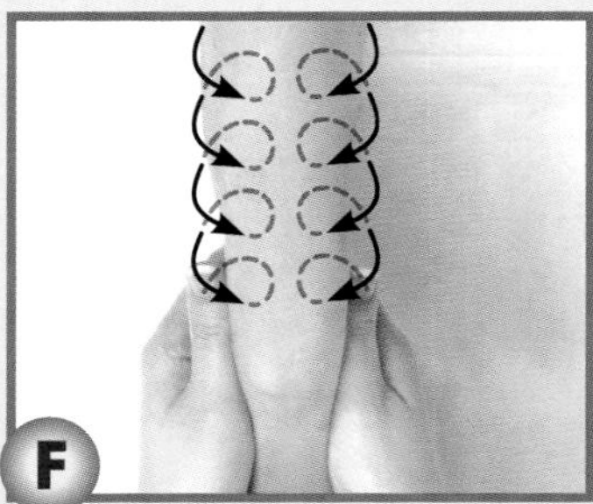

F

Continue circular rotation down to wrist. **Repeat two times**, turn arm and repeat this same step to underside of arm.

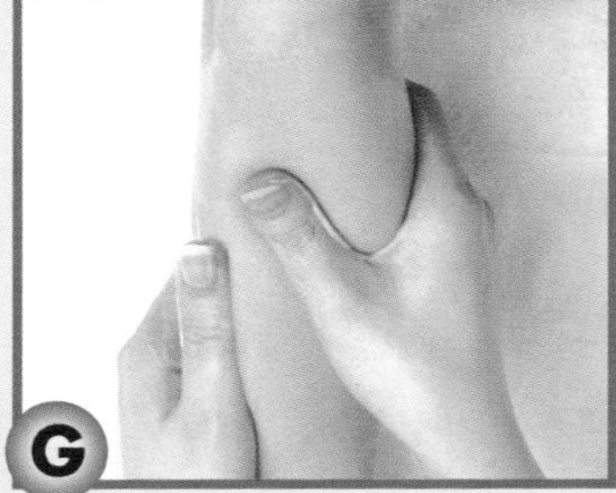

G

**Petrissage movement:** Starting on topside of elbow, wrap both hands around arm and squeeze.

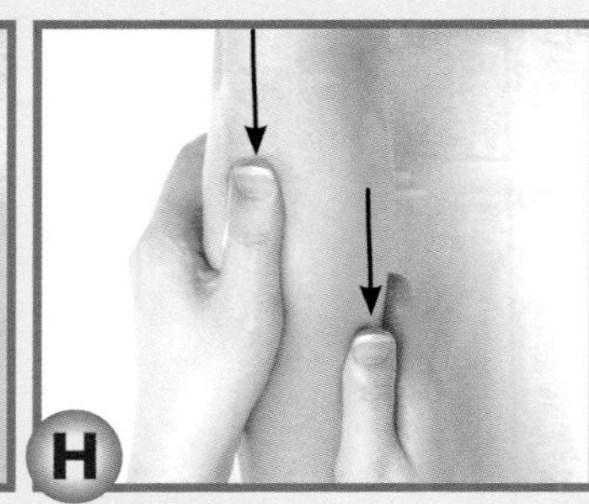

H

Squeeze arm consistently as you move down to wrist, **repeat two times.**

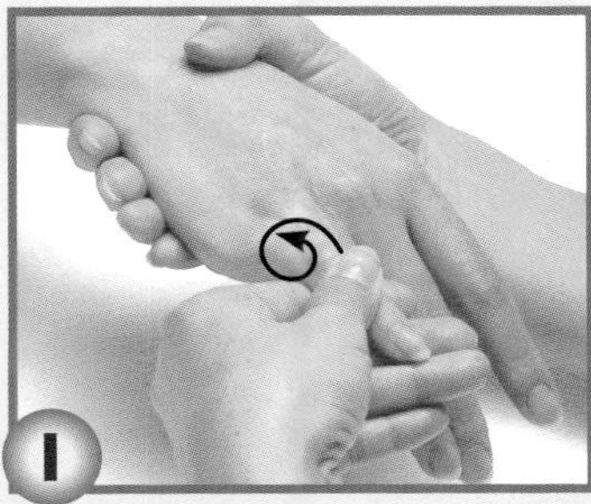


**Friction movement:** Beginning with little finger at fingertip, apply a circular rotation.

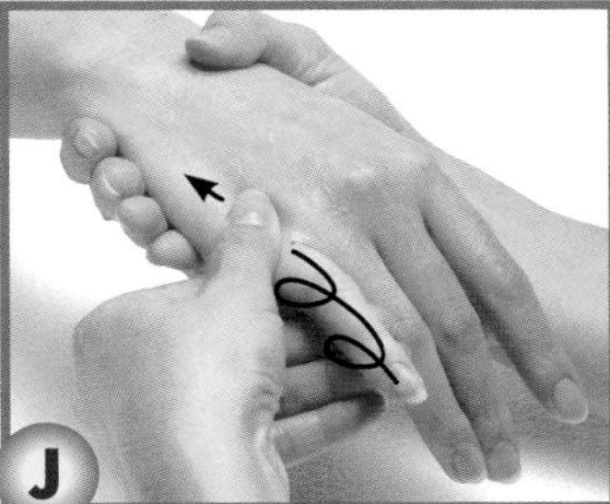


Using your thumb, continue a circular movement over finger rotating to knuckle.

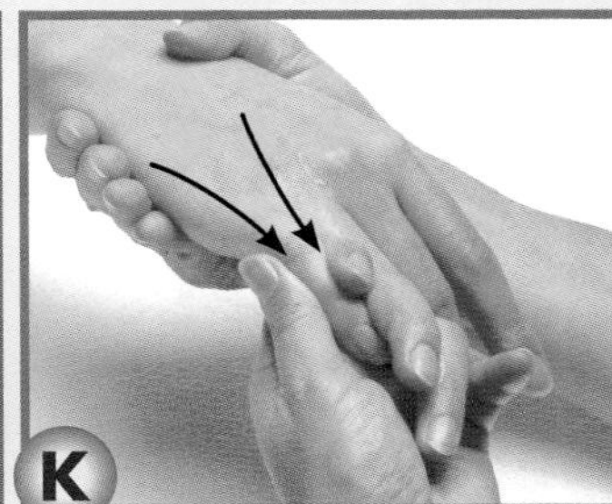


Slide down to fingertip and **repeat two times.** Continue rotation on all fingers.

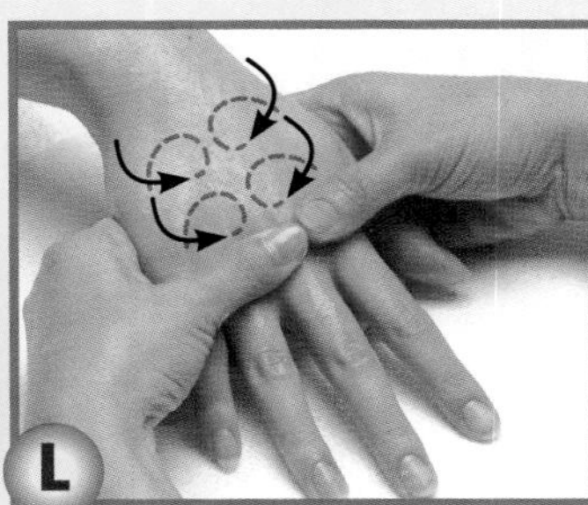


**Effleurage movement:** Place thumbs on top of hand. Starting at middle knuckle, apply a circular rotation.

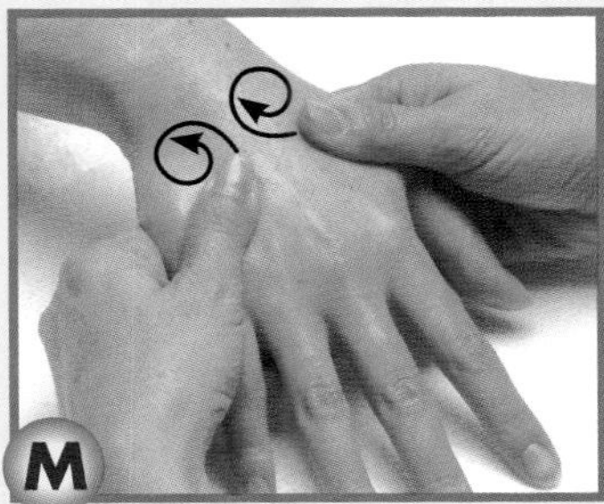


Continue circular movement to wrist, slide thumbs down to knuckles and repeat movement to wrist. **Repeat two times.**

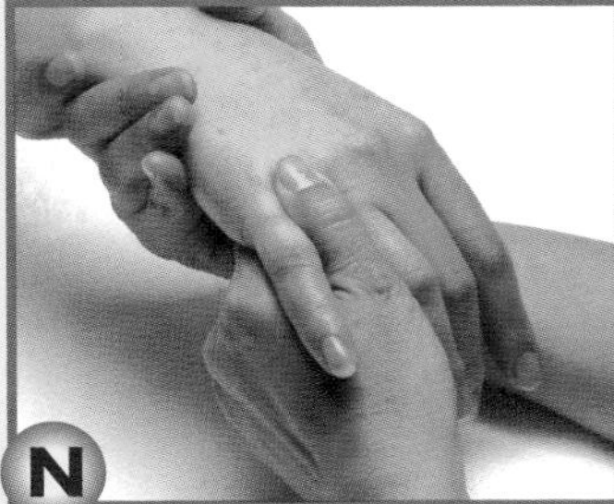


**Petrissage movement:** Starting on client's little finger web, grip web with your thumb and bent index finger.

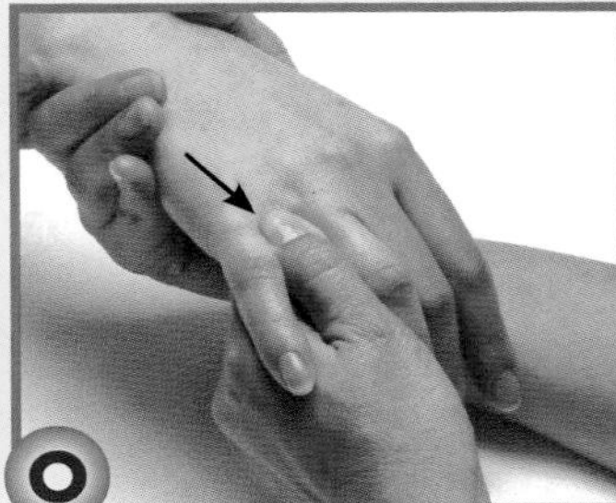


Squeeze web with a slight pull in between each finger, continue on each finger web. **Repeat two times.**

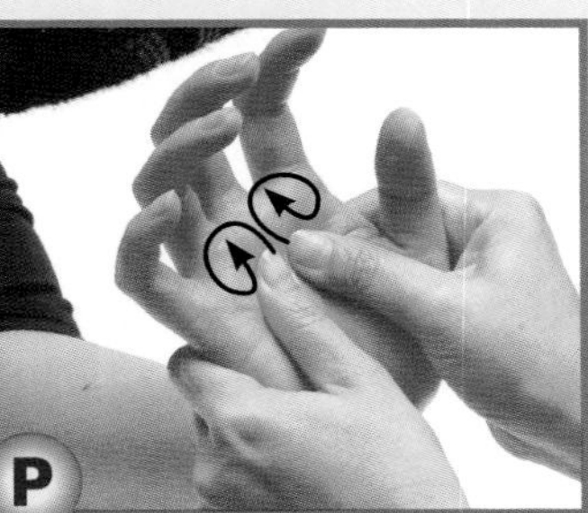


**Friction movement:** Place thumbs below client's fingers in palm of hand and perform a firm circular movement.

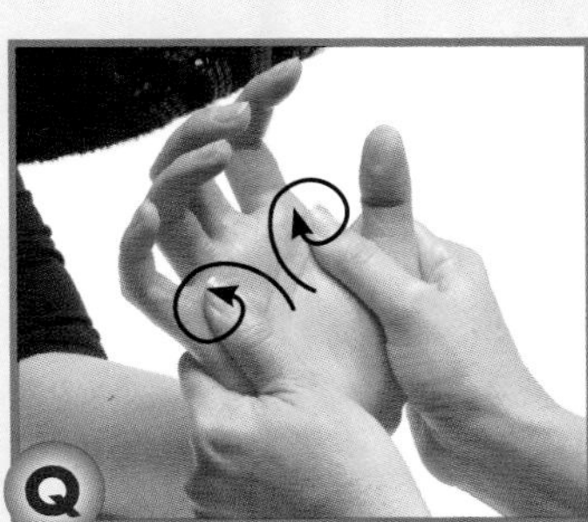


Create larger rotations to encompass entire palm area. **Repeat two times.**

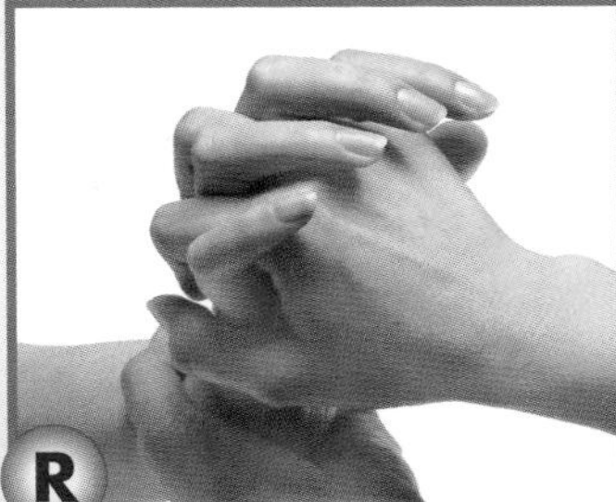


**Effleurage movement:** Interlock your fingers with client's fingers; your opposite hand is holding client's wrist.

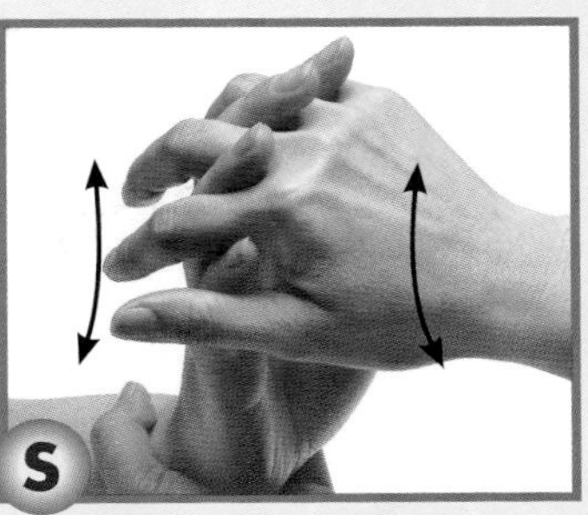


Stroke your fingers to top of client's fingers (slight pulling effect). Slide down and **repeat two times. Repeat Steps A thru S on left arm and hand.**

**Hand and arm massage techniques:**
- **Petrissage**
- **Effleurage**
- **Friction**

17

## EVALUATION

**GRADE** STUDENT'S NAME ID#

SIMPLE LAB PROJECT

# Basic Pedicure

## OBJECTIVE

To improve the cosmetic appearance of the feet, toes and toenails.

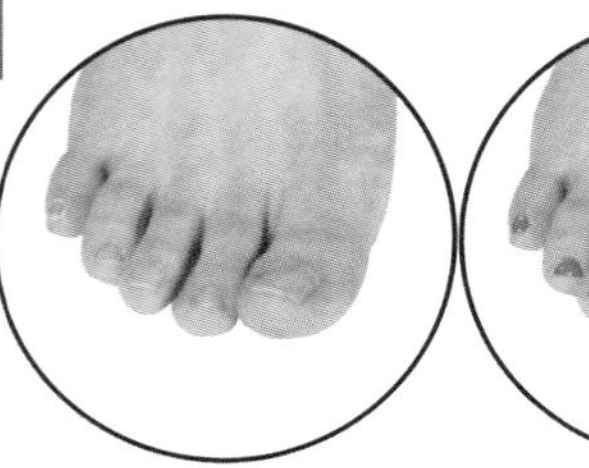

Before

After

## TOOLS & MATERIALS

- Large towels
- Foot basin/bath
- Hand gel sanitizer
- Cuticle remover
- Base coat
- Polish dryer (liquid/spray)
- Cuticle cream or oil
- Plastic container
- Client profile card/file
- Wet disinfectant jar
- Cleansing treatment
- Files
- Cuticle pusher
- Top coat
- Foot soak
- Waste receptacle
- Toe separators
- Nail wipes or cotton
- Polish remover
- Manicure stick
- Cuticle nipper
- Color polish
- Disinfectant
- Nail brush
- Nail clipper

## PROCEDURE

**"The client consultation is an important part of your professional service. Be sure to complete this step prior to each client service you provide. Your successful retail sales and customer satisfaction rates depend upon it!"**

RETAIL • RE-BOOK • REFERRAL

1. Cosmetologist sanitizes hands.
2. Sanitize and set up table.
3. Sanitize foot basin.
4. Prepare foot basin with sanitizing foot soak.
5. Soak both feet in foot basin for 5 to 10 minutes.
6. Follow procedure as shown
7. Allow client sufficient drying time of nails.
   ***Optional:*** Apply a polish dryer (liquid or spray) on all nails.
8. Suggest appropriate retail tools for the client's at-home nail maintenance.
9. Follow standard cleanup procedures.
10. Document client profile card/file.

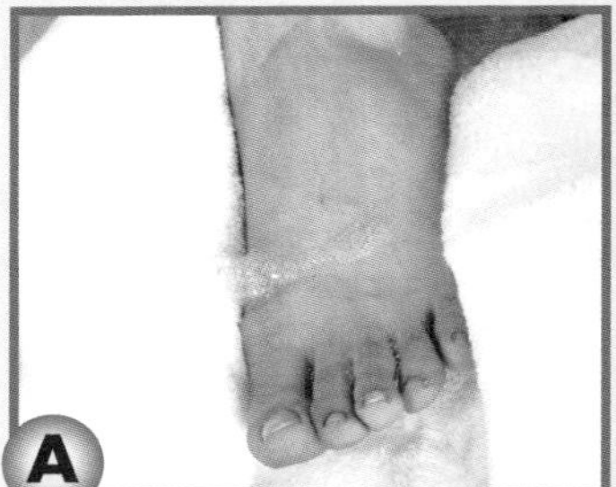

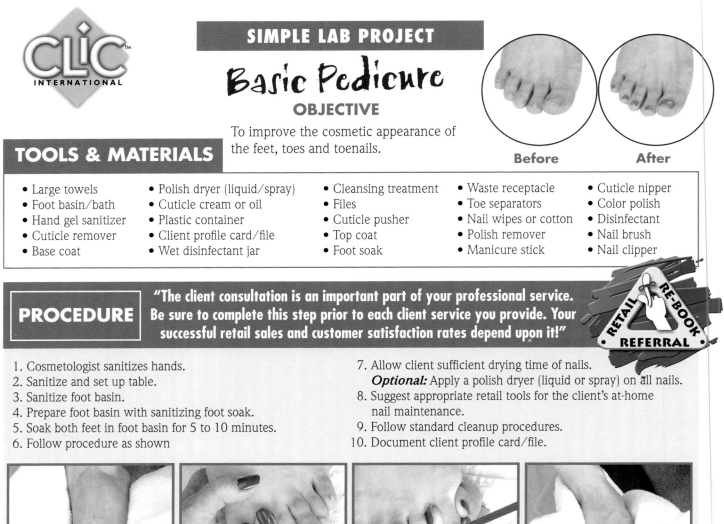

**A** Remove client's **left** foot from basin and place on towel-covered footrest. Dry foot.

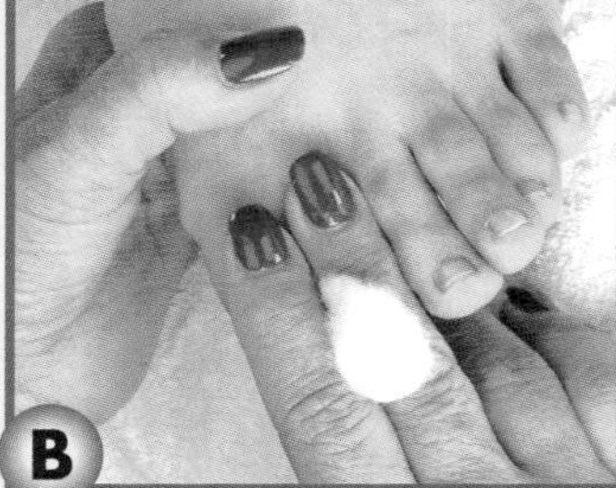

**B** Remove all nail polish. Perform a visual examination of foot and nails.

**C** Cut and/or shape free edge of toenails, being careful not to file into corners of nail.

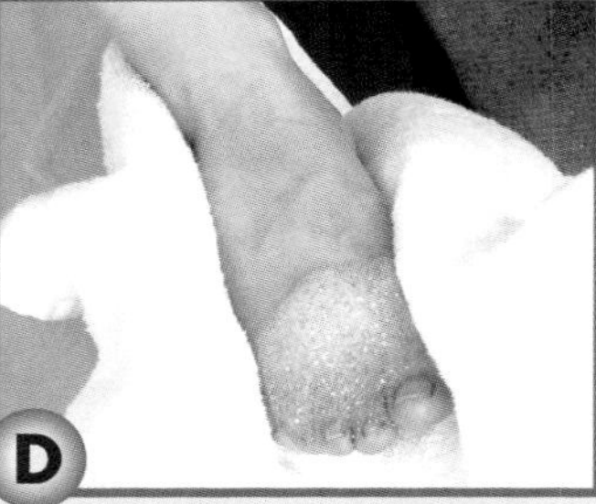

**D** Remove client's **right** foot from basin and place on towel-covered footrest. Dry foot.

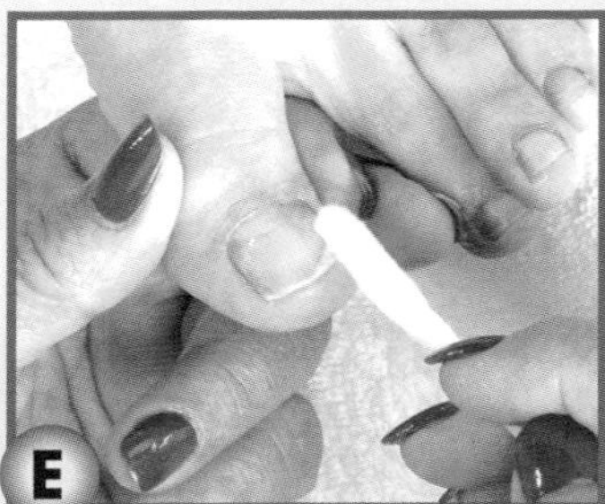

**E** Empty basin and fill with a cleansing treatment. Apply cuticle remover to the cuticle area of left foot.

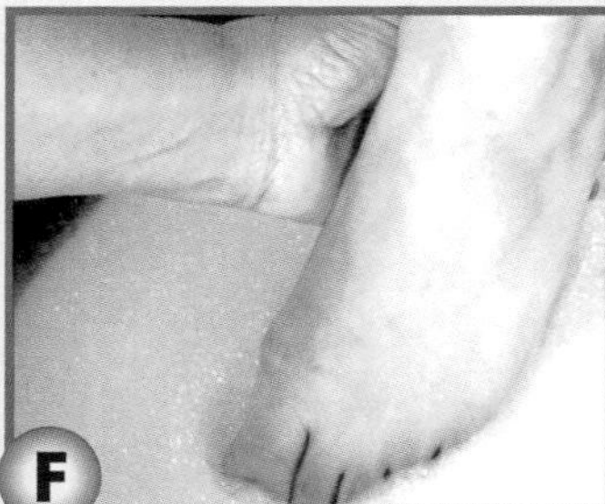

**F** Soak left foot in basin. **Repeat Steps A thru C, E and F on right foot.**

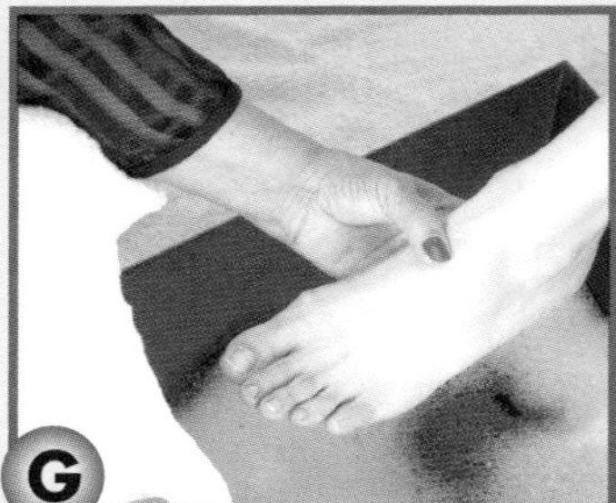

**G** Remove left foot from cleansing treatment and dry foot. Immerse right foot into cleansing treatment.

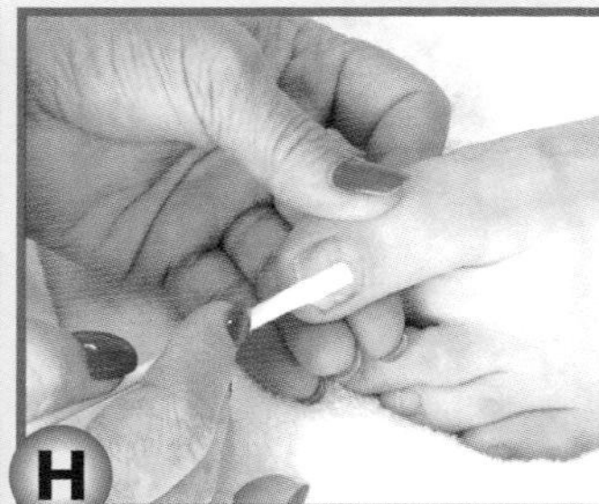

**H** **Gently** push back cuticles (slightly lifting cuticle away from the nail plate), using cuticle pusher or cotton-wrapped manicure stick to all toenails of left foot.

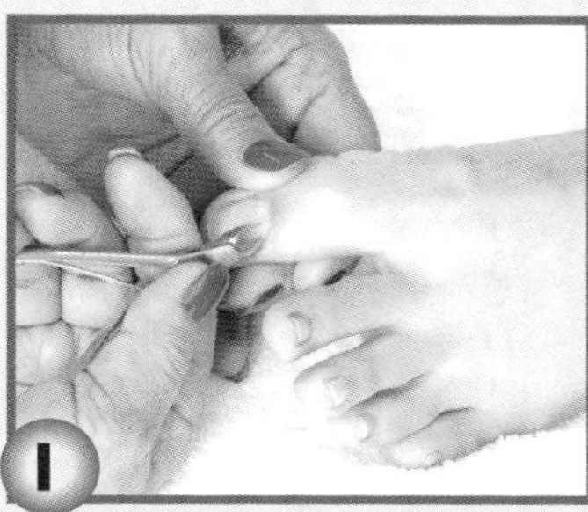
I
**Optional:** Cut **only excess** cuticle from the toenails using a cuticle nipper.

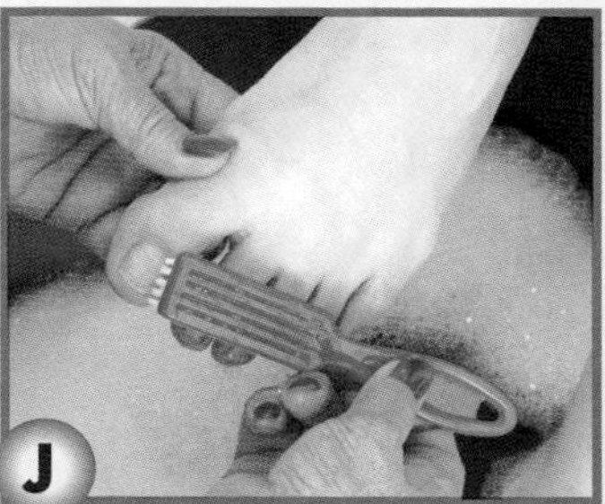
J
Using the nail brush, dip into cleansing treatment and brush the nails, moving from cuticle area outward to the free edge.

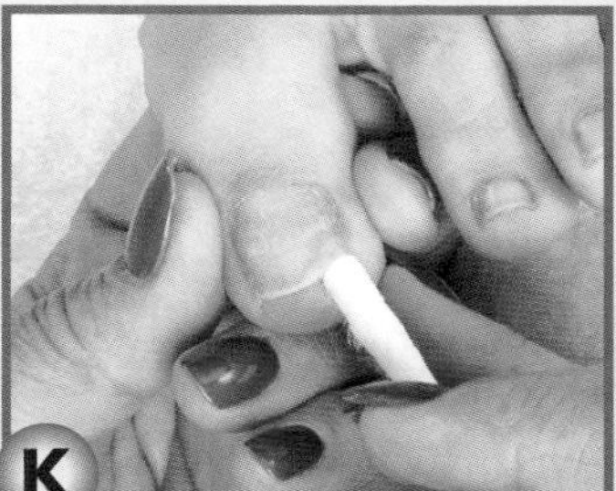
K
Clean under free edge of nail using cotton-wrapped manicure stick.

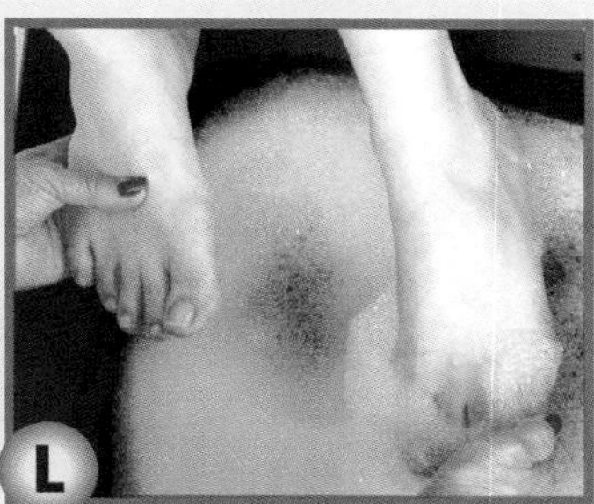
L
Remove right foot from basin, dry and **Repeat Steps H thru K.**

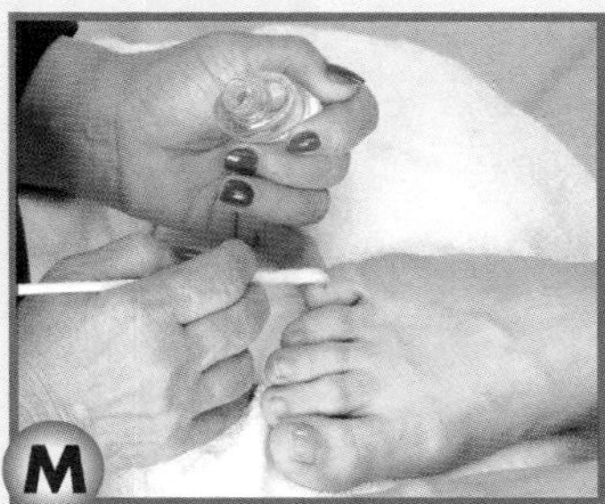
M
Apply a cuticle cream or oil at cuticle area.

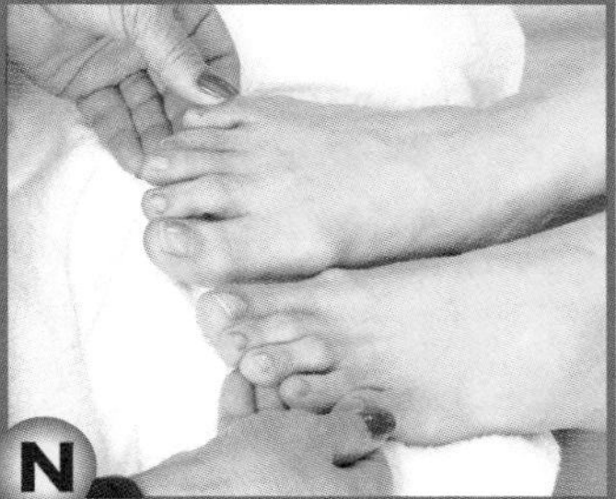
N
Starting with the little toes, massage cuticle cream or oil into cuticle area working toward the big toes.

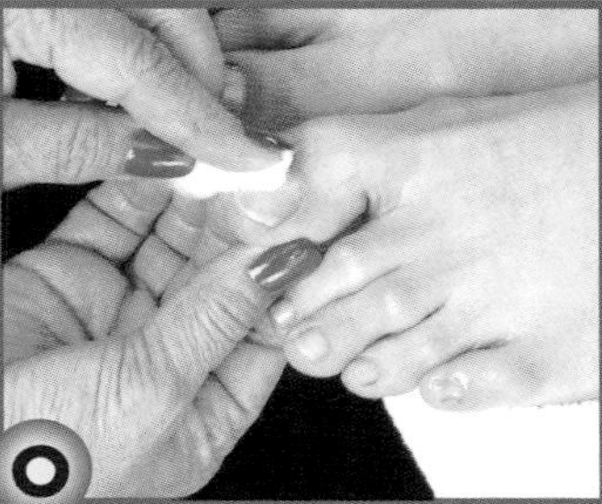
O
Remove oily residue from the nail plate with cotton saturated in polish remover.

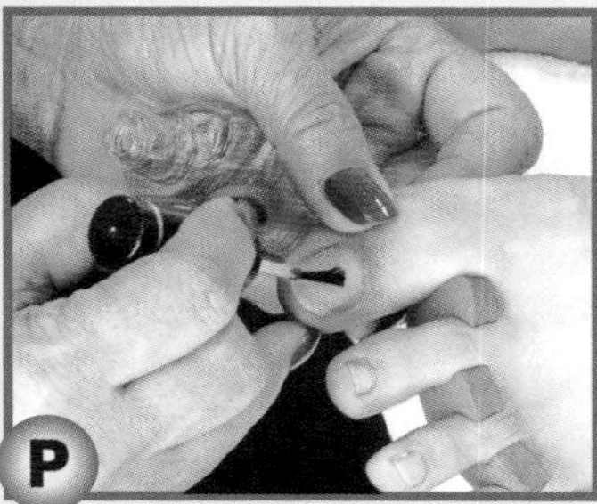
P
Apply toe separators. Cover each nail with a base coat.

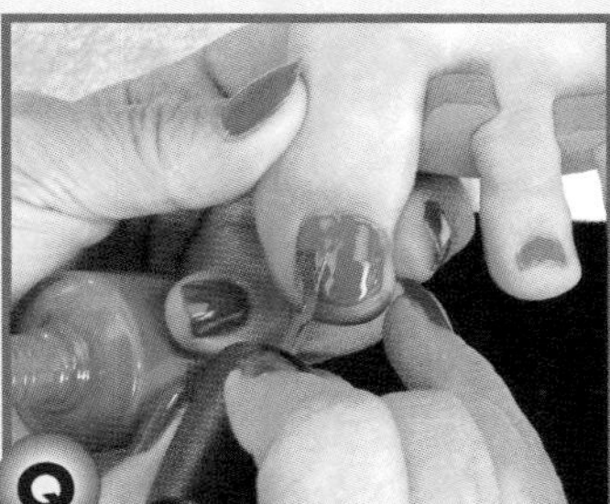
Q
Apply two coats of color polish on all nails.

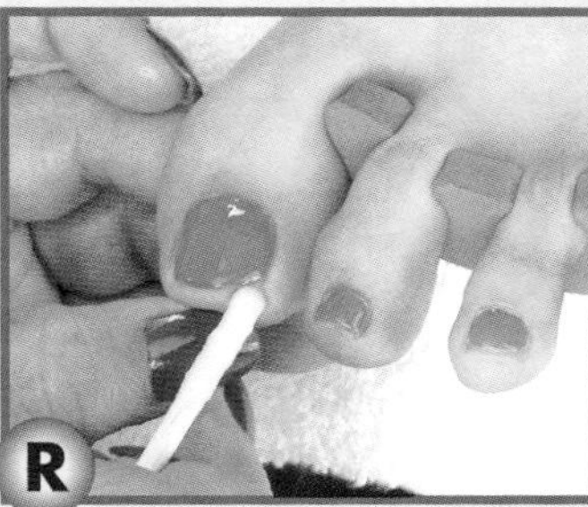
R
Clean any excess polish off skin using cotton-wrapped manicure stick saturated in polish remover.

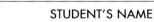

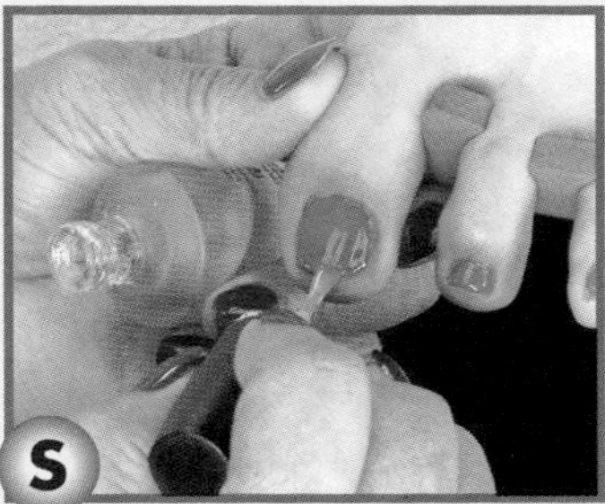
S
Apply one covering of top coat to all nails.

*Recommend monthly pedicure treatments to maintain healthy feet and toenails.*

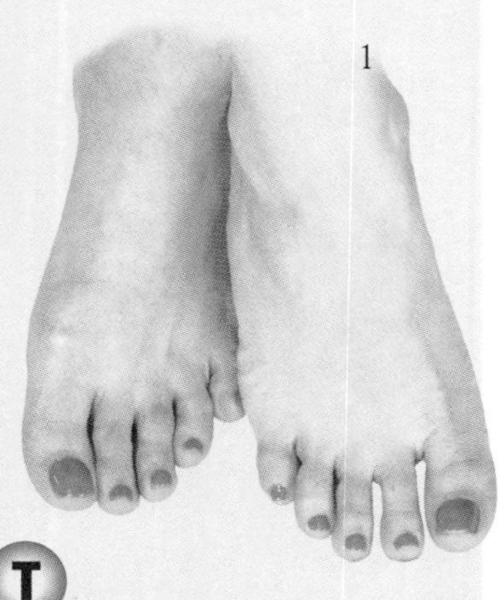
T
**Completed basic pedicure.**

17

**EVALUATION** ____________________

**GRADE** ______ STUDENT'S NAME ______ ID# ______

INTERMEDIATE LAB PROJECT

# Spa Manicure with Paraffin

## OBJECTIVE

To increase the benefits of a manicure by adding the hydrating effects of a paraffin wax.

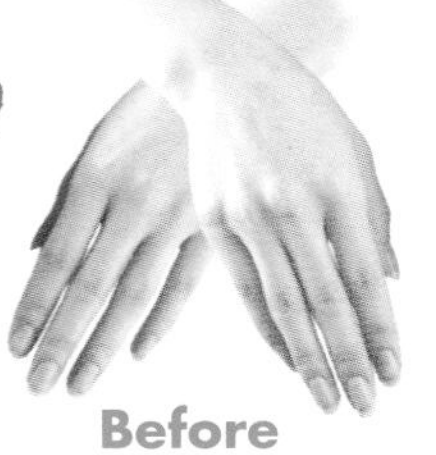

Before

After

## TOOLS & MATERIALS

- Towels
- Manicure bowl
- Hand gel sanitizer
- Cuticle remover
- Base coat
- Polish dryer (liquid/spray)
- Waste receptacle
- Paraffin therapy bath
- Mitts
- Wet disinfectant jar
- Cleansing treatment
- Files
- Cuticle pusher
- Top coat
- Disinfectant
- Nail brush
- Paraffin wax
- Nail clipper
- Cotton or nail wipes
- Polish remover
- Manicure stick
- Cuticle nipper
- Color polish
- Cuticle cream or oil
- Plastic container
- Plastic bags
- Client profile card/file

## PROCEDURE

"The client consultation is an important part of your professional service. Be sure to complete this step prior to each client service you provide. Your successful retail sales and customer satisfaction rates depend upon it!"

RETAIL • RE-BOOK • REFERRAL

1. Cosmetologist sanitizes hands.
2. Sanitize and set up table.
3. Client sanitizes hands.
4. Remove polish from nails.
5. Perform a visual examination of hands and nails.
6. Follow procedure as shown.
7. Allow client sufficient drying time of nails. ***Optional:*** Apply a polish dryer (liquid or spray) on all nails.
8. Suggest appropriate retail tools for the client's at-home nail maintenance.
9. Follow standard cleanup procedures.
10. Document client profile card/file.

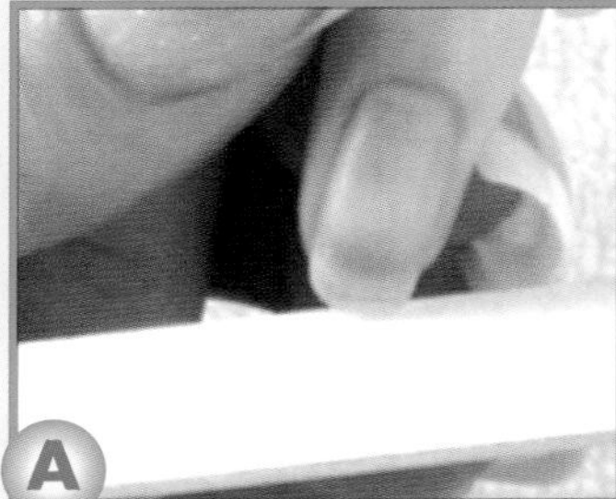

A — Cut and/or shape free edge, on little finger on client's left hand moving to thumb.

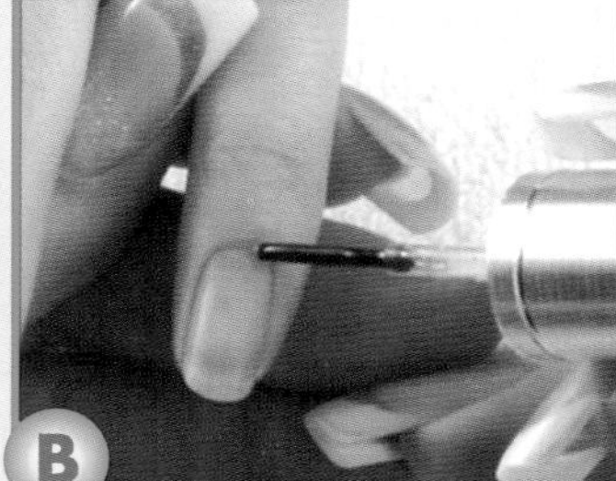

B — Apply cuticle remover to cuticle area of left hand.

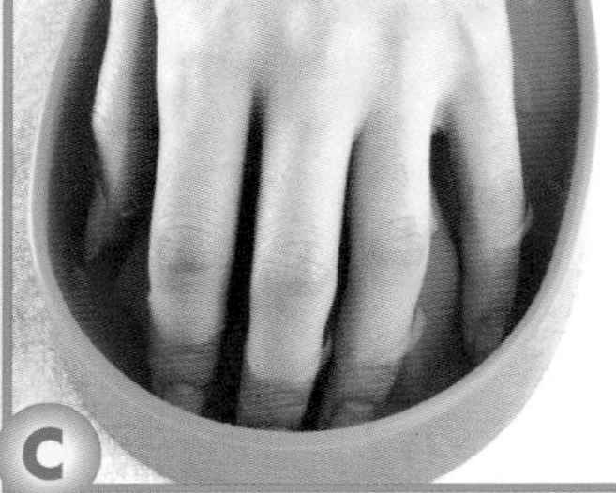

C — Soak fingers of left hand in cleansing treatment in manicure bowl. **Repeat Steps A and B to right hand.**

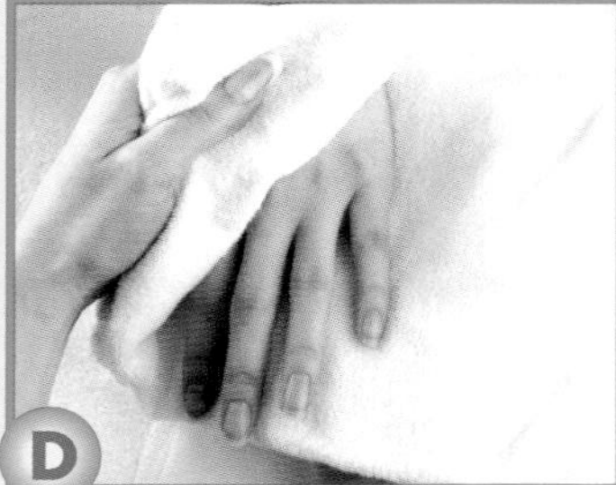

D — Remove left hand from manicure bowl; place on towel and dry fingers. **Repeat Step C to right hand.**

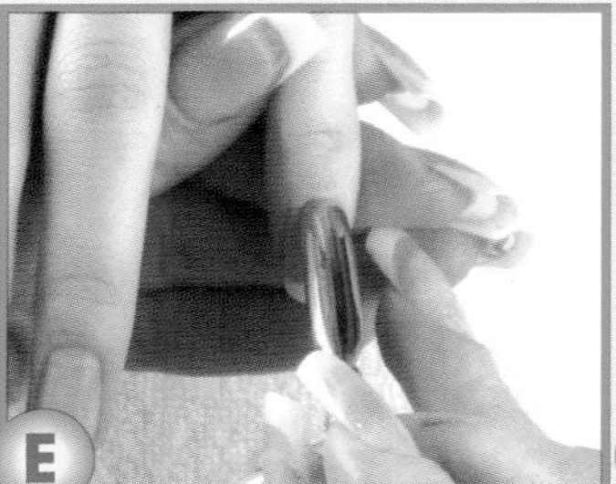

E — On left hand, **gently** push back cuticles using cuticle pusher. **Reminder:** hold pusher at a 30-degree angle.

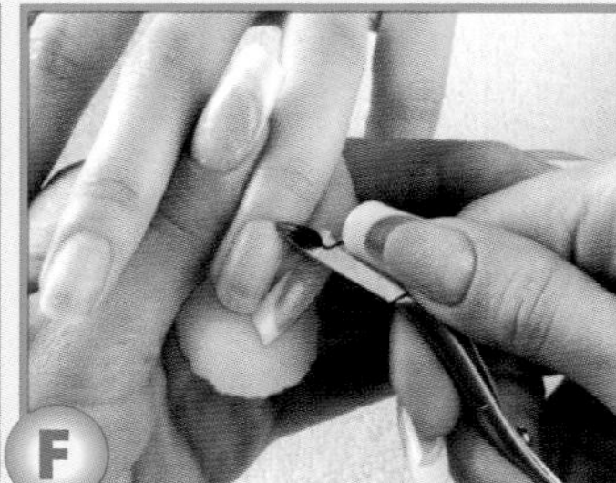

F — A moist cotton ball is placed in opposite hand for holding excess cuticle. Cut cuticle using a cuticle nipper, **carefully removing only cuticle skin.**

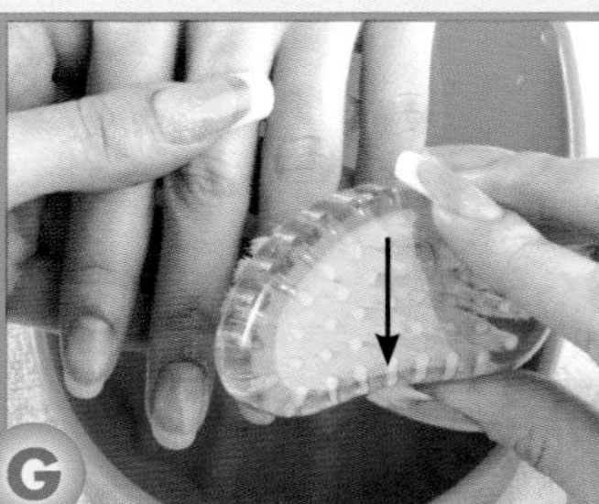

G — Use nail brush and dip into cleansing treatment. Brush nails, moving from cuticle outward to the free edge. Dry fingers with towel.

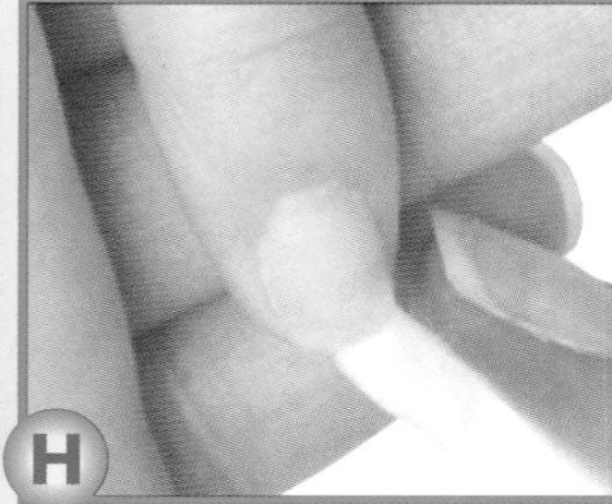

H — Clean under free edge of nail with cotton-wrapped manicure stick. **Repeat Steps D thru H on right hand.**

17

# Spa Manicure with Paraffin

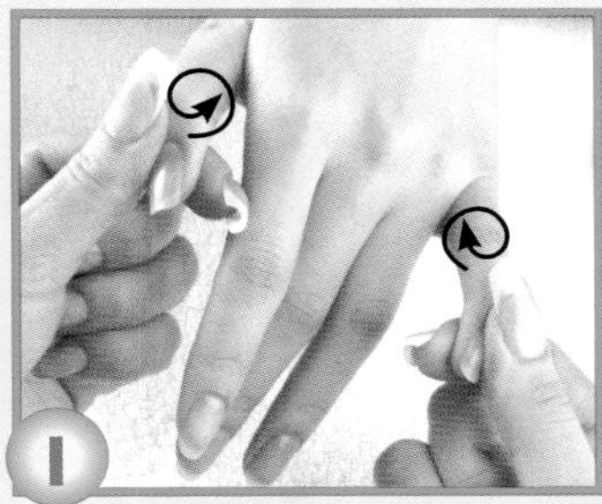

**I** Apply cuticle cream or oil on both hands at cuticle area, starting with the little fingers. Massage cuticle cream into cuticle area working toward thumbs.

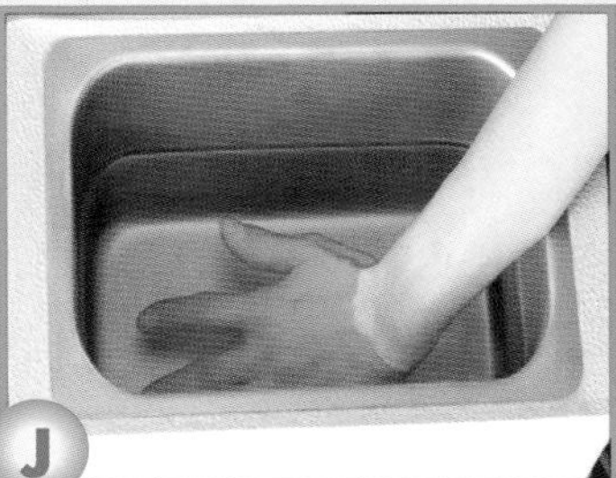

**J** Paraffin is applied to both hands; immerse entire hand into liquid.

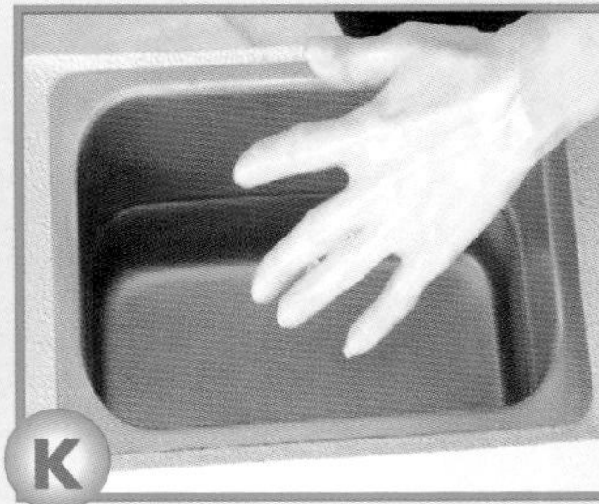

**K** Build layers by dipping three to five times, allow the wax to solidify after each dip before dipping hand again.

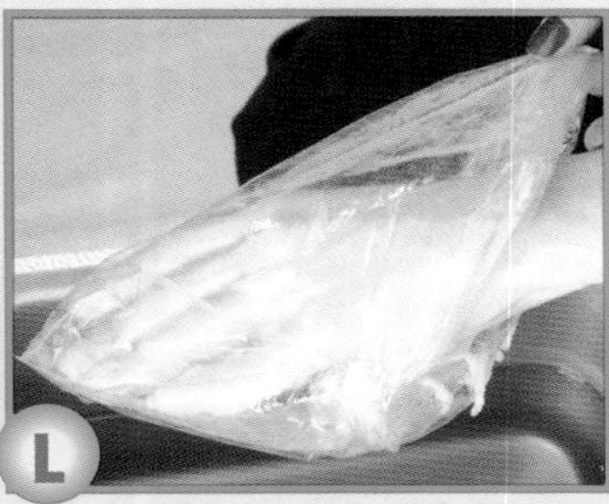

**L** Cover each hand with a plastic bag.

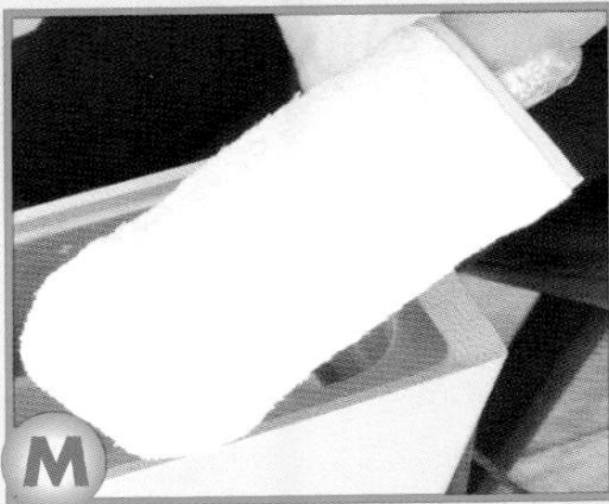

**M** Cover hands with mitts, wait 5 to 10 minutes.

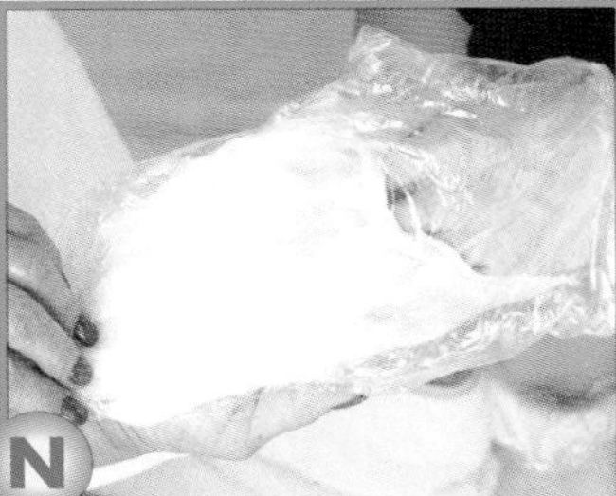

**N** Paraffin is removed by using the plastic bag and rolling the paraffin from the wrist outward to the fingertips into the bag.

**O** Completed paraffin treatment to hand. Remove oily residue from nail plate with cotton or nail wipe saturated in polish remover.

**P** Apply one covering of base coat on all nails.

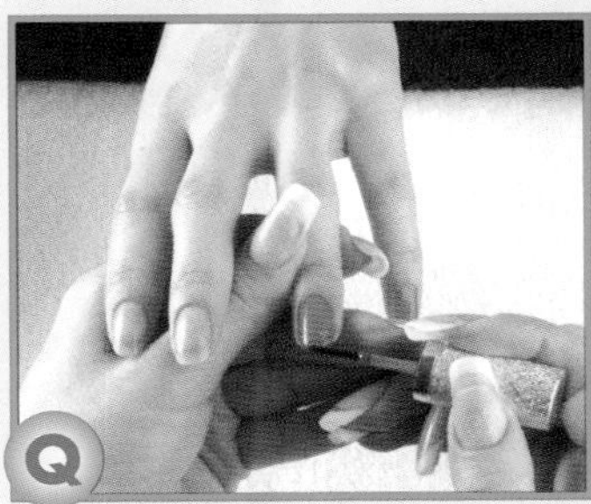

**Q** Apply two coats of color polish on all nails.

**R** Clean any excess polish off skin using tip of brush or cotton-wrapped manicure stick saturated in polish remover.

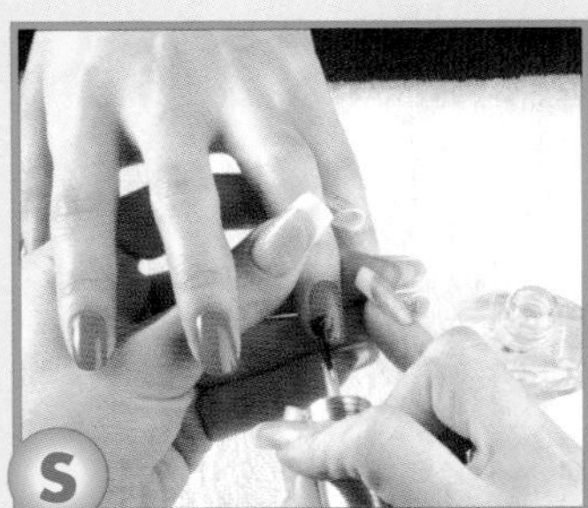

**S** Apply one covering of top coat to all nails.

**T** **Completed spa manicure with paraffin treatment.**

## EVALUATION

______________________________

______________________________

**GRADE** ______ STUDENT'S NAME ______ ID# ______

INTERMEDIATE LAB PROJECT

# Spa Pedicure with Paraffin

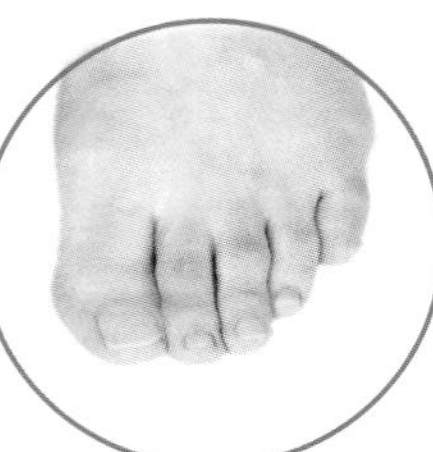
Before

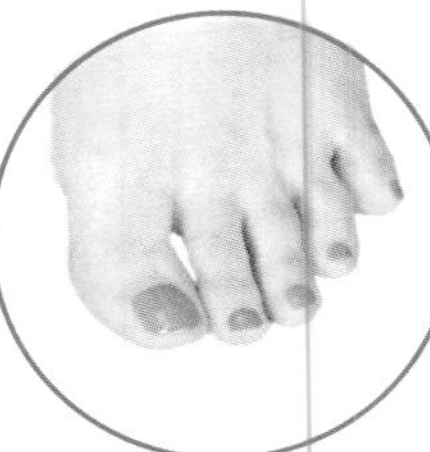
After

## OBJECTIVE

To increase the benefits of a pedicure by adding the hydrating effects of a paraffin wax.

## TOOLS & MATERIALS

- Large towels
- Foot basin or bath
- Hand gel sanitizer
- Cuticle remover
- Base and top coat
- Polish dryer (liquid/spray)
- Cuticle cream or oil
- Nail brush
- Foot file
- Paraffin therapy bath
- Client profile card/file
- Wet disinfectant jar
- Cleansing treatment
- Files
- Cuticle pusher
- Foot soak
- Waste receptacle
- Plastic container
- Scrub gel
- Plastic bags
- Cotton or nail wipes
- Polish remover
- Manicure stick
- Cuticle nipper
- Color polish
- Disinfectant
- Toe separators
- Paraffin wax
- Booties
- Nail clipper

## PROCEDURE

**"The client consultation is an important part of your professional service. Be sure to complete this step prior to each client service you provide. Your successful retail sales and customer satisfaction rates depend upon it!"**

RETAIL • RE-BOOK • REFERRAL

1. Cosmetologist sanitizes hands.
2. Sanitize and set up table.
3. Sanitize foot basin.
4. Prepare foot basin with sanitizing solution.
5. Soak both feet in foot basin for 5 to 10 minutes.
6. Follow procedure as shown.
7. Allow client sufficient drying time of nails. ***Optional:*** Apply a polish dryer (liquid or spray) on all nails.
8. Suggest appropriate retail tools for the client's at-home nail maintenance.
9. Follow standard cleanup procedures.
10. Document client profile card/file.

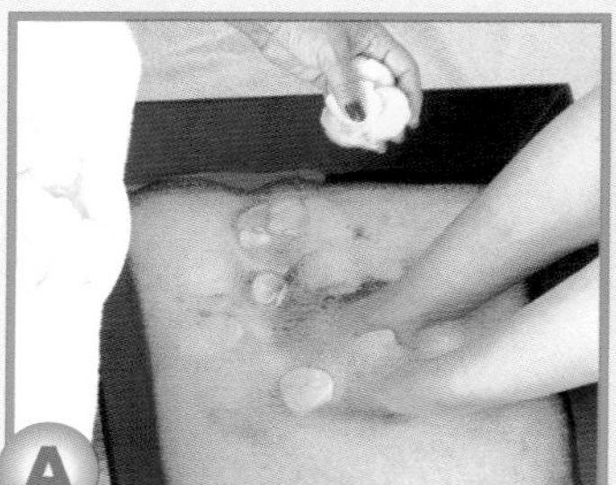
A Remove client's left foot from basin and place on towel-covered footrest.

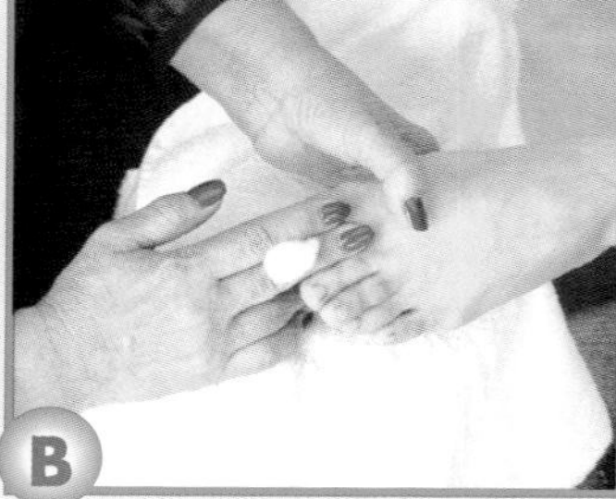
B Dry foot and remove nail polish. Perform a visual examination of foot and nails.

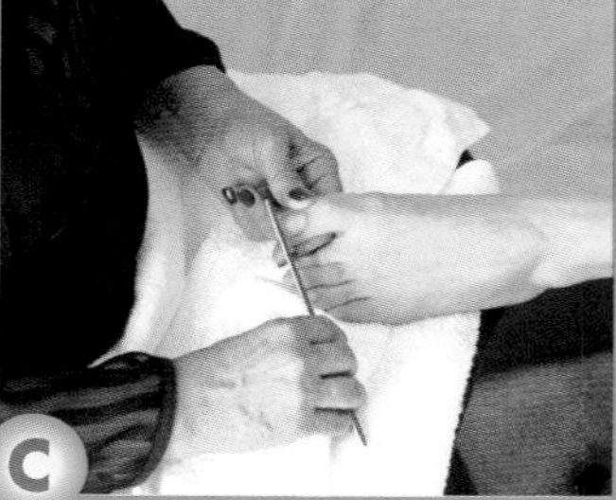
C Cut and/or shape free edge of nails, being **careful not to file into corners of nails**. Apply cuticle remover to the cuticle area of nails on left foot.

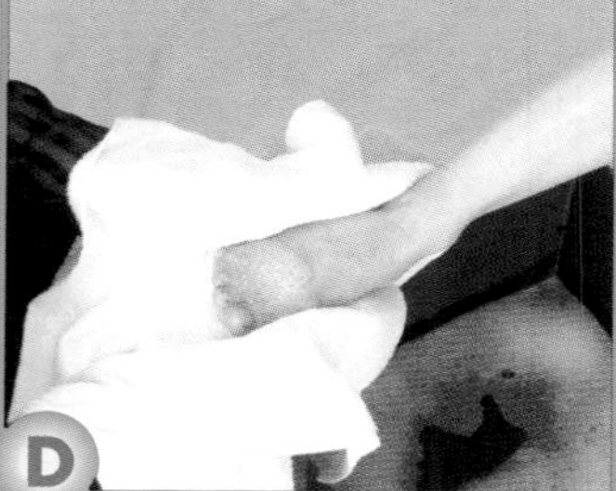
D Remove client's right foot from basin and place on towel-covered footrest.

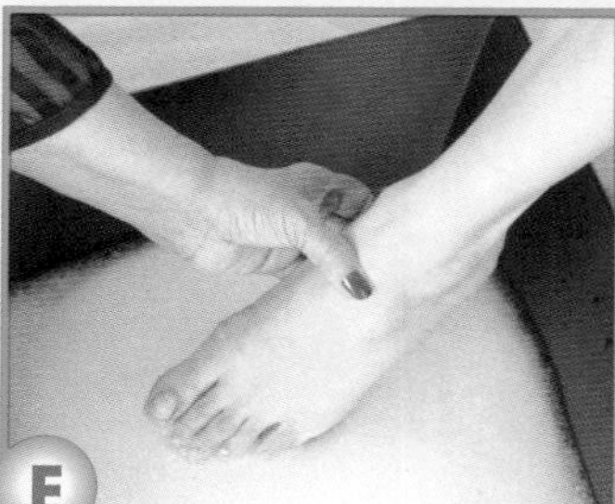
E Empty basin and fill with cleansing treatment. Soak left foot in cleansing treatment and **Repeat Steps B and C on right foot.**

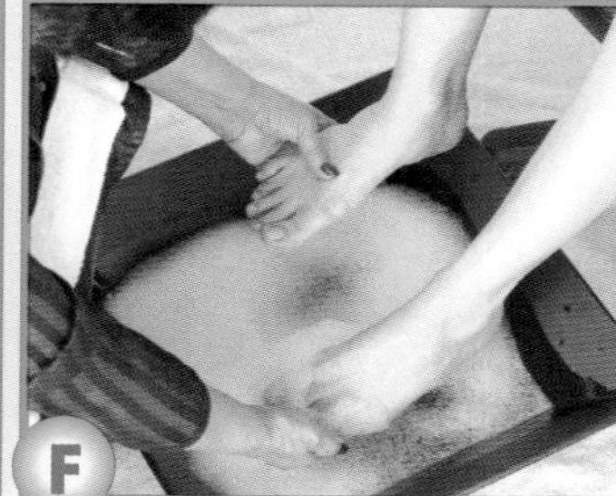
F Remove left foot from cleansing treatment and dry foot. **Immerse right foot in basin.**

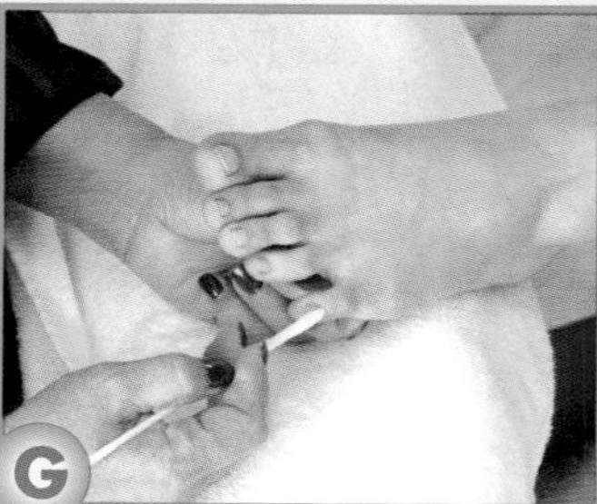
G **Gently** push back cuticles using cuticle pusher or cotton-wrapped manicure stick. **Optional:** Cut **only excess** cuticle from the toenails.

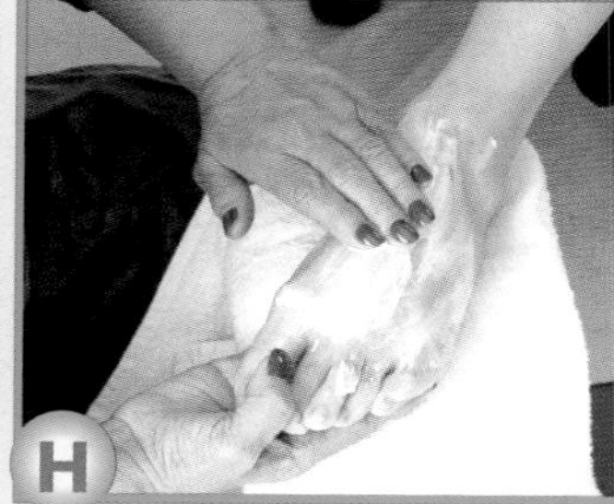
H Apply scrub gel lightly on both sides of left foot. **Optional:** a foot file assists in softening hardened skin. **Repeat Steps G and H on right foot.**

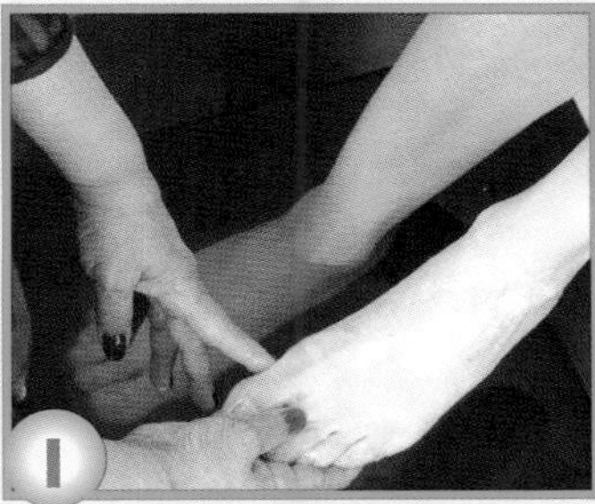

I

**Immerse both feet in basin and rinse left foot.** Remove left foot and dry; continue soaking right foot. Clean under free edge of nail with tip of cotton-wrapped manicure stick.

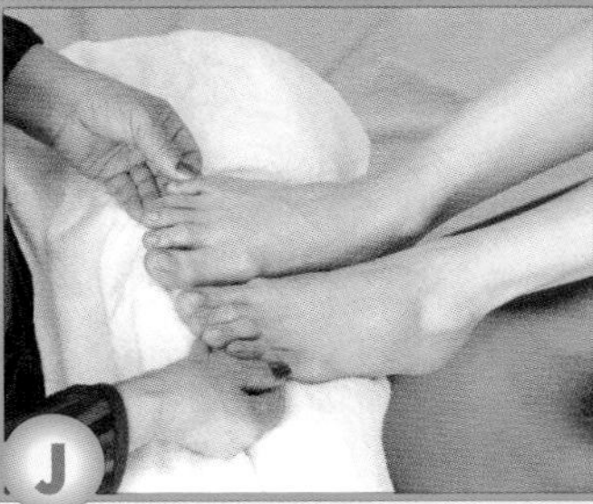

J

Remove right foot from basin, dry and **Repeat Step I.** Apply cuticle cream or oil on both feet at cuticle area. Starting with the little toes, massage cream into cuticle area working toward the big toes.

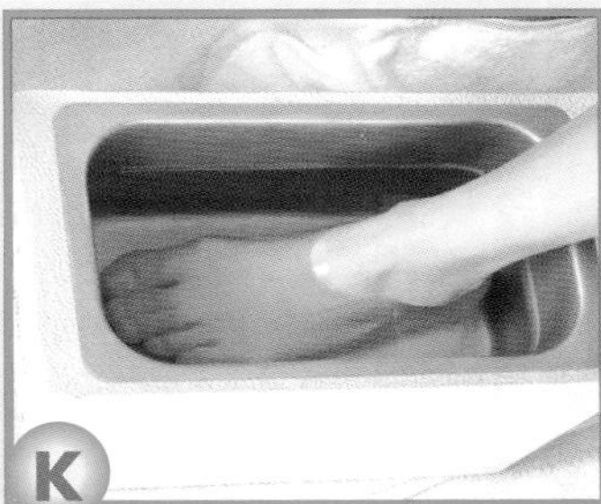

K

Paraffin is applied to both feet; immerse entire foot into paraffin bath.

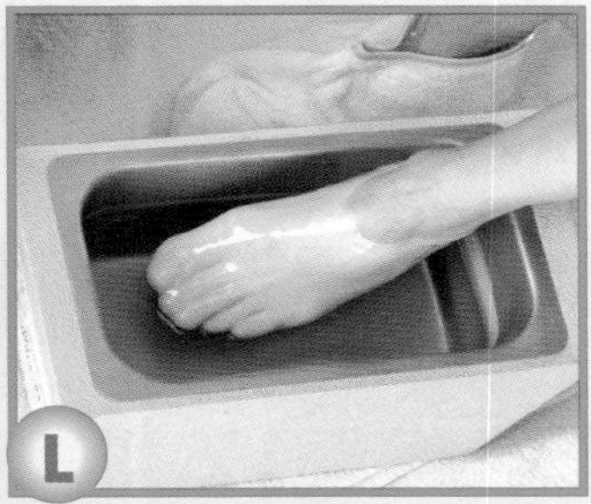

L

Build layers by dipping three to five times. After each layer, allow the wax to solidify before applying next layer.

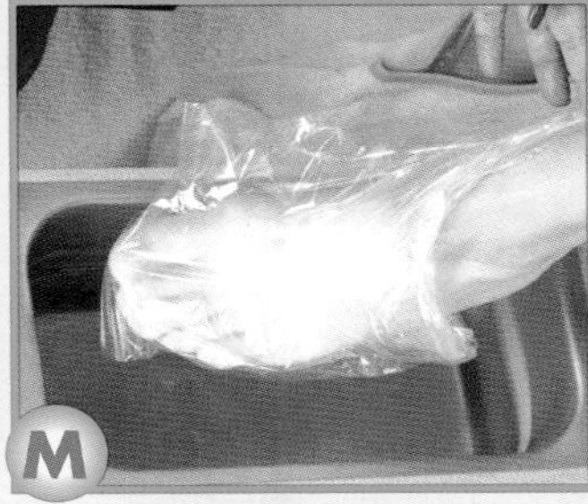

M

Cover each foot with a plastic bag.

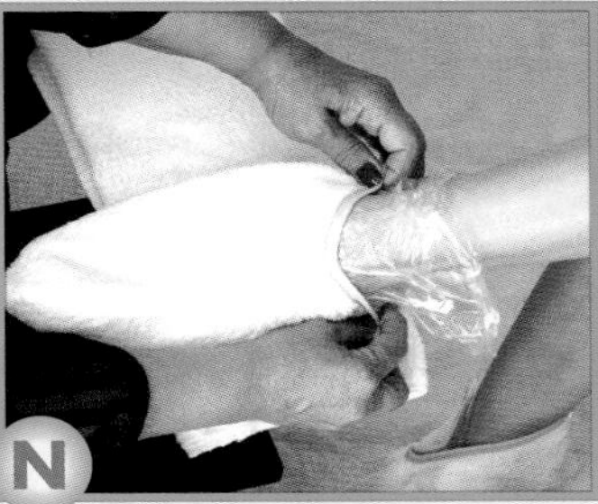

N

Apply a bootie to each foot, wait 5 to 10 minutes.

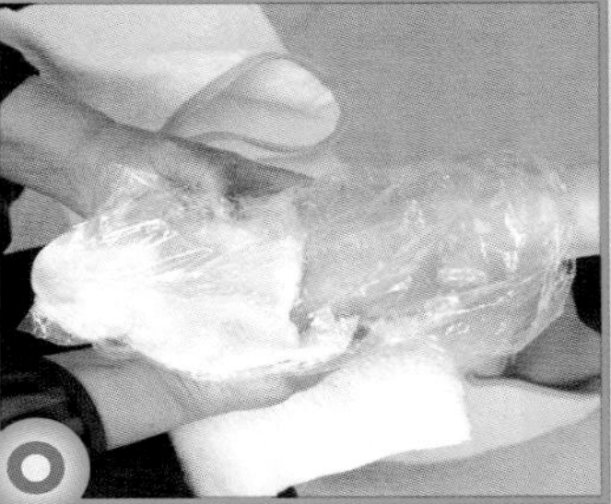

O

Paraffin is removed by using the plastic bag and rolling paraffin from the ankle outward to the toes into the bag.

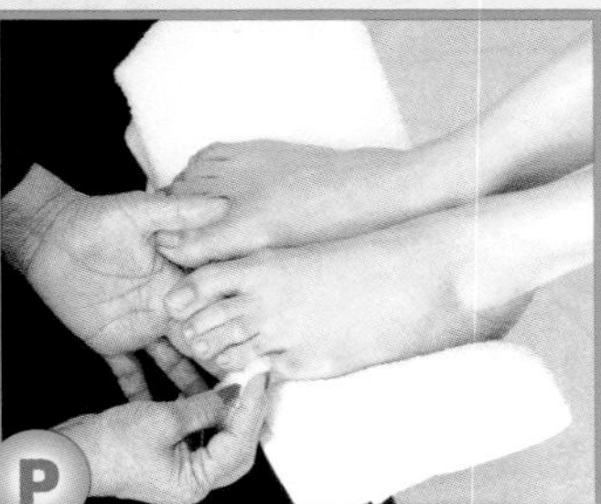

P

Remove oily residue from nail plate with cotton saturated in polish remover.

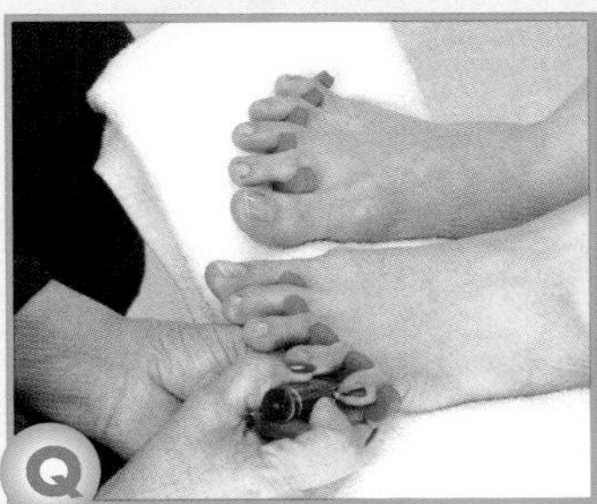

Q

Apply toe separators and cover each nail with a base coat.

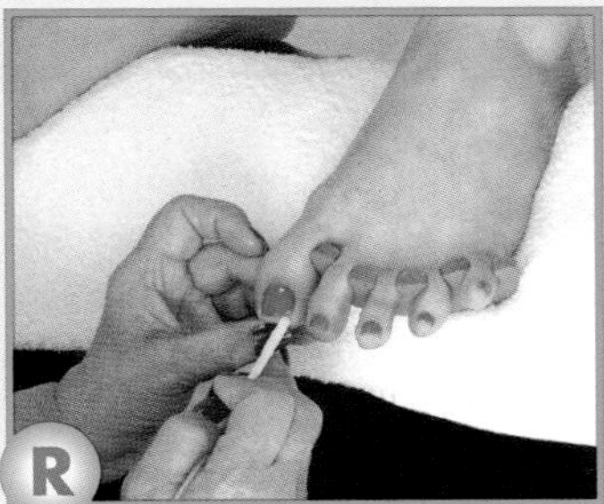

R

Apply two coats of color polish on all nails. Clean any excess polish off skin using cotton-wrapped manicure stick saturated in polish remover.

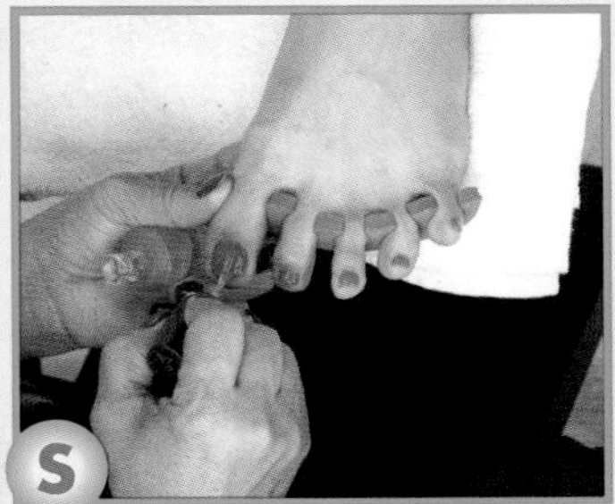

S

Apply one covering of top coat to all nails.

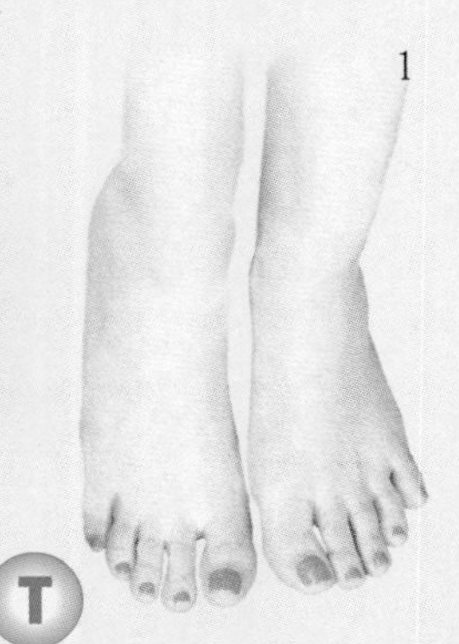

T

**Completed spa pedicure with paraffin.**

17

**EVALUATION** ______________________

______ GRADE ______ STUDENT'S NAME ______ ID#

## INTERMEDIATE LAB PROJECT

# Foot and Leg Massage

### OBJECTIVE

To promote additional benefits of relaxation with any foot nail service.

## TOOLS & MATERIALS

- Towels
- Disinfectant
- Client profile card/file
- Foot and body lotion
- Foot powder
- Foot basin
- Cotton or nail wipes
- Spatula
- Files
- Polish Remover

## PROCEDURE

**"The client consultation is an important part of your professional service. Be sure to complete this step prior to each client service you provide. Your successful retail sales and customer satisfaction rates depend upon it!"**

RETAIL • RE-BOOK • REFERRAL

1. Cosmetologist sanitizes hands.
2. Sanitize and set up table.
3. Sanitize foot basin.
4. Prepare foot basin with sanitizing solution.
5. Soak both feet in foot basin for 5 to 10 minutes.
6. Follow procedure as shown.
7. Suggest appropriate retail tools for the client's at-home nail maintenance.
8. Follow standard cleanup procedures.
9. Document client profile card/file.

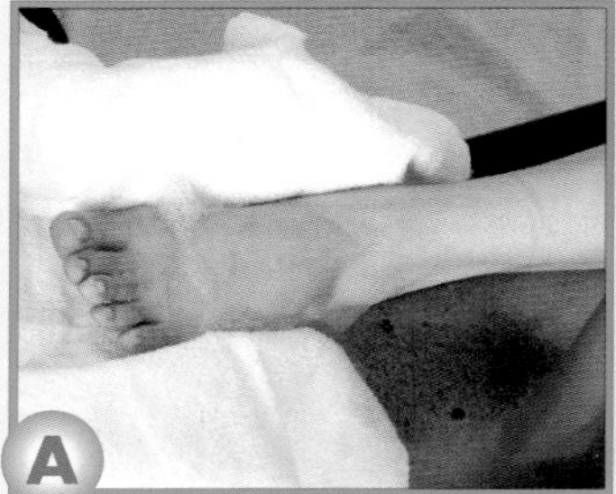

A: Remove client's left foot from basin and place on towel covered footrest. Dry foot and remove nail polish; perform visual examination of foot and nails.

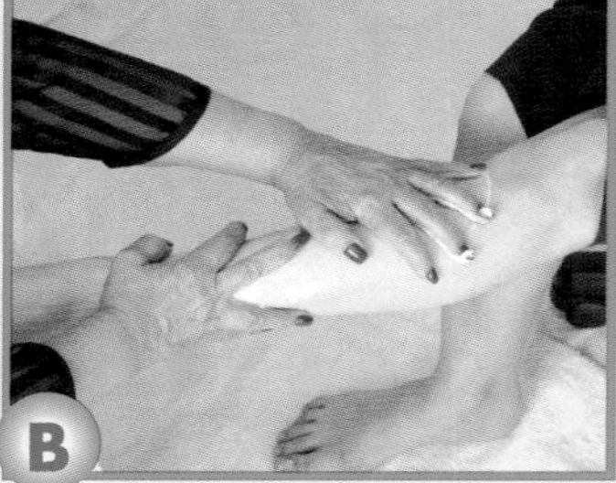

B: Distribute lotion to left leg and foot.

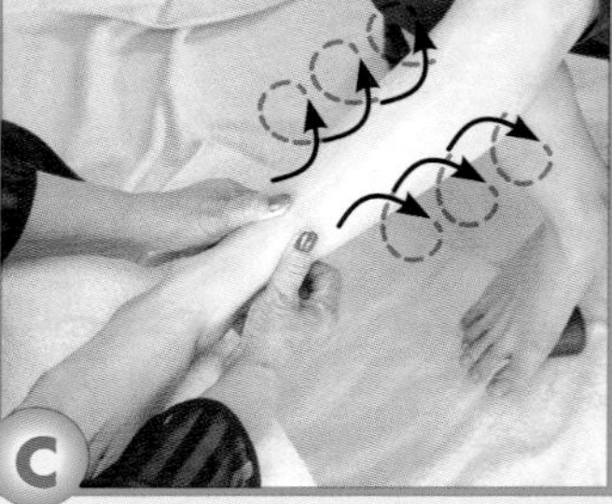

C: **Effleurage movement:** Place thumbs on topside of ankle, simultaneously apply a circular rotation, moving up to top of leg.

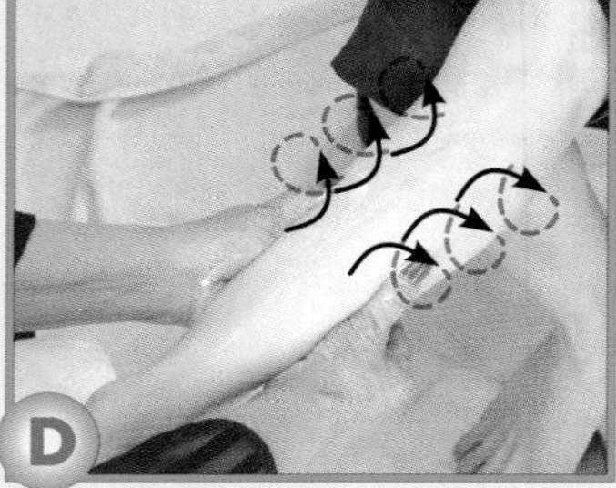

D: **Effleurage movement:** Slide thumbs down and continue circular rotation moving up side of leg.

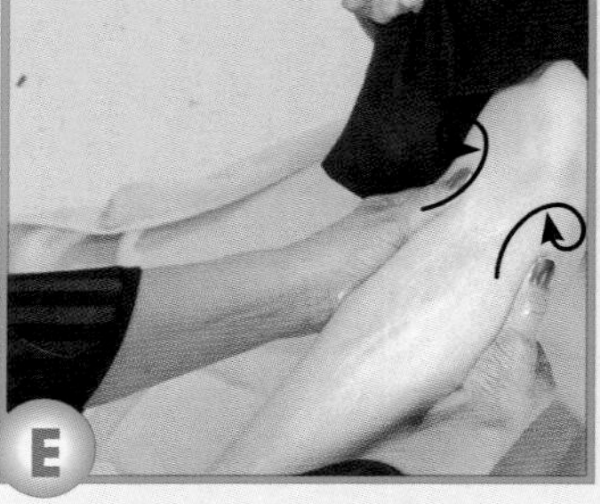

E: **Effleurage movement:** Continue movement to top of leg (bottom of knee). Slide down to ankle and **repeat two times**.

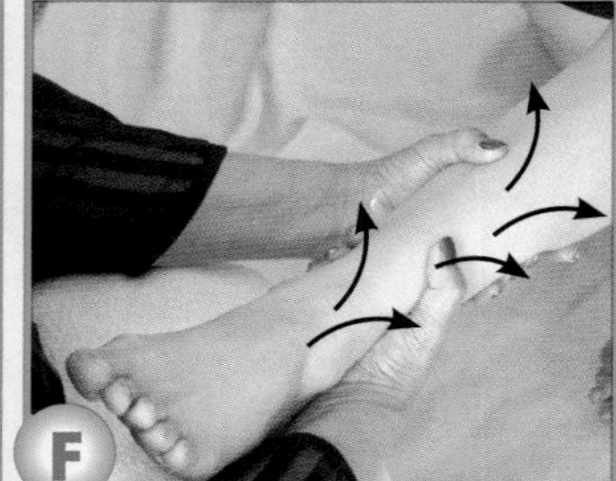

F: **Petrissage movement:** Start at ankle, wrap both hands around leg and twist out.

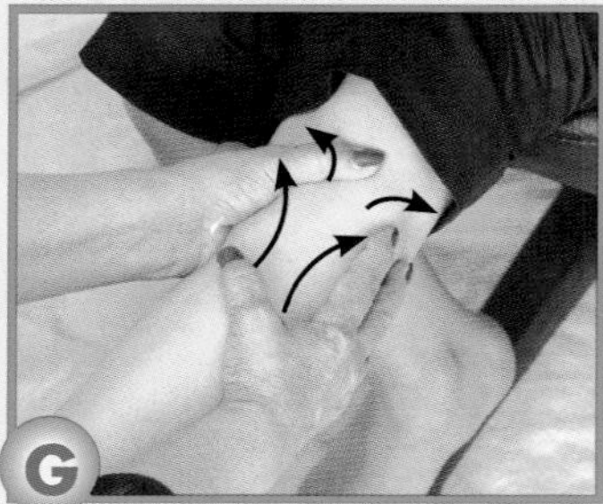

G: **Petrissage movement:** Continue twisting up leg to bottom of knee. Slide down to ankle and **repeat two times.**

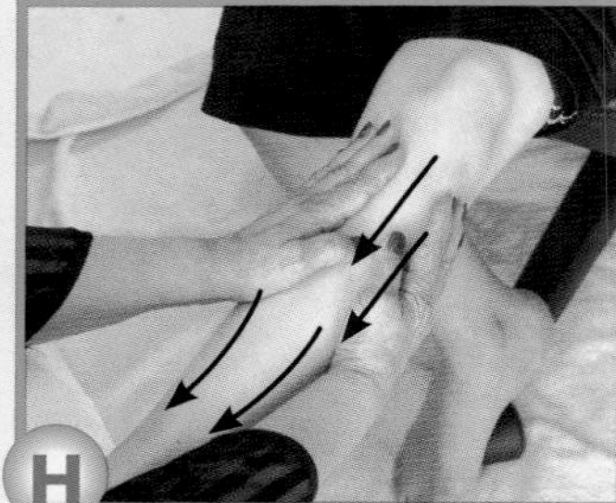

H: **Effleurage movement:** Start at bottom of knee, place hands palm down on top of leg, alternate hands using a gliding motion down the leg.

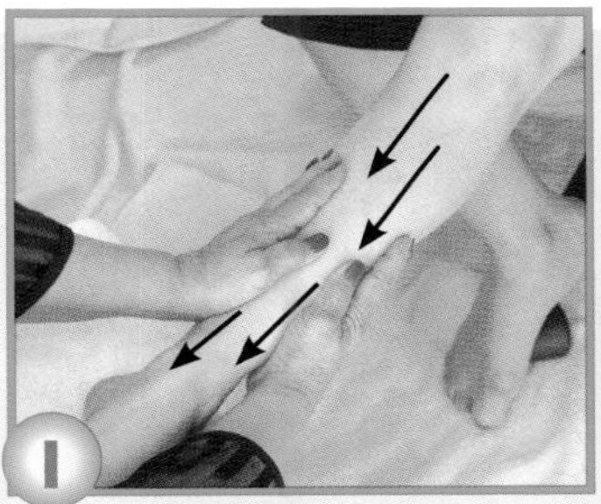


**Effleurage movement:** Continue gliding down to ankle until reaching foot (apply more lotion to foot if necessary). Proceed to foot massage.

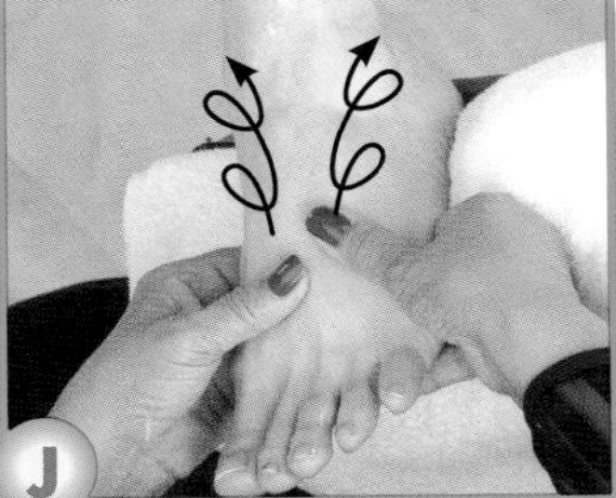


**Effleurage movement:** Place thumbs on topside of foot. Begin at base of toes; simultaneously apply a circular rotation.

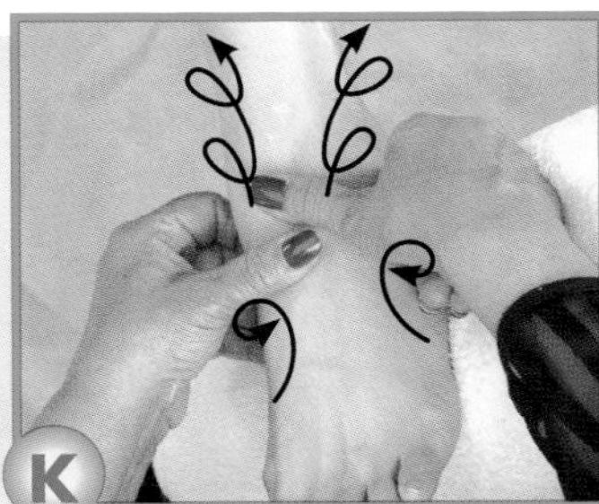


**Effleurage movement:** Continue circular rotation to the ankle. Slide down to base of toes and **repeat two times.**

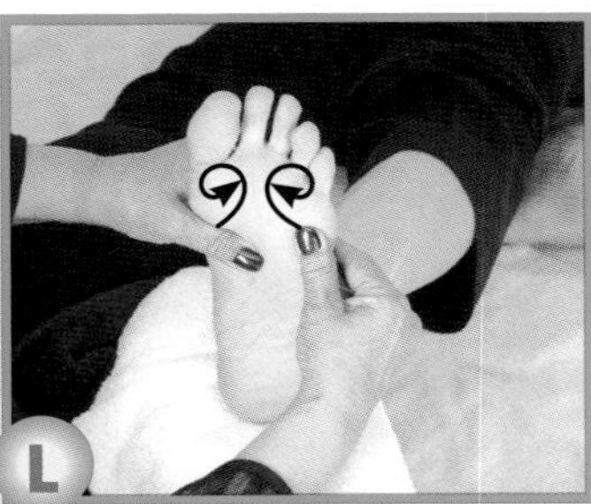


**Effleurage movement:** On underside of foot, place thumbs at base of toes, apply a circular rotation.

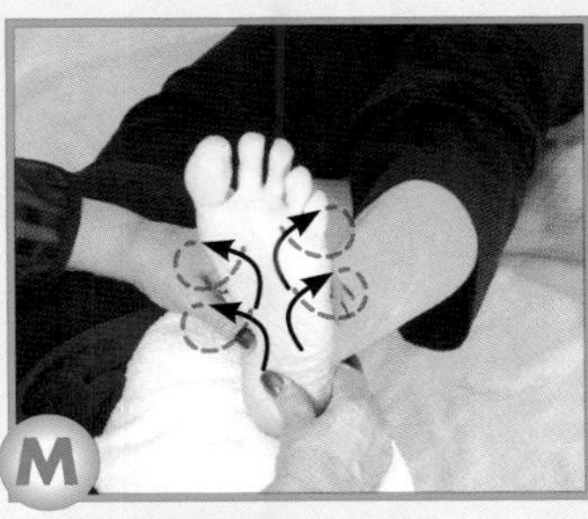


**Effleurage movement:** Continue movement to heel of foot. Slide thumbs to base of toes and **repeat two times.**

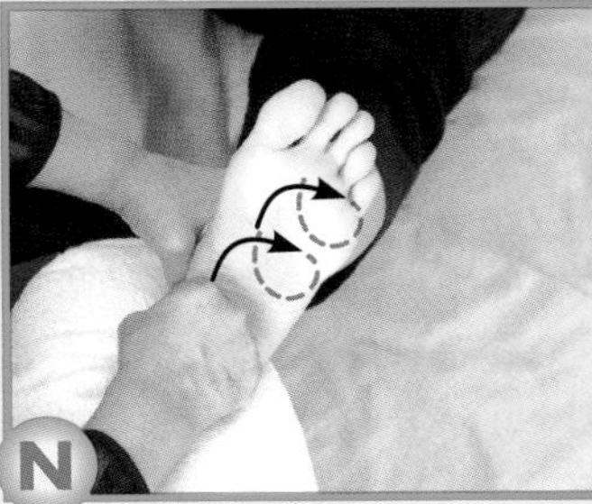


**Friction movement:** Place fist of either hand at center of underside of foot.

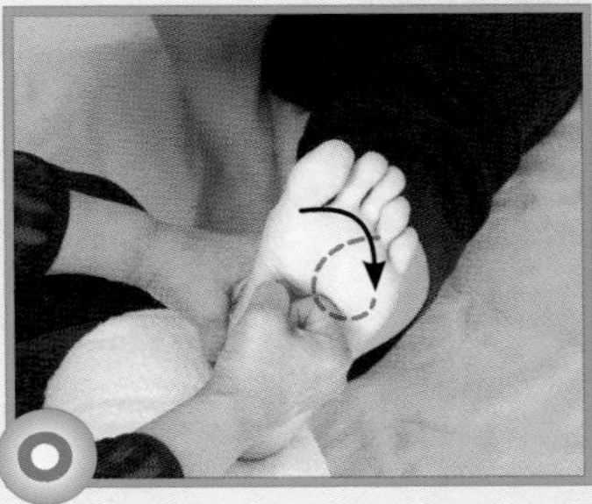


**Friction movement:** Turn fist in a clockwise motion and apply pressure.

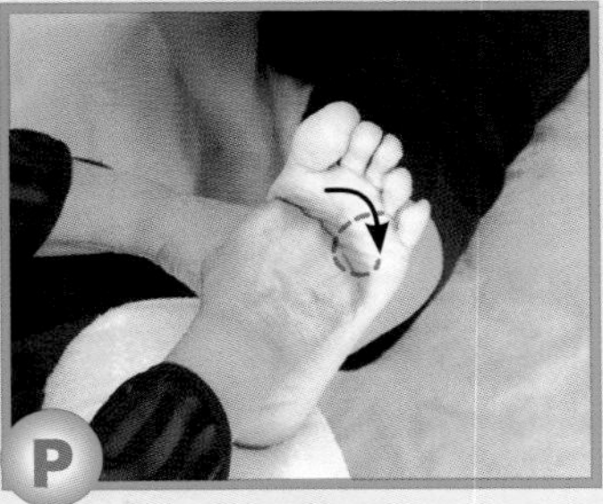


**Friction movement:** Continue twisting, moving up toward base of toes. **Repeat two times.**

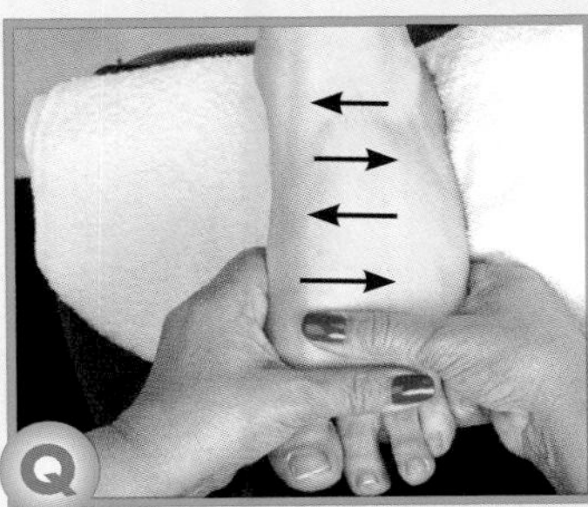


**Petrissage movement:** Place thumbs on topside of foot. Begin at base of toes and simultaneously apply a cross over with thumbs.

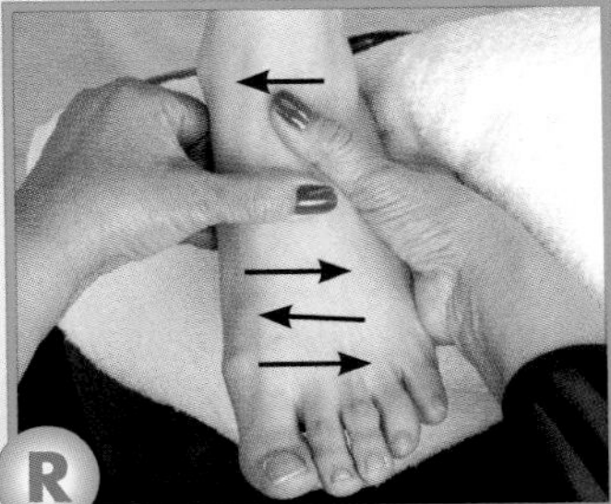


**Petrissage movement:** Continue to cross over moving to ankle. Slide to base of toes and **repeat two times.**

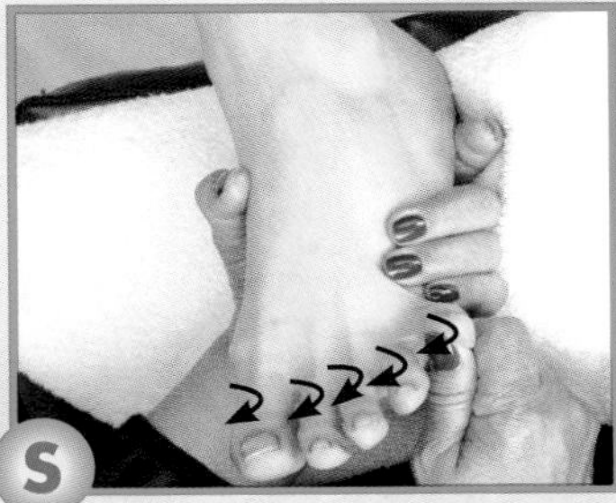


**Effleurage movement:** Start at little toe and **rotate toe three times** in a clockwise circular motion.

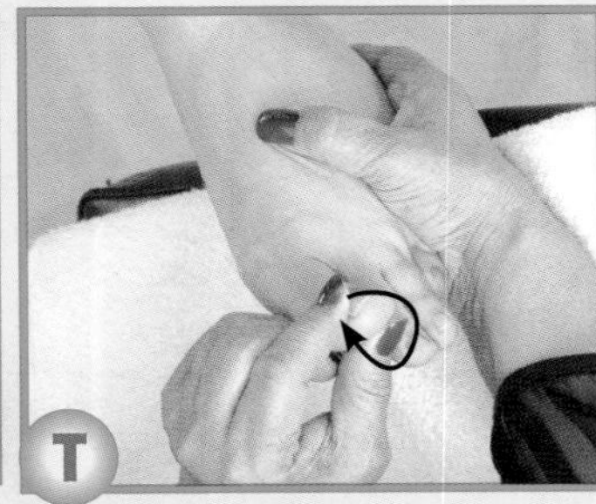


**Effleurage movement:** Continue circular rotation on each toe. **Rotate each toe three times. Repeat Steps A thru T on right leg and foot.**



**EVALUATION** ______________________________

______ GRADE ______ STUDENT'S NAME ______ ID#

RA

INTERMEDIATE LAB PROJECT

# Nail Tip Application

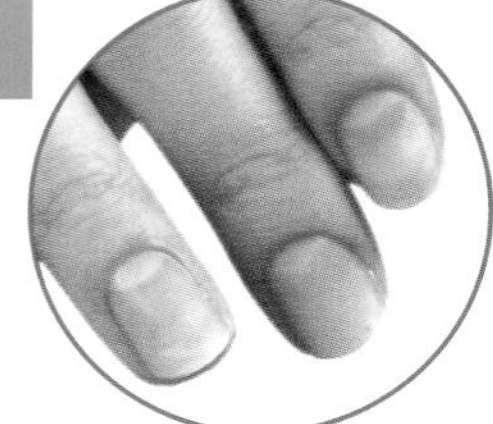

Before

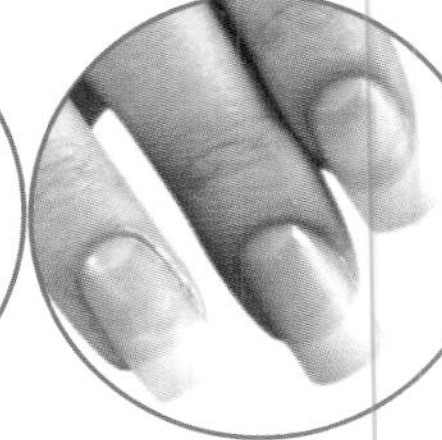

After

## OBJECTIVE

To increase the free edge length by using artificial nail tips.

## TOOLS & MATERIALS

- Towels
- Disinfectant
- Client profile card/file
- Waste receptacle
- Tip cutter
- Goggles
- Wet disinfectant jar
- Manicure stick
- Hand gel sanitizer
- Plastic container
- Nail tips
- Cotton and nail wipes
- Files and buffers
- Polish remover
- Cuticle pusher
- Nail clipper
- Nail adhesive
- Dehydrant

## PROCEDURE

**"The client consultation is an important part of your professional service. Be sure to complete this step prior to each client service you provide. Your successful retail sales and customer satisfaction rates depend upon it!"**

RETAIL • RE-BOOK • REFERRAL

1. Cosmetologist sanitizes hands.
2. Sanitize and set up table.
3. Client sanitizes hands.
4. Remove polish from nails.
5. Perform a visual examination of hands and nails.
6. Follow procedure as shown.
7. Suggest appropriate retail tools for the client's at-home nail maintenance.
8. Follow standard cleanup procedures.
9. Document client profile card/file.

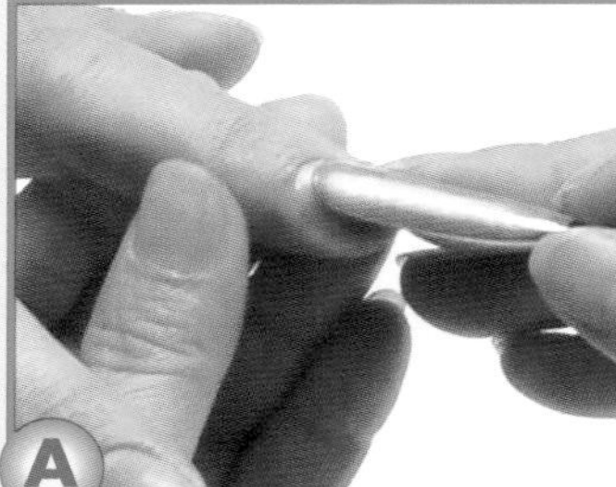

A — Use cotton-wrapped manicure stick or cuticle pusher to **gently** push back cuticles.

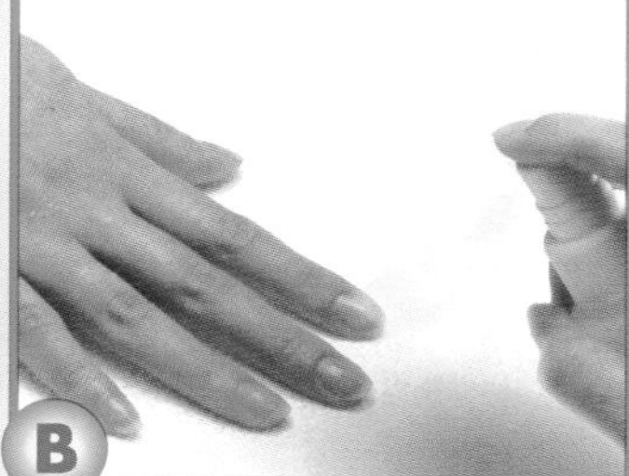

B — Apply a nail antiseptic to the natural nail; either spray on or wipe over nail with nail wipe.

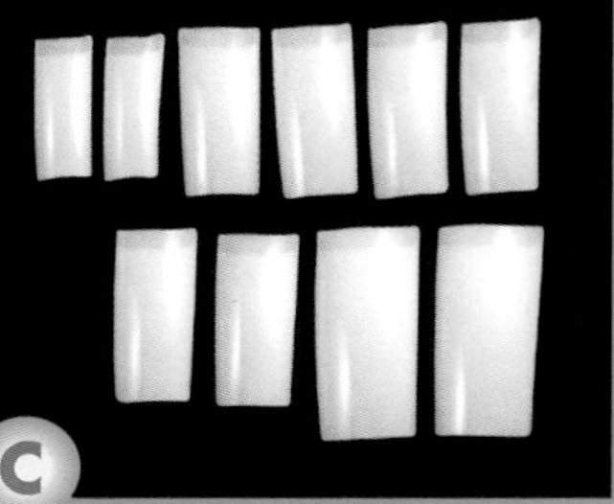

C — Choose the proper nail tip size and shape ensuring 1/2 of the natural nail is exposed when tip is placed.

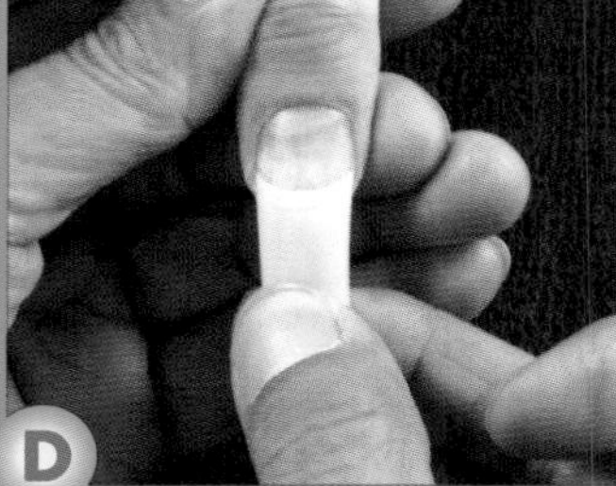

D — Match tip to client's natural nail contour and width, ensuring tip aligns sidewall to sidewall.

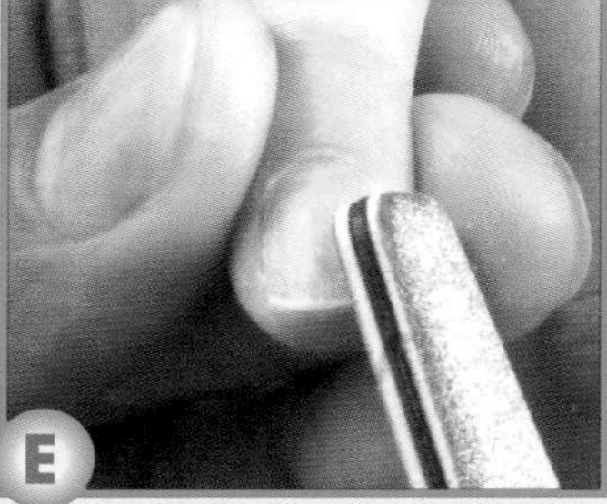

E — Shape and buff the free edge of natural nail. Buff entire top of nail to remove shine or natural oils, which will allow proper adhesion.

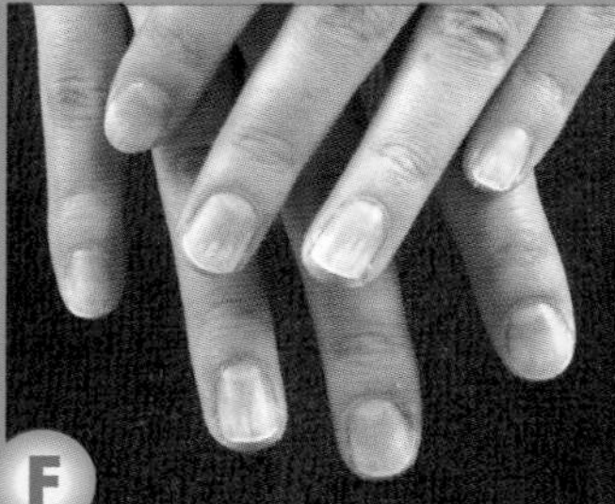

F — Natural nails after buffing, with no shine on nail plates.

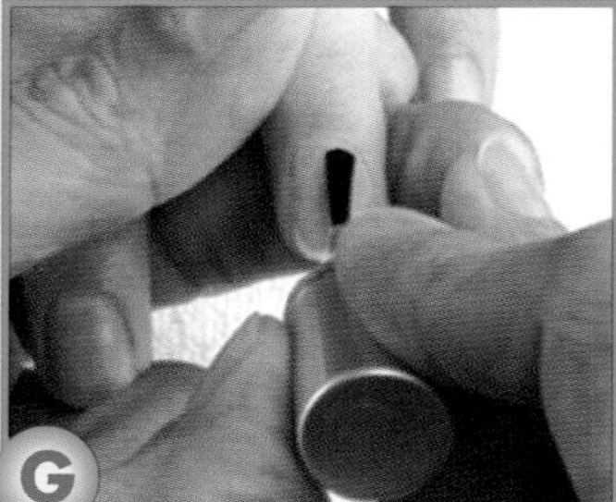

G — Apply a nail dehydrant to natural nail plate **only**. This removes moisture from nail plate to improve adhesion of nail tip to natural nail.

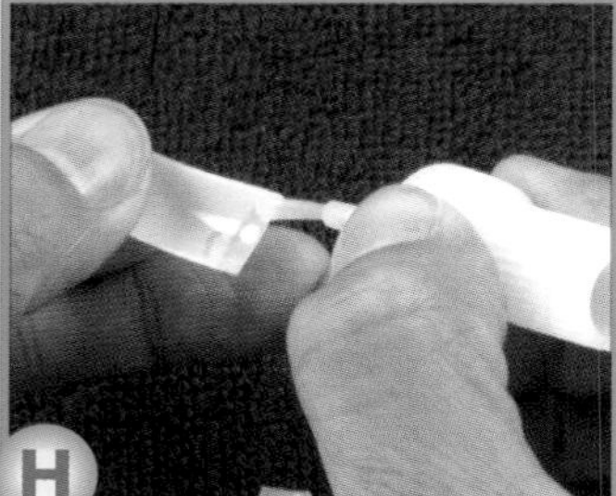

H — Apply a thin layer of adhesive to underside (concave) well of tip. **NOTE:** Excessive use of adhesive will prevent tip from adhering to natural nail and possibly force adhesive onto the skin.

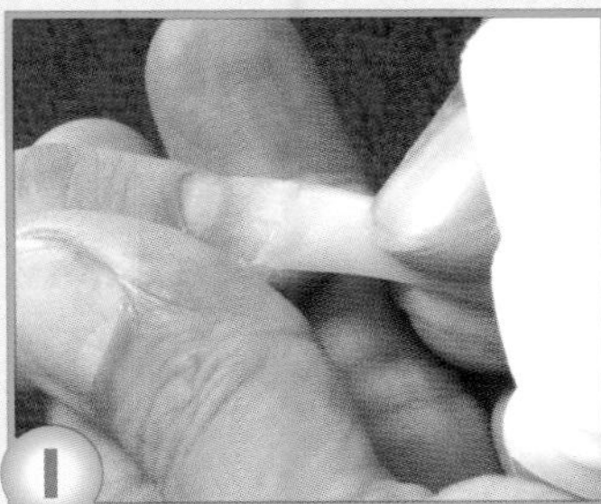
**I** Hold client's finger at a 90-degree angle, place stop point of tip against free edge at a 45-degree angle.

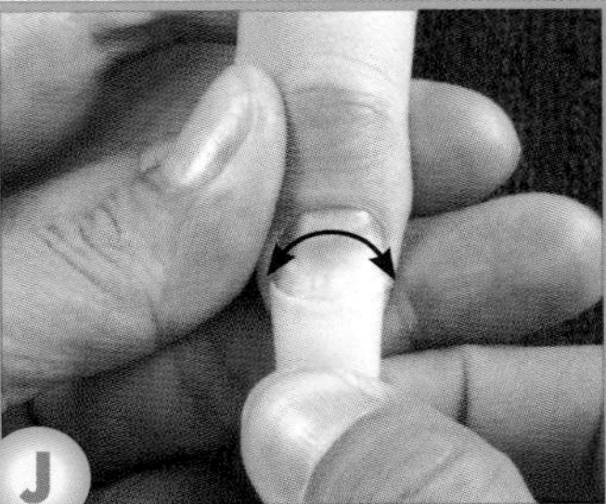
**J** Slowly elevate tip upright to align with nail using a slight rolling motion to prevent trapped air bubbles between tip and natural nail.

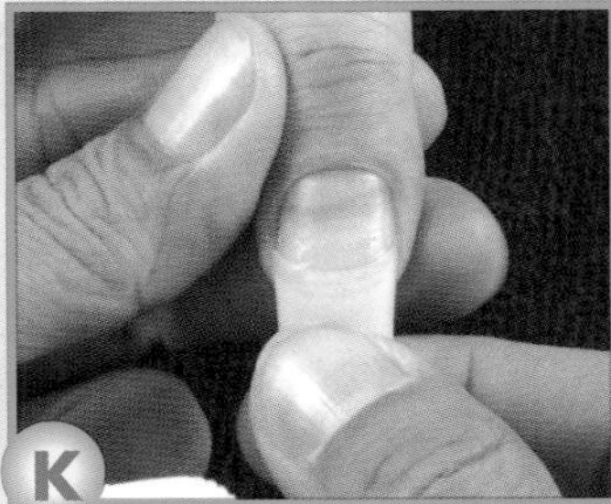
**K** Hold nail tip in place for 10 seconds to allow adhesive to cure (set). Three step action for tip application: **stop, roll and hold.**

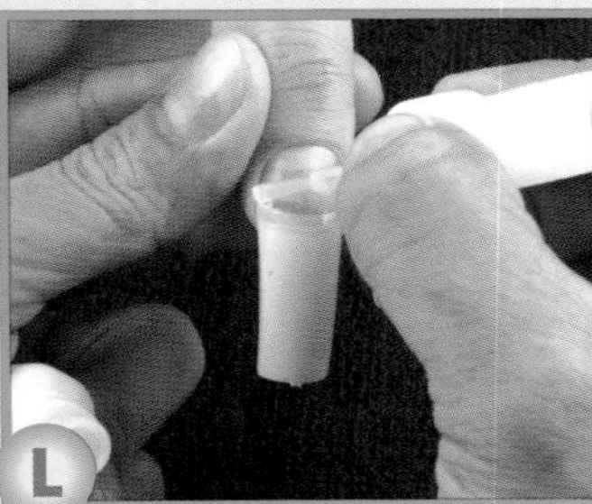
**L** **Optional:** Apply a very small amount of adhesive to the seam, where the well connects with the natural nail to provide additional strength to stress area.

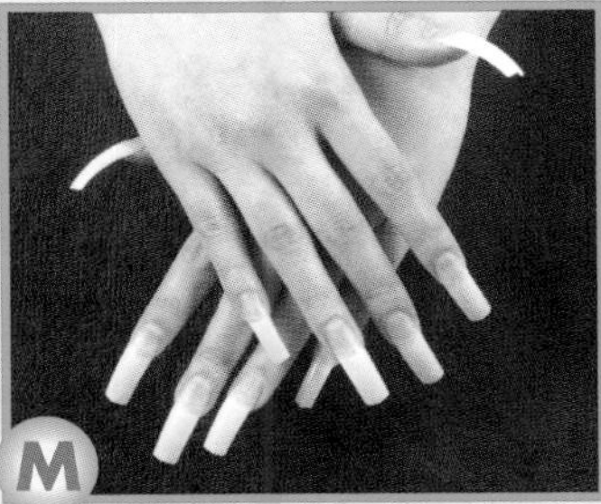
**M** Apply nail tips on both hands.

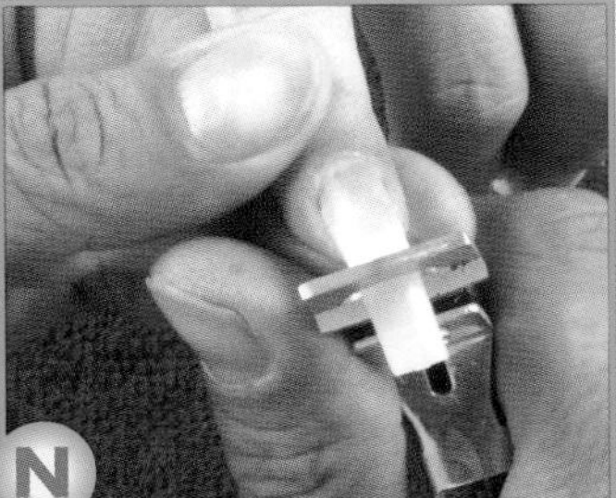
**N** Using a nail tip cutter or nail clippers, cut the nail tip to a desired length.

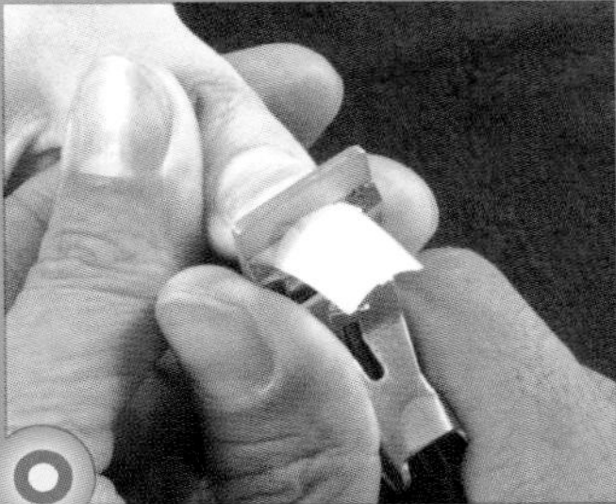
**O** Control removal of excess tip by positioning the tip cutter at a 45-degree angle.

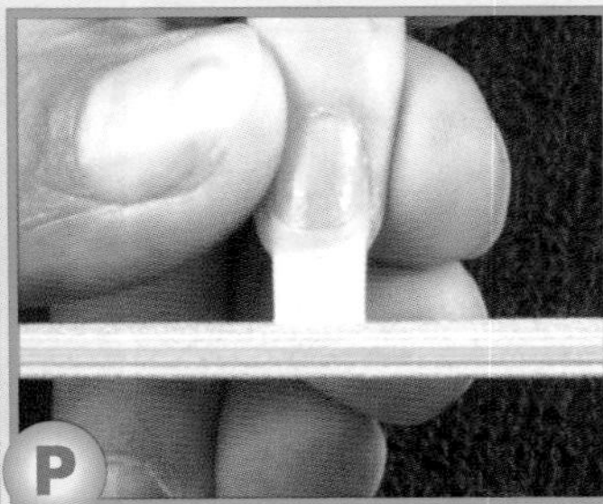
**P** Shape and buff free edge of nail tip.

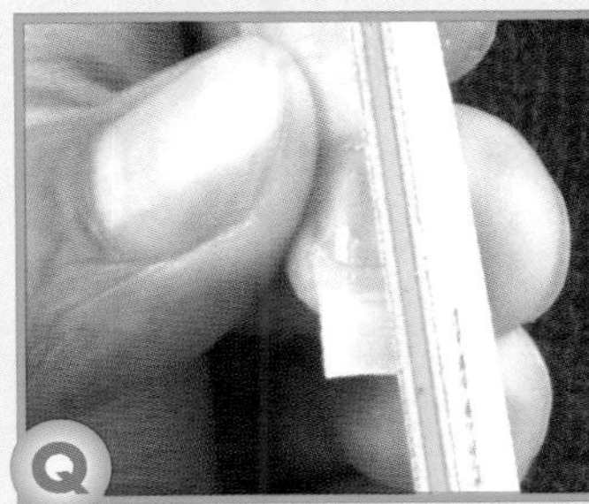
**Q** Blend seam of tip at well area into natural nail using a medium abrasive to create the appearance that nail and tip are a single unit.

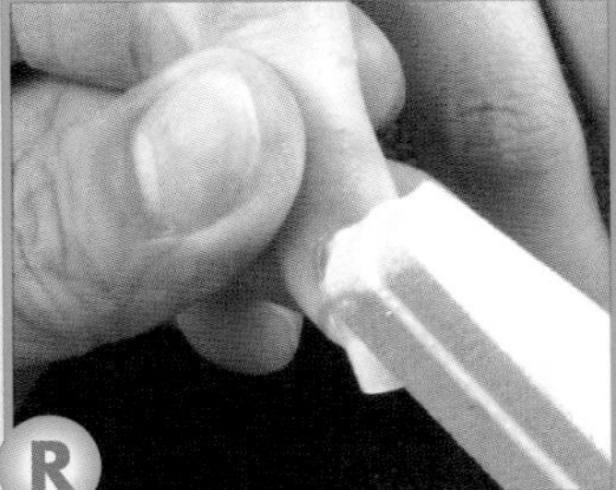
**R** Use a fine grit abrasive for gentle buffing and a buffer/shiner for smoothing nail.

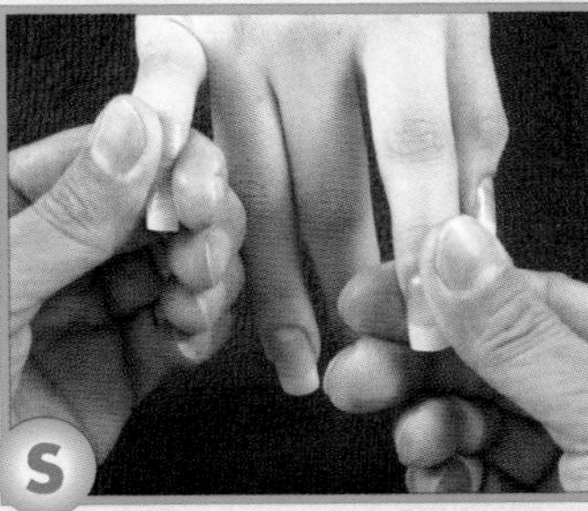
**S** Complete nails by massaging cuticle oil into surrounding skin for a natural finish.

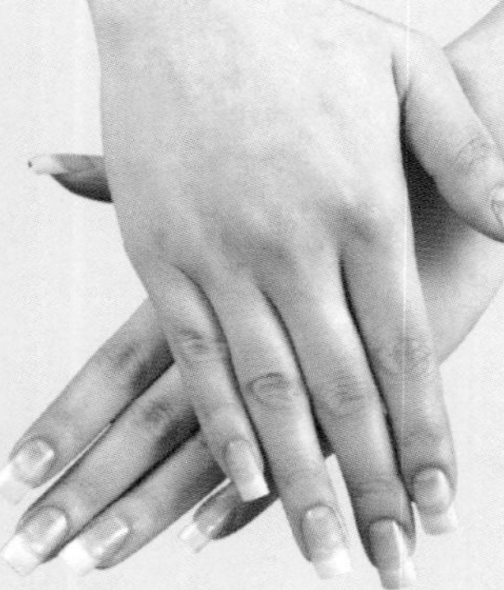
**T** **Completed nail tip application**. You are ready to proceed with acrylic overlay, fabric wrap or gel system.

**CAUTION:** To remove adhesive on skin, immerse finger(s) in warm soapy water to soften area, then apply a small amount of acetone polish remover to assist in removing adhesive. **Gently** rub over area until adhesive is detached from skin.

**NOTE:** To customize a nail tip when nail tips sizes do not match the nail plate, use a medium abrasive and smooth lower arch area of well or contact area of tip. Slowly remove part of tip continuously checking with the natural nail for an accurate match.

**EVALUATION** ______________________________

**GRADE** ________ STUDENT'S NAME ________ ID# ________

CLIC INTERNATIONAL

RA

INTERMEDIATE LAB PROJECT

# Fabric Wrap

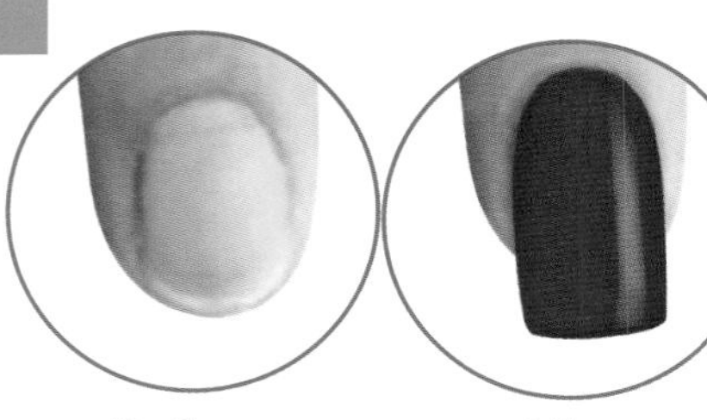

Before After

## OBJECTIVE

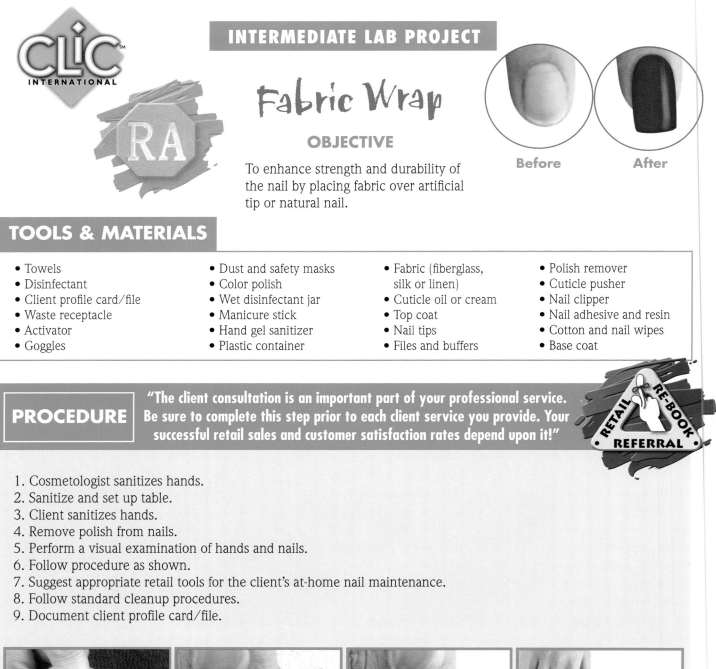

To enhance strength and durability of the nail by placing fabric over artificial tip or natural nail.

## TOOLS & MATERIALS

- Towels
- Disinfectant
- Client profile card/file
- Waste receptacle
- Activator
- Goggles
- Dust and safety masks
- Color polish
- Wet disinfectant jar
- Manicure stick
- Hand gel sanitizer
- Plastic container
- Fabric (fiberglass, silk or linen)
- Cuticle oil or cream
- Top coat
- Nail tips
- Files and buffers
- Polish remover
- Cuticle pusher
- Nail clipper
- Nail adhesive and resin
- Cotton and nail wipes
- Base coat

## PROCEDURE

**"The client consultation is an important part of your professional service. Be sure to complete this step prior to each client service you provide. Your successful retail sales and customer satisfaction rates depend upon it!"**

1. Cosmetologist sanitizes hands.
2. Sanitize and set up table.
3. Client sanitizes hands.
4. Remove polish from nails.
5. Perform a visual examination of hands and nails.
6. Follow procedure as shown.
7. Suggest appropriate retail tools for the client's at-home nail maintenance.
8. Follow standard cleanup procedures.
9. Document client profile card/file.

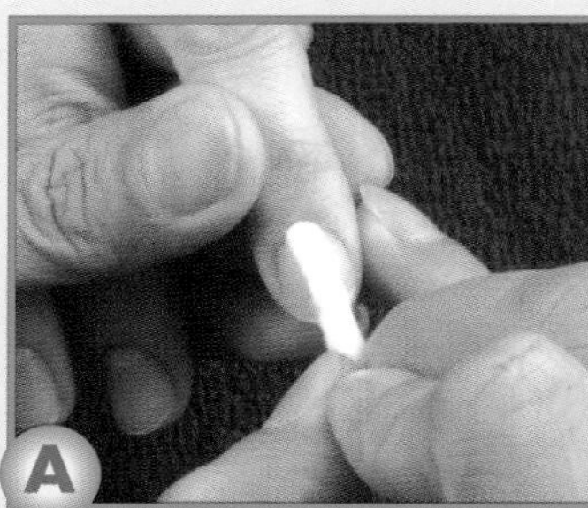

A Use cotton-wrapped manicure stick or cuticle pusher to **gently** push back cuticles. Apply a nail antiseptic to the natural nail; spray on or wipe over nail with nail wipe.

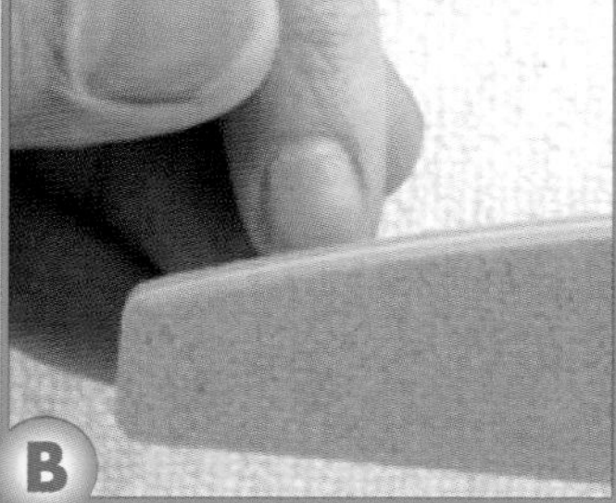

B Shape and buff the free edge of natural nail. Buff entire top of nail to remove shine or natural oils, which will allow proper adhesion.

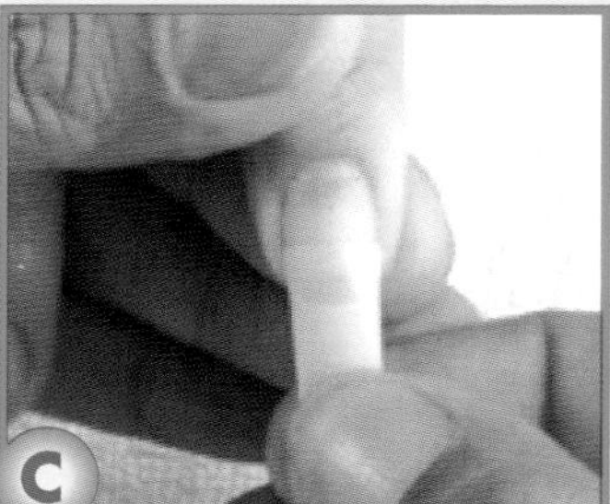

C Perform a tip application following previous procedure in this chapter.

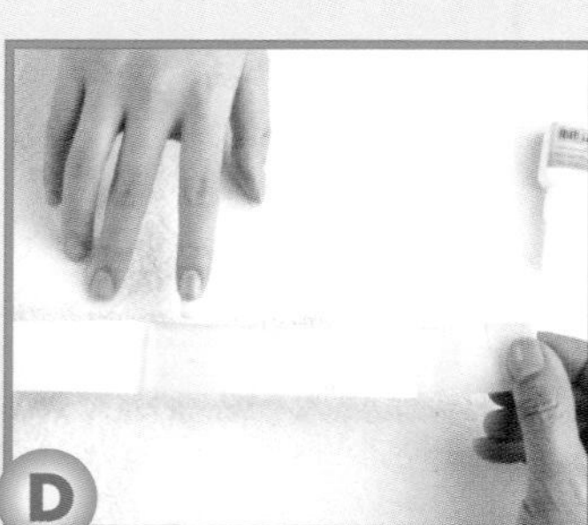

D Determine the type of fabric used, depending on service provided.

## Fabric Wrap

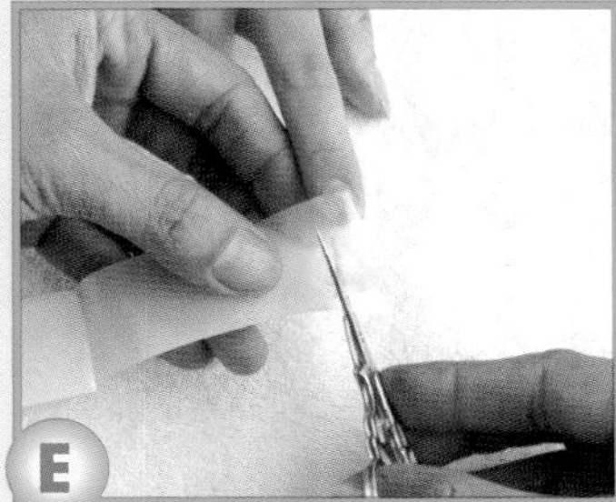

**E** Size fabric according to nail width and length, using a fabric scissors. **NOTE:** Fabric will need to be slightly smaller than actual nail size. Fabric must not touch skin.

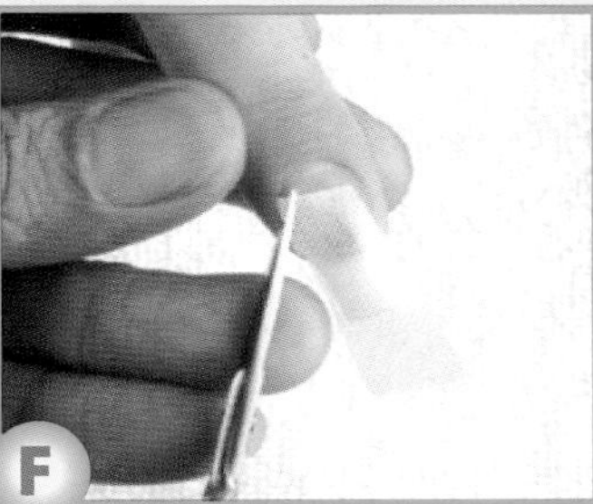

**F** Apply fabric over nail, adhesive side down onto nail plate. For a non-adhesive fabric, spread small amount of adhesive on nail plate, then apply fabric.

**G** Be careful to keep fabric **1/16 (0.15cm) of an inch away from skin** surrounding nail in order to prevent lifting of fabric.

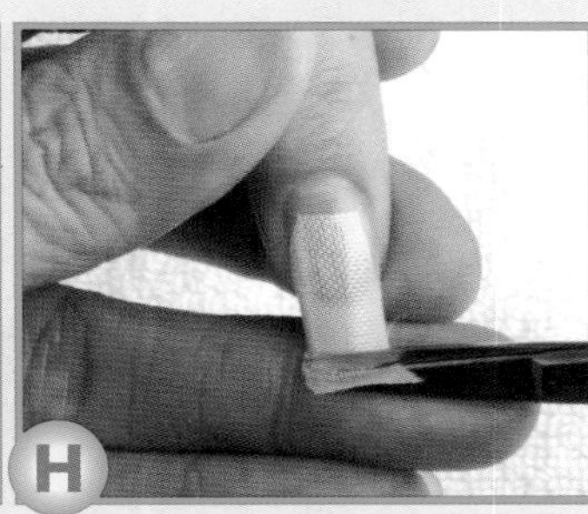

**H** Trim fabric if necessary to allow an exact covering over nail plate and free edge.

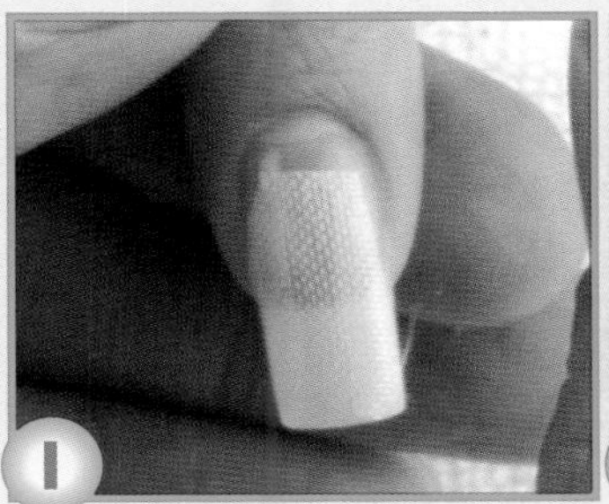

**I** Press fabric firmly to nail using a nail wipe or a small piece of plastic, adhering fabric to nail completely. **NOTE: DO NOT use fingers** to adhere fabric to nail. Oils from skin touching fabric will hinder adhesion.

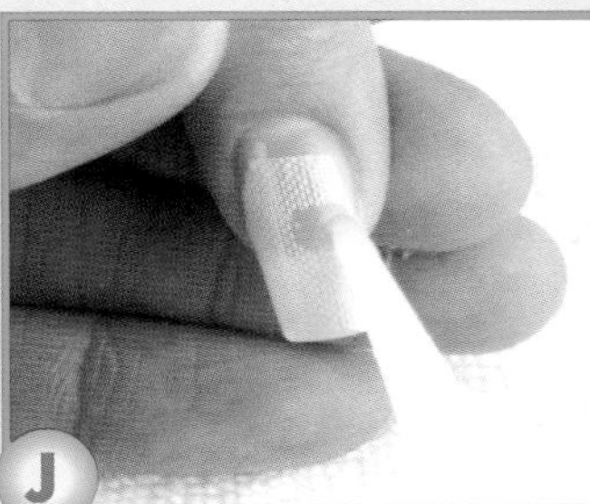

**J** Apply first application of adhesive at center of fabric.

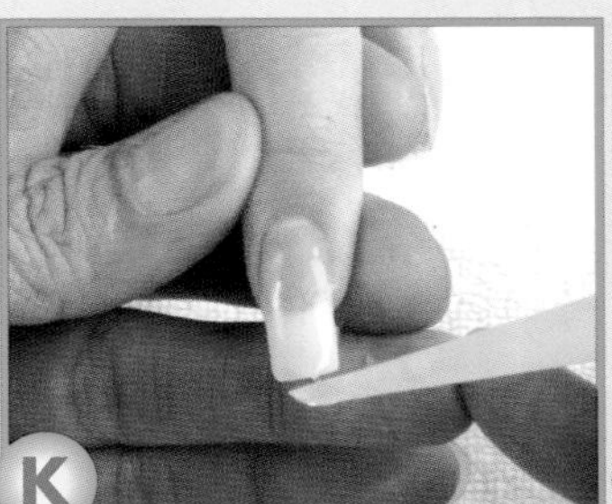

**K** Spread adhesive across nail in a side-to-side motion using extender tip on bottle. **Optional:** A brush-on adhesive is an alternative to replace extender tip applications.

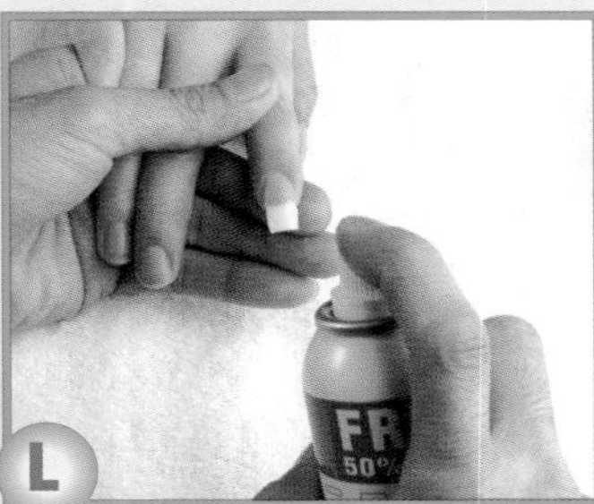

**L** Apply a spray-on or brush-on activator to assist in the adhesive drying time.

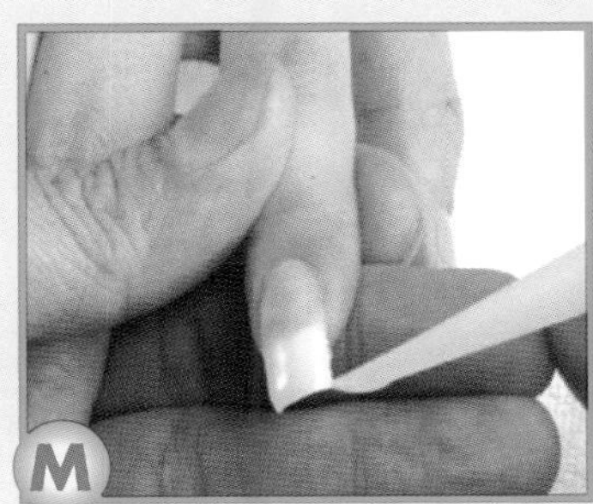

**M** Continue with second application of adhesive and activator **repeating Steps J thru L.** Always follow manufacturer's directions.

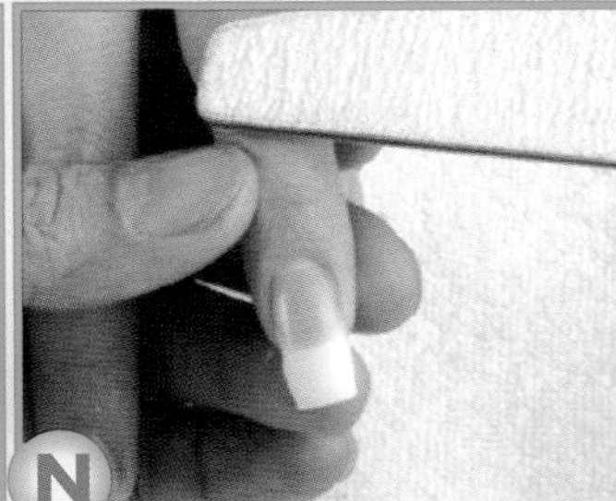

**N** Use a medium abrasive and gently smooth over the nail plate to create an evenly shaped nail.

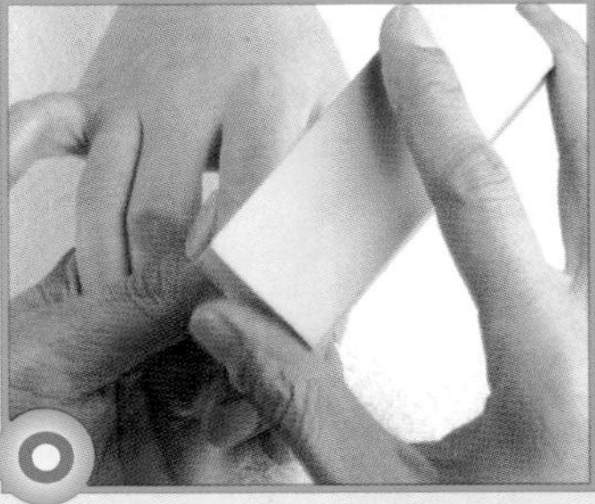

**O** Lightly buff nails with buffer/shiner to provide a natural finish to the nails. Ask client to wash hands to remove any dust filings or product residue. Complete nails by applying cuticle oil for a natural finish.

**P** **Completed fabric wrapped nails with color polish.**

17

**EVALUATION** ______________________

______________________

**GRADE** ____________ STUDENT'S NAME ____________ ID# ____________

## INTERMEDIATE LAB PROJECT

# Fabric Wrap Refill

Before

After

### OBJECTIVE

To provide continual wear of fabric wrap by maintaining the new growth area of the nail.

## TOOLS & MATERIALS

- Towels
- Disinfectant
- Client profile card/file
- Waste receptacle
- Activator
- Goggles
- Dust and safety masks
- Color polish
- Wet disinfectant jar
- Manicure stick
- Hand gel sanitizer
- Plastic container
- Fabric (fiberglass, silk or linen)
- Cuticle oil or cream
- Top coat
- Files and buffers
- Polish remover
- Cuticle pusher
- Nail clipper
- Nail adhesive and resin
- Cotton and nail wipes
- Base coat

## PROCEDURE

**"The client consultation is an important part of your professional service. Be sure to complete this step prior to each client service you provide. Your successful retail sales and customer satisfaction rates depend upon it!"**

RETAIL • RE-BOOK • REFERRAL

1. Cosmetologist sanitizes hands.
2. Sanitize and set up table.
3. Client sanitizes hands.
4. Remove polish from nails.
5. Perform a visual examination of hands and nails.
6. Follow procedure as shown.
7. Suggest appropriate retail tools for the client's at-home nail maintenance.
8. Follow standard cleanup procedures.
9. Document client profile card/file.

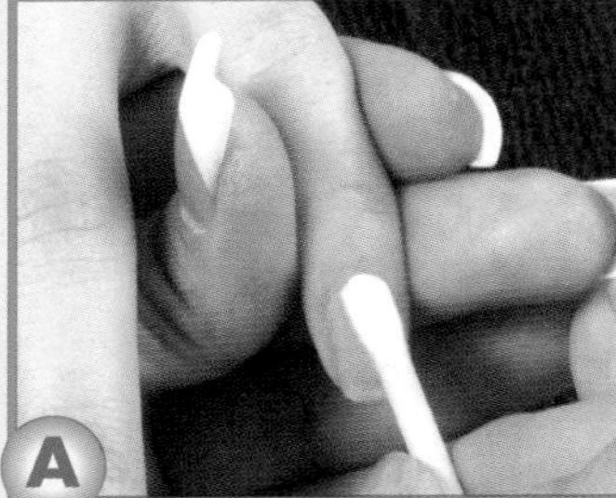
A
Use cotton-wrapped manicure stick to **gently** push back cuticles. Apply a nail antiseptic to the natural nail; spray on or wipe over nail with nail wipe.

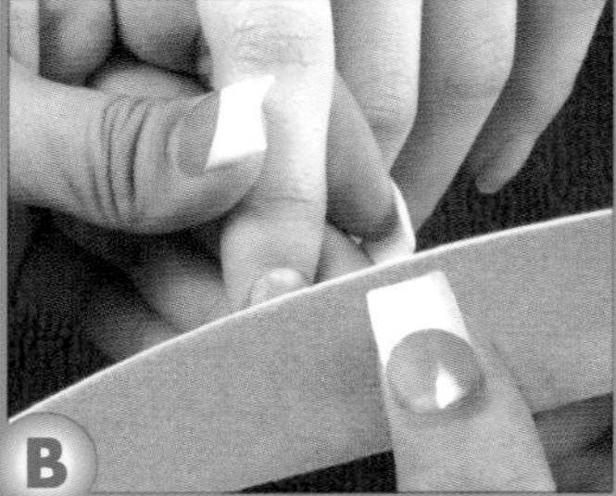
B
Shape free edge of natural nail and buff new growth area to remove line of demarcation, shine or natural oils. This will allow proper adhesion and blending.

C
Cut a ¼ (0.6cm) inch strip of fabric to cover entire new growth area.

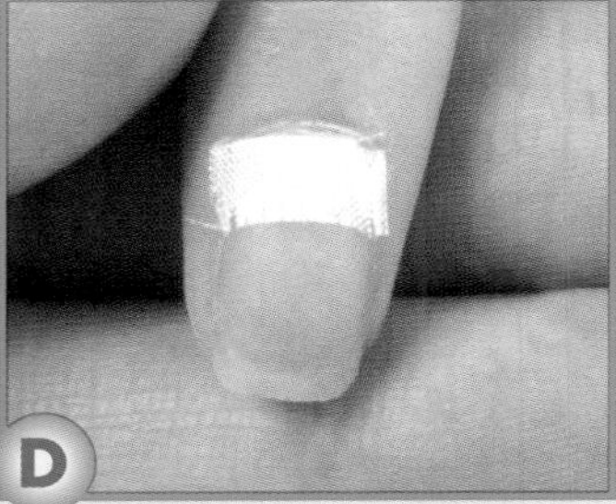
D
Apply fabric over refill area of nail **only.**

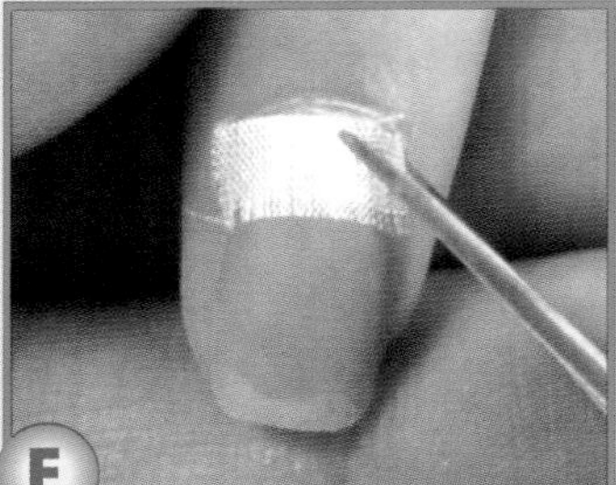
E
Keep fabric **1/16 (0.15cm) of an inch away from skin** surrounding nail in order to prevent lifting of fabric.

F
Trim fabric if necessary to allow an exact covering over new growth area.

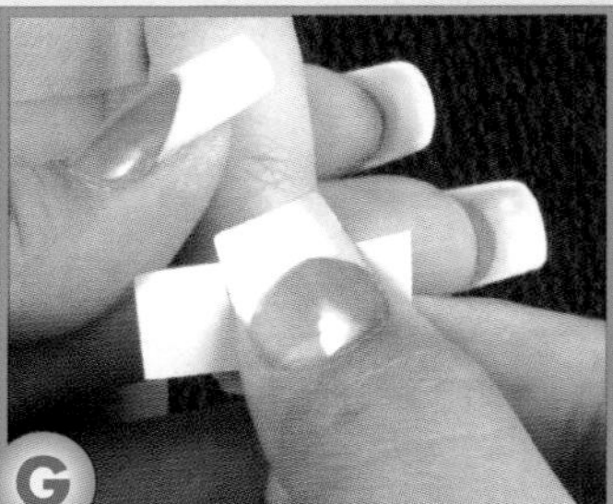
G
Press fabric firmly to nail using a nail wipe, adhering fabric to nail completely. **DO NOT use fingers** to adhere fabric to nails. Oils from skin touching fabric will hinder adhesion.

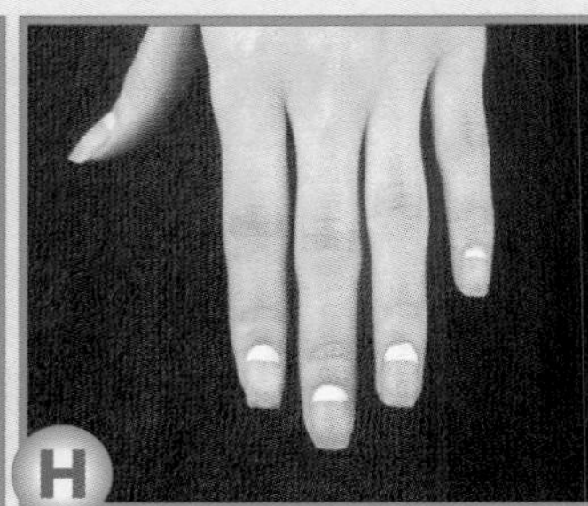
H
**Repeat Steps C thru G** on other fingers.

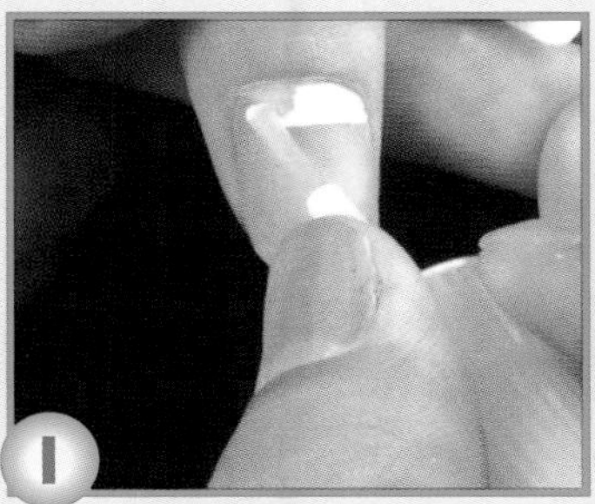

I — Apply a small amount of brush-on adhesive to new growth area, carefully spread to cover entire area. **Optional:** An alternative is adhesive in a bottle with an extender tip.

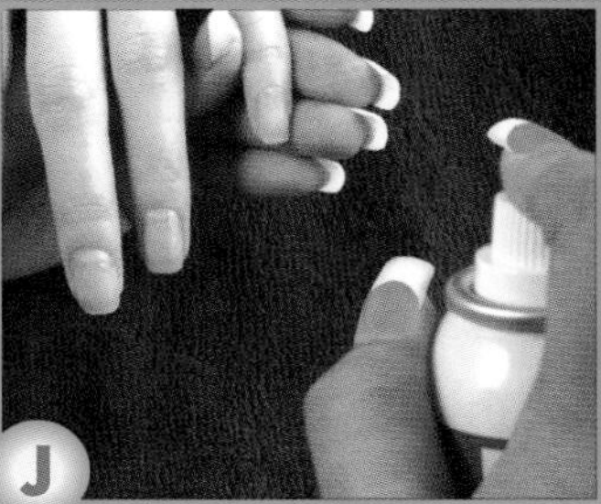

J — Apply a spray-on or brush-on activator to assist in the adhesive drying time.

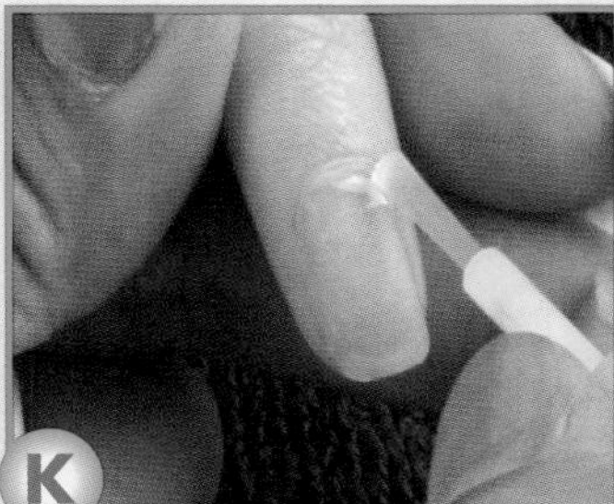

K — Apply a second application of adhesive and activator **repeating Steps I and J.** Always follow manufacturer's directions.

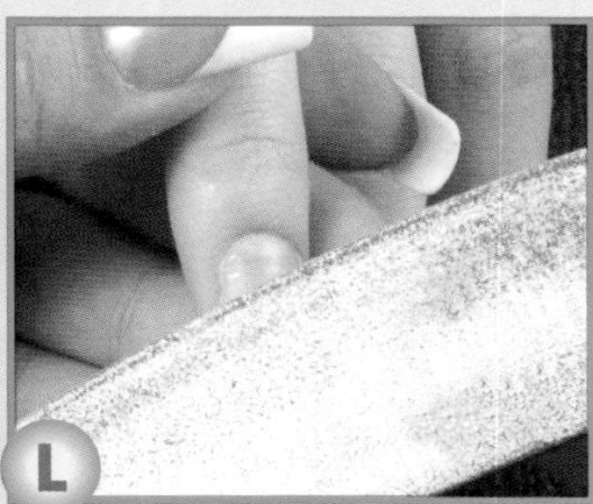

L — Use a medium abrasive and gently smooth over the nail plate (new growth area) to produce a blended smooth nail.

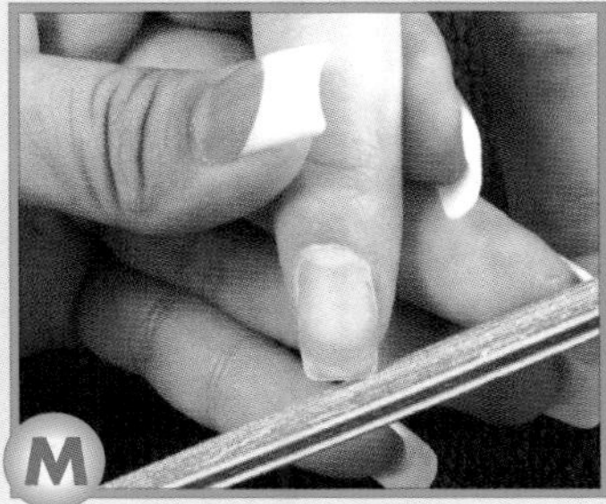

M — Continue with the medium abrasive and shape the free edge of nail.

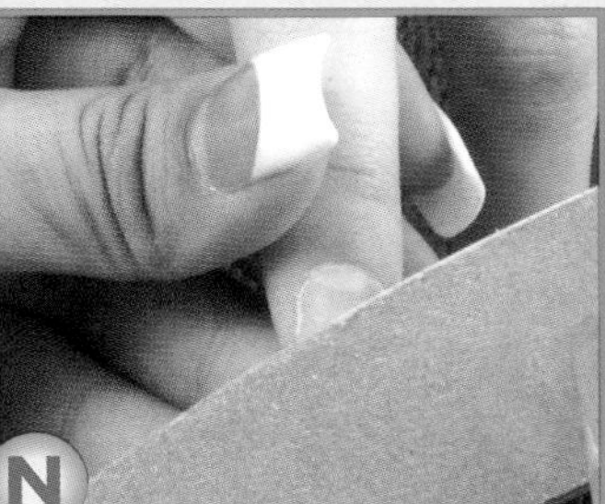

N — Lightly buff nails using a buffer/shiner to provide a natural finish to the nails. Ask client to wash hands to remove any dust filings or product residue.

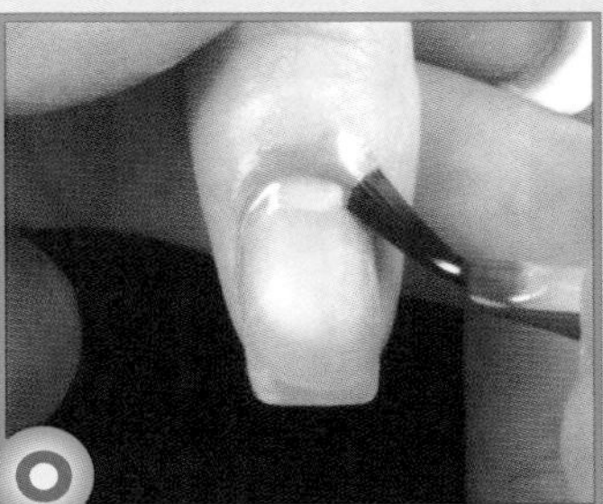

O — Complete nails by applying cuticle oil.

P — Massage cuticle oil into surrounding skin.

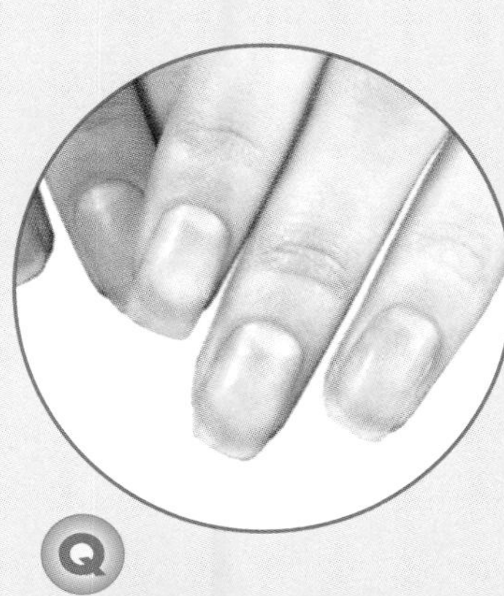

Q — **Completed fabric wrapped refill nails with no polish.**

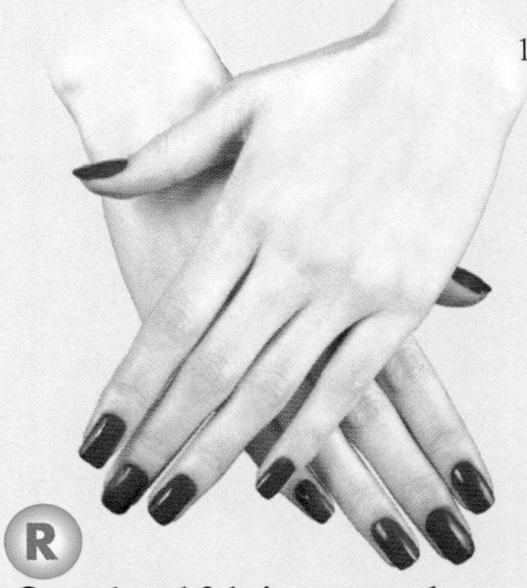

R — **Completed fabric wrapped refill nails with color polish.**

*Nail wraps are serviced for maintenance every two weeks with adhesive fill and every four weeks for fabric fills.*

**EVALUATION**

**GRADE** STUDENT'S NAME ID#

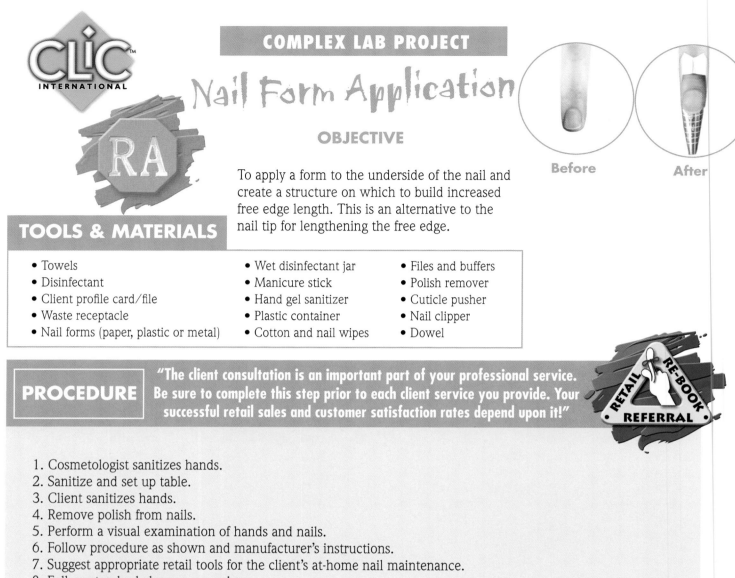

COMPLEX LAB PROJECT

# Nail Form Application

RA

## OBJECTIVE

To apply a form to the underside of the nail and create a structure on which to build increased free edge length. This is an alternative to the nail tip for lengthening the free edge.

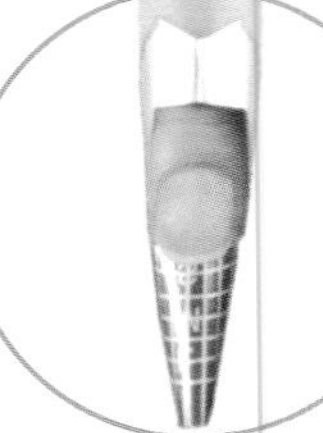

Before

After

## TOOLS & MATERIALS

- Towels
- Disinfectant
- Client profile card/file
- Waste receptacle
- Nail forms (paper, plastic or metal)
- Wet disinfectant jar
- Manicure stick
- Hand gel sanitizer
- Plastic container
- Cotton and nail wipes
- Files and buffers
- Polish remover
- Cuticle pusher
- Nail clipper
- Dowel

## PROCEDURE

"The client consultation is an important part of your professional service. Be sure to complete this step prior to each client service you provide. Your successful retail sales and customer satisfaction rates depend upon it!"

1. Cosmetologist sanitizes hands.
2. Sanitize and set up table.
3. Client sanitizes hands.
4. Remove polish from nails.
5. Perform a visual examination of hands and nails.
6. Follow procedure as shown and manufacturer's instructions.
7. Suggest appropriate retail tools for the client's at-home nail maintenance.
8. Follow standard cleanup procedures.
9. Document client profile card/file.

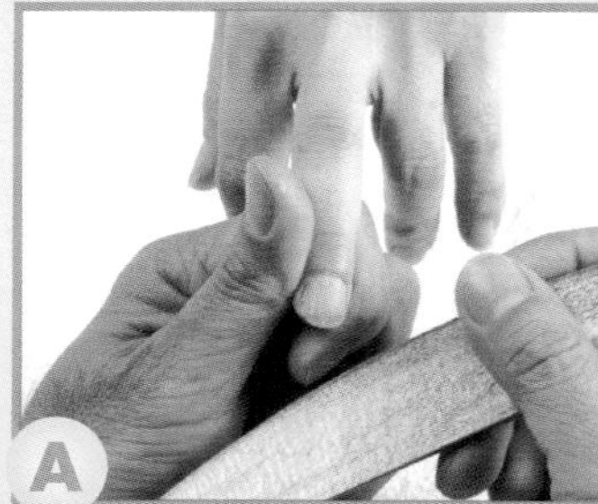

A

Shape and buff nails vertically following natural grain of nail to remove shine or natural oils. This will allow proper adhesion of acrylic.

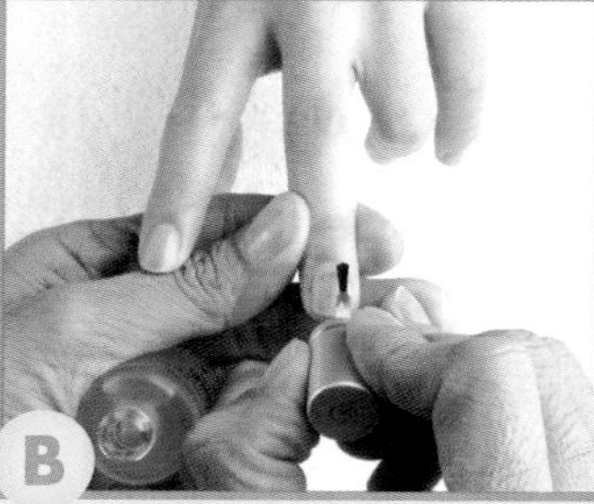

B

A minimum amount of primer is applied to the natural nail **only** to ensure proper acrylic adhesion. **NOTE:** Excess primer can burn nail plate and cuticle skin.

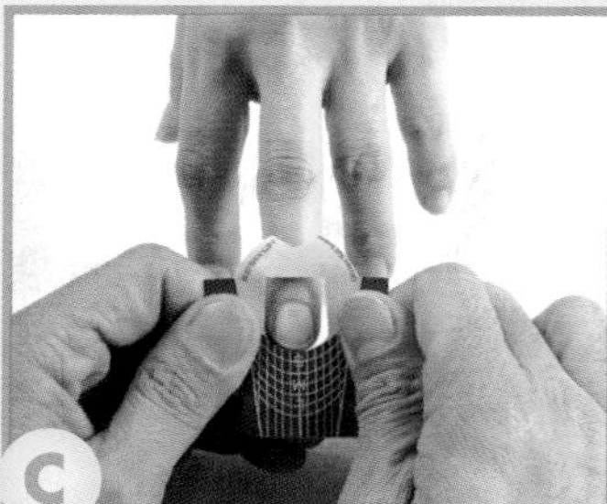

C

Position form under free edge until aligned with nail; form must be even with free edge. **NOTE:** Be careful not to force nail form under free edge to prevent injury to hyponychium.

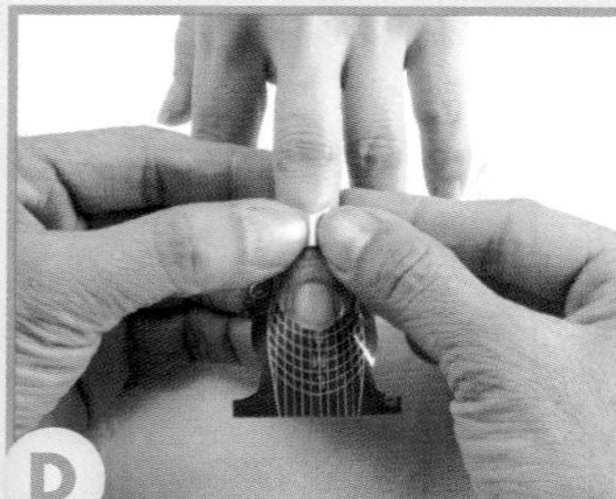

D

Whether using a **reusable or disposable** nail form, an arch needs to be created to conform to free edge curve.

# Nail Form Application

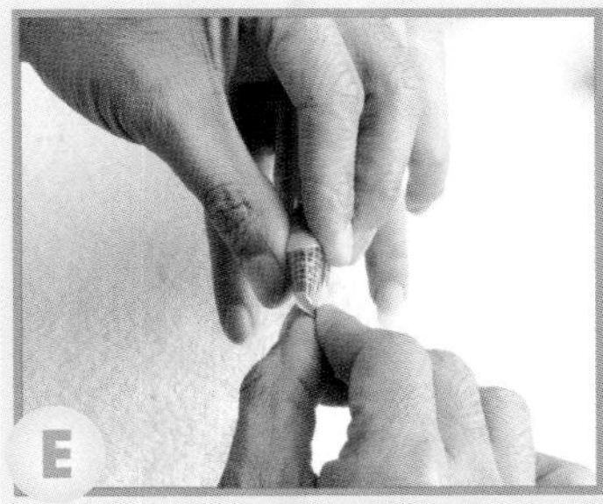


Create a c-curve by bending each side of form down until compatible with nail's natural curve.

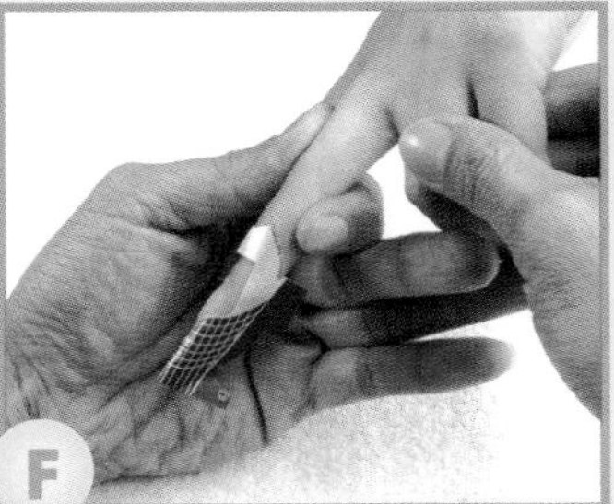


Secure **disposable** form along sides or underside of finger by lightly squeezing tabs against the skin.

Secure **reusable** form by lightly squeezing prongs of form along sides of fingers.

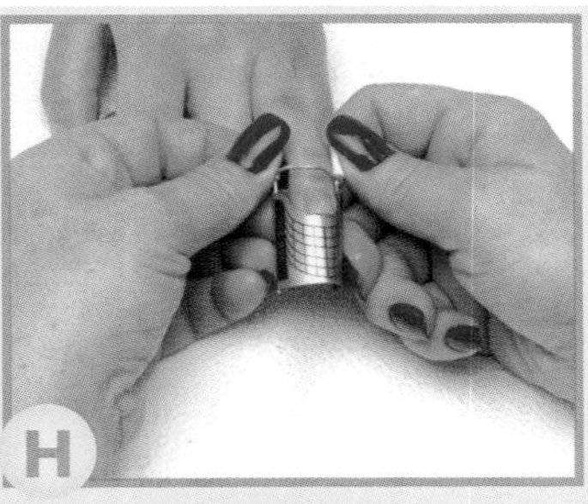


A comfortable but snug fit is important to assure a **stationary** nail form.

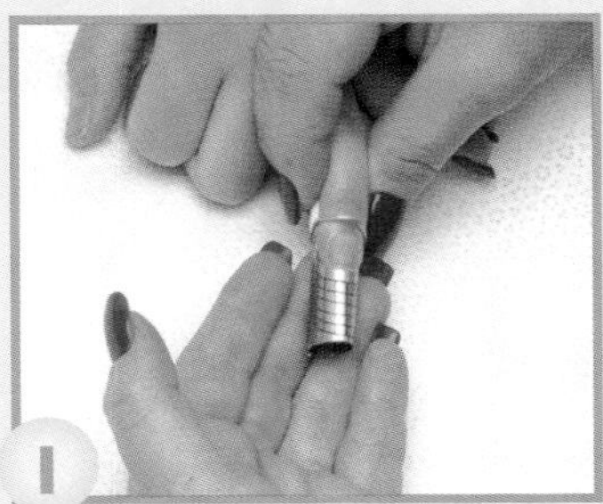


A secured **reusable** form.

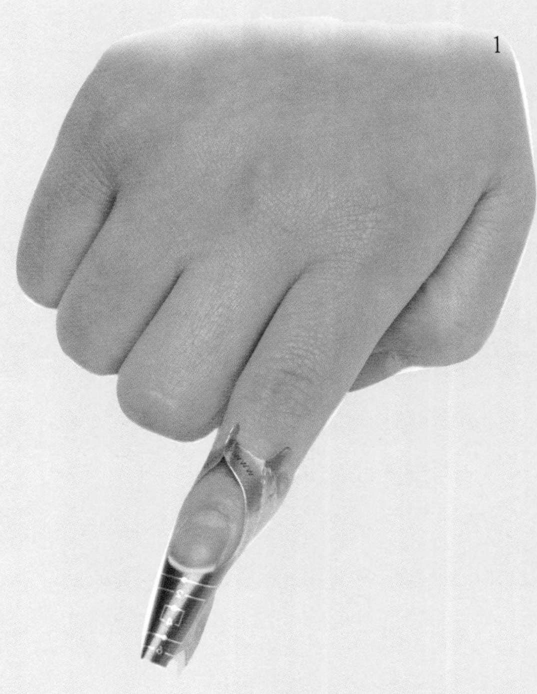

J

**Completed disposable** form fit. You are ready to proceed to an acrylic overlay, fabric wrap or gel application.

"The type of form used is dependent upon the desired nail enhancement service."

**EVALUATION** ______________________________

______ **GRADE** ______________________ STUDENT'S NAME ______________________ ID#

COMPLEX LAB PROJECT

# Acrylic Nails or Free Form

Before

After

RA

## OBJECTIVE

To increase the free edge length and durability by creating an acrylic nail over existing natural nail.

## TOOLS & MATERIALS

- Towels
- Disinfectant
- Client profile card/file
- Waste receptacle
- Sculpting brushes
- Goggles
- Primer
- Polymer
- Top coat
- Wet disinfectant jar
- Manicure stick
- Hand gel sanitizer
- Plastic container
- Dappen dishes
- Cuticle oil or cream
- Dehydrant
- Monomer
- Base coat
- Files and buffers
- Polish remover
- Cuticle pusher
- Nail clipper
- Pipette and scoop
- Dust and safety masks
- Nail forms (paper, plastic or metal)
- Cotton and nail wipes
- Color polish

## PROCEDURE

**"The client consultation is an important part of your professional service. Be sure to complete this step prior to each client service you provide. Your successful retail sales and customer satisfaction rates depend upon it!"**

RETAIL RE-BOOK REFERRAL

1. Cosmetologist sanitizes hands.
2. Sanitize and set up table.
3. Client sanitizes hands.
4. Remove polish from nails.
5. Perform a visual examination of hands and nails.
6. Follow procedure as shown and manufacturer's instructions.
7. Suggest appropriate retail tools for the client's at-home nail maintenance.
8. Follow standard cleanup procedures.
9. Document client profile card/file.

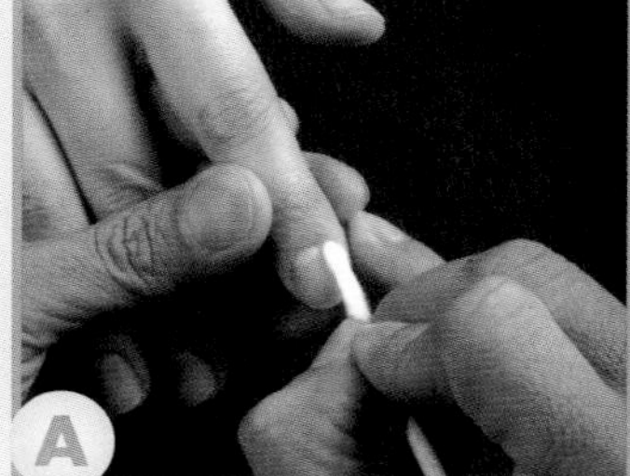

A Use cotton-wrapped manicure stick and **gently** push back cuticles. Apply a nail antiseptic to the natural nails; spray on or wipe over nail with nail wipe.

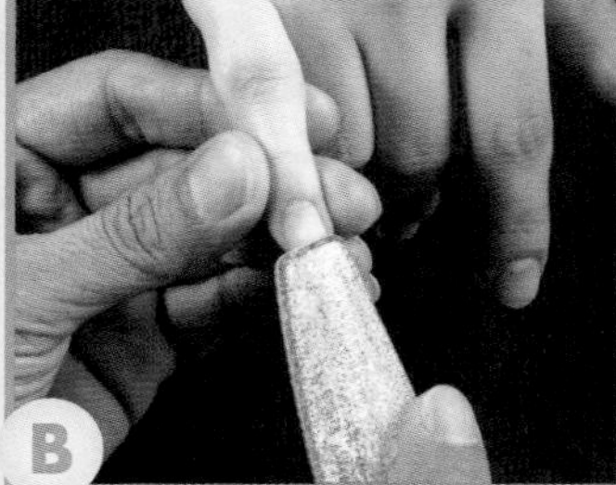

B Shape and buff the natural nail in a vertical direction following natural grain of nail.

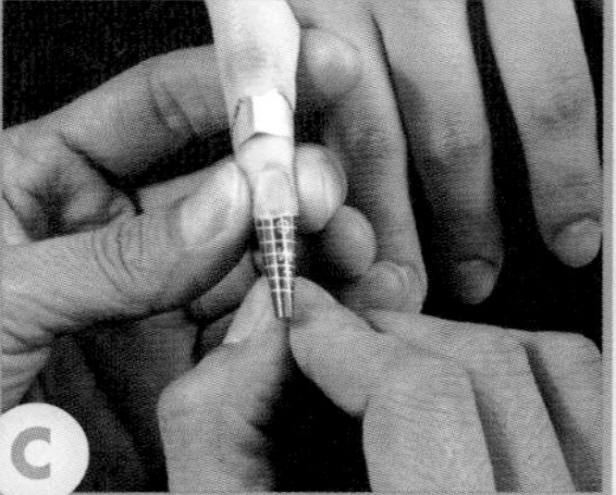

C Apply a minimal amount of primer to natural nails to ensure adhesion. Apply nail forms to all nails; refer to procedure in this chapter.

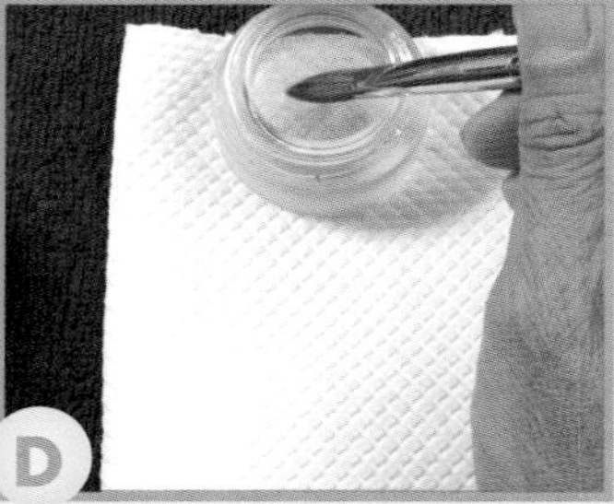

D Prime the acrylic brush in monomer to soften flags and prepare for product application.

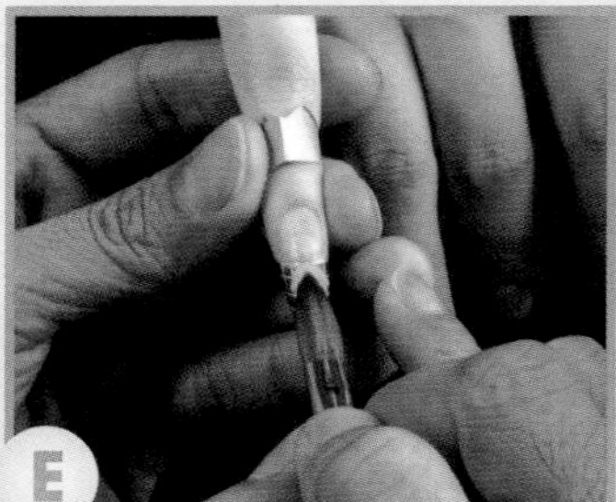

E Using a three acrylic ball method, place acrylic ball starting at zone 1/free edge area on form.

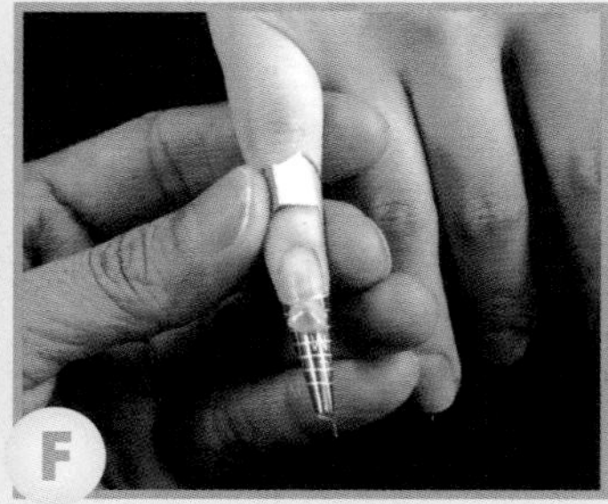

F Size and placement of ball is dependent upon desired length of free edge.

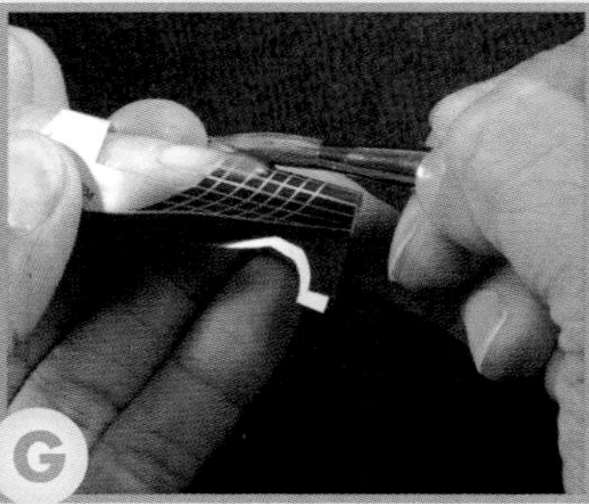

G Holding brush at a **0-degree angle**, flatten and press ball to form the **free edge**. Create a **smile line** using a **45- to 90-degree angle.**

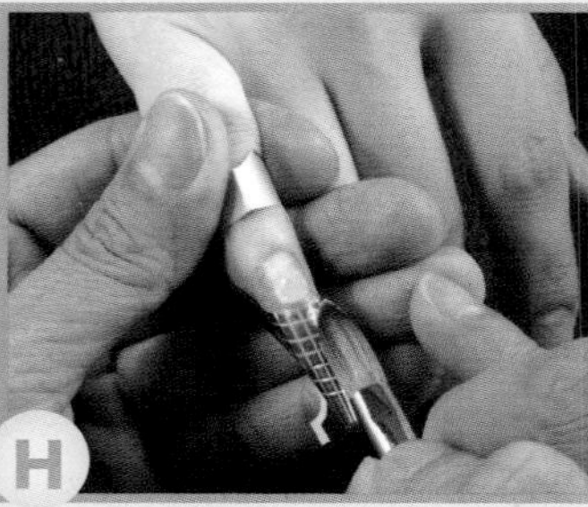

H Continue with acrylic ball application at **zone 2/stress area.**

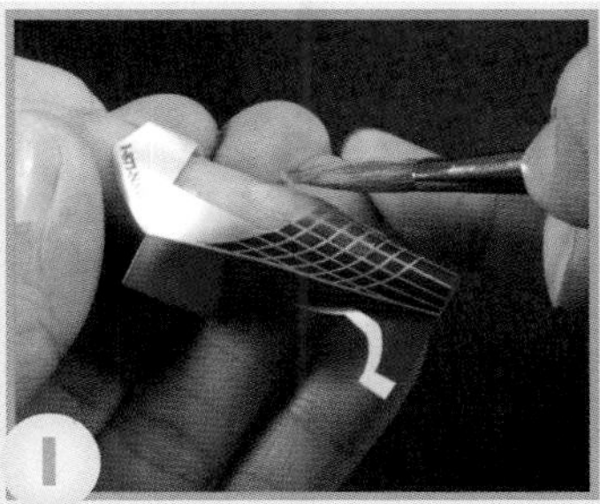


Holding brush at a **45-degree angle**, pat and press ball into shape and lightly glide product over **zone 1** for blending of acrylic.

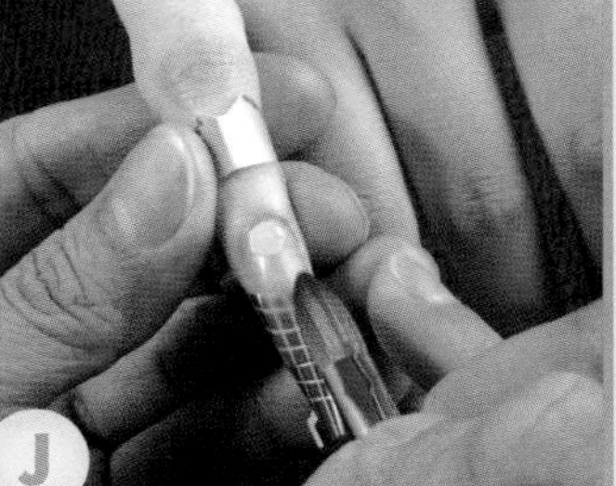


Place acrylic ball at **zone 3/cuticle area.**

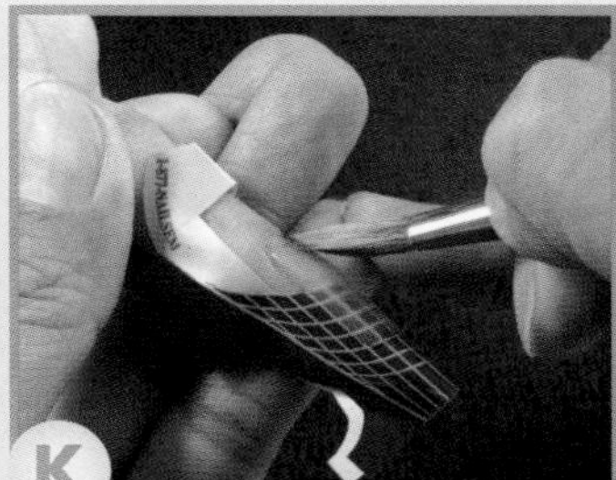


Holding brush at a **45- to 90-degree angle, lightly** press around **cuticle** keeping 1/16 (0.15cm) of an inch away from skin. **Lightly** glide product over **zone 2** for blending.

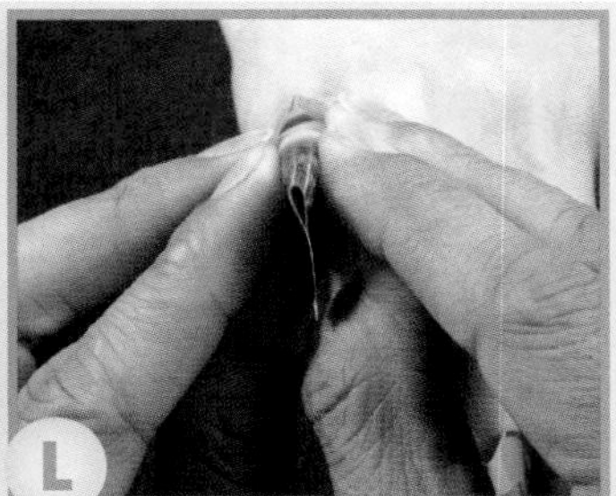


Check side and front views of nail for proper proportion and balance.

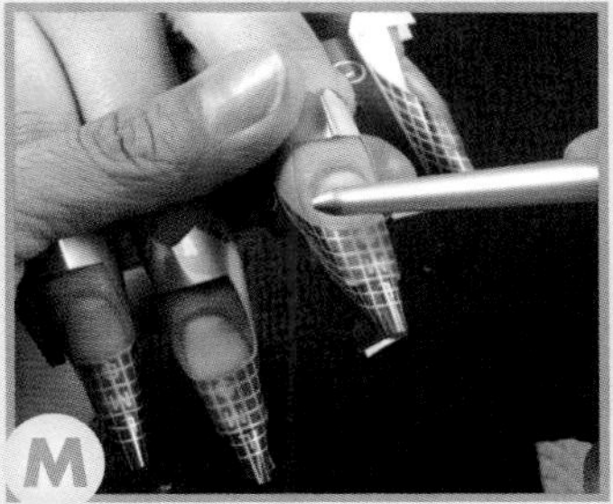


Allow to cure. Using handle of brush, lightly tap on nail to determine if product is hardened. When acrylic is hard, a **"clicking"** sound is heard and **ONLY then is form removed.**

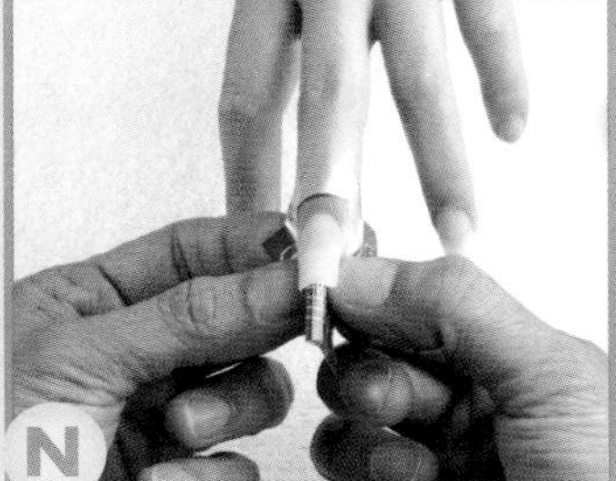


Loosen form underneath free edge by pinching form together.

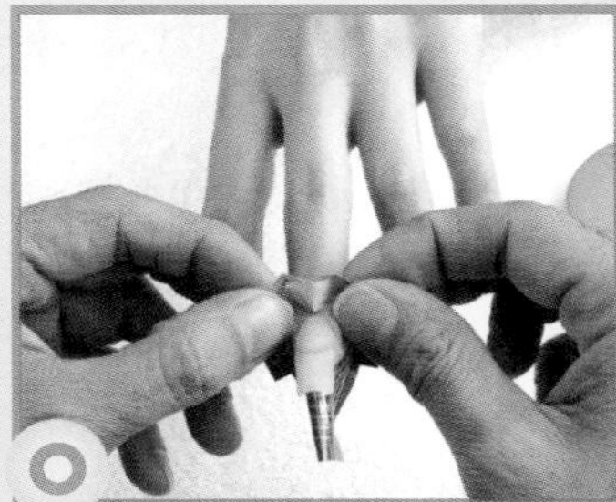


Peel disposable form off skin and discard.

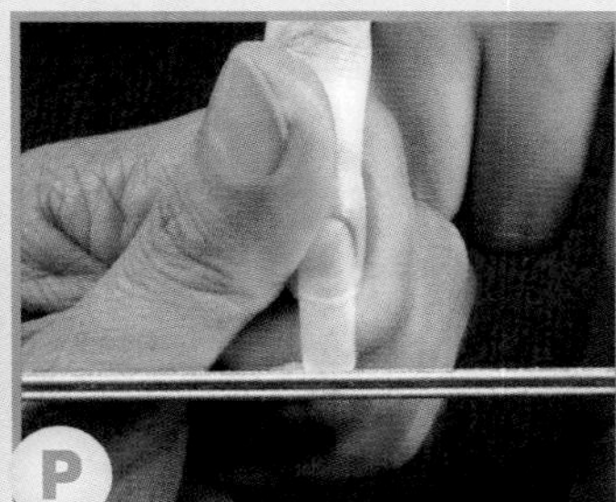


Use a coarse or medium abrasive to shape and smooth free edge.

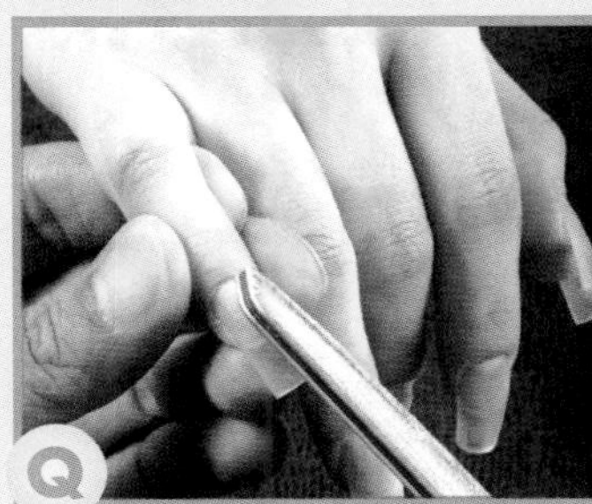


Smooth over surface of nail with a medium or fine abrasive. When completed, remember to view all sides of nail for proper proportion.

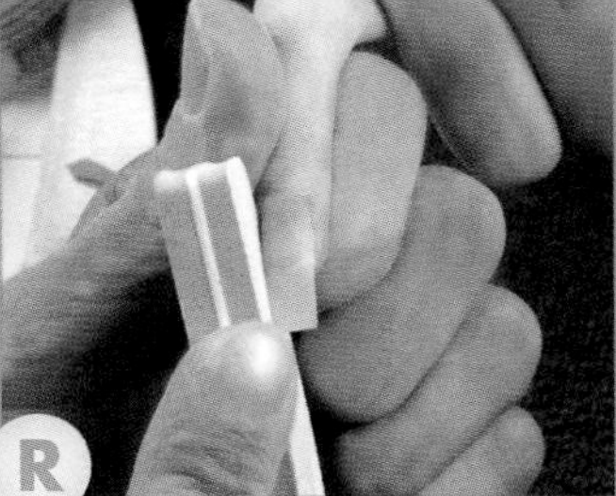


Use a buffer/shiner on surface of nail to produce a natural finish. Ask client to wash hands to remove product residue and filing dust.

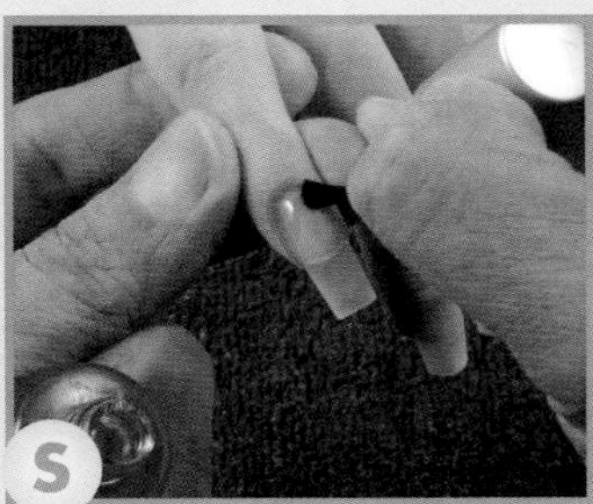


Massage cuticle cream or oil into skin surrounding nails. (Remove oil from nails with polish remover.)

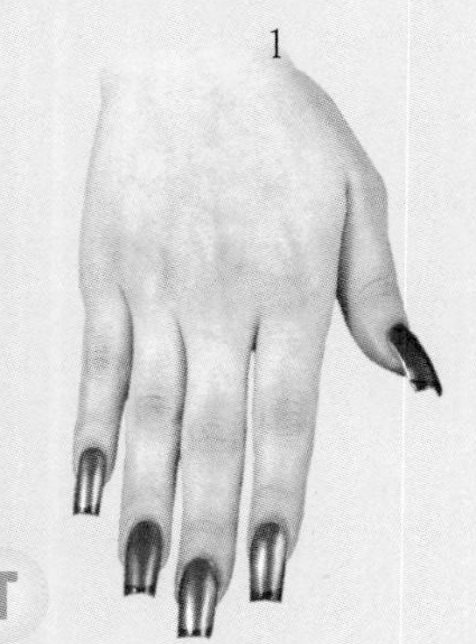


**Completed acrylic nails** with color polish.

*For the first four to six weeks, promote weekly visits to the salon for maintenance of nails by offering free polish change with a paid refill service.*

"To prevent contamination and to control evaporation of odor, cover polymer and monomer dappen dishes when not in use!"

GRADE STUDENT'S NAME ID#

17

## COMPLEX LAB PROJECT

# Acrylic Refill

### OBJECTIVE

To maintain proper balance and proportion to the nail by applying acrylic to the new growth area of the nail.

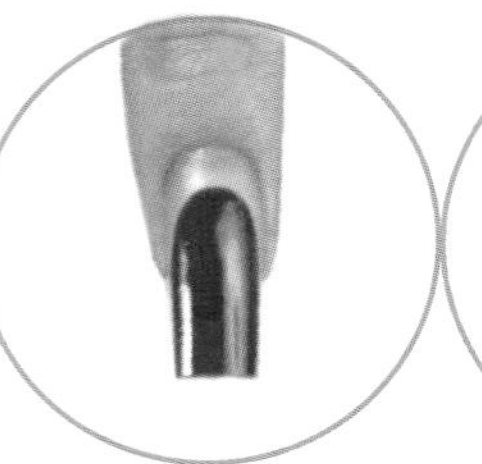

Before

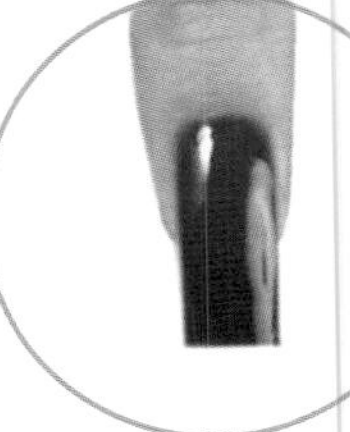

After

## TOOLS & MATERIALS

- Towels
- Disinfectant
- Client profile card/file
- Waste receptacle
- Sculpting brushes
- Goggles
- Primer
- Polymer
- Top coat
- Wet disinfectant jar
- Manicure stick
- Hand gel sanitizer
- Plastic container
- Dappen dishes
- Cuticle oil or cream
- Dehydrant
- Monomer
- Base coat
- Files and buffers
- Polish remover
- Cuticle pusher
- Nail clipper
- Pipette
- Scoop
- Cotton and nail wipes
- Color polish
- Dust and safety masks

## PROCEDURE

**"The client consultation is an important part of your professional service. Be sure to complete this step prior to each client service you provide. Your successful retail sales and customer satisfaction rates depend upon it!"**

RETAIL • RE-BOOK • REFERRAL

1. Cosmetologist sanitizes hands.
2. Sanitize and set up table.
3. Client sanitizes hands.
4. Remove polish from nails.
5. Perform a visual examination of hands and nails.
6. Follow procedure as shown.
7. Suggest appropriate retail tools for the client's at-home nail maintenance.
8. Follow standard cleanup procedures.
9. Document client profile card/file.

A — The pointer shows fill-in area of nails.

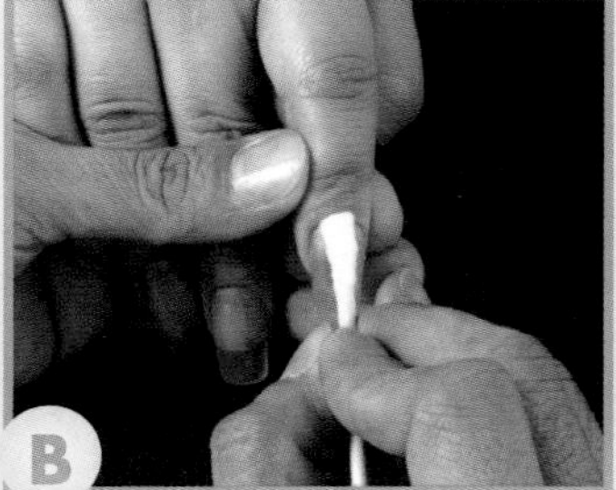

B — Use cotton-wrapped manicure stick and **gently** push back cuticles. Apply a nail antiseptic to the nails; spray on or wipe over nail with nail wipe.

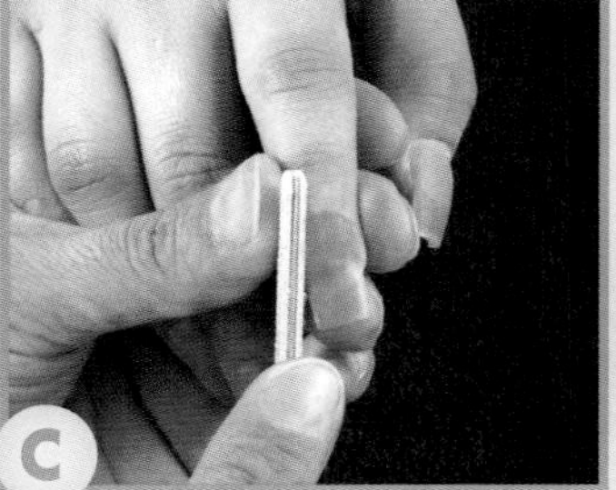

C — Shape free edge of nails and buff entire new growth area to remove line of demarcation, shine or natural oils to ensure adhesion.

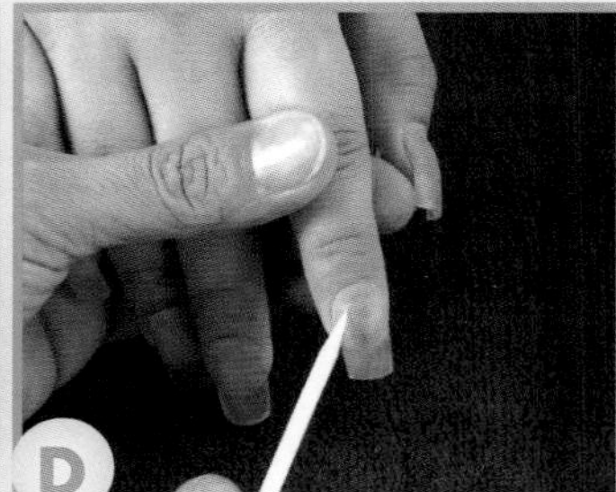

D — Pointer shows removed refill line.

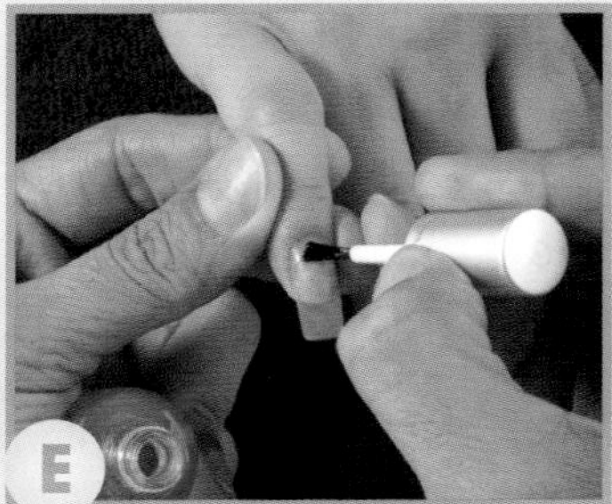

E — Apply primer to natural nail at new growth area **only** to enhance adhesion.

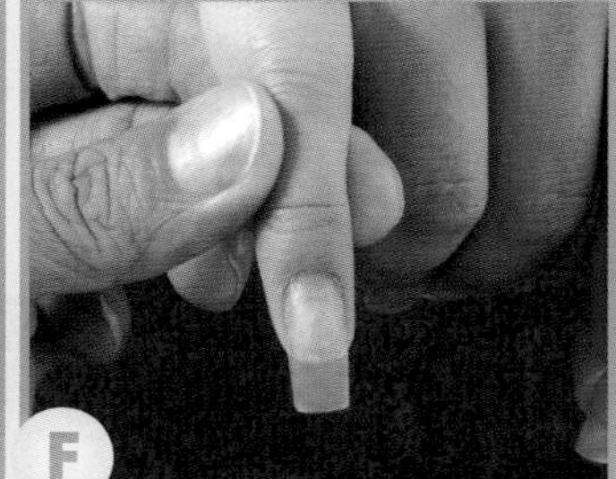

F — Primer appears chalky white when dry. Avoid excess use of primer. **Optional:** A dehydrant may be used to reduce moisture on nail plate.

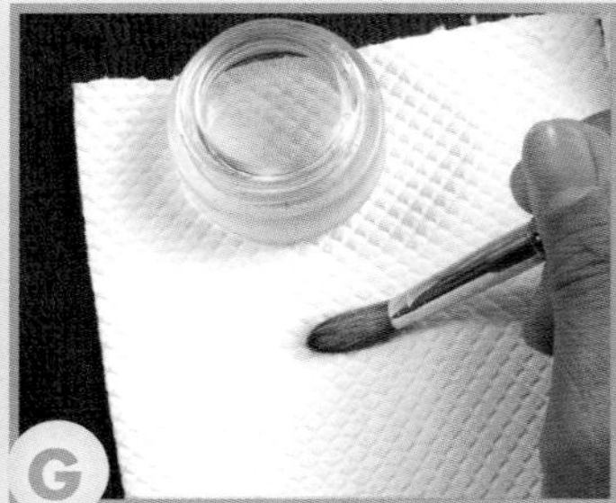

G — Prime the acrylic brush in monomer to soften flags and prepare for product application.

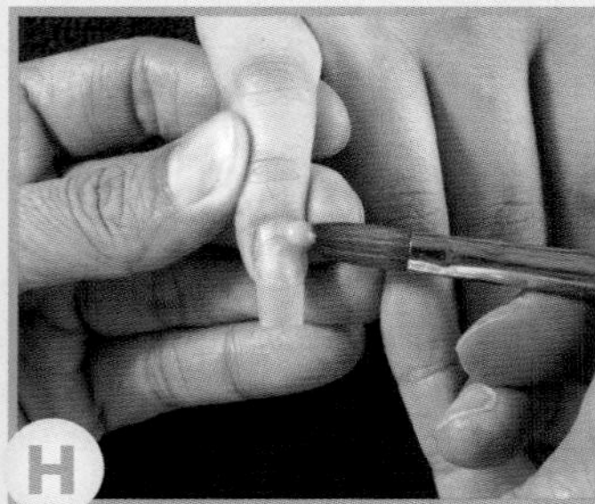

H — Place a small acrylic ball at new growth area **(zone 3/cuticle area)**.

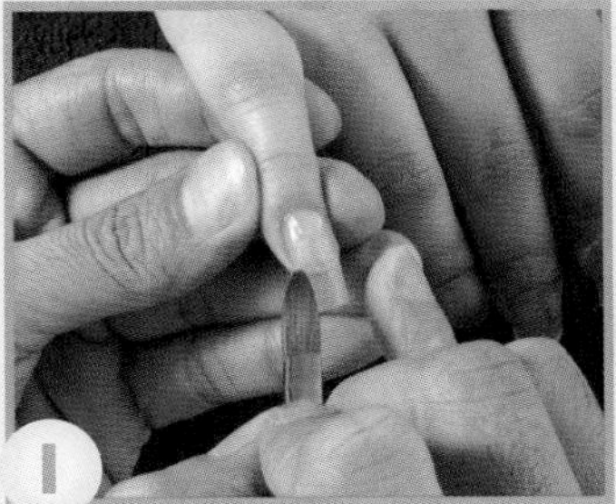
I — Pat and press into place. Keep product from contacting skin; product should be thinnest in this area.

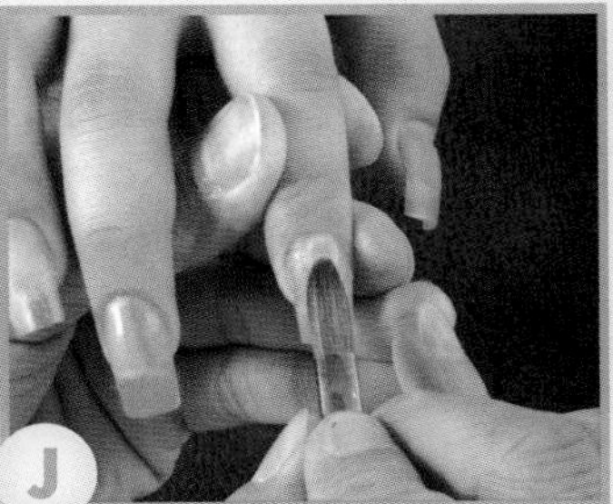
J — Place another acrylic ball of medium size at **zone 3/cuticle area** to build acrylic durability.

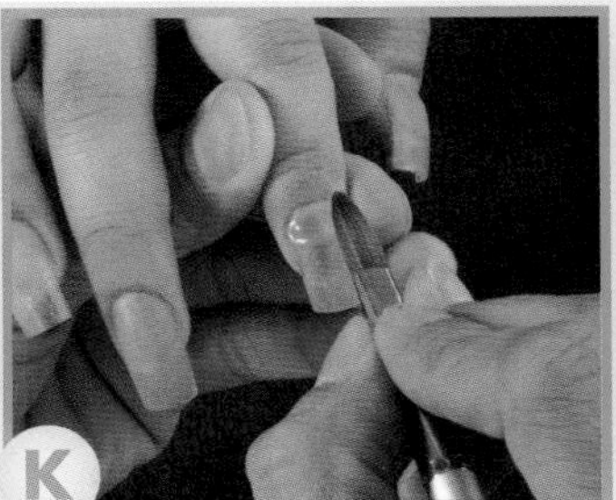
K — Holding brush at a **90-degree angle**, pat and press into cuticle area, keeping acrylic thin around skin.

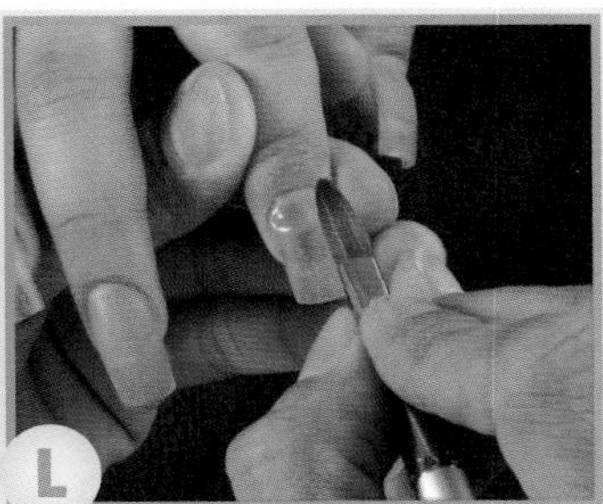
L — **Lightly** glide acrylic over **zone 2.**

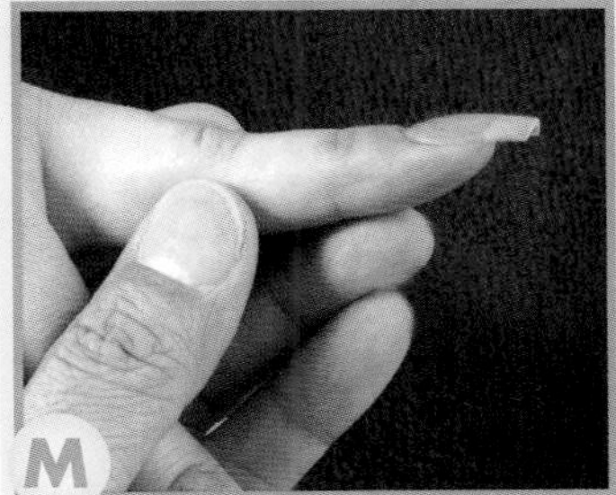
M — Check side and front views of nail for proper blending and proportion.

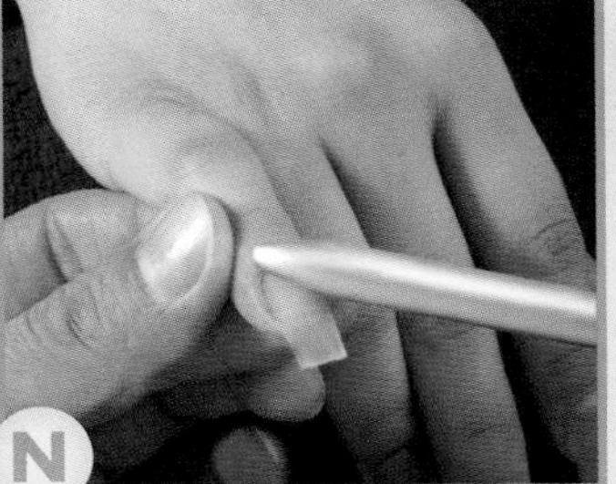
N — Allow to cure. Using handle of brush, lightly tap on nail to determine if product is hardened. Acrylic is cured when a **"clicking"** sound is heard.

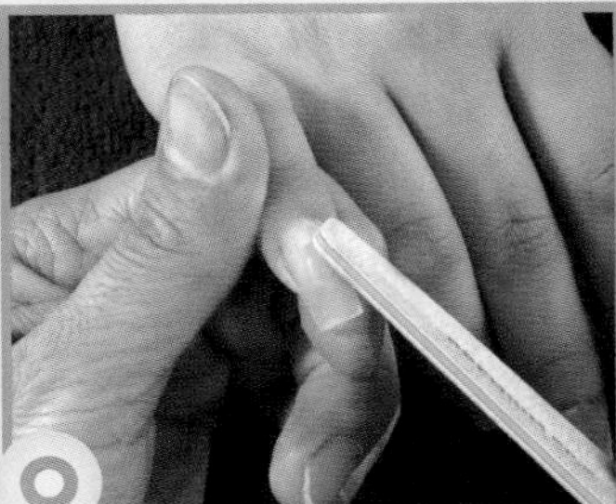
O — Use a medium abrasive and gently smooth over the nail plate (new growth area) to provide an evenly shaped nail. Remember to view sides of nail for proper proportion.

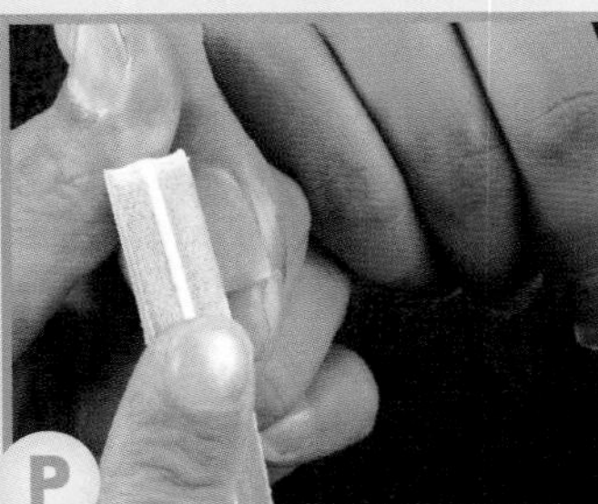
P — Use a buffer/shiner on surface of nail to produce a natural finish. Ask client to wash hands to remove product residue and filing dust.

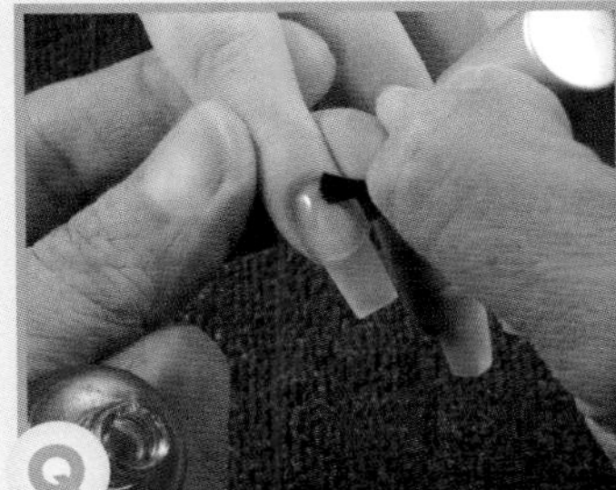
Q — Massage cuticle cream or oil into skin surrounding nails. (Remove oil from nails with polish remover.)

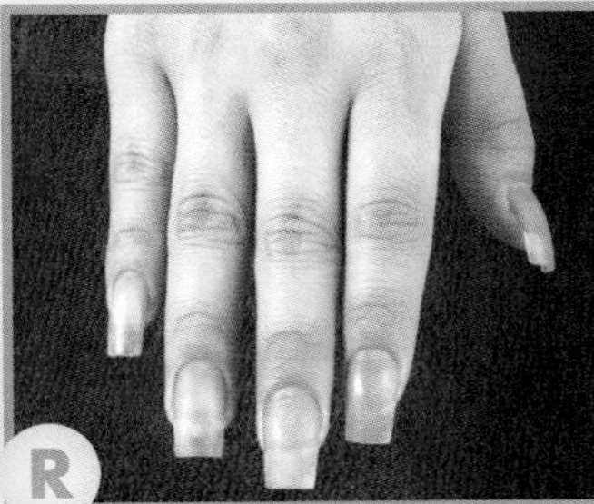
R — **Completed acrylic refill nails** with natural finish.

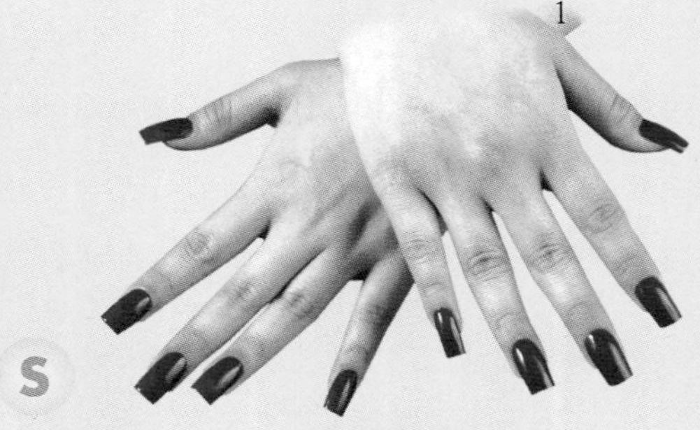
S — **Completed acrylic refill nails** with color polish.

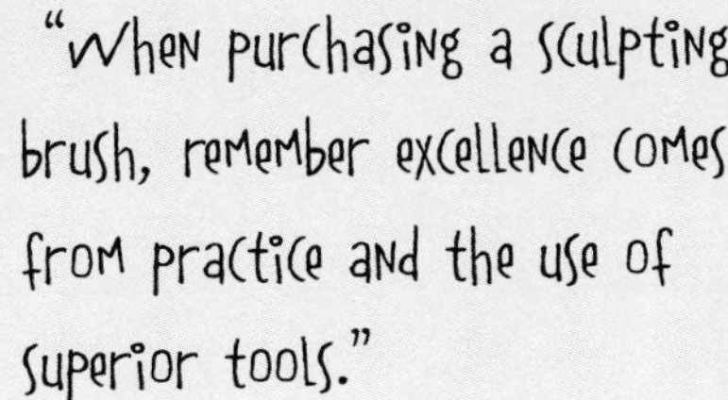

"When purchasing a sculpting brush, remember excellence comes from practice and the use of superior tools."

*Acrylic fills are serviced with maintenance or refills every two to three weeks depending on amount of new growth.*

**EVALUATION** ______________________________

______ GRADE ______ STUDENT'S NAME ______ ID#

COMPLEX LAB PROJECT

# Acrylic Removal

**NOTE:** This procedure applies to fabric wrap, overlay and free form acrylics.

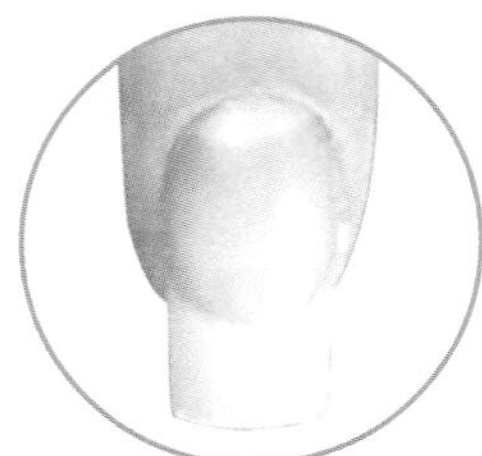
Before

## OBJECTIVE

To remove acrylic effectively and safely from the natural nails.

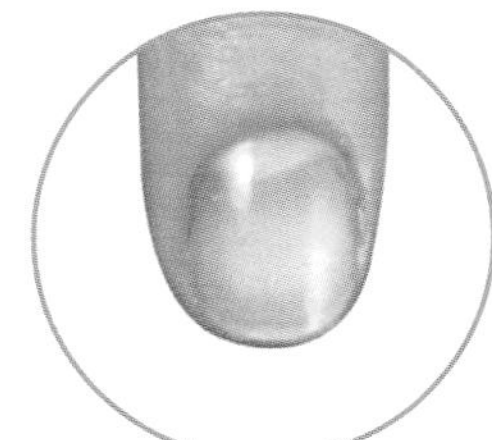
After

## TOOLS & MATERIALS

- Towels
- Disinfectant
- Client profile card/file
- Waste Receptacle
- Goggles
- Nail enhancement remover or acetone remover
- Top coat
- Wet disinfectant jar
- Manicure stick
- Hand gel sanitizer
- Plastic container
- Cuticle oil or cream
- Cotton and nail wipes
- Base coat
- Files and buffers
- Polish remover
- Cuticle pusher
- Nail clipper
- Glass bowl
- Dust and safety masks
- Color polish

## PROCEDURE

"The client consultation is an important part of your professional service. Be sure to complete this step prior to each client service you provide. Your successful retail sales and customer satisfaction rates depend upon it!"

1. Cosmetologist sanitizes hands.
2. Sanitize and set up table.
3. Client sanitizes hands.
4. Remove polish from nails.
5. Perform a visual examination of hands and nails.
6. Follow procedure as shown.
7. Suggest appropriate retail tools for the client's at-home nail maintenance.
8. Follow standard cleanup procedures.
9. Document client profile card/file.

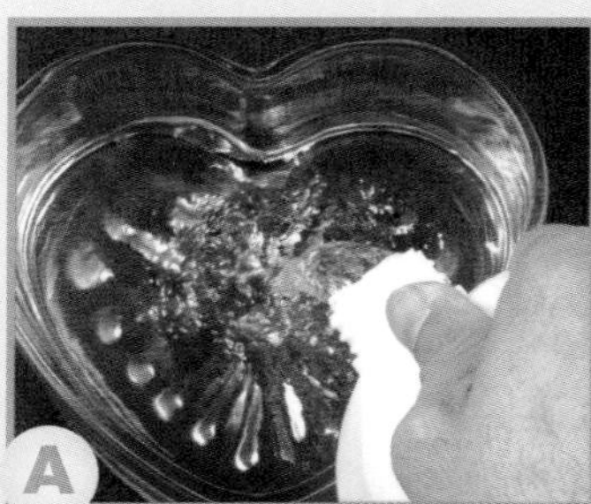
A
Place nail enhancement remover or acetone remover in a glass bowl. Amount to use is determined by estimating amount needed for complete nail coverage.

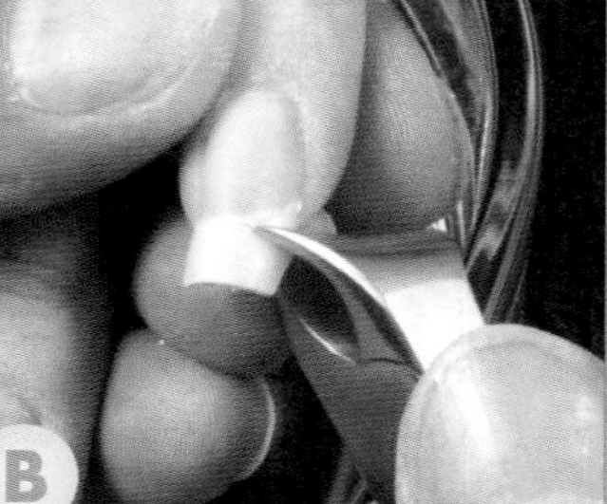
B
Use acrylic nippers and trim excess free edge length.

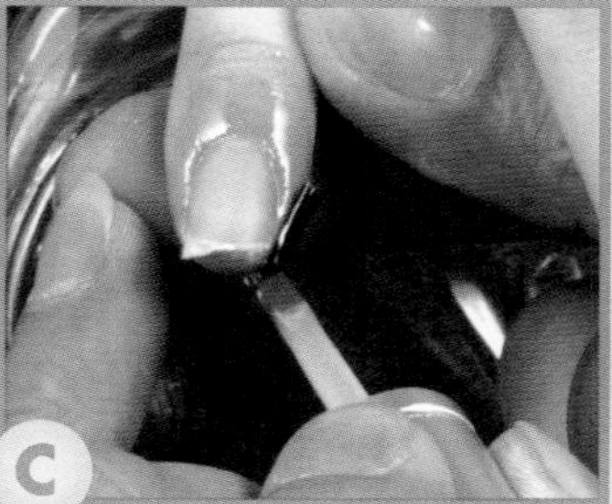
C
Apply cuticle oil to skin surrounding nails.

D
Immerse fingers in solution, ensuring all nails are covered in liquid.

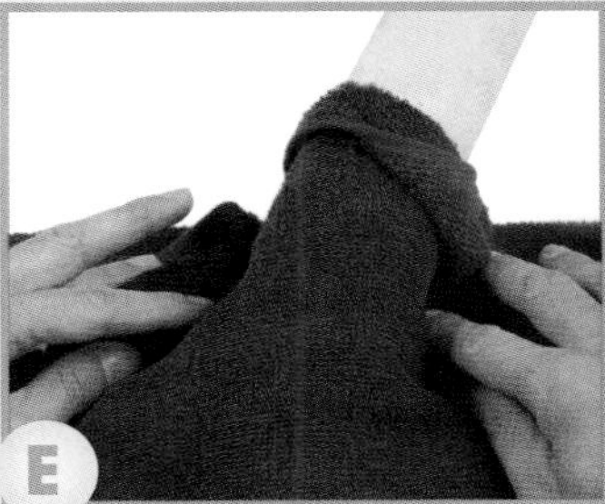


Cover hand in bowl with a towel to help contain body heat for faster softening of acrylic and controlling odor.

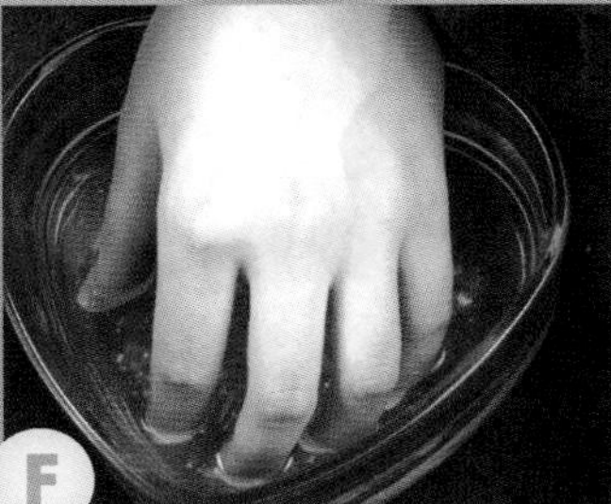


Soak nails for allotted time determined by manufacturer's directions or periodically checking every five minutes for acrylic softening.

Lift hand out of solution to see if product has softened enough to loosen the nails.

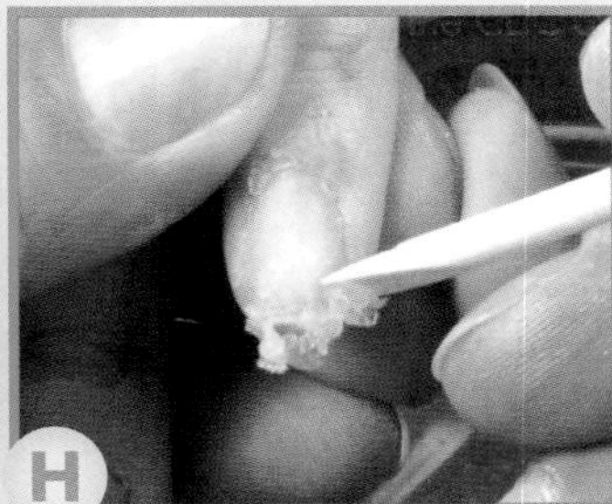


Using a manicure stick, **carefully** and **gently** work product from nails.

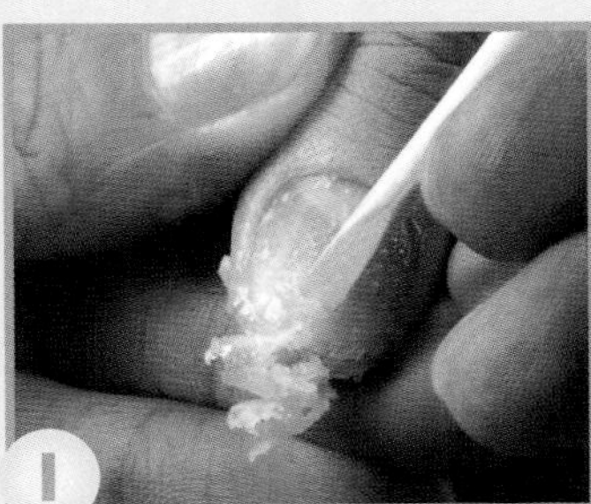


Continue soaking until all acrylic is softened and removed from nails. When product is removed from nails, ask client to wash hands to eliminate enhancement remover residue.

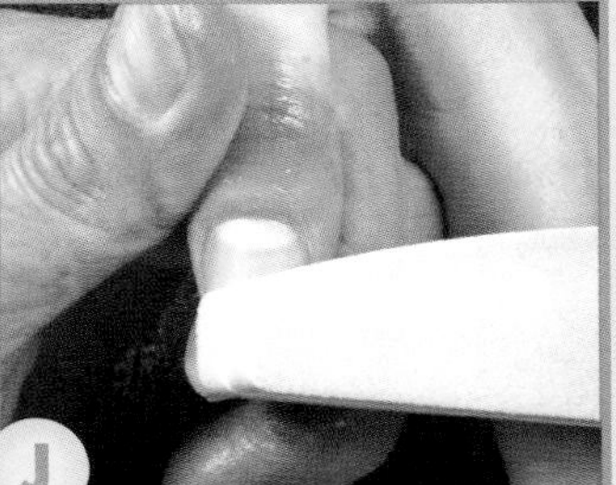


Lightly buff nails using a buffer/shiner to remove any additional acrylic or adhesive product and provide a natural finish to the nails.

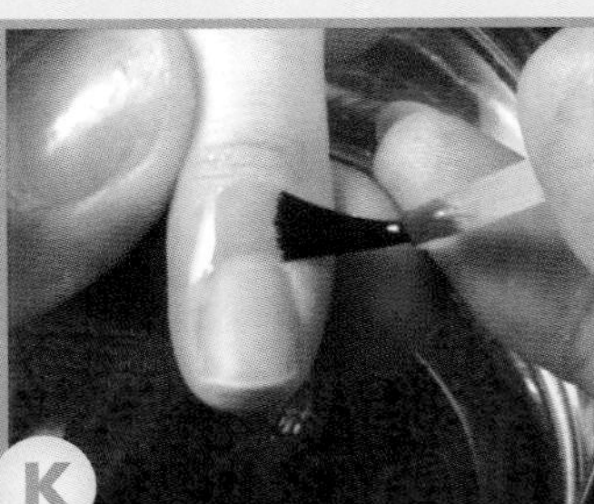


Massage cuticle oil or cream into the skin surrounding nail.

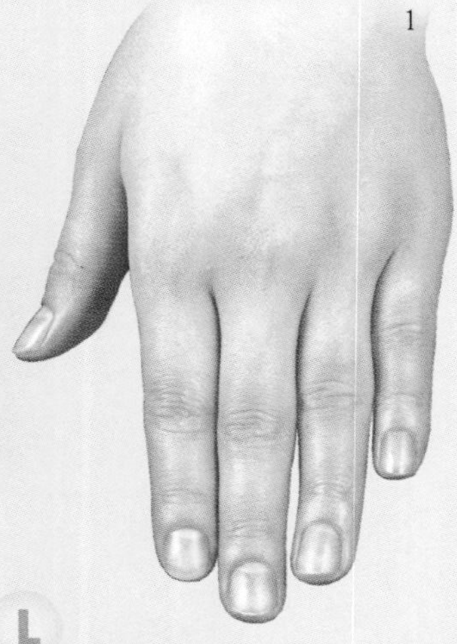

L

**Completed acrylic nail removal with natural finish.**

"The amount of time allotted for soaking the nails is determined by manufacturer's directions and type of enhancement used on nails."

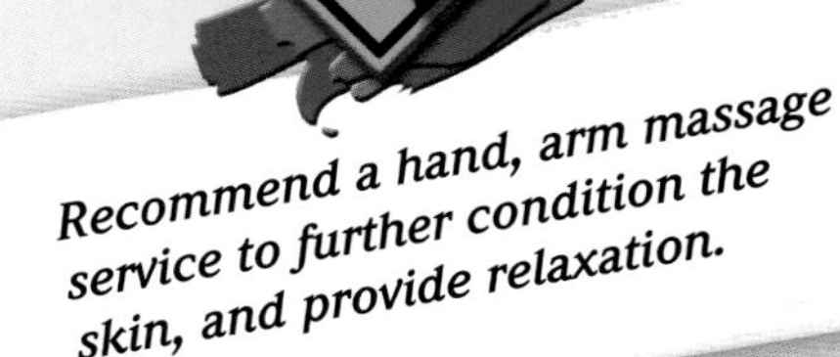


*Recommend a hand, arm massage service to further condition the skin, and provide relaxation.*

**EVALUATION**

**GRADE** STUDENT'S NAME ID#

COMPLEX LAB PROJECT

# Flat Art Painting

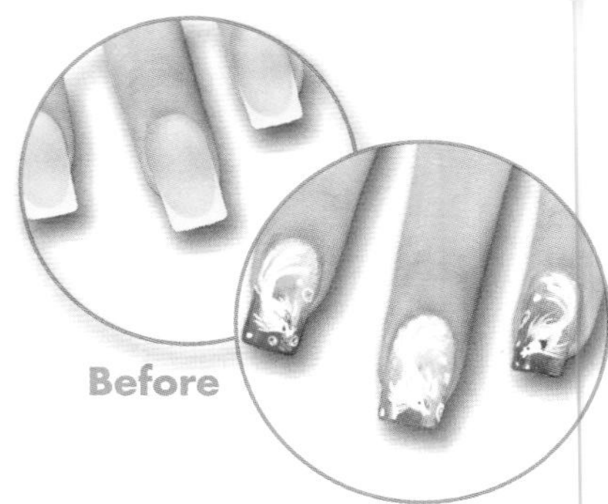


## OBJECTIVE

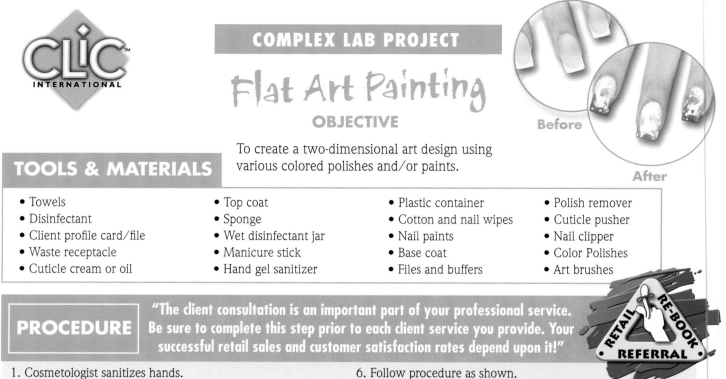

To create a two-dimensional art design using various colored polishes and/or paints.

## TOOLS & MATERIALS

- Towels
- Disinfectant
- Client profile card/file
- Waste receptacle
- Cuticle cream or oil
- Top coat
- Sponge
- Wet disinfectant jar
- Manicure stick
- Hand gel sanitizer
- Plastic container
- Cotton and nail wipes
- Nail paints
- Base coat
- Files and buffers
- Polish remover
- Cuticle pusher
- Nail clipper
- Color Polishes
- Art brushes

## PROCEDURE

**"The client consultation is an important part of your professional service. Be sure to complete this step prior to each client service you provide. Your successful retail sales and customer satisfaction rates depend upon it!"**

RETAIL • RE-BOOK • REFERRAL

1. Cosmetologist sanitizes hands.
2. Sanitize and set up table.
3. Client sanitizes hands.
4. Perform a visual examination of hands and nails.
5. Complete desired nail service.
6. Follow procedure as shown.
7. Suggest appropriate retail tools for the client's at-home nail maintenance.
8. Follow standard cleanup procedures.
9. Document client profile card/file.

A — Select paint to be used as a background for art. Using a small sponge, you will place four shades of selected color on each nail. (For the first nail we have selected blue.)

B — Imagine the nail is divided into three equal sections from top (cuticle) to bottom (free edge). Starting with light blue, sponge paint on top third of nail.

C — Sponge a medium blue on middle third of nail, overlapping onto the light blue color. Place a blue-green color below the medium blue, always overlapping previous color for blending.

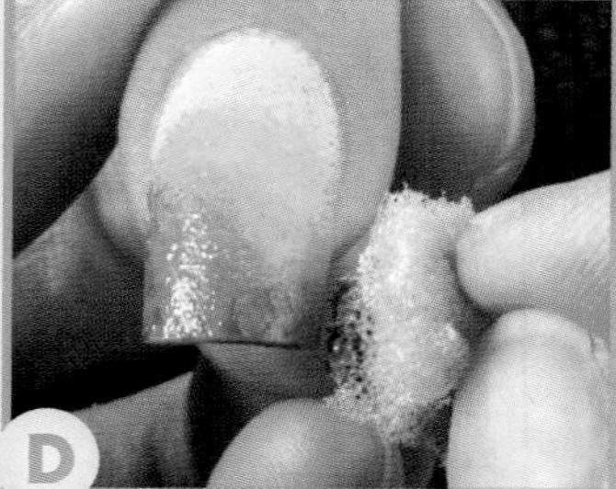

D — Finish background by sponging a dark blue on free edge of nail.

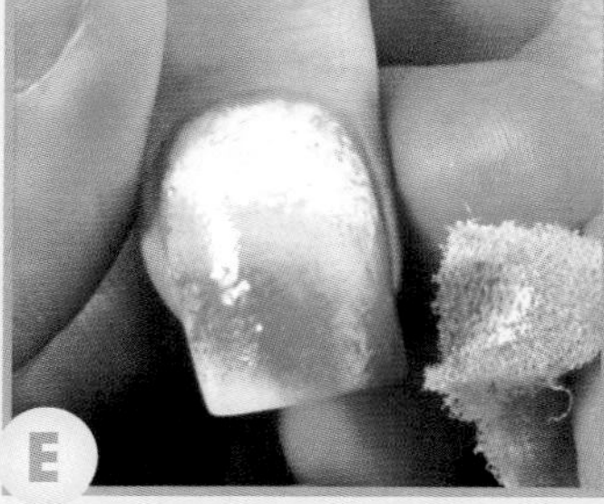

E — Choose contrasting colors as background for the other nails.

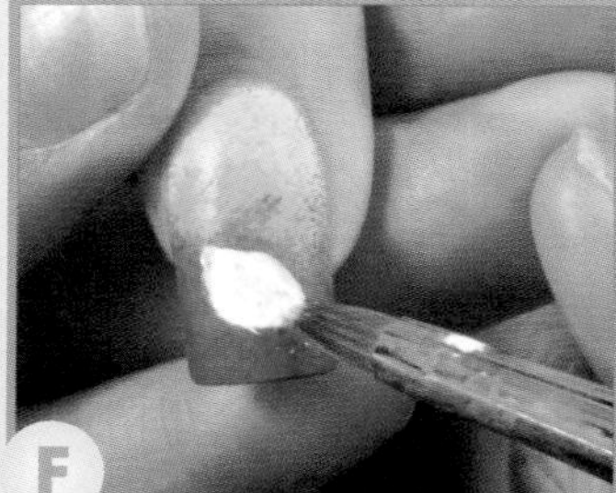

F — Use tip of brush dipped in white paint, draw your design. (In this case, a fish body, drawn with an elongated oval shape.)

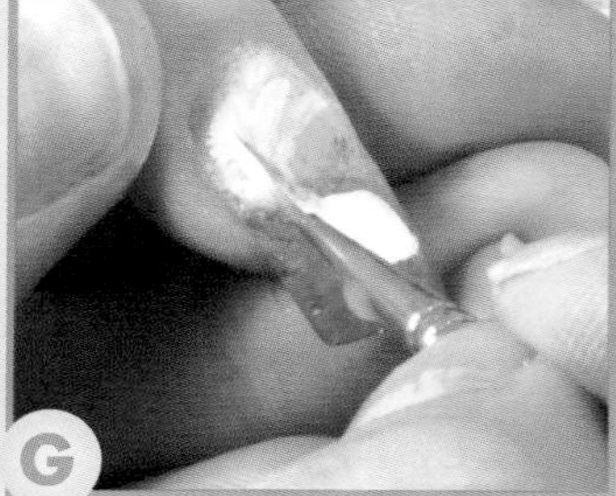

G — Continue with white paint to create the fish tail, using long curved lines and a thin art brush.

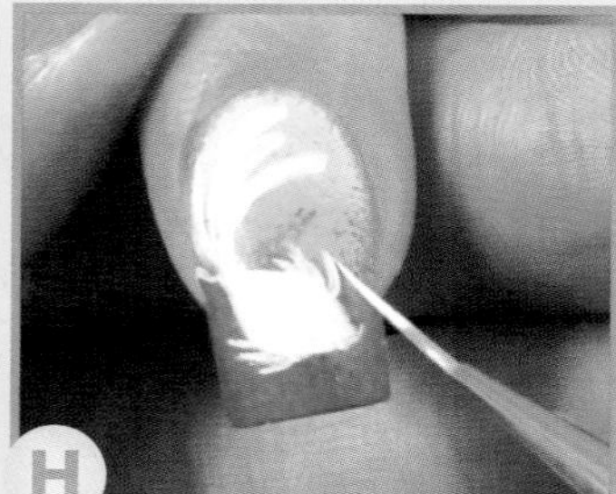

H — Short white curved lines are used to create the fish fins.

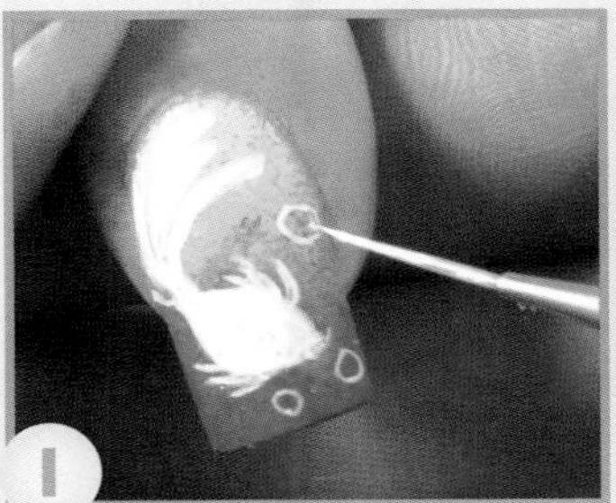

I

Use the white paint and a thin art brush to draw water bubbles around the fish.

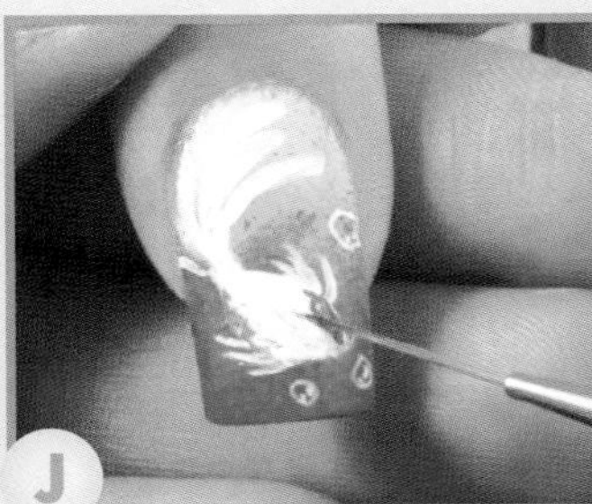

J

Apply final details by placing contrasting colors of red and orange inside the fish.

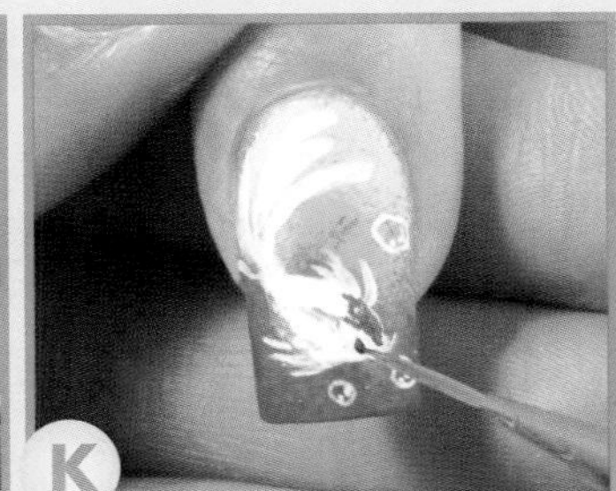

K

Use black for the eye of the fish.

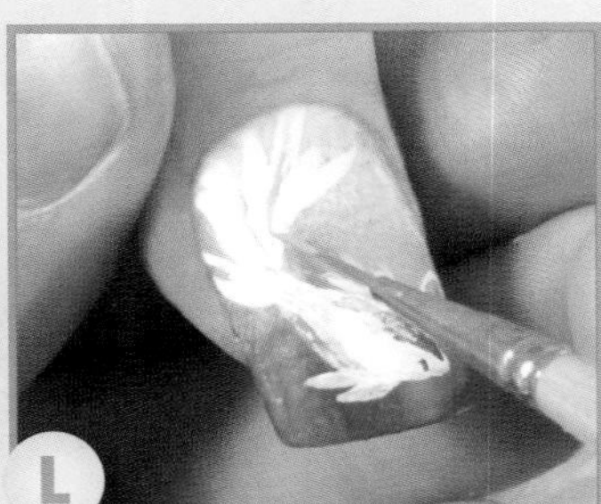

L

**Repeat Steps F to K** on all nails, using a variety of colors and fish designs.

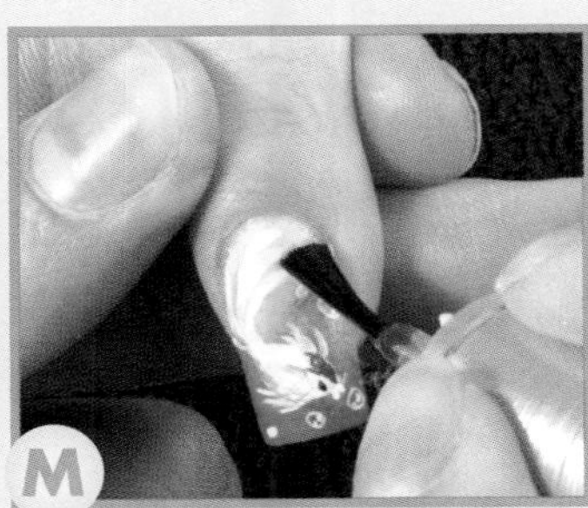

M

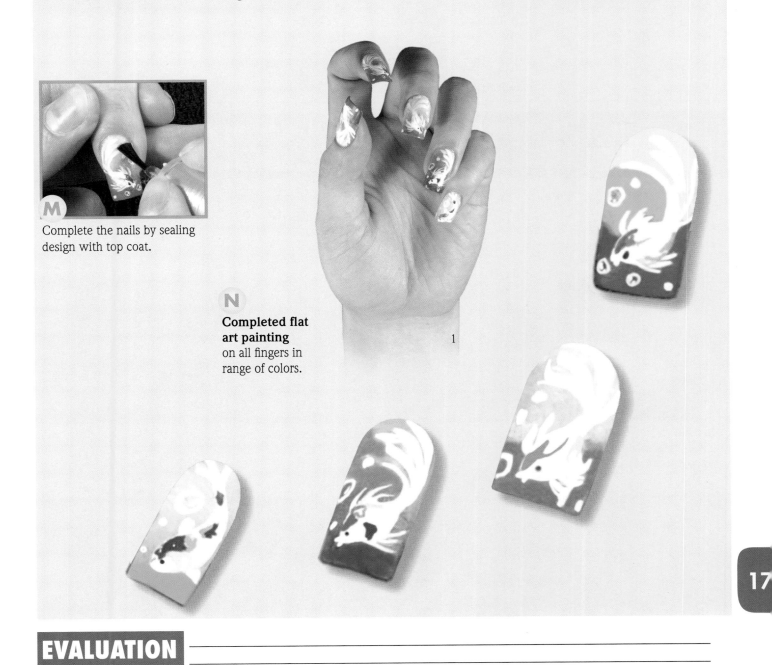

Complete the nails by sealing design with top coat.

N

**Completed flat art painting** on all fingers in range of colors.

1

17

## EVALUATION

GRADE

STUDENT'S NAME

ID#

COMPLEX LAB PROJECT

# Jeweled Nail Art

Before

After

## OBJECTIVE

To create a three-dimensional design by transforming the nails with glitter, gems and rhinestones.

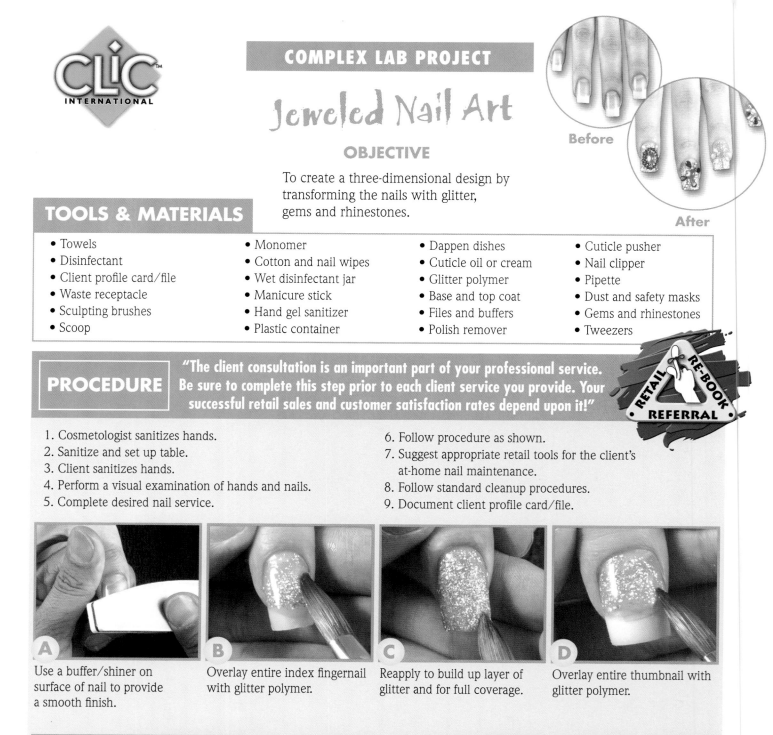

## TOOLS & MATERIALS

- Towels
- Disinfectant
- Client profile card/file
- Waste receptacle
- Sculpting brushes
- Scoop
- Monomer
- Cotton and nail wipes
- Wet disinfectant jar
- Manicure stick
- Hand gel sanitizer
- Plastic container
- Dappen dishes
- Cuticle oil or cream
- Glitter polymer
- Base and top coat
- Files and buffers
- Polish remover
- Cuticle pusher
- Nail clipper
- Pipette
- Dust and safety masks
- Gems and rhinestones
- Tweezers

## PROCEDURE

"The client consultation is an important part of your professional service. Be sure to complete this step prior to each client service you provide. Your successful retail sales and customer satisfaction rates depend upon it!"

RETAIL • RE-BOOK • REFERRAL

1. Cosmetologist sanitizes hands.
2. Sanitize and set up table.
3. Client sanitizes hands.
4. Perform a visual examination of hands and nails.
5. Complete desired nail service.
6. Follow procedure as shown.
7. Suggest appropriate retail tools for the client's at-home nail maintenance.
8. Follow standard cleanup procedures.
9. Document client profile card/file.

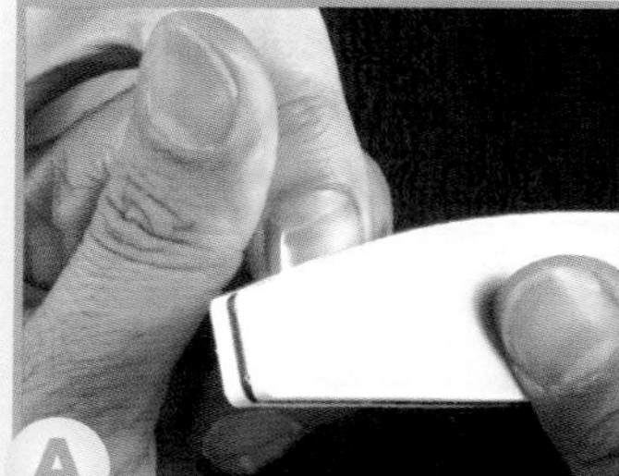

A Use a buffer/shiner on surface of nail to provide a smooth finish.

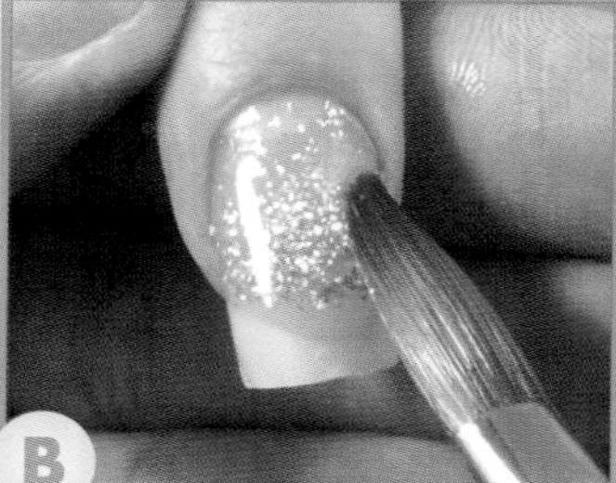

B Overlay entire index fingernail with glitter polymer.

C Reapply to build up layer of glitter and for full coverage.

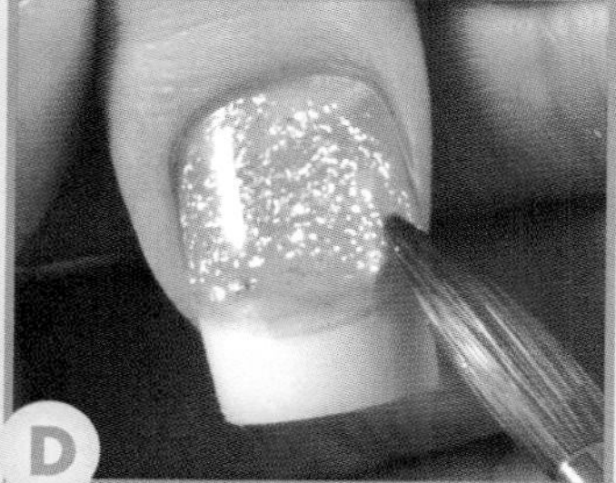

D Overlay entire thumbnail with glitter polymer.

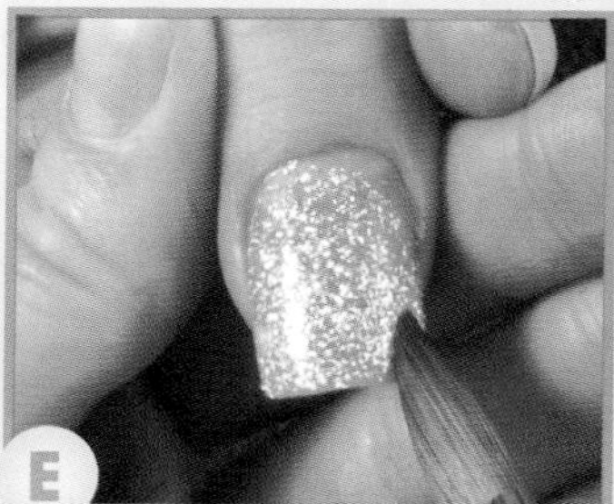

E Reapply to build up layer of glitter and to provide full coverage. **Repeat Steps D and E on all fingernails.**

F Using a tweezers, center a gem on index fingernail. Secure gem on nail using a manicure stick.

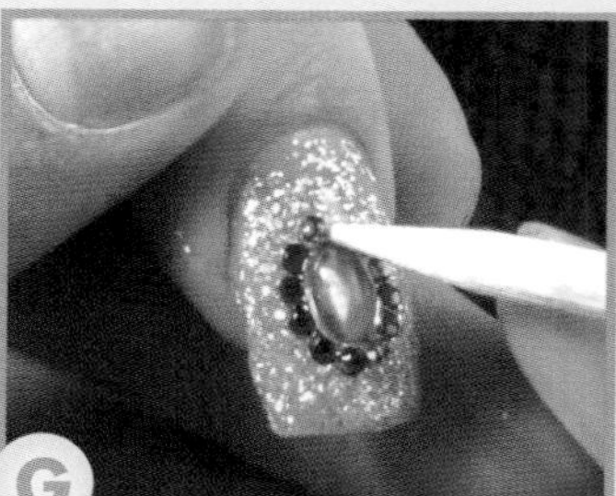

G Enclose gem with a circle of small rhinestones. Use a manicure stick to secure stones on nail.

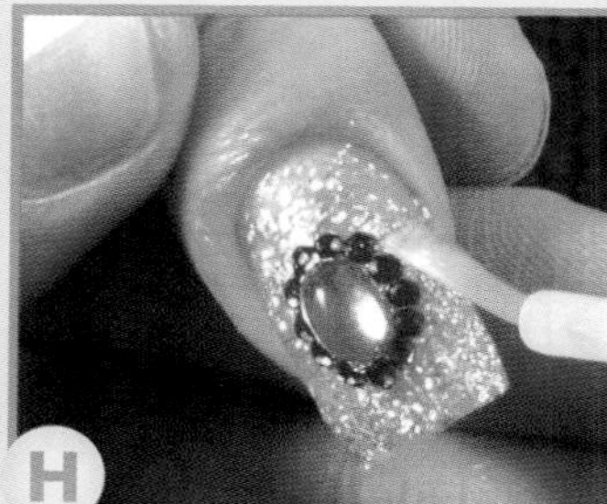

H Apply a small amount of base coat on outside of rhinestone circle.

I
Surround first rhinestone circle with another circle of small rhinestones.

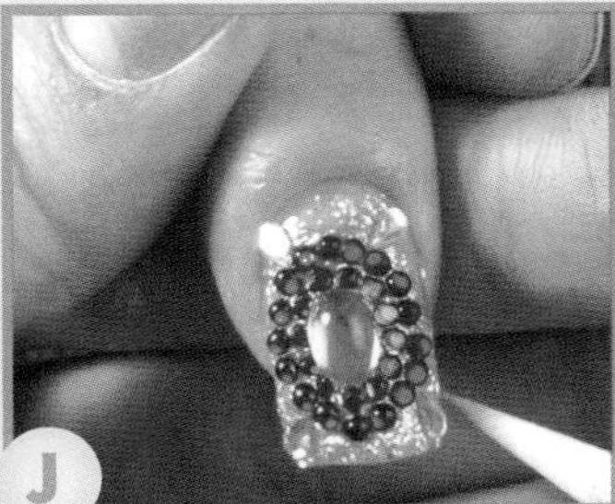
J
Place teardrop rhinestones at the four corners of the nail.

K
Center a gem on thumbnail and place small rhinestones around it. Use a manicure stick to secure stones on nail.

L
Place teardrop rhinestones on all four corners of the centered gem. Continue to place gem and rhinestone designs on all nails.

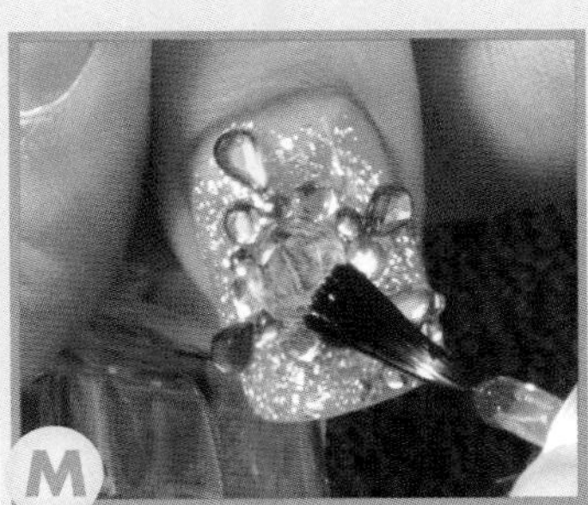
M
Complete each nail by sealing design with top coat.

N
**Completed jeweled nail art.**

**EVALUATION** ______________________________

______________________________

**GRADE** ______ STUDENT'S NAME ______ ID# ______

# Nail Treatments REVIEW QUESTIONS

## MULTIPLE CHOICE

1. What recommended cutting tool shortens fingernail length?
   A. nail clippers B. cuticle nippers C. fabric scissors
2. How many methods of acrylic ball applications are there?
   A. one-ball B. two-ball C. three-ball
3. What is the name of the acrylic powder that combines with monomer?
   A. polymer B. resin C. gel
4. Which liquid tool is applied under polish color to help seal in wavy ridges on the nail?
   A. ridge filler B. top coat C. nail strengthener
5. If the grit number on a file is **high**, the abrasive is considered?
   A. fine B. medium C. coarse
6. At what degree is the sculpting brush held to create an artificial nail on the free edge?
   A. 45-degree B. 15-degree C. 0-degree
7. Which nail shape is more susceptible to breakage?
   A. triangular B. squoval C. square
8. Which file smoothes the surface of the nail and provides shine?
   A. block buffer B. diamond file C. crystal file
9. Which product is used as a gentle exfoliate for the feet during a pedicure?
   A. sea salt B. feet soak C. foot powder
10. If the grit number is **low**, the abrasive is considered?
    A. fine B. medium C. coarse
11. What bonding agent allows a nail tip to adhere to the natural nail?
    A. dehydrant B. primer C. adhesive
12. What determines the coarseness to fineness of a file or buffer?
    A. core material B. size of file C. grit number
13. The three types of fabric wraps are fiberglass, silk and?
    A. paper B. linen C. rayon
14. What liquid tool helps to revitalize and moisturize the skin during massage?
    A. foot powder B. sloughing lotion C. massage lotion or oil
15. Which nail shape is a common choice for men or children?
    A. triangular B. square C. round
16. The cylinder-type rod used to reinforce the arch in a sculptured nail is?
    A. dowel B. manicure stick C. spatula
17. What are the plastic extensions applied to the top of the natural nail to create length?
    A. forms B. nail tips C. fabric wraps
18. The degree or amount by which something is raised or angled is referred to as?
    A. ratio B. elevation C. dimension
19. What chemical process will remove dirt and reduce the number of pathogenic bacteria?
    A. sterilization B. sanitation C. disinfection
20. How many nail surface divisions are there for artificial nail placement?
    A. one B. two C. three

STUDENT'S NAME DATE GRADE

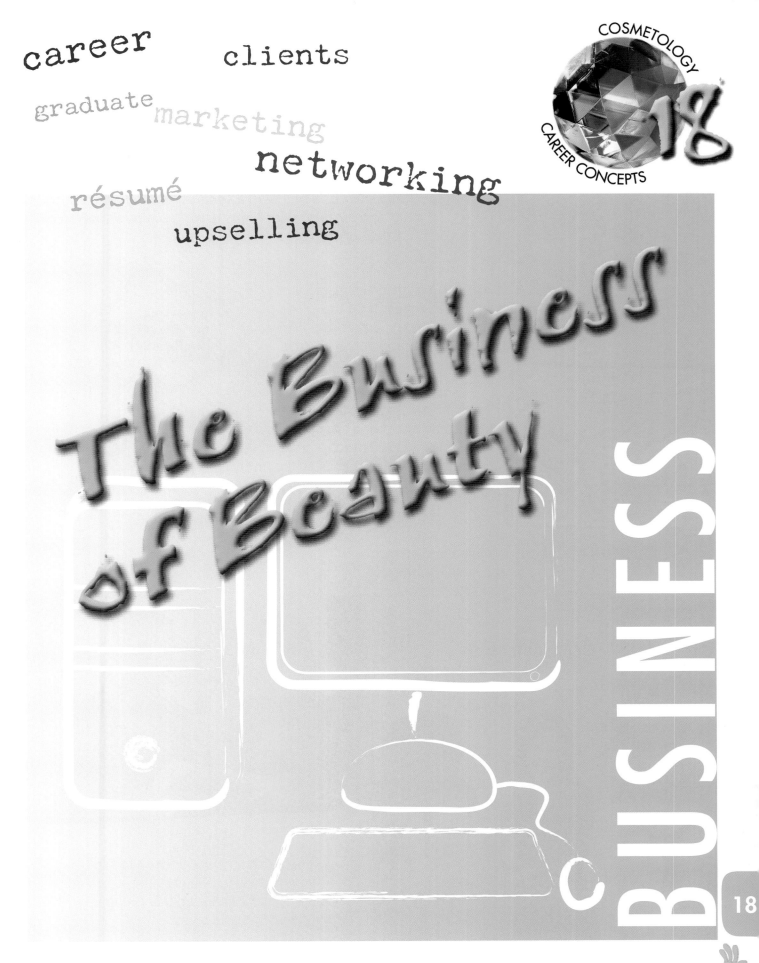


career clients

graduate marketing

networking

résumé

upselling

# The Business of Beauty

BUSINESS

18

# Terminology ...

**As with** *all the chapters in this book, there are certain industry words that are repetitively used in relationship to the chapter's subject, and it is helpful to understand them. Below is a list of those words along with a summarized definition to acquaint you with terms used in the business aspect of the cosmetology industry.*

**Accounting** is maintaining and organizing business records for the purpose of reporting taxes, preparation of forms and other financial accounts.

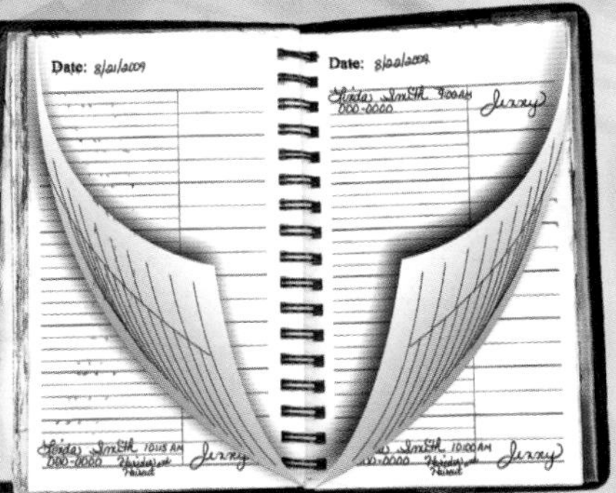

**Brand** is a "mental imprint" characterized by a symbol or logo that is earned and belongs to a product, service, organization, individual and/or event.

**Client Retention** is when the customer continuously returns for scheduled services, remaining loyal to salon and professional.

**Communication** is the process through which people exchange information.

**Fashion Image Fingerprint** is your particular style of clothing, hair and application of makeup that is uniquely presented through you.

# Terminology . . .

**Franchised Chain Salons/Spas** are part of a large chain salon/spa group but are locally owned and operated, with the owner paying a franchise fee.

**Goal** is a "target" that is planned, monitored and reached within a scheduled time frame.

GOAL!

*5-Year Goal*
Consider specializing in a selected area of cosmetology or operating your own business.

*3-Year Goal*
Work successfully in a salon/spa building your customer base.

*1-Year Goal*
Graduate cosmetology school, get licensed and locate a professional job.

**Independent Salon/Spa** is solely owned and operated by a person or a partnership.

**Résumé** is a communication tool that catalogs and summarizes your education, employment history and professional accomplishments.

Resume

**Style** is an outward representation of your fashion attitude to others both physically and verbally.

18

# Beauty Industry ...

*The beauty industry encompasses numerous areas within the field. An individual has multiple opportunities to succeed, whether it is to work in the salon, be a product distributor/manufacturer, or a salon owner, platform artist, educator, etc. Along with these many roles come numerous titles associated with the beauty industry professional ... an individual that has become successful through hard work, motivation and persistence.*

## When someone asks you what you do for a living, what is your response?

"I am an esthetician."

"I am a stylist."

"I am a haircutter."

"I do nails."

"I make people feel good about themselves."

"I am a makeup artist."

"I am a color specialist."

"I am a cosmetologist."

## What exactly does the individual that works in a salon/spa accomplish on a daily basis?

**Response:** "I make people look good and feel better, thus creating an image of how others will see you and in turn how you will see yourself." Plus, "I inspire confidence and instill self-esteem in each individual, thereby helping to create opportunities for that person to go out and possibly achieve his or her long awaited dream!

So, essentially the people that work within the beauty industry are successful professionals licensed to touch and change the lives of everyone they meet!

# Career Preparation . . .

*In order to get started in the beauty industry, one must attend a licensed beauty school that educates the student in the arts of cosmetology.*

## Pre-Grad Cosmetology Student (while still in school)

### What area of the beauty industry most excites and interests you?

- **New career opportunities** in the professional beauty industry are created all the time. (A partial list of career options is in chapter one.) You are ONLY limited by your thinking … the beauty industry offers alternative career paths for those willing to explore them.

### What skills are needed to support your goals: Technical and Communication!

- It is believed by some that **80 percent of your long-term success** will come from your ability to communicate well with your clients and **20 percent from your technical skills**. Others believe it is really the other way around. What can best be stated is that you will need **both** throughout your career to be successful. In the beginning of your career as a professional cosmetologist, you will need to focus more on your technical skill development. As those skills improve, you will start to integrate the ability to communicate while performing the hair- and skin-care services, resulting in a **professional balance between the two skills**. Performing highly technical services while maintaining dialog with the client equals success.

"Get involved in an internship program to better understand the beauty industry through a real work experience while in school. Positions can be found in either an area salon/spa or in a distributor of professional beauty products."

*When close to graduation, the next step is to prepare for the salon/spa search and interview. An* ***interview*** *is a* ***conversation*** *that occurs between the prospective employee and employer. It is important to be punctual and bring all supporting paperwork with you. It would also be a good idea to bring an image portfolio to showcase your skills through photos of your work.*

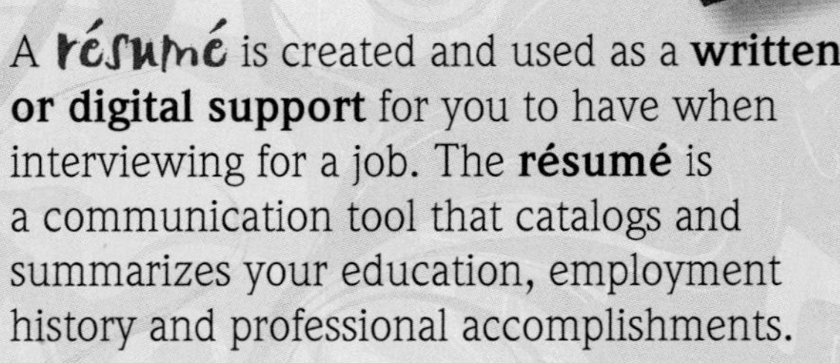


A **résumé** is created and used as a **written or digital support** for you to have when interviewing for a job. The **résumé** is a communication tool that catalogs and summarizes your education, employment history and professional accomplishments.

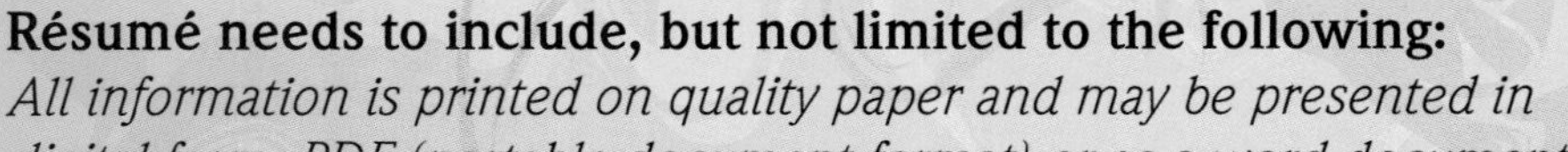

**Résumé needs to include, but not limited to the following:**
*All information is printed on quality paper and may be presented in digital form, PDF (portable document format) or as a word document.*

1) Your name, full address of current residence, phone number and email address
2) List a summary statement
3) List most recent work experience
4) Significant education and name of school from which you graduated and any advanced classes related to the job you are seeking; keep it simple to allow for fast and easy reading
5) List ONLY the most important and necessary accomplishments pertaining to the career you are pursuing; use numbers or percentages when detailing any achievements
6) Three to five professional references with their contact information; place this information on the last page of your résumé

"Keep résumé short, but detailed!"

# Career Preparation ...

**Résumé example:** This is a basic outline, which can be artistically altered to reflect your personal style.

Page 2

**PROFESSIONAL REFERENCES**

**Name, Address, Phone number**
**Name, Address, Phone number**
**Name, Address, Phone number**

Page 1

**NAME**

**Address**
**Phone Number**
**Email Address**

**SUMMARY STATEMENT**

**WORK EXPERIENCE**

**20XX-present** ORGANIZATION, City, State
Job title
**19XX-XX** ORGANIZATION, City, State
Job title
**19XX-XX** ORGANIZATION, City, State
Job title

**SIGNIFICANT EDUCATION AND ADVANCED CLASSES**

Degree, Major [if relevant], 20xx
School, City, State

**COSMETOLOGY ACCOMPLISHMENTS**

Award, competition name, date

"Make sure all words are spelled and sentences are punctuated correctly!"

18

# Career Preparation ...

**When** the résumé is completed, a **cover letter** is written and attached to the résumé. A **cover letter** is an **introduction to the employer from the prospective employee** requesting an interview. An employer might use the cover letter as criteria to screen out applicants that are not sufficiently qualified for the open position. Cover letters along with résumés are presented in both written and electronic format in today's digital world.

**Cover letters are generally one page long and consist of the following:**
*All information should be printed on quality paper.*

**Greeting:** If no specific name was given as a contact, use "Dear Director" or "Dear Professional" in the greeting.

**Header:** Begin cover letter with sender and recipient contact information and date.

**Introduction:** The opening paragraph specifies requested position you are applying for. Express interest in position and capture employer's attention. Keep brief, averaging two to three sentences.

**Body:** The second paragraph includes a highlight of your skills/ qualifications for the open position. List a few of your experiences relating to the position supported by specific evidence such as past jobs projects, etc. This is the longest paragraph of the cover letter and may be separated into two paragraphs if becoming too lengthy for easy reading.

**Closing:** The final paragraph is a summary of body and intent to contact for an interview. Last sentence should thank the prospective employer for his or her time in reading the letter. Finish letter with a valediction such as, "sincerely" followed by your signature in preferably black ink along with your printed name.

**Optional:** May use the abbreviation, "encl." to indicate the résumé enclosure

**Exercise:**
Below is an example of a basic cover letter. Review the letter then create your own letter to use when you are ready to interview for a job. Remember, a cover letter may also be artistically altered to reflect your personal style.

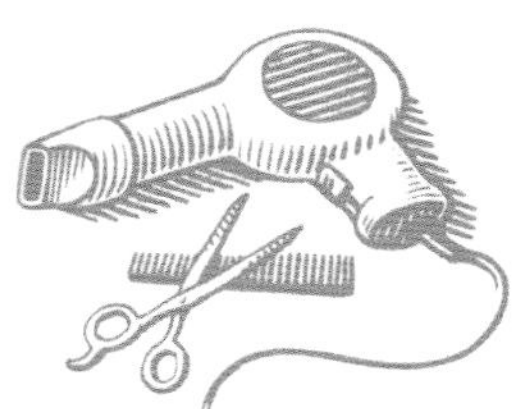

Your name
Mailing address
City, state, and zip
Telephone number(s)
Email address

Today's date

Your addressee's name
Professional title
Organization name
Mailing address
City, state and zip

Dear Mr. (or Ms. ) last name,

Start your letter with a grabber - a statement that establishes a connection with your reader, a probing question, or a quotable quote. Briefly say what job you are applying for.

The mid-section of your letter should be one or two short paragraphs that make relevant points about your qualifications. You should not summarize your resume! You may inncorporate a column or bullet point format here.

Your last paragraph should initiate action by explaining what you will do next (e.g., call the employer) or instigate the reader to contact you to set up an interview. Close by saying " thank you."

Sincerely yours,

*Your handwritten signature*

Your name (printed)

Enclosure: resume

"Cover letters must be grammatically correct and without punctuation errors. The cover letter represents your writing skills."

## Post-Grad Cosmetology Professional (licensed to practice)

*Once you have graduated, the next step is to become licensed in order to work legally as a cosmetologist in a salon/spa. Licensing in the beauty industry usually requires taking a written and practical exam.*

***Each state licensure will vary. Check with your state's regulatory agency for current license information.***

A written exam consists of a **series of multiple choice and true/false questions** pertaining to your area of study. To prepare for any written test, practice **effective study habits** by taking accurate notes and reviewing past materials. Study and know the material well!

### Some test-taking strategies are:

- When answering true/false questions the entire question **must be accurate** in order for it to be marked true. To help determine if question is true, look for **key words** such as all, sometimes, never, no, less, always, etc.
- For multiple choice questions, **read the question and choices carefully** and use the process of elimination or **deductive analysis** to rule out any incorrect options first. If more than one choice is correct, **choose the best answer**.

A practical exam consists of **performing the actual hands-on skills** appropriate to your area of study. Selected services are performed either on a model or mannequin and generally are mocked or not completed in the full capacity. This is not a day at the salon or spa; it is a test to determine if students are proficient enough in their area of study to be licensed to perform legally in a salon/spa.

"Practice, practice, practice is your best strategy to passing the practical examination!"

# Questions and Answers ...

Randy Rick
Founder/Creator
of the CLiC System

The following questions with accompanying answers are most frequently posed to **Randy Rick** by cosmetology students. These questions/answers may help direct you to a better understanding of what a **Burgeoning Hair Artist** needs to become successful.

**QUESTION:** *What advice would you give to a recent graduate of beauty school?*

**ANSWER:** Be honest – always honor your employer, co-workers and customers. Remember honesty is always the best policy! Be passionate about your career and the work of art you create. Communicate through creative hairstyles. Love your work, and then it will never be a job. Be inspired by other stylists you admire. Be trendy – learn new fashions and hairstyles quickly. Do not get stuck on outdated styles that "look alike." Learn to wear what is hot and stay away from what is not!

**QUESTION:** *What type of salon should I work for?*

**ANSWER:** Throughout my career, I always found that the greatest salons provide the cornerstone to your personal success. These are the salons that offer continuous advance education and a strong advertising presence. They have great furnishings, professional products and are located in populated areas with plenty of parking.

**QUESTION:** *What does success mean to you?*

**ANSWER:** Success cannot be measured by money! It is about being able to give back to the industry and fellow hair artists. Communicating what inspires me and sharing that creative result, technique or innovation with others is extremely exciting and very rewarding.

**QUESTION:** *How do you feel your awards, books and inventions have improved the cosmetology students and educators of today?*

**ANSWER:** Beauty school students and educators need to have modern day technology, tools and books to meet the demands of today's progressive clients and salons. Learning techniques that are 40 to 50 years old cannot produce the international skills needed to keep you competitive with the rest of the world. The CLiC system was developed to meet the demands of the ever-changing beauty industry and future professionals.

**QUESTION:** *What are the most rewarding achievements in your career?*

**ANSWER:** This is not a one answer question, since I have had many complex artistic aspirations. My early career achievement was in the hair competition arena winning three gold medals for the U.S.A. in the Open Championships at HairWorld. This was the most memorable award amongst my eighty-plus awards. My greatest personal reward was developing the CLiC system. This by far is probably the greatest highlight of my life because the books consist of the written documentation that will live on forever in helping to upgrade artists' skills and provide for their success.

# Career Preparation ...

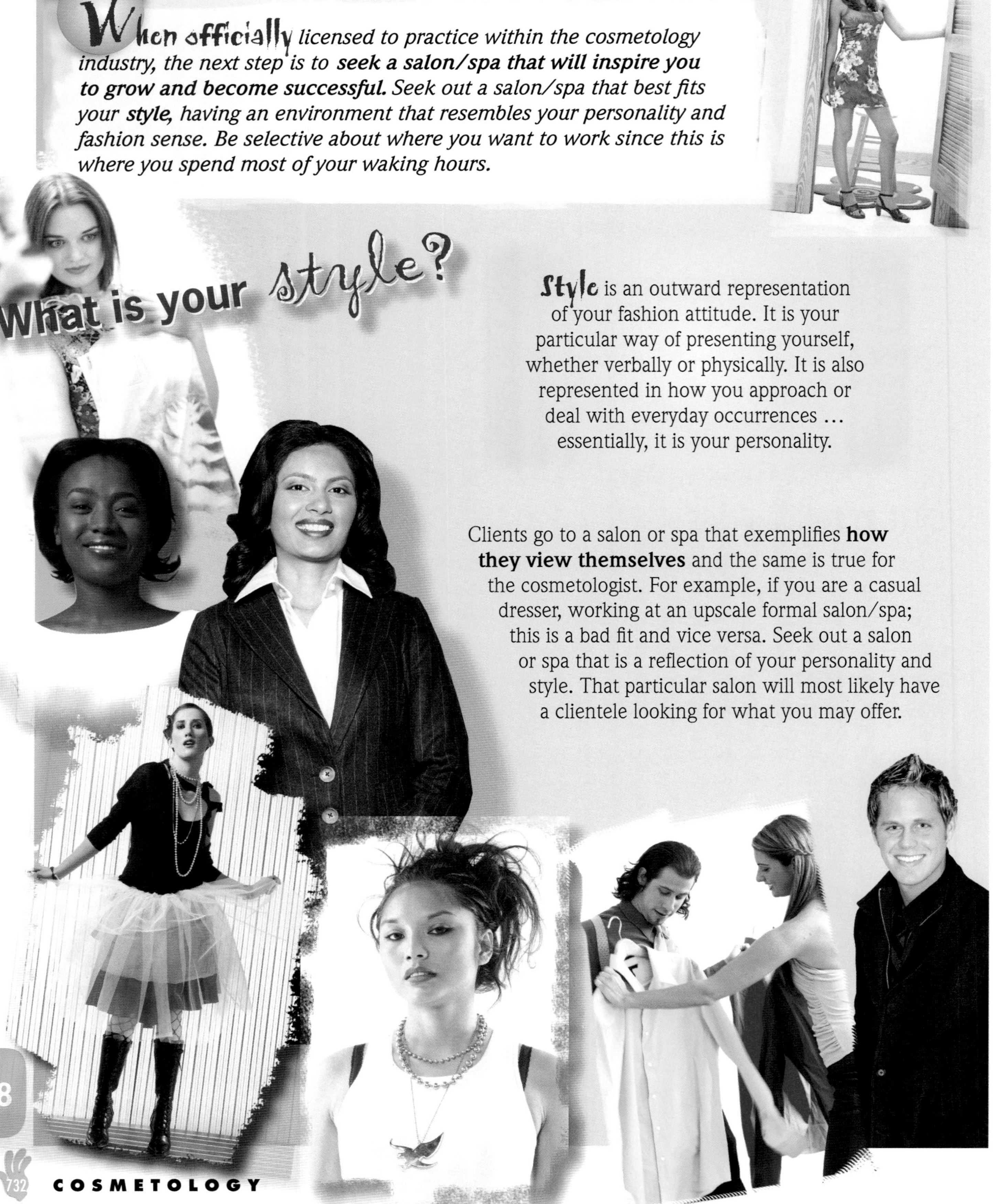

**When officially** *licensed to practice within the cosmetology industry, the next step is to* ***seek a salon/spa that will inspire you to grow and become successful.*** *Seek out a salon/spa that best fits your* ***style****, having an environment that resembles your personality and fashion sense. Be selective about where you want to work since this is where you spend most of your waking hours.*

## What is your style?

**Style** is an outward representation of your fashion attitude. It is your particular way of presenting yourself, whether verbally or physically. It is also represented in how you approach or deal with everyday occurrences ... essentially, it is your personality.

Clients go to a salon or spa that exemplifies **how they view themselves** and the same is true for the cosmetologist. For example, if you are a casual dresser, working at an upscale formal salon/spa; this is a bad fit and vice versa. Seek out a salon or spa that is a reflection of your personality and style. That particular salon will most likely have a clientele looking for what you may offer.

18

# Career Preparation . . .

**First impression** is the immediate, total perception of how **others view who you are** ... your look, how you think, what you like and even your attitude/behavior, which is shown once you "greet" someone. First impressions are a critical beginning in establishing a clientele base.

Have you ever heard the expression, **"never judge a book by its cover"?** Well that is exactly what happens when people are about to meet you, either through an interview or if you are servicing them. The unfortunate news is it happens within the first 15 seconds! So remember you only have one chance to make a really good first impression, after that it is only a matter of correction.

## When **greeting** a prospective or existing client,

Approach them with a **smile**

Make **eye contact**

Extend right hand for **handshake**

Welcome your client by **introducing yourself**

This will make the first client-to-professional connection.

**First Impressions happen in less than 15 seconds upon initial greeting!**

* **70% Visual**
* **20% Verbal**
* **10% Emotion**

**Optional:** Find a salon/spa that offers a **mentoring** program. A new stylist/technician **mentors or advises** under an "advanced" technician by helping to develop his or her skills or business knowledge through hands-on experience. This will gradually increase the new stylist's technical and people skills while in a real life work environment.

# Career Positioning . . .

*The selection of your first professional career destination is one of the most important decisions you will make. This will set you on a path that will determine the rest of your working career. Along that path you will have numerous **opportunities to network** with other people, co-workers and customers, which in turn will influence you toward your future endeavors.*

## Entry Level Career Positions

**"Choose a job you love, and you will never have to work a day in your life."**
—Confucius

Start by **networking** or interacting with people in any social setting. This will create contacts to be pursued for possible salon visitation or interviewing. Each contact or person met could possibly be a future employer or customer.

Selecting the right place to work that will help achieve your goals is a decision that should be made carefully. Remember, location, client base, style and opportunity for growth are all important factors – as well as salary and benefits – in helping to make this decision.

# Career Positioning...

The **most common entry level career positions** for a new cosmetology graduate is to work for a regional or national chain salon, a franchise chain salon group or work for a local independent salon owner.

**Chain salons/spas** are usually **multiple salons of five or greater,** which can be classified as an independent chain or a national chain. This type of salon is owned and operated either by **one individual, partners or as a corporation** out of a central headquarters. This type of salon may operate as a full-service salon or spa, or incorporate both types of services. Chain salons can range from offering low - to high-priced services and are usually located in malls and shopping centers surrounded by other businesses.

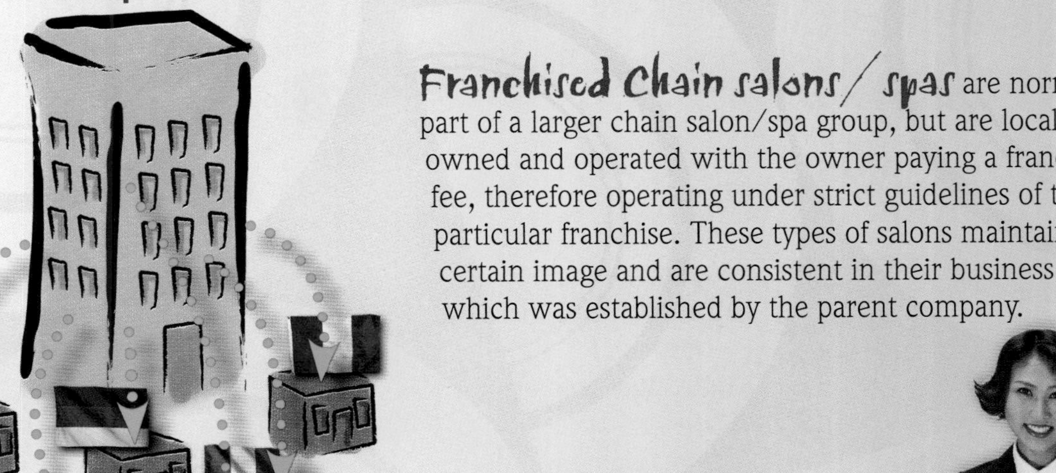


**Franchised Chain salons/spas** are normally part of a larger chain salon/spa group, but are locally owned and operated with the owner paying a franchise fee, therefore operating under strict guidelines of that particular franchise. These types of salons maintain a certain image and are consistent in their business plan, which was established by the parent company.

**Independent salons/spas** are **solely owned and operated by a person or partnership** and usually have less than 10 salon locations in a regional area. The owner is typically the cosmetologist who manages the salon as well as provides services to his or her own clientele. Everything within the salon is a reflection of the owner's experience in the beauty industry.

# Career Positioning . . .

*Once established within the salon of choice, you may decide to explore other areas of the cosmetology industry. You might find that a certain hair service generates more excitement and desire for knowledge and you would like to specialize in that particular area.*

**Primary and Advanced Level Career Positions** (refer to Chapter 1 for detailed explanation of each):

- Cosmetologist, barber, esthetician, nail technician, educator, platform artist
- Service specialist: color consultant, electrologist, massage therapist, reflexologist
- Salon coordinator, sales representative, cruise ship stylist, film and theater stylist or makeup artist

1

With the proper education, the **opportunities are limitless** for the individual seeking growth and success. The right amount of technical and people skills will "open the door" to positions that are available for your choosing.

2

# Career Positioning . . .

**Booth rental** or chair rental is **renting an area in a salon to perform cosmetology services.** The person renting is responsible for supplies, clients, finances, insurances and taxes.

RA *Check with local regulatory agency to see if booth renting is legal in your area.*

**Managing a salon,** whether it is one or multiple salons, involves many areas to **oversee such as staffing, inventory, payroll, benefits and other related expenses** that need to be supervised on a daily basis. This position requires efficient business skills, which can be taught through advanced training courses, books, materials and online resources.

**Salon/Spa Owner** is when a stylist/technician decides to **purchase his or her own establishment.** This is a huge commitment and as an owner, you will need to be competent in both your technical skills as well as business skills to run a salon efficiently. It is always recommended to gain experience first by practicing the trade in an established salon prior to operating your own business.

*Check with your local regulatory agency before managing or purchasing your own salon/spa for the guidelines set up in your area.*

# Job Fundamentals . . .

*As part of the interviewing process the following areas need to be addressed in order to decide if this salon is the right one for you.*

To function efficiently within a salon/spa, a **job description** is given to the professional to preview prior to employment. The **job description** is a record stating all the responsibilities and tasks for each individual position. This should be presented to the prospective employee at the interview in case he or she has questions. Reviewing the job description would eliminate any expectations upon hire as well as deciding in taking the position.

Salons/spas receive their revenue from the customers for payment of services performed by the professionals who work there. **Revenue or gross income** is the **initial income without deductions** such as taxes or insurances, etc. Another **source of income for the salon is retailing,** which is when the cosmetologist markets products to the customer for home use.

**Compensation** is receiving **payment for hours worked**, beauty services rendered and products sold. This is a necessary resource for survival in order to pay for life's necessities.

**There are three basic methods of payment when working in a salon/spa:**
**salary**, **commission** and **salary with commission (normally 40-60 percent).**

**Salary** is when the professional receives a **periodic payment using an hourly rate**, which is based on minimum wage or wage set by salon owner. A salary provides a steady income as the new professional builds a client base. Some salons/spas will offer a slightly higher wage to encourage new hires.

**Example:** If wage is \$9 an hour, working 40 hours equals a salary of \$360 without deductions.

**WAGE x HOURS = SALARY**
**\$9.00 x 40 hours = \$360.00**
**(without deductions)**

"Remember, taxes, health benefits and other withdrawals are deducted from the total earnings."

NOTE: The commission paid out must always be equal or higher than the current minimun wage multiplied by the hours worked per week.

# Commission

is a **percentage of the revenue generated from the services rendered** by the professional within the salon/spa. A commission is generally only offered once the professional has built up a loyal clientele. The amount of compensation received is derived from taking a percentage of total dollars brought into salon/spa from client services and products sold. This percentage can range anywhere from 25 to 60 percent depending on experience and performance level.

**Example:** If the total of services rendered equals $500, at a 50 percent commission, the total income is $250 without deductions.

# Salary with Commission

**Salary with Commission** is when an **hourly wage is given along with a commission percentage from total services rendered**. This type of payment method provides incentive to complete more services in a week's time.

**Example:** If the gross revenue of services rendered on a weekly basis averages $800 after earning a weekly salary of $400, the employer might offer 40 to 60% on any **services amounting to over** the $800. That extra amount is added to the hourly income. Also, a commission may be offered for the amount of retail products sold, typically 10 to 15 percent.

# Tipping

NOTE: Tips are considered a form of income and must be reported to the IRS, (Internal Revenue Service).

**Tipping** (also referred to as gratuity) is when the customer gives the professional some **extra money to express appreciation for a service well done.** Some salons/spas have a "no-tipping" policy while others suggest a small percentage of the customer's service cost. Keep accurate records of income and expenses. The word tip comes from the old English term of upper royalty whom demanded prompt service. **(T – To, I – Insure, P- Promptness).**

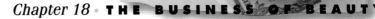

# What is Branding?

**A brand is a mental imprint** that is earned and belongs to a product, service, organization, individual and/or event. It is the sum of all tangible and intangible characteristics. A brand is what an **audience thinks and feels** when it hears a name or sees a logo, a product and/or a place of activity.

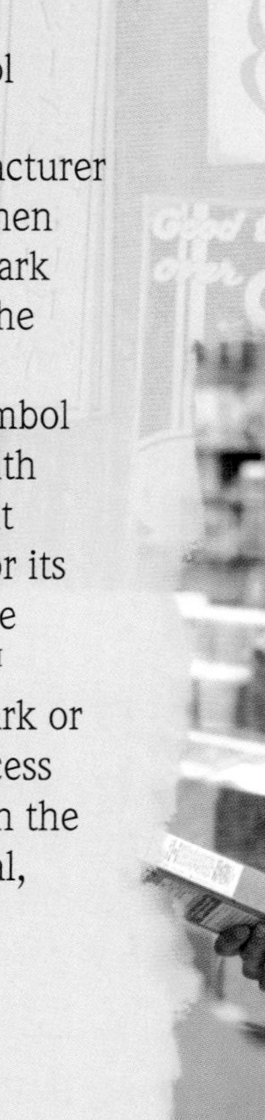

In most incidences, the branding logo or symbol becomes the exclusive property of that manufacturer or company, which is then designated by a trademark or registered symbol. The **registered symbol ®** means the branding symbol was legally recorded with the United States Patent and Trademark Office or its foreign counterpart. The **trademark symbol ™** means the branding mark or logo may be in the process of legal registration with the USPTO and once official, the ™ is replaced with the ® symbol.

# Branding your Career ...

**Products that became the Brand Leaders**
**Examples of some products:**
*(Note these items are either trademarked - ™ or registered- ®)*

**Tissues - Kleenex®**

**Soda- Coca-Cola/Pepsi®**

**Photocopiers - Xerox®**

**Adhesive memo notes - Post-its®**

**Liquid Paper Corrector - Wite•out®**

**Lip Balm - Chapstick®**

**Tape - Scotch®**

**Ketchup - Heinz®**

**Lighter - Bic®**

**Some of the most recognized brands and symbols in the world:**

McDonalds
Nike
Coca-cola
Pepsi
Apple Macintosh
Microsoft Windows
Disney
Lexus or Mercedes-Benz cars

# Branding your Career ...

**F**amous stars *of the film and music industry usually have their* ***own brand of style.*** *History remembers these personal brands for many years after that person is no longer an influence or has passed away. Each had a unique brand that* ***represented their character and persona and was all their own.*** *Many have grown their brand beyond themselves to include a clothing line, perfume and so much more.*

**Examples of a few notable people as brands:**

**Elvis Presley,** a young, good-looking and charismatic singer/songwriter of the 1960s, known to all as "The King of Rock 'n' Roll"

**Marilyn Monroe,** a beautiful and sensual movie star of the 1950s, best known as the "blonde-bombshell"

**Kurt Cobain,** an influential singer/songwriter of the "grunge" and "alternative rock" music movement and leader of the band Nirvana

**"The Beatles,"** is one of the most popular bands of all time and set a brand standard with hair and fashion

**Jacqueline Kennedy,** the quiet and reserved First Lady of the 35th President of the United States; known for importing high fashion clothing and accessories

**Tiger Woods,** one of the world's top ranked professional golfers of all time, an endorsed spokesperson for major top brands throughout the world

**Britney Spears,** child star, singer and entertainer, and clothing, perfume and assorted marketing mega sales spokesperson

**Beyonce Knowles,** singer, entertainer, movie star, and spokesperson for several companies such as L'Oréal and Pepsi

**Miley Cyrus,** the famous "Hanna Montana" movie star, singer/songwriter and teenage icon sensation, who has become one of the largest brands of the world since 2005

# Branding your Career ...

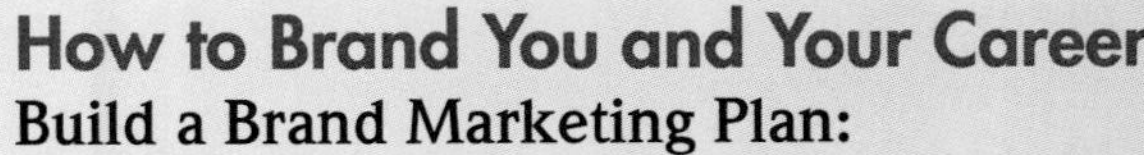

## How to Brand You and Your Career

**Build a Brand Marketing Plan:**

### Be consistent

Always dress, speak and promote the same **"Fashion Image Fingerprint,"** which is your particular style of clothing, hair and makeup application. It is how others view you!

### Know who you are

Be comfortable in your style and who you are … it must be the **"real you"** or it will be viewed as a false expression. The **"real you"** is always the most comfortable and natural way to project to others.

### Be unique

Find out what makes you different or unique from other people and use that to your advantage. **Expand and deliver upon this unique gift in your technical services.**

### Connect with customers who want what you have

This is all about servicing clients who have the **same sense of style** and wish to have the look you have. Remember your total look is your best way to promote your business to potential clients.

### Deliver a great experience

Make the service **memorable** … offer a haircut with a relaxing shampoo. Interact with the client so that you really get to know his or her likes and dislikes. Remember your clients' names, genuinely greet them, go **"above and beyond"** to make their visit memorable and wanting to come back for more.

### Add value by listening to customers' needs

When making a service valuable, it helps to enhance the visit by **suggesting the client indulge further into their beauty needs. Listening** is the key factor in bringing value to the client's services. It was once said, "Since we have two ears and only one mouth, we should always listen twice as much as we speak."

# Client Retention . . .

*When starting in a salon, one of the priorities is to build your client base, which will ensure you a steady income.* ***Retention*** *is keeping and maintaining something or someone, whether physically or mentally or both.* ***Client retention*** *is when the* ***customer continuously returns*** *for scheduled services, remaining loyal to a cosmetologist and salon. This is an art to be learned and mastered, for it will be one of the most important factors that will impact your success as a professional.*

## Top seven reasons customers choose a particular salon:

### 1) LOCATION AND CONVENIENCE

Local salons normally win a percentage of clients due to the convenience of **being close to home**. Many customers however will not continue with the salon if expectations are not met regardless of the convenience factor. Clients will travel great lengths to go to a salon that makes them look and feel their best despite the distance or costs.

### 2) REPUTATION FOR SERVICES

Satisfaction of services rendered builds a **content and confident clientele**. The clients will be your source of advertisement, which will market your abilities to others and possibly bring profits to your salon/spa.

### 3) PRICE VS. VALUE

When clients' expectations are meant **"above and beyond," it adds "value"** to their service and they feel they got a great deal. When the client is disappointed with the service, the value goes down and then he or she will feel misled or deceived.

## 4) IMAGE AND FASHION SENSE

The salon must **mirror the image of the client** along with the staff. The client will only go where he or she feels surrounded by others who share the same sense of ideals.

## 5) CLEANLINESS

The salon/spa needs to present itself in a **clean, orderly fashion following the highest standards of sanitation.** This represents concern for the welfare of each staff member and client that is serviced. Maintenance to the exterior of the salon is equally important for the safety of the public as well as providing a visual marketing tool for advertisement.

## 6) PEOPLE SKILLS

People skills are when the cosmetologist is **actively listening** to the customer's concerns about his or her beauty needs. It is important to make the client feel welcomed by providing an environment that is friendly and caring.

## 7) A PERSONAL CONNECTION

**Connect or bond with your client** by getting to know his or her likes and dislikes. **Build a rapport to gain trust** by allowing the customer to express his or her concerns or needs. This is the customer's time to talk and your time to listen in order to provide the most successful service. Your reward will be customer loyalty and continued patronage.

# Client Retention ...

## "It is all about you!"

The science behind client retention is the how and why clients select you ... and continue to make a regular "ongoing" decision to consistently seek your professional services and not go elsewhere.

### Here are some reasons why customers choose YOU as their hair stylist:

- Your style/image – representation of your fashion attitude
- Your listening skills – clients want to be heard
- You offer new or fresh ideas – attend shows, classes to stay abreast of the newest trends
- You treat them with respect – build a loyal customer base
- You remember their name and interests – personalize the service
- You understand their lifestyle – design the hairstyle that suits their needs
- When a close friend recommends you – "word-of-mouth" advertising
- When your work advertises itself – your image is branded

### Here are some reasons why customers STOP coming to you:

- When the client no longer can relate to your style/image
- When people skills are lacking
- When new or fresh ideas are not being offered
- When the client feels neglected or not valued
- When client personalization is weakened
- When the client moves farther away from salon location
- When the client becomes bedridden or passes away
- When your service prices increase or the client's lifestyle changes such as job layoff or losing job

### Here are some reasons why customers choose ANOTHER salon:

- Location salon/spa is no longer convenient
- The beauty services no longer meet customer's expectations
- Price of services rendered outweighs the "value" the client feels at completion of service
- Image of salon no longer reflects the client's personality
- The salon/spa standards for sanitation and safety are low
- People skills are diminished or absent

# How to Have a Successful Career . . .

"The road to success is always under construction."
—Dale Carnegie

## Plan Your Journey and Continue Your Goal Setting

Planning your professional journey takes a combination of clear goals on what you wish to achieve, a vision to see where you want to go, a plan on how to get there and a map showing you the way. Remember that the journey itself may be the most fun and rewarding part of your professional career.

"Creating the roadmap to success is all about having a vision and setting reachable goals."

## Listed below are career suggestions:

1) Build upon your technical skills by working in a salon/spa to gain experience.
2) Expand upon your people or communicational skills in the salon/spa by establishing a loyal client base.
3) Obtain a managerial position at a salon/spa to accomplish the business side of the industry.
4) Represent a manufacturer by promoting a product line at a salon/spa or beauty shows.
5) Establish your own salon/spa and hire people to work for you.

# How to Have a Successful Career . . .

*As with any* ***successful career-minded individual,*** *it is important to* ***monitor and track your growth within the salon/spa.*** *Keep* ***score*** *on how well you are doing on your career journey.*

**There are five key factors of importance when measuring your growth as a stylist.**

## 1. Active Number of Clients:

Active clients are those who schedule at least four appointments or visits per year. A typical female client will normally visit a salon every four to six weeks. Most male customers visit a salon/spa on an average every two to four weeks due to maintenance of short hair. If the client does not continue to visit the salon at least four times per year, he or she is considered in-active.

## 2. New Clients per Month:

Most salons/spas and designers alike will lose a small percentage (normally 5%) of clients over the course of a year, therefore it is most important to always attract new people to replace the ones lost. Everyone you meet or have contact with has the potential to be a new client (also sometimes called a guest).

## 3. New Client Retention Percentage:

The key to most thriving businesses is to maximize the ability to keep as many new clients coming back as possible. Salons typically fail in this area because owners do not realize that this should be a major focus and should be measured on a daily basis. Most salons keep less than 20 percent of all new clients over the course of a year or longer, which means 80 percent of their new clients are not maintaining active status, therefore seeking another salon/spa for their hair-, nail-and skin-care needs.

## 4. Frequency of Visits:

The frequency of visits is determined by the average number of appointments or visits made within 52 weeks. The average number of visits for a female client is nine to 13 per year, with an increase of 10 to 14 by encouraging add-on services. For the male customer, the average number of visits is 13 to 26, with an increase of 14 to 27 by encouraging add-on services.

## 5. Average Ticket per Visit:

If the client normally spends $30 (not counting gratuity) per visit for a basic cut and style, your goal would be to offer add-on services or products to increase the total amount spent per visit. Adding a home care product at a $20 dollar value would increase the total ticket cost to $50. If you add a highlight service for an additional $40, the ticket increases to $90. The average ticket value is determined by adding all totals and dividing it by the number of visits for an entire year.

# Owning a Business . . .

*If desiring to own a business, there are many important factors to consider. Enough money, or capital, will be needed for the first five years to cover all expenses. The largest expense, which averages about 50 percent of the salon's budget, will go toward employee salaries. The employee must be paid first before any other expenses.*

If needing financial assistance, it is important to have a **business plan or a written report**, which describes the **current and projected future** of the business. This plan needs to include an operational plan, projected income, expenses and location demographics.

A Demographic study is reviewing the area's local number of businesses, average income and offered services. This helps determine if there is enough of a need for another business of a certain type.

**Location, location, location** is always the most important factor when **opening a salon. It needs good visibility and must be easily accessible.** It should have a large area for parking with adequate distance from other area salons to avoid too much competition.

Purchase malpractice, property, burglary, fire and theft **insurances** to cover all monetary demands. Review and abide by all **disability policies.**

Check with the local authorities to observe all business codes from the **local, state and federal regulations and laws.** Keep current and accurate records within business.

Comply with the federal **Occupational Safety and Health Administration** guidelines and the **Material Safety Data Sheets** for all products used in the business.

Establish **business policies** for employees as well as customers to follow and keep detailed and complete financial records of the business. **Personal records of each employee** must be maintained with the salary, social security number and length of employment according to state and federal law.

## Types of Business Ownerships

**An individual type of ownership** is when **one person is the sole proprietor**. That person accepts full responsibility for all the expenses, policies, making decisions, profits and losses. Generally this individual will be the owner as well as the manager.

**A partnership type of ownership** is when **two or more persons share responsibilities**. The advantage is that two people bring more capital to the business and the duties of running the day-to-day operations are shared.

**A corporation type of ownership** is when a **group of stockholders have proprietary interest** in the company. This is an excellent choice for protecting one's own assets and limiting personal loss.

### Optional:

**Leasing** is an alternative to **owning a business**, but includes **not owning the building** in which the business is located. The owner of building charges the lessee a fee each month for using the space in the building. An agreement is written that will detail who is responsible for expenses, repairs and exactly what each person owns.

*Accounting is maintaining and organizing business records for the purpose of reporting taxes, preparation of forms and other financial accounts. This also provides a "clear picture" of exactly ALL the money coming in (revenue) and going out (expenses and debt).*

**NOTE:** In keeping accurate records, identify your personal life budget from your business budget.

## Categories of Accounts:

**Budgeting** is a list of all estimated monthly expenditures added together and subtracted from the month's total income. A separate budget may be created for both personal and business records. **Financial planning** is managing your money to know exactly how much money is spent, saved or borrowed.

**Banking** is to have a clear understanding of how to manage your savings, checking or any other bank accounts. **Debt** can occur by **borrowing money** through obtaining a loan whether it is for buying a house, car or a business. If loans are not paid back, it is referred to as a **"default,"** which may result in ruining your credit.

PROFITS

**Profit & Loss Record** (P&L) is based on money gained or lost over a certain period of time. If you spent more money than made, than you are losing money **(negative gain)**, but if you made more money than spent, you are making money or a profit **(positive gain)**.

**Accurate Income and Tax Records** are reliable sources to obtain bank loans or make purchases on credit. A portion of income for the individual practicing cosmetology is generated from tips/gratuities and is considered a part of the income.

**Consult a professional Certified Public Accountant (CPA)** to maximize your ability to save and invest, borrow and manage your money. A CPA will know how to get the best tax return and guide you to invest toward the future in achieving your financial goals.

# Business Basics . . .

In order to **operate a business efficiently and successfully,** an owner should have some basic knowledge of certain industry tools. These tools may involve **legalities in protecting** you as well as clients and employees and will also assist in effectively **managing the operations** of the business.

As a business owner, know and follow the **state laws** that are established within the cosmetology industry and the municipality of your location. This will **protect all persons** working in the establishment as well as customers receiving services. Whether styling hair or becoming a salon/spa owner, each area comes with a set of rules and regulations to follow in order to stay within the **legalities of servicing the public.**

**Insurance** protects your investment and may be obtained to replace all assets (tools, equipment, furniture, etc.) if damaged or stolen. It is also used to protect yourself and clients from accidents, lawsuits, injury, etc. There are a multitude of insurances such as malpractice, fire, burglary, property, etc. A premium is paid monthly or quarterly to an insurance company from which you receive a policy that lists everything covered.

**Computer Skills** are a necessity in keeping with the modern technology of today. Computers streamline appointment scheduling, client service record storage, email marketing/advertising, inventory, product ordering/purchasing, etc. Basic PC or Mac skills and a computer with Internet service will make organizing the business more efficient and will save space in the salon by eliminating paper records.

**Investing in you or the business** is when a certain percentage of the total business income is put back into the business either for renovations to the building (whether inside or out), advertising or upgrades on products. Investment also consists of allotting a percentage of the monies taken in to the owner for a salary.

Today, many companies offer employees the opportunity to join and invest in **retirement planning**. The **401K is currently the most common plan,** which allows you to elect to have a pre-taxed amount deducted from your pay and deposited into another company account. When done privately without another company component, it is referred to as an **IRA or a ROTH IRA.** All these plans put your money into some form of investment tool with the objective of earning interest on the investment until you reach a federal/state listed retirement age (typically 65 to 70 years old). An early withdrawal would result in a penalty, which consists of a specialty tax deducted from your accrued total amount.

**Advertising/Marketing** *is used to* ***acquire more clients through public promotion of business, products and services.*** *The success of the business is dependent upon the approach of marketing, whether utilizing one or all three of the options. The average amount of income spent on advertising is generally no greater than 3 percent. The best marketing choice would be to use all three forms in order to reach all types of customers, businesses and organizations of past, present and future.*

## The Most Common Styles of Advertising/Marketing are:

### 1) One to One

The best option for the beauty industry is **"word of mouth"** advertisement, which allows your **existing customers to be your "lead generators" for acquiring new customers.** A satisfied client will generate other clients to the salon. Cell phones and email are both personalized and targeted ways to communicate with people, whether it is family, friends or acquaintances.

### 2) Business to Business

Partner and exchange with area businesses that have a similar customer base for customer lists and or services. A special savings can be offered to area businesses, organizations and groups like the Chamber of Commerce, Rotary, Ladies Auxiliary, etc. Another option is to join a club, Web community or social networks to gain access to potential new customers and "loyalty programs."

### 3) Business to Customer

Partner with your customer to be your main supplier of new customers by creating a rewards program to help provide new customer leads. For example, the business card referral technique can be offered to expand clientele. Have your existing customers hand out your business cards and in turn for every client referred, the existing customer will receive a discount on his or her next salon visit. This also builds loyalty between cosmetologist and client. Other industry markets can be used to locate and connect to potential customers that could employ your services.

# Business Basics ...

***Marketing** is a method of reaching out to potential customers and make them aware of the services and products that are available for purchase. Understanding the difference between **Mass vs. Niche marketing** will help you successfully target potential customers during your professional career.*

**Mass Market** is the process of reaching as many people as possible regardless of whether they become potential customers or not. **Example:** Web advertising reaches the entire world, but 99 percent of those reached will never become an "actual" client.

How it works:

- Shoot first, then aim!
- Target everyone that may become your customer.
- Establish a Web site and use other broad sites that are viewed by everyone.
- Promote and support a "need" or "foundation" that represents your beliefs and the salon/spa in which you work. Promote the foundation's message. **Example:** The term "Green Salon" denotes "Environmentally and Earth Friendly."

**Niche Market** is the process of narrowing the marketing strategy to small demographic areas or targeting a particular group of people. **Example:** Web advertising allows you to select options that reach people in a certain state, region or county, which increase the percentage of the viewers that could be potential customers.

How it works:

- Aim first, then shoot!
- Concentrate your target to select a few population segments that might have a better chance of becoming your customer.
- Use the Web to focus on small groups of people by geography, age, income level and any other relative factor.

"Remember it is easier to keep an existing customer than to find a new one ... client retention!"

**Special Event Marketing** is remembering and acknowledging special days or holidays in the lives of clients as well as fellow co-workers. Use these events to promote add-on services or discounts on services for a limited time.

*During the month of Diane's (client's name) birthday, we are offering Diane (client's name) a 20 percent discount on all her haircoloring services.*

## Create a Special Events Calendar

To increase sales, create gift opportunities by marking your calendar with the following special events and/or holidays.

- Birthdays
- Anniversaries
- Graduations
- Back to school
- Vacation
- All major holidays

Acknowledge life changing events for clients or co-workers:

- Weddings
- Relocation/new house
- Divorce
- New baby
- Health-related concerns
- Retirement

How the acknowledgement is delivered is dependent upon the salon/spa, professional and the event. Is it going to be a small, personable message or large group acknowledgment?

## Selecting a Delivery Method

- Print – greeting card
- Radio
- Web/Internet
- Verbal
- Gift – complimentary service, free product or discount on service

# Business Basics ...

*Selling* ***is a major part of the beauty industry, whether it is convincing the customer to receive a certain service or suggesting that he or she purchase a cosmetic product.*** *It all begins when you appear and greet the customer because at that moment the selling begins ... you want them* ***to like and trust you*** *so they will return for future visits.*

The professional's selling approach and technique may be adapted depending on the client's needs and personality. A **"soft sell" or consultative approach** is used to inform the client of the recommended products to be used, but does not pressure a purchase. A **"hard sell" or prescriptive approach** will emphasize the importance of purchasing the product, plus list the possible results if the customer chooses not to buy.

BUY NOW

Once the client **gains assurance of your abilities and sincerity**, he or she will not hesitate to purchase products or receive the recommended beauty services. The most important fact is to **always be honest and considerate** when giving advice on clients' beauty care needs. Another convincing factor is for the professional to have had the experience of receiving the services that are suggested for their clients. This allows you to advertise the results of any proposed service.

# Business Basics . . .

**Retailing** *is the act of* ***requesting the client purchase cosmetic products*** *for home use. Always state the* ***results and benefits*** *of the cosmetic products that are being offered for the client to purchase. Set the example by using the products on yourself, which enforces your support and belief in their benefits and results.*

**Upselling or ticket upgrading** is when the professional advises the client to **receive additional beauty services** to either accentuate beauty or remedy a problem thereby increasing your sales. The best time to upsell is while the client is getting her hair shampooed or while in the professional's chair. It is also recommended to re-book client for her next appointment before leaving the salon.

**Inventory records** provide a clear and concise list of all products located within the salon/spa. Update inventory records periodically to determine over- or under-stocking of products, which will alert of any possible internal theft.

**Consumption supplies** are any products used in the daily operation of the salon/spa.

**Retail supplies** are the products sold to the customers.

**Client record cards** are reminders on each client's product purchase as well as the services he or she received. Keep all cards centrally located either in a filing cabinet or electronically stored in the computer within the salon/spa for easy access. These cards also help in product consumption and re-stocking and if the product is available for client's next buy or salon's next use.

# To Master Success ...

## "Failure to try is true failure."

—Unknown

*As with most endeavors you choose to pursue and achieve in life, it all starts with a great education and a natural progression of small successful steps. The following summarizes eight steps of how you can master success.*

**STEP ONE** is conquering your **Technical and Artistic Skills.**

1. **Mastering the simple skills** of hair-, nail- and skin-care services along with the proper handling and function of tools used to perform each service is the beginning of developing your technical abilities. Achieving the simple skills first with accuracy and assurance strengthens your confidence to move to the next level of learning.

2. **Mastering the intermediate skills** is when you begin to add or blend what you learned on the simple skill level and expand upon it to include variables of each hair-, nail- and skin-care service. Example: The basic manicure will include a hand massage for the intermediate skill level. You may also start to include some small creative components to the work performed in each service.

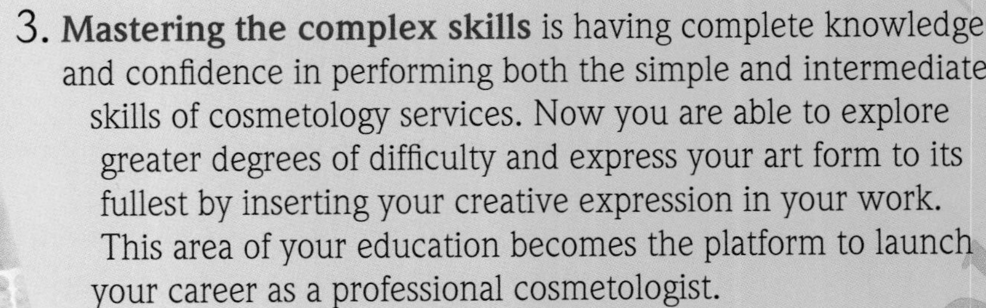

3. **Mastering the complex skills** is having complete knowledge and confidence in performing both the simple and intermediate skills of cosmetology services. Now you are able to explore greater degrees of difficulty and express your art form to its fullest by inserting your creative expression in your work. This area of your education becomes the platform to launch your career as a professional cosmetologist.

Simple

Intermediate

Complex

**Optional: Create a "Before and After" Image Portfolio consisting of photos, illustrations, accomplishments and/or documents that showcase your skills acquired within the beauty industry.**

This is a simple and effective way to build your career by **cataloging your talents**, which will lend support in building your career. The **before/after images** of everyday clients have the most impact to future customers because they share your abilities to transform someone's life. This book may also contain awards, diploma, résumé and letters of employment references.

# To Master Success ...

## STEP TWO is establishing solid Communicational Skills.

**Master your ability** to communicate and relate to the customer. **Communication** is the process through which people exchange information, also referred to as **"human skills" or people skills"** in the beauty industry. Communication is two parts listening and one part talking, which will establish a rapport between you and the client. Clients will gain the confidence to share valuable insight about their hair-care challenges and you can present solutions to those challenges by offering new ideas for them to consider. Remember clients come to you for professional advice and direction as to what is best for their hair.

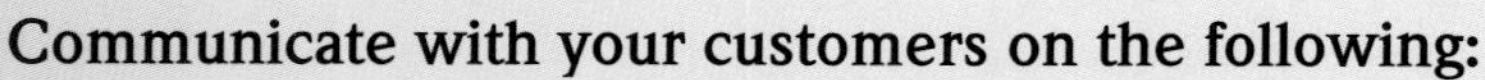

## STEP THREE is getting to Know Your Customers.

**Communicate with your customers on the following:**

1) **Hair-, Nail- and Skin-Care Needs:** Client has dry hair, dandruff, oily scalp, hair too curly and wants straight hair or vice versa, or wants a different haircolor, etc. Skin is dry, experiences frequent break outs, is a nail biter, or nails are yellow or weak nails, etc.

2) **Lifestyle Issues:** Client is getting married, divorced, or is pregnant, active in sports, or a stay at-home mom, etc.

"Avoid using the word '<u>problems</u>,' which comes across negative, instead use the word '<u>challenges</u>.'"

# To Master Success ...

3) **Challenges:** Client has limited funds, has a hard time making appointments, or lives far away, works an outdoor job, or is under medical care, etc.

4) **Client Goals:** What does the client want to accomplish? Set benchmarks for each visit to work toward **achieving the goal over a period of time**.

A **goal** is a "target" that is **planned, monitored and reached** within a scheduled time frame. Maybe the client's goal is to grow her hair long, so begin the process now by **realistically** stating that hair typically grows ½ inch (1.25 cm) per month. Depending on her current length, she may not have "long hair" for two years. In between those two markers, you need to support the goal and help the client maintain "a look" that they can live with during the growing-out stage. Maybe another type of goal would be to return to a "natural haircolor" or "remove curl by relaxing the hair." Regardless of the goal, you must determine a realistic one, agree to the terms in achieving the goal and most importantly, **keep the goal reasonable and attainable**.

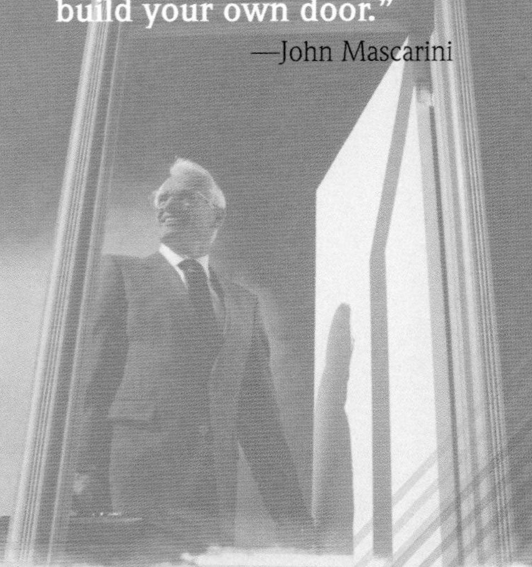

"If opportunity doesn't knock ... build your own door."
—John Mascarini

## STEP FOUR is to become Self Motivated:

**Self-motivated** is when an individual is a **"self-starter,"** does not require direction or someone to lead them ... and **takes the initiative** to get the task completed. It is important to become self-motivated to succeed on your own. A self-motivator is not dependent on someone else to wake them in the morning, instead sets an alarm clock to get the day started on time, whether going to work or school. Self motivation and a "work ethic" are human traits that must be part of your daily plan to be successful in any career. Success is earned, based on your ability to perform **"above and beyond"** to get the job done.

## STEP FIVE is to become aware of your Image, Fashion and Market Conscience:

*"If fashion is the language, then your clothes, hair and makeup is the vocabulary, your style is a recognizable fingerprint."*
—Mary McFadden

**Fashion Image Fingerprint** is your particular style of clothing, hair and application of makeup that is uniquely presented through you. Make sure your ***Fashion Image Fingerprint*** matches with the customers you desire to gain as a clientele.

There is a **distinction between personal attire and fashion attire**. What is acceptable for home wear might not be acceptable to wear in a professional environment. Present yourself according to the standard of **clients you wish to attract.** Jeans and tee shirts will not work in an upscale salon/spa catering to high-income clients and the same is true in reverse.

# To Master Success ...

## **STEP SIX** is developing **Self-Confidence.**

The more knowledge and experience gained by you, the more valuable you become to an employer and your customers. That is true with most careers and holds true for the cosmetology field as well. **Learning is a life-long journey** ... it does not end at graduation. Attend hair shows/events or hold classes within the salon to keep you abreast of the current hair trends and beauty products being used. An increase in compensation will only occur as you continue to develop through knowledge and experience.

"Knowledge is power. Education is the fuel to advancement during your career journey!" ©

## **STEP SEVEN** is having **Realistic and Attainable Goals:**

**Goals** can be both **personal and professional** to include higher grades, graduating, income level, title of position, or lifestyle changes such as eating healthy and daily exercise. It is always recommended to write goals down on paper for confirmation and to ensure direction.

The most successful goal planning is making a **one-, three-, and five-year goal plan**. This may be referred to as **short term (1 year), intermediate (3 year) and long term (5 year)** goals. This plan is also used by major companies around the world to forecast their future growth and budget. It would be updated every year as goals are accomplished and new ones are established. Accomplishing a goal is not the only reason goals change ... new ambitions, lifestyle adjustments or different priorities require goal modifications.

Goals may also be **measured daily/weekly/monthly** to further break down the steps necessary to reach yearly goals. Be able to distinguish between a goal and a "wish or a dream!" A goal that is not actively measured is not a goal, it is a wish.

# To Master Success ...

Below is an **example of a goal sheet** to get you started in writing down your one-, three- and five-year plan. This same example can be used to create a weekly and monthly goal sheet.

Goal Sheet:

| One-Year Goals | Three-Year Goals | Five-Year Goals |
|---|---|---|
| Example: Graduate cosmetology school, receive license and locate first professional job | To work successfully in a salon as a cosmetologist and build a loyal client base | To work as a platform artist for a product manufacturer or open my own salon business |
| | | |
| | | |
| | | |
| | | |
| | | |
| | | |

**STEP EIGHT** is to acquire good **Work Ethics and Morals:**

A career in the service business requires a high standard of work ethics and morals in order to maintain customer loyalty. Customer loyalty is when the client continuously comes to you and the salon for hair, nail, and skin services. This builds a consistent client base, resulting in a steady income.

**Work Ethics** are implementing a behavior of decency or respect to fellow co-workers and customers.

**Moral** is a standard of right or wrong behavior based on an individual's principles or beliefs.

# To Master Success ...

## Some Ethics and Moral Standards to follow:

- Client and salon requests come first before your needs or desires.
- Respect the rules or policies of the salon whether agreeing or disagreeing.
- Recognize and solve problems constructively.
- Arriving to work on time and being punctual for each client is a major part of success for the business.
- Always be honest with recommendations or services offered.

"Go out and 'makeover' the world one person at a time."


— John Mascarini

Never **"Burn any Bridges,"** which means **keep a friendly working relationship** with all people met within the beauty industry ... never knowing when your paths will cross again. These people will **encourage and support** you in future endeavors as you move forward in your career.

Continue your education as part of your lifelong career journey. It will always support you every step of the way.

"The Golden Rule: 'Treat others as you would like to be treated.'"

# The Business of Beauty REVIEW QUESTIONS

## FILL-IN-THE-BLANKS

| | |
|---|---|
| A. | Advertising |
| B. | Branding |
| C. | Client Retention |
| D. | Commission |
| E. | Compensation |
| F. | Consumption Supplies |
| G. | Cover Letter |
| H. | Default |
| I. | Goal |
| J. | Leasing |
| K. | Location |
| L. | Mass Market |
| M. | Moral |
| N. | Practical Exam |
| O. | Registered Symbol |
| P. | Résumé |
| Q. | Retailing |
| R. | Revenue |
| S. | Style |
| T. | Upselling |

1. ________ is a mental imprint that is earned and belongs to a product or individual.
2. ________ is the most important factor when opening a salon.
3. ________ on a loan means it was not paid back.
4. ________ is a communication tool that catalogs and summarizes your education, employment and accomplishments.
5. ________ consists of performing the actual hands-on skills appropriate to your area of study.
6. ________ is a standard of right or wrong behavior based on an individual's principles of beliefs.
7. ________ is used to acquire more clients through public promotion of business, products and services.
8. ________ is an outward representation of your fashion attitude.
9. ________ is a target that is planned, monitored and reached within a scheduled time frame.
10. ________ is initial income without tax deductions.
11. ________ is when customers continuously return for scheduled services.
12. ________ is receiving payment for hours worked.
13. ________ is to own the business, but not owning the building in which the business is located.
14. ________ is the process of reaching as many people as possible.
15. ________ is a percentage of the revenue generated from services rendered.
16. ________ is the act of requesting the client purchase cosmetic products for home maintenance.
17. ________ means the branding symbol was legally recorded with the USPTO or its foreign counterpart.
18. ________ is when the professional advises the client to receive additional beauty services.
19. ________ is an introduction to the employer from the prospective employee requesting an interview.
20. ________ are any products used in the daily operation of the salon/spa.

STUDENT'S NAME DATE GRADE

## A

# Index

## C

# Index ...

# Index

## F

# Index ...



## G

## L

## M

# Index . . .

## N

# O

## Q



## R

## S

# Index . . .

# U



# V

# CLiC Classmates Sign In . . .

School ______________________ Class of ______________________

Thank you for joining our professional team
of great cosmetologists!